A Lexicon
to the Latin Text of
the Theological Writings of
Emanuel Swedenborg
(1688-1772)

A Lexicon to the Latin Text of the Theological Writings of Emanuel Swedenborg (1688-1772)

EDITORS

Dr John Chadwick

Dr Jonathan S Rose

The Swedenborg Society

20-21 Bloomsbury Way

London WC1A 2TH

2010

Edited by Dr John Chadwick and Dr Jonathan S Rose

First edition (in loose-leaf format), 1975-90
Second edition, 2008
Second printing of second edition, 2010

Published by:
The Swedenborg Society
Swedenborg House
20-21 Bloomsbury Way
London WC1A 2TH

Book design: Stephen McNeilly

Typeset at Swedenborg House
Printed and bound in Great Britain by TJ International Ltd,
Padstow, Cornwall

ISBN 978-085448-153-8
British Library Cataloguing-in-Publication Data
A catalogue record for this book is available
from the British Library

CONTENTS

PREFACE

A very full account of the life and work of John Chadwick has been provided by two of his closest friends, Professor J T Killen and Professor A Morpurgo Davies, in the *Biographical Memoirs of Fellows, I*, which form part of *The Proceedings of the British Academy, 115*. John's two friends set out in detail his many achievements as a scholar in the field of classical Greek and Latin; and they speak with authority about that for which he was specifically renowned, namely his contribution to the decipherment and understanding of the Minoan script known as Linear B. But in their 'biographical memoir' the two professors also indicate their friend's less well-known achievements as an editor and translator of the works of Emanuel Swedenborg. They state that John 'produced new translations of no fewer than eight of Swedenborg's works, six of them in his later years when retirement gave him time for it... He was legitimately proud of his Swedenborg lexicon (1975-90), a unique example, as he rightly said, of a lexicon of eighteenth-century Latin'.

John Chadwick came from a family of Swedenborgians. In his early years, he and his older brother Kenneth went with their parents Margaret and Fred to Sunday services held in places of worship connected with the General Conference of the New Church, a national body consisting of Christian congregations that subscribe to the teachings contained in the religious works of Emanuel Swedenborg. John's father Fred was also an active lay preacher, and in his later years a lay pastor.

But Fred Chadwick's more notable contribution to Swedenborgianism lay in his service to the Swedenborg Society, a publishing house which had been established in 1810. Having served for eight years as a member of the governing Council, he was appointed Honorary Secretary in 1933. His greatest achievement during the ten years he served as the Secretary was undoubtedly the organization of the two hundred and fiftieth anniversary celebrations of Swedenborg's birth. Chief among these celebrations were the birthday meeting held in Queen's Hall on 29 January 1938, and in the same year the publication, in twenty different languages, of new translations of *De Nova Hierosolyma et ejus Doctrina Coelesti*. Now in his teens, John would have been aware of much of what his father was doing as Secretary to prepare for these 1938 celebrations. He was present at that birthday meeting and was probably called on by his father to act as one of the ushers. But how much interest did the seventeen-year-old John, already reading Swedenborg in Latin, take at this time in the translation work of the Society?

Though he ceased to be Secretary of the Swedenborg Society in 1943, Fred Chadwick continued to serve on its governing Council for a further eleven years, at the end of which he had been a member for almost three decades. His two sons were no less devoted to the work of the Society, for in 1946 Kenneth was elected to the governing Council and after ten years appointed the Chairman, a position he held for another ten years. But also in 1946 John accepted an invitation to join the Advisory and Revision Board, of which he remained a member for the rest of his life, that is, for more than half a century. For several years he served as Chairman of that board. In 1988, when the three hundredth anniversary of Swedenborg's birth was being celebrated, John was elected President of the Swedenborg Society; but ill health prevented him from serving for more than one year.

Professors Killen and Morpurgo Davies tell us that John Chadwick's 'chosen specialisation' while a student at Cambridge was Classical Linguistics, and that very soon after his graduation in 1946 he was appointed by the Clarendon Press to serve as 'Assistant to the Editor' of the *Oxford Latin Dictionary*. For six years this was his full-time occupation. Thus expertise as a lexicographer was one of the many talents John brought to the Swedenborg Society when he joined its Advisory and Revision Board. Early on he taught members of the Board how to record on a slip of paper any unusual Latin word, or any seemingly special meaning given to a word, that appeared in the religious works of Emanuel Swedenborg. For about twenty-five years such slips of paper were being assembled; they were inserted alphabetically into appropriately-shaped green boxes. Then in the early 1970s—with the aid of these assembled slips of paper, and also word lists such as those to be found on pages 793-858 of volume six of John F Potts's *The Swedenborg Concordance*—John began to create what he entitled *A Lexicon to the Latin Text of the Theological Writings of Emanuel Swedenborg (1688-1772)*. It was published in eight parts, one after another, during the years 1975-1990—in type written, loose-leaf form. Additions or supplements to the already published sections were also issued from time to time. John would I'm sure have wished me to mention that the typing over these years was ably carried out by Miss Madeline Waters, and that he was aided in so many ways by the Revd Norman Ryder, and latterly by the Revd Dr Jonathan Rose, who was to succeed him as the editor of the work.

John Chadwick died on 24 November 1998, while on his way to the headquarters of the Swedenborg Society in London to discuss the future publication of the Lexicon. As his two academic friends have observed in their biographical memoir, in retirement he had more time to devote to the translation of Swedenborg's works; no doubt there would have been more than the half a dozen he produced in his later years, had he not been taken from us so suddenly. Not only in those later years however, but also throughout his busy life before retirement, he would respond promptly to anyone who sought his opinion or advice. It was always a joy to receive a letter from him, composed in his neat and distinctive handwriting. John was unstinting also in his support of those engaged in the task of editing and/or translating the Latin texts of Swedenborg's works. As general editor of the Latin/English and Swedish/English volume *Small Theological Works and Letters*, published by the Swedenborg Society in 1975, I myself relied very much on him; indeed he was the translator of several documents included in that publication. And during the many years when I was engaged in the translation of *Arcana Coelestia*, John never failed to answer a call for help.

Twenty years ago, while visiting a museum in Crete where artefacts belonging to the Minoan civilization were displayed, my wife and I saw the name John Chadwick on some of the cards explaining the exhibits there. His name was known not only to academics but also to all who had an interest in that civilization, in particular its written language. People from various walks of life who had gone on one of the Swan Hellenic Tours on which John was a speaker have told me how much they enjoyed listening to him. They also enjoyed his company, and that of Joan his wife who accompanied him and who lovingly cared for him when he was at home in Cambridge.

John Chadwick was indeed renowned throughout the world; yet fame never went to his head. I knew him to be a quiet, humble, and sincere Christian. Even so, he could speak his mind when it was necessary to do so, and there was no false modesty in him. As two of his closest friends have stated, he was 'legitimately proud of his Swedenborg lexicon'. I pray that he would be no less proud of it in the form in which it is now being presented to the world, about ten years after his death in his seventy-ninth year.

Among John's favourite hymns was that composed by Peter Abelard nine centuries ago, which begins,

> O quanta qualia sunt illa sabbata,
> Quae semper celebrat superna curia,
> Quae fessis requies, quae merces fortibus,
> Cum erit omnia Deus in omnibus!

How close do the following English versions come to what John saw in those words or to what he felt as he sang them?

O what their joy and their glory must be,
Those endless Sabbaths the blessed ones see!
Crown for the valiant; to weary ones rest;
God shall be all, and in all ever blest.

J M Neale

Oh what high holiday, past our declaring,
Safe in his palace God's courtiers are sharing,
Rest after pilgrimage, spoil after fighting!
God, all in all, is their crown and requiting.

R A Knox

John no doubt acquired his affection for *O quanta qualia* while he was a pupil at St Paul's School in London. Even during his schooldays perhaps, the hymn encapsulated for him something of what he heard at home or in church, or else was reading about in Swedenborg's Latin works concerning life both in this world and in the next. At the end of their life on earth, 'weary ones' seeking 'rest' from the trials and temptations they have been undergoing during their earthly 'pilgrimage' will not be disappointed. They will come among 'the blessed ones' in heaven who enjoy 'endless Sabbaths' of rest from the wearisome and seemingly unending task of fighting against evil and selfishness. We pray that John himself has entered into that rest in which God is his 'all in all'.

John Elliott
President of the Swedenborg Society
London, 2008

EDITOR'S INTRODUCTION

This Lexicon was first assembled and edited by John Chadwick (about whom see the Preface earlier in this volume). After he gathered and evaluated information from various sources, which are noted in his Preface to the First Edition, reproduced below on pages xxxvii-xlii, he circulated it in eight sections issued between 1975 and 1990. It contained over thirteen thousand entries. He also circulated a supplement in 1990 with over six hundred additions and changes.

Chadwick is now well known as a Perceval Maitland Laurence Reader in Classics at Cambridge and a decipherer, scholar, and presenter of Linear B, but he started his professional career as a lexicographer. He is named on page vii of the *Oxford Latin Dictionary* as a member of its editorial staff.

Chadwick allowed the Swedenborg Society, of which he was an active member throughout his adult life, to circulate in an unpublished form his Lexicon to Swedenborg's theological Latin in order to invite corrections and additions before going to press. He intended to publish it eventually in type conventions similar to those of the *Oxford Latin Dictionary*. He was standing on a platform to take a train to the Swedenborg Society's headquarters at Swedenborg House in London to discuss publication of his Lexicon when he suddenly passed away.

I had first become involved in the Lexicon as a reference checker in the early 1980s, paid by a grant from the General Church of the New Jerusalem's Translation Committee, based in Bryn Athyn, Pennsylvania. Perhaps because of my youth as much as anything, Chadwick named me as his successor as editor for the project.

With characteristic humility but also with a realization of the magnitude of his task, Dr Chadwick had expressed regret in his Preface for the limitations of his Lexicon. Although I have enjoyed the privilege of standing on his broad shoulders and have had, as Chadwick had, the assistance of many scholars and printed resources, programmers and computers, this Lexicon remains but a humble beginning. As with Chadwick's mimeographed original, this first true publication, produced in Chadwick's memory, will hopefully lead to another round of helpful criticism and supplementation. (The address to which to send corrections and suggestions appears on the title page.)

The primary aim of the Lexicon is to serve those who are studying and translating Swedenborg's theological works. While those works might seem a narrow focus—just one part of the lifetime work of a single author—they nevertheless constitute a corpus of 4.5 million Latin words on a wide range of topics:

> biblical and ecclesiastical studies, liturgy and rubric, as well as study of world religions contemporary and ancient; philosophy; geometry, calculus, and other forms of mathematics; anatomy, astronomy, botany, chemistry, metallurgy, and other sciences; classical literature and mythology, oratory, poetry, narrative, simile, dialog, drama, music, art, and sculpture; sports; education, history, geography, agriculture, economics, politics, law, business, trade, and travel; and the domestic world of marriage, home, and family. [1]

A secondary aim, or perhaps wish, of this Lexicon is to assist in the much larger task, now energetically undertaken by members of the International Association for Neo-Latin Studies, of documenting and supplying reference tools for the vast literature of Neo-Latin, the dialect of Latin that developed, loosely speaking, out of the Renaissance, and was furthered by the scientific revolution.

In addition to circulating the Lexicon, the Swedenborg Society also provided for its improvement by allowing the General Church of the New Jerusalem and its educational arm, the Academy of the New Church, to scan the Lexicon into machine-readable form for the purposes of developing NeoSearch, search and morphological analysis software for Swedenborg's theological corpus.

As it turned out, this act of generosity eventually brought an ample reward back to the Lexicon itself.

Chadwick's material served as a basis for teaching the computer Latin, so to speak. The Lexicon's lemmas were culled and broken apart to form stem- and ending-sets. The resulting search software allowed for some 1,800 substantial improvements to be made to the Lexicon: it found over 450 new entries to be added to the Lexicon itself; over 500 changes that needed to be made in declension, principal parts, gender, and so on, to entries already in the Lexicon; and 850 proper nouns and adjectives to be placed in an appendix.

For instance, Chadwick had given ***fulcio*** and ***fulgeo*** their classical principal parts of ***fulcio*** *fulcire fulsi fultum* and ***fulgeo*** *fulgere fulsi*; he noted in a cross reference that *fulsi* could therefore be from either verb. When the computer found the strings *fulcivi* and *fulcivit* and was unable to place them, an investigation showed that Swedenborg actually never used *fulsi* as the perfect of

fulcio; he consistently used the non-classical form *fulcivi* as its perfect instead, and therefore *fulsi* in his Latin always comes from ***fulgeo***.

The computer was not the only form of assistance. In accordance with Chadwick's wishes, slips of paper and later on e-mails kept coming in over the years from scholars from various parts of the world. They supplied another 50 new entries and more than 150 changes that lay beyond the computer's vigilance. Since the cut-off point for this edition some time ago, information has been accumulating for another edition. To reiterate, we invite and appreciate your input. Although it has been a blessing to be able to further Chadwick's work and bring it quite a bit closer to being exhaustive, it is nevertheless striking that the second edition team has been able to add only ten per cent to what Chadwick and his first edition team achieved.

Content of entries

Each article consists of:

1. The lemma or headword in boldface type.
2. An indication of its inflectional type. This is normally the genitive of substantives, the feminine and neuter nominative of adjectives (unless both of these forms are the same as the masculine, when the genitive is given instead); the infinitive, perfect active, and supine (if any) of verbs, with appropriate forms for deponent verbs. These are generally abbreviated, as is also the word when it appears in quotations, by a swung dash representing the unchanging part of the stem (see below pages xvii-xx). Because Swedenborg's Latin morphology is not identical to that of classical Latin, I have included on pages xxi-xxxv below a list of all sets of substantival endings that occur more than once in Swedenborg's theological Latin.
3. An abbreviation specifying the part of speech (*a.* = adjective, *adv.* = adverb, and so on), the gender of a substantive (*m.* = masculine, *f.* = feminine, *neut.* = neuter), and in the case of verbs, whether it is transitive (*tr.*) or intransitive (*intr.*).
4. Its derivation, if any, from other entries in the Lexicon (pf. pple. of **compono**) or from other languages, mainly Hebrew (Hebr.) and Greek (Gk.).
5. Alternative spellings of the lemma, if any (e.g., **lachryma** also **lacrima**). In the main text of the Lexicon the alternative spellings have the same declension as the lemma unless otherwise noted. In the section Proper Nouns, however, information about the declension of alternative spellings is generally given even if it matches the lemma, since in many cases the declension would not otherwise be obvious.

6. Alternative or unusual forms, if any (pf. act. also *~sidi*), including in the case of adjectives and adverbs the comparative and superlative.
7. The meaning or meanings, distinguished by boldface arabic numerals for major divisions and letters of the alphabet for minor ones. Where necessary, the first part of the definition is intended to be a precise statement of the meaning, and is followed by possible translation equivalents. Although one could often increase the number of meanings by analysing in more detail, the aim has been to present enough information without trying to imitate the precision of the largest dictionaries.
8. For each meaning one or more references to Swedenborg's theological writings, and wherever helpful and informative a short quotation. These quotations are frequently abbreviated by the omission of words not directly relevant to the sense; the user is advised to consult the whole passage when in doubt. In a few cases the quotation, or part of it, is translated, where it might otherwise be obscure, especially to students. The references use the abbreviations given below, pages xliii-xliv. The numbers following the abbreviations are section numbers, not page numbers. (In his published theological works, Swedenborg invariably used sequential arabic numerals for the sections of his work, which are therefore uniform in all editions. In the case of the theological works Swedenborg did not publish, however, different editors have sometimes introduced different numbering systems; for more on this, see Appendix II.) If in this Lexicon the number is followed by a full stop and another number, the number after the full stop indicates a subsection. (For more on this referencing system and its abbreviations, see below in Chadwick's Preface, pages xli-xlii)

In the alphabetical sequence of the Lexicon, hyphens or spaces in the headword or words have been treated as non-existent. For example, the sequence is ***Baal***, ***Baal-Hanan***, ***Baalhazor***, ***Baalpeor***, ***Baal-Zephon***.

This Lexicon is based on multiple editions of Swedenborg's Latin texts. It aims to be inclusive so that readers who discover a form in a second or third edition can find it in this Lexicon, even if that form never occurs in a first edition. Some of these forms, therefore, are not well-attested Neo-Latin but simply the best guess of a more recent editor. Although a great deal of checking and care has gone into these quotations, I too, like Chadwick, have not been able to compare all the quotations in all editions.

Changes have been made to the punctuation in quotations for the sake of consistency and ease of reading in a lexical format. These changes have not been noted. Any additions or omissions to the wording are however indicated. Additions are noted with brackets [sc. *amoris*] and omissions are represented by ellipses (. . .).

The abbreviations of Swedenborg's titles have been based on the Latin titles (see the table of abbreviations). For the biblical quotations, however, because there are significant differences between

English and Latin Bibles in the naming and versification of books, it seemed best to keep to English abbreviations and versification, as they are presumably more accessible to students and scholars. A deviation from this versification policy occurs in references to Exodus, chapters 7-8, in *Arcana Coelestia*, where the nature of Swedenborg's text dictates that we follow him (and the majority of his editors and translators) in giving the Latin versification.

Although the proper nouns and adjectives in the Lexicon are not always labelled as to their origin, it is safe to assume that most of them were not originally Latin, but were borrowed and Latinized.

The particles and 'little words' are perhaps the weakest part of this Lexicon. Much further study is needed on words like ***enim*** and ***etiam***. The meanings and roles assigned to them by this Lexicon do not work for all contexts in which they appear, but the exact nuances they do convey have not been properly researched and documented yet.

Differences between the first and second editions

Since some aspects of the first edition, introduced by Chadwick's original Preface which is reproduced below, are no longer in place, it seems useful to list and briefly explain those changes.

1. *Proper nouns are now thoroughly represented.* Chadwick makes it clear on page xxxix below that his first edition did not aim for anything like thoroughness in its inclusion of proper nouns, especially in the case of biblical names that occur infrequently, and easily recognizable contemporary names. This decision has been reversed for the second edition, largely because computers have reduced some of the tedium and brought a thorough accounting of alternate spellings within reach. This material not only makes Swedenborg's intended meaning that much more available to the reader and lets the reader know who is who when there is more than one person with the same name, but also provides a fascinating insight into the struggle Swedenborg and his contemporaries faced to transliterate Hebrew words using the Roman alphabet, a struggle that has a parallel in English even up to the present day. (As of this writing, there is still no fixed and universally agreed upon method of transcribing Hebrew into English.)
2. *Accents in lemmas have been removed.* Chadwick's first edition was unusual among Latin dictionaries and lexicons for including *accents* on the lemmas. They were offered, of course, as a guide to pronunciation. The practice of classical Latin dictionaries in this regard has generally been to give an indication instead of the *length* of all the vowels, wherever those vowels may occur in the word, as an aid primarily in the scanning of poetry, but also as a

guide to pronunciation, and occasionally as a method of distinguishing two otherwise identical words. The user of those volumes could derive the accented syllable of each word from the vowel lengths. In this edition, however, we have elected to present neither accents nor syllable lengths. Swedenborg's theological works contain no poetry per se and were left in written form and distributed to readers all over Europe, where there were four markedly different, in some ways even incompatible, general approaches to Latin pronunciation, with further national and regional variations. The many loanwords from other languages, especially Hebrew, supplied a further complication. It is not known, and is difficult to reconstruct, exactly how Swedenborg pronounced the Latin he wrote; we do know that if a nobleman in England, a scientist in Germany, and a cleric in Spain read his works out loud, they will have done so in strikingly different ways. Since pronunciation was not a significant factor in the original communication of Swedenborg's theology, indications of pronunciation have been omitted as non-essential in this second edition of the Lexicon.

3. *Appendices have been added.* The fact that the proper nouns were likely to be less often consulted, and that they were of greater abundance in this edition, recommended that we place in a separate section all but the most crucial and most frequently occurring. Other appendices have been added to show the various editions of Swedenborg's works referenced herein, to note differences in numbering between some of those editions, to elucidate the reason for the dotted ḥ in some words, and to provide some background information on the Latin Bible of Sebastian Schmidt that Swedenborg often consulted.
4. *English abbreviations of titles have been replaced with Latin abbreviations.* In the first edition of the Lexicon, abbreviations for the titles of Swedenborg's works were based on their common English short titles, since these would be familiar to most readers. As we prepared the Lexicon for wider publication, however, it struck us as inconsistent in a Lexicon otherwise based on the original Latin to identify Swedenborg's works using abbreviations of English titles; therefore abbreviations based on the original Latin titles have been adopted instead.
5. *Priority and popularity of first edition spellings.* Although this Lexicon has been based on multiple editions of Swedenborg's works, we have followed John Chadwick's wishes, and further striven in the preparation of this second edition of the Lexicon, to give priority to the spellings printed in Swedenborg's first editions (for the published works) and written in the manuscripts (for the posthumously published works). Where more than one spelling is used by Swedenborg across the first editions, priority is given to the more common spelling, and this will be the headword. Alternative spellings are listed in alphabetical order after the headword (disregarding whether they come from first or later editions).

Nevertheless, we decided not to delete or alter anything in Chadwick's Preface to the First Edition. We have preserved it as it originally was, both as an important part of the history of this volume and as an acknowledgement of his immense contribution to the project as a whole.

The swung dash (~) and how to determine the letters it stands for

In the mimeographed original version of the Lexicon, Chadwick followed the standard Latin lexicographical practice of saving space by using a line to indicate whatever portion of a given headword remained unchanged. Since his was a typescript, he used a hyphen. For publication he intended to use the swung dash (~) instead. He also followed the standard Latin lexicographical approach to the use of the swung dash.

Although paper is not as expensive at it was centuries ago, the swung dash is still useful for saving space; and it also serves in a quotation to make the word that is the subject of the entry easy to find.

As mentioned above, Chadwick's Lexicon was scanned into the computer and analysed for the purposes of building NeoSearch morphological analysis software. In the process, the fact that the computer was unable to analyse certain forms made me realize that the traditional use of swung dashes is inconsistent and even somewhat illogical. As I will argue just below, correctly interpreting which letters the swung dash represents in forms such as ***ars*** *~tis*, ***icio*** *~ere*, ***nux*** *~cis*, ***praeceps*** *~ipitis*, and ***sapio*** *~ere ~ui* requires prior knowledge of Latin, which seems less than ideal in a work that may be used by students and beginners. Now that Latin is no longer as widely known as it was in centuries past, a more consistent approach to the swung dash seems desirable.

To illustrate the problem with the standard approach, how is someone with little knowledge of Latin to determine which letters the swung dash in ***ars*** *~tis* stands for? With third declension forms like this it is of course especially important to be able to tell, because the genitive, not the nominative, yields the stem on which all other endings are placed. Does the swung dash in this case imply that the genitive singular is *arstis*, *artis*, or *atis*? If one guesses or learns from elsewhere that the correct answer is *artis* and one presumes that the swung dash in other cases represents everything up to but not including the final letter of the headword, then one would correctly divine that the swung dash in ***nux*** *~cis* leads to a genitive singular of *nucis*, but one would incorrectly divine ***praeceps*** *~ipitis* to mean a genitive singular of *praecepipitis*. Similarly, if one has no prior knowledge of the Latin word ***icio***, how does one guess whether the swung dash in ***icio*** *~ere* represents *ic* or *ici*? The traditional approach is not as valuable as it could be if one has to already know the Latin word one is looking up in order to answer these questions.

In this Lexicon we have reduced the many inconsistent and seldom explained rules of the traditional approach to two universal rules, one for vowels and one for consonants.

How to reconstruct what a swung dash stands for in this Lexicon

To take the information in the Lexicon and reconstruct the unchanging element at the beginning of the form—the portion represented by the swung dash—one needs first to see if the portion after the first swung dash in a given entry begins with a **vowel** or a **consonant**.

amo ~**a**re ~avi ~atum	*vowel*
beatitudo ~**i**nis	*vowel*
bombyx ~**y**cis	*vowel*
cometes ~**a**e	*vowel*
invehor ~**h**i ~ctus sum	*consonant*
jubilaeus ~**a** ~um	*vowel*
lego ~**g**ere ~gi ~ctum	*consonant*
praeceps ~**i**pitis	*vowel*
pulcher ~**c**hra ~chrum	*consonant*
redigo ~**d**igere ~degi ~dactum	*consonant*
rumor ~**o**ris	*vowel*
sapio ~**p**ere ~pui	*consonant*
supellex ~**e**ctilis	*vowel*

If the portion after the first swung dash begins with a **vowel** (a, e, i, o, u, y), the part of the headword that does not change goes up to but does not include **the last vowel in the headword**, regardless of whether it is the same vowel as the one that begins the latter portion of the form or not.

am**o** ~are ~avi ~atum
beatitud**o** ~inis
bomb**yx** ~ycis
comet**es** ~ae
jubilae**us** ~a ~um
praec**eps** ~ipitis
rum**or** ~oris
supell**ex** ~ectilis

In effect, you cut off the last syllable of the headword beginning with its final vowel.

<table>
<tr><td>amo ~are ~avi ~atum</td><td>am|o</td></tr>
<tr><td>beatitudo ~inis</td><td>beatitud|o</td></tr>
<tr><td>bombyx ~ycis</td><td>bomb|yx</td></tr>
<tr><td>cometes ~ae</td><td>comet|es</td></tr>
<tr><td>jubilaeus ~a ~um</td><td>jubilae|us</td></tr>
<tr><td>praeceps ~ipitis</td><td>praec|eps</td></tr>
<tr><td>rumor ~oris</td><td>rum|or</td></tr>
<tr><td>supellex ~ectilis</td><td>supell|ex</td></tr>
</table>

Then you take the remaining portion after any other swung dash in the entry—regardless of whether the number of syllables or even the vowel immediately after that swung dash differs—and add it to the first portion so derived.

<table>
<tr><td>amo ~are ~avi ~atum</td><td>am|o am|are am|avi am|atum</td></tr>
<tr><td>beatitudo ~inis</td><td>beatitud|o beatitud|inis</td></tr>
<tr><td>bombyx ~ycis</td><td>bomb|yx bomb|ycis</td></tr>
<tr><td>cometes ~ae</td><td>comet|es comet|ae</td></tr>
<tr><td>praeceps ~ipitis</td><td>praec|eps praec|ipitis</td></tr>
<tr><td>rumor ~oris</td><td>rum|or rum|oris</td></tr>
<tr><td>supellex ~ectilis</td><td>supell|ex supell|ectilis</td></tr>
</table>

From then on in that entry, any swung dash consistently represents that same first portion of the headword. In the case of ***supellex***, for instance, *~ectilia* in a quotation would stand for *supellectilia*.

If on the other hand the portion after the first swung dash begins with a **consonant**, the part of the headword that does not change goes up to but does not include **the last instance of that same consonant in the headword**.

inve**h**or ~**h**i ~ctus sum
le**g**o ~**g**ere ~gi ~ctum
pul**c**her ~**c**hra ~chrum
re**d**igo ~**d**igere ~degi ~dactum
sa**p**io ~**p**ere ~pui

In effect, you cut off a portion of the headword starting at the point just before this consonant.

<table>
<tr><td>lego ~gere ~gi ~ctum</td><td>le|go</td></tr>
<tr><td>invehor ~hi ~ctus sum</td><td>inve|hor</td></tr>
<tr><td>pulcher ~chra ~chrum</td><td>pul|cher</td></tr>
<tr><td>redigo ~digere ~degi ~dactum</td><td>re|digo</td></tr>
<tr><td>sapio ~pere ~pui</td><td>sa|pio</td></tr>
</table>

Again, you take the remaining portion after any other swung dash in the entry—regardless of whether the number of syllables or even the consonant immediately after that swung dash differs—and add it to the first portion so derived.

<table>
<tr><td>lego ~gere ~gi ~ctum</td><td>le|go le|gere le|gi le|ctum</td></tr>
<tr><td>invehor ~hi ~ctus sum</td><td>inve|hor inve|hi inve|ctus sum</td></tr>
<tr><td>pulcher ~chra ~chrum</td><td>pul|cher pul|chra pul|chrum</td></tr>
<tr><td>redigo ~digere ~degi ~dactum</td><td>re|digo re|digere re|degi re|dactum</td></tr>
<tr><td>sapio ~pere ~pui</td><td>sa|pio sa|pere sa|pui</td></tr>
</table>

From then on in that entry, any swung dash consistently represents that same first portion of the headword. In the case of ***invehor***, for example, *~cti* in a quotation would stand for *invecti*.

Please note, however, that to talk of these as 'stems' and 'endings' is not at all appropriate: ***rumpo*** *~mpere ~pi ~ptum* stands for ***rumpo*** *rumpere rupi ruptum*; but in no sense is *ru-* here a Latin stem or *-mpere* a Latin ending.

There is such a thing as an unchanging portion that is too short to be replaced by a swung dash. To serve any purpose the swung dash needs to replace two or more letters. For example, irregular verbs such as ***eo*** *ire ivi itum* cannot be served by a swung dash in this system; and in words such as ***dux*** *ducis*, the swung dash would replace only one letter. In such cases, all forms are spelled out in full.

Even if the headword is indeclinable, a swung dash is still used in its quotations. I have generally followed Chadwick's lead in using the final syllable, or sometimes the final letter if it is a consonant, as the material after the swung dash. Since the whole word is clearly spelled out in the headword, there is no difficulty in reconstructing the form.

A morphology of Swedenborg's Neo-Latin

By the time Swedenborg used it to write theology, the Latin language had been in existence for many centuries. Although his Neo-Latin has a morphology that is generally the same as that of classical Latin, it exhibits a sufficient number of changes to warrant clearly spelling out the endings implied in this Lexicon. (Since the morphology of the Latin verbs used in Swedenborg's theological works is largely identical with that of classical Latin verbs, it has not been covered exhaustively here; but two minor departures from classical practice have been noted. A full description of Swedenborg's Latin syntax is not attempted, but two key points are briefly covered.) For the meaning of the swung dash (~) in this Introduction and throughout the Lexicon, see the section just above.

1. Nouns

1.1 *First Declension*

1.1.1 First Declension f. regular (some m. words)

e.g.: **adhaerentia** ~ae, *f.* **advena** ~ae, *m.* **idea** ~ae, *f.* **inertia** ~ae, *f.*

	nom.	-a		nom.	-ae
	gen.	-ae		gen.	-arum
sg.	dat.	-ae	pl.	dat.	-is
	acc.	-am		acc.	-as
	abl.	-a		abl.	-is

1.1.2 First Declension f. irregular (abl. pl. -*abus*)

The only such forms in Swedenborg's theological works are **anima** ~ae, *f.* **asina** ~ae, *m.* **dea** ~ae, *f.* and **filia** ~ae, *f.*

	nom.	-a		nom.	-ae
	gen.	-ae		gen.	-arum
sg.	dat.	-ae	pl.	dat.	-abus
	acc.	-am		acc.	-as
	abl.	-a		abl.	-abus

1.1.3 First Declension f. Gk. I

e.g.: **anatome** ~es, *f.* **chymice** ~es, *f.* **ode** ~es, *f.* **systole** ~es, *f.*

	nom.	-e		nom.	-ae
	gen.	-es		gen.	-arum
sg.	dat.	-ae	pl.	dat.	-is

	acc. -en		acc.	-as
	abl. -e		abl.	-is

1.1.4 First Declension m. Gk. II

e.g.: **Andreas** ~ae, *m.* **Elias** ~ae, *m.* **Messias** ~ae, *m.* **Pythagoras** ~ae, *m.*

	nom.-as		nom.	—
	gen. -ae		gen.	—
sg.	dat. -ae	pl.	dat.	—
	acc. -am		acc.	—
	abl. -a		abl.	—

1.1.5 First Declension m. Gk. III (some f. words)

e.g.: **cometes** ~ae, *m.* **dynastes** ~ae, *m.* **geometres** ~ae, *m.* **selenites** ~ae, *f.*

	nom.-es		nom.	-ae
	gen. -ae		gen.	-arum
sg.	dat. -ae	pl.	dat.	-is
	acc. -am		acc.	-as
	abl. -a		abl.	-is

1.1.6 First Declension m./f. Hebr. I

e.g.: **gerah** ~ae, *m.* **Jehovah** ~ae, *m.* **minchah** ~ae, *f.* **Silpah** ~ae, *f.*

	nom.-ah/-a		nom.	-ae
	gen. -ae		gen.	-arum
sg.	dat. -ae	pl.	dat.	-is
	acc. -am		acc.	-as
	abl. -ah/-a		abl.	-is

1.1.7 Heteroclite m. Hebr./Gk. I

e.g.: **Moscheh** ~is, *m.* (**Moscheh** varies between first and third declensions. Although it is a law unto itself, it is included here because of its sheer frequency of occurrence. The third Latin edn. of AC occasionally implies a declension of proper nouns in *-eh -es*, which is unattested by the first editions. Examples include **Niniveh** ~es, *m.* and **Rabshakeh** ~es, *m.* The declension of such nouns in the third Latin edn. of AC differs from the first edn. only in having a nom. sg. in *-eh* rather than *-e*; in other respects, in both editions they take the endings listed in 1.1.3 above.)

	nom.-eh		nom.	—
	gen. -is		gen.	—
sg.	dat. -i	pl.	dat.	—

	acc. -en		acc. —
	abl. -e/eh		abl. —

1.2 *Second Declension*

1.2.1 Second Declension m. regular (some f. words)

e.g.: **mundus** ~i, *m.* **oceanus** ~i, *m.* **paragraphus** ~i, *f.*

	nom.-us		nom.-i
	gen. -i		gen. -orum
sg.	dat. -o	pl.	dat. -is
	acc. -um		acc. -os
	abl. -o		abl. -is

1.2.2 Second Declension m. with anomalous nom. sg.

e.g.: **aper** apri, *m.* **hexameter** ~tri, *m.* **Lamech** ~chi, *m.* **puer** ~eri, *m.*

	nom.—		nom.-i
	gen. -i		gen. -orum
sg.	dat. -o	pl.	dat. -is
	acc. -um		acc. -os
	abl. -o		abl. -is

1.2.3 Second Declension neut. regular

e.g.: **lucrum** ~i, *neut.* **malum** ~i, *neut.* **microscopium** ~i, *neut.* **pendulum** ~i, *neut.*

	nom.-um		nom.-a
	gen. -i		gen. -orum
sg.	dat. -o	pl.	dat. -is
	acc. -um		acc. -a
	abl. -o		abl. -is

1.2.4 Second Declension neut. Gk.

e.g.: **analogon** ~i, *neut.* **phaenomenon** ~i, *neut.* **sceleton** ~i, *neut.*

	nom.-on		nom.-a
	gen. -i		gen. -orum
sg.	dat. -o	pl.	dat. -is
	acc. -on		acc. -a
	abl. -o		abl. -is

1.3 *Third Declension*

1.3.1 Third Declension m./f. regular non i-stem with anomalous nom. sg.

e.g.: **gigas** ~antis, *m.* **helix** ~icis, *f.* **Laban** ~anis, *m.* **nux** nucis, *f.*

	nom.	—		nom.	-es
	gen.	-is		gen.	-um
sg.	dat.	-i	pl.	dat.	-ibus
	acc.	-em		acc.	-es
	abl.	-e		abl.	-ibus

1.3.2 Third Declension f. regular non i-stem in *-as* (some m. words)

e.g.: **charitas** ~atis, *f.* **cupiditas** ~atis, *f.* **primas** ~atis, *m.* **serenitas** ~atis, *f.*

	nom.	-as		nom.	-ates
	gen.	-atis		gen.	-atum
sg.	dat.	-ati	pl.	dat.	-atibus
	acc.	-atem		acc.	-ates
	abl.	-ate		abl.	-atibus

1.3.3 Third Declension f. regular non i-stem in *-do* (some m. words)

e.g.: **albedo** ~inis, *f.* **ordo** ~inis, *m.* **similitudo** ~inis, *f.* **tendo** ~inis, *f.*

	nom.	-o		nom.	-ines
	gen.	-inis		gen.	-inum
sg.	dat.	-ini	pl.	dat.	-inibus
	acc.	-inem		acc.	-ines
	abl.	-ine		abl.	-inibus

1.3.4 Third Declension f. regular non i-stem in *-o* (some m. words)

e.g.: **actio** ~onis, *f.* **bubo** ~onis, *m.* **ostensio** ~onis, *f.* **papilio** ~onis, *m.*

	nom.	-o		nom.	-ones
	gen.	-onis		gen.	-onum
sg.	dat.	-oni	pl.	dat.	-onibus
	acc.	-onem		acc.	-ones
	abl.	-one		abl.	-onibus

1.3.5 Third Declension m. regular non i-stem in *-or*

e.g.: **fulgor** ~oris, *m.* **labor** ~oris, *m.* **moderator** ~oris, *m.* **rumor** ~oris, *m.*

	nom.	-or		nom.	-ores
	gen.	-oris		gen.	-orum
sg.	dat.	-ori	pl.	dat.	-oribus

	acc. -orem		acc. -ores
	abl. -ore		abl. -oribus

1.3.6 Third Declension m. parisyllabic non i-stem in ***-is*** *~is* (some f. words)

The only such forms are **apis** ~is, *m.* **canis** ~is, *m.* **juvenis** ~is, *m.* **neptis** ~is, *f.* **panis** ~is, *m.* and **proneptis** ~is, *f.*

	nom.-is		nom.-es
	gen. -is		gen. -um
sg.	dat. -i	pl.	dat. -ibus
	acc. -em		acc. -es
	abl. -e		abl. -ibus

1.3.7 Third Declension m./f. regular mixed i-stem with anomalous nom. sg.

e.g.: **ars** artis, *f.* **dens** dentis, *m.* **lis** litis, *f.* **sal** ~lis, *m.*

	nom.—		nom.-es
	gen. -is		gen. -ium
sg.	dat. -i	pl.	dat. -ibus
	acc. -em		acc. -es
	abl. -e		abl. -ibus

1.3.8 Third Declension m./f. parisyllabic mixed i-stem in ***-is*** *~is*

e.g.: **finis** ~is, *m.* **orbis** ~is, *m.* **ovis** ~is, *f.* **phrasis** ~is, *f.*

	nom.-is		nom.-es
	gen. -is		gen. -ium
sg.	dat. -i	pl.	dat. -ibus
	acc. -em		acc. -es
	abl. -e		abl. -ibus

1.3.9 Third Declension f. parisyllabic mixed i-stem in ***-es*** *~is* (some m. words)

e.g.: **aedes** ~is, *f.* **fames** ~is, *f.* **Johannes** ~is, *m.* **sedes** ~is, *f.*

	nom.-es		nom.-es
	gen. -is		gen. -ium
sg.	dat. -i	pl.	dat. -ibus
	acc. -em		acc. -es
	abl. -e		abl. -ibus

1.3.10 Third Declension f. parisyllabic pure i-stem in ***-is*** *~is*

The purest examples are **pelvis** ~is, *f.* **securis** ~is, *f.* **sitis** ~is, *f.* and **turris** ~is, *f.* (**cidaris** ~is, *f.* and

cutis ~is, *f.* take these but also other forms. Note that even the purest third declension i-stem forms have -*es*, never -*is*, in nom. and acc. pl.)

	sg.		pl.
	nom.-is		nom.-es
	gen. -is		gen. -ium
sg.	dat. -i	pl.	dat. -ibus
	acc. -im		acc. -es
	abl. -i		abl. -ibus

1.3.11 Third Declension f. Gk. i-stem in ***-is*** *~eos*

e.g.: **Apocalypsis** ~eos, *f.* **Genesis** ~eos, *f.* **haeresis** ~eos, *f.* **hypocrisis** ~eos, *f.* (**basis** ~eos is irreg. for occasionally having -*is* in gen. sg.)

	sg.		pl.
	nom.-is		nom.-es
	gen. -eos		gen. -ium
sg.	dat. -i	pl.	dat. -ibus
	acc. -in		acc. -es
	abl. -i		abl. -ibus

1.3.12 Third Declension m./f. i-stem with pl. forms only

e.g.: **fides** ~ium, *f.* pl. **fores** ~ium, *f. pl.* **Hamburgenses** ~ium, *m. pl.* **nates** ~ium, *m. pl.*

	sg.		pl.
	nom.—		nom.-es
	gen. —		gen. -ium
sg.	dat. —	pl.	dat. -ibus
	acc. —		acc. -es
	abl. —		abl. -ibus

1.3.13 Third Declension neut. non i-stem with anomalous nom./acc. sg.

e.g.: **idioma** ~atis, *neut.* **jus** juris, *neut.* **latus** ~eris, *neut.* **mel** mellis, *neut.*

	sg.		pl.
	nom.—		nom.-a
	gen. -is		gen. -um
sg.	dat. -i	pl.	dat. -ibus
	acc. —		acc. -a
	abl. -e		abl. -ibus

1.3.14 Third Declension neut. non i-stem in ***-en*** *~inis*

e.g.: **agmen** ~inis, *neut.* **inguen** ~inis, *neut.* **nomen** ~inis, *neut.* **tutamen** ~inis, *neut.*

	sg.		pl.
	nom.-en		nom.-ina
	gen. -inis		gen. -inum
sg.	dat. -ini	pl.	dat. -inibus

	acc. -en		acc. -ina
	abl. -ine		abl. -inibus

1.3.15 Third Declension neut. mixed i-stem with anomalous nom./acc. sg.

The only such forms are **cor** cordis, *neut.* **os** oris, *neut.* and **os** ossis, *neut.*

	nom.—		nom.-a
	gen. -is		gen. -ium
sg.	dat. -i	pl.	dat. -ibus
	acc. —		acc. -a
	abl. -e		abl. -ibus

1.3.16 Third Declension neut. pure i-stem with anomalous nom./acc. sg.

The only such forms are **par** paris, *neut.* and **supellex** ~ectilis, *neut.*

	nom.—		nom.-ia
	gen. -is		gen. -ium
sg.	dat. -i	pl.	dat. -ibus
	acc. —		acc. -ia
	abl. -i		abl. -ibus

1.3.17 Third Declension neut. pure i-stem in ***-e*** *~is*

e.g.: **altare** ~is, *neut.* **conclave** ~is, *neut.* **mare** ~is, *neut.* **ovile** ~is, *neut.*

	nom.-e		nom.-ia
	gen. -is		gen. -ium
sg.	dat. -i	pl.	dat. -ibus
	acc. -e		acc. -ia
	abl. -i		abl. -ibus

1.3.18 Third Declension neut. pure i-stem in ***-al*** *-alis*

e.g.: **animal** ~lis, *neut.* **cervical** ~lis, *neut.* **tribunal** ~lis, *neut.* **vectigal** ~lis, *neut.*

	nom.-al		nom.-alia
	gen. -alis		gen. -alium
sg.	dat. -ali	pl.	dat. -alibus
	acc. -al		acc. -alia
	abl. -ali		abl. -alibus

1.3.19 Third Declension neut. pure i-stem in ***-ar*** *~aris*

e.g.: **exemplar** ~aris, *neut.* **lacunar** ~aris, *neut.* **pulvinar** ~aris, *neut.* **torcular** ~aris, *neut.*

	nom.-ar		nom.-aria
	gen. -aris		gen. -arium

sg.	dat.	-ari	pl.	dat.	-aribus
	acc.	-ar		acc.	-aria
	abl.	-ari		abl.	-aribus

1.4 *Fourth Declension*

1.4.1 Fourth Declension m. (some f. words)

e.g.: **caetus** ~us, *m.* **influxus** ~us, *m.* **quercus** ~us, *f.* **reditus** ~us, *m.*

	nom.	-us		nom.	-us
	gen.	-us		gen.	-uum
sg.	dat.	-ui	pl.	dat.	-ubus/-ibus
	acc.	-um		acc.	-us
	abl.	-u		abl.	-ubus/-ibus

1.4.2 Fourth Declension neut.

e.g.: **cornu** ~u, *neut.* **gelu** ~u, *neut.* **genu** ~u, *neut.* **penu** ~u, *neut.* (**tonitru** often has irregular gen. sg. *-ui*. Note that the gen. sg. is *-u*, not *-us*. In Swedenborg's day the fourth declension neuter was considered indeclinable in the singular.)

	nom.	-u		nom.	-ua
	gen.	-u		gen.	-uum
sg.	dat.	-u	pl.	dat.	-ubus/-ibus
	acc.	-u		acc.	-ua
	abl.	-u		abl.	-ubus/-ibus

1.5 *Fifth Declension*

1.5.1 Fifth Declension f. (one word that is usually m.)

e.g.: **astuties** ~ei, *f.* **dies** ~ei, *m.* or *f.* **facies** ~ei, *f.* **pernicies** ~ei, *f.*

	nom.	-es		nom.	-es
	gen.	-ei		gen.	-erum
sg.	dat.	-ei	pl.	dat.	-ebus
	acc.	-em		acc.	-es
	abl.	-e		abl.	-ebus

2. Adjectives and participles

2.1 *First and Second Declension Adjectives and Participles*

2.1.1 First and Second Declension regular adjectives and participles

e.g.: **faciendus** ~a ~um (from *facio*), **perpetuus** ~a ~um, **respectivus** ~a ~um, **separatus** ~a ~um

		m.	f.	neut.
	nom.	-us	-a	-um
	gen.	-i	-ae	-i
sg.	dat.	-o	-ae	-o
	acc.	-um	-am	-um
	abl.	-o	-a	-o
	nom.	-i	-ae	-a
	gen.	-orum	-arum	-orum
pl.	dat.	-is	-is	-is
	acc.	-os	-as	-a
	abl.	-is	-is	-is

2.1.2 First and Second Declension regular adjectives with anomalous m. nom. sg.

e.g.: **aeger** ~gra ~grum, **miser** ~era ~erum, **pulcher** ~chra ~chrum, **stellifer** ~era ~erum

		m.	f.	neut.
	nom.	—	-a	-um
	gen.	-i	-ae	-i
sg.	dat.	-o	-ae	-o
	acc.	-um	-am	-um
	abl.	-o	-a	-o
	nom.	-i	-ae	-a
	gen.	-orum	-arum	-orum
pl.	dat.	-is	-is	-is
	acc.	-os	-as	-a
	abl.	-is	-is	-is

2.1.3 First and Second Declension irregular adjectives

The only such forms are **nullus** ~a ~um, **solus** ~a ~um, **totus** ~a ~um, **ullus** ~a ~um, and **unus** ~a ~um

		m.	f.	neut.
	nom.	-us	-a	-um
	gen.	-ius	-ius	-ius
sg.	dat.	-i	-i	-i
	acc.	-um	-am	-um
	abl.	-o	-a	-o
	nom.	-i	-ae	-a
	gen.	-orum	-arum	-orum
pl.	dat.	-is	-is	-is
	acc.	-os	-as	-a
	abl.	-is	-is	-is

2.1.4 First and Second Declension irregular adjectives with anomalous m. nom. sg.

The only such forms are **alter** ~era ~erum, **neuter** ~tra ~trum, and **uter** utra utrum

		m.	f.	neut.
	nom.	—	-a	-um
	gen.	-ius	-ius	-ius
sg.	dat.	-i	-i	-i
	acc.	-um	-am	-um
	abl.	-o	-a	-o
	nom.	-i	-ae	-a
	gen.	-orum	-arum	-orum
pl.	dat.	-is	-is	-is
	acc.	-os	-as	-a
	abl.	-is	-is	-is

2.2 *Third Declension Adjectives*

2.2.1 The Third Declension three-termination pure i-stem adjectives with anomalous m. nom. sg. These have apparently all but ceased to be. The only partial one left in Swedenborg is ***acer*** *acris acre*, which also has *acris* as m. nom. sg. ***Acer*** occurs but twice, AM 363 and 374. *Acris* occurs once as m. nom sg: *humor acris, qui...* VR 665.4. Swedenborg gives no other classical three termination adjectives an *-er* m. nom. sg. form.

2.2.2 Third Declension two-termination non i-stem comparative adjectives and participles

e.g.: **anterior** ~or ~us, **beatior** ~or ~us (from *beatus*), **compositior** ~or ~us (from *compositus*), **eminentior** ~or ~us (from *eminens*). (The abl. sg. simply varies; *-i* and *-e* seem to be interchangeable. For example see AM 33 1st edn.)

		m.	f.	neut.
sg.	nom.	-ior	-ior	-ius
	gen.	-ioris	-ioris	-ioris
	dat.	-iori	-iori	-iori
	acc.	-iorem	-iorem	-ius
	abl.	-iori/-iore	-iori/-iore	-iori/-iore
pl.	nom.	-iores	-iores	-iora
	gen.	-iorum	-iorum	-iorum
	dat.	-ioribus	-ioribus	-ioribus
	acc.	-iores	-iores	-iora
	abl.	-ioribus	-ioribus	-ioribus

2.2.3 Third Declension two-termination pure i-stem adjectives

e.g.: **essentialis** ~is ~e, **forensis** ~is ~e, **habilis** ~is ~e, **immunis** ~is ~e

		m.	f.	neut.
sg.	nom.	-is	-is	-e
	gen.	-is	-is	-is
	dat.	-i	-i	-i
	acc.	-em	-em	-e
	abl.	-i	-i	-i
pl.	nom.	-es	-es	-ia
	gen.	-ium	-ium	-ium
	dat.	-ibus	-ibus	-ibus
	acc.	-es	-es	-ia
	abl.	-ibus	-ibus	-ibus

2.2.4 Third Declension one-termination non i-stem adjectives

The only such forms are **alipes** ~edis, **diversicolor** ~oris, **dives** ~itis, **ingens** ~ntis, **pauper** ~eris, and **vetus** ~eris. (In the abl. sg. **dives** and **pauper** always take an *-e*; **ingens** and **vetus** predominantly take *-i*, although *-e* also occurs.)

		m.	f.	neut.
sg.	nom.	—	—	—
	gen.	-is	-is	-is
	dat.	-i	-i	-i
	acc.	-em	-em	—
	abl.	-e/-i	-e/-i	-e/-i
pl.	nom.	-es	-es	-a
	gen.	-um	-um	-um
	dat.	-ibus	-ibus	-ibus
	acc.	-es	-es	-a
	abl.	-ibus	-ibus	-ibus

2.2.5 Third Declension one-termination mixed i-stem half-frozen[2] substantives

The only such forms are **adolescens** ~ntis, **infans** ~ntis, **parens** ~ntis, **potens** ~ntis, **sapiens** ~ntis, **serpens** ~ntis, and **suaviloquens** ~ntis. As for the abl. sg., *-e* occurs much more often than *-i* does; and for gen. pl. only **potens** and **sapiens** often use *-ium*, although they do so even in a substantival usage.

		m.	f.			m.	f.
sg.	nom.	-ns	-ns	pl.	nom.	-ntes	-ntes
	gen.	-ntis	-ntis		gen.	-ntum/-ntium	-ntum/-ntium
	dat.	-nti	-nti		dat.	-ntibus	-ntibus
	acc.	-ntem	-ntem		acc.	-ntes	-ntes
	abl.	-nte/-nti	-nte/-nti		abl.	-ntibus	-ntibus

2.2.6 Third Declension one-termination pure i-stem adjectives

e.g.: **anceps** ~ipitis, **atrox** ~ocis, **coelebs** ~ebis, **dispar** ~aris, **felix** ~icis, **hebes** ~etis

		m.	f.	neut.
sg.	nom.	—	—	—
	gen.	-is	-is	-is
	dat.	-i	-i	-i
	acc.	-em	-em	—
	abl.	-i	-i	-i
	nom.	-es	-es	-ia
	gen.	-ium	-ium	-ium

pl.	dat. -ibus	-ibus	-ibus
	acc. -es	-es	-ia
	abl. -ibus	-ibus	-ibus

2.2.7 Third Declension one-termination pure i-stem pres. participles and adjectives

e.g.: **amans** ~ntis, **inferens** ~ntis (from *infero*), **jacens** ~ntis (from *jaceo*), **livens** ~ntis

Most of these only have abl. sg. in *-e*; about one out of seven abl. sg. instances of **sequens** reads *sequenti*.

		m.	f.	neut.
	nom.	-ns	-ns	-ns
	gen.	-ntis	-ntis	-ntis
sg.	dat.	-nti	-nti	-nti
	acc.	-ntem	-ntem	-ns
	abl.	-nte(-nti)	-nte(-nti)	-nte(-nti)
	nom.	-ntes	-ntes	-ntia
	gen.	-ntium	-ntium	-ntium
pl.	dat.	-ntibus	-ntibus	-ntibus
	acc.	-ntes	-ntes	-ntia
	abl.	-ntibus	-ntibus	-ntibus

Any set of substantival endings that occurs more than once I have included here. Many interesting irregularities that occur with only one word I have omitted. These are noted below in the main text of the Lexicon.

3. Two notes on verbs

Swedenborg's verbs follow classical morphology exactly. Only two things need to be noted: contracted perfect and pluperfect forms; and the supine.

3.1 *Contracted Perfects and Pluperfects*

The first conjugation alone frequently contracts perfects and pluperfects. (There are only two occurrences of contracted perfects and pluperfects of other conjugations: **capesso** has *capesserint* once for *capessiverint* and **divido** has *divissent* once for *divisissent*.)

In effect the following endings are placed on the *present* stem. For example, the ordinary 2nd sg.

pf. act. ind. of **amo** would be *amavisti*; putting the ending below on the present stem (*am-*) results in the contracted form, *ama(vi)sti* or *amasti*. The same applies to all first conjugation verbs.

3.1.1 Perfect Active Indicative

	1st	—		1st	—
sg.	2nd	-asti	pl.	2nd	-astis
	3rd	—		3rd	-arunt

3.1.2 Perfect Active Subjunctive

	1st	—		1st	—
sg.	2nd	—	pl.	2nd	—
	3rd	—		3rd	-arint

3.1.3 Perfect Active Infinitive

-asse

3.1.4 Pluperfect Active Subjunctive

	1st	-assem		1st	-assemus
sg.	2nd	-asses	pl.	2nd	-assetis
	3rd	-asset		3rd	-assent

3.2 *The Supine*

My research on this point is not exhaustive, since the accusative form of the supine as a defective fourth declension noun is identical with the pf. pple. My current findings are that Swedenborg never uses the accusative supine, and that the ablative supine occurs with only four adjectives and six verbs as follows. They occur in either possible word order and can be translated with a present participle or infinitive—'worth mentioning', 'necessary to know', 'amazing to observe', 'foul to hear'.

tetrum auditu (AC 5568)
dignum lectu (SE 81; VR 181)
dignum memoratu (25x with various endings on *dign-*)
dignum observatu (7x, once with *dignius*)
dignum relatu (AM 73.2)
dignum scitu (AM 73.2)
mirabile observatu (ES 1940)
necessarium scitu (DP 60)

An oddity is ES 761½'s *observatu memorandum* ('something that I/one ought to remember to observe'?).

4. Two notes on syntax

A thorough accounting of Neo-Latin syntax will not be attempted here; but two points seem essential for the user's comprehension of the quotations.

4.1 *Indirect Discourse*

In expressing indirect discourse, Swedenborg's theological Latin displays a strong preference for the conjunction **quod** with a verb in the subjunctive mood. Relatively rarely does he use the more classical form of an accusative with an infinitive.

4.2 *Ellipsis of the Verb To Be*

Swedenborg exceeds normal Latin usage and comes closer to imitating the Old Testament in the remarkable degree to which he omits the verb to be, and other verbs as well. Without this knowledge many of the quotations in this Lexicon would be difficult for readers to scan. Most common are relative clauses without verbs, such as *verum quod fidei* for *verum quod est fidei.*[3]

Acknowledgements

I am grateful to John Chadwick for seeing the need and having the vision for this Lexicon, initiating it, and doing the lion's share of the work, taking on both the tedium of gathering and assembling entries and the challenge of discerning just how the Latin words are being used and how to render them in accessible English. His mentoring has also meant a great deal to me personally. I am thankful to the Swedenborg Society as a whole for its long-standing commitment to the Lexicon; and specifically to the Rev. N Ryder, whose tremendous care and diligence in reading over the entries has benefited both editions of the Lexicon; to John Elliott, for bringing his wisdom and lifetime of working with Swedenborg's Latin publications, manuscripts, and Bibles to this edition; and to Stephen McNeilly and James Wilson, whose design, formatting, typesetting, and attention to detail have benefited this edition's every page.

I am also thankful to Gudmund Boolsen, Lisa Hyatt Cooper, George Dole, John Elliott, Kurt Nemitz, N Bruce Rogers, and Stuart Shotwell for sending in additions and corrections for this second edition; to Carolyn Andrews Cole, Anastasia Synnestvedt, and James Wilson for research and verification; and to Bjornar Larsen for computer programming for NeoSearch that in turn benefited the Lexicon. The generosity of the aforementioned General Church Translation Committee made my participation and that of Carolyn Andrews Cole and Anastasia Synnestvedt possible; and its support of the creation of NeoSearch turned out to be of benefit to the Lexicon as well. Mine is the responsibility for any problems or errors that remain.

Jonathan S Rose
Bryn Athyn, Pennsylvania
October 2007

1 Jonathan S Rose, 'Swedenborg's Garden of Theology: An Introduction to Swedenborg's Published Theological Works', in *Emanuel Swedenborg: Essays for the New Century Edition on His Life, Work, and Impact*, ed. Jonathan S Rose, Stuart Shotwell, and Mary Lou Bertucci (West Chester, PA: Swedenborg Foundation, 2005), p. 92.

2 By 'half-frozen' I mean that from their origin as adjectives or participles (which would take a gen. pl. ending of *-ium*) they seem part way solidified into nouns (which would take a gen. pl. ending of *-um*).

3 For statistics and more on both of these points, see Jonathan S Rose, 'Latin styles of Swedenborg and his contemporaries: early spadework', in *The New Philosophy*, vol. CI, nos. 3-4, July-December, 1998, pp. 247-302.

PREFACE TO THE FIRST EDITION

All who have ever set their hand to the task of translating Swedenborg's Latin, into whatever language, must have repeatedly regretted the absence of a guide to the vast vocabulary that he employs. It is not as if there were satisfactory dictionaries of seventeenth- or eighteenth-century Latin, to which we might add some notes on peculiar Swedenborgian uses of words. We have to use dictionaries devised for very different purposes and compiled from authors of other periods; for it goes without saying that no other Latin author deals in the same way with the same subject matter.

It therefore seemed to me that the best way to improve our translations would be to compile an exhaustive Lexicon of Swedenborg's Latin, and in this project I have been encouraged and supported, first over a long period of years by the Advisory and Revision Board of the Swedenborg Society, and latterly by interest shown in other countries. Indeed, the task has become so pressing that I do not think it is enough to continue merely to collect materials, it is time to put our materials to work, and to make from them not the complete and perfect work we should all like to see, but at least a first draft to which additions and corrections can be made, and which will in the meantime serve for some of the uses the work is intended to fulfil.

While the assistance of the translator is of course the chief aim, we must not forget the student. In these days when the study of classical Latin is diminishing, many who would study Swedenborg may come to him largely unprepared; and even those who have become familiar with the classical authors will sometimes find themselves puzzled and even misled by some of the words they find in the theological works of Emanuel Swedenborg. Thus this Lexicon is addressed simultaneously to two classes of user: the scholar and the student. We hope that the features included for the benefit of one will not impede the other.

By writing the definitions in English, we address ourselves primarily to speakers of that language, but with the consciousness that it is also the most widely known language in other parts of the world. It is therefore our hope that it may be of use to scholars and students all over the world, and thus contribute to the dissemination of the Writings to an ever greater public.

Acknowledgements

This work, imperfect as it is, would have been impossible to achieve so rapidly were it not for the labours of our predecessors. Above all, we must record a deep debt of gratitude to J F Potts, whose *The Swedenborg Concordance* contains at the end of the sixth volume a Vocabulary of Swedenborg's Latin made for the purposes of the Concordance. That it is incomplete and occasionally in error is no shame; it is a pioneering work which has vastly lightened the labours of all who come after. The other vocabularies that exist, especially that of W C Dick to *The True Christian Religion* and *Divine Providence*, have at times been consulted with profit; but their scope and purpose is so different that I have relied much more upon independent study of the material. Likewise translations have occasionally contributed helpful suggestions; but the aim of the lexicographer must be to use his own judgement on the material before him, not to compile an index of other people's judgments. If I differ occasionally from the opinions of my august predecessors, I am nonetheless in their debt, and I may have overlooked much in their work which might improve my own. This is not the result of arrogance, but simply of lack of time for the necessary research.

Other dictionaries which have been consulted include: *Oxford Latin Dictionary*; Lewis and Short's *Latin Dictionary*; *Thesaurus Linguae Latinae*; A Souter's *Glossary of Later Latin*; and Ducange's *Glossarium mediae atque infimae Latinitatis*.

The collection of material has been spread over a long period of time. The majority of the slips were laboriously written out by hand, and we must record here the great contributions made in this way by the late E C Mongredien. The labours of the Rev. N Ryder in supplying materials based on lists of desiderata must also be mentioned here. Other slips were made by cutting up proof sheets of the Third Latin Edition of *Arcana Caelestia*. But the latest contribution has come from the Literary and Linguistic Computing Centre of the University of Cambridge, where a whole volume was put on tape and a computer program devised by means of which a slip was printed for every different word form by the University computer. We are grateful to those who accepted and carried out this project, and to the Swedenborg Scientific Association and the Translation Committee of the General Church of the New Jerusalem, who made a grant in support of this work. It is hoped to extend the coverage of works by this project before the Lexicon is finished.

My greatest debt is to the Rev. N Ryder for the work he has put into checking and criticizing the preliminary draft. Dictionaries are not inspiring works to read through, but the care and patience which he has devoted to this irksome task have resulted in improvements and corrections on every page. He bears, however, no responsibility for the surviving blemishes. I should also like to thank Miss Madeline Waters, Secretary of the Swedenborg Society, for having undertaken the difficult task of typing this complicated text for reproduction.

Scope and limitations

It is possible to write a dictionary on any scale the lexicographer chooses, even though certain limits may be dictated by the material. All lexicography is in consequence a process of choice, the selection of the details judged to be most useful to the prospective users. This Lexicon is in no way exempt from this process; it could have been made considerably larger, it could have been shorter and less informative. We hope the choice made will render it useful without being unwieldy.

It aims to include every Latin word used by Swedenborg in his theological works, that is to say, from the time of the opening of his spiritual sight in 1745 to his death in 1772. The unpublished manuscripts he left are as valuable as sources as the books printed in the author's lifetime; indeed they are in some ways more authentic than the first editions, which were much at the mercy of the printer. Interesting and useful as it would have been to extend its purview to include the earlier works, this is a task which must be left to others.

It is not easy to decide what is a Latin word; as a rule, words of other languages are excluded, but in a few cases notes have been included; and the famous words of the 'spiritual' language are indexed. Proper names are more difficult. There seems no point in listing every historical character mentioned in these books, especially if the name appears in the customary form or with a Latin *~ius* ending. But where it might occasion doubt, it is included; and wherever an adjectival form is used it is indexed, since its form is then specifically Latin. However, large numbers of Hebrew and Greek names from the Bible have been omitted, since no further information on them is required for purposes of translation; though here too some discretion has been used, and names which have peculiar Latin forms are listed.

With these exceptions, our intention is to give every word, though of course inflected forms will be found under the customary headword; a number of cross references are included which may help the student, even if superfluous for the scholar. Adverbs are treated separately from the corresponding adjective. Perfect participles are given separate entries if they have become virtual adjectives, but here the line of division is often tenuous. Words and usages occurring in the Latin versions of the Scriptures quoted by Swedenborg are included, but where there is evidence that Swedenborg himself used them without allusion to a biblical passage, these references are preferred. The coverage of biblical Latin is probably inadequate.

It is inevitable that our collection of material is incomplete, though sampling has shown that the number of words omitted is very small. More difficult to detect are the cases where we have overlooked a meaning of a word. The Editor would be very glad to receive notes of omissions in either of these categories, but would like to point out that what constitutes a separate meaning is often a matter of opinion. The subdivision of meaning could often be taken further, but scale and usefulness must decide what finally appears in the Lexicon. Numerous entries in Potts's Vocabulary may not be found owing to the different criteria adopted in determining how to treat a word. It perhaps needs to be remarked that the Editor is not interested in differences between his interpretation of a word and that of previous translators, unless a case can be presented to demonstrate that he is wrong. It is our hope and intention to correct errors that have occurred in the existing translations, and to open the way to further improvements.

Content of entries

Each article consists of:

1. The lemma or headword, printed in capitals owing to the lack of other means of typographic distinction.
2. An indication of its inflectional type; this is normally the genitive of substantives, the feminine and neuter of adjectives (unless both are the same as the masculine, when the genitive is given instead); the infinitive, perfect active and supine (if any) of verbs, with appropriate forms for deponent verbs. These are abbreviated, as is also the word when it appears in quotations, by a hyphen representing the unchanging part of the stem.
3. An abbreviation specifying the part of speech (a. adjective, adv. = adverb), the gender of a substantive (m. = masculine, f. = feminine, n. = neuter), and in the case of verbs whether it is transitive (tr.) or intransitive (intr.).
4. Alternative spellings and any special forms, including in the case of adjectives and adverbs the comparative and superlative, if recorded in our material. It must not be supposed that their absence is evidence that they are not used.
5. An indication of the origin of words borrowed from other languages, mainly Hebrew (Hebr.) or Greek (Gk.).
6. The meaning or meanings, distinguished by arabic numerals and letters of the alphabet. Where necessary, the first part of the definition is intended to be a precise statement of the meaning, and

is followed by possible translation equivalents. One might often increase the number of meanings by analysing in more detail. The aim has been to present enough information without trying to imitate the precision of the largest dictionaries.

7. For each meaning one or more references to the Writings is supplied, and wherever helpful and informative a short quotation is given. These quotations are frequently abbreviated by the omission of words not directly relevant to the sense; the user is advised to consult the whole passage when in doubt. In a few cases the quotation, or part of it, is translated, where it might otherwise be obscure, especially to the student.

In 1 and 2 above, the position of the accent has been noted, since Latin in Swedenborg's time was certainly pronounced in accordance with accent, though the distinctions of vowel length, which play a part in determining the position of the accent, were no longer observed. The rules of the accent may accordingly be specified as follows: disyllabic words accent on the first syllable; polysyllabic words on the penultimate or antepenultimate syllable. Only polysyllabic words therefore are marked to show where the accent falls; in the case of abbreviated words in 2, the accent is marked if it falls upon the part of the word given. Thus the infinitive of a second conjugation verb is shown as *~ére*, that of a third conjugation verb as *~ere*. In capitals the accent is shown before the vowel which it affects; in lower case as an acute mark on the vowel (e.g., AFF'ECTIO, *affectiónis*).

References

References to Swedenborg's works have been given in accordance with the two letter system laid down in the Preface to the third Latin edition of *Arcana Caelestia* and subsequently expanded. Unfamiliar as this may seem, it has considerable advantages over the single letter system adopted by Potts. But some of the minor works still require longer abbreviations. The English titles of the works have been used as the basis of the abbreviations, since HH will be immediately identifiable by English users, while CI would not.

The sub-paragraph numbers introduced by Potts and appearing in recent editions and translations are given where possible. For typographical reasons they are shown as ordinary numerals following the paragraph number after a point (e.g. AC 904.3). The first sub-section is indicated by 1. Where the Latin text is not numbered, the numbers in the English translations are used; note especially that LO and WI are numbered as in the 1963 English edition (*On the Divine Love and on the Divine Wisdom*).

References to Swedenborg's quotations of biblical texts are given by the book, chapter and verse, with the Swedenborg reference added in parentheses; only one such reference is given, no matter how many times the passage is quoted. In the case of the chapters of Scripture in the expository works the biblical reference is followed simply by the abbreviation for the work in question; e.g., Gen. 3.4 (AC) means that this is to be found where AC quotes the whole of chapter 3 of Genesis.

Spelling

It is the aim of this Lexicon to prefer the spellings adopted by Swedenborg himself to the more familiar 'modern' spellings of some texts, notably the third Latin edition of AC. Since the materials have inevitably been assembled from the latest available Latin editions, it has not been easy to find all these changes and to restore the original forms, and corrections to matters of spelling will be welcome. In general, the spellings *e*, *ae* and *oe* were in Swedenborg's time all pronounced alike, and the choice of spelling was often dictated by spurious etymologies (e.g., in Swedenborg's time *coelum* was regularly used for classical *caelum* owing to an erroneous belief that the word was derived from Greek *koilos* 'hollow'). In some cases Swedenborg uses a single consonant for an original double consonant (*imo*, *quatuor*). There are also doubtful cases where assimilation may or may not take place (e.g., *affectio*, not *adfectio*, but *adsto*, not *asto*). Where either the 'modern' or the manuscript spelling is likely to cause confusion, cross references are inserted.

Conclusion

We are well aware that many imperfections will be found in this work; but it is being published in parts in a format which will allow for easy revision in the light of criticism. It is our wish to invite constructive criticism, and also offers of help with the complicated processes involved in editing the material. A few jobs are of a mechanical nature, but for others some knowledge of Swedenborg's Latin and an acquaintance with his theological works is necessary. The Editor would be particularly grateful for offers from scholars able and willing to devote time to serious criticism of the preliminary draft. However, we trust no one will be deterred from offering assistance by a feeling of his own inadequacy. Swedenborg himself has left us in no doubt of the very humble use performed by makers of dictionaries (SD 805), and those of us who cannot aspire to theology may yet contribute at the linguistic level to the great task of disseminating the knowledge of the Writings.

John Chadwick
Cambridge, January 1975

ABBREVIATIONS OF SWEDENBORG'S THEOLOGICAL WORKS

AC *Arcana Coelestia*
AC Appendix *Appendix* to *Arcana Coelestia*
AC Codex 8 Autograph MS of *Arcana Coelestia* forming Codex 8
AD *Adversaria*
AE *Apocalypsis Explicata*
AM *Delitiae Sapientiae de Amore Conjugiali*
AR *Apocalypsis Revelata*
AS *Sapientia Angelica de Divino Amore et de Divina Sapientia*
AT *De Athanasii Symbolo*
CA *Colloquia cum Angelis*
CC *De Commercio Animae et Corporis*
CH *De Charitate*
CI *De Coelo et ejus Mirabilibus, et de Inferno*
CJ *De Conjugio II*
CN *Canones Novae Ecclesiae*
CO *Coronis seu Appendix ad Veram Christianam Religionem*
CS *De Consummatione Saeculi*
DA *De Divino Amore*
DC *Documents concerning Swedenborg*
DD *Doctrina Novae Hierosolymae de Domino*
DI *Dicta Probantia Veteris et Novi Testamenti*
DO *De Domino*
Doc RC *Doctrinalia Ecclesia et Religionis Catholico Romanae* (in AR)
Doc Ref *Doctrinalia Ecclesia et Religionis Reformatorum* (in AR)
DP *Sapientia Angelica de Divina Providentia*
EA *De Equo Albo*
ES *Experientiae Spirituales*
ES(M) *Experientiae Spirituales (Minores)*
FC *Index ad Formulam Concordiae*
FI *Doctrina Novae Hierosolymae de Fide*
HE *Historia Ecclesiastica Novae Ecclesiae*
IB *Index Biblicus*
IM *Index Memorabilium* in *Vera Christiana Religione*
JU *De Justificatione*
ME [*Quinque*] *Memorabilia*
MI *De Miraculis*
MI(F) *Fragmentum de Miraculis*
NE *Invitatio ad Novam Ecclesiam*
NH *De Nova Hierosolyma et ejus Doctrina Coelesti*
PD *De Praeceptis Decalogi*
PM *Pro Memoria*
PP *Summaria Expositio sensus interni Librorum Propheticorum ac Psalmorum*
QN *Questiones Novem*
RE *Responsum ad Ernesti*
SA *De Divina Sapientia*
SE *Summaria Expositio Doctrinae Novae Ecclesiae*
SS *Doctrina Novae Hierosolymae de Scriptura Sacra*
SS(P) *De Scriptura Sacra seu Verbo Domini* [posth.]
TE *De Telluribus in Mundo nostro Solari*

UJ	*De Ultimo Judicio*	VI	*Doctrina Vitae pro Nova Hierosolyma*
UJ(C)	*Continuatio de Ultimo Judicio*		
UJ(P)	*De Ultimo Judicio* [posth.]	VR	*Vera Christiana Religio*

ABBREVIATIONS OF BIBLICAL BOOKS

Old Testament

Gen.	Genesis
Exod.	Exodus
Lev.	Leviticus
Num.	Numbers
Deut.	Deuteronomy
Josh.	Joshua
Judg.	Judges
Ruth	Ruth
1 Sam.	1 Samuel
2 Sam.	2 Samuel
1 Kgs.	1 Kings
2 Kgs.	2 Kings
1 Chr.	1 Chronicles
2 Chr.	2 Chronicles
Ezra	Ezra
Neh.	Nehemiah
Esther	Esther
Job	Job
Ps., Pss.	Psalms
Prov.	Proverbs
Eccles.	Ecclesiastes
S. of S.	Song of Songs / Song of Solomon / Canticles
Isa.	Isaiah
Jer.	Jeremiah
Lam.	Lamentations
Ezek.	Ezekiel
Dan.	Daniel
Hos.	Hosea
Joel	Joel
Amos	Amos
Obad.	Obadiah
Jonah	Jonah
Mic.	Micah
Nahum	Nahum
Hab.	Habakkuk
Zeph.	Zephaniah
Hag.	Haggai
Zech.	Zechariah
Mal.	Malachi

New Testament

Matt.	Matthew
Mark	Mark
Luke	Luke
John	John
Acts	Acts of the Apostles
Rom.	Romans
1 Cor.	1 Corinthians
2 Cor.	2 Corinthians
Gal.	Galatians
Eph.	Ephesians
Phil.	Philippians
Col.	Colossians
1 Thess.	1 Thessalonians
2 Thess.	2 Thessalonians
1 Tim.	1 Timothy
2 Tim.	2 Timothy
Titus	Titus
Philem.	Philemon
Heb.	Hebrews
Jas.	James
1 Pet.	1 Peter
2 Pet.	2 Peter

1 John	1 John	Jude	Jude
2 John	2 John	Rev.	Revelation
3 John	3 John		

Apocrypha

1 Esdr.	1 Esdras	S. of III Ch.	Song of the Three Children
2 Esdr.	2 Esdras	Sus.	Susanna
Tobit	Tobit	Bel & Dr.	Bel and the Dragon
Judith	Judith	Pr. of Man.	Prayer of Manasses / Prayer of Manasseh
Rest of Esth.	Rest of Esther	1 Macc.	1 Maccabees
Wis.	Wisdom	2 Macc.	2 Maccabees
Ecclus.	Ecclesiasticus / Sirach		
Baruch	Baruch		

Other miscellaneous abbreviations

Sym. Ap.	*Symbolum Apostolicum*
Sym. Ath.	*Symbolum Athanasii*
Sym. Nic.	*Symbolum Nicaenum*
BCP	The English *Book of Common Prayer*
Book of Concord	The Lutheran statement of doctrine promulgated in German in 1580, in Latin in 1584, that Swedenborg refers to as *Formula Concordiae*

GENERAL ABBREVIATIONS

a.	adjective
abl.	ablative
absol.	absolute(ly)
acc.	accusative
act.	active
AD	anno Domini
ad.	adapted from
adj.	adjective
adv.	adverb, adverbial
alt.	alternative
anat.	in anatomy
app.	apparently
Arab.	Arabic
BC	before Christ
Bibl.	biblical, in the Bible
c.	circa
cent.	century
cf.	compare
cm	centimetre
compar.	comparative
conj.	conjunction
dat.	dative
def.	defining
dep.	deponent
dir.	direct
dist.	distinguished
edn., edns.	edition, editions
ellipt.	elliptically
esp.	especially
etc.	et cetera
EVV	English versions
expr.	expression
f., fem.	feminine
fig.	figurative(ly)
freq.	frequently
fut.	future
gen.	genitive
geom.	in geometry
Gk.	Greek
Hebr.	Hebrew
i.e.	id est (that is)
impers.	impersonal
impf.	imperfect
indecl.	indeclinable
indef.	indefinite
indic.	indicative
indir.	indirect
inf.	infinitive
interj.	interjection
interr.	interrogative
intr.	intransitive (verb)
irreg.	irregular
Ital.	Italian
l.	line
Lat.	Latin
m	metre
m., masc.	masculine
Mt.	Mount or Mountain
myth.	in mythology
n.b.	nota bene (mark well)
neg.	negative
neut.	neuter
no.	number
nom.	nominative
obj.	object
opp.	opposed
orig.	originally
p.	page
pass.	passive
perh.	perhaps

pers.	person
pf.	perfect
phr.	phrase
pl.	plural
plupf.	pluperfect
poss.	possibly
pple.	participle
praef.	praefatio (preface)
prec.	preceding
pred.	predicative
prep.	preposition
pres.	present
prob.	probably
pron.	pronoun, pronominal
prov.	proverbial
qu., qus.	question, questions
quot.	quotation
q.v.	quod vide (which see)
ref.	reference
refl.	reflexive
reg.	regular
rel.	relative
sb.	substantive
sc.	scilicet
Schm.	Sebastian Schmidt or Schmidius
sg.	singular
sim.	similar
spec.	specific(ally), special(ly)
St	Saint
subj.	subjunctive
superl.	superlative
s.v.	sub voce or sub verbo (under the word)
Swed.	Swedish
tr.	transitive (verb)
transf.	in transferred sense
usu.	usually
vb.	verb
voc.	vocative
vol.	volume
w.	with
*	The asterisk indicates a word that does not have its own entry in this Lexicon.

A

a, ab, *prep. w. abl.* see also **abs**. (n.b. *a* is used before consonants, *ab* before vowels or h.) **1** (to denote motion) Away from: *ab iis discedere* AC 182; *a super* (Hebr.), from on, off: Exod. 3.5 (AC 1748.2); *ab invicem*, from one another: AC 1159.3. **2** (to denote change of state or activity) From: *a communicatione removebar* AC 171; *abstinet a malo* AC 7051.1. **b** from among: *nihil perdit a suis facultatibus* ES 662. **3** (to denote difference) From: *diversus...a genio eorum* AC 310.1. **4** At, on (a position): *a lateribus* AC 7077. **b** *a parte* (w. gen.), on the part (of): VR 2.3; *ab una parte...ab altera,* on the one side...on the other: AC 9391.18. **c** (to denote the province of counsellors): *consiliarii a latere...a cameris* AM 14.1. **5** (to denote time) From: *a tempore Domini* VR 4; *ab aeterno* VR 82. **6** (to denote the starting point of a series) Starting from, from: *a reginis...usque ad ancillas* VR 12.9. **7** (to denote origin) From: *calor qui ab Ipso...venit* AC 7083; *illa...quae trahunt a materiali* CI 464; also, *a cum* (Hebr.): *ros a cum Jehovah* Mic. 5.6 (AC 468.3). **b** (w. words denoting knowledge): *constat a significatione* AC 398; *a se sequitur* AM 489. **8** (to denote cause) **a** (w. pass. vb. to mark the agent) By: *Homo...creatus a Domino* AC 69. **b** under the impulse of, as a result of: *pulmo respirat ex se a corde* VR 154.3; *nudus ab ebrietate* AC 1073. **c** (Hebr., w. vbs. of fearing): Job 5.22 (AC 46.2). **9** (to denote membership of a group) From, of: *illi qui ab Ecclesia sunt* VR 113.8. **b** in favour of: *qui a decretis illius Synodi fuerunt* VR 487.1. **10** *Ab extra*, from without: ES 1751; *ab intra*, from within: *ab intra fibras* ES 1799; ES 1803.

abactio ~onis, *f.* A driving away: AC 6912.

abactus ~a ~um: pf. pple. of **abigo**.

abalienabilis ~is ~e, *a.* (compar. *~ior*) That may be taken away, removable: VR 352.

abalienatio ~onis, *f.* **1** A taking away, removal: AC 9018. **2** A removal from association, alienation, estrangement: AC 4844.1.

abalieno ~are ~avi ~atum, *tr.* **1** To transfer (property) to another, alienate: AC 4098. **2** To take or drive away, remove, repel: AC 9092; AM 167.2. **3** To remove from association with, estrange: AC 5280.4; VR 678.

ab ante, *prep. w. acc.* In front of: *profecta columna nubis ab ante illos* Exod. 14.19 (AC).

abba, *indecl.* (Aramaic) Abba, the Aramaic word for father: Mark 14.36 (AC 1787.2).

abbas ~atis, *m.* An abbot: VR 683.

abbrevio ~are ~avi ~atum, *tr.* To shorten, cut short: Isa. 1.2 (AE 328.14); Matt. 24.22 (AR 9).

abdicatio ~onis, *f.* A renunciation, repudiation, forswearing: AC 6143; VR 685; the resignation (of an office): AR 153.7.

abdico ~are ~avi ~atum, *tr.* **1** To renounce, repudiate, forswear: DP 121.1; AM 155; (also, refl. w. dat.): AC 995.2. **2** (w. dat. of refl. pron.) To divest oneself of: AE 114.9. **3** (w. dat.) To deprive (someone of office): *papae qui dominio ~averunt imperatores* AM 265.

abdite, *adv.* (compar. *~ius*) In a secret place, secretly: ES 639.

abditum ~i, *neut.* (pf. pple. of **abdo**) *In ~o*, in a secret place, in hiding (from): Ps. 31.20 (AE 412).

abdo ~ere ~idi ~itum, *tr.* To keep from sight, hide: AC 32.

abdomen ~inis, *neut.* The abdomen, belly: AC 1120.

abdominalis ~is ~e, *a.* Abdominal: *aliae varietates respirationum interiorum, sicut ~es* ES 3325.

abduco ~cere ~xi ~ctum, *tr.* **1** To lead away, carry off: DD 52. **2** To withdraw, lead away, divert (from a state): *~ci a corpore* CI 440; *~cuntur ne cadant in gravissima mala* NH 163. **b** to withhold (from an action): *~xerit a loquendo* DP 236.

abductio ~onis, *f.* **1** A leading away, carrying off: DP 246. **2** A withdrawal, withholding: DP 183.1.

abeo abire abivi, *intr.* **1** To go away, depart: VR 136.1. **b** (of roads) to lead away, run: CI 534. **2** To be changed, be turned, dissolve (into): *ut inclinatio...abeat in calorem* AM 155.1; VR 30.2. **3** To depart, diverge (from a belief): *quod...populi abiverint et abeant in diversum* VR 5.

aberratio ~onis, *f.* A wandering away, straying: *~o et abalienatio a Divino Vero* AC 4790.

aberro ~are ~avi, *intr.* To make an error, go astray: DP 333.3; AC 409.

abhinc, *adv.* also spelled as two words **ab hinc**. From this place, from here, hence: VR 160.7; from this time, hence: DD 9.

abhorreo ~rere ~rui, *tr.* To shrink from, abhor: AC 865.2.

abhorresco ~ere, *tr.* To abhor, disdain: *quod non ederet panem et biberet aquam apud Jerobeamum, significabat quod ~eret bonum ibi et quoque verum, quia erant prophanata* AC 9323.3.

Abib, *indecl.* Abib, the first month of the Hebrew sacred year: Exod. 13.4 (AC).

abies ~etis, *f.* A fir tree: AC 643.1.

abigo abigere abegi abactum, *tr.* To drive away: CI 299.

abinde, *adv.* From there, thence: VR 76.5.

abjectio ~onis, *f.* A throwing away, rejection: AC 8939.

abjicio ~jicere ~jeci ~jectum, *tr.* (superl. of pf. pple. *~jectissimus*) To throw away: AM 7.4.

ablactatus ~i, *m.* A weaned child: Isa. 11.8 (VR 789.2).

ablacto ~are ~avi ~atum, *tr.* To wean: Gen. 21.8 (AC).

ablatio ~onis, *f.* A taking away, removal: AC 2256.2.

ablatus ~a ~um: pf. pple. of **aufero**.

ablegatio ~onis, *f.* A sending away, banishing: *hi ideo separati sunt, et emissi ad angulos; datum est videre separationes post Ultimum Judicium et ~ones* AR praef.

ablego ~are ~avi ~atum, *tr.* To banish: *spiritus ille ~atus est in abyssum* VR 110.7; to choose out, depute: *judicialis hic caetus ~avit unum intelligentem, qui nos...instrueret* AM 77.4; to send out (as an envoy): *quod ex urbe Athenaeo frequenter ~entur studiosi ad literatos ex Christianis* AM 151[a].2.

abluo ~ere ~i ~tum, *tr.* To clean by washing: VR 331.3; to remove by washing, wash away: AM 525.2.

ablutio ~onis, *f.* A cleansing: VR 510.2.

abnegatio ~onis, *f.* A giving up, rejection: *mundi* ES 2652.

abnego ~are ~avi ~atum, *tr.* **1** To deny knowledge of: *ter Ipsum ~aturus esset* Matt. 26.34 (AE 9). **2** To disown, renounce: *qui non ~at omnes suas facultates* Luke 14.33 (AC 4599.5); *~et semetipsum* Matt. 16.24 (AE 122.4).

aboleo ~lere ~lui ~litum, *tr.* To do away with, destroy: *~lere ideam* VR 23.1.

abolitio ~onis, *f.* A destroying, destruction: *faederis conjugialis* AM 468.

abominabilis ~is ~e, *a.* (compar. *~ior*, superl. *~issimus*) Abominable: AS 130.

abominabiliter, *adv.* In an abominable manner: ES 3811.

abominatio ~onis, *f.* That which is abominated, an abomination: AC 7454.

abominor ~ari ~atus sum, *tr.* To loathe, abominate: AM 433.

abortiens ~ntis, *f.* A woman who miscarries: Exod. 23.26 (AC).

abortio ~tire ~tivi, *intr.* To miscarry: *~tiverunt greges* AS 345.

abortus ~us, *m.* A monstrosity, abortion: VR 367.

abrado ~dere ~si ~sum, *tr.* To scrape off: VI 10; to shave off (hair): SS 35.

abrech, *interj.* (Hebr.) Bend your knees (a Hebrew command): *abrech...in lingua originali est 'flecte genua'* AC 5323.1.

abripio ~ripere ~ripui ~reptum, *tr.* To take or carry away: AC 10542; VR 146.

abrogatio ~onis, *f.* A giving up, abrogation: *ritualium* AM 340.3; a taking away, deprivation: *per... castigationes, paenas, ~ones* CH 79 (= iv.2).

abrogo ~are ~avi ~atum, *tr.* **1** To dismiss from office: AR 153.6. **2** To put an end to: *de lege talionis, quae non a Domino ~ata est sed explicata* AC 8223.3; Jer. 25.10 (AE 274).

abrumpo ~rumpere ~rupi ~ruptum, *tr.* To tear off: *pulvillos* Ezek. 13.20 (AC 1178.2); to break off, stop: *sermonem* AM 477.3.

abrupte, *adv.* In a disjointed manner, disconnectedly: AC 6195.

abruptio ~onis, *f.* A breaking away: *regni Israelis a Schaule* AC 9825.2.

abs, *prep. w. abl.* (variant of **ab**) Away from: Matt. 5.29 (AC 10061.5).

abscedo ~cedere ~cessi, *intr.* To go away, depart: AM 214.3; (transf., of a church) AC 2243.7.

abscendo ~ere, *intr.* To rise away, spread upwards and outwards: *ex toto illo tractu ~ebat fumus* UJ 61.

abscessus ~us, *m.* An abscess: AM 253.2.

abscindo ~ndere ~di ~ssum, *tr.* To cut off: AC 7045.

abscissio ~onis, *f.* A cutting off: AC 7049.

absconditio ~onis, *f.* A hiding away, concealment: AM 167.1.

absconditus ~a ~um, *a.* (compar. *~ior*) Hidden, concealed: AC 960; *in ~o*, in concealment: AC 9013.2; CI 469.

abscondo ~dere ~didi ~ditum, *tr.* To hide away, conceal: CI 341.

absconsio ~onis, *f.* A hiding away, concealment: CI 594.2.

absens ~ntis, *a.* (pres. pple. of **absum**) (compar. *~ntior* AC 981.1) Not present, absent: AM 293.3.

absentia ~ae, *f.* Absence: AM 291.

absimilis ~is ~e, *a.* (usu. following *non*, w. dat.) Dissimilar (to), different (from): CI 221.

absimiliter, *adv.* In a dissimilar manner, differently: AC 1983.

absinthium ~i, *neut.* Wormwood: Amos 6.12 (AC 1488.2); Rev. 8.11 (AR 410).

absolute, *adv.* Completely, utterly: AM 324.1; without restraint, absolutely: VR 73.1.

absolutio ~onis, *f.* Absolution (by a priest): VR 562.2.

absolutus ~a ~um, *a.* (pf. pple. of **absolvo**) **1** Complete, total: *identitas* AM 186.2. **2** (of power) Unhindered, absolute: VR 57.

absolvo ~vere ~vi ~utum, *tr.* **1** To complete, finish (a task, structure, etc.): *~uti sunt coeli et terra* Gen. 2.1 (AC); AE 128. **2** To discharge (an obligation): *paenitentialia* AC 3993.10. **3** To absolve, forgive: *ex significatione 'justificare' quod sit insontem declarare et ~vere* AC 9264. **4** To go through, complete (a period of time): AM 78.

absonus ~a ~um, *a.* Absurd: AC 446; AC 8918.1.

absorbeo ~bere ~psi ~ptum, *tr.* **1** To swallow up: CI 229. **2** To make imperceptible, swallow, absorb: *sensationem* AM 178; *bona* AC 571; *radios lucis* AC 1042.2.

absorptio ~onis, *f.* A swallowing up: VR 31.2.

absorptor ~oris, *m.* One who swallows up: *procul aberunt ~ores tui* Isa. 49.19 (AC 5376.5).

absque, *prep. w. abl.* Without: *charitate* AC 1076.2; (w. *ut*) *absque ut curent conjugia* ES 230; (w. *quod*) *absque quod...percipiat* AC 10684.

abstergo ~gere ~si ~sum, *tr.* **1** To wipe away: *lachrymas* VR 126; to clean by wiping: *~sus et ablutus aquis* AC 868.1. **2** To remove utterly, wipe out: *peccata* VR 71.2.

absterreo ~rere ~rui ~ritum, *tr.* To frighten off, deter: AC 1983.1.

abstersio ~onis, *f.* The action of wiping away: AC 2039.1.

abstinentia ~ae, *f.* A refraining, abstinence: *a... scortationibus* AM 105.

abstineo ~nere ~nui, *intr.* (w. *ab*) To refrain, abstain (from): CI 522.

abstracte, *adv.* (w. *ab*) Without reference (to): *qui... ~e a corpore cogitant* CI 438; in an abstract sense: *illi...vocantur spiritus scientiarum et ~e scientiae* AM 461.3.

abstractio ~onis, *f.* A removing, abstraction: *cogitationum a mundanis* CI 360.

abstractus ~a ~um, *a.* (pf. pple. of **abstraho**) **1** (of persons) Distracted: *a variis negotiis ~us* AC 1295; VR 178.2. **2** (of things, w. *ab*) Separated (from): *rebus ~is a persona* AM 34; (absol.) abstract: *in sensu ~o* VR 76.4.

abstraho ~here ~xi ~ctum, *tr.* (compar. of pf. pple. *~ctior*) To draw away, remove: Luke 22.41 (AC 1787.2); (transf.) *a Divinitate ~hunt spatia et tempora* VR 31.2.

abstrusus ~a ~um, *a.* Recondite, abstruse: *in religione ~a* AE 455.12; (neut. as sb.) *~a scientiarum indagare* AC 4096.3.

abstuli: pf. of **aufero**.

absum abesse afui, *intr.* **1** To be absent: AC 654. **2** (Hebr.) *absit a Jehovah mihi,* Jehovah forbid me: 1 Sam. 24.6 (AE 375.22). **3** To be remote (from): *quae ...tam longe absunt a veritate* ES 556.

absumo ~ere ~(p)si ~(p)tum, *tr.* To consume, destroy: *cum coelo quod prius ~etur* NE 34.

absurditas ~atis, *f.* An absurdity: *se in ~ates conjuciunt* ES 3596.

absurdus ~a ~um, *a.* Absurd: NE 19.

abundanter, *adv.* (compar. *~ius*) In abundance, abundantly: Matt. 13.12 (CI 349).

abundantia ~ae, *f.* Fullness, abundance: *~ae annonae* Gen. 41.29 (AC 5275.1); *ex ~a cordis* Matt. 12.34 (VI 28); AE 118.

abunde, *adv.* Abundantly: AM 369.

abundo ~are ~avi, *intr.* (compar. of pres. pple. *~antior*)

1 To be present in large amounts, be abundant: Matt. 5.20 (VI 2); AS 125. **2** To be richly endowed, abound: Matt. 25.29 (AE 193); (w. abl.) CI 357.

abusus ~us, *m.* Misuse, abuse: *ex imbecillitate oriunda vel ex morbo vel ex ~u* AM 494.2.

abutor ~ti ~sus sum, *intr.* (w. abl.) To misuse, abuse: *qui ~si sunt Verbo* AE 66.

abyssus ~i, *f.* An abyss: *caligo super faciebus ~i* Gen. 1.2 (AC); (transf., as a type of impenetrable area) *quid inde nisi ~us caliginum?* AC 206.2; VR 32.8.

ac, *conj.* **1** And: *incipiunt angi ac interius cruciari* CI 400; (connecting another clause) *quod Dominus... convocaverit...discipulos...,ac illos...emiserit* VR 4.1; (dist. from **et**) *distinximus inter Esse Dei et Essentiam Dei..., ac infinitas applicate dicitur de Esse Dei* VR 36. **2** (w. exprs. denoting likeness) Compared with, as: *tam sensibiliter ac in societate humana* ES 1532; *homo... aeque ac angelus* CI 57. **3** (w. exprs. denoting difference) Than: *homo non potest...aliter ac malum facere* AC 233.3.

academia ~ae, *f.* A university, academy: CH 78 (= iv.2).

acarus ~i, *m.* (Gk. *akarí*) A tiny insect, mite: *blattae, pediculi, ~i* AS 338.

accedo ~dere ~ssi ~ssum, *intr.* **1** To come near, approach: AM 21.1; (implying a change of state) *gentes quae ~ssurae ad verum cultum Dei* AE 50. **b** (w. *in* + acc.) to come into: *in regionem hanc quotidie ~dunt novi e tellure* AM 77.11. **2** To become similar in quality, approach: *status tranquillus ~dens...ad statum pacis* AC 1275; *ut [equi] ad camelorum proceritatem ~dant* ES 632. **b** to accede (to), go along (with an opinion): *si unus ad alterius sententiam non ~deret* AC 6628; *allectamentum ad ~dendum ad tua nova* AM 82.1. **3** To be added: *quantum cognitiones ~dunt* CI 352. **b** *~dit quod*, there is also the fact that, an additional fact is that: *~dit quod homo natus sit facultas sciendi* AM 122.

accelero ~are ~avi ~atum, *tr.*, *intr.* **1** (tr.) To move (something) quickly: *~averunt eum e fovea* Gen. 41.14 (AC); (pass.) to be speeded up: *~atur defectus* AM 304. **2** (intr.) To proceed faster, hasten: *puella...pergens cito...paulum ~ans* AC 1872.

accendo ~dere ~di ~sum, *tr.* **1** To set fire to, light: *Non ~detis ignem* Exod. 35.3 (AC); *[lychnariis] ~sis* AM 20.1. **2** To arouse, fire (an emotion): *~sa cupidine* AC 963; to arouse (a person) emotionally, inflame, fire: *~debar desiderio audiendi* VR 25.1.

accensio ~onis, *f.* A kindling: *~o Divini Amoris* AC 10034.

accentus ~us, *m.* The tone or method of pronunciation (of speech): *loquela...in fine cujusvis sensus terminatur quoad ~um in unum* VR 8.2; AC 1758; ES 2414.

acceptatio ~onis, *f.* An acceptance: AM 300.3.

accepto ~are ~avi ~atum, *tr.* To receive willingly, take, accept: *qui bona faciunt ~entur* VI 2; *tribus...~ata loco primogenitorum* AC 352.

acceptus ~a ~um, *a.* (pf. pple. of **accipio**) (superl. *~issimus* ES 4284) **1** Acceptable: *annum Domini ~um* Luke 4.19 (DD 11); AC 2974. **2** *~um fertur*, is to be attributed (to): *quod mens...talis sit, ~um fertur binis facultatibus* DP 104.2; also, *~us deberi*: *quod salvatio illorum unice ~a debeatur a Domino* AC 7935.

accessibilis ~is ~e, *a.* Capable of being approached, approachable: *Dominus...Se fecit visibilem...et sic ~em* AR 962.6.

accessio ~onis, *f.* A coming near, approach: *non est recessio seu disjunctio, sed ~o seu conjunctio* AC 3730.

accessorius ~a ~um, *a.* Additional, accessory, incidental, subsidiary: *bono ~o* VR 389.5; AM 5.3; (w. dat.) *sunt modo ~a gaudiis cordium nostrorum* AM 12.2; (w. gen.) *[gaudia illa] non sunt nisi quam ~a caelestium* VR 734.3.

accessus ~us, *m.* **1** An approach: *modum ~us* AM 56.1; *~um illorum ad Ecclesiam* AE 406.6. **2** A means of approach, access: *ut ad illud ~us sit homini* AC 3441.1.

accidens ~ntis, *a.* (pres. pple. of **accido**) **1** Happening by chance, accidental: *quod omne malum, etiam ~ns, ab inferno veniat* ES 224; (neut. pl. as sb.) *per ~ntia, ut per infortunia, morbos, et similia* AC 7761. **2** (neut. as sb.) A non-essential characteristic: *de qualitatibus, ~ntibus, viribus, substantiis, et similiter* ES 2263.

accidentalis ~is ~e, *a.* Supplemental, additional, incidental: *causae ~es* AM 234; *hoc ~e dicitur, quia addit se frigori intrinseco ut causa, et adstipulatur ei ut ratio* AM 256.

accido ~dere ~di, *intr.* To happen, befall: AE 434; (impers., w. *quod*) it happens that: *~dit quod post mortem amici conveniant* AM 273.3.

accinctus ~us, *m.* A state of preparedness: *cum violator in ~u est* AM 512.1.

accingo ~gere ~xi ~ctum, *tr.* **1** To gird on: *~ge gladium Tuum super femur Tuum* Ps. 45.3 (AE 131); (w. abl.) to dress (a person with a girdle): *~xi te bysso* Ezek. 16.11 (CI 180); (transf.) *~ges Me robore* Ps. 18.39 (DD 14). **2** (refl.) To gird oneself, prepare for action:

~xerunt se, et comitati sunt angelum AM 14; (pf. pple.) *~ctus*, prepared, eager, zealous: AM 17.2.

accipio ~cipere ~cepi ~ceptum, *tr.* **1** To have given to one, receive: *postquam reges ~ceperunt, facti sunt populus* AC 1259.7; (dist. from **recipio** 'welcome', cf. sense 3) *cum homo bonum charitatis ~cipit et recipit* AC 880.1. **2** To take hold of: Matt. 24.17 (CI 208); to take (a wife): Gen. 11.29 (AC). **3** To give hospitality to, receive (a person): *mendicant, sed nullus eos ~cipit* ES 476. **4** To understand (a word or phrase in a stated manner): *tertius dies in Verbo ~cipitur pro septimo* AC 720; *terra...~cipitur varie* AC 1066.1. **5** To adopt, assume, take: *si veritas pro thesi ~cipitur* ES 1312.

accipiter ~tris, *m.* A hawk: VR 72.3.

accitus ~a ~um, *a.* (pf. pple. of **accio***) Summoned: *volebat illum videre, quare ~us ex inferno* ES 5833.

acclamatio ~onis, *f.* A crying out, shout: *vocem ~onis* 1 Sam. 4.6 (AC 1343.4).

acclamo ~are ~avi ~atum, *intr.* To cry out, shout: *~ate Deo Jacobi* Ps. 81.1 (AE 323); (impers. pass.) *a quodam praecone ~atum est* AM 7.2.

acclino ~are ~avi, *intr.* (w. *ad*) To become mentally disposed (to), incline (to): *quod...ad unam...faeminam intendat mentem et ~et* AM 108.

acclivitas ~atis, *f.* A piece of rising ground, rise, slope: *~as lente surgens* AM 76.1.

acclivum ~i, *neut.* A rise, slope: *per longum ~um ascendimus* AM 76.3.

accola ~ae, *m.* One who lives near, a neighbour: ES 6020.

accommodate, *adv.* (w. *ad*) In a manner suited (to): *~e ad captum hominis* CI 545.

accommodatio ~onis, *f.* A making suited, adjustment: *~o voluntatis* AM 220.1.

accommodatus ~a ~um, *a.* (compar. *~ior*) (w. abl. or *ad*) Suited, adjusted (to): *hi angeli ~iores illis sunt* CI 515; *~a ad receptionem* AE 78.

accommodo ~are ~avi ~atum, *tr.* To make suitable, adjust: *cum homo se ~at et disponit ad receptionem* VR 150.

accrementum ~i, *neut.* That which is acquired by growth: *quicquid...adjicitur est matris, nam aliunde ~um non habet* AC 1815.

accresco ~rescere ~revi ~retum, *intr.* To become greater, increase, grow: *aequilibrium...diminuitur et ~rescit* CI 593; *murmur...~rescens* AM 316.5.

accubo ~are ~ui ~itum, *intr.* To lean or recline (upon): *Johannes ~uit ad pectus...Domini* AE 9; (of stones) to be set or laid: *~are faciam in carbunculo lapides tuos* Isa. 54.11 (AC 1298.3).

accumbo ~ere, *intr.* To take one's seat, recline (esp. at table): *agricola...cum ~it ad mensam* DP 254.4; *~ent cum Abrahamo...in regno Dei* Luke 8.11 (AE 146).

accumulatio ~onis, *f.* A piling up, accumulation: AS 269.

accumulo ~are ~avi ~atum, *tr.* (w. abl.) To provide lavishly, heap (with): *~aret bonos honoribus* DP 216.1.

accurate, *adv.* Carefully: AC 153.

accuratus ~a ~um, *a.* Carefully executed: *distinctio ~a* AC 471.

accurro ~rere ~ri ~sum, *intr.* To move (into another's presence) with haste, run or rush up: *tunc ~rit unus ex curia cum mandato* AM 10.2; (w. *ad*) to run or hurry (towards): *ad cadaverosa et stercorea advolant et ~runt* CI 429.

accusatio ~onis, *f.* An accusing: AM 524.4.

accusator ~oris, *m.* An accuser: Rev. 12.10 (AR).

accuso ~are ~avi ~atum, *tr.* To accuse (w. gen. of crime): *~are adulterii* AM 469.

acer acris acre, *a.* (nom. masc. sg. also *acris* VR 665.4) (superl. *acerrimus*) **1** (of sounds) Sharp, penetrating: *sonus loquelae...altus, vehemens, acer et asper* AM 363; (also, of substances) pungent, sharp: *humor acris, qui fibras ibi vellicat* VR 665.4. **2** Shrewd, keen: *acerrimus...defensor...dogmatum* VR 796.1.

acerbe, *adv.* Bitterly: *~e lamentantur* CO 19.6.

acerbitas ~atis, *f.* Sharpness, bitterness: *ex tentationis ~ate* AC 8351.

acerbus ~a ~um, *a.* (of sensations) Sharp, keen, bitter: *per influxus veritatum ~os* AC 5563; (also, of the voice) complaining, sharp: *~a voce* ES 2905.

acerra ~ae, *f.* A container for incense, censer: Num. 16.37 (AE 324).

acervatim, *adv.* In large numbers, in heaps or crowds: *spiritus mali...qui ~im influunt* AC 842.1.

acervus ~i, *m.* A heap or pile: *posuisti de urbe in ~um* Isa. 25.2 (AC 402.5).

acescens ~ntis, *a.* Becoming sharp or sour: *humus ~ns aut putrescens* VR 41.3.

acetabulum ~i, *neut.* The cotyloid cavity in a joint, socket: Gen. 32.25 (AC 5051.1); AC 9496.2.

acetosus ~a ~um, *a.* Sour, vinegary: *vinis ~is* AS 342.

acetum ~i, *neut.* Vinegar: VR 38.2.

achates ~is, *m.* A precious stone, agate: Exod. 28.19. (AC).

aciarium ~i, *neut.* A needle-case: Isa. 3.22 (AC 2576.11).

aciditas ~atis, *f.* Acidity: *ventriculi tetram ~atem* ES 1272.

acies ~ei, *f.* **1** The cutting edge (of a sword): *~em gladii* Ezek. 21.15 (AE 131.5). **2** *~es oculorum,* the power or direction of sight, gaze: *quocunque vertimus ~es oculorum nostrorum* AM 13.3; so *~es* alone: *intendi ~em* VR 697.1; *~e aquilae pollere* 'to have as keen sight as an eagle' VR 40. **3** The power or keenness (of the senses or mental faculties): *sensus ~es ascendunt secundum gradus* 'the powers of the senses increase by degrees' ES 1343; *acutae ~ei* CI 97.2; *~em ingenii* VR 35.6.

acinus ~i, *m.* A berry: *ex uvis, cerasis et ~is* AM 8.2.

aconitum ~i, *neut.* Poison: *Cerberus...ex triplici suo ore exspumans ~a* CO 40; VR 380.4.

acontias ~ae, *m.* (Gk.) A small kind of snake: VR 380.4.

acquiescentia ~ae, *f.* Satisfaction: AE 348.

acquiesco ~quiescere ~quievi, *intr.* To be satisfied: AC 8176; (w. *in* + abl.) *~quiescimus in effatis illorum* AM 79.7; (w. dat.) AM 332; (w. *quin*) *ne tunc quidem ~quiescerent quin flagrarent* AC 695.

acquiro ~rere ~sivi ~situm, *tr.* To acquire, gain: *~sivit decem minas* Luke 19.16 (AE 112.5); *proprium ex amore sui... ~situm* CI 277.

acquisitio ~onis, *f.* A thing acquired, acquisition: Gen. 12.5 (AC).

acrimonia ~ae, *f.* Pungency: *humorum* AM 253.2.

acris: see **acer**.

acriter, *adv.* (compar. *acrius*) Sharply, keenly: *~er ratiocinantur* VR 77.1.

acta ~orum, *neut. pl.* Deeds: AC 1396; *~a Apostolorum*, the Acts of the Apostles: VR 4.1.

actio ~onis, *f.* **1** The process or fact of acting, action: *~o et reactio* CI 589. **2** An instance of this, an action: *ex voluntate...fluant ~ones* AM 220.1. **3** *Gratiarum ~o*, the giving of thanks, thanking: AC 1096.1.

actiuncula ~ae, *f.* A small action: AC 6622.

active, *adv.* In an active manner, actively: *sphaera... operans admodum ~e* ES 930.

activitas ~atis, *f.* The fact of being in action, activity: *systolica ~ate cordis* VR 87; *ad...synchronas ~ates* AM 310.1.

activus ~a ~um, *a.* (superl. *~issimus* 2AD 143) Engaged in action, active: *quod Dominus...solus ~us sit* VR 110.6; (neut. as sb.) an active principle, motive force: *est...amor ipsum vitae ~um* AM 183.3.

actualis ~is ~e, *a.* Realized in action, put into practice: *quod nondum...irradicatum sit malum ex ~i vita* CI 330; *~e peccatum* AC 313; (neut. as sb.) practice: AC 482.2.

actualitas ~atis, *f.* A putting into practice, realization in action: *ex ~ate et habitu* AC 831; *cupidines per ~ates firmatae* AM 454.

actualiter, *adv.* In actual fact, actually: *ut ~er [Deus] etiam homo fieret* VR 89.

actuo ~are ~avi ~atum, *tr.* To cause to function, activate: *vita Divina quae per influxum ~at hominem* VR 34.3.

actus ~us, *m.* An action: AM 90.3; *~u*, in action: *fides ~u* AC 342.

actutum, *adv.* Immediately, at once: AM 7.2; *~um ut advenit* 'as soon as it arrives' VR 16.1.

aculeatus ~a ~um, *a.* Equipped with sharp points, spiky: (neut. as sb.) *per mucrones ensium...et per ~a* AE 560.3.

aculeus ~i, *m.* A small sharp point, spike, spine: *fibrilla ~o tacta* AE 162.2; the sting (of an insect): AC 9331.1.

acumen ~inis, *neut.* **1** The point (of a sword or sim.): ES 934. **2** The power of mental perception, sharpness of intellect: *quod...noverint de Deo...non fuit...ex proprio illorum ~ine* SS 117.

acuminatim, *adv.* In a point: *variis formis, partim desinentibus ~im* ES 2274.

acuminatus ~a ~um, *a.* Pointed: *in modum coni sursum ~i* AC 958.

acumino ~are ~avi ~atum, *tr.* To make pointed: *conus qui sursum ~atur* [unless *~atus* should be read here] ES 870.

acuo ~ere ~i ~tum, *tr.* **1** To sharpen (the tongue): *~ere [linguas] in dicteria* VR 74.3; to make (the mind) penetrating: *~itur ingenium* ES 400. **2** To treat in a subtle fashion, refine: *~itis et sublimatis nimis hanc rem* AM 79.8.

acupictor ~oris, *m.* An embroiderer: *opere ~oris* Exod. 26.36 (AC).

acupictura ~ae, *f.* Embroidery: Ezek. 27.7 (AC 1156).

acupictus ~a ~um, *a.* Embroidered: *alari...insignito stellis ~is* AM 15; (neut. as sb.) an embroidered garment: Ezek. 16.10 (AC 297).

acupingo ~ngere ~nxi ~ctum, *tr.* To embroider: AC 9688.2.

acus ~us, *m.* A needle: *per foramen ~us* AC 233.1.

acustice ~es, *f.* (Gk.) The science of acoustics: SS(P) 51 (= 19.3).

acusticus ~a ~um, *a.* Of or belonging to hearing, acoustic: (neut. pl. as sb.) DA 14 (= v.[3]).

acute, *adv.* (compar. *~ius*) With keenness of intellect, acutely: *spiritus ~ius ratiocinantur quam homines* CI 320.

acutio ~onis, *f.* The process of refining: AM 145.2.

acutus ~a ~um, *a.* (pf. pple. of **acuo**) (compar. *~ior*, superl. *~issimus*) **1** Pointed, sharp: *nasus ~ior* ES 1376. **2** Capable of penetration: *per ~ius microscopium* 'by a more powerful microscope' AC 1869.2. **3** (of mental powers) Penetrating, subtle: *~issimo ingenio* VR 17.1. **4** Possessed of penetrating mental powers, sharp: ES 897.

ad, *prep. w. acc.* **1** (implying motion) In the direction of, towards, to (a place): *abeamus ad caelicolas* AM 77.1. **2** (w. vbs. of saying) To: *Dives dixit ad Abrahamum* Luke 16.24 (AC 6832.9). **3** (w. expr. implying a change of state) Towards, to: *Dominus...progressus est ad coelestia et in coelestia* AC 1554. **b** (ellipt.) let us proceed to: *sed ad seria* VR 80.2. **4** (w. expr. implying inducement or tendency) To: *quod...ad usum...conducat* CI 465; *ad serviendum adigere* AC 6850. **b** tending to: *ad perniciem hominis...foret* ES 1088. **5** (w. expr. denoting limitation) Up or down to, as far as (a point in space or time): *usque ad lumbos* CI 65; *permanent...ad septimanas* CI 426. **6** Up or down to, to the point of (a degree or term in a series): *percutiunt, sed non ad sanguinis effusionem* AC 821.2; *ab homine usque ad bestiam* Gen. 7.23 (AC); *ad omnem apicem* 'down to the last jot' VR 110.5. **b** up to the number of: *congregatos ad centenos vidi* VR 76.1. **7** (w. no motion) At, towards, near (a place): *sedebant ad septentrionem* VR 48.2; *ad distantiam,* at a distance: AC 1274. **8** Upon, at (a point of time): *ad praesentiam eorum* ES 5939. **b** *ad tempus,* for a while: AC 948. **9** In response to, in reply to: *serviant illis ad nutus* AM 11; *ad haec...siluit* VR 137.11. **10** With respect to, in so far as concerns: *paenitentiam ad Deum* Acts 20.21 (VR 4.1); *quod ad me,* as far as I am concerned: VR 12.8. **b** (w. words implying respect): *respective ad* CI 462. **c** (w. words meaning belonging): *pertinent ad classem* AC 10624. **11** In accordance with; *ad amussim,* precisely, exactly: VR 32.2; *ad vivum,* in a vivid manner, to the life: AM 189; *ad instar* (w. gen.), on the model (of), analogously (with): VR 583. **12** With a view to, for the purpose of, for: *haec duo...unum ad salvationem faciunt* VR 126; *difficile est ad captum dicere* AC 634.1; *arborem...bonam ad cibum* Gen. 2.9 (AC).

adactio ~onis, *f.* The action of driving or impelling: *~o in reciprocas vibrationes* ES 1073; AR 417.8.

adaequate, *adv.* (compar. *~ius*, superl. *~issime* ES 4377) In a suitable manner, evenly, suitably: *ut ~e correspondeant* AC 1832.4.

adaequatus ~a ~um, *a.* Evenly matched, fully suitable: *ut amiciant spiritualia vestibus ~is...ad operandum fines* AM 233; *~a...captui simplicium* SS 40.

adaequo ~are ~avi ~atum, *tr.* (compar. of pf. pple. *~atior*) To make equal; (pass.) to be matched or suited: *quod suo genio favet et ~atur* VR 154.2.

adama: Hebr. word for 'earth' VR 48.13.

adamantinus ~a ~um, *a.* Made of or decorated with diamonds: *~is orbiculis* AM 7.2; as of diamonds: *aura ~a* AC 154.

adamas ~antis, *m.* A diamond: VR 8.4; (as a type of unyielding hardness) *cor suum posuerunt ~antem* Zech. 7.12 (DD 51).

Adamicus ~a ~um, *a.* Of or belonging to Adam: *Ecclesia* CO 4.

adamo ~are ~avi ~atum, *tr.* To love: *verum quod ~atur* VR 660.2; Ezek. 23.15 (AC 9828.8).

adaptate, *adv.* In a fitting manner: *tam correspondenter et ~e* AC 1637.2.

adaptatio ~onis, *f.* A making suitable, fitting: *~onem ad recipiendum* AC 9399; VR 588.2.

adapto ~are ~avi ~atum, *tr.* To make suitable, fit: *continue ~antur* CI 282; *particularia...~ant se suo communi* VR 47.

adaugeo ~gere ~xi ~ctum, *tr.* To increase further: *expectatio...~get* [*anxietatem*] AM 29; (pass.) to be increased, grow: VR 121.2.

adblandimentum ~i, *neut.* An endearing action or word: AC 1517.

adblandior ~diri ~ditus sum, *intr.* (w. dat.) To make oneself agreeable (to): *cui ~diuntur sub amicitiae specie* AC 1088.2; (of things) to be alluring (to), appeal (to): *talia quae ~diuntur sensibus corporis* AM 187; (w. no dat.) Hos. 10.2 (AE 391.25); (in a pass. sense) to be soothed, calmed: *redarguit et increpat illam...sed usque ~ditur per id quod...* AS 419.

adblanditio ~onis, *f.* An endearing action: ES 2973.

addicabilis ~is ~e, *a.* That may be assigned, attributable: VR 640.

addicatio ~onis, *f.* **1** Assignment, attribution: *~onem omnium quae fidei...Domino* AC 10214. **2** Commitment, devotion: *constricta ~o amoris unius ad amorem alterius* AM 306.

addico[1] ~cere ~xi ~ctum, *tr.* **1** To assign, attribute, allot: *angelus ~xit illis loca* AM 23. **2** To hand over, submit: *si se ~xerat negotio* VI 39; *corpus...spontaneis ~ctum* ES 498. **3** To commit, devote: *regna illi religioni ~cta* SS(P) 39 (=16).

addico[2] ~are ~avi ~atum, *tr.* Variant form of **addico**[1] in all its meanings: AC 8042; CI 230; AM 194.2; VR 108.

addictio ~onis, *f.* A transferring, reassigning (of income): *~ones redituum aliunde qui sunt juris alieni* AR 799.2.

addisco ~discere ~didici, *tr.* To acquire by learning: *artificia in mundo ignota quae ibi ~discunt* AC 831.2; AC 1050.2.

additamentum ~i, *neut.* An addition: *Humana... Essentia fuit modo ~um ad Ipsius Divinam* AC 1461.

addo ~ere ~idi ~itum, *tr.* **1** To add: *'H' quod ~itum est nominibus* SS 90; to say in addition, add: *velim his ~ere cur...* AE 31. **2** (ad. Hebr., w. inf.) To say in addition, repeat: *~idit parere fratrem ejus* Gen. 4.2 (AC); *cecidit, non ~et surgere virgo* Amos 5.2 (AC 576.2).

addoctus ~a ~um, *a.* Learned in addition: *scientiae ~ae* ES 1053.

adduco ~cere ~xi ~ctum, *tr.* **1** To lead towards, bring: Zeph. 3.20 (DD 4). **2** To bring about, produce: *~cens diluvium aquarum* Gen. 6.17 (AC). **3** To bring forward, adduce (an example, argument, etc.): *ab exemplis e Verbo ~cendis* SS 7; *~cam memorabile hoc* VR 12.1. **4** (w. *ut*) To induce, impel (to): *partes malae in corpore, quae variis modis ~cuntur ut adjungantur* ES 1711.

adductio ~onis, *f.* A bringing together: *toni discordes qui per solertes ~ones...trahuntur in harmoniam* AM 243.

adeo[1] adire adivi aditum, *tr.* To go to, approach, turn to (for help): *adi Dominum* FI 12; *ut possit adiri* VR 107.1.

adeo[2], *adv.* (w. *ut*) To such an extent (that), so (that): [*Ecclesia*] *devastata erat...adeo ut...* DD 15; *usque adeo ut...* CI 35.

adeps ~ipis, *m.* The fat (of meat): *quod...~eps adoleretur super altari* AC 10033; (ad. Hebr.) the juicy part (of wheat): Deut. 32.14 (AC 3941.2).

adf-: see **aff-**.

adhaerentia ~ae, *f.* Stickiness, tenacity: *quod... vastationes...fiant diversimode secundum ~am malorum et falsorum* CI 513 note z.

adhaereo ~rere ~si, *intr.* (w. dat.) **1** To stick together, cling, adhere: *viscera ~rentia cordi* VR 12.3. **2** To be closely associated: *spiritus quibus...terrestres ideae ~rent* AC 1376. **3** (of persons) To associate oneself (with), cleave (to): *~rebit uxori suae* Gen. 2.24 (AM 156[a].1).

adhaeresco ~ere, *intr.* To begin to adhere, stick, cling: *~it malum ex haereditario* AC 2410.

adhaesio ~onis, *f.* A sticking together, adhesion: *~o ac conjunctio...est amor* AC 3325.9.

adhibeo ~bere ~bui ~bitum, *tr.* To bring into play, apply, use: *judicium ad duas...res ~buimus* AM 112; *voces quae hic ~bentur* AC 209.

adhorreo ~rere ~rui, *intr.* To feel revulsion, shudder (at something): *vincula externa non nescit spiritus dein sed usque ita ~rent ut...* ES 3849.

adhortatio ~onis, *f.* An exhortation, encouragement: AC 2542.

adhortor ~ari, *tr.* To urge, exhort, incite: AC 4734.

adhuc, *adv.* **1** Henceforth: *~c...dies et nox non cessabunt* Gen. 8.22 (AC). **2** Up to that time, still: *hominum ~c viventium spiritus* VR 14.4. **3** Despite this, still: *qui innumera scit et ~c non bonus est* AC 1100. **4** (w. compar.) Even more, still: *~c manifestius* AC 119; *posteriora sunt receptacula priorum, et haec ~c priorum* VR 33. **b** (w. no compar.) in addition, further: *hoc ~c patet* VR 85.2. **5** After that, afterwards: *~c coram illis lectum est* VR 111.8; *post diem ~c* 'a day later' AM 77.1.

adiaphoron ~i, *neut.* (Gk.) also **adiaphorum** ~i, *neut.* (AR 161). A matter of indifference: *fiunt ~a, deinde sicut nauci* AM 5.4.

adiaphorum: see **adiaphoron**.

adigo adigere adegi adactum, *tr.* To impel, drive: *omnipotentiam adigere ad faciendum ita* VR 74.1; *superficiem* [*cordis*] *adigere, ut se elevet sursum* VR 151.

adimo adimere adem(ps)i adem(p)tum, *tr.* To take away, remove: *quod paene adempta esset respiratio* CI 449; (w. dat.) *Dominus omnem potentiam Diabolo... ademerat* DD 17.

adimpleo ~lere, *tr.* To fill up: *plures paginae recensione... ~leri possunt* AM 227.

adinvenio ~nire ~ni ~ntum, *tr.* To find in addition: *sicut novum quoddam ~nissent* AC 340.

adipiscor ~ci adeptus sum, *tr.* To acquire, gain: *homo... ~citur virtutem* AM 109; *vita quam adepti per cognitiones* CI 518.

adipsus ~it, *m.* (Gk.) One who does not suffer thirst: *sunt ~i* [*etiam* Hindmarsh] *qui absque terrestri victu, ita solo atmosphaerico diu vixerunt* SA 121 (= x.3).

aditus ~us, *m.* A means or way of approaching, approach, entrance: *~us communicativus occlusus est* AM 344.

adjacens ~ntis, *a.* Situated close at hand, adjacent, near: *intellectuale...est ~ns et inserviens* AC 10150.

adjectio ~onis, *f.* An adding, addition: AC 2950.

adjectivum ~i, *neut.* An epithet: *infinitum fit ~um Essentialium et Attributorum Dei* VR 36; AR 10.1.

adjicio ~jicere ~jeci ~jectum, *tr.* **1** (w. dat.) To put together (with), add (to): *cum doctrinalia fidei ~jiciuntur* AC 581.1. **2** To induce in addition: *nusquam ...fidem ~jicerent* ES 244. **3** To add in speaking or writing: *his ~jicere licet aliqua loca* DD 6; (w. *quod*) AM 3.6.

adjudicatio ~onis, *f.* The action of judicially assigning; (w. *paenae*) sentencing: AC 9160.

adjudico ~are ~avi ~atum, *tr.* To condemn judicially, sentence: *morti* VR 57.

adjumentum ~i, *neut.* Help, aid, assistance; *~o esse*, to be of help: AC 8719.

adjunctio ~onis, *f.* A joining on: *haec ~o fit a Domino* CI 295; (dist. from **conjunctio** as less intimate) *non conjunctio in unum, sed ~o* AM 158.

adjunctivus ~a ~um, *a.* Joined on; (neut. as sb.) an adjunct: VR 36.

adjungo ~ngere ~nxi ~nctum, *tr.* **1** To join on, attach: *affectio veri...~ncta cognitionibus* AE 208. **2** To give (credence): *quod...tu illis fidem ~ngas* VR 16.1. **3** To associate (persons): *angeli...homini a Domino ~ncti sunt* CI 165; *~ngit sibi septem spiritus* Matt. 12.45 (DD 48).

adjuramentum ~i, *neut.* A sworn covenant: Deut. 29.12 (AC 2838.3).

adjuratio ~onis, *f.* A swearing (by): AC 3023.

adjutorium ~i, *neut.* Assistance, aid: AC 6128.2.

adjuro ~are ~avi ~atum, *tr.* **1** To swear (to): *~avit ei super verbo hoc* Gen. 24.9 (AC). **2** To charge solemnly, adjure: *~o te per Deum viventem* Matt. 26.63 (DD 26).

adjutrix ~icis, *f. adj.* Helping, assisting, auxiliary: *~icem operam* DA 13 (= v.[3]); SA 90 (= vi.[6]).

adjuvo ~vare ~vi ~tum, *tr.* To help, aid: *~vit terra mulierem* Rev. 21.16 (FI 58); AC 1271.

admetior ~tiri ~nsus sum, *tr.* To measure out, mete out: Isa. 65.7 (AC 6960.5).

adminiculum ~i, *neut.* A thing which serves for a purpose, a necessary piece of equipment, aid: *quis potest balaenas...captare absque...~is accommodatis ad capturam?* VR 124.1; *rationis ~o* 'by the aid of reason' AC 1231.

administer ~tra ~trum, *a.* Helping, assisting, auxiliary: *media ~tra* AC 5131.2; (neut. as sb.) a tool: *naturale est modo ~trum et instrumentale* UJ 30.

administratio ~onis, *f.* **1** The action of administering: *~o ritualium* AC 1795.1. **2** A position of responsibility (over others), responsibility: *sunt in coelis sicut in terris plures ~ones, nam sunt ecclesiastica, ...civilia, et...domestica* CI 388. **3** The governing or ordering (of a society): *variae ~ones sunt societatum* CI 217.

administrator ~oris, *m.* An administrator, governor: AM 207.6.

administratrix ~icis, *f.* A female official, manageress: ES 2500.

administratura ~ae, *f.* An administrative office, ministry: AM 207.3.

administro ~are ~avi ~atum, *tr.* To serve as a means to bring about, administer, perform: *~at sacerdos desponsationes* AM 21.4; ES 162.

admirabilis ~is ~e, *a.* Worthy of wonder, wonderful: Rev. 15.1 (AC 395.2).

admiratio ~onis, *f.* **1** Wonder, surprise: *erant in ~one quod...* AM 44. **2** Admiration, awe: *caeca ~o sapientiae* AC 7643.9; *timor sanctus...est ~onis pro Divino* AC 3718; *studuerunt eloquentiae eo fine ut, omnia sint in sui ~onem* AC 1514.

admiror ~ari ~atus sum, *intr.*, *tr.* (intr.) To be surprised, wonder: *ut eruditi...~ati sint et adplauserint* AM 233.2; (tr.) to wonder at, look on in awe at, admire: *visus ocularis superficiem ~atur* ES 252.

admisceo ~scere ~scui ~xtum, *tr.* To mix in: *propriae cupiditates se ~scent* AC 874.

admissio ~onis, *f.* An allowing to enter, admission: *portae...significant ~onem* AE 208; *Dominus...disponit omnia...sed quaedam ex permissione, quaedam ex ~one, quaedam ex venia* AC 1755.

admitto ~mittere ~misi ~missum, *tr.* **1** To allow to enter, admit: *vidi...hos in caelum ~missos* SS 61. **2** To allow to enter (the mind): *non potui in mentem meam aliam ideam...~mittere* VR 16.2; cf. *placuit...in hoc* [sc. *Humanum*] *~mittere homines* VR 135.4. **3** (w. *in se* and sim.) To expose oneself to, undergo (temptation): *tentationes in Se ~missas* AC 8321.1. **4** To permit, allow of: *non ~mittunt loquelam...de vero* AC 1384.

admodum, *adv.* Very much, greatly: *non communicabant nisi ~m remote* AC 920.3; *~m falli* ES 921.

admoneo ~nere ~nui ~nitum, *tr.* To admonish, warn: *nec ~nueris illum* Ezek. 3.18 (AE 186); *nusquam aliquid ~neant* 'never utter a warning' AM 221.

admonitio ~onis, *f.* Admonition, warning: AM 406.

admotio ~onis, *f.* A moving towards, bringing into contact: VR 48.8.

admoveo ~vere ~vi ~tum, *tr.* To bring close (to): *serpens ~tus igni* AM 10.5.

adn-: see also **ann-**.

adnatus ~a ~um, *a.* Acquired by birth: *bonitas...~a a parentibus* VR 537; (w. dat.) associated by birth (with): *quae [mala] inclinationibus ~a sunt* AM 146.

adnumero ~are ~avi ~atum, *tr.* To count along (with), include (among): *quod Ecclesia Noach dicta non ~anda sit Ecclesiis quae ante diluvium* AC 535; (w. *inter*) *illa ~ant inter charitatis opera* VR 453.

adoleo ~lere ~lui, *tr.* To burn (sacrifices): *in sacrificiis ~lebantur [renes]* AE 167; *suffimenta ~luit* Hos. 2.13 (AC 10402.3).

adolescens ~ntis, *m.* or *f.* Someone between the onset of puberty or twenty years of age and full adult life on one's own, a young adult: *puer...~ns, vir, senex* CI 330; *cum ~ns ex proprio intellectu incipit cogitare et agere, ac vox loquelae ejus incipit fieri masculina* AM 444[a]; VR 476; (as adj.) *~ntis virginis* AM 250; *~ns sponsus* AM 108.

adolescentia ~ae, *f.* An age of human life starting as early as the onset of puberty (AM 444[a]) or as late as twenty years of age (AC 10225.1), and ending at the age of full adult responsibility (VR 476), young adulthood: *status...ab anno aetatis vigesimo ad sexagesimum... est status intelligentiae, et vocatur ~a, juventus, et virilitas* AC 10225; *infantia, pueritia, ~a, juventus* AM 185.1; *nulla idea...aetatum hominis, nempe infantiae, pueritiae, ~ae, adultae aetatis, et senectutis* AC 3254.

adolescentilis ~is ~e, *a.* Of or typical of a young adult: *in statum...~em* ES 3146 (Tafel).

adolescentula ~ae, *f.* A young woman of marriageable age: *aliae ~ae quae nubiles* TE 178.

adolesco ~lescere ~levi, *intr.* To grow up, mature: *homo...gestatur, nascitur, ~lescit* CI 269; (w. abl.) *sicut ~lescit et perficitur [homo] intelligentia* AE 150.

adolitio ~onis, *f.* The burning (of a substance as a sacrifice): *per pinguedinem et ejus ~onem* AC 5943.5.

Adonis ~is, *f.* (app. used in error as fem., as a type of loveliness): *ab mea Adonis* VR 80.1. (In ancient mythology Adonis was a youth loved by Venus.)

adoptatio ~onis, *f.* Adoption: *cum rejectione veteris Ecclesiae et ~one novae* AC 4423.1.

adoptio ~onis, *f.* Adoption (as): (w. gen.) *[ut] omnes ~onem filiorum reciperent* SE 4(a); (w. *in* + acc.) *~o in filios* Council of Trent in SE 11(c).

adoptivus ~a ~um, *a.* Adoptive: *~us Filius Dei* UJ(P) 38.

adopto ~are ~avi ~atum, *tr.* To adopt: *quod... infantes...~entur a Domino* CI 416.

adoratio ~onis, *f.* Adoration, worship: *cecidi ad pedes Ipsius significat ~onem* AE 75.

adorator ~oris, *m.* One who worships, worshipper: *sculptilis ~or* AC 2598.

adoratorius ~a ~um, *a.* Of or relating to worship; *lapillos ~os*, prayer beads, a rosary: ES 5407.

adorea ~ae, *f.* A mark of distinction, prize, reward: *meta, ubi ~a ad quam cursum direxit* VR 721.

adorior adoriri adoritus sum, *tr.* To attack: VR 510.1.

adorno ~are ~avi ~atum, *tr.* To trim (lamps): *~arunt lampadas suas* Matt. 25.7 (SS 17.1); to decorate: *denuo ~abis tympana tua* Jer. 31.4 (AC 8337.3); *omnia...quae superficiem ejus* [sc. *mundi*]*...~ant* CC 9.1.

adoro ~are ~avi ~atum, *tr.* To adore, worship: *quo supplicantes et ~antes illos venerunt* AM 265; *hoc [bonum] quoque ~at* AC 81.1.

adp-: see **app-**.

adramandoni See quot.: *Dixit 'adramandoni', quod est delitium amoris conjugialis* AM 183.

ads-: see also **as(s)-**.

adscisco ~scere ~vi ~tum, *tr.* also **as-**. **1** To take to oneself, associate (with): *numerum [uxorum] quem polygamus potest ~scere* AM 345.2; (w. *sibi*) *coeleste naturale quod rationale sibi ~vit* AC 2180.1. **2** (pass.) To be substituted (for), take the place (of): *quod loco eorum qui adorantur alii ~sci possint* ES 2921 titulus; ES 2922.

adscititius ~a ~um, *a.* also **as-**. **1** Assumed or adopted from without: *sunt desumpta e marito et sic ~a* AM 199.1; (neut. as sb.) *qui ex haereditario et inde ~o mites...sunt* AC 5032.2. **2** Supplemental, additional: *hujus voluminis ~i* CO 8.

adscribo ~bere ~psi ~ptum, *tr.* also **as-**. **1** To assign, attribute: *illis tot oculi ~buntur* AE 152.15. **2** To assign the reason of, ascribe, attribute: *omnia naturae ~bunt* AM 416.3.

adsisto ~ere adstiti, *intr.* also **ass-**. **1** To take up a position near, stand by: *ab angelis qui ~unt* ES 1742. **2** (w. dat.) To help, assist: *~ere...oesophago in munere ejus deglutitionis* DA 13 (= v.[3]).

adstans ~ntis, *m.* or *f.* (pres. pple. of **adsto**) also **as-**. A bystander: VR 16.4.

adstipulor ~ari ~atus sum, *intr.* also **as-**. **1** To join in asserting: *gentes reliquae...~antur, quod Deus unus sit* VR 9.2. **2** To give support (in an argument): *hoc...a me tradendum est; at usque ita ut quoque ratio ~etur* AM 45.

adsto ~are ~iti, *intr.* also **asto**. To stand by: *non auditur ab illis qui ~ant* CI 248; (w. dat.) *~abant illis a tergo* AM 16.1.

adstringo ~ngere ~nxi ~ctum, *tr.* also **as-**. To restrain, compel: *faedus...libertinos ad obsequium... ~ngit* AM 307.

adstruo ~ere ~xi ~ctum, *tr.* also **as-**. To build on: *ex columnis muro ejus ~ctis* VR 353.2.

adsuesco ~scere ~vi ~tum, *intr.* also **ass-**. To become accustomed, get used: AC 2294.

adsum adesse adfui, *intr.* (fut. pple. *affuturus*) To be present: (of persons) *in infantia adsunt spiritus* CI 295; (of things) *nisi adsint vera et bona* AC 711; (of times) *ultimum vastationis tempus adesse debeat* AC 411; (w. dat.) to be present or associated (with): *similia quae solent adesse memoriae locorum* ES 1434.

adulator ~oris, *m.* A flatterer: DP 224.1.

adulter ~era ~erum, *a.* Practising adultery, adulterous: *gens ~era et peccatrix* Mark 8.38 (AE 222.7); AM 247; (masc. as sb.) an adulterer: AC 827; (fem. as sb.) AC 6311.

adulteratio ~onis, *f.* A making impure, corruption, adulteration: *~o boni* SS 18.3.

adulterinus ~a ~um, *a.* Of or belonging to adultery, adulterous: *sphaeram ~am foedam* ES 4406.

adulterium ~i, *neut.* Extramarital sexual relations by or with a married person, adultery: SS 67.3; (w. pl.) an instance of this: *~a et scortationes* AE 141.3.

adultero ~are ~avi ~atum, *tr.* **1** To make impure, corrupt, adulterate: *duo...mala...unum quod ~at bona...et alterum quod falsificat vera* FI 49. **2** (pass.) To commit adultery: VI 53.

adultus ~a ~um, *a.* (compar. *~ior* and *~erior*) **1** Of full age, grown up, adult: *progeniem suam ~am* AM 399; *virginis ~ioris* ES 951. **2** (of age) Mature, full: *cum ad ~am aetatem venit* AC 677.

adumbratio ~onis, *f.* An outline sketch: AC 4644.1.

adumbro ~are ~avi ~atum, *tr.* **1** To cast a shadow upon, overshadow, put in the shade (usu. transf.): *quae* [sc. *fama*] *non modo ~at, sed etiam exstinguit lucem* VR 112.5; *virtus Altissimi ~abit te* Luke 1.35 (AE 328.21; VR 112.5). **2** To form an outline sketch of, foreshadow: *quod lavationes...figuraverint et ~averint, hoc est, repraesentaverint lavationes spirituales* VR 671.

adunatio ~onis, *f.* Union: *'esse' talis societatis etiam est conjunctio seu ~o* AC 5002.2.

adunio ~nire ~nivi ~nitum, *tr.* To join or unite to: *cujus animae suam animam ~nit* AM 447.2.

aduno ~are ~avi ~atum, *tr.* To join, unite: *non ~aberis cum iis* Isa. 14.20 (AC 6767.4).

aduro ~rere ~ssi ~stum, *tr.* To subject to intense heat, burn: *laterificemus lateres et ~ramus in ~stum* Gen. 11.3 (AC).

adustio ~onis, *f.* A burning: AC 1297.

adustus ~a ~um, *a.* (of wine) Mulled: DP 254.4.

advectus ~a ~um, *a.* (app., of age) Advanced, i.e., adult: *pueri...ante ~am* [perh. read *adultam*] *aetatem dum suae intentionis fiunt* VR 527.1.

advena ~ae, *m.* One who comes or arrives, visitor, stranger: CI 35; esp. *novus ~a*, a newcomer: AC 1631.

advenio ~nire ~ni, *intr.* To approach, come: ES 226; (w. acc.) to arrive (at): Matt. 2.1 (AE 422.20).

advento ~are ~avi, *intr.* To approach, come close: AC 925.2.

adventus ~us, *m.* An arrival, coming: VR 12.1; esp. the Lord's coming into the world, advent: VR 3.1; or the Lord's coming into a specified state: *~um Ipsius in gloriam* AC 728.1.

adversarius ~i, *m.* An opponent, adversary: Matt. 5.25 (VI 73); VR 409.

adversatio ~onis, *f.* An opposing: AC 3429.

adversitas ~atis, *f.* A state of misfortune, adversity: *consolationes ~atum Ecclesiae* VR 434.

adversor ~ari ~atus sum, *intr.* To show opposition: ES 4223; (w. dat.) to oppose: *amori ejus* AE 159.1.

adversus[1] ~a ~um, *a.* **1** Opposite, opposed: *in ~um*, in the opposite direction: AM 203. **2** (transf.) Contrary, opposing: *sphaerae...~ae et discordes* AM 171.1.

adversus[2], *prep. w. acc.* **1** Opposite, over against: *~us Gilgal* Deut. 11.30 (AC 1443). **2** Against, contrary to: *habeo ~us te quod...* Rev. 2.4 (AR).

advertentia ~ae, *f.* Notice, observation: *hoc absque ~a* AC 5798.5.

adverto ~tere ~ti ~sum, *tr.*, *intr.* **1** To turn towards: *~te aurem* Ps. 80.1 (AE 448.13). **2** To pay attention to, notice, observe, remark: *Dominus ~tit eos* AC 2387; (intr.) to pay attention: AC 8514; (w. *ad*) CI 493. **3** To call to attention, remind, warn: *dum ~tuntur [mariti] ab uxoribus de amore* AM 208.4. 4 (intr., of a state) To change: AC 3614.1.

advincio ~cire ~civi ~ctum, *tr.* To tie on, attach: *odiis suis etiam alios spiritus tenaciter sibi ~ctos tenuit* ES Index s.v. 'odium' (p. 128 Tafel), referring to ES 1267-81.

advocatus ~i, *m.* An advocate, counsel: VR 603.2.

advoco ~are ~avi ~atum, *tr.* To call upon, invoke: *~ans [adorans* Rogers] *solum Dominum* UJ(P) 61 (Tafel, p. 20).

advolo ~are ~avi, *intr.* To come flying, fly in: VR 69.2; *~arunt juvenes sicut ex caelo* AM 7.2.

advolvo ~vere ~vi ~utum, *tr.* To roll towards: AC 3769.1.

adytum ~i, *neut.* (Gk.) 1 The innermost or central part of a temple, inner sanctum, holy of holies: *sicut templum...et in medio ejus ~um* SS 33; *quod Arca ...~um seu intimum Templi Hierosolymitani fecerit* AR 669 (Worcester). 2 Any particularly sacred place, shrine: *hostias...ex ~is altarium depromunt* VR 159.4; (transf.) *in ~o mentis* AM 98.2.

aecumenicus: see **oecumenicus**.

aedes ~is, *f.* A large building, hall: *~em conventus* AM 2.2.

aedicula ~ae, *f.* A small hall: AM 56.1.

aedificatio ~onis, *f.* The action of building: VR 721; (transf.) *in ~onem corporis Christi* Eph. 4.12 (VR 379.1).

aedificium ~i, *neut.* A building: ES 4575.

aedifico ~are ~avi ~atum, *tr.* 1 To build, construct: *~are significat exstruere id quod lapsum est* AC 153. 2 (fig., pass., of a woman having a child by proxy): *forte ~abor ab ea* [sc. *ancilla*] Gen. 16.2 (AC).

aeger ~gra ~grum, *a.* 1 Sick, ill: *~ger opinatur se esse sanum* SE 40; *~gro animo,* sick at heart: *bellum ...non ~gro animo...tulisset* 3AD 613. 2 Accomplished with pain or difficulty, hard, troublesome: *hoc... ~grum illis est* AE 342.12.

aegre, *adv.* (compar. *~grius*, superl. *~gerrime*) With difficulty, hardly: *haec ~gre cadunt in ideam hominis* CI 15.

aegritudo ~inis, *f.* 1 Difficulty, effort: VR 69.1. 2 Sickness, illness: Jer. 14.18 (AE 131.9).

aegrotatio ~onis, *f.* The state of being sick, illness: AC 6221.1.

aegroto ~are ~avi, *intr.* To be sick, be ill: CI 470.

aegrotus ~a ~um, *a.* Diseased, sick, ill: *quod... sanaverit ~os per tactum* AM 396.3; (neut. as sb.) a sickness: *animi ~um* AC 227.

Aegyptiacus ~a ~um, *a.* Egyptian: *idola ~a* AC 1195.

Aegyptius ~a ~um, *a.* Egyptian: *hieroglyphica ~orum* SS 20.

aemulatio ~onis, *f.* Rivalry: *~o uxorum pro honore* AM 78.5.

aemulor ~ari ~atus sum, *tr., intr.* 1 (tr.) To imitate: *ex amicitia...simulata quae ~ari vult sinceram* CI 406. 2 (intr.) To contend in rivalry, strive: *Ephraim non ~abitur cum Jehuda* Isa. 11.13 (SS 15); (w. dat.) *~atae sunt illi...arbores* AE 110.

aemulus ~a ~um, *a.* (w. gen.) Imitating: *amores ...~i caloris genuini amoris* AM 271; (masc. as sb.) a rival: *ut...prae aliis seu ~is excellat* AC 3518.2.

aeneus ~a ~um, *a.* also **aheneus**. 1 Made of bronze: *murus ~us* AC 699. 2 (of the third age) *Saeculum ~um*, the Bronze Age: *tertium saeculum ~um seu cupreum* AE 70.1.

aenigma ~atis, *neut.* (Gk.) A riddle: *~ata proposuit [regina Schebae]* 1 Kgs. 10.1 (AC 117.2).

aenigmaticus ~a ~um, *a.* Speaking in riddles, enigmatic: *vox obscura et ~a ex tripode...emissa* DP 340.2.

aenum ~i, *neut.* also **ahenum**. A vessel made of bronze, cauldron, copper: ES(M) [4737].

aequalis ~is ~e, *a.* 1 Equal, identical: *longitudo, latitudo et altitudo ~es* Rev. 21.16 (CI 307.1); (w. dat.) *Dominum...~em Deo Patri* AM 332.2; (w. abl.) *~is Patre quoad Divinum* DD 35.1. 2 Regular, even: *pulsus...~is* ES 1101.

aequalitas ~atis, *f.* Equality: AM 291.2.

aequaliter, *adv.* Regularly: SA 88 (= vi.[2]).

aequatio ~onis, *f.* A making equal, equalizing: *~o caloris et lucis* AM 222.4.

aequator ~oris, *m.* The Equator: ES 566; also, the Celestial Equator: ES 4673.

aeque, *adv.* Equally: AM 273.2; (w. *ac*) VR 77.3; (w. *quam*) AE 1170.4.

aequilibratio ~onis, *f.* The action of holding equally balanced, balancing: *per ~onem inter binos...influxus* AC 6308.

aequilibris ~is ~e, *a.* Evenly balanced: *sententia super lance ~is* VR 48.2.

aequilibrium ~i, *neut.* Equality of balance, equilibrium: *de ~o inter caelum et infernum* VI 20.

aequilibro ~are ~avi ~atum, *tr.* To hold the balance even, balance: *nihil...quod non ~atur a suo opposito* AC 689.

aequinoctialis ~is ~e, *a.* Of the equinox, equinoctial: AM 104.

aequinoctium ~i, *neut.* One of the two times of the year when day and night are of equal length, equinox: CI 141.

aequiparo ~are ~avi ~atum, *tr.* To compare: (w. dat.) *amor et sapienta...~ari possunt calori et luci* VR 67.

aequitas ~atis, *f.* **1** Due proportion, balance: *ut... teneantur in aequilibrio, hoc est, in ~ate cogitandi, loquendi agendique* ES 2361. **2** Fair behaviour, impartiality, equity: *secundum ~atem naturalem* VR 413.

aequivaleo ~lere ~lui, *intr.* To be of equal strength: (w. dat.) *unius vis ~let vi alterius* CI 537.2.

aequivocus ~a ~um, *a.* Of ambiguous meaning, equivocal: *de formulis ~is* ES 1304; (neut. as sb.) an ambiguous statement, equivocation: *~a seu lusus verborum* ES 805.

aequo ~are ~avi ~atum, *tr.* To be equal to, equal: *facie, cujus latitudo ~at quatuor...facies aliorum* AC 830; to make equal: CI 593.

aequus ~a ~um, *a.* **1** Equal: (neut. as sb.) *lux... ~um seu unum agit* AM 188.1; *ex ~o*, equally: VR 41.2. **2** Fair, equitable: (neut. as sb.) *justum et ~um* CI 468.2.

aër aëris, *m.* (Gk.) The earth's atmosphere, air: *loquela... influit primum in aërem* CI 248; (dist. from **aether**) the lowest stratum of the atmosphere: *datur...aura suprema, aether sub illa, et aër infra hunc* VR 32.8.

aerarium ~i, *neut.* A treasury: *ex publico ~o* VR 430.

aereus[1] ~a ~um, *a.* Made of bronze; (of the third age) *saeculum ~um*, the Bronze Age: AC 1551.1.

aëreus[2] ~a ~um, *a.* Belonging to or composed of air, airy: *effigies ~ae* AM 182.7; ES 222.

aërifer ~era ~erum, *a.* Carrying air: *vasa quae vocantur ~era* [i.e., air vessels] AS 412.

aeruginosus ~a ~um, *a.* Of copper rust: *in ferruginosum et ~um [colorem]* AM 115.1.

aerugo ~inis, *f.* Copper rust, verdigris: Matt. 6.19 (DP 217.6).

aerumna ~ae, *f.* Trouble, distress: AM 294.8.

aerumnosus ~a ~um, *a.* Wretched, distressed: Rev. 3.7 (AR 208).

aes aeris, *neut.* The metal bronze: *aes et ferrum* SS 84.2; (as the metal of coinage) *quod non possiderent aurum nec argentum nec aes* Matt. 10.9 (AE 242.22).

aesculus ~i, *f.* A horse chestnut tree: AM 78.2; VR 815.

aesophagus: see **oesophagus**.

aestas ~atis, *f.* Summer: CI 105.

aestimatio ~onis, *f.* **1** Reckoning, judgment, estimation: *~o veri* SS 12.2. **2** Good opinion, esteem: *non plus in ~one sunt* CI 526.4.

aestimatus ~a ~um, *a.* (superl. *~issimus*) Highly esteemed: AC 2540.2.

aestimo ~are ~avi ~atum, *tr.* **1** To assess the worth of, value: *aurata...~antur secundum artem* VI 10; *vitam suam pro vili ~ant* AM 333.1. **2** To reckon, judge: *nihil ibi ~etur secundum spatia* CI 198. **3** To hold in esteem, value: *quisque sua ~at et amat* CI 292.

aestivus ~a ~um, *a.* Of or belonging to the summer: *caloris...~i* AE 59.

aestrum: see **oestrus**.

aestrus: see **oestrus**.

aestuo ~are ~avi ~atum, *intr.* **1** To be excessively hot, burn: *~averunt homines aestu magno* Rev. 16.9 (AR); AM 235.3. **2** (of emotions) To be roused: *~arunt paenitudines meae* Hos. 11.8 (AC 588.3); (of persons) to be inflamed with emotion: *cum ~averint* Jer. 51.39 (AE 481.5).

aestuositas ~atis, *f.* Excessive heat: *~as brutalis* 2AD 2125.

aestuosus ~a ~um, *a.* Excessively hot: (neut. as sb.) *~um...et salsuginosum...destruunt terram* AC 1666.4; (fig.) *ardor veneris...~us* AM 459.2.

aestus ~us, *m.* **1** Heat, hot weather: *neque percutiet eos ~us aut sol* Isa. 49.10 (AE 386.27). **2** The heat or fire of passion: *visi sunt nigri ex ~u cupiditatum* AC 1063.2; (dist. from **calor**) AM 155.1.

aetas ~atis, *f.* **1** The length of time one has lived, age: *annorum numerus non significat ~atem vitae* AC 515. **2** Appropriate age: *cum ad ~atem suam provecta est [soboles apium]* VR 12.7; old age: *ex ~ate* VI 111. **3** A person of a particular age: [*in caelo*] *omnis ~as juvenescit* VR 137.4. **4** A period of life: *in prima et secunda ~ate* VR 159.7; *cum quatuor ~atibus hominis* CI 166. **b** one of the four traditional ages of mankind: SS 117; also, the people of a particular age: *~ates sequentes...non potuerunt videre* VR 37.1.

aeternitas ~atis, *f.* Infinite time, eternity: VR 27; *dies ~atis* 'the most ancient time' AC 16.

aeterno ~are ~avi ~atum, *tr.* To confer immortality on, perpetuate, eternalize: *jucundum caeleste...~at illa* AM 18.3.

aeternus ~a ~um, *a.* **1** Everlasting, eternal: *in ignem ~um* Matt. 25.41 (VI 2); *vitae ~ae* John 6.68 (SS 2.3). **2** (neut. as sb.) Eternity: *~um est infinitum temporis* AM 185.3; *in ~um*, for ever: VR 2.2.

aether ~eris, *m.* (Gk.) **1** An invisible and intangible atmosphere believed to surround the earth, the ether: *~er in terris et aquis per quem orbis...circumagitur* VR 30.2; (conceived as higher or more subtle than the air) VR 32.8; AC 827; AC 6057.1. **2** (pl.) The skies: *usque ad ~eres* Ps. 36.6 (AC 9857.6); Ps. 78.23 (AE 146.4).

aethereus ~a ~um, *a.* Made of ether, ethereal: *formae illae ~ae* VR 79.6.

aevum ~i, *neut.* A particular period of time, age: *~i Saturnini seu saeculi aurei* AM 153[a].2; *in sequenti ~o* VR 9.3.

affabilis ~is ~e, *a.* Easy to converse with, approachable, affable: AM 182.1.

affabilitas ~atis, *f.* Affability: AM 16.3.

affabiliter, *adv.* Affably: *loqui ~er* ES 5692.

affatim, *adv.* In a large quantity, amply: AC 824.

affectatio ~onis, *f.* (w. gen.) A striving after, seeking: *officiorum* AC 1509.

affectio ~onis, *f.* **1** The state of being acted upon or affected: *hic sensus* [sc. *gustus*] *est modo ~o substantiae et formae, quae sunt linguae* AS 41; *~o mentis* AM 155[a].1. **2** (w. adj.) A physical condition or ailment: *~o caeliaca* AM 253.2. **3** A permanent or ongoing attribute of the will or heart, love: *~o seu amor dominans* CI 236.3; *quantum ducit illum ~o* CI 358; *voluntatis ~o est finis a quo* DP 178.2; (also, in animals) *~ones connatae* AM 134.2. **b** a disposition or inclination: *~o amandi scientiam, intelligentiam et sapientiam* AM 91. **c** a specific love, passion, or interest that forms part of one's central love: *omnis ~o...in sua essentia est amor subalternus derivatus ab amore vitae* DP 195.1; *~o amoris caelestis* DP 74.2. **d** (w. gen. denoting the object of affection) love, affection (for): *derivationes amoris caelestis sunt ~ones boni et veri* DP 106.2; *~o sciendi* AS 410; *ex ~one honoris, gloriae et lucri* AS 416; *in ~one sinceritas* DP 146; *~o justitiae* VR 186.2; (also, w. *pro*) AC 831.2. **4** A temporary state or condition of the will, emotion, feeling: *omnium ~onum et cogitationum communicatio et perceptio exquisitissima datur in altera vita* AC 549; *per status ~onis pudoris* AC 1641.2; CI 168.3; *mirati sunt quod sculptilis adorator tanta misericordiae et innocentiae ~one moveretur* CI 324; *~o desiderii* CI 479; *~o laetitiae,... ~o doloris* DP 49.

affectionalis ~is ~e, *a.* Of or concerned with the affections: *hoc genus hypocritarum est ~ium* ES(M) 4653.

affectiuncula ~ae, *f.* A small affection: AC 2367.1; ES 433.

affecto ~are ~avi ~atum, *tr.* **1** To seek after, strive for, aim at: *~are bonum* ES 570; *mutationem sui status* VR 12.6; (w. inf.) to seek or strive (to): *~at imperare* VR 45. **2** To pretend to have, feign: *quod amor conjugialis, ubi non genuinus est, usque ~andus sit* AM 276.1.

affectus ~us, *m.* An emotion, feeling: *voluntas...non est nisi quam ~us et effectus alicujus amoris* AM 461.6; CI 324.

affero afferre attuli allatum, *tr.* also **adfero** in pres. system. **1** To bring to, inflict, apply: *reges afferent gloriam* Rev. 21.24 (AE 31.4); *si non...medela affertur* VR 73.1; *nullum alicui incommodum afferunt* AC 1125. **2** To adduce, cite, quote: *ex Verbo afferentur loca* VR 93.

afficio ~ficere ~feci ~fectum, *tr.* **1** To act upon, affect: *omnia...~ficiunt internum hominem* VR 24.1. **b** (pass., w. abl.) to be subjected (to): *verberibus ~ficerentur* ES 1788. **2** To produce an emotional effect upon, move: *est usus qui nos ~ficit* AM 16.3; (pass.) *corde ~ficitur* VI 89. **3** (w. abl.) To cause to be affected (by), inspire, fill (with): *pulchritudo...~ficiens charitate...vitam mentis* AC 553.2; (pass.) *pudore ~fici* AC 217. **4** (pass., w. abl.) To feel affection (for): *qui amant vera et ~ficiuntur illis* SS 91.

affigo ~gere ~xi ~xum, *tr.* To attach, affix: *his amorem suum adjungunt, ~gunt, et agglutinant* AM 405.2.

affinis ~is ~e, *a.* (compar. *~ior*) **1** (masc. as sb.) A relation, relative: VR 120.1. **2** (transf.) Similar in nature, akin: *in ~i bono* AE 16.2.

affinitas ~atis, *f.* A relationship, affinity: *propinquitates et ~ates amoris* AM 158.1.

affirmans ~ntis, *a.* (pres. pple. of **affirmo**) (neut. pl. as sb.) Supportive arguments: *inde sic ~ntia trahunt* ES 1737.

affirmatio ~onis, *f.* An affirmation: AM 258.

affirmative, *adv.* In an affirmative manner: *quidam dubitative, quidam ~e jactant et spargunt talia* ES 1571.

affirmativus ~a ~um, *a.* Affirmative: *sententiae ~ae* AE 147.

affirmo ~are ~avi ~atum, *tr.* To assert as true, affirm: *~ari sicut vera* AE 1; (w. *quod*) SS 23.4; to give an affirmative answer, say Yes: *~abant tandem cum dicerem folia ficus* AC 8377.

affixio ~onis, *f.* A fastening: *paxilli seu clavi ~onem seu adjunctionem* AC 8990.5.

affixus ~a ~um: pf. pple. of **affigo**.

afflatus ~us, *m.* A breathing on, breath: *ex ~u caloris coelestis* CI 525.

afflictio ~onis, *f.* Affliction: Matt. 24.21 (AM 80.3).

afflicto ~are ~avi ~atum, *tr.* To afflict repeatedly: *malos paupertate* DP 216.1.

affligo ~gere ~xi ~ctum, *tr.* To distress, afflict: *mens... ~gitur a falsis* AE 47.

afflo ~are ~avi ~atum, *tr.* To breathe or blow upon: *si...~aret [Deus] illos* VR 124.1; (of things) to be felt like a breath: *jucunda...~averunt illos* VR 79.8.

affluentia ~ae, *f.* A flowing towards, tide: Deut. 33.19 (AE 445. 5); (transf., of people) the gathering of a crowd: *viderunt ~am ex omni angulo terrae* AM 9.1.

affluo ~ere ~xi, *intr.* **1** To gather in crowds: *~ebat turba* CI 344. **2** To be rich: *tunc videbis et ~es* Isa. 60.5 (AC 489.1).

affluxus ~us, *m.* A flowing towards, afflux: *caloris* CI 135; approach (of crowds): *via ~us* VR 160.3.

affor ~ari ~atus sum, *tr.* To speak to, address: CC 19.1.

affore: fut. inf. of **adsum**.

affulgeo ~gere ~si, *intr.* (w. dat.) To shine (upon): *illis...lux ~get* CI 265; (transf., of hope) ES 220.

affundo ~ndere ~di ~sum, *tr.* To add or apply copiously, heap on: *corporea...~ndunt umbras* AC 4027.2.

Africanus ~a ~um, *a.* African; (masc./fem. as sb.) an inhabitant of Africa, African: VR 64.

agapae, *f. pl.* The reading is almost certainly unsound; J Elliott suggests emending to *cryptae* (cf. CI 488.2): CO 45.

agens ~ntis, *neut.* (pres. pple. of **ago**) An acting force, agent: *quae ~ntia si auferrentur, substantiata...concidерent* VR 30.2; *~ns seu actio* AM 293.5.

agentia ~ae, *f.* Activity, action: CI 589.1.

ager agri, *m.* **1** Cultivable land, the field: *ex messibus agri* VR 12.9; *distinguitur...inter bestias...terrae ac inter bestias...agri* AC 46.3. **2** A piece of such land, a field: *agri et novalia* FI 63.1; CI 104; (w. epithet of place) *de agris Gomorrhae* Deut. 32.32 (SS 51.9). **3** *Agri sylvae*, the woods: Ps. 132.6 (DD 6).

agger ~eris, *m.* **1** An earthwork for purposes of war, ramp: *poneret vallum et ~erem contra Hierosolymam* Ezek. 4.2 (SS 16). **2** A breakwater, mole: AC 1661.3.

agglutino ~are ~avi ~atum, *tr.* To fasten on with glue, stick on: *ova ~ant foliis [papiliones]* VR 361.3; (transf.) to join indissolubly: *his amorem suum adjungunt, affigunt, et ~ant* AM 405.2.

aggravo ~are ~avi ~atum, *tr.* **1** To weigh down, make heavy: ES 436; (transf.) *aures ejus* [sc. *populi*] *~a* Isa. 6.10 (AC 303.1); *~avit Jehovah spiritum...regis* Deut. 2.30 (DD 48.2). **2** To make worse, aggravate: *~et damnationem* BCP (VI 6); *dolores...~abantur* ES 153. **3** To annoy, aggravate: *quae...~arunt et offenderunt spiritus* ES 2293.

aggredior ~di ~ssus sum, *tr.* **1** To attack, assault: *urbem munitam ~di* VR 84; *inferna... ~diantur coelum* CI 595. **2** (w. inf.) To set oneself (to), attempt (to): *~ssi aedificare turrim* AC 1283.

aggrego ~are ~avi ~atum, *tr.* (refl.) To flock together (with), join oneself (to): *se ~ant hircis* VR 536.3; (of things) UJ(P) 291.

aggressio ~onis, *f.* Attack, aggression: CH 164 (= vii.[5]).

aggressor ~oris, *m.* An attacker, aggressor: CH 164 (= vii.[5]).

aggressus ~us, *m.* An attack, assault: AC 1820.5.

agilis ~is ~e, *a.* Agile: *facere pedes sicut cervarum ~es et ad currendum habiles* AC 6413.2.

agitatio ~onis, *f.* **1** A setting in violent motion, agitation: *sanguinis motus seu ~o* 3AD 2342. **2** (Bibl.) A wave-offering: Exod. 29.24 (AC).

agito ~are ~avi ~atum, *tr.* **1** To set in rapid or violent motion, shake, toss: *~antibus eum aquis* AC 891. **2** To argue about, discuss: *post subtilitates inaniter ~atas* AM 111.

agmen ~inis, *neut.* **1** A column of troops, line: *quis rex...non convocat ~ina* CO 13. **2** (of things) A mass, accumulation: *quod post mortem [animae] evolent ad ~en prius* IM 12.

agminatim, *adv.* In columns: *spiritus...turmatim et ~im circum volitant* ES 2393.

agna ~ae, *f.* A ewe-lamb: CI 110.

agnatus ~i, *m.* A blood relation, relative: AM 282.2.

agnellus ~i, *m.* A young lamb: Isa. 40.11 (AC 1736.3); ES 330.

agnitio ~onis, *f.* Recognition, acknowledgment: *Dei* VR 5; (w. *quod*) AM 153[a].2.

agnitor ~oris, *m.* One who acknowledges: DP 236.

agnosco ~noscere ~novi ~nitum, *tr.* (contracted pf. 3rd pers. pl. *~norunt*) **1** To recognize (a person) as known to one, acknowledge: *per signari...significatur ~nosci a Domino* SS 11; (w. predicate) to recognize as: *~noscebant se feras* ES 229. **2** To acknowledge the existence of, recognize: *Deum* VR 5; *Dominum* DD 15.2. **3** To recognize (a fact) as true, acknowledge: *aliud est* *veritates scire et veritates ~noscere* AC 896.1; (w. *quod*) AM 69.1.

agnus ~i, *m.* A lamb: AM 75.3; (used of the Lord) DD 46.5.

ago agere egi actum, *tr.* (*intr.*) **1** To set in motion, impel, drive: *ovem* VR 57; *latas radices agunt* 'spread their roots widely' ES 1436; (absol.) *navis in torrente contra viam ejus agente* VR 57; cf. *finis qui agit et ducit media* VR 13.3. **2** To stir (a person or his mind) emotionally, rouse, drive: *zelo...agi* AC 593; *mentes...per id in tale delirium actae sunt* VR 4.2; *vincula quibus agitur* [*homo*] AC 81.3. **3** To perform, execute, do: *ut redemptionem ageret* VR 83; *paenitentiam* Luke 13.3 (VI 103); *bonum* AC 503. **b** *gratias agere* (w. dat.), to thank: AM 25. **c** to lead (a life): *piam egerunt vitam* ES 274. **d** to keep (a festival): Gen. 5.1 (AC). **4** (intr.) To act (in a specified manner): *ex libero agere* AE 9.4; *absolute* VR 73.1. **b** *unum agere*, to act as one or in concert: *unum agunt ut causa et effectus* SS 5; (w. *cum*) VI 1. **5** To play (a part): *amor principale agat* AC 63; *primas partes* VR 105. **b** to play the part of, act: *agit hypocritam* VR 14.4. **6** (intr., of things, w. *in* + acc.) To exercise an effect, act (upon): *binae rotae...in se mutuo agerent* VR 57; *malum...agit in homine et in hominem* VR 154.4. **7** (intr., of speakers, writers, books, etc., w. *de*) To deal (with), treat (of), discuss: *Verbum...non de mundanis agit* AC 1151.2; (impers. pass.) *de quibus ...agendum est* CI 67; *negotia de quibus agebatur* CI 563. **8** *Actum est* [*de*], it is all over (with): *prorsus actum fuerit de Ecclesia* DD 55.4; AC 582.

agon ~onis, *m.* (Gk.) The struggle (for life), (mortal) agony: *usque ad vitae ~onem* AM 292.2; *in ~one mortis* AC 6571.2.

agrestis ~is ~e, *a.* (of plants, etc.) Not cultivated, wild: *pabulum* AC 274; *mel* Matt. 3.4 (DD 15.8).

agricola ~ae, *m.* A farmer: *parabola de ~is in vinea* VI 2.

ah, *interj.* also **ahah** (Jer. 14.13 (AC 2799.9)). Ah, oh: *ah Deus, misereatur nostri* AC 699.

ahah: see **ah**.

aheneus: see **aeneus**.

ahenum: see **aenum**.

aio: see **ajo**.

ajo (no inf. or pf.), *intr.* also **aio**. To say: (w. dir. speech) AM 44.2; (w. *quod*) CI 9; (w. acc. and inf.) AC 680.1.

ala ~ae, *f.* **1** The wing (of a bird, flying insect, etc.): *~ae aquilae* Rev. 12.14 (AR); (transf.) *~ae venti* 'the wings of the wind' Ps. 104.3 (AE 36.3); (fig.) *~is spiritualibus per quas res quae cogitatur elevatur e memoria* AC 6200.1; also, a sail (of a windmill): *ad ~as molae* VR 364.3. **2** The outer edge (of a flowing garment), skirt, hem: *periculamentum super ~is vestium* Num. 15.38 (VI 2); Zech. 8.23 (DD 4); the wing (of a collar): VR 137.1. **b** a side-piece, wing (on either side of the gate of the court of the tabernacle): Exod. 27.14 (AC). **3** A squadron (of cavalry): *Gomer et omnes ~ae ejus* Ezek. 38.6 (AC 1151.2).

alabastrum ~i, *neut.* (Gk.) Alabaster: AM 76.3.

alacer ~cris ~cre, *a.* (compar. *~crior*) Lively, keen: CI 403.

alacritas ~atis, *f.* Liveliness, keenness: AM 164.

alacriter, *adv.* In a lively manner, keenly: *sic ut recipiant satis ~er* ES 2955.

alapa ~ae, *f.* A slap: Matt. 5.39 (AC 9049.4).

alatus ~a ~um, *a.* **1** Endowed or equipped with wings, winged: *equum* AM 182.2; (w. abl.) *Auroram ~am pennis argenteis* VR 112.1; (neut. as sb.) AC 776.1. **2** (of sounds) As if made by wings, vibrant: *loquela...~a* ES 412; *ex...sono canoro ~o* AC 418.2; CI 339.

albe, *adv.* Whitely, palely: ES 548; ES 2866.

albedo ~inis, *f.* Whiteness: AC 1126.

albens ~ntis, *a.* White: *~ntis faciei* TE 76.

albescens ~ntis, *a.* (pres. pple. of **albesco**) Whitening, whitish: *pileo...~nte* AC 830.

albesco ~ere, *intr.* To become white: *peccata...sicut nix ~ent* Isa. 1.18 (VI 30); AM 233.4.

albo ~are ~avi ~atum, *tr.* To make white, whiten: AE 476.

albugo ~inis, *f.* A white spot in the pupil of the eye, leucoma, albugo: ME 2.

albus ~a ~um, *a.* **1** White, light-coloured: *vestes candidae et ~ae absque splendore* AM 178; *veste ~a coerulea* [i.e., light blue] ES 1080; (neut. as sb.) the colour white: AC 731; white garments: AC 1269. **2** (of persons) Light-skinned, white: ES 432.

alchymia ~ae, *f.* Alchemy: SS(P) 19 (= 7.5).

alcohol ~lis, *neut.* Alcohol: VR 98.1; AM 145.2.

Alcoranum ~i, *neut.* (Arab.) see also **Coranum**. The Koran: AM 342.1.

alea ~ae, *f.* **1** A game of chance, dice: *ludum familiarem ~ae* AC 6494. **2** Risk, chance: *extra omnem dubitationis ~am* VR 369.1.

aleph, *indecl.* (Hebr.) The first letter of the Hebrew alphabet, aleph: AR 38.

ales ~itis, *m.* A large bird, bird of prey: AM 416.2.

Alexandrinus ~a ~um, *a.* Of Alexandria: *Arii presbyteri ~i* VR 632.

alga ~ae, *f.* Seaweed: Jonah 2.5 (AC 1691.5); water plants: Exod. 2.3 (AC).

algebraicus ~a ~um, *a.* Of algebra, algebraic: ES(M) 4578.

alias, *adv.* At another time: *de quo* [sc. *statu*] *alias* ES 164.

alibi, *adv.* In another place, elsewhere: SS 23.1; in another passage (of a book): AM 414.

alicubi, *adv.* In some place, somewhere: *~i et non ubivis* AM 315.8; (w. neg.) anywhere: *quod non possit dari ~i unum idem cum altero* AS 155.

alienigena ~ae, *m.* A foreigner, stranger: AC 1097.1.

alienus ~a ~um, *a.* Of or belonging to another, not one's own: *mulieres ~as* AM 208.4; (w. *ab*) different (from), foreign (to): *qui vident ~a a fide* CI 535.1.

alimentum ~i, *neut.* (sg. or pl.) Food, nutriment: VR 12.5.

alimonia ~ae, *f.* Food: VR 48.8.

alioqui: see **alioquin**.

alioquin, *adv.* also **alioqui**. **1** If this were not so, otherwise: *dicetur quid correspondentia, ~in non comprehendi potest quale est Verbum* AE 1080.2. **2** At other times: ES 243; at other places (in a book): *~in sex in Verbo occurrunt* AC 737.3.

aliorsum, *adv.* To another place, elsewhere: *quandoque in caput, quandoque ~um* AC 1381; AS 23.

alipes ~edis, *a.* Wing-footed: *qui* [*equi*] *sic excurrebant sicut ~edes* AM 103.1.

aliqualis ~is ~e, *a.* Of a certain sort, some: *purificationem* AE 386.30; *ad ~em distantiam* AC 822.

aliqualiter, *adv.* To a certain extent, somehow: *quae si ~er modo exponerentur* AC 2574.2.

aliquamdiu, *adv.* For a certain length of time, for some time: *potui ~u teneri in spiritu* AM 155[a].1.

aliquando, *adv.* At times, from time to time: *haec urbs iis ~o apparet magnifica* ES 751.

aliquantillus ~a ~um, *a.* Of any small amount or extent: *nec recipiat ~um influxum* AE 982.5.

aliquantisper, *adv.* For a short time, for a while: AM 7.1; to some slight extent: CI 210.

aliquanto, *adv.* (w. compar.) To some extent, somewhat: *remotiorem* AC 1153.3.

aliquantulus ~a ~um, *a.* Of some small amount or extent, some little: *remissionem* ES 157; (neut. as sb.) a small quantity: AC 884; (neut. as adv.) to some small extent: AS 341.

aliquantum, *adv.* To some extent, somewhat: *~um comprehendi potest* CI 47; *quidam mihi ~um notus* ES 758.

aliquantus ~a ~um, *a.* Some, a certain: *ad ~am distantiam a nostra tellure* TE 105; *post ~am commorationem separantur* CI 494.

aliquatenus, *adv.* Within certain limits, to some extent: AM 189; CI 459.

aliquis ~a (*or* ~ae) ~id (*or* ~od), *pron.* and *adj.* (app. no difference in usage of *~id* and *~od*, both being used as pron. and adj.) **1** (pron.) **a** (masc. and fem.) Someone; (esp. w. neg., virtual neg., questions or conditions) anyone: CI 183.1; *quomodo ~is potest effugere mala...?* VR 535. **b** (neut.) something: *~id nunc dicetur* DD 17.1; (w. neg., etc.) anything: *nec ~id cogitationis* AM 354.1; *si...offendit ~od* VR 525. **2** (adj.) Some: *~a vena* AM 6.6; *~is amor* AM 243; (w. neg., etc.) *~id verum* AC 2906.1; *~od coelum* AC 3482; *vix ~ae reliquiae* VR 4.1.

aliquot, *indecl. adj.* Some number of, several: *ante ~t menses* VR 4.1.

aliquoties, *adv.* A number of times, several times: VR 25.1.

aliter, *adv.* In another way, otherwise: CI 96; *non possunt ~er ac scire* 'they cannot help knowing' AC 408.

aliunde, *adv.* From another place: AC 1115; from another source: *cognitiones...discant ~e* AC 1198; to another place: *~e postea transferuntur* ES 669; ES 3133.

alius ~a ~ud, *a.* (gen. sg. *~us*, dat. sg. *~i*) **1** Not the same, different, other: *~um angelum* Rev. 7.2 (AR). **2** (masc. as sb.) Another person: *non sui et ~us gratia* AC 1088.2; (neut. as sb.) another thing: AC 4044. **3** *~us...et ~us*, of one sort...and of another, one... and different: [*lux*] *~a...est in regno coelesti...et ~a in unaquavis societate* CI 128; (neut. as sb.) *~ud intelligere et ~ud velle* CI 425. **4** *~i aliter*, some in one way, some in another: CI 488.6.

allabor ~bi ~psus sum, *intr.* To move smoothly (towards): *~psus ille ad pectus Jesus, dicit* John 13.25 (AC 6960.4).

allaboro ~are ~avi, *intr.* (w. inf.) To strive (to): *~ant...illos abducere* AC 6663.1; VR 56.

allapsus ~us, *m.* A gliding towards: ES 542.

allatus ~a ~um: pf. pple. of **affero**.

allectamentum ~i, *neut.* A thing which allures, enticement: *~um ad accedendum* AM 82.1.

allectatio ~onis, *f.* An enticing: AC 9348.1.

allecto ~are ~avi ~atum, *tr.* To allure, entice: *~averunt illos ad matrimonium* AM 275.

allectrix ~icis, *f. adj.* Alluring, enticing: AM 155.1.

allegatio ~onis, *f.* A citing, quotation: CO 59.1.

allego ~are ~avi ~atum, *tr.* To cite in evidence, quote: *in supra ~ato loco* AC 7553.3.

allegoricus ~a ~um, *a.* (Gk.) Allegorical: (neut. as sb.) VR 810.

alleluia: see **alleluja**.

alleluja, *interj.* (Hebr.) also **alleluia, halleluia, halleluja, hallelu-Jah, halleluJah** (Schm. **halelu-Jah**, see AC 8331 3rd edn.). Hallelujah: Rev. 19 (AR); AC 8267.2; ES 4779; Rev. 19.6 (AE 273.6).

allevo ~are ~avi ~atum, *tr.* To lift up, raise: CI 335.

allicio ~licere ~lexi ~lectum, *tr.* To obtain by enticement, attract: *aliorum bona* ES 909; *affectionem ad se ~licit* AM 272; to win over (a person): ES 381.

allido ~dere ~si ~sum, *tr.* To strike against, dash in pieces: Isa. 13.16-18 (AC 8902.2).

alligamentum ~i, *neut.* An ornament tied on, sash: AM 300.2; Isa. 3.20 (AC 2576.11).

alligatio ~onis, *f.* A binding on: AC 396.2.

alligo ~are ~avi ~atum, *tr.* **1** To bind or tie on, tie up: *~abat armillas super poplites manuum* AM 20.3; *~at ad vitem asellum suum* Gen. 49.11 (AC). **2** (transf., w. dat.) To attach (to): *~ant ideas suas objectis* AC 1644; *mali... ~antur societati infernali* CI 427.

allium ~i, *neut.* (pl.) Garlic: Num. 11.5 (AE 513.6).

alloquor ~qui ~quutus (*or* ~cutus) sum, *tr.* To speak to, address: CI 438.

alluo ~ere ~i, *intr.* To arrive: [*navicula*] *per undas ~it* VR 119.2; *spiritus ex mundo ~entes* AC 454; *verum quod ~it* AC 798.

alo ~ere ~ui ~tum, *tr.* **1** To give nourishment to, feed: CI 108.3; (transf.) *homo regeneratur et quoque ~itur* AE 175.4. **2** To allow to exist, harbour (suspicions, etc.): AM 374.

aloe ~es, *f.* (Gk.) The juice of the aloe plant: AC 10252.7.

alpha: see **alphah**.

alphabeticus ~a ~um, *a.* Of the alphabet, alphabetical: *litera* VR 19.2.

alphabetum ~i, *neut.* (Gk.) The alphabet: AM 326.5.

alphah ~ae, *f.* also **alpha**. The first letter of the Greek alphabet, alpha: VR 19.2.

altare ~is, *neut.* An altar: *quid ~e nisi lapideum quid?* AC 922.1; AC 9714.10.

alte, *adv.* (compar. *~ius*, superl. *~issime*) **1** In or to a high position: *supra caput ~issime* AC 1115; (transf.) *non ~ius se elevare* [*sensualibus*] *permittendum* AC 746. **2** In a loud voice, loudly: VR 72.2. **3** At a great remove, deeply: *causa ~ius latuit* AC 999.2. **4** (of thinking, knowing, etc.) Profoundly, deeply: *qui ~ius cogitat* AC 241; *orbis... ~e ignorat* AC 2.

alter ~era ~erum, *a.* (gen. sg. *~erius*, dat. sg. *~eri*) **1** The other (of a pair): *quantum...homo est in uno...tantum non potest esse in ~ero* VI 18; *~er...~er*, the one...the other: *dictamen ~erius in ~ero* FI 1; *~era vita*, the other life: AC 5. **2** Second: *in primo...in ~ero...in tertio* AC 1802.1. **3** *Unus et ~er* or *unus ~erve*, one or two: VR 32.4; CI 258.

alteratio ~onis, *f.* A change (for the worse), alteration: ES 490.

altercatio ~onis, *f.* A dispute, quarrel: AR 435.

altercor ~ari ~atus sum, *intr.* To dispute, quarrel: *~antur de omni re num ita sit* AR 435.

alternatim, *adv.* Alternately: AC 8607.

alternatio ~onis, *f.* Alternation: AC 933.4.

alternative, *adv.* Alternately, by turns: ES 4629.8.

alternis, *adv.* Alternately, by turns: AM 271.

alterno ~are ~avi, *intr.* (*tr.*) To exist by turns, alternate: *~at nulla vita et ipsa vita* AC 933.2; *~ant status* AE 481.2; (tr.) *vices ~are*, to alternate: CI 159; (pass.) to alternate: [*status*] *quovis anno ~antur et quovis die* AC 8211.2.

alternus ~a ~um, *a.* Successive: (neut. pl. as sb.) *judicamus...constantias ~orum ejus* [sc. *amoris*] AM 110.

altero ~are ~avi ~atum, *tr.* To make different, change, alter: CI 48.

alteruter ~tra ~trum, *a.* One or other (of two): AC 9331.

altitudo ~inis, *f.* **1** Vertical measurement, height, depth: Rev. 21.16 (AR). **2** Exalted station: *ex persuasione suae ~inis et praeeminentiae* AC 580. **3** Penetrating quality, depth (of thought, feeling, etc.): *~o et profunditas...cum praedicatur de sapientia* AC 1613.3; *perspicere res in eadem ~ine* AM 175.3.

altus ~a ~um, *a.* (compar. *~ior*, superl. *~issimus*) **1** High, lofty: *montem* AC 920.1; (neut. as sb.) a high place: Isa. 26.5 (AC 258); *in ~o*, on high: VR 69.2. **2** (masc. as sb.) Exalted: *sic dixit ~us et Excelsus* Isa.

57.15 (AC 795.5). 3 (of sounds) Loud: *~a voce* VR 74.2; AM 17.1. 4 (of sleep) Profound, deep: *in ~o sopore* AC 1072.6.

alumna ~ae, *f.* A nurse: *infantes cum ~is illorum* AM 13.1.

alumnus ~i, *m.* One who is reared or fostered, ward, charge: VR 459.8.

alveare ~is, *neut.* A beehive: VR 12.7; ES 3340.

alveus ~i, *m.* The bed (of a river or sea): Ezek. 6.3 (AC 1292.4); Ps. 18.15 (AC 8286.4).

alvus ~i, *m.* The intestine, stomach: *~o ruminatorio* DP 233.8; *excrementa ~i* VR 569.5.

amabilis ~is ~e, *a.* (compar. *~ior*) Fit to be loved, lovable: *pulchra uxor ~is viro ex castitate* VI 46.

amabilitas ~atis, *f.* The quality of being fit to be loved, lovableness: AM 211.

amaene, *adv.* also **amoene**. Pleasantly: EA 11.

amaenitas ~atis, *f.* also **amoenitas**. Pleasantness, loveliness: *ab omni pulchritudine, ~ate et jucunditate* CI 56.2; (pl.) *cum delitiis et ~atibus* CI 517.3.

amaeno ~are ~avi ~atum, *tr.* also **amoeno**. To make pleasant: AM 285.2; AE 365.14.

amaenus ~a ~um, *a.* also **amoenus**. (compar. *~ior*, superl. *~issimus*) Giving pleasure, pleasant, lovely: *victu ~o et dulci* VR 12.6; AC 996.1; (neut. as sb.) a pleasant sensation, pleasure: *hoc ~um, dum percipitur, est verum ex bono* VR 38.1.

amando ~are ~avi ~atum, *tr.* To send away, banish: AM 406.

amans ~ntis, *a.* (pres. pple. of **amo**) (compar. *~ntior*) Loving: AM 94.

amare, *adv.* (superl. *~issime*) Bitterly: *~e flent* CI 287.1; ES 220.

amarico ~are ~avi ~atum, *tr.* To make bitter: Rev. 10.9-10 (AR).

amaritudo ~inis, *f.* Bitterness: AM 364; Hos. 12.15 (AC 1232).

amaror ~oris, *m.* A bitter herb: Exod. 12.8 (AC).

amarus ~a ~um, *a.* 1 Bitter to the taste: AC 3470.2. 2 Acrimonious, bitter: *gentem ~am* Hab. 1.6 (AC 1613.2); *verbo ~o* Ps. 64.3 (AE 131.17).

amasius ~i, *m.* A lover: AM 333.2; Lam. 1.19 (AC 680.4).

amatio ~onis, *f.* The action of loving: AM 401.

amator ~oris, *m.* One who loves, a lover: *sapientiae* VR 48.1.

amatorium ~i, *neut.* The action of a lover, making love, embrace: *dilexerunt ~a uxorum suarum* AM 433.

amaurosis ~eos, *f.* (Gk.) Loss of sight from disease of the optic nerve, amaurosis: VR 346.2.

ambages ~um, *f. pl.* A circuitous route: *circumduxit illos per ~es a plaga in plagam* AM 8.1.

ambigo ~ere, *intr.* To be in two minds, doubt: *~unt de justo* AM 207.4.

ambigue, *adv.* Ambiguously, doubtfully: VI 77.

ambiguitas ~atis, *f.* A state of doubt, ambiguity: AM 532.4.

ambiguus ~a ~um, *a.* 1 In a state of doubt, doubtful: *facti sumus ~i de felicitate aeterna* AM 8.3; (neut. as sb.) *in ~o*, in doubt: VR 35.10. 2 (of words or statements) Of uncertain meaning, ambiguous: *vox* AC 519.2.

ambio ~bire ~bivi, *tr.*, *intr.* 1 (tr.) To surround: *tres athmosphaerae ~bientes priores illas* VR 76.3. 2 To pay attention to, court: *quod virum oporteat ~bire et rogare faeminam de conjugio* AM 297. 3 (tr.) To seek after, strive for: *dignitates... ~bivimus* AM 266.3; VR 98. 4 (intr., w. inf.) To seek or strive (to): *ut maximus ~biat esse* AC 1419; (w. *in* + acc.) to seek to reach: *~biebant in coelum* AC 538.

ambitio ~onis, *f.* A seeking after: *famae* AM 377.2.

ambitus ~us, *m.* 1 The surrounding region: *locum sortitae in ~u* VR 79.3; AM 115.1. b a surrounding part, edge, parapet: *facies ~um tecto* Deut. 22.8 (AC 10184). 2 A seeking after, striving for: *in ~u honoris* CI 236.3.

ambo ~ae ~o, *pl. adj.* and *pron.* Both: *~as illas conjungunt* AM 293.3; *~o similem vitam...egerunt* CI 531.3.

ambrosia ~ae, *f.* (Gk.) (in classical mythology) The food of the gods, ambrosia: AC 4966.2.

ambulacrum ~i, *neut.* A place for walking, promenade, walk: *~a circumcincta arbustis* AM 326.1.

ambulatio ~onis, *f.* The action of walking or an instance of this: AC 1379.

ambulatorium ~i, *neut.* A covered place for walking, gallery: *~um palatii* AM 14.1.

ambulo ~are ~avi, *intr.* (fut. pple. *~aturus*) 1 To walk: *claudi ~ant* Matt. 11.5 (SS 17.4). b (w. internal acc.): *via quam ~ant* 4AD Jer. 7.24. 2 To walk (in a specified manner, often as the equivalent of to live): *homo...~at medio inter caelum et infernum* VR 69.2; *post baales non ~avi* Jer. 2.23 (AC 1292.3); AC 519.1. 3 (of things) To proceed, advance: *fides et vita pari passu ~ant* VI 52.

ambustus ~a ~um, *a.* (pf. pple. of **amburo***) Superficially burnt, scorched: *~is uvis* VR 328.

amen, *interj.* (Hebr.) Verily: *in Hebraea lingua veritas et fides una vox sint, quae vocatur amuna seu amen* FI 6.

amens ~ntis, *a.* Out of one's mind, distracted, mad: AM 212.

amenter, *adv.* In a distracted fashion, madly: CC 4.4.

amentia ~ae, *f.* Unsoundness of mind, madness: Zech. 12.4 (AC 2761.7).

Americus ~a ~um, *a.* American: ES 3194.

amethystus ~i, *f.* (Gk.) A precious stone of blue colour, amethyst: Rev. 21.20 (AR); AC 9870.

amianthus ~i, *m.* (Gk.) A mineral, amianthus: VR 192.

amica ~ae, *f.* A female friend: AC 4054.1.

amice, *adv.* In friendly fashion: AM 292.1.

amicio ~cire ~civi ~ctum, *tr.* **1** To clothe, dress: *vestes quae ~ciunt* SS 40.1; (refl.) to put on clothes, clothe oneself: AM 7.2. **2** To cover as with clothing: *spiritus corpore ~ctus* AC 69; VR 38.3; VR 60.

amicitia ~ae, *f.* Friendship: *in ~a aut in amore* AC 1038.1; *~a non est charitas* AC 1158.2.

amictus ~us, *m.* Clothing, dress: *solicitudo...de victu et ~u* CI 277.2; *corpus quod est ~us animae* AC 1073.

amiculum ~i, *neut.* A cloak, robe: Ezek. 26.16 (AE 275.5); a covering, dress: [*calor et lux naturalis*] *inserviant calori et luci spirituali pro ~o et adminiculo* VR 75.2.

amicus ~a ~um, *a.* (superl. *~issimus*) **1** (adj.) Friendly: *virgines...~ae* Ps. 45.15 (AM 21.3); VR 12.5; *vultum ~um, imo ~issimum* AC 4327.2. **2** (masc. as sb.) A friend: AE 25.1; (voc. as a mode of address) FI 43.

amissio ~onis, *f.* The act of losing, loss: *~onis possessionum* AC 6914.4.

amita ~ae, *f.* A father's sister, paternal aunt: Exod. 6.20 (AC).

amitto amittere amisi amissum, *tr.* To lose: *postquam amiserat imaginem Dei* AM 132.4; (also w. inf.) to lose the power (of): *timor...quod amitterent vivere* ES 2899.

amo ~are ~avi ~atum, *tr.* (compar. of pres. pple. *~antior*) **1** To have a liking for, be fond of: *notum est quod infantes ~ent lac* ES 2084. **2** To experience a deep affection for, love: *coeleste...est ut ~et Dominum et ~et proximum* AC 1894.1; *quod...~et verum* FI 12. **b** (of God): *Ecclesia a Domino ~ata* AC 414.4. **3** (of human relationships): *~avit et desponsavit sibi filiam* Mal. 2.11 (AC 4434.3). **b** *sexum ~are*, to make love: *de modis ~andi sexum* VR 48.8; AM 55.7.

amoen-: see **amaen-**.

amor ~oris, *m.* **1** Love regarded as an active principle which directs life: *ad producendum illa quae ~or vult* VR 35.6; *~or...non aliud est quam nisus ad conjunctionem* VR 43.3; *~or facit totum hominem* AE 6. **2** Love as an attribute of and the essence of God: *quod...Deus sit Ipse ~or et Ipsa Sapientia* VR 3.1; *Domini ~or fuit salus universi generis humani ardentissimus* AC 1820.5; *Divinus ~or* SS 3. **3** Love directed towards a particular object, love of a specified sort: *~orem erga proximum* AC 1153.1; *cognoscit unus alterum...ex similitudine ~oris* CI 427; *~ores sunt multiplices* DP 106.1; *hic ~or...est ~or malus* AM 88.2; *~or conjugialis* AC 2039.1. **b** love directed towards God: *~orem in Dominum* AC 1153.1. **c** love directed towards abstract qualities: *~orem pro bono et vero* AC 8897; *~or, qui est affectio boni, producit fidem* FI 13. **4** Love as an emotion experienced by one individual for another: *~or viri ad faeminam* AM 55.6; *qui...in casto ~ore conjugii vixerunt* CI 489.7. **b** *~or sexus*, the sexual expression of love: *~or sexus, qui...vocatur fornicatio* AM 447.1; *quod bestiae...nascantur...in omnia quae ~oris sexus* VR 48.9.

amotio ~onis, *f.* A moving away, removal: *peccatorum* VR 135.5.

amoveo ~vere ~vi ~tum, *tr.* To move away, remove: *mala* AE 240.4.

amphitheatrum ~i, *neut.* (Gk.) An amphitheatre: AM 231.2.

ample, *adv.* (compar. **amplius** q.v.) To a large extent, extensively: AM 171.3.

amplector ~cti ~xus sum, *tr.* **1** To embrace: AM 216.2. **2** To take up, embrace (a principle, etc.): *fidem* AC 409; *haereses* SS 52. **3** (w. abl.) To surround (with): *circumdare significat cultu ~cti* AE 391.12.

amplexatio ~onis, *f.* An embracing: AC 3807.

amplexor ~ari ~atus sum, *tr.* To embrace: ES 228.

amplexus ~us, *m.* (of things) Close juxtaposition, embrace: *quod origo Ecclesiae et origo amoris conjugialis sint in eadem sede, et ibi in mutuo ~u* AM 238.3.

amplificatio ~onis, *f.* A making larger, enlargement, increase: *rei familiaris* AM 274.

amplifico ~are ~avi ~atum, *tr.* To make larger, enlarge: *dominium* AM 267.3.

amplificus ~a ~um, *a.* Magnificent: *ex ~o horto* VR 365.4.

amplio ~are ~avi ~atum, *tr.* To make larger, enlarge, increase: *dominatus...~andus* VR 819.

amplitudo ~inis, *f.* **1** Fullness of extent, amplitude: *libertas...perspiciendi res in sua ~ine* VR 814. **2** Dignity, rank (of official position): *secundum ~inem officiorum* VR 281.6.

amplius, *adv.* (compar. of **ample**) **1** At greater length, further: *~us describi nequit* AC 200; *~us dixerunt* CI 270.5. **2** (w. neg.) Henceforward, hereafter, any more: *ut non sint duo ~us* AM 306; VR 14.2. **3** (w. neg.) Otherwise, further: *non ~us Deus praeter Me* Isa. 45.21 (VR 6.3).

amplus ~a ~um, *a.* (compar. *~ior*, superl. *~issimus*) Large in size or extent, extensive: *~issimum templum* AM 9.1; (neut. as sb.) VR 31.

amputo ~are ~avi ~atum, *tr.* To cut short, cut off: *hastam* Ps. 46.9 (AC 1664.7); to amputate (a limb): *si dextra manus scandalizaverit te, ~a illam* Matt. 5.30 (AM 316.5).

Amstelodamensis ~is ~e, *a.* Of Amsterdam: ES 339.

amuna See quot.: *quod in Hebraea lingua veritas et fides una vox sint, quae vocatur amuna seu amen* FI 6.

amurca ~ae, *f.* Lees of oil: (pl.) VR 519; ES 3811.

amussis ~is, *f.* (acc. sg. *~im*) **1** A straight edge, ruler: *describit illud ~i* Isa. 44.13 (AC 9424.10). **2** *Ad ~im*, exactly, precisely: VR 32.2.

amygdala ~ae, *f.* An almond (kernel): Gen. 43.11 (AC).

amygdalatus ~a ~um, *a.* Made to resemble almonds, almond-shaped: *scyphi* Exod. 25.33 (AC).

amygdalinus ~a ~um, *a.* Of almonds: *placentas* ES 3858.

amygdalum ~i, *neut.* (Gk.) An almond (kernel): AM 109.

amygdalus ~i, *f.* An almond tree: AC 5622.2.

an, *particle.* **1** (introducing a dir. qu.): *an potes cogitare aliquid?* AS 1. **2** (introducing an indir. qu.) Whether: *non scio an queat ad captum exponi* AC 1043.1. **b** (following *utrum*, to introduce 2nd part of a double qu.): *vix scire potui utrum essem in corpore an extra corpus* ES 1706.

analogia ~ae, *f.* An analogy: *quod similitudo et ~a sit inter formationem hominis...et inter ejus reformationem* SA 84 (= iv titulus).

analogice, *adv.* By analogy: AC 4570.2.

analogicus ~a ~um, *a.* Analogical; (neut. pl. as sb.) AC 4570.2.

analogon ~i, *neut.* (Gk.) (w. gen.) That which stands instead (of), an analogue (of): *~on perceptionis* AC 1442; *illa tria [essentialia] vertantur in ~a* AM 183.3; *per ~on*, by analogy: AM 238.1.

analogus ~a ~um, *a.* (w. gen.) Analogous (to): *in statum...~um status caelestis* VR 12.6.

analysis ~eos, *f.* (Gk.) (acc. sg. *~in*) An analysis (of arguments, etc.): *per varias ~es rationales* CI 500.

analytice, *adv.* In an analytical manner: *~e cogitare* VR 12.8.

analyticus ~a ~um, *a.* (Gk.) Capable of analysis, analytical: *mens...summe ~a* VR 28; (neut. as sb.) an analytical argument: AC 1072.2.

anastomosis ~eos, *f.* (Gk.) (anat.) A connecting vessel or orifice, anastomosis: VR 60.2.

anataria ~ae, *f.* A bird of prey, (perhaps) vulture or owl: *etiam platea et ~a in malogranatis ejus pernoctabunt* Zeph. 2.14 (AC 1188.4).

anathema ~atis, *neut.* (Gk.) A curse, anathema: *~ate percussi* VR 688.

anathematizo ~are ~avi ~atum, *tr.* To subject to a curse, anathematize: VR 380.2.

anatome ~es, *f.* (Gk.) Dissection, anatomy: ES 1625; AM 416.2.

anatomia ~ae, *f.* Anatomy: AS 399.

anatomicus ~a ~um, *a.* Of or relating to anatomy: CI 353.1; (masc. as sb.) an anatomist: DP 180.3.

anceps ~ipitis, *a.* **1** Two-edged: *romphaea ~eps* Rev. 1.16 (AR). **2** (of persons) Uncertain, doubtful: *qui haerent ~ipites in dubitatione et affirmatione* CO 9; (of propositions, attitudes, etc.) wavering, doubtful: *quod ita sit, apparet adhuc sicut ~eps* AS 218; *ex ~ipiti fide* CC 3; *in ~ipiti*, in doubt: *qui in ~ipiti de religione haerent* VR 820.2.

anchora ~ae, *f.* An anchor: VR 57.

ancilla ~ae, *f.* A female servant, maid: AM 250.

angelice, *adv.* In an angelic manner: ES 1221 ½.

angelicus ~a ~um, *a.* Of or belonging to angels, angelic: *loquelam ~am* CI 245; *sapientia ~a* FI 4; (of a certain heaven) *e caelo ~o* AM 316.5; *spiritus ~us*, a spirit of the second heaven: AC 1642.

angelus ~i, *m.* (Gk.) **1** A messenger (of God): *mitto ~um meum* Mal. 3.1 (DD 6); cf. VR 92; (of the devil) Matt. 25.41 (VI 2). **2** An angel: *quod...non sit unus ~us qui a principio creatus est* CI 311.2.

angina ~ae, *f.* Angina pectoris: VR 482.2.

Anglicanus ~a ~um, *a.* Anglican: *Ecclesiae ~ae* AE 885.3.

Anglicus ~a ~um, *a.* English: AM 326.4.

ango ~gere ~xi, *tr.* To cause pain, hurt: *mala ~gunt et cruciant* AC 6997.4; (refl. and pass.) to feel pain, be hurt: (refl.) ES 527; (pass.) *incipiunt ~gi ac interius cruciari* CI 400.1.

angor ~oris, *m.* Intense pain, anguish: CI 400.1.

anguiculus ~i, *m.* A small snake: ES 3810.

anguis ~is, *m.* A snake: AC 831.3.

angularis ~is ~e, *a.* Placed at the corner: *in termino ~i* AC 941.1; (masc. as sb.) a cornerstone: Isa. 19.13 (AC 1462.2).

angulatus ~a ~um, *a.* Having sharp corners: ES 1995; (neut. pl. as sb.) AC 5981.

angulus ~i, *m.* **1** A corner: *in quatuor ~is* AM 20.1; *in ~is susurrant in aures* CI 488.2. **2** (geom.) An angle: *secundum ~um incidentiae* AS 41.

angustatio ~onis, *f.* A compressing or restricting, restriction: ES 241.1.

angustator ~oris, *m.* One who causes distress, oppressor: *Ubi ira ~oris?* Isa. 51.13 (AC 4728.6).

angustia ~ae, *f.* Distress: *~a respirationis* AC 1119; Job 5.19 (AC 737.2).

angusto ~are ~avi ~atum, *tr.* To distress, trouble: *cor mulieris ~atae* Jer. 48.41 (AC 583).

angustus ~a ~um, *a.* (compar. *~ior*) **1** Narrow: *~am viam* CI 428; *flumen ~um* Isa. 59.19 (DD 50.1). **2** Restricted: *~a respiratio* AC 1119.

anhelatio ~onis, *f.* Panting: ES 307.

anhelitus ~us, *m.* Shortness of breath: *deficientes ~u* VR 136.5.

anhelo ~are ~avi, *tr., intr.* **1** (tr.) To draw (breath) in gulps, inhale: *onagri...~arunt ventum* Jer. 14.6 (AE 419.10); (transf.) *~avimus devotionem* VR 159.3. **2** (intr.) To pant: *ut spiritus illorum ~arent* AM 7.2. **3** To yearn, pant (for): *homo...~at semper versus infimum infernum* DP 183.1.

anhelus ~a ~um, *a.* Gasping, panting: *quosdam sicut ~os ad loquendum* AM 5.1.

anima ~ae, *f.* (dat. and abl. pl. *~abus*) **1** Breath: *Deus...dat ~am populo* Isa. 42.5 (DD 49.1). **b** (ad. Hebr.) a creature: *factus est homo in ~am viventem* Gen. 2.7 (AC). **2** The immortal part of the human personality, soul: *~a est intimum et supremum hominis* VR 8.1; VR 103.1. **b** (Bibl., used of God): *in quo beneplacitum habet ~a mea* Isa. 42.1 (DD 6). **3** A soul freed from the body: *vitam ~arum seu recentium spirituum post mortem* AC 320; *~ae vocantur ii qui nondum locum sortiti sunt in maximo corpore* ES 2547. **4** The animating and essential principle of anything, inspiration, soul: *ut sanguis dici queat ~a corporea* AC 1001.6; *agnitio Dei...est ipsa essentia et ~a omnium in...theologia* VR 5.

animadversio ~onis, *f.* = **animadvertentia**: ES 720.

animadvertentia ~ae, *f.* A taking notice, noticing: *conscientia seu interna ~a* AC 219.

animadverto ~tere ~ti ~sum, *tr.* (*intr.*) **1** To be aware of, notice, remark: *correspondentias ~ti in coelo* CI 109; *influxum* VR 12.8; (w. acc. + inf.) BCP (VI 6). **2** (intr., w. *ad*) To pay attention (to), remark (on): *secundum ea ad quae prius ~tebam* ES 195 (J D Odhner).

animal ~lis, *neut.* A living creature, animal: *hominum, et in genere ~lium* AM 380.12; (dist. from man) a beast: *distinguitur...homo ab ~li per id quod ei mens spiritualis sit* VI 86; (of the creatures in Revelation) Rev. 4.6 (AR); (seen by Ezekiel) AC 2162.6.

animalculum ~i, *neut.* A small animal or insect: AM 329.1; (of a locust) AC 7643.10.

animalis ~is ~e, *a.* **1** Of or proper to a beast, animal: *homo qui...est...~is cum spectat deorsum* AC 1702.2; *ex tribus regnis naturae, quae vocantur ~e, vegetabile et minerale* SS 66. **2** Of or relating to the physical principle of life, vital, animate: *corporis ~is* CI 103; *spiritus ~is* 'animal spirit' AC 4227.3.

animans ~ntis, *neut.* A living creature: *~ntia terrae* AC 4525.

animatio ~onis, *f.* The action of breathing, a breath: AS 383.3.

animatorius ~a ~um, *a.* Of or relating to breathing, respiratory: *motus systolicus et ~us* SA 100 (= vii.3.[2]).

animatus ~a ~um, *a.* Possessing life, animate: *principium ~um* CI 602.

animo ~are ~avi ~atum, *tr., intr.* **1** (intr.) To draw breath, breathe: *spiritum ducere seu ~are* ES 1614; AM 115.3. **2** (tr.) To give life to, animate: *internum...quod ~et et vivificet* AC 1795.2. **3** (tr.) To draw in as breath, breathe in, absorb: *~arem illa* [sc. *gaudia*] *in aeternum* AM 10.3.

animositas ~atis, *f.* Courage, spirit: ES 996.

animosus ~a ~um, *a.* (superl. *~issimus*) Brave, courageous, spirited: AM 209; ES 1153; also, puffed up, inflated: *ii ~i, sicut colon suo vento* ES 993.

animus ~i, *m.* **1** The mind as the seat of consciousness and means of thought: *qui in contextu historico tenent ~um* AC 1143; *versare ~o*, to turn over in the mind, think of: CI 532.2; (cf. w. sense 3) *interiora quae mentis seu ~i sunt* CI 480. **2** A particular state of mind: *si...hilari ~o est* AC 5576.3. **3** (dist. from **mens**) The lower, more external or natural mind: *mens inferior seu naturalis, vulgo ~us* 1AD 61; *interiora hominis quae ejus mentis et ~i sunt* CI 30; *mentes exhilarant, ~os oblectant* AM 5.4. **4** The mind as typical of the individual, character: *alium quasi ~um sibi assumit* AC 3527.1; *quia diversis ~is erant ex vita in mundo* CI 427; *quot capita, tot ~i* VR 32.2. **5** An intention, inclination, propensity: *per ~os intelliguntur affectiones et inde inclinationes externae* AM 246.2; (w. gen.) *~us erat...necandi* AC 959; *~us odii...elucet* AC 1079.2. **b** *~o*, with the intention (of): *ut ~o sint occidere* AC 391; *~o ut offenderent* AC 950; *~o me suffocandi* AC 1879.1.

ann-: see also **adn-**.

annales ~ium, *m. pl.* Chronicles, annals: CO 35.2.

annascor ~sci ~tus sum, *intr.* To be born or arise in addition: *id [verum] quidem ~scitur malo* AC 2689.4; (w. dat.) to be born along with: *quod homini non ~scatur [reflexio continua]* ES 4226.

anne, *particle* and *conj.* **1** (to introduce a dir. qu.): *si animam suam in vita corporis destruit, anne eam in aeternum?* AC 794.2. **2** (to introduce an indir. qu.) Whether: *ei respondere dabatur...anne sciat quod...* AC 444.

annecto ~ctere ~xi ~xum, *tr.* (w. dat.) To link on, join: AC 9236.

anniculus ~a ~um, *a.* One year old: *agnum ~um* AC 3994.7 (Autograph).

annihilatio ~onis, *f.* Annihilation: AE 355.28.

annihilo ~are ~avi ~atum, *tr.* also **adnihilo**. To reduce to nothing, annihilate: CI 538; VR 134.3.

annon, *particle.* **1** (to introduce a dir. qu. expecting an affirmative reply) Surely: *~n sic essentiam... Divinam dividitis?* VR 16.3. **2** (in indir. qus.) Whether ...not: *expende...~n...unum expungit alterum* VR 4.2.

annona ~ae, *f.* Corn for sale: *vidit Jacob, quod esset ~a in Aegypto* Gen. 42.1 (AC); cf. AC 5405.1.

annosus ~a ~um, *a.* (superl. *~issimus*) Having lived many years, aged: VR 137.2.

annoto ~are ~avi ~atum, *tr.* To write a note on: ES 350.

annuentia ~ae, *f.* Assent, agreement: AC 2433.

annullo ~are ~avi ~atum, *tr.* To render of no account, annul: ES [6098.2].

annulus ~i, *m.* **1** A ring worn on the finger: *imposuit digito ejus ~um aureum* AM 20.3. **2** A ring used for other purposes: Exod. 25.26 (AC); Exod. 28.23 (AC).

annuntiatio ~onis, *f.* An announcement: *~one adventus Domini* AC 220.

annuntiatum ~i, *neut.* A thing announced or reported, announcement: AC 10240.2.

annuntio ~are ~avi ~atum, *tr.* To announce, report: *~ate Johanni quae auditis et videtis* Matt. 11.4 (SS 17.4); (of a statement) AC 1731; (absol.) *~abo de statuto* Ps. 2.7 (DD 6).

annuo ~ere ~i, *intr.* (fut. pple. *~iturus*) To assent, agree, allow: *quod Filius ~erit* VR 134.2; *~erunt manibus, quod liceret* AM 113.

annus ~i, *m.* A year: AS 73; the year of one's life, age: *~um Noachi* AC 755.5.

annuus ~a ~um, *a.* Lasting a year: *~um tempus* AC 1636; (of the motion of planets around the sun) annual: *motus ~us Jovis est 12 annorum* ES 583.

anodynon: see **anodynum**.

anodynum ~i, *neut.* (Gk.) also **anodynon** ~i, *neut.* A painkilling remedy, anodyne: VR 665.6.

anomalia ~ae, *f.* An irregularity, anomaly: ES 2414.

ansa ~ae, *f.* An opportunity, chance: *privaretur ~is inde profitendi* ES 927.

anser ~eris, *m.* A goose, gander: AM 246.3.

ansula ~ae, *f.* A clasp, fastening: Exod. 26.11 (AC).

antagonista ~ae, *m.* (Gk.) An antagonist, opponent: ES(M) [4804]; ES 4549.

ante, *prep. w. acc.* also *adv.* see also **ab ante**. **1** In front of, before: *~e fores* VR 3.1. **2** Previous to, before (in time): *~e tempus meridiei* AM 11; *~e aliquot menses* 'some months ago' VR 4.1. **3** Before (in sequence): *~e capita Libri Exodi* AC 6627. **4** (adv.) In front, before: *cum...cogitarem...de praecipitio quod ~e erat* ES 3406.

antea, *adv.* Previously, before: *saepius ~a dictum est* AM 130.1.

anteactus ~a ~um, *a.* Previously engaged in, preceding: *vita ~a* AE 125; (neut. pl. as sb.) preamble: *in ~is hujus capitis* AC 137.

antecedens ~ntis, *a.* (pres. pple. of **antecedo**) Preceding, previous: DD 31; (masc. as sb.) a predecessor: *ab...avo, proavo, atavo et ~ntibus* AC 313; (neut. pl. as sb.) preceding remarks: AC 6845.

antecedo ~dere ~ssi, *intr.* To precede: AC 2430.

antecessus ~us, *m.* *In ~um*, as a preliminary, in advance: *in ~um memorare licet...* DD 37.1.

antedictus ~a ~um, *a.* Previously stated: (neut. pl. as sb.) CC 15.6.

antediluvianus ~a ~um, *a.* Existing before Noah's flood, antediluvian: *Ecclesiae ~ae* AC 635; (masc. pl. as sb.) AC 259.2; (as a kind of wicked spirit) *hodierni ~i* AC 2754.

anteeo ~teire, *tr.* To precede, go before (in time): *libido ...~teit sapientiam* AM 108.

antefero ~rre, *tr.* To prefer: *agni sunt mitissimi, et omnibus ~rendi* 2AD 2185.

antehac, *adv.* Before the present time, previously: *quod haec in Ecclesiis ~c non data sint* VR 789.3; earlier (in a book): DP 193.2.

antemurale ~is, *neut.* A fortification constructed in front of a wall, bulwark: *instar ~is seu munimenti* AE 365.35; AC 402.2.

antenuptialis ~is ~e, *a.* Previous to marriage, premarital: *faedus ~e* AM 307.

antepono ~nere ~sui, *tr.* To prefer: *quod status virginitatis et caelibatus ~nendus sit statui conjugiali* AR Doc RC.7.

antequam, *conj.* Before: (w. indic.) *~m haec sciunt* AC 692; *~m venit dies Jehovae* Joel 2.31 (DD 4); (w. ellipse of vb.) *in damnationem veniunt, ~m in infernum* AC 8333; (w. subj.) *~m mundus esset* John 17.5 (AC 1603.2).

anterior ~or ~us, *compar. a.* Of the front, front, leading: *~or pars...zonae* AM 15; (neut. pl. as sb.) the front parts: *~ora...equi* VR 113.3.

anterius, *compar. adv.* Nearer to the front: *in infernis ~us* CI 123.

antesignanus ~i, *m.* A leader, protagonist: AC 1879.2; CI 74.2.

anthrax ~acis, *m.* (app.) Charcoal or coal: *consumti ~ace* [*combusti pruna* Autograph] Deut. 32.24 (AC 4832).

anthropophagus ~i, *m.* (Gk.) A cannibal: *spirituales ~i* VR 380.4.

antichristus ~i, *m.* A being diametrically opposed to Christ, antichrist: *non potest nisi ab ~o negari* VR 167; (pl.) UJ(P) 297.

anticipo ~are ~avi ~atum, *tr.* To perform hastily or before due time, hasten on: *conjugia* AM 459.1; *in via, quae contracta et ~ata erat* AM 78.2.

anticuria ~ae, *f.* An outer court or hall: AM 11.

anticus ~a ~um, *a.* Frontal, forward: *a parte ~a* CO 52.

antiecclesia ~ae, *f.* The opposite of a church: *connubium mali et falsi est ~a* AM 497.

antipathia ~ae, *f.* (Gk.) Mutual hostility, antipathy: AM 272.

antipathicus ~a ~um, *a.* Antipathetic, hostile: [*inclinatio*] *discors et ~a* AM 47[a]; (neut. as sb.) AM 171.1.

antipodes ~um, *m. pl.* (Gk.) The people on the other side of the globe: *quod ~es nusquam stare possent pedibus* AC 1378.2; AS 275.5.

antiquitas ~atis, *f.* Ancient time, antiquity: *dies ~atis* AC 16; the people of antiquity, the ancients: *prima ~as vidit* VR 37.1.

antiquitus, *adv.* In ancient times, formerly: AC 96.

antiquor ~are ~atus sum, *intr.* To decay with age, be worn out: *omnia* [*in mundo naturali*]...*~antur et consumuntur* VR 756.

antiquus ~a ~um, *a.* (superl. *~issimus*) **1** (of time) Remote in the past, ancient: *ab ~issimis temporibus* AC 8317; (neut. as sb.) *ab ~o* Mic. 5.2 (DD 6). **2** Of or belonging to antiquity, of ancient times: *sapientes ~i* AM 182.4; (superl.) most ancient (as dist. from ancient): *quod Ecclesia ante diluvium appelletur Ecclesia ~issima* AC 1148; (masc. as sb.) *~issimi in saeculo aureo* VR 9.2; (also) *~issima Ecclesia*, the earliest Christian Church: FC s.v. 'Christus'. **3** *~us dierum,* the Ancient of Days (as a divine title): Dan. 7.13 (AC 49.3); VR 15.2.

antistes ~itis, *m.* A leader (of the Church), prelate, dignitary: *~ites Ecclesiae* AM 126; *~ites qui nullam fidem habent...possunt praedicare Evangelium* AE 114.5; CO 17.1.

antithalamus ~i, *m.* An anteroom: AM 20.1.

antlia ~ae, *f.* (Gk.) *~a pneumatica*, an air pump: CI 54.

antrorsum, *adv.* In a frontal direction, frontwards: *quod spectaret sursum, vel ~um* AC 248; CI 3; in a forward position: *~um in capitis facie sunt quinque hominis sensoria* AM 315.5.

antrorsus, *adv.* = **antrorsum**: ES 1848.

antrum ~i, *neut.* A cave: CI 429.

anus[1] ~i, *m.* (anat.) The anus: AC 4632.

anus[2] ~us, *f.* An old woman, hag: *vetulae et ~us* DD 324.4.

anxietas ~atis, *f.* Anxiety, worry: *~as, dolor animi*

ac tristitia CI 299; (w. pl.) an instance of this: *nec sunt tentationes, sed solum ~ates* AC 847.2.

anxius ~a ~um, *a.* (compar. *~or ~or ~us* AM 182.5) **1** Worried, anxious: *~us de futuro statu* AC 1778. **2** Causing anxiety, worrying: *gaudia...fiunt...demum tristia et ~a* AM 5.4; (neut. as sb.) *~um appercepi in inferiore parte ventriculi* AC 5179.

aorta ~ae, *f.* (Gk.) The aorta: AM 315.7.

aper apri, *m.* A wild boar: Ps. 80.13 (AE 388.4); ES 1602.

aperio ~rire ~rui ~rtum, *tr.* (fut. pple. *~rturus*, but *~riturus* UJ 28, AR 24, AR 110) **1** To make open, open: *~rire os* VR 6.3; (absol.) to open a door: *Domine...~ri nobis* Luke 13.25 (VI 2). **2** To make accessible, open the way to: *Verbum...~rit caelum* SS 3.1; (pass., of rooms, w. *in* + acc.) to open (into): *atria...quae in se continuantur seu ~riuntur* ES 850. **3** To activate by opening, open (the mind): *interiora mentis...~ruit* AM 1. **4** To disclose, reveal (opinions): *caeperunt...~rire suam mentem, et dixerunt* VR 48.10; (also refl.) *quiddam ...loquelae demittebatur e medio, sicut se ~riret quid* ES 3241. **5** To reveal (facts): *cultum internum, quem Dominus ~ruit* VR 109.2; (w. indir. qu.) *licet ~rire quomodo se res habet* AC 32.

aperitio ~onis, *f.* **1** The action of opening: *~o... portarum* AE 86.3; *~o sigillorum* SS 12.1. **2** The enlightenment (of a person or his mind): *~ones mentis* AM 188.3; CI 267. **3** Revelation, disclosure: *~o Verbi* DD 26.1.

aperitor ~oris, *m.* One who opens or reveals: *revelatorem occultorum et ~orem futurorum* AC 5331.

aperte, *adv.* (compar. *~ius*) Without concealment, openly: *~e loquuntur* AM 153.2; AC 302.

apertibilis ~is ~e, *a.* Capable of being opened: *caelum clausum est et non ~e illis* VR 720.

apertilis ~is ~e, *a.* That is or may be opened: *ideae [infantum]...~es usque ad Dominum* AC 2291.

apertio ~onis, *f.* The action of opening: *~onem oris* Ezek. 29.21 (AC 2832.5).

apertura ~ae, *f.* **1** An opening, aperture, orifice: *magna ~a supra in medio tecti* VR 134.1. **2** (ad. Hebr.) *~a florum*, open flowers: 1 Kgs. 8.29 (SS 47); *~a uteri*, that which opens the womb: Exod. 13.2 (AC).

apertus ~a ~um, *a.* (pf. pple. of **aperio**) (compar. *~ior*) In senses of verb, esp. **1** Unconcealed, open: *artibus occultis et ~is* AC 6832.9; *in ~o*, without concealment: AC 7102.9. **b** clearly stated or revealed: *quomodo...Ultimum Judicium peractum est, ~um feci* VR 115. **2** (of the mind or its powers) Enlightened: *quo...interiora ~iora ad Dominum sunt* CI 33.

apex ~icis, *m.* **1** The tip or summit: *super uno ~ice capilli* VR 29.2; (of a tree) VR 601. **2** A part of a letter of the alphabet, tittle: *quod Verbum Divinum sit quoad omnem ejus ~icem* CI 260; SS 90.1.

apiarium ~i, *neut.* A beehive: AE 1198.4.

apiarius ~a ~um, *a.* Of or belonging to bees: *favus ~us* 'honeycomb' Luke 24.42 (AC 5620.14).

apis ~is, *m.* (gen. pl. *~um* AM 397, abl. sg. *~e* VR 785) A bee: *sciunt ~es legere mella* CI 108.1.

Apocalypsis ~eos, *f.* (Gk.) (acc. sg. *~in*) The last book of the Bible, the Revelation: *cum scripsit [Johannes] ~in* AM 30.

apollyon, *m.* (Gk.) The destroyer (in Gk. pple. of vb.): Rev. 9.11 (AR); SE 93.

apologia ~ae, *f.* (Gk.) A defence, apologia: AM 105.

apoplexia ~ae, *f.* (Gk.) A stroke, apoplexy: AM 253.2.

apostasis ~eos, *f.* (Gk.) Rejection of God, apostasy: AM 464.

apostasia ~ae, *f.* Apostasy: *a frequente ~a illorum ad cultum aliorum deorum* AC 8301.4.

apostata ~ae, *m.* (Gk.) An apostate: 3AD 4502.

apostema ~atis, *neut.* (Gk.) A gathering of pus, aposteme: AM 253.

Apostolicus ~a ~um, *a.* (Gk.) Of or belonging to the Apostles, Apostolic: *Symbolum ~um* VR 81; *Patres ~i* VR 137.1; *Ecclesiam ~am* VR 174.1.

apostolos ~i, *m.* (Gk.) An apostle: Rev. 2.2 (AR); one of the Twelve Apostles: AC 3858.16; Paul: VR 154.

apothecarius ~i, *m.* A dealer in drugs, pharmacist, apothecary: ES 3349.

apotheosis ~eos, *f.* (Gk.) The act of making into a god, deification: DP 274.2; VR 177.4.

apparatus ~us, *m.* The furnishing or equipping (of a table): AM 14.2; (pl.) furnishings, equipment: *omnes ~us et ornatus splendent ex auro* AE 1191.2.

apparens ~ntis, *a.* (pres. pple. of **appareo**) (compar. *~ntior* AC 1116) Seeming, apparent (but not real): *~ns homo et tamen non homo* AM 267.3; (neut. as sb.) an appearance: *hoc ~ns vitae* CI 474.

apparenter, *adv.* (compar. *~ius*) In appearance, seemingly, apparently: *non ita actualiter, sed usque ~er* VR 29.1; *ut nihil ad vivum ~ius dari queat* AC 1116.

apparentia ~ae, *f.* **1** Outward seeming, appearance: *in ~a sicut dracones* FI 56; *Verbum in litera apparet...sicut ad ~am sunt scripta saeculi* SS 1. **2** A thing which appears, appearance: *inverterent judicia* *in ~as justitiae* AM 231.3; *ex ~is in spirituali mundo* AE 36.1.

appareo ~rere ~rui, *intr.* (fut. pple. *~riturus* ES 2498) **1** To be seen, appear: *~rebit signum* Matt. 24.30 (DD 26.1); *modo sol ortus sit, et in mundo ~reat* SS 109. **2** To have a specified appearance, look (like): *estis, sicut ~retis* AM 315.11; *~rentes ut inquilini* AM 14.2. **3** To have an appearance differing from reality, seem: *quae...possunt ~rere sicut aurum* VI 10; *hoc ~ret sicut non aliquid sit* CI 265; *~ret quod* 'it looks as if' AC 6322.1.

apparitio ~onis, *f.* A coming into view, appearance: *~o Divini Veri* CI 1.

apparo ~are ~avi ~atum, *tr.* To make ready, prepare: *~antur...aulae vestrae* AM 7.2; AM 14.2.

appellatio ~onis, *f.* The giving of a name, naming: AC 1931.

appello[1] ~are ~avi ~atum, *tr.* (*intr.*) **1** (w. pred.) To name, call: *Dominus Jehovam ~at Patrem* DD 20. **2** (intr., w. *ad*) To call (upon), bid: *~o ad sapientes, ut expendant num...* SE 69.2.

appello[2] ~pellere ~puli ~pulsum, *intr.* To come close (to), approach: *unus...~pulerit clanculum ad me* ES 291; ES 277.

appendentia ~ae, *f.* An appendage: *sunt omnia, quae in corpore ejus sunt, ~ae* VR 224.2.

appendicula ~ae, *f.* A small appendage, appendicle: *fibrae et ~ae, quae...sunt circa unumquodvis sensorium* AC 6322.1.

appendix ~icis, *f.* **1** A final part, appendage: *quae* [sc. *cauda*] *est ultima ~ix eorum* [sc. *cerebri et cerebelli*] AC 10071. **2** An appendix (to a book): VR 15.2. **3** Something appended, a derivative: *~icem facimus operationem Spiritus Sancti* VR 74.2.

appendo ~dere ~di ~sum, *tr.* **1** To hang on: *laqueum...~dit in arbore* VR 72.3; AM 300.2. **2** To weigh: *numeratus, ~sus, divisus* Dan. 5.25 (AE 242.23); to weigh out (money in payment), pay: *quare ~ditis argentum in quod non panis?* Isa. 55.2 (AC 353.2).

apperceptibilis ~is ~e, *a.* Capable of being perceived, perceptible: AC 5337.

apperceptibiliter, *adv.* So as to be perceived, perceptibly: AC 2094.3.

apperceptio ~onis, *f.* The action or power of perception: *aliquid ~onis veri* AE 163.3; (dist. from **perceptio** as being less penetrating) *quid non in altera vita, ubi perceptio multis excedit ~onem talem?* AC 1640.3.

apperceptivus ~a ~um, *a.* (neut. as sb.) Power of perception, perceptivity: AC 10050.2.

appercipio ~cipere ~cepi ~ceptum, *tr.* **1** To apprehend with the bodily senses, perceive: *venena ita clandestine...infundunt, ut non ~cipi possit* AC 947; *~cipiunt quasi olfactu* AC 1820.2; *aedificia...quorum tecta non ~cepi* ES 844. **2** To apprehend mentally, perceive: *~cipit bonum* AC 1614; *~cipere ideas angelicas* AC 1875; (w. indir. qu.) *~cipitur illico num mens...consentit* AC 1680.3.

appetibilis ~is ~e, *a.* To be sought after, desirable: *vidit mulier...quod ~is ea* [sc. *arbor*] *oculis* Gen. 3.6 (AC).

appetitio ~onis, *f.* A seeking after: AC 4017; AC 6110.1.

appetitus ~us, *m.* A longing, appetite (esp. for bodily satisfaction): *~us...est edendi bibendique* ES 741; AC 714.

appeto ~ere ~ivi ~itum, *tr.* To have a desire for, long for: *mortem ~unt* AC 825; *~unt vera* AE 455.9; (esp. of bodily appetites) *~ens victum* FI 31; cf. *~ere seu appetitus dicitur corporis* ES 1568.

applano ~are ~avi ~atum, *tr.* To make smooth: *sic ~at Deo viam* VR 73.2.

applaudo ~dere ~si ~sum, *intr.* also **adp-**. To applaud, clap: *plerique...illis meis effatis ~serunt* VR 16.1; AM 521.2.

applausibilitas ~atis, *f.* The possibility of gaining applause: ES 2993.

applicabilis ~is ~e, *a.* (compar. *~ior*) Capable of being applied: *contendentes non ~em esse...vocem* AC 196.2; (w. dat.) *ideis...~ior* AC 1118; (w. *ad*) *cum varietate...~i hic ad Ecclesiam* AC 765.

applicate, *adv.* With special reference, in a particular application: *infinitas ~e dicitur de Esse Dei* VR 36; (w. *ad*) *longitudo ~e ad tempus significat perpetuum* AC 650.

applicatio ~onis, *f.* also **adp-**. An applying, application (in senses of vb.): *per ~ones scientiarum* VR 48.15; *Judaei...vera Verbi falsificarunt per ~onem ad se* AE 177.7.

applico ~are ~ui ~atum, *tr.* also **adp-**. **1** To bring into contact, apply: *~ui manum* ES 1667; (w. dat.) *quidam spiritus se ~uit lateri meo sinistro* AC 537. **2** To bring into relationship, apply: (w. dat.) *in voluntate ~ata intellectui sui viri* AM 379.1; (w. *ad*) *hoc ~are ad se* VR 11.1. **3** To apply (a term): (w. *ad*) *~uerunt singula...ad...status Ecclesiae* AE 1; (w. dat.) *misericordia ~atur illis qui coelestes sunt* AC 598.2. **4** To make conformable, apply (to a purpose): *artifex...~at illum* [sc. *adamantem*] *ad recipiendum...splendorem lucis* VR 110.5; SS 96.

appono ~nere ~sui ~situm, *tr.* also **adp-**. **1** To put close (to), place (on), apply: *~e cor tuum ad semitam* Jer. 31.21 (AE 219.3); *arcentur ab aspectu...per fenestras, ~sitis cancellis* AM 375.1. **2** To serve (food): VR 331.3.

apporto ~are ~avi ~atum, *tr.* To carry towards, bring: *~abant vestes byssi* AM 14.1.

appositus ~a ~um: pf. pple. of **appono**.

apprehendo ~dere ~di ~sum, *tr.* **1** To lay hold of, grasp: *~debant brachia illorum* AM 9.3; (of fire) to set alight: *quando...ignis...~derit spinas* Exod. 22.5 (AC); (fig.) *ne tenebrae vos ~dant* John 12.35 (AC 1839.10). **2** To grasp with the mind, apprehend: *veritates* VR 589; CC 15.2.

apprime, *adv.* Above all, chiefly: *Hoc ~e se manifestat in altera vita* AC 10130.2 (3rd edn.).

apprimis, *adv.* (cf. **imprimis**) Above all, chiefly: *~is notum est ex simulatoribus* CI 499.1.

apprimum, *adv.* = **apprimis** (poss. so to be read): AC 9300.2 (Autograph).

approbatio ~onis, *f.* Approval: AC 10410.

approbo ~are ~avi ~atum, *tr.* **1** To express approval of, approve: AE 555.17. **2** To prove (a statement): *~are quod ita sit* AE 1170.3.

appropinquatio ~onis, *f.* The action of coming close, approach: *de ~one regni Dei* AE 100.2; (pl.) CI 193.

appropinquo ~are ~avi, *intr.* (*tr.*) **1** To come near, approach: *cum ~ant ad aliquam societatem coelestem* CI 400.1. **2** To come close in time, be at hand: *~avit...regnum coelorum* Matt. 4.17 (AE 447.5). **3** (pass.) To be brought close: *per quae...~atur regnum Dei* AE 1002.

appropriatio ~onis, *f.* The action of making one's own, appropriation: *per ~onem affectionum mariti* AM 184; VR 48.18.

approprio ~are ~avi ~atum, *tr.* also **adp-**. **1** (w. *sibi*) To make one's own, take (to oneself), appropriate: *internus ~at sibi interiorem...et suum facit* AC 1707.4; (pass., w. dat.) to be made the property (of): *ut sapientia viri...~etur uxori* AM 172. **2** (pass., w. *ad*) To be in keeping with, match: *veste concinne ad pectorale quoddam ~ata* AC 1644.

approximatio ~onis, *f.* **1** The action of coming close, approach: *status...mutationes...sunt...~ones ad Divinum* AC 4111.3. **2** A stage in approaching (a state), approximation: *quod ~ones dentur in infinitum...et nusquam tamen pertingant* ES 883.

approximo ~are ~avi, *intr.* To come near, approach: *ad primum limen...~are* AC 34.1; CI 385.

appulsus ~us, *m.* Approach: *ad primum ~um* ES 1583.

apricum ~i, *neut.* Sunshine: *in ~o solis* VR 57.

Aprilis ~is, *m.* The month of April: ES 5762.

apsis ~idis, *f.* (Gk.) The felloe or rim of a wheel: Ezek. 1.18 (AC 8215.4).

aptabilis ~is ~e, *a.* That can be applied, suitable: *scientificum...verum et ~e* AC 6112.

aptatio ~onis, *f.* The action of fitting or making suitable: AC 9670.6.

apte, *adv.* (compar. *~ius*) Fittingly, suitably: AC 5114.4.

aptitudo ~inis, *f.* A propensity or suitability (for): *~o ad verum* ES 3918.

apto ~are ~avi ~atum, *tr.* To fit, shape: *per quod lapides secantur et ~antur in formam* AC 8942.

aptus ~a ~um, *a.* (compar. *~ior*) Fitted or suitable: (w. *ad*) *juvenis ad nuptias ~us* AM 229; (w. gen.) *~us percipiendi interiora coeli* ES 759.

apud, *prep. w. acc.* **1** In the presence of, with: *erant apud me Africani* ES 5947; *impurum apud sanguinem* AC 5182. **b** (implying possession) under the control of, in the hands of: *quamdiu sunt [bestiae] apud matres et patres* VR 106; *gazae apud Regem Persiae* VR 245.2; *Verbum erat apud Deum* John 1.1 (VR 3.1). **c** (implying control) acting upon: *angelos qui apud hominem* CI 166; *quod sint a Domino apud illum et per illum* VR 3.2. **2** In the works of (an author): *apud Johannem* VR 2.3. **3** In the time of, with: *apud posteros* AC 54. **4** On the part of: *apud Dominum nusquam est irasci* AC 1093.1; *fieri plus homo apud uxorem* AM 200. **5** In the case of: *finis apud hominem est ipsa ejus vita* AC 1317; *quid is repraesentat apud Dominum* AC 1547.

aqua ~ae, *f.* Water: *fons cujus ~a est impura* VI 25; (pl.) the waters of springs or rivers: *ad fontes et ~as salientis venae* AM 8.2; (Bibl.) *~a vivens,* living water: John 4.10 (SS 2).

aquaeductus ~us, *m.* An aqueduct: Deut. 3.17 (AE 435.6).

aqualiculum ~i, *neut.* A water channel: AC 3095.

aqualis ~is, *m.* A water basin: AC 4017.

aquarius ~i, *m.* One who draws water, a water-carrier: ES 151.

aqueus ~a ~um, *a.* Of or associated with water, watery, aqueous: *infima [athmosphaera] est ~a* AM 188.3; (neut. as sb.) VR 22.3; *serpens ~us,* a water snake: Exod. 7.9 (AC).

aquila ~ae, *f.* An eagle: *~a...in vertice arboris cubans* AM 15; (as a type of sharp sight) *hominem...donare visu ~ae* VR 58.2; (Bibl., as translation of Hebr. *nesher*, perh.) vulture: Deut. 28.49 (ES 2229).

aquilinus ~a ~um, *a.* Of or belonging to an eagle: *~os pullos* AM 15.

ara ~ae, *f.* An altar in a pagan temple (cf. **altare**): *sicut adytum et ~a in templo* VR 163.

Arabicus ~a ~um, *a.* Arabian, Arabic: [*linguam*] *~am* AM 326.4.

arachnipara ~ae, *f.* A mother-spider: *quot araneolae sunt in glomere ab una ~a* VR 178.2.

arachnoideus ~a ~um, *a.* (anat.) Of the arachnid, arachnoidal: *tunica* NE 49.

Aramaeus ~a ~um, *a.* Of Aram or Syria, Aramaean: Gen. 28.5 (AC).

aranea ~ae, *f.* A spider: *involvunt id ratiociniis, sicut ~a capturas filis* AM 231.4.

araneola ~ae, *f.* A small spider: VR 178.2.

aratio ~onis, *f.* Ploughing: Gen. 45.6 (AC).

arator ~oris, *m.* A ploughman: Isa. 28.24 (AE 374.9).

aratrum ~i, *neut.* A plough: Luke 9.62 (AC 5895.5).

arbiter ~tri, *m.* An umpire, judge (of a contest): AM 315.2.

arbitrarius ~a ~um, *a.* Discretionary, arbitrary: *jura...~a* AR 799.1.

arbitratus ~us, *m.* *~ui relinquere*, to leave to (someone's) discretion: *vitam suam relinquit ~ui illorum* CO 59.4.

arbitrium ~i, *neut.* **1** An arbitrary choice: *quod judicia illorum non essent judicia justitiae, sed ~a* AM 231.2; *ex ~o*, at will, arbitrarily: AC 1178.1. **2** *Sui ~i esse*, to be capable of choosing for oneself, be one's own master: VR 17.3. **3** *Liberum ~um*, the power of free choice: *homini est liberum ~um comparandi sibi cognitiones* VR 24.2.

arbitror ~ari ~atus sum, *intr.* **1** To be of the opinion, think: *~ati venisse in paradisum* AC 540; *prius, ut ~or, dictum est* ES 197. **2** To make a choice, judge: *vos...~amini et eligite quid potius* AM 315.6.

arbor ~oris, *f.* A tree: SS 18.2; (w. def. gen.) *~ores olei...~ores vini* AM 13.2; *~or vitae* AE 109.2.

arboretum ~i, *neut.* **1** A plantation of trees: *~a, floreta et vireta* VR 66. **2** (app.) = **arbustum**: *papyri erant ~a Aegypti, ex quibus codices facti* 4AD Isa. 19.7.

arboreus ~a ~um, *a.* Made of trees: *~as aedes* ES 1684; AM 13.2.

arbuscula ~ae, *f.* also **arbusculum** ~i, *neut.* (VR 491). A shrub, bush: AC 6832.1.

arbusculum: see **arbuscula**.

arbustum ~i, *neut.* A shrub: *omnis arbor, omne ~um, virgultum* VR 54.

arca ~ae, *f.* **1** A box, cabinet: *~a confecta ex jaspide* VR 192. **2** The Ark (of the Testimony, etc.): Jer. 3.16 (DD 4). **3** (Noah's) ark: Gen. 6.14 (AC). **4** A coffin: Gen. 50.26 (AC).

arcanista ~ae, *m.* One who specializes in mysteries: VR 385.2.

arcanus ~a ~um, *a.* (compar. *~ior*, superl. *~issimus*) **1** Hidden from common perception or knowledge, secret: *venenis ~is* ES 642; *causa...~issima est* AC 784.2. **2** (neut. as sb.) A secret, mystery, arcanum: *~a coelestia* ES 1329; *~a in Verbo* AE 9.1; (compar.) *patet quod ~iora involvant* AC 293; (superl.) AC 67. **3** *~a Coelestia* (as the title of Swedenborg's work): CI 1.

arceo ~cere ~cui, *tr.* (*intr.*) To hold back, restrain: *praesentia Domini...~cet* AC 8206.2; (w. *ab*) *homo non ~ceri potest a malo* CI 295; (w. *quin*) *sive...locus et occasio ~cuerint quin in actum prodierint* ES 865.

arcesso ~ere ~ivi ~itum, *tr.* To summon: *~it... spiritus ab inferno* AC 9009.1.

archangelus ~i, *m.* (Gk.) An archangel (see quot.): *non est aliquis ~us in coelis* AE 735.2.

archiclitinus: see **architriclinus**.

archididascalus ~i, *m.* (Gk.) A senior teacher: AM 261.2.

archidux ~ducis, *m.* An archduke: CH 164 (= vii.[5]).

archiepiscopus ~i, *m.* (Gk.) An archbishop: AM 9.4.

archipelagus ~i, *m.* (app. Ital.) The islands of the Aegean: AE 50.1.

archisynagogus ~i, *m.* (Gk.) The ruler of a synagogue: Mark 5.36 (AC 2826.14).

architectonice, *adv.* In a masterly style of architecture: *palatia magnifica constructa ~e* AM 355.1.

architectonicus ~a ~um, *a.* Of architecture: *ars ~a* AM 12.2; (neut. as sb.) a masterpiece of architecture: *talia sunt ~a coeli* CI 185.

architectura ~ae, *f.* A style of architecture: AC 1628; ES 1681.

architectus ~i, *m.* A designer of buildings, architect: ES 1344; AC 6486.

architriclinus ~i, *m*. The master of ceremonies (at a feast): John 2.8 (AE 376.29 Worcester). (n.b. Autograph and Hindmarsh have *archiclitinus*.)

arcte, *adv*. (compar. *~ius*) Closely, tightly: *~e unitus* AC 176; *~ius conjunctos* AE 485.

arcticus ~a ~um, *a*. (Gk.) Of the extreme north, arctic: *climata ~a* VR 527.3.

arctus ~a ~um, *a*. also **artus**. (compar. *~ior*, superl. *~issimus*) **1** (of bonds) Tight, close: *ligationem ~iorem* AM 217; *~a conjunctio* AC 5835.1. **2** (of a room) Narrow, confined: *in ~o conclavi* AC 788.2.

arcuatus ~a ~um, *a*. (of a roof) Arched, vaulted: *tectum...~um* AR 875.5; (of a room) having a vaulted ceiling: *atria...~a* AC 1629.

arcula ~ae, *f*. A small box, casket: VR 527.2; (of the basket in which Moses was hidden in the bulrushes) *capsae seu ~ae* AC 6723.1.

arcus ~us, *m*. **1** A bow (as a weapon): AE 131.2. **2** A rainbow: Gen. 9.13 (AC); *~um irideum* AM 294.1.

ardea ~ae, *f*. A heron: AE 1100.22.

ardens ~ntis, *a*. (pres. pple. of **ardeo**) (compar. *~ntior*, superl. *~ntissimus*) **1** Burning hot, fiery: *~ntissimus [sol]* CI 120. **2** (of emotions) Intense, burning: *[zelus] ~ntior* VR 146; *ex ~ntissimo amore sui* AC 10430.

ardenter, *adv*. (compar. *~ius*) Intensely: AC 1820.2; VR 132.1.

ardeo ~dere ~si, *intr*. **1** To be on fire, burn: Isa. 62.1 (DD 64.2); AM 304.2. **2** To be inflamed (with passion): *quod cupiditate ~derem* ES 597. **3** (w. inf.) To be eager, burn (to): *genus humanum, quod...salvare ~deret [Dominus]* AC 2253.

ardesco ~ere, *intr*. To become inflamed (with passions): ES 597; VI 67; VR 309.

ardor ~oris, *m*. **1** Heat: *ignis talis ~oris* AC 6834. **2** Intense desire, passion: *~or qui defervescit* AM 78.5; (w. gen.) *inditur iis ~or se evolvendi* AC 964.

arduus ~a ~um, *a*. (of roads) Leading uphill, steep: *via ~a* AM 75.1.

area ~ae, *f*. **1** A plot of ground, court: *extra ~am sui gymnasii* AM 380.13; (in a garden) a bed: *floreta et vireta in ~as pulchre distincta* CI 489.4. **2** A threshing floor: Matt. 3.12 (AE 374.14). **3** A surface: *non est facies, solum ~a lata faciei* ES 4150. **4** Extent, area: *aedificium magnae ~ae* ES 845.

arefacio ~facere ~feci ~factum, *tr*. To make dry, dry up, parch: *ventus...~fecit fructum* Ezek. 19.12 (AC 7679.2); John 15.6 (VI 29).

arefactio ~onis, *f*. A drying up: AE 419.26.

arefio ~fieri, *intr*. To become dry, wither: *nisi quis manserit in Me, ejicietur foras sicut palmes et ~fiet* John 15.6 (AC 9258.4).

arena ~ae, *f*. Sand: *pulsatis ~am* AM 232.4; (pl.) AE 109.2. **b** (as a type of infertility): *semen injectum ~ae* CI 475. **c** (as a type of instability): *aedificavit domum super ~a* Matt. 7.26 (AE 212.2). **d** (as a type of multitude): *congessit...frumentum, sicut ~am maris* Gen. 41.49 (AC). **e** (used to soak up a liquid): AR 655.1.

arenarius ~a ~um, *a*. Sandy: *~us campus* VR 484.2; (neut. as sb.) a sandpit: UJ(P) 217.

arenosus ~a ~um, *a*. Abounding in sand, sandy: *in campo ~o, ubi nec gramen* SS 96.

arens ~ntis, *a*. Dry, parched: *loca ~ntia* DD 48.6.

arenula ~ae, *f*. A grain of sand: *non foret metallum, nec lapis, imo ne quidem ~a* VR 499.2.

areola ~ae, *f*. A small plot of ground, garden bed: *ex ~is plantationis ejus* Ezek. 17.7 (AE 281.2).

aresco arescere arui, *intr*. To become dry, dry up: *aruerunt aquae* Gen. 8.13 (AC); *brachium ejus arescendo arescet* Zech. 11.17 (AC 878.2).

argenteus ~a ~um, *a*. **1** Made of silver: *patina ~a* SS 40.1. **2** Relating to silver, silvery: *coloris ~i* AM 15. **b** (of the second age) *saeculum* or *aevum ~um*, the Silver Age: CI 115; AM 76.3.

argentum ~i, *neut*. **1** Silver: *aurum commixtum ~o* VI 10. **2** Silver coin: *per quindecim [nummi] ~i* Hos. 3.2 (DD 15.6). **3** *~um vivum*, mercury, quicksilver: VR 11.3.

argilla ~ae, *f*. Clay: *ferrum commixtum cum ~a* AM 73.1; *num ~a increpatura est figulum...?* VR 72.1.

argillaceus ~a ~um, *a*. Of clay: *ultima [aetas] ferrea et ~a* AC 1837.

argumentatio ~onis, *f*. A line of argument: *~ones ex fallaciis* SS 13.3.

argumentor ~ari ~atus sum, *intr*. To derive arguments, argue: *ratiocinantur et ~antur ex illis* AR 450.2.

argumentum ~i, *neut*. A proof: *~is demonstrativis ...confirmabitur* AM 63; *vis ~i* ES 3374.

arguo ~ere ~i ~tum, *tr*. **1** To bring a charge against, accuse: *potest jure ~ere Deum immisericordiae* VR 341. **2** To put to the test, try: *Ego quoscunque amo, ~o et castigo* Rev. 3.19 (AR).

argute, *adv*. Shrewdly, cleverly: *hae ~e inspectabant oculos meos* AM 155[a].2.

argutiae ~tiarum, *f. pl.* Verbal trickery, sophistry: *illa...sunt merae ~tiae et astutiae* VR 389.5.

arida ~ae, *f.* Dry land: *appareat ~a* Gen. 1.9 (AC).

ariditas ~atis, *f.* Dryness, drought: Isa. 58.11 (AC 149.1).

aridus ~a ~um, *a.* Dry: *ligna ~a* AM 477.3; *in ~o*, on dry land: Exod. 14.16 (AC).

aries ~etis, *m.* A male sheep, ram: CI 110.

ariolus: see **hariolus**.

arista ~ae, *f.* An ear of corn: [*messis*] *crescit in ~as et spicas* VR 571.

aristocraticus ~a ~um, *a.* (Gk.) Of the aristocracy, aristocratic: *de regimine ~o* VR 133.

Aristotelicus ~a ~um, *a.* Of or typical of the Greek philosopher Aristotle, Aristotelian: AC 4966.1.

arithmetica ~orum, *neut. pl.* (Gk.) Arithmetic: VR 184.

arithmetice, *adv.* Arithmetically: ES 2927.

arma ~orum, *neut. pl.* Weapons, arms: *omnia ~a belli* AE 131.2.

armamentarium ~i, *neut.* An armoury, arsenal: *~a...sunt ubi reconduntur arma belli* AC 6661.2.

armatus ~i, *m.* An armed man: *~i et jaculatores arcus* Ps. 78.9 (VR 247.1).

armentum ~i, *neut.* A herd (of large cattle): *~a et greges* FI 63.1; *~a ex bobus et vitulis, tum ex camelis et mulis* VR 78.1.

armilla ~ae, *f.* A bracelet: Ezek. 16.11 (AE 126.3); AM 20.3.

armo ~are ~avi ~atum, *tr.* To arm, equip, furnish: *constare potest ex vitris opticis, per quae ~andi sunt* [*homines*], *ut solum illa quae proxime interioris naturae sunt videant* AC 9577.2.

armus ~i, *m.* The hindquarter (of an animal): *quod ~i sint partes posteriores animalis* AC 10075; *~um sublationis* Lev. 7.34 (AE 375.14); the shoulder (of a man): ES 1349.

aro ~are ~avi ~atum, *tr.* To plough (land): (absol.) *num ~abit bobus?* Amos 6.12 (AE 355.34); (fig.) *~are sulcum* VR 137.8; *~astis impietatem* Hos. 10.13 (AC 1179).

aroma ~atis, *neut.* (Gk.) A fragrant substance, perfume: *Aethiopia abundabat...~atibus* AC 117.1.

aromataria ~ae, *f.* A female maker of perfumes, perfumer: 1 Sam. 8.13 (AC 2567.9).

aromatarius ~i, *m.* A maker of perfumes, perfumer: Ezek. 17.4 (AC 10199.5).

aromaticus ~a ~um, *a.* Sweet-smelling, aromatic: *cera ~a* AC 5621.1; (neut. as sb.) *sentitum est ~um* AM 266.3.

aromatopolium ~i, *neut.* (Gk.) A shop which sells perfume, perfumery: VR 834.

arrhabo ~onis, *f.* (Gk.) A pledge: Gen. 38.17 (AC).

arrideo ~dere ~si ~sum, *intr.* **1** To smile, grin: *quaedam facies ~debant* ES 583; AC 8246. **2** (of things) To be pleasing, be welcome: *falsa...iis maximopere ~dent* ES 2481.

arrigo ~rigere ~rexi ~rectum, *tr.* To cause to stand erect, prick up (one's ears): *nonne cum...superbus audit laudes...~rigit aures?* VR 696.2; *mens ~rigit aurem ad audiendum* AS 387.

arripio ~ripere ~ripui ~reptum, *tr.* **1** To catch hold of, seize, grasp: *~ripit frondes...arboris* VR 127. **b** to catch (fire): *facile ~ripit ignem* [*sulphur*] AC 643.1. **2** To take to oneself mentally, seize upon intellectually: *quod amat homo, hoc libenter ~ripit* AC 1016.3; *~ripere et credere falsum ac verum* CI 352.1.

arroganter, *adv.* Arrogantly: AC 4156.2.

arrogantia ~ae, *f.* Arrogance: *~ae et jactationis variae species* AC 6203.

arrogo ~are ~avi ~atum, *tr.* (w. *sibi*) To lay claim to, arrogate to oneself: *sibi libertatem dimittendi uxores...~avit* AM 276.1; *Divinam Domini potestatem sibi ~ant* VI 79.1.

ars artis, *f.* **1** Craftsmanship, skill: *est...ipsa ars ibi in sua arte* AE 1191.2; AM 130.2. **b** *arte factus*, artificial: *aurum arte factum...non est bonum* VI 10. **2** A particular craft, art or science: *in arte botanica* AE 1203.2. **3** Ingenuity, art: *quod verum vertatur in falsum...vel ex dolo...vel ex arte* ES 1994. **4** (pl.) Tricks, devices: *artes, astutiae et ligae* CI 229.

arteria ~ae, *f.* (anat.) An artery: CI 95.

arteriola ~ae, *f.* A small blood vessel: VR 54.

arteriosus ~a ~um, *a.* (of blood) Arterial: AS 420.

articulate, *adv.* In articulate speech, articulately: *~e loqui* AM 521.2.

articulatim, *adv.* In a series of articles, point by point: *hoc fiet ~im in hoc* SE 109.

articulatio ~onis, *f.* A structure composed of separate elements, articulation: *quot sunt momenta, ~ones et generationes fidei ibi* VR 57; *~onis sonorum* AM 440.

articulatum ~i, *neut.* = **articulatio**: VR 626.

articulo ~are ~avi ~atum, *tr.* **1** To equip with a

jointed structure: *loquitur per os ~atum* [*statuae*] VR 23.2. **2** To divide (sounds) into speech, articulate: *nec ~are sonum in aliquam vocem humanam* VR 48.8; *loquela...non ~ata..., sed...tacita* AC 1118.

articulus ~i, *m.* **1** A joint: *statua facta cum ~is mobilibus* VR 23.2. **2** A section of a written work, paragraph, article: *in ~is praecedentibus* CI 101.

artifex ~icis, *m.* A skilled worker, craftsman: *quemadmodum ~ex secat adamantem* VR 110.5.

artificialis ~is ~e, *a.* Artificial: *quod lapides... significarent ~ia et sic fictitia cultus* AC 1298.2; *~es caelos* UJ(C) 57; *cogitare ab ~i* AC 521.

artificialiter, *adv.* **1** Artificially: *est...later ~er factus apis* AC 1296. **2** Artfully, craftily: [*affectiones*] *flectit...~er in malum* ES 617.

artificiose, *adv.* (compar. *~ius*, superl. *~issime*) Skilfully: *aranea ~issime texit telam* VR 335.3.

artificiosus ~a ~um, *a.* **1** Skilfully constructed: *in aranea...est...inclinatio ad struendam telam ~am* VR 785; (neut. as sb.) a trick: AC 5188.1. **2** (of a person) Skilled, artful: ES 3750.

artificium ~i, *neut.* **1** An artifice, device, trick: *possunt...mali spiritus ~is suis producere calorem* AC 1773.3. **2** A craft: *quod ibi* [sc. *in caelo*] *sint...~a et operae* AM 207.3.

artus[1] ~us, *m.* **1** (anat.) A joint: *distorsio...~uum* ES 870; AC 5323.1. **2** A limb: *calor...inflammet illorum facies et ~us* AM 380.12.

artus[2]: see **arctus**.

arundo ~inis, *f.* A reed: *cannae seu ~inis* AE 627.13.

arvum ~i, *neut.* A ploughed field, arable land: AM 522.

arx arcis, *f.* A citadel: Ps. 144.2 (AC 1788.2).

Asasel, *indecl.* and ~lis, *m.* also **Azazel**, *indecl.* (AC 3147.10 3rd edn.). The Hebrew name for the scapegoat: *remotio peccatorum...repraesentata est in Ecclesia Judaica per hircum ~lem vocatum* AC 9937.8.

ascendo ~dere ~di ~sum, *intr.* (*tr.*) **1** To go up, rise, climb: *~dunt...versus caelum* VI 25; *nimbus ex inferis ~dens* AM 7.2; (w. *super*) *si...~dero super spondam strati mei* Ps. 132.3 (DD 6). **b** (tr.) to climb (a mountain): *~damus Sionem* Jer. 31.6 (DD 4). **2** (of a journey from Egypt to Palestine) To go up: *~dit Abram ex Aegypto* Gen. 13.1 (AC). **3** (of rivers) To rise: *aquae ~dentes ex septentrione* Jer. 47.2 (FI 53); (of plants) to grow, come up: *nec ~det...ulla herba* Deut. 29.23 (AC 1666.4). **4** To rise to a higher degree, increase in scale: *perfectiones ~dunt ita sicut exteriora se habent ad interiora* AC 1642.

ascensio ~onis, *f.* Ascent, rising: *gradus ~onis a mundo ad coelum* AC 9435.

ascensus ~us, *m.* **1** A going up, ascent, rise: *~us in superius caelum* AM 343. **2** A rise to a higher degree: *cognitiones, per quas fit intellectui humano ~us* VR 24.2.

ascisco: see **adscisco**.

ascititius: see **adscititius**.

ascribo: see **adscribo**.

asellus ~i, *m.* A young ass: Gen. 49.11 (AC).

Asiaticus ~a ~um, *a.* Of Asia, Asiatic: *orbis ~i* AE 391.31.

asina ~ae, *f.* (dat. and abl. pl. *~abus*) A she-ass: AE 31.7.

asinarius ~a ~um, *a.* Of or worked by asses: *mola ~a* Matt. 18.6 (AC 9755.15).

asininus ~a ~um, *a.* Of or belonging to an ass: *pulli ~i* Isa. 30.24 (AC 566.5).

asinus ~i, *m.* An ass: *satius foret nasci ~us quam homo* AM 182.5.

Asmodeus ~a ~um, *a.* Of or typical of Asmodeus (cf. Tobit 3.8), Asmodean: *daemonia ~a* AE 1003.3.

aspectabilis ~is ~e, *a.* That may be seen, visible: *in mundo ~i* VR 12.1; *novum caelum ~e* VR 768; (neut. as sb.) AE 232.1.

aspecto ~are ~avi ~atum, *tr.* also **ads-**. To look upon, regard (in a specified manner): *amaenis oculis ~abant pueros* AM 218.2.

aspectus ~us, *m.* also **ads-**. **1** The action of looking, sight: *non solum ex ratione, sed etiam ex ~u* ME 15. **2** The direction of looking, line of sight: *secundum hominis ~um* AC 1582; VR 151. **3** Appearance, aspect: *similitudo sicut ~us Hominis* Ezek. 1.26 (AC 49.3); *flores ~u pulcherrimi* AM 137.1. **b** (Bibl.) fair appearance, beauty: *vidimus Ipsum, sed non ~us* Isa. 53.2 (DD 6).

asper ~era ~erum, *a.* (compar. *~erior*) Rough, harsh, prickly: *quod vir sit facie ~eriore* CI 368; (fig.) *intelligentia virorum...gravis, ~era, dura* AM 209.

aspere, *adv.* Roughly: *literas consonantes ~e* SS 90.2; *~e inter rogavit* AM 82.2.

aspergo ~gere ~si ~sum, *tr.* To sprinkle, splash: *quod ~gerentur aqua expiationis* Num. 8.7 (AE 475.4); (impers. pass.) *quod ~sum fuerit de sanguine ejus ad parietem* 2 Kgs. 9.33 (AE 160.1).

asperitas ~atis, *f.* Roughness, harshness: SS 90.2.

aspernor ~ari ~atus sum, *tr.* To reject scornfully, spurn: *rationalia...~antur et...rejiciunt* AM 442.

aspero ~are ~avi ~atum, *tr.* To make rough or harsh: *dum externum...se ~at* AM 365; AM 378.

aspersio ~onis, *f.* A sprinkling on: *per ~onem aquae* AE 475.4.

aspicio ~picere ~pexi ~pectum, *tr.* **1** To turn one's gaze upon, look at: *angelus...~pexit illum* FI 43; (absol.) *~pexi, et ecce nubes candida* Rev. 14.14 (AE 36.3). **2** To regard in a specified manner: *illum dura fronte ~picere* VR 56; *uxor ~picitur ut scortum* AM 247.

aspiratio ~onis, *f.* **1** A breathing upon: *~o erat signum...Divinae inspirationis* VR 140. **2** An influence: *secundum affectionis ~onem omnia fiunt* AC 1016.2; ES 542. **3** The action of aspiring, aspiration: *~o ad honores* AM 274.

aspiratus ~us, *m.* **1** The action of blowing upon: *~um aëris* AC 7768; breathing: DP 338.6. **2** Influence: ES 3809.

aspiro ~are ~avi ~atum, *tr., intr.* also **adspiro**. **1** (tr.) To breathe on: *quod Dominus ~averit discipulos* VR 140. **2** (intr.) To exert an influence: *percepi...quod Deus... jugiter ~aret* ES 170; *~ante perpetuo vere* AM 3.4. **3** (intr., w. *ad*) To aspire (to), seek (for): *~ant ad honores* AC 7377.

aspis ~idis, *f.* A poisonous snake, asp: *fel ~idum* Deut. 32.33 (SS 51.9).

assarius ~i, *m.* A coin of small value, penny: Luke 12.6 (DP 332.4).

assecla ~ae, *f.* An adherent, follower (of a school of thought): *illi* [sc. *Plato et Aristoteles*] *et illorum ~ae* AM 151[a].1.

assensio ~onis, *f.* An assenting, agreement: AC 379.

assensus ~us, *m.* Assent: *pleno ~u* VR 16.2.

assentatio ~onis, *f.* Insincere agreement, flattery: *simulationes, ~ones et hypocrises* VR 147.

assentator ~oris, *m.* One who agrees insincerely, flatterer, toady: CI 499.1.

assentior ~tiri ~sus sum, *intr.* (pf. act. also *~serunt* VR 666.4) **1** To give assent, agree: *loquendo ad favorem et ~tiendo* AC 5388. **2** (of ideas) To receive assent, be approved: *faciunt ut omnia faveant et ~tiantur* AC 570; AM 156.2.

assentor ~ari ~atus sum, *intr.* To agree insincerely, flatter: *laudes ~antium* SE 19.

assequor ~qui ~quutus (*or* ~cutus) sum, *tr.* **1** To overtake: *~quutus Laban Jacobum* Gen. 31.25 (AC). **2** To attain to, achieve: *haec duo* [sc. *eminentiam et opulentiam*] *non ~quitur* AM 267.2. **3** To grasp mentally (a fact): *~quetur..quod illud sit Ipsum* AS 45; (w. indir. qu.) *qui non ~quuti, seu non intellexerunt, quomodo fides conjungi potest cum bonis operibus* AE 802.1.

asser ~eris, *m.* A plank, board: *planitiem stratam ~eribus* AM 6.1; VR 152.

asserinus ~a ~um, *a.* Made of or resembling boards: *apparent humeri sicut nudi ~i* ES(M) 4576.

assero ~ere ~ui ~tum, *tr.* **1** To claim as true, assert (a fact): *veritates...~tae* SE 29; (w. *quod*) *~ere quod unaquaevis persona...sit Deus* VR 17.1. **2** (w. pred.) To claim (as), assert (to be): *proprietates...quas ~it incommunicabiles* VR 135.2.

assertio ~onis, *f.* An assertion, claim: AM 315.7.

assertor ~oris, *m.* One who claims as true, a proponent: *a fidei istius ~oribus* VR 451.

asseveratio ~onis, *f.* A strong assertion, asseveration: AC 1037.

assevero ~are ~avi, *intr.* To assert strongly, insist: *~o in veritate quod non sint inventa* AM 1; CI 311.2.

assideo ~sidere ~sedi, *intr.* also **adsideo**. (w. dat.) To sit near or by: *angeli...bini prope caput, cui ~sidebant* CI 449.1.

assidue, *adv.* Persistently, regularly: *in Verbo satis ~e legerat* ES 1663.

assiduitas ~atis, *f.* Persistence, constancy: *~atem instruendi* AE 94.

assiduus ~a ~um, *a.* Persistent, constant: *~i comites* AM 156.1; AE 98.5.

assigno ~are ~avi ~atum, *tr.* To attribute, assign, place: *qui ~avit animae sedem...in quadam glandula* AS 365.8.

assimilo ~are ~avi ~atum, *tr.* To treat as similar, compare, liken: *Dominus ~avit regnum caelorum decem virginibus* VI 61; AC 97.

assisto: see **adsisto**.

asso ~are ~avi ~atum, *tr.* To roast, grill: *~atum piscem* Luke 24.42 (AC 7852.2).

associabilis ~is ~e, *a.* Capable of being associated: ES 809.

associatio ~onis, *f.* The act or process of becoming a member of a community, association: *eorum adventum et ~onem audivi* ES 1743.

associo ~are ~avi ~atum, *tr.* also **adsocio**. (w. dat.) To bring into society, associate (with): *tales spiritus mali ei ~antur* AC 653.

assuefacio ~facere ~feci ~factum, *tr.* To make accustomed: *qui spurca et obscoena loqui...~fecerunt* [*assueverunt* Tafel] *se* ES 2307 titulus.

assuefactio ~onis, *f.* The act of becoming accustomed, habit: ES 3003.

assuefactus ~a ~um, *a.* (pf. pple. of **assuefio**) also **adsuefactus**. Acquired by habit, customary: *erectio corporis...docta et ~a* ES 567; (masc. as sb.) one who is accustomed: *~us vehi curru* VR 563.

assuefio ~fieri ~factus sum, *intr.* (w. dat.) To become accustomed (to): *quod draco ~fieret dolis* ES 253.

assuesco: see **adsuesco**.

assuetudo ~inis, *f.* The process of becoming accustomed, habituation: *ex ~ine trahit aliquem habitum*: CI 533.

assugo ~gere ~xi ~ctum, *tr.* To draw up by sucking, suck up: ES 1128.

assultus ~us, *m.* An attack, assault: *ut* [*bona*] *in tuto possint subsistere, ac inhibere ~um* VR 604.

assumo ~mere ~m(p)si ~m(p)tum, *tr.* **1** To take into a group, select: *unus ~metur, alter relinquetur* Luke 17.34 (AC 931.3); *~me aliquos ex satellitio meo* AM 11; *quae...ex Arcanis Coelestibus ~mpta et collata sunt* CI 78. **2** To take upon oneself, adopt, assume: *quod...~mserit Humanum* VR 3.1; *quod angeli...~mserint humanam formam* AE 53.2. **3** To give attention to, take up (a subject): *~me...ideam unius Dei* VR 16.2; *~mserunt primum subjectum ventilationis* VR 48.2. **4** To put into use, introduce: *numerus...quadraginta pro...quadraginta duo ~mtus est* AC 730.3.

assum(p)tio ~onis, *f.* The action of taking upon oneself, assumption: *per ~onem Humani* Sym. Ath. (DD 56).

assuo ~ere ~i ~tum, *tr.* To sew on: *~ere vel committere unum alteri* AC 9212.7.

assurgo ~rgere ~rrexi, *intr.* **1** To rise up: *vidi ~rgentem diabolum* AM 269.4; (of things) *quod aquae successive ~rgant* VR 119.2. **2** To come about, happen, arise: *obstantia...quae continue ~rgunt et remorantur* AE 98.5. **3** (of numbers) To add up to, reach (a total): *anni aetatum illorum ne quidem ad 430 ~rgunt* AC 7985.

assus ~a ~um, *a.* Roast: *~am igne* Exod. 12.8 (AC).

Assyrius ~a ~um, *a.* Assyrian: Ezek. 23.5 (AE 141.4).

ast, *conj.* But, however: [*spiritus*] *affecti sunt novo gaudio...; ast haec delectatio persistebat per menses* AC 1880.3; VR 16.4.

astans: see **adstans**.

asterismus ~i, *m.* (Gk.) A constellation: *equitare ad quendam ~um in caelo* VR 137.3.

asthma ~atis, *neut.* (Gk.) Shortness of breath, asthma: VR 482.2.

astipulor: see **adstipulor**.

asto: see **adsto**.

astrifer ~era ~erum, *a.* Bearing the stars, starry: *in caelo ~ero* VR 32.5.

astringo: see **adstringo**.

astroites ~ae, *m.* (Gk., prob. error for *astriotes* Pliny the Elder, *Naturalis historia* 37.133) A precious stone, perh. moonstone: AM 109.

astrologus ~i, *m.* (Gk.) An astrologer: *sicut audirent...nugas ex ~is* VR 695.3.

astronomicus ~a ~um, *a.* Of or relating to astronomy, astronomical: [*scientia*] *~a* CI 353.1.

astronomus ~i, *m.* (Gk.) An astronomer: *secundum observationes ~orum* VR 176.2.

astrum ~i, *neut.* (Gk.) A star: *ajunt se esse ab ~is seu ~orum mundis* ES 1594; Luke 21.25 (AE 175.12).

astruo: see **adstruo**.

astuosus ~a ~um, *a.* (superl. *~issimus*) Deceitful: AC 6666.2; (neut. as sb.) a trick: ES 5635.

astus ~us, *m.* Guile, trickery, deceit: *blanda voce in qua intus erat ~us* VR 71.3; (pl.) *quod...nihili fecerint ...~us* AE 231.2.

astute, *adv.* In a deceitful manner, guilefully: *a quodam nebulone ~e loquente* AM 216.2.

astutia ~ae, *f.* **1** The quality of being deceitful, deceitfulness: *fiunt...vulpes quoad ~am* VR 13.4. **2** (pl.) Trickery, wiles: *~as fallendi* SS 13.3.

astuties ~ei, *f.* = **astutia**: ES 2663.

astutus ~a ~um, *a.* (compar. *~ior*, superl. *~issimus*) Deceitful, wily: *~i et dolosi* CI 535.

asylum ~i, *neut.* (Gk.) also **azylum**. A place of refuge, asylum: *quaesiverunt...scrobes, ut ~a* AM 71.3.

asymptota ~ae, *m.* (Gk.) A line which continually approaches a curve without meeting it, asymptote: *sicut inter ~as parabolae* ES 883.

at, *conj.* (cf. **ast**) But, however: *usque percipiunt, at cum differentia* AC 1384; *at vero*, but on the other hand: VR 441.1.

atavus ~i, *m.* A great-great-grandfather: *ab ejus avo, proavo, ~o* AC 313; (more generally) an ancestor: AC 6716.2.

ataxia ~ae, *f.* (Gk.) Inability to control the movements of the body, ataxy: VR 665.4.

atechnicus ~a ~um, *a.* (Gk.) Not having a profession, unskilled: ES 4373.

ater atra atrum, *a.* Pitch-black: *lumbi erant...atri sicut fuligo* AM 264.1; (transf., of evils) *purificare...impium ab atris ejus malis* VR 90.

Athanasianus ~a ~um, *a.* Of or belonging to Athanasius, Athanasian: *in Symbolo ~o* VR 4.3.

atheismus ~i, *m.* (Gk.) Disbelief in God, atheism: *totum Christianismum invaderet ~us* VR 628.

atheista ~ae, *m.* (Gk.) An atheist: ES 4769.

atheisticus ~a ~um, *a.* Atheistic: *de turba ~a* ES 4769.

atheus ~i, *m.* (Gk.) One who does not believe in God, an atheist: VR 12.10.

athleta ~ae, *m.* (Gk.) One who takes part in games, an athlete, sportsman: *inter se pugillant sicut duo ~ae* AM 55.6.

athmosphaera ~ae, *f.* (Gk.) also **atmo-**. The gaseous layer surrounding the Earth or other planets, atmosphere: *suprema regio ~ae* AE 304.2; VR 32.8; also, in the spiritual world: AS 173.

athmosphaericus ~a ~um, *a.* also **atmo-**. Of or belonging to the atmosphere: *caelum...~um* DD 62.1; *ideas...~as et materiales* VR 24.2; (neut. as sb.) a vapour, gas: *admittebant...quoddam ~um, apparens usque ut tenue aqueum* AM 412.

atmo-: see **athmo-**.

atomus ~i, *f.* (Gk.) An atom: *in Epicuri ~is* CC 17.2.

atque, *conj.* (= **ac**, usually preferred by Swedenborg himself) And: *Schimeon et Levi postquam occiderant omne masculum in urbe atque Chamorem et Schechemum* AC 4503.1; ES 192; (Bibl.) *Ego feram, atque eripiam* Isa. 46.4 (AC 9937.10).

atqui, *conj.* Yet, however: AM 498.

atramentarium ~i, *neut.* The equipment of a scribe, pen and ink: *~um scribae in lumbis ejus* Ezek. 9.2 (AC 7601.4); VR 483.1.

atramentum ~i, *neut.* Ink: AM 207.5.

atratus ~a ~um, *a.* (pf. pple. of **atro**) Blackened: *sicut pictura ~a* VR 681.

atresco ~rescere ~rui, *intr.* To become black, wear mourning: *~ruerunt ad terram* Jer. 14.2 (AC 2851.13).

atrium ~i, *neut.* A porch, forecourt, entrance: *porticus seu ~a longa, arcuata* AC 1629; (fig.) the outermost region (of heaven): *in primum ~um coeli sublati* AC 65; (transf.) an entryway (into the mind): *intrat per oculos sicut fores in mentem, et sic per visum ut ~um in cogitationes* AM 191.2.

atro ~are ~avi ~atum, *tr.* To make dark, darken, blacken: *~abo stellas* Ezek. 32.7 (VR 198); (transf.) *verum ~at oculos illorum sicut umbra noctis* AM 79.6.

atrocitas ~atis, *f.* The quality of being horrifying, atrocity: *quantus...est amor, tanta ~as est* AC 1820.5.

atrociter, *adv.* In a horrifying manner, atrociously: *quod Christum...e mundo ~er sustulerint* AM 340.2.

atrophia ~ae, *f.* (Gk.) Atrophy: *~a oculi et inde jactura visus* VR 346.2.

atror ~oris, *m.* Blackness, darkness: *vestiam coelos ~ore* Isa. 50.3 (AC 40.1); *~or sutorius,* shoe-blacking: CO 22.

atrox ~ocis, *a.* (compar. *~ocior*, superl. *~ocissimus*) Causing severe mental distress, horrifying, atrocious: *~oces illae tentationes* AE 365.31.

attamen, *conj.* Yet, however: AC 8705.5.

attendo ~dere ~di ~tum, *tr.*, *intr.* **1** (tr.) To make receptive, direct (the mind or senses): *tunc ~dit aurem, sed ridens* VR 35.8; *ad quae primum ~debam mentem* ES 228. **2** (intr.) To pay attention: *quod quisque scire potest si modo velit ~dere* AC 678; *~de paulum, et visurus es...currus* AM 103.2; (w. *ad*) *non ~dendum ad talia* AC 1082. **3** (tr.) To pay attention to: *sensus solum ~debatur* ES 2414.

attente, *adv.* (compar. *~ius*, superl. *~issime*) Attentively: *qui...ad sensum...~e advertit* AC 241.

attentio ~onis, *f.* Mental concentration, attention: *erat ~o avida* AM 183.1.

attentus ~a ~um, *a.* (compar. *~ior*) Attentive: *~iores aures* ES 634.

attenuo ~are ~avi ~atum, *tr.* To make thin or fine: *sicut caenum platearum ~abo eos* Ps. 18.42 (DD 14.6); *~atur nubes* AC 1044.2.

attero ~ere attrivi attritum, *tr.* To wear away, wear down, crush: *sanctos ~et* Dan. 7.25 (AC 2832.13); *~etur gloria Jacobi* Isa. 17.4 (DD 4).

attestor ~ari ~atus sum, *tr.* **1** To bear witness, attest: *~ari faciendo testes* Jer. 32.44 (AE 449.6). **2** To call to witness: *~or vos, ut credatis* ES 228.

attineo ~nere ~nui, *tr.* *Quod* [*aliquid*] *~net*, as concerns, as for (something): *quod stellas ~net, sunt illae modo luminaria* VR 79.3.

attingo ~tingere ~tigi, *tr.* **1** To touch: *ne...~tingeret aliquid* CI 335; *cum ~tigerit eam ventus orientalis* Ezek. 17.10 (AE 419.26); (transf.) to succeed without a break: *sanguines sanguines ~tingunt* Hos. 4.2 (AE 342.9). **2** To attain to, reach: *non ~tigerunt dies annorum vitae patrum meorum* Gen. 47.9 (AC).

attollo ~ere, *tr.* To lift up, raise: *stagna e quibus crocodili ~ebant capita* AM 79.2; *~ite portae capita vestra* Ps. 24.7 (AE 208.12); *...quod faciem ~at super aliquem* AC 1054.

attonitus ~a ~um, *a.* Amazed, astonished: *vidi omnes...~os et mutatos facies* VR 137.12.

attractio ~onis, *f.* The action of drawing towards, attraction: *hoc...erat ex ~one caelestis athmosphaerae* AM 10.3; *dolorem tanquam ~onis syringicae* [i.e., suction] AC 1763.1.

attractivus ~a ~um, *a.* Exerting attraction, attractive: *vis...~a* ES 1130.

attractus ~us, *m.* Attraction: *sentiebam quendam ~um* ES 1886.

attraho ~here ~xi ~ctum, *tr.* **1** To draw to oneself, attract: *ex quo [nimbo] ~cto* AM 7.2. **2** To acquire (a quality): *inde ~xerunt naturam saevam* CI 488.6.

attribuo ~ere ~i ~tum, *tr.* To ascribe, attribute: *quantum ~unt omne bonum...Domino* CI 154[a].

attributum ~i, *neut.* An attribute: *per tres personas intelligam tria ~a Divina procedentia* VR 26.

attritus ~a ~um: pf. pple. of **attero**.

attuli: pf. of **affero**.

auceps ~upis, *m.* A bird-catcher, fowler: *sonus fistulae ~upis* VR 452.

auctor ~oris, *m.* also **autor**. A creator, maker: *ex suo ~ore, qui est Dominus* AM 64.1; the maker of a work of literature, author: *~orum classicorum* ES 805.

auctoramentum ~i, *neut.* **1** A piece of evidence, proof: *plura sunt ~a...quod Deus...operetur omnia* VR 12.9; AE 802.3. **2** A recompense, reward: *diplomata, ~a et praemia* VR 181.2.

auctoritas ~atis, *f.* also **aut-**. **1** The guidance of an influential person, authority: *ab aliorum ~ate... dependent* ES 5577. **2** The quality of possessing influence, prestige, authority: *ex ore viri ~atis* DD 168.5; *sphaeram supereminentiae et ~atis contraxit* AC 1507; *~atem...Verbi infirmant* SS 115.1.

aucupatio ~onis, *f.* A seeking, hunting: *vel ex fastu vel ex ~one famae* VR 425.

aucupium ~i, *neut.* **1** A trap for catching birds, snare: *affersne hoc ut ~um et allectamentum...?* AM 82.1. **2** A seeking after, hunting for: *propter ~um famae* AM 495.2.

aucupo ~are ~avi ~atum, *tr.* also **aucupor**. **1** To seek after, hunt for: (act.) *qui eruditionis famam... ~averunt* CI 309; (dep.) *famam...~ati* ES 302. **2** To acquire, gain: *si non ~ant honores* VR 441.2.

aucupor: see **aucupo**.

audacia ~ae, *f.* Boldness, audacity: *eo ~ae et impudentiae sunt* AC 8295.1.

audacter, *adv.* Boldly: *si ~er instat* AM 287.

audax ~acis, *a.* (abl. sg. *~ace* and *~aci*) Audacious, bold, presumptuous: *audivimus ab ~ace praecone peccati* AR 531.3.

audeo ~dere ~sus sum, *intr.* (fut. pple. *~surus*) **1** To dare: *non possunt aut non ~dent corpore* AM 153.2; (w. inf.) *propalare illa...non ~det* AE 182.2. **2** (subj. in archaic forms *~sim, ~sis, ~sit, ~sint*): *~sim dicere* VR 15.1; *quod infernales non ~sint...accedere* AC 7568.

audibilis ~is ~e, *a.* That may be heard, audible: *cogitatio...tacita est ~is spiritibus* AC 6624.

audio ~dire ~divi ~ditum, *tr.* **1** To perceive by the hearing, hear: *quae nusquam auris ~divit* CI 176; (w. *de*) *nihil...de Verbo ~diverunt* SS 17.4. **2** To hear and attend to, listen to: *~di Israel* Deut. 6.4 (VR 6.3); *~diunto illos* Luke 16.29 (DD 9). **3** To be called, have the reputation of being: *ex jucundo trahit quod sit et ~diat voluptas* AC 995.1; *~dit...draco* ES 508.

auditio ~onis, *f.* **1** The action of hearing: *ex ~one praedicationum* AE 232.3. **2** That which is heard, rumour: *veniet in anno ~io et violentia in terra* Jer. 51.46 (AC 623.2).

auditor ~oris, *m.* One who hears, hearer, listener: AM 315.2.

auditorium ~i, *neut.* A lecture room, hall: VR 694.1.

auditus ~us, *m.* The faculty of hearing: *sensus ~us* AE 14.1.

aufero ~rre abstuli ablatum, *tr.* **1** To carry away: *~rri in sinum Abrahami* AC 6960.3. **b** to distract, divert [*spiritus mali*] *~rebant oculos meos in omnia talia* ES 2843. **2** To take away, remove: *si...vitam ~rs* AM 5.4; *Dominus ~rt eorum conatus* AC 695.

aufugio ~gere ~gi, *intr.* To run away, flee: *ad primum tactum...~giunt* CI 18; *~gerunt domum* AM 5.4.

augeo ~gere ~xi ~ctum, *tr.* To make larger, increase: *numerum...ad aliquot millia ~gere* CI 269.3; *affectionem...pro varia excitamenta ~ctam* FI 26.

augesco ~ere, *intr.* To become greater, increase, grow: *felicitas...in ratione plurium ~it* AC 549.

augmentum ~i, *neut.* Increase: *'prolongari'... praedicatur de bono et ejus ~o* AE 304.42.

Augsburgensis ~is ~e, *a.* Of Augsburg in Bavaria; *Confessio ~is*, the Augsburg Confession, compiled by Lutherans at Augsburg in 1530: VR 640.

augurator ~oris, *m.* One who foretells the future, seer: AC 3698.2.

augurium ~i, *neut.* A prediction of the future, prophecy: *~a veterum ex volatu avium* VR 631.2.

auguror ~ari ~atus sum, *tr.* To conjecture, guess, surmise: *~atur quae credit realia esse, cum tamen sint ludicra* VR 127; (w. *quod*) AM 22.

Augustanus ~a ~um, *a.* = **Augsburgensis**: VR 111.10.

augustus ~a ~um, *a.* **1** Of imposing appearance, august: *porticus ~i* AM 355.1. **2** (as the name of a month) August: ES 2721.

aula ~ae, *f.* **1** A large room, hall: *templa et ~ae* VR 12.9. **2** The court (of a monarch): *alios qui componebant ~am ejus* [sc. *Jovis*] VR 9.3.

aulaeum ~i, *neut.* A curtain: *theatrum cui appendit ~a picta* VR 136.3.

aulicus ~i, *m.* The attendant of royalty or a magnate, courtier: *venturi sunt ~i cum satellitiis* AM 7.2.

aura ~ae, *f.* **1** A breeze: *ad ~am diei* Gen. 3.8 (AC). **2** An atmosphere, air: *~a suprema, aether sub illa et aër infra hunc* VR 32.8; *puram et lenissimam ~am* AC 545.2. **3** A visible luminance, radiance: *vivunt in ~a lucis...splendentis margariticae* AC 1116. **4** A visible presence, aura: *nimbus...erat ~a phantasiae* AM 7.2.

aurantia ~ae, *f.* An orange tree: VR 78.2.

aurantium ~i, *neut.* An orange: *olivas, uvas, ~a et citros* AM 8.3.

aurantius ~a ~um, *a.* also **orantius** (ES 1679, ES 1681 Autographs, J D Odhner). Of orange: *in colores coeruleos et ~os* AC 10514; *coloris ~i obscurioris* ES 1679; (of the fruit) *pomis ~is* AM 42.5 (Rogers).

auratus ~a ~um, *a.* Gilded, gilt: *~um argentum... ~um lignum* VI 10.

auree, *adv.* In a golden fashion: *ad angelos ~e coeruleos* ES 525.

aurelia ~ae, *f.* The pupa of an insect undergoing metamorphosis: VR 12.6.

aureus ~a ~um, *a.* **1** Made of gold, golden: *altare ~um* SS 33; of golden colour: *athmosphaera sicut ~a* AM 20.1. **2** (of the first age) *Saeculum ~um*, the Golden Age: AC 1551.1; VR 9.2.

auricula ~ae, *f.* **1** The lobe of the ear: *applicant se...sinistrae ~ae* AC 1763. **2** (anat.) The auricle of the heart: AS 403.

auricularis ~is ~e, *a.* Of the lobe of the ear; (masc. pl. as sb.) the name given to certain spirits (see quot.): *mittuntur inter ~es, seu qui constituunt cartilagineam cutem auriculae sinistrae* ES 4194.

auriga ~ae, *m.* A charioteer: CC 9.4.

aurigo ~inis, *f.* Mildew: Deut. 28.22 (AC 8364.3).

auris ~is, *f.* The external organ of hearing, ear: *obturaverunt ~es* FI 46; (as the means of judging musical pitch) *cujus ~is in harmonico et consono est* VR 61.1; (w. reference to the character of the hearer) *sunt illorum ~es castae* AM 155[a].2.

aurora ~ae, *f.* **1** The dawn: *sicut mane seu ~a tempore veris* CI 289. **2** (in ancient mythology, personified as a goddess): *quod finxerint ~am alatam pennis argenteis* VR 112.1.

aurum ~i, *neut.* Gold: *idolum ex ~o* VR 7.

auscultata ~orum, *neut. pl.* That which is listened to, orders: *secundum ~a* VR 16.2.

auscultatio ~onis, *f.* The action of listening: AE 1080.2.

auscultator ~oris, *m.* A listener: VR 796.1.

ausculto ~are ~avi ~atum, *intr.*, *tr.* **1** (intr.) To listen, hearken: *ut videam et ~em* VR 48.2; (w. dat.) *non permisisset Adamo ~are serpenti* VR 58.2. **2** (tr.) To listen to: *devote ~at praedicationes* VI 25.

ausim: irreg. subj. of **audeo**.

auspicium ~i, *neut.* **1** The ancient practice of divination by watching the flight of birds: ES 4849. **2** Control, guidance: *diversitas ~orum* [sc. in Germany] VR 813; *sub ~o*, under the guidance of: *quantum homo sub ~o Divino vivit, hoc est, patitur se duci a Deo* VR 20; also, *ex ~o*: AC 3191.

auspicor ~ari ~atus sum, *intr.* To be inaugurated, be started: *quod...nullum doctrinale fidei ~ari, minus condi possit* AC 2516.2; AM 342.4.

austerus ~a ~um, *a.* **1** Sour to the taste, bitter: *cibus ...durus, mollis, ~us, dulcis* ES 1742. **2** Austere, severe: *quod inde vir...sit torvus, ~us, siccus et inamabilis* AM 56.4.

austrinus ~a ~um, *a.* Southern: *plaga ~a* AC 9668.1 (Autograph).

austrum ~i, *neut.* **1** The south: *angulum ~tri versus meridiem* Ezek. 47.19 (AC 1678.2); *ad ~trum respective ad Habitaculum* AC 9742. **2** The south wind: Luke 12.55 (AE 644.20).

ausus ~us, *m.* An act of boldness: *non potuerunt in illo ~u esse fari cum uxoribus nisi amice* AM 292.1.

aut, *conj.* **1** (to put mutually exclusive alternatives)

Or instead, or: *accedendo ad bonum aut ad malum* VR 476. **2** (to introduce an alternative description) Or it may be, or: *per viam externam, seu sensuum aut sensualem* AC 609.

autem, *conj.* (as 2nd word in clause) But, however: *quod...perficiantur...per auditum, non autem per visum* CI 271.

automaton ~i, *neut.* (Gk.) (gen. pl. *~um*) A self-moving figure, automaton, robot: *stat sicut ~on nihil videns et nihil agens* VI 96; CI 472.1.

autopsia ~ae, *f.* (Gk.) **1** Personal observation: *hoc videt et ex ~a agnoscit unusquisque* VR 35.8. **2** Inspection of anatomical specimens, dissection: AS 366; NE 14.

autopsicus ~a ~um, *a.* Based upon personal observation: *documenta ~a* AM 39.

autor: see **auctor**.

autoritas: see **auctoritas**.

Autumnus ~i, *m.* Autumn: CI 417.

autumo ~are ~avi ~atum, *intr.* (*tr.*) To conjecture, guess: *quod forte ~ent quod...loquantur mecum vernacula mea* CI 246.2; (impers. pass.) *~atum est, quod passio crucis fuerit ipse actus redemptionis* VR 95; (tr.) *quis aliud ~at?* AC 4.

auxiliaris ~is ~e, *a.* Assisting, auxiliary: *~es spiritus* ES 266.

auxiliator ~oris, *m.* One who assists, helper: Ezek. 30.8 (AE 654.38).

auxiliatrix ~icis, *f. adj.* Assisting, auxiliary: *absque viribus succenturiatis et ~icibus* AE 1211.4.

auxilior ~ari ~atus sum, *intr.* To give help, assist: *Aegyptii vane...~abuntur* Isa. 30.7 (AC 2781.2); (w. dat.) Isa. 41.14 (AC 1736.1).

auxilium ~i, *neut.* **1** Help, assistance: *mutuo ~o* AM 137.3. **2** One who helps, a helper: *faciam ei ~um tanquam apud illum* Gen. 2.18 (AC).

avare, *adv.* In miserly fashion, greedily: *~e...conquirendo opes* AM 496.

avaritia ~ae, *f.* Miserliness, avarice, greed: *~a, quae est amor divitiarum absque usu* CI 363.

avarus ~a ~um, *a.* (superl. *~issimus*) Miserly, greedy: *~i omnium sordidissimi sunt* AC 938.

avello ~ere avulsi avulsum, *tr.* To pull or tear away: *cum se a sacerdotibus ~ere conati sunt* AM 9.3; (transf.) *quod...sibi impresserat, hoc...non potest ~i* VR 110.2.

avenae ~narum, *f. pl.* Oats: VR 531.

aveo avere, *tr.* To desire ardently, long for: *qui avent sapientiam* AM 98.1; (w. inf.) *ab iis discedere avet* AC 182.

aversatilis ~is ~e, *a.* Repulsive: AC 7409.

aversatio ~onis, *f.* Repulsion, aversion: *omnis ~o est ex contrarietate affectionum* CI 194; *~oni esse,* to be repugnant: CI 429.

aversio ~onis, *f.* A turning away from: *~o et remotio a Domino* AE 78.4.

aversor ~ari ~atus sum, *tr.* To turn away from, reject, repel: *si...mentes conjugum...se interius ~atae fuerunt* CI 494; *fugit et ~atur mala ut peccata* FI 32.

aversus ~a ~um, *a.* (pf. pple. of **averto**) In senses of verb esp. **1** (w. *ab*) Turned away (from), having one's back (to): *~i ab oriente...prospiciebant ad occidentem* AM 268.2. **2** Estranged: *revertimini filii ~i* Jer. 3.14 (AC 983.1); *~um spirituale ab interno* AC 5584.

averto ~tere ~ti ~sum, *tr.* **1** To turn away: *eum oportet ~tere faciem* CI 223. **2** To keep apart, keep off: (absol.) *angeli solum ~tunt et defendunt* AC 1683. **3** (w. *ab*) To direct (the attention) away (from): *~terunt mentem a cogitando de Divino* VR 12.3; (esp. refl.) *~tit se a caelo* VI 19.

avicula ~ae, *f.* A small bird: AC 3324.2.

avide, *adv.* Eagerly: *sermoni quem...tam ~e hausi* AM 294.2.

aviditas ~atis, *f.* Eagerness, avidity: *~as praedandi* VR 498.2.

avidus ~a ~um, *a.* **1** (w. gen.) Ardently desirous (of), eager (for): *lucri ~i* AC 548.3. **2** Eagerly given, keen: *erat attentio ~a* AM 183.1.

avis ~is, *f.* A bird: *~ibus et feris rapacibus* CI 429.

avocamentum ~i, *neut.* A distraction: *vocant... divitias...~a seu media removentia hominem a coelo* AC 5008.4.

avolatio ~onis, *f.* The action of flying away: AE 1100.4.

avolo ~are ~avi, *intr.* To fly away: *columba fenestrae nostrae...~avit* AM 155[a].5.

avulsio ~onis, *f.* A pulling or tearing away: *~o et liberatio...ab inferno* AC 6368.

avus ~i, *m.* A grandfather: *cum similitudine ~i et atavi* AM 466.2.

axilla ~ae, *f.* The armpit, axilla: ES 4642; *~a manus*, the wrist: Ezek. 13.18 (AC 1178.2).

axioma ~atis, *neut.* (Gk.) An axiom: AE 1207.3.

axis ~is, *m.* (Gk.) (gen. sg. *~eos* AC 829.1) **1** The imaginary line about which a body rotates, axis: *quod* *tellus circum ~em suum rotet* VR 29.1; *in modum ~eos* 'axially' AC 829.1. 2 (transf.) The centre line of anything: *ex septo nasi, ut ex ~e faciei, reliqua pendent* ES 1126 1/2. 3 An upright post, pole: *alligatus cuidam longo palo seu statuto ~i* ES 3006. 4 (transf.) A cardinal point, pivot: *Ecclesia antiqua servavit suum ~em, qui erat Noachus* ES 4071.

Azazel: see **Asasel**.

azyga ~ae, *f.* (ad. Gk.) (anat.) The vena cava: *arteriae ...oriundae ex ~a seu vena cava et aorta* AS 405.

azylum: see **asylum**.

azymus ~a ~um, *a.* (Gk.) Unleavened: *placentas ~as* Exod. 12.39 (AC); (neut. pl. as sb.) unleavened bread: *festum ~orum* SS 20.2.

B

Babelicus ~a ~um, *a.* Of or belonging to Babel: AR 47.4; (masc. pl. as sb.; cf. **Babylonia** in Proper Nouns): ME 24.

Babylonicus ~a ~um, *a.* Babylonian: *captivitatis ~ae* AC 728.4.

baca: see **bacca**.

bacca ~ae, *f.* also **baca**. A berry: VR 78.2.

bacchans ~ntis, *m.* A reveller: *sonos sicut ~ntium in lupanaribus* ME 21.

bacillus ~i, *m.* A rod, stick: ES 2763.

baculus ~i, *m.* A stick for walking, staff: CC 7; (as a badge of office) *custodes cum ~is* AM 500.7; (as used by magicians) *magi repraesentantur per ~os in manu* AC 4013.1; *~um panis* (ad. Hebr.), the staff of bread: Ezek. 4.16 (DD 16).

badius ~a ~um, *a.* Chestnut-coloured, light brown: *in togis coloris ~i* AM 15.

bajulo ~are ~avi, *intr.* To carry a burden: Gen. 49.15 (AC).

bajulus ~i, *m.* One who carries loads, a porter: VR 563.1.

balaena ~ae, *f.* A whale: AC 819; (as a type of great size and strength) *pulex contra ~am* VR 68.

balbus ~a ~um, *a.* Stammering: AC 7225.3; (masc. pl. as sb.) Isa. 32.4 (AR 282.2).

balneum ~i, *neut.* A bathhouse, bathroom: CI 571.

balsamice, *adv.* In the manner of balsam: VR 568.2.

balsamicus ~a ~um, *a.* Of or made of balsam: *arbustis ~is* VR 537; (neut. pl. as sb.) substances smelling of balsam: VR 759.3.

balsamum ~i, *neut.* An aromatic ointment, balsam, balm: VR 148.

balteum: see **baltheus**.

balteus: see **baltheus**.

baltheum: see **baltheus**.

baltheus ~i, *m.* also **balteum** ~i, *neut.*, **balteus**, and **baltheum** ~i, *neut.* A belt: *ex significatione ~i seu cinguli, quod sit commune vinculum* AC 9828.1.

baptisma ~atis, *neut.* (Gk.) Baptism: Luke 3.3 (DD 18.4).

baptismus ~i, *m.* (Gk.) Baptism: AC 870.1.

Baptista ~ae, *m.* (Gk.) *Johannes ~a*, John the Baptist: AC 6752.1.

baptizatio ~onis, *f.* The action of baptizing: AC 10239.1.

baptizo ~are ~avi ~atum, *tr.* To baptize: AC 870.1.

barathrum ~i, *neut.* (Gk.) An abyss, chasm: *~um aperiebatur in medio urbis* VR 567.2.

barba ~ae, *f.* A beard: AE 66.2; (of a lion or bear) 1 Sam. 17.35 (AR 573.1).

barbare, *adv.* In an uncivilized manner, barbarously: VR 683.

barbaricus ~a ~um, *a.* Foreign, strange: Ps. 114.1 (AC 2830.7).

barbarus ~a ~um, *a.* **1** Uncivilized, barbarian: *gens tam ~a* DP 322.2. **2** Savage, cruel, barbarous: *ut semet ...~o modo crucient* ES 661; AM 105.

barbatus ~a ~um, *a.* (superl. *~issimus*) Bearded: *mento ~o* VR 137.1; ES 470.

basiliscus ~i, *m.* (Gk.) A poisonous snake, basilisk: VR 124.1.

basis ~eos, *f.* (Gk.) (acc. sg. *~in* AC 947) **1** A stand, pedestal: 1 Kgs. 7.43 (AE 70.4); AC 947. **2** A fundamental entity, foundation, basis: *quod sit [ultimum] ~is et fundamentum* CI 304.2.

bassus ~a ~um, *a.* (of the voice) Low-pitched, deep: *loquuti sono ~o sicut gigantes* AC 941.2.

bath: see **bathus**.

bathus ~i, *m.* also **bath**, *indecl.*, and **batus**. A Hebrew liquid measure, a bath: Isa. 5.10 (AC 576.1).

batus: see **bathus**.

bdellium ~i, *neut.* A precious stone, bdellium: Gen. 2.12 (AC).

beate, *adv.* (compar. *~ius*) In a happy manner, blessedly: AC 2654.3.

beatificatio ~onis, *f.* **1** The action of making happy: *omnium ~o est a Solo Deo* VR 46.3. **2** A thing which causes gratification: *reportant...~ones ut merita* AR 786.2.

beatifico ~are ~avi ~atum, *tr.* To make happy: *amor conjugialis...~at hominem* AM 78.5; to call happy: *~abunt me filiae* Gen. 30.13 (AC).

beatitudo ~inis, *f.* A state of being happy, blessedness: *~inem aeternam hominum* VR 13.2; (w. pl.) an instance of this: *de ~inibus illius amoris* AM 291.1.

beatus ~a ~um, *a.* (compar. *~ior*, superl. *~issimus*) Happy, blessed: *~i pauperes* Luke 6.20 (SS 51.4); (neut. as sb.) blessedness: *inde...est angelis omne ~um* CI 286.

Belgicus ~a ~um, *a.* Belgian: SE 38.

belial ~lis, *m.* and *indecl.* (Hebr.) Belial, a generic name for ungodliness: Ps. 18.4 (AR 409).

bellicus ~a ~um, *a.* Of war; *navis ~a*, a warship: VR 112.2.

bellua ~ae, *f.* also **belua**. A beast of prey, wild beast: VR 488.

bellum ~i, *neut.* Warfare, war: *arma ~i* AC 6661.2; (w. pl.) a war: FI 50; *~a Jehovae*, the Wars of Jehovah (a book of the Ancient Word): AM 77.2.

bellus ~a ~um, *a.* Beautiful, pretty: *foemina satis ~a facie* ES 4832.9.

belua: see **bellua**.

bene, *adv.* (compar.: see **melius**, superl.: see **optime**) **1** Properly, fully, well: *~e scrutari* AC 6704; (as interj.) good: VR 26. **2** In a moral fashion, correctly, well: *qui ~e vivit* CI 470.

beneacta ~orum, *neut. pl.* also spelled as two words **bene acta**. Good deeds: CI 10.

benedico ~cere ~xi ~ctum, *intr.* (w. dat.) To pronounce a blessing (on), bless: *~xit Deus Noacho* Gen. 9.1 (AC).

benedictio ~onis, *f.* **1** The action of blessing: *signum ~onis e caelo* VR 747.3. **2** The formula used in blessing: AC 6674.8. **3** A thing which confers a blessing: *eris ~o* Gen. 12.2 (AC).

benedictus ~a ~um, *a.* Blessed: *~a inter mulieres* Luke 1.28 (DD 19.2); (as the name of a Pope) AE 114.9.

benefacio ~facere ~feci ~factum, *intr.* To do good: *in amando et ~faciendo* FI 21; (w. dat.) to confer benefits (on), do good (to): *cui dives...~facere potest* CI 361.

benefactor ~oris, *m.* One who confers benefits, benefactor: AC 6429.

benefactum ~i, *neut.* A kindness, benefit: AC 6429.

beneficium ~i, *neut.* **1** A good deed, kindness, benefit: VI 114. **2** *~o* (w. gen.), by the grace (of), with the aid (of): *~o lucis...sistantur videnda mirificissima* AC 1534; *mentis intellectualis ~o mentiri bonum* ES 191.

benefio ~fieri, *intr.* (used as impers. pass. of **benefacio**): AC 5008.3.

beneplacentia ~ae, *f.* Good pleasure: *quod salvatio non sit nisi quam ~a Divina* CI 521.

beneplaceo ~cere ~cui ~citum, *intr.* **1** (w. *in* + abl.) To take pleasure (in), be pleased (with): *~cebit Jehovah in te* Isa. 62.4 (DD 64.2). **2** (impers. w. dat.) It is pleasing to: *cum ~cet Domino* CI 171; (w. *ut*) AC 471.

beneplacitum ~i, *neut.* That which is pleasing, a decision, good pleasure: *in ~is mariti* AM 209; *ex ~o*, at will: *quod solum sit intromissio...ex ~o* CI 420; *~i alicujus est*, it is someone's pleasure: AM 207.4.

beneventote, *interj.* Welcome!: AM 56.1.

benevolentia ~ae, *f.* Good will, benevolence: *~am ini cum adversario tuo* Matt. 5.25 (VI 73); (w. pl.) a kindly act, kindness: *ad grate recipiendum ~as oblatas* AM 285.2.

benevolo ~velle ~volui, *intr.* To be well disposed: *si ~vis* AC 361; (w. dat.) CI 359.

benevolus ~a ~um, *a.* Well-disposed, benevolent: AM 365.

benigne, *adv.* In a friendly or kindly fashion: *hic nos ~e excepit* AM 78.4.

benignitas ~atis, *f.* Kindness: CH 40 (= ii.7).

benignus ~a ~um, *a.* Friendly, kindly: AC 2927.

beo ~are ~avi ~atum, *tr.* (w. abl.) To endow (with a blessing), bless (with): *illum ~are omni gloria* AC 6645.2.

beryllus ~i, *m.* (Gk.) A precious stone, beryl: Rev. 21.20 (AR).

bestia ~ae, *f.* An animal as distinct from a human being, beast: *discrimen inter hominem et inter ~am* VI 15; AC 45; (as dist. from wild beast) VR 373; (of the Beast in Rev.) Rev. 17.3 (AR); *homines ~ae*, beast-people: VR 160.7.

bestiarium ~i, *neut.* A place where animals are kept, zoo: VR 57; VR 798.8.

bibitio ~onis, *f.* The action of drinking: AC 5165.1.

bibliotheca ~ae, *f.* (Gk.) A library: AM 207.5.

biblium ~i, *neut.* (Gk.) A book: *in ejus ~is Naturae* AM 416.2; *~a sancta* 'the Bible' ES 895; so *~ium* alone: *in ~is illorum* AE 768.3.

bibo ~ere ~i ~itum, *tr.* To drink: *~ere aquam ex fonte* AM 182.2; (absol.) *acetum ad ~endum* VR 130.3.

biceps ~ipitis, *a.* Two-headed: *canes... ~ipites* AM 79.2.

biduum ~i, *neut.* A space of two days: *post ~um ab obitu* CI 312.4.

biennium ~i, *neut.* A space of two years: AM 522.

bifidatio ~onis, *f.* A splitting into two: *~o loquelae* ES 3096.

bifide, *adv.* With splitting into two parts: *loquebatur ...quasi ~e* AC 5056.1.

bifidus ~a ~um, *a.* Split into two parts: *sono rauco sicut ~o* AC 1763.2.

bifurcatus ~a ~um, *a.* Bifurcated, forked: *~a lingua* ES 570.

biga ~ae, *f.* A pair (of horses): *currus cum ~a equorum* AC 6212.2. (In ES 2276 perh. *binis* should be read; cf. ES 2275.)

bihorium ~i, *neut.* A space of two hours: AM 103.2.

bilanx ~ncis, *f.* A pair of scales, balance: VR 72.1.

biliaris ~is ~e, *a.* Of or for bile: *ductus...~ares* AC 10030.1.

bilifer ~era ~erum, *a.* Carrying bile: ES 1015 ½.

biliosus ~a ~um, *a.* Abounding in bile, bilious: AM 357; (neut. pl. as sb.) VR 42.

bilis ~is, *f.* The bile, esp. any one of its three types: *~e atra, flava aut viridi* VR 665.5; AC 1103.2.

bini ~ae ~a, *pl. adj.* Two: *de ~is his regnis* VI 32.1; *~i ~i*, two by two, in twos: Gen. 7.9 (AC); (sim.) *~i et ~i* ES 1529.

binus ~a ~um, *a.* Twofold, double: *quod naturale sit ~um* AC 5649.2.

bis, *adv.* Twice: AC 737.1; *semel aut bis*, once or twice: AM 529; *bis aut ter* or *bis et ter*, two or three times: DP 298.2; CI 441.

bisseco ~are ~ui ~tum, *tr.* To cut in half: VR 74.2.

bitumen ~inis, *neut.* Asphalt, bitumen: Gen. 6.14 (AC); DP 215.13.

bituminatio ~onis, *f.* Treatment with bitumen: AC 639.1.

bitumino ~are ~avi ~atum, *tr.* To treat with bitumen, caulk: Gen. 6.14 (AC).

bituminosus ~a ~um, *a.* Abounding in bitumen: *taedas sulphuratas et ~as* AM 231.2.

bivium ~i, *neut.* A place where two roads meet, a parting of the ways: CI 534; (fig.) *quia pectus est in ~o* AM 179.

blande, *adv.* With agreeable mildness, mildly: *quaesivimus ~e* VR 35.5.

blandiloquium ~i, *neut.* Agreeable speech, soft words: *in risibus amaenitatis ex ~is et facetiis* AM 3.2.

blandior ~diri ~ditus sum, *intr.* To use flattery, cajole: ES 466; *jucunda ~dientia* ES 5943.

blanditer, *adv.* With flattery: *jam ~er* [*blanditur* Tafel], *jam cum precibus* ES 466.

blanditiae ~tiarum, *f. pl.* Flatteries: VR 331.3.

blandus ~a ~um, *a.* Agreeably mild, gentle: *taciti sunt ~i* ES(M) 4705; *vocis ~ae* AM 17; easy to bear: *jugum Meum ~um est* Matt. 11.30 (AC 905).

blasphematio ~onis, *f.* A speaking ill (esp. of the Divine), blaspheming: *secundum qualitatem...~onis et prophanationis* AC 1878; a blasphemous utterance, blasphemy: CI 462[a].5.

blasphemator ~oris, *m.* One who speaks ill of, a slanderer: BCP (VI 6); *~or proximi* VR 481.

blasphemia ~ae, *f.* (Gk.) A blasphemous utterance, blasphemy: *~a contra Spiritum Sanctum* DD 50.2.

blasphemo ~are ~avi ~atum, *tr.* To speak ill of, slander: (esp. against God) *~are Dominum et Verbum* SS 67.5; (absol.) to blaspheme: *~ant et prophanant* AC 301.

blasphemus ~a ~um, *a.* Slandering, blasphemous: [*malum*] *~um* CH 207 (= Articulus Primus.7).

blateratio ~onis, *f.* A talking nonsense, prating, babbling: AC 1094.1.

blatero ~are ~avi, *intr.* To talk nonsense, babble, prate: *qui...~arunt et nihil cogitaverunt quid dixerant* AC 5557.

blatta ~ae, *f.* A destructive insect, clothes moth grub, bookworm, cockroach, etc.: *sicut lanam comedet eos ~a* Isa. 51.8 (AC 9331.7); *~am currentem super charta mea* AM 329.1.

boatio ~onis, *f.* A lowing (of cattle): *vaccarum ~o* VR 203.

bolus ~i, *m.* (Gk. *bolos*) A lump, clod: *qui projicit grandinem...sicut ~os* Ps. 147.17 (AC 7553.5); *grandinis ~i*, hailstones: AC 7553.7.

bombarda ~ae, *f.* A cannon: VR 123.3.

bombyx ~ycis, *m.* A silkworm: VR 687.3.

bonitas ~atis, *f.* **1** The quality of being good, goodness: *haec ~ate differunt ab ipso auro* VI 10. **2** (w. pl.) A good quality, virtue: *amor est complexus omnium ~atum* VR 38.1.

bonum ~i, *neut.* **1** That which is good in an absolute sense, esp. of the Divine, goodness: *quod...Deus...sit Ipsum ~um et Ipsum Verum* VR 3.1; *affectio ~i* FI 13; *indignantur* [*angeli*]...*si quis ~um illis tribuit* CI 9.2. **2** That which is good in a relative sense, a particular kind of goodness: *~um veri* AM 83; *omnes quicunque in terris differunt ~o* AC 6706. **3** Goodness or a particular kind of good as an attribute of individuals or groups, a good quality: *~a Ecclesiae* VR 38.1; *unusquisque angelus est sicut suum ~um* CI 41. **4** Goodness in action: *velle et facere ~um ex amore* CI 15; *si dicit se cogitare ~um et vivit male* AC 379; (w. pl.) a good deed: [*homo*] *producit ~a* AC 9; *~a charitatis seu opera* VR 506.8. **5** A desirable thing, advantage, benefit, good: *propter commune ~um* CI 64.2; *per benedictionem significatur omne ~um mundanum, corporeum et terrestre* AC 1096.1; *quod aliquis amat, hoc ei ~um est* CI 23; *~o cedere*, to be of advantage: *quod cedat ~o famulis si ab heris suis...castigantur* VR 459.15. **6** (pl.) Property, goods: *depopulantur incolarum ~a* VR 117.1; *~a mundi* VR 661.3; (also sg.) *ut...fruantur ejus ~o* ES 2500.

bonus ~a ~um, *a.* (compar.: see **melior**, superl.: see **optimus**) **1** In good condition, sound, whole: *et vidit Deus quod ~um* Gen. 1.12 (AC). **2** (of things) Desirable, satisfactory: *arbores tam malas quam bonas* VR 459.5; *in ~o sensu* AC 1159.3. **3** Good (for a specified purpose or in respect of a quality): *arborem...~am ad cibum* Gen. 2.9 (AC); *puella ~a aspectu* Gen. 24.16 (AC). **4** Good at a specified action, efficient, competent: *pastor ~us* John 10.14 (AC 6806.2). **5** (of persons or spirits) Morally good, upright: *mali...malefaciunt...sed ~i benefaciunt* AC 6703. **6** (of actions, states, etc.) Induced by or productive of good: *de ~is operibus* VR 462.3; *affectiones...~as* ES 1889; *si cogitatio et voluntas ~ae sunt, tunc facta et opera sunt ~a* CI 472.1.

boo ~are ~avi, *intr.* (of cattle) To low: *vaccas, quae ~abant in via* VR 203.

borborygmus ~i, *m.* (Gk.) A rumbling of the belly: VR 798.8.

borealis ~is ~e, *a.* Of the North Wind, northerly: *spiritus ~es* VR 185.1; *in terris ~ibus* VR 385.4.

bos bovis, *m.* or *f.* (gen. pl. *boum*, abl. pl. *bovibus* and *bobus*) A bull or cow, ox: AM 342.3; *frustum bovis*, a joint of beef: DP 254.4.

botanicus ~a ~um, *a.* Of botany, botanic: *in arte ~a* AE 1203.2.

botrus ~i, *f.* (ad. Gk. *botrus*) A cluster or bunch of grapes: AC 1071.1; VR 348.

bracchium: see **brachium**.

brachiolum ~i, *neut.* A small arm: *quod* [*infans*] *~a moveret* ES 4322.

brachium ~i, *neut.* also **bracchium**. **1** An arm (of the human body): CI 65; (Bibl. as a symbol of strength) Isa. 51.5 (AE 50.2). **2** An arm-piece (of a garment): *sicut vestium ~a* ES 1485. **b** the arm (of a chair): ES 4458. **3** A sail-arm (of a windmill): VR 482.3.

bractea ~ae, *f.* A thin metal plate worn as an ornament: *~a aurea adamantibus circumobsita* AM 20.2.

bracteola ~ae, *f.* = **bractea**: Isa. 3.19 (AC 2576.11).

bravo, *interj.* (Ital.) Bravo: AM 521.2.

brevi, *adv.* In a short time, shortly, soon: *quod ~i venturus sit in alteram vitam* AC 5075.6.

breviarium ~i, *neut.* A summary: SE 1.

brevis ~is ~e, *a.* (compar. *~ior*, superl. *~issimus*) **1** (of space or time) Short: *~e tempus* John 12.34 (AE 63.2). **2** (of narratives, etc.) Brief: AM 515.

breviter, *adv.* (compar. *~vius*, superl. *~vissime*) **1** For a short while: ES 466. **2** In a few words, briefly: *~viter describere* DP 299.

breviusculus ~a ~um, *a.* Fairly short: *intra ~um tempus* AC 698.

bronchia ~orum, *neut. pl.* (Gk.) (anat.) The bronchial tubes, bronchia: AS 405.2.

bronchiae ~chiarum, *f. pl.* = **bronchia**: VR 462.6.

bronchialis ~is ~e, *a.* Of the bronchia, bronchial: [*venae*] *~es* AS 504.2.

bruchus ~i, *m.* (Gk.) The wingless larva of the locust: Nahum 3.15 (AE 543.10).

bruma ~ae, *f.* Winter: *fides...exspirat sicut avis in intensa ~a* VR 385.

brumalis ~is ~e, *a.* (neut. as sb.) Wintertime: *sicut ~e in zonis calidis* AS 102.

brunee, *adv.* With brown colour: *sphaera...~e colorata* ES 4196.

bruneus ~a ~um, *a.* Brown: *color aedificiorum... lateritius seu ~us obscurus* ES 844.

brutesco ~ere, *intr.* To become brutish: *quod* [*vita*] *...depravetur et ~at* SA 124 (= x.6.[1]).

brutus ~a ~um, *a.* **1** *~a animalia*, animals other than man, beasts: VR 12.8; (neut. as sb.) ES 1827. **2** Of or appropriate to beasts; brutish: *adulteria...non rationalia sed ~a* AM 105.

bubo ~onis, *m.* A horned owl (dist. from **noctua**): VR 61.2.

bubulcus ~i, *m.* A herdsman: ES 1451.

bucca ~ae, *f.* The mouth: *qui cibaria...ingerunt in ~am* VR 527.3.

buccina ~ae, *f.* A kind of trumpet, horn: *tuba seu ~a* AE 55.1.

buccinator ~oris, *m.* A horn blower, trumpeter: *vox...~orum* Rev. 18.22 (AR).

bulbus ~i, *m.* (anat.) The glans penis: ES 3453.

bulla ~ae, *f.* **1** A bubble: *~a aquea* VR 159.7. **2** A papal bull: VR 90; SE 2.

bullatus ~a ~um, *a.* Producing bubbles, bubbling: *aliquid ~um seu ebulliens* ES 2380; cf. *similaginem ~am* Lev. 7.12 (AC 3880.8).

bullitio ~onis, *f.* A forming into bubbles, bubbling: *nubium ~ones* ES 2380.

bullula ~ae, *f.* A small bubble: ES Index s.v. 'spiritus' (p. 335 Tafel), referring to ES 433.

bursa ~ae, *f.* A pocket (in a garment): *in ~a togae* VR 137.3.

bustum ~i, *neut.* A tomb: *non procul a ~o Lutheri* VR 137.8.

butyrum ~i, *neut.* (Gk.) Butter: AC 1002.

buxus ~i, *f.* A box tree: Isa. 41.19 (AE 109.4); (sg. as collective) *campi...circumcincti ~o* AM 78.3.

byssinus ~a ~um, *a.* Made of fine linen: *vestimenta...~a* CI 180 (cf. Rev. 4.4); (neut. as sb.) SS 9.

byssus ~i, *f.* (Gk.) Fine linen: *vestes ~i* AM 14.1.

C

cacabus ~i, *m.* (Gk.) A cooking pot: *a mincha quae conficiebatur in ~o* Lev. 2.7 (AC 7356.3).

cachexia ~ae, *f.* (Gk.) An unhealthy state of the body, cachexy: VR 665.5.

cachinno ~are ~avi ~atum, *intr.* also **cachinnor** ~ari ~atus sum, *intr.* To laugh loudly, guffaw: *quis non ~aret ad tres Deos?* VR 172.2; (dep.) *ad haec plures ... ~ati sunt* AM 79.7.

cachinnor: see **cachinno**.

cachinnus ~i, *m.* A loud laugh, guffaw: *reliqui in ~is applaudebant manibus* AM 521.2.

cacochymia ~ae, *f.* (Gk.) An unhealthy state of the bodily humours, cacochymy: VR 665.5.

cacodaemon ~onis, *m.* (Gk.) An evil spirit: CO 33.2.

cacumen ~inis, *neut.* The peak (of a mountain), summit: AC 9434.

cadaver ~eris, *neut.* A dead body, corpse: *corpora hominum...vel ~era* AM 182.6; (prov.) *ubi ~er ibi aquilae* AC 1667.4.

cadaverosus ~a ~um, *a.* Of or resembling a corpse, cadaverous: *in inferno... ~o* AC 814.1; (neut. pl. as sb.) *avibus...qui...ad ~a...advolant* CI 429.

cado ~ere cecidi casum, *intr.* **1** To fall over, collapse: *homo ~eret mortuus* VR 118; *arbor ubi ~it, ibi jacet* DP 277[a]. **2** To fall to the ground or downwards, drop: *stellae...ceciderunt in terram* Rev. 6.13 (AR); *bos in puteum ~it* Luke 14.5 (AC 9086.2); *a procella deorsum ~ente* VR 108. **3** To fall to pieces, collapse: *decima pars urbis cecidit* Rev. 11.13 (AR). **b** (of cities, states, etc.) to be destroyed, fall: *cecidit, cecidit Babylon* Rev. 14.8 (AR); *societas, respublica et regnum absque illis legibus ~erent* VI 53. **4** (of the face) To assume a look of dismay, fall: Gen. 4.5 (AC). **5** To become ineffectual, fail: *~unt apud me omnia illa quae dixisti* VR 16.2. **6** (of conditions) To come on, happen: *~ere fecit Jehovah Deus soporem super hominem* Gen. 2.21 (AC). **7** (w. *in* + acc.) To become subject (to), fall (into): *~unt in perceptionem num vera sint vel non* FI 3; *facile in errorem...possit ~ere* SS 1; *~it in gravia falsa* AE 644.24. **8** (w. *in* + acc.) To deteriorate (into), lapse (into): *~it...spirituale in suum correspondens naturale* AE 8.1; *~it idea in nullum* AC 6876.3. **9** (w. *in* or *sub* + acc.) To be applicable (to), suit, match: *talia vix ~unt in hominem probum* VR 132.2; *quod regnum Domini...non sub mensuras terrestres ~at* AC 648.1.

caducus ~a ~um, *a.* **1** Falling: *stella ~a* VR 82.1; *foliorum ~orum* ES 269. **2** Liable to fall: *homo ~us sicut in morbo* ES 4572. **3** Liable to perish, transient: *quia dignitates...illae pereunt, dicuntur temporariae et ~ae* DP 217.6; VR 375.1.

cadus ~i, *m.* (Gk.) A jar, pot: *ex ~o aceti* VR 132.3.

caece, *adv.* also **coece**. Blindly: *~e obedit* AM 492.

caecitas ~atis, *f.* Blindness: Zech. 12.4 (AE 152.9); (fig.) *in... ~ate de statu vitae post mortem* CI 312.5.

caecus ~a ~um, *a.* also **coecus**. (compar. *~ior*) **1** Not having the power of sight, blind: *quod ~i receperint visum* SS 17.4. **2** Intellectually blind, unable to perceive: *quoad intellectum... ~ae sunt* AM 134.4. **3** (of things) Not accompanied or controlled by perception, blind: *credit quod omnia sint fluxus ~i* AC 6692.2; *ex ~a scientia* VR 48.13; *fides ~a* FI 1.

caecutio ~tire ~tivi, *intr.* To be without sight or mental perception, be blind: *~tiunt in tantum ut non sciant quid Deus* CI 86.

caedes ~is, *f.* Slaughter, murder, carnage: *ad evitandum cruentas ~es* AM 107.

caedo ~dere cecidi ~sum, *tr.* **1** To strike, hit: *unum ceciderunt virgis* Matt. 21.35 (AE 122.3). **2** To quarry, cut to shape (stone): *ex lapide integro, non ~so* 1 Kgs. 6.7 (SS 47); to fell (timber): AC 9011.4. **3** To cut (hair): *comae circumcirca sunt ~sae* ES 1347.

cael-: see **coel-**.

caen-: see **coen-**.

caepi: see **coepi**.

caerimonia: see **ceremonia**.

caerulescens ~ntis, *a.* Becoming blue, bluish: *indumentum factum ex...cortice ~nte* AC 8245.

caerulescentia ~ae, *f.* Pale blueness, azureness: *adamas...ad ~am interiorem accedit* AC 9868.5.

caeruleus ~a ~um, *a.* also **coeruleus**. Blue, azure: *in colore...flammeo vel ~o* CI 356; (neut. as sb.) *in ~o, quale est coeli nocturni* AC 3221.

Caesar ~aris, *m.* One of the Roman emperors: *ante ~arum tempora* VR 141; any emperor or absolute ruler: *aliquem ~arem, regem aut principem* VR 161.3; *milites custodes ~aris sui* UJ(P) 86.

caesius ~a ~um, *a.* Grey: *facie sicut chalybea, coloris ~i* AM 78.4.

caesor ~oris, *m.* One who cuts, a hewer: *~ores lignorum* Josh. 9.27 (AC 1097.2).

caespes: see **cespes**.

caeteroquin, *adv.* also **cet-**. In other respects, otherwise: AC 468.2.

caeterum, *conj.* also **cet-**. And further: *~um Verbum caro factum est* John 1.14 (DD 1); in other respects: *et ~um vivere sicut in corpore* ES 3502.

caeterus ~a ~um, *a.* also **cet-**. The rest of, the other (usu. pl. as sb.): *faemella...ponit ova, ~i ministrant* CI 108.1; *~a...quae non concordant, rejicit* CI 18.1.

caetus ~us, *m.* also **coetus**. A gathering, collection (of people): *~us gentium* SE 66; *~us angelorum* CI 51.

calamitas ~atis, *f.* Disaster, misfortune: AR 416.

calamus ~i, *m.* (Gk.) **1** A reed or cane: *ex meris cannis et ~is* VR 676; (used as a weapon) *quod caput ~o percusserint* DD 16.5. **b** sweet flag (used for its perfume): *~us optimus e terra longinqua* Jer. 6.20 (AC 1171.5). **2** A pen: *quosdam cum ~is sub sinistri temporis crinibus* AM 151[a].2. **3** A stalk: *septem aristae ascendentes in ~o uno* Gen. 41.6 (AC); each of the branches of a multiple candlestick: *candelabrum instructum septem ~is et schyphis ex auro* AM 20.1.

calathus ~i, *m.* (Gk.) A basket: *in ~is portantes [fructus]* AM 8.2.

calcaneum ~i, *neut.* also **calcaneus** ~i, *m.* The heel of the foot: *planta pedis et ~um* AC 1748.1; the fetlock (of a horse): *mordens ~os equi* Gen. 49.17 (AC).

calcaneus: see **calcaneum**.

calcareus: see **calcarius**.

calcarius ~a ~um, *a.* also **calcareus** (ES 1248). Of lime: *instar cujusdam ~i* ES 1884; *ex lapide ~o* limestone AM 78.3; white as lime, chalky: *facie ~a* AM 514.3.

calcatio ~onis, *f.* A trampling underfoot: (by sheep) *~o ovis* Isa. 7.25 (AE 304.12).

calceamenta ~orum, *neut. pl.* Footwear, shoes: *~a ...lignea* ES 992.

calceo ~are ~avi ~atum, *tr.* To equip with footwear, shoe: *~avi te taxo* Ezek. 16.10 (AE 195.7).

calceus ~i, *m.* A covering for the foot, shoe, sandal: *cujus ego non sum dignus ut solvam Ipsius corrigiam ~i* John 1.27 (DD 37.2); *~i ex holoserico* AM 42.3.

calcitro ~are ~avi ~atum, *intr.* To kick: DP 300.

calco ~are ~avi ~atum, *tr.* **1** To trample on, tread: *~are et terere unam glebam* AM 232.2; (in a wine press) *sicut ~antis in torculari* Isa. 63.2 (DD 14.2). **2** To walk over (a path): *per viam nusquam prius ~atam* ES 3340.

calculo ~are ~avi ~atum, *intr., tr.* **1** (intr.) To make a calculation, do sums: ES 1114; ES 5956. **2** (tr.) To discover by calculation, calculate: *materialia collata... ad palatium, quae ~ata ab architecto* ES 3724.

calculus ~i, *m.* **1** A pebble (used in voting): *dabo illi ~um album* Rev. 2.17 (AR); a vote: AM 315.6. **2** A calculation: *qui ~um init* CI 415; VR 32.3; ES 3482.

calefacio ~facere ~feci ~factum, *tr.* To make warm: *se ~facere student* ES 575.

calefio ~fieri ~factus sum, *intr.* To become warm: *per laborem... ~fieri* ES 271.

caleo ~lere ~lui, *intr.* To be hot: *~lent toto corpore* AM 44.7.

calesco ~ere, *intr.* To become hot: *corda illorum ex se frigida ~ant* AM 56.4.

calidus ~a ~um, *a.* Hot, warm: *in aqua ~a balnei* AM 339.3; (of persons) *novi...quod nec frigidus [sis] nec ~us* Rev. 3.15 (AR); (neut. as sb.) warmth: *quod ii... ~um spirent* ES 954.

caliga ~ae, *f.* A boot: *~ae seu calcei* 3AD 5910.

caligatio ~onis, *f.* Obscuration of the mind, mental darkness: *fit...caligo, et inde infatuatio et ~o* CI 572.

caliginosus ~a ~um, *a.* Full of thick darkness, murky: *sol mundi apparet angelis ut ~um quid* CI 122.

caligo[1] ~inis, *f.* Thick or dense darkness, murk: *est... sicut ~o ad lucem* SS 3; mental obscurity: *patet...in qua ~ine sunt de spiritualibus* VR 12.4; (dist. from **tenebrae**) AC 1860.3.

caligo[2] ~are ~avi, *intr.* To be in darkness: *ad influxum lucis coeli incipiebant ~are oculis* CI 518.

calix ~icis, *m.* A cup: *~ix auri* Jer. 51.7 (AC 1072.4).

calleo ~lere ~lui, *tr.* (w. acc.) To be skilled in, know: *dicens quod ~leret artem* AC 816; (w. inf.) to possess the skill (to), know how (to): *~lent viros jugo...subjicere* AM 292.2; *quod ars musica ~leat exprimere affectionum varia genera* CI 241.

callide, *adv.* (compar. *~ius*) Skilfully: *~e mentiri innocentiam* AM 514.2.

calliditas ~atis, *f.* Skill, cunning: *qui ~ate et artibus praevalent* CI 543.

callidus ~a ~um, *a.* (compar. *~ior*) Cunning, skilful: *quod velint videri ~i* AC 830; (of actions) *~as expurgationes* AM 469.

callositas ~atis, *f.* A callosity: *~as eorum apparet dura* CI 466.

callosus ~a ~um, *a.* Covered in calluses: *caput... apparet ~um, sicut ex ebeno, quod pertingit usque in nasum* CI 354.

callus ~i, *m.* A hard piece of skin, callus: CI 466; ES 358.

calo ~onis, *m.* A soldier's servant: VR 388.4.

calor ~oris, *m.* Heat, warmth: *cum ~ore...ex sole mundi* SS 109; (in heaven) *elevari in ~orem caeli, qui est amor* VI 15.

calumnia ~ae, *f.* A slanderous report, calumny: *ex ~a imposita nomini zelotypiae* AM 376.

calumnior ~ari ~atus sum, *intr.* To utter slanders, calumniate: Jer. 9.4 (AC 6756.3).

calvaria ~ae, *f.* The skull: *ossa ~ae nostrae* VR 185.6.

calvities ~ei, *f.* **1** Baldness: VR 74.5. **2** The scalp: *ut quasi...comprimant ~em capitis* ES 542.

calvitium ~i, *m.* **1** Baldness: *~um sibi inducere* SS 35.2. **2** The scalp: *avellere ~um capitis* ES 358.

calvus ~a ~um, *a.* Having no hair on the head, bald: 2 Kgs. 2.23 (AE 66.2); (of parts of the body) hairless: *mento ~o* VR 137.1.

calx[1] ~lcis, *f.* **1** The heel: *a capite ad ~lcem* CI 527. **2** The end (of a book): *vide infra ad ~lcem hujus libri* 3AD 3333.

calx[2] ~lcis, *f.* Lime: *lapides ~lcis* Isa. 27.9 (AE 391.14); (used on walls) *casis structis ex juncis et calamis ~lce incrustatis* AR 442.3.

camaena ~ae, *f.* also **camoena**. A female author: *per scripta a quibusdam eruditis ~is* AM 175.3.

camara: see **camera**.

cambium ~i, *neut.* A place of exchange: *intellectus humanus est sicut ~um, in quo fit permutatio* VR 11.3.

camela ~ae, *f.* A female camel: Gen. 32.15 (AC).

camelinus ~a ~um, *a.* Of camel: *Johannes...habebat vestimentum ex pilis ~is* AC 3301.2 (Matt. 3.4).

camelus ~i, *m.* (Gk.) A camel: *~um intrudere per foramen acus netoriae* AM 240.

camera ~ae, *f.* also app. **camara** (ES 3993). **1** A room in a building, chamber: *in domo erant plus quam quinquaginta ~ae* AM 5.1. **b** *consiliarii a ~is*, councillors of the treasury, treasurers: AM 14.1. **2** (anat.) A cavity in the body, chamber: *~am thoracis* ES 1723; *auris internam ~am* ES 1751; *in interiore ~a oculi* ES 3213. **3** A region of hell: *e ~a infernali* AC 817.

cameratus ~a ~um, *a.* (of a vehicle) Covered: *super rhedis ~is* Isa. 66.20 (AE 355.15); vaulted, ceilinged: *~as eductiones, quae erant sicut conclavia juxta fenestras* AM 103.4; (neut. as sb., perh.) a covered vehicle: *sicut fluctus volvebatur...quandoque sicut ~o* ES 1386.

caminus ~i, *m.* **1** A furnace: *in ~o igniti* Rev. 1.15 (AR). **2** A chimney: *fuliginarius qui in furvo ~i haeret* VR 61.2.

camoena: see **camaena**.

campana ~ae, *f.* A large bell, church bell: *ad ~arum sonos* ES 721; *~a urinatoria*, a diving bell: VR 125.

campanatus ~a ~um, *a.* Provided with bells, belled: ES 2972.

campanula ~ae, *f.* A small bell: *~is quibus solent equi...praediti esse in Anglia* ES 2862.

campanulatus ~a ~um, *a.* Equipped with small bells: ES 2862.

campestria ~um, *neut. pl.* Flat stretches of countryside, plains: *~a obsita arbustis* AM 231.1.

campus ~i, *m.* **1** A plain: *in ~o arenoso* SS 96; *~us, in quo sunt multi currus* ES 302; *~i Elysii*, the Elysian Fields (as the home of the blest): AM 182.6. **2** A field of activity: *~us illorum objectorum est memoria* AC 4301.4; AC 5089.2.

Canaanaeus: see **Cananaeus**.

Canaanitis ~idis, *f. adj.* Of Canaan: *ex muliere ~ide* AE 433.36.

canaliculus ~i, *m.* A small channel for water: Exod. 2.16 (AC).

canalis ~is, *m.* A channel or runnel for water, trough: *~is ligneus in quem hauritur aqua...ad potandum greges* AC 6777; (anat.) a passage in the body carrying fluids, duct: ES 831.

Cananaeus ~a ~um, *a.* also **Canaanaeus**. Of or belonging to Canaan: *in terra ~a* AC 1444.4; (masc. as sb.) an inhabitant of Canaan: Zech. 14.21 (DD 4).

cancelli ~orum, *m. pl.* Lattices: *orchestrae circumductae ~is consertis ex vitibus* AM 17.1.

cancer ~cri, *m.* **1** A crustacean, crab, lobster: *~cro, qui vadit promovendo gradus per caudam* CC 9.5; AM 295.1. **2** A malignant growth, cancer: VR 120.2.

candela ~ae, *f.* A candle: AM 380.4; (app. used for lamp) *sunto... ~ae lucentes* Luke 12.35 (AE 252.4); Luke 15.8 (AE 675.10).

candelabrum ~i, *neut.* A candlestick or lamp-stand: AC 552; Exod. 25.31 (AC).

candens ~ntis, *a.* (compar. *~ntior*) White-hot, shining: *igneum Gehennae...factum est ~ntius* AC 826.

candeo ~dere ~dui, *intr.* To be white or brilliant: *charitas rubet, et fides ~det* VR 360.3.

candescens ~ntis, *a.* (pres. pple. of **candesco**) Brilliant white, shining: *circum columnam erat lucidum, quod variegabatur per quoddam ~ns* AC 4328.2.

candesco ~ere, *intr.* To become white, brighten: *lux nostra ~it plus et plus* AM 56.1; *modo sicut sues,...pilis detraheretur...sic utique ~eret* ES 1294.

candicans ~ntis, *a.* Whitish: *circa finem mundi nostri solis apparuit primum nubes ~ns sed densa* TE 128.

candidus ~a ~um, *a.* (compar. *~ior*, superl. *~issimus*) **1** Brilliant white, shining: *lux flammea et ~a* SS 73; *super asinabus ~is* Judg. 5.10 (AE 31.7); (neut. as sb.) *indutus ~o* AC 788.2. **2** (fig.) Pure: *quod animae eorum ~ae sint* ES 453.

candor ~oris, *m.* **1** Brightness, brilliance: *~ori lucis* AM 10.4; *simplices Ipsum...vident sicut Antiquum in ~ore* CI 82. **2** Purity: *quod...induant ~orem animae* ES 454.

canis ~is, *m.* A dog: *triticum...projicitur ad ~es* AM 161.3; (used in hunting) a hound: *odorant sicut ~es in sylvis feras* CI 579.

canistrum ~i, *neut.* A basket: AM 137.1.

canities ~ei, *f.* Whiteness of the hair, hoariness: ES 588.

canna ~ae, *f.* **1** A small reed, cane: *qui naviculam contexunt ex juncis et ~is* VR 342.3; *per calamum seu ~am* AR 485.2. **2** Anything shaped like a hollow reed, tube: *candelabrum cum suis ~is* ES 2646.

canneus ~a ~um, *a.* Made from reeds: *pileus ~us* 'a straw hat' ES 2498; also AC 830, where *carneo* should be emended to *canneo* (L H Cooper).

cano ~ere cecini ~tum, *intr., tr.* **1** To sing: *ut una cum illis ~erent* SS 108; (w. acc.) to sing (a song): *~entes dulces odas* AM 8.2. **2** (of birds) To chirp, sing: ES 4176; (of a cock) to crow: Matt. 26.34 (AE 9.2).

canon ~onis, *m.* (Gk.) A rule, canon: *inter ~ones Ecclesiae Christianae*: VR 11.1; ES 2884; (as title of a book) *~ones Novae Ecclesiae* CN titulus.

canonicus[1] ~a ~um, *a.* Regular, prescribed: *~as... loquelas* VR 815.2.

canonicus[2] ~i, *m.* A minister of religion, clergyman: *fuerunt ~i, et unus ex illis episcopus* VR 16.1.

canorus ~a ~um, *a.* **1** Of song, singing: *per aves ~as* VR 42.2; *sono ~o alato* AC 418.2. **2** Accompanied by song: *repraesentationes ~as* ES 512. **3** Musical: *vox ~a sibili* VR 347.2.

cantatio ~onis, *f.* The act of singing: AC 5618.

cantharis ~idis, *f.* The blister beetle, Spanish fly: *~idibus quae fulgent sicut ex auro* VR 590.2.

canthus ~i, *m.* (Gk.) A tyre: 1 Kgs. 7.33 (AC 8215.5).

canticum ~i, *neut.* A song: *cantabitur ~um hoc* Isa. 26.1 (DD 4); AM 6.5; *~um ~orum*, Solomon's Song of Songs: AC 1756.2.

cantilena ~ae, *f.* A little song, ditty: *uxores...quae concinebant ~am* AM 55.1.

cantio ~onis, *f.* Singing: *suavitas ~onis* AM 55.1.

canto ~are ~avi ~atum, *intr., tr.* **1** (intr.) To sing: *~abunt omnes arbores sylvae* Ps. 96.12 (AC 368); *~ate Deo* Ps. 68.4 (AE 36.3). **2** (tr.) To sing (a song): *~abitur canticum hoc* Isa. 26.1 (DD 4); to express in song: *affectio...quae quovis mane ~atur* AM 17.2.

cantor ~oris, *m.* One who sings, a singer: AM 17.1.

cantrix ~icis, *f.* A woman who sings, a female singer: AM 17.1.

cantus ~us, *m.* The action of singing: *vox ~us* Isa. 51.3 (SS 87); (w. pl.) an instance of this: *interjectis ~ibus odarum suavissimis* AM 3.3.

canus ~a ~um, *a.* (of hair) White, hoary: *quendam barba ~a virum* ES 5082.

capacitas ~atis, *f.* Ability to comprehend, capacity: *secundum ~atem ejus* AC 545.2.

capapellum ~i, *neut.* ? A hood?: *quoad caput tectus ~o* VR 595.3. (*Capapellis* is quoted by Du Cange; but perhaps we should read *capello* 'with a hat'?)

capax ~acis, *a.* **1** Of large capacity, capacious: *stagnum...quod ~ax est* AC 819. **2** (w. gen.) Capable of holding: *templum... ~ax circiter trium millium* AM

23; capable of doing: *nullius rei ~ax foret* ES 507. 3 (w. inf.) Capable (of): *nequicquam ~ax est videre infinitatem Dei* VR 28.1; (w. gerund) *nec inquietari volunt similibus, quae non ~aces sunt intelligendi* ES 1140.

capella ~ae, *f.* A young female goat, kid: AC 10042.8.

caper ~pri, *m.* A he-goat: Gen. 30.35 (AC).

capesso ~ere ~ivi, *tr.* (contracted pf. subj. *~erint* AM 292.3) To acquire, gain: *regiminis aliquid in me ~ere* ES 1809; VR 80.4.

capillaceus ~a ~um, *a.* Resembling hair, hairy: *apparet* [*callositas*] *~a et hirsuta* CI 466.

capillamentum ~i, *neut.* 1 The hair of the head: *~is trahunt* ES 593. 2 A wig: *~a pulchre cincinnata ...super capite calvo* VR 810.

capillaris ~is ~e, *a.* Of or resembling hair, hairy: *cerebrum hirsutum, ~e et tenebricosum* AC 4319.2; of the thickness of a hair, capillary: *vascula minima sanguinis quae vocantur ~ia* VR 665.5.

capillitium ~i, *neut.* 1 The hair of the head: *cranium cum ~o* ES 1024. 2 A wig: *~is ex crine muliebri cincinnatis* VR 137.1.

capillus ~i, *m.* A hair: (usu. pl.) *~os sicut ~os mulierum* Rev. 9.8 (AR); (also, anat.) a capillary: *ipsi ~i, ut vocantur, etiam trahunt principiis istis suam naturam* ES 1075.

capio capere cepi captum, *tr.* 1 To take possession of, seize, capture: *cum ceperunt urbem Jericho* AE 55.2. b *captus oculis,* blind: Isa. 61.1 (AE 811.18); *captus mente,* mentally disturbed, mad: ES 2097. c (of emotions): *cepit timor omnes* Luke 7.16 (DD 15.3). 2 To have given or added, receive: *loquela vocum incrementa cepit* AC 8250.1. 3 To apprehend by means of the bodily senses, perceive: [*oculi*] *formati sunt ad capienda terrestria et corporea* AC 9577.2. 4 To apprehend mentally, grasp, understand, take in: *non possunt... capere aliquod spirituale* SS 24; (w. indir. qu.) *non capere potest quomodo coeli distincti sunt* CI 38.1. 5 To understand in a specified manner, take: *qui aliter rerum existentias et ortus capiunt* AC 775.2. 6 To adopt, take up (an idea, view, etc.): *ex una capta haeresi nascuntur plures* AC 400; *ideas...quas cepistis* VR 16.1.

capistratus ~a ~um, *a.* Equipped with halters: *equos varie... ~os* AM 76.2.

capistrum ~i, *neut.* A halter, headstall (for a horse): VR 113.1.

capitalia ~um, *neut. pl.*: misdivision of **subcapitalia**.

capitellum ~i, *neut.* A small head: AM 293.7.

capitium ~i, *neut.* Prob. error for **capillitium**, wig: VR 460.3.

Capitolinus ~a ~um, *a. Mons ~us,* one of the seven hills of Rome, the Capitoline Hill: ES 5210.

capra ~ae, *f.* A she-goat: AC 3519.1.

caprea ~ae, *f.* A roe deer: 1 Kgs. 4.23 (AC 2165.1).

caprinus ~a ~um, *a.* Of goats: *de lana ~a* VR 72.2; (prov.) nothing: *rixamini de nihilo, aut sicut dicitur, de lana ~a* VR 335.2.

capsa ~ae, *f.* A chest, box: (used of the ark in which the infant Moses was placed) Exod. 2.3 (AC).

capsula ~ae, *f.* (anat.) *~ae renales,* the renal capsules: ES 968.

captio ~onis, *f.* An instance or act of deception, ensnarement, entrapment: *quod laqueus in spirituali sensu sit...allectatio et deceptio malorum...nam illaqueationes et ~ones non aliunde sunt* AC 9348.6.

captiosus ~a ~um, *a.* Intended to deceive; (neut. pl. as sb.) snares: *quo sciunt ~a...callidius et vafrius componere* AE 978.2.

captivatio ~onis, *f.* A making captive: *~o verorum a falsis* AE 122.3.

captivitas ~atis, *f.* The state of being a captive, captivity: *septuaginta anni ~atis Babylonicae* AC 728.4; (Bibl.) captives: *ducet rex Aschuris ~atem Aegypti* Isa. 20.4 (AE 240.3).

captivo ~are ~avi ~atum, *tr.* To make captive, capture, enslave: *~abuntur inter omnes gentes* Luke 21.24 (AC 1857.5); (transf.) *quod cogitationes...violenter ~entur* AM 375.2.

captivus ~a ~um, *a.* Made captive, enslaved: *~as duxerunt omnes foeminas* Num. 31.9 (AE 140.2); (masc. as sb.) AM 79.5; (transf.) *talia ~um tenent animum* ES 1247.

capto ~are ~avi ~atum, *tr.* 1 To seize, grasp: *inde ~are stellam* VR 137.3. b to hold (in a specified state): *dogma, quod intellectus ~andus sit sub obedientia fidei* VR 338.2. 2 To seek for, aim at: *ut... ~ent famam eruditionis* AE 109.3. 3 To grasp mentally: *illa quae ~anda sunt fide et non intellectu* AM 39; (w. acc. + inf.) VR 665.6. 4 To form, adopt (an idea): *quod... materialem ideam ~averis* VR 16.2. 5 To try to win over, captivate, entice: *~are potuerat animos loquendo ad favorem* AC 5388.

captura ~ae, *f.* 1 Capture, seizing: *adminiculis accommodatis ad ~am* [*balaenarum*] VR 124.1. 2 That which is captured, prey: *involvunt id ratiociniis, sicut aranea ~as filis* AM 231.4.

captus[1] ~a ~um: pf. pple. of **capio**.

captus[2] ~us, *m.* Mental grasp, understanding: *quae... adaequata sunt ~ui simplicium* SS 40.1.

capulus ~i, *m.* The hilt (of a sword): ES 4733.

caput ~itis, *neut.* **1** The head (of a human being or animal): *draconis ~ut* FI 56; *supinati ~ite deorsum ad infernum* CI 558[a]; *a ~ite ad calcem* AS 268. **b** *supra ~ut,* overhead: VR 57.1. **2** (as the part which contains the mind) Head: *fatuitates...per ~ita instauratorum in Ecclesiam irrepserunt* VR 52; *quot ~ita, tot animi* VR 32.2; *ex ~ite,* in one's head, mentally: ES 2927. **3** The top or summit (of anything): *pendet sicut catena a suo ~ite* VR 163; *super ~ite seu vertice collis* VR 48.1. **4** A branch (of a river): *[fluvius] separabatur, et erat in quatuor ~ita* Gen. 2.10 (AC). **5** The chief part (of anything): *quod sit omne Ecclesiae seu... ~ut Ecclesiae* AC 770; *lapis...factus est in ~ut anguli* Matt. 21.42, Luke 20.18 (CI 534.3); *dicitur quod rex sit ~ut et subditi corpus* AS 24. **6** A source, fount, origin: *quod [hi amores]...sint ~ita omnium amorum Inferni* AR 502.2. **7** A chapter of a book: CI 171.

carbasa ~orum, *neut. pl.* (Gk.) Linen garments: Isa. 3.22 (AC 10540.4).

carbo ~onis, *m.* A piece of charcoal; (esp. pl.) burning charcoal, coals: *sicut lux ex ignitis ~onibus* CI 481.4.

carbonareus: see **carbonarius**.

carbonarius ~a ~um, *a.* also **carbonareus**. Produced by charcoal: *ignis ~i* AC 1527.

carbonicus ~a ~um, *a.* Of coals: *igni... ~o* ES 2672.

carbunculus ~i, *m.* A precious stone of red colour, carbuncle: Isa. 54.12 (AE 208.12).

carcer ~eris, *m.* **1** A place of confinement, prison: *ad educendum e ~ere vinctum* Isa. 42.7 (DD 6); *in ~ere infernali* AM 54; (transf.) *quia vera sunt sicut in custodia aut in ~ere* AE 122.1. **2** Imprisonment: *tempus ~eris...variatur* ES 409. **3** The starting gate of a racecourse: *signabat locum ubi excursus statio seu ~er baculo* ES 4652.

carchesium ~i, *neut.* (Gk.) A drinking cup, goblet: CO 33.2.

cardiacus ~a ~um, *a.* (Gk.) Of or belonging to the heart: *motus ~us* AS 381; CI 212; also, of a region of heaven: AS 381.

cardialgia ~ae, *f.* (Gk.) Heartburn: VR 665.5.

cardinalis ~is ~e, *a.* **1** Principal, cardinal: *de duodecim communibus seu ~ibus rebus* AC 3913.1. **2** (masc. as sb.) A cardinal (of the Roman Catholic Church): AR 752.2.

cardo ~inis, *m.* **1** A hinge (on which a door is mounted): *janua...cum ~ine obice chalybeio praestructa* CO 28; VR 381.4. **2** A natural joint, hinge: *~ini lumborum* ES(M) [4786]. **3** (transf.) A turning point, pivot: *~o determinationum vertitur introrsum* AC 9730.2; *~o Ecclesiae* HE 2.

carduus ~i, *m.* A thistle: AC 273.

carentia ~ae, *f.* (w. gen.) Absence, lack: *~a intelligentiae et sapientiae* AC 3993.6.

careo ~rere ~rui, *intr.* (fut. pple. *~riturus*) (w. abl.) To be without, lack: *~ret...experientia* AM 108; (absol.) to be in want: *pastor meus, non ~rebo* Ps. 23.1 (AC 57).

carina ~ae, *f.* The keel of a ship: CO 57.3.

caritas ~atis, *f.* Scarcity, dearness: *in anno ~atis* Jer. 17.8. (AC 885.2).

carnalis ~is ~e, *a.* Of the flesh, fleshly, carnal: *amor ille ~is* AM 79.10.

carneolus ~i, *m.* A red stone, carnelian: VR 669.1.

carneus ~a ~um, *a.* **1** Made of or resembling flesh, fleshy: *non apparebant ut facies humanae ~ae* AC 546. **2** Unable to rise above the flesh, carnal: *~us homo* VR 381.1.

carnifex ~icis, *m.* An executioner or torturer: ES 1065.

carnificina ~ae, *f.* A place of execution or torture: *reliquos ejicit in ~am* VR 798.9.

caro ~rnis, *f.* **1** Flesh: *ii qui comedunt ~rnes humanas* AC 819; (as typical of man and his lower self) *Verbum ~ro factum est* John 1.14 (CI 137.1); *e voluntate ~rnis* John 1.13 (VI 17). **2** (Bibl.) The human race, mankind: *videbunt omnis ~ro simul* Isa. 40.5 (DD 6). **3** The pulp (of a fruit): AC 9258.2.

carotides ~um, *f. pl.* (Gk.) (anat.) The carotid arteries: AM 315.7; ES 831.

carpo ~ere ~si ~tum, *tr.* **1** To pluck (fruit): *~entes malvam super frutice* Job 30.4 (AC 2682.1). **2** To press on with, cover fast (a journey): *~ere viam* VR 563.1; ES 5485. **3** To find fault with, criticize: *nec quicquam erat...quod non ~erent intra semet* ES 1824.

carta: see **charta**.

cartilaginee, *adv.* In a gristly manner: *loquuntur tunc quasi ~e* ES 4194.

cartilagineus ~a ~um, *a.* Made of or resembling cartilage, gristly: *ab amore lascivo corporeo et carneo fit ~us et osseus* AM 511.

cartilago ~inis, *f.* (anat.) A cartilage: *~ines et ossa quae fulciunt...omnia quae in corpore sunt* AC 5552.

carus: see **charus**.

casa ~ae, *f.* A crude dwelling, hut: *sicut qui non extra suas ~as sylvae fuerunt* AC 692.

caseus ~i, *m.* Cheese: DP 254.4.

casia ~ae, *f.* An aromatic plant, cassia: Ezek. 27.19 (AC 426.1).

cassis[1] ~idis, *f.* A helmet: *super equitum capitibus ... ~ides crispatae* AM 103.1.

cassis[2] ~is, *m.* A spider's web: AC 5984.

casso ~are ~avi ~atum, *tr.* To break in pieces, shatter: *ova...deciderent in terram et ~arentur* VR 375.1.

cassus ~a ~um, *a.* (w. abl.) Deprived (of), lacking: *~i memoria* AM 152ª.1; VR 367.6.

castanea ~ae, *f.* A chestnut tree: VR 78.2.

caste, *adv.* In a chaste manner: *agit...mens casta ~e* AM 191.2.

castellum ~i, *neut.* A fort, castle: Gen. 25.16 (AC, but see especially AC 3271).

castigatio ~onis, *f.* **1** Punishment, chastisement: *~o pacis nostrae super Illo* Isa. 53.5 (DD 15.1). **2** (in chemistry) A refining process, purification: AM 145.2.

castigator ~oris, *m.* One who chastises: AC 7801.

castigo ~are ~avi ~atum, *tr.* **1** To refine, purify: *cibus in via ~atur leniter* ES 1742. **2** To correct, emend: *quod ~aturus sit mala* AE 176.1. **3** To chastise, punish: *sicut pater [amat] filium quem ~at* AC 4730.3.

castitas ~atis, *f.* Chastity: *uxor amabilis viro ex ~ate* VI 46.

castra ~orum, *neut. pl.* A camp: AM 75.3.

castrametatio ~onis, *f.* Encamping: AC 8193.

castrametor ~ari ~atus sum, *intr.* To pitch one's tent, encamp: *vos ~amini foris extra castra septem dies* Num. 31.19 (AC 901.3).

castus ~a ~um, *a.* Chaste: (of persons) SS 26.3; (of love) *amor sexus ~us* AM 22; (of homes) *~as domos fugiunt* CI 488.6.

casus ~us, *m.* **1** An overthrow, fall: *a voce ~us Edomi* Jer. 49.21 (AE 400.10). **2** An accidental happening, chance: *ex aliquo ~u* AM 216.1. **3** A particular circumstance, case: *quandoque, in certis ~ibus* ES 933.

cataracta ~ae, *f.* (Gk.) **1** A violent downpour of water, flood, cataract: *~ae coeli apertae* Gen. 7.11 (AC). **2** A disease of the eye, cataract: VR 346.2.

catech-: see **cathech-**.

catellus ~i, *m.* A young dog, puppy: *~i etiam edunt de micis quae cadunt de mensa* Matt. 15.27 (AC 7784.3).

catena ~ae, *f.* **1** A chain: *connectit per ~as* AE 237.1; (used to confine prisoners) *vinctorum ~is et pedicis* AM 182.5. **2** A string (of pearls): AR 926.2. **3** Anything which confines or restricts: *obstringere Deum...legum ~is* VR 73.1.

catenatus ~a ~um, *a.* Connected as by a chain, linked: *quod spirituum societates sint series ~ae* ES 2316.

catenula ~ae, *f.* A small chain: Exod. 28.14 (AC).

caterva ~ae, *f.* **1** A group of animals, herd, flock, drove: Gen. 29.2 (AC). **2** A troop of persons: *~ae prophetarum* ES 2521.

catervatim, *adv.* In crowds or swarms: *~im alluunt* AC 2122.

cathechesis ~eos, *f.* (Gk.) also **catech-**. A religious book of instruction, catechism: AM 521.5.

cathechismus ~i, *m.* (Gk.) also **catech-**. A religious book of instruction, catechism: VR 14.3.

cathedra ~ae, *f.* (Gk.) A chair, seat: *~as vendentium columbas* Matt. 21.12 (AE 840.4); esp. a formal chair for a teacher: AM 315.2.

cathedralis ~is ~e, *a.* Of a chair; *vir ~is*, the chairman (of a meeting): VR 137.4.

Catholicus ~a ~um, *a.* (Gk.) **1** Of the whole Church: *fidem... ~am* Sym. Ath. (DD 56). **2** Of the Roman Church, (Roman-) Catholic: *religionis ~ae* AM 513.

catinus ~i, *m.* A melting pot, crucible: *argentum conflatum in ~o terrae* Ps. 12.6 (AC 1551.4); ES 5419.

catulus ~i, *m.* The young of an animal, whelp, cub: *~us leonis* Gen. 49.9 (AC); *ursus cum ~is* CO 59.4; *~os ovium* CC 14.5.

cauda ~ae, *f.* **1** The tail (of an animal): *~as similes scorpiis* Rev. 9.10 (AR). **2** The tail (of a comet): VR 80.4. **3** (anat.) *~a equina,* the leash of nerves at the end of the spinal cord, horsetail: AC 5389; ES 869.

caudex ~icis, *m.* (also spelled **codex** q.v., esp. in sense 2) **1** The trunk or stem of a plant: *~ices et ramos arborum* VR 78.4; VR 519. **2** A book formed of wooden tablets: *[scripturae] super ~icibus levigatis* AM 77.6.

caudicillus ~i, *m.* (cf. **codicillus**) A small stem (of a plant): VR 585.2.

caula ~ae, *f.* A sheepfold, pen: *habitaculum seu ~a pecoris* AC 415.1.

caulis ~is, *m.* The stem or stalk (of a plant): FI 16.

caupona ~ae, *f.* A stand for the sale of goods, stall: *charta quae venditur in ~is* VR 582.1.

causa ~ae, *f.* **1** (in philosophy) A cause (dist. from effect): *unum agunt ut ~a et effectus* SS 5. **2** (generally) A reason, cause: *~a quod spiritualia comprehendantur est quia...* FI 3; *ob ~am ut...* VR 4.3. **b** *in ~a esse*, to be responsible, be the cause: *malum est in ~a* AC 391. **c** *~a* (w. gen.), on account (of), because (of): *distinctionis ~a* CI 140.

causatum ~i, *neut.* An event which is caused, result: *principiata faciunt principia et ~a causas* VR 37.3.

causor ~ari ~atus sum, *tr.* To be the cause of, cause: *tepidum... ~atur evomitionem* AE 235.1.

causticitas ~atis, *f.* The quality of being burning: *in igne sunt duo, ~as et splendor* VR 39.

causticus ~a ~um, *a.* (Gk.) Of or for burning: *in medium focum speculi ~i* [i.e., of a burning glass] CO 51.1.

caute, *adv.* Cautiously: *~e loquendum* ES 410.

cautela ~ae, *f.* Carefulness, caution: *~a et prudentia* AM 445.

cautes ~is, *f.* A rock, crag: *~es et scopuli* UJ(P) 302 Rogers.

cautus ~a ~um, *a.* (pf. pple. of **caveo**) Cautious, careful: *~us in loquendo* ES 3171.

cavea ~ae, *f.* A cage for keeping wild animals: *sicut in unam ~am committerentur lupi et oves* VR 604.

caveo ~vere ~vi cautum, *intr.* (*tr.*) **1** To take precautions, guard: *nisi...ne quis talia faciat per leges ~verent* VI 53; (impers. pass.) *~vetur a Domino ne spiritus sciant* CI 292. **b** (pass.) *quod hoc solum ~vendum sit* AE 172. **2** *Sibi ~vere*, to take one's own precautions, guard oneself, keep oneself: (w. *ab*) *~veant sibi ab opinione falsa* AC 322.1; (w. *ne*) *~vete vobis ne mentes vestrae...indurescant* AM 232.4; (w. inf.) *quod populus ~veat sibi prophanare sancta* 3AD 5618.

caverna ~ae, *f.* An underground chamber, cavern, cave: *aufugiunt in ~as et occludunt januas* AM 212.

cavernosus ~a ~um, *a.* Full of caves: *planum ~um* ES 3221.

cavernula ~ae, *f.* A small hole, aperture: *~ae in extima cute capitis* ES 3719.

cavillor ~ari ~atus sum, *intr.* To jest, make fun: *ad haec plures...irriserunt et ~ati* AM 79.7.

cavitas ~atis, *f.* An empty space, hollow, cavity: ES 2812.

cavus ~a ~um, *a.* **1** Hollow: *~um tabulatum facies* Exod. 27.8 (AC). **2** (neut. as sb.) An empty space, void, hollow: *miserunt tres illas [schedulas] in ~um pilei, et elegerunt unum* VR 696.5; *deduxerunt me ad ~um* AM 232.2.

-ce: deictic particle that appears in forms such as **ecce**, **ejuscemodi**, **hicce**, and **hujuscemodi**.

cedens ~ntis, *a.* (pres. pple. of **cedo**) Yielding: *charitas cum fide est ~ns et mollis* AC 8321.2.

cedentia ~ae, *f.* The quality of yielding, lack of resistance: *absque ulla ~a* AC 7298.2; ES 2591.

cedo ~ere cessi, *intr.* (compar. of pres. pple. *~entior*) **1** To yield to the touch, give: *quo plus ~it...ac...mollius, eo firmius constat* ES 241. **2** To give way, yield: *quod ~ant seu fugiant* ES 1724. **3** To be given or assigned, pass, fall: *cesserunt primogenito binae partes ex haereditate* AE 28.2; *provisum est ut piscis ~eret pisci in escam* VR 32.3. **4** (w. *in* or *ad* + acc.) To result (in), turn (to): *conspiratio quae in irritum cessit* ES 458; *providet ut omnia... ~ant ei ad bonum* AC 6306.

cedrinus ~a ~um, *a.* (Gk.) Of cedar wood: AC 643.4.

cedrus ~i, *f.* (Gk.) A cedar tree: *parietes...erant ex ~is* AM 103.3.

celebratio ~onis, *f.* The process of making famous, celebration: *quod Deus nec opus habeat laudibus et ~one* CI 404; *nominis quandam ~onem apud mortales* ES 780.

celebratus ~a ~um, *a.* (pf. pple. of **celebro**) (compar. *~ior*, superl. *~issimus*) Famous, celebrated: AC 4948; AM 2.1.

celebris ~bris ~bre, *a.* (superl. *~berrimus*) Famous, celebrated: *qui ~bres eruditione...fuerant* VR 77.5.

celebro ~are ~avi ~atum, *tr.* **1** To make famous, praise: *ut laudarent et ~arent Deum* CI 404. **2** To hold or celebrate (a feast or festival): *festiva repotia ~are* AM 8.1.

celer ~eris ~ere, *a.* (compar. *~erior*) Fast-moving, swift: *~eres sunt prae aquilis equi ejus* Jer. 4.13 (AE 281.10).

celeritas ~atis, *f.* Swiftness, speed: *ideae...excipiunt una alteram tali ~ate ut...* AC 6599.

celeriter, *adv.* (compar. *celerius*) Quickly, swiftly: AC 6811.

celeusma ~atis, *neut.* (Gk.) (app.) A shout of joy or triumph (used to translate Hebr. *hedad*): *per 'hedad' significatur finis, quando super peracta vindemia et collecta messe solebant ovare et ~a edere* AE 911.10; *'hedad'...vertitur ~a* 4AD Isa. 16.18 (= EVV 16.9).

cella ~ae, *f.* **1** A small room, cubicle: AM 106; ES 384. **2** A cell in a honeycomb: VR 12.7.

cellarium ~i, *neut.* A storeroom: *in ~is apud pharmacopolas* VR 834.

cellula ~ae, *f.* A small room, cell: *mapalia...divisa in ~as* AR 421.2; a cell (in a beehive): VR 12.7.

cellulosus ~a ~um, *a.* Consisting of an aggregate of small cavities, alveolar: *videri potest in pulmone ex substantia ejus ~a, quae consistit ex continuatis bronchiis usque ad folliculos minimos, qui sunt receptiones aëris* AS 413.

celo ~are ~avi ~atum, *tr.* To keep concealed, hide: *non ~abit amplius occisos suos* Isa. 26.21 (AE 315.18); *cogitata ~are* CI 492.

celsitudo ~inis, *f.* Loftiness, height, exaltation: *~ines Dei in gutture eorum* Ps. 149.6 (AE 131.5).

celsus ~a ~um, *a.* (superl. *~issimus*) Of exalted quality, high: *~issimae pretiositates* VR 618.1.

cen-: see also **coen-**.

censeo ~sere ~sui ~sum, *tr.* **1** To count, number: *e qua* [sc. *creatione*] *~sentur sex millia annorum* AM 29. **2** To reckon, regard (as): *vix...quicquam ut proprie theologicum...hodie ~setur* VR 343.

census ~us, *m.* **1** A contribution imposed by authority, tax: *a quibus accipiunt tributa aut ~um...?* Matt. 17.25 (AC 6394). **2** Financial means, income: *ex suo ~u et reditu sustentare domum* AM 287.

centeni ~ae ~a, *pl. adj.* A hundred: *erant aliquot ~i stantes in uno loco* AM 232.2; *aliquot ~a millia* AC 6927.

centesimus ~a ~um, *a.* Hundredth: *in ~um annum* AC 2213.

centies, *adv.* A hundred times: *~es si non millies vidi...* AC 7137.

centralis ~is ~e, *a.* Central: *a peripheria ad ~em locum* ES 2824; (neut. as sb.) centre: *in intimum ~e grani...penetrare* VR 499.2.

centripetentia ~ae, *f.* Tendency towards the centre: CI 142.

centripetus ~a ~um, *a.* Tending towards the centre, centripetal: ES 3727.

centrum ~i, *neut.* **1** The centre point, centre: *procedunt omnia...e ~o in peripherias* AE 63.1; the central region: *quod...succus...distribuatur in omnia ejus* [sc. *arboris*] *meditullia ac ~a* ES 251. **2** (transf.) A focal point, centre: *ut unusquisque sit quasi ~um omnium* AC 549; *ubicunque Dominus est, ibi est ~um* AC 1582; *~a...actionis* ES 1254.

centum, *indecl.* A hundred: AE 336.2.

centuplus ~a ~um, *a.* One hundred times as much: *dederunt fructum, aliud ~um, aliud sexagecuplum* Matt. 13.8 (AC 3310.2).

centuria ~ae, *f.* A group of a hundred: *~ae sapientum* AM 478.2.

centurio ~onis, *m.* An officer commanding a unit of 100 men, centurion: Matt. 8.8 (AE 815.3).

cepa ~ae, *f.* An onion: Num. 11.5 (AE 513.6).

cephalalgia ~ae, *f.* (Gk.) A headache: VR 665.6.

cepi: pf. of **capio**.

cera ~ae, *f.* Beeswax: AM 419; (pl.) VR 12.7; also, any similar substance: *~a aromatica* AC 5621.1.

cerasus ~i, *m.* A cherry: AM 8.2.

cerebellulum ~i, *neut.* A small cerebellum (in an embryo): AS 432.

cerebellum ~i, *neut.* (anat.) One of the two main parts of the brain, the cerebellum: VR 160.8.

cerebrositas ~atis, *f.* An attack of madness, brainstorm: *quosdam* [*invadunt*] *~ates in religiosis* VR 665.4.

cerebrosus ~a ~um, *a.* Maddened, crazy: *ex ~o ratiocinio volunt explorare quid spiritus* AC 448.2.

cerebrum ~i, *neut.* Either of the two main parts of the brain: *quod homini duo ~a sint* VR 160.8; the cerebrum (dist. from the cerebellum): *alterum in frontispicio, quod vocatur ~um* VR 160.8.

ceremonia ~ae, *f.* also **caerimonia**. A ceremony, ritual: VR 667.1.

ceremonialis ~is ~e, *a.* Of or relating to ceremonies, ceremonial: *plura quae externa et ~ia sunt* AC 1175.2.

cereus ~a ~um, *a.* Made of beeswax: *lumina...~a* ES 3410; (masc. as sb.) a wax taper: *in delitiis vivunt ad ~os* ES 3212.

cerevisia ~ae, *f.* Beer: DP 254.4.

cerno ~ere crevi cretum, *tr.* To perceive, discern: *videndo videbitis et non ~etis* Matt. 13.14 (VR 7).

certamen ~inis, *neut.* A contest: *~ina palaestrica* AM 17.4.

certe, *adv.* (superl. *~issime*) To be sure, for certain: *~e non es in statu vitae nostratium* AM 326.1.

certitudo ~inis, *f.* A state of being certain, certainty: *qui in ~ine est de victoria* AC 1787.1.

certo[1] *adv.* As a certain fact, for certain: *quae...vera esse...~o confirmare possum* ES 179.

certo[2] ~are ~avi ~atum, *intr.* To compete, struggle: *~ate intrare* Luke 13.24 (AE 208.12).

certus ~a ~um, *a.* (superl. *~issimus*) **1** Firmly persuaded, sure: *voluit ~us fieri quod...* AC 1781. **2** Firmly established, fixed, certain: *~a et immutabilis lex* VR 100. **b** *pro ~o*, as a certain fact, for certain: *pro ~o asseverare* AC 59.2; *pro ~issimo scire* ES 1910. **3** A particular, certain: *bonum... ~o modo se sistit videndum* VI 43.2.

cerva ~ae, *f.* A female deer, hind: Ps. 29.9 (SS 18.4).

cervical ~lis, *neut.* A pillow: AC 3695.

cervinus ~a ~um, *a.* Of or relating to deer: *accedens ...ad speciem ~am* ES 3262.

cervix ~icis, *f.* **1** The neck: *a ~ice ad lumbos* AM 231.5; *~icem vestram non indurate amplius* Deut. 10.16 (FI 54). **2** (anat.) The cervix (of the bladder or uterus): ES 867; ES 875.

cervus ~i, *m.* A deer, stag: *~os cum cornibus* AM 76.2.

cespes ~itis, *m.* also **caespes**. A piece of turf, sod: *~ites ex humo* VR 113.5.

cessatio ~onis, *f.* **1** A ceasing, stopping: *ad ~onem totalem cordis* CI 447. **2** A ceasing from work, holiday: *non odorabor ~ones vestras* Amos 5.21 (AC 925.4).

cessio ~onis, *f.* The action of yielding: AM 292.2.

cesso ~are ~avi, *intr.* (fut. pple. *~aturus*) **1** To come to an end, cease, stop: *...cum ~ant inimicitiae* CI 290. **2** (w. *ab* or inf.) To cease (from an action): *~at excitator a subigendo massam ejus* Hos. 7.4 (AC 7356.2); *~averunt esse habitacula Dei* AM 153[a].2. **b** (w. *ab*) to leave alone, let be: *~avit ab illo* Exod. 4.26 (AC).

ceter-: see **caeter-**.

cetus ~i, *m.* (Gk.) A sea monster: *quod Jonas fuerit in ventre ~i* SS 29.

ceu, *particle.* As if: *justitiam accipientes, eam ceu primam stolam...jubentur...conservare* Council of Trent in SE 5(d).

chaenix: see **choenix**.

chajoth, *indecl.* (Hebr.) Chajoth, a Hebrew word meaning animals (see quot.): *leo, bos, homo, et aquila in lingua Hebraea...vocantur ~oth, quae vox quidem significat animalia sed derivatur a chaja, quae est vita, ex qua etiam Adami uxor vocata est Chaja* AR 239.1.

chalcedonius ~i, *m.* (Gk. *khalkedon*) A precious stone, chalcedony: Rev. 21.19 (AR).

chalcolibanum ~i, *neut.* (Gk. *khalkolibanos*) A kind of yellow metal, perhaps brass: Rev. 1.15 (AR); *aes ut ~um significat naturale* AR 49.8.

chalybeius: see **chalybeus**.

chalybeus ~a ~um, *a.* also **chalybeius** (CO 28 Worcester). Made of steel: *facie sicut ~a* AM 78.4.

chalybs ~bis, *m.* (Gk.) Steel: *ex polito ~be* VR 332.5.

chameleo ~onis, *m.* (Gk.) A chameleon: *ursi, viperae, ~ones* SA 121 (= x.3).

chaos ~i, *neut.* (Gk.) A state devoid of order, chaos: *quod primum in confusum quoddam quasi ~os redigantur* AC 842.3; (as the primal state of the universe) VR 76.1.

character ~eris, *m.* (Gk.) **1** A special sign, mark: Rev. 13.16 (AR). **2** A character in a writing system: *non erant ~eres peregrini, sed stylus ex literis Latinis* ES(M) [4830]. **3** The mental disposition (of a person), character: *quia notus, et ~eris non boni* ES 1296.

characteristicon ~i, *neut.* (Gk.) A characteristic: *ob naturale ~on illorum* [sc. *virorum*] AM 285.1; a special sign: *praeficitur...descriptioni cuivis Ecclesiae Divinum ~on, quod indicat de quo agitur* AE 96.

characteristicus ~a ~um, *a.* Distinguishing, differentiating, characteristic: *quod...a parentibus suis trahant...tales notas ~as ut ex facie et pluribus aliis dignosci queant* AC 471.

charitas ~atis, *f.* (orig. not dist. from **caritas**, but influenced by Gk. *kharis*) **1** Charity: *~as non aliud [est] quam bonitas* VR 142; *~as est...amor erga proximum* AC 615. **2** A particular kind or act of charity: *quod ~atem tuam primam reliqueris* Rev. 2.4 (AR); *eorum opera sunt ~ates* ES 413.

charta ~ae, *f.* also **carta**. **1** A sheet of paper, esp. for writing: *~ae exaratae scripturis* CI 258; *~a sigillo obsignata* VR 48.1. **2** (pl.) Playing cards: CH 189 (= xi).

chartaphylacium ~i, *neut.* (Gk.) A piece of furniture for keeping papers, desk, bureau: VR 797.2.

chartula ~ae, *f.* A small sheet of paper: *ad me e caelo missa est ~a* SS 90.1; *~ae lusoriae*, playing cards: DP 212.1.

charus ~a ~um, *a.* also **carus**. (compar. *~ior*, superl. *~issimus*) Dearly beloved, dear: *sunt favores illi ~iores et pretiosiores quibuscunque donis* AM 300.2; ES 2889.

cherub: see **cherubus**.

cherubim: see **cherubus**.

cherubinus ~a ~um, *a.* Of or belonging to cherubim, cherubic: *sphaera quae... ~a...vocanda* ES 255.

cherubus ~i, *m.* (Hebr.) also **cherub**, *indecl.* (pl. *~im* AE 282.9). A living creature, cherub: *quatuor animalia, quae erant ~i* DD 52 (Ezek. 1, 10).

chiliarchus ~i, *m.* (Gk.) A commander of a thousand men: *ut comedatis...carnes ~orum* Rev. 19.18 (AR).

chilias ~adis, *f.* (Gk.) A group of one thousand: AM 500.1.

chiliasta ~ae, *m.* One who holds that Christ will reign in person on earth for a thousand years, chiliast: *usque adhaeserint ~arum seu millenariorum conjecturis* AR 842.

chimaera ~ae, *f.* (Gk. *khimaira* 'goat', mythological monster) A wild fancy, chimera: *concipiunt ~as et parturiunt larvas* VR 37.3.

chimaericus ~a ~um, *a.* (Gk.) Chimerical: *id quod concionator profert est...imaginarium et ~um* VR 525.

chippod, *indecl.* (Hebr.) A hedgehog or porcupine: Zeph. 2.14 (AC 655.2).

chirurgus ~i, *m.* (Gk.) A surgeon: VR 665.5.

Chittaeus ~a ~um, *a.* also **Ḥittaeus**. Hittite: AC 1203; (masc. as sb.) a Hittite: AC 4429.3.

Chivaeus ~a ~um, *a.* also **Ḥivaeus**. Hivite: AC 4431; (masc. as sb.) the Hivite (collective sg.), a people descended from Canaan: AC 4447.3.

chlamys ~ydis, *f.* (Gk.) A royal robe, mantle: *in ~yde Imperatoris* VR 669.1; *[angelus] indutus erat ~yde* AM 2.1.

chocolad App. intended for English *chocolate*, cf. German *schocolade*: UJ(P) 292.

choenix ~icis, *f.* (Gk.) also **chaenix**. A Greek dry measure, corresponding approximately to one litre: Rev. 6.6 (AR).

cholericus: see **colericus**.

chomer ~eris, *m.* (Hebr.) also **ḥomer**. A large measure of volume used for liquids, homer: AE 373.1.

chorda ~ae, *f.* (Gk.) A string (of a musical instrument): *musici cum instrumentis ~ae* AM 17.1.

chordaceus ~a ~um, *a.* (of musical instruments) Stringed: AC 418.1.

chorea ~ae, *f.* (Gk.) A dance: *ludi ac ~ae virginum et juvenum saltantium ad modos symphoniarum* AM 3.3; *Viti chorea*, St Vitus's dance, chorea: ES 3895 (Tafel).

choroideus ~a ~um, *a.* (strictly incorrect for *chorioideus*, Gk. *khorioeides*) (anat.) Choroid: *a plexu ~o* ES 831.

chorus ~i, *m.* (Gk.) An organized group of singers, choir, chorus: AC 418.2.

Christiane, *adv.* In a Christian manner: *discrimen inter vivere civiliter et moraliter bene, et ~e bene* ES 5396.

Christianismus ~i, *m.* **1** Belief in Christ, Christianity: *si quis totum terrarum orbem converteret ad ~um* ES 2451. **2** The Christian world or society, Christendom: *ex tot haeresibus quae in ~o fuerunt* SS 92; *apud plures hodie in ~o* VR 7.

Christianus ~a ~um, *a.* **1** Composed of followers of Christ, Christian: *Ecclesia ~a* VR 4.1; *in toto ~o orbe* DD 21; (masc. as sb.) a Christian: SS 24. **2** Belonging to or typical of Christians, Christian: *fides ~a* FI 34; *iis bene velle ~um est* ES 1246.

Christus ~i, *m.* (Gk., = English 'anointed') The title given to Jesus, Christ: *Deus et Homo unus sit ~us* Sym. Ath. (VR 4.3).

chronicus ~a ~um, *a.* (Gk.) (of diseases) Long-lasting, chronic: AM 253.2.

chronologia ~ae, *f.* (Gk.) An account of the sequence of events in time, chronology: VR 466.

chronologicus ~i, *m.* (Gk.) A writer of annals, chronicler: *ut patet...a ~is Scripturae Sacrae* AC 7985.

chrysallis ~idis, *f.* The chrysalis of an insect: CI 108.2.

chrysolithus ~i, *m.* (Gk.) also **chrysolitus**. A precious stone, chrysolite: Rev. 21.20 (AR).

chrysolitus: see **chrysolithus**.

chrysoprasus ~i, *m.* (Gk.) A precious stone, chrysoprase: Ezek. 27.16 (AC 1232); Rev. 21.20 (AR).

chrystallinus ~a ~um, *a.* (Gk.) also **crystallinus**. Made of crystal: *vas ~um* VR 38.2; (anat.) *lens ~a*, the crystalline lens (of the eye): ES 1075.

chrystallum ~i, *neut.* (Gk.) also **crystallum**. Rock crystal: VR 34.3; AM 12.1.

chylifico ~are ~avi, *intr.* To make bile: *mesenterium ~at* DP 336.

chylus ~i, *m.* (Gk.) The juice produced by the digestion of food, chyle: *ex cibo, cum factus est chylus* SS 66.

chymice ~es, *f.* (Gk.) Chemistry: *omnia arcana... ~es* AC 6057.1.

chymicus ~a ~um, *a.* (Gk.) Of or belonging to chemistry, chemical: *[scientia] ~a* AM 163; (masc. as sb.) a chemist, pharmacist: *quae fiunt a ~is* AM 145.2.

cibarium ~i, *neut.* Plain food, victuals: AM 6.4.

cibatio ~onis, *f.* Feeding: AE 730.30.

cibatus ~us, *m.* Food: *omnem ~um spiritualem* VR 23.2.

cibo ~are ~avi ~atum, *tr.* To provide with food, feed: *quis ~abit nos carne?* Num. 11.4 (AC 999.1).

cibus ~i, *m.* **1** Food: *~um qui manet in vitam aeternam* John 6.27 (DD 27); (w. pl.) a particular kind of food: *edules ~os* SS 40.1; cf. *coelestis homo... delectatur coelestibus, quae...vocantur ~i coelestes* AC 56. **2** Fuel (for a fire): *factus est populus sicut ~us ignis* Isa. 9.19 (AC 1861.2).

cicatrix ~icis, *f.* A scar: AC 9103.2.

cicer ~eris, *neut.* The chickpea, *Cicer arietinum*: ES(M) [4731].

ciconia ~ae, *f.* A stork: Jer. 8.7 (AC 9857.4).

cicurus ~a ~um?, *a.* Tame, domesticated: *omnium... bestiarum, tum ~arum, tum ferarum* Gen. 3.14 (1AD 52). (n.b. Classical form is *cicur, cicuris.*)

cicuta ~ae, *f.* Hemlock: VR 595.2.

cidaris ~is, *f.* (acc. sg. both *~im* and *~in*; abl. sg. *~i*) **1** An exotic headdress, turban, tiara: Exod. 28.39 (AC); Isa. 28.5 (DD 4); AM 20.2. **2** The mitre of a bishop: *qui spectat primatem Ecclesiae solum ex ~i ejus et clenodiis in illa* CO 51.3.

cilicinus ~a ~um, *a.* Made of goat's hair: *saccus ~us* Rev. 6.12 (AE).

cilicium ~i, *neut.* A cloth made of goat's hair: *in ~o candidissimo* ES 4133.

cimeliarchium ~i, *neut.* A place for keeping valuable objects, treasure-house: AM 77.6.

cimelium ~i, *neut.* (Gk.) **1** A valuable object, treasure: *conclavia intus sicut ~is pretiositatum referta* AM 443. **2** A treasure-house, treasury: *qui in ~is viderunt cylindros opticos* AC 1871; ES 5999.1.

cincinnatus ~a ~um, *a.* Furnished with curls, curly: *capillitiis ex crine muliebri ~is* VR 137.1.

cincinnus ~i, *m.* A lock of hair, ringlet: *Delilah vocavit virum qui rasit septem ~os capitis ejus* Judg. 16.19 (AC 5247.4).

cinctura ~ae, *f.* **1** A girdle, belt: AC 7863. **2** A collar, ruff: *in ~a coronali* VR 137.3. **3** A band (round a column): Exod. 27.10 (AC); (in a building) *mansiones columbarum...cum lapideis introitibus et ~is* ES 4142. **4** A halo: *vidi...solem...et circumcirca illum ~am* VR 112.1.

cinereus ~a ~um, *a.* (neut. pl. as sb.) Ash-coloured garments: ES(M) [4723] (Tafel).

cineritius ~a ~um, *a.* (anat., of the substance of the brain) Cineritious: VR 351.3.

cingo ~gere ~xi ~ctum, *tr.* **1** To surround with a belt, gird: *~gebas te ipsum* John 21.18 (AE 9.3); esp. *~ctus*, girt: *~ctus erat fascia ex pyropis* AM 2.1. **2** To surround (with anything): *unus...permultis spiritibus ... ~ctus* ES 602.

cingulum ~i, *neut.* **1** A garment worn about the waist or loins, belt, girdle: *fecerunt sibi ~a* Gen. 3.7 (AC); *erit justitia ~um lumborum Ejus* Isa. 11.5 (DD 6). **2** Anything ring-shaped, a halo, ring: *~um album circumvelat caput meum* AM 269.5; (of the ring of Saturn) AC 6697.

cinis ~eris, *m.* Ash: *latet...sicut ignis in ligno sub ~ere* VI 67.

cinnamomum ~i, *neut.* Cinnamon: *ligni ~i* AM 439.

cio cire civi citum, *tr.* To arouse, provoke: *vomitus ciunt* AS 341.

cippus ~i, *m.* A coffin: *in ~o argenteo* VR 595.1.

circa, *prep. w. acc.* **1** (in space) Around: *~a pedes* VR 48.20. **2** (in time) Around, about: *~a autumnum* VR 12.7. **3** In connection with, in the case of: *appercipere ideas angelicas... ~a haec verba* AC 1875.

circinnatus ~a ~um, *a.* Error for **cincinnatus**: VR 508.6.

circiter, *adv.* Approximately, roughly: *per decem horas ~er* AC 10734; *ibi ~er est civitas malorum* ES 750.

circueo ~cuire ~cuivi, *intr.* see also **circumeo**. To go around: *~cui urbem* Isa. 23.16 (AC 420.5); *~cuibat porticus* AM 56.1.

circuitio ~onis, *f.* A going round, spiral: *labyrintheae ~ones vasorum* ES 1075.

circuitus[1] ~us, *m.* **1** A roundabout route, circuit: *duxit...comites suos per ~us huc illuc* AM 8.3. **2** The surrounding region, surroundings: *congregate vos a ~u ad sacrificium meum* Ezek. 39.17 (SS 15.3).

circuitus[2], *adv.* From around: *iris ~tus throni* Rev. 4.3 (AR).

circularis ~is ~e, *a.* Circular: ES 208.

circulatio ~onis, *f.* A circular motion, revolution, circulation: AM 78.8; (of the blood) AC 6948.4; (of thoughts in the spiritual world) ES 2730.

circulo ~are ~avi, *intr.* To go round in a circle, circulate: *dum sanguis purior ~aturus est* ES 968.

circulus ~i, *m.* **1** (geom.) A circle: *de quadrando ~o* DP 335.3. **2** A circular object, ring: *habent ~um...cui affixi aculei* AC 814.2. **3** A ring (of light), halo: *splendor, qui abiit in latum ~um circum chartam; ~us ille seu ambitus apparuit inde sicut apparet aurora verno tempore* AM 115.1. **4** A zone or region extending outwards from a single point: *sol ille* [sc. *mundi spiritualis*] *est ~us proximus ambiens*

Dominum VR 365.2. **5** A closed and repeating series, cycle: *~us amoris ad cogitationes et a cogitationibus ad amorem ab amore* DP 29.3; *~us vitae hominis est scire, intelligere, velle et facere* AE 242.4.

circum, *prep. w. acc.* and *adv.* **1** (prep.) Surrounding, around: *apparuit columna lucis ~um nos* VR 159.2. **2** (adv.) Around: *tunc maligni spiritus ~um irati* ES 2119.

circumactio ~onis, *f.* Rotation: *apparebat ut sphaera horizontalis ~onis...a dextro ad sinistrum* ES 2824.

circumaffundo ~ndere ~di ~sum, *tr.* To pour round about: *ut fides in Ipsum ~ndatur* ES 1534.

circumago ~magere ~megi ~mactum, *tr.* To move in a circle, move round: *per vexillum ~mactum* AE 411.18; (pass.) to revolve, turn: *aether...per quem orbis ... ~magitur* VR 30.2.

circumambio ~bire ~bivi, *tr.* To surround completely, encompass: *Divinum...Bonum est flamma, et Divinum Verum est lux inde, haec ~bit et sic circumtegit illam* AC 8764.4; ME 17.

circumambulo ~are ~avi ~atum, *tr.* To walk around: *putant...orbem quendam ~are* ES 285.

circumamicio ~cire ~civi ~ctum, *tr.* To clothe all round: *quatuor Seniores... ~ctos vestibus albis* Rev. 4.4 (AR); Rev. 18.16 (AR).

circumcaelatus ~a ~um, *a.* Engraved all round: *patinae... ~ae similibus formis* AM 14.2.

circumcido ~dere ~di ~sum, *tr.* To circumcise: FI 51; (also, fig.) to purify spiritually: *ut fructus arborum ... ~derentur* AE 109.6 (see Lev. 19.23).

circumcingo ~gere ~xi ~ctum, *tr.* To go around, surround: *~xerunt me aquae* Jonah 2.5 (AC 756.1); esp. *~ctus* (w. abl.), surrounded (by): *pileis ~ctis serico* VR 74.1.

circumcirca, *adv.* and *prep. w. acc.* also spelled as two words **circum circa**. **1** (adv.) Round about: *haec [sphaera] se extendit... ~a in longum et in latum* CI 49. **2** (prep.) Surrounding, about: VR 16.1.

circumcircum, *adv.* Round about: ES 2138.

circumcisio ~onis, *f.* Circumcision: *nusquam coelum intelligit ~onem carnis, sed ~onem cordis* AC 1025.5.

circumcursio ~onis, *f.* The act of running around: ES 436 titulus.

circumcursito ~are ~avi, *intr.* To keep running round: ES 436.

circumdo ~are ~edi ~atum, *tr.* **1** To go around, surround: *ex terris quas ~abant fluvii* AC 567. **2** (w. abl.) To surround, encircle (with): *maceria ~abo maceriam* Hos. 2.6 (AE 237.6); (pass.) *~abuntur carne et ossibus* AM 44.1.

circumduco ~cere ~xi ~ctum, *tr.* **1** To lead by a roundabout route, lead around: *quod populus Israeliticus... ~ctus fuisset in deserto* AC 730.4. **2** To cause to move in a circle, rotate: *ubi sicut rota... ~ceretur in orbem* ES 276. **3** (w. abl.) To surround (with): *orchestrae ~ctae cancellis* AM 17.1.

circumductio ~onis, *f.* A leading round: *~onem filiorum Israelis* AE 730.31.

circumeo ~mire ~mivi ~mitum, *tr.*, *intr.* see also **circueo**. To go round: **1** (tr.) *~mibitis urbem* Josh. 6.4 (AE 700.15). **2** (intr.) *~mibit ad te calix...Jehovae* Hab. 2.16 (AE 235.6).

circumextendo ~dere ~di ~sum, *tr.* To stretch around, wrap around: *repraesentative sicut serpens ~ditur, qui cingit omnes sicut globum confasciculatum* AC 2756.

circumferentia ~ae, *f.* A peripheral region, circumference: *ultimam ~am constituunt gentes...in Asia* SS 105.3; *lux candidissima cincta quadam ~a* AC 1624.

circumfero ~ferre ~tuli ~latum, *tr.* **1** To carry around: *corpus quod ~tulit in mundo* AC 10758.2. **2** (pass.) To travel in a circle, revolve: *tellus circumvolvitur quotidie et ~fertur quotannis* SS 95.2.

circumflecto ~ctere ~xi ~xum, *tr.* To bend round, make curved: *formis inflexis et ~xis* CI 260.1.

circumflexio ~onis, *f.* A bending round, involution: CI 260.1.

circumfluo ~ere ~xi, *intr.* To flow around: *illa quae ~unt in aëre* AM 210.

circumfluus ~a ~um, *a.* Flowing around, ambient: *~a gaudia* AM 10.6.

circumfluxio ~onis, *f.* A flowing around: *~ones [cogitationum]* AC 6607.

circumfulgeo ~gere ~si, *tr.* To surround with radiance, shine round about: *et gloria Domini ~sit illos* Luke 2.9 (AC 2921.5).

circumfundo ~ndere ~di ~sum, *tr.* **1** To pour out or shed around: *gloriam famae suae effudit et ~dit* VR 35.3; (refl.) to spread around: *sicut sonus...se ~ndit in aëre* DP 296.6. **2** To surround, bathe: *tertius [sol]...qui ~ndit angelos et homines* VR 141; (pass., w. abl.) *felicitatum aura ~nderer* AM 10.2.

circumfusio ~onis, *f.* A surrounding: *~o ab aquis* AC 8137.3.

circumgestio ~tire ~tivi, *tr.* (perh. better **circumgesto** ~are, *tr.*) To carry about: *corpus quod ~tit* AC 4364.4 (perh. to be emended to *circumgestat*, from **circumgesto** ~are; cf. **gesto**).

circumgesto: see **circumgestio**.

circumgyratio ~onis, *f.* A movement in a circular orbit, revolution: *quod tellus faciat motum...per circumrotationes et ~ones* AC 5084.2.

circumgyratus ~a ~um, *a.* Formed by movement in a circle, circumvoluted: ES 155.1.

circumgyro ~are ~avi, *intr.* To move in a circular path, gyrate: ES 3222.

circuminduco ~cere ~xi ~ctum, *tr.* To surround with a covering: [*apes*] *~cunt illa* [sc. *ova*] CI 108.1; (w. abl.) *sceleta aliqua cute ~cta* AE 233.4.

circuminduo ~ere ~i ~tum, *tr.* To clothe around, invest: *nisi corpore rursus ~atur* AC 5084.4.

circumitio ~onis, *f.* A going round, circumperambulation: *~onem urbis* AE 700.16.

circumjacens ~ntis, *a.* Lying around, surrounding, neighbouring: *quamdiu cor integrum est, ~ntia viscera possunt vivere* AC 468.2; (neut. as sb.) VR 61.2.

circumjaceo ~cere ~cui, *intr.* To lie round about: NH 5.

circumlatio ~onis, *f.* A carrying around: *quod per ~onem ejus* [sc. *arcae*] *muri Jerichuntis ceciderint* VI 55.3; the orbital motion (of the Earth): *Tellus per circumrotationes et ~ones suas facit illa tempora* VR 71.3.

circumligo ~are ~avi ~atum, *tr.* To tie around, bind: *funis quo... ~ati sunt* CI 479.3; ES 2867.

circumlino ~linere ~levi ~litum, *tr.* To daub around, surround with: [*apis*] *ponit ova quae turba sequens ~lit* VR 12.7.

circumluceo ~cere, *intr.* To shine around: *quod* [*lignum*] *luce fatua ~cet* CO 30.

circummoveo ~vere ~vi ~tum, *tr.* To move in a circle, move around: *quomodocunque ~ventur oculi* ES 2850.

circumobsideo ~sidere ~sedi ~sessum, *tr.* To besiege on all sides: *quae terra ~sessa erat ab infernis* AC 6854.2.

circumobsitus ~a ~um, *a.* also spelled as two words **circum obsitus** (AR 926.3). Besprinkled: *bractea aurea adamantibus ~a* AM 20.2.

circumpono ~nere ~sui ~situm, *tr.* To place round: *sepem ei* [sc. *vineae*] *~suit* AC 124.

circumpremo ~mere ~ssi ~ssum, *tr.* To exert physical pressure on from all sides, surround with pressure: [*coelum*] *innititur illi* [*bono*]...*sicut extrema corporis aëri et aetheri ~menti* AC 9490.

circumpressio ~onis, *f.* Pressure exerted on all sides: *ex ~one aëris* AC 6057.

circumprojectio ~onis, *f.* The action of casting in all directions: *quod...se extorqueat per ~onem a societate* ES 2991.

circumquaque, *adv.* Around in all directions, all around: *ut* [*arbores*] *ramos... ~que diffundant* ES 1681.

circumrepo ~ere ~si, *intr.* To move slowly or gradually around (a centre), creep around: *delicta...sunt sicut ulcera, quae nisi aperiuntur et sanantur, colligitur inibi sanies, quae corrumpit vicinias, ac serpentis instar ~it* VR 459.12.

circumrotatio ~onis, *f.* Rotary motion, rotation: AC 5084.2.

circumroto ~are ~avi ~atum, *tr.* To cause to rotate, twist: *quod... ~entur sicut volumen* AC 829.1.

circumsaepio: see **circumsepio**.

circumscribo ~bere ~psi ~ptum, *tr.* To confine, circumscribe: *es tu qui ~psisti Deum legibus...?* VR 74.2.

circumsepio ~pire ~psi ~ptum, *tr.* also **circumsaepio**. To surround with a fence or hedge, hedge about: *quod mons ~ptus fuerit ne quis accederet* VI 55.1; *coelum...undequaque ~ptum est* CI 428.

circumspargo ~gere ~si ~sum, *tr.* To scatter around: *odor... ~gi ex rore* CI 289.

circumsparsio ~onis, *f.* A scattering around: AM 309.

circumspecte, *adv.* With circumspection, carefully: *~e posuit id* Ezek. 17.5 (AE 281.2).

circumspectio ~onis, *f.* **1** Looking around: *quoad ~onem undequaque* AE 276. **2** Caution, circumspection: *causae quae...sunt prudentiae et ~onis uxorum* AM 161.1.

circumspectus ~a ~um: pf. pple. of **circumspicio**.

circumspicio ~picere ~pexi ~pectum, *intr.*, *refl.* To look around: (intr.) *cum ~peximus, visi sunt ibi ursi* AM 78.2; (refl.) *datum...est...me ~picere undequaque* CI 184; AC 314; (pf. pple.) given careful consideration: *ex ~pectis rationibus* AM 108.

circumstans ~ntis, *a.* Standing around: *spiritibus ~ntibus* ES 315; (masc. pl. as sb.) bystanders: AM 6.2.

circumstantia ~ae, *f.* A circumstance, detail, particular: *quae nusquam relata fuissent...et fere cum similibus ~is, nisi...* AC 1502.2.

circumstipo ~are ~avi ~atum, *tr.* To crowd round about, throng: *quod sphaera illa ~et hominem* AM 171.2; *malis... ~atus* AC 59.2.

circumsto ~are ~eti, *tr.* To stand around, surround: AC 8206.1.

circumtego ~gere ~xi ~ctum, *tr.* To surround with a covering, envelop: *quod mens naturalis... ~gat et includat mentem spiritualem* AS 260; *lectica nigris pannis ~cta* AC 817.

circumtexo ~ere ~ui ~tum, *tr.* To construct or weave (an elaborate structure) around (a centre), weave around: *amor infernalis...comparari potest araneae et ejus telae ~tae* DP 107; VR 353.

circumtorqueo ~quere ~si ~sum, *tr.* To twist around: ES 745.

circumtraho ~here ~xi ~ctum, *tr.* To draw around: 4IB s.v. 'Immundum' (p. 289 Kahl).

circumustus ~a ~um, *a.* Burnt on the outside, charred: *ex ramis arborum ~is* AM 79.4.

circumvado ~dere ~si, *intr.* To go around: *~dit et inquirit ubinam sua domus est* IM 61.

circumvagator ~oris, *m.* One who wanders around, itinerant: DA 32 (= xii.[1]).

circumvagor ~ari ~atus sum, *intr.* To wander around: *permittebatur ~ari* CI 6; (of the mind) *studium ...continet mentem ne diffluat et ne ~etur* AM 16.3.

circumvehor ~hi ~ctus sum, *intr.* To travel around: ES 309.

circumvelatio ~onis, *f.* A surrounding with a veil, veiling: *~o amoris conjugialis* AM 475.3.

circumvelo ~are ~avi ~atum, *tr.* To surround with a veil or means of concealment: *malum... ~atum et obvolutum jacuit externa probitate* CI 577.2.

circumvenio ~nire ~ni ~ntum, *tr.* To get the better of by craft or fraud, deceive: *eludimus et ~nimus quoscunque ex sua concupiscentia, hos ludibriis, hos assentationibus, hos astutiis, hos simulata amicitia, hos ficta sinceritate* VR 665.3.

circumversio ~onis, *f.* An instance or an ongoing state of turning around: *ibi quod ad dextram est apparet ad dextram in omni versura seu ~one* AC 8613; *non...cogitant de solis statione et telluris ~one* AS 349.

circumverto ~tere ~ti ~sum, *tr.* To turn round: *illi ~terunt illos* VR 160.7; (refl. and pass.) to turn: *utcunque se ~tit* CI 479.2; AC 1274.

circumvestio ~tire ~tivi ~titum, *tr.* To cover completely as with clothing: *corpus...cingit et ~tit animam* AC 2973.4; AC 3570.3.

circumvolito ~are ~avi, *intr.* To fly around, flit about: *in caverna ~ant sicut larvae* AM 514.3.

circumvolutio ~onis, *f.* A rotation: *apparet sol per apparentes ~ones facere dies et annos* AC 7381.3; a wrapping around, turn: *cum involutus est homo panno et quidem per aliquot ~ones* ES 1372.

circumvolvo ~vere ~vi ~utum, *tr.* To cause to turn on its axis, rotate: *tellus ~vitur quotidie* SS 95.2; *~utus*, wrapped around, twisted: *retia ~uta sicut in nodum inexplicabilia* VR 74.2.

circuo ~ere, *tr.* To encircle, surround: *intimum... centrum tenet, interiora quae sub intimo, ~unt centrum, et exteriora faciunt peripherias* AC 6451.2.

circus ~i, *m.* Anything of circular shape, a ring: (of hanging lamps) *e longinquo ab hoc ~o* VR 16.1; *~us gramineus* AM 183.1.

cis, *prep. w. acc.* and *adv.* **1** (prep.) On this side of: *cis et trans Jordanem* CI 327. **2** (adv.) *Cis et retro*, to and fro, back and forth: *per violentas collisiones partium cis et retro* AC 959; AC 4050.3.

cista ~ae, *f.* A treasure-chest, strongbox: *ut pecunia esset non ita in ~is...sed in negotiatione* ES 3500.

cisterna ~ae, *f.* **1** A tank for storing water, cistern: *implet ~am aquis faeculentis* AM 480. **2** (anat.) The *cisterna chyli*, Pecquet's Cistern: AC 5180; DP 164.6.

citatio ~onis, *f.* A reference to a passage in a book, citation: AC 9372.9.

cithara ~ae, *f.* (Gk.) A lyre: *habentes unusquisque ~as* Rev. 5.8 (AR).

citharaedus: see **citharoedus**.

citharoedus ~i, *m.* (Gk.) also **citharaedus**. One who sings to the lyre, minstrel: *vocem... ~orum pulsantium in citharis suis* Rev. 14.2 (AR).

cito[1], *adv.* (compar. *~ius*, superl. *~issime*) Swiftly, quickly: *venio ~o* Rev. 22.12 (AR); *serius aut ~ius*, sooner or later: CI 159.

cito[2] ~are ~avi ~atum, *tr.* To refer to (a passage in a book), quote, cite: *ex ~atis in Verbo locis* AC 82.

citra, *prep. w. acc.* On this side of: *~a Jordanem* 3AD 4560.

citreum ~i, *neut.* A citrus fruit, citron: AC 8603.2; ES 3898.

citrus ~i, *f.* A citron tree, poss. used for lemon: *olivae, aurantii et ~i* AM 8.3.

citus ~a ~um, *a.* (compar. *~ior*) **1** (of persons) Quick in action or thought: *in...cogitando loquendoque promptiores et ~iores sunt* AC 6921; ES 1821. **2** (of actions) Quickly performed: *hoc quod homini apparet tam ~um et momentaneum* ES 2010.

civilis ~is ~e, *a.* **1** Of or belonging to a state, civil: *ex lege ~i* VI 12; *ex ordine ~i* VR 74.1; (neut. pl. as sb.) civic matters: *in politicis...et in ~ibus...et in domesticis* VR 508.3. **2** Of or proper to a citizen, polite, civil: *ex amicitia ~i et simulata* AC 548.3; *qui moralem et ~em vitam vixerunt* AC 1835.3; (neut. pl. as sb.) AM 292.2.

civilitas ~atis, *f.* **1** Politeness, civility: *amicitia non est charitas, minus adhuc ~as* AC 1158.2. **2** Good citizenship: *non ita sapientes sunt, sed solum ex moralitate et ~ate externa apparent sicut sint* AM 18.2.

civiliter, *adv.* In a polite manner, civilly: AM 297.

civis ~is, *m.* A citizen: VI 12; AM 18.1.

civitas ~atis, *f.* A large town, city: *respublica, ~as, domus* VR 55; *quod sciant* [*apes*]*...struere cellas...et disponere illas in formam ~atis* VR 12.7.

clades ~is, *f.* A disaster: *pugnae, victoriae, ~es* AC 8261.3.

clam, *adv.* Secretly, privately: *in latibulo seu clam* ES 639.

clamo ~are ~avi ~atum, *intr.* To cry out, shout: *~avit voce magna* Rev. 19.17 (AR); (impers. pass.) AM 7.2.

clamor ~oris, *m.* A cry, shout: *media...nocte ~or factus est* Matt. 25.6 (SS 17.1).

clanculum, *adv.* Secretly, stealthily: *unus...appulerit ~um ad me* ES 291.

clandestine, *adv.* With concealment, secretly: *vicinum ~e necavit veneno* CI 462[a].7.

clandestinus ~a ~um, *a.* Secret, concealed: *ex ~is artibus* AM 292.1.

clango ~gere ~xi, *intr.* To sound a blast (on a trumpet): *angelus...cui tuba erat in manu et ad os, qui ~xit versus septentrionem* AM 2.1.

clangor ~oris, *m.* The sound made by a trumpet, blast, blare: *audivi ~orem tubae tuae* AM 2.1.

clare, *adv.* (compar. *~ius*, superl. *~issime*) Clearly, plainly: *ut hoc ~ius sciatur* AC 788.1; *quod... ~e docet Dominus* AC 36.

claresco ~rescere ~rui, *intr.* To become bright or clear: VR 335.7.

clarifico ~are ~avi ~atum, *tr.* To make clear or transparent: *cum ~atur mustum vini* AM 272.

claritas ~atis, *f.* Brightness, brilliance: *ex luce fatua, quae...est similis ~ati* VR 155.

clarus ~a ~um, *a.* (compar. *~ior*, superl. *~issimus*) **1** (of light) Unobscured, clear, bright: *lux intelligentiae ~a* AE 21. **2** (of vision or perception) Penetrating, clear: *~is oculis viderunt* SE 34; *in perceptione ~a* CI 148. **b** (of sounds) clear: *viva et ~a voce* ES 2367. **3** Brightly illuminated, bright: *quod...transeant a vita obscura in ~am* AC 1854.1. **4** Clearly perceived, clear, plain: *hoc...ita ~um visum est...ut nusquam posset negari* ES 1076.

classicum ~i, *neut.*? A bugle: *canebant tuba, ~o, etc.* 3AD 3391.

classicus ~a ~um, *a.* Of the classical age (of Greece and Rome), classical: *lectiones autorum ~orum* ES 805.

classificatio ~onis, *f.* Classification: AC 4647.

classifico ~are ~avi ~atum, *tr.* To put into classes, classify: *spiritus ~ati sunt* ES 167.

classis ~is, *f.* **1** A group of persons or things sharing a common attribute, class: AC 1153.3; a social class: *quomodo charitas exercenda esset erga illos qui in una ~e* AC 6705. **2** A fleet: *milites super navibus bellicis cum vident ~em hostilem* VR 112.2.

claudicatio ~onis, *f.* Limping, lameness: *laedere ut inde ~o* AC 4317.1.

claudico ~are ~avi, *intr.* To walk lamely, limp: *is ~ans super femore suo* Gen. 32.31 (AC).

claudo ~dere ~si ~sum, *tr.* **1** To close, shut (a door): *januis ~sis* John 20.26 (DD 35.9). **2** To stop up, shut (an orifice): *~dent reges os suum* Isa. 52.15 (AE 31.5); to block up, close (a way): *via ad animam ~sa est* AM 183.8. **3** To render inaccessible, shut off, close: *homo ...sibi coelum ~sit* AC 1880.3; *internum ejus... ~sum est* CI 202. **4** To confine, shut up (a person): *~dentur in claustro* Isa. 24.22 (AC 6854.5).

claudus ~a ~um, *a.* Lame: *~i ambulant* Matt. 11.5 (SS 17.3).

claustrarius ~i, *m.* A maker of door-bolts, locksmith: *faber et ~us* Jer. 24.1 (3IB s.v. 'claustrarius').

claustrum ~i, *neut.* A place of confinement, prison: *in ~o seu in carcere* AC 5089.2; *e domo ~i* Isa. 42.7 (AE 152.13); also, an enclosure: *intra ~um seu latum pulpitum* ES 3396.

clausula ~ae, *f.* A final phrase, conclusion: *ultimo loco seu ut ~a dicitur* AE 340.1.

clausura ~ae, *f.* Anything which encloses, enclosure: *facies ei* [sc. *mensae*] *~am palmi circumcirca* Exod. 25.25 (AC); *gentes...sicut serpentes terrae* *commovebuntur e ~is suis* Mic. 7.17 (AC 249); *ultra ~am cordis* AM 44.5.

clausus ~a ~um: pf. pple. of **claudo**.

clavichordium ~i, *neut.* A clavichord: ES 4482.

claviger ~eri, *m.* A key-bearer: AM 3.6.

clavis ~is, *f.* A key: *~is ad aperiendum* VR 7.

clavus ~i, *m.* **1** A wooden peg, tent peg: *non removebuntur ~i ejus in perpetuum* Isa. 33.20 (AE 799.10); AM 431 (Deut. 23.13). **2** The tiller attached to a rudder: *~um gubernaculi* VR 434.2.

clemens ~ntis, *a.* (superl. *~ntissimus*) Gentle, mild: *bonum... ~ns* AE 427.9; *substantiae formae fiunt lenes, blandae, ~ntes* AM 361.2.

clementer, *adv.* Gently, mildly: *quisquam...comprimit et elevat pulmonem secundum...influxum affectionis ex amore, lente, festine, cupide, ~er, attente* AS 382.

clementia ~ae, *f.* Mildness, clemency: AM 12.2.

clenodium ~i, *neut.* (Medieval Latin; cf. German *Kleinod*) A precious object, jewel, gem: *colligunt ~a auri et argenti* VR 527.2; VR 669.1; (fig.) *conjugiale...est ~um vitae humanae* AM 444[a].

clericus ~i, *m.* A man in holy orders, clergyman, clerk: AM 39.

clerus ~i, *m.* (Gk.) The clergy: *aliqui ex ~o* AM 463.3.

clibanus ~i, *m.* (Gk.) An earthenware baking dish, oven: AC 7356.1.

cliens ~ntis, *m.* A member of one's household or group, dependant, supporter: *de tyranno qui ~ntes in urbem admittit* VR 798.9; *~ns procus*, a suitor who has proposed: *aliter prorsus fieret si filia ex se, inconsultis parentibus...ad ~ntem procum consentit* AM 299.

clientela ~ae, *f.* The relationship of a dependant: *si parentelae et ~ae sint uxori* AM 469.

clima ~atis, *neut.* (Gk.) A region with reference to its prevailing weather, climate: *in ~atibus calidis* AC 7177; CI 157.

clipeus: see **clypeus**.

clitellae ~larum, *f. pl.* A packsaddle (of a camel): *Rachel sumsit theraphim, posuitque eos inter ~las cameli* Gen. 31.34 (1AD 1295).

clivosus ~a ~um, *a.* Having slopes, sloping: *per tramitem ~um* AM 11.

clivus ~i, *m.* A hill, slope: AM 76.1.

cloaca ~ae, *f.* (anat.) The cloaca: *diaboli sedes in homine repraesentatur per posteriora, ubi ~a* 3AD 2230.

clunis ~is, *m.* or *f.* (in pl.) The buttocks, haunches: *capite deorsum et ~ibus sursum* AM 269.3.

cluo ~ere, *intr.* (impers.) It is reckoned, it is said: *inde ~it quod aliae mutationes sint* AM 187.

clypeus ~i, *m.* also **clipeus**. A shield: VR 84; (fig.) *Ego ~us tibi* Gen. 15.1 (AC).

coacervatim, *adv.* In heaps: *tantus terror invasit, ut ~im ruerent ad portas* VR 136.5.

coacervatio ~onis, *f.* The act of heaping up, accumulation: *quod ex illa substantia per ~ones existant substantiata* AS 229.

coacervo ~are ~avi ~atum, *tr.* To heap or pile up: *~atae sunt aquae* Exod. 15.8 (AC); (fig.) to increase in amount or number: *homo... ~at illa* [sc. *mala et falsa*] AC 698; *fastidium... ~atur usque ad nauseam* AM 509.

coacte, *adv.* Under compulsion: ES 489.

coactio ~onis, *f.* Compulsion: *ex ~one illa se exsolvere nequicquam possunt* AC 7218.

coactus ~a ~um, *a.* (pf. pple. of **cogo**) Performed under compulsion, forced: *cohabitatio... ~a et non libera* AM 234; (neut. as sb.) *quod internum...renuat ~um ab externo* DP 136.1.

coadjutor ~oris, *m.* A helper, assistant: AE 834.

coaeternus ~a ~um, *a.* Equally eternal, coeternal: *Deus Filius et Deus Spiritus Sanctus... ~i cum Patre* VR 159.3.

coagmento ~are ~avi ~atum, *tr.* To make by fastening together, construct: Eph. 2.21 (CO 2.3).

coagulatus ~a ~um, *a.* Coagulated, curdled: *quoddam... ~um lacteum* ES 3791; formed into a lump, massed together: *cum quibus in societate quasi ~i* ES 266.

coalesco ~lescere ~lui, *intr.* (fut. pple. *~liturus*) (w. *cum*) To combine, coalesce (with): *quod...cadavera ... ~litura sint cum suis animabus* AM 182.6; SS 116.2.

coalitio ~onis, *f.* A combining, growing together: *~onem seu reunionem animarum cum suis cadaveribus* IM 71.

coangelus ~i, *m.* A fellow angel: AM 216.2.

coaptabilis ~is ~e, *a.* That may be fitted together, matching: *formae mutuae et ~es* AM 44.2.

coapto ~are ~avi ~atum, *tr.* To fit together, assemble: *quod tunc corporea...rursus ~arentur in corpus* AM 532.3.

coarctatio ~onis, *f.* A pressing together, compression: *~o dolorifica circa medium ventrem* AC 7810;

DP 319.1; (transf.) repression: *dies angustiae et ~onis* Zeph. 1.15 (AC 1839.5).

coarcto ~are ~avi ~atum, *tr.* To confine, compress: *ita ~abatur et angustabatur* ES 291; *quae... ~ant et...retardant visum internum* AC 6811.

coarguo ~ere ~i, *tr.* To make manifest, expose: *ne ~antur opera ejus* John 3.20 (VI 2).

coaxo ~are ~avi, *intr.* (of frogs) To croak: AC 7352; AR 702.

coccineus ~a ~um, *a.* Scarlet: *chlamyde ~a* AM 20.2; *si fuerint peccata vestra sicut ~a* Isa. 1.18 (VI 30); (neut. as sb.) Lev. 14.4 (AC 7918.2).

coccinum ~i, *neut.* Scarlet colour: *angelos in purpura et ~o* AM 183.1.

coccus ~i *m.* The insect *coccus ilicis* or the scarlet dye derived from it: *~us vel purpura* 2AD 371.

cochlaca ~ae, *f.* A pebble: *ludunt cum ~is inter digitos* VR 695.4.

cochlea ~ae, *f.* (Gk.) A snail: AM 268.2.

cochleare ~is, *neut.* A spoon: *~e ebenum* CI 325.

cochlearis ~is ~e, *a.* Shaped like a snail's shell, spiral: *per scalam ~em* AM 270.6.

cochleatim, *adv.* In a spiral motion: *saccum varie circumagebat dextrorsum, sinistrorsum, ~im...* ES 4361.

coctio ~onis, *f.* Cooking: *per aquas...in quibus fit ~o* AC 10105.1.

codex ~icis, *m.* see also **caudex**. **1** A book formed of wooden tablets: *ars scribendi...primum super ~icibus, dein super membranis* AC 9353. **2** A book, volume: *ut...correspondentias...in ~icem conferrent* AE 728.2; *dilataretur hoc opus in tam amplum ~icem ut...* AM 209.

codicillus ~i, *m.* A small volume: *in ~o De Commercio Anime et Corporis* VR 33.

coec-: see **caec-**.

coelatura ~ae, *f.* also **cael-**. Carving: *decoramenta ~ae inimitabilis* AM 12.1.

coelebs ~ebis, *a.* also **caelebs**. Unmarried, celibate: *qui in mundo ~ibes vixerunt* AM 54.3.

coelestis ~is ~e, *a.* also **caelestis**. (compar. *~ior*, superl. *~issimus*) **1** Of the sky: *coloris ~is* AC 184; *sidus ~e* AC 530.2. **2** Of the heavens, heavenly: *apud angelum ...etiamsi ~issimum* AC 633; *de gaudio ~i* AM 2.1; *ex conjugio ~i* AC 6794; (masc. pl. as sb.) *sub intuitu ~ium* AC 6914.2; (neut. pl. as sb.) *~ia illis curae sunt* AC 6810. **3** (as opp. to **spiritualis**) Of the highest heaven, celestial: *amor ~is* AC 6804.11; *loquela angelorum ~ium* CI 241; *vocatur id Divinum ~e, spirituale et naturale* VR 6.1; (neut. as sb.) *e ~i nascitur spirituale* AC 1025.7; *~e ejus* [sc. *hominis*] *moritur* AC 80. **b** (coupled w. *spiritualis*): *a ~i spirituali origine* AC 91; *societates...quae vocantur ~es spirituales* CI 27; (also w. *naturalis*) *~es naturales vocantur qui influxum recipiunt ex coelo tertio* CI 31.

coeliacus ~a ~um, *a.* (Gk.) also **cael-**. Of the belly, coeliac: *affectio ~a* AM 253.2.

coelibatus ~us, *m.* also **caelibatus**. Celibacy: *sphaera perpetui ~us* AM 54.5.

coelicola ~ae, *m.* also **caelicola**. An inhabitant of heaven: CI 115.

coelifico ~are ~avi ~atum, *tr.* also **cael-**. To make heavenly: *nec vocant id mori, sed potius ~ari* ES 623.

coelitus, *adv.* also **cael-**. From heaven: *hoc dictum est ~us* ES 1340.

coelum[1] ~i, *neut.* also **caelum**. (pl. uses *~i ~orum* masc. endings) **1** The visible sky: *~um cum...astris* AC 5084.2; *omnis avis ~i* VR 54. **2** Heaven: *de ~o et Inferno* DD praef.; *nisi revelatio fit e ~o* AE 2. **b** (used collectively for its inhabitants): *qui in sensu interno sunt, ut totum ~um* AC 1025.4. **3** (w. pl.) One of the three separate parts making up heaven, a heaven: *quod tres ~i sint, nempe interius, intimius et intimum* ES 2191; AC 6706. **b** (w. ref. to Rev. 21.1): *per primum ~um intelligitur id quod conflatum ex aliis quam qui angeli facti sunt* UJ 66.

coelum[2] ~i, *neut.* also **caelum**. A chisel: *~um...est ferrum per quod lapides secantur* AC 8942.

coena ~ae, *f.* also **caena**, and **cena**. **1** A dinner: *beati qui ad ~am nuptiarum Agni vocati sunt* Rev. 19.9 (AR). **2** *Sancta* or *Sacra ~a*, the rite of the Eucharist, the Holy Supper: AC 6789.3; AE 475.21; AC 1727; CI 111.

coenaculum ~i, *neut.* also **caenaculum**, and **cenaculum**. **1** A dining room: *janitorem inducere in ~um ad mensam* VR 459.3. **2** (Bibl.) An upper storey, attic: *fenestrae apertae illi in ~o* Dan. 6.10 (AC 2788.9).

coeno ~are ~avi, *intr.* also **caeno**, and **ceno**. To dine, sup: *~abo cum illo, et ille Mecum* Rev. 3.20 (AR); AM 19.

coenosus ~a ~um, *a.* also **caenosus**. Muddy, mucky: (neut. pl. as sb.) *in stagneis, ~is et excrementitiis degere* AC 1666.1.

coenum ~i, *neut.* also **caenum**. Foul-smelling mud or muck: *sicut ~um platearum* Ps. 18.42 (DD 14.6);

hoc putet in caelo sicut putre ~um platearum AM 500.6; (pl.) AM 430.

coeo coire coivi, *intr.* **1** To come together, unite, join: *mapalia...visa...coire et conjungi in formam urbis* AM 79.4. **2** To have sexual intercourse: *mixtim coeunt* ES 2867.

coepi ~isse ~tum, *intr.* also **caepi**. (used only in pf. act. and pass.) To have begun: *posteri... ~erunt imagines ...colere* SS 23.1; (w. ellipse of *esse*) *et ~it Noach vir humi* Gen. 9.20 (AC); (impers. pass.) *~tum est demonstrare* DD 37.1.

coeptus ~a ~um, *a.* (pf. pple. of **coepi**) Commenced, begun: AM 110.

coerceo ~cere ~cui ~citum, *tr.* To put under restraint, restrain, repress: *voluptates... ~cendae sunt* AC 1547; *per paenas... ~citi et refraenati sunt* VR 79.8.

coercitio ~onis, *f.* Restraint, repression: *nimia ~o amoris sexus* AM 450.

coeruleus: see **caeruleus**.

coetus: see **caetus**.

coexisto ~ere, *intr.* To come into existence simultaneously, arise together: *haec tria...unum fiunt et ~unt* VR 370.3; *partes...ex quibus commune ~it* AM 10.8.

cogitabilis ~is ~e, *a.* That can be thought about, conceivable: *quod nihil ejus [status]...expressibile sit nec ~e* CI 412.

cogitata ~orum, *neut. pl.* Things thought about, thoughts: *~a celare* CI 492.

cogitatio ~onis, *f.* **1** The process of thinking, thought: *quis potest comprehendere Ipsum Divinum aliqua ~one?* AC 6804.4. **b** thought (as opposed to action, etc.): *non sciunt aliter quam quod [fides] sit mera ~o* AC 36. **c** (w. object of thought specified): (w. gen.) *~o veri* VI 36; (w. *in* + acc.) *~o in Dominum* AC 36; (w. *quod*) *~o quod ita sit* FI 1. **2** The faculty of or power of thought: *quia hominis ~o cohaeret cum ejus memoria* CI 246.1; *mali...habent ~onem* AC 978.1. **3** The result of thinking, a particular thought: *angeli...nusquam determinant suas ~ones ad singulares personas* AC 6804.2; *~ones veri* AC 745; *~onem de sanctis Ecclesiae* AC 6787.

cogitative, *adv.* By a process of thought, cogitatively: ES 5915.

cogitativus ~a ~um, *a.* Of or relating to thought, cogitative: *vita ~a* AM 315.9; *ex fide ~a* AE 76.2; *loquelam... ~am* AC 174; (neut. as sb.) AC 3599.2.

cogito ~are ~avi ~atum, *tr., intr.* **1** (tr.) To form an idea of, hold in the mind, think of: *~abam urbes* ES 2581; *ut...pateat...quid ~ant* AC 6655. **2** (tr.) To form an intention of, have in mind, contemplate: *liberum ~andi volendique malum* AC 6657.1; (intr., w. inf.) *dum... ~avi ea verbis describere* ES 1086. **3** (intr.) To form an idea in the mind, conceive, think: *qui...ex se et suo proprio... ~at* SS 1; (w. *de*) *qui bene vivit, bene ~et...de Deo* VI 1; (w. *quod*) *quis... ~are potest quod tam immensum medium factum sit pro tam parvo...fine* AC 6698; (w. acc. and inf.) *potuisset homo... ~are se justificatum* DD 18.3.

cognatio ~onis, *f.* Relationship: *ex una familia aut in aliqua ~one* AC 157.

cognatus ~a ~um, *a.* Related: *doctrinalia ~a* AC 3052; (neut. as sb.) something related: *a repraesentatione Nachoris quod sit ~um* AC 3052; (masc. as sb.) a relative: *parentes, ~i, et amici* AM 287.

cognitio ~onis, *f.* **1** The fact of knowing, knowledge: *absque ~one corporis humani* ES 1145 ½; *~o omnium quae complectitur doctrina fidei, et eorum agnitio* AC 36; *agnitio Dei ex ~one Ejus* VR 5. **2** The individual's faculty of knowing, knowledge, cognizance: *nusquam ad alicujus hominis ~onem...venerunt* AC 5; AC 67. **3** A particular item or arrangement of knowledge, concept: *postquam perire coepit ~o illa* AC 1409.2; *absque illa ~one praevia* CI 67; (usu. pl.) items of information, concepts: *omnes ~ones cujuscunque generis* AC 3020.2; *congregationem scientificorum seu ~onum* AC 991; (w. gen.) *~ones mundanorum* AC 1453.1; *~ones sunt memoriae naturalis hominis* AC 9544; (w. *de*) *quod ~ones de Deo sint specula Dei* VR 11.3; (w. indir. qu.) *secundum ~ones quid peccatum* VR 525. **4** (pl., as dist. from *scientifica*) Concepts about interior things: *distinguit...inter ~ones quae sunt apud hominem internum et scientifica quae sunt hominis externi* AC 24.1; *scientifica ex Verbo seu ex doctrina Ecclesiae quae ~ones veri et boni vocantur* AC 9723.1; *quod ~ones apud hos sint scientifica* AC 1193.

cognitivum ~i, *neut.* An item of knowledge: *omne ~um boni* AC 7671; CI 365.3.

cognitus ~i, *m.* (pf. pple. of **cognosco**) An acquaintance: *quisnam ex meis ~is...esset* ES 890.

cognominatio ~onis, *f.* The attribution of a distinguishing name, naming: *a ~one Abrami quod hic dicatur Hebraeus* AC 1702.1.

cognomino ~are ~avi ~atum, *tr.* To attribute a name to, name: Isa. 45.4 (AC 145).

cognoscibilis ~is ~e, *a.* Capable of being known: *alia non ~ia quod a tali origine* ES 4404.

cognosco ~noscere ~novi ~nitum, *tr.* (superl. of pf. pple. *~nitissimus*) **1** To know (a person) by his appearance, recognize: *apparent sibi e longinquo esse, nec* *ita ~noscunt se* AC 6806.3. **2** To be acquainted with, know (a person): *~nosco Meos et ~noscor a Meis* John 10.14 (AC 6806.2); *~noscite Jehovam* Jer. 31.34 (FI 5); *omnes quos ~noverunt in mundo* AC 1114. **3** To have carnal knowledge of: *homo ~novit Chavam uxorem suam* Gen. 4.1 (AC); Luke 1.34 (VR 82.3). **4** To have cognizance of, know about (a fact): *erat desiderium ~noscendi conjugia antiquissimorum* AM 75.5; (w. *quod*) *atmosphaera ~nita est, quod efficiat auditum* ES 222; (w. indir. qu.) *ad ~noscendum quid fieret illi* Exod. 2.4 (AC). **5** To recognize (a thing for what it is): *jucundum ~noscitur ex suo bono* CI 288.2.

cogo ~ere coegi coactum, *tr.*, *intr.* To force, compel: **1** (tr.) *quod faciem suam non ~ant, sed libere eam emittant* ES 530; (w. *ad*) *~i non possit ad bonum* CI 293; *~ere os suum ad edicendum* VR 111.6. **2** (intr.) *permittendo et patiendo...at nusquam ~endo* AM 208.2; (w. inf.) *quod...coacti sint stricte observare* AE 433.38; (w. *ut*) *~it ut unum sit* VI 44.

cohabitatio ~onis, *f.* The action or fact of living together as man and wife, cohabitation: *post brevem ~onem* CI 379.2; *~o spiritualis* AM 158.2.

cohabito ~are ~avi ~atum, *intr.* To live together in one place: *qui ab Antiquissima Ecclesia fuerunt, etiam in coelo ~ant* AC 483.2; (of man and wife) *~are, hoc est, simul esse in una domo inque cubiculo et toro* AM 50.

cohaerens ~ntis, *a.* (pres. pple. of **cohaereo**) Closely joined, cohering: *opus ~ns a centro ad superficiem* AM 314.2.

cohaerentia ~ae, *f.* The quality of being closely joined or compacted: ES 242; coherence: *~a causarum* AM 234.

cohaereo ~rere ~si, *intr.* **1** To be closely joined or inseparable, cohere: *quod apud hominem...nihil Ecclesiae ~reat* VR 5; (w. dat.) *falsa...ipsi vitae hominis ~rent* AC 1679.2. **2** To form an organized series, cohere, hang together: *haec tria genera homicidiorum unum faciunt et ~rent* VI 67; (w. *cum*) *haec ~rent cum supra explicatis* AM 169.

cohibeo ~bere ~bui ~bitum, *tr.* To put under restraint, restrain, check: *amorem sexus ~bere* AM 446.

cohobatio ~onis, *f.* Repeated distillation, cohobation: AM 145.2.

cohobo ~are ~avi ~atum, *tr.* To cohobate, concentrate: *vasa spermatica...in quibus semen ~atur et decantatur* SA 76 (= iii.2).

cohorresco ~rescere ~rui, *intr.* To shudder, shiver: *reges...~ruerunt horrore* Ezek. 27.35 (AE 406.2).

cohors ~rtis, *f.* A group, band (of persons): *perplures tales, integrae ~rtes* ES 1571; AM 2.3.

coincido ~ere ~i, *intr.* To be in exact agreement: *hoc...~it cum veterum sapientia* VR 33; (w. *in* + acc.) to join in referring (to): *quae sequuntur, ~unt in inimicum* 3AD 43.

colaphus ~i, *m.* (Gk.) A blow with the fist, punch: VR 130.3.

colatorium ~i, *neut.* A filter: *pulmones quoad sanguinem agunt ~um* DA 12 (= v.[2]).

colericus ~a ~um, *a.* also **chol-**. Constitutionally short-tempered, choleric: ES 825.

coli: gen. sg. of **colon**.

colica ~ae, *f.* The colic: ES(M) 4680.

colicus ~a ~um, *a.* (Gk.) Of the colon, colic: ES 1035.

collabor ~bi ~psus sum, *intr.* To fall down, collapse: *sicut domus in terrae motu, dum ~buntur* VR 79.2; (fig.) *ex otio ~bitur mens et non expanditur* AM 207.3.

collaboro ~are ~avi ~atum, *intr.* To work together, collaborate: ES 2991.

collarium ~i, *neut.* A collar: *in ~is ex alis* VR 137.1; a necklace: *~um ex unionibus* AM 20.3.

collateralis ~is ~e, *a.* Indirect, collateral: *in linea obliqua seu ~i* AC 3665.4.

collateraliter, *adv.* In a collateral manner: AC 9836.3.

collatio ~onis, *f.* **1** A bringing together: *~onem in unum* AC 10403. **2** A comparison: *~o...falsificatorum bonorum...cum bonis...genuinis* AC 4774.

collatus ~a ~um: pf. pple. of **confero**.

collaudo ~are ~avi ~atum, *tr.* To join in praising, praise together: *quod mille...~ent Deum* ES 356.

collecta ~ae, *f.* A contribution of goods for religious purposes, collection, offering: *accipiant Mihi ~am* Exod. 25.2 (AC).

collectaneus ~a ~um, *a.* (neut. pl. as sb.) A collection of sayings: IM 24; ES 2476.

collectim, *adv.* Collectively: AC 10083.1.

collectio ~onis, *f.* A bringing together, gathering, collection: *~onem omnium ex sepulchris die ultimi judicii* AM 182.5; *solum sensui literae Verbi Domini student, et ~ones inde faciunt* ES 2391 titulus.

collectus ~a ~um: pf. pple. of **colligo**[2]. (neut. pl. as sb.) Collected passages: CI 78.

collegium ~i, *neut.* A place of higher education, college: *musaea, gymnasia et ~a* AM 207.6.

colliculus ~i, *m.* A hillock: *cespites ex humo sicut ~i* VR 113.5.

collido ~dere ~si ~sum, *intr.* To come into violent contact, collide: *vortices qui inter se ~serunt* VR 79.2; (also pass.) *~detur cum eo rex meridiei* Dan. 11.40 (AC 3708.23); (transf.) to conflict: *interiora...contra se mutuo ~dunt et pugnant* CI 380.3.

colligamentum ~i, *neut.* A binding: AC 9895.

colligatio ~onis, *f.* A tying together as in bundles: *~ones bonorum et malorum* VR 38.3; a joining in association: *~o illa est qualis latronum* AC 7773.

colligo[1] ~are ~avi ~atum, *tr.* To fasten, tie: *veste... quam anterius ~abant rubini* AM 42.4.

colligo[2] ~ligere ~legi ~lectum, *tr.* **1** To bring together, collect, gather: *in quem [mundum]... ~liguntur omnes mortales* AM 2.2; *quod sciant [apes] ex...floribus ~ligere ceram* VR 12.7. **b** (pass.): (Bibl.) *~ligi ad patres*, to be gathered to one's fathers: AC 1854.1. **2** To take (a person) into one's home, welcome: *peregrinus fui et ~legistis Me* Matt. 25.35 (VI 2). **3** To deduce, infer: *ex illis ~legi quod de Deo...naturalem... ideam...foveas* VR 16.2.

collimatio ~onis, *f.* The action of aiming a weapon: DP 202.3.

collimo ~are ~avi ~atum, *intr.* To take aim (with a weapon): *si jaculator aut sclopetarius ~aret ad scopum* DP 333.3; (transf.) to aim: *quae varietates ad...unum amorem ~ant* VR 15.1.

collineo ~are ~avi, *intr.* To aim: *quod haec Ecclesia sit ad quam sicut ~arunt* [Worcester for *collinuarunt*; perh. read *collimarunt*] *omnes Ecclesiae* CN prologus.

colliquefio ~fieri ~factus sum, *intr.* To melt away: *~facti omnes habitatores Canaanis* Exod. 15.15 (AC).

colliquesco ~ere, *intr.* To become liquid, melt: *ut ~at cor* Ezek. 21.15 (AE 131.19).

collis ~is, *m.* A hill: AM 2.1.

collisio ~onis, *f.* A striking together, clash, conflict: *apparentiae pugnae et ~onis argumentorum* VR 77.1.

collisus ~us, *m.* A striking together (in quot., perh. w. ref. to the clicks of some African languages): *sermo eorum* [sc. *spirituum ex Africa*] *est conjunctus cum quodam ~u, quasi panni* ES 453.

colloco ~are ~avi ~atum, *tr.* To set (in a specified place), place: *quod extra velum... ~ata fuerint* VI 55.1; VR 79.2.

collocutio: see **colloquutio**.

colloquium ~i, *neut.* A conversation: AM 5.2; ES 226.

colloquor ~qui ~quutus (*or* ~cutus) sum, *intr.* To hold speech, converse: *~quuntur inter se* CI 377.

colloquutio ~onis, *f.* also **collocutio**. The action of speaking with, conversing: *~o cum Domino est per Verbum* AC 6752.9; (w. pl.) an instance of this, conversation: *velim ~ones illorum hic afferre* FI 41.

colludo ~dere ~si, *intr.* **1** To play together: *ibi pueri ... ~debant* AM 218.2. **2** To act together, harmonize: *in fine se conjungunt et ~dunt* [*duae opiniones*] VR 631.2. **3** To form a conspiracy, conspire: *quidam qui ~serat cum altero* ES 4701.

collum ~i, *neut.* The neck: *caput usque ad ~um* CI 65.

colluvies ~ei, *f.* A jumbled heap: *~es insectorum* AC 9331.2.

colluxatio ~onis, *f.* The dislocation (of a joint): AC 829.2.

collyra ~ae, *f.* (Gk.) A kind of cake: *~a ex squamis piscis* VR 453; Hos. 7.8 (AE 540.4).

collyrium ~i, *neut.* An ointment for the eyes, eyesalve: *quod sacerdotes parent ~a ex Verbo...quae super oculos...illinunt* VR 134.5.

colo ~ere ~ui cultum, *tr.* **1** To till (land): *secundum hominem qui illum* [sc. *hortum*] *~it* AC 225. **2** To pay divine honours to, worship: *qui naturam pro Deo... ~it* SS 1; *quomodo Divinum ~endum est* CI 319.1; *fides et charitas quibus Dominus ~itur* AC 6674.2. **3** To treat with deference, pay respect to: *pro inimicis reputando illos...qui illos non ~uerunt* ES 4587.

colochyntis: see **colocynthis**.

colocynthis ~idis, *f.* (Gk.) also **colochyntis**, **colychyntis**, and **colycinthis**. A bitter apple, colocynth: VR 148.1 (2 Kgs. 4.39).

colon ~i, *neut.* (Gk.) (perh. ~onis, *m.* ES 1062 J D Odhner) (anat.) The large intestine, colon: ES 1062.

colonus ~i, *m.* A tiller of the soil, husbandman, farm worker: AM 522.

color ~oris, *m.* A colour: *simile auro ex ~ore* VI 10.

coloratio ~onis, *f.* Colouring: AC 4530.

coloratus ~a ~um, *a.* (pf. pple. of **coloro**) Coloured: *aves pulcherrime ~as* VR 78.1; *instar arcus ~i* [i.e., a rainbow] AC 1043.1.

colorificatio ~onis, *f.* Colouring: *per avem similium ~onum* AC 7743.

colorificus ~a ~um, *a.* Producing colours: *variationes ~ae* AC 1625.

coloro ~are ~avi ~atum, *tr.* To colour: *~ando illam*

telam postea ex succis herbaceis TE 146; *~are fucis*, to colour with rouge; (transf.) to mispresent: *quod possent res cujusvis quaestionis ~are fucis, et eis inducere species secundum favorem* VR 332.2.

colubellus ~i, *m.* A small snake: VR 258.2.

coluber ~bri, *m.* A snake: *quoad pedes sicut ~bri* AM 231.5.

columba ~ae, *f.* A pigeon, dove: *emisit ~am...ad videndum* Gen. 8.8. (AC); AM 155[a].4.

columbarium ~i, *neut.* A dovecote: *sicut accipiter in ~o* VR 383.

columbus ~i, *m.* A male pigeon: CI 110.

columna ~ae, *f.* **1** An upright member of a building, pillar, column: *vincentem faciam ~am in templo Dei Mei* Rev. 3.12 (AR); (used as a platform) *stetit rex super ~a* 2 Kgs. 23.3 (AC 1038.5). **2** (transf.) Anything resembling a pillar: *~as fumi* Joel 2.30 (CI 570.2); *~a lucis* VR 159.2.

columnatim, *adv.* In the manner of a column: *~im perterebrans* ES 3218.

colychyntis: see **colocynthis**.

colycinthis: see **colocynthis**.

coma ~ae, *f.* (Gk.) The hair (of the head): AE 66.2 (Num. 6.5).

comaedum ~i, *neut.* (Gk.) also **comoedum**. A comedy: *tunc ~um eorum fit tragicum* VR 148.2.

comaedus ~i, *m.* (Gk.) also **commaedus**, **commoedus**, and **comoedus**. A comic actor, comedian: *spectacula ~orum super theatris* AM 17.5; VR 381.4; ES 4315.

comatus ~a ~um, *a.* Having the head covered in hair: *decenter ~i* AC 5247.1.

combinatio ~onis, *f.* A joining together, union: AE 802.1.

combino ~are ~avi ~atum, *tr.* To join together, unite, combine: *non potestis vos ~are in unum hominem eruditum* VR 17.2; (esp. in pf. pple.) *arbores... ~atae in transtra* CI 176; *vocum ~atarum seriebus* AC 607.2.

comburo ~rere ~ssi ~stum, *tr.* To destroy with fire, burn: *irruit in ignem et ~ritur* AM 365; (neut. pl. of pf. pple. as sb.) *~sta*, burnt objects: CI 571.

combustibilis ~is ~e, *a.* Easily set alight, combustible: *materiae ~es* AM 360.

combustio ~onis, *f.* Burning: *spiritu ~onis* Isa. 4.4 (AC 374.2).

comedo ~dere ~di ~stum (*or* ~sum), *tr.*, *intr.* also **commedo**. **1** (tr.) To eat: *adipem ~ditis* Ezek. 34.3 (AE 67.2); ES 2251. **b** (intr.): *delectant se diu ~dendo* ES 633. **2** (tr.) To consume, devour: (of fire) *ignis... ~det terram et proventum ejus* Deut. 32.22 (AC 1691.4); (of digestion) *escis non ~sis in ventriculis ruminatoriis* AE 242.4.

comes ~itis, *m.* **1** A companion: *duxit angelus ~ites suos...huc illuc* AM 8.3; (fig.) *sunt scientia et amor individui ~ites* VR 48.12. **2** A count: *in domo ~itis equestris ordinis* ES 4151.

comesio ~onis, *f.* The action of eating: *quomodo nunc ~o haec significat ~onem* 3AD 2485.

comessatio ~onis, *f.* also **commessatio**. A feast, banquet: *in voluptate ~onum* AR 952.2; *~ones ex sacrificiis* AE 141.1.

comestio ~onis, *f.* The action of eating, a meal: AC 4211.1.

cometes ~ae, *m.* (Gk.) A comet: *~ae cum longa cauda* VR 80.4.

comitas ~atis, *f.* Courtesy, graciousness: *ex... consortiis...amabilibus et ~ate plenis* AM 290.

comitatus ~us, *m.* An accompanying group of persons, retinue, entourage: AM 9.2; (of bees) VR 12.7.

comiter, *adv.* Pleasantly, courteously: *quod...uxores cum illis ~er loquantur* AM 292.1.

comitialis ~is, *m.* A member of a committee: IM 50.

comitium ~i, *neut.* A meeting, assembly: AM 112.

comitor ~ari ~atus sum, *tr.* **1** To go along with, accompany: *ille ~atus est nos extra atrium* VR 35.13. **2** (of things) To be present together with, accompany: *~ante innocentia* CI 279.

comma ~atis, *neut.* (Gk.) A mark of punctuation indicating the end of a phrase, comma: ES 2631.

commaedia: see **comoedia**.

commaedus: see **comaedus**.

commedo: see **comedo**.

commemoro ~are ~avi ~atum, *tr.* To relate, tell of: *~ate...aliqua de gaudiis ejus* AM 17.1.

commendo ~are ~avi ~atum, *tr.* To commit for safe keeping, entrust: *in manum Tuam ~o spiritum meum* Ps. 31.5 (DD 49).

commentatio ~onis, *f.* A piece of reasoning, argumentation: *ad illud confirmandum peculiari ~one non opus est* AM 181.

commentator ~oris, *m.* A recorder: *Joachus...~or* Isa. 36.22 (AC 4763.1).

commento ~are ~avi ~atum, *tr.* To comment on, discuss: *ex illis quae... ~ata sunt* VR 456.2.

commentum ~i, *neut.* A fabrication, fiction: AM 182.4.

commercium ~i, *neut.* **1** An exchange (of words): *cum quibus aliqua...intercesserunt ~a sermonis de statu* AC 448.1; *~um...loquelae* ES 164. **2** Social contact between persons, dealings with others: *~um... regnorum Europae...cum gentibus extra Ecclesiam* SS 108; *ut angeli unius coeli non sociare possint ~um cum angelis alterius* CI 37. **3** The mutual influence or interplay (of soul and body): *De ~o Animae et Corporis* CC titulus; AC 657; VR 154.6.

commessatio: see **comessatio**.

commilito ~are ~avi, *intr.* To serve as fellow soldiers, join in warlike activity: *quod sint socii qui ~ant* AC 6657.1.

comminatio ~onis, *f.* The act of threatening, threat: *~onem quod plene rejicerentur* DP 243.

comminor ~ari ~atus sum, *tr.* To threaten: *quod ~etur incolas regionis* ES 872.

comminuo ~ere ~i ~tum, *tr.* To break in pieces, crush: *frumentum...per molas ~itur in farinam* AC 7780; (transf.) *ut ~as populos multos* Mic. 4.13 (AC 7770.5).

commisceo ~scere ~scui ~xtum, *tr.* **1** To combine (substances), mix: *aurum ~xtum argento* VI 10. **2** To bring into close contact or relation, mix: *fibrae plures...inibi se ~scent* CI 212; (w. dat.) *si prophana sanctis ~sceant* AC 301; (w. *cum*) *quod non ~scerent vitam hanc novam...cum vita mala* AC 1000. **3** (Bibl.) To set (one man against another), embroil (with): *~scebo Aegyptum cum Aegypto* Isa. 19.2 (AC 6756.3).

commiseratio ~onis, *f.* The action of pitying, pity: AC 6737.

commiseror ~ari ~atus sum, *intr.* To feel pity: AC 6737.

committo ~mittere ~misi ~missum, *tr.* **1** To bring together, collect: *quod causae...in unum caput ~mittantur* AM 234. **2** To commit (a crime or offence): *tametsi non ~miserat homicidia, adulteria, furta* VI 63.2.

commixtio ~onis, *f.* The action of mixing together, mixing: *non per confusionem (alii, ~onem) substantiae* Sym. Ath. (DD 56); the quality of mixture: *aurum commixtum argento est...bonum secundum ~onem* VI 10.

commixtura ~ae, *f.* A mixture: *~a affectionum* AM 207.1.

commodato, *adv.* As a loan: *et quando ~o petiverat vir ex socio suo* Exod. 22.14 (AC).

commodo ~are ~avi ~atum, *tr.* To supply for payment, hire out: *propter lucrum ~are vera* AC 9210.4; *terminos ~atos ex arte methaphysica* VR 17.4.

commodum ~i, *neut.* An advantage: AM 320.2.

commodus ~a ~um, *a.* Of use, suitable, fit: [*sal*] *neque in terram neque in sterquilineum ~um est* Luke 14.35 (AC 9207.4).

commoedus: see **comaedus**.

commolitorius ~a ~um, *a.* Of milling or grinding: *sonus... ~us* ES 910.

commolo ~ere ~ui ~itum, *tr.* To grind up: *scorpiones ~iti* ES 3913; *ut...quasi ~at illum* [*amorem*] *in pulverem* AM 509.

commonefacio ~facere ~feci ~factum, *tr.* To remind, advise: *Ille... ~faciet vos de omnibus quae dixi* John 14.26 (AC 6788); ES 546.

commoneo ~nere ~nui ~nitum, *tr.* To point out consequences firmly, warn: *postquam illi qui ibi visitati, informati et ~niti sunt...usque permanent in suis malis* AR 515.

commonstro ~are ~avi ~atum, *tr.* To make known, reveal: *illa quae vidistis... ~ant adventum Domini* ME 18.

commoratio ~onis, *f.* A period of time spent in a place, stay: *per ~onem in Aegypto* VR 19.1; *ante ~onem trium dierum* AM 9.2.

commoror ~ari ~atus sum, *intr.* To remain in a place, stay: *in hunc collem, ubi tu ~aris* AM 2.1; *~antur...una* CI 494.

commotio ~onis, *f.* **1** A violent movement, stir: *audivi... ~onem sub planta pedis* ES 2662. **b** (Bibl.) *~o viscerum*, a movement of the bowels (as an expression of compassion): Isa. 63.15 (AC 1803.3). **2** An emotion (of the mind): *~onem animi eorum percipere datum est* CI 325.

commoveo ~vere ~vi ~tum, *tr.* **1** To move violently, shake: *num propter hoc non ~veatur terra* Amos 8.8 (AC 6693.5); *~vebar per totum corpus* ES 228. **2** To disturb, upset: *virtutes caelorum ~vebuntur* Matt. 24.29 (SS 112). **3** To excite emotionally, rouse: *interius ~ti sunt* CI 325; (w. *ad*) *misericordia, ad quam Deum... credunt... ~veri* CI 526.1.

commune ~is, *neut.*: see **communis**.

communicabilis ~is ~e, *a.* Capable of being shared or communicated: *ut omnia bona sint ~ia* AC 1388.

communicans ~ntis, *m.* (pres. pple. of **communico**) One who takes Holy Communion, communicant: VR 722.3.

communicatio ~onis, *f.* A means of communicating, communication: *quod... ~o facta sit cum caelis* SS 64; *omnes spiritus... ~onem habent cum coelo* CI 294.

communicativus ~a ~um, *a.* Serving for the purpose of communication: *alioquin non foret verbum ~um cum angelis* AE 98.5; *perceptiones ~ae* AC 685.

communicator ~oris, *m.* One who communicates, communicator: ES 2552.

communicatorius ~a ~um, *a.* Serving for communication: *in ~o illo loco* ES 4969.

communico ~are ~avi ~atum, *tr., intr.* **1** To impart a share of, share: *Divinam sapientiam... ~atam illis qui in amore...sunt* AE 149; *cum quibus ~ari potuit sermo* ES 293; (absol.) *amor talis est ut velit cum altero, quem...amat, ~are* AM 180. **2** To pass on, transmit, communicate (information): *ut... ~entur omnia quae norunt* AC 6813; *velim ~are quae ab angelo...audivi* FI 41. **3** (intr.) To be in communication: *ita scientia cognitionum fidei est distincta a scientia rerum naturalium ut vix ~ent* AC 1198; to serve as means of communication: *Verbum per illum sensum ~at cum caelis* SS 5.

communio ~onis, *f.* **1** The fact of having in common, sharing: *pro principio habent omnium ~onem, sic etiam uxorum* ES 2867. **2** Communion, partnership: *in plena ~one agunt* AM 441. **3** The state of being in communication, contact: *quod hic amor in ~onem secum ferat omnes supradictos sensus* AM 210; *ille in ~one sanctorum in terris est* VR 15.1. **4** *Sancta ~o*, Holy Communion: AR 531.5. **5** The generality of people, crowd: *amat... ~o inerudita imagines* VR 80.3; *~o plebeja* VR 159.5.

communis ~is ~e, *a.* (compar. *~ior*, superl. *~issimus*) **1** Shared between two or more parties, held in common: *quid sol... ~e habet cum regimine...?* VR 12.8; (neut. as sb.) something in common: *idea...spiritualis...non ~e habet cum spatio* VR 30.1. **2** Belonging to the community at large, common, general: *a ~i bono est bonum singulis* CI 418; (neut. as sb.) the common interest: *student sibi et mundo, raro ~i et coelo* AC 946. **3** Commonly found, common, ordinary: *quod aquae significent cognitiones..., ~issimum est in Verbo* AC 28; *in ~i sermone* AC 671; (neut. as sb.) *~e ex jugi licito* AM 256. **4** Generally shared, universal (as opposed to particular): *hae sphaerae sunt ~es, pariter sunt sphaerae particulares* AC 6657.1; (neut. as sb.) that which is universal, a general principle, generalization: *differt...ut ~e a particulari* CI 140; *cum dicuntur ~ia, intelliguntur etiam particularia quae sub illis et in illis* AC 8276; *in ~i*, in general: *vita hominis in ~i* DD 46.7. **5** *Sensus ~is*, common sense: *ex confusione boni et veri per philosophica; quibus inde minus sensus ~is* AC 5556. **6** Lacking detail or precision, general: *bonum quod influit fit ~e, ita obscurum* AC 6775; *quo ~ius aliquid est, eo minus percipit singularia* AC 6686.

communitas ~atis, *f.* A whole composed of various parts, partnership: [*si*] *non penderet ~as eorum* [sc. *omnium in corpore*] *ab uno corde et pulmone* VR 679.1.

communiter, *adv.* (superl. *~nissime*) **1** In a general way, without details: *ex quibus ~niter quid bonum et verum illis nosse datum* AC 597.2; AC 272. **2** As a general rule, commonly: *quod ~niter vocatur resurrectio* CI 447; *circulationes istae mirabiliores sunt quam usquam aliquis ~nissime comprehendere capax sit* ES 2730.

commuto ~are ~avi ~atum, *tr.* To change completely, turn: *quod totus Adam...in deterius ~atus fuerit* Council of Trent in SE 3(a); *si...quis negat liberum arbitrium in spiritualibus... ~at liberum spirituale in liberum mere naturale* VR 494.

comoedia ~ae, *f.* also **commaedia**. Comedy: ES Index ii s.v. 'comoedus, comoedia' (p. 22 Tafel).

comoedum: see **comaedum**.

comoedus: see **comaedus**.

comosus ~a ~um, *a.* Abounding in foliage, leafy: *'mons Seir'...significat tale, nempe ~um* AC 3527.2.

compages ~is, *f.* A composite structure: *cerebrum... erat ~es ex...sphaerulis contiguis* SA 78 (= iii.4); AM 361.1; *serteae ~es ornatissimae* ES 4354.

compaginatio ~onis, *f.* A fastening together, combination: *in... ~onibus, confasciationibus et congregationibus* AS 190; CC 13.

compagino ~are ~avi ~atum, *tr.* To fit together, interlace: *portam ex ramis... ~atis exstructam* AM 8.1; CI 212.

compar ~aris, *a.* Matching, corresponding: *cupido cum ejus ~are scientia* DP 96.4; (masc. or fem. as sb.) a partner, mate, match: *ex illa unione...cum suo ~ari foemina nascatur* AM 173; *ex quodam instinctu cognoscant, quod sint ~res* AM 229.

comparabilis ~is ~e, *a.* Admitting comparison, comparable: *aurum...quod cum bono Pharisaico ~e est* VI 10.

comparatio ~onis, *f.* **1** The process of comparing one thing with another, comparison: *illustrari haec possunt per ~onem cum arbore* FI 16. **2** (w. pl.)

An instance of comparing, comparison: *apparentiae veri, ac sicut similitudines et ~ones* SS 40.1; VR 48.10. **3** Acquisition: *hic...agitur de ~one seu addicatione scientificorum* AC 4968.

comparative, *adv.* As or by a comparison: *se habet voluntarium sicut ~e flamma* CI 32.

comparativus ~a ~um, *a.* (neut. as sb.) A thing instanced by way of comparison: *Dominus...non per repraesentativa et significativa ita loquutus est, sed per ~a* AC 4424.1; CI 270.2.

compareo ~rere ~rui, *intr.* To become manifest, appear: *historica...qualia in sensu literae ~rent* AC 66.2.

comparitio ~onis, *f.* A manifestation, appearance: *comparent [affectiones] in umbra, quae ~o non ita persuadet* 3AD 2999.

comparo ~are ~avi ~atum, *tr.* **1** To obtain for oneself, acquire, get: *qui aedificat domum, primum ~at sibi materias ad illam* VR 152; *intellectus non ~ari potest nisi per scientias et cognitiones* AC 1555.3. **2** To liken, compare: (w. dat.) *quod coelum... ~etur conjugio* CI 371.

compasco ~pascere, *intr.* (of beasts) To feed together: *quod recubare et ~pascere queant [mali spiritus] cum iis qui sunt fideles, secundum Es.xi. 4-7* ES 154 titulus.

compello ~pellere ~puli ~pulsum, *tr.* To compel, force, constrain: *sicut singulatim unamquamque personam Deum et Dominum confiteri Christiana veritate ~pellimur, ita tres Deos aut tres Dominos dicere Catholica Religione prohibemur* Sym. Ath. (VR 172.1).

compendiarius ~a ~um, *a.* Shortened: *per viam ~am* 'by a quick route' ES 1021.

compendium ~i, *neut.* An abridged form, compendium: *ut aliquid in brevi ~o...dicatur* AM 61.

compenso ~are ~avi ~atum, *tr.* To make up for, compensate: *~abo vobis annos quos consumsit locusta* Joel 2.25 (AR 447).

comperio ~rire ~rii ~rtum, *tr.*, *intr.* (pf. act. also *~rui* ES 180) **1** To acquire knowledge of, learn (a fact): *quod manifeste ~rui dum expergefactus* ES 180; ES 3068; (w. *quod*) *~ries quod ne hilum credant* AC 3865.2. **2** (pass. as dep.): *~rtus sum quod...* VR 19.2; (impers.) *~rtum est quod interiora...clausa sint* CI 313.

compes ~edis, *m.* A fetter: Ps. 105.18 (AE 448.16).

compesco ~ere ~ui, *tr.* To restrain, control, check: *furorem ~ere et violentiam domare* VR 84.

competo ~ere ~ivi ~itum, *intr.* (w. dat.) To be appropriate (to): *cui nulla alia attributa ~unt* AC 1735.1; AC 8263.

compilo ~are ~avi ~atum, *tr.* To put together from various sources, compile: *~arunt fidem imputativam meriti* VR 489.1; ES 1605.

compingo ~pingere ~pegi ~pactum, *tr.* **1** To compress, confine: *vir...qui in tonnam... ~pingebat humanam carnem* ES 2615; *de illis quae in unam vocem ~pinguntur* AE 102.2. **b** to make by pressing, mould: *~pingunt illam [sc. ceram] in varias formas* VR 184. **2** To compose, construct: *falsa...quae Judaei... ~pegerunt ex sensu literae Verbi* AE 540.6.

compitum ~i, *neut.* A crossroads: *in vicis et ~is* ES 420.

complacentia ~ae, *f.* Pleasure, liking: *num ~a Jehovae in holocaustis et sacrificiis...?* 1 Sam. 15.22 (AC 922.3).

complaceo ~cere ~cui, *intr.* (impers.) It pleases: (w. dat.) *Filius Meus dilectus, in quo ~cuit Mihi* Matt. 3.17 (DD 19.10).

complacitum ~i, *neut.* = **beneplacitum**: Gen. 49.6 (AC 4433.3).

complano ~are ~avi ~atum, *tr.* To make smooth or level: *~ate in solitudine semitam Deo nostro* Isa. 40.3 (VR 81.1).

complaudo: see **complodo**.

complector ~cti ~xus sum, *tr.* **1** To grasp with the mind, embrace: *plura quam homo potest... ~cti et effari* AE 17. **2** To include, embrace: *infernum ~ctitur omnes istos, qui se reges...universi appellant* 4AD Isa. 14.9.

complementum ~i, *neut.* Fulfilment, completion: *mors est ~um ejus [sc. hominis]* AE 128; AM 44.8.

compleo ~lere ~levi ~letum, *tr.* **1** To make up to a sufficient number, complete the tale of: *usque dum ~lentur et conservi eorum* Rev. 6.11 (AR). **2** To bring to fulfilment: *requisita, quae promovent et ~lent illum [sc. amorem conjugialem]* AM 295.2.

completus ~a ~um, *a.* (pf. pple. of **compleo**) Complete, finished: *quod in omni re ~a sit trinum* SS 28.

complexus ~us, *m.* A composite structure, complex: *quod mundus sit ~us usuum* VR 13.2; *in [suo] ~u*, taken as a whole: *amor...qui in suo ~u vocatur amor conjugialis* AM 188.1; *omnia vera et bona...in ~u* AE 9.1.

complico ~are ~avi ~atum, *tr.* To fold or wind together, interweave: *sedilia formata ex... ~atis propaginibus arborum* AM 13.2; to clasp (one's hands in an attitude of prayer): *~abant manus et simul susurrabant laudem votivam ad Dominum* AM 16.1.

complodo ~dere ~si ~sum, *tr.*, *intr.* also **complaudo**.

(tr.) To clap (the hands): *~serunt palmas* VR 137.3; (intr.) to clap (with the hands): *arbores agri ~dent vola* Isa. 55.12 (AC 795.4).

complosio ~onis, *f.* A knocking together, clapping: *per horum* [sc. *pedum*]...*~ones* CO 30.

compono ~nere ~sui ~situm, *tr.* **1** To make out of parts or ingredients, compound: *cur non ex elementis...* [*Deus*] *~suit corpus* VR 90.1; (pass.) to be composed (of): *spiritus ejus formatur et ~nitur ex illis quae homo cogitat et vult* AE 86; (also, of parts) to make up, compose: *sunt innumerabilia quae ~nunt* [*hepar*] ES 2216. **2** To modify, compose (one's expression): *~nit faciem ad devotionem* CI 531.1.

comporto ~are ~avi ~atum, *tr.* To collect by transporting, bring together, amass: *quod lateres, argillae, arenae, lapides...~entur non in eo ordine quo construenda domus* AC 6487; *omnem praedam...~abis in medium plateae* Deut. 13.16 (AC 9193.1).

compos ~otis, *a.* (w. gen.) In control of, capable of: *ut homo...amplius nullius ~os esset* ES 2043; *sui ~os*, in control of oneself: CI 527.

compositio ~onis, *f.* A putting together, composition: *malorum...mera congeries et ~o* AC 761; *ex... concinnitate ~onis vocum* AM 175.3.

compositor ~oris, *m.* A writer, composer: *Proverbiorum ~ores* SS 103.2.

compositus ~a ~um, *a.* (pf. pple. of **compono**) (compar. *~ior*) Made up of several parts or members, collective, composite: *de...societate, quae homo ~us ...vocatur* AC 1030.2; *a singulis minimis ad ~iora* ES 1112; (of numbers) AC 487.2; *in ~o,* taken as a group: *soni...in simplici et in ~o* AE 323.11.

comprehendo ~dere ~di ~sum, *tr.* **1** To seize hold of, grasp, clutch: *persequar hostes meos, et ~dam eos* Ps. 18.37 (DD 14.6). **2** To grasp with the mind, comprehend: *quod qui universalia scit, postea possit ~dere singularia* AM 261.2; (w. *quod*) *quod ita se res habeat, nequaquam possunt ~dere* AC 6639.3. **3** (of words or ideas) To include, take in: *infinitas ~dit et immensitatem et aeternitatem* VR 27.

comprehensibilis ~is ~e, *a.* Capable of being grasped mentally, comprehensible: *adorant Divinum... ut ~e per humanam formam* AC 6700.

comprehensibiliter, *adv.* In such a way as to be readily comprehended or understood, comprehensibly: *si...providentia visibiliter et ~er ageret, discrimen foret* AC 5508.2.

comprehensio ~onis, *f.* **1** The action of being taken together, grouping, summary: *in summaria ~one* AM 130.4. **2** Comprehension: *supra sphaeram ~onis hominis* AC 3404.2.

compressio ~onis, *f.* Compression: *~o a cingulo acuto* AC 7810; *sensu ~onis et attractionis durae* ES 2248.

comprimo ~rimere ~ressi ~ressum, *tr.* (compar. of pf. pple. *~ressiores*) **1** To press together: *~rimere labia* VR 111.2. **2** To restrain, suppress: *ut nescirent... quomodo ~rimerent corpus* CI 400.3; *~ressos pectore* AM 9.2. **3** To ravish (a woman): *quod qui ~ressit virginem dotem daret* AC 4444.3.

comprobo ~are ~avi ~atum, *tr.* To prove (a fact): *veritas propositionis ita ~ata est* VR 48.9.

comptus: see **comtus**.

computo ~are ~avi ~atum, *tr.* To calculate, reckon: *~et numerum bestiae* Rev. 13.18 (AR).

computresco ~rescere ~rui, *intr.* To become rotten, rot: Exod. 16.20 (AC).

computus ~i, *m.* A calculation, reckoning: AC 487.2.

comtus ~a ~um, *a.* also **comptus**. Well-arranged, dressed: *ex crinibus quasi ~is* ES 5925.

conamen ~inis, *neut.* An effort, endeavour: *in... singulis ~inibus voluntatis* AC 1040.2.

conatus ~us, *m.* An attempt, effort: *omnis ~us eorum est malum* AC 986.3; *sphaera communis ~uum ab inferno* AC 6657.1; (w. gen.) *~us producendi fructum* FI 16; *~us subjugationis* AC 6800.

concatenatus ~a ~um, *a.* Joined as in a chain, linked: *corollis...simul ~is* ES 166; AS 392.

concateno ~are ~avi ~atum, *tr.* To join together as in a chain: *quae series cum ~atur* ES 4578.

concedo ~dere ~ssi ~ssum, *tr., intr.* **1** To allow, permit: (w. dat.) *qui uxoribus ~dunt licentiam* AM 376; (impers. pass.) *ei ~ditur* AC 139; (w. inf.) *cum illis loqui ~ditur* AC 6695; (w. *ut*) *~ssum erat a Domino ut venirent* AC 7252. **2** (w. *quod*) To grant, concede (a proposition): *~do quod formae...ab aethere...formatae fuerint* VR 79.6. **3** (intr.) To yield ground, retreat, withdraw: *~ssit in Aegyptum* Matt. 2.14 (AC 1462.6).

concelebro ~are ~avi ~atum, *tr.* To join in praising: *sanctorum...Jehovam Deum ~antium* 1AD 317.

concelo ~are ~avi ~atum, *tr.* To hide, conceal: *quae in propheticis Verbi sub figuris ~ata sunt* VR 123.2.

concento ~are ~avi, *intr.* To sing or howl together: *quod...discorditer ~ent* [*dracones, ululae*] VR 133.1.

concentratio ~onis, *f.* The direction of mental powers to a single object or an instance of this, concentration:

ut servire possint [*spiritus*] *pro subjectis ~onum* ES 400.

concentro ~are ~avi ~atum, *tr.* **1** To bring into a narrow compass, concentrate: *potuisset universum illud...super uno apice capilli ~ari* VR 29.2. **2** To direct (mental powers or emotions) to a single object, concentrate: *haec mentem quasi ~at* ES 769; *qui...non illam* [sc. *ideam*] *in Domino unam fecerunt et ~averunt* CI 2; *quod...dum sola uxor amatur, amor ~etur* AM 161.3.

concentus ~us, *m.* **1** Concord of sounds, harmony: *in loquela angelica est quidam ~us* CI 242. **2** Agreement (of other things): *illae* [sc. *jucunditates*]...*fluunt...ex ~u et harmonia plurium concordantium* CI 56.

conceptibilis ~is ~e, *a.* Capable of being imagined, conceivable: *in Divino prorsus non ~e est aliquid amoris sui* AC 5957.

conceptio ~onis, *f.* The act of conceiving, conception:VR 88.

conceptor ~oris, *m.* One who devises a concept, framer, inventor: *~ores Symboli Athanasiani* VR 110.3.

conceptus ~us, *m.* **1** That which is conceived, foetus: *~us...et partus Ecclesiae...nominati sunt filii* AC 489.1. **2** A mental idea, concept: *qui nullum ~um de vita...post mortem habent* AC 1053.2.

concerno ~ere, *tr.* To be concerned with: *omnia statuta...quae cultum et vitam illorum ~ebant* SS 20.2; *quod ~it,* as concerns, as regards: AC 7248; VR 55.

concha ~ae, *f.* (Gk.) **1** A mollusc, shellfish: *captavi rhombos et ~as* VR 381.3. **2** A seashell: *simulachrum... cum magna ~a...in manu* VR 803. **3** The shell of a tortoise or similar animal: VR 443.3.

conchilium ~i, *neut.* (Gk. *konkhulion*) also **conchylium**. A seashell: *testae...rutilae sicut ~a* AM 364; AM 380.2; AM 443.

conchylium: see **conchilium**.

concidentia ~ae, *f.* A collapse: *~a artuum in confinio...ita ubi genua* AC 5323.1.

concido[1] ~ere ~i, *intr.* To fall down or in ruins, collapse: *quod...muri Jerichuntis ~erunt* VI 59; (transf.) *numne...vitalis expansio faciei ~erit* AM 207.3.

concido[2] ~dere ~di ~sum, *tr.* To cut up: *vituli quem ~derunt in duas* Jer. 34.18 (AE 279.7).

conciliabulum ~i, *neut.* A meeting, assembly: *in Conciliis et ~is...ante Nicaenum* VR 503.1.

concilio ~are ~avi ~atum, *tr.* **1** To procure, obtain: *scientia correspondentiarum...~avit nobis intelligentiam* AM 76.4. **2** To reconcile (ideas): *num aliter ~ari possunt...?* DP 191.2.

concilium ~i, *neut.* A meeting, council: VR 16.3; esp. one of the Councils of the Church: *~um Nicaenum* VR 94.2; *edicta omnium ~orum* VI 27.

concinne, *adv.* (compar. *~ius*) Smartly, neatly: *per crines decoros et ~e positos* AC 3301.1; ES 3757.

concinnitas ~atis, *f.* Smartness, neatness: *ex elegantia et ~ate compositionis vocum* AM 175.3.

concinno ~are ~avi ~atum, *tr.* To make, construct (any regular structure): *ad ~andum varia quae operarum muliebrium sunt* AM 370; to compose, compile (literary works, speeches, etc.): *cum...praedicationes ~arent et elimarent* VI 7; AC 1756.2; ES 805.

concinnus ~a ~um, *a.* (compar. *~ior*) Smart, neat, elegant: *~o verborum nexu* ES 424.

concino ~ere ~ui, *tr.* To join in singing: *uxores... quae ~ebant cantilenam* AM 55.1.

concio ~onis, *f.* also **contio**. **1** A meeting, assembly: *loquere ad universam ~onem filiorum Israelis* Lev. 19.2 (AE 204.8). **2** An address given to a meeting, sermon, speech: *finite ~ones* AM 9.2; VR 134.1.

concionata ~orum, *neut. pl.* also **cont-**. Preachings, sermons: *recitaturi ~a* AM 9.1.

concionator ~oris, *m.* also **cont-**. A preacher: VR 381.2.

concionor ~ari ~atus sum, *intr.* also **cont-**. To preach: *dum ex zelo ~antur* VR 146.

concipio ~cipere ~cepi ~ceptum, *intr.*, *tr.* **1** (of women or female animals) To conceive: (intr.) *virgo ~cipiet* Isa. 7.14 (DD 6); (pass., of offspring) *Dominus ... ~ceptus...erat a Jehovah* AE 31.8. **2** (w. reference to regeneration): *quomodo spiritualis homo e novo ~cipitur* CI 269.3. **3** To form in the mind, conceive (ideas): *a jucundis mali...quae ~cepit et parturivit apud se* VR 14.3; cf. VR 37.3.

concisus ~a ~um, *a.* Terse, concise: [*stylus propheticus*] *tam ~us est, ut nisi suppleantur, sensus inde non possit elici* 3AD 7704.

concito ~are ~avi ~atum, *a.* To stir up, arouse: *universalia mentis ~ant* ES 866.

concivis ~is, *m.* A fellow citizen: *quod...amet patriam, ~es, proximum* AM 34.

conclamatio ~onis, *f.* The sounding of an alarm: AC 3708.15 (Num. 10.6).

conclamo ~are ~avi ~atum, *tr.* To shout out, cry: *~a et convoca sapientissimos* AM 2.2; to sound the alarm: *quod quando venirent in bellum... ~arent tubis* Num. 10.9 (AR 397.1).

conclave ~is, *neut.* **1** A private room with lock and key (as opp. to *atria*, more accessible areas of the house): *super mensa in quodam ~i, quod illico conclusit, et porrexit mihi clavem* AM 43; *~ia seu penetralia* AC 3900.6. **2** An apartment or suite of rooms with a single key: *distribue cuivis suum ~e cum suo cubiculo* AM 11. **3** (transf.) Any room: *in arcto ~i* AC 788.2; *sicut quis per fores intrat in ~e* CC 19.

conclavium ~i, *neut.* = **conclave**, sense 1: *effugiunt ...in ~um* AM 512.1.

concludo ~dere ~si ~sum, *tr.*, *intr.* **1** To confine, shut up: *~sit illos ad custodiam* Gen. 42.17 (AC); to lock up (a room): *in quodam conclavi quod... ~sit* AM 43. **2** To place under restraint, subject (to): *quod Deus... ~serit illud* [sc. *genus humanum*] *sub damnatione universali* VR 132.1. **b** (w. *ab*) to prevent (from): *~sit me Jehovah a pariendo* Gen. 16.2 (AC). **3** To arrive at a conclusion, infer: *quod ratio humana... ~dere possit quod Deus sit* VR 5; (impers. pass.) *ex supradictis possit ~di quod...* SS 32; (w. indir. qu.) *ex his... ~di... potest, num homo sit Christianus* VI 77. **4** (of facts) To lead to a conclusion, prove: *haec omnia ~dunt quod Divinum...sit Humanum* CI 78. **5** To decide: *conclusio et rei ~sae exequutio* AC 5124.1.

conclusio ~onis, *f.* An inference, conclusion: *~o cogitationis seu responsum* AC 2552; *quae judicii sunt et ~onum ex cognitionibus* AC 6814.

conclusum ~i, *neut.* An inference, conclusion: *~um ex his sequitur quod...* VI 52; *ut ex ventilatis fieret ~um* AM 134.6.

concomitantia ~ae, *f.* The coexistence of the body and the blood of the Lord in both elements of the Holy Supper (asserted by the Council of Trent), concomitance: *quod...corpus* [*contineatur*] *sub specie vini, et sanguis sub specie panis, ac anima sub utraque, vi naturalis connexionis et ~ae* AR 795.

concordantia ~ae, *f.* The assonance or harmony (of sounds): *~as articulationis sonorum in loquelis* AM 440; agreement, concord: *correspondentiam et ~am externi hominis cum interno* AC 1568.3.

concordia ~ae, *f.* Agreement, concord: *~a oris nihil est cum discordia cordis* AC 1322; *Formula ~ae*: see **formula**.

concorditer, *adv.* Agreeably, in harmony (with): *ad cogitandum ~er et congrue suo amori* VR 571.1.

concordo ~are ~avi, *intr.* To be in agreement, harmonize: *recipit omnia vera quae ~ant* AE 6; (w. *cum*) *unanimitas...non ~at cum unitate Dei* VR 25.2; (w. dat.) *quod omnia... ~ent sapientiae eorum* CI 266.2.

concors ~rdis, *a.* **1** Of agreeable sound, harmonious: *instrumentis non ~rdibus sed rudis soni* ES 887. **2** Of agreeable nature, fitting, suitable: *inclinatio... ~rs et sympathica* AM 47[a]; (w. *cum*) *respirationem... ~rdem et similem cum respiratione angelorum* AC 805.2; (w. dat.) *illa in ordinem ~rdem universali...reducere* VR 56.1.

concredo ~ere ~idi ~itum, *tr.* To entrust, confide: *~imus maritis arcana* AM 155[a].3; CI 564.3.

concreo ~are ~avi ~atum, *tr.* To create as an original part of (human beings): *quod...sit totalis carentia seu privatio ~atae in paradiso justitiae originalis seu imaginis Dei* Book of Concord in VR 464.10.

concresco ~scere ~vi, *intr.* To grow together, coalesce: *dum ~scere incipiunt partes* ES 242.

concretus ~a ~um, *a.* **1** Solidified: *musta vinorum ~a* AM 14.2. **2** (neut. as sb.) *In ~o,* concretely: VR 156.1.

concubina ~ae, *f.* A concubine: *non sum amplius uxor, sed ~a* AM 216.3.

concubinatus ~us, *m.* Concubinage: AM 251.

concubitus ~us, *m.* A lying together: *venerunt ad illam...ad ~um amorum* Ezek. 23.17 (AE 141.4).

concubus ~a ~um, *a.* Lying together: *faemina... ~a spondae conjugialis* AM 465.

conculcatio ~onis, *f.* A trampling: *dies tumultus et ~onis* Isa. 22.5 (AC 1292.3).

conculco ~are ~avi ~atum, *tr.* To crush underfoot, trample upon: *quod...projecerit eum in terram et ~averit eum* Dan. 8.7 (FI 65); ES 2801.

concumbo ~mbere ~bui, *intr.* (w. *cum*) To lie (with) carnally: *ut...non ~mbat cum alterius uxore* AC 5060.3.

concupiscentia ~ae, *f.* A strong desire, lust, concupiscence: *~ae carnis* AE 182.3; *adulteria, furta...cum ~a ad illa* VI 62 titulus.

concupisco ~scere ~vi ~tum, *tr.* To desire strongly, lust for, covet: *homo... ~scit honores* AM 267.2; (neut. pl. of pf. pple. as sb.) *~ta*, things desired: *paret ~tis ex sensibus, et nondum desideriis ex mente elimata* AM 299.

concurro ~rere ~ri ~sum, *intr.* **1** To run together: *in globo ~rerunt ad portas* AM 9.2. **2** (transf.) To come rapidly together, be united: *quod in una cogitatione... ~rant...myriades influentiae* ES 237. **3** To act together: (w. *cum*) *cum aguntur* [*affectiones*] *ut ~rant cum interiore homine* AC 1713; (w. *ad*) *musculi et fibrae motrices ad unam actionem ~rent* ES 1760. **4** To be in agreement, concur: *Deus...nunquam aliter ~rit cum tentationibus* AC 2768.2.

concursus ~us, *m.* A coming together, coincidence: *per reactionem et ~um actionis* ES 635.

concussio ~onis, *f.* A shaking, disturbance: *Ecclesiae ~ones* AR 711.

concutio ~tere ~ssi ~ssum, *tr.* To cause to tremble, shake: *~tietur terra e loco suo* Isa. 13.13 (AE 304.5).

condemnatio ~onis, *f.* Condemnation: *de salvatione et de ~one hominis* CI 471.

condemno ~are ~avi ~atum, *tr.* **1** To condemn (in a court of law): *a senioribus comprehensus et ~atus* DD 16.5. **2** To condemn to hell, damn: *haec mala ~ant* AC 7272.3; *~ari propter statum vitae* AE 222.6.

condensatio ~onis, *f.* The action of making dense: *~onem falsi ex malo* AC 8197.1.

condensatus ~a ~um, *a.* Thickened, thick: *nubes nigra et ~a secundum gradum mali* CI 549.

condenso ~are ~avi ~atum, *a.* To thicken, make dense: [*mali spiritus*] *confirmant ea quae perversa sunt, et ~ant sic umbras* 4AD Jer. 5.6.

condescendentia ~ae, *f.* Deference: AC 4755.

condescendo ~dere ~si, *intr.* To show oneself complaisant, defer: *ad externa filiorum Jacobi ~debat* AC 4472; AC 6954.

condicio: see **conditio**.

condignus ~a ~um, *a.* Worthy; *ex ~o*, in accordance with worth: SE 14(l) (Book of Concord).

condimentum ~i, *neut.* A seasoning (used as a medicine): VR 665.6.

condio ~dire ~dii ~ditum, *tr.* **1** To flavour, season: *mel pro ~diendis cibis* CI 108.1. **2** To embalm (a corpse): *odor...cadaveris ~diti* AC 175.

conditio ~onis, *f.* also **condicio**. **1** State of being, condition: *talis est ~o hominis quod...* AC 933.3. **2** Social rank, status, condition: *foeminae...ex sordida et vili ~one divites factae* AC 944; also, high rank: *qui ~onis homines fuerunt* ES 2120.

conditura ~ae, *f.* **1** A seasoned food, sweetmeat: *parvis pyramidibus cum ~is* AM 6.2. **2** The embalming (of a corpse): *~ae fiebant ut corpus praeservaretur a putredine* AC 6503.

condo ~ere ~idi ~itum, *tr.* **1** To construct, build: *sciunt apes... ~ere cellulas ex cera* CI 108.1; *ex his ~it* [*Deus*] *caelum* VR 74.5. **2** To devise, construct, frame (an idea): *ad ~endum doctrinam in qua mere falsa* AE 453.12; *~ere hypotheses* AS 394.

condoleo ~lere ~lui, *intr.* To share grief, condole (with): *quis ~leat tibi?* Isa. 51.19 (AE 386.5).

condonatio ~onis, *f.* The pardoning (of sins): *~o peccatorum* AC 10042.5.

condono ~are ~avi ~atum, *intr.* (w. dat.) To grant pardon (to): *non ~abo illis* FI 44; *cui urbi ~atum* AC 1188.2; (pass., of sins) to be pardoned: *qui credunt peccata ~ari posse ab hominibus* AC 7272.3.

conducibilis ~is ~e, *a.* Tending to one's good, beneficial, fitting, suitable: *quod non sciat* [*infans*]... *alimoniam sibi ~em* VR 48.8.

conduco ~cere ~xi ~ctum, *tr.*, *intr.* **1** (tr.) To hire: Gen. 30.16 (AC); 1 Sam. 2.5 (AE 386.23); to make conducive, prepare: *non opus habent...dapibus ut emant, aut ~cant* ES 2449. **2** (intr.) To be of use or advantage, be suitable, conduce: *quod tantum recipiant quantum ~cit* CI 278.1; (w. *ad*) *ad quem* [*sensum*] *concinnandum unaquaevis vox...~cit* SS 13.4; (w. dat.) *cum tamen...*[*veritates*] *~cant tantum confirmandis...veritatibus spiritualibus* ES 2634.

condus ~i, *m.* A storehouse, store: *ex meo promo et ~o aperiam mentem* AM 315.9.

confabulatio ~onis, *f.* A conversation, chat: *suavissimae ~ones* AM 3.2.

confabulor ~ari ~atus sum, *intr.* To converse, chat: *~ari de rebus mundi* CI 358; to speak in myths: *ex fonte de quo vetusti ~ati sunt* AM 182.2.

confaederatio ~onis, *f.* also **confoederatio**. An alliance: CO 50.

confaedero ~are ~avi ~atum, *tr.* also **confoedero**. To join in alliance: *primaria quae ~ant, consociant et in unum congregant animas* AM 176.

confarcio ~cire ~si ~ctum, *tr.* (pf. pple. also *~tum* AS 315) To make by cramming together, throw together: *sic dissolvuntur societates spirituum male ~ctae* AC 842.2; cf. ES 2122; *concordiae in domibus ~ciantur* [*consarciantur* Rogers] *propter necessitates* AM 283; to join by cramming, string together: *~ciunt illa...cum vocibus* AR 417.8.

confarctio ~onis, *f.* A cramming together: ES(M) [4814].

confasciatio ~onis, *f.* A tying together: DP 180.4.

confasciculatio ~onis, *f.* A bunching: *altera substantia...constat ex perpetuis ~onibus fibrillarum* VR 351.3.

confasciculatus ~a ~um, *a.* Bunched together: ES 2867.

confascio ~are ~avi ~atum, *tr.* To bind together,

tie: *ut plurimum externa ~ant illos* AM 320.3; *paradoxa... ~ata sicut in unum fasciculum* SE 56.

confectio ~onis, *f.* A putting together, making: *ad ~onem suffitus* AC 10177.11 (Autograph).

confectus ~a ~um: pf. pple. of **conficio**.

confero ~rre contuli collatum, *tr.* **1** To bring together: *nomina locorum et personarum collata* SS 51.1. **2** *Se ~rre*, to take oneself, proceed, go: *se contulerunt ad coelum unde erant* CI 35; *amor et sapientia...evolant, nisi in usum se ~rant* VR 67. **3** To present, confer (benefits): *munera... ~rre* AM 300.3; *in hominem... omnia...collata sunt* CI 30. **b** to contribute (to an effect): *nihil ad salutem ~rt* VR 96.1. **4** To compare: *contulimus illa inter se* AM 3.4; *si haec loca ~rantur cum aliis* AC 6788.

confertim, *adv.* In dense crowds: *in quam* [*urbem*] *~im alluunt* AC 940.2.

confertus ~a ~um, *a.* Packed full, teeming: *sylvam ex variis arborum generibus ~am* AM 75.2.

confessio ~onis, *f.* **1** An admission: *ab omnium ~one, quod...*VR 8.1; *~one unius Dei* DD 55.3. **2** An admission of guilt, confession: *oralis ~o, quod peccator sit* VR 562. **3** A statement of belief, creed: *ex ~one Athanasiana* AM 341.1. **4** Thanksgiving: Isa. 51.3 (AC 100).

confessionarius ~i, *m.* A confessor: VR 665.7.

confessor ~oris, *m.* **1** One who proclaims a belief, a proponunt: *~or et cultor naturae* VR 12.8. **2** One who hears confessions, confessor: AC 3993.10.

confestim, *adv.* Hurriedly: AC 7997.

conficio ~ficere ~feci ~fectum, *tr.* **1** To prepare, make (confections, dishes, garments, etc.): *lautitiis ex pane et vino ~fectis* AM 14.2; *species minchae ...~fectae per oleum* AE 324.14; *vestibus quae ex fibris...arborum ~ficiunt* AC 7485. **2** To wear out, exhaust: *quae seniles ac senio ~fectae mortuae sunt* AC 553. **3** To destroy, kill: *~ficiam oppressores tuos* Zeph. 3.19 (DD 4).

confidenter, *adv.* With confidence, confidently: *ut amice et ~er...consortium teneant* AM 502.1.

confidentia ~ae, *f.* Confidence, trust: *ex fiducia seu ~a* CI 526.3.

confido ~dere ~si ~sum, *intr.* To be confident, trust: *~dite, Ego vici mundum* John 16.33 (DD 13); (w. dat.) to have trust (in), rely (on): *~sa est* [*uxor*] *suo viro* AM 325.1; (w. *in* or *super* + abl.): *beati omnes ~dentes in Ipso* Ps. 2.12. (DD 6); *~dunt super curru* Isa. 31.1 (VI 30.2).

configuratio ~onis, *f.* An object of a particular form, shape, figure: *~ones repraesentativae variarum virtutum moralium* AM 76.1.

confingo ~ngere ~nxi ~ctum, *tr.* To forge, fashion, invent: *in Nicaea urbe... ~cta et conflata est haeresis* VR 489.

confinium ~i, *neut.* A border region, frontier: *ex terra Canaane et ex ~is ejus* SS 102.1; AM 76.1.

confirmabilis ~is ~e, *f.* Capable of being confirmed: AC 6865.3.

confirmantia ~um, *neut. pl.* Confirmatory passages, proofs: *quod...conquisiverint ~a ex Verbo* AC 4738.3.

confirmatio ~onis, *f.* **1** A strengthening (of a person in a quality): *~onem in bono* AC 6787. **2** A confirmation of a fact or belief, proof: *quod hi contra amorem ...sint, manifesta ~o seu evictio datur* AM 212; (pred. dat.) *quod...etiam haec ~oni sint* AC 662; *caveat...sibi a ~onibus pro natura* VR 12.10.

confirmative, *adv.* With the use of proofs: *de illis qui negant Deum ~e* ES 5150 titulus.

confirmativus ~a ~um, *a.* Serving to confirm, proving: *causa ~a* AM 314.1; (neut. as sb.) a proof: AM 239.

confirmator ~oris, *m.* One who proves or confirms (by fallacious arguments): AM 233.1.

confirmatum ~i, *neut.* *Ex ~o*, as the result of a hardened attitude, by conviction, deliberately: AM 431.

confirmo ~are ~avi ~atum, *tr.* **1** To establish firmly: *ut regnum ~ent sancti* Dan. 7.22 (DD 4); to make strong: *oves infirmas non ~astis* Ezek. 34.4 (AC 8364.4). **2** To reinforce, strengthen (a promise, attitude, etc.): *~abo foedus Meum vobiscum* Lev. 26.9 (AC 6804.10); *fides...quae si ~atur fit persuasio* FI 11; *~ant illa apud se* DD 15.1. **3** To adduce evidence in support of, demonstrate, prove: *explicat Verbum ad ~andum Ecclesiae quoddam dogma* SS 5; *cognitiones per quas ~ant principia falsa* AC 6723.1; (absol.) *scientifica ~antia* AE 417.7; (w. *quod*) *velim...per plura ~are quod per sanguinem significetur verum* AE 30.3. **4** To give (a person) confidence, strengthen mentally: *~a te* Isa. 41.6 (AC 6756.3); (w. *in* + abl.) *quod ~aturi sint suos in hac veritate* AM 154[a]; (w. *pro*) *possunt ex permultis...se ~are pro Deo* VR 12.1; VR 35.2.

confiteor ~fiteri ~fessus sum, *tr.*, *intr.* **1** To acclaim, praise: **a** (tr.): *~fitebuntur coeli mirabile Tuum* Ps. 89.5 (AE 205.4); *~fitebuntur Te populi* Ps. 67.3 (SS 86). **b** (intr., w. dat.): *~fitemini Jehovae* Isa. 12.4 (DD 4). **2** (intr.) To make a declaration, say earnestly: *~fitebor illis, non novi vos* Matt. 7.23 (VI 2); (w. *quod*) *hic*

~fessus est quod non crediderit vitam post mortem AM 182.7. **b** to make confession (to a priest): *non ausus ~fiteri sacerdoti* ES 1261. **3** To proclaim belief in, confess: *qui solam fidem... ~fessi sunt* AC 7112; *~fitebuntur Dominum* AC 6988.1.

conflagro ~are ~avi, *intr.* To be destroyed by fire, burn up: *~abit terra* AC 3353.1.

conflator ~oris, *m.* One who melts precious metals, refiner, goldsmith: *pudefactus omnis ~or a sculptili* Jer. 51.17 (AC 215).

conflictio ~onis, *f.* A clash, conflict: *inde ~o jucunditatum seu affectionum* AC 8352.2.

conflictus ~us, *m.* A clash, conflict: *ex ~u cogitationum* AE 498.

confligo ~gere ~xi ~ctum, *intr.* To clash, conflict: *quod homo qui est finis malus nequaquam possit esse inter illos qui sunt fines boni...fines enim ~gunt* AC 6571.2; (w. *cum*) *rationale ~git cum phantasiis ex sensibus externis* ES 3330.

conflo ~are ~avi ~atum, *tr.* **1** To melt down (metals): *ex argento ~ato cum auro* AM 12.1; *~abo eos juxta ~are argentum* Zech. 13.8 (AC 901.5). **2** To fashion from molten metal, cast: *scrinium ~atum ex auro* VR 137.4; *catenas argenti ~ans* Isa. 40.19 (AC 424). **3** To fashion from any material, form: *hanc [laurum]...per artem suam ~avit* VR 80.2; *tentorium...ex simili materia ~atum* ES 548. **4** To compose, make up: *compilantem ex Verbo quibus ~et figmentum* AC 424; *totus homo ex meris cupiditatibus ~atus est* AC 59.1.

confluo ~ere ~xi ~xum, *intr.* To come together as in a stream, flock together: *quod hoc in ordinem a se ~xerit* VR 35.7; *ubi omnes hominum animae... ~unt* AC 969.

confluxus ~us, *m.* A flowing together: *de ~u elementorum in talem formam* VR 20.2.

confodio ~dere ~ssi ~ssum, *tr.* To pierce, run through: *~ssum gladio* Num. 19.16 (AE 79.4); *~ssus ob praevaricationes nostras* Isa. 53.5 (DD 15.1).

confoederatio: see **confaederatio**.

confoedero: see **confaedero**.

conformatio ~onis, *f.* An organized form, structure, conformation: AC 5114.4.

conformis ~is ~e, *a.* (compar. *~ior*) In keeping (with), agreeable (to): (w. dat.) *id solum credentes verum quod persuasionibus eorum ~e* AC 573; (w. *cum*) *haec...collata sunt cum Verbo...et cum illo ~ia sunt* SS 97.5.

conformitas ~atis, *f.* Conformity, compliance; an instance of this: *quod talis ~as...cum Romano-Catholicis sit Protestantibus* SE 20; (w. pl.) *per ~ates in rebus Ecclesiae* AM 228.

conformiter, *adv.* In keeping, agreeably, conformably: *ad ~er praestandum illis usus* CI 60.

conformo ~are ~avi ~atum, *tr.* **1** To give shape to, form, mould: *tanquam viscerula quae ~ant corpus* ES 2212; (transf.) *ut imagines...quae simul ~ant cultum Ipsius* AM 78.7. **2** To bring into conformity, harmonize, reconcile: *haec absque doctrina non ~antur* SS 51.2.

conforto ~are ~avi ~atum, *tr.* **1** To make strong, strengthen: *~asti Tibi [manum]* Ps. 80.17 (AC 8281.5). **2** (pass.) To be encouraged, take heart: *~amini et estote in viros* 1 Sam. 4.9 (AC 1703.1).

confossio ~onis, *f.* A piercing: *gladius ~onis* Ezek. 21.14 (AE 131.5).

confossus ~a ~um: pf. pple. of **confodio**.

confractio ~onis, *f.* A breaking, shattering, ruin: *super ~one Josephi non afficiuntur dolore* Amos 6.6 (AE 163.4); a breaking wave, breaker: *omnes ~ones Tuae et omnes fluctus Tui* Ps. 42.7 (AC 756.1).

confrater ~tris, *m.* A colleague; (pl.) brethren: *~tres...et consocii...vix sciunt aliter* AM 266.3; VR 138.

confringo ~ringere ~regi ~ractum, *tr.* To break in pieces, shatter: *os non ~ringetis Ipsius* John 19.36 (DD 11); *ut posset ~ringere omne obvium* CI 231.

confugio ~gere ~gi, *intr.* To take refuge (in), have recourse (to), resort (to): *ad supplicationes... ~giunt* ES 149.

confundo ~fundere ~fudi ~fusum, *tr.* **1** To turn upside down: *~fundetur terra* Isa. 24.3 (AE 223.6). **2** To make unclear, confuse: *~fundamus ibi labium eorum* Gen. 11.7 (AC); *solent ita plagae ~fundi, ut boni vix sciant ubi oriens eorum est* CI 152. **3** (refl.) To make oneself confused: *erant spiritus qui se ~fundebant ex iis, quod non scirent...* ES 3591.

confuse, *adv.* Without clear distinction, confusedly: *vident...formas indistincte et colores ~e* VR 61.2.

confusio ~onis, *f.* A mingling, mixing together: *per ~onem...substantiae* Sym. Ath. (DD 56); confusion: *nihil nisi turba, ~o et condemnatio apparet* ES 409.

confusus ~a ~um, *a.* (pf. pple. of **confundo**) **1** Unclear, obscure, confused: *sicut abyssus seu ~um obscurum quid* AC 18; *nam auditur ~um murmur* ES 1316. **2** *~us oculo*, having sight impaired: Lev. 21.20 (AE 152.14).

congelo ~are ~avi ~atum, *tr.* To make to freeze: *~atae abyssi* Exod. 15.8 (AC).

congeries ~ei, *f.* A random collection, heap, pile: *ex ~e inordinata rerum* CI 466; (of abstract objects) *~es idearum* VR 154.5.

congero ~gerere ~gessi ~gestum, *tr.* To heap or pile together: *ex ~gestis lapidibus* AE 411.20; (abstract objects) *ratiocinia ex se...plura ~gerunt* AC 735.

congestio ~onis, *f.* A random collection of material, heap: ES 5325.

congestus ~a ~um, *a.* (pf. pple. of **congero**) Casually composed, of random structure: *quod Verbum...sit visionarium et ~um quid* VR 14.3.

conglobatim, *adv.* In the form of a ball or sphere: *sed emissi sunt, ~im* ES 3416.

conglobatio ~onis, *f.* A forming into a ball, conglomeration: AS 195.

conglobo ~are ~avi ~atum, *tr.* To form into a ball, roll together: *ipsum malum est harum* [sc. *concupiscentiarum*] *~ata congeries seu glomus* AM 427; ES 431.

conglomeratio ~onis, *f.* A forming into a rounded mass, conglomeration: *congeriem illam seu ~onem illorum* SE 56.

conglomero ~are ~avi ~atum, *tr.* To form into a rounded mass: *per quod tellus ~ata sit in orbem* VR 29.1; (transf.) *~atae concupiscentiae* AM 440.

conglutinatio ~onis, *f.* A mass formed by adhering: *parva ~o similium quasi bacillorum* ES 2763.

conglutino ~are ~avi ~atum, *tr.* To cause to adhere, stick together: *charta longa...a pluribus chartis ~ata* AC 6930; *quod uniantur arctius, sic ut quasi ~entur* ES 2130.

congratulor ~ari ~atus sum, *tr.* To greet, welcome: CI 494.

congredior ~di ~ssus sum, *intr.* **1** To come together, meet (in argument): *cum quibus ratiocinando de Deo...licet ~di* VR 77.2. **2** To meet in hostile fashion, clash: *jucunda...amorum...necant se cum ~diuntur* AM 10.8. **3** To engage in sexual intercourse, copulate: *antequam illi* [sc. *Josephus et Maria*] *~derentur* Matt. 1.18 (DD 21).

congregatim, *adv.* In a group: *dicebatur de illis quod ~im veniant* AC 5189.2.

congregatio ~onis, *f.* **1** A coming together in a crowd, meeting: *post ~onem* AM 2.3. **2** An assembly, group, society (of persons): *quod modo sit* [*Ecclesia*] *~o simplicium* VR 14.3. **3** An assemblage, gathering (of things): *~onem aquarum vocavit maria* Gen. 1.10 (AC).

congrego ~are ~avi ~atum, *tr.* **1** To bring together as in a flock, assemble (persons): *~abo omnes gentes* Joel 3.2 (DD 4); *postquam ~ati sunt* AM 24. **2** To bring together, gather (things): *in fibras ~atas* CI 413; (masc. of pf. pple. as sb.) *tumultus inter ~atos* VR 71.1.

congressus[1] ~us, *m.* Sexual intercourse, copulation: *raro infantes ex talium ~u nascuntur* AC 828; (of birds) AM 417.

congressus[2] ~a ~um: pf. pple. of **congredior**.

congrue, *adv.* (w. dat.) In accordance (with), in keeping (with): AM 446.

congruenter, *adv.* Appropriately, suitably: *non ~er nisi cognitiones...sint veritates* AC 1900.3.

congruentia ~ae, *f.* Agreement in form or nature, congruence: AC 9496.1.

congruo ~ere ~i, *intr.* To be in keeping, agree: *quod prima lingua hominum... ~erit* CI 237; (w. dat.) AM 225.

congruus ~a ~um, *a.* Agreeing, in keeping (with): *per receptionem religionis ~ae cum alterius* AM 241.

congyratus ~a ~um, *a.* Formed into a loop, twisted together: ES 155.

conitor: see **connitor**.

conjectio ~onis, *f.* A throwing or casting (into prison): *haec ~o in custodiam a diabolo* AE 122.2.

conjecto ~are ~avi, *intr.* To make a guess: ES 1569.

conjectura ~ae, *f.* Guessing, conjecture: *ex ~a* AC 8377; a guess, conjecture: *una cum ratiociniis et ~is de eventibus* AM 5.1.

conjecturalis ~is ~e, *a.* Arrived at by conjecture: *quod ~ia sint quae de anima venditata fuerunt* AC 6053.

conjecturo ~are ~avi, *intr.* To make a guess: *curiositas ~andi quid...inter se colloquuti sunt* VR 183.3.

conjicio ~jicere ~jeci ~jectum, *tr.* **1** To throw, cast, hurl: *~jecerunt lapides post me* VR 333.4; (refl.) *ita perculsi sunt ut se praecipites retro ~jicerent* AC 538. **2** To throw, propel, cast (to a destination implying a change of state): *arbor...in ignem ~jicitur* Matt. 7.19 (VI 2); *in infernum ~jecti sunt* FI 64.1. **3** To bring, cast (into a new state): *phantasiae in quas se ~jiciunt* VR 31.4.

conjugalis ~is ~e, *a.* Probably misprint for **conjugialis** in all cases, but this can be disputed in some: AM 98.1; AM 203; VR 805; VR 847. (Schm. has *debitum conjugale* in Exod. 21.10; cf. 3AD 890, 891.)

conjugialis ~is ~e, *a.* **1** Of or appropriate to marriage: *spondae ~is* AM 465; *vinculum ~e* VR 41.3. **2** (esp.) *Amor ~is*, the love peculiar to marriage, conjugial love: *voluptas amoris ~is cum a vero amore ~i trahit originem* AC 995.3; *amores ~es* ES 2572; (neut. as sb.) the inclination towards marriage: AM 64.2.

conjugialiter, *adv.* In a manner appropriate to marriage, conjugially: *vere ~er amare conjugem* AM 193.2.

conjugium ~i, *neut.* **1** Marriage: *quod verum ~um sit unius viri et unius uxoris* AC 865.2. **2** *~um coeleste*, the heavenly marriage (of good and truth, love and wisdom, the Lord and the church): *conjunctio boni et veri...vocabitur ~um caeleste* VI 33; *ex ~o amoris et sapientiae in usu* AM 8.5; *~um Domini cum caelo et Ecclesia* SS 17.2.

conjuncte, *adv.* = **conjunctim**: *qui ~e* [*conjuncti* Tafel] *vivere possunt* ES 438.

conjunctim, *adv.* (superl. *~issime*) In conjunction, jointly: *illud coelum ~issime constituunt* AC 6701; *scintillulae quae ~im flagrant* VR 159.1; (w. *cum*) *~im cum uxore* AM 462.

conjunctio ~onis, *f.* **1** A joining together, union: *insitus est utrique amor ~onis in unum* AM 32; *agent in ~one* FI 15; the point of joining: *ad nervi optici... ~onem* ES 3840. **2** (esp.) Union as a spiritual process, conjunction: *~o Domini cum Ecclesia* SS 18.1; *~o...cum malis spiritibus* CI 295; *quod...habuerit in Se illa quae impedirent ~onem* AC 1659.2.

conjunctivus ~a ~um, *a.* Tending to union, uniting: *inclinatio ~a* AM 46; (neut. as sb.) a uniting principle, tendency to union: *quod in conjugiali masculino sit ~um cum conjugiali faeminino* AM 316.4.

conjunctus ~a ~um, *a.* (pf. pple. of **conjungo**) (compar. *~ior*, superl. *~issimus*) Closely associated, united, tied: *angeli...Ipsi propiores et ~iores* CI 25; *~issimi amici* AM 292.3.

conjungibilis ~is ~e, *a.* (compar. *~ior*) Capable of union: *Se fecit* [*Deus*] *visibilem, accessibilem et ~em* VR 538.

conjungo ~gere ~xi ~ctum, *tr.* **1** To combine into one, unite: *~gite illa tria* [*arcana*] *in unam sententiam* VR 48.2. **2** To bring into spiritual union, conjoin: *malum et verum non...possunt ~gi* AC 3110; (w. dat.) *Verbum...~git hominem Domino* SS 3.2; (w. *cum*) *verum quod ~gitur cum bono* AC 6717.3.

conjunx: see **conjux**.

conjuratio ~onis, *f.* A conspiracy, plot: *~onem facere contra bonos* ES 750.

conjuro ~are ~avi ~atum, *intr.* (of things) To act together, conspire: *tunc intimum in universali... ~at* ES 241.

conjux ~jugis, *m.* or *f.* also **conjunx** ~jugis, *m.* or *f.* **1** A married partner, spouse: *par ~jugum* AM 42.1. **2** (transf.) A thing standing in the relationship of husband or wife: *quod...bonum et verum sint ~juges* AE 46; *haec* [sc. *natura*] *ut universi ~junx concipit* VR 80.2.

conl-: see **coll-**.

connascor ~sci ~tus sum, *intr.* To be born together, arise simultaneously: *quod ex illo ~scatur et facultas et inclinatio ad sapiendum* AM 142; (w. dat.) *bina haereditaria sunt quae ~scuntur homini* AC 1414.

connatus ~a ~um, *a.* Born together, connate, innate: *ex ~a timiditate* AM 292.3.

connecto ~ctere ~xi ~xum, *tr.* **1** To link together, join, connect: *per...sculptilia quae artifex... ~ctit per catenas* AE 237.1. **2** (transf.) To bring into a connected whole, join, string together: *argumenta ~ctere* AC 7601.2; *quae* [*arcanissima*]*...se in continua serie ~ctunt cum illis quae sequuntur* AC 1659.1.

connexio ~onis, *f.* That which connects, a connective: ES 809.

connexus ~us, *m.* The act of linking together, connection: *ex ~u plurium* AC 793.

connisus ~us, *m.* A moving with concentrated effort, struggle: *~um ascensus eorum sentire dabatur* AC 4949; AC 3079.1.

connitor ~ti ~xus sum, *intr.* also **conitor**. To exert oneself, strive: (w. inf.) *quod quisque ~tatur...excludere illa* AE 381.3; AC 6716.2; (w. *in* + acc.) *ut ~tantur in conjunctionem* AM 46.

conniventia ~ae, *f.* Connivance: *cum mariti venia aut ~a* ES [6103.2].

conniveo ~vere, *intr.* (of the eyes) To be shut: *non ~vebunt oculi videntium* Isa. 32.3 (AE 152.5).

connubialis ~is ~e, *a.* Relating to the mating of animals, of pairing: *ex amore polygamico, qui est ~is* AM 78.5; (of the inhabitants of the sixth earth) *domum... ~em* AC 10837.

connubium ~i, *neut.* The mating of animals, pairing: *quod... ~a jungant* [*aves*] VR 12.5.

connubo ~bere ~psi ~ptum, *tr.* To join as in mating, mate, marry: *spiritum quem ~bant chylo* ES 1137.

connumero ~are ~avi ~atum, *tr.* To count, number: *~ati ad centum et viginti* AM 14.1.

conor ~ari ~atus sum, *intr.* (usu. w. inf.) To attempt, try (to): *~antur agere similia* CI 507.

conp-: see **comp-**.

conquasso ~are ~avi ~atum, *tr.* To shake violently: *montes...vidi... ~atos ab uno fine ad alterum* CI 229.

conqueror ~queri ~questus sum, *intr.* To complain: *multum ~questi sunt* AM 161.2; (also tr.) to complain about: *quod ii ~questi* ES 2089.

conquestus ~us, *m.* A complaint: ES 3110.

conquiro ~rere ~sivi ~situm, *tr.* To gather, acquire: *fraudulenter ~rendo opes* AM 496; (w. immaterial objects) *in se ~rit rationes quae confirmant* NH 180.

conquisitio ~onis, *f.* That which is acquired, acquisitions, possessions: *quia fuit ~o eorum multa prae habitare simul* Gen. 36.7 (AC).

consacro: see **consecro**.

consanguineus ~a ~um, *a.* Related by blood, akin: *illa quae in medio sunt vocantur ~a* AC 5530.1; (masc. as sb.) a blood relation: AC 685.

consanguinitas ~atis, *f.* Blood relationship, consanguinity: *~ates et affinitates* AC 917.

consarcio ~cire ~si ~tum, *tr.* To bring together again by mending, repair, restore: *concordiae in domibus ~ciantur propter necessitates* AM 283 (Rogers).

conscendo ~dere ~di ~sum, *tr.* To climb into, mount (a vehicle, etc.): *~de currum* Ps. 45.4 (AE 131.5).

conscientia ~ae, *f.* **1** Awareness, consciousness: *absque ulla hominis ~a* IM 50. **b** (w. dependent gen.): *qui ~am veri et boni a Domino acceperunt* AC 762. **c** (w. *quod*): *accipit ~am quod conjugium cum pluribus uxoribus sit peccatum* AC 865.2. **2** The faculty of distinguishing good and evil, conscience: *~ae morsus* VR 665.4; *non spirituales sunt, nec habent ~am* AE 107.4.

conscientiosus ~a ~um, *a.* Possessing a conscience, conscientious: AM 271.

conscio ~cire ~civi, *intr.* To be aware, have knowledge: *de quo mens non ~cit* AC 9165.

conscius ~a ~um, *a.* Having knowledge, aware: *non ~o viro nec ~a uxore* AM 193.2; (w. gen.) *sicut solent ~i mali* AC 222.

conscribo ~bere ~psi ~ptum, *tr.* To compose, write (a book): *Verbum... ~ptum est per meras correspondentias* CI 1.

consecratio ~onis, *f.* A ritual for making sacred, dedication, consecration: *pro ~one altaris* AC 10042.7.

consecro ~are ~avi ~atum, *tr.* also **consacro**. To make sacred, dedicate, consecrate: *ut conjugia a ministris Ipsius ~entur* AM 308.

consectarium ~i, *neut.* A consequence, corollary: *quod ut ~um...ex illa fide effluxerit* SE 66; AM 303.

consedeo ~dere ~di, *intr.* see also **consido**. To take a seat, sit down: *quod [Dominus] sublatus in caelum ~deat a dextris Dei* Mark 16.19 (VR 136.1 1st edn.); Matt. 24.3 (VR 764 1st edn.); (of a people) to set up camp: *ubi [filii Israelis] congregati ~debant vocabantur 'castra'* AR 862.2.

consedi: pf. of **consedeo** or **consido**.

consenesco ~nescere ~nui, *intr.* To grow old: Ps. 92.10 (AE 375.23).

consensio ~onis, *f.* Agreement, concord: *~o doctrinalium cum sensu literali Verbi* AC 3452.

consensus ~us, *m.* **1** The action of agreeing, consent: *nisi detur ~us in voluntate* VI 52; a formal declaration of consent: *sacerdos... ~um audit* AM 21.4. **2** The agreement or concord of things: *quod omne unum formetur ex ~u harmonico plurium* CI 405.

consentaneus ~a ~um, *a.* (w. dat.) In agreement (with), conformable (to): *per moralem [vitam] ~am bonis dogmatibus* CI 516.

consentienter, *adv.* In agreement, conformably: *respondebunt ~er* VR 646.2.

consentio ~tire ~si ~sum, *intr.* **1** To express agreement, concur, consent: *ut lector...videat veritates, et sic ~tiat* AM 295.1; (w. *ad*) *~timus ad illa quae fratres nostri loquuti sunt* VR 48.14. **2** (of a proposition) To be in agreement: *quod... ~tit cum fide...recepta* AE 250.5; (neut. of pres. pple. as sb.) *forma ~tientium* ES 158.

consequela ~ae, *f.* A consequence, result: *ratiocinia ...ex effectibus...procedunt ad aliquas ~as* AM 385.

consequens ~ntis, *neut.* A consequence: *hoc fluit ut ~ns ex antecedentibus* AM 199.1.

consequenter, *adv.* As a consequence, consequently: *quae [turba]...mundum spirituum, et ~er genus humanum, aggressa est perdere* AC 1675.2.

consequentia ~ae, *f.* A logical deduction, consequence: *quod talis amor non detur...non valet ~a* AM 333.2.

consequor ~qui ~quutus (*or* ~cutus) sum, *tr.*, *intr.* **1** To come after, follow: *ab illis quae praecedunt et ab illis quae ~quuntur* AC 1725.1. **2** To follow as a consequence: *idem etiam ~quitur ex unione utriusque* VR 101; (impers., w. *quod*) it follows (that): VR 47. **3** To attain to, achieve: *ut...felicitatem ~quantur* AC 59.2.

consero[1] ~ere ~ui ~tum, *tr.* To fasten together: *cancellis ~tis ex vitibus* AM 17.1; to clasp (hands): *~ere manus* VR 125.

consero[2] ~serere ~sevi ~situm, *tr.* To plant (trees, etc.): *arbores...in continua serie ~sitae* AM 13.2; to plant (land): *quodque sex annis ~sererent terram* AC 737.2; *tractus...arboribus ~situs* ES 2072.

consertio ~onis, *f.* A connection: AS 432.

conserto ~are ~avi ~atum, *tr.* (refl.) To form a connection, connect: *quomodo illae [fibrae] iterum se ~ant in corpore* CI 212.

conservatio ~onis, *f.* Conservation, preservation: *~o est perpetua creatio* VR 46.3.

conservator ~oris, *m.* One who preserves, preserver: *a Domino Creatore et ~ore universi* AM 400.3.

conservo ~are ~avi ~atum, *tr.* **1** To keep in existence, preserve: *quod id Verbum adhuc apud illos ~atum sit* SS 102.1. **2** To keep alive, save: *circumcincti tunc fuerunt columna spirituum, et sic ~ati* AE 78.3.

conservus ~i, *m.* A fellow slave: AE 397.1.

consessus ~us, *m.* A sitting together, assembly, meeting: *in ~u senum* Ps. 107.32 (AC 6524.2).

consideratio ~onis, *f.* A being taken into account, regard, consideration: *in multo majori ~one esse* ES 2514.

considero ~are ~avi ~atum, *tr.* **1** To take into consideration, contemplate: *~avimus, Deus, misericordiam Tuam* Ps. 48.9 (AE 313.5); (w. *quod*) *ille non ~at quod Ipse Jehovah...loquutus sit Verbum* SS 2.1. **2** To regard in a specified manner, look on, consider: *non ~atur homo in coelo ab externis sed ab internis* AC 1003.

consido ~sidere ~sedi, *intr.* see also **consedeo**. **1** To take a seat, sit down: AM 20.3; (of a people) to establish itself: *~sedit Israel in Schittim* Num. 25.1 (AE 141.1). **2** To subside, be reduced: *hoc spiculum ~sidebat in formas* ES 2763.

consiliarius ~i, *m.* An adviser, counsellor: *~i a latere* AM 14.1; *ut ~us Ejus* [sc. *Patris*] *sit* [*Filius*] VR 136.2.

consiliator ~oris, *m.* Adviser, counsellor: *video...et nullus ~or* Isa. 41.28 (AC 3134).

consilior ~ari ~atus sum, *intr.* To take counsel: Isa. 40.14 (AC 627.3).

consilium ~i, *neut.* **1** Advice, counsel: *ex ~o Bileami* Num. 31.16 (AE 140.2); *gens perdita ~is* Deut. 32.28 (AC 7051.3). **2** An intended course of action, plan: *quod ~um inirent...contra illos* AC 6681. **3** A group of advisers, council: *e secretis ~is* AM 5.1.

consimilis ~is ~e, *a.* Very similar: *quod hodie sit* [*gens Judaica*] *~is patribus suis* AM 202.2.

consimiliter, *adv.* In a very similar manner: VR 80.4.

consistentia ~ae, *f.* Firm establishment: *quod omnium ~a pendeat ab ordine* VR 679.1; AC 9657.

consisto ~ere, *intr.* (n.b. pf. *constiti* may belong to **consto**) **1** To stand firm: *ut ~erent super pedes suos* Rev. 11.11 (AE 183.5); (esp. in the face of an adversary) *quis ~et cum apparuerit?* Mal. 3.2 (DD 4); *infernales...ad praesentiam boni ~ere nequeunt* AC 6677. **2** (of things) To be firmly established, remain stable: *ut ratio constet, ac ita coelum ~at* AC 6807; *omnia... ~unt ex aequilibrio* CI 592. **3** (w. *ex*) To be composed (of): *homo ex utraque* [*vita*] *~it* AC 801. **4** (w. *in* + abl.) To consist in: *vita eorum in male faciendo ~it* AC 6666.2; *sapientia angelica in eo... ~it, ut videant* FI 4.

consistorium ~i, *neut.* A papal council, consistory: AR 734.

consitus ~a ~um: pf. pple. of **consero**[2].

consobrina ~ae, *f.* A female cousin: 1IB s.v. 'Amram'.

consocia ~ae, *f.* A female companion: AM 155.3.

consociabilis ~is ~e, *a.* Capable of associating, companionable: ES 298; (of affections) leading to association: AM 393.1.

consociabilitas ~atis, *f.* The quality of being an agreeable companion, sociability: AM 253.1.

consociatio ~onis, *f.* **1** Companionship: *foedera... fiunt...amicitiae, ~onis, ita conjunctionis gratia* VI 60. **b** the association of angels with men: CI 304.1. **2** A group of companions, company: *spirituum Jovialium ~o ad me venit* ES 613.

consocietas ~atis, *f.* Companionship, association: *cum in caelo percipitur ~as illa* AM 273.3.

consocio ~are ~avi ~atum, *tr.* **1** To join in (conversation): *animae post mortem... ~antes sermonem* ES 290. **2** To join in association: *quod ibi ~ent tales qui conveniunt animis* AC 7363; (pass.) to be formed into societies: *quod in coelo omnes ~ati sint secundum affinitates spirituales* AE 46; to be matched in marriage: *~abantur comparibus* AM 216.3.

consocius ~a ~um, *a.* **1** Sociable: *~am vitam vivunt* AM 279. **2** (masc. as sb.) A companion, fellow: *~us in afflictione* Rev. 1.9 (AR); *loquuntur cum ~is urbanis* VR 22.2; (of birds) VR 12.5.

consolatio ~onis, *f.* The act of consoling, consolation: *~ones post tentationes* AC 1863.

consolido ~are ~avi ~atum, *tr.* To make firm or solid: *receptacula illa... ~antur et indurescunt* SA 86 (= v.[3]).

consolor ~ari ~atus sum, *tr.* To give comfort to, console: *~abitur Jehovah Zionem* Isa. 51.3 (AE 110.2).

consonans ~ntis, *a.* (pres. pple. of **consono**) (of a letter) Having a consonantal value: SS 90.2; (fem. as sb.) a consonant: *duplicatio durior ~ntium* AC 1759; ES 1147; (also, masc. as sb.) ES 1645.

consono ~are ~avi, *intr.* To agree in sound, chime in (with): *loquela...eorum* [sc. *angelorum*] *talis est ut ~et cum affectionibus* CI 269.1.

consonus ~a ~um, *a.* Agreeing in sound, concordant: *clamor...non...dissonus, sed ~us* AM 207.1; (neut. as sb.) *in ~o*, in tune: VR 61.1.

consors ~rtis, *a.* Held or possessed in common, shared: *~rtem vitam cum sui similibus* AM 10.6; (fem. as sb.) a consort, mate: AM 52.

consortium ~i, *neut.* **1** A state of social contact, living together: *in ~o esse cum angelis* SS 70; *non simul sunt, nec ~um inter se habent* CI 27; (w. pl.) an instance of this: *quod Dominus...doceat hominem...per loquelas et ~a* AE 1175.4. **2** *~um tori*, sleeping together as man and wife, intercourse: AM 306.1; also *~um* alone: AM 51.

conspectus ~us, *m.* The range of sight, view: *in ~um illorum venerunt duo angeli* AM 44.10; *bonum amoris erat in ~u Domini* AE 9.5.

conspergo ~gere ~si ~sum, *tr.* To besprinkle: *~sit illud* [sc. *sertum*] *aqua fontis* AM 293.7; (w. retained acc.) *~sus vestes* 'with his clothes sprinkled' Isa. 63.1 (VR 116.1).

conspersio ~onis, *f.* A sprinkling, scattering: *per ~onem pulveris* AC 247.

conspicio ~picere ~pexi ~pectum, *tr.* **1** To see, witness, view: *~piciuntur* [*spiritus*] *ab hac...parte* AC 8947; *charitatis forma...ad vivum ~picitur in coelo* CI 414. **2** To discern mentally; (esp. pass.) to be plainly discerned: *status...non describitur sed usque ~picitur a sequentibus* AC 507. **3** (of things) To be related to: [*historica et universalia*] *se...mutuo aliter ~piciunt* AC 1222.

conspicor ~ari ~atus sum, *tr.* To catch sight of, see: *haec dum ~atus sum* VR 508.2.

conspicue, *adv.* Evidently, obviously: VR 343.

conspicuus ~a ~um, *a.* Plain to view, clearly seen: *planetae coram oculis... ~i* CI 417; perceptible (mentally): *Dei...coram mentibus ~i* VR 159.3.

conspiratio ~onis, *f.* A conspiracy: AC 1879.1.

conspirator ~oris, *m.* A conspirator: ES 5093.

conspiro ~are ~avi, *intr.* **1** To form a conspiracy, combine for evil purposes: *in inferno socii ~ant simul in malum* AC 5764. **2** To act in harmony, agree: *quia sic vivebant absque amore, ~avit tam amor sui quam phantasia inde* AC 362; (w. *ad*) *ad talem...sapientiam ~at quoque id* CI 266.2.

conspuo ~ere ~i ~tum, *tr.* To spit upon: AE 83.2 (Luke 18.32).

conspurcatio ~onis, *f.* A making filthy, defilement: AE 235.6.

conspurco ~are ~avi ~atum, *tr.* To make filthy, defile, pollute: *quod...foret ~are sanctum prophanis* DD 18.3.

constabilio ~lire ~livi ~litum, *tr.* To make firm or well-founded, establish securely: *quod non detur imperium...civitas, domus, quae non ~liuntur per leges* VR 55; *unio sicut animae et corporis ~ita est in Symbolo Athanasii* VR 98.2.

constabilitio ~onis, *f.* A making firm, establishment: *ex ~one faederis* AM 217.

constans ~ntis, *a.* (compar. *~ntior*, superl. *~ntissimus*) **1** Unchanging, constant: *quod ita se res habeat, ~ns est veritas* AC 1676.2. **2** (of persons) Persistent, resolute, steadfast: [*homo*] *manebit ~ns in bono usque ad finem vitae* AC 8394. **3** (w. *ex*) Composed (of): *in solido ex tribus illis gradibus ~nte* AS 205; (also w. abl.) *id quasi ~ns filis clausis, seu reti quodam* ES 1629.

constanter, *adv.* (compar. *~ius*, superl. *~issime*) Without change, unvaryingly: *illa quae in domibus nostris sunt... ~er ibi manent* VR 78.2.

constantia ~ae, *f.* The quality of being unchanging, constancy: *~am in veris* AE 129; (applied to persons) *hi...constantiores fiunt aliis, adeo ut dici queant ~ae* UJ(C) 49.

consternatio ~onis, *f.* Dismay, consternation: *in terrore et ~one sunt* AC 9330.2.

consterno[1] ~are ~avi ~atum, *tr.* To terrify, dismay: *spiritus... ~abantur et anxii facti* AC 546.

consterno[2] ~sternere ~stravi ~stratum, *tr.* To spread, scatter, or strew all over, cover: *illa in pulverem et cinerem redacta sunt, et per ventum orientalem... super inferna eorum ~strata* AR 772.1.

constipatio ~onis, *f.* The state of being tightly surrounded, crowding: *conjectio in infernum est ~o a falsis e malo* AC 8210.2.

constipo ~are ~avi ~atum, *tr.* To pack tightly, fill completely: *est spirituale quo...illas* [sc. *formas*] *~at materiis ex tellure* AS 340; (pass.) to be closely surrounded, be crowded or thronged: *quando ab illis* [sc. *falsis*] *ibi ~ati sunt* AC 8232.

constipulatio ~onis, *f.* A bargain, covenant: *~ones seu pacta* AC 6804.5.

constipulor ~ari ~atus sum, *intr.* To make a bargain: [*fides*] *in Deum Filium ut intercedat et ~etur* VR 177.1; (impers.) *sic ex proviso ~atum* AC 3951.1.

constituo ~ere ~i ~tum, *tr.* **1** To make to stand, place, set: *~it super petra pedes meos* Ps. 43.2 (AC 6669.3). **2** To appoint (to an office or dignity): *omnes praedicatores sunt ~ti a Domino* CI 226; *qui in nulla dignitate ~ti sunt* AM 292.1. **3** To appoint, fix (a time): *~tum tempus* Lam. 1.15 (AE 863.2). **4** To compose, make up, constitute: *illi omnes Ecclesiam Domini ~unt* AE 21; (pass., w. *ex*) *ex illis... ~itur Ecclesia* AC 6637.2.

constitutio ~onis, *f.* Organized character, situation, constitution: *secundum eorum interiorem ~onem* ES 3203; *mutabatur ibi ~o sphaerae* AC 1270.3.

consto ~are ~iti, *intr.* **1** To be placed, stand: *quo plus cedit...eo firmius ~at* ES 241. **2** (of accounts) To tally, balance: *ut ratio ~et* AC 6807. **3** (w. *ex*) To be composed, consist (of): *societatem ex aliquot millibus angelorum ~antem* VR 65; (w. *in* + abl.) to consist (in): *perceptio Ecclesiae ~at in eo ut percipiant...quid bonum* AC 495; (w. abl.) *aliter in spiritibus, qui carne et ossibus...non ~ant* 1AD 1148. **4** (w. clause as subject) To be established as a fact, be evident: (w. *ex*) *quod identitas trium Essentiarum Divinarum sit...scandalum, ~itit mihi ex angelis* VR 23.2; *quod...haec spiritualiter intelligenda sint ~are potest ex eo, quod...* SS 10; *...qualis differentia est... ~are potest ex illis quae...* AE 1. **b** (impers.) it is evident: *~at ex apparitionibus Divini coram Abrahamo* CI 84.

constrepitus ~us, *m.* Concomitant noise: ES 187.

constrictio ~onis, *f.* Compression, tightening: ES 1944.

constrictorius ~a ~um, *a.* Pressing together, squeezing: *motum ~um et restrictorium* AC 958.

constrictus ~a ~um, *a.* (in senses of vb., esp.) Restricted, bound: *amor conjugialis...determinatus, ~us* AM 107.

constringo ~ngere ~nxi ~ctum, *tr.* (compar. of pf. pple. *~ctior*) **1** To make tight or compressed, tighten: *~ngitur vinculum* ES 193; to make solid, bind: *in humo ~cta gelu* AE 365.3. **2** To exert pressure on, compel: *vinculum ad justum conjugium mentes ~ngens* AM 307.

constructio ~onis, *f.* Construction, building: *~one novi templi* AE 422.8.

construo ~ere ~xi ~ctum, *tr.* To build, construct: *domus in quibus angeli habitant non ~untur sicut domus in mundo* CI 190.

constupro ~are ~avi ~atum, *tr.* To ravish, debauch: *vide ubi non ~ata fueris* Jer. 3.2 (AC 2466.6).

consubstantialis ~is ~e, *a.* (w. dat.) Having the same substance or essence as, consubstantial: *credo in...Jesum Christum...Deum de Deo ~em Patri* Sym. Nic. (VR 632).

consuetudo ~inis, *f.* Habit, custom: *ex ~ine* CI 458; (pl.) AM 246.2.

consuetus ~a ~um, *a.* Accustomed to obedience, trained (of animals): *sicut vitulus non ~us* Jer. 31.18 (AC 5354.9); (neut. as sb.) custom, usage: *juxta ~um Legis* Luke 2.27 (DD 9).

consul ~lis, *m.* One of the two senior magistrates of the Roman Republic, consul: VR 141.

consulo ~ere ~ui ~tum, *tr.*, *intr.* **1** (tr.) To go to for advice, consult: *~at se quisque...num aliam ideam...foveat* VR 94.1; to be guided by: *~ere scientifica* AC 6723.1; *~e rationem et perspice num...* VI 91. **2** (intr., w. dat.) To give advice (to), advise: *~imus vobis ut vivatis monogami* AM 77.4. **3** (intr., w. dat.) To consult the interests (of), take thought (for), care (for): *qui sibi et suis non ~it* AC 1076.2; *saluti suae... ~ere* VR 119.2.

consultatio ~onis, *f.* Consultation: AM 478.2.

consulto ~are ~avi, *intr.* To take counsel: *dominatores ~arunt una contra Jehovam* Ps. 2.2 (AE 375.19).

consultum ~i, *neut.* **1** *Ex ~o*, as the result of deliberate thought, from premeditation: *adulteri ex ~o* AM 432.3. **2** *~um ducere*, to think it advisable: *~um duxi aliquam sciagraphiam ejus emittere* SE 1.

consummatio ~onis, *f.* An ending, finishing off: Zeph. 1.18 (DD 4); esp. *~o saeculi*, the consummation of the age: Matt. 24.3 (AC 6895.1).

consummatus ~a ~um, *a.* (pf. pple. of **consummo**) (superl. *~issimus*) (in senses of verb, esp.) Brought to completion, perfected: *~issima sapientia* AM 111.

consummo ~are ~avi ~atum, *tr.* **1** To bring to completion, finish: *cum absolvisset Moses scribere verba...usque dum ~avit illa* AC 6752.4. **2** To put an end to, finish off: *Ecclesia...in tantum ~ata est, ut vix aliquae reliquiae ejus supersint* VR 4.1; *phthises, ex quibus corpus ~atur* AM 253.2.

consumo ~ere ~(p)si ~(p)tum, *tr.* To eat up, destroy, consume: *corpora...putredine ~ta* CI 312.2; *~am hominem et bestiam* Zeph. 1.3 (AE 280.8); *rubus nullatenus ~ebatur* AC 6828.

consumptio: see **consumtio**.

consumtio ~onis, *f.* also **consumptio**. A consuming, destruction: AE 131.12.

consuo ~ere ~i ~tum, *tr.* To sew together: *~erunt folia ficus* Gen. 3.7 (AC).

consurgo ~rgere ~rrexi ~rrectum, *intr.* To rise up (in opposition): *~rgent liberi contra parentes* Mark 13.12 (AC 6767.4).

contabesco ~bescere ~bui, *intr.* To waste away: *ut... ~bescant propter iniquitatem eorum* Ezek. 4.17 (VR 130.2).

contactus ~us, *m.* The action of touching, contact: *ad ~um alicujus mali* VR 56.2.

contagio ~onis, *f.* Contact as a source of infection, contagion: AC 10130.10.

contagiosus ~a ~um, *a.* Infecting by contact, contagious: *omnia...mala sunt ~a* VR 120.2.

contagium ~i, *neut.* = **contagio**: *totum corpus inficitur in tantum, ut lethale ex ~o inducatur* AM 253.1; (transf.) *ex ~o libidinis* AM 464.

contaminatio ~onis, *f.* Contamination: AC 2056.1.

contamino ~are ~avi ~atum, *tr.* To make foul, defile: *terra ~abitur* Isa. 24.5 (AC 1066.1); (transf.) to besmirch, befoul: *pervertunt et ~ant sancta et vera fidei* AC 1071.6; *lasciva quae amorem... ~ant* AM 102.

contego ~gere ~xi ~ctum, *tr.* To cover over: *sicut aquae mare ~gunt* Isa. 11.9 (AE 71.2); *illa quae sunt voluntatis...sint...quasi ~cta et reservata ne quicquam eam tangeret* AC 641.

contemno ~nere ~(p)si ~(p)tum, *tr.* To hold in contempt, despise, look down on: *qui ~nunt Verbum* SS 35.4.

contemplatio ~onis, *f.* Contemplation: *illam* [sc. *triarchiam*] *suae ~oni sistere* VR 171.1.

contemplator ~oris, *m.* One who considers or contemplates: *patet cuivis ~ori ex ratione* AM 85.

contemplo: see **contemplor**.

contemplor ~ari ~atus sum, *tr.* perh. also **contemplo** (ES 3581). **1** To gaze upon, look at: *cum quis ~atur oculis corporis coelum stelliferum* AC 1806. **2** To contemplate mentally, consider: *quod universum consistat ex...usibus... omnis sapiens potest ~ari* VR 47; (w. *ut*) *~ari universum creatum ut opus cohaerens* VR 13.2.

contemptibilis: see **contemtibilis**.

contemptor: see **contemtor**.

contemptus: see **contemtus**.

contemtibilis ~is ~e, *a.* also **contemptibilis**. Contemptible, despicable: ES 1249.

contemtor ~oris, *m.* also **contemptor**. One who despises: *~ores proximi* ES 4746.

contemtus ~us, *m.* also **contemptus**. Contempt, despising: *~us aliorum, inimicitiae, odia* CI 481.5.

contendo ~dere ~di ~tum, *intr.* To strive, contend: *~dite cum matre vestra* Hos. 2.2 (AE 240.5).

contentio ~onis, *f.* Quarrelling, contention: *ne quaeso sit ~o inter me et inter te* Gen. 13.8 (AC); (w. pl.) an instance of this: Ps. 18.43 (AC 1259.5).

contentum ~i, *neut.* That which is contained in something, contents: *quot viscerula intra quodlibet ~um visceris* AC 7836.2; (esp. pl.) the contents (of a book, etc.): AC 6 titulus.

contentus ~a ~um, *a.* Satisfied, content: *~i paucis et pusillis* CI 277.2; (w. inf.) *qui nusquam ~i scire quid fides* ES 1595.

conterminus ~a ~um, *a.* Having common boundaries, adjacent: *ad regionem ~am occidenti* AM 79.2.

contero ~terere ~trivi ~tritum, *tr.* To crush, pound: *ex quibus* [sc. *scorpiis*] *~tritis et oleo mixtis* ES 2743; (transf.) *~teret et consumet omnia illa regna* Dan. 2.44 (AM 81.1).

contestatio ~onis, *f.* The action of solemnly claiming, attestation: *quod ~ones fiant per elevationes manuum ad coelum* AE 607; a protest: *verum falsificatum...super quo ~o et indignatio* AE 223.6.

contestor ~ari ~atus sum, *tr.* **1** To affirm solemnly, attest, proclaim: *tam certo confirmare possum, ut maxime id ~ari liceat* ES 179; *Paulus ~atus et Judaeis et Graecis paenitentiam in Deum* Acts 20.21 (VR 107.2). **2** *~ari litem*, to engage in a lawsuit: *quod vir timeat cum uxore ~ari litem* AM 469. **3** (w. *quod*) To claim, protest: *~atus quod talis non fuerit* ES 3814.

contexo ~ere ~ui ~tum, *tr.* **1** To make by weaving, weave: *tunica... ~ta* John 19.23 (AE 64.3); *florum serta mirabiliter ~ta* AC 1629. **2** To make as by weaving, construct: [*corpus*] *~tum ex talibus quae e mundo naturali sunt* VR 103.1; (abstract things) *integrum systema doctrinae ex Verbo ~ere* AC 794.2.

contextura ~ae, *f.* **1** A piece of weaving, woven cloth, fabric: *~a ex filis...lini* AC 7601.3. **2** The coachwork, fabric (of a vehicle): AC 8215.2. **3** The manner of construction, structure: *quod...formae membrorum... quoad ipsam ~am sint ex fibris oriundis ex principiis suis in cerebris* AS 370.

contextus ~us, *m.* **1** Logical connection, coherence: *ex ipsa serie ~us rerum* AC 905. **2** A whole made up of parts, complex, structure: *quod ~us illi correspondeant vitae in ultimo gradu* VR 12.4; SA 79 (= iii.4.[1]).

conticeo ~cere ~cui, *intr.*, *tr.* (intr.) To keep silence, remain unspeaking: *angelus his auditis diu ~cuit* VR 134.3; (tr.) to keep silent about: *facit horrenda...quae ~cenda sunt* ES 4684.

conticesco ~ticescere ~ticui, *intr.* To fall silent, cease to speak: *ad haec ~ticuerunt uxores* AM 330.4.

contigno ~are ~avi ~atum, *tr.* To furnish with beams: *~at aquis triclinia sua* Ps. 104.3 (AE 283.8).

contiguitas ~atis, *f.* Nearness, contiguity: AR 55.

contiguus ~a ~um, *a.* **1** Adjacent, contiguous: *urbes cum palatiis magnificis, ~is* AC 1626; (w. dat.) AM 13.1. **2** Following without a break, run on: *loquelae ideae seu voces non ~ae* ES 1648.

continens ~ntis, *a.* **1** (of land) Forming a continuous expanse: *terra pro ~nte ubi humus* AC 566.2. **2** Not separated by a break, immediately accessible: *in terram quae mihi ~ns erat* AM 2.1. **3** (w. gen.) Serving as container (of), containant: *communia sunt ~ntia singularium* CI 267; *qui* [sc. *aquales*]*...sunt ~ntes aquae* AC 4017; *opus ~ns finium, causarum, et effectuum* VR 47.

continenter, *adv.* Without a break, immediately: *quod exteriora cohaereant interioribus ~er* AC 5146.2; *ex verbis quae ~er sequuntur* AM 41.2; continuously: *quod...spes salutis ~er adesset* ES 170.

continentia ~ae, *f.* A holding together: *facies illis baltheos significat ~am in nexu* AC 9941.

contineo ~nere ~nui, *tr.* **1** To hold firmly, preserve: *ut Deus possit...* [*universum*] *ut unum ~nere in perpetuum, quod est conservare* VR 13.1. **2** To have within itself, contain, hold: *sicut vasa quae includunt et ~nent* SS 40.1; *doctrina...~nebat leges vitae* AC 6705; (w. *in se*) *coelestis amor in se ~net omnia quae boni et veri sunt* AC 5701; (pass.) *quae in hoc versu ~nentur* AC 1063.1. **3** To hold back, restrain: *amor usus...~net mentem ne diffluat* AM 16.3; *qui se ~net* AC 5697.

contingens ~ntis, *a.* Happening by chance, accidental: *quomodo omnia ~ntia sint Providentiae* ES 213; liable to happen, not necessary; (neut. as sb.) an accidental happening: *num* [*insit*] *hilare ex naturali aut ~nte* AC 6616. *series ~ntium* ES 2483.

contingo ~ngere ~gi, *tr.*, *intr.* **1** (tr.) To touch: *Jehovah...non potest ~ngere aliquem diabolum* VR 84. **2** (intr.) To happen, come about: *per quae...nusquam talia ~gissent* AC 1183; (w. dat.) to befall: *morbi ...qui...conjugi...~ngunt* AM 253.1. **3** (intr., w. dat.) To fall to the lot of: *non ~git Levitis pars* Deut. 10.9 (AE 444.4); (also w. inf.) *ut...eos interrogare ~ngat* ES [972 ½].

continuatio ~onis, *f.* That which continues, a continuation: *quod mors...significet...~onem vitae* CI 445; *quod fructificationes...sint ~ones creationis* AM 183.5; (esp. w. ref. to a written work) *~o de Ultimo Judicio* UJ(C) titulus.

continue, *adv.* (compar. *~ius*) Without interruption, continuously: *per 26 annos ~e* VR 12.8; *quod angeli ...usque ~e perficiantur sapientia* CI 271; *loquebantur adhuc ~ius et plenius* AC 8024.

continuitas ~atis, *f.* Continuity: *a ~ate causarum et effectuum a primo usque ad ultimum* AE 1207.4; AC 6465.2.

continuo[1], *adv.* App. used as equivalent of **continue**: *quod angeli ~o* [*continue* 3rd edn.] *defendant hominem* AC 761; AC 986.1; AC 1047.

continuo[2] ~are ~avi ~atum, *tr.* **1** To keep on performing, go on with, continue: *ut non possem ~are somnum* ES 228; *~avimus dicendo* VR 35.8. **2** (pass.) To remain in existence, continue: *Antiquissima Ecclesia...~abatur post diluvium* AC 407. **3** (pass., of topics) To be further discussed: *quae nunc de Abramo ~antur* AC 1540; (impers.) *~atur ad finem capitis de infestatione illa* AC 6635. **4** (pass.) To extend, stretch: *porticus...~atus usque ad ejus* [sc. *collis*] *caput* VR 48.1.

continuum ~i, *neut.* **1** A continuation, extension: *cupiditates quae sunt ~a amorum istorum* AC 760. **2** *Ex ~o*, immediately, at once: *omne delitium absque sua...anima ex ~o elanguescit* AM 8.4.

continuus ~a ~um, *a.* **1** Uninterrupted, unbroken, continuous: **a** (in space): *aedificia ~a altissima* ES 844; cf. *tunc apparerent serpentes ~i* [i.e., all over, totally] ES 2497. **b** (in time): *in ~o conatu subjugandi sunt* AC 6666.1. **c** (in order): *scientifica...in ~as series disposita sunt* AC 6690. **2** Continuously present, permanent: *sunt in coelo...~a repraesentativa Domini* AC 1619. **3** Forming a continuous series, constantly repeated: *per ~as tunc victorias* DD 33.1.

contio: see **concio**.

contionata: see **concionata**.

contionator: see **concionator**.

contionor: see **concionor**.

contorqueo ~quere ~si ~tum, *tr.* **1** To twist, screw up: *~serunt et plicaverunt labia in plures sinus* VR 111.2; *quod...serpentis modo ~querent se in orbes* CI 400.3. **2** To distort the form or meaning of, twist: *quod omnia cupiverint ~quere* ES 933.

contorsio ~onis, *f.* A twisting together: AC 829.2.

contortim, *adv.* With unnatural twisting, contortedly: *sicut manci, qui modo una manu ~im operantur* CC 7.

contortus ~us, *m.* A twist (forming a knot): VR 74.2.

contra[1], *prep. w. acc.* **1** In opposition to, against: *doctrina...pugnans ~a falsa* SS 12.1; *quid exercitus valeret ~a hostes absque duce?* VR 10. **2** To the detriment of, against the interests of: *ita facere non potest ullus herus probus ~a famulos suos* VR 134.3. **3** Not in conformity with, contrary to: *~a Divinum ordinem* CI 296; *rationalia ~a apparentias...aspernantur* AM 442. **4** With regard to, towards: *amorem ~a illum declarant* AC 3427.2.

contra[2], *adv.* On the other hand: *~a venient ab ortibus et occasibus* Luke 13.28 (AC 1032.3); *dum ~a ii qui instructi, indignati* ES 204.

contractio ~onis, *f.* A contraction: *dextrae parti capitis...inducebant speciem ~onis cum dolore* AC 6811.

contractus ~a ~um, *a.* (pf. pple. of **contraho**) In senses of vb., esp. **1** Contracted: *iris et pupilla nunc dilatata, nunc ~a* AE 37. **2** Restricted in ability, poor, feeble: *loco spiritus ~i* Isa. 61.3 (VR 156.2).

contradico ~cere ~xi ~ctum, *tr.* To contradict: *possunt loqui et non ~ci* FI 9; (also w. dat.) to speak against: *cui [cultui] ~cere...non ausi fuerint* AC 4227.2; (absol.) *in se ~cunt* ES 2383.

contradictio ~onis, *f.* A contradiction: *omnipotentia limitata est ~o* VR 74.4.

contradictorius ~a ~um, *a.* Internally inconsistent, contradictory: *~um prorsus est quod malum dominari possit super malum* AC 987.3.

contraho ~here ~xi ~ctum, *tr.* **1** To draw together, contract: *quicquid recondere vult homo, hoc ~hit faciem ejus* AC 4799.3. **2** To restrict, limit: *stellae ~hent splendorem suum* Joel 2.10 (SS 14.3); *quae* [sc. *cogitatio*]... *~hitur ad particularia* AC 6804.2. **3** To enter upon, take up, contract: *quod...matrimonium ~heret* AC 471; *natura quam ~ximus in mundo* VR 79.8. **4** To have befall one, incur, contract (evils): *~here delirium* VR 31.2; *~hunt...horrores pro talibus* AC 955.

contranitor ~ti ~xus (*or* ~sus) sum, *intr.* To exert force or influence in opposition, strive against, resist: *non possunt aperire os...aura enim caelestis...~titur* VR 6.3; (w. dat.) *~titur flumini* ES 2384.

contrarietas *~atis, f.* A spirit of opposition, resistance: *quodcunque non favet amori proprio...hoc excitat ~atem* AC 357.

contrarior ~ari ~atus sum, *intr.* To be in opposition, go against: *ut ne quidem audire velint aliquid quod ~atur* AC 806; (w. dat.) AC 357.

contrarius ~a ~um, *a.* **1** Acting in opposition, opposed, hostile: *binae rotae in ~o versu* VR 57.2; *sphaerae...spirituales...sunt paene ~ae* AC 6816; (w. dat.) *vitam ~am vitae spirituali* AC 6685. **2** Of opposite nature, reverse, contrary: *in sensu ~o* AC 1005; (neut. as sb.) the reverse, opposite: *hoc confirmatur etiam ex suo ~o* VI 45; *qui non in bono charitatis vixerunt, sed in ~is* AC 6692.1.

contravenio ~nire ~ni, *tr.* To speak in opposition, contradict, dispute: *quod Ecclesiae sit judicare de vero sensu...Scripturae Sacrae, et quod qui ~niunt... puniendi sint* AR Doc RC.9.

contravolutio ~onis, *f.* A rolling in the opposite direction: ES 1373.

contrecto ~are ~avi ~atum, *tr.* **1** To search by touching or handling: *~abat Laban omne tentorium* Gen. 31.34 (AC 4152); *quia ~asti omnia vasa mea, quid invenisti?* Gen. 31.37 (AC). **2** To handle amorously, caress, fondle: *ibi compressa sunt ubera earum, et ibi ~arunt mammas virginitatis earum* Ezek. 23.3 (AC 6432.4); to handle, feel: *~abat Laban omne tentorium* Gen. 31.34 (AC).

contremisco ~miscere ~mui, *intr.* To be shaken, tremble, quake: *~miscet terra e loco suo* Isa. 13.13 (AC 23); Ps. 18.7 (AE 304.15).

contribuo ~ere ~i ~tum, *intr.* To make a contribution (towards a stated result): *varietates...quae ~unt ad perfectionem totius* AC 1285.3; (w. acc.) *non quod coelum aliquid ex se ~erit* AC 6720.

contristo ~are ~avi ~atum, *tr.* To make sad, depress: *laetificant animum, et non ~ant* AM 355.5.

contritio ~onis, *f.* **1** Crushing: *per ~onis modum crudelem* ES 3298. **2** Mental self-abasement, contrition: VR 512.

contritus ~a ~um, *a.* (pf. pple. of **contero**) **1** Contrite: *in ~o et humili spiritu* Isa. 57.15 (DD 49). **2** (ad. Hebr.) *~us contritione*, castrated: Deut. 23.1 (AC 2468.15).

controversia ~ae, *f.* A controversy: *haereses et ~ae* AC 2120.

controverto ~tere ~ti ~sum, *intr.* To engage in controversy, dispute: *minus de aliquo vero ~tunt* CI 270.2.

contubernalis ~is, *m.* One who shares one's dwelling: AS 432.2.

contubernium ~i, *neut.* An assembly of persons living together: *nos populares in nostro ~o convenimus* AM 105.

contuli: pf. of **confero**.

contumacia ~ae, *f.* An instance of contumacious conduct ES 4478.

contumaciter, *adv.* (superl. *~cissime*) Contumaciously: *se ex semet vivere ~citer instant* AC 150.

contumax ~acis, *a.* (compar. *~acior*, superl. *~acissimus*) Resistant to authority, contumacious, stubborn: *tam ~aces sunt, ut nusquam velint desistere* AC 5185; *oppugnationes charitatis quae ~aces* AC 8096.2.

contumelia ~ae, *f.* A severe insult, contumely: AM 469.

contumeliose, *adv.* Insultingly: *ne ~e loquantur de Christo* UJ(C) 79.

contumeliosus ~a ~um, *a.* Severely insulting: *ideo ~um erat scissis vestibus ire* AC 4763.7.

contundo ~ndere ~di ~sum, *tr.* To pound up: *quod posset ossa mea minutim ~ndere* CI 231; to bruise: *calamum ~sum* Isa. 42.3 (AC 25); (transf.) to smite, break (people): *fortes eorum ~si sunt* Jer. 46.5 (DD 14.4).

conturbatio ~onis, *f.* Disorder, confusion: *mittet Jehovah in te maledictionem, ~onem et increpationem* Deut. 28.20 (AC 8364.3).

conturbo ~are ~avi ~atum, *tr.* **1** To set in disorder, derange, upset: *~asti flumina tua* Ezek. 32.2 (AC 7293.2); (enemies) *~avit illos* Ps. 18.14 (DD 14.6). **2** To disturb mentally, trouble: *illa... ~ata est super verbo ejus* Luke 1.29 (DD 19.2).

contus ~i, *m.* (Gk.) A pole: *demiserunt ~um transversum* ES 1553.

contusio ~onis, *f.* A striking: *cum ~one incudis* Isa. 41.7 (AC 3527.3).

conus ~i, *m.* (Gk.) A cone (as a geometrical figure): AC 5389.

convalesco ~lescere ~lui, *intr.* To become healthy, be cured: *quod...a morbis spiritualibus... ~lescerent* AE 706.14.

convello ~vellere ~vulsi ~vulsum, *tr.* To tear from its position, pull up, uproot: *ne quid...subintret quod ~vellit ejus funes et palos* VR 758.2; to convulse: *ut spiritus eorum ~vulserit omne eorum corpus* ES 3767; (fig.) *in...veritatibus quae infirmari, ~velli et impugnari nequeunt* SE 16.

conveniens ~ntis, *a.* (pres. pple. of **convenio**) (compar. *~ntior*) Fitting, suitable: *quod...detur viro uxor ~ns* AM 45; *non ~ns est prophetam interire extra Hierosolymam* Luke 13.33 (DD 15.3); (w. dat.) *affectio veri ~ntis usui* CI 517.3.

convenienter, *adv.* (compar. *~ius*, superl. *~issime*) Fittingly: *quod...altera [vis] recipiat et ~er cedat* CI 589.2; AC 7408.2.

convenientia ~ae, *f.* The quality or fact of being fitting, suitability: *~a et repugnantia* ES 482; *per quae [sc. cantica] ~ae rerum cum sonis affectionum formabantur* AE 326.2.

convenio ~nire ~ni ~ntum, *intr.* (*tr.*) **1** To come together, assemble, meet: *ut in hunc collem... ~niant* AM 2.1. **b** (tr.) to encounter, meet (a person): *pauperes etiam perplures ~ni* ES 766. **2** To come to an agreement, agree: *nos ~nimus cum sodalibus nostris ...quod homo non nascatur in ullum amorem* VR 48.13. **b** (tr.) to agree on, reach (an agreement): *post pacta ~nta* VR 730.1. **3** To be suitable, suit, fit: *transire in aliam [vitam] quae non ita ~nit* CI 49; (impers. w. inf.) *quod nequaquam ~niat homini...in solis cognitionibus subsistere* AC 6815.

conventiculum ~i, *neut.* A small assembly: ES 3766.

conventio ~onis, *f.* An agreement: *post ~onem inter illos tacitam* AM 248.2.

conventus ~us, *m.* **1** A coming together, meeting: *in medio intellectu fit ~us influxuum* VR 11.3. **2** A meeting of persons, assembly: *ad locum ~us* AM 25; *tentorium ~us* Exod. 28.43 (AC).

conversabilis ~is ~e, *a.* (of persons) Sociable: *quia ~is erat et flexilis* ES 1172.

conversatio ~onis, *f.* Social intercourse, meeting: *voluptates amicitiae et ~onis cum sociis* AC 994.2; ES 294.

conversim, *adv.* With interchange, crosswise: (of crossing hands) *~im misit manus suas* Gen. 48.14 (AC).

conversio ~onis, *f.* **1** A turning (of oneself or a part of the body): *vertunt...faciem ad Ipsum...de qua ~one videatur...* AE 37; *per ~onem a Deo ad semet* AM 444.4. **2** A change (of one thing into another): *non per ~onem Essentiae Divinae in corpus* Sym. Ath. (DD 56); VI 8; *~o status vitae* AR 84.

conversor ~ari ~atus sum, *intr.* To have social intercourse, consort: *inter se ~antur angeli in summa felicitate* AC 1521; *cum quibus ~atus sum et saepe loquutus* AC 7801.

converto ~tere ~ti ~sum, *tr.* **1** To direct, turn (oneself or one's face in a specified direction): *~timus facies ad orientem* AM 75.2; *cum angeli se ~tunt ad hominem* CI 252; (pass. as refl.) *~sus Petrus videt discipulum* John 21.20 (AE 9.3). **2** To convert (to a new belief): *ad fidem in Dominum prius ~tes lapides quam illos* AC 8301.6. **3** To change, convert (into something different): *~tere diabolos et satanas in angelos* VR 58.1.

convibratio ~onis, *f.* Vibration: ES 1651.

convicior ~ari ~atus sum, *tr.* also **convitior**. To insult, abuse: *~ari et blasphemare Deum* VR 298.

convicium ~i, *neut.* also **convitium**. An insult: *duo illa ~a declarata sunt pro mendaciis* IM 21; VR 300.

convictio ~onis, *f.* A strongly held belief, conviction: *ut ~o evidens fiat quod sit flagitium* AM 501.

convictrix ~icis, *f. adj.* Serving to convince, convincing: *num aliqua sapientia dabilis sit, quae ~ix quod...* AM 478.2.

convinco ~ncere ~ci ~ctum, *tr.* To impart a firm belief to, convince: *ille sensus potest... ~ncere etiam hominem naturalem* SS 4; (esp. pass.) *~cti sunt quod illis...perceptio esset* VI 7; *dum ratio humana ex Verbo... ~ncitur* VR 4.3.

convitior: see **convicior**.

convitium: see **convicium**.

conviva ~ae, *m.* A fellow banqueter, table companion: AM 16.3.

convivium ~i, *neut.* A ceremonial meal, feast, banquet: *comessationes et ~a* AM 6.5.

convivo ~vere ~xi, *intr.* To live together: AM 224.

convivor ~ari ~atus sum, *intr.* To partake of a banquet, feast: AC 3832.1.

convocatio ~onis, *f.* **1** A call to assemble, invitation: *de ~one omnium ad regnum Domini* SS 15.3. **2** An assembly, meeting: *~ones...fiebant ad quodlibet festum* AC 7891. **3** A place of assembly: *creabit Jehovah...super ~ones ejus nubem* Isa. 4.5 (AE 294.10).

convoco ~are ~avi ~atum, *tr.* To call together, summon: *quod Dominus... ~averit duodecim Suos discipulos* VR 4.1.

convolutio ~onis, *f.* A winding around, twist: ES 231.

convolutus ~a ~um, *a.* (pf. pple. of **convolvo**) Wound around, twisted: *~o pileo sicut Turcarum* ES 723.

convolvo ~vere ~vi ~utum, *tr.* **1** To twist together, screw up: *~vi me sicut serpens admotus igni* AM 10.5; [*natura*] *~vit se in vortices* VR 79.2. **2** To roll up (a scroll): *~vens librum* Luke 4.20 (DD 11); AE 299.3.

convulsio ~onis, *f.* A convulsion: *per lethiferas corporis ~ones* VR 500.2.

convulsivus ~a ~um, *a.* Convulsive: *~os motus agere* UJ(C) 87.

cooperatio ~onis, *f.* A working together, cooperation: CI 453.3.

cooperativus ~a ~um, *a.* (neut. as sb.) The ability to cooperate: *aufer homini activum et ~um tunc, annon etiam aufers receptivum?* VR 505.3.

cooperatrix ~icis, *f. adj.* Working together, cooperating: *~ice vi* ES 655.

cooperor ~ari ~atus sum, *intr.* To work together, cooperate: *Divinum...adjuvit et ~atum est* VR 97.

coopertus ~a ~um, *a.* Covered over: *omnes* [*aperturae*] *sunt ~ae* CI 585.

coopto ~are ~avi ~atum, *tr.* To admit as a member of a group, induct, co-opt: *quod baptismi...finis sit ut homines...in Christianam communionem ~entur* AR Doc Ref.7.

coordinatio ~onis, *f.* Combination in a regular structure, coordination: [*variorum*] *harmonica ~o et dispositio ad unum* AM 524.2.

coordino ~are ~avi ~atum, *tr.* To arrange in regular structure, coordinate: *omnes...secundum Divinum ordinem ~ati et subordinati sunt* CI 392; AM 249.1.

cophinus ~i, *m.* (Gk.) A large basket, hamper: Matt. 14.20 (AE 430.15).

copia ~ae, *f.* **1** Amount, quantity, number: *in majore aut minore ~a* FI 26. **2** Large amount or number, abundance: *documenta...propter ~am hic non possunt adduci* AM 39; *verum...in ~a* AC 6745.2. **3** Opportunity, scope, ability: *quod...detur ~a bono ut succedat* AM 147; (w. gen. of gerund) *cum...datum est aliquid ~ae loquendi* CI 343; (app., w. inf.) *~a aliquid dicere* [*dicendi* Tafel] ES 1073. **4** A copy (of a book, document, etc.): *Joschua scripsit super lapide altaris ~am Legis Mosis* Josh. 8.32 (AC 6752.6).

copiose, *adv.* In large amounts or numbers, copiously: *haec...ab angelis ~e et plene* [*percipiuntur*] AC 167.

copiosus ~a ~um, *a.* (compar. *~ior*) Present in large amounts, abounding, copious: *~iorem multo et meliorem intellectum rerum* ES 1923.

copula ~ae, *f.* A thing which joins, link, connection: *~a est rupta* AC 1096.3; *ne* [*filia*] *invita feratur ad ~am cum viro inamato* AM 299.2.

copulatio ~onis, *f.* **1** Sexual intercourse, copulation: *~ones extraconjugiales* AM 320.2; (transf.) *omnium...est conjugii instar seu ~o, ut verorum cum bonis* AC 747. **2** A wedding: *ex ritualibus desponsationum et ~onum* AC 5317.

copulatus ~a ~um, *a.* Intimately connected, coupled, linked: (w. dat.) *cum intellectus voluntati ~us est* AC 55.2; (w. *cum*) *spiritualis homo faedere matrimoniali ~us cum naturali* AM 282.1.

copulo ~are ~avi ~atum, *tr.* To connect intimately, couple, link: *cum fide erronea non potest charitas... ~ari* SE 50.

coqua ~ae, *f.* A female cook: 1 Sam. 8.13 (AC 2567.10).

coquo ~ere coxi coctum, *tr.* (*intr.*) **1** To prepare (food) by means of heat, boil, bake: *azyma coxit* Gen. 19.3 (AC); *non ~es hoedum in lacte matris suae* Exod. 23.19 (AC). **b** to boil (as dist. from baking): *distinguitur assatum a cocto* AC 7852.1. **c** (as a kind of torture): *unus alium ~it in aqua calida fervente* ES 2711; AC 941.1. **2** (intr., fig. of hatred) To be in ferment, seethe: ES 1276.

coquus ~i, *m.* A cook: ES 2500.

cor cordis, *neut.* **1** (anat.) The heart: *sicut cor et pulmo in thorace* SS 33. **2** The heart regarded as the seat of the will: *amabis Dominum...ex toto corde tuo* Matt. 22.37 (AC 6632); *ut corda auditorum ad pietatem moveant* AC 6914.3. **b** *cordi esse*, to be pleasing or agreeable: *quid plus homini cordi esse debet...?* AC 794.2. **3** The heart regarded as the seat of the intellect: *ne...corde intelligant* Matt. 13.15 (VR 7).

corallium ~i, *neut.* A coral: *a ~is in fundo marium* AS 61.

coram, *prep. w. abl.* and *adv.* **1** In the sight or presence of, before the eyes of: *cum transformatus fuit [Dominus] ~m...discipulis* VR 104; *nonne tota terra ~m te?* Gen. 13.9 (AC). **b** before (someone's eyes): *~m oculis nostris* AC 6697. **2** In the mental perception of, in the estimation of: *humiliationis ~m parentibus* VR 106.1; *in Deo et ~m Deo...non fuerunt spatia et tempora* VR 30.2. **3** From the point of view of, regarded from: *quod...fabulosum sit ~m ratione* VR 82.1. **4** (adv.) Openly, to view: *sistitur pars inimica ~m* AC 1044.3; *ut sisteretur ~m quomodo se habent* ES 3328.

Coranum ~i, *m.* see also **Alcoranum**. The Koran: ES 5666[a].

corbis ~is, *f.* A basket: Jer. 24.1 (AE 403.18).

corculum ~i, *neut.* A tiny heart (of an insect): VR 12.4.

coriaceus ~a ~um, *a.* Made of leather: *quia [tympanum] est ~um* AC 8337.3.

coriandrum ~i, *neut.* (Gk.) Coriander: Exod. 16.31 (AC).

corium ~i, *neut.* Tanned hide, leather: *sonus pulsati ~i* VR 391.1.

cornea ~ae, *f.* (anat.) The cornea: VR 346.2.

corniculum ~i, *neut.* A small projection (on a Hebrew letter): Matt. 5.18 (AC 6752.2); *literae...inflexae cum ~is sursum vergentibus* SS 90.1.

cornu ~u, *neut.* (gen. sg. *~u* ES 3498, AC 5573, AC 9081, and 1st and 2nd edns. of AM 439; gen. sg. *~us* in 3rd and 4th edns. of AM 439) **1** The horn of an animal: *~ibus vestris feritis...oves* Ezek. 34.21 (AC 1085.1); *~u magnum hirci* Dan. 8.8 (FI 65). **2** A horn as a symbol of power: *crescere faciam ~u domui Israelis* Ezek. 29.21 (DD 4); cf. *vinea...in ~u filii olei* Isa. 5.1 (AC 9139.4). **3** A horn used as a container for liquids: *fiebat hoc per oleum ex ~u* AE 316.28. **4** Anything shaped like a horn: **a** the infundibulum of the brain: ES 915. **b** each of the projections on the altar: Exod. 27.2 (AC).

cornucopia ~ae, *f.* (in mythology) The horn of plenty: *est...quodvis [dogma] sicut ~a, ex qua quisque depromit quod suo genio favet* VR 154.2.

cornuferio ~rire, *tr.* To strike with the horn, gore: Deut. 33.17 (AC 2832.4), but better as two words, cf. Exod. 21.31 (AC).

cornupeta ~ae, *m.* One who strikes with the horn: (of an ox) Exod. 21.29 (AC).

cornutus ~a ~um, *a.* Having horns, horned: AE 316.1; AR 417.4.

corolla ~ae, *f.* A small wreath or chaplet of flowers worn round the head: *~ae ex floribus decorabant capita illorum* AM 137.1; AC 546.

corollarium ~i, *neut.* (in logic) A corollary: CI 78; (also, more generally) an additional detail, appendage, pendant: *~i loco, licet hoc memorandum adjicere* AC 5061.

corona ~ae, *f.* **1** A crown (worn as a symbol of royalty): *quod rex...portaret ~am ex auro* AE 31.6. **2** A final and culminating part, culmination, crown: *ex Verbo, quod est revelationis ~a* VR 11.1; *quod Nova haec Ecclesia sit ~a omnium Ecclesiarum* VR 787.

coronalis ~is ~e, *a.* **1** Of or resembling a crown: *in cinctura ~i circum collum erant* 'wore collars with ruffs' VR 137.3. **2** Culminating: *appendix ~is* JU (ad finem).

coronamentum ~i, *neut.* A decoration worn like a crown on the head: *visus est sicut columba volans, sed cum ~o super capite* AM 293.7.

coronarius ~a ~um, *a.* Culminating: SE 116 titulus.

coronatio ~onis, *f.* The formal attribution of a crown to a new monarch, coronation: AE 31.6; VR 721.

coronis ~idis, *f.* (Gk.) A concluding section, tailpiece, conclusion: *~idis loco ad hoc opus* VR 795.

corono ~are ~avi ~atum, *tr.* **1** To crown (a monarch): AE 31.6. **2** To endow (with an attribute) as with a crown: *quos...vita aeterna ~aturi sint* VR 16.1. **3** To add a finishing touch to, crown: *rogatus ut ~aret responsa dixit...* VR 160.6.

corporalis ~is ~e, *a.* Of or pertaining to the body, bodily, corporeal: *omnia quae ex illo [sc. amore sui] sequuntur, quod sint ~ia...quia homo hujus amoris ...cogitationes mentis suae immergit corpori* CC 17.

corporaliter, *adv*. In bodily form: Col. 2.9 (VR 101).

corporatura ~ae, *f.* Bodily form, embodiment: *spirituales maritorum jucunditates induunt naturalem quasi ~am apud nos* AM 155[a].4; ES 1038.

corporee, *adv*. In a bodily or material form: *homines idem intelligerent naturaliter et ~e* ES 1221.

corporeus ~a ~um, *a*. **1** Of or relating to the body, bodily, corporeal: *in amoribus ~is* AC 7041.2; (neut. as sb.) *materialia, mundana, ~a et terrestria* AC 6816. **2** (of persons) Concerned only with bodily matters: *fieri ~us, sicut fuit ante regenerationem* AC 305; (neut. as sb.) the bodily part of the human personality: *quod ~um hominis perdiderit omnem intellectum veri* AC 625.

corpulentus ~a ~um, *a*. (of persons) Stout, corpulent: ES 1515.

corpus ~oris, *neut*. **1** The body (of a human being): *quod is vult, hoc agit ~us* CI 228; (esp., dist. from **anima**) *sicut anima in ~ore* AE 10.1. **b** the trunk (as dist. from head and limbs): *circum caput, ad aures, circum ~us, ad pedes* ES 406. **2** The body as the visible part of the human being: *qui ~ore apparet ut homo* AC 288. **3** The body as representative of the state of life on earth: *in mundo, ubi sum ~ore* VR 160.1; *dum vivit in ~ore* [*homo*] AC 6639.2. **4** A material object, body: *quod haec* [sc. the planets] *inania ~ora sint* AC 6697; *~us consonans* ES 2003. **b** (anat.) a body of tissue: *~us medullosum* ES 862; (of the brain) *in ~oribus striatis* AM 315.5. **5** The material part of anything: *verbis...quae sunt ~us loquelae* ES 895. **6** A group of persons organized after the fashion of the human body: *~us maximum, quod est mundus spirituum* ES 2439; cf. *quod illi qui ab Ecclesia sunt faciant Christi ~us* VR 113.8.

corpuscularis ~is ~e, *a*. Of or relating to a small body, corpuscular: *se induere ~i forma in ovulo* AC 1815.1.

corpusculum ~i, *neut.* A corpuscule: *quod anima hominis...possit omnipraesens esse ubivis in suo ~o* ES 4016.

corrado ~dere ~si ~sum, *tr.* To scrape together, assemble laboriously: *priusquam...omnium...opes ~serit* AC 987.2; *~dit et cumulat confirmantia* AC 589.

correctio ~onis, *f.* Chastisement, correction: *in die ~onis* Hos. 5.9 (AC 5354.4).

correptio ~onis, *f.* A rebuking, chastening: Ps. 73.14 (AE 475.16).

correspondens ~ntis, *neut.* That which corresponds: *quod...jucunda...vertantur in ~ntia* CI 485.

correspondenter, *adv.* In a corresponding fashion: *media...se habebunt ad primum et ultimum ~er* AC 10259; AS 412.

correspondentia ~ae, *f.* **1** A mutual relationship of one thing with another, correspondence: *quod ~a sit omnium quae in naturali mundo sunt cum omnibus quae in spirituali* CI 303. **2** The relationship between natural objects and spiritual ideas, correspondence: *scientia ~arum* AM 342.2; *quid 'os'...significat non constare potest nisi ex ~a* AC 6987.1. **3** An object which serves to convey a corresponding spiritual idea: *etiam ~ae sunt quae ab industria humana...ad usum parantur, sicut...cibi, vestes...* CI 104.

correspondeo ~dere ~di, *intr.* **1** To be in agreement or harmony, suit, fit (w. dat.): *ibi 'aurum, aes et lignum' sibi ~dent* AC 643.1. **2** (of things on the natural and spiritual planes) To have a special correspondence, correspond: *intellectus...~det pulmoni, et voluntas cordi* VI 46; *os cum labiis ~det loquelae interiori* AC 6987.1.

corrigia ~ae, *f.* A cord used to tie footwear, lace: Gen. 14.23 (AC); John 1.27 (DD 37.3).

corripio ~ripere ~ripui ~reptum, *tr.* **1** To seize upon, attack: *lumbos ejus plagis ~ripit* VR 122. **2** (pass., w. abl.) To be seized (with pain, fear, etc.): *dolore ~ripientur* Isa. 23.5 (AE 275.4); *~ripiuntur terrore* AC 1740.3; (w. *ab*) *zelus a quo multi ~ripiuntur* VR 146. **3** *Viam ~ripere*, to hasten away, start suddenly: ES 1110.

corroborate, *adv.* (compar. *~ius*) With strength, strongly: ES 1364.

corroboratio ~onis, *f.* A strengthening: AE 819.2.

corroboro ~are ~avi ~atum, *tr.* To give strength to, strengthen: *sic ~abuntur socii* AC 6657.1; *haec idea ~atur indies* VR 8.2.

corrodo ~dere ~si ~sum, *tr.* To gnaw away, corrode: *quod...~dat et perdat omnia* [*in corpore*] ES 1801; *falsum...~dit...et sic cruciat* AC 8481.

corrugatio ~onis, *f.* A making wrinkled, wrinkling: *~o et horripilatio* AC 4180.4.

corrugo ~are ~avi ~atum, *tr.* To make wrinkled: *quod facies...ex lugubri statu animi se ~et* AC 10492.2.

corrumpo ~mpere ~pi ~ptum, *tr.* **1** To make worse, spoil: *quod* [*cingulum*]...*invenit ~ptum* Jer. 13.7 (DD 15.4); VR 378. **2** To spoil morally, defile: *altera ~pit amorem suum plusquam illa* Ezek. 23.11 (AE 141.4).

corruo ~ere ~i, *intr.* To fall down, collapse: *urbes gentium ~erunt* Rev.16.19 (AE 223.4).

corruptela ~ae, *f.* A means of corrupting morally,

corrupting influence: *quod prandia et caenae...sint ~ae ad trahendum in partes* VR 433.1.

corruptio ~onis, *f.* Corruption: *~o et praevaricatio in cultu* AC 10420.1.

corruptor ~oris, *m.* One who corrupts or spoils: *vae...filiis ~oribus* Isa. 1.4 (AE 768.24).

cortex ~icis, *m.* **1** The bark (of a tree): *~ices circum arbores* AM 232.1; ES 251. **2** The superficial part of anything: *docti...amant...solum in ~ice errare* AC 3677.2.

corticalis ~is ~e, *a.* **1** Of or relating to bark: *per ~ia putamina* ES 1475. **2** (anat.) Of the cortex of any organ, cortical: VR 351.3; ES 999.

corticeus ~a ~um, *a.* Taken from or made out of bark: *vestiuntur ibi vestibus quae ex fibris ~is quarundam arborum conficiunt, quae illam consistentiam habent ut contexi queant et quoque conglutinari* AC 7485.

cortina ~ae, *f.* A tent curtain: *extendit coelos sicut ~am* Ps. 104.2 (AE 283.8).

corus ~i, *m.* (Hebr.) A Hebrew measure of capacity equivalent to a homer: Hos. 3.2 (AE 374.13).

coruscans ~ntis, *a.* (superl. *~ntissimus*) Gleaming: ES 4639.

coruscatio ~onis, *f.* The action of glittering: *~o ut solis* AE 391.13.

corusco ~are ~avi, *intr.* To glitter, gleam: *quod... lampades...~arent* VR 16.1; *vestimenta Ipsius facta sunt ~antia* Mark 9.3 (AE 67.1).

coruscus ~a ~um, *a.* (neut. as sb.) A gleam of light, flash: *cave...ne ~um...penetret interius* AM 42.2.

corvus ~i, *m.* A raven: *quod ~us sit albus et non niger* AM 233.4.

corylus ~i, *f.* A hazel tree: AC 4013.2.

costa ~ae, *f.* **1** (anat.) A rib: AC 147; SS 33. **2** The front or back members of a structure: *super duabus ~is ejus* [sc. *altaris*] Exod. 30.4 (see AC 10189.1).

costum ~i, *neut.* (Gk.) An aromatic plant, but app. used to mean a scented ointment, pomade: *ad emendum ~um* ES 2954.

cotidianus: see **quotidianus**.

cotidie: see **quotidie**.

cottidianus: see **quotidianus**.

cottidie: see **quotidie**.

coturnix ~icis, *f.* A quail: VR 810.

counio ~nire ~nivi ~nitum, *tr.* To join into one, unite: *Divinus Amor...tria illa ~nit apud hominem* AE 1084.2; *~nitus fascis* AM 427.

coxendix ~icis, *f.* (anat.) The hip: ES 884.

crabro ~onis, *m.* A hornet: VR 69.2.

cranium ~i, *neut.* (Gk.) A skull: *in ~is a cerebro vacuis* AM 186.1.

crapulo ~are ~avi, *intr.* To suffer from the after-effects of intoxication, have a hangover: *vinum urget in illos qui ~ant* VR 459.7.

cras, *adv.* Tomorrow: AM 21.1; (as indecl. sb.) *ad cras* Exod. 8.19 (AC).

crassamentum ~i, *neut.* A thick layer or deposit, impurity, dregs: *sphaera quae circumfundit illos apparet sicut ~um* AC 4949; AM 495.3; (transf.) *nec vitam...inquinaverunt ~is ex honoribus et divitiis* CI 515.

crasse, *adv.* (compar. *~ius*, superl. *~issime*) Grossly: *voces...~ius materiales* AC 1876.2; *perquam ~e cogitaretur de Divino* AC 5943.2.

crassesco ~ere, *intr.* To become gross: *illi in descensu ~unt et fiunt materiales et corporei* AS 274.2.

crassities ~ei, *f.* Grossness: *~e ingenii* ES 169.

crassitudo ~inis, *f.* **1** Density, thickness: *cujus* [*faciei*] *magnitudo et ~o* [*crassa talis* Autograph] *tanta erat* ES 2498. **2** Mental dullness: *quod redigerentur in talem ~inem* ES 3927.

crassiuscule, *adv.* In a rather gross manner: ES 3923.

crassiusculus ~a ~um, *a.* Rather gross: *modo... regulari, sed ~o* ES 1819.

crassus ~a ~um, *a.* (compar. *~ior*, superl. *~issimus*) **1** (of solids) Thick, dense, heavy: *argenti laminam ~iorem* ES 4045; *~o corpore* AM 178.1. **2** (of liquids) Thick, viscous: *succum ~iorem* SS 66; (also, of dust) *~us et pungens grumus* AC 545.2. **3** (of sounds) Dull, heavy: *~um murmur sicut molae ingentis* ES 910; AC 826. **4** Lacking in subtlety, coarse, gross: *dicebant quod illa quae scriberem admodum ~a essent* AC 6929; *non in tam ~is affectionibus...possunt esse* CI 345; *~a est falsitas* AC 892.1. **5** (of persons, their minds or senses) Unable to perceive fine distinctions, gross, crass: *quod visus oculi tam ~us...sit, ut plura insectula spectet ut unum obscurum* VR 12.4; [*spiritus*] *redacti in statum ~issimum* ES 3927.

crastinus ~a ~um, *a.* *~us dies*, the next day, the morrow: Gen. 30.33 (AC); (so, also) *~um*: CI 278.2.

crater ~eris, *m.* (Gk.) A mixing bowl: Exod. 24.6 (AC).

crates ~is, *f.* A grating, framework: (used of teeth) *ingluvies...in qua apparuit dentium ~es* ES 763; ES 1157.

creabilis ~is ~e, *a.* Capable of being created: VR 40.1.

creatio ~onis, *f.* **1** The act of creating, creation: *per ~onem coeli et terrae* AE 29; *Liber ~onis*, the Book of Genesis: CI 137.4. **2** The moment of creation: *a ~one insitus est utrique amor* AM 32. **3** A created thing, creation: *si ~onem creaverit Jehovah* Num. 16.30 (AC 8306).

creator ~oris, *m.* (as epithet or attribute of God) The Creator: *~or et Dominus universi* AC 6876.3.

creatrix ~icis, *f.* A creator: *quod natura sit... ~ix universi* VR 35.2.

creatum ~i, *neut.* A created thing, creation: *Deus... non potest ab ullo ~o videri* VR 6.1.

creatura ~ae, *f.* A living being, creature: AC 772.

creber ~bra ~brum, *a.* Often repeated, frequent: *per ~bros actus* AC 7051.4.

crebro, *adv.* Frequently: *id quod in antecedentibus ~o dictum est* AM 130.4.

credenda ~orum, *neut. pl.* Things which ought to be believed: *cognitio ~orum* AC 654.

credere, *indecl.* (inf. of **credo**) The creed: *qui non dicunt quod vocant Credere* AC 1798.5.

credibilis ~is ~e, *a.* Worthy of belief, credible: *~e...est quod...* AC 7363.

creditor ~oris, *m.* One to whom money or its equivalent is owed, creditor: *duo debitores erant cuidam ~ori* Luke 7.41 (AC 10253.4).

credo ~ere ~idi ~itum, *tr.*, *intr.* **1** To believe, be persuaded of (a fact): **a** (absol.): *~e et non dubita* FI 1; *scire non est ~ere* ES 2467; *quod multi aliter ~iderint* DD 8. **b** (w. acc.): *non ~erent aliquam resurrectionem* AC 6945.3; (pass.) *ut nihil ~atur nisi falsum* AC 6729. **c** (w. *quod*): *~ebant quod Jehovah irasceretur* AC 6997.3; (impers. pass.) *quod ab homine ~i queat quod plures tellures in universo sint* AC 6698. **d** (w. inf. or acc. + inf.): *discipulis... ~entibus videre spiritum* VR 109.1; *qui... ~unt talia vim miraculosum habere* ES 269. **2** To believe in the existence or power of, believe in: **a** (w. *in* + acc.): *quisquis ~it in Me* John 7.38 (SS 2.3); *non ~idit in nomen...Dei* John 3.18 (AC 6674.7); VR 2.1. **b** (w. dat.): *cum simpliciter ~it Verbo* AC 1043.3.

credulus ~a ~um, *a.* Believing: *non esto incredulus sed ~us* John 20.27 (DD 35.9); prone to belief, credulous: ES 1728.

cremasteres ~um, *m. pl.* (Gk.) (anat.) The cremaster muscles: AM 107.

cremo ~are ~avi ~atum, *tr.* To destroy by fire, burn: *de...caminis in quibus [scripta mea] ~ata sint* ES 3296; (in sacrifice) AE 768.25; (as a torture) AC 941.1.

cremor ~oris, *m.* *~or lactis*, cream: ES 6029.

creo ~are ~avi ~atum, *tr.* **1** (of God) To cause to come into existence, create, make: *in Verbo accurata fit distinctio inter ~are, formare et facere* AC 472. **b** (w. pred.) *homo ita ~atus est ut nexum...habeat cum Domino* CI 304.1. **2** (generally) To bring about, produce: *talia quae ~ant stuporem* VR 12.3.

crepitus ~us, *m.* A crackling sound, crackle: 2AD 1957.

crepo ~are ~ui, *intr.* To make an ugly sound, squeak, croak: *cantus ille...coram incastis... ~uit ita discors...* AM 55.8.

crepor ~oris, *m.* A sharp sound, crack: *~or aëris sicut tonitru* VR 77.1.

crepusculum ~i, *neut.* Twilight, dusk: Isa. 5.11 (AE 376.37); (of daybreak) *status qualis ~i matutini* AC 865.1; cf. **diluculum**.

crescentia ~ae, *f.* The process of increasing, increase, growth: *in ~a seu progressione* AM 216.1.

cresco ~ere crevi, *intr.* **1** (of living things) To increase in size by natural processes, grow: *et crevit natus* Exod. 2.10 (AC); *ut ~ere facerent comam* SS 35.3; *calor ...qui facit ut gramina... ~ant* AC 1016.2. **2** (of other things) To increase in size, number or degree, grow, develop: *quod...bonum ~at per vera* AC 6647; *quod ... ~at conjunctio mentium* AM 209.

cribro ~are ~avi ~atum, *tr.* To put through a sieve, sift: *quod sensualia admittant quae e mundo alluunt et quasi ~ent illa* VR 565.3.

cribrosus ~a ~um, *a.* Resembling a sieve, full of holes: *laminam ~am* ES 1793.

cribrum ~i, *neut.* A sieve: *transfluit sicut aqua per ~um* AC 4167.1; a grating, grid (for an altar): Exod. 27.4 (AC).

crimen ~inis, *neut.* An unlawful act, crime: *qui negaverunt sua ~ina et flagitia* CI 462[a].1.

criminosus ~a ~um, *a.* Criminal: AM 459.5.

crinis ~is, *m.* The hair (of the head): **a** (sg.): *quod... consecraret ~em suum* AE 66.3. **b** (pl.): *quod potentia ejus in ~ibus fuerit* SS 49.3.

crinitus ~a ~um, *a.* Covered in hair, hairy: *apparent quoad...faciem ~i* AC 3301.1.

crisis ~eos, *f.* (Gk.) A critical state, crisis: *cum in hac ~i sunt* VR 665.4.

crispo ~are ~avi ~atum, *tr.* (refl.) To become

puckered: *quod amor...substantias formae suae... erigat quasi in cristas...hoc est, ~et se* AM 361.2; *~atus*, having a wavy edge or rim: *pilei naviculares ~ati* 'sailors' cocked hats' AM 78.4; *cassides ~atae* AM 103.1.

crista ~ae, *f.* A crest, ridge (on the head of a bird): *super quarundam [avium] capitibus erant ~ae* VR 71.1; (elsewhere) AM 361.2; AR 438.1. (In VR 331.2 *cristas* is a misprint for *aristas*.)

criterion ~i, *neut.* (Gk.) A mark which permits judgment, criterion: 3AD 5570.

criticus ~a ~um, *a.* (Gk.) Concerned with criticism, critical: *arti ~ae* ES 1950; CI 353.1; (masc. as sb.) a critic: ES 2040.

crocito ~are ~avi, *intr.* (of birds) To croak: *~abant et ululabant aves noctis ferales* AM 521.1.

crocodilus ~i, *m.* (Gk.) A crocodile: AM 79.2; VR 13.4.

cruciatio ~onis, *f.* Torment: *conscientiae ~one* ES 218.

cruciatus ~us, *m.* Torment, torture: *per mille punitionum ac ~uum modos* AC 8232.

crucifigo ~gere ~xi ~xum, *tr.* To nail to a cross as a means of execution, crucify: *quod Dominus sit ~xus* AE 83.1.

crucifixio ~onis, *f.* Crucifixion: AE 655.4.

crucio ~are ~avi ~atum, *tr.* To inflict tortures upon, torment: *ignis...qui ~at illos qui in infernis* AC 6832.9; *hoc ~abit conscientiam* AC 6997.2.

crudelis ~is ~e, *a.* (compar. *~ior*, superl. *~issimus*) **1** (of persons) Delighting in the infliction of pain, cruel: *filia populi Mei ~is* Lam. 4.3 (AC 6745.6). **2** (of things, actions) Characterized by cruelty: *~i cupidine nocendi* CI 283.

crudelitas ~atis, *f.* Cruelty: *utuntur...omni ~ate* AC 6666.2.

crudeliter, *adv.* In a cruel fashion: *~er...tractare* AC 3605.4.

crudus ~a ~um, *a.* **1** (of food) Uncooked, raw: Exod. 12.9 (AC). **2** Not treated, undigested: *chylum qui ~us...influit* ES 1033. **3** Caused by indigestion: *ructus... olidi, ~i* AM 253.2.

cruentus ~a ~um, *a.* Characterized by the shedding of blood, bloody: *~as caedes* AM 107.

crumena ~ae, *f.* A small bag for holding money, purse: *magnas ~as, apparentes sicut sacci, in quibus reconditum fuit argentum* SS 26.3.

cruor ~oris, *m.* Spilt blood, gore: *sanguis...separatus a carne est ~or* VR 367.5.

crus cruris, *neut.* The leg: *statuam...cujus crura ex ferro* AM 78.1.

crusta ~ae, *f.* **1** The shell (of a nut or sim.): *sicut amygdalum intus in ~a* AM 109; *~is ostreae* ES 3611. **2** Any hard outer covering, crust: *venenis obductis ~is saccharinis* VR 148; ES 250.

crustaceus ~a ~um, *a.* Of or belonging to a shell: *hic [amor] vocari potest ~us non nucleatus* AM 312; (neut. as sb.) *sunt quasi ~a seu squamosa* AC 1500; AC 4844.13.

crustatenus, *adv.* In regard to its shell, outwardly: *amygdalae ~us apparentes integrae sed intus a vermibus plane corrosae* AS 424.2 1st edn. and Rogers.

crux crucis, *f.* **1** A cross (as an instrument of execution): *sequere Me, tollens crucem* Mark 10.21 (VI 66.1); esp. that on which the Lord was crucified: *passio crucis* DD 3.6. **2** *In crucem*, to form a cross, crosswise: ES 3404.

crypta ~ae, *f.* (Gk.) An underground room, cellar, crypt: *aufugiunt in ~as et se abscondunt* AM 514.3.

crystall-: see **chrystall-**.

cubatio ~onis, *f.* A lying down: AC 3696.

cubicularius ~i, *m.* An attendant of the bedroom, eunuch: Gen. 37.36 (AC).

cubiculum ~i, *neut.* A bedroom: CI 184; *frigus invaderet maritos, et separaret a toro, ~o et aspectu* AM 155ª.3.

cubicus ~a ~um, *a.* (Gk.) Cubic: *spatium 3 ulnarum ~arum* CI 417.

cubile ~is, *neut.* **1** A bed, couch: Exod. 7.28 (AC); (spec.) the marriage bed: *ascendisti ~ia patris tui* Gen. 49.4 (AC). **2** The lair, den (of an animal): *~e ferae* Zeph. 2.15 (AE 388.11).

cubitum, supine of **cubo**. Only in phr. *~um ire*, to go to bed: AM 23; CO 59.4.

cubitus ~i, *m.* **1** The elbow: *in medium brachium sinistrum, seu in ~um ejus* ES 3405. **2** A measure of length, cubit (about 1 1/2 feet or 45 cm): *mensus est murum ejus, centum quadraginta quatuor ~orum* Rev. 21.17 (AR); AM 7.2.

cubo ~are ~ui ~itum, *intr.* To lie down, recline: *quod ~aret super latere suo* Ezek. 4.4 (SS 16); AM 8.2; (also, of beasts) *balaena...quae ~at in medio fluviorum suorum* Ezek. 29.3 (AC 7293.2).

cubulus ~i, *m.* A small cube: *panis...in tessulas scissus quasi cultris, in ~os* ES 2627.

cucumis ~eris, *m.* A cucumber: Num. 11.5 (AE 513.6).

cucurbita ~ae, *f.* A gourd: Num. 11.5 (AE 513.6).

cudo ~ere, *tr.* To strike (coins): *monetas ~unt, inaurant illas* VR 320.

cujusmodi, *adv.* Of which kind, of a quality: [*apparuerunt vestimenta*] *splendentia, candida valde sicut nix, ~i fullo super terra non potest dealbare* Mark 9.3 (AC 5319.1).

culina ~ae, *f.* A kitchen: AC 2125.

culinaris ~is ~e, *a.* = **culinarius**: ES 3923 (Autograph and Tafel).

culinarius ~a ~um, *a.* Of or belonging to a kitchen: *calor ~us* ES 2711.

culmatus ~a ~um, *a.* (of plants) Having a stalk: *~i sicut hordeum* 2AD 2070.

culmen ~inis, *neut.* A peak, summit: *et ecce ~en ejus non erat ~en, sed planities* AM 77.2.

culmus ~i, *m.* The stem of a cereal grass, stalk: Exod. 9.31 (AC).

culpa ~ae, *f.* **1** Responsibility for wrongdoing, blame, fault: *non...eorum ~a est* AE 452; *in quod conjicere ~am possent* ES 3688. **2** The state of having done wrong, guilt: *sistere illum in ~a* AC 5650.

culpabilis ~is ~e, *a.* Deserving of blame, culpable: *neque foret ~is homo* VR 154.4.

culpo ~are ~avi ~atum, *tr.* To blame, accuse: *~avi illos, qui dixerunt quod...* VR 162.7.

culter ~tri, *m.* **1** A knife: *se ~tris percutere videntur* AC 818. **2** *~ter putatorius*, a pruning hook: Isa. 2.4 (AE 734.2).

cultor ~oris, *m.* One who worships, worshipper: *naturae ~ores* AC 6832.10; *~ores Mahumedis* ES 344; *~ores sui et mundi* CI 327.

cultrarius ~i, *m.* One who uses a knife as a weapon, knifer: *spiritus mali qui vocantur ~i* AC 2799.22.

cultus ~us, *m.* Worship: *templum in quo ~um agit* FI 48; (w. pl.) a particular kind of worship, cult: *sibi novos ~us fingunt* AC 1134.

cum[1], *prep. w. abl.* Placed after personal pronouns: *mecum, tecum, vobiscum*, etc. **1** In company with, together with: *ad...societates...cum quibus non prius fuerat* AC 8367. **b** (Bibl.) *a cum*, from the presence of: *ros a cum Jehovah* Mic. 5.6 (AC 468.3). **2** Simultaneously with, at the time of: *cum quibus* [sc. *imperiis*] *inceperunt amores mundani* VR 9.2. **3** (w. exprs. denoting joining, identity, similarity, etc.) With, as: *communicatio cum bono* AC 8349; *illa unam rem constituunt cum interno* AC 1576. **4** (w. exprs. denoting speech) With: *loquutus est cum nobis* VR 35.13. **5** Regarded together with, combined with: *os cum labiis correspondet loquelae interiori* AC 6987.1. **b** *quid* [*alicui*] *cum...?*, what has (anyone) to do with...?: *quid mihi juveni cum tam sublimi theoremate?* VR 697.6. **6** In possession of, having: *quod Dominus* [*discipulos*] *...emiserit cum mandato ut...* VR 4.1. **7** In agreement with, in keeping with: *respirabant...cum angelis in quorum consortio fuerunt* AC 1119; *non cum veris... sed contra illa* AE 1170.5. **8** In the case of, with: *cum Ecclesiis post diluvium ita se res habuit* AC 1327.1.

cum[2], *conj.* also **quum**. **1** (w. indic.) On all occasions when, whenever: *angeli, cum de infernis cogitant...de falsis et malis abstracte...cogitant* AC 8343. **2** At the time when, when: **a** (w. subj.): *cum viderent illos ita ambulantes* AC 8375. **b** (w. indic.): *cum descendimus...dedit hospes nobis botrum* AM 76.8. **3** (w. indic.) Seeing that, since, as: *cum ita est, videri potest quod...* AM 260; *cum...charitas...est bene velle* VR 408. **4** *Cum tamen* (w. indic.), although: *quod regeneratio non sit scibilis...cum tamen Dominus dicit quod...* VR 591.2.

cuminum ~i, *neut.* (Gk.) Cummin: Isa. 28.25 (AC 10669.4).

cumprimis, *adv.* Above all, especially: *apud omnes qui in coelo, ~is qui in coelo intimo...sunt* AC 7055.3.

cumprimum, *adv.* = **cumprimis**: ES 910; 2AD 52.

cumulo ~are ~avi ~atum, *tr.* To heap or pile up, amass: *opes ~are* CI 358; *~are falsa super falsis* AE 237.6.

cumulus ~i, *m.* A heap, pile: *colligit sicut ~um aquas maris* Ps. 33.7 (AE 275.11).

cuncti ~ae ~a, *pl. adj.* All: (neut. as sb.) *~a quae existunt nascuntur* VR 12.1.

cunctor ~ari ~atus sum, *intr.* To delay, hesitate: Isa. 29.9 (AE 376.32).

cupediae ~diarum, *f. pl.* also **cuppediae**. Foods delightful to the taste, dainties, delicacies: *opimae dapes, ~diae et lautitiae* AM 6.5.

cupedium ~i, *neut.* A dainty, delicacy: *viri...spectant virginitatem sponsae...ut ipsum ~um, ex quo delitiae illius amoris inchoaturae...sunt* AM 503.

cupide, *adv.* Eagerly: AC 4802.1.

cupiditas ~atis, *f.* An intense desire arising in the natural mind, longing, yearning: *~as gloriae* CI 354; *~as malum faciendi* AC 7110; *cupere seu ~as est animi* ES 1568; *~ates seu affectiones malae* AC 744.

cupido ~inis, *f.* Strong desire, longing: *talis illis est ~o cognitionum* AC 6811; *in iis* [sc. *comis*] *~inem habent* ES 1228.

cupidus ~a ~um, *a.* (compar. *~ior*) Desirous, longng,

eager: *~os ad sciscitandum* AM 5.1; also, desired: *ut voluntas non sentiat aliquid lautius et ~ius* AM 495.3.

cupiens ~ntis, *a.* (compar. *~ntior*) Desirous, longing: *ut me multo essent ~ntiores* ES 2169.

cupio ~pere ~pivi (*or* ~pii) ~pitum, *tr.* To wish for in the natural mind, long for, want. **1** (w. acc.): *~piebat coelum* AC 537; *vindictam ~pere* SS 67.4; (pass.) *ex finibus... ~pitis* ES 930; (neut. pl. of pf. pple. as sb.) things wished for, aims: *dolent si ~pitis non potiuntur* AC 8478.2. **2** (w. inf.): *~piunt venire in coelum* AC 7042. **3** (w. preps. and ellipse of vb. of motion) To want to go: *~pit...ab angelorum consortio* AC 315; *in coelum ~piunt* AC 546; *quod ad coelum ~piat* ES 875.

cupisco ~ere, *tr.* = **concupisco**: CH 208 (= Articulus Primus.8).

cuppediae: see **cupediae**.

cupreus ~a ~um, *a.* **1** Made of or characterized by copper: *lamellae ~ae* AM 182.8. **2** (of the third age) *Saeculum ~um*, the Copper Age: CI 115.

cuprum ~i, *neut.* Copper: VI 10; AM 73.2.

cur, *interr.* and *rel. adv.* For what reason, why? **1** (In direct qu.): *quaesivi, 'Cur domus hic ligneae sunt?'* AM 77.2. **2** (In indirect qu.): (w. subj.) *quaesitus est... cur non...scriberet* VR 797.2; (w. indic.) *inde...patet, cur tres coeli sunt* CI 65.

cura ~ae, *f.* **1** Anxiety, trouble, care: *~am pro crastino* CI 278.2; (w. pl.) a source of anxiety: *a ~is in mundo...detenti* FI 30. **2** *~ae esse* (w. gen.), to be a matter of concern (to): *non illorum ~ae est discernere* AM 151; (also, w. dat.) *cum interiora...non ita iis ~ae sunt* ES 3239. **3** *~am habere* (w. gen.), to take care (of), look after: *illorum ... ~am multam Dominus habet* AC 1110.

curabilis ~is ~e, *a.* That may be cured, remediable: *plaga non ~i* Isa. 14.6 (SS 86).

curatio ~onis, *f.* A treatment to restore health, healing, cure: *morborum ~ones seu sanationes* AC 9031.3; *~o palliativa*, a superficial or temporary medical treatment: AE 1152.2; CH 25 (= ii.4); NE 25.

curator ~oris, *m.* One who looks after, caretaker, curator: *quod...fuerit modo ~or alicujus domus* AM 263.2.

curia ~ae, *f.* A meeting house, hall of assembly: *gymnasia...sunt ~ae, ubi conveniunt eruditi* VR 136.1.

curiositas ~atis, *f.* Eagerness for knowledge, curiosity: *ex insita ~ate volebant adhuc plura scire* ES 1628.

curiosus ~a ~um, *a.* **1** Eager for knowledge, curious: *quod ~i sint et cupidi sciendi quales sint* ES 885. **2** Exciting interest, curious: (neut. pl. as sb.) *a quibus audiverunt ~a* AM 151[a].2.

curo ~are ~avi ~atum, *tr.* (*intr.*) **1** To heal, remedy: *malum malo ~atur* ES 2874. **2** (w. acc.) To concern oneself with, take thought for, bother about: *cum nihil ~at coelestia et spiritualia* AC 1707.3; *se modo amant, ac proximum non ~ant* AC 1150. **b** (w. inf.): *nec tantopere ~ant instrui* CI 33. **3** (intr.) To be concerned, care: *non ~ant si illa...vera...sint* AE 115.

curriculum ~i, *neut.* also **curriculus** ~i, *m.* *~um vitae*, the course of life: *in sequente vitae ~o* AM 487.

curriculus: see **curriculum**.

curro ~ere cucurri cursum, *intr.* **1** (of persons or animals) To run: *~entes, ludentes, saltantes* AM 8.2. **2** (of inanimate things) To travel fast, rush: *vox curruum... ~entium in bellum* Rev. 9.9 (AR).

currus ~us, *m.* **1** (in antiquity) A chariot: *vecti in ~u igneo sicut Elias* AM 266.5. **2** (in modern times) Any horse-drawn passenger vehicle, coach: *me versus ~um agere tentant* ES 253.

cursim, *adv.* Hastily, cursorily: *cum aliquid... ~im legerem* ES 2885.

cursitatio ~onis, *f.* A running about: *~o ad aliquam metam* VR 730.

cursito ~are ~avi, *intr.* To run to and fro, scurry: ES 917.

cursor ~oris, *m.* A runner; esp. a messenger, footman: *venit ~or...ac invitavit illos* AM 19; VR 825.

cursorius ~a ~um, *a.* Of runners, running: *ludi ~i* AM 17.4.

cursus ~us, *m.* **1** Fast movement, running: *festino ~u aufugerunt domum* AM 6.4. **2** Movement in a specified direction, course: *solis motum et ~um* SS 95. **3** *Vitae ~us*, the course of one's life: *per totum vitae suae ~um in mundo* AC 6977.

curtus ~a ~um, *a.* Truncated, short: *sceptrum quod est ~us baculus* AC 7026.

curva ~ae, *f.* A curved line, curve: *in circulo et ~is quae se ad circulum referunt* ES 3484; ES 4174.

curvatura ~ae, *f.* A curved line, curve: *inflexionibus et ~is literarum* CI 260.

curvo ~are ~avi ~atum, *tr.* (refl.) To bend oneself, stoop: *~avit se, cubuit sicut leo* Gen. 49.9 (AC).

curvus ~a ~um, *a.* (neut. as sb.) What is curved, bent, or crooked: *ut rectum appareat ~um ac ut ~um appareat rectum* AE 1019.2; (neut. as sb.) a curve: *magnus draco cum cauda in ~um extensa* UJ(C) 28.

cuspis ~idis, *f.* The point or tip (of a sword or spear): ES 929; ES 4198.

custodia ~ae, *f.* **1** Watchfulness, protection: *Dominus quoad providentiam et ~am* AE 69.3. **b** that which gives protection, a guard: *~ae a Domino positae sunt* SS 26.2. **2** One of the periods into which the night is divided, a watch: *nox divisa fuit in ~as* AC 8211.5. **3** A place of confinement, prison: *in ~a fui et venistis ad me* Matt. 25.36 (VI 2); AM 406.

custodio ~dire ~divi ~ditum, *tr.* **1** To keep safe, protect, guard: *ad ~diendum te in via* Exod. 23.20 (AC); *vera scientifica a Divino ~diebantur* AC 6689. **2** To control, guard (a passage): *per cherubim ~dita est via* AM 353. **3** To act in accordance with, observe, keep (a rule, promise, covenant, etc.): *~dire quod Divinum praecepit* AC 6678; *omnia ordinis ~dienda* CI 213. **b** (w. inf.) to take care (to): *si ~dias facere omnia verba Legis hujus* Deut. 28.58 (AC 6752.4). **4** To keep holy, observe (the Sabbath): *quisquis ~dit Sabbathum a prophanando illud* Isa. 56.6 (AC 923).

custoditio ~onis, *f.* A guarding, protection: *~o per angelos caeli* AR 545; a keeping, observance: *~o praeceptorum* AC 6678.

custos ~odis, *m.* A protector, guard: *traduntur angelis ~odibus* CI 519; a watchman: *~os, quid de nocte?* Isa. 21.11 (AE 179.9).

cutaneus ~a ~um, *a.* Of or relating to the skin: *quia ~i sunt, ratiocinantur ex fallaciis sensuum* AM 510.3.

cuticula ~ae, *f.* An outermost covering, skin, peel: *~ae seu involucra in quae fructus aut semina desinunt* AC 501; *quum homo talis est ut ~am curet nimium* ES 1743.

cuticularis ~is ~e, *a.* Of or relating to the skin: *~i corpore* ES 440; superficial, skin-deep: *quod libido illa...tandem fiat ~is* AM 509.

cutis ~is, *f.* (acc. sg. *~im* in 1st edns.; AC 3rd edn. changes acc. sg. to *~em*) The outermost part of the body, skin: *corpus humanum absque integumentis quae vocantur ~es* SS 33.

cyaneus ~a ~um, *a.* Dark blue: *botri coloris ~i* AM 75.3; purplish blue: AM 76.6.

cyanus ~i, *m.* (Gk.) A precious stone, lapis lazuli: Exod. 28.19 (AC).

cyathus ~i, *m.* (Gk.) A cup: *exprimentes mustum ...in cyathos et genialiter bibentes* AM 8.2.

cygnus ~i, *m.* (Gk.) A swan: AM 270.2.

cylindrus ~i, *m.* (Gk.) A cylinder, tube: *~os opticos* AC 1871.

cymba ~ae, *f.* (Gk.) A small rowing boat, skiff: *agi... sicut ~a in mari a procellis* VR 68.2.

cymbala ~orum, *neut. pl.* (Gk.) Cymbals: AE 323.1.

cysticus ~a ~um, *a.* (Gk.) Of the bladder: *ductum ~um* AC 5185.

cystis[1] ~is, *f.* *~is nautica*, a mariner's compass: VR 620.2.

cystis[2] ~idis, *f.* (Gk.) (anat.) The bladder: ES 1035.

D

dabilis ~is ~e, *a.* Capable of existing, possible: *species arborum...nusquam visae nec ~es in mundo* CI 176.

daemon ~onis, *m.* (Gk.) An evil spirit, demon: *hominem mutum a ~one obsessum* Matt. 9.32 (AC 6988.2); AM 431.2.

daemonium ~i, *neut.* (Gk.) = **daemon**: *etiam ~a obediunt nobis* Luke 10.17 (AC 6674.5).

daemonophonia ~ae, *f.* (Gk., but app. not in use) The killing of demons, sorcery: *exorcismos, incantamenta...et plures alias ~as* CO 45.

dama ~ae, *f.* A small deer, gazelle: 2 Kgs. 4.23 (AC 2165.1).

damnabilis ~is ~e, *a.* **1** Capable of causing damnation: *ei nihil ~e esse potest* ES 327; AM 463.3. **2** Liable to be damned: *non ~es propter ullam rem* AE 239.2.

damnatio ~onis, *f.* **1** Disapproval, condemnation: *de ~one polygamiae* AM 332.2. **2** Condemnation to hell, damnation: *vivere post mortem in ~one aeterna* AC 304; *totalis ~o* VR 3.1.

damno ~are ~avi ~atum, *tr.* (superl. of pf. pple. *~atissimus*) **1** To condemn by judicial process: *quod Messias se passus est... ~ari* 3AD 4522. **2** To disapprove, condemn: *cur conjugia polygamica...plane ~ata sunt* AM 332.1. **3** To condemn to hell, damn: *mori spiritualiter seu ~ari* AC 7021.2; *quod non bonum opus salvet, nec malum ~et* FI 39; (masc. of pf. pple. as sb.) ES 487.

damnosus ~a ~um, *a.* (compar. *~ior*, superl. *~issimus*) Inflicting damage, injurious, harmful: *cohors ~a* AM 406; *haeresis ~a* AE 427.5; VR 489.1.

damnum ~i, *neut.* Damage, injury, harm: *ei ~um inferre* CI 283; (w. pl.) an instance of this: *fugiunt amores extraconjugiales...sicut ~a animae* AM 71.1; (pred. dat.) *hoc iis maximo ~o esset* ES 4259.

daps dapis, *f.* A feast, banquet: AM 6.5; DP 254.4.

dare: pres. inf. of **do**.

datum ~i, *neut.* A thing given, gift: *ex ~is dives factus* ES 777.

datus ~a ~um: pf. pple. of **do**.

Davidicus ~a ~um, *a.* Of David: *haec jam stirps... postmodum dicta est ~a* 1AD 459.

Davus ~i, *m.* The name often given to slaves in comedy, used as a type of stupidity with ref. to Terence, *Andria* 194: *auscultatori ~o infundere intelligentiam antistitis Oedipi* CO 54.3.

de, *prep. w. abl.* **1** Concerning, about, of: *nihil sciunt de Verbo* AC 6637.2; (ellipt.) *qualis...ordo est, manifestabitur...quando de miraculis Divinis* VR 91. **2** From (a point in space); *de sub*, from under: *de sub coelis* Gen. 6.17 (AC); *de sub se* 'from under his own roof' Exod. 10.23 (AC). **3** From (a point in time): *de die in diem* 'from day to day' Ps. 96.2 (AC 1422.2). **4** From (a source): *dabo illi edere de arbore vitae* Rev. 2.7 (AR); from among (a group): *angelo qui perdidit de populo* 2 Sam. 24.16 (CI 229).

dea ~ae, *f.* (dat. and abl. pl. *~abus*) A goddess: *ut affectiones quascunque sicut deos et ~as sisterent* AC 1756.2.

dealbo ~are ~avi ~atum, *tr.* To make white, whiten: *qualia non potest fullo... ~are* Mark 9.3 (CI 129); VR 16.1.

deardeo ~dere ~si, *intr.* To become exhausted by burning, burn down; (transf., of passions): *sicut in principio arsit, ita subito ~det* AM 304.2.

dearo ~are ~avi ~atum, *tr.* To bury by ploughing, plough in: *sicut qui seminat et sementem ~at* VR 347.3.

deaster ~tri, *m.* A minor deity: *tunc crederet se ~trum aut numen, possidentem partem potentiae Divinae* VR 503.3; VR 459.7.

debello ~are ~avi ~atum, *tr.* To defeat in war, wage war successfully on, vanquish: *quod Dominus... ~averit et evicerit persuasionum falsi genera omnia* AC 1654.

debeo ~bere ~bui, *intr.* **1** (w. inf.) To be obliged or compelled (to): *sanctum nusquam potest esse cum prophano...sed discedere unum ab altero ~bet* AC 1326.1. **2** (w. inf.) To be under a moral obligation (in translation usu. 'ought'): *quod homo fugere ~beat mala quia peccata sunt* VI 22. **3** (pass., w. dat.) To be owing (to): *quod salvatio illorum unice accepta ~beatur Domino* AC 7935.

debilis ~is ~e, *a.* Lacking strength, weak: *Leam ~em oculis* AC 422.

debilitas ~atis, *f.* Weakness: *quod...angi sit ~as et aegritudo animi* AC 7217.2; *~ates mentium* ES 3625.

debilito ~are ~avi ~atum, *tr.* To make weak, weaken, impair: *voluptatum quae...obscurant et ~ant intellectum* CI 462.2.

debitor ~oris, *m.* One who owes money or its equivalent, debtor: *Dominus per parabolam loquitur de ~oribus* AC 2636.6; (w. gen. of what is owed) *in parabola Domini de oeconomo qui dixit ad ~orem olei* AC 2252.5.

debitum ~i, *neut.* **1** A sum of money owed, debt: VR 317; (transf.) *quando ultimum ~i solverint* ES 261. **2** That which one ought to do, obligation, duty: *cogitant...de ~o, quod ita facere deceat civem* VR 423; *quod ex ~o mariti sit...sustentare domum* AM 287; *~um conjugiale* 'the duty of a spouse' ES 3197. **3** That which one ought to receive, right: *~um conjugiale ejus non diminuet* Exod. 21.10 (AC).

debitus ~a ~um, *a.* Merited, due: *praestigiatrix ...poenae ~ae tradita* ES 232.

decachordium ~i, *neut.* (Gk.) A musical instrument having ten strings, lyre: Ps. 33.2 (AC 8261.6).

decachordus ~a ~um, *a.* (Gk.) Having ten strings: *in nablio ~o* Ps. 33.2 (AC 420.1).

Decalogus ~i, *m.* (Gk.) The Ten Commandments, Decalogue: *decem praecepta seu ~us* AC 6804.6.

decalvatio ~onis, *f.* A making bald or bare, stripping: *ejus* [sc. *arboris*] *denudatio et ~o ab omni folio et fronde* VR 41.2.

decalvo ~are ~avi ~atum, *tr.* To make bald or bare: *Dominus ~abit verticem filiarum Zionis* Isa. 3.17 (AE 240.7).

decantatio[1] ~onis, *f.* Celebration in song: *'~o'... derivatur a cantatione* AC 5618; choice products: *accipite ex ~one terrae in vasis vestris* Gen. 43.11 (AC).

decantatio[2] ~onis, *f.* The action of purifying a liquid by pouring it off to leave a deposit, decanting: AM 145.2.

decanto[1] ~are ~avi ~atum, *tr.* To sing the praises of, celebrate: *productiones ~atas et laudatas* AC 5618.

decanto[2] ~are ~avi ~atum, *tr.* To purify (a liquid) by pouring off, decant: VR 585.2; (transf.) to purify, cleanse: *sanctitas...quae continue ~at et purificat illum* [*amorem*] AM 64.1.

decas ~adis, *f.* (Gk.) A group of ten, decade: AM 8.2.

decaudo ~are ~avi ~atum, *tr.* To remove the tail of; (fig.) to kill off and remove like a tail: *memento...quod* [*Amaleck*] *occurrerit tibi in via, et ~averit in te omnes infirmos* Deut. 25.18 (AC 8593.3).

decedo ~dere ~ssi, *intr.* **1** To go away, depart: *in mundo e quo ~ssimus* AM 44.3; *cum amor ~dit* CI 159. **2** To die: *infantes qui... ~sserunt* AC 1637.1.

decem, *indecl. adj.* Ten: AM 14.2.

December ~bris, *m.* December: ES 282.

decens ~ntis, *a.* **1** Of fitting appearance, smart, tidy: *chartam... ~ntem et nitidam* AC 6930; *in ~ntibus comis* SS 35.4. **2** Respectable, proper: *mores ~ntes* CI 277.3.

decenter, *adv.* Fittingly, properly: [*infantes*] *nudi sertis ~er ornati* AM 137.1.

deceptio ~onis, *f.* The action of deceiving, deception: *ex allectatione et ~one malorum* AC 9348.1; ES(M) 4706.

deceptor ~oris, *m.* A deceiver, esp. the devil: *insinuatur in singulis verbis animus et mens ~oris* 1AD 1268; 3AD 1100.

deceptorius ~a ~um, *a.* Deceptive: *bona hypocritica, quae ~a et fraudulenta* VI 9.

deceptrix ~icis, *f.* A female deceiver: *sunt inter ~ices* ES 3294.

decerno ~ere decrevi decretum, *tr.* **1** (impers. pass.) To come to a decision, decide, decree: *in concilio quando decretum de bina natura Domini* AC 4738.3. **2** To decide upon, decree: *decretam sententiam inscribite chartae* AM 103.4.

decerpo ~ere ~si ~tum, *tr.* **1** To pluck off, pick: *folium olivae ~tum* Gen. 8.11 (AC). **2** To take away, detract: *tantum ex amore ad uxorem ~it* AM 466.1.

decertatio ~onis, *f.* The accomplishment of a competition: *non...datur...praemium nisi quam post ~onem* VR 721.2.

decessus ~us, *m.* Departure from the natural world, death: *quod post ~um sint primum...inter spiritus* AC 8029.

decet ~ere ~uit, *impers. vb.* It befits, it is fitting (for): **a** (tr.): *non ~et me aperire illa* AM 166. **b** (intr.): *dictum est et quod hoc non ~eat* AC 6813; *sicut ~et* CI 322.3.

decido[1] ~dere ~di, *intr.* **1** To fall down: *quod Dagon ...in terram ~derit* 1 Sam. 5.4 (VI 59); *ergastula, in quae ~derent illi* AM 264.3; *~dit sicut exanimis* CI 203.3. **b** to fall off: *sicut squamae ~dunt* AC 7790. **2** (w. *in* + acc.) To enter (upon) by chance, fall (into): *in cogitationes ~di de rebus mundanis* ES 185.

decido[2] ~dere ~di ~sum, *tr.* **1** To cut, hew: *si ~derit ad dextram, esuriet tamen* Isa. 9.20 (AE 386.2). **2** To mark out: *septimanae septuaginta ~sae sunt* Dan. 9.24 (AC 728.2).

deciduus ~a ~um, *a.* Transitory: *id...in terminis ut ~um moratur* AS 368.2.

decies, *adv.* Ten times: ES 1377.

decimae ~marum, *f. pl.* Tithes: VI 61.

decimarius ~a ~um, *a.* Of or relating to the number ten: *numerus ~us sanctus* AC 468.4.

decimatio ~onis, *f.* The action of taking a tenth, tithing: AE 675.18.

decimo ~are ~avi ~atum, *tr.* To subject to a tithe, take a tenth of: *gregem vestrum ~abit* 1 Sam. 8.17 (AC 2567.9).

decimus ~a ~um, *a.* **1** Tenth: *usque ad ~um annum aetatis ejus* AC 2280.2. **b** (masc. as sb.) the tenth day: *in ~o mensis hujus* Exod. 12.3 (AC). **c** (fem. as sb.) a tenth part: *duarum ~arum erit placenta una* Lev. 24.5 (AC 7978.2). **2** (Combined with other ordinal numerals): *decimoquarto die* 'the fourteenth day' AC 7842.

decineratio ~onis, *f.* A removing of ashes: *lebetes sunt talia per quae remotio, quoniam per illos ~o* AC 9723.1.

decinero ~are ~avi ~atum, *tr.*, *intr.* (tr.) To remove ashes from: *quod cum sacerdos ~aret altare* AC 9723.3; (intr.) to remove ashes: *ex significatione lebetum ad ~andum quod sint removentia post usus* AC 9723.1.

decipio ~cipere ~cepi ~ceptum, *tr.* **1** To mislead, deceive: *si quis ipsius uxorem...tali modo ~cepisset* AM 481; *scientifica quae ~ceperunt Antiquissimam Ecclesiam* ES 3760. **2** To cheat the expectations of, let down: *clamavi ad amatores meos, illi ~ceperunt me* Lam. 1.19 (AE 270.4).

decipula ~ae, *f.* A trap, snare: *quid miracula...aliud quam laquei et ~ae?* NE 52.2.

decisio ~onis, *f.* The action of deciding, a decision: *quod...nusquam fieri possit ~o quid verum* ES 5545.

decisum ~i, *neut.* A thing decreed, decision: *narravit illi ~a illorum de anima* VR 79.7.

declaratio ~onis, *f.* Public proclamation, declaration: AM 167.2.

declaro ~are ~avi ~atum, *tr.* To announce publicly, declare: (w. pred.) *~ati sunt sponsi et sponsae* AM 300.3; *infidelem ~are fidelem* VR 57; (w. indir. qu.) *finis ~at quomodo quisque sibi proximus erit* AC 6935.

declinatio ~onis, *f.* Decline, recession: *agitur de ~one Ecclesiae* AC 1292.2.

declino ~are ~avi, *intr.* **1** To slope downwards: *terra ~abat oblique in vallem* AM 78.3. **2** (of the day) To approach sunset, decline: *~avit dies* Jer. 6.4 (AC 23). **3** To refuse to go forward, turn aside: *nisi asina ~asset coram me* Num. 22.33 (AE 140.4); (transf.) *a vero ~abunt* AC 8091; *spiritus...non probi volebant ~are* ES 3053. **4** (of a dispute, w. *in* + acc.) To be reduced (to), come down (to): *~abat lis in hoc primum* VR 162.1.

declivis ~is ~e, *a.* (compar. *~ior*) Sloping downwards, descending: (neut. as sb.) *per longum ~e descendimus* AM 79.4; *per ~iora* ES 1907.

declivitas ~atis, *f.* A downward slope: AC 1270.3.

decollatio ~onis, *f.* The act of breaking the neck: AC 9262.6 (Deut. 21.4).

decollo ~are ~avi ~atum, *tr.* To break the neck of: *vitulum... ~arent* AC 6767.5 (Deut. 21.4).

decor ~oris, *m.* see also **decus**. A pleasing appearance, beauty: *tota...facies fuit unus splendens ~or* AM 42.3.

decoramentum ~i, *neut.* A decoration, adornment: *sub tectis ~a caelaturae inimitabilis* AM 12.1.

decorate, *adv.* (superl. *~issime*) Decoratively: *infantes ~issime amictos* CI 37.

decore, *adv.* In a seemly manner, properly: *in externa forma ~e et civiliter agere* AC 4612.3.

decoro ~are ~avi ~atum, *tr.* To adorn, decorate: *ad ~andum se* AM 91.

decorticatio ~onis, *f.* The action of stripping off bark, peeling: *~ones albas* Gen. 30.37 (AC).

decortico ~are ~avi ~atum, *tr.* To strip off bark, peel: *baculos quos ~avit* Gen. 30.38 (AC).

decorum ~i, *neut.* That which is becoming, propriety: *ultra limites ~i et honesti* CI 504; (w. pl.) an instance of this: *ex ~is et honestis quae ex infantia didicit* AM 267.2.

decorus ~a ~um, *a.* Beautiful in appearance, lovely: *ut... ~i amictus [amiciunt] virginem* SS 40.1.

decrementum ~i, *neut.* Decrease: *secundum incrementa et ~a virium* AM 160.

decrepitus ~a ~um, *a.* Worn out by age, broken down, decrepit: *senes ~i* AM 137.7.

decrescentia ~ae, *f.* Decrease: *~a lucis vergentis ad umbram* CI 275.

decresco ~rescere ~revi, *intr.* To grow less, lessen, decrease: *homo, cum fit senex, etiam ~rescit corpore* CI 278.3; *sapientia...successu temporis ~revit* AC 6630.

decretum ~i, *neut.* An agreed resolution of a council, decree: *demum factum est ~um hoc* AR 962.12; VR 487.1.

decrevi: pf. of **decresco** or **decerno**.

decumbo ~mbere ~bui, *intr.* To lie down: *is in lecto ~mbit* ES 462.

decursus ~us, *m.* A running or rushing down, downward flow: *~um fluviorum qui declinavit ad habitari Ar* Num. 21.15 (AC 2897).

decurtatus ~a ~um, *a.* Mutilated: 3AD 5938.

decurto ~are ~avi ~atum, *tr.* To make shorter, shorten: *via protrahitur et ~atur* CI 195.

decus ~oris, *neut.* Beautiful physical appearance, glory: *sibi inducere...floridum puellare ~us* AM 505.2. (n.b. It is not always possible to distinguish **decus** from **decor** q.v.)

decussatim, *adv.* So as to form a cross, crosswise: *sedent quoad pedes ~im* AC 8373.

decussio ~onis, *f.* A shaking down: *~o oleae* Isa. 17.6 (AC 649).

decusso ~are ~avi ~atum, *tr.* To cross (the legs): *sedentes ut solent Indiani pedibus ~atis* ES 6067.

dedecus ~oris, *neut.* A disgrace, reproach: *grande ~us erat calvitium sibi inducere* SS 35.2; (pred. dat.) *quae nomini ejus ~ori et infamiae forent* AM 286.

deditus ~a ~um, *a.* (pf. pple. of **dedo**) (w. dat.) Much occupied (with), given (to): *~us studiis* ES 2053.

dedi: pf. of **do**.

dedo ~ere ~idi ~itum, *tr.* To surrender, hand over: *quod...se ~at cupiditatibus et voluptatibus* AC 1679.3.

deduco ~cere ~xi ~ctum, *tr.* **1** To conduct, lead, bring: *~ctus sum ad principem* VR 76.1. **2** To derive the origin of: *qui creationem non a Divino Amore... ~cunt* VR 13.3. **b** to derive (the origin): *quod... non...originem illius amoris inde ~xerit* AM 83. **3** To bring down, reduce (to a lower plane): *angelorum cogitationes nec ~cuntur ad terrestria et materialia* CI 266.3. **4** To bring forth, produce: *ita ex insaniis ...laetitiae et jucunditates... ~ci...possunt* ES 231.

deductio ~onis, *f.* The drawing of an inference, deduction: *absque multa explicatione et ampla ~one* AC 4264.1; an inference, deduction: *ex ~onibus analytice ex Verbo...formatis* VR 131.

defaecatio ~onis, *f.* also **defecatio**. The action of cleansing from impurities, defecation: AM 145.2.

defaeco ~are ~avi ~atum, *tr.* also **defeco**. To purify, purge: *~abit eos sicut aurum* Mal. 3.3 (AC 349.2); *ex specubus mentis nondum ~atis* AM 108.

defaedo ~are ~avi ~atum, *tr.* also **defoedo**. To make ugly, disfigure: *si...facies ~ata est* AM 253.1.

defatigatio ~onis, *f.* Weariness, tiredness: *ut animi relaxentur a ~one* AM 17.1.

defatigo ~are ~avi ~atum, *tr.* To make weary, tire out: *a continuis sermocinationibus ~ati sumus* AM 5.2; (w. inf.) *ut ~arentur audire* VR 113.8.

defecatio: see **defaecatio**.

defeco: see **defaeco**.

defectio ~onis, *f.* The act of deserting an allegiance, defection: *praevaricationes...sunt trangressiones et ~ones* AC 9156.3.

defectus ~us, *m.* **1** Failure to be available, lack, absence: *a ~u veri apud docentes* FI 30; *secundum ~um et jacturam amoris conjugialis* AM 209. **2** A physical defect: *si vir dederit ~um in proximo suo* Lev. 24.19 (AC 8223.1).

defendo ~dere ~di ~sum, *tr.* **1** To fight in defence of, defend: *zelus amoris boni...se ~dit contra malum* AM 365; *quisque...vitam suam ~dit* AC 6705. **2** (w. *ab*) To protect (from): *quae...usque in ossa fatiscunt, et ab insultibus ~dunt* ES 3913. **3** To say by way of defence, make one's defence: *inde est quod ~dant quod naturalis homo non capere possit ea quae fidei sunt* AC 9300.5.

defensio ~onis, *f.* The action of defending, defence: *~o falsi ex fallaciis* AC 6978.

defensionalis ~is ~e, *a.* Of or relating to defence; (neut. as sb.) means of defence: *unumquodvis animal habet suum ~e* ES(M) 4675.

defensor ~oris, *m.* A defender: *~or et tutor amoris* AM 358.

defero ~rre detuli delatum, *tr.* **1** To carry, take (a person): *sublatus sum...et delatus in diversorium* AM 10.5. **2** To carry down, transport (goods): *oleum in Aegyptum ~rtur* Hos. 12.1 (SS 79.5). **3** To communicate (to a lower plane), impart: *non potuerit aliqua doctrina...per coelum ad homines... ~rri* CO 20.1.

defervesco ~rvescere ~rbui, *intr.* To go off the boil, stop boiling; (transf.) to calm down, be assuaged: *amor...fit ardor qui ~rvescit et transit* AM 78.5.

deficientia ~ae, *f.* A failing, lack: *~a spirituum* AC 5323.1.

deficio ~ficere ~feci ~fectum, *intr*. **1** (of persons) To lose consciousness, faint: *~ficient...juvenes siti* Amos 8.13 (DD 4); ES 4374. **b** (of parts of the body) to cease to function, fail: *lingua eorum siti ~ficit* Isa. 41.17 (AE 71.2). **2** (of things) To be missing or absent, fail: *~fecerat iis oleum in lampadibus* ES 701; (transf.) *amor ille ~ficit et frigescit* AM 44.8; (w. abl.) *quod tunc melior sanguis ~ficiat massa sanguinis* ES 972.

defiguratio ~onis, *f.* Disfiguring, deformation: *propter hanc transfigurationem et ~onem coelestium* CO 43.

definio ~nire ~nivi ~nitum, *tr*. **1** To establish the limits of, determine: *quod apud unumquemvis ~niantur [bona] cum vivit in mundo* AC 8533. **2** To establish, ordain: *ut... ~nitam damnationem in se susciperet* VR 132.1. **3** To give an exact description of, define: *ita omnes primores Ecclesiae Personam ~niunt* VR 17.3.

definitio ~onis, *f.* A definition: *per philosophiae humanae terminos et ~ones* AC 1626.

definitus ~a ~um, *a*. (pf. pple. of **definio**) Subject to limits, limited, restricted: *multitudo ~a* CI 420.

defio ~fieri, *intr*. To be lacking, fail: *~fiunt iis voces* ES 3097.

deflagro ~are ~avi, *intr*. **1** To be consumed by fire, burn up: [*vermiculi*] *momento cum strepitu ~abant* ES 397. **2** (of fire, and transf. of love) To burn out: *zelus amoris... ~at et mitescit* AM 365.

deflammor ~ari ~atus sum, *intr*. (of fire or love) To burn out: *at ille [zelus] ~atur et sedatur* VR 408.

deflecto ~ctere ~xi ~ctum, *intr*., *tr*. **1** (intr.) To turn aside: *ab his ~xi ad primum* AM 231.2. **2** (refl.) To bow down, bend: *et ~xerunt se et incurvarunt se* Gen. 43.28. (AC). **3** (tr.) To deflect: *quod... [visus internus] ~ctatur a coelo* CI 532.1.

defleo ~lere ~levi ~letum, *tr*. To shed tears for, mourn: *~lebo fletu Jaeserem* Isa. 16.9 (AE 484.4); Rev. 18.9 (AR).

deflexio ~onis, *f.* A turning aside, bending: *est... ~o minor gradus incurvationis* AC 5682.

defloratio ~onis, *f.* The violation of virginity, defloration: AM 319.

defloro ~are ~avi ~atum, *tr*. **1** (pass.) To lose flowers: *quae* [sc. *tulipae*] *post mensem dierum ~antur et emarcescunt* VR 316. **2** (act.) To violate, deflower (virgins): AC 828.

defluo ~ere ~xi, *intr*. **1** (of fluids or their courses) To flow down: *ubi venae majores ~erent juxta collum* ES 1289. **2** (of solid objects) To collapse, fall down: *montes ~xerunt* Judg. 5.5 (AC 1675.4). **3** To come down from a higher plane, descend, flow down: *~xit super nos maledictio* Dan. 9.11 (AC 6752.6); *quod loquela angeli ... ~at usque in aurem ab interiore* CI 248.

defluxus ~us, *m*. A flowing down, descent: AE 1147.4.

defodio ~dere ~di ~ssum, *tr*. To put in the ground by digging, bury: *quod excrementa... ~derent et contegerent* Deut. 23.13 (VR 569.5).

defoedo: see **defaedo**.

deformis ~is ~e, *a*. (compar. *~ior*, superl. *~issimus*) Badly shaped, deformed, ugly: *faciei ~i inducere fucum* VI 112; *ut nullam cogitationis ideam sistere amplius potuissent nisi ~issimam* AC 607.3.

deformitas ~atis, *f.* Ugliness: *ut ob ~atem non queant...spectari* ES 574; (w. pl.) an instance or example of ugliness: *quod...mulieres pulchrae fiant ~ates* AM 330.1.

deformiter, *adv*. In an ugly manner: *corpus ~er nigrum* VR 595.1.

deformo ~are ~avi ~atum, *tr*. To deform, disfigure: *~assent illa* [sc. *revelata*] CO 54.2.

defraudatio ~onis, *f.* Fraud: *simile est cum...furtis et ~onibus* VI 112.

defraudator ~oris, *m*. One who tricks or cheats: AM 269.4.

defraudo ~are ~avi ~atum, *tr*. To defraud, cheat: *aliquem virum ~are* AM 460.2.

defunctus ~a ~um, *a*. Physically dead: *postquam ~i sunt* CI 312.4.

degener ~eris, *a*. Ignoble: *adulteria...vertunt homines in ~eres hos gradus* AM 496.

degeneratio ~onis, *f.* A falling away from an earlier standard, deterioration, degeneration: *de ~one Ecclesiae Antiquissimae* AC 337.

degenero ~are ~avi ~atum, *intr*. also **degeneror**. To become worse with time, degenerate: **a** (act.): *omnes hae Ecclesiae... ~averunt in binos enormes errores* AE 817.2. **b** (dep.): *Ecclesia...Antiqua a cultu quodam interno ~ata est* AC 1356.1.

degeneror: see **degenero**.

deglutio ~tire ~tivi ~titum, *tr*. To swallow up: *balaenae...quae ~tiunt hominem et evomunt* AC 819; *haec [cupiditas]...inhibet influxum amoris conjugialis, absorbet illum, et ~tit illum* AM 375.3.

deglutitio ~onis, *f.* The action of swallowing up: AC 8325.3.

dego ~ere ~i, *intr*. To pass one's time, live (in specified places or conditions): *populus... ~it in septentrione* AM 78.1; *si...in odiis, in vindictis... ~at* AC 1077; *postquam hanc vitam ~erunt* ES 393.

dehortor ~ari ~atus sum, *tr*. To exhort or urge (one to desist from something): *ad ~andum impium a via ejus mala* Ezek. 3.18 (AE 186.2).

dein, *adv*. Thereafter, subsequently: *primum aperte, et dein tacite* VR 442; (w. *inde*) AC 1438.

deinceps, *adv*. From that time on, thenceforward: *homo ~ps purificatur...jugiter* AC 10266.

deinde, *adv*. Thereafter, subsequently: *inficit primum lumbos, et ~de viscera* VR 119.2.

Deipara ~ae, *f*. The Mother of God: VR 111.11.

dejectio ~onis, *f*. A throwing or casting down: *per ~onem in terram* AE 304.6; *~o in infernum* AC 7844.2.

dejectus ~a ~um, *a*. (pf. pple. of **dejicio**) (superl. *~issimus*) **1** Of low status, depraved: *quod gentiles tot deos agnoverint...et ~issimi idola* ES 169. **2** Downcast, dejected: *cum aliquis equus minaretur malum, subito erant ~i* ES 4138.

dejero ~are ~avi, *intr*. To take an oath, swear: *aliqui ~ant et clamant, 'certe est ulula'* VR 803.

dejicio ~jicere ~jeci ~jectum, *tr*. To throw or cast down: *~jiciuntur profunde in infernum* AC 6677; *turmam... ~jicere in fugam* VR 87.2; to direct downwards, cast down (the eyes): *~jectis aut subductis oculis* AM 207.3.

delabor ~bi ~psus sum, *intr*. **1** To fall down or off: *vidi stellam e caelo ~psam* Rev. 9.1 (AR); *crederent ...nautas cum in opposito sunt ~bi* 'would believe that sailors on the opposite side of the world fall off' AC 1378.2; to fall apart, collapse: *~berentur omnia momento* ES 4016. **2** To come down: *voces quae ex illo coelo ~buntur* AE 353.1; (transf.) *sapientia a suo culmine ... ~psa est* AM 130.1. **3** To fall away, lapse (from belief): *ab omni fide ~psi sunt* AC 7290.3.

delapsus ~us, *m*. A falling down, fall: *ubi ~um ejus* [sc. *meteori*]*...vidi* VR 110.1.

delasso ~are ~avi ~atum, *tr*. To tire out, weary: *~atur visus videndo* AM 8.3; VR 361.3.

delator ~oris, *m*. One who lays information against another, an informer: ES 1571.

delectabilis ~is ~e, *a*. (compar. *~ior*) Giving delight, delightful: *quod iis ~e quam maxime erat* AC 66.1.

delectamentum ~i, *neut*. Delight, pleasure: *ut in illis omne suum ~um posuerint* ES 4428.

delectans ~ntis, *a*. (pres. pple. of **delecto**) (compar. *~ntior*) Delightful: ES 1964.

delectatio ~onis, *f*. An experience of pleasure, delight: *felicitatem...percipiebant...in ~one ex pluribus* [*uxoribus*] AC 162.2; (pred. dat.) *sunt...cognitiones illis ~oni* AC 6814.

delecto ~are ~avi ~atum, *tr*., *intr*. **1** To give pleasure: *usum bonum propter quem opulentia ~at* AC 7377; (tr.) to give pleasure to: *nihil...infernales ~at* AC 7392.2. **2** (pass. or refl.) To experience pleasure, feel gratified (at), delight (in): (w. abl.) *~ari cognitionibus* AC 6815; *~ant se diu comedendo* AC 8377; (w. *ex*) *angeli ex hoc sermone ~ati* VR 160.1; (w. *in* + abl.) *~ati sunt in eo quod...* AC 755.1; (w. inf.) *is non ~atur nosse, sed facere bonum* AC 503.

delectus ~us, *m*. Selection, choice: *absque ~u sive sunt viri aut si pueri* ES 1063.

delego ~are ~avi ~atum, *tr*. To send away, banish: *quod pellices...ad gynaecea... ~entur* AM 370; *~antur e caelo* DP 279.3; *mala...modo removentur et ad latera ~antur* DP 283.

deleo ~lere ~levi ~letum, *tr*. **1** To delete, rub out, wipe out (writing): *non ~lebo nomen ejus e libro vitae* Rev. 3.5 (AR); cf. *quod quae audivit...memoriae internae...inscripta sint; et quod illa quae ibi nusquam ~leantur* CI 463. **2** To destroy, do away with: *religiosum Mahumedanum...religiosa...priora ~lerit* SS 117.

deletio ~onis, *f*. The action of destroying, wiping out: *~o eorum qui...semet perdiderunt* AC 727.

deliberatio ~onis, *f*. Debate, consideration: AM 82.2; AR 962.7.

deliberativus ~a ~um, *a*. Deliberative: *cogitatio ~a* VR 31.3.

deliberatus ~a ~um, *a*. (cf. **delibero**) Influenced by consideration, deliberate: *qui non ~o animo facit* AC 1327.3; (neut. as sb.) a considered decision: *illis non est...propositum et ~um* CI 277.2.

delibero ~are ~avi, *intr*. **1** To engage in debate, consider: *quod...oporteat...apud se ~are, antequam consentit* AM 295.3. **2** To set free, liberate: *petit ~ari a quodam* ES 3766; ES 3483 (reading *deliberarentur* for *delibarentur*).

delicate, *adv*. In a refined or luxurious manner: *~e edere et bibere* CI 358.

delicatus ~a ~um, *a*. (superl. *~issimus*) **1** Refined, luxurious: *edulia ~a et opipara* AM 3.3; *~am et otiosam vitam* ES 592. **2** (of persons) Given to soft living: *tales sunt qui cuticulam nimium curant...qui alioquin vocantur ~i* ES 1746; ES 4458.

delici-: see **deliti-**.

delictum ~i, *neut.* A fault, offence: *remitte nobis ~a nostra* Matt. 6.12 (VR 459.12); VR 562.2.

deligo ~ligere ~legi ~lectum, *tr.* To select from a range of choices, choose: *quod...humana voluntas habeat libertatem...ad ~ligendum res rationi subjectas* AR Doc Ref.9.

delineamentum ~i, *neut.* An outline, drawing: *~a primorum staminum licet vascula appellare* AC 5726.

delineatio ~onis, *f.* An outlining, drawing: *cum ~one subtili alicujus faciei* AS 432.2.

delineatus ~a ~um, *a.* (app.) Measured out with a line (referring to land occupied): *gens ~a et conculcata* Isa. 18.2 (SS 86).

delineo ~are ~avi ~atum, *tr.* To draw, depict: *formae...quae non possunt...ulla arte ~ari* AM 477.5.

delinio ~nire ~nii ~nitum, *tr.* To soothe: *~niebat sicut odor totum hominem* 3AD 2336.

delinquo ~nquere ~qui ~ctum, *intr.* To commit an offence, misbehave: *sicut nos remittimus ~nquentibus contra nos* Matt. 6.12 (VR 459.12).

deliquium ~i, *neut.* A state of unconsciousness, fainting: *tales sphaerae ut ~um causentur* AC 1512; *caput...in ~um cadit* VR 119.1.

deliratio ~onis, *f.* A disturbance, unhingeing (of the mind): *per insaniam intelligitur ~o mentis ex falsis* AM 212.

delirium ~i, *neut.* **1** A state of mental disturbance, madness: *contrahere ~um* VR 31.2; *mentes...in tale ~um actae* VR 4.2; (as the result of fever) UJ(C) 62. **2** An irrational belief, madness: *caveant...sibi a tali ~o* SS 118; VR 23.1.

deliro ~are ~avi, *intr.* To go out of one's mind, become mad: *ex illecebris mundi...aliquoties ~avit* AM 48[a].4.

delirus ~a ~um, *a.* (of the mind or senses) Deranged, crazy: *quosdam ~os oculis* 'having visual hallucinations' AM 9.2.

delitesco ~tescere ~tui, *intr.* To hide oneself: *ibi ~tuit per multum tempus* VR 798.3.

delitiae ~tiarum, *f. pl.* also **deliciae**. (for the sg. see **delitium**) A source of intense pleasure, delight: *summae illorum felicitates et ~tiae erant conjugia* AC 54; *arbores fructuum et flores ~tiarum* AM 3.4.

delitiatio ~onis, *f.* also **deliciatio**. The act of taking pleasure, delightful play: *~o caloris spiritualis cum luce spirituali* AM 189.

delitior ~ari ~atus sum, *intr.* also **delicior**. To take pleasure, be delighted: *ad angelum qui ~abatur cum sua consorte* AM 71.3.

delitiosus ~a ~um, *a.* also **deliciosus**. (compar. *~ior*, superl. *~issimus*) Giving intense pleasure, delightful: *jucunditates ~issimas* AC 1123; *sicut ~a vena fontis ejus transfluit* AM 68.1; (neut. as sb.) ES 3380.

delitium ~i, *neut.* also **delicium**. (for the pl. see **delitiae**) Intense pleasure, delight: *quod gaudium et ~um sicut a corde veniret* AC 545.2.

deludo ~dere ~si ~sum, *tr.* To delude, deceive: *sciunt ...quid phantasia et quid reale, adeo ut non ~di possint* UJ(P) 20; ES 3206.

demando ~are ~avi ~atum, *tr.* To pass on, channel: *ut [chylus] ~etur versus cor* AC 5180.

demens ~ntis, *a.* Out of one's mind, mad: *ut gererent se sicut ~ntes* CI 54.2.

demensum ~i, *neut.* (app. for **dimensum***) That which is measured out; a prescribed number or amount: *et ~um laterum...ponetis super illos* Exod. 5.8 (AC); VR 364.3; (in doubtful sense) *rex Tyri, tu obsignans ~um tuum* Ezek. 28.12 (SS 45).

dementer, *adv.* In an insane way: *foret sicut cum caput delirat, unde corpus fertur ~er et insane usque in sui perniciem* AC 10452.3.

dementia ~ae, *f.* Derangement of the mind, madness: *hos...invadunt diversi generis phantasiae, ~ae et deliria* VR 665.4.

demento ~are ~avi ~atum, *tr.* To make insane, drive mad: *quod ~averit gentes in Samaria* Acts 8.9 (NE 52.1).

demeo ~are ~avi, *intr.* To go down, descend: *quod hoc frigus inceptet ibi et successive in consequentia ~et* AM 236.

demergo ~gere ~si ~sum, *tr.* To press down: *et in funem ~ges linguam ejus?* Job 41.1 (AE 455.18).

demersio ~onis, *f.* An immersion, plunging: *~ones in infernum* AC 7032.3.

demeto ~tere ~ssui ~ssum, *tr.* To mow, reap: *et ~ssa est terra* Rev. 14.16 (AR).

demiexpergefactus ~a ~um, *a.* Half-awake: *mox ~us videbam mare istud* ES 243 (J D Odhner). (Cf. Medieval *demivirgata* for *semi-*.)

demihora ~ae, *f.* A half-hour: ES 5101 (*semihoram* Tafel).

demimortuus ~a ~um, *a.* Half-dead: ES 5496 (*semimortui* Tafel).

demissio ~onis, *f.* A letting down, lowering: AC 7077.

demisupinatus ~a ~um, *a.* Half lying on one's back: *sedent [foeminae] ~ae in solio* AC 10164; cf. **demiexpergefactus**.

demitto ~mittere ~misi ~missum, *tr.* To cause to descend, send down, let down: *funiculos... ~mittebant quibus Dominum allevarent* CI 335; (from heaven) *ne verbulum...quod non ~missum sit e coelo* AC 1659.2; (refl.) *quod Se ~mitteret ad illos ad eximendum e potentia falsorum* AC 6850.

demo ~ere ~(p)si ~(p)tum, *tr.* To take away, remove: *haec ~unt lucem* AC 6829.

demolior ~liri ~litus sum, *tr.* To pull down, demolish: *dum ~litus est murum* CO 57.3.

demonstratio ~onis, *f.* A demonstration, proof: *quod non aliae proles nascantur...non ~one eget* AM 120.

demonstrativus ~a ~um, *a.* Serving to demonstrate or prove: *argumentis ~is* AM 63.

demonstro ~are ~avi ~atum, *tr.* **1** To point out, indicate: *quis ~avit vobis fugituros a futura ira* Matt. 3.7 (AC 6997.6). **2** To demonstrate, prove (a proposition): *de unitate Dei quae in ordine... ~abitur* VR 5; (w. *quod*) VI 36.

demoror ~ari ~atus sum, *tr.* To remain in a place, stay: *ibi dicebantur spiritus aliquantum ~ari* ES 262.

demum, *adv.* As the last in a series, finally: *frigus invaserit pedes meos, et successive lumbos et ~um pectus* VR 385.3.

denarius ~i, *m.* A small bronze coin of the Roman Empire, penny: *chaenix tritici ~o* Rev. 6.6 (AR).

denascor ~sci ~tus sum, *intr.* To decrease with age, wither away: *arbor...procedit ad staturam plenam, et successive ~scitur* VR 756.

denego ~are ~avi ~atum, *tr.* To refuse the attribution of, deny: *quando charitas...homini ~atur* VR 631.2.

denigro ~are ~avi ~atum, *tr.* To make black, darken: *flumina ~abant, ut aqua non limpida appareret* AC 7071; (transf.) to defile, sully: *aliquid hominis...in fidem suam intraret, et ~aret illam* VR 515.

denique, *adv.* As the last in a series, finally: *tum etiam de Spiritu Sancto, et ~que de Divina Trinitate* VR 369.1.

denominatio ~onis, *f.* **1** The action of assigning a name, naming: *haec causa ~onis sit pro illis in mundo qui non ultra sensum literae Verbi cogitant* AE 314.1. **2** A given name: *similiter...se habet cum aliis ~onibus* AC 6653.

denomino ~are ~avi ~atum, *tr.* To assign a name to, name: AE 388.22.

denoto ~are ~avi ~atum, *tr.* To denote, mean: *vox ...edere in lingua originali ~at consumere* AC 5149.1.

dens dentis, *m.* A tooth: *stridor dentium* CI 245.

dense, *adv.* Densely, thickly: *quod sphaera illa circumstipet hominem...tenuiter a tergo, ~e autem a pectore* AM 171.2.

densitas ~atis, *f.* Density, thickness: *sylvam...ex ~ate illarum* [sc. *arborum*] *opacam* AM 75.2.

denso ~are ~avi ~atum, *tr.* To make dense, thicken: ES 1267.

densus ~a ~um, *a.* (compar. *~ior*, superl. *~issimus*) **1** Thickly packed, dense: *vapor ~us terrestris in serena aura* AC 6639.2; *in densis sylvis* DP 3785. **2** (of falsities) Impenetrable, obscure: *~issimum falsum* AC 1858; (neut. pl. as sb.) obscurities: *innumera...involvunt ~is quae sunt ex curis in mundo* CI 576.

dentatus ~a ~um, *a.* Provided with teeth, toothy: *crocodili... ~is rictibus...hiabant* AM 79.2.

denudatio ~onis, *f.* A laying bare, stripping, denudation: [*arboris*] *~o et decalvatio ab omni folio* VR 41.2.

denudo ~are ~avi ~atum, *tr.* To lay bare, strip: *nuda et ~ata* Ezek. 16.7 (AC 213); *vox Jehovae... ~at sylvas* Ps. 29.9 (SS 18.4).

denuntiatio ~onis, *f.* A proclamation as a threat, threatening: *~o mortis* AC 7810.

denuntio ~are ~avi ~atum, *tr.* To proclaim as a threat, threaten: *ideo ~ata est illi mors* AE 324.4.

denuo, *adv.* A second or further time, again: *cum ~o dicitur* AC 6881; *quaesiverunt ~o, cur...* AM 21.3.

deorsum, *adv.* also **deorsus** (ES 3406 Tafel). In a downward direction, downwards, down: *amare mundana est spectare ~um* AC 760; *homo stans super...palmis manuum capite ~um et clunibus sursum* VR 507.2.

deorsus: see **deorsum**.

deosso ~are ~avi ~atum, *tr.* To remove the bones of, bone: Jer. 50.17 (AC 1186.4).

depasco ~scere ~vi ~stum, *tr.* To use as pasture, feed off: *pascuum bonum ~scitis* Ezek. 34.18 (FI 68); (transf.) *~scent terram Aschuris* Mic. 5.6 (AC 1186.5).

depastus ~a ~um, *a.* (pf. pple. of **depasco**) (of land) Having had its pasture eaten, used up: *separat campum virentem a ~o* CO 13.1.

depaupero ~are ~avi ~atum, *tr.* To make poor: *~abit urbes...gladio* Jer. 5.17 (AE 911.14).

depello ~pellere ~puli ~pulsum, *tr.* To drive off: *et venerunt pastores, et ~pulerunt illas* Exod. 2.17 (AC).

dependentia ~ae, *f.* A state of being dependent, dependence: *in tali subordinatione et ~a* AC 8728.

dependeo ~dere ~di, *intr.* **1** To hang down: *pili ~dent* ES 4357. **2** (w. *ab*) To be dependent (on): *mundus ~det a coelo* AE 306.

deperditus ~a ~um, *a.* No longer known, lost: *scientia illa tam prorsus ~a est...* CI 87; [*Verbum*] *in regnis Asiae ~um est, et modo in Tartaria Magna reservatum* AM 77.2.

deperdo ~ere ~idi ~itum, *tr.* To lose: *dicunt imaginem Dei ~itam esse in primo homine* AC 1013.1.

dephlegmatio ~onis, *f.* The removal of phlegm: SA 124 (= x.6.[2]).

dephlegmo ~are ~avi ~atum, *tr.* To remove the phlegm of: *sanguis cordis in pulmone ~atur* SA 124 (= x.6.[2]).

depictum ~i, *neut.* An artistic representation, picture, carving, etc.: *~um super pariete* Ezek. 8.10 (AC 994.7).

depilo ~are ~avi ~atum, *tr.* **1** To remove the hair of: *omnis humerus ~atus* Ezek. 29.18 (SS 35.4). **2** To despoil, rob: *qui avaritiam exercent in ~andis aliis* ES 908.

depingo ~ngere ~nxi ~ctum, *tr.* To represent in a picture, portray: *si...describeret aut repraesentaret aut... ~ngeret odium* AC 1860.2.

deploro ~are ~avi ~atum, *tr.* To show regret for, deplore: *~et vitiosam suam naturam* 'bewail one's own sinfulness' BCP (VI 6); the parallel English quotation given in VI 5 (1st edn.) reads 'bewail your own sinfullness [sic]'.

depluitio ~onis, *f.* A falling down like rain: *~o ignis et sulphuris* ES(M) [4800].

deplumo ~are ~avi ~atum, *tr.* To remove the feathers of, pluck (a bird): *~are corvum* VR 125.

depluo ~ere ~i, *intr.* To fall like rain: *~ere fecit super eos man* Ps. 78.24 (AE 146.4); AC 7290.3.

depluvium ~i, *neut.* A falling of rain: *sub utraque* [*nube*] *sicut ~um* VR 112.7.

depono ~nere ~sui ~situm, *tr.* To lay aside, put off: *externum ~nit cum corpore cum moritur* VI 68; *~sito corpore* ES 2255.

depopulatio ~onis, *f.* The action of ravaging, ruination: *~onem ex falsis mali* AE 403.3.

depopulor ~ari ~atus sum, *tr.* **1** To plunder thoroughly: [*praedones*] *incendunt domos, ~antur incolarum bona, et dividunt praedes inter se* VR 117. **2** To wipe out, destroy: *quod...* [*cupidines*] *amorem conjugialem ~entur* AM 454.

deportatio ~onis, *f.* Removal, deportation: *ante ~onem* [*Judaeorum*] AE 403.18.

deporto ~are ~avi ~atum, *tr.* **1** To carry down, bring down: *cum* [*Moses*] *illas* [sc. *tabulas Legis*]*...e monte ~avit* VI 55.1. **2** To carry away, take off: *angeli... chartam in caelum ~abant* VR 48.20; *ut me... ~arent in meam lucem* AM 10.4.

depositio ~onis, *f.* A laying aside: *~ones quasi vestium* ES 4480.

depositum ~i, *neut.* A quantity kept in store, reserve: *sit cibus ad ~um terrae* Gen. 41.36 (AC).

depraedatio ~onis, *f.* The action of robbing, despoiling: *de ~one Aegyptiorum* AC 6914.2; VR 612.

depraedator ~oris, *m.* A despoiler, plunderer, robber: *mox remissus est in statum priorem, in quo fuit ~or, adulter et blasphemator proximi* VR 481.

depraedor ~ari ~atus sum, *tr.* **1** To seize the possessions of, despoil, rob: *~abimini Aegyptios* Exod. 3.22 (AC). **2** To carry off as booty, steal: *aurum et argentum ~atum a gentibus* AC 6917.3; cf. *~arentur omnium facultates* AC 7032.3.

depravo ~are ~avi ~atum, *tr.* To make crooked, corrupt: *quod verae fidei cognitiones ~averint* AC 560.

deprecatio ~onis, *f.* A prayerful, earnest urging, beseeching: *quod ~o ne abalienetur significet continuam sollicitationem* AC 5471.

deprecor ~ari ~atus sum, *tr.* **1** To attempt to mollify, placate: *cum ~atus* [*Moses*] *facies Jehovae* AC 588.2. **2** To beg to have taken away, beg off: *quia hoc ~atus est* Ezek. 4.15 (DD 15.7); *quod Pharao ~atus sit malum ranarum* AC 7392.2.

deprehendo ~dere ~di ~sum, *tr.* **1** To discover, catch (in specified circumstances): *mulierem in adulterio ~sam* John 8.3 (AE 222.7). **2** To disclose, reveal: *si suspicio fota ~derit causam* AM 375.1. **3** To grasp mentally, perceive: *~dentes quod ita sit* VR 16.2.

depressio ~onis, *f.* A pushing down, lowering: *per ~onem ventris usque ad terram* AC 247.

deprimo ~rimere ~ressi ~ressum, *tr.* **1** To pull or cast down, make lower: *pileus... ~ressus super frontem usque ad oculos* AM 263. **2** (transf.) To abase, humble, humiliate: *~rimetur altitudo virorum* Isa. 2.11 (AC 1306.1).

deprivatio ~onis, *f.* A being deprived, deprivation: *in timore ~onis possessionum* AC 6914.3.

deprivo ~are ~avi ~atum, *tr.* (w. abl.) To deprive, strip (someone of something): *qui affinem ~avit haereditate sua* CI 462[a].6; VR 12.7.

depromo ~ere ~(p)si ~(p)tum, *tr.* **1** To take out of a store, draw: *argentum ibi repositum ~ere* SS 26.3; *voces...quae excitant seu ~unt e memoria hominis* AC 1638. **2** To express, display, bring out: *bonum...non ridet, sed jucundum et hilare suum in facie, loquela et gestu alio modo ~it* AC 2216.

depso ~ere ~ui, *tr.* To knead: *mulieres ~unt massam ad faciendum placentas* Jer. 7.18 (AC 4581.7).

depuratus ~a ~um, *a.* Purified, refined: *obtexit illud auro ~o* 1 Kgs. 10.18 (AC 5313.15).

derasio ~onis, *f.* A shaving off: *per pilorum ~onem* AC 939.

derelinquo ~linquere ~liqui ~lictum, *tr.* To abandon, forsake, leave behind: *vir ~linquet patrem et matrem* Gen. 2.24 (AM 112); *~lictum*, an abandoned place: *erunt urbes refugii...in ~licta sylvae* Isa. 17.9 (DD 4).

derepente, *adv.* Suddenly: *caput...retraxerunt ~te* ES 5363.

derideo ~dere ~si ~sum, *tr.* To laugh at: *~det equum* Job 39.18 (AC 2762.3).

derisio ~onis, *f.* Contemptuous or jeering laughter, derision: *ponam eas in desolationem, et in ~onem* Jer. 25.9 (AC 5376.11).

derisus ~us, *m.* Contemptuous or jeering laughter, derision: *~ui habentur* TE 70.

derivate, *adv.* In a line of descent, derivatively: NH 21.

derivatio ~onis, *f.* **1** The source from which a word is formed, derivation: *trahit etiam vox 'spiritus' ~onem suam a 'respiratione'* DD 47.1. **2** Anything produced from a given source, a derivative: *omnia viscera...ex corde et pulmone per varias ~ones vitam trahunt* CI 308; *~ones doctrinalium et cultuum* AC 1145.

derivativus ~a ~um, *a.* Derivative, secondary: *vera et bona ~a seu descendentia* AC 8042.2; (neut.as sb.) *filii...sunt ~a illius rei quae per parentem repraesentatur* AC 6583.

derivo ~are ~avi ~atum, *tr.* **1** To cause to flow, channel: *cibus qui...in ventriculum ~atur* ES 1742; (transf.) *nec quod peccata in Se ~averit* AC 1846.3. **2** (pass.) To be drawn (from a source), be derived: *vile...a vero ~atum* AC 6715; *ab antiquis temporibus ~atum est, quod reges...insignirentur talibus* AE 31.6; *~ata*, things derived, derivatives: *~ata non sunt nisi quam formae successivae inde* AC 7004.2.

derogatio ~onis, *f.* A lessening, disparagement, depreciation: *annihilatio gratiae et misericordiae Divinae, rejectio reformationis et regenerationis per Divina media,... ~o meriti et justitiae Domini Dei Salvatoris, quae sibi vindicant* VR 439.

derogo ~are ~avi ~atum, *tr.* (w. dat.) To take away, subtract (from): *qui sanctum Verbo...corde ~ant* VR 148.2.

derutus ~a ~um, *a.* Fallen down, collapsed: *ex camino ~o* ES 3967.

descendo ~dere ~di, *intr.* (*tr.*) (fut. pple. *~surus*) **1** To go to a lower level, go down, descend: *~dit filia Pharaonis ad lavandum ad flumen* Exod. 2.5 (AC); *~damus in hanc aream, et dimicemus* VR 17.3. **b** (implying a change of state): *~surus es in infernum* Ezek. 31.15 (DD 4); *quod... ~derit et assumserit humanum* VR 3.1. **2** (w. acc., Bibl.) To go down into: *cum ~dentibus foveam* Ezek. 26.20 (AC 7090.2). **3** To descend to a lower plane or degree: *quod Divinum procedens a Domino ad ultima sua ~dat per tres gradus* SS 6; *ex bonis coelestibus et spiritualibus...existunt et ~dunt bona...naturalia* AC 775.2. **4** To be transmitted to a later time, come down: *ex quo cultu, quum tempore ~dit, exorta est idololatria* VR 159.5.

descensus ~us, *m.* The action of coming down, descent: *vidi ~um tuum per aërem* AM 2.1; *Domini ~um ad vinctos* CI 335.

descisco ~scere ~vi, *intr.* **1** To defect: *qui... ~verit ad Chaldaeos obsidentes vos* Jer. 21.9 (AC 7102.7). **2** To depart (from a standard), fall away: *cum Ecclesia ~scere incipit a bono charitatis* AC 2406.1; *patet quantum Ecclesia haec... ~verit in cultum idololatricum* AC 1356.2.

describo ~bere ~psi ~ptum, *tr.* also **discribo**. **1** To relate in words, describe: *hi sunt qui a Domino ~buntur apud Matthaeum* VR 7; (w. indir. qu.) *~bitur...qualis fides futura est* AE 9.4. **2** To enter in a book, register: *Jehovah numerabit in ~bendo populos* Ps. 87.6 (AE 850.8). **3** To compose, write (a book): *in quodam opusculo ex visis ~pto* VR 32.5.

descriptio ~onis, *f.* A description: *~one varietatum* AM 227.

desero ~ere ~ui ~tum, *tr.* **1** To depart from, abandon: *~et homo patrem et matrem* Matt. 19.5 (AM 112); *oravit ne Pater Ipsum ~eret* DD 35.3. **2** To cease from, give up: *scortationes suas...non ~uit* Ezek. 23.8 (VI 79.2).

desertio ~onis, *f.* Desertion (of a wife): *malitiosa ~o* AM 468.

desertor ~oris, *m.* One who forsakes something or someone to which one has a duty or responsibility, deserter: *vae pastori vani, ~or gregis* Zech. 11.17 (AC 2799.17); *~ores Jehovae consumentur* Isa. 1.28 (AC 4552.4).

desertus ~a ~um, *a.* Deserted, uninhabited: *in loco*

~o CI 249; (esp. neut. as sb.) a desert: *per tentationes Ipsius in ~o* DD 12.

deservio ~vire ~vivi, *intr*. (w. dat.) To be of service (to), serve: *dixit...quod...iis ~vire vellet* ES 1583.

desiderabilis ~is ~e, *a*. Desirable: *omnem arborem ~em aspectu* Gen. 2.9 (AC).

desideratus ~a ~um, *a*. (superl. *~issimus*) Highly desired: *~issima eorum non prosunt* Isa. 44.9 (AC 10406.5).

desiderium ~i, *neut*. A desire, wish: *hoc scire ~um meum fuit* AC 6695; *secundum ~um* CI 195; *in continuo ~o bonum faciendi* AC 8223.2.

desidero ~are ~avi ~atum, *tr*. **1** To wish for, desire: *coepi ~are cognitionem...de statu utriusque* AM 261.2; (w. inf.) *~at loqui* AE 25.1; (absol.) *cuivis si ~at cum illis loqui conceditur* AC 6695. **b** to wish to go: *in devia, a quibus ~avi in viam* ES 4566. **2** (Specifically defined as a function of the rational mind): *~are...est mentis interioris seu rationalis* ES 1568.

desido ~sidere ~sedi, *intr*. To sink down, be lowered: *valles ~sidunt in paludes* AE 413.4.

designatio ~onis, *f*. A specification: *~o quantitatis et mensurae per numeros toties apud Moschen* AC 10262.6.

designo ~are ~avi ~atum, *tr*. **1** To specify, prescribe: *~are tempora et nomina* AC 755.1; *ad locum ~atum* CI 441. **2** To mark out, destine: *statim ~atur homo vel ad coelum vel ad infernum* AE 413.1.

desino ~sinere ~sii, *intr*. (fut. pple. *~siturus*) **1** To have an end, finish: *formis... ~sinentibus acuminatim* ES 2274; (w. *in* + acc.) to end in: *spiritualia ~sinunt in naturalia* AE 30.2; *quod [Ecclesia]...recedat a vera fide et tandem in nullam ~sinat* AC 407. **2** To cease to be, go out of existence, come to an end: *cum ~siit Antiqua Ecclesia* AC 6738; cf. *ex significatione 'mori' quod sit ~sinere esse* AC 6799.

desisto desistere destiti, *intr*. (fut. pple. *destiturus*) **1** To cease, desist (from a course of action): *nusquam desistunt, nisi per graves punitiones* AC 7032.2; (w. *ab*) *desistere a peccatis* VI 64; *quod desisterent ab illis infestandis* AC 7088; (w. inf.) *num possent desistere aggredi* ES 2872. **2** (Bibl., see quot.): *desistite vobis ab homine* 'cease to have anything to do with man' Isa. 2.22 (AC 477.4).

desolatio ~onis, *f*. **1** The state of being desolate: *apud hominem qui regeneratur sunt, tentationes, apud hominem qui non regeneratur, sunt ~ones* AC 705.3. **2** A desolate place: *habitare fecero te in terra inferiorum in ~onibus* Ezek. 26.20 (AC 7090.2).

desolo ~are ~avi ~atum, *tr*. **1** To leave alone, abandon: *ut... ~entur vir et frater* Ezek. 4.17 (AE 71.2). **2** To render empty, void: *hominem vastatum quoad bonum et ~atum quoad verum* AC 6826.

desopio ~pire ~pivi ~pitum, *tr*. To render quiescent, lull to sleep: *usque dum jucundum mali ~pitum sit* ES 4199.

despectio ~onis, *f*. The action of despising: ES 3123 ½.

despecto ~are ~avi ~atum, *tr*. To look down upon, despise: *~ant tanquam nauci omnes sub pedibus suis* ES 388.

despector ~oris, *m*. One who despises: *~ores sexus faeminini* AM 504.3.

despectus ~us, *m*. Contempt, disdain: *cum ~u aspicientes omnes qui in seriis functionibus* AC 1509.

desperatio ~onis, *f*. An absence of hope, hopelessness, despair: *anxietates...quae inducunt statum ~onis de fine* AC 1787.1; (w. gen.) *~onem amplificandi dominium* AC 8310.

desperatus ~a ~um, *a*. (app.) Reckless from despair, desperate: *de magicis subtilioribus et temerarie ~atis* ES 3135 titulus.

despero ~are ~avi, *intr*. To lose hope, despair: *de cujus ope ~ant* AC 8567; *ut ~ent quod usquam salvari possent* AC 2694.4; *~are incepi, num remaneret iis diu vita* ES 3551.

despicio ~picere ~pexi, *intr*. To look down: *ne aliquis angelus superioris coeli ~piciat in societatem inferioris* CI 208.

despolio ~are ~avi ~atum, *tr*. To rob, plunder, despoil: *fur aufert opes et ~at domum* AE 1005.1; *annon ...se...usque ad femoralia despoliarent?* VR 574.2.

despondeo ~dere ~di, *tr*. *Animum ~dere*, to be despondent, despair: *terrentur et tremiscunt...sic ut illico ~deant animum* ES 149.

desponsatio ~onis, *f*. A betrothal: *administrat sacerdos ~ones* AM 21.4.

desponso ~are ~avi ~atum, *tr*. To promise in marriage, betroth: *ad virginem ~atam viro* Luke 1.27 (DD 19.2); *quod...se ~ent* AM 229; (transf.) *quomodo amor... ~at sibi sapientiam* AS 402.

despoticus ~a ~um, *a*. (Gk.) Authoritarian, despotic: *Germani sub regimine ~o...in quovis ducatu sunt* VR 814.

despumo ~are ~avi ~atum, *tr*. To remove the scum from: *quis non ~at crudam carnem coctione, antequam illa [ille 1st edn.] fit edulis...?* VR 331.3.

desquamo ~are ~avi ~atum, *tr*. To remove the scales of, scale (a fish): *~are piscem* VR 125.

destillo ~are ~avi, *intr*. To allow rain to fall, shower: *~ate coeli superne* Isa. 45.8 (AE 36.4).

destino ~are ~avi ~atum, *tr*. To assign to a fate, destine: *~e eos ad diem occisionis* Jer. 12.3 (AC 6767.2); *quod Dominus...damnationem praevisam aut ~atam abstulerit* DD 18.2.

destituo ~ere ~i ~tum, *tr*. (w. abl.) To deprive (of): *qui... ~itur illis non vitam habet* AC 680.1; (pass.) to be abandoned: *~tus...a sociis* AC 1506.

destructio ~onis, *f*. The action of destroying, destruction: *ad ~onem genuini veri* SS 92.

destructivus ~a ~um, *a*. (w. gen.) Causing the destruction (of), destructive (of): *quod sit [amor sui] ~us amoris in Dominum* AM 267.4.

destructor ~oris, *m*. One who destroys, destroyer: *homicida est ~or veri Ecclesiae* AE 122.5.

destruo ~ere ~xi ~ctum, *tr*. **1** To pull down, raze, destroy (physical structures): *~am munimenta tua* Mic. 5.11 (AC 7297.3). **2** To reduce to nothing, destroy: *~ere potentiam* DD 14.8; *quibus falsificatis...totum Verbum ~ctum est* SS 35.4; *id foret ~ere totum hominem* AC 59.1.

desub, *prep. w. abl*. Under: *duos annulos...desub limbo ejus* [sc. *altaris*] Exod. 30.4 (AC).

desubter, *adv*. and *prep*. (adv.) Below, beneath: *quae in coelis desuper, et quae in terra ~er* Exod. 20.4 (AC); (prep. w. abl.) below: *sepeliebatur ~er Bethel* Gen. 35.8 (AC).

desuefio ~fieri ~factus sum, *intr*. To become unaccustomed: *~factus in vita corporis talibus* ES 3138.

desuesco ~scere ~vi, *intr*., *tr*. (intr., w. abl.) To cease to be accustomed (to), lose the habit (of): *paenas subeunt usque dum ~scant talibus* AC 961; *quod adulti ~scant lacte* ES 2084; (pass.) to cease to be customary: *id [malum] apparet...quod ~sci possit* ES 2457.

desuetudo ~inis, *f*. Lack of practice, disuse: *~o inveterat hominem* VR 561.

desum deesse defui, *intr*. To be lacking or absent: *ut primum deest alicubi quale aut quantum correspondentiae* AC 6807; (w. dat.) *palatium cui deest basis* SS 39.

desumo ~ere ~(p)si ~(p)tum, *tr*. **1** To take (from a store or collection), choose out: *ex aulicis meis ~e aliquos* AM 11; *fructum ex arbore scientiae boni et mali ~ere* VR 58. **2** To draw (from a source): *naturalis homo ex sua ratione non aliud potest ~ere* VR 22.1.

desuper, *prep. w. abl*. and *adv*. also spelled as two words **de super**. **1** (prep.) From upon: *calceum exueret ~r pede suo* DD 15.3 (Isa. 20.2). **2** (adv.) From above: *omne bonum et verum ~r venit* CI 9.2.

desupinatus ~a ~um, *a*. Prob. error for **demisupinatus** (cf. AC 10164): TE 146.

detectio ~onis, *f*. The action of revealing: *~o causarum* AM 484.

detego ~gere ~xi ~ctum, *tr*. To make known, reveal (a previously hidden fact): *~xerunt fallacias* AC 7127.3; *causas per quas hoc arcanum evolverent et ~gerent* VR 48.9; (w. indir. qu.) *~gebat quid scirent* AC 7077.

detentio ~onis, *f*. A state of being restrained, restraint: *~o a malo et falso* AC 929.

detergeo ~gere ~si ~sum, *tr*. To wipe off, wash away, purge: *cum abluet Dominus sordes filiarum Zionis, et sanguines Hierosolymae ~serit e medio* Isa. 55.4 (AC 374.2).

deterior ~or ~us, *compar. a*. Worse: *societas major et ~or* ES 1204; (neut. as sb.) *in ~us*, for the worse: *quod totus Adam...in ~us commutatus fuerit* SE 3(a) (Council of Trent).

determinate, *adv*. In a determinate manner: *qui...cogitant de Deo, cogitant de Ipso ~e* AC 8705.5.

determinatio ~onis, *f*. **1** The bounding, delimitation (of a thing): *secundum formam et partium dispositionem et ~onem* AC 681. **2** The direction (of thought, etc. to a particular object): *~o cogitationis ad aliquem populum* AC 6653. **3** The action or fact or being directed to an object: *quod ordo sit qualitas dispositionis, ~onis et activitatis partium* VR 52. **4** A decision, determination: *quod ~ones relinquendae sint beneplacitis mariti* AM 221.

determinatus ~a ~um, *a*. (pf. pple. of **determino**) Precisely limited, defined, determinate: *non sunt plagae ~ae sicut in mundo naturali* CI 123; *in sensu ~o* AC 7269.

determino ~are ~avi ~atum, *tr*. **1** To direct (vision, thought, etc. towards a particular object): (w. *ad*) *intellectus... ~at...hunc* [sc. *visum*] *ad objecta* AE 37; *cogitationes ad interiora... ~ant et elevant* AC 762; *spiritus qui,...non se ~are possunt, ad aliquid possidendum* ES 3970; *omnia quae ab anima et mente ~antur in corpus* AM 179. **2** (w. indir. qu.) To decide, determine: *liquet quod quale boni Christiani ~et in quo gradu unusquisque est proximus* AC 6707. **3** To make determinate: *formae sunt subjecta ~antia* AC 7408.2.

deterrefacio ~facere ~feci ~factum, *tr*. To frighten off: *a quibus [monstrosis] tamen non ~facti sunt* VR 797.4.

deterreo ~rere ~rui ~ritum, *tr.* To restrain by fear, deter: *per quos* [*timores*]... *~rentur a malis faciendis* CI 543.

detestabilis ~is ~e, *a.* (compar. *~ior*) Loathsome, detestable: AM 462; AC 916.3.

detestatio ~onis, *f.* A detestable thing: *quod... imagines abominationum ~onum suarum fecerint ex eo* Ezek. 7.20 (AE 827.5).

detestor ~ari ~atus sum, *tr.* To loathe, detest: *nigredinem corporis ~antur* [*Africani*] ES 453.

detineo ~tinere ~tinui ~tentum, *tr.* **1** To keep from going away, hold back, detain: *in tali carcere toties ~tinentur* AE 122.1; AC 7090.1. **2** To keep (in a specified state), hold: *animus ~tinetur in litera* AC 755.4. **3** To keep (from an action), hold back, restrain: *~tinentur a nefandis suis dolis* AC 6914.2; *~tinet illos amor sui et mundi* AC 7032.3.

detondeo ~dere ~di ~sum, *tr.* To cut off the hair of, crop: *tempore illo ~debit Dominus...caput et pilos pedum* Isa. 7.20 (AE 66.5); ES 3355.

detorqueo ~quere ~si ~tum, *tr.* To twist out of shape, distort: *forma...est depravata ac, ut ita dicatur, ~ta* AC 4317.5; to twist the meaning of, distort: *an ulla haeresis est quae non...quae non consentiunt...diversimode explicat et ~quet ut non dissentiant?* AC 794.1.

detractio ~onis, *f.* The action of drawing away: *si homo...sentiret hanc* [sc. *per Divinam Providentiam*] *~onem aut abductionem* DP 183.1.

detraho ~here ~xi ~ctum, *tr.* **1** To pull off, remove: *~he calceos tuos a super pedibus tuis* Exod. 3.5 (AC). **2** To pull down, drag down: *illas prehendebant ~hentes in cavernam* AM 521.1; (transf.) *quos divitiae seduxerunt et a coelo ~xerunt* CI 362. **3** To take away, remove: *nihil ~hetur e servitio vestro quicquam* Exod. 5.11 (AC); *ita ~hit Domino quod Ipsius est* AC 1316.1.

detrecto ~are ~avi ~atum, *tr.* To disparage, belittle: (absol.) *is non ~at lingua sua* Ps. 15.3 (VI 84.1).

detrimentosus ~a ~um, *a.* Causing damage, harmful: *effluvia ~a* AM 253.1.

detrimentum ~i, *neut.* Damage, loss: *ne coeli priories... ~um paterentur* AE 258.

detritus ~a ~um, *a.* (pf. pple. of **detero***) Worn-out; (neut. pl. as sb.) worn-out clothing: *veteramenta ~orum* Jer. 38.11 (AE 537.17).

detrudo ~dere ~si ~sum, *tr.* **1** To push down: *quod ~derent caput usque ad pedes* CI 400.3. **2** (transf.) To push down (to a lower level): *se in miserias...sponte ~dunt* AC 995.1; *~di in infernum* AC 582.

detrusio ~onis, *f.* The action of pushing down: *~o in infernum* AC 6907.2.

deturbo ~are ~avi ~atum, *tr.* To thrust down: *quum ~atus esset draco de coelo* ES 526.

deturpo ~are ~avi ~atum, *tr.* To make foul: Jer. 14.21 (AE 253.5).

Deus ~i, *m.* (nom. pl. *dii*, dat. and abl. pl. *diis*) **1** The Supreme Being, God: *agnoscunt Dominum pro unico ~o* AC 6700. **2** (usu. lower case) Any being regarded as divine, a god: *simulachra pro diis colunt* VR 9.1; *usque ut velint esse dii* AM 262.3.

Deuteronomium ~i, *neut.* Deuteronomy, the fifth book of Moses: *legebam caput primum ~i de populo Judaico* AC 3474.

devastatio ~onis, *f.* **1** The action of laying waste, devastation: *~o a Schaddai veniet* Isa. 13.6 (DD 4); *quod Jehovae...tribuatur malum, ira, furor, ~o* AC 7032.1. **2** Utter destruction: *~onem veri* AC 7027. **3** The act of rendering totally devoid of good qualities: *~o Ecclesiae per falsificationes veri* FI 52; *tentatio fidelium et ~o infidelium* AC 755.3.

devasto ~are ~avi ~atum, *tr.* **1** To render uninhabitable, lay waste: *dum ~abuntur urbes ut sint sine habitatore* Isa. 6.11 (AE 223.5). **2** To destroy utterly (spiritual qualities): *~ata charitas* AC 427; *~ato vero* AC 7102.1. **3** To make (persons) devoid of good qualities: *illi ~antur prorsus quoad verum* AC 7039.2.

deveho ~here ~xi ~ctum, *tr.* To carry across, transport, convey: *jucunda sunt quae aperiunt meatus seu ductus qui recipiunt et ~hunt in sanguinem, injucunda autem claudunt* AC 5147.3.

devenio ~nire ~ni, *intr.* To be reduced to, become: *quales ~niunt mihi ostensum est* ES 1866.

deviatio ~onis, *f.* A turning aside, deviation: *non aliquod semen potuisset...excrescere absque ulla ~one a primo stamine usque ad fructus* VR 470.3; AM 385.

devigoro ~are ~avi ~atum, *tr.* To deprive of strength, weaken, impair: *quod...virtus, quae vocatur virilis, ~etur ad nullam* AM 433.

devincio ~cire ~xi ~ctum, *tr.* To attach by moral ties: *haeredes...quibus secundum legem, ut apparet, ~ctus erit* ES 1240.

devinco ~ncere ~ci ~ctum, *tr.* To conquer, subdue: *~cit et subjugavit inferna dirissima* AE 918.11.

devio ~are ~avi, *intr.* To go astray, wander, err: *quod ~averint a vero* AE 94.

devius ~a ~um, *a.* Off the beaten track, out of the way: (neut. as sb.) *in ~a, a quibus desideravi in viam* ES 4566.

devolo ~are ~avi, *intr*. To fly down: *quod cum videt, ad hoc ~at* AM 495.2.

devolutio ~onis, *f.* That which derives from a higher plane: *~ones infiniti* AT 190.

devolvo ~vere ~vi ~utum, *tr*. **1** To roll down: *~vam te de petris* Jer. 51.25 (AC 1298.5). **2** To roll away: *ii quasi ~vere volunt tunicas...ab oculo* ES 1106.

devoratio ~onis, *f.* The action of eating up, devouring: AE 614.1.

devoro ~are ~avi ~atum, *tr*. To eat up, devour: *ferae dabo illum ad ~andum illum* Ezek. 33.27 (AC 7102.3); to destroy: *gladius Jehovae ~ans* Jer. 12.12 (AE 131.5).

devote, *adv*. In a devout manner, devoutly: *oravit ~e ad Deum* AM 461.1.

devotio ~onis, *f.* **1** A devout attitude, devotion: ES 732; *libros ~onis* 'devotional books' AE 1061.2. **2** Perdition, destruction: *quod gentes ~oni darentur* AE 193.9.

devotus ~a ~um, *a*. Devout: *honesti, sapientes, ~i* AC 1010.2.

devoveo ~vere ~vi ~tum, *tr*. **1** To vow as an offering, devote: *et ~vi quaestum eorum Jehovae* Mic. 4.13 (AC 7770.5). **2** To consign to perdition, curse: *usque dum ~verit omnes habitatores Ajae* Josh. 8.26 (AC 878.6); *contra ~vebit Jehovah linguam maris Aegypti* Isa. 11.15 (SS 15.2); (w. dat., or w. *in* + acc.) *damnare homines et ~vere illos inferno* FI 45; *~vere aliquem in infernum* ES 1495. **3** To abominate, abhor: *hi si non spiritu... ~vet* [*~vent* Rogers] *adulteria, usque adulteri sunt* AM 153.2.

dexter ~tra ~trum, *a*. also **dexter** ~tera ~terum. (superl. *~terrimus*) **1** Right (as opp. to left): *oculus... ~ter* AC 7078; *a ~tra parte* CI 118. **b** *ad ~trum* or *a ~tris*, on the right-hand side, on the right: *vidi... flumen...ad ~trum ad multam satis distantiam* AC 6699; *dicet ovibus a ~tris* Matt. 25.34 (VI 2). **2** Skilled, clever: *confirmatores ~terrimi* DP 318.8.

dexteritas ~atis, *f.* Skill, cleverness: ES 512.

dextra ~ae, *f.* The right hand: *est in ~a mea fulmen excommunicandi* AM 264.1.

dextre, *adv*. Skilfully, cleverly: *quod etiam sirenes ~e callent* VR 80.1.

dextrorsum, *adv*. Towards the right: *spiritus... ~m abiit* AC 1396; *apparuit ille in aliqua altitudine ~m* AC 7077.

diabolicus ~a ~um, *a*. (Gk.) Of or belonging to devils, devilish: *in forma humana, sed dira et ~a* CI 314; *amor ~us est amor sui* VR 45.

diabolus ~i, *m*. (Gk.) **1** An evil spirit, devil: *vidi ascendentem ex inferno ~um* AM 263.1. **2** The supreme evil spirit, Satan, the Devil: *quod non facienda sint mala, quia sunt ~i et a ~o* VR 3.2; *creditur...quod ~us seu Satanas fuerit lucis angelus* CI 311.1.

diaconus ~i, *m*. (Gk.) A deacon: *cardinales, episcopi, ~i* ES 5079.

diadema ~atis, *neut*. (Gk.) (app.) A precious stone, gem: *sensus literae translucet a sensu spirituali...sicut ~a a luce* AR 823; AR 540.1; *flores ex ~atibus* AM 42.4. (n.b. The ordinary meaning of the word in Latin as in Greek is 'diadem', 'crown', but the passages quoted leave little doubt of the meaning. In AM 42.4 A Acton emended to *adamantibus*.)

diagnosticum ~i, *neut*. (Gk.) A means of discrimination, choice: *~a astrologorum ex astris* VR 631.

diamantinus ~a ~um, *a*. Of diamond: *fulgurant ...sicut a ~is sphaerulis* AC 1621.

diameter ~tri, *f.* (Gk.) The diameter (of a circle): AC 5291.10; *e ~tro*, diametrically opposite: *sol...sub terra est e ~tro oppositus suae meridiei* AM 152ª.1; (fig.) *est...e ~tro contra Verbum* VI 31.

diametraliter, *adv*. On the line of a diameter, diametrically: *antra...tendentia introrsum, ac inde quoque in profundum oblique vel ~er* CI 586.

diaphanus ~a ~um, *a*. (Gk.) Allowing the passage of light, diaphanous: [*lucis*] *influxu in objectum ~um* VR 34.3.

diaphragma ~atis, *neut*. (Gk.) (anat.) The diaphragm: VR 119.2; ES 983.

diastole ~es, *f.* (Gk.) (anat.) The dilatation (of the heart, etc.), diastole: VR 37.2.

diastolicus ~a ~um, *a*. (Gk.) Characteristic of the periodic relaxation and dilatation of the heart chambers, diastolic: *quod pulsus cardiaci coeli...correspondentiam habeant cum corde, et cum ejus systolicis et ~is motibus* AC 3884.4.

dibaphus ~a ~um, *a*. (Gk.) Twice-dyed: *coccineo ~o* Exod. 28.6 (AC).

dicatus ~a ~um, *a*. (w. dat.) Assigned, devoted (to): *in organis generationi ~is* AM 310.2; ES 495.

dico[1] ~are ~avi ~atum, *tr*. To devote, dedicate: *coeperunt ipsum solem et lunam colere...usque adeo ut illis templa ~arent et statuas ponerent* AC 2441.7.

dico[2] ~cere ~xi ~ctum, *tr., intr*. **1** To utter in words, say, speak: *ita ~xit Jehovah* Exod. 4.22 (AC); (w. dat.) *amen ~co vobis* Matt. 25.40 (VI 2); (w. *ad*) *cur Dominus ad Petrum ~xit* AE 9.2; *secum ~cere* 'to say to oneself' SS 1. **b** (w. *quod*): *quod Jehovah Moschi ~ceret* *quod reverteretur Aegyptum* AC 7019. **c** (w. acc. and inf.): *quod... ~cat se non esse virum verborum* AC 6982. **d** (w. indir. qu.) To say by way of question, ask: *sed iis... ~ctum...an alium Dominum habuerint* ES 1113; *~cebatur a quibusdam num Judaei... praerogativam haberent* ES 2935. **2** To state (in writing): *ad finem sequentis capitis ~cetur de spiritibus planetae Mercurii* AC 6702; *quid correspondentia, in praecedente articulo ~ctum est* CI 103; (pass.) *difficillime haec possunt ~ci quomodo se...habent* AC 111. **3** (w. pred.) To call (by a name): *virgines quae Vestales ~ctae sunt* AC 6832.7; (pass.) to be named: *~citur doctrina Novae Hierosolymae* DD praef. **4** (pass., w. inf.) To be said (to): *~cuntur e longinquo venire* AC 6740.

dictamen ~inis, *neut.* **1** A formal statement, dictate: *quod ~en Papae sit nullius rei* SS 24. **2** An internal voice conveying orders, dictate: *haec [Ecclesia habuit]...non perceptionem, sed loco ejus aliud quoddam ~en quod vocari potest conscientia* AC 607.1; *internum ~en* VR 9.1.

dictatio ~onis, *f.* The act of formally stating, dictation: *in se etiam reflexio et perceptio est indicatio et ~o interna* AC 2862.

dictator ~oris, *m.* One who makes an authoritative statement, dictator: VR 112.3.

dicterium ~i, *neut.* An unkind remark intended to provoke ridicule, witticism, jest (at someone's expense): *volentes acuere illas* [sc. *linguas*] *in ~a* VR 74.3; *eos... ~is laedunt et persequuntur* AC 1844.

dictio ~onis, *f.* **1** The action of saying: *post gratiarum ~onem* AM 25. **2** A way of speaking: *~o et sermo inde est naturalis* AE 236.1. **3** A thing said, saying: *omnis ~o contra id est sicut stimulus in naribus illorum* VR 110.1.

dictionarium ~i, *neut.* A book giving the meaning of the words of a language, dictionary: ES 805.

dicto ~are ~avi ~atum, *tr.* **1** To utter (words) for another to write down, dictate: *illi* [sc. *prophetae*] *scripserunt sicut spiritus a Divino ~avit* AC 7055.3. **2** To state with authority, lay down: *credunt verum esse, quia ~atum a viro auctoritatis* VR 42.2; (w. *quod*) *idea spiritualis...interius ~at quod hoc...verum sit vel non* FI 5.

dictus ~a ~um, *a.* (pf. pple. of **dico**²) **1** Stated, mentioned: *ex malo cupiditatum ~orum amorum* AC 6859; *ita ~us,* so-called: *ut servirent falsis ita ~is* AC 7123. **2** (neut. as sb.) A thing said, saying: *recitant ...aliquot ~a ex sensu literae Verbi* SS 64.

didascalus ~i, *m.* (Gk.) A teacher: AM 153ª.2; *doctores ~i* VR 803.

didrachma ~ae, *f.* (Gk.) A coin worth two drachmas or half a shekel, bekah: Exod. 38.26 (AC).

diduco ~cere ~xi ~ctum, *tr.* **1** To cause to spread out, pull apart: *obduxit auro, ita ut ~ceret super cherubos* 1 Kgs. 6.32 (AC 8369.3); *~cto ore* VR 16.4. **2** To treat at greater length, extend the discussion of: *illa hic amplius ~cere non opus est* FI 37.

diductio ~onis, *f.* The action of pulling apart: *~ones et coarctationes lobulorum ejus* [sc. *pulmonis*] *reciprocae* DP 319.1.

dies ~ei, *m.* (also, *f.* ES 932) **1** A period of 24 hours, day: *non per ~em aut septimanam, sed per plures menses* AC 6695; *nondum est meridies ~ei* AM 13.1. **b** *in ~em* or *per ~em*, daily, day by day: Gen. 19.36 (AC); AC 6699. **2** A day as a point of time: *in ~e illo, quo descensurus est Pharao in infernum* Ezek. 31.15 (AC 6693.5); (pl.) a period: *post afflictionem ~erum illorum* Matt. 24.29 (SS 14.1); *~ebus vitae suae* ES 3113. **b** (Bibl.) *Antiquus ~erum*, the Ancient of Days (as a divine title): Dan. 7.9 (AC 934.2). **3** The light of day, daylight: *laetati quod in ~em venirent et lucem conspicerent* ES 271; (transf.) *progressione in ~em sapientiae* AC 1807.2.

diffamatio ~onis, *f.* The action of defaming: *timor ~onis sui nominis* AM 373.

diffamia ~ae, *f.* Ill repute, notoriety: CJ 9.

diffamo ~are ~avi ~atum, *tr.* To impugn the reputation of, defame: *quum... [Josephus] non vellet illam ~are* Matt. 1.19 (DD 21); AM 474.

differenter, *adv.* In a different way, differently: AC 4411.

differentia ~ae, *f.* A measure of difference: *~a est qualis inter vesperam et mane* SS 99; *'creare, formare et facere'...significant regenerare, cum ~a* AC 16.

differo ~rre distuli, *intr.* (*tr.*) **1** To be different, differ: *quod bonum illud ubivis ~rat et varium sit* CI 51; (w. abl. of quality in respect of which the difference exists) *~runt etiam gestibus et moribus* AM 33; (w. *ab*) *qui [stylus spiritualis] prorsus ~rt a stylo naturali* SS 71.1. **2** (tr.) To make later in time, keep back, delay: *primitias vini tui non ~res* Exod. 22.29 (AE 28.3).

differtus ~a ~um, *a.* Stuffed, crammed: *stomachus biliosis ~us* VR 42.2.

difficile, *adv.* (compar. *~ius*) With difficulty: ES 4597.

difficilis ~is ~e, *a.* (compar. *~ior*, superl. *~limus*) Hard to accomplish, difficult: *de ~i investigatione* AM 183.2.

difficultas ~atis, *f.* A difficulty: *sola ~as est, posse resistere amori sui* CI 359.

difficulter, *adv*. With difficulty: *loqui potuit sed ~er* AC 6985.

diffido ~dere ~di, *intr*. To lack confidence, distrust: *timere...significat ~dere, aut fidem et amorem non habere* AC 2826.14.

diffindo ~ndere ~di ~sum, *tr*. **1** To split into pieces, break up, divide: *~dit petras in deserto* Ps. 78.15 (AE 411.5); *~ndebantur aquae* Exod. 14.21 (AC). **2** To tear apart (persons): *fera agri ~ndet eos* Hos. 13.8 (AC 908.3).

difflo ~are ~avi ~atum, *tr*. To blow in different directions, scatter: *induxistis in domum, et ~avi id* Hag. 1.9 (AC 1488.2).

diffluo ~ere ~xi, *intr*. **1** To lose coherence, collapse, fall apart: [*statuae*] *sic accensae igne intestino ~ebant* VR 110.8. **2** (w. *in* + acc.) To dissolve (into): *mens... ~eret sicut bulla in aërem* VR 30.2; *quod ea* [sc. *poena*] *sensim ~eret in serpentes* ES 232. **3** To become diffuse, lack concentration: *amor usus...continet mentem ne ~at, et ne circumvagetur* AM 16.3.

diffringo ~ringere ~regi ~ractum, *tr*. To break open or apart: *securi parietem ~ringere* ES 262; (transf.) *hi veram fidem ~ringunt per divisionem unitatis Dei* VR 379.4.

diffundo ~ndere ~di ~sum, *tr*. **1** To cause to spread, diffuse, scatter: *quod ~nderent mentem naturalem undequaque* AC 7123. **2** (refl.) To spread out, extend: *evolabant...aves noctis, quae se ~ndebant ad sinistrum* VR 71.1; *quae opinio tam late se ~dit* AC 1850.1.

diffusio ~onis, *f*. The manner of spreading out: *ex coma, ejus colore, longitudine, ~one* ES 1229.

diffusus ~a ~um, *a*. (pf. pple. of **diffundo**) Not concentrated, diffuse: *cogitatio quae non determinatur ad aliquam speciem est ~sa quaquaversum* AE 151.1.

digero ~rere ~ssi ~stum, *tr*. **1** To digest (food): DP 296.14. **2** To arrange, classify: *ut...* [*ideas*] *analytice ~rat in ordine* 3AD 2655.

digestio ~onis, *f*. The process of digestion: ES 1272.

digitus ~i, *m*. A finger: *sunt pauci qui ~o attingunt illum* [*amorem*] AM 318.3; a toe (of the foot): *~is plantae pedis sinistri* AC 5714; a claw (of a beast): *~i scorpionis* ES 2748.

digne, *adv*. In a worthy manner, worthily: *qui ad Sanctam Caenam ~e accedunt* VR 719.1.

dignitas ~atis, *f*. Eminent position, rank, dignity: *unicuivis functioni adjuncta est ~as secundum ~atem usus* CI 389.

dignor ~ari ~atus sum, *tr., intr*. **1** (tr.) To deem fit, judge worthy: *quid facilius Deo est, quam omnes ~ari fide...?* VR 72.1. **2** (intr., w. inf.) To see fit, deign (to): *Ipse ~atus est dicere* AC 29.2; (also absol.) *~ante Domino* ES 2939.

dignosco ~scere ~vi ~tum, *tr.* also **dinosco**. To tell apart, distinguish: *per receptionem...cognoscitur et ~scitur amor vere conjugialis ab amore conjugiali spurio* AM 224; *ut nihil ~scere possint inter vitam eorum in corpore et post corporis mortem* ES 2355.

dignus ~a ~um, *a*. (compar. *~ior*, superl. *~issimus*) **1** Deserving, worthy: *ambulabunt Mecum...quia ~i sunt* Rev. 3.4 (AR); (w. abl.) *fructus ~os paenitentia* Luke 3.8 (DD 18.4); *quae scire datum ~a memoratu sunt* AC 6695. **2** Of high rank or status, exalted: *quod ~ior esset rege* AM 263.2.

digredior ~di ~ssus sum, *intr*. To depart from one's subject, digress: *non licet a materia hic proposita abire, et sic ~di* AM 156[a].3.

dijudicatio ~onis, *f*. The process of distinguishing by judgment: AC 9159.

dijudico ~are ~avi ~atum, *tr., intr*. **1** (tr.) To judge to be different, distinguish: *quod...inde falsa ~ent* AC 6766.2. **2** (intr.) To make a judgment, decide: *et ~ent inter ambos nos* Gen. 31.37 (AC).

dilabor ~bi ~psus sum, *intr*. **1** To slip away: *quod is miratus est, et postea ~psus* ES 282. **2** To fall to pieces, dissolve, collapse: *sceleton... ~psum in pulverem* AM 182.5. **3** (of abstract things) To break down, collapse: *ejus doctrinae verum et bonum, quae non consistunt sed ~buntur* AE 223.19.

dilaceratio ~onis, *f*. The action of tearing in pieces, rending: *continuis ictibus et ~onibus* ES 284.

dilacero ~are ~avi ~atum, *tr*. To tear in pieces, rend: *~ando vestes ejus* AM 512.1.

dilaniatio ~onis, *f*. The action of tearing to pieces: *pugnas et ~ones* CI 380.3.

dilanio ~are ~avi ~atum, *tr*. To tear to pieces, butcher: *sicut ferae, unus alterum ~ent* AC 1844.

dilatatio ~onis, *f*. An expanding, dilatation: DP 319.1.

dilatio ~onis, *f*. A stretching or enlarging of a part of the body, dilation: *per ~onem oris seu regionis labiorum ac genarum* ES 626.

dilato ~are ~avi ~atum, *tr*. **1** To make broader, widen: *~atis faucibus* VR 31.4; *plateae...angustae, sed in progressu ~atae* AM 79.4; (refl.) to expand (in pride): *~abit se cor tuum* Isa. 60.5 (AC 489.1). **2** (Bibl.) To increase the territory of: *~et Deus Japhetum* Gen. 9.27 (AC).

dilectio ~onis, *f*. The action of loving: *~o seu amor facit conjunctionem* AE 213; VR 388.6.

dilectus ~a ~um: pf. pple. of **diligo**.

diligens ~ntis, *a*. Diligent: *pauperes...in suo opere seduli et ~ntes* CI 364.

diligenter, *adv*. Diligently: AC 1175.2.

diligentia ~ae, *f*. Diligence: ES 5668.

diligo ~ligere ~lexi ~lectum, *tr*. (superl. of pf. pple. *~lectissimus*) To delight in, love: *quod ~ligat aut amet illud* AC 1001.1; *inter gentes in coelo maxime ~liguntur Africani* CI 326; *~lexerunt homines magis tenebras quam lucem* John 3.19 (DD 1); (w. inf.) *quod in sentinis... ~ligant versari* ES 414.

diluculum ~i, *neut*. The period of twilight before dawn: *in ~o ante mane* AC 879; *~um, nam tunc finitur nox et incipit dies* AC 8211.1.

diluo ~ere ~i ~tum, *tr*. **1** To dissolve: *aqua...facit ut ~atur...cibus* AC 4976.1; to dissipate: *columna...nigra quae sic ~i et temperari non possit* ES(M) 4713. **2** To expiate, wipe out (a crime): *ut...nefas, sic ~atur* VR 134.4.

diluvium ~i, *neut*. **1** An inundation, flood: *tentationes...in Verbo comparantur ~is seu inundationibus aquarum* AC 705.1. **2** The great flood in the time of Noah: *Ecclesia Antiqua dicitur, quae fuit post ~um* CI 327.

dimensio ~onis, *f*. **1** Extension in space in one particular plane: *trina ~o omnium est in terrestribus* AC 650. **2** Measurements, size: *si arca, cum ejus bituminatione, ~one et constructione, ut et diluvium, non plus...significarent* AC 639.1. **3** Scope or extent (of immaterial things): *ut adulteria quoad utramque ~onem noscantur* AM 478.3.

dimetior ~tiri ~nsus sum, *tr*. To measure carefully or thoroughly: *partiar Schechemum, et vallem Succoth ~tiar* Ps. 60.6 (AC 1441).

dimicatio ~onis, *f*. The action of fighting, combat: AM 248.2.

dimico ~are ~ui, *intr*. **1** To engage in physical combat, fight: *vidi puerulos inter se ~antes* CI 344. **2** (of things) To be at variance, quarrel: *apparuit nubes candida absque striis seu radiis inter se ~antibus* AM 315.12.

dimidiatio ~onis, *f*. A splitting (of something) into two parts: *illustratum et ostensum per ~ones cum inirentur foedera* AC Index 1 s.v. 'Tabulae'.

dimidiatus ~a ~um, *a*. Divided in two, halved: *homo divisus seu ~us* AM 37.

dimidio ~are ~avi ~atum, *tr*. To divide into two, halve: *~avit populum* Gen. 32.7 (AC); *cum ~antur [numeri]* AC 10255.

dimidius ~a ~um, *a*. Half: *quod hic non sit nisi quam ~us homo* AM 432.2; (neut. as sb.) a half: *per unum diem et ~um* AM 8.3; *~um temporis* Rev. 12.14 (AR); also, the midpoint (of anything): *per ~um femoris* ES 1686; (so, also as adj.) *versus ~am faciem* 'towards the middle of the face' ES 439.

diminuo ~ere ~i ~tum, *tr*. To cause to decrease in number or extent, lessen, diminish: *aequilibrium ... ~itur et accrescit secundum numerum illorum qui intrant* CI 593; (refl. and pass.) to become less, diminish: *delitiae hujus amoris...se exaltant et diminuunt* AM 293.2; AC 8054.3.

diminutio ~onis, *f*. A lessening, diminution: *per ~onem sociorum ad paucos* SD 696.

diminutivum ~i, *neut*. A form of smaller size, diminutive: *generatio quarta significat idem ac quadraginta...; est ~um quoddam inde* AC 1856; AC 1748.1.

dimissio ~onis, *f*. The act of sending away, dismissal: *~o propter hanc causam est plenaria separatio mentium* AM 255.2; the act of leaving alone: AC 9274.1.

dimitto ~mittere ~misi ~missum, *tr*. **1** To allow to depart, let go: *~missi...aufugerunt domum* AM 6.4; *divites ~misit inanes* Luke 1.53 (AE 118.5). **2** To put away, divorce (a wife): *quicunque ~miserit uxorem* Matt. 19.9 (AM 255.2). **3** To leave alone or untouched: *septimo [anno] intermittes eam* [sc. *terram*] *et ~mittes eam* Exod. 23.11 (AC).

dimoveo ~vere ~vi ~tum, *tr*. **1** To move from its place, remove: *montes recedent et colles ~vebuntur* Isa. 54.10 (AC 1038.2); *ab homine usque ad bestiam se ~vebunt* Jer. 5.3 (AC 1326.6). **2** To break or end (an agreement): *foedus pacis Meae non ~vebitur* Isa. 54.10 (AC 6804.10).

dinosco: see **dignosco**.

dioecesis ~eos, *f*. (Gk.) A diocese: AR 716.4.

diploma ~atis, *neut*. (Gk.) A document granting privileges, charter, diploma: *quid eminens administratio in regno absque ~ate* VR 730.2.

dire, *adv*. In a dreadful manner: *~e cruciantur* AC 6849.4.

directe, *adv*. (compar. *~ius*) **1** Straight ahead: *~e et quidem in crucem* ES 3404. **2** Directly, immediately: *unum [tentorium] ~e supra locum* VR 110.1; *qui Ipsum ~e adeunt* AM 71.1.

directio ~onis, *f*. **1** The action of directing: *bonum...quia absque aliqua ~one in via, vertitur in spurcum* AC 5145.3. **2** A specified direction: *interiora...mentis illorum...inflexa sunt in ~onem obliquam* AM 153[a].2. **3** A tendency to move or face in a specified direction: *quod ad centrum commune sit omnis ~o etiam in tellure, notum est* CI 142; *non possunt aliter loqui quam secundum ~onem vasorum* ES 3759.

directus ~a ~um, *a.* **1** Moving or facing straight forwards, straight: *conjugem intueri facie ~a* AM 241. **2** Direct, straightforward, immediate: *sub cogitationem ~am* CI 183.2.

direptio ~onis, *f.* The action of plundering, looting: *erunt opes eorum in ~onem* Zeph. 1.13 (AC 1488.2).

dirigo ~rigere ~rexi ~rectum, *tr.* **1** To guide, direct: *~rigere iis concedebatur manum meam dum haec scriberem* ES 288; *~rexit gressum ad me* AM 2.1; (w. *ne*) *~rigere ne praecipitet se in...malum* AC 50.2. **2** (Bibl.) To open (a way): *~rexit viam irae Suae* Ps. 78.50 (AC 7102.10). **3** To turn towards a stated aim, direct: *ex fide ~recta in Ipsum* DD 32.7.

dirimo ~rimere ~remi ~remptum, *tr.* **1** To pull apart, separate: *societates...ab illis non ~rimuntur; sed successive separantur* AC 7502.3; VR 447. **2** To put an end to, settle (a dispute): *ut lis hujus arcani ~rimeretur* AM 161.2.

diripio ~ripere ~ripui ~reptum, *tr.* To plunder, loot (treasure): *argentum...depromere, imo ~ripere* SS 26.3; to rob (persons): *alios defrauderent, ~riperent et spoliarent* CI 530.2.

diritas ~atis, *f.* The quality of being dreadful: *~as eorum crescit, sicut propinquiora sunt* CI 587.4; an instance of this: *secundum ~ates cordis* AC 819.

diruo ~ruere ~rui ~rutum, *tr.* To ruin, destroy: *~ruentur montes* Ezek. 38.20 (AC 1691.3).

dirumpo: see **disrumpo**.

dirus ~a ~um, *a.* (compar. *~ior*, superl. *~issimus*) Exceedingly unpleasant, dreadful, frightful: *~ae aves noctis* AM 264.4; *se mutuo ~is modis torquent* AC 5071.

dirutus ~a ~um, *a.* Ruined: *ad templum ~um* ES 4179.

discalceatio ~onis, *f.* The action of removing shoes: *'exuitio calcei' seu ~o* AC 1748.4.

discalceatus ~a ~um, *a.* Wearing no shoes, unshod: Isa. 20.3 (VR 130.1).

discalceo ~are ~avi ~atum, *tr.* To remove shoes from: *~are plantas pedis* AE 240.3.

discantum ~i, *neut.* An accompanying melody, descant: *sic ut consentiant cum ~o respective* ES 5113.

discedo ~dere ~ssi ~ssum, *intr.* **1** To go away, depart: *quibus exploratis ~dunt* AC 6813. **2** (of things) To be separated, recede: *affectiones ab invicem ~dunt* AM 244.2; *sensus eorum verborum...admodum ~dit a sensu literae* AC 5307.1.

disceptatio ~onis, *f.* A quarrel, dispute: *~o fuit, cur Deus non omnibus...imputat meritum...Filii Sui* VR 72.1.

discepto ~are ~avi ~atum, *intr.* (*tr.*) **1** To be at variance, quarrel, dispute: *miratus quod ita ~arent* CI 320; *coeperunt inter se ~are de intelligentia et sapientia* AM 354.1. **2** (tr.) To make the subject of a dispute, argue about: *tam multa ~ata et ratiocinata* ES 4441; (impers. pass.) *~abatur quisnam eorum major esset* AC 8301.4.

discerno ~cernere ~crevi ~cretum, *tr., intr.* **1** (tr.) To tell apart, distinguish: *quod homo...ne quidem sciat ~cernere sexum* AM 133.1; ES 207. **2** (intr., w. *inter*) To make a distinction, distinguish (between): *quod ~cernat Jehovah inter Aegyptios et inter Israelem* AC 7774. **3** (tr.) To separate, secrete: *renes...~cernunt liquida obsoleta...a sanguine* ES 959.

discerpo ~ere ~si ~tum, *tr.* **1** To rend in pieces, tear apart: *quod...pueri ~ti fuerint ab ursis* 2 Kgs. 2.24 (AE 66.2). **2** To reduce to fragments, pull apart: *sic etiam ~sisti fidem nostram* VR 74.2.

discerptio ~onis, *f.* The action of tearing apart: AC 955.

discerptor ~oris, *m.* One who tears apart: AC 957.

discessio ~onis, *f.* The action of going away, departure: *reconciliationes quae fiunt post ~ones* AM 289.

discessus ~us, *m.* A going away, departure: *~um quaerit* CI 548; departure (from a standard): *si vel minimus ~us verborum* ES 2120.

discidium: see **dissidium**.

discindo ~ndere ~di ~ssum, *tr.* **1** To part violently, tear apart, split: *quo plus se dissolvere cupiunt seu ab invicem ~ndere, eo arctius ligantur* AC 960; *quod aquae Jordanis ~ssae sint* VI 55.3. **2** To set at variance: *divide et impera, hoc est, ~ndere animos* VR 133.

disciplina ~ae, *f.* **1** Correction, punishment, discipline: *~am non acceperunt* Jer. 2.30 (AE 131.9). **2** A branch of science, discipline: *studia omnium ~arum* AM 207.2.

discipulus ~i, *m.* A pupil or follower of a teacher, disciple: *ad ~os Johannis* SS 17.4; esp. the Lord's disciples on earth: AC 577.

discissio ~onis, *f.* A tearing apart, splitting: *~o per gladios* AE 315.8.

disco ~ere didici, *tr.* To implant in the mind, learn: *veritates quas ex Verbo ~it* VR 6.2; *lingua ibi non ~itur*

CI 236.1; (absol.) *qui ~unt et ducuntur ad bonum charitatis* AC 6778; (w. inf.) [*infans*] *~it loqui* VR 79.5; (w. indir. qu.) *ut... ~at quid verum et quid bonum* AC 7122.2.

discontinuo ~are ~avi ~atum, *tr*. To make discontinuous, interrupt: *~atur...uxoris cogitatio de marito per domestica* AM 169.

discontinuus ~a ~um, *a*. Discontinuous, interrupted: *si ~um, periisset homo* AC 8054.2.

disconveniens ~ntis, *a*. (pres. pple. of **disconvenio**) Unfitting, unsuitable: *quicquid iis apparet ~ns et coram iis reprobum* ES 1221.

disconvenientia ~ae, *f*. Unfittingness, unsuitability: *per convenientias et ~as perceptas* AC 1641.2.

disconvenio ~nire ~ni, *intr*. Not to be in accordance (with), to be inharmonious, ill-suited, unfitting (to): *rationalis bonum non...appropriat sibi alia...quam quae bono suo conveniunt...; quicquid ~nit rejicit* AC 3570.1; (w. dat.) *si angelus traheret minutissimum ex calore et luce naturali, periret, prorsus enim ~nit vitae ejus* AS 90.

discooperio ~rire ~rui ~rtum, *tr*. To uncover, lay bare: *~rtus fuit in medio tentorii sui* Gen. 9.21 (AC).

discordantia ~ae, *f*. Lack of harmony, disagreement: *videbis ~am illorum cum ipsa veritate* FI 46.

discordia ~ae, *f*. Lack of agreement, discord: *quod nulla ~a debeat esse inter utrumque* AC 1575; *cum cessant inimicitiae et ~ae inter homines* CI 290.

discorditer, *adv*. Inharmoniously, discordantly: VR 133.

discordo ~are ~avi, *intr*. To be at variance, clash: *duo conjuges qui discrepant animis et ~ant affectionibus* AM 171.2; *haec non ~ant, sed concordant per doctrinam* SS 51.2.

discors ~rdis, *a*. Disagreeing, clashing: *inclinatio ... ~rs et antipathica* AM 47[a].

discrepantia ~ae, *f*. Disagreement: *propter ~am affectionum internarum* AM 275.

discrepo ~are ~avi, *intr*. To be at variance, differ in nature: *duo conjuges qui ~ant animis* AM 171.2; VR 61.

discrete, *adv*. In separate groups, separately: *angeli, ~e et distincte, imo distinctius, habitant quam homines* VR 29.2.

discretim, *adv*. Separately, discontinuously: *sunt... tres athmosphaerae...discretim distinctae* CC 16.

discretio ~onis, *f*. The act of distinguishing, distinction: *nec habuerit ~onem, num esset maritata vel non* ES 1663.

discretus ~a ~um, *a*. Separated into parts, not continuous: *ad Trinitatem ~am et non ad conjunctam* VR 108; (esp. of degrees) discrete: *gradus non continui sed ~i* CI 38.2.

discribo: see **describo**.

discrimen ~inis, *neut*. **1** That which allows one thing to be distinguished from another, difference: *hoc facit ~en inter hominem et bestiam* VI 15. **2** A difference of attitude: *internae Ecclesiae homo cum ~ine, ita cum intelligentia, hoc agit* AC 6704. **3** A danger, risk, peril: *ut sic eorum felicitas in ~en agatur* ES 1490; *cum ~inibus quasi vitae* AC 828.

discriminatio ~onis, *f*. The action of distinguishing, distinction: *nisi sciret homo a ~onibus soni doctis per usum* AC 1378.1.

discrimino ~are ~avi ~atum, *tr*. To distinguish, separate: *quae [fides] parum ~atur a fide in nullum Deum* VR 8.4.

discriminosus ~a ~um, *a*. Full of danger, dangerous, perilous: ES 611.

discubitus ~us, *m*. A reclining or sitting down together for a meal: *numerus centum, ut et quinquaginta, qui fuit ~uum* AC 5291.7.

discumbo ~mbere ~bui, *intr*. To recline at table, be seated for a meal: *faciet ut ~mbant* Luke 12.37 (AE 187.3); *~buerunt viri cum patribus illis* AM 6.2; also, in a church: *~mbunt in forma circi* CI 223.

discupio ~pere ~pivi ~pitum, *intr*. To desire passionately: *~pit ille regere caelum e mundo* VR 598; to desire passionately to go: *e statu rationali suo in statum insanum suum ~piunt* AM 269.1.

discurro ~ere ~i, *intr*. To run in different directions, run about: *~unt huc illuc* AC 963; AC 940.2.

discursito ~are ~avi, *intr*. To keep running about: *~abunt ad quaerendum Verbum Jehovae* Amos 8.12 (AC 7668.4).

discussio ~onis, *f*. The act of breaking up, dispersal: *aliqua umbrae ~o* ES 3180.

discutio ~tere ~ssi ~ssum, *tr*. **1** To dispel, banish, remove: *Dominus... ~tit nubem et aperit mentem spiritualem* VI 86.4; *fallaciae...facile ~tiuntur* AC 1408.3; *dum ignorantiam ~timus* VR 160.7. **2** To inquire, examine: *~tiunt illico num ita sit* AC 4329.3.

disharmonia ~ae, *f*. Lack of harmony, discord: *quod mundus spirituum in tali ~a sit* ES 2180.

disharmonicus ~a ~um, *a*. Lacking in harmony, dissonant: *exacte animadvertit ~um et dissonum, quantum et qualiter discrepant* VR 61.

disjicio ~jicere ~jeci ~jectum, *tr*. To cause to go in all directions, scatter: *sicut palea e ventilabro in aërem ~jiciatur* VR 176.

disjunctio ~onis, *f.* A failure of union, disjunction: *charitas...est quae conjungit hominem Domino; absque charitate est ~o* AC 389.

disjunctivus ~a ~um, *a*. Tending to separation: *status mutationes...vel conjunctivae vel ~ae mentium* AM 191.1.

disjungo ~gere ~xi ~ctum, *tr*. To put apart, separate: *quia diversis animis erant...post breve tempus ~cti sunt* CI 427.

dispar ~aris, *a*. Unequal: *inclinationes ad ineundum conjugia...cum ~aribus* AM 246.2.

disparatio ~onis, *f.* Disappearance: *propter hanc discordantiam et ~onem unius e conspectu alterius* SE 42; AC 8204.

dispareo ~rere ~rui, *intr*. To disappear: *coram angelis...quicquid est materiae... ~ret* AC 488.3.

disparor ~ari ~atus sum, *intr*. To be dispersed, scatter, vanish: *vidi...ideas...ablatas sicut vento...et ~atas* VR 26; *quod haec fides...recipiatur, dum prior fides... ~atur* SE 42.

dispello ~pellere ~puli ~pulsum, *tr.* To drive away, scatter: *circulus... ~pulit nimbum* AM 115.5.

dispendium ~i, *neut*. Expenditure, loss: *absque ~is fortunarum* AM 450; AM 474.

dispensatio ~onis, *f.* **1** The action of apportioning, dispensing: *~ones mercedum sibi arrogant* AC 2371.2. **2** A dispensation from a rule granted by authority: *per ~ones papales* DP 280; AR 784.1.

dispensator ~oris, *m*. One who administers another's property, steward: *non est ~or, sed est fur* DP 316.

dispenso ~are ~avi ~atum, *tr*. **1** To apportion, give out, dispense: *haec* [sc. *athmosphaera*] *non ~at partem sui ad respirationem hominis, adque volatum avis* VR 364.3; *novit ~are bonum diversimode secundum usus* AC 4988.3. **2** To adminster, control: *servus et minister, qui fideliter ~at bona domini sui* DP 210.1; *affectiones... ~at mirabiliter* ES 617.

disperdo ~ere ~idi ~itum, *tr*. To destroy, ruin: *obest uxoribus amorem suum ~ere apud viros* AM 379.1; *quod imago Dei possit ~i ab homine* VR 48.4.

dispergo ~gere ~si ~sum, *tr*. **1** To spread in all directions, scatter: *quod ~si ab hostibus recolligerentur* AC 1228.2; *ab illis* [sc. *filiis Noachi*] *~sa est tota terra* Gen. 9.19 (AC); (refl.) *fons...cujus vena ex summitate pyramidis ~sit se* AM 14.2. **2** (transf.) To dispel, dissipate: *quod prorsus ~serit et charitatem et fidem* FI 67.

dispersio ~onis, *f.* The action of scattering, dispersion: *~onem omnium falsorum* AE 60.

dispertio ~tire ~tivi ~titum, *tr*. To divide into parts, split: *transactio de illa* [sc. *paenitentia*] *~tienda est in articulos* VR 509.

dispesco ~cere ~cui ~tum, *tr*. To divide, separate: *expositio... ~cetur in canones seu articulos* VR 114; ES 413; *ex Divinis veris analytice in formas ~tis* VR 350.

dispicio ~picere ~pexi ~pectum, *tr*. To scrutinize, investigate: *qui in ~piciendis rebus...acuta acie sunt* AM 103.2; (w. *ut*) *interest personis magistratus ~picere et prospicere, ut sit et servetur ordo* AM 283.

displicentia ~ae, *f.* Displeasure: AC 6288.

displiceo ~cere ~cui, *intr*. To be displeasing: *inferebant talia quae ~cerent* AC 8027; (w. dat.) *quod maxime iis ~cet* ES 152.

dispono ~nere ~sui ~situm, *tr*. **1** To arrange (in a specified form): *quod habitacula eorum ~sita sint in formas civitatum* AE 223.1; *quod...illam* [sc. *faciem*] *~nerent ridentem* AC 8113; (transf.) *quod in coelestem formam ~nerentur...vera* AC 6690. **b** to set (in order): *lux intellectus...in ordines analytice ~nit* [*vera*] CI 130. **2** To render suitable or agreeable, accommodate, condition: *intimum et intimius coelum... ~nunt ac ministrant ea quae a Deo Messia praevidentur et providentur* ES 224; (w. *ad* + acc.) *interius...externum ad sui nutum ~nit* AC 6724.2; *ut homo ~nat se ad receptionem Dei* VR 105. **3** To control, rule: *quod Dominus regat et ~nat omnia et singula* AC 592.1; *haec* [sc. *mens casta*] *~nit corpus, at illa* [sc. *mens lasciva*] *~nitur a corpore* AM 191.2; (absol.) *persona magistratus...quoties ~nit et judicat, bonum opus facit* VI 72.

disposite, *adv*. (superl. *~issime*) In good order or arrangement: *quia spiritualia et coelestia ibi suo ordine ~issime consequuntur* AC 2953.

dispositio ~onis, *f.* **1** Arrangement, ordering: *per quos* [*colores*], *secundum ~onem...pulchra..., sistuntur* AC 731. **2** Conditioning, disposition: *qualis* [*hominis*] *~o est, talis fit receptio* VR 8.1.

dispunctio ~onis, *f.* A separation into points: *a radice pullulat malum continuo, inde continua ~o* 3AD 2537.

dispungo ~gere ~xi ~ctum, *tr*. To mark off, separate: *si quidquam non verum inest, id ejicitur et ~gitur* 3AD 7089.

disputatio ~onis, *f.* A debate, disputation: *~ones de fide* ES 4676.

disputo ~are ~avi ~atum, *intr*. To debate, dispute: *~ant num sit* AM 232; (impers. pass.) *quod ~atum sic inter mala et bona de possessione eorum* ES 698.

disquiro ~rere ~sivi ~situm, *intr*. To investigate, inquire: *si quaversum ~rat* AM 333.2; *~rebatur inter spiritus de discipulis* ES 1216.

disquisitio ~onis, *f*. An investigation, inquiry: *~ones hominum de Divino Vero* AC 3385.

disrumpo ~mpere ~pi ~ptum, *tr*. also **dirumpo**. To break asunder, break open: *~mpitur vinculum inter Dominum et hominem* AC 379; *in die hoc ~pti sunt omnes fontes abyssi magnae* Gen. 7.11 (AC); to tear (clothes): Gen. 44.13 (AC).

disruptio ~onis, *f*. A tearing off: *quod ~o alae pallii Samuelis significaret abruptionem regni Israelis a Schaule* AC 9825.2.

disseco ~are ~ui ~tum, *tr*. To cut apart: *~abunt te gladiis* Ezek. 16.40 (AC 7456.3).

dissemino ~are ~avi ~atum, *tr*. To spread abroad, disseminate: *ne ~ent falsa per ratiocinia* CI 464.6.

dissensio ~onis, *f*. Dissension, quarrelling: [*hoc*] *significat ~onem et pugnam* FI 59.

dissensus ~us, *m*. Lack of consent, dissent: *libido... recedit ex consensu et exasperatur ex ~u* AM 511; (w. pl.) an instance of this: *unde divaricationes, ~us, haereses et schismata* VR 11.1.

dissentio ~tire ~si, *intr*. To differ in opinion, dissent: *ad illa quae non concordant ~tiunt* SS 59.

dissero ~ere ~ui ~tum, *intr*. To discuss: *de veris ~it* AC 2709.1; (w. indir. qu.) *~it num ita sit* AC 2715.6.

dissidentia ~ae, *f*. A disagreement: *~ae mentium inter se et conjugem* AM 271; AC 7046.2.

dissideo ~sidere ~sedi, *intr*. To be at variance: *si hae* [sc. *affectiones internae*] *~sident* AM 271; (w. *ab*) to be at variance (with), differ (from): *cum...intellectus ~sidet a voluntate* AC 35.

dissidium ~i, *neut*. also **discidium**. A difference of opinion, disagreement: *ex quo ~o resultat quod nullus Deus sit* VR 4.2.

dissilio ~lire ~lui, *intr*. To spring apart: [*ranae*] *congregatae in unum... ~liebant cum sonitu* 2AD 1957.

dissimilis ~is ~e, *a*. Unlike: *angeli...non in simili sapientia sunt, sed in ~i* CI 275.

dissimiliter, *adv*. In an unlike manner, dissimilarly: *consiliarii...non ~er amicti* AM 15.

dissimilitudo ~inis, *f*. The quality of being dissimilar, unlikeness: *de similitudine et ~ine inter conjuges* AM 209.

dissimulatio ~onis, *f*. The concealment of one's real wishes, dissimulation: *ex simulatione et ~one* AM 195.

dissimulo ~are ~avi ~atum, *tr*., *intr*. **1** (tr.) To pretend to have: *~arunt sancta Ecclesiae* AE 426.2; to pretend to be: *~are potest omnes, nunc se fingit hunc, nunc alium* ES 937. **2** (intr.) To make a pretence: *~amus sicut non sciamus illas* AM 208.2.

dissipatio ~onis, *f*. The action of driving away, dispelling: *~o falsi ignorantiae et illustratio* AE 239.9.

dissipo ~are ~avi ~atum, *tr*. **1** To scatter in all directions, disperse: *quod...* [*Spiritus Sanctus*] *~et peccata, sicut ventilator fumum e fornace* VR 16.1; *Dominus infernum dejecit et ~avit* VR 123.1. **2** (transf.) To reduce to nothing, scatter: *ut cogitationes...concentrentur, alioquin ~arentur* AC 7111.2.

dissitus ~a ~um, *a*. Remote, distant: *qui ~i sunt 1000, vel si foret 1,000,000 milliaribus* ES 2771; (neut. pl. as sb.) distant places: *quod colles et montes...e suis locis evulserit, et in ~a transtulerit* VR 124.3.

dissociatio ~onis, *f*. The breaking of an association, dissociation: AE 129.

dissocio ~are ~avi ~atum, *tr*. To exclude from association, dissociate, separate: *cum anima se ita ~at* AC 316; *~antur ac ~ati conferunt se in loca deserta* CI 360.1.

dissolutio ~onis, *f*. A breaking up, dissolution: *~ones conjugiorum* AM 276.2; ES 676.

dissolutus ~a ~um, *a*. **1** (w. *ad* or *in* + acc.) Abandoned (to): *~us est ad omnes lascivias amoris scortatorii* AM 426; ES 379. **2** Morally lax, dissolute: *vidit Moscheh populum quod ~us ille* Exod. 32.25 (AC); *libido scortationis prorsus ~a* AM 507.

dissolvo ~vere ~vi ~utum, *tr*. **1** To unfasten, ungird: *quod ~veret saccum desuper lumbis* Isa. 20.2 (SS 16). **2** To reduce (a composite structure) to its constituent parts: *si* [*Deus*] *adiret hominem, ~veret illum sicut ignis lignum* VR 135.4; (transf.) *conjunctiones solum naturales post mortem ex se ~vuntur* AM 320.3.

dissonantia ~ae, *f*. A combination of discordant sounds, dissonance: *innumerae sunt ~ae in quovis tono* [*sono* Tafel] ES 2178 (J D Odhner).

dissonus ~a ~um, *a*. Discordant: *clamor... ~us* AM 207.1; (neut. as sb.) *cujus auris in harmonico et consono est, exacte animadvertit disharmonicum et ~um* VR 61.

dissuadeo ~dere ~si ~sum, *tr*. To persuade one against: *commoda quae ~dent separationem a domo* AM 469.

dissuasio ~onis, *f.* The act of dissuading, opposition: *propter discordantiam et ~onem naturalis hominis* AC 4302.6.

dissuo ~ere ~i ~tum, *tr.* To undo the sewing of, rip apart: *vestes vestras non ~etis* Lev. 10.6 (AC 9960.5).

distans ~ntis, *a.* (superl. *~ntissimus*) Far removed, distant: ES 984.

distantia ~ae, *f.* The amount of separation between two things, distance: *~a inter solem et lunam ibi est triginta graduum* CI 146; *ad multam satis ~am* AC 6699.

distendo ~dere ~di ~tum, *tr.* To cause to swell, distend: *quod...hoc aequilibrium ~datur et impleatur a malis* CN De Redemptione v.4.

distentus ~a ~um, *a.* Bulging, distended: *crumenae ~ae* AM 268.2; ES 2864.

distermino ~are ~avi ~atum, *tr.* To separate as a boundary: *a terris quas fluvius iste terminat et ~at a terra Canaane* AC 1866.2.

distincte, *adv.* (compar. *~ius*, superl. *~issime*) With distinction, separately: *quod Jehovah et Sanctus Israelis unum sint, tametsi ~e nominantur* DD 40; *universum coelum... ~issime ordinatum est* AC 111.

distinctim, *adv.* = **distincte**: AM 444[a].

distinctio ~onis, *f.* **1** The action of keeping apart, separation: *~o per commata* ES 2631; *~one coelorum* AE 342.3. **2** The action of treating as separate, distinction: *charitas potest exerceri...absque ~one aeque erga malos quam erga bonos* AC 6703. **3** Importance, eminence: *aulici variae ~onis, et ultimo satellites* AM 14.1.

distinctus ~a ~um, *a.* (compar. *~ior*, superl. *~issimus*) **1** Occupying different places, separate: *habitationes in mundo spirituali sunt omnes ~ae secundum vitas* AE 133. **2** Different in nature, distinct: *tres illi gradus inter se prorsus ~i sunt* SS 7; (neut. as sb.) a distinction: *commune quoddam obscurum absque ~o quodam* AC 522.

distineo ~nere ~nui, *tr.* To hold apart: *post magnum desertum...ut plene ~neantur et separentur ab incolis saeculorum antecedentium* AM 79.3; ES 2737.

distinguens ~ntis, *neut.* A distinguishing mark, separation: *sit ~ns inter aquas aquis* Gen. 1.6 (AC).

distinguo ~guere ~xi ~ctum, *tr.* **1** To make a division, separate: *~xit Deus inter lucem et inter tenebras* Gen. 1.4 (AC). **2** (w. *in* + acc.) To divide, separate (into parts): *qui aedificat domum... ~guit in cameras* VR 152; (transf.) *qui Deum in tres Personas ~guunt* VR 15.2. **3** To keep apart mentally, distinguish: *hi bini status prophetarum probe ~guendi sunt* DD 52; (w. *ab*) *in eo ~guuntur miracula Divina a miraculis diabolicis* AC 6988.3; (w. *inter*) *sicut nec ~guit [lingua Hebraea] inter voces* AC 618.

disto ~are, *intr.* **1** To be distant: *longissime a sole ~at [planeta Saturnus]* AC 6697. **2** To be remote in nature, differ: *inde patet quantum ~at sensus spiritualis a sensu literae* AE 131.8.

distorqueo ~quere ~si ~tum, *tr.* To twist out of shape, distort: *ordinem spiritualem ~quere et destruere* VR 678.2.

distorsio ~onis, *f.* The action of twisting in different directions: *reciproca ~o omnium in spiritu qui torquetur* ES 870.

distortus ~a ~um, *a.* Twisted out of shape, distorted: *misere erat a pluribus spiritibus ~us* ES 2243; *ossa ...cum luxata aut cum ~a* AC 8005.

distractio ~onis, *f.* The action of pulling apart: *cum ~one dolorifica* AC 829.1.

distractivus ~a ~um, *a.* Tending to pull apart or distract: *sphaera...est ~a ita ut nihil sit ibi nisi inimicum et hostile* AC 2027.2.

distractus ~a ~um, *a.* Far-flung, dispersed: *populus ~us* Isa. 18.2, 7 (AE 331.5).

distraho ~here ~xi ~ctum, *tr.* **1** To pull apart, separate: *dum binae partes unitae ~herentur* AM 368.3; *merces... ~ctae a piscibus* VR 378.1. **b** (Bibl.) to scatter (seed): *~hentem semen* Amos 9.13 (AE 376.6). **2** To draw away, divert, distract (the mind or a person): *quae animum reddant inquietum, ~hunt et turbant* AM 285.1; *qui non ~cti a negotiis mundi possunt videre* SS 59.

distribuo ~ere ~i ~tum, *tr.* **1** To send in various directions: *cum visum ~i ad cameratas eductiones* AM 103.4. **2** To allot, distribute (into classes): *quod spiritus secundum genera et species in classes ~ti sunt* ES 197.

distributio ~onis, *f.* The process of distributing, distribution: ES 197.

disturbo ~are ~avi ~atum, *tr.* To disturb, disrupt: *hymni...non potuerunt ~ari a phantasiis* ES 490.

disunio[1] ~onis, *f.* Lack of union, disunion: *'separari vir a fratre' est ~o* AC 1594.1; *~o humani generis et coeli* ES 4394.

disunio[2] ~nire ~nivi ~nitum, *tr.* To disunite: *malum, quod solum ~nit* AC 1607.3.

ditesco ~ere, *intr.* To become rich: *ex bonis aliorum ~ere* AC 8118.1.

ditio ~onis, *f.* An area of land subject to a single authority, region, province: [*Germania*] *divisa in plures ~ones* VR 813; *angeli sciunt in qua ~one alicujus partis hominis habitant* VR 65.

dito ~are ~avi ~atum, *tr.* To make wealthy, enrich: *profecto ~atus sum, inveni opes mihi* Hos. 12.8 (AC 10227.15); (transf.) *quod inde ~arent doctrinam charitatis* AC 6777.

diu[1], *adv.* (compar. *diutius*) For a long time: *hoc perstabat diu, per horas* ES 4420; *cum spiritibus ...diutius sociare commercium datum est* AC 7799.

diu[2], *adv.* By day: *sidus lucens...diu et noctu* VR 503.2. **b** *sub diu*, in the open air: *pulpitum sub diu variis exposita violentiis* VR 55.

diurnus ~a ~um, *a.* Of or belonging to a day, daytime: *lumen ~um a sole* AC 7233.2.

diutinus ~a ~um, *a.* Long-lasting, lengthy: *per ~am conversationem cum spiritibus* AC 8111.

diutior ~or ~us, *compar. a.* Longer lasting, more prolonged: *cruciatibus ~oribus torquentur* ES 2532.

diuturnitas ~atis, *f.* Length of time, long duration: *propter ~atem temporis* ES 760.

diuturnus ~a ~um, *a.* (compar. *~ior*) Long-lasting: ES 854; ES 4634.

divagor ~ari ~atus sum, *intr.* **1** To wander apart or in different directions, stray: *a voce tumultus ~entur populi* Isa. 33.3 (AE 331.11). **2** To err in belief, go astray: *nec sinunt ~ari alterum a sua idea* AC 5180; *habent ...suas meditationes...fixas...sic non ~antur* ES 1125.

divaricatio ~onis, *f.* A diverging, splaying, splitting into several: *in quo...interiora...fulciuntur ne fiat ~o* AC 8005; (w. pl.) VR 11.1.

divarico ~are ~avi ~atum, *tr.* To cause to diverge, splay, spread out: *nervus...in plures fibras ~atur* AC 5189.2; *via...quae in ascensu ~atur in plures* CI 429; *~ando oculos* VR 641.3; (transf.) *mens...in otio ~atur ad varia mala* ES 6088.4.

divello ~vellere ~vulsi ~vulsum, *tr.* To tear apart or away, rend: *quod Dagon...deciderit, et...jaceret ~vulsus a capite* VI 55.3; *homo...est...ita consociatus, ut non possit ~velli ab illis* [sc. *angelis*] AM 28; *ne consociatio ~vellatur* VR 12.7.

diversicolor ~oris, *a.* Of various colours: *flores ~ores in serto* VR 62.

diversicoloratus ~a ~um, *a.* = **diversicolor**: ES 4029.

diversiformis ~is ~e, *a.* Of various shapes or types: *currus ~es* AM 76.2.

diversimode, *adv.* In various manners, differently: *omnes hi salvati sunt, sed ~e* VR 580.2; *unum* [*membrum*] *~e agit ac alterum* AC 1285.2.

diversimodus ~a ~um, *a.* Of various kinds, differing: *loquutio cum spiritibus exstitit ~a* ES 2868.

diversitas ~atis, *f.* The quality of being different, variety: *apparentiae oriundae ex ~ate affectionum* AE 282.10; AC 7800.

diversorium ~i, *neut.* **1** A lodging place for travellers, inn: *et fuit in via in ~o* Exod. 4.24 (AC); AM 10.5. **2** (pl.) Entertainments, amusements: *haec...sunt ~a utilia ad recreandum animos* CH 189 (= xi); VR 433 titulus.

diversus ~a ~um, *a.* **1** Different one from the other, various, diverse: *quod...appareant...ad ~as plagas* AC 7078; CI 303. **2** *In ~um*, in different directions, apart: *quod qualis ille Deus unus est, gentes...abiverint...in ~um* VR 5.

diverto ~tere ~ti ~sum, *intr.* To turn away (from): *'secedere'...est ~tere a cogitatione in qua est* AC 6836.

dives ~itis, *a.* (compar. *ditior*, superl. *ditissimus*) Rich, wealthy: *quod pauperes recipiantur et non ~ites* CI 357; *ut maximus sit et ditissimus* AC 987.2.

divido ~dere ~si ~sum, *tr.* (contracted plupf. subj. *~ssent* DP 259) **1** To separate into parts, divide, split up: *vestimenta Domini ~serunt* AE 38; *mare Suph ~sum* AC 7290.3. **2** To spread disunity among, divide: *quod...mentes non conjungantur sed ~dantur* CI 380.2; *sicut dicitur, ~de et impera* VR 133.

dividuus ~a ~um, *a.* Capable of being divided, divisible: *quod unaquaevis mica cogitationis...sit ~a usque ad infinitum* AM 329.2.

divinatio ~onis, *f.* The action of predicting a future event, divination: *magicis artibus dediti sunt, ~onibus et similibus* ES 3137.

divinator ~oris, *m.* One who practises divination, diviner: *~ores et magi* SS 102.1.

divinitas ~atis, *f.* **1** The quality of being divine, divinity: *de Verbi ~ate et sanctitate* SS 4. **2** The divine essence of God: *tres Personae in una ~ate* Sym. Ath. (DD 56); VR 8.3.

divinitus, *adv.* From the Divine, divinely: *Verbum... ~us inspiratum* SS 1; *cavetur ~us ne...labantur* ES 623.

divino ~are ~avi ~atum, *intr.* **1** To form a conjecture, guess: *~abant varia* AM 55.1; (w. *quod*) *quis ~aturus est quod illa verba talia significent* AC 10582.4; (w. indir. qu.) *quid hoc, ~a si potes* AM 294.1. **2** To practise divination: *is ~ando ~at in hoc* Gen. 44.5 (AC).

Divinum ~i, *neut.* That which is divine: *quod a Deo est, non vocatur Deus sed vocatur ~um* VR 25.3; *Jehovah Deus...sic rediit in Suum ~um in Quo ab aeterno fuit* VR 3.1.

Divinus ~a ~um, *a.* (compar. *~ior*) **1** Of or peculiar to God, divine: *verum ~um* AC 6714; *~us amor, ~a sapientia et ~us usus* AM 183.2; *cultus ~us* AC 6674.4. **2** Typical of God, divine: *si...nec coelestius quid aut ~ius amori inesset* AC 714.

divisibilis ~is ~e, *a.* Capable of being divided, divisible: *quod omnia et singula ~ia sint in infinitum* VR 33.

divisio ~onis, *f.* The action of dividing, division: VR 41.2.

divisus ~a ~um, *a.* Divided: *non licet ita ~am habere mentem* AM 48ª.2.

divitiae ~tiarum, *f. pl.* Riches, wealth: *ut ditescat ...solum ~tiarum causa* AC 6935.

divortium ~i, *neut.* **1** Divorce (of married partners): AM 59.1. **2** (transf.) Lack of harmony, dissent: *apud tales dissidia et ~a sunt* ES 1794.

divulgo ~are ~avi ~atum, *tr.* To make publicly known, divulge: *ex timore ne ~arentur* AM 521.3.

divulsio ~onis, *f.* The action of tearing apart: AC 7791.

divum ~i, *neut.* *Sub ~o*, in the open air, under the sky: ES [5513ª.13] (Tafel).

do dare dedi datum, *tr.* **1** To give, grant: *dedit servis suis decem minas ad negotiandum* Luke 19.13 (AE 223.23); *quod illae* [sc. *cognitiones*] *darentur bonis* AC 7770.4; (of inanimate things) *cingulum* [*Saturni*] *...multam lucem...telluri illi dat* AC 6697. **2** To give in marriage: *et dedit Zipporam filiam suam Moschi* Exod. 2.21 (AC). **3** (in special phrs.) **a** *morti dare*, to put to death: AC 7791. **b** *in effectum dare*, to put into practice: AM 280. **c** *in publicum dare*, to make public, publish: VR 123.2. **4** (Bibl.) To place, put: *et accipient de sanguine, et dabunt super binos postes* Exod. 12.7 (AC). **b** to make: *en testem populis dedi Ipsum principem* Isa. 55.4 (AC 6804.2). **5** To make possible, grant (an action): *quae dat unde habeant quod possint cogitare* ES 3762; *cum datur iis reflexio* ES 4301; *quod dat se percipi et sentiri* DP 11.2. **b** (impers. pass.): *hoc quod ita sit, datum est scire ex multa experientia* AC 6639.2. **6** (pass.) To have being, exist: *patet quod correspondentia detur* AC 2989; *num dari queat aliquod Esse quod non existit* AS 14.

doceo ~cere ~cui ~ctum, *tr.* **1** To cause (someone) to learn, teach, instruct: *Ipse* [*Dominus*] *illos ducit ac in rebus vitae ~cet* CI 214; (absol.) *in plateis nostris ~cuisti* Luke 13.26 (AC 6806.2). **b** (w. two accs.): *Ille vos ~cebit omnia* John 14.26 (AC 6788); (pass.) *haec ~ctus sum ab iis* ES 336. **2** (w. thing taught as obj.) To convey, impart (information): *qui illa investigabant et ~cebant* AC 7296; (w. *quod*) *quod Dominus sit in bono, Ipse Dominus ~cet* AC 6711. **3** (of documents or doctrines) To teach: *quod tota Scriptura Sacra ~ceat quod Deus sit* VR 6.1; AE 10.2.

docilis ~is ~e, *a.* Capable of being taught, teachable: *didici...quod spiritus ~es sint* ES 263.

docilitas ~atis, *f.* The capability of being taught, receptiveness to teaching: *de ~ate spirituum* ES 263.

docte, *adv.* In a learned manner, learnedly: *extulerunt vocem dicentes '~e, ~e'* AM 315.7.

doctor ~oris, *m.* One who teaches, instructor, teacher: *nolite vocari ~or, quia unus est ~or vester, Christus* Matt. 23.8 (SS 51.6); AE 250.3; *quidam ~or...qui se prae aliis eruditum putavit* ES 4440.

doctoratus ~us, *m.* The degree or status of doctor granted by a university, doctorate: *insigniuntur pileis ~us ac palliis episcopatus* SE 59; AR 606.

doctrina ~ae, *f.* **1** The process of learning: *qui ~a et studio hausit numeros harmonicos* AM 424. **2** A branch of learning, science: *~a cognitionum* AC 1462.7. **3** The teaching of the church on a particular point, doctrine: *~a Ecclesiae illorum continebat leges vitae* AC 6705; *~as ex falsificatis veris* AC 6650. **4** (as the title of various works by Swedenborg): *in ~a Novae Hierosolymae De Domino* SS 2.2.

doctrinale ~is, *neut.* A matter of doctrine: *~ia, quae in se non aliud sunt quam scientifica* AC 1597; *secundum ~e Ecclesiae* AC 7005.

doctus ~a ~um, *a.* (compar. *~ior*, superl. *~issimus*) (of persons) Learned: *in mundo ut ~i celebrati sunt* SS 61.1; *~iores ponunt apud hos conatum ad bonum* FI 39.

documentum ~i, *neut.* A piece of convincing evidence, proof: *~a experientiae* CI 184; *per ~a autopsica* AM 39.

dodim: see **dudim**.

Dodracenus ~a ~um, *a.* also **Dodrechtanus**, **Dodrectanus**, **Dordracenus**, **Dordrechtanus**, and **Dordrectanus**. Of Dordrecht or Dort in the Netherlands: *synodus ~a*, the Synod of Dort (1618-19): SE 38; VR 803.

dodrans ~ntis, *m.* A small coin, farthing: *donec persolveris ultimum ~ntem* Matt. 5.26 (VI 73); ES 589.

Dodrechtanus: see **Dodracenus**.

Dodrectanus: see **Dodracenus**.

dogma ~atis, *neut.* (Gk.) An agreed belief on a point of theology, dogma: *vocantes illorum ~ata somnia* AM 380.1; *consentaneum bonis ~atibus religionis eorum* CI 516.

dogmaticus ~a ~um, *a.* (Gk.) **1** Of or concerned with dogma: *in libro Evangelicorum ~o* VR 798.10; (neut. as sb.) a formula containing a dogma: *naturalia sunt omnia, quae Ecclesiae capita et membra in suis ~is tradiderunt* VR 133. **2** (masc. as sb.) One devoted to dogma, dogmatic: FI 4.

doleo ~lere ~lui, *intr.* (*tr.*) **1** To experience pain: *in esse illos ~lentes* Gen. 34.25 (AC). **2** To be sad, grieve: *spiritus probi... ~luerunt corde* CI 77; (w. *quod*) *~lentes quod sic amitterent suos* ES 3032; (w acc. and inf.) *quod ~lerem, tales dari in altera vita* ES 231. **3** (tr.) To grieve over: *quod nihil possint ~lere mortem corporis* ES 4430.

dolo ~are ~avi ~atum, *tr.* To shape by cutting, hew: *~a tibi duas tabulas lapidum* Exod. 34.1 (AC).

dolor ~oris, *m.* **1** Physical discomfort, pain: *quia mater...cum ~ore pepererat illos* AM 284; (distinguished as exterior and interior) AC 5563. **2** Interior or mental distress, grief: *~orem...ob non eminentiam super alios* AC 10535.

dolorificens ~ntis, *a.* (compar. *~ntior*) Causing pain: *infernum habuissent multo ~ntius* ES 1720.

dolorificus ~a ~um, *a.* Causing pain, painful: *cum distractione ~a* AC 829.1.

dolose, *adv.* (superl. *~issime*) Deceitfully: *~issime inficiunt et infestant* AC 1820.3.

dolosus ~a ~um, *a.* (compar. *~ior*, superl. *~issimus*) **1** (of persons) Given to deceit, guileful: *in mundo interius ~i fuerant* AM 407. **2** (of actions) Characterized by deceit, deceitful: *sub praetextu ~o* CI 462ª.6.

dolus ~i, *m.* Deceit, trickery, guile: *utuntur...omni astu et fraude, omni ~o* AC 6666.2; *fiunt...pardi quoad ~um* VR 13.4; (w. pl.) an instance of this: *detinentur a nefandis suis ~is* AC 6914.2.

domatio ~onis, *f.* The act of taming: *cum illarum* [sc. *ferarum*] *strage et ~one* VR 123.4.

domesticus ~a ~um, *a.* Of or belonging to a household, domestic: *in rebus ~is* AM 271; *canis ~us* ES 3679; *pediculi ~i* ES 4570; (masc. as sb.) a household servant: VI 72; (transf.) *bonum naturale ~um est id bonum quod homo a parentibus trahit* AC 3518.1.

domi, *adv.* (locative of **domus**) At home: *cum ~i eram* AM 10.3.

domicilium ~i, *neut.* A dwelling place, domicile, home: *ad ~a scribarum* AM 207.5; (of insects) VR 12.7; ES 3719.

domina ~ae, *f.* **1** A female superior, mistress: *dic regi et ~ae* Jer. 13.18 (AE 272.6); [*apes*] *praeficiunt...sibi ~am sicut reginam* VR 12.7. **2** (as fem. adj.) Dominant: *versavimus causas...et vidimus illarum hanc ~am* AM 106.

dominans ~ntis, *a.* Dominant: *amor ~ns* AC 6690.

dominatio ~onis, *f.* The act of dominating: AM 78.4.

dominator ~oris, *m.* One who dominates, master: *mittite agnum ~oris terrae de petra* Isa. 16.1 (DD 6).

dominatus ~us, *m.* The position of master, dominion: *qui... ~um quaerunt* AE 405.6; *~um extendit in coelum* CI 559.

Dominicus ~a ~um, *a.* Of or belonging to the Lord; *Oratio ~a*, the Lord's Prayer: VR 112.6; *in ~a die*, the Lord's day, Sunday: Rev. 1.10 (AR).

dominium ~i, *neut.* **1** The exercise of control, power, dominion: *~um super omnia terrae* AC 257; *qui ~a sua extendunt usque in coelum* CI 544; (esp. of the Pope) *ex ~o papali* SS 24. **2** An area controlled by a single authority, realm: *in ~o ubi est* VR 508.3.

dominor ~ari ~atus sum, *intr.* **1** To exercise control, have dominion, rule: *luminare magnum ad ~andum die* Gen. 1.16 (AC); (w. dat.) *Jehovah... ~ans cum ira gentibus* Isa. 14.6 (SS 86); (w. *in* + acc.) *~abuntur in pisces maris* Gen. 1.26 (AC). **2** (of abstract things) To be dominant, reign: *cum fallaciae sensus... ~antur* AC 6948.4; (w. *super*) *ne apud illos infernum aliquo modo ~etur super talia quae sunt coeli* AC 7040.2.

Dominus ~i, *m.* **1** The Lord: *per ~um unice intelligitur Salvator mundi Jesus Christus, et ~us appellatur absque caeteris nominibus* AC 14. **2** (usu. lower case) A person of high rank, lord, master: *quia etiam illi se dicunt ~os* AC 8735; (as a respectful term of address) *assume, ~e, si placet, ideam Unius Dei* VR 16.2; *dicentes, ~e, etiam daemonia obediunt nobis* Luke 10.17 (AC 6674.5).

domo ~are ~ui ~itum, *tr.* (pf. pple. *~atus* AC 857.1; AC 868.2; ES 1742 Autograph) To reduce to subjection, tame, subdue: *ut unus illorum millia infernalium ~are possit* AC 6677; *illecebrae...quas intelligentia non ~at et refraenat, sed diligit* VR 41.3; *aegritudines corporis...quae...vitam ejus voluptatum... ~ant et frangunt* AC 762.

domula: see **domulus**.

domulus ~i, *f.* perh. also **domula** ~ae, *f.* A small house: *inhabitare parvas ~os* [*~as* J D Odhner; *domunculas* Tafel] ES 392; ES Index s.v. 'diabolus' (p. 208 Tafel), referring to ES 392-3.

domuncula ~ae, *f.* A small house, hut: *palatia sensim dissipantur, et fiunt ~ae* AC 1631; *~as hortulanas* AM 8.2; *quod sciant* [*apes*]*...struere cellas sicut ~as* VR 12.7.

domus ~us, *f.* (dat. sg. *~ui*, abl. sg. *~o*, nom. pl. *~us*, acc. pl. *~us* or *~os*, gen. pl. *~uum* or *~orum*, dat. and abl. pl. *~ibus*) see also **domi**. **1** A house: *in ~o in qua non sunt fenestrae* FI 48. **b** one's own house, home: *abivi ~um* ME 3; *scire viam ~um* 'to know the way home' ES 2209; see also **domi**. **2** A household: *quod praefectus sit ~ui Pharaonis* AC 6643; *~um constituerunt conjuges cum liberis et cum servis et ancillis* AC 1159.3. **3** A family: *nec datur electio nisi...limitata ad ~us quae cognoscuntur* AM 49.

donarium ~i, *neut.* An offering dedicated in a church: *~a...quae salutis causa impendunt simulacris miraculosis* VR 453.1; VR 459.10.

donatio ~onis, *f.* The action of giving, gift: *~ones...receptae usu fuerunt* AM 300.3.

donec, *conj. w. subj.* Until: *gladio...visitabo super gentem hanc, ~c consumam eos* Jer. 27.8 (AC 1327.5); *jotha unum...non praeteribit de Lege, ~c omnia fiant* Matt. 5.18 (DD 11).

dono ~are ~avi ~atum, *tr.* **1** To convey as a gift, make a present of: *quod ~averit Dominus aliam fidem* AC 437; (neut. of pf. pple. as sb.) *qui delectantur raptis et praedatis, et non ~atis* AM 511. **2** (w. abl.) To endow (with): *plures alios...etiam divinitate ~averunt* VR 9.3; (esp. pass.) to be endowed (with): *quod homo ~ari bono spirituali a Domino non possit* AC 8307; *qui in altera vita ~antur coelo* AC 6775.

donum ~i, *neut.* A thing given, gift: *accessit rex...tenens in manu duo ~a* AR 341.1; (esp. as a quality conferred by the Lord) *quod amare possit alium plus quam se, quod sit ~um Domini* AC 1594.5; *in ~o praedicandi sunt* CI 226.

Dordracenus: see **Dodracenus**.

Dordrechtanus: see **Dodracenus**.

Dordrectanus (n.b. usually spelled **Dodr-** in 1st edn. of VR, also SE 66.2; but the town is **Dordrectum** in VR 487.1): see **Dodracenus**.

dormio ~mire ~mivi (*or* ~mii) ~mitum, *tr.* **1** To sleep: *viderunt plerosque ~mientes* AM 9.2; *aliqui bene ~miverunt* ES 2437; *antequam ~mitum irem* AC 3891.2. **2** (Bibl., w. acc.) To sleep the sleep of (death): *ne forte ~miam mortem* Ps. 13.3 (AC 212); (also, absol.) to lie dead, sleep awaiting resurrection: *multa corpora ~mientium sanctorum suscitata sunt* Matt. 27.52 (AC 8018.2); Dan. 12.2 (AC 8018.3).

dormitatio ~onis, *f.* Slumbering: *si dedero somnum oculis meis, palpebris meis ~onem* Ps. 132.4 (AC 4594.3).

dormitio ~onis, *f.* The state or act of sleeping, sleep: *cubatio...et ~o* AC 3696.1; *~o et somnus* AR 158.

dormito ~are ~avi, *intr.* (*tr.*) To be drowsy, doze: *tardante vero sponso ~arunt omnes* Matt. 25.5 (SS 17.1); *somnum ~are*, to be in a deep sleep: Jer. 51.57 (AC 150).

dorsalis ~is ~e, *a.* Of or relating to the back, dorsal: *nervis ~ibus* ES 153.

dorsum ~i, *neut.* The back (of a human being or animal): *instar ~i humani* ES 848; *bestiae quae resupinae incumbent ~is* [i.e., lie upside down on their backs] AM 79.3.

dos dotis, *f.* **1** A dowry: *dos quae dabatur virgini desponsandae* AC 4456. **2** A natural quality or faculty, endowment, gift: *illi...dote ratiocinandi prae aliis pollent* AC 6949; *uteris illis meis donis et dotibus sicut tuis* SE 52.

doto ~are ~avi ~atum, *tr.* (w. abl.) To endow (with): *~avit me Deus me dote bona* Gen. 30.20 (AC).

drachma ~ae, *f.* (Gk.) A Greek coin, drachma: Luke 15.8 (AE 675.10).

draco ~onis, *m.* (Gk.) **1** A kind of poisonous snake, serpent: *serpentes venenati, scorpii, crocodili, ~ones* AS 338; *cum ovo ~onis* DP 233.9; CO 30.2. **2** A dragon, esp. that described in Rev. 12: *quod viderit...~onem et ejus pugnam cum Michaele* AM 26.

draconicus ~a ~um, *a.* Of or relating to the Dragon (see Rev. 12): *Fides illa ~a* SE 89; (masc. as sb.) a follower of the Dragon: *vox audita est inde a quodam ~o* VR 110.8; FI 56.

dromas ~adis, *f.* (Gk.) A dromedary: *~ades Midianis et Ephae* Isa. 60.6 (AC 113).

dualitas ~atis, *f.* The quality of being two, duality: *~atem Christi* AR 839.2.

dubitatio ~onis, *f.* The act of doubting, doubt: *ut non sit relicta aliqua ~o* AC 7298.2; *negativa ~o quod dabilis sit* AM 243.

dubitative, *adv.* In a doubting manner: *etiam de veris...sentit ~e* AC 5657.

dubitativus ~a ~um, *a.* Relating to doubt, doubtful: *in statu ~o* AC 5657; (neut. as sb.) *in ~o manet* AC 2338.

dubito ~are ~avi, *intr.* To be in doubt: *crede et non*

~a FI 1; (w. *quin*) *nemo ~aret quin Dominus resurrexerit* DD 35.9.

dubium ~i, *neut.* **1** A state of uncertainty, doubt: *aliquod...quod facit ~um* AC 7298.2; *nisi...fidem servaverit...integram absque ~o* Sym. Ath. (DD 56); *homo in ~o esset, quin Verbum sit* SS 4. **2** The condition of being held to be uncertain, doubt: *de re evidente et nullius ~i* CI 98; *quod anima sit a patre, a nullo sapiente in ~um vocatur* AM 206.

dubius ~a ~um, *a.* Of uncertain value, doubtful: *vertuntur in res ~as* CI 435; (neut. as sb.) AC 6839; *procul ~o*, without doubt, undoubtedly: ES 339.

ducatus[1] ~i, *m.* A ducat: ES 4813.

ducatus[2] ~us, *m.* A dukedom, duchy: VR 55; (also, generally) leadership, control: *non sub alius ~u tentari potest, quam sub diaboli* 3AD 5620.

ducenti ~ae ~a, *pl. adj.* Two hundred: *dies mille ~i nonaginta* Dan. 12.11 (DD 4).

duco ~cere ~xi ~ctum, *tr.* **1** To lead, conduct: *~cebar per planitiem ad collem* VR 48.1. **b** (of a road): *pons qui ab urbe ~cebat versus Gehennam* ES 853; *choream ~cere*, to be the leader of a dance: 3AD 3386. **2** (transf.) To direct, guide: *probi a Domino per angelos ~cti* AC 7127.3; (w. *ad*) *~citur a Domino ad bonum agendum* AC 24.3; (of things) *in omnibus mediis est finis, qui agit et ~cit media* VR 13.3; *~cente eo tempore* ES 221. **3** To marry (a wife): *non licet...plures uxores ~cere* AM 47[a]. **4** To develop (cracks): *quod illud chaos rimas ~xerit* VR 79.3. **5** To derive, draw (from a source): *originem proximi ~cent ab Ipso* AC 6711; *haec conjugia ~cunt principium et ortum suum a conjugio coelesti* AC 718. **6** (in mathematics) To multiply: *componitur* [*octoginta*]...*ex decem et octo in se ~ctis* AC 7284; VR 32.3. **7** (w. pred.) To consider, hold: *pro enormi re ~cebant aliud facie ostendere, aliud cogitare* AC 358.

ductor ~oris, *m.* One who leads, a guide: *angelus ~or* AM 9.1.

ductrix ~icis, *f. adj.* Leading, guiding: *absque doctrina regulatrice et ~ice* AC 9409.4.

ductus ~us, *m.* **1** The action of leading, guidance: *sub auspicio et ~u Domini* CI 63. **2** A channel (for water): *rivi, ~us aquarum* Isa. 30.25 (AC 1306.2); (anat.) a duct: ES 1058.

dudaim, *pl.* (Hebr.) Mandrakes: Gen. 30.14 (see AC 3942.1).

dudim, *indecl. pl.* (Hebr.) perh. also **dodim** (see AC 3942.1 Autograph). See quot.: *ex derivatione illius vocis* [sc. *dudaim*] *in lingua originali, derivatur enim a voce ~im, quae significat amores et per illos conjunctionem* AC 3942.1.

duellium ~i, *neut.* A duel: *in praeliis, ~is, naufragiis...* DP 140.

dulce, *adv.* Sweetly: ES 231; ES 2436.

dulcedo ~inis, *f.* Sweetness: *inspirat illis amoris ~ines* AM 162.

dulciaria ~orum, *neut. pl.* A musical instrument, prob. castanets: *cum ~is et cum cymbalis* 2 Sam. 6.5 (AE 323.11).

dulcis ~is ~e, *a.* Agreeable to the senses, sweet: *~es odas* AM 8.2; *odores...tetros et ~es* ES 2392; (neut. as sb.) *a ~ibus eorum* [sc. *corporum*] *transeunt ad posteriora eorum* ES 3205.

dulciter, *adv.* (compar. *~cius*) Sweetly: *quod sphaera ...percipiatur sicut ~citer fragrans* AM 171.3.

dum, *conj. w. indic.* (or sometimes *w. subj.*) **1** So long as, while: *ille dum supra terram illam erat, percurrit viam stratam* VR 71.1; *de Domini instructione dum puer* AC 1542.1. **2** At the time when, when: *ut homo, dum ad adultam aetatem venit, possit esse homo* AC 1050.1; *dixit ad Mosen, dum supplicavit ut videret gloriam Jehovae* VR 6.1. **3** *Dum modo*: see **dummodo**; but each word may have its separate force. **4** *Usque dum*, up to the time when, until: *et hoc usque dum angelus avertit oculos* CI 232; (w. subj.) *usque dum praetereat coelum et terra* Matt. 5.18 (AC 6752.2).

dumetum ~i, *neut.* A clump of bushes, thicket: *post sylvam apparuerunt ~a* AM 78.3.

dummodo, *conj. w. indic.* also spelled as two words **dum modo** (q.v. **dum**, sense 3). On condition that, so long as: *intellectus in...luce potest esse, dum modo amores naturales...removentur* VR 79.7; VR 41.1. (*Dummodo* in CI 384 should be split into two words.)

dumtaxat: see **duntaxat**.

dumus ~i, *m.* A thorn bush: *bonus eorum sicut spina rectus ut ~us* Mic. 7.4 (AC 4843.3).

duntaxat, *adv.* also **dumtaxat**. **1** Up to the point of, as far as: *~at aliquantulum constare potest* AC 1590. **2** No more than, just: *hoc* [sc. *corpus*] *~at est indumentum ejus* [sc. *animae*] VR 103.1; *est...verum absque bono ~at scientificum* AC 7724. **3** (introducing a limiting clause) Provided that, so long as: *sunt ~at casti illi* AM 155.2.

duo duae duo, *pl. adj.* (fem. acc. *duas*, reg. masc. acc. *duos*, irreg. masc. acc. *duo* ES 579; masc. and neut. abl. *duobus*, fem. abl. *duabus*) Two: *duo priora sunt fidei* VR 3.2; *super duas tabulas lapidum* Deut. 4.13 (AC 6804.6).

duodecies, *adv.* Twelve times: *~es duodecim* AC 7973.4.

duodecim, *indecl. adj.* Twelve: *~im Suos discipulos* VR 4.1.

duodecimus ~a ~um, *a.* Twelfth: *~a hora* AE 194.2 (w. ref. to Matt. 20.1-16).

duodenarius ~a ~um, *a.* Relating to the number twelve: *numerus ~us* 3AD 4475.

duodenus ~a ~um, *a. Intestinum ~um*, the first portion of the small intestine, duodenum: AC 10030.1.

duplex ~icis, *a.* **1** Twofold, double: *quod sapientia ...sit ~ex, rationalis et moralis* AM 163. **2** (of persons) Prone to duplicity, two-faced: *quod sit* [*hic homo*] *~ex et ille modo simplex* VR 147.

duplicatio ~onis, *f.* A doubling, reduplication: *~o durior consonantium* AC 1759.

duplicatura ~ae, *f.* A fold: *cum...ureteribus...quae in ~is ejus* [sc. *peritonaei*] *sunt* ES 993.

duplicatus ~a ~um, *a.* Doubled: *~a et triplicata felicitas* ES 289; AM 478.3.

duplicitas ~atis, *f.* The quality of being doubled: *quod ~as et triplicitas sit in omni creato* VR 147.

dupliciter, *adv.* In two ways: *quod...una res ~er describatur* AC 683.

duplico ~are ~avi ~atum, *tr.* **1** To fold, double over: *et ~abis aulaeum sextum e regione facierum tentorii* Exod. 26.9 (AC). **2** To make double: *atria longa, arcuata, quandoque ~ata* AC 1629.

duplus ~a ~um, *a.* Double: *is numerus* [*24*] *est ~us numeri duodecim* AE 253.6; *gigantes proceritatis ~ae supra humanam* AM 77.1.

durabilis ~is ~e, *a.* Capable of lasting, durable: *quo ens minus cohaerens est...eo magis ~e* ES 242.

duratio ~onis, *f.* The length of time occupied, duration: *significant ~onem prioris status* AC 862; *tentationes et illarum ~ones* AC 8098.

dure, *adv.* (compar. *~ius*) **1** In a hard manner: *apparet illa* [sc. *memoria*] *sicut ~e ossea* CI 466. **2** Harshly: *dum externum se tutandi gratia asperat...et sic ~e agit* AM 365; *quod spiritus iste interloquatur ~ius* ES 1656.

duresco ~ere, *intr.* To become hard, harden: *affectio veri et boni obfirmatur et ~it extrinsecus ex zelo* AE 412.34.

duriter, *adv.* Harshly: *~er et saeve afflixit filios Israelis* AC 6652; ES 453.

durities ~ei, *f.* The quality of being hard, hardness: *~es lapidis* VR 16.1; (fig.) *ob ~em cordis* Matt. 19.8 (AM 340.2).

duro ~are ~avi, *intr.* To occupy a period of time, last, endure: *quae pugna ~at quamdiu homo tenetur in suo malo* AC 6657.2; *~ante statu desponsationis* AM 304.2.

durus ~a ~um, *a.* (compar. *~ior*, superl. *~issimus*) **1** Unyielding to the touch, hard, unbending: *semina alia ceciderunt super viam ~am* Matt. 13.4 (VI 2); *stant erecti sicut ~i* AC 7068; (transf.) *illum ~a fronte aspicere* VR 56. **b** (anat.) *~a mater*, the outermost of the three membranes enclosing the brain and spinal cord AM 315.5. **2** Resistant to change, hard, tough: *verum...est in se ~um* AC 7068; *intelligentia virorum ...gravis, aspera, ~a* AM 209. **3** Difficult, hard: *~us est hic sermo* John 6.60 (AC 680.2); *quod non posse loqui...sit ~um illis* VR 111.2. **4** Unpleasant to suffer, harsh: *post eventus illos ~os* AC 1865.2; *~ior sors est illorum* AC 6959.2; (neut. pl. as sb.) *satis ~a patiuntur* AC 1106.

dux ducis, *m.* **1** A guide: *vae vobis duces coeci* Matt. 23.16 (AE 220.6). **2** A governor, controller, ruler: *per Moschen futurum illius* [*gentis*] *ducem* AC 7043. **3** (as a title of nobility) A duke: *reges regum, duces ducum* AM 263.2; VR 106. **4** A military commander, general: *quid exercitus valeret...absque duce...?* VR 10.

dynastes ~ae, *m.* (Gk.) A potentate: AE 783.3; *ab...~is Ecclesiae* VR 633.1.

E

e, *prep. w. abl.*: see **ex**[1].

ea: fem. of **is**.

eapropter, *adv.* On that account, therefore: ES 1261.

ebenum ~i, *neut.* Ebony: *caput eorum etiam apparet callosum sicut ex ~o* CI 354; *cornua eboris et ~um...per '~um' quod insulae adducunt* AE 1146.2 (Ezek. 27.15).

ebenus ~a ~um, *a.* (app.) Made of ivory: *apud eos apparet illa* [sc. *callositas*] *sicut ossea et ~a quae reflectit radios lucis* AC 2492; *cochleare ~um* CI 325; AM 344; *thronum ~um* 1 Kgs. 10.18 (AE 253.7). (Emended by some editors to *eburneus*, but confusion of *ebenus* 'ebony' with *ebur* 'ivory' is ancient.)

ebibo ~ere ~i, *tr.* To drink up, drain: *lagenam vini rubri...quod ~ebat* ES 3801.

ebrietas ~atis, *f.* Drunkenness: AM 252; ES 2422.

ebriosus ~a ~um, *a.* Addicted to alcohol; (masc. as sb.) a drunkard, an alcoholic: *bibere cum ~is* Matt. 24.49 (AC 4422).

ebrius ~a ~um, *a.* Intoxicated, drunken: *fiunt sicut ~i* SS 118.

ebullio ~lire ~livi, *intr.* To give off bubbles, froth: *imber...penetravit...statuam, quae... ~liebat* VR 110.8; (transf.) *malum...quod continuo ~lit* ES 3547.

ebullitio ~onis, *f.* The emission of bubbles, frothing: *conatus illorum enitendi apparent sicut ~ones* AC 8273.4; CI 595.

ebur ~oris, *neut.* Ivory: AE 1146.2.

eburneus ~a ~um, *a.* Made of ivory: *ossea sicut ~a* CI 466.

ecce, *interj.* Behold, see, lo: *ducebar...ad collem, et ~e ad pedem collis porticus* VR 48.1.

Ecclesia ~ae, *f.* (Gk.) **1** A group of people sharing a particular religion or faith, church: *doctrina in Antiquis ~is* AC 6628; *~a Judaica* ES 4250; *angelo Ephesinae ~ae* Rev. 2.1 (AR); also in modern times, the congregation of a particular parish: *a...potestate nominandi coram rege modo unum ad ~as* AR 716.4. **2** The whole Christian community upon earth, the Church: *~a est coelum Domini in terris* CI 374; *verum ~ae* AC 6727. **3** The state of a regenerate person: *antequam fit ~a, hoc est, antequam regeneratus est* AC 1083.1.

ecclesiasticus ~a ~um, *a.* Of or belonging to a church, ecclesiastic: *ex ordine ~o* VR 74.1; *amor sui ~us* AM 264.4; (neut. pl. as sb.) AC 575.

echidna ~ae, *f.* (Gk.) A viper: *subrepserunt hydrae et ~ae* AM 79.4.

echo, *f. indecl.* (Gk.) An echo: *ex repercussione soni...potest sentire sicut echo* VR 577.3.

eclipsis ~eos, *f.* (Gk.) An eclipse (of a celestial body): DP 190.1.

ecliptica ~ae, *f.* (Gk.) The apparent orbit of the sun, the ecliptic: *quod tellus...quotannis feratur secundum ~am* SS 95.2.

ecstasis: see **exstasis**.

ecstaticus: see **exstaticus**.

edico ~cere ~xi ~ctum, *tr.* **1** To utter aloud, proclaim: *his ~ctis* AM 3.4; *quia non talis, non potuit ~cere* ES 4316. **2** To state fully, enumerate: *arcana plura hic continentur quam usquam cogitari et ~ci potest* AC 1414; CI 269.1.

edictio ~onis, *f.* A judicial proclamation, edict: AM 470.

edictum ~i, *neut.* An authoritative statement, edict: *~a omnium conciliorum* VI 27; *~um Apostoli Pauli* AM 24.

edilis ~is ~e, *a.* Prob. error for **edulis**: AM 364.

edissero ~ere ~ui ~tum, *tr.* To relate: 3AD 7612 (*edissere* Tafel and Autograph, prob. an error for *edisserere*).

edite, *adv.* (compar. *~ius*) At a great elevation, high: *angeli interiores habitant ~ius super montibus* AC 10608.2.

editio ~onis, *f.* A published form of a book, edition: *in mea ~one* VR 503.4.

editus ~a ~um, *a.* (compar. *~ior*, superl. *~issimus*) Situated at a great elevation, high, lofty: *montes erant ~issima terrae* AC 795.1; *angeli...habitant...in ~ioribus locis* CI 188.

edo[1] ~ere ~i esum, *tr., intr.* To eat: *ne aliquid praeter panem ~erent* AC 7810; (intr.) *delicate ~ere et bibere* CI 358; *equus qui inde* [sc. *ex praesepi*] *~it* SS 26.4.

edo[2] ~ere ~idi ~itum, *tr.* **1** To put forth, utter (sounds): *angeli in sua athmosphaera...~unt voces* CI 235; to produce (results) *quod eae* [*repraesentationes*] *similem effectum ~erent* ES 269. **2** To publish (a book): *in codicillo...Londini Anno 1769 ~ito* VR 33.

edoceo ~cere ~cui ~ctum, *tr.* To teach thoroughly: *quae a pueritia ~cta sunt* AE 401.34; (pass. of persons) *antequam ~cti aliquam linguam* AC 1637; (w. inf.) *qui ~cti sunt recondere interiora sua* CI 48.

educatio ~onis, *f.* The bringing up, education (of children): AM 174.

educator ~oris, *m.* One who brings up or educates: *marito solum manente prolis ~ore* AC 829.2.

educatrix ~icis, *f.* A woman who brings up children: *infantes...a sua ~ice discunt loqui* AM 411.

educo[1] ~are ~avi ~atum, *tr.* To bring up, educate: *quod unusquisque infans...in coelo ~etur* CI 329; ES 3621.

educo[2] ~cere ~xi ~ctum, *tr.* **1** To bring or lead out: *ad ~cendum e carcere vinctum* Isa. 42.7 (DD 6); *fuci...~cuntur et deprivantur alis, ne redeant* VR 127. **2** To render active, bring out: *quae* [sc. *imago patris*] *jugiter allaborat se ~cere* VR 103.2; *interna ~cuntur cum quis...cogitat de regno Domini* AC 1806. **3** (app.) = **educo**[1]: *quod...~cantur* [perh. read *educentur*] *ab illis et instruantur* AM 4.2.

eductio ~onis, *f.* **1** The action of bringing out: *per resuscitationem intelligitur ~o spiritus hominis a corpore* CI 447. **2** A projection: *a latere postium ~ones e parietibus sicut camerae supra fornicatae* AM 103.3.

eductor ~oris, *m.* One who brings out: *Tu ~or meus* Ps. 71.6 (AC 8043.4).

edulcoratus ~a ~um, *a.* Sweetened: *venenis ~is* VR 324.

edulis ~is ~e, *a.* Eatable, edible: *~es cibos* SS 40.1.

edulium ~i, *neut.* A foodstuff, comestible: *~a delicata et opipara* AM 3.3; *habetisne aliquid ~i hic?* Luke 24.41 (DD 35.10).

effabilis ~is ~e, *a.* That may be spoken: *quod talis esset felicitas ut nusquam ore ~is sit* ES 288; (neut. as sb.) *voces ineffabiles, quae...articulabantur in hoc ~e* VR 135.1.

effatum ~i, *neut.* An utterance, statement, saying: *secundum Domini ~um* CI 505; *plerique...illis meis ~is adplauserunt* VR 16.1.

effective, *adv.* In effect, effectively: *quod inde fiat ~e unio animarum* AM 172.

effectivus ~a ~um, *a.* Put into effect, effective: *in ~um amorem* AM 301.

effectrix ~icis, *f. adj.* (of causes) Efficient: *causa media promotrix et ~ix* CO 40.

effectuatio ~onis, *f.* The act of putting into effect: *imputatio, justitia imputata et ~o* VR 633.2; AM 190.

effectus ~us, *m.* The result of a process, effect: *finis, causa et ~us* VI 14; *fructus...sunt ultimi ~us conatus fructificandi in arbore* FI 16; *in ~um dare*, to put into practice: AM 280.

effero ~rre extuli elatum, *tr.* (compar. of pf. pple. *elatior*) **1** To bring out: *ex terra inferiore...se extulit spiritus* VR 71.1. **b** to carry out for burial: *si viderent sacerdotem excitantem mortuum elatum* ES 3521. **2** To bring forth, utter (a sound): *aliqui extulerunt vocem* AM 315.7. **3** (refl.) To be exalted in spirit, be proud, exult: *non...ob causam ut se submittat, sed ne ~rat se* AC 1594; CI 555; (w. *ad*) to aspire (to the position of): *extulit se ad principem exercitus* Dan. 8.11 (FI 65). **4** *Laudibus ~rre*, to praise greatly: 3AD 7565.

effervescens ~ntis, *a.* Boiling over (in quot. fig.): *~ns lascivia* AM 466.1.

effervescentia ~ae, *f.* A boiling over, effervescence: *~a ex fecibus* AE 1143.5; *libidinum ~ae* AM 440.

effervesco ~ere, *intr.* To boil over, effervesce: *quod receptum sit dicere...~ere, ignescere, cum de affectionibus* CI 134.

effetus ~a ~um, *a.* also **effoetus**. Exhausted, used up: *~os halitus illaqueare* DA 13 (= v.[3]) Worcester; (neut. pl. as sb.) *ex effluviis immundis quae ex ~is in corpore exspirant* AE 1057.6.

efficacia ~ae, *f.* The power to produce effects, efficacy: *sibi tribuerunt ~am salvationis* AC 1110; ES 3546.

efficaciter, *adv.* (compar. *~cius*) Effectively: *ut eo ~cius suas artes exercerent* ES 292.

efficax ~acis, *a.* Effective: *sphaeram satis ~acem habent* ES 2740; ES 2765.

efficiens ~ntis, *a.* Causing an effect, efficient: *effectus ex sua causa ~nte* CI 89.

efficio ~ficere ~feci ~fectum, *tr., intr.* **1** To produce, bring about: *ut operentur et ~ficiant effectus suos* AM 178.2; *erit...conjunctio quae... ~ficiet vitam coeli* AC 7022. **2** (intr., or w. indef. obj.) To be effective, act: *ut ~ficere possint [inferna], emittunt a se emissarios* AC 7111.2; *vera apud malos nihil prorsus ad emendationem vitae eorum ~ficiunt* AC 7332; *videatur...quid boni ~ficiunt* VI 100. **3** (pass. w. pred.) To be made, become: *ut... ~ficiamini discipuli Mei* John 15.8 (AE 33).

effigies ~ei, *f.* A form bearing a specified appearance, effigy: *~es seu species humanas* AM 182.6; *caelum est in maxima ~e forma Divini Ordinis* VR 65; (dist. from **imago**) *spiritualis homo est imago, coelestis autem homo est similitudo seu ~es* AC 51; AC 473.

effigio ~are ~avi ~atum, *tr.* To render apprehensible by means of a likeness: *quod...id possit...eloqui ex ore corporis, et simul id ~are gestu* AM 260; *quod ipsa charitas sit quae ~at et ~atur* AC 553.2.

effingo ~ngere ~nxi ~ctum, *tr.* **1** To devise, invent: *quod...talem loquelam ~nxerint* AC 7745; *quod infernum sit fabula ~cta a clero* VR 160.3. **2** To simulate, pretend: *quia innocentiam ~ngere didicit in vita* ES 4374.

efflagito ~are ~avi, *tr.* To insist, demand: *usque fides ~et ut non tres Dii nominentur* VR 165.1.

efflagro ~are, *intr.* To burst into flames: *quod zelotypia spiritualis sit sicut ignis ~ans* AM 368.2; *faculae cereae, quae admoto igne ~ant* VR 455[a].

efflo ~are ~avi ~atum, *tr.* To breathe out: *~are seu emittere animam* AM 315.9; to say with difficulty, gasp: *tunc diducto ore ~avit tres Deos* VR 16.4.

effloreo ~rere ~rui, *intr.* To grow and spread in the manner of a plant, flourish: *~rebunt sicut vitis* Hos. 14.7 (AC 5113.7).

efflorescentia ~ae, *f.* The process of coming into blossom, efflorescence: AM 301.

effloresco ~rescere ~rui, *intr.* **1** (of plants) To come into flower, blossom: *~ruit virga* Ezek. 7.10 (DD 4); (transf.) *incipit amor germinare et ~rescere, sicut pomarium* AM 147. **2** (of leprosy) To break out: *si ~rescendo ~ruerit lepra* Lev. 13.12 (AC 6963.4). **3** (of persons) To become eminent: *sapientes...qui...ingenii laude apud suos ~ruerunt* AM 103.2.

effluo ~ere ~xi, *intr.* **1** To flow out, stream forth: *findet petram ut ~ant aquae* Isa. 48.21 (AE 71.2); *halitus ~ens e coelo* CI 429. **2** To emanate, come forth, arise: *quod inde... ~at contemtus* AM 247.

effluviosus ~a ~um, *a.* Abounding in effluvia: *aliquod ~um exsurgens ex cadavere* VR 80.4; AM 495.3.

effluvium ~i, *neut.* An emanation of liquids or gases, effluvium: *morbi...ex quibus exhalantur ~a detrimentosa* AM 253.1; ES 931.

effluxus ~us, *m.* That which flows forth, emanation, efflux: *~us caloris et lucis ejus* [sc. *solis*] *prorsus mortui* VR 12.5; *ex cujus* [sc. *Domini*] *~u seu Divina sphaera* ES 4403.

effodio ~dere ~di ~ssum, *tr.* **1** To produce by digging, dig up: *per aquam, fontem, puteum, quae ~diuntur* AC 7343.3; *ex montibus ~ditur cuprum* Deut. 8.9 (AE 304.59). **2** To pierce by digging, dig through: *per ~ssum parietem* Ezek. 12.5 (DD 15.5).

effoetus: see **effetus**.

effor ~ari ~atus sum, *tr.* To utter, speak out, declare: *quinta cohors... ~ata est hoc* AM 3.5; *quae lingua nusquam ~ari...potest* ES 288.

efformo ~are ~avi ~atum, *tr.* To form, compose: *tanquam segmentum...circuli ~ent* ES 813; (refl.) to form oneself (into): *spiritus qui se in angelum lucis ~are potuit* VR 71.1.

effossio ~onis, *f.* A digging out: Isa. 51.1 (AE 411.6).

effractor ~oris, *m.* One who breaks open: *veniantque in illud ~ores* Ezek. 7.22 (AC 623.1).

effraene, *adv.* also **effrene**. In an unrestrained manner: *homo...rueret ~e in omnia nefaria* UJ 10.2.

effraenis ~is ~e, *a.* also **effrenis** = **effraenus**: AM 459.1.

effraenus ~a ~um, *a.* also **effrenus**. Unrestrained, unchecked: *de ~o amore sui* AM 267.4.

effrene: see **effraene**.

effrenis: see **effraenis**.

effrenus: see **effraenus**.

effringo ~ringere ~regi ~ractum, *tr.* To break open: *concurrerunt ad portas, ~regerunt illas* AM 9.2; AM 79.5.

effugio ~gere ~gi, *intr.* (*tr.*) To run away, flee: *~giunt sicut ex terrore in conclavium* AM 512.1; (tr.) to run away from, escape: *~gere omnia illa quae futura sunt* Luke 21.36 (AE 187.5).

effulgeo ~gere ~si, *intr.* To shine out: *lux ~sit super eos* Isa. 9.2 (AE 97).

effulguratio ~onis, *f.* A flash (of light): *per ~ones varias lucis tulerunt responsa* AC 6640.2.

effundo ~ndere ~di ~sum, *tr.* **1** To pour out (liquids): *~ndam aquam super sitientem* Isa. 44.3 (AC 8043.2); to empty (a vessel): *sextus angelus ~dit phialam suam* Rev. 16.12 (AR). **2** To spread out, diffuse: *gloriam famae suae ~dit* AM 380.3; *~nde cogitationem quaquaversum* VI 13. **b** (refl. and pass.) to go in different directions, spread out: *tres equites ~derunt se in tres plagas* AM 103.1; (transf.) to become diffused: *cum in Ens universale... ~nditur cogitationis idea* AC 6876.3. **3** (refl.) To proceed, descend (to an action): *Dominus moderatur ne in vituperia se ~ndant* AC 7250.

effusio ~onis, *f.* The act of pouring out, shedding: *non ad sanguinis ~onem* AC 821.2.

effusor ~oris, *m.* One who pours out or sheds: *~or sanguinis seu occisor* AC 1011.

effutio ~tire ~tivi ~titum, *tr.* To utter foolishly, babble: *vir qui vagabundus spiritu et mendacium ~tit* Mic. 2.11 (VR 156); ES 2307.

egenus ~a ~um, *a.* Lacking in material wealth, needy: *homo...opitulatur ~is* VI 9; (transf.) lacking in resources, poor: *fides fit pusilla et ~a* FI 28; ES 226.

egeo egere egui, *intr.* (w. abl.) To stand in need (of), require: *quod propositio illa egeat...multa inquisitione* VR 333.3; (w. clause as subject) *quod non aliae proles nascantur...non demonstratione eget* AM 120.

egerminatio ~onis, *f.* Sprouting, germination: CI 464.6.

egermino ~are ~avi ~atum, *intr.* (*tr.*) (of plants) To put forth shoots, sprout: *fructu...qui ex terra illorum ~at* AC 7484; (fig.) *ex insaniis...laetitiae...deduci et quasi ~are possunt* ES 231.

egero egerere egessi egestum, *tr.* To bring forth: *libertatis eloquendi et egerendi cogitata* VR 814; DP 184.

egestas ~atis, *f.* Lack of material wealth, poverty: *quod homo...quia in ~ate est in coelum recipiatur* CI 357; (transf.) *~as spiritualis* AC 6915.

egestio ~onis, *f.* The act of bringing out, emission, ejection: *sicut qui ex commotione viscerum...exciuntur ad ~onem* SE 62; AS 347.

egi: pf. of **ago**.

eglomero ~are ~avi ~atum, *tr.* To separate by forming into a mass, gather into a mass: *cum aether ex magno illo chao se ~avit* VR 79.6.

ego mei, *1st pers. sg. pron.* I: *nos sumus cultores Domini, ego princeps societatis, alter...sacerdos* AM 266.1; (reinforced with *-met*) *in memet influere* ES 217.

egredior ~di ~ssus sum, *intr.* **1** To step outside, go out: *in ~diendo dixit mihi angelus...* AM 78.3. **2** To proceed, emerge, go forth: *ex omni verbo ~diente ex ore Dei* Matt. 4.4 (SS 69); (i.e., born of) *omnis anima ~ssae femur Jacobi* Exod. 1.5 (AC). **3** To change one's nature, step outside: *Deus... ~di ex Se non potest* VR 56.

egregie, *adv.* In an outstanding manner, excellently: *~e de charitate docuit* VR 796.5.

egregius ~a ~um, *a.* Outstandingly good, excellent: *~a charitatis documenta* VR 459.17.

egressio ~onis, *f.* The act of going out: *~o e monumentis* AC 8018.2.

egressus ~us, *m.* A going out: *sicut aurora paratus ~us Ipsius* Hos. 6.3 (AC 93); VR 335.4.

egurgitatio ~onis, *f.* The action of belching forth, egurgitation: AC 1763.2.

egurgito ~are ~avi ~atum, *tr.*, *intr.* To belch forth, egurgitate: *ventriculum...ex quo expromunt et ~ant talia* VR 146; (intr.) to emerge as by belching: *vociferationes quae sicut per aquas ~abant ex inferis* AM 231.1.

egyratio ~onis, *f.* A winding outwards, spiral: *ingyrationes et ~ones vorticillares* DP 319.2.

ejaculo ~are ~avi ~atum, *tr.* To hurl forth: *ignis emotus et se ~ans contra infestantes* AM 368.2.

ejectio ~onis, *f.* The action of throwing out, ejection: *~ones extra se* CI 580; AC 8079; a heaving up: *~ones dorsi* AC 8273.4.

ejicio ejicere ejeci ejectum, *tr.* **1** To remove by force, throw out: *si ejicerentur domo* AM 292.2; *scrobem coepit ejicere* AC 817; to push forth: *ne quidem ausit ejicere inde unum digitum* CI 400.4. **2** To expel, put away: *per nomen Tuum daemonia ejecimus* Matt. 7.22 (AC 6806.2); *creditur quod illa quae intrant prorsus obliterata et ejecta sint* AC 7398.

ejulatio ~onis, *f.* A wailing, shrieking: *vox clamoris a porta piscium, et ~o a secundaria* Zeph. 1.10 (AC 2240.2).

ejulatus ~us, *m.* A wailing: *usque ad Eglaim ~us ejus* Isa. 15.8 (AE 393).

ejulo ~are ~avi, *intr.* To wail, howl: *~ate naves Tharschischi* Isa. 23.1 (AC 1156); *inceperunt ~are, dicentes quod non possint vivere amplius* AM 216.2.

ejus: gen. sg. of **is**.

ejuscemodi, *indecl. a.* (*ejus*, gen. sg. of **is**, + particle *-ce* and gen. sg. of **modus**) Of that sort: *~i visiones sunt tales* ES 1752; AC 3477.

ejusmodi, *indecl. a.* (*ejus*, gen. sg. of **is**, + gen. sg. of **modus**) see also **ejuscemodi**. Of that kind, such: *quod homo, qui in tali amore est, non sciat quod ~i* *vesana absque limite cupido in illo lateat* VR 400.7; ES 2521.

El, *indecl.* (Hebr.) see also **Elim**, **Eloah**, **Elohe**, and **Elohim**. The singular form of the Hebrew word for God: *in Verbo Jehovah seu Dominus plurimis in locis nominatur El in singulari, etiam Eloah, et quoque nominatur Elohim in plurali* AC 4402.4.

elabor ~bi ~psus sum, *intr.* To slip away, fall out: *dum aliquid ~bitur ex ordine* VR 74.4; *si minimum tale ~beretur ex ore illarum* AM 155[a].3.

elaboro ~are ~avi ~atum, *tr.* To cultivate, work (land): *~are agrum* VR 336.2; (transf.) to make by hard work: *viscera...sanguinem ~ant* DP 180.7.

elambo ~ere ~i, *tr.* To lick up, lap: *aves...quae... ~ebant viscum* ME 23.

elanguesco ~guescere ~gui, *intr.* To become weak, languish, slacken, fail: *omne delitium...ex continuo ~guescit et torpescit* AM 8.4.

elapido ~are ~avi ~atum, *tr.* To free from stones, clear: *vinea...quam... ~avit* Isa. 5.2 (AE 375.31).

elapsus ~us, *m.* The passing, lapse (of time): *post brevem temporis ~um* VR 79.8.

elasticitas ~atis, *f.* Elasticity: *ex jactura... ~atis nervorum* AM 253.2.

elasticus ~a ~um, *a.* (Gk.) Elastic: *sicut globulus ~us cadens in petram* AM 526.

elater ~eris, *m.* (Gk.) A spring: *repellunt omne verum sicut ~er osseus id quod incidit* CI 354; (in a clock) VR 364.1.

elatio ~onis, *f.* **1** The action of raising, arousing: *in ~onem maris* Ps. 89.10 (AE 275.8). **2** *~o animi*, the lifting up of the mind, elation, exultation: *super ~onem animi in externis, quae superbia vocatur* CI 555.

elatus ~a ~um, *a.* (pf. pple. of **effero**) In senses of vb., esp. **1** Lifted up, elevated: *super throno alto et ~o* Isa. 6.1 (AE 220.5). **2** *~us animo* (or *spiritu*), in an exalted state of mind, elated, exultant: AC 795.1; so *~us* alone: *si vel ~i vel submissi* AC 7372; (of the mind) ES 4069.

electio ~onis, *f.* **1** The action of choosing, choice: *a libera ~one hominis* VR 154.4; *quod ~o sit viris* AM 295.2. **b** the choice of followers exercised by God, election: *ex statuta ~one Dei* VR 628. **2** A chosen group: *~o ducum tertianorum submersi in mari Suph* Exod. 15.4 (AC).

elector ~oris, *m.* (as title of a German prince) Elector: IM final paragraph.

electus ~a ~um, *a.* (pf. pple. of **eligo**) **1** Chosen, selected: *musculi et fibrae motrices...quorum... myriades sunt, sparsim ~ae per totum corpus* ES 1760; (usu. masc. or fem. as sb.) *nonne...adhaereret ~ae?* AM 333.2. **2** Specially chosen, elect: *~us meus, in quo beneplacitum habet anima mea* Isa. 42.1 (DD 6); *non nisi quam ~i* CI 420.

eleemosina: see **eleemosyna**.

eleemosyna ~ae, *f.* (Gk.) also **eleemosina**. A charitable gift, alms: *si quis pauperi...dat ~am* ES 2657.

elegans ~ntis, *a.* (compar. *~ntior*) Graceful, elegant: *patet quam ~ns et jucunda est loquela illorum* [sc. *angelorum*] CI 238; AC 8971.1.

eleganter, *adv.* Elegantly: *hoc nimis ~r* AC 6924; AR 875.5.

elegantia ~ae, *f.* Elegance, gracefulness: *affectationes ~ae sermonis et eruditionis* AC 6924; (w. pl.) an instance of elegance, elegant phrase: *loquebantur ~as cum illis* AM 17.1.

elementaris ~is ~e, *a.* Of or relating to the elements, elemental: *quod ignis vitalis...sit ex alia origine quam ignis ~is* AC 6832.9.

elementum ~i, *neut.* **1** Any one of the four substances (earth, air, fire, water) originally conceived as the constituents of matter, an element: *ne quidem potest piscis vitam trahere in aëre, sed in ~o vitae ejus applicato* VR 838.2. **2** (more scientifically) A simple substance out of which compounds are made: *ab exuviis, quae fuerunt compositae ex ~is in aquis et terris* AM 192; CO 17.2.

elephantinus ~a ~um, *a.* (Gk.) Made of ivory: *omne vas ~um* Rev. 18.12 (AC 4748.5).

elephantus: see **elephas**.

elephas ~antis, *m.* (Gk.) also **elephantus** ~i, *m.* (ES 1641). An elephant: *locusta contra ~antem* VR 68.2.

elevabilis ~is ~e, *a.* Capable of being raised: *nostine quod mens humana sit ~is supra sensualia...?* VR 35.6; AM 269.6.

elevate, *adv.* (compar. *~ius*) In a lofty manner: *qui ~ius, hoc est, interius in rationali cogitant* DP 48.1.

elevatio ~onis, *f.* **1** The act of raising, lifting: *secundum rerum ~ones* AC 6947; *~ones et inclinationes magneticas* ES 222. **b** a raised part, projection: *pons erat...sed utrinque ~o sic ut tutissime transiri posset* ES 853; VR 48.20. **2** The fact of being raised up (to heaven): *status ~onis illorum in coelum* AC 7860. **3** The uplifting (of the mind, thoughts, etc): *~o mentis eorum ad interiora* AC 6629; *a facultate ~onis intellectus in lucem caeli* VI 86.5; *~o cordis ad Deum* AM 3.6.

elevator ~oris, *m.* One who lifts or raises, lifter, elevator: *musculi ~ores auriculae* ES 2667.

elevatus ~a ~um, *a.* (compar. *~ior*, superl. *~issimus*) **1** On a higher level, raised: *humus ~a formabat sicut theatrum* VR 48.1; *in loco ~iori* ES 1881. **2** Raised in quality, lofty: *mens humana, etiam summe analytica et ~a* VR 28.

elevo ~are ~avi ~atum, *tr.* **1** To lift up, raise: *~avi manum meam ad Jehovam* Gen. 14.22 (AC); *qui in arca fuerunt et ~ati supra aquas* AC 791; *quasi alae quae ~abant* AC 7039.2. **2** To raise (to heaven): *qui ~andi sunt in coelum* AC 6639.2. **3** To raise (the mind, thoughts, etc. to a higher plane): *quia...minime ~ant suas cogitationes* AC 938; *quod mens eorum ~ata sit supra sensualia* AC 6925; *quod naturalis homo possit se ~are supra naturam* VR 22.2. **4** To make superior in rank: *astutias excogitarunt ad se ~andos supra alios* AC 6692.2.

elicio ~cere ~cui ~citum, *tr.* To extract, elicit: *in... locis...ex quibus non aliquis sensus potest ~i* SS 51.1; *qui ~ciunt aliorum arcana fine nocendi* AC 1763.2.

eligo eligere elegi electum, *tr.* To give preference to, choose, select: *quod gens illa iterum eligetur* AC 7051.2; *loca arenosa, quae eligunt prae campestribus* CI 488.2.

Elim, *indecl.* (Hebr.) see also **El**, **Eloah**, **Elohe**, and **Elohim**. Hebrew word meaning gods: AC 4402.7.

elimate, *adv.* With keen discrimination, sharply: *qui ~e et distincte intuentur res* AM 463.2.

elimatio ~onis, *f.* The act of refining: *per ~ones et abstractiones intellectus a fallaciis sensuum* AM 145.3.

elimatus ~a ~um, *a.* Discerning, keen: *ratio ~a potest videre* AM 87.1.

elimo ~are ~avi ~atum, *tr.* To refine, extract: *nihil aliud ab hominis cogitatione ~ant [angeli]* AC 1645; *cum sermones suos...concinnarent et ~arent* VI 7.

elixatio ~onis, *f.* The act of boiling: AC 8496.

elixo ~are ~avi ~atum, *tr.* To prepare (food) by boiling, boil: *quod ~abitis ~ate* Exod. 16.23 (AC); to remove by boiling: *dum nutritium ejus* [sc. *cibi*] *~atum est* CO 47.

Eloah ~ae, *m.* (Hebr.) see also **El**, **Elim**, **Elohe**, and **Elohim**. An alternate Hebrew term for God (see quot.): *Jehovah seu Dominus plurimis in locis nominatur El in singulari, etiam Eloah...; quod El involvat aliud, et Eloah aliud* AC 4402.4.

elocutio: see **eloquutio**.

Elohe, *indecl.* (Hebr.) see also **El**, **Elim**, **Eloah**, and **Elohim**. God (see quot.): *El Elohe in lingua originali significat Deum Deum, et stricte secundum verba, Deum deorum* AC 4402.4.

Elohim, *indecl.* (Hebr.) see also **El**, **Elim**, **Eloah**, and **Elohe**. The usual Hebrew word for God: *quod in lingua originali Deus dicatur Elohim in plurali* AC 7268.2; AE 24.

elongatio ~onis, *f.* The action of withdrawing, withdrawal: *quod ~o sit aversatio* AC 9261.

elongatus ~a ~um, *a.* Remote, distant: *insulae maris ~ae erant a terra Canaane* AE 1024.1; ES 3606.

elongo ~are ~avi ~atum, *tr.* **1** To cause to depart, send away, remove: *~abit Jehovah hominem* Isa. 6.12 (AC 477.4); (fig.) *amor adulterii...detrahit et ~at illam* [sc. *mentem*] *e caelo* AM 497. **2** (refl. and pass.) To take oneself off, retreat: *~abant se adhuc magis* AC 6811; ES 522.

eloquentia ~ae, *f.* Eloquence: AC 1514.

eloquium ~i, *neut.* **1** A piece of oratory, speech: *congeries expressionum, quales sunt ~orum* AC 2184.3. **2** Eloquence: *verum possunt loqui...cum ~o et apparente zelo* AC 1321.2; AM 354.1.

eloquor ~qui ~quutus (*or* ~cutus) sum, *tr.* To speak, utter: *quod angeli non possint ~qui unam vocem linguae humanae* CI 246.2; (absol.) *non permissum erat ei ~qui, sed modo cogitare* ES 775.

eloquutio ~onis, *f.* also **elocutio**. Utterance: *ex ~one eorum* [sc. *verorum*] AE 365.4.

eluceo ~cere ~xi, *intr.* **1** To shine forth, be radiant: *Divinum... ~cet sicut lux per formas crystallinas* VR 6.2; *~xit ex illis [faciebus] sincerum et modestum* AC 8242. **2** To be revealed, appear: *timent ne quicquam quod cogitant... ~ceat* AC 6655; *inde ~cet error illorum* VR 144; (impers.) *ex quo potest ~cere, quod Ipse sit* DD 37.2.

elucentia ~ae, *f.* A shining forth, appearance: *coruscatio cutis facierum Moschis est ex ~a* [*elucescentia* Autograph] *ab interno* AC 10691.

elucescentia: see **elucentia**.

elucesco ~ere, *intr.* To begin to shine forth, appear: *incipit ab obscuro...lux veritatum sensim ~ere* ES 3904; *genuinum humanum in facie ejus ex loquela et ex moribus ejus ~it* AM 432.1.

elucidatio ~onis, *f.* The act of making plain: *propter ~onem hujus arcani* AM 116.

elucido ~are ~avi ~atum, *tr.* To make plain or clear to the comprehension, elucidate: *haec non amplius adhuc ~ari possunt* CI 143.

elucubro ~are ~avi ~atum, *tr.* To produce (a book or similar) with expenditure of lamplight, burn the midnight oil over: *in Arcanis Coelestibus...per octennium ~atis* CO 23.1.

eludo ~dere ~si ~sum, *tr.* **1** To deceive, trick: *~dimus et circumvenimus quoscunque ex sua concupiscentia* VR 665.3. **2** To escape by trickery, evade: *~dere tentabant paenam* AC 959; ES 4514.

elusio ~onis, *f.* The act of tricking, deception: *maritorum ~ones* AM 477.1.

Elysius ~a ~um, *a.* (Gk.) *Campi ~i*, the Elysian fields (in Gk. mythology, the abode of the blest after death): VR 453.2; ES 1232.

emachinor ~ari ~atus sum, *tr.* To devise, work out: *plures dolos ~ati sunt ut imperarent* AC 6312.

emacio ~are ~avi ~atum, *tr.* To cause to waste away, make thin: *Jehovah ~abit omnes deos terrae* Zeph. 2.11 (AE 50.2); (pass.) to become thin: ES 4150.

emancipo ~are ~avi ~atum, *tr.* (w. dat.) To make subservient (to): *~atur vir alicui scorto* AM 54; AM 155.3.

emano ~are ~avi ~atum, *tr.* **1** To flow forth, flow out: *flumen ignis ~ans et exiens a coram Ipso* Dan. 7.10 (AE 336.9). **2** To be spread (from a source), emanate: *e qua* [*Ecclesia*] *religio ~avit ad plures gentes* CI 322.1; VR 4.2.

emarcesco ~cescere ~cui, *intr.* To wither away: *quae* [*tulipae*] *post mensem dierum deflorantur et ~cescunt* VR 316; ES 3100.

emarcidus ~a ~um, *a.* Wasted: *facies eorum detestabilis, non facies, sed ~um quid* ES 1866.

emblema ~atis, *neut.* (Gk.) A symbol, badge: *per interpretationem sicut ~atum* AC 4581.3; AC 9011.7.

embryo ~onis, *m.* (ad. Gk.) A foetus at an early stage of development, embryo: AM 401.1; VR 87.

emendabilis ~is ~e, *a.* Capable of being corrected, corrigible: *quod ii in altera vita ~es sint* ES 3910.

emendatio ~onis, *f.* Correction, improvement: *ex causa ~onis mali* AC 592.2; *ad ~onem vitae* AC 7332.

emendo ~are ~avi ~atum, *tr.* To correct, put right, improve: *ut... ~entur ut inserviant alicui vili usui* AC 986.3; *voluntas non ~ari potest* AE 140.7; *cum pleno proposito ~andi vitam* BCP (VI 6); to correct, cure (a fault): *si quae mala et falsa vident, ea... ~are student* AC 1079.1.

emergo ~gere ~si, *intr.* **1** (of floods) To become high, rise: *cum* [*aquae*] *ad altitudinem, in qua ipse stat, ~gunt* VR 119.2; (fig.) *falsum...et malum quae apud illum ~gunt* AC 6828; CI 595. **2** To be liberated, emerge (from affliction): *cum...homo ex tentatione ~git* AC 6829.

emersio ~onis, *f.* Emergence: *~onem e nocte* AC 2961; AC 6607.

emeticus ~a ~um, *a.* (Gk.) Provoking vomiting, emetic: (neut. pl. as sb.) *ex ~is et ex cibis affatim ingestis* ES 1278.

emico ~are ~ui, *intr.* To flash forth: *ab oculis ejus ~abat lux scintillans* AM 42.3.

emigro ~are ~avi, *intr.* To move to another country, emigrate: *quod cum opibus conquisitis ~arent* ES 3516; (transf.) *cum per mortem* [*anima*] *a naturali mundo ~at in suum spiritualem* CC 11.3.

eminens ~ntis, *a.* (compar. *~ntior*, superl. *~ntissimus*) **1** Exceeding, surpassing: *~ns potentia* AC 8281.1; *in ~nti sensu* CI 278.3; *deliratio ~ns est deliratio mentis ex falsificatis veris* AM 212. **2** (of persons) Of high rank or reputation, eminent: *putant se reliquis esse majores et ~ntiores* ES 2514.

eminenter, *adv.* (superl. *~issime*) In an outstanding degree, surpassingly, exceedingly: *ille ~er amat proximum* VR 419.

eminentia ~ae, *f.* High rank or reputation, eminence: *~am et opulentiam pro mediis habent* AC 7820; AM 267.2.

emineo ~nere ~nui, *intr.* **1** To be conspicuous by reason of height, stand out: *chorus, e quo deus tutelaris ...quoad caput ~nuit* AM 78.3. **2** To possess high rank or reputation, be eminent: *ut ~neant super alios* CI 362.

emissarius ~a ~um, *a.* Sent forth as an agent: *Deus per spiritum ~um Suum operatur* VR 159.3; (masc. as sb.) an emissary: *emittunt a se ~os per quos agunt* AC 7111.2; a missionary: *conversi sunt ad religionem Christianam per ~os* ES 4676.

emissio ~onis, *f.* The act of sending forth: *~onem et praesentiam illorum qui...infestant* AC 7123; the putting forth (of one's hand): *per ~onem manus ad virum Dei* AC 878.8; the shedding (of blood): AE 476.

emitto emittere emisi emissum, *tr.* **1** To put or send forth, emit: *vox quae emissa ore dissipatur* AC 6880; *'emittere animam' est non amplius animare* FI 19.1; *ex illo* [sc. *sole*] *emittit calorem et lucem* VR 63. **2** To despatch, send out (persons): *ad discipulos quos emisit* [*Dominus*] CI 287.2; also, to let go, release: *impense rogamus ut emittamur* AM 6.4.

emo ~ere ~i ~(p)tum, *tr.* To acquire by payment, buy: *ad frumentum ~endum* AC 6638; VI 39.

emolior ~liri ~litus sum, *tr.* To remove with effort, heave out the way: *templi custodes ~liebantur nivem* VR 185.2.

emollesco ~ere, *intr.* To become soft, soften: [*calli*] *qui duri sunt, ~ent* ES 958.

emollio ~lire ~livi ~litum, *tr*. To make soft or mild: *forma illa remittit se, ~lit se* AM 361.2; *per affectiones, quae... ~liunt voces* AC 1759.

emollitio ~onis, *f*. Softening: AC 3318.3; ES(M) 4597.

emolumentum ~i, *neut*. Gain, profit: *sibi persuadent omne ~um proprium esse bonum commune* AC 1673.4; CI 56; *~o esse*, to be profitable: AM 446.

Emoraeus: see **Emorraeus**.

emorior emori emortuus sum, *intr*. To die off: *in hyeme, quando...omnia et singula torpent et emoriuntur* AC 34.2.

Emorraeus ~a ~um, *a*. also **Emoraeus**. Amorite: *per gentem ~am repraesentatum sit malum* AC 6306.2; (masc. as sb.) an Amorite: Gen. 15.16 (AC); Exod. 3.17 (AC).

emotio ~onis, *f*. The act of stirring, excitation: *fit ~o et dolor* VR 110.1; *~o animi* AM 358.

emotor ~oris, *m*. One who prods or stirs: *sicut flamma ex igne erumpens in ~orem ejus* AM 359.2.

emoveo ~vere ~vi ~tum, *tr*. **1** To move from its place, remove: *quod ~verentur damnata* AC 7410; *radix mali manet insita, et non est ~ta* VI 108. **2** To arouse, excite: *ignis ~tus* AM 368.2; *quod...illas affectiones ~veant* AC 8337.2.

emphasis ~eos, *f*. (Gk.) (acc. sg. *~im* or *~in*) Emphasis: *ob majorem ~im rei* AC 4137.3; AC 4691.

emplastrum ~i, *neut*. (Gk.) (in medicine) A plaster: VR 665.6; (fig.) *~um, quod super vulnera a dogmatibus illorum inflicta ponunt* VR 134.5.

emptio: see **emtio**.

emptor: see **emtor**.

empyema ~atis, *neut*. A collection of pus, empyema: VR 665.5.

emtio ~onis, *f*. also **emptio**. The act of buying, purchase: VR 730; also, a thing bought: *omnis servus viri, ~o argenti* Exod. 12.44 (AC).

emtor ~oris, *m*. also **emptor**. A buyer, purchaser: VR 701.1.

emulgentia ~um, *neut. pl*. (anat.) The emulgent vessels (of the kidneys): *ex ~bus descendunt spermatica vasa* ES 960.

emulsum ~i, *neut*. An emulsion: VR 160.5; VR 665.6.

emunctorium ~i, *neut*. That which serves to remove waste products, a cleaner: *quod [forcipes] sint ~a* AC 9572; an organ of the body serving to discharge waste matter: *per poros cutis, et alia ~a, ut nares* ES 3124.

emunctus ~a ~um, *a*. (of a candle) Snuffed: *quia illa* [sc. *candela*] *non erat ~a, illuminabat parum* VR 35.4.

emundo ~are ~avi ~atum, *tr*. To make clean, purify: *conflans et ~ans argentum* Mal. 3.3 (AC 1551.4).

emurmuro ~are ~avi ~atum, *tr*. To mutter, murmur: *in abeundo ~abant aliquos terminos commodatos ex arte methaphysica* VR 17.4.

en, *interj*. Lo!, behold!: (w. nom.) *en Ego mittens vobis Eliam prophetam* Mal. 4.5 (AC 6752.10); (w. acc.) *en novum hospitem* AM 10.2.

enarro ~are ~avi ~atum, *tr*. To relate, tell: *plura...ex ore angelorum ~ata* AM 69.2.

enascentia ~ae, *f*. The fact of being born, origin: *ex ~a eorum ex foetore fluviorum* AE 410.6.

enascor ~sci ~tus sum, *intr*. (of plants) To spring up, grow: *simul ~tae spinae suffocarunt illud* Luke 8.7 (VI 90); AM 3.4; (transf.) *inde ~tae sunt dirae haereses* VR 489.1.

enato ~are ~avi, *intr*. To swim out, float off: *halitus...qui...e ventriculo... ~ant ad capitis provincias* ES 2336.

enavigo ~are ~avi, *intr*. To sail away: *videt reliquos nautas in naviculis... ~are* VR 504.4.

encomium ~i, *neut*. (Gk.) A eulogy: (in quot. in doubtful sense, poss. erroneous) *quod...caelestes beatitudines animarum illorum recesserint ab intimis ad extrema corporis illorum..., et simul cum illis ~a virilitatis* AM 75.9.

eneco ~are ~avi (*or* ~ui) ~atum, *tr*. To kill off: *si modo afflaret [Deus] illos qui in inferno sunt, momento ~aret illos* VR 124.1; ES 4501; AR 875.16.

enervo ~are ~avi ~atum, *tr*. To cut the sinews of, hamstring: *~arunt bovem* Gen. 49.6 (AC); to take away the strength of, emasculate: *~antur vires* AM 456.

enim, *conj*. (placed after the first word or phrase of a clause) (to give a reason for a preceding statement) For: *amor sui est qui omnium minime concordat cum vita coelesti; omnia enim inde mala* AC 1307.

enitor ~ti ~sus (*or* ~xus) sum, *intr*. To struggle out: *ad quos David ~sus* ES 3664; *a falsis, e quibus tamen ~ti volunt, tenentur* AC 6854.5.

enixus ~us, *m*. Parturition, delivery: AS 401.

enodo ~are ~avi ~atum, *tr*. To free from knots, unravel; (transf.) to solve, make plain: *illud magnum mysterium... ~avi* VR 16.1; *hic sensus aegre potest ~ari* SS 19.

enormis ~is ~e, *a.* also **inormis**. (compar. *~ior*) **1** Of abnormal appearance, disfigured, ugly: *facies...ex pustulis...et ulceribus ~es* CI 553.2. **2** Outstandingly bad, heinous, gross: *de Divino vel nullas vel ~es ideas haberent* AC 7091.1; *~e peccatum* AM 513.

enormitas ~atis, *f.* Deviation from a standard of rectitude, enormity: *ob, quae ~as* VR 135.1; *excommuni hoc...plures ~ates influxerunt in Ecclesiam* VR 94.

enormiter, *adv.* Grossly, heinously: *quod... ~er peccaverint* AC 4489.4.

ens entis, *neut.* An entity, being: *absque hoc est bonum ens nullius nominis* AM 87.1; *Jehovah...significat supremum et unicum ens* VR 9.3; *ens rationis*, an entity only existing in the mind, an imaginary thing: *quid essentia absque forma aliud quam ens rationis...?* AM 315.10; *quod Deus non sit ens rationis* VR 159.7.

ensis ~is, *m.* A sword: *arma belli, sicut ~es, hastae, clypei et similia* AE 131.18.

enthusiasmus ~i, *m.* (Gk.) Belief in divine inspiration, enthusiasm: *in similem ~um veniunt post mortem* UJ(C) 83.

enthusiasta ~ae, *m.* (Gk.) One who believes he is divinely inspired, enthusiast: *visionarii et ~ae* CI 249.

enthusiasticus ~a ~um, *a.* (Gk.) Given to belief in divine inspiration: *spiritus ~i* CI 249; of or belonging to such a belief: *si interrogarentur num scirent quid perceptio...vocarent ~um quid* AC 206.2.

entitas ~atis, *f.* An entity: *res exprimere meris terminis scholasticis, ut... ~atibus et similibus* ES 3960.

enucleo ~are ~avi ~atum, *tr.* To remove obscurities from, make clear, expound: *illud per sensum spiritualem ~are* CO 1.

enumeratio ~onis, *f.* The act of counting: *per ~onem earum* [sc. *felicitatum*] ES 906.

enumero ~are ~avi ~atum, *tr.* To relate fully, list, count: *per gentes...quae ~antur hic* AC 6858; *dolos eorum ~are foret innumeras membranas implere* ES 617.

enunc-: see **enunt-**.

enuntiabilis ~is ~e, *a.* That can be expressed in words, expressible: *per alia indicia non ita ~ia* AC 1758; ES(M) 4668.

enuntiatio ~onis, *f.* The expressing of a thought in words, utterance: *intuitio, apperceptio et ~o* AC 1757.

enuntiator ~oris, *m.* One who utters or proclaims; (in pl., as the title of the Prophetic books of the Ancient Word): *propterea dicunt ~ores* Num. 21.27 (SS 103.2).

enuntiatum ~i, *neut.* An utterance, expression: *illis non aliud est Deus quam duntaxat ~um oris* VR 7; (in pl., as the title of the Prophetic books of the Ancient Word): *Verbum historicum vocatum est Liber Bellorum Jehovae, et Verbum propheticum ~a* AC 8273.4; SS 103.2.

enuntio ~are ~avi ~atum, *tr.* To express in words, utter: *loquela angelica...sonore ~atur et sonore auditur* CI 235.

eo[1] ire ivi itum, *intr.* **1** To be in motion, move, go: *in eundo vidi...tres pueros* AM 75.4; (w. place specified) *cum in platea irem* ES 2911; *ivit arca super faciebus aquarum* Gen. 7.18 (AC); (w. acc. of the way) *hanc viam eamus* VR 79.8; (w. destination specified) *angeli in medium plani ad mensam ibant* VR 482; (impers. pass.) *quo profundius itur* ES 4545. **2** (w. destinations implying a special purpose) To go: *cum irem in lectum* ES 3851; *ito in salutem nobis* Ps. 80.2 (AE 448.13); *obviam ire Deo et influxum recipere* VR 11.1; (w. supine in *~um*): *quod...destructum iret* [*caelum*] VR 121.1. **3** To go away, depart: *cum itis, non ibitis vacui* Exod. 3.21 (AC); *num ibo et vocabo tibi mulierem nutricem...?* Exod. 2.7 (AC). **4** To go (in a specified manner): *Jehovah ibat ante illos interdiu in columna nubis* Exod. 13.21 (AC); *pedibus ire*, to walk: AC 188. **5** To behave, act, live (in a specified manner): *quod...iret nudus et discalceatus* Isa. 20.2 (SS 35.1); *ituri continue in pia meditatione* CI 528; *altius it sua phantasia quam alii* ES 2621; *obviam ire* (w. dat.), to take action against: *nisi prudenter et severe obviam irent...amori sui* AC 7364. **6** (of persons or their faculties) To take action, proceed, act: *ne in universalia eat* [*mens*] ES 769; *nec in arcana ulterius eundum* ES 1601; *aliis quorum captus non ultra it* ES 4525. **b** (of actions) to proceed, take place: *omnia et singula vult Dominus, ut secundum ordinem eant* ES 1509. **7** (of plants) To grow: *ibunt rami ejus* Hos. 14.6 (AC 886.2); Jer. 12.2 (AC 348). **8** (of things, w. abl.) To be running (with): *colles ibunt lacte* Joel 3.18 (AC 2184.6).

eo[2], *adv.* **1** By so much, to that extent: *quod quo distinctius duo sunt, eo perfectius unum possint facere* DP 4.4. **2** To that place or point, thither: *cum indoles perversa est, sequitur quod reliqua...eo flectantur* ES 233. **3** *Eo quod*, by reason of the fact that: *nec potuit Moscheh intrare, eo quod habitaret super eo nubes* Exod. 40.35 (AC 10574.13).

eo[3], eorum, eos: see **is**.

eousque, *adv.* To such an extent, so far: *non licet ante tempus meridiei; sunt omnes ~e in suis officiis* AM 11; *~e ut...* AC 878.6.

epha ~ae, *f.* also **ephah**. A measure of capacity, ephah: Deut. 25.15 (AE 304.42); Isa. 5.10 (AC 576.1); Zech. 5.6 (DD 52).

ephah: see **epha**.

ephatah, *indecl.* also **ephathah**, and **ephphathah**. 'Be opened' (see quot.): *Jesus assumens surdum aegre loquentem, injecit digitum suum in aures ejus, et...dixit ei, Ephatah, hoc est, aperitor* Mark 7.32-34 (AE 455.21).

ephathah: see **ephatah**.

ephebatus ~us, *m.* The period of a man's life immediately following puberty, youth: *usque ad ~um, adolescentiam et juventutem* VR 106.

ephebus ~i, *m.* (Gk.) A boy immediately after puberty, youth: *puer qui in ~is adhuc est* AC 5497.1; AM 111.

Ephesinus ~a ~um, *a.* (Gk.) Of Ephesus: Rev. 2.1 (AR).

ephod: see **ephodum**.

ephodus: see **ephodum**.

ephodum ~i, *neut.* (Hebr.) also **ephod**, *indecl.*, and **ephodus** ~i, *m.* A priestly garment, ephod: *Aharonis... ~um* SS 16; *sponsus indutus erat pallio...et tunica ...cum ~o* AM 20.2.

ephphathah: see **ephatah**.

Ephrataeus ~a ~um, *a.* Of Ephrata: *ut Bethlechem ~a* Mic. 5.2 (DD 6).

epigastricus ~a ~um, *a.* (Gk.) (anat.) Of the epigastrium: AC 7803.

epilepsia ~ae, *f.* (Gk.) Epilepsy: AM 253.2.

episcopatus ~us, *m.* The office and dignity of a bishop, episcopate: *insigniuntur pileis doctoratus ac palliis ~us* SE 59.

episcopus ~i, *m.* (Gk.) A bishop: AM 9.4.

epistola ~ae, *f.* (Gk.) A letter: *~ae et schedulae* CI 462[a].6; esp. one of the letters incorporated into the New Testament: ES 4824.

epitaphium ~i, *neut.* (Gk.) An inscription on a tomb, epitaph: *sepulchrum ornatum ~o hoc*: VR 636.1.

epithetum ~i, *neut.* (Gk.) An extra name, title: *Antiqua Ecclesia, a qua ~a illa emanaverunt, nusquam nisi quam unum Deum sub tot nominibus veneratum coluit* AC 2724.3.

epitome ~es, *f.* (Gk.) An abridged version, epitome: *supersedetur demonstrari in hac ~e, verum adducentur et demonstrabuntur in ipso opere* SE 69.

epocha ~ae, *f.* (Gk.) A period of time, epoch: *hujus* [*Ecclesiae*] *binae ~ae fuerunt* VR 760.

epoto ~are ~avi ~um, *tr.* To swallow (a liquid), drink down: *quomodo aliquis Aegyptius factus mumi, et a pharmacopola immixtus extractis vel emulsis, ~is aut comestis, redire et aliquid narrare?* VR 160.5.

epotum ~i, *neut.* A dose of liquid, draught: VR 160.5.

epulae ~larum, *f. pl.* A feast, banquet: AM 3.3.

epularis ~is ~e, *a.* Of feasting: *~es scenae* AM 6.3; (neut. pl. as sb.) CO 57.

epulatio ~onis, *f.* The holding of a feast, feasting: *~ones cum Abrahamo, Isaco et Jacobo* AM 3.3.

epulor ~ari ~atus sum, *intr.* To attend a banquet, feast: *ditescere, ~ari, habitare et vestiri splendide* CI 359.

eques ~itis, *m.* The rider of a horse, horseman: AM 103.1.

equestris ~is ~e, *a.* Of knights, knightly: *in domo comitis ~is ordinis* ES 4151; *in ~i vestitu* UJ(P) 238.

equinus ~a ~um, *a.* Of horses, equine: *bina capita ~a* ES 4018; (anat.) *cauda ~a*, the horsetail: see **cauda**.

equitatio ~onis, *f.* The action of riding an animal: *Domini ~o super pullo asinae* AE 31.7.

equitatus ~um, *m.* A band of horsemen, group of cavalry: VR 113.1.

equito ~are ~avi, *intr.* (fut. pple. *~aturus*) To ride on horseback: *tam impossibile est, ut est ~are ad quendam asterismum* VR 137.3; (on other animals and fig.) *~are fecit illos super asino* Exod. 4.20 (AC); *Jehovah ... ~avit super cherubo* Ps. 18.10 (SS 97.4); *~antem super nubibus* Ps. 68.4 (AC 8267.2).

equus ~i, *m.* A horse: AM 342.3; (esp.) one of the four horses mentioned in Rev. 9.17: Rev. 9.17 (AR).

eradiatio ~onis, *f.* The emission of rays: *ex ~one inde cutis* AM 42.3.

eradico ~are ~avi ~atum, *tr.* To pull up by the roots, uproot: *omnis plantatio... ~atur* Matt. 15.13 (AE 254.3); (fig.) *haereditarium malum...nusquam ~ari potest* AC 1573.3.

eradior ~ari ~atus sum, *intr.* To radiate: *in quod corpus... ~antur radii amoris* 3AD 1326.

Ereb, *indecl. f.* (app.) Hebr. = foreigners: Ezek. 30.5 (AC 1164.2).

erecte, *adv.* Upright: *ire feci vos ~e* Lev. 26.13 (AC 248).

erectim, *adv.* Upright: *~im ambulare* AC 8374.

erectio ~onis, *f.* An upright posture: *~o corporis* ES 567.

erectus ~a ~um, *a.* Standing upright: *~us super pede vadit huc illuc* AM 2.1.

ereptio ~onis, *f.* A snatching away, rescue: *~o et liberatio ab inferno* AE 278.2; AC 7770.3.

ereptor ~oris, *m.* One who snatches away, rescuer: *~or meus* Ps. 144.2 (AC 1788.2).

erga, *prep. w. acc.* Directed at, towards: *amor ~a proximum* CI 238; *ex amore Dei ~a totum genus humanum* VR 43.2.

ergastulum ~i, *neut.* A place of confinement accompanied by hard labour, labour camp: *hi...sunt in infernis inclusi ~is* FI 63.2.

ergo, *adv.* (usu. second word in phr.) Therefore, consequently, then: *cum ~o homo...in tentationem venit* AC 6657.2; *a quo et in quo ~o est causa damnationis...?* VR 72.1.

erigo erigere erexi erectum, *tr.* **1** To cause to stand upright, raise up (persons): *in die tertio eriget nos* Hos. 6.2 (DD 4); to make superior, exalt: *Pharao qui erexit Josephum super terram Aegypti* AC 1361.2. **2** To set up, raise, erect, establish: *erigite signum Zionem versus* Jer. 4.6 (AE 55.2); (fig.) *erigam foedus Meum tecum* Gen. 6.18 (AC). **3** To excite, arouse: *qui spe patitur se erigi* AC 2338.

eripio eripere eripui ereptum, *tr.* **1** To take away by force, snatch away: *ne...sua bona aliis eripiant* AC 7364. **2** To remove violently, snatch away, rescue (from danger): *Lot...ereptus incendio Sodomae* AC 1589.1.

Eris ~idis, *f.* (Gk.) Strife (personified): *pomum ~idis* VR 112.1.

erodo ~dere ~si ~sum, *tr.* To gnaw away: *nucleus ... ~sus a vermibus* VR 435.1.

errans ~ntis, *a.* Wandering: *stellae ~ntes* [i.e., planets] AC 1808.1.

erraticus ~a ~um, *a.* Not firmly established, erratic: *fides ~a* VR 345; AC 2679.

erratilis ~is ~e, *a.* Wandering: *fasciola in qua stellae coruscantes ~es* TE 50.

erratum ~i, *neut.* An error, mistake: *quod absque ~o esse velint* ES 454.

erro ~are ~avi ~atum, *intr.* **1** To depart from the correct path, wander, stray: *quod ~averim a domo* ES 4554; (fig.) *~at eorum cogitatio ab uno ad alterum* CI 2. **2** To be in error, be wrong: *patet quantum ~ant qui credunt quod gens illa iterum eligetur* AC 8301.6.

erronee, *adv.* Incorrectly, erroneously: *videri potest quam ~e cogitant illi* AC 4847.3.

erroneus ~a ~um, *a.* Incorrect, mistaken, wrong: *ab ~o et falso hoc principio* AC 8094.2; *in sua ~a fide* CI 312.2; (neut. pl. as sb.) *quod hodie abdicaverit sua ~a* VR 137.8.

error ~oris, *m.* A mistaken belief or action, error: *quod...facile in ~orem...possit cadere* SS 1; *mens... prona in ~ores* SS 52.

erubesco ~bescere ~bui, *intr., tr.* **1** (intr.) To blush: *et fuerunt ambo nudi...et non ~buerunt* Gen. 2.25 (AC); *~bescet luna* Isa. 24.23 (DD 4). **2** (tr.) To be ashamed at: *nec ~bescunt nuditatem* AC 8375.

eruca ~ae, *f.* A caterpillar: *oleas vestras comedit ~a* Amos 4.9 (AE 403.8); (app. as a stage in the growth of a locust) Joel 2.25 (AC 9331.5); (as a stage in the development of butterflies) *ut... [larvae] fiant chrysallides, aureliae, ~ae, nymphae, et demum papiliones* AS 354.

eructatio ~onis, *f.* An emission of wind from the mouth, belch: *~ones ex pulmone saucio* VR 108.

eructo ~are ~avi ~atum, *tr.* To emit (wind, etc.) from the mouth, belch: *ex ore ~abat fumum* AM 263.1; (absol.) Ps. 59.6 (AC 7784.4).

erudio ~dire ~divi ~ditum, *tr.* (compar. of pf. pple. *~ditior*, superl. *~ditissimus*) To instruct, train: *non ex Divino ordine est per scripta ~diri e coelo* CI 258.

erudite, *adv.* (compar. *~ius*) In a learned fashion: *qui ex scientiis ~ius hoc facere possunt* AC 10227.3.

eruditio ~onis, *f.* The quality of being learned, learning: *celebratissimos ~one* AM 2.1; learning relating to a specific subject, knowledge: *quaesivi quam ~onem de Deo...secum ferrent* VR 12.1; the opinion of the learned: *quod non detur illa identitas... ~o humana ex ratione vidit* VR 32.1.

eruditus ~i, *m.* A learned person: *a regula ~is in mundo nec ignota* AC 7270.4; SS 28.

erumpo ~mpere ~pi, *intr.* (fut. pple. *~pturus*) To emerge violently, break out: *subito tunc vir e sinistro caetu ~pit* VR 137.12; *non potui amplius retinere risum quin ~mperet* VR 80.4; *ut primum aliquid copiae datur, ~mpit inde effectus* AC 8209.1; (w. *in* + acc.) *si dissidentiae mentium illorum in apertas inimiticias ... ~mperent* AM 286.

eruo ~ere ~i ~tum, *tr.* To pull out: *si oculus dexter scandalizaverit te, ~e eum* Matt. 5.29 (AE 152.12).

eruptio ~onis, *f.* The action of breaking out: AM 521.3.

esca ~ae, *f.* The food (of an animal): *omne viride herbae in ~am* Gen. 1.30 (AC); CI 479.5.

esculentum ~i, *neut.* A substance fit for eating, food: *de...aliquo ~o* AM 478.1; ES 939.

esio ~onis, *f.* The act of eating: *~o Paschatis* 2AD 2183.

esse, *indecl. neut.* (inf. of **sum**) Being (in its most general sense), existence: *Dominus dat omne posse et omne esse in adoratione* AC 1150; *Esse est universalius quam Essentia* VR 18.

essentia ~ae, *f.* **1** The quality which makes anything be what it is, essence: *charitas et fides faciunt* *unum sicut ~a et forma* FI 18.2; *ipsissimum essentiale, ex quo sunt omnes ~ae rerum in utroque mundo* AC 8200.2; *~a Divina et Natura Humana* DD 35.1. **b** *in sua ~a*, in essence, essentially: SS 4. **2** An essential oil, essence: *sensus spiritualis comparari potest nutritione ejus* [sc. *arboris*] *ex variis succis et ~is* SS(P) 53 (= 19.5).

essentialis ~is ~e, *a.* (superl. *~issimus*) (app. used only in neut. as sb.) The essential part or component: *quae* [sc. *flamma*] *est ~e caloris et lucis* AC 365; *quod amor in Dominum et charitas erga proximum sint principalia et ~ia Ecclesiae* AC 7233.3; *~issimum cultus est agnitio quod Dominus sit solus Deus* AC 7550.

essentialiter, *adv.* Essentially: *amor et sapientia, quae ~er faciunt hominis vitam* VR 35.10.

esuries ~ei, *f.* A state of ravenous hunger, starvation: *in egestate et in ~e solitarius* Job 30.3 (AC 2682.1).

esurio ~rire ~rivi, *intr.* (*tr.*) To feel hunger, be hungry: *quod mater potius famem patiatur quam ut videat infantem ~rire* AC 548.3; AM 182.3; (w. inf.) *omnes spiritus quasi ~riunt et sitiunt scire* ES 1055; (w. acc.) *sitiunt et ~riunt bona et vera* ES(M) 4583.

esuritio ~onis, *f.* The fact of being hungry, hungering: *~o et sitis spiritualis* AE 480.

esus ~us, *m.* The act of eating: *cogitavi in platea de ~u, seu quid ederem* ES 4295; VR 48.2.

et, *conj.* **1** (to correlate two or more items) And: *calor et lux* AS 5; *conceptio primae et purissimae formae* AS 6; *quando homo scit, intelligit et sapit* DP 151; *et quia homo vult quod amat, et cogitat quod intelligit, ideo omnia voluntatis se referunt ad amorem, et omnia intellectus ad sapientiam; et quia haec duo non dari possunt...nisi...* DP 157.5. **b** *et...et*, both...and: *quia cor...regit et corpus et caput* AM 315.7. **2** (to correlate alternatives) Or: *bis et ter* AC 1884; *qui interius magis et minus recipiunt Divinum* CI 21. **3** Also: *quod etiam patet ex cujusvis inclinatione, ut et forma* CI 368. **4** And also: *quod nemo possit videre Deum et vivere* VR 6.1; (w. *non*) *subjugare Indos, et non transferre illuc milites per naves* VR 84.

etc., abbreviation for *et caetera*: ES 2742; ES(M) 4589.

etenim, *conj.* (as second word in clause) For, since: *nec permittuntur* [*tentationes*] *ut olim, quia homo non in veritate fidei est, sic ~im succumberet* AC 762.

ethicus ~a ~um, *a.* (Gk.) Concerned with morals, ethic: *scientiae...ut...~a* AM 163.

ethnicus ~i, *m.* (Gk.) A heathen: *quod pejor ~o sit* AC 1076.2; *loquutus cum gentibus qui fuerunt ~i* ES 4330.

etiam, *particle.* **1** As well, also: *quod cum de intellectualibus, ~m de voluntariis agatur* AC 1190. **2** Even: *dracones et viperae ~m suam progeniem ament* VR 44. **3** Even so, yes: *erit sermo vester, ~m ~m, non non* Matt. 5.37 (AC 202).

etiamsi, *conj.* Even if: *quod usque non credituri essent... ~si ipsi visuri* CI 456.3.

etsi, *conj.* Even if: *qui credit in Me, ~i moritur, vivet* John 11.21 (AC 10817).

etymologia ~ae, *f.* (Gk.) Etymology: *non quaesivimus de ~a vocis conscientiae, sed de conscientia* VR 665.2.

Eucharistia ~ae, *f.* (Gk.) The Eucharist: VR 111.11.

eucharisticus ~a ~um, *a.* Of thanksgiving, eucharistic: *holocausta et sacrificia ~a* Num. 10.10 (AE 55.2); (neut. as sb.) the Eucharist: *cum receperunt ~um* UJ(P) 216.

euge, *interj.* (Gk.) Well done, good!: *~e bone serve* Luke 19.12 (AC 5291.5); *dixit Tyrus super Hierosolymam, ~e fracta est,...traducta est ad me* Ezek. 36.2 (AE 208.11).

eum: acc. of **is**.

eunuchus ~i, *m.* (Gk.) A eunuch: Matt. 19.12 (AC 394); AM 138; a castrated singer, castrato: *Itali ~i* AM 156.2.

Europaeus ~a ~um, *a.* also **Europeus**. Of Europe, European: *in toto ~o orbe* VR 159.3; *spiritus quidam ~i* AC 8383.

Europeanus ~a ~um, *a.* = **Europaeus**: ES 453.

Europeus: see **Europaeus**.

Eurus ~i, *m.* The east wind: Hos. 12.1 (SS 79.5).

Eustachianus ~a ~um, *a.* (anat.) *Tuba ~a*, the Eustachian or pharyngo-tympanic tube: AC 1118; ES 3322.

Euxinus ~a ~um, *a.* (Gk.) *Pontus ~us*, the Black Sea: CO 39.

evacuatorius ~a ~um, *a.* Of or for voiding, evacuant: (neut. pl. as sb.) *purificatoria et ~a* AC 9572.

evacuo ~are ~avi ~atum, *tr.* **1** To make empty: *~abitur terra* Isa. 24.3 (AE 223.6); *~atur omne interstitium* VR 110.7. **2** To void, empty out (waste products): *qui renum provinciam constituunt, quia sera immundiora ~ant* ES 992. **3** To unsheathe, draw (a sword): *per evaginatum seu ~atum gladium* AC 8294.

evado ~dere ~si, *intr.* **1** (w. pred.) To become by a process of change, turn into: *quod...ei...dolorificum ~dat* AC 543; *membranae omnes ~dunt perfectiores* ES 1741. **2** (w. *in* + acc.) To change (into), end up (as): *cogitationes...in repraesentationes obscenas ~dunt* AC 829.1; AM 374. **3** To escape: *ut urbs non ~dat* Jer. 48.8 (AE 223.8).

evagino ~are ~avi ~atum, *tr*. To unsheathe, draw (a sword): *gladium ~abo post illos* Ezek. 12.14 (AC 8294).

evagor ~ari ~atus sum, *intr*. To wander away: *~ati sunt, abiverunt* Jer. 9.10 (AC 776.3).

evanesco ~nescere ~nui, *intr.* (fut. pple. *~niturus*) To disappear, vanish: *haec lux coram oculis nostris illico ~nuit* VR 35.3; *omnia interna successu temporis ~nescunt* AC 7996.

evangelicus ~a ~um, *a*. Evangelical: *omnes Protestantes, sive dicantur ~i sive Reformati* VR 154.2.

Evangelista ~ae, *m*. Any of the writers of the Gospels, Evangelist: DD 2.1.

Evangelium ~i, *neut.* (Gk.) The Good News of Christ's coming, the Gospel: *ut ~um e novo ibi praedicarent* VR 4.1.

evangelizatio ~onis, *f.* The preaching of the Gospel: AE 418.5.

evangelizatrix ~icis, *f.* She who preaches the Good News: *~ix Zion* Isa. 40.9 (AC 795.4).

evangelizo ~are ~avi ~atum, *intr.*, *tr*. **1** (intr.) To bring good news: *en super montibus pedes ~antis* Nahum 1.15 (AC 7093.5); *ad docendum et ~andum de Domino* AE 100.2. **2** (tr.) To bring good news of, proclaim, preach: *abhinc regnum Dei ~atur* Luke 16.16 (DD 9).

evanidus ~a ~um, *a*. Disappearing, fading from sight: *hic amor assimilari potest chrystallo nigricanti, qui suffocat lucem et non variegat illam in colores nisi pullos et ~os* VR 404.2.

evaporatio ~onis, *f.* An evaporated substance, vapour: *~o spiritualis e singulis vitae* AC 6571.2; AS 313.

evasio ~onis, *f.* **1** The act of escaping: *ne sit illi ~o* Jer. 50.29 (AE 357.16). **2** That which escapes, the remnant: *comedet* [*locusta*] *residuum ~onis relictae vobis a grandine* Exod. 10.5 (AC).

evasor ~oris, *m*. One who escapes, survivor: *mittam ex illis ~ores ad gentes* Isa. 66.19 (AC 1151.7).

eveho ~here ~xi ~ctum, *tr*. **1** To transport away, carry (persons): *in coelum ~cti sunt* CI 54. **2** To advance to higher states, exalt, promote: *ut gentem illam ~heret super omnes in universo* AC 6963.2; VR 57. **3** To excite, carry away: *spiritum tuum in hunc gradum vesaniae ~xeras* AM 264.2.

evello ~ere evulsi evulsum, *tr*. To tear out, pull away: *crania ~unt* ES 593; (transf.) *si idea aeterni ~eretur* AM 216.1.

evenio ~nire ~ni ~ntum, *intr*. To come about, happen: *quia praedictum hoc tempus...vident non ~nire nec instare* AC 1850.1; (w. dat.) *mala quae malis ~niunt* AC 8227.1.

eventus ~us, *m*. An outcome, result: *certitudo de ~u praecedit victoriam* AC 1820.1.

eversio ~onis, *f.* The act of overturning: *per ~onem collium* AE 405.43.

eversor ~oris, *m*. One who overturns: *si fures venerint tibi, si ~ores noctu* Obad. 5 (AE 193.6).

everto ~tere ~ti ~sum, *tr*. To overturn, overthrow: *ut...altaria ~terent* Exod. 34.13 (SS 101.1); *si aliquid ibi resistit...dejiciunt et ~tunt solum per nisum voluntatis* CI 229.

evestigo ~are ~avi ~atum, *tr*. To track down: *illi qui ~aret secretum mox proponendum* AM 103.3.

evibratio ~onis, *f.* A projection (of light): *~ones lucis in formas imaginum* AM 231.2; *a...lucis ~one quae emicat* AC 4407.

evibro ~are ~avi ~atum, *tr*. To project, cast (light): *luces in parietes... ~atae sistebant imagines picturatas avium* AM 231.2; ES 3646.

evictio ~onis, *f.* A conclusive proof: *manifesta confirmatio seu ~o datur* AM 212; AM 485.2.

evidens ~ntis, *a*. (compar. *~ntior*) Clearly apprehensible, evident, manifest: *ut haec res ~ntior fiat* AC 10603.3; *~ns...est quod...* DD 53.1.

evidenter, *adv*. (compar. *~ius*, superl. *~issime*) Manifestly, evidently: *ex his paucis ~er videri potest quod...* SS 16; *infinitas Dei adhuc ~ius mihi constitit* VR 32.6; ES 3535.

evidentia ~ae, *f.* The state of being evident: *ut in ~a videri potest* AM 518; *haec in ~am sistentur* CO 8.

evigilatio ~onis, *f.* An awakening: (fig.) VR 160.7.

evigilo ~are ~avi ~atum, *tr*. To awake from sleep, rouse: *~atus e somno* VR 77.1; (fig.) *tunc memoria naturalis sopitur et ~antur in memoriam interiorem* CI 467.

evigoro ~are ~avi ~atum, *tr*. To endow with strength, strengthen, invigorate: *quod sapientia...vitam intellectualem... ~et* AM 433.

evilesco ~ere, *intr*. To become utterly worthless: *~et laus Moabi* Isa. 16.14 (AC 2468.8).

evinco ~ncere ~ci ~ctum, *tr*. **1** To overcome completely, master: *mala contra quae pugnavit et quae ~cit* AC 1444.1. **2** To prove convincingly: *volui pluribus ~ncere quod non ita sit* CI 246.3; *ad ~ncendum quales sunt* ES 326; (impers. pass.) *in hoc capite ~ctum est quod...* VR 101. **3** (pass.) To be convinced: *priusquam ipse scit ac interius ~ctus est quod in malo sit* AC 7795.2.

evitabilis ~is ~e, *a.* That may be avoided, avoidable: *lethum non ~e inducit* VR 524.1.

evitatio ~onis, *f.* An avoiding: *~ones infamiae* AM 271.

evito ~are ~avi ~atum, *tr.* To avoid: *illi qui ~ant actualia mala* VR 535; (w. *quin*) *ut nusquam aliquis homo...possit ~are quin...captivatus sit* ES 4479.

evocatio ~onis, *f.* A summoning up or calling forth: *per ~onem mortuorum quos cognoverant* VR 500; (transf.) *absque ~one illorum ex memoria* AC 10295; *absque libero nusquam aliqua productio veri in naturali homine, nec ~o inde in rationalem* AC 3145; *datum est percipere ipsum influxum, ~onem verorum quae apud me, applicationem ad objecta orationis* AC 10299.3.

evoco ~are ~avi ~atum, *tr.* To summon out, call forth: *ne adeamus illos, sed ~emus e caetu unum* AM 233.2; *angelus spiritualis ~at spirituale* SS 65.

evolo ~are ~avi ~atum, *tr.* To fly out or away: *sicut palea in vento quae... ~at* AC 6631; *examen... ~at ad investigandum sibi domicilium* VR 12.7.

evolutio ~onis, *f.* **1** The act of unrolling, unfolding: *~o illa a facie* CI 450. **2** Emergence, evolution: *~o et exsertio graduum in potentiam* AS 220. **3** The act of explaining, exposition: *~o [sensuum spiritualis et caelestis] est instantanea* SS 63.

evolvo ~vere ~vi ~utum, *tr.* **1** To unroll, unfold, roll back: *~vere tunicam oculi...versus septum nasi* AC 183; (a scroll or book in roll form) *tenens...membranam quam ~vebat* AM 43; Luke 4.17 (DD 11). **2** (refl.) To emerge by rolling, roll out: *sic tandem se ~vunt iis sepulchris* AC 938; (fig.) *ex his duabus ideis mentes nostrae nondum se potuerant ~vere* VR 76.1. **3** To make known by exposition, explain: *arcana...quae nunc ventilarent et ~verent* VR 48.2; *paradoxon erat, sed ~utum per id quod...* ES 226.

evomitio ~onis, *f.* A vomiting forth: *tepidum... causatur ~onem* AE 235.1.

evomo ~ere ~ui ~itum, *tr.* To vomit forth, spew out: *infantem qui lac ore ~ebat* AC 546; (absol.) *habebat effectum in ventriculum ut ~erem* AC 814.1.

evulgatio ~onis, *f.* The act of making public: *declarationem et ~onem amoris illarum* AM 167.2.

evulgo ~are ~avi ~atum, *tr.* To make public, publish: *silere et sic non ~are mentis suae cogitata* VR 111.1.

evulsio ~onis, *f.* A tearing out: *sicut ~o interiorum quae mentis meae* CI 449.3.

ex[1], *prep. w. abl.* also **e** (but not before vowels or h). **1** (to denote motion or extension) Out of, from: *quod ex seminulo jacto in terram exeat radix* AS 351; *telum ex arcu emissum* DP 202.3; *petras e loco movere* ES 282. **2** (to denote position) *E longinquo*, a long way off: Exod. 2.4 (AC); *e diametro*, diametrically: *scortatio e diametro est opposita vitae amoris conjugialis* AM 468; *ex opposito*, in the opposite position or manner: AM 530.2. **3** (to denote membership of a group or class) From among, of: *multi ex illis* AS 432; *potentiores ex diabolis* DD 185; *illi qui e nova Ipsius Ecclesia erunt* VR 154.6. **4** (to denote composition) Composed of, made of: *vincula sicut ex molli lana* DP 296.3; *[caelum] ex myriadibus myriadum angelorum consistit* DD 19. **b** *ex aequo*, in equal amounts, equally: *ubi calor ex aequo unitus est luci* AM 137.4. **5** (to denote change) Out of (a state or condition), from: *gentes e captivitate sua solvendae* ES 214; *somnium...e quo...expergefactus* ES 228. **6** (to denote substitution) In substitution for, instead of: *ex mollibus [vincula] fiunt dura* DP 296.3; cf. *eque tenebris oculi caecorum videbunt* Isa. 29.18 (DD 4). **7** (to denote distance from a point in time) From: *ex nativitate* DP 210.2. **b** *e novo*, anew, again: *illos qui e novo creantur* AC 1022; *ut evangelium e novo ibi praedicarent* VR 4.1. **8** (to denote source or origin) Arising from: *calor et lux...existunt ex sole mundi* AC 7083; *illa...quae trahunt a materiali, eque tempore et spatio* CI 464; *quod [Dominus] filius Mariae ex Josepho fuerit* VR 94; *Pen ex quo Pensilvania* ES 3814. **b** by inference from: *ex his patet...* AM 461.6; *exque ipsis locis...cognosci potest* AC 7111.2. **9** (to denote motivation) Under the influence of, moved by: *ut ex laeto animo colant Dominum* AC 7093.1; *ex libero*, of one's own free will, freely: DP 200; *ex lubitu*, at will: AM 513; *ex professo*, deliberately: AM 187; *ex spontaneo*, spontaneously: AM 500.4. **b** *ex se*, of one's own motion, by oneself: *apparet sicut corpus agat ex se* AS 25. **10** (to denote causation) As a result of: *aliter facere nequeunt ex continuo usu* AC 7074; (w. participial phr.) *separantur paleae a tritico ex ventilabro agitato* VR 26.

ex.[2] Abbreviation of *exempli* (see **exemplum**): ES 4140.

exacerbatio ~onis, *f.* The process of making angry, exasperation: AM 361.2.

exacerbo ~are ~avi ~atum, *tr.* To make angry, irritate, exasperate: *cum amor impugnatur, tunc se ~at* AM 360; *audi vocem ejus, ne ~es eum* Exod. 23.21 (AC).

exacte, *adv.* (superl. *~issime*) Precisely, exactly: *cujus auris in harmonico...est, ~e animadvertit disharmonicum* VR 61; ES 297.

exactio ~onis, *f.* Enforcement: *~onem sustinuit et afflictus est* Isa. 53.7 (AE 314.9).

exactitudo ~inis, *f.* The fact of being exact, precision: *hoc fit ~ine sicut ad libram* AC 6663.1.

exactor ~oris, *m*. A person in charge, ruler, overseer: *praecepit Pharao... ~oribus in populo* Exod. 5.6 (AC); Isa. 60.17 (AC 643.1).

exactus ~a ~um, *a*. **1** (of time) Past, over: *post ~um tempus* AM 229; AE 413.1; *~a nocte* CI 289. **2** Accurate, exact: *libratio...praecisa et ~a* ES 193.

exacuo ~ere ~i ~tum, *tr*. To sharpen: *gladius ~tus* Ezek. 21.9 (AC 309); (transf.) *exacerbatur cor meum, et renibus meis ~o me* Ps. 73.21 (AE 167.4).

exaequo ~are ~avi ~atum, *tr*. To make equal, measure: *quis...coelos spithama ~avit?* Isa. 40.12 (AE 373.4).

exaestuo ~are ~avi ~atum, *tr*. To cause to boil or be in ferment, excite violently: *si uxor...captat animum viri... ~ando usque dum impos judicii evadit* AM 488.

exaggeratio ~onis, *f*. A heaping up of words: *alioquin foret unius rei repetitio, seu ~o inanis* AC 1860.3.

exaggero ~are ~avi ~atum, *tr*. To heap up, pile up: *immundi spiritus...excitant mala et falsa...et ~ant usque ad desperationem* AC 5246.2.

exagito ~are ~avi ~atum, *tr*. To disturb continually, harass: *a phantasiis... ~antur* CI 354.

exaltatio ~onis, *f*. **1** The act of raising, lifting: *per... ~onem ejus in lucem superiorem* AM 57. **2** The act of praising, exaltation: *laetitia cordis cum ~one Domini est quae intelligitur per glorificationem* AC 8261.5. **3** A state of high excitement, exaltation: *ne credatis, quod haec...sint solum verba ~onis* VR 137.6.

exalto ~are ~avi ~atum, *tr*. **1** To raise, lift up: *si ~atus fuero e terra* John 12.32 (AC 7093.6). **2** To raise in power or status, exalt: *Messiam qui illos super omnes gentes in universo mundo ~aret* SS 23.4; to ascribe power to, exalt: *cum dicitur de homine quod ~abit Jehovam* AC 8271. **3** To raise to a higher plane: [*homo*] *recipit scientias et ~at illas in intelligentiam* VR 48.14; *quod percipiant* [*angeli*] *delitias illas apud se ~ari et impleri* AM 144.

examen ~inis, *neut*. **1** A swarm (of bees): *~en se primum colligit in turmam* VR 12.7. **2** A trial, test: *ex scrutinio et ~ine illorum perspici potest* VR 46; *lis illa in ~en missa est* FI 70.

examinator ~oris, *m*. One who tries or tests, examiner: ES 924.

examino ~are ~avi ~atum, *tr*. To put to the trial, test: *quod ~andi* [*peregrini*], *unde illi, et quid negotii hic* AM 77.3.

exanclo: see **exantlo**.

exanimis ~is ~e, *a*. Dead, lifeless, inanimate: *ex loquela illorum vix aliquid vitale percepi; loquuti sicut adigerent statuas ~es* [*inanimes* Tafel] *loqui* UJ(P) 191 (Rogers); ES 3551.

exanimo ~are ~avi ~atum, *tr*. To cause to lose consciousness, make faint: *jucundum conjugii...paene ~abat illos* AM 500.7; (transf.) to deprive of life: *loquelam ~are, et illam facere instar simulachri* AC 7745.

exanimus ~a ~um, *a*. Lifeless: *simile obscurum ~um osseum* ES 3853.

exantlo ~are ~avi ~atum, *tr*. also **exanclo**. **1** To draw out (fluid): *quasi aliquid ~aretur ex puteo* ES 913; to pump out (air): *sicut ~atur aër* VR 28. **2** To exhaust, use up: *quod...amor...decerpatur, ~etur et exinaniatur* AM 466.2. **3** To perform laboriously: *post ~atum laborem* CI 108.2.

exardeo ~dere ~si, *intr*. To be passionately angry, blaze: *~dere* [*significat*] *destructionem per mala* AE 863.6.

exardesco ~descere ~si, *intr*. (of emotions) To become violent, blaze up: *super pastores ~sit ira Mea* Zech. 10.3 (FI 68); *ignis...in quem ~descit amor...polygamicus* AM 370.

exarefacio ~facere ~feci ~factum, *tr*. To make completely dry, dry up: *aliud* [*semen*]*... ~factum est* VI 90 (Matt. 13.6, etc.).

exarescentia ~ae, *f*. The fact or condition of drying up: *quod siccitas et ~a sit ubi non verum* AE 131.4.

exaresco ~rescere ~rui, *intr*. **1** (of liquids) To dry up: *fluvius exsiccabitur et ~rescet* Isa. 19.5 (AC 28). **2** (of plants) To die from lack of moisture, wither: *vitis ~ruit et ficus languet* Joel 1.12 (AC 8369.2).

exaro ~are ~avi ~atum, *tr*. **1** To plough up: *desertum illud potest ~ari et excoli in arva* VR 531. **2** To cover (with writing): *chartula ~ata literis Hebraicis* SS 90; CI 258. **3** To record in visible form, write, draw: *secunda aetas ~averit suas scripturas super membranis* AM 77.6; *formae...quae...non aliqua arte ~ari, nec voce describi possunt* AM 14.2; *ea quae typo ~ata* [i.e., printed] ES 3262.

exaspero ~are ~avi ~atum, *tr*. **1** To make sharp or intense, whet: *libido... ~atur ex dissensu* AM 511. **2** To make angry, annoy: *quod quia detectum erat, ~ati sunt* ES 5886.

exaudio ~dire ~divi ~ditum, *tr*. To listen attentively to, hearken to: *Ego Jehovah ~diam illos* Isa. 41.17 (AE 118.3); *omnis...homo...qui non credit in Dominum posthac nec ~ditur* VR 108.

excaeco ~are ~avi ~atum, *tr*. To take away the sight from, blind: *~avit oculos* John 12.40 (CI 456.4).

excandescentia ~ae, *f*. Passionate anger, wrath:

quod ~a, ira et vindicta Deo sit AE 250.1; *cum in statu ~ae super id esset* CI 385; VR 146.

excandesco ~descere ~dui, *intr.* (of anger) To become intense, blaze: *~descet ira Mea* Deut. 31.17 (AE 412.18); (of persons) to become intensely angry: *~descit turba, fit brevi tumultus* AM 79.8.

excarnifico ~are ~avi ~atum, *tr.* To torment, torture: *quod...velint socios...mactare, securi dividere, ~are, cruciare* ES 377.

excavatio ~onis, *f.* The fact of being hollowed out: VR 160.8.

excavo ~are ~avi ~atum, *tr.* **1** To make hollow, hollow out: *possunt pedibus ~are solum* AM 232.2; *occipitia... ~ata* VR 160.7. **2** To remove by hollowing out, dig out: *interiores hominis substantiae ~arentur* ES 1582.

excedo ~dere ~ssi, *tr., intr.* **1** (intr.) To go away, depart: *qui e mundo ~dit* CI 330. **b** *vita ~dere*, to die: ES 386. **2** (tr.) To go beyond, surpass, exceed: *quae lux multum ~dit lucem mundi* AC 6832.2; *homines ...numerum illarum* [sc. *animarum*] *~sserunt* VR 79.6. **3** (intr) To be excessive: *si praesentia [Domini] ~dit, fit angustia* AE 80; *quod excedit* 'which is more than usual' ES 621; ES 1908; ES 3510.

excellens ~ntis, *a.* (compar. *~ntior*, superl. *~ntissimus*) Of high quality, superior, excellent: *utcunque sublimis et ~ns apparet [stylus]* SS 3.1; *gaudia caeli, et ~ntiora quam usquam cogitare potuistis* AM 16.2.

excellentia ~ae, *f.* High quality, superiority, excellence: *amor qui omnes alios amores ~a et amaenitate superscandit* AM 333.1.

excello ~ere ~ui, *intr.* To be superior, excel: *patet quantum ~et homo* CI 576.

excelsum ~i, *neut.* A high place, height: *ascendam supra ~a nubis* Isa. 14.14 (AC 7375); (esp. as a place of worship) *ritus sacrificandi super montibus et exstruendi ~a* AC 796.

excelsus ~a ~um, *a.* (superl. *~issimus*) **1** High, lofty: *per ~am portam* AM 8.1; *manu ~a* 'with their hand raised aloft' Exod. 14.8 (AC). **2** (Bibl., as epithet of God): *sic dixit Altus et ~us habitans in aeternum* Isa. 57.15 (AC 795.5); Ps. 78.35 (DD 34.2).

excentricum ~i, *neut.* Eccentricity: *~um ejus* [sc. *telluris*] *in polis* VR 32.1.

excerno ~ere excrevi excretum, *tr.* To excrete: *processus mammillares... ~unt eam* [sc. *pituitam*] *in nares* ES 939.

excerpo ~ere ~si ~tum, *tr.* **1** To pluck out: *aves ...foliola ~entes rosis* VR 78.1; *sol... ~sit ex se flammulas lucentes* VR 79.3. **2** To extract (from a book), excerpt: *quum ~erem quae continentur Es.xxxiv de vastatione* ES 189.

excessus ~us, *m.* A going out, departure: *post ~um ...e corpore* AC 1769.1; *post ~um...e mundo* CI 354.

excidium ~i, *neut.* Destruction, ruin: *~um a septentrione venit* Jer. 46.20 (AC 8002.5).

excido[1] ~ere ~i, *intr.* **1** To fall out or away, slip: *plura adhuc observata sunt, quae ~erunt memoria* ES 152; *~it ex statu integritatis* AM 135.3. **2** (w. abl.) To be deprived (of), fall short (in): *quod Deus Pater ~erit gratia erga genus humanum* VR 161.1.

excido[2] ~dere ~di ~sum, *tr.* To cut out: *Jehovah ~det implexa sylvae ferro* Isa. 10.34 (SS 15); to cut off: *~sus est e terra viventium* Isa. 53.8 (DD 15.1).

excio ~cire ~civi ~citum, *tr.* To stir up, arouse: *quae... non ex sensibili revocatione ex memoria ~ciuntur* AC 7398.

excipio ~cipere ~cepi ~ceptum, *tr.* (*intr.*) **1** To receive, accept, take over: *jucundum auditus et jucundum visus...modo ~cipiunt illa quae inservitura sunt pro usibus* AC 7038.2. **2** To make welcome, receive (guests): *quisquis non ~ceperit vos* Matt. 10.14 (AC 7418.2); *spiritus... ~cipitur a spiritibus bonis* CI 450. **3** To leave out of account, except: *genus humanum nullo ~cepto salvavisset* VR 58.2; ES(M) 4630. **4** (intr.) To come next in order, succeed: *post has ~cipiebant arbores olei* AM 13.2; (esp. in speaking) to take up the tale: *meridionales ~ceperunt, et ediderunt suum effatum* VR 48.12.

excisio ~onis, *f.* **1** A cutting off, destruction: *inundatio grandinis, procella ~onis* Isa. 28.2 (AC 739.3); *vastatio...et desolatio...tum consummatio et ~o* AC 411. **2** The point at which a thing is cut off, base, root: *ad ~ones montium descendi* Jonah 2.6 (AC 1691.5).

excisor ~oris, *m.* One who cuts out or off: *cum securibus venerunt, sicut ~ores lignorum* Jer. 46.22 (AR 847).

excitamentum ~i, *neut.* That which arouses or excites: *secundum affectionem sciendi connatam, et per varia ~a auctam* FI 26.

excitatio ~onis, *f.* The act of exciting, arousal: *vitae ~o* DD 48.1; a state of excitation: *quod uxores in nulla ~one sint sicut viri* AM 219.

excitator ~oris, *m.* One who excites or arouses: *cessat ~or a subigendo massam ejus* Hos. 7.4 (AC 7356.2).

excitatorius ~a ~um, *a.* Serving to excite: *plura*

alia quae sunt ~a habilitatum in pueris latentium AM 17.4.

excitatrix ~icis, *f. adj.* Exciting, arousing: *ex turba illa ~ice* ES 5103.

excito ~are ~avi ~atum, *tr.* **1** To render active, arouse, stir up: *quod propheta ~aretur e medio fratrum* Deut. 18.15 (DD 15.3); *~abitur gens contra gentem* Matt. 24.7 (AE 48.2); *qui statim post vitam corporis ~antur* ES 299; *quandoque ~ata est urina apud me* ES 3189. **2** To arouse, stir up, call forth (ideas, emotions, etc.): *spiritus...intrant in...memoriam, et ~ant inde sibi convenientia* AC 6811; *mali continue ~abant mala et falsa* AC 8321.1; *hic conatus ~atus a calore* FI 16. **3** *Semen ~are*, to raise up seed, propagate the lineage: *qui primum nati sunt...erant...ejus cujus semen ~abant* AC 4818.2.

exclamatio ~onis, *f.* A loud utterance, cry, shout: *ex hac Ipsius ~one super cruce* VR 126.2; ES 4452.

exclamo ~are ~avi ~atum, *intr., tr.* **1** (intr.) To cry aloud, shout: *~a et jubila, filia Zionis* Isa. 12.6 (DD 40); *quo facto ~avit dicens...* AM 477.4. **2** (tr.) To utter loudly, shout: *Romano-Catholici missas suas latino idiomate ~ant* VR 159.4.

excludo ~dere ~si ~sum, *tr.* **1** To shut out, exclude: *quod ~dant bona charitatis, credendo quod homo absque illis salvetur per fidem* AC 8313.1; *~dunt operationem angelorum* ES 266. **2** To hatch out (eggs or young): *calor qui ~dit ova* DP 292.2; [*aves*] *~dunt pullos* VR 12.5. **3** To devise, think up: *propositiones a cerebro eorum ~sas* ES 1467; *qui...primum ~serunt talem ideam* CI 74.2; (w. *ex*) *contradictoria ex phantasia ~dere* VR 90.1.

exclusio ~onis, *f.* The hatching (from an egg): *cum omni progressione post ~onem usque dum fiat avis* VR 12.3.

exclusivus ~a ~um, *a.* Exclusive, debarring: *nemo...in sensu interno est negativum, ita ~um ab omni alio* AC 5310.

excogitatio ~onis, *f.* Devising, invention: *ad excogitandum ~ones* Exod. 31.5 (AC); AC 9915.2.

excogitator ~oris, *m.* One who devises, inventor: *opere ~oris* Exod. 26.31 (AC); AC 9915.2.

excogito ~are ~avi ~atum, *tr.* To devise, invent, think up: *~ant artes* AM 513; VR 11.2.

excolo ~ere ~ui excultum, *tr.* (compar. of pf. pple. *excultior*) **1** To cultivate, till: *'desertum'...significat parum habitatum et excultum* AC 6828. **2** To improve by training, cultivate: *homo...potest sicut humus ~i* AM 134.1; *timent ~ere intellectuale per scientias* AC 8361. **3** To practise devotedly, develop (a science): *quod scientia correspondentiarum in multis regnis Asiae non modo nota fuerit, sed etiam exculta* SS 21.

excommunico ~are ~avi ~atum, *tr.* To cut off from communion, excommunicate: *quod Deus... ~averit illud* [sc. *genus humanum*] VR 161.2; *quia ~atus ab Ecclesia, ille etiam ~atus est e caelo* VR 14.1.

excoriatio ~onis, *f.* The removal of a layer (of hair), scraping off: *per talem pilorum ~onem* ES 1295.

excorio ~are ~avi ~atum, *tr.* To remove the hair from, scrape: *vapor ex suibus ~atis* AC 939; to excoriate, flay: *prope pollicem pedis, qui nondum erat ~atus* ES 3752.

excors ~rdis, *a.* Disheartened, dejected: *dux...fit exspes et ~rs* CO 59.

excrementicius: see **excrementitius**.

excrementitius ~a ~um, *a.* also **excrementicius**. Of or resembling dung, excrementitious: *in infernum sub natibus, quod est mere ~um* AC 943; (neut. pl. as sb.) CI 488.5.

excrementosus ~a ~um, *a.* Full of excreted matter: *ut humor* [*humus* Tafel] *~us cerebri stagnet* ES 1793.

excrementum ~i, *neut.* Excrement, dung: *quo tegerent ~um suum* Deut. 23.14 (AM 431); *cum ~is bovis* Ezek. 4.15 (DD 15.7).

excrescentia ~ae, *f.* An external growth, excrescence: *similes sunt ~is arborum* ES(M) [4739].

excresco ~scere ~vi ~tum, *intr.* **1** To grow up, mature: *semina a pluvia ~scunt in segetem* VR 347.3. **2** To emerge by growth, grow out: *tumoribus, qui ~scunt extra corpus* ES(M) [4740].

excretio ~onis, *f.* **1** The process of excreting: *media separationis, purificationis, ~onis* DP 296.10. **2** An excreted substance, excretion: *quod secretiones et ~ones sint...a renibus in vesicam* AC 5380.

excretorium ~i, *neut.* An excretory organ: *sunt ...alibi in corpore secretoria et ~a* AC 5386; (transf.) *patet quod cogitatio sit purificatorium et ~um malorum* VR 659.

excubiae ~biarum, *f. pl.* A guard, picket: *quae... muniunt variis modis, etiam per ~bias maleficas* [*maleficorum* J D Odhner] ES 5792.

excudo ~dere ~di ~sum, *tr.* **1** To make by striking, hammer out: (transf.) *ordo...cujus imperfectionem insania rationis ex cupiditate ~dit* VR 52. **2** To print: *e libro...Lipsiae... ~so* VR 137.7.

exculpatio ~onis, *f.* The act of excusing, exculpation: AM 452.3.

exculpo ~are ~avi ~atum, *tr.* To make an excuse for, excuse: *ita possunt naevos suos ~are* AC 6813; *non amplius possunt ~ari apud semet, nec apud alios* AC 7273.1.

excurro ~rere ~ri ~sum, *intr.* **1** To run out: *decimus ~rit ex ordine in medium* VR 160.6; AM 103.1. **2** To extend, run outwards: *quomodo inde ~rant* [*fibrae*] ES 3607. **3** To be excessive: *per integram horam, quod ~rit, repraesentabatur quod transirent Jordanem* ES 2289.

excursio ~onis, *f.* (in military use) A raid, foray: *quod quotannis ~ones fecerint et depraedati gentes* AC 7249.

excursus ~us, *m.* An outburst, incursion, raid: *procellae, nimbi...conspiciuntur, sed usque post eorum ~um...rediguntur ad quietem* ES 418; cf. *in corporis omnia est ~us ejus* [sc. *mentis*] DA 40 (= xiii.[4]).

excusabilis ~is ~e, *a.* Deserving to be excused, excusable: *ob plures causas etiam ~es* 3AD 4499.

excusatio ~onis, *f.* **1** The act of excusing: *propter ~ones naevorum* AM 271. **2** A reason alleged as an excuse: *audivi... ~ones a mulieribus illis* AM 292.3.

excuso ~are ~avi ~atum, *tr.* **1** To make excuses for, excuse: *si quae mala et falsa vident, ea ~ant* AC 1079.1. **2** (refl.) To refuse an invitation, excuse oneself: *quod ~averint se omnes qui vocati* Luke 14.18 (AE 252.2).

excussio ~onis, *f.* A shaking off: *per ~onem illorum* [sc. *vermiculorum*] VR 117.

excutio ~tere ~ssi ~ssum, *tr.* **1** To remove by shaking, shake or cast off: *~tite pulverem pedum vestrorum* Matt. 10.14 (AC 7418.2); *quod Jehovah... ~sserit illos in medium maris* AC 8211.3; to knock out: *si dentem servi sui... ~sserit* Exod. 21.27 (AC); to dispel: *angeli ~sserunt ignorantiam* VR 160.7. **2** To free by shaking, shake free: *~te te a pulvere* Isa. 52.2 (DD 64.4); *dum ex suis jucundis ~titur* AM 358; cf. *~tit manus suas ne sustineant munus* Isa. 33.15 (VI 84.1).

exec- : see also **exsec-**

executio ~onis, *f.* The act of putting into effect, execution: *~o judicii* AC 1320.

exedo ~dere ~di ~sum, *tr.* To eat up, devour: *serpentes qui pectora...mordent et ~dunt* ES 3206; *corpus a vermibus ~sum* VR 160.5.

exemplar ~aris, *neut.* **1** A specimen to be imitated, pattern, exemplar: [*vir ut uxor*] *~ar sunt coelestis hominis* AC 162.1; *vita Domini in mundo fuit ~ar secundum quod victuri homines Ecclesiae* AE 254.2. **2** A copy (of a book): *adhuc ~aria in copia Londini apud typographum reservata sunt* VR 123.1.

exemplum ~i, *neut.* An instance or case used as an illustration, example: *velim etiam rem illustrare ~o* CI 269.3; *ab ~is e Verbo... adducendis* SS 7. **b** *pro ~o*, as an example: *sint...pro ~o, prophetae...* AC 7055.3; AM 233.4; (so, also) *in ~um*: AC 714.

exem(p)tio ~onis, *f.* Removal, taking away: *liberatio seu ~o ab infestationibus* AC 7200.

exem(p)tus ~a ~um: pf. pple. of **eximo**.

exeo exire exivi exitum, *intr.* (pf. act. also *exii*) **1** To go out, depart: *ad dicendum vinctis 'exite'* AC 6854.4; *portae...tenentur clausae pro exituris* AM 5.2; (w. *ab*) *in infernum a quo non amplius exibunt* AC 6657.2; (w. *ex*) *cum exibant ex Aegypto* AC 7093.6. **2** To go forth (in order to take action): *exivit seminans ad seminandum* Matt. 13.3 (VI 2); *circa medium noctis Ego exibo in medium Aegypti* Exod. 11.4 (AC). **3** To grow out, proceed: *quod ex seminulo...exeat radix* VR 12.2. **4** To issue, proceed, go forth: (w. *ex*) *super verbis...exeuntibus ex ore Ipsius* Luke 4.22 (AE 22.2); (w. *ab*) *Divinum Verum exit a Divino Humano Domini* AC 6685. **5** To depart from (one's character and sim.): *quod omnipotentia Divina nequaquam possit a Se exire* VR 56.2.

exequiae ~quiarum, *f. pl.* also **exsequiae**. Funeral rites, obsequies: CI 312.4.

exequor: see **exsequor**.

exerceo ~cere ~cui ~citum, *tr.* **1** To put into effect, practise, use, exercise: *actualiter potentia per baculos ~cetur* AC 7026; *universo...in quo* [*potest Deus*] *illum* [sc. *amorem suum*] *~cere* VR 46; *in illos vindictas ~cent* CI 220; *charitatem, justitiam, castitatem ~cent* VI 108. **2** To perform, undertake (actions): *~cent charitatis opera* AC 989; *postquam militiam spiritualem ~cuerunt* AC 7236.1. **3** To harass, worry: *sic ~citus usque ad indignationem* ES 1559.

exercitatio ~onis, *f.* Exercise: *~ones et palaestrae spirituales* AM 207.6.

exercitium ~i, *neut.* also **exertitium**. The putting into effect, practice, exercise (of qualities, skills, etc.): *quod homo in nullum ~um vitae...nascatur* AC 1050.2; *corpus quod impediit ~um interius ejus facultatum* AC 1853; (pl.) *~a charitatis* AC 6705; *~a pietatis* VI 25.

exercitus ~us, *m.* **1** A large military force, army: *quid ~us valeret contra hostes absque duce...?* VR 10; CI 229. **2** Any large body of individuals, host: *et absoluti sunt coeli et terra, et omnis ~us eorum* Gen. 2.1 (AC); *~us qui in caelo sequebantur Ipsum super equis albis* Rev. 19.14 (AR).

exertitium: see **exercitium**.

exfascio ~are ~avi ~atum, *tr.* To peel off (wrappings): *pupae illae ~abantur* ES 4598; *sicut ordine evolvuntur seu ~antur externa* AC 996.1.

exhalatio ~onis, *f.* An emanation of vapour, exhalation: *quae* [sc. *pestis*] *ex sola aspiratione et ~one inficit* VR 120.2; *~ones ex vita illorum* AC 8146.2.

exhalativus ~a ~um, *a.* Of or produced by exhalations: *loquelam... ~am* ES 2869; ES 4627.1.

exhalo ~are ~avi ~atum, *intr.* (*tr.*) To proceed as an exhalation, emanate: *amor ab illis non modo elucet sed etiam ~at* AC 6872.3; *ex praesentia spirituum... sphaera scortationis nefanda ~at* AE 141.16; (also in pass.) *morbi...ex quibus ~antur effluvia detrimentosa* AM 253.1; CI 384.

exhaurio ~rire ~si ~stum, *tr.* To use up fully, exhaust: *quod forma coelestis talis sit, ut non possit ...usquam ~riri* CI 212; ES 3050.

exhibeo ~bere ~bui ~bitum, *tr.* To present to view, show, exhibit: *ros...qui...speciem pluviae aureae coram visu meo ~bebat* AM 155[a].1; *quaedam sciagraphia ejus in sequente lemmate... ~bebitur* VR 54; (refl.) *ut Deum Hominem...Se ~buerit videndum* VR 90.1.

exhilaratio ~onis, *f.* The act of making joyful: *~ones mentis per colloquia* VR 434.1.

exhilaro ~are ~avi ~atum, *tr.* To make joyful, gladden: *consortia quae angelorum mentes ~ant* AM 5.4.

exhinc, *adv.* **1** From there, thence: *eduxit Jehovah vos ~c* Exod. 13.3. (AC). **b** *~c... ~c*, on one side...on the other side: *et Aharon et Chur sustentabant manus illius, ~c unus et ~c unus* Exod. 17.12 (AC). **2** From that time on, henceforward: *~c nunc erit Filius Hominis sedens a dextris virtutis Dei* Luke 22.69 (AC 1607.1).

exhorreo ~rere ~rui, *tr.* To feel horror at, shudder at: *quod...casta et pudica...fugiant et ~reant* AM 429.

exhorresco ~ere, *intr.* To shudder with fear, be terrified: *~ent cum volare fecero gladium Meum praeter facies eorum* Ezek. 32.10 (AE 131.19).

exhortatio ~onis, *f.* Exhortation, admonition: *~ones et minae nihil prorsus faciunt* AC 7032.2.

exhortor ~ari ~atus sum, *tr.* To admonish, urge, exhort: *ille ~atus est fratres suos* AE 434.9; (used as pass.) *cum...non potuissent se retinere...tametsi ~ati ut desisterent* ES 1183.

exigo ~ere exegi exactum, *tr.* **1** To demand payment of, exact: *~ebant tributa* AC 6852. **2** To spend, pass (time): *exegimus vitam desiderii nostri* AM 5.2; *post aetatem hanc primam exactam* CI 334. **3** To complete, accomplish: *post exactam unitionem* CN De Deo Redemptore viii titulus.

exiguitas ~atis, *f.* Smallness: *e monte ~atis* Ps. 42.6 (AC 1585.3).

exiguus ~a ~um, *a.* (superl. *~issimus*) Small in size or amount: *dividebant se in ~as turmas* AM 326.1; *cum ~a differentia* VR 22.3; *homo est sicut quoddam ~issimum coelum* AC 644.

exilis ~is ~e, *a.* Small in size or quantity, slight, scanty: *apparuit... ~is...incepit tunc...major fieri* ES 4265; *in tam ~i perceptione veri, ut vix in aliqua* SS 107.

exilium ~i, *neut.* also **exsilium**. Banishment from one's native land, exile: *rex eorum in ~um abiit* Jer. 49.3 (AE 237.4); (transf.) *cum charitas in ~um mittitur et exstinguitur* AC 379; VR 23.1.

eximius ~a ~um, *a.* (compar. *~ior*) Remarkable, notable: *erant in ~a a me distantia* DP 312.4.

eximo ~ere exemi exem(p)tum, *tr.* **1** To take out, bring forth: *~itur ex inferno et introducitur in caelum* SS 49.1. **2** To take away, release (from a state): *illi qui ab infestationibus ~untur* AC 8099.2. **3** To exclude from reckoning, leave out of account, exempt: *totum humanum genus nullo exempto* VR 502.

exinanio ~nire ~nivi ~nitum, *tr.* To make empty: *Jehovah evacuans terram et ~niens eam* Isa. 24.1 (AE 304.4); (w. abl.) *amor ~nitus suae vitae essentia* AM 44.4; also, to discharge completely, empty out: *quod usque ad mortem ~niverit animam suam* Isa. 53.12 (VR 104).

exinanitio ~onis, *f.* The state of being emptied, exinanition: *status humiliationis seu ~onis* DD 35.3; VR 104.

exinde, *adv.* As a consequence of this, hence: *constat ex illis quae prius...dicta, tum ~de quod 'maledictus' dicatur* AC 1093.1; *~de patuit* VR 14.4.

exinter, *prep. w. acc.* From among: *ignis exivit e Chesbone, et flamma ~er Sichonem* Jer. 48.45 (AC 2897).

existentia ~ae, *f.* **1** The act or fact of coming into existence: *constat ex significatione 'parere' quod sit ~a* AC 6719; *de ~a naturae a natura* VR 35.9. **2** The fact of existing, existence: *quod homo absque Verbo scire posset ~am Dei* SS 115.1; (as a quality of things) *jucundum usus trahit suam essentiam ex amore et ~am ex sapientia* AM 5.3; (dist. from **existere**) *distinguendum est...inter Existere et ~am, sicut inter prius et posterius* VR 21.

existere, *indecl.* (inf. of **existo**) (as a philosophical term) The result of coming into existence, existing: *quod* *tria illa nominari possint finis, causa et effectus, tum esse, fieri et ~ere* SS 28; *substantiae Ipsius ~ere est Divinum Verum* AM 115.3; VR 21.

existimo ~are ~avi ~atum, *tr.* **1** To think, believe: *ne ~ate quod venerim ad mittendum pacem* Matt. 10.34 (AC 8159.4); *~avi quod esset probus* AC 5187. **2** To hold an opinion of, judge (a person): *hi vocantur egeni...et ita ~antur ab aliis* ES 620.

existo ~ere exstiti, *intr.* also **exsisto**. (fut. pple. *exstiturus*) **1** To come into being, arise, be created or produced: *universum...aspectabile est medium ut ~ant tellures* AC 6698; *quod mala...post creationem exstiterint* VR 53; *ens ex quo omne est, quod in universo est et ~it* VR 9.3. **b** to arise (from a source), spring (from): *omnis lex...ex coelesti et spirituali, ut a suo vero principio, ~it* AC 266; *indicium quod omnia ex amore et sapientia exstiterunt* VR 38.1. **2** (of events) To come about, happen: *si aliquid determinatum ~it* AC 6692.2; *hoc saepissime... ~it, quod quidam e coelo exterminentur* ES 2597. **3** (w. pred.) To turn out to be, become: *precando quod divites ~ant* ES 472; ES 2044.

exitiabilis ~is ~e, *a.* Capable of causing death, deadly: *~e facinus moliti* ES 3680.

exitialis ~is ~e, *a.* Causing death, destructive, deadly: *ab homine quem occiderit...per ~e quoddam a tergo* AC 816.2.

exitium ~i, *neut.* Destruction, disaster, ruin: *nisi praeviderint... ~um suum* AM 292.3; *lata enim est porta et spatiosa via quae ducit ad ~um* Matt. 7.13 (CI 534.3).

exitus ~us, *m.* **1** The act of going out, departure: *per ~um filiorum Israelis ex Aegypto* AC 7844.1; *Paracletum...quem Dominus post ~um Suum misit* VR 85.2. **2** A way out, exit: *illi ~us ac hi introitus ...vocantur portae inferni et coeli* CI 428. **b** *~us aquarum*, a place from which water issues forth, spring, well: *Jehovah ponit fluvios in desertum, et ~us aquarum in siccitatem* Ps. 107.33 (AC 7324.2). **3** Origin, source: *cujus ~us ab antiquo* Mic. 5.2 (DD 6). **4** Final state, result, end: *~us eorum est quod teneantur in... cupidine* AC 951.

exlex ~egis, *a.* Outside the law, outlaw: *vivunt sicut ~eges* VR 382.

Exodus ~i, *f.* (Gk.) The name of the second book of the Pentateuch, Exodus: AC 6703; AM 156ª.3.

exoneratio ~onis, *f.* The act of discharging a burden, easing: *quod ~ones spiritualis hominis fiant in naturalem* NH 48.7.

exonero ~are ~avi ~atum, *tr.* **1** To free from a burden, ease: *difficultates ~andi alvum* ES(M) 4680. **2** To get rid of, discharge, expel (a burden): *quod mala... purificet, et non convenientia amandet, et per ignotas vias ~et* DP 296.8.

exopto ~are ~avi ~atum, *tr.* To desire vehemently, long for: *quod in vita ~averint* ES 1909; ES 2659.

exorcismus ~i, *m.* (Gk.) Exorcism: UJ(P) 212; CO 45.

exordior ~diri ~sus sum, *tr.*, *intr.* To commence, begin: *ut ~diamini beatitudines felicitatis aeternae vestrae* AM 8.1; (w. inf.) *~sus sum respondere* VR 16.2; (w. *ab*) *quod omnis annus ~diatur a vere* VR 762.1.

exordium ~i, *neut.* A beginning, commencement: *inde fit novum ~um vitae* AC 316.

exorior exoriri exortus sum, *intr.* (fut. pple. *exoriturus*) **1** To come into view above the horizon, rise: *lux exorta illis est* Matt. 4.16 (SS 111); (of Jehovah or the Lord) *super te exorietur Jehovah* Isa. 60.2 (AC 31.2); CI 141. **2** To come into being, arise: *pro primo statu exorientis Ecclesiae* AC 7844.5; *postquam exorta sunt* [*mala et falsa*] AM 479.

exornatio ~onis, *f.* Adornment: CO 50.

exorno ~are ~avi ~atum, *tr.* To adorn, decorate: *horum* [sc. *foliorum*] *oras ~atas smaragdis* AM 13.1; *lapides pretiosi, quibus uxores... ~antur* VR 78.2.

exoro ~are ~avi ~atum, *tr.* To move by prayer, prevail upon: *et ~atus illi Jehovah* Gen. 25.21 (AC).

exorsus ~a ~um: pf. pple. of **exordior**.

exortus ~us, *m.* The act of rising: *obtenebrabo solem in ~u suo* Isa. 13.10 (CI 119); the act of coming into being, originating: *de ~u hominum* VR 20.

exosus sum, *tr.* (used only as pf. pass.) To hate, loathe: *quia amaverunt falsa, et exosi sunt vera* CI 488.1; ES 3384; (Bibl.) to be hated: *eritis exosi omnibus propter Nomen Meum* Matt. 10.22. (AE 102.3).

expando ~dere ~si ~sum, *tr.* To make to extend, spread out: *Ego Jehovah... ~dens coelos* Isa. 44.24 (AC 8043.3); *calor...disponit...semina in naturales suas formas, ~dendo et aperiendo* CI 567.3; (parts of the body) *quando ~ditis manus vestras* Isa. 1.15 (VI 30.1); (as a sign of joy) *~dimus vultus facierum nostrarum* VR 159.4; *olor ~sit alas et evolavit* AM 155ª.5.

expansio ~onis, *f.* **1** The act of spreading out: *~o manuum versus coelum* AC 7596; cf. *amor sexus angelicus...est ~o amaenissima omnium mentis* AM 44.3. **2** That which is spread out, an expanse: *byssus ...fuit ~o tua* Ezek. 27.7 (AC 1156).

expansum ~i, *neut.* A large extent, expanse: *laudate Ipsum in ~o roboris Ipsius* Ps. 150.1 (AC 8330.5); esp.

the expanse of heaven, the sky, firmament: *sit ~um in medio aquarum* Gen. 1.6 (AC); *sicut de natura universi...ita sicut de ejus ~o* VR 20.

expavesco ~ere, *intr*. To become afraid: *coepit ~ere et valde angi* Mark 14.33 (AC 1787.2).

expec-: see also **exspec-**.

expectoro ~are ~avi ~atum, *tr*. To bring from the heart, divulge: [*boni*] *nihil plus desiderant quam ~are quicquid sciunt* ES 4154.

expedio ~dire ~divi, *tr*., *intr*. **1** (tr.) To prepare for use, make ready: *Abram... ~divit initiatos suos* Gen. 14.14 (AC). **2** (intr., impers.) It is expedient: (w. inf.) *non ~dit matrimonium contrahere* Matt. 19.10 (AM 276.1); (w. *ut*) *~dit ut principium ejus...lustretur* AM 444[a].

expedite, *adv*. Without impediment, freely: *in... vernacula, quam... ~e et solerter loquuntur* AC 1637; ES 4369 titulus.

expeditus ~a ~um, *a*. Well-prepared, ready: *stylus scribae ~i* Ps. 45.1 (AC 1288.3).

expello ~pellere ~puli ~pulsum, *tr*. To drive out, expel: *gentes...quas filii Israelis ~pulsuri erant* AC 8317; *ut irascantur malo et velint id ~pellere* AC 1580.

expendo ~dere ~di ~sum, *intr*. also **exsp-**. **1** To weigh: Isa. 33.18 (AE 453.11). **2** To weigh in the mind, consider, ponder: *dum illa videt et rite ~dit* VR 12.2; *~dite, et percipietis* AM 44.6; (w. *quod*) *illi nec ~dunt quod in Verbo sit sensus spiritualis* AC 7051.3; (w. indir. qu.) *non ~dit num verum sit* AC 6717.1; VR 4.2.

expergefacio ~facere ~feci ~factum, *tr*. To arouse from sleep, wake up: *quodam mane suavissimus cantus...me ~fecit* AM 155[a].1; CI 506.1.

expergefactio ~onis, *f*. An awakening: *post aliquot vices ~onis* ES 228.

expergiscor ~gisci ~rectus sum, *intr*. To be roused from sleep, wake up: *in media nocte ~rectus e somno* AM 115.1; SS 17.2.

experientalis ~is ~e, *a*. Relating to experience: (neut. as sb.) *nisi ~ia ducant quasi manum hominis* UJ(P) 323.

experientia ~ae, *f*. **1** The act or fact of experiencing, experience: *hoc datum est mihi scire ex multa ~a* FI 3; *ex pluribus et rationis et ~ae documentis concluserunt* AM 220.1; (w. pl.) an experience: *hoc per ~as plures mihi scire datum est* AC 6762. **2** An experiment: *facta ...est ~a in mundo spirituali* DP 294.5.

experimentalis ~is ~e, *a*. Of or concerned with experiment, experimental: CI 353.1.

experimentum ~i, *neut*. An experiment: *de ~is, e quibus causas elicere nequeunt* ES 1967.

experior ~periri ~pertus sum, *intr*. To learn by experience: (w. *quod*) *quod res ita se habeat centies...vidi, et quoque ~pertus sum* AC 7137; *~pertus quod nihil ex me possem* CI 228.

expers ~rtis, *a*. Having no part (of), devoid (of): (w. gen.) *forma...paene vitae ~rs* AC 8250.1; *brachia eorum pendent...sicut ~rtia virium* CI 3; (w. abl.) *considerant eam* [sc. *faciem*] *sicut ~rtem musculis* ES 547; AE 326.11.

expeto ~ere ~ivi ~itum, *tr*. To seek earnestly: *paene omnes id ~unt* CI 400.2.

expiatio ~onis, *f*. The act of expiating, expiation: *absque illa ~one, satisfactione et propitiatione* DD 18.1; AE 316.28.

expiator ~oris, *m*. One who expiates: *ut...fieret ~or, Mediator, Propitiator et Intercessor* VR 135.2.

expiatorius ~a ~um, *a*. Expiatory: *processus ~us* AC 4503.11.

expilatus ~a ~um, *a*. Having the hair removed, shaven: *populus distractus et ~us* Isa. 18.7 (SS 86).

expio ~are ~avi ~atum, *tr*. (*intr*.) **1** To cleanse ceremonially, make ritually clean: *omnis tangens mortuum, et non ~averit se* Num. 19.11 (AE 79). **2** To atone for, expiate (an offence): *nisi violationem grandi mercede ~et* AM 512.1. **3** (intr.) To make expiation, atone: *quod Dominus missus sit...ut ~aret pro genere humano* DD 18.1.

expiro: see **exspiro**.

expiscor ~ari ~atus sum, *tr*. To seek to learn by wiles, angle for: *ad ~andum talia quae familiaria...suo proco sunt* AM 299.

explano ~are ~avi ~atum, *tr*. **1** To make flat or smooth, smooth out: *ita ~at viam per quam Deus descendat* VR 24.2. **2** To render easy to understand, make plain: *illa correspondentia in singulari paragrapho... ~abitur* AM 62.

expleo ~lere ~levi ~letum, *tr*. To have one's fill of, be sated with: *~levimus gaudia nostra, cibi facti sunt nobis insipidi* AM 6.4.

explicabilis ~is ~e, *a*. Capable of being interpreted or explained, explicable: *vox una eademque ad quodcunque tempus ~is est* AC 618; AE 95.

explicate, *adv*. In an unfolded manner: *quae* [*series muscularium fibrarum*] *si evolverentur, et sic ~e et libere agerent* AC 4799.1.

explicatio ~onis, *f*. The process of explaining, exposition: *quod significet multiplicationem...constat absque ~one* AC 1610.1; an exposition, interpretation: *causa quod ~ones...tales sint, est quia...* AE 1.

explicator ~oris, *m.* One who expounds, expositor: *~ores [Apocalypseos] conjecturarunt varia* AR praef.

explico ~are ~ui (*or* ~avi) ~atum, *tr.* To give a detailed account of, expound, interpret: *leges doctrinae in sui favorem vel ~at vel immutat* AC 6705; *postquam Dominus ~uit propheticum Esajae* AE 22.2; *cum ~arem Verbum quoad sensum ejus internum* AC 6929.

explodo ~dere ~si, *intr.* (*tr.*) To express disapproval by clapping: *his dictis adplaudebant qui in sola fide erant, sed ~debant qui in charitate* VR 460.4; (tr.) *quod phrases de bonis operibus...non docendae...sed potius... ~dendae* Book of Concord in SE 12(k).

exploratio ~onis, *f.* The process of investigating, investigation: *visitatio est ~o hominis...qualis est* AE 144.

explorativus ~a ~um, *a.* Concerned with investigation, investigative; (neut. as sb.) an investigation: *significatur ~um num aliquid veri inde conjungi posset* AC 3089.

explorator ~oris, *m.* An investigator: *licet ~ores non inveniunt causas, usque credimus* ES 2432; one who spies out territory, spy: *~ores illius terrae* AE 403.11; AM 79.6.

exploro ~are ~avi ~atum, *tr.* **1** To subject to investigation, examine: *Deus... ~at unumquemque post mortem* VR 74.5; *aurum ~atum igne* Rev. 3.18 (AR). **2** To seek out (facts) by inquiry, inquire into, investigate: *scientificis per quae ~are volunt spiritualia* AC 1151.5; (w. indir. qu.) *~are quomodo cum illis...se habet* AC 6808. **b** *in ~ato esse*, to be established by investigation: AM 397.

explosio ~onis, *f.* An explosion: *effluxit ignis...et facta est ~o cum fragore* AR 566.7.

expolio ~lire ~livi ~litum, *tr.* To make to shine, burnish, polish: *gladius...ut sit ei splendor ~litus est* Ezek. 21.15 (AE 131.5); Jer. 46.4 (AC 1788.6).

expono ~nere ~sui ~situm, *tr.* **1** To render visible, display: *Deum nemo vidit unquam...Filius...Ille ~suit* John 1.18 (AC 6849.5); *quod... ~nant idola eorum in quolibet templo* ES 420. **2** To cast out unprotected, expose: *quod hostes...occisos non sepelirent, sed ~nerent avibus et feris devorandos* AC 908.3; ES 2166. **3** (w. dat.) To make subject (to), render liable (to), expose (to): *sic ~nerer eorum subsannationi* AC 448.2; *corpus... ~neretur aestui* VR 55. **4** To set forth in words, expound: *qui librum hunc propheticum... ~suerunt* AE 1; (w. indir. qu.) *licet adhuc paucis ~nere quid sit* AC 6685.

exporrectio ~onis, *f.* The act of stretching forth: *per ~onem manus dextrae* ES 4900.

exporrigibilis ~is ~e, *a.* Capable of being stretched forth, extensible: *ingluvies cum faucibus, quae ~es sunt* ES 4573.

exporrigo ~rigere ~rexi ~rectum, *tr.* To stretch forth, extend: *~rexi manum* VR 137.12.

exporto ~are ~avi ~atum, *tr.* To carry or take out: *sententiae ~abantur ad clientes* AM 231.3; ES 2206.

expositio ~onis, *f.* An exposition: *in ~one articuli* AM 149.

expostulatio ~onis, *f.* The act of demanding, insistence (upon): *proterva ~o debiti conjugialis* AM 472.

expostulo ~are ~avi ~atum, *tr.* To ask for insistently, demand: *quod...non voluerit supplicando rogare Ipsum de ope, sed quod ~averit* AC 8588.2.

expresse, *adv.* (compar. *~ius*) With precision, distinctly: *quod ~e nominata sint* AC 1823.1; *cum tamen prius ~e mandaverit, ut iret* AC 7041.1.

expressibilis ~is ~e, *a.* Capable of being expressed, describable: *quae non adequata erant ideis cogitationis naturalis, ita non ~ia* CI 239.2; ES 591.

expressio ~onis, *f.* A form of words used for a particular purpose, expression: *omnes hae ~ones forent voces vanae* SS 10.

expressivus ~a ~um, *a.* (superl. *~issimus*) Rich in means of expression, expressive: *loquela angelorum ~issima est* ES 4411.

expressus ~a ~um, *a.* (pf. pple. of **exprimo**) Distinctly expressed: *in lingua Hebraea vocales non ~ae sunt* CI 241; (neut. pl. as sb.) expressions, phrases: *in Verbo regni caelestis sunt ~a bona amoris* SS 74.

exprimo ~rimere ~ressi ~ressum, *tr.* **1** To bring forth by pressing, press out: *~rimentes mustum ex uvis* AM 8.2; *teneritudinem...talem ut ~rimeret lachrymas ex oculis meis* AC 7251. **2** To give expression to, make manifest: *per inflatoria [instrumenta] ~rimebantur affectiones boni* AC 8337.2; (esp. of words or language) *constanter illa [vox] adhibetur quae proprie rem de qua, ~rimit* AC 621. **3** To express in words, describe, relate: *vox per quam in lingua originali ~rimuntur promptuaria etiam significat armamentaria* AC 6661.2; *aeternum non alia voce in coelo ~rimi potest* AE 23.2.

expromo ~ere ~(p)si ~(p)tum, *tr.* **1** To bring out of store: *si ~seris famelico animam tuam* Isa. 58.10 (AC 1458.2). **2** To make manifest, disclose, reveal: *ut... tuam meditationem ~as* VR 76.1; AM 2.

expugno ~are ~avi ~atum, *tr.* To take by storm: (fig.) *quod nusquam ~ari possit [forma interiorum]* ES 241 titulus.

expulsio ~onis, *f.* The act of ejecting, expulsion: *~onis [e] sinistra aure* ES 266.

expungo ~gere ~xi ~ctum, *tr.* To wipe out, erase, expunge: *interior...idea...exterminavit et ~xit ideam hanc novam* VR 111.7; VR 4.2.

expuo ~ere ~i ~tum, *tr., intr.* also **exspuo**. (fut. pple. *~turus* AC 934, DP 231.8, VR 437 and *~iturus* DP 18) **1** (tr.) To spit out, spew forth: *~am te ex ore Meo* Rev. 3.16 (VI 71). **2** (intr.) To eject saliva, spit: *~ent in Ipsum* Mark 10.34 (DD 24).

expurgatio ~onis, *f.* **1** A cleansing, purification: *per spiritum ~onis* Isa. 4.4 (AE 329.23). **2** A justification, excuse: *timet...callidas ~ones suae meretricis* AM 469.

expurgatorius ~a ~um, *a.* Of or relating to purification, purificatory: *processus inquisitorius et ~us sanguinis innocentis effusi* AC 9262.3.

expurgo ~are ~avi ~atum, *tr.* To cleanse: *telum ~atum* Isa. 49.2 (AE 357.9); to declare clean: *~antem omnes cibos* Mark 7.19 (AE 622.5).

exquiro ~rere ~sivi ~situm, *tr.* To seek out: *nec ~runt sensum internum* AC vol. iii, praef.1.

exquisite, *adv.* (superl. *~issime*) With fine appreciation, sensitively: *~e attendere ad affectionem* AM 155^a.1; AC 301.

exquisitus ~a ~um, *a.* (pf. pple. of **exquiro**) (compar. *~ior*, superl. *~issimus*) Capable of fine appreciation, sensitive, accurate: *angelis sunt omnes sensus qui homini, imo multo ~iores* CI 170; *quam ~a perceptio angelorum sit* AC 228.

exsanguis ~is ~e, *a.* Lacking circulation, bloodless: *digiti...sicut forent mortui et ~es* ES 3363.

exsatio ~are ~avi ~atum, *tr.* To satiate: *ad comedendum, ad ~andum se* Isa. 23.18 (AC 6917.3).

exscindo ~ndere ~di ~ssum, *tr.* **1** To destroy by cutting, cut down, cut off: *omnis arbor non faciens fructum bonum ~nditur* Matt. 3.10. (AC 1861.10); *praeputia...erant ~ndenda* ES 2113. **2** To remove violently, cut out: *ad ~ndendum ex ea* [sc. *Hierosolyma*] *hominem et bestiam* Ezek. 14.21 (AC 7102.2). **3** To destroy utterly, cut down: *~ndet te gladius* Nahum 3.15 (AC 6669.2); *hostes Jehudae ~ndentur* Isa. 11.13 (SS 15.2).

exscribo ~bere ~psi ~ptum, *tr.* To copy in writing, copy out: *canones ~pti ex tabulis lapideis* AM 77.6; *scientifica quae conscripsit et ~psit* CI 464.5.

exsculpo ~ere ~si ~tum, *tr.* To form by sculpture, carve out: *currus...~tos sicut aquilas* AM 76.2.

exsecrabilis ~is ~e, *a.* also **execr-**. (superl. *~issimus*) Detestable, execrable: *praedestinationis ~e dogma* VR 798.11.

exsecratio ~onis, *f.* also **execr-**. A curse, imprecation: *in intentionibus malis, quae sunt ~ones* VR 297.

exsecror ~ari ~atus sum, *tr.* also **execr-**. To curse: *principem...non ~aberis* Exod. 22.27 (AC).

exsequiae: see **exequiae**.

exsequor ~qui ~cutus (*or* ~quutus) sum, *tr.* also **exequor**. To carry out, execute: *tertia Persona quae decreta... ~quetur* VR 135.2.

exsero ~ere ~ui ~tum, *tr.* To put forth, display, exercise: *si quis [fera] minacem vultum ~it* VR 123.4; *conatur omne suum malum... ~ere* ES 3291; (esp. refl.) to be displayed, emerge, appear: *bona charitatis se ~unt in affectionibus* AC 984; (w. *in* + acc.) *influxus ...se ~it in faciem* ES 3861.

exsertio ~onis, *f.* **1** The act of putting forth, exertion: *~o virium corporis* AE 79. **2** A part put forth, process: *involucrum...per ~ones a se intrat in omnia interiora* DP 180.2.

exserto ~are ~avi ~atum, *tr.* To thrust or put out: *omnes illi qui in speluncis et in petris sunt non audent pedem ex illis efferre, ne quidem digitum ~are* AR 339.1.

exsibilatio ~onis, *f.* A noise made by hissing: *ad audiendum ~ones gregum* Judg. 5.16 (AE 6390).

exsibilo ~are ~avi ~atum, *tr.* To express contempt for by hissing or whistling, hiss at, whistle at: *quis...non illa ut absona et ridicula ~aturus est?* VR 356.

exsiccatio ~onis, *f.* The drying up (of fluids): *usque ad ~onem aquarum de super terra* Gen. 8.7 (AC); *~o et induratio humoris chrystallini* VR 346.1.

exsicco ~are ~avi ~atum, *tr.* To make dry, dry up (fluids): *nonne Tu ~as mare?* Isa. 51.10 (AC 8278.2); (fig.) *obturatur vena et ~atur fons* AM 313.3.

exsilio ~lire ~lui, *intr.* To leap up, jump up: *senex ille excanduit in tantum, ut ~liret solio* VR 161.3.

exsilium: see **exilium**.

exsisto: see **existo**.

exsolvo ~vere ~ui ~utum, *tr.* To release from bonds, untie, free: *funis quo quasi circumligati sunt...et a quo se ~vere nequeunt* CI 479.3; to liberate, set free: *qui...monasteriis inclusi sunt... ~vuntur et emittuntur* AM 54.4.

exspatiatio ~onis, *f.* A walking about: ES 3416.

exspatior ~ari ~atus sum, *intr.* **1** To walk out, stroll: *~ari in paradisos quaquaversum* CI 270.4. **2** To extend, spread out: *cogitatio, quae in universum ~ari potest* ES 4139. **3** To speak or write at length, be prolix: *sed eo usque nondum licet ~ari* AE 8.2.

exspectatio ~onis, *f.* also **expectatio**. **1** The act of waiting for, expectation: *in... ~one Jesu Christi* Rev. 1.9 (AR); *in ~one videndi praesules mensarum* AM 6.2. **2** That which is expected, expectation, hope: *norunt quod illa ~o vana sit* AC 7051.2; *ecce... ~o nostra* Isa. 20.6 (DD 4).

exspecto ~are ~avi ~atum, *tr., intr.* also **exp-**. **1** (tr.) To wait for, expect: *staret sicut inanimatus... ~ans influxum* VI 107; *annon per saecula frustra ~atus est [dies judicii]*? CI 312.3. **2** (intr.) To be in expectation, wait: *ut diu ~are deberem antequam colligerem sensum* AC 8021; *~avi, et ecce post semihoram vidi duas turmas* AM 2.3; (w. *ad*) *~ate ad diem Ultimi Judicii* VR 160.4; (w. *ut*) *quod homo... ~et, ut Deus... peccata abstergat* VR 71.2.

exspendo: see **expendo**.

exspes ~ei, *a.* Devoid of hope, hopeless: *dux...fit ~es et excors* CO 59.

exspiratio ~onis, *f.* **1** The emission of breath, vapour or the like, exspiration, exhalation: *ex ~one halituum e vegetabilibus* VR 470.3; ES 3296. **2** The act of breathing one's last, expiring, death: *ante ~onem* AC 7272.2.

exspiratorium ~i, *neut.* Something breathed out or emitted, an exhalation: *effluviosum seu ~um* AC 10130.2.

exspiro ~are ~avi ~atum, *tr., intr.* also **exp-**. **1** (tr.) To emit, exhale (scents, vapours, etc.): *vas...ex quo aperto ~atur suaveolentum* VR 38.2. **2** (intr.) To breathe one's last, expire, die: *quod homo, dum ~at, dicatur...emittere animam* AM 315.9; VR 28. **3** (intr.) To collapse, fail: *repraesentativa Ecclesia tunc ~avit* ES 3675; (also pass.) *~ata sunt imaginaria nostra gaudia* AM 8.3.

exsplendeo ~dere ~dui, *intr.* To radiate light, shine forth: *elucens et ~dens* AC 9908; *quod... ~dere de montes Paran...significet...coelestia humanae Domini essentiae, ex qua praedicatur quod Jehovah exortus et ~duerit* AC 1675.3.

exsplendescentia ~ae, *f.* The radiation of light, radiance: *'Urim' est ignis lucens, et 'Thumim' ~a in lingua angelica* SS 44.3; AE 268.3.

exsplendesco ~descere ~dui, *intr.* To radiate light, shine forth: *luna ultra modum ~duit* CI 159; AC 6723.3.

exspumo ~are ~avi ~atum, *tr.* To emit like froth, foam with: *Cerberus...ex triplici suo ore ~ans aconita* CO 40.

exspuo: see **expuo**.

exstans ~ntis, *a.* (compar. *~ntior*) Plain to see, evident, obvious: *vidi...cincturam primum tenuem et postea ~ntiorem* VR 112.1; (transf.) *quid ~ntius est, quam quod natura sit omne in omnibus?* VR 77.2.

exstanter, *adv.* (compar. *~ius*, superl. *~issime*) Manifestly, evidently, obviously: *omnia vidi tam ~er, ut nusquam oculis corporis ~ius spectari possint* ES 4437; *quod zelotypia...sit... ~issime apud gallos* AM 378.

exstasis ~eos, *f.* also **ecstasis**. Ecstasy: *in statu somni seu ~eos* ES 2083; ES 2231.

exstaticus ~a ~um, *a.* also **ecstaticus**. Ecstatic: *non eram in quadam idea ~a, sed in corpore* ES 1609; ES 4488.

exstimulo ~are ~avi ~atum, *tr.* To provoke by stimulation, excite: *annon ille amor...quoque per pharmaca potest corroborari et ~ari?* AM 79.10.

exstinctio ~onis, *f.* The act of causing a thing not to exist, annihilation, exstinction: *~onem interioris vitae* AM 361.2; *~o omnis veri* AE 275.3.

exstinguo ~guere ~xi ~ctum, *tr.* also **extinguo**. **1** To extinguish, put out (fire, light, etc.): *lampades nostrae ~guuntur* Matt. 25.8 (SS 17.1); VR 79.5; (fig.) *ne frigus...caloris ejus scortatorii focum ~guat* AM 294.6. **2** To deprive of life, kill, wipe out: *quod homo se ~gueret* AC 592.1; *quando lux frigida est, tunc torpent omnia et jacent ~cta* CI 13. **3** To annihilate, destroy, extinguish: *verum a falso ~ctum* AC 6767.5; *vita...incipit ~gui* AC 6677; *flagrat...ira...et vult nomen Ipsius ~guere* VI 67.

exstirpatio ~onis, *f.* Total removal, extirpation: *per ~onem gentium in terra Canaane* AC 4057.

exstirpo ~are ~avi ~atum, *tr.* **1** To remove totally, root out (a plant or sim.): *si non illa radix ~aretur* VI 93; Matt. 21.19 (VR 106). **2** To remove totally, extirpate (other things): *gentes quae non ~averunt illam ideam* AE 522; *incolae terrae...partim ~ati fuerunt* AC 1205.

exstiti: pf. of **existo**.

exsto ~are, *intr.* **1** To be exposed or exhibited: *ubi esculenta faetida veno ~ant* VR 834; *quod Verbum ac doctrinalia ita ~ent vulgata* AC 8385. **2** To be clearly perceptible, be manifest: *ut videat...Divina Vera, ubi ~ant et ubi latent* SS 41; *talis numerus nusquam apud Prophetam ~aret nisi arcana...involveret* AC 755.3.

exstructio ~onis, *f.* The act of building, construction: *cum ~one templi* VR 336.2.

exstruo ~ere ~xi ~ctum, *tr.* **1** To construct, build: *Templum a Salomone ~ctum* AE 220.12. **2** To build up the character of, develop (a person): *per illa* [sc. *scientifica*] *~ere externum hominem et aedificare illum* AC 1488.

exsufflo ~are ~avi ~atum, *tr.* **1** To inflate, puff up: *haec memoria sic ~ata est quasi callus* ES 358. **2** (app.) To sniff at: *~atis nomen Meum...cum adducitis raptum, claudum et aegrotum* Mal. 1.13 (VR 298).

exsugo ~gere ~xi ~ctum, *tr.* also **exugo**. To suck out: *quod sciant* [*apes*] *ex...floribus...~gere mel* VR 12.7; (w. dat.) *ut...non aliud ~gant homini quam...* ES 2743.

exsul-: see **exul-**.

exsumo ~ere ~(p)si ~(p)tum, *tr.* To take from store, take out: *constanter id quod ~itur e novo reficitur* AM 148.3; AE 242.4.

exsumptio ~onis, *f.* A taking away: *non est ~o partis, sed est productio totius* AM 220.2.

exsurgo ~gere ~rexi, *intr.* also **exurgo**. **1** (of plants) To grow up, rise: *dum vegetabile ex semine ~git* VR 106; *floreta e quorum areis ~gebant oleae* AM 42.5. **2** (of persons) To get out of bed, get up: *hoc mane antequam ~gerem* ES 221. **3** To come into existence, arise, spring up: *dum e novo Ecclesia Domini ~git* AC 482.2. **4** To arise, spring (from a specified source): *cum iris...sit quoddam ~gens ex modificatione radiorum lucis* AC 1042.1; *a voluntate omnia ~gunt* AC 808. **b** (in mathematics) to be produced, amount: *numeri 72, 144...ex 12 per multiplicationem ~gunt* AE 39.3; *quorum numerus ad quartam...partem totius generis humani...~git* CI 416.

exsuscitatio ~onis, *f.* The act of raising up (of the dead): *per ~onem mortuorum e monumentis* AC 8018.2.

exsuscito ~are ~avi ~atum, *tr.* **1** To make active, stir up: *Ego ~ans Chaldaeos* Hab. 1.6 (AC 1613.2); *quae* [*vita*] *tamen apud eos ~atur* ES 3758. **2** To raise (from the dead), resuscitate: *Lazarum quem...~avit a mortuis* AE 137.2. **3** To cause to grow or appear, raise: *quod Jehovah...vellet...aliam gentem ex Mosche ~are* AC 7043 (Num. 14.12); *virgultum ex cinere ~atum* AM 151[a].5; *solvite templum hoc, et in tribus diebus ~abo illud* John 2.19 (SS 47).

ext-: see also **exst-**.

exta ~orum, *neut. pl.* Entrails: *qui...ab ~is augurati sunt* VR 669.

extemplo, *adv.* Immediately, at once: *surrexit ~o* Luke 8.55 (DD 47.2).

extendo ~dere ~di ~sum, *tr.* (pf. act. also *~si* AM 79; pf. pple. also *~tum* AC 1664.3; compar. of pf. pple. *~sior*) **1** To stretch out, put forth (a part of the body or object held): *~des manus tuas* John 21.18 (AE 9.3); *draco cum ~sa cauda versus caelum* FI 56; *contra gladium ~sum* AC 8282. **2** To cause to stretch, make wider, spread out: *manus Meae ~derunt coelos* Isa. 45.12 (AC 49.2); *argentum ~sum* 'beaten silver' Jer. 10.9 (AC 424); *~dere...limites* AM 267.3; (refl. and pass.) to stretch, extend: *quod infernum hoc...~dat se satis late versus sinistrum* AC 8099.2; *inferna...~sa ad multam distantiam* AC 6692.2. **3** To give wider scope to, enlarge, extend, spread: *qui ulterius ~dunt ideas* AC 680.1; *in quod* [sc. *universum*] *potest* [*Deus*] *amorem Suum ~dere* VR 46; (refl. and pass.) *amor Dei vadit et ~dit se...ad bonos* VR 43.2; CI 169.

extense, *adv.* (compar. *~ius*) Extensively: *a centro ad peripherias...successive adhuc ~ius* AC 3833.2; ES 1846.

extensio ~onis, *f.* **1** The act of stretching forth: *per ~onem manus et baculi* AC 7417. **2** The increase of power or range, extension: *ex eo fit ~o visui spirituali quoad verum illud* AC 7298.2. **3** The region occupied or covered by extension, extent, range: *ea sapientia ~onem habet in universum coelum* AE 99; *intra sphaeram ~onis boni* VR 56. **4** A development resulting from extension, product: *quod inde ~ones falsi ex malo relaberentur super illos* AC 8207.

extensus ~a ~um, *a.* (pf. pple. of **extendo**) (compar. *~ior*) Having extension in space, extensive: *civitas ~a et spatiosa* AM 77.2; *Deus non est ~us, et usque implet omnia ~a universi* VR 63; (neut. as sb.) a space, extent: *quod non sint* [*animae*] *in aliquo ~o* VR 29.2; a plane, level: *quid tunc Deus nisi intimum ~um naturae* CC 9.

extentus ~a ~um, *a.* Made taut, stretched out, drawn: *coram gladio extenso et coram arcu ~o* Isa. 21.15 (AC 1664.4).

exter ~era ~erum, *a.* Foreign: *si quis in ~eras regiones proficiscitur* ES 1240.

exterior ~or ~us, *a.* **1** Situated on the more remote side, outer: *ejicientur in tenebras ~ores* Matt. 8.12 (VI 65); (neut. as sb.) the outside: *purgatis ~us poculi* Matt. 23.25 (VI 30.1). **2** Externally perceptible, outward: *~or loquela est soni articulati* AC 7359. **3** (as opp. to interior) Of the external man, external: *humiliatio ~or* AC 7068; (esp. neut. sg. or pl. as sb.) the external part or parts of the human personality: *sunt...apud unumquemvis hominem interiora et ~ora* AC 1029.

exterius, *compar. adv.* More externally: *quo ~us cogitat* AC 6612; AM 248.

exterminatio ~onis, *f.* Banishment, exile: *dissipatio, ~o, et separatio a bono et vero Ecclesiae* AE 373.3.

extermino ~are ~avi ~atum, *tr.* **1** To send into exile, banish, expel: *e societate aliorum ~ati sunt, quia mali* AC 7812; *falsitas eos ex societate ~at* ES 2555. **2** (transf.) To send away, remove, banish, expel: *ipsa vera foras ~antur* AC 6652; *interior idea... ~avit et expunxit ideam hanc novam* VR 111.7.

externe, *adv.* On or from the outside, externally: *pomum, quam modo ~e videmus* ES 2877.

externum ~i, *neut.* **1** The outward or external part: *ea quae crescunt a seminibus ab interno incipiunt et ad ~a adolescunt* ES 252. **2** The external or corporeal part: *quod homini internum et ~um sint* AE 98.1; *quod illis modo naturale seu ~um fidei esset* VI 49. **3** (pl.) Things of the physical world: *erat prorsus in ~is et in nulla fide* AC 6692.3.

externus ~a ~um, *a.* **1** Outwardly perceived, exterior, external: *similia quoad formam ~am, non autem quoad formam internam* AC 7297.1; *sensus internus Verbi...qui sensui ~o...inest* SS 4. **2** Of or relating to the external or physical world, external, bodily: *fallaciae sensuum ~orum* AC 7344; *causae frigorum... ~ae* AM 234; *illa quae plane ~a sunt, ita sensualia* AC 6693.4. **3** (of persons or their states) Concerned with bodily and worldly matters, external: *tunc homo est ~us seu corporeus* AC 268; *~ae Ecclesiae homo* AC 6704; *status ~i ejus* AC 6645.1.

extersio ~onis, *f.* A wiping away: *excrementitias ~ones* ES 3350.

extime, *adv.* On the outside, superficially: *cerebrum ... ~e induratum* ES 1623.

extimesco ~mescere ~mui, *intr.* To become terrified: *~mui propter iram et excandescentiam qua iratus fuit Jehovah contra nos* Deut. 9.19 (AC 9143).

extimus ~a ~um, *a.* Outermost: *~a cutis pectoris* ES 3673; *circulum ejus ~um* AM 294.1; (neut. as sb.) *ab intimis usque ad ~a* SS 38.1.

extinguo: see **exstinguo**.

extollo ~ere, *tr.* **1** To lift up, raise: *~ere manum* AC 6947; *~imini ostia mundi, ut ingrediatur Rex gloriae* Ps. 24.7 (DD 33.4); *nec potest [bestia]...illum* [sc. *vultum*] *~ere ad caelum* VR 69.1. **2** To utter loudly, lift up (one's voice): *~ant vocem desertum et urbes ejus* Isa. 42.11 (AC 8261.4); *soni musici illuc se ~unt* CI 241. **3** To praise, extol: *~ite equitantem super nubibus* Ps. 68.4 (AC 8267.2); *~e illum supra ordines* AM 499.

extorqueo ~quere ~si ~sum, *tr.* **1** To expel by twisting: *quod...homo...se ~queat per circumprojectionem a societate* ES 2991. **2** To extract by force, wring out: *consensus invitus seu ~sus* AM 299.

extra, *adv.* and *prep. w. acc.* **1** (adv.) Outside: *opposita...sunt quae ~a sunt* VR 62; *ab ~a*, from outside: *voluntas ab intra agit, et intellectus ab ~a* AM 490.3. **2** (prep.) Outside: *quod coelum sit intra unumquemvis et non ~a illum* CI 33; *amare alios ~a se* VR 36. **b** *~a semet*, not in full control of oneself, beside oneself: ES 3768. **3** (prep.) Without: *~a subtilitates illas video...quod* VR 17.4; *~a timorem* ES 2919.

extraconjugialis ~is ~e, *a.* Outside marriage, extramarital: *quod vester amor sexus sit amor ~is* AM 44.6.

extractio ~onis, *f.* A drawing out, extraction: *~onem talium ex sensu literae Verbi* AC 10402.1.

extractum ~i, *neut.* A drug extracted from a substance, extract: *a pharmacopola immixtus ~is vel emulsis* VR 160.5.

extraho ~here ~xi ~ctum, *tr.* **1** To drag out or away, pull out or back: *arbor...ex humo per radicem ~hit et evocat succum* SS 66; *quod Deus non potuerit...a damnatione et inferno ~here illos* VR 84. **2** To prolong, drag out: *dies...non ~hentur* Isa. 13.22 (DD 4).

extraneus ~a ~um, *a.* Strange, peculiar: *modis ~is, ita aliter quam fieret si ex propria voluntate* CI 504; AE 232.1; (masc. as sb.) a foreigner: *non patiantur ut ~i ad illos intrent* AR 11.2.

extraordinarius ~a ~um, *a.* Abnormal, extraordinary: *bina genera visionum sunt quae ~a* AC 1882; ES 2951.

extravagor ~ari ~atus sum, *intr.* To wander outside, roam, stray: *vincula quae tenent eos ne ~entur* ES 3093; *extra quorum sphaeram nusquam possunt cogitata... ~ari* ES 4190.

extravasatio ~onis, *f.* An extravasation (of blood): ES 2841.

extravasatus ~a ~um, *a.* Allowed to escape from its proper vessels, extravasated: *sanguis ~atus* ES 2841.

extremitas ~atis, *f.* **1** A furthest end, extremity: *ab ~ate terrae* Isa. 43.6 (AC 489.1); *facies binos cherubos...a duabus ~atibus propitiatorii* Exod. 25.18 (AC); *in una ~ate mundi spiritualis* VR 31.4. **2** A remote time: *in ~ate dierum* Jer. 23.20 (DD 4). **3** An extreme state, extreme: *illa per adulteria, usque ad illas ~ates illorum, conspurcaverunt* AM 512.2.

extremum ~i, *neut.* **1** An end, extremity: *ab uno ~o universi ad alterum* ES 979; *ut intingat ~um digiti sui in aquam* Luke 16.24 (AC 6832.9). **2** The lowest or ultimate part: *quod interiora...influant in externa, usque in ~um seu ultimum* AE 41; *tunc Ecclesia in ~is fuit* AC 637.2; *mala...quae in ~is mentis naturalis* AC 7441. **3** The end of life, death: *exspectavi ~um* SE 114.1.

extremus ~a ~um, *a.* **1** Most remote in space, outermost: *usque ad ~as fibras corporis* AC 8261.3. **2** Last in a temporal series: *in ~o die* John 12.48 (VR 652). **3** Last in rank or order, lowest: *et ecce sunt ~i qui erunt primi* Luke 13.30 (AC 1032.3); *Antiquissimi sensualia hominis...compararunt...reptilibus...quia ~a sunt* AC 746. **4** Of the highest degree, extreme: *qui in ~is falsis doctrinae sunt* VR 146.

extrico ~are ~avi ~atum, *tr.* **1** To free from knots, unravel: *nec potest ~ari e nodo isto* AC 8325.2; *muscularium fibrarum hodie non ~atarum series sunt* AC 607.2. **2** (transf.) To free from difficulty or obstruction, extricate: *quia non cogitare potest nisi ex spatio et tempore, non possit se inde ~are ex se* AC 8325.3.

extrinsecus[1], *adv.* On the outside, externally: *in vulnere solum ~us sanato* AM 149; *qui ~us sicut oves apparent* VR 120.1; *ab ~us,* from without: *sicut tenear in fide ab ~us* ES 1534.

extrinsecus[2] ~a ~um, *a.* External, outward: *non audita per viam ~am auris* ES 3322; (neut. as sb.) *cum ~um exuitur, quod fit post mortem* VI 45.

extrorsum, *adv.* In an outward direction, outwards: *quod suprema...versa sint sursum ad Deum, media ~um ad mundum* AM 269.6; ES 564.

extrorsus, *adv.* = **extrorsum**: 3AD 5481 (*extrorsum* Tafel).

extrudo ~dere ~si ~sum, *tr.* To push out, put forth: *et ecce termites illi [ex vite]... ~serunt uvas* VR 461.8.

extubero ~are ~avi, *intr.* To bulge: *sicut orbita primum plana, quae mox in circumrotatione ~ant* ES 1763.

exturbo ~are ~avi ~atum, *tr.* To drive out, expel: *illum...ex possessione sua ~ant* ES 5569.

extus, *adv.* Outwardly, externally: *utcunque apparet ~us alius* AC 1861.9; *quod non sit ulla pars intus in homine, nec ulla ~us, quae se non renovat* AM 171.2.

exu- : see also **exsu-**.

exubero ~are ~avi, *intr.* To be present in excessive amounts, abound: *quod...concupiscentiae... ~ent* DP 112.3.

exugo: see **exsugo**.

exuitio ~onis, *f.* The action of taking off: *~o calcei* AC 1748.4.

exulceratio ~onis, *f.* The condition of being ulcerated: *corporis eorum ~o, scabies, lepra* ES 654.

exul ~lis, *m.* A banished person, exile: *afflictos ~les introducere domum* Isa. 58.7 (AE 386.26).

exulo ~are ~avi, *intr.* also **exsulo**. To be banished: *cum...idea conjunctiva cum hoc ~at* AM 55.5; *~abit laetitia terrae* Isa. 24.4 (AE 304.4).

exultatio ~onis, *f.* also **exsultatio**. Exceeding joy, exultation: *laetitiam ~onis meae* Ps. 43.4 (AC 922.5); *ecce Ego creaturus Hierosolymam ~onem* Isa. 65.18 (DD 64.3).

exulto ~are ~avi, *intr.* also **exsulto**. **1** To leap out: *~are suo pariete volebant* ES 993. **2** To leap with joy, rejoice greatly, exult: *ex his auditis... ~avit cor meum* AM 81.5.

exundo ~are ~avi, *intr., tr.* **1** (intr.) To issue in waves, well out: *inde tantus foetor ~at* AC 814.1; *quod sphaera boni amoris ex illis ~et* AC 8370. **2** (tr.) To send forth in waves: *ut... ~ent torcularia mustum et oleum* Joel 2.24 (AE 375.29).

exuo ~ere ~i ~tum, *tr.* **1** To take off, remove (clothes): *~ere calceos* AC 6844.3; *quod ~ant et induant illas* [sc. *vestes*] CI 181. **2** To strip (a person): *~ite illum nudum* AM 10.2; (w. abl.) *externis iis ~tis, dum fit spiritus* ES 2255. **3** To divest oneself of, put off (the body or its attributes): *dum ~unt corpus et fiunt spiritus* AM 267.3; *usque dum corporea...aversantur, et sic ~unt* AC 6928; *cum Dominus... ~erit humanum ex matre* AE 183.11; *ut ibi ~ant principia falsi* AC 1106.

exurgeo ~gere, *tr.* To force out: *ut nequicquam possem ~gere aliquid vocis* ES 4566.

exurgo: see **exsurgo**.

exuro ~rere ~ssi ~stum, *tr.* To destroy by burning, burn up: *ignis solis... ~reret et consumeret omnia* AC 8328.2; AM 182.5.

exuviae ~viarum, *f. pl.* The sloughed skin (of a snake, insect, etc.): *dum [vermes] ~vias deponunt et fiunt papiliones* VR 106; AM 31; ES 4351.

Ezra, *indecl. m.* The Old Testament book of Ezra: AC 4818.2.

F

faba ~ae, *f.* A bean: *ex triticis, miliis, hordeis, et ~is* VR 78.1.

faber ~bri, *m.* A craftsman, maker: *~ber fecit et non Deus* Hos. 8.6 (AE 279.9); (prov.) *quod quisque sit ~ber suae fortunae* ES 4909.

fabrica ~ae, *f.* **1** The process of construction, building: *ligni utiles ad ~as* AM 13.2. **2** The style of construction, build: *quod ~a pulmonis talis sit ut respirare possit* AS 417. **3** A device, plan, trick: *non nisi quam ~as et latrocinia cogitat et molitur* AE 978.3.

fabricator ~oris, *m.* One who constructs, craftsman, maker: *sculpsit illud ~or ejus... ~or mendacii sui* Hab. 2.18 (AE 587.8).

fabrico ~are ~avi ~atum, *tr.* To construct, make, forge (manufactured objects): *~at ferrum forcipe* Isa. 44.12 (AE 386.4); *haec...non sunt aliqua manu angelica facta et ~ata* AM 12.2; ES 718; (w. *in* + acc.) *haec* [sc. *massa auri*] *~ata in pulchras formas* VR 701.3.

fabula ~ae, *f.* An empty tale, fiction, nonsense: *quod infernum sit ~a efficta a clero* VR 160.3; *haec vocantur hodie ~ae, sed fuerunt correspondentiae* AM 182.2.

fabulor ~ari ~atus sum, *intr.* To talk nonsense, tell fictions: *quod ~entur de diabolo* ES 190; (w. acc.) *de quibus multi multa ~antur in hoc mundo* VR 80.2.

fabulosus ~a ~um, *a.* Fictitious, nonsensical: *per confirmationes ~ae fidei suae de tribus personis Divinis* VR 121.2; (neut. as sb.) a myth: *unde orta sunt ~a illorum, ut de Deucalione et Pyrrha* VR 58; SS 20.2.

facere, *indecl.* (inf. of **facio**) The act of doing: *inde ejus fides fit viva et salvifica, et ejus ~ere fit charitas* VR 74.3.

facesco: see **facesso**.

facesso ~ere ~i, *intr.* also **facesco**. To depart, cease: *qui amor* [sc. *sexus*] *post votum ~it* AM 214.2; (w. *in* + acc.) to disappear into: *talis calor est qui putrescit, et ~it in excrementitium* AC 1773.3.

facetiae ~tiarum, *f. pl.* Jokes, witticisms: *in risibus amaenitatis ex blandiloquiis et ~tiis* AM 3.2; VR 151.

facetus ~a ~um, *a.* Well-mannered, courteous, polite: *tametsi...apparuerint sicut boni, jucundi, ~i* AC 4054.2; *~a voce se primum salutabant* VR 696.2; *e caelo meridionali...non audiebatur nisi quam ~um murmur* AM 81.1.

facies ~ei, *f.* **1** The countenance, face (of a person or animal): *patet...ex ~e, quod viri sint duriore, obnixiore* AM 218.1; *~e ferina* AC 5717.1; (Bibl., in pl.) *non novit quod coruscaret cutis ~erum ejus* Exod. 34.29 (AC). **2** The face (as indicating the direction of facing), view, sight: *quod...jaceant ~e et ventre deorsum* AC 5188.3; *nisus procidendi super ~es* AR 926.4; *ut volaret in desertum...a ~e serpentis* Rev. 12.14 (AR); *sicut pulverem coram ~ebus venti* Ps. 18.42 (DD 14.6). **b** *~e ad ~em*, face to face: Judg. 6.22 (AC 6849.2); VR 107.1. **3** The face (as the means of expressing emotion or character): *sicut cogitatio in oculis et affectio in ~e* SS 5; *per labiorum motiunculas et correspondentes ~ei mutationes* AC 7361.2; cf. *cum Domini ~es sit misericordia, pax et omne bonum* AC 223; *quis potest credere, quod homo malus intra ~em suam talis sit...?* DP 298.2. **4** The face (as a means of recognition), features: *quod...sint* [*Judaei*]*...diversa ~e a reliquis* AC 788.2; *quod non modo...consimiles sint mentibus, sed etiam ~ebus* AM 202.2. **5** (Bibl., pl.) The surface of anything: *super ~ebus abyssi* Gen. 1.2 (AC); *super ~ebus humi* Gen. 6.1 (AC); *expandentes rete super ~es aquarum* Isa. 19.8 (AC 6693.2). **6** Superficial appearance, outward looks: *duo illi mundi prorsus similes quoad externam ~em sunt* AS 163; *sunt binae ~es istius fidei* SE 42; *fides...praemittitur,...sicut ~es ante opus quod sequitur* VR 1.

facile, *adv.* (compar. *~ius*, superl. *~lime*) Easily: *non ~e sciri potest* AC 6690; *quod... ~e in errorem...possit cadere* SS 1; *tunc mala... ~ius profugantur* AC 1835.1.

facilis ~is ~e, *a.* (compar. *~ior*) **1** (of tasks, events, etc.) Easy to bring about or accomplish: *~ius est caelum et terram transire* Luke 16.17 (DD 10); *~i opera* CI 262. **2** (of persons or their minds) Easily influenced, susceptible: *quod adulterae seu ~es pellici se ad adulteria patiantur* ES 3611; (w. *ad*) liable (to), apt (to): *mens...prona in errores, et quoque ~is ad haereses* SS 52; VR 14.3. **3** Skilful, deft: *et quoque erat ~is, et simul in artificio admodum ingeniosus* ES 4561.

facilitas ~atis, *f.* Ease, facility: *habilitas et ~as ad conjungendum bonum vero* AM 204.

facilito ~are ~avi, *tr.* To make easy, facilitate: *promovent concordes...vocari quasi possunt unguenta, quia ~ant* ES 809.

facinorose, *adv.* In a criminal manner, outrageously: *vocantur...diaboli qui ~e vixerunt* VR 35.2.

facinorosus ~a ~um, *a.* (compar. *~ior*, superl. *~issimus*) **1** (of persons) Prone to crime or outrage, criminal, outrageous: *inter ~os* AC 817; ES 4396. **2** (of actions) Criminal, outrageous: *multa quae quoque spurca, obscaena, prophana et ~a sunt* CI 532.2; (neut. as sb.) ES 232.

facinus ~oris, *neut.* A criminal act, crime, outrage: *omnia mala, ~ora, latrocinia, artes, doli* CI 462[a].8; *simulatio...illis fuit ~us enorme* AC 7361.2.

facio ~cere feci ~ctum, *tr.* (n.b. in pass. **fio** is used, except in the pf. system, but fut. pass. *~cietur* 3AD 3383) **1** To make, construct, build: *deos fusiles... ~ctos ab Aharone* AC 8301.5; *et fecit illis domos* Exod. 1.21 (AC); *fit distinctio inter creare, formare et ~cere* AC 472. **b** (of living things) to produce (offspring, fruits, etc.): *arbores vitae ~cientes fructus quovis mense* AM 26. **c** to make up, invent (a story and sim.): *fuerunt historica non vera sed historica ~cta* AC 1403. **d** to acquire, get: *fecisti tibi opes* Ezek. 28.4 (AC 1551.3). **2** To bring about, cause (a state, result, etc.): *cum haec conjunctio ~cta est* AC 6717.2; *quod [tellures] circum axem suum... rotentur, et inde ~ciant dies* AC 6697; *magnam molestiam fecerunt* ES 4307. **3** To constitute, compose, make up: *mundana, corporea et terrestria, quae nusquam ~cere possunt Verbum Domini* AC 1540; *humus quae ~ciebat tectum super illos* VR 71.1. **b** *unum ~cere*, to make a single unit, be indivisible: *spatia et tempora unum ~ciunt* AS 77; *charitas et fides ~ciunt unum* FI 18.1. **4** To be a determining feature of, make up: *bonum et verum quae ~ciunt Ecclesiam* AC 6652; *internum ejus ~cit hominem* VR 14.4. **5** (w. pred.) To render, make: *fecistis vos pares bestiis* VR 77.3; *ut certus ~ctus sim quod ita sit* ES 4646; *~ctus sum in spiritu* VR 76.1. **6** (w. pred.) To change into, make: *aquae...non ~ctae sanguis* AC 7343.1; *quomodo Ipse quoad Humanum lex Divina ~ctus est* AC 6714; (w. *in* + acc.) *et ~ctus homo in animam viventem* Gen. 2.7 (AC); *quod sic illa ~ciant in vestem* ES 4673. **7** To bring it about (that), cause (to): (w. inf.) *occidere ~ciam solem in meridie* Amos 8.9 (AC 6693.5); *~cere arbores crescere* VR 84; (w. *ut*) *ille sensus... ~cit ut Verbum sit spirituale* SS 5; (w. *quod*) *haec cupido ~cit...quod jucundum modo ponant in scientia* AC 1472. **8** To perform, accomplish, do (an action): *solem quotidie circum tellurem nostram ~cientem gyrum* AC 8282; *ex...miraculis ~ctis in Aegypto* AC 6910; *scire...quid ~cerent* ES 4663. **b** (w. object specifying the quality of the action): *quod opera charitatis non ~cienda* AC 7318.1; *malum ~cere* ES 4633. **c** to perform the action indicated by another verb in the context, do: *legunt quae ibi sunt quasi e libro; spiritus Mercurii hoc solertius... ~ciebant* AC 6811; *ut...illum mundum describerem, quod ~ctum est in opere De Coelo et Inferno* AS 85. **9** To perform, do (the action appropriate to or defined by the object): **a** *vasa ~cere*, to pack one's bags: *vasa migrationis fac tibi habitatrix filia Aegypti* Jer. 46.19 (AC 6729). **b** to sacrifice (a victim): *princeps... ~ceret juvencum peccati* AC 2830.4. **c** to celebrate, hold (a festival): *praecepit rex...ut ~cerent Pascha Jehovae Deo* 2 Kgs. 23.21 (AC 6804.7). **d** to conclude, make (an agreement): *sirenes...cum variis infernis pactum ~ciunt* ES 4635. **e** to carry out, perform (orders): *per ~cere illas...leges* VR 71.3. **f** (w. verbal nouns): *quod mansionem ~ciat [Dominus] apud illos qui amant Ipsum* John 14.23 (AS 111). **10** (absol.) To act, behave (in a specified manner): *quare ~cis sic servis tuis?* Exod. 5.15 (AC); *externae Ecclesiae homo... indiscriminatim ~cit* AC 6704; *quod...non ~ciat contra alterum* ES 4658; *male ~cere*: see **malefacio**. **b** (to repeat a more specific verb): *quod non recipiant amorem Dei...similiter ut ~cit spina et urtica cum calore solis* VR 43.2. **11** To regard (as): *quod...homines ~ciant animantia illius regni sui similia* AS 61. **b** (w. gen.) to value (at): *quod parvi ~ciat scientifica* AC 1557; *nihili ~cit violentias inferre* VR 120.2. **12** (absol.) To make a difference, matter: *distantia loci in altera vita nihil ~cit* AC 1274; ES 4017; (w. *ad*) *nihil est quod non scire cupiant, sive ad rem eorum ~ciat, sive non* ES 178; ES 2319.

factitius ~a ~um, *a.* Artificial, made up: *charitas et fides cum illarum ideis ~is* VR 375.2.

factor ~oris, *m.* One who makes, maker: [*Deus*] *creator, formator et ~or universi* VR 29.3; *respiciet homo ad ~orem suum* Isa. 17.7 (DD 4); one who perpetrates (a crime), author: *~or inculpatur et punitur ex lege* AM 486.

factum ~i, *neut.* A deed, action: *in ~is est voluntas omne* AE 15; *homo secundum ~a judicabitur* CI 358.

facula ~ae, *f.* A torch: *facies...quorundam instar ~arum igneae* CI 553.2; AM 500.5.

facultas ~atis, *f.* **1** A physical resource, supply, wealth: *~ates tuas, omnes thesauros tuos in praedam dabo* Jer. 17.3 (AC 368); *depraedarentur omnium ~ates* AC 7032.3. **2** A possibility, chance: *omnem ~atem emendationis eorum auferrent* ES 4690. **3** A propensity, ability: *quod...haereditent...modo inclinationes et quoque ~ates ad illas [affectiones]* AM 202.1; *~as ad sciendum* VR 48.11; (w. gen.) *~ate judicii* AC 6814; *~as loquendi* AC 6982; *~as vegetandi* FI 16. **4** A mental quality or part of the mind, faculty: *homini binae ~ates sunt, voluntas et intellectus* AC 35; *quod homo ex tribus distinctis ~atibus consistat* ES 205.

facundia ~ae, *f.* Ease of utterance, fluency: *non judicii et sapientiae, sed ingenii et ~ae* AM 175.3.

fae-: see also **foe-**.

faeculentus ~a ~um, *a.* (superl. *~issimus*) Of or resembling lees of wine or dregs: *cum ~is jucunditatibus amoris scortatorii* AM 441; ES 585.

faed-: see **foed-**.

faem-: see **foem-**.

faen-: see **foen-**.

faet-: see **foet-**.

faex faecis, *f.* also **fex**. Lees of wine, dregs: *vinum ...clarescit faecibus ad fundum decidentibus* AC 7906.2; also, any kind of excretion: *quod exhalent quoque subtiliores faeces* ES 1738; (transf.) *castigatur [conjugiale externum] et purificatur e suis faecibus ab interno* AM 148.1.

fagus ~i, *f.* A beech tree: AM 78.2.

fallacia ~ae, *f.* **1** A false appearance, deception: *apparet quasi voces loquelae forent in cogitatione, sed est ~a* AC 6987.2; *~a...est, quod fides producat bonum* FI 17. **2** A mistake, error: *~ae sensuum* AC 735; *quod singula...recenserentur absque omni ~a* ES 4703.

fallaciter, *adv.* With false appearances, mistakenly: *quod...sic vere et non ~er appareant* AM 57.

fallax ~acis, *a.* Deceptive, fallacious: *causas...spurias et ~aces* AM 474; AC 6948.5; (of persons) *~aces homines* ES 634.

fallo ~lere fefelli ~sum, *tr.* **1** To persuade of an untruth, deceive: *~lere et seducere alios* AC 7356.1; *qui...proximum fefellerunt* AC 7097.3; (absol.) *per simulationem innocentiae et charitatis ~lunt* AC 6914.2. **2** (of things) To lead into error: *opinio me fefellit* ES 2524; (pass.) to be deceived, be wrong: *qui credit...multum ~litur* AC 7038.

fallopius ~a ~um, *a.* (anat.) *Tuba ~a,* (app.) the canal of the facial nerve: *sic penetrat [loquela] per tubam ~am* ES 1541.

falsarius ~i, *m.* A counterfeiter, falsifier: *illi qui falsa loquuntur ex dolo aut proposito et illa sono aemulo affectionis spiritualis pronuntiant...ab antiquis dicti sunt incantatores,...hi ~i, mendaces et dolosi...* VR 324; AR 462.2; AR 137.1.

false, *adv.* Contrary to truth, falsely: *quod ~e credant quod Dominus pugnaverit...ut maximus esset* AC 1813.2; *~e testari* VI 53.

falsificatio ~onis, *f.* The process of falsifying, falsification: *~onem intellectus Verbi* SS 79.5; (w. pl.) an instance of this: *scortationes spirituales non aliud sunt quam ~ones veri* AE 141.3.

falsificator ~oris, *m.* One who practises deception: AC 7337.1.

falsifico ~are ~avi ~atum, *tr.* **1** To cause (a thing) to appear what it is not, counterfeit: *num aurum... bonum est, num commixtum et ~atum* VI 11. **2** (esp.) To falsify (truths): *~atur verum cum...dicitur quod... bonum nihil faciat ad salutem* AC 7318.1; *qui ~arunt vera et adulterarunt bona* AC 7089.1.

falsiloquium ~i, *neut.* The speaking of falsehoods, lying: *horror...per ~a fallendi* AC 957; AR 624.

falsiloquus ~a ~um, *a.* Speaking falsehoods, lying: ES 824.

falsitas ~atis, *f.* A false statement or belief, falsity: *ex quo patet quam enormes ~ates fides caeca potest producere* FI 8; *internus homo dominatur...super ejus cupiditates et ~ates* AC 986.1.

falsum ~i, *neut.* False belief or principle, falsity: *cultum ex ~o* AC 6728; *quid ~um et malum* CI 351.2; (w. pl.) an instance of this: *doctrina...fidei pugnans contra ~a* SS 12.1.

falsus ~a ~um, *a.* (superl. *~issimus*) Not true or correct, wrong, false: *ex principiis ~ae religionis* AC 8318.3; *dignoscitur amor vere conjugialis ab amore conjugiali spurio, ~o et frigido* AM 224; *se abdicare jucundis vitae...hoc ~um est* AC 945.

falx ~lcis, *f.* A cutting tool used in agriculture, sickle, pruning hook, bill: *contundent...hastas suas in ~lces* Isa. 2.4 (AC 1664.3); Rev. 14.14 (AR).

fama ~ae, *f.* **1** A report, rumour: *ut audiat ~am et revertatur in terram suam* Isa. 37.7 (DD 48.2). **2** A person's reputation, repute, esteem: *timent jacturam ~ae* AC 7032.3; *propter ~am, ut evehantur ad honores* AM 266.5.

famelicus ~a ~um, *a.* Exceedingly hungry, starving:

dum ~i edunt grana ES 4176; (masc. as sb.) *desiderant illas* [sc. *intelligentiam et sapientiam*] *sicut ~us cibum* AE 117.1.

fames ~is, *f.* 1 Desire for food, hunger: *sicut homo, qui in ~e est,* [*appetit*] *cibum* CI 274; *non ~em ad panem...sed ad audiendum verbum Jehovae* Amos 8.11 (AE 71.2). 2 Lack of food, starvation: *qui defecerunt per ~em* Lam. 2.19 (AE 187.7); famine: *si venirent septem anni ~is* 2 Sam. 24.13 (AC 7102.8).

famigeratus ~a ~um, *a.* (superl. *~issimus*) Renowned, famous: *propter eruditionem ~issimus fuit* TE 38.1; AC 1114.

familia ~ae, *f.* (gen. sg. *~as* used w. *pater*, *mater*, etc. AM 402) 1 A group of related persons living in close proximity, family in an extended sense: *~am constituerunt domus pauciores aut plures quarum una non procul ab altera habitavit* AC 470; AC 1159.3; *~a Levi* AC 7231.2. 2 Any cognate group: *e ~a sirenum* ES 3123; *dantur etiam ~ae regionum* AM 375.

familiaris ~is ~e, *a.* (compar. *~ior*, superl. *~issimus*) 1 Of or belonging to one's household; *res ~is*, private property: *rei ~is amplificatio per opes* AM 274; AM 290. 2 Closely associated, intimate, familiar: *~es sibi faciunt...cum iis qui disponunt domini bona* ES 2500. 3 Commonly known or experienced, familiar: *terminis orbi erudito ~ibus* AC 129; *inde...est, quod ~e sit homini dicere...* CI 97; (neut. as sb.) *ex assuetudine ab infantia et inde ~i* AE 182.4.

familiaritas ~atis, *f.* Intimate association, familiarity: *cum amicis...ligant ~atem* VR 808.

familiariter, *adv.* (compar. *~liarius*) In a familiar manner: *caepit ~liarius mecum loqui* VR 796.3.

famositas ~atis, *f.* The quality of being famous: *quod...mereatur ~atem in vita civili* 3AD 5563.

famosus ~a ~um, *a.* (superl. *~issimus*) Famous: ES 3191.

famula ~ae, *f.* A female servant, maid: *clamando...ad ~as pro opitulatione* AM 512.1; VR 110.8.

famulitium ~i, *neut.* A servant: *is non amat illa aliter quam ~a quia serviunt sibi* CI 557; *intellectus ...non est nisi quam ministerium et ~um voluntatis* AM 196; (also, collectively) a household: *servus...quem constituit dominus ejus super ~um suum* Matt. 24.45 (AC 4422.1).

famulor ~ari ~atus sum, *intr.* (w. dat.) To act as servant (to), serve: *cui non ~ari vellet* AC 370; *intellectuali parti...~antur* AC 7038.2.

famulus ~i, *m.* A servant: *est ibi herus et sunt ~i* CI 219; AM 10.3.

fanaticus ~a ~um, *a.* 1 (of persons) Crazed by erroneous belief, fanatic: *Mahumedani...vocant...illos ~os* VR 831. 2 Characterized by such belief: *enormes et ~os errores* VR 628; (neut. as sb.) VR 58.

fanatismus ~i, *m.* Erroneous religious belief: *~us quod Filius Mariae ex Josepho fuerit* VR 94.1.

fanum ~i, *neut.* A shrine, temple: *~a ex lapide calcario caeso* AM 78.3; *~a idolorum* VR 84.

farcio ~cire ~civi, *tr.* To fill to bursting point, stuff: *qui ~civerant ventres cibariis usque ad nauseas* AM 6.4; *quid plus...libros orthodoxorum implet et ~cit?* VR 132.1.

farina ~ae, *f.* 1 Meal or flour: *frumentum...per molas comminuitur in ~am* AC 7780. 2 (transf., of character) A type, sort, batch (cf. Ital. *farina*, French *farine*, Spanish *harina*): *praeter plura similis ~ae alia* VR 77.2; *pessimae hujus ~ae* [*uxores*] AM 292.2.

farrago ~inis, *f.* 1 Mixed grain as food for beasts, fodder: *boves et asini...~inem meram comedent* Isa. 30.24 (AC 9272.6). 2 A mess, hotchpotch: *redegit omnia illa quae dicta sunt in insulsam ~inem* IM 12.

fas, *indecl.* That which is morally right, just behaviour: *per fas aut nefas* AC 953; ES 3462; *si potestatem suam ultra fas in nefas extendunt* AM 291.2.

fasces ~ium: see **fascis**.

fascia ~ae, *f.* 1 A band (of cloth or similar material): *cinctus erat ~a ex pyropis et sapphiris* AM 2.1; *pilei quorum limbos ornabant ~ae ex auro* VR 48.20; (of swaddling clothes) *quem ad modum vestes quae amiciunt, ut ~ae infantem* SS 40.1. 2 A band, strip, line: *per quasi ~as obscure coeruleas* AC 1512. **b** (anat.) *~a alba*, the fascia which swathes the abdominal muscles: AC 9236.

fasciatim, *adv.* In the manner of bands, ringwise: *serta quibus ornarent...~im pectora puerorum* AM 8.2.

fascicularis ~is ~e, *a.* Formed of bundles, fasciculate: *in formas hasce ~es* AC 5881.

fasciculatim, *adv.* In bundles: *scientifica et vera cohaerent ~im* AC 5881; AC 7379.

fasciculatio ~onis, *f.* A grouping into bundles: *~o illa imprimis sistitur videnda in cerebro* AC 7408.1.

fasciculatus ~a ~um, *a.* Formed into bundles: *per meninges et fibras ~as* ES 1267.

fasciculus ~i, *m.* A bundle, bunch: *accipietis ~um hyssopi* Exod. 12.22 (AC); *desumpsit ex arbore aliquot termites et ligavit in ~um* AM 77.7; *ex ~is fibrarum* VR 147.

fascinatio ~onis, *f.* The act of bewitching, magic,

spell: *si per tales ~ones non patiuntur se...abduci* AM 505.3; ES 3090.

fascinator ~oris, *m.* One who bewitches, wizard, warlock: ES 3137.

fascino ~are ~avi ~atum, *tr.* To bewitch, enchant: *mali spiritus...illudunt...et ~ant eos qui in altera vita sunt* ES 755; (fig.) *vos potestis autumare, quod talia ~ent oculos nostros* AM 12.2.

fascinum ~i, *neut.* An evil spell: *quod religio...non sit nisi quam ~um plebis* VR 80.3.

fascio ~are ~avi ~atum, *tr.* To wrap in swaddling clothes, swaddle: *ex indefessa opera ~andi et mundandi illos* [sc. *infantes*] AM 396.2.

fasciola ~ae, *f.* A band, bandage (used as swaddling clothes): *manu tenentes ~am, sic projiciendo infantem* ES 2642; any narrow strip: *~a in qua stellae coruscantes* AC 8112.

fascis ~is, *m.* **1** A bundle: *cohaerent sicut ~es colligati* AM 406. **2** (pl.) The bundles of rods and axes carried before Roman magistrates as the symbol of their authority (in quot. fig.): *apud uxores, post obtentos imperii ~es ab illis, remanet cupido* AM 291.2.

fastidio ~dire ~divi ~ditum, *tr.* **1** To reject (food): *cibi facti sunt nobis insipidi... ~dit illos stomachus* AM 6.4. **2** To feel disgust at, loathe: *post paucum tempus eam* [*vitam*] *~dirent et nausearent* AC 454; *qui ~dit propter lucrum oppressiones* Isa. 33.15 (VI 84.1).

fastidiose, *adv.* With disgust, distastefully: *qui ~e spectabant faeminas* AM 55.2.

fastidiosus ~a ~um, *a.* Distasteful: *spectat consortem...sicut ~am anum* AM 226.

fastidium ~i, *neut.* A feeling of distaste, disgust, loathing: *vos tunc in statu ~i sexus...fuistis* AM 55.5.

fastigium ~i, *neut.* The top, summit, peak: *amor possidendi opes...crevit in ~um, ut possidere omnium aliorum opes vellet* DP 215.5; Ezek. 31.3 (AE 388.12).

fastosus: see **fastuosus**.

fastuosus ~a ~um, *a.* also **fastosus**. (compar. *~ior*, superl. *~issimus*) Haughty, proud: *senes...ex quadam opulentia prae caeteris ~i* AM 6.3; CI 587.3.

fastus ~us, *m.* Improper pride, haughtiness: *mansit apud illos ~us, sicut forent aliis sapientiores* CI 464.3; *in sordida avaritia, in odio et in ~u* AC 7051.1; (w. gen. of cause of pride) *ex ~u propriae intelligentiae* FI 49.

fatalis ~is ~e, *a.* Causing or capable of causing death, deadly, fatal: *morbi gravissimi et ~es* AC 4227.3.

fateor ~teri fassus sum, *tr.*, *intr.* **1** To grant (a statement) to be true, admit: *hoc ~tentur ipsi* [*angeli*] SS 73; (w. *quod*) *tandem fassi sunt quod non possent amplius* AC 8383; to admit (an error): AC 444. **2** To accept as an item of belief, profess: *qui solam fidem ex doctrina fassi sunt* CI 482.

fathisco ~ere, *intr.* also **fatisco**. **1** To become exhausted, weaken, fail: *quod quando illa* [*viscera*] *~unt, cor incipiat palpitare* VR 119.2. **2** To be broken up, dissolve: *cibus...~it in sterquilineum* CO 47; *ex vegetabili et animali in minutissimum pollinem ~entibus* AS 65; ES 3811.

fatigatio ~onis, *f.* Tiredness, fatigue: *nec ~o ulla percipitur* AC 1884.

fatigo ~are ~avi ~atum, *tr.* To make tired, weary: *dissensio...~abat mentem meam* ES 158; *Jehovah... non ~atur* Isa. 40.28 (AE 294.8).

fatisco: see **fathisco**.

fatue, *adv.* Foolishly: *dicunt se ~e cogitavisse* CI 313; also, in a deceptive fashion, like a will-o'-the-wisp: *aufugerunt in tenebras suas, quae coram oculis illorum ~e lucebant* AR 566.5.

fatuitas ~atis, *f.* Foolishness, silliness, folly: *fit in ~ate* VR 40; (w. pl.) an instance of this: *quot et quales ~ates in mentes humanas...irrepserunt* VR 52.

fatum ~i, *neut.* **1** The predestined order of things, fate: *quod...virgo...et...juvenis...sicut ex ~o alicubi conveniant* AM 229. **2** (also pl.) That which befalls one, fate: *narrabit tunc quisque sua ~a alteri* VR 160.4.

fatuus ~a ~um, *a.* **1** Foolish, silly: *fassus errorem suum et miratus quod tam ~us fuerit* AC 444; *quare seditis ita ~i...?* AM 7.3; (of things) *phantasia...tam simplex et ~a* ES 2930. **2** Feeble, weak: *visio ex luce ~a in tenebris* VR 346.2. **b** *Ignis ~us*, a will-o'-the-wisp: *lumen sicut ex igne ~o* FI 63.2; VR 110.1.

fauces ~ium, *f. pl.* (also abl. sg. *~e*) **1** The jaws: *oves...e ~ibus leonis...eripit* VR 122; VR 31.4; (sg.) *caput draconis cum ~e magna* ES 936. **2** A gaping pit resembling the jaws of a beast: *interponunt sibi quasi ~es inter binos montes* ES 2653.

faunus ~i, *m.* A faun: *quod...sint sicut ~i cum tribus cornibus* VR 831.

faustitas ~atis, *f.* Extreme happiness, blissfulness: *ex vita aeterna, quae est beatitudo, ~as et felicitas absque fine* VR 43.3; (pl.) *homo in mundanis bonis et ~atibus ponit benedictionem Divinam* AC 7007.3.

faustus ~a ~um, *a.* (compar. *~ior*) Extremely agreeable, blissful: *aliqua quae illa gaudia reddunt ~a et felicia* AM 17.1; (neut. as sb.) *laetitia probi...fit ~um coeleste* AC 7007.3; AE 375.24.

fautor ~oris, *m.* One who favours another's views, supporter: *sententiae exportabantur ad clientes amicos et ~ores* AM 231.3.

faventer, *adv.* Favourably: *ut conjux spectet conjugem benigne et ~er* AM 284.

faventia ~ae, *f.* An instance of showing favour, approval: *per increpationes et alternas ~as* AM 292.2.

faveo ~vere ~vi, *intr.* (compar. of pres. pple. *~ventior*) **1** (of persons, w. dat.) To be favourably disposed (to): *in perniciem omnium qui sibi non ~vent* AC 7032.3. **b** to express agreement: *animadverti quod omnes pleno assensu ~verent* VR 16.2; VR 48.7. **2** (of things) To be in accord, be consonant: *quod ament mala, et inde falsa quae ~vent* VI 65; (w. dat.) *omnia quae amoribus istis ~vent* AC 20.

favilla ~ae, *f.* The ashes of a fire: *sicut ignis [dissolvit] lignum, et redigit illud in ~am* VR 135.4.

favor ~oris, *m.* **1** Good will, favour: *~or deficiens apud uxorem* AM 290; *agere ex beneplacito secundum ~orem* CI 563. **2** *Ad* or *in ~orem* (w. gen.), in favour (of), to suit: *leges doctrinae in sui ~orem...explicat* AC 6705; AE 163.1. **3** Partiality: *praejudicium cum ~ore* AM 231.4.

favus ~i, *m.* A honeycomb: *de ~o apiario* Luke 24.42 (DD 35.10); ES 4027.

fax facis, *f.* A torch: *diabolus cum facibus in manu* VR 72.3; ES 3539; (fig.) *haec [potentia] post nuptias faces suas mutat, ac decrescit et increscit* AM 108.

febra ~ae, *f.* A fever: *~ae malignae et pestilentiales* AM 470.

febricitans ~ntis, *a.* Fevered, feverish: *visui oculi ~ntium, qui unum objectum...vident ut tria* VR 184; ES 4571.

febrilis ~is ~e, *a.* Of or appropriate to a fever, feverish: *quod infundant calorem ~em* ES 4571.

febris ~is, *f.* A morbid condition characterized by high temperature, fever: *~es malignae et pestilentiales* AM 253.1; *sicut qui correpti sunt a ~i gelida* CI 572.

Februarius ~i, *m.* February: ES 654.

fec-: see foec-.

fel fellis, *neut.* Gall, bile: *de vesica fellis* ES 1012; (esp. as a type of bitterness) *uvae ejus uvae fellis* Deut. 32.32 (SS 51.9).

feles ~is, *f.* A cat: *sicut ~es tractant mures* ES 4369; AM 246.3.

felicitas ~atis, *f.* **1** The state of being happy, happiness, joy: *in eminentia et opulentia est ~as mundana* AC 7007.3; *quod caelum sit ~as aeterna* VI 94. **2** An instance of happiness, cause of joy: *angeli...omnem ~atem habent ex usibus* AC 7038.1; *jucunditates et ~ates in altera vita* AC 1392.

feliciter, *adv.* Happily, with good luck, fortunately: *dicunt quidem, cum res ~er succedunt, quod hoc a Deo* AC 8717.3.

felix ~icis, *a.* (compar. *~icior*, superl. *~icissimus*) **1** (of persons) Affected by joy, happy: *quod probi ~ices in mundo essent prae improbis* AC 7007.1; AC 8113. **2** (of things) Causing joy, happy: *optabam ~icem adventum* VR 12.1; *existunt omnes status ~ices ex amore* AC 925.3; (neut. as sb.) *Divinum Bonum et Divinum ~ix* AC 8114; *in ~icia coeli venerunt* CI 18; AC 1470; *ad quos...veniunt...amici, ~icia optandi causa* [i.e., to wish them happiness] AM 316.1.

felleus ~a ~um, *a.* Of or resembling gall: (neut. as sb.) *ab urinariis...et ~is cystidis* ES 1035.

fem-: see also **foem-**.

femoralia ~um, *neut. pl.* A garment to cover the loins, drawers, pants: *et fac eis ~a lini...a lumbis et usque ad femora erunt* Exod. 28.42 (AC); *~a et tibialia* AM 15; ES 3515.

femur ~oris, *neut.* also ~inis, *neut.* (Bibl.) The thigh: *venter [statuae] et ~ora ex aere* Dan. 2.32 (AM 78.1); *erit...veritas cingulum ~inum Ejus* Isa. 11.5 (DD 6); (Bibl. as standing for parenthood) *et reges e ~inibus tuis exibunt* Gen. 35.11 (AC 3021.2).

fenestra ~ae, *f.* A window: *templum...et non aliquae ~ae in parietibus* VR 134.1; *per ~as apertas* AM 270.2.

fera ~ae, *f.* A wild animal: *'~a' quid dignius et excellentius involvit quam bestia* AC 774; AC 908.1; *~a mala* AC 7102.2; *rex mutatus ab homine in ~am* AE 220.8; *~ae domesticae*, harmless wild animals: AE 388.24.

feralis ~is ~e, *a.* Of or relating to death, deadly: *aves noctis ~es* AM 521.1; *occidunt sicut stylis aut simili ~i instrumento* ES 1863; *~is lectica* or *mensa*, a bier: AC 817; CI 433.

ferculum ~i, *neut.* A dish served at table: *apparebant omnes mensae plenae ~is* AM 6.2.

fere, *adv.* Almost, nearly: *funiculos ~e inconspicuos* AM 412; *qui angeli ~e sunt* ES 1652; *ubivis ~e in propheticis* AC 16.

feretrum ~i, *neut.* A coffin: *cum duobus...loquutus sum eodem die cum sepelirentur, et cum uno qui per meos oculos vidit suum loculum et ~um* AC 4622.4.

feria ~ae, *f.* A day of festival, holy day: *in ~a ad diem festi nostri* Ps. 81.3 (AE 448.15).

ferinus ~a ~um, *a.* Of or resembling a wild beast, savage: *exuit naturam humanam, et induit ~am* AC 6952.6; (neut. as sb.) *~um intraret homines* VR 74.5.

ferio ~rire ~rii, *tr.* **1** To strike, smite, hit: *hircos cum duobus cornibus quibus...~rierunt oves* FI 63.4; (transf.) *cum ~riit illum halitus effluens e coelo* CI 429. **2** *Foedus ~rire*, to enter into a treaty, make a covenant: *et ~riam illis foedus...cum fera agri* Hos. 2.18 (AC 40.3).

ferior ~ari ~atus sum, *tr.* To celebrate, keep as a festival: *et ~abimini illum [diem] festum Jehovae* Exod. 12.14 (AC); (absol.) *tribus vicibus ~aberis Mihi in anno* Exod. 23.14 (AC).

feritas ~atis, *f.* The quality of being wild, savagery: *ex crudelitate et ~ate [hominis]* AC 5393.1.

fermentatio ~onis, *f.* The fermentation (of wine, etc.): *vinum, quod post ~onem clarescit* AC 7906.2; DP 284; (transf.) *pugnae spirituales seu tentationes sunt ~ones in spirituali sensu* AC 7906.3; DP 25.

fermentatum ~i, *neut.* Food prepared with yeast, leavened bread: *omnis comedens ~um* Exod. 12.15 (AC); *non sacrificabis super ~o sanguinem sacrificii Mei* Exod. 23.18 (AC).

fermento ~are ~avi ~atum, *tr., intr.* To treat with yeast, leaven, ferment: *donec ~aretur totum* Matt. 13.33 (AC 7906.3); (intr.) to work like leaven: *sic ut vita sic quasi ~at* ES 789.

fermentum ~i, *neut.* Yeast: *quod regnum caelorum sit simile ~o* SS 29 (Matt. 13.33); AC 1327.2.

fero ~rre tuli latum, *tr.* (compar. of pf. pple. *latior*, superl. *latissimus*) **1** To come having, bring: *quaesivi quam eruditionem...secum ~rrent* VR 12.1; *qui extrinsecus ~runt faciem et vitam honestam* AC 821.1; (esp.) to bring (help): *quod Dominus...omnibus opem ~rat* AC 6852; *si auxilium ~rret* AC 7877.5. **2** To have (in one's mind or heart), bear: *non aliud animo ~rebat* ES 3290; *in corde suo ~runt quod ipsi domini velint fieri* AC 1594.3. **3** To have given to one, receive: *naturale quod a matre tulit* VR 103.1; *spiritus...~rt...judicium secundum fidem et opera* ES 2340. **b** *responsum ~rre*, to receive a reply: *per effulgurationes lucis tulerunt responsa* AC 6640.2. **4** To endure, suffer, bear: *morbos nostros Ipse tulit* Isa. 53.4 (AC 1846.3). **5** To tolerate, bear: *non ~rebat illos terra ad habitandum simul* Gen. 13.6 (AC); *novi...quod non possis ~rre malos* Rev. 2.2 (AR). **6** To bring forth, produce (fruit and sim.): *hic ~rt fructum multum* John 15.5 (DD 32.6); *~rt multum semen* ES 4637; (transf.) *ludi infantiles...qui usum ~runt* ES 2290. **7** To carry, pass (a law): *leges ordinis in Verbo latas* VR 74.3; AC 8080.4; to pass (judgment): *cum judice qui ex amicitia...judicia ~rt* DP 168.4. **8** To cause to go, direct, lead: *finis...~rt unius animam contra alterum* ES 3112; (transf.) *se in errores...~rre* AC 1072.1; (pass.) *quod bestiae ad illas [scientias] ~rantur paene sicut caeci...a canibus* VR 48.13; (absol.) *sicut ~rt natura* ES 4659. **b** (pass. w. abl.) to be impelled (by): *qui cupiditate ~runtur examinandi ...qualis est* ES 2305; ES 4395. **9** (pass.) To travel, move, go: *quod illae [sc. planetae]...circum solem ~rantur* AC 6697; *secundum odorem ~runtur [crabrones]* ES 2901. **10** To utter, express: *non ~res nomen Jehovae Dei tui ad vanum* Exod. 20.7 (AC); *ut vix rear posse in numeris ~rre, quae objecta tunc memoriae meae offenderunt* ES 3671. **b** *ore ~rre*, to proclaim, announce: *ita alia corde gererent et aliud ore ~rrent* AC 8383; (w. inf.) *Judaei...ore ~rentes occidere, mactare, cremare* AC 941.2; (w. *quod*) *qui ore ~runt, quod sola fides salvificet* AC 369. **c** (intr., of a book): *libri ita scripti sunt ut aliter ~rrent in sensu interiore quam in litera* AC 1540. **d** *acceptum ~rtur*, is to be attributed (to): see **acceptus**.

ferocia ~ae, *f.* Fierceness, ferocity: *fiunt...lupi quoad ~am* VR 13.4; AC 1690.6.

ferocitas ~atis, *f.* Fierceness, ferocity: *furor et ~as* AM 407.

ferociter, *adv.* (compar. *~cius*) Fiercely, ferociously: *os dire et ~citer diductum* AC 5566.

ferox ~ocis, *a.* (compar. *~ocior*, superl. *~ocissimus*) Fierce, savage, ferocious: *ferarum ~ocissimarum* ES 374; *~oci animo* AM 407.

ferreus ~a ~um, *a.* **1** Made of iron: *virga ~a* Rev. 2.27 (AR). **2** (of the last of the four ages) *Saeculum ~um*, the Iron Age: *saecula aurea, argentea, aerea et ~a* AC 1551.1; AM 73.1.

ferruginosus ~a ~um, *a.* Of iron rust, rusty: *a colore aureo in argenteum...et demum in ~um* AM 115.1.

ferrum ~i, *neut.* **1** Iron: *argentum, cuprum, ~um, stannum* VI 10; *aes [significat] bonum naturale...et ~um verum ejus* AE 70.1. **2** An iron implement: *Jehovah excidet implexa sylvae ~o* Isa. 10.34 (SS 15.1).

fertilis ~is ~e, *a.* Fertile: *in humum ~em* VR 38.2; AC 8116.

fertilitas ~atis, *f.* Fertility: *[aurora] dat ~atem humo* CI 289.

ferus ~a ~um, *a.* (compar. *~ior*) Wild, savage: *si ~us vocatur ursus seu lupus* CI 110.

fervens ~ntis, *a.* Scalding, boiling: *unus alium coquit in aqua calida ~nte* ES 2711.

fervesco ~vescere ~vui, *intr.* To become extremely hot: *ut incalescat et ~vescat aes ejus* Ezek. 24.11 (AC 4744.2).

fervidus ~a ~um, *a.* Hot (in quot. transf.): *si calor voluntatis...est ~us ex concupiscentia mali* DP 297.

fervor ~oris, *m.* **1** Agitated motion, seething, agitation: *lapides grandinis in ~ore* Ezek. 13.11 (AC 739.2); *accedente illo falso ad bonum fit ~or* AC 9992.2. **2** Emotional ardour, passion, heat: *~or Jehovae contra omnes gentes* Isa. 34.2 (AC 3614.3); *oravit Deum...cum tali ~ore, ut vix alii ardentius* UJ(P) 245.

fessus ~a ~um, *a.* Weary, tired: *~us sum anhelitu meo* Ps. 6.6 (AE 484.4).

festalis ~is ~e, *a.* Of or proper to festivals, festal, ceremonial: *~ia loca Dei* Ps. 74.8 (AE 504.29).

festinatio ~onis, *f.* Haste: *comedetis illam in ~one* Exod. 12.11 (AC); (w. gen.) the hastening on (of an event): *ex nimia protractione, et quoque ex nimia ~one temporis desponsationum* AM 305.2.

festine, *adv.* Hurriedly, in haste: *quod non tarde sed ~e fit* AC 9223.1; ES 3081.

festino ~are ~avi ~atum, *tr., intr.* **1** (tr.) To hasten on, perform urgently: *~ans justitiam* Isa. 16.5 (DD 6); *consummationem ~atam* Zeph. 1.18 (DD 4). **2** (intr.) To act hastily, hurry: *ero testis ~ans contra praestigiatores* Mal. 3.5 (AC 7297.3); (w. *ad*) *~avit Pharao ad vocandum Moschen* Exod. 10.16 (AC); (w. inf.) *quapropter ~astis venire hodie?* Exod. 2.18 (AC). **3** (intr.) To go hastily, hurry: *~abat a luce in lucem* AC 1872; VR 160.7.

festinus ~a ~um, *a.* Hurried, rapid, fast: *~o cursu* AM 6.4; *circumgyratione quae tam ~a est, ut...* ES 579.

festivitas ~atis, *f.* Festivity: *quod ludere sit quod est ~atis interioris* AE 223.9; a festival: *palmae adhibebantur in ~atibus sanctis* AC 8369.1; AM 10.1.

festivus ~a ~um, *a.* Festive: *~a repotia celebrare* AM 8.1.

festuca ~ae, *f.* A piece of straw: *cur cernis ~am quae in oculo fratris tui* Matt. 7.3 (AC 9051.3).

festum ~i, *neut.* A festival, feast, holiday: *et ~um agant Mihi in deserto* Exod. 5.1 (AC); *in ~o Tabernaculorum* AE 109.6 (Lev. 23.39).

festus ~a ~um, *a.* Of festival; *dies ~us*, a holiday: AC 7882.

fet-: see **foet-**.

fex: see **faex**.

fibra ~ae, *f.* (anat.) A fibre (as part of the body): *per ~as nerveas et motrices* CI 95; *ad extremas corporis ~as* AC 8261.3; (in an insect) *quod praeditum sit* [*insectulum*] *~is et vasis* VR 12.4.

fibricus ~a ~um, *a.* (anat.) Of a fibre, fibrous: ES 2562.

fibrilla ~ae, *f.* A fibril: *omnis nervus...consistit a fibris, et fibra a ~is* VR 147; *~as purissimas pectoris et cordis* AC 233.1.

fibrillaris ~is ~e, *a.* Fibrillar: *altera* [*substantia cerebri est*] *~is et vocatur medullaris* VR 351.3.

fibrosus ~a ~um, *a.* Resembling fibres, fibrous: *per transitus sicut ~os* AC 8603.3.

fibula ~ae, *f.* A pin, clasp, brooch: *viri cum foeminis ...adduxerunt ~am, et inaurem, et annulum, et cingulum* Exod. 35.22 (AC 10083.3).

ficticius: see **fictitius**.

fictilis ~is ~e, *a.* Made of pottery, earthenware: *vasa ~ia* Rev. 2.27 (AE); ES 3486.

fictio ~onis, *f.* An invented tale, fiction: *poesi...in qua nihil nisi ~ones verbosae* ES 1045.

fictitius ~a ~um, *a.* also **ficticius**. Invented, fictitious: *artificialia, et sic ~a cultus* AC 1298.1; *fallacia et ~a falsa* AC 7086.

fictor ~oris, *m.* One who shapes, sculptor, maker: *sculpsit illud ~or ejus* Hab. 2.18 (AC 586.2).

ficus ~us, *f.* **1** A fig tree: *in parabola de ~u* VI 2; AM 155^{a}.5. **2** The fruit of the fig tree, a fig: *non ~us in ficu* Jer. 8.13 (AC 5117.4).

fidelis ~is ~e, *a.* **1** Observing promises, faithful: *qui justi et ~es sunt* AE 208.4; VI 84.2; (as a title of the Lord) *qui sedens super eo* [sc. *equo*] *vocabatur ~is et Verus* Rev. 19.11 (AR). **2** (masc. pl. as sb.) The loyal followers of the Lord, the faithful: *liberatio ~ium a Domino* AC 7823; DD 14.7.

fidelitas ~atis, *f.* The quality of being faithful, faithfulness, loyalty: *integritas, justitia, ~as et rectitudo* VI 83; (w. pl.) an instance of this: *gens justa, custodiens ~ates* Isa. 26.2 (AC 402.5).

fideliter, *adv.* Faithfully: *qui ~er usus faciunt* AM 7.3.

fides[1] ~ei, *f.* **1** A firm belief, persuasion: *qui...in illa ~e se confirmaverunt, quod bonum...et verum...sint a semet* CI 10; *nec aliquis sibi ~em inducere potuerat, quod...* AM 12.1; *~em habere* (w. dat.), to believe (in): *veritatum...quibus ~em habuit* AC 896.1. **2** (w. *in* + acc.) Belief (in the Lord): *qui fuerunt in ~e in Dominum* AC 477.3; VR 4.1. **3** Belief in the Lord as Saviour, true faith: *~es non aliud est quam veritas* VR 142; *alterius ~em destruere* AC 6754; *docent quod sola ~es salvet* VI 4; cf. *per ~em hodie non aliud intelligitur, quam cogitatio quod ita sit, quia Ecclesia docet* FI 1. **4** A declaration of faith: *~es novi caeli et novae Ecclesiae...haec est...* VR 2.

fides[2] ~ium, *f. pl.* A stringed musical instrument: *laudate Ipsum cum ~ibus et organo* Ps. 150.4 (AC 8337.5); ES 1996.

fido ~ere, *intr.* (w. dat.) To have confidence (in), trust (to): *qui sibi ~unt suaeque sapientiae in spiritualibus* AC 8185.2; (impers. pass.) *sensuale hominis cui ~itur* AC 194.

fiducia ~ae, *f.* Confidence, trust: *ne ~am ponite in duce* Mic. 7.5 (AC 6960.2); *~am habere quod Ipse salvet* FI 36; (w. gen.) *cum plena ~a acceptionis precum* AM 3.6.

fidus ~a ~um, *a.* Worthy of trust: *haec verba vera et ~a sunt* Rev. 21.5 (AR).

figmentum ~i, *neut.* **1** That which is fashioned or moulded: *~um dixerit de figulo suo* Isa. 29.16 (AE 177.6). **2** That which is devised in the mind, a figment: *omne ~um cogitationum cordis ejus solummodo malum* Gen. 6.5 (AC); *quod essent ~a et inventa* AM 182.7.

figo ~gere ~xi ~xum, *tr.* **1** To establish firmly, make immovable, fix: *eorum effectus est, ut ~gant caetera* ES 1812; *hic ecce ~xus auro et argento* Hab. 2.19 (AC 643.2); (transf.) *non potuit amor ille...se firmare et ~gere* AM 401.1; *in externo homine ideas ~gunt quod ita sit* AC 7290.2. **b** *radicem ~gere*, to strike root: *quod nihil boni...adhuc potuisset radicem ~gere* AC 873; ES 227. **2** To direct steadfastly, fix (one's gaze): *in loco ubi ~gitur seu terminatur aspectus* CI 121; *~xi intuitum in luce illa* VR 25.1; *dum in solum Deum Messiam intuitum internum ~gerem* ES 256.

figulinus ~a ~um, *a.* Of pottery, earthenware: *vasa ~a* Rev. 2.27 (AR); ES 2068.

figulus ~i, *m.* A potter: *num argilla increpatura est ~um quod ex se testam lotii faciat* VR 72.1.

figura ~ae, *f.* **1** Shape, form: *secundum templi ~am* AM 23; *humana ~a* ES 355. **2** A likeness, model: *~ae locustarum* Rev. 9.7 (SS 13.1). **3** An appearance serving to denote something else, figure: *cultus...constiterit in typis et ~is* VR 109.2; *plura quae in propheticis Verbi sub ~is concelata sunt* VR 123.2.

figurate, *adv.* Under another appearance, disguisedly: *ne aliquid oppositi...nisi ~e et sicut e longinquo exhibeant* AM 17.5.

figuratio ~onis, *f.* The use of one thing to denote another: *propter eam ~onem jussus est Abraham peregrinari in Philisthaea* AC 9340.11.

figuro ~are ~avi ~atum, *tr.* To represent in visible form, body forth: *haec [Ecclesia] talis fuit ut ~aret Ecclesiam venturam Christianam* VR 670; *[sirenes] ~ant pulchritudinem Veneris* VR 80.1.

filamentosus ~a ~um, *a.* Full of threads, stringy: *materiale quoddam ~um* AC 671.2.

filamentum ~i, *neut.* A thread: *'marionettes'...cum ~is pendulis ad manus* ES 4529; AS 190.

filia ~ae, *f.* (dat. and abl. pl. *~abus*) A daughter: *~a Pharaonis* Exod. 2.5 (AC); AM 184; (in Bibl. phr.) *~a Gallim* Isa. 10.30 (SS 15.1); *atrium ~abus noctuae* Isa. 34.13 (AC 7293.3).

filialis ~is ~e, *a.* Of or proper to sons or daughters, filial: *reverentiam ~em erga parentes* ES 3151.

filiolus ~i, *m.* A little son, little child: *~i, cavete vobis ab idolis* 1 John 5.21 (VR 560).

filius ~i, *m.* **1** A male child, son: *omnem ~um qui nascitur, in flumen projicietis illum* Exod. 1.22 (AC); *a ~is et filiabus ad nepotes et neptes* AM 402. **2** (of the Lord): *Deum Patrem et Deum ~um* FI 39; *~us Dei et Unigenitus* AC 2628.2; *~us Hominis* Matt. 16.27 (VI 2). **3** (Bibl.) **a** (to denote age): *et fuit Noach ~us quingentorum annorum* Gen. 5.32 (AC); Exod. 7.7 (AC). **b** (w. gen. to denote nature): *~is mortis* Ps. 102.20 (AC 8330.5); *a ~o irae facere ~um gratiae* VR 58. **4** (pl.) The members (of a stated group): *~i Israelis* 'the children of Israel' Gen. 32.32 (AC); *ab Antiquissimae Ecclesiae ~is* AC 1121; *~i regni* ES 4139; *plures ex vetutis Sophis, et illorum ~is, hoc est, discipulis* AM 151[a].1.

filum ~i, *neut.* A thread or anything resembling one: *involvunt id...sicut aranea capturas ~is* AM 231.4; *~um lini* Ezek. 40.3 (AE 70.4); *hae* [sc. *meninges cerebri*] *per ~a a se excerpta in...glandulas intrant* VR 60.2.

fimbria ~ae, *f.* A fringe: *ut saltem tangerent ~am vestimenti Ipsius* Mark 6.56 (AC 10130.7).

fimbriatus ~a ~um, *a.* Fringed: *baculus...crassius* [*crassus* J D Odhner] *~us* ES [4567] ½.

fimus ~i, *m.* Excrement, dung: *potest...~us induci auro* VI 10; ES 2901; (pl.) *~i et stercora* AC 1103.2.

finalis ~is ~e, *a.* **1** Of or relating to the end, last, final: *exploratio et manifestatio ~is* AR 477. **2** Of or relating to the end or purpose: *ubi pecunia est amor ~is* VR 801.

finaliter, *adv.* As end or purpose: *omne creatum est ~er propter hominem* AS 170.

findo ~ere fidi fissum, *tr.* To split, cleave: *~et petram ut effluant aquae* Isa. 48.21 (AE 71.2); *atra illa nubes ~ebatur in medio* VR 134.1.

finga ~ae, *f.* A member of the ape family, prob. chimpanzee: *sicut ~ae astutae, quae fingunt actus similes humanis* VR 568.4.

fingo ~gere ~xi fictum, *tr.* **1** To make by the use of the imagination, devise: *quod alii... ~xerint imagines ex sole et luna* VR 11.2; *baculum fictum* ES 4595. **2** To invent, devise (that which is false): *falsa quae ~xerunt* AC 6650; *ne ~gerent sibi cultum ex proprio* AE 324.19. **3** (w. pred.) To imagine or portray as, pretend to be: *se lucis angelos ~gunt* AC 875.5; *in hac* [sc. *glandula pineali*] *~xerunt sedem animae* AM 315.4; *~xerunt Auroram alatam pennis argenteis* VR 112.1.

finio ~nire ~nivi ~nitum, *tr.* **1** To bring to an end, conclude, finish: *voluit praeses oratione ~nire synedrium* VR 137.12; AM 9.2; *excipiebat usus quae alius ~niebat* ES 2419. **b** (pass.) to come to an end, finish: *tunc ~nitur nox et incipit dies* AC 8211.1. **2** To impose bounds upon, limit: *una cum illo mundo creata sunt spatia et tempora, et haec ~niunt illum* VR 27; *determinatio cogitationis ad aliquem populum... limitat et ~nit ideas* AC 6653.

finis ~is, *m.* **1** The outermost part, edge, end: *ab uno ~e universi ad alterum* AC 1380; ES 1513. **2** The last period, conclusion, end: *vetus...Ecclesia ad ~em suum pervenit* VI praef.; *in ~e saeculorum* AC 530.2. **3** The last item in sequence, end: *ad ~em capitum sequentium* AC 6695. **4** An end in view, purpose, aim: *pro ~e habuit praeeminentiam sui prae aliis* AC 952; *intentio seu ~is* AC 2364; (in philosophy, dist. from cause and effect) *sicut ~is, causa et effectus* VI 14. **b** *~e* (w. gen.), with the intention (of): *captando homines ~e perdendi* AC 830; AM 242; cf. *eo ~e, ut neminem lateret* ES 2148.

finitio ~onis, *f.* The quality of being finite: *ibi* [sc. *in sole spirituali*] *et inde est primum ~onis* VR 29.3.

finitus ~a ~um, *a.* (superl. *~issimus*) Having bounds, finite, limited: *mens humana...est ~a* VR 28.1; (neut. as sb.) *nequaquam aliquam ideam habere possit de Infinito, nisi per simile ~o* AC 6876.2; *ratiocinationem a ~issimis* ES 3476.

fio fieri, *intr.* (*factus sum*, see **facio**, is used as pf.) **1** To come about, take place, happen: *influxus fit per correspondentias* AS 88; *quod non fierent mala* AC 7007; *convivia fiebant apud antiquos* AC 6791; (w. dat.) *ad cognoscendum quid fieret illi* Exod. 2.4 (AC). **2** To come into existence, arise: *ex plane nihilo nihil fit* AS 55; *fiet in eo fons aquae salientis in vitam aeternam* John 4.14 (SS 2.2). **3** (w. pred.) To become: *apud illos qui fiunt angeli* AS 67; *per id fit angelus sapiens* AS 115; *Divinum verum cum fit vitae fit bonum* CI 348; *illa quae audiunt...fiunt vitae* CI 271; (w. *in* + acc.) *aquae...quae fient in flumen inundans* Jer. 47.2 (FI 53).

firmamentum ~i, *neut.* **1** That which makes firm or secure, foundation, support: *naturale est instar ~i aut baseos spirituali* AC 8106.4; *amor mutuus, qui est ~um coeli* AC 2733.2. **2** The container of the visible universe, sky, firmament: *stellae in ~o mundi* VR 74.5.

firmatio ~onis, *f.* The act of making firm, securing: AE 783.1; AE 799.5.

firme, *adv.* (compar. *~ius*) Securely, firmly: *quo plus cedit...eo ~ius constat* ES 241; confidently: *quod satis ~e cupiebat affirmare* ES 292.

firmitas ~atis, *f.* Stability, strength: *cum ~ate templi ex lapidibus disposite connexis* VR 353.2.

firmiter, *adv.* Securely, firmly: *omnes qui sibi ~er impresserunt quod...* AC 6692.8; AM 9.1.

firmitudo ~inis, *f.* Stability, strength: *quod sint* [*anguli*] *robur et ~o* AC 9494.1; AC 9538.

firmo ~are ~avi ~atum, *tr.* **1** To establish securely, make firm: *~atus est per misericordiam thronus* Isa. 16.5 (AC 414.1); *~abo semen tuum* Ps. 89.4 (AE 205.4). **2** To render strong, confirm: *~antur vera et bona* AC 6663.1; *quae spes...amorem...lactat et ~at* AM 254. **3** To confirm (a person in a belief or sim.): *ita se in sententia sua ~at* AC 6663.2.

firmus ~a ~um, *a.* (compar. *~ior*) Not easily abolished, strong, firm, definite: *misericordias Davidis ~as* Isa. 55.3 (DD 43): *quod viris sit* [*gestus*] *fortior et ~ior* AM 218.1.

fissura ~ae, *f.* A cleavage, fissure: *per foramina et ~as sicut rupium* CI 428; *nubes findebatur...et per ~am visi sunt angeli* VR 134.1.

fistula ~ae, *f.* **1** A wind instrument, pipe: *nablia, citharae, ~ae, cymbala* AE 323.1; AM 86. **2** (anat.) A windpipe: *quod praeditum sit* [*insectulum*]... *~is pulmonicis* VR 12.4.

fixatio ~onis, *f.* The act of fixing or making permanent: AS 346.

fixe, *adv.* In an unchanging manner, unwaveringly, fixedly: *tenent animum ejus in cogitatione alicujus rei ~e et continenter* AC 1967; ES 4343.

fixo ~are ~avi ~atum, *tr.* To make permanent, solidify, fix: *si illa avis...foret impleta materiis correspondentibus ex tellure et sic ~ata, quod foret avis perdurans* AS 344; AS 370; *interiora mentis illorum ~ata et constabilita sunt* VR 720; *simile est cum omnibus, quae persuasio et confirmatio ~ant, quae apparent demum sicut picti tapetes parieti...multis clavis affixi* VR 639.

fixus ~a ~um, *a.* (pf. pple. of **figo**) Unmoving, fixed: *stellae ~ae* AC 7803; unchanging, stable: *hoc ~um manet* CI 345.

flaccesco ~ere, *intr.* To become weak, fail, droop: *inde ~unt nervi et cadunt vires* AC 8316; AM 107.

flaccide, *adv.* Limply: *ibi pendent [mala], sed ~e, deorsum* AC 5356.2.

flagellatio ~onis, *f.* A whipping, flogging: *~o monachi pro toto caetu* VR 582.

flagello ~are ~avi ~atum, *tr.* To flog, whip: *postquam Illum ~averint* Luke 18.33 (AE 83); VR 130.3; ES 3550.

flagellum ~i, *neut.* A whip: *tunc excitabit Jehovah ...contra Aschurem ~um* Isa. 10.24 (SS 15.1).

flagitiosus ~a ~um, *a.* (superl. *~issimus*) (of actions) Criminal: *~is lenociniis* AM 468; (neut. pl. as sb.) *sirenes...ad ~issima progressae* ES 4452.

flagitium ~i, *neut.* A wicked action, crime: *ut... liberius possint animum ~is dare* CI 362; AM 501.

flagito ~are ~avi, *intr.* To ask imperiously, demand: *cum desiderio... ~abat intense* ES 874; *~ante aliqua necessitate* CI 428.

flagratio ~onis, *f.* A blazing, burning: *~o seu flamma illius amoris* AM 357.

flagro ~are ~avi, *intr.* (*tr.*) **1** To burn brightly, blaze: *flamma satis candide ~ans* AC 6922; (fig.) *calores... ~antes dum instant nuptiae* AM 275. **2** (w. abl., of persons) To be consumed (with), burn (with): *incipiunt ~are odio* AE 121; *~are vindicta* VI 67; ES 4496. **3** (tr.) To desire ardently, long for: *quod non aliud cuperent et ~arent quam eos cruciare* AC 699; *cujus* [sc. *generis humani*] *salutem... [Dominus] unice desideravit et ~avit* AC 1813.1.

flamen ~inis, *m.* A clergyman of the lowest rank: CO 9; CO 17.

flamma ~ae, *f.* A flame: *oculi Ipsius tanquam ~a ignis* Rev. 1.14 (AR); *facile arripiunt ~am* ES 808; (fig.) *ut sic amor conjugialis a primo suo calore rite progrediatur usque ad ~am nuptialem* AM 301.

flammans ~ntis, *a.* Producing flames, blazing: *in luce fulgurante et quasi ~nte* AC 7059.2.

flammeus ~a ~um, *a.* Resembling flame, flaming, fiery: *lux ~a et candida* SS 73; *amictus toga lanea fulgente ex ~a purpura* AM 266.1; (neut. as sb.) *decidit ~um intensum ante oculum* AC 1524.

flammula ~ae, *f.* A small flame: *sol...excerpsit ex se ~as lucentes* VR 79.3; VR 111.12; ES 808.

flatus ~us, *m.* A blowing, breath: *~us Jehovae sicut flumen sulphuris ardentis* Isa. 30.33 (AC 643.3); *instrumenta ~us* 'wind instruments' AC 420.2. (n.b. At AM 183.4 *flatus mentis* was rightly emended by A Acton to *status mentis*.)

flavedo ~inis, *f.* Yellowness: *~ine auri* Ps. 68.13 (AE 283.4).

flavescens ~ntis, *a.* Yellowish: *lux ~ns, qualis est aurorae post solis exortum* VR 136.1; *punctulis ~ntibus sicut stellulis* AC 1624; ES 2866.

flavesco ~ere, *intr.* To turn yellow: *folia arborum primum ~unt ac postea decidunt* CO 7.

flavidus ~a ~um, *a.* (compar. *~ior*) Yellowish: *cum punctulis ~ioribus sicut stellulis* ES 3636.

flavus ~a ~um, *a.* (compar. *~ior*) Yellow, tawny: *lux ...satis ignea et ~a* AC 9695; *quod viri sint [facie]... asperiore, ~iore, etiam barbata* AM 218.1.

flecto ~ctere ~xi ~xum, *tr.* **1** To bend: *quod... ~ctenda sint genua* FI 47; *genu ~xus*, kneeling: ES 423. **2** To direct towards a new object, deflect: *~ctunt suas facies et sua corpora quaquaversum* CI 143; (transf.) *nisi Divinum continue hominis liberum regat et ~ctat* AC 7007.3; *Dominus illorum cogitationes...ad Se ~ctit et determinat* AE 151.2. (n.b. In AM 8.2 *flectentes serta* should perhaps be emended to *plectentes serta* 'weaving garlands'.)

fleo flere flevi, *intr.* To weep, cry: *qui flent ad omnia* AM 182.8; *cum quis...videt aliquem in miseria, ut hic filia Pharaonis natum...flentem* AC 6737.

fletus ~us, *m.* Weeping, crying: *cum ~u venient* Jer. 31.9 (AE 71.2); AM 182.8.

flexibilis ~is ~e, *a.* (compar. *~ior*) That may be bent, flexible: *inde ~is redditur homo* ES 468; *~iores eorum animi* AC 1835.1.

flexilis ~is ~e, *a.* That may be bent, flexible: ES 3431; (of persons) capable of being influenced, impressionable: *quia non ~es et dociles* ES 546.

flexio ~onis, *f.* **1** A bending: *~onem genuum, procumbentiam super genubus, et quoque prostrationem corporis usque ad terram* AC 5323.1; VR 767.3. **2** A redirecting toward a new object: *sanctum cultus ab infantia irradicatum hoc secum habet quod non patiatur violentiam, sed ~onem lentam et clementem* AC 1992.4.

flexura ~ae, *f.* A curve: *quod illos* [sc. *sensus*] *scirent imprimis ex ~is linearum et apicum literae* SS 90.1.

flexus ~us, *m.* A winding course, bend, turn: *quae [lux] per spirales ~us se devolvens secum tulit... sertum* AM 461.8.

flo flare flavi, *intr.* To blow: *flare naribus seu spirare* AC 8286.4; (of winds) *sunt sicut venti qui flant et transeunt* AM 232.1.

floccipendo ~ere ~i, *tr.* To regard as worthless, attach no value to: *apud illos qui Verbum ~unt* VR 146; AM 466.3.

floccus ~i, *m.* A fine particle, esp. of fibrous material: *possunt...dissipari, vix aliter ac floccus in aëre per ventum oris* AC 9327.3; AE 1050.2.

florens ~ntis, *a.* (superl. *~ntissimus*) Flourishing: *campum ~ntissimum* CO 33; *de ~ntissimo ejus statu* AC 137.

floreo ~rere ~rui, *intr.* **1** (of plants) To be in flower, bloom: *in regno vegetabili sunt omnia quae...crescunt et ~rent* CI 104; AC 7083; ES 269. **2** (transf.) To flourish, be vigorous: *~rebit in diebus Ipsius justus* Ps. 72.7 (DD 4); *quod tunc germinent, ~reant et fructificent [mentes] sicut arbores* AM 201.

florescentia ~ae, *f.* The state of blooming, blossoming: *[arboris] germinatio, ~a et fructificatio* VR 41.2.

floresco ~ere, *intr.* **1** To develop flowers, blossom, bloom: *facit ut germinent, ~ant, et fructificent* VR 44; *~unt antequam pariunt fructus* AC 10185.2. **2** (fig. of a time of life) To blossom, flourish: *in aetatem hanc ~entem reducti* AM 137.7.

floretum ~i, *neut.* A flower garden, flower bed: *hortos, arboreta et floreta* AC 1807.2.

floridus ~a ~um, *a.* **1** Covered in flowers, flowery: *campi ~i et virides* FI 63.3. **2** At its acme, flourishing: *~um puellare decus* AM 505.2; AC 4676.1.

florifer ~era ~erum, *a.* Flowery: *campi ~eri* AM 430.

florificatus ~a ~um, *a.* Decorated with flowers, flowered: *amicti ~is vestibus* AM 137.2.

floriformis ~is ~e, *a.* In the form of a flower, flower-shaped: *adamantes secti ~es* VR 48.20.

flos floris, *m.* **1** A flower: *rubus...producit flores et baccas* AC 6832.1; VR 12.7; (sg. as collective) *arborem...cujus...folium pulchrum, flos multus* Dan. 4.12 (AE 109.4); *in floribus*, in flower, flowering: AM 183.1. **2** A representation of a flower: *candelabrum cum suis lucernis et floribus* AC 552. **3** The season or state of highest excellence, acme, flower: *puella... aetate ut in primo flore* AC 1872; *in juventutis et adolescentiae florem veniunt* CI 414; *virginitatis florem furati* AC 828.

flosculus ~i, *m.* **1** A small flower, floweret: *serta ex ~is* DP 205. **2** A rhetorical ornament, grace: *cogitationes ...quas... ~is concinnant* AE 763.3.

fluctuatio ~onis, *f.* The state of being tossed upon waves, tossing: *quod ~ones ejus* [sc. *arcae*] *ita increbruerint* AC 785.

fluctuo ~are ~avi, *intr.* To be unsteady, waver: *qualis ejus [Ecclesiae] fuerit, quod ~ans* AC 703; *Judaei...prae aliis ~ant inter verum et falsum* AC 788.2.

fluctus ~us, *m.* A wave: *mare...cum ~ibus in altum surgentibus* ES 243.

fluentia ~ae, *f.* A fluency: *quia apparet ~ia, ut dictum* AC 5558.

fluentum ~i, *neut.* A body of running water, stream: *eduxit ~a e petra* Ps. 78.16 (AC 8278.1); Isa. 44.3 (AE 71.2).

fluide, *adv.* (compar. *~ius*) Fluently: *~ius agunt soli* ES 3423.

fluiditas ~atis, *f.* Liquidity, smoothness: *~as et amaenitas loquelae* AC 1759.

fluidus ~a ~um, *a.* (compar. *~ior*, superl. *~issimus*) **1** Of a liquid nature, fluid: (neut. as sb.) *mala sanguinis et ~orum corporis temperie* AC 847.2; *quod ~iora se ex his secreverint...unde maria* VR 79.2; *~um vitale*, vital fluid: ES 2298. **2** Resembling a liquid, fluid, fluent: *sermo...solito ~ior* ES 1840; *quo mollior [est homo] ...seu ~ior, eo est perfectior* ES 2250.

fluito ~are ~avi, *intr.* To move freely in space, float: *quod sic ~ent [spiritus] in universo* ES 3685.

flumen ~inis, *neut.* **1** A river: *descendit filia Pharaonis ad lavandum ad ~en* Exod. 2.5 (AC); (used of a flood) *descendit imber, et venerunt ~ina* Matt. 7.25 (AE 644.24). **2** (transf.) Anything resembling a river, stream: *quod in homine...nihil sit nisi ~en fluidum* ES 242; *loquelae ~en* ES 1840; *non est in ~ine eorum vitae* ES 3843.

fluo ~ere ~xi, *intr.* **1** (of liquids) To flow: *aqua ~ens* AC 8026. **b** (w. abl.) to abound (in liquids), flow (with): *ad terram ~entem lacte et melle* Exod. 3.8 (AC). **2** (of things) To move with a sinuous motion, flow: *indutus erat chlamyde, quae ex volatu ~ebat retrorsum* AM 2.1; *capillis ~entibus* ES 2241. **3** To be inconstant, change, fluctuate: *facies...penes eos libere ~it* ES 530. **4** To be derived, flow (from a source): *omnis loquela ~it ex cogitatione* AC 7745; *cogitationes angelorum vadunt et ~unt secundum formam coeli* AE 27.1; *[nervi] ~unt ex cerebris* ES 2561. **b** (impers.) it follows as a consequence, it comes: *ex quo ~it quod homo sit homo* VR 48.5; ES 3024.

fluor ~oris, *m.* A flow, flux: *ad imitationem istius ~oris qui in ventriculis [cerebri] est* ES 915; ES 1889; CC 12.3.

fluvialis ~is ~e, *a.* Resembling a river, stream-like: *modo ~i* ES 1183 ½.

fluviatilis ~is ~e, *a.* = **fluvialis**: AC 1761.

fluvius ~i, *m.* **1** A river: *fontes et ~i* AM 182.3; *~us aquae vitae* Rev. 22.1 (AR). **2** Any succession resembling a river, stream: *~us ignis emanans* Dan. 7.10 (AC 934.2); *~us idearum* ES 1146; *in ~o sermonis* ES 2042.

fluxio ~onis, *f.* A flowing movement, flux: *per fibrarum ~ones in nostro corpore* ES 3607; ES 2173.

fluxus ~us, *m.* **1** *~us sanguinis*, an emission of blood, haemorrhage: Luke 8.44 (AE 79). **2** A stream-like movement, flux, flow: *credit quod omnia sint ~us coeci* AC 6692.2; *mollis quidam ~us sermonis eorum* ES 1621.

focalis ~is ~e, *a.* Of or belonging to a hearth: *ministri ~es* AM 231.2; *igne ~i* CJ 9.

focus ~i, *m.* **1** A place where a fire is lit, fireplace, hearth: *ignis sicut ~i* AM 264.1; (for cooking) *piscem superpositum ~o* Luke 24.42 (AC 7852.2); (an area in the spiritual world) *ejiciuntur in ~os occidentis* AM 77.5. **2** The focus of a lens or mirror: *in medium ~um speculi caustici* CO 51; CC 9.3.

fodina ~ae, *f.* A digging for the extraction of minerals, mine: *de ~a adamantina* AR 655.7; CI 586; VR 534.2.

fodio ~dere ~di ~ssum, *intr.* (*tr.*) **1** To dig: *~dit et in profundum penetrat* Luke 6.48 (AC 705.2); (tr.) to produce by digging, dig for: *et ~derunt...Aegyptii circum fluvium aquas ad bibendum* Exod. 7.24 (AC). **2** To pierce: *quidam ex militibus...latus Ipsius ~dit* John 19.34 (AE 329.16).

foecunditas ~atis, *f.* also **fec-**. Fruitfulness, fertility: AC 3985.

foecundo ~are ~avi ~atum, *tr.* also **fec-**. To make fruitful, fertilize: ES 2660.

foecundus ~a ~um, *a.* also **fec-**. Fruitful, fertile: *filius ~ae Joseph* Gen. 49.22 (AC).

foede, *adv.* also **faede**. Foully: *~e scortatorius erat* AM 477.4.

foederatus ~a ~um, *a.* Bound by a treaty or covenant, allied: *quod...dixerint...~os...socios* AC 2360.5.

foedifragus ~i, *m.* also **faedifragus**. One who breaks a treaty, renegade: *cum ~is, qui violant pacta* VR 316.

foeditas ~atis, *f.* Foulness or an instance of this: *ne inter se etiam ~ates sint* CI 553.4.

foedo ~are ~avi ~atum, *tr.* also **faedo**. To make foul or dirty, befoul, pollute: *~antur corpore et facie* AC 956; (transf.) *~are cultum Domini naturalismo* VR 137.9; *quod verum fidei ~averint* AC 4504.

foedus[1] ~a ~um, *a.* also **faedus**. (compar. *~ior*, superl. *~issimus*) Foul, noisome: *halitus ~i et putres* AM 253.2; (transf.) *vidi rem ~am* Hos. 6.10 (SS 79.6); *persuasiones ...quae ex amore sui sunt ~issimae* AC 1675.7.

foedus[2] ~eris, *neut.* also **faedus**. **1** A treaty, pact, agreement: *ex ~eribus inter regna* AC 6804.5; *~us conjugiale pactum in mundo* AM 45. **2** The pact between God and man, covenant: *arca ~eris Jehovae* Jer. 3.16 (DD 4); cf. *dabo te in ~us populi* Isa. 42.6 (CI 129). **3** One of the two covenants described by the two divisions of the Word: *in sacris utriusque ~eris scriptis* 1AD 61; AM 128; cf. *vocatur illa [lex] '~us et Testimonium'* VI 57.

foemella ~ae, *f. adj.* also **faem-**, and **fem-**. Female: *pecudes ~ae* AC 7838; CI 108.1.

foemina ~ae, *f.* also **faemina**, and **femina**. A woman, female: *masculus et ~a praedicatur de intellectualibus* AC 725; *satanas...ascendit una cum ~a* VR 80.1; ES 2618.

foemininus ~a ~um, *a.* also **faem-**, and **fem-**. Of women, female: *ex sexu ~o* CI 332; *a ~o amore* ES 3177.

foeneratio ~onis, *f.* also **faen-**. The taking of excessive interest upon money lent, usury: *furta non manifesta, sicut ~ones et lucrationes illicitae* AE 967.3; the improper gaining (of other advantages): *propter ~onem lucri aut honoris* AC 7757.

foenerator ~oris, *m.* also **faen-**. One who lends money at excessive interest, usurer, moneylender: *~or concredit pecunias alteri propter usuram* AC 9210.1.

foeneror ~ari ~atus sum, *tr.* also **faen-**. To have lent to one, obtain as a favour: *tandem ~antur visum noctuarum similem* VR 7; *hoc arcanum ~abitur lucem in sequentibus* VR 50.

foenum ~i, *neut.* also **faenum**. Mown grass, hay: *~um tectorum* Isa. 37.27 (AC 996.3); *~um pro eorum bestiis* ES 2707.

foenus ~oris, *neut.* also **faenus**. Interest, profit: *cum ~ore...negotiando* AM 453.

foeta ~ae, *f.* also **feta**. A female person or animal having recently given birth: *in brachium suum colliget agnos...~as leniter ducet* Isa. 40.11 (AC 343).

foeteo ~tere ~tui, *intr.* also **faeteo**, and **feteo**. To emit an unpleasant smell, stink: *~tuit flumen* Exod. 7.18 (AC 6693.6).

foetide, *adv.* also **fet-**. In an ill-smelling manner, stinkingly: *in stagnis ~e olentibus* AC 820.

foetidus ~a ~um, *a.* also **fet-**. Evil-smelling, stinking: *calidum balnei ~um* AM 344.

foetificatio ~onis, *f.* A reproductive process: *ut vix scirent eam [sc. animam humanam] distinguere ab anima vilissimorum insectorum...quia similes ~ones ibi vident* 2AD 1076.

foetifico ~are ~avi, *intr.* also **fet-**. To give birth to offspring: *ut ~ent et multiplicentur* Jer. 23.3 (AC 415.1).

foetor ~oris, *m.* also **faetor**, and **fetor**. A foul smell, stench, stink: *~or graveolentus sicut a cadaveribus* AC 814.1; AM 461.7.

foetus ~us, *m.* also **faetus**, and **fetus**. **1** The young of men or animals, offspring: *quid mater aliud cogitat dum peperit ~um...?* VR 44.1; VR 48.9. **2** (transf.) Progeny, offspring: *quod ex fide hodiernae Ecclesiae enati sint... ~us enormes* SE 64; VR 75.7.

foliaceus ~a ~um, *a.* Abounding in leaves, leafy: *arbores solum ~ae et absque fructibus* AE 109.2; VR 78.1.

foliolum ~i, *neut.* A petal: *quod non aliquid ibi sit, ne quidem ~um...* AM 8.5; VR 78.1.

foliosus ~a ~um, *a.* Resembling a leaf or leaves, foliate: *~a nubes* ES 2931.

folium ~i, *neut.* **1** A leaf (of a tree or plant): *arbor luxurians ~is* VI 46; AC 7966.2. **2** A sheet of paper: *cum de formis scripserim in ~o* ES 3484.

follicularis ~is ~e, *a.* (anat.) Follicular: *substantia... ~is* AS 413.2.

folliculus ~i, *m.* (anat.) A small sac, follicle: AS 413.2; ES 2298.

follis ~is, *m.* A pair of bellows: *sicut ventosum ex ~e* VR 154.5.

fomentator ~oris, *m.* One who applies a poultice: *aegrotus arcessit ~ores* ES 4571.

fomento ~are ~avi ~atum, *tr.* To kindle or feed (a fire): *ignem, ad quem diabolus cum facibus in manu stat et ~at* VR 72.3; (fig.) *talis ignis non datur...nisi ~atus sit subter ab honore* DP 250.3; (transf.) *omne malum... ~at se* DP 278[a].5.

fomentum ~i, *neut.* A piece of kindling, firewood: *sunt...illa sicut totidem ~a* AM 360; (transf.) anything which excites or arouses: *~a spei continue recreantis mentes illorum* AM 304.1.

fomes ~itis, *m.* Firewood, kindling; (in quot. transf.) that which arouses, stimulus: *quod omnis homo ex ~itibus et inde incitamentis...ad unam...faeminam intendat mentem* AM 108.

fons ~ntis, *m.* **1** A source of running water, spring: *ad ~ntes et aquas salientis venae* AM 8.2; (fig.) *in die illo ~ns erit apertus domui Davidis* Zech. 13.1 (DD 4); (Bibl.) *omnes ~ntes abyssi magnae* Gen. 7.11 (AC). **2** A point of origin, source: *in ipsis ~ntibus et originibus vitae...sunt* AC 1647. **3** (anat.) *~ns pulsatilis*, the anterior fontanelle: AC 10381; ES 1675.

fontanella ~ae, *f.* (anat.) A fontanelle: *supra caput juxta fontem pulsatilem, qui ~a vocatur* AC 10381.

fonticulus ~i, *m.* A small spring: *~us ex fortitudine venae saliens in altum* AM 183.1.

for fari fatus sum, *intr.* To speak, say: *'si de hoc aliquid novisti, fare'; et respondi 'fabor'* VR 136.4; (w. acc.) *fatus est haec* VR 134.3.

foramen ~inis, *neut.* An opening, hole: *in ~ine petrae* Exod. 33.22 (AC 6849.2); *demittuntur deorsum per tenebrosissimum ~en versus infima terrae* AC 815; ES 4027; the eye (of a needle): *per ~en acus netoriae* AM 240; the socket (of the eye): *oculi ejus contabescent in ~inibus suis* Zech. 14.12 (AE 152.8); (anat.) *~en ovale*, the opening into the vestibule of the ear, *fenestra ovalis*: ES 2477.

foraminosus ~a ~um, *a.* Full of holes: *domus ~a* VR 390.1.

foraminulum ~i, *neut.* A tiny hole: *per ~um non visibile* ES 2609; AC 4627.1.

foras, *adv.* To the outside (of a building), out of doors: *educens illum ~as* Gen. 15.5 (AC); (esp. with implication of throwing away) out, away: *ejectus est ~as sicut palmes* John 15.6 (VI 29); *ipsa vera ~as exterminantur* AC 6652; *atrium...ejice ~as, et ne illud non metiaris* Rev. 11.2 (AR).

forceps ~ipis, *f.* A pair of tongs or pincers: *fabricat ferrum ~ipe* Isa. 44.12 (AE 386.4); a pair of scissors (glossed as Swedish *sax*): ES(M) 4575.

fore: fut. inf. of **sum** (alternative form for *futurum esse*): CI 464; ES 3678.

forem ~es ~et, etc. (alternative form of *essem, ~es, ~et*): see **sum**.

forensis ~is ~e, *a.* Relating to public life, public: *retentione a domesticis et ~ibus* AM 9.3; ES 1011; (of law) statutory, criminal: *ex lege ~i...ex lege civili* VR 432.

fores ~ium, *f. pl.* Double doors: *apertae sunt ~es* AM 14.1; (fig.) *totalis damnatio ante ~es stetit et imminuit* VR 3.1.

forinsecus[1], *adv.* **1** To the outside: *quod corporea... ~us seu deorsum tendant* 3AD 5481; *non...venit in aurem ~us sed...ab intrinseco* 3AD 6966. **2** Away from home: *faemina...si lasciviam exercet cum introducto aliquo viro in atrium per astum, aut ~us, puniatur morte* AM 369.

forinsecus[2] ~a ~um, *a.* External: *si administrationes ~ae abstrahunt mentem a familiaribus domus* AM 321.7.

foris, *adv.* Outside: *quae [sepulchra] ~is quidem apparent pulchra* Matt. 23.27 (VI 30.1); *~is stant* CI 38.3.

forma ~ae, *f.* **1** Outward appearance, shape, form:

externa ~a apparuerunt honesti AC 1010.2; *in his est similiter Divinum, sed in alia ~a* VR 6.1; *sub humana ~a* AE 27.1. **2** Form as imparting a specific quality: *quod haec* [sc. *loquela*] *non aliud sit quam ~a soni* AR 875.2; *omnes spiritus in infernis...apparent in ~a sui mali* CI 553.1. **b** (as philosophical term) form (as distinct from essence): *charitas et fides faciunt unum sicut essentia et ~a* FI 18.2; *quod...Deus sit...ipsa ~a* VR 20.1. **3** An object of a specified form, shape: *~ae regni animalis, quae una voce vocantur animalia* AC 1757; *Divinum...elucet sicut lux per ~as chrystallinas* VR 6.2. **4** A manifestation: *verum est modo ~a boni* AC 668; *omnes...qui ibi* [sc. *in coelo*] *sunt ~ae amoris et charitatis* CI 17. **5** A verbal expression, form (of words): *ideae cogitationis fiunt discretae ita ut pro ~is loquelae distinctis inserviant* AC 1757; AC 2643. **6** (Bibl.) Beauty, comeliness: *non ~a ipsi* Isa. 53.2 (DD 6).

formabilis ~is ~e, *a.* Capable of being moulded: *lutum...quod non ~e est ad aliquod vas* VR 393.2.

formabilitas ~atis, *f.* The quality of being capable of receiving a form: *est in omni homine ~as* SA 109 (= viii.2.[5]).

formalis ~is ~e, *a.* **1** Of or concerned with form, formal (as dist. from essential): *affectio veri est ~is, affectio boni est essentialis* ES 4399; (neut. as sb.) *quod...praeferant...~ia prae essentialibus* AC 1175.1. **2** Of shape: *ex sphaera pulchri ~is* AC 1517; cf. ES 1047.

formaliter, *adv.* With due ceremony, formally: *inter essentialia, quae solenniter manifestanda sint et ~er celebranda* AM 306.

formatio ~onis, *f.* **1** The process of being formed, formation: *de ~one faeminae a viro* AM 195; *dum* [*mens*] *in ~one est* CI 430. **2** A thing formed by a derivative process, formation: *quod substantia...sit modo unica, et quod reliqua sint ~ones inde* AC 7270.4.

formator ~oris, *m.* One who moulds or forms: *Ipse ut creator, ~or et factor universi* VR 29.3.

formatus ~a ~um, *a.* Given a specific shape, formed: *per viam doctrinae ~ae* AC 521; (neut. as sb.) *amor ...continens ~a in nexu* VR 37.1.

formica ~ae, *f.* An ant: *sicut ~as, quae repunt humi et terunt stratam viam* AM 380.1.

formidabilis ~is ~e, *a.* Inspiring fear, frightening: *transivimus ~em sylvam* AM 79.2; *~is Jehovah super illis* Zeph. 2.11 (AC 1158.4).

formido[1] ~inis, *f.* Intense fear, fright, dread: *cecidit super illos ~o et pavor* Exod. 15.16 (AC); *timor diffamationis...ac ~o ne res domesticae labefactentur* AM 373.

formido[2] ~are ~avi, *tr.* To feel intense fear, be frightened, dread: *ne turbator cor vestrum, neque ~et* John 14.27 (AE 365.6).

formo ~are ~avi ~atum, *tr.* **1** To produce by forming, form: *accurata fit distinctio inter creare, ~are et facere* AC 472; *tentoria...~are et mundare* AC 8379; *splendor lucis...cherubos volantes ~avit in aëre* VR 73.4; *vera ex quibus jucundum amoris...nutritur et ~atur* VI 39; *homo...ideas suas ~averat ex illis quae in natura sunt* AC 7381.2. **2** To change the shape or nature of, form in a specific manner: *facies ~ata est prorsus ad effigiandum illa quae homo cogitat* AC 8249; *quod ~et* [*homo*] *animam suam* AC 5847; (w. *in* + acc.) *quod faemina actualiter ~etur in uxorem* AM 193.1. **3** (of constituent parts) To make up, compose: *spiritus... ~ant quasi globum* AC 6926.

formositas ~atis, *f.* Beauty, loveliness: *in aliquo flore ejusque ~ate* AC 1807.2; (w. pl.) an instance of this: *virgines, quae erant ~ates* AM 477.6.

formosus ~a ~um, *a.* (compar. *~ior*, superl. *~issimus*) Beautiful, lovely: *binae mulieres ~ae* AC 7337.3; (neut. as sb.) AM 42.4.

formula ~ae, *f.* **1** A regular form of speech, stock phrase: *haec loquutionis ~a non est qualis sonat* AM 528; *pro ~is irrisionis* AC 1878; *ut ~a ei familiaris fuerit diabolum nominare* ES 4050. **2** *~a Concordiae*, the Lutheran statement of doctrine promulgated in German in 1580, in Latin in 1584: VR 101.1.

fornax ~acis, *f.* A furnace: *fumus ~acis magnae* Rev. 9.2 (AR); ES 2641.

fornicatio ~onis, *f.* Fornication: *per ~onem intelligitur libido...juvenis cum faemina maecha ante conjugium* AM 444[a].

fornicator ~oris, *m.* A fornicator: AM 448.

fornicatorius ~a ~um, *a.* Of or relating to fornication, fornicatory: *amor ~us* AM 423.

fornicatus ~a ~um, *a.* Covered with arches, vaulted: *e parietibus...camerae supra ~ae* AM 103.3.

fornicor ~ari ~atus sum, *intr.* To fornicate: AM 445.

forsan, *adv.* Perhaps: *cogitant...de influxu vini in cyathos... ~an de influxu aëris in pulmonem* VR 695.4.

forsitan, *adv.* Perhaps: VR 173.2.

fortasse, *adv.* Perhaps: ES 404; ES 1421.

fortassis, *adv.* Perhaps: VR 665.5; ES 4440.

forte, *adv.* **1** (to express doubt) It may be, perhaps:

quod incredibile ~e sed usque verissimum AC 41; *Jovem, ita ~e vocatum a Jehovah* VR 9.3. **2** (w. ref. to the past) As it so happened, by chance: *tunc ~e duo spiritus...illis occurrebant* AM 44.2; ES 4494.

fortifico ~are ~avi ~atum, *tr*. To make strong: *vox buccinae vadens et ~ans se valde* Exod. 19.19 (AC).

fortis ~is ~e, *a*. (compar. *~ior*) **1** Possessing great physical force, strong, powerful: *sicut flumen ~e* Amos 5.24 (AC 922.3); (masc. as sb.) *ut manducetis...carnes ~ium* Rev. 19.18 (AR); (neut. as sb.) *ecce Dominus Jehovih in ~i venit* Isa. 40.10 (AM 81.4). **2** (of abstract things) Possessing powerful influence, strong, intense: *a vi ~iore retinentur* AC 8287; DP 250.3; *quod ~iorem talem venenatam odii sphaeram haberet* ES 1282.

fortiter, *adv*. (compar. *fortius*) With force, strongly, intensely: *resistunt vero et bono fortius* AC 7710; *intendi fortiter aciem oculi ad videndum quid facerent* AM 293.1.

fortitudo ~inis, *f*. Physical strength, force, power: *fonticulus ex ~ine venae saliens in altum* AM 183.1; ES 255; a mighty deed: *dextra Jehovae fecit ~inem* Ps. 118.15 (AC 8281.4).

fortuito, *adv*. By a random process, fortuitously: AM 380.9.

fortuitus ~a ~um, *a*. **1** Random, haphazard, fortuitous: *fortuna...apparet sicut casus ~us quia non sciunt unde* AC 6493. **2** (neut. as sb.) A random event, chance: *fortuna, quae in mundo apparet sicut ~um* ES 4562; *ex ~o*, fortuitously: *de confluxu elementorum in talem formam ex ~o* VR 20.2.

fortuna ~ae, *f*. **1** Chance, fortune: *lusi ludum ~ae* ES 4567; *quod caetera vocent ~am ac casum* AC 7007.1; (worshipped as a deity) *quod Gentiles olim ~am agnoverint, et templum ei struxerint...notum est* DP 212.2. **2** Good fortune, prosperity: *ut in amplificato statu ~ae sint* AM 274; (w. pl.) a piece of good fortune: *ex ~is variis et infortuniis* ES 4423.

fortunatus ~a ~um, *a*. Endowed with good fortune, lucky: (neut. as sb.) *dicebant quod ~um illis repraesentaretur per nubem candidam* AC 6494.

forum ~i, *neut*. A place of public assembly, meeting place: *quae viderant...in ~o et in plateis* AM 5.1; AM 17.1; CI 184.

fossa ~ae, *f*. A ditch: *restituetur et aedificabitur platea et ~a* Dan. 9.25 (AC 2336.3).

fossula ~ae, *f*. A small ditch: *si perrumperetur agger rima seu ~a* AC 1692.2; AC 10754.

fovea ~ae, *f*. **1** A large hole in the surface of the earth, pit: *vulpes ~as habent, et volucres nidos* Matt. 8.20 (DD 27); *Amora, locus derelictus urticae, et ~a salis* Zeph. 2.9 (AC 1666.3); AC 6854.2. **2** (anat.) A depression, pit (in the bones): *in partem occipitis supra ~am* ES 2865.

foveo ~vere ~vi fotum, *tr*. **1** To tend carefully, cherish, nurture: [*aves*] *excludunt pullos, quos...sub alis ~vent* VR 12.5. **2** To hold eagerly, entertain (ideas): *ex idea cogitationis meae, quam nunc ~veo* VR 111.11; *quod quisque suam sententiam ~veat* ES 262; to cherish (hatred and sim.): *nectunt insidias, ~vent odia* CI 508.2; *ab invidia...quae intus fota* ES 2079 1/2.

fractio ~onis, *f*. The act of breaking: *'annona' in lingua originali exprimitur per vocem quae significat ~onem* AC 5405.1.

fractor ~oris, *m*. One who breaks, breaker: *societas tutelam...faederis in se suscepit, et indixit paenas ~oribus ejus* AM 307.

fractura ~ae, *f*. **1** The act of breaking: *iniquitas... franget eos sicut ~a utris figulorum* Isa. 30.14 (AE 177.7). **2** The result of breaking, a fracture, breach: *~a pro ~a* Lev. 24.19 (AC 8223.1); *obligabit Jehovah ~am populi Sui* Isa. 30.26 (VR 109.3); (transf.) *amor conjugialis in ~a ejus* [sc. *unionis*] *perit* AM 460.5.

fractus ~a ~um: pf. pple. of **frango**.

fraeno ~are ~avi ~atum, *tr*. also **freno**. To restrain, inhibit: *ut bonum duceret malum, et ~aret illud* AC 10808.

fraenum ~i, *neut*. also **frenum**. **1** A bridle (for horses): *usque ad ~a equorum* Rev. 14.20 (AR). **2** A restraint, inhibition, check: *amores crescunt quantum illis laxantur ~a* AC 7375; *cum...libere et absque ~o cogitavit* CI 502; *cupiditas in ~o tenetur per timores* AC 6977.

fragilis ~is ~e, *a*. Liable to break, fragile: *verum absque bono est durum, at usque ~e* AE 411.33.

fragmentum ~i, *neut*. A broken piece, fragment: *unde non invenietur in ~o ejus testa* Isa. 30.14 (AE 177.7); a rag: *cum ~is teterrimis vestium* ES 431.

fragor ~oris, *m*. The noise as of breaking, crash, roar: *facta est explosio cum ~ore* VR 162.7; VR 209.3.

fragrans ~ntis, *a*. (superl. *~ntissimus*) Sweet-smelling, fragrant: *cornua germinantia et ~ntia* AE 316.28; *suffitibus ~ntissimis* AM 3.6.

fragranter, *adv*. With a pleasing smell, fragrantly: *percipitur sicut athmosphaera ~er olens quae pleno spiritu attrahitur* DP 296.9.

fragrantia ~ae, *f*. A sweet smell, fragrance: AM 189; AM 210; AS 420.

fragro ~are ~avi, *intr*. To smell sweetly: *ex arbore... cujus succus ~at ex balsamo* AM 77.7.

frangibilis ~is ~e, *a*. Capable of being broken, breakable: ES 242.

frango ~ere fregi fractum, *tr*. **1** To break in pieces: *vox Jehovae ~ens cedros* Ps. 29.5 (SS 18.4); *quod fracta sit virga* Isa. 14.29 (FI 53); esp. to break (bread): *ecce Ego ~ens baculum panis* Ezek. 4.16 (VR 130.2); *fractus panis non scissus* ES 2626. **2** To injure by breaking, break: *non ~erent os ejus* AC 7831; *fractus seu vulneratus pes* ES 2458; *fregisti capita balaenarum* Ps. 74.13 (AC 7293.3); [*ovem*] *fractam non obligastis* Ezek. 34.4 (AC 8364.4). **3** To break in spirit, break down: *ad obligandum fractos corde* Isa. 61.1 (AC 6854.5); *sic ~untur* [*sirenes*] ES 4278. **4** To destroy the resistance of, break down (abstract objects): *fallacias non ~it* AC 25; *ipsum spirituale... ~itur* ES 241; *contumaciae ~endae erunt* ES 4478.

frater ~tris, *m*. **1** A son of the same parents, brother: *loquutus est cum ~tre suo* AC 2304. **2** (in an extended sense) A member of the same group, comrade: *consentimus ad illa quae ~tres nostri loquuti sunt* VR 48.14.

fraternitas ~atis, *f*. A brotherly relationship: *~as illarum* [sc. *charitatis et fidei*]*...repraesentata fuit per Esavum et Jacobum* AC 367.1; *nec sciunt quid frater, nisi ex ~ate qualis est in coelo* AC 1434; brotherly feeling: *recepti cum amicitia et ~ate* ES 709.

fraternus ~a ~um, *a*. Of brothers, fraternal, brotherly: *ex tanto amore ~o mutuo ut frater nequaquam potuisset resistere quin lachrymaret* AC 2304.

fratria ~ae, *f*. The wife of a brother: *accedet ~a ejus ad eum* Deut. 25.9 (AC 1748.4).

fraudo ~are ~avi ~atum, *tr*. To deprive through deception, cheat, defraud: *quare ~asti me?* Gen. 29.25 (AC).

fraudulenter, *adv*. Deceitfully: *quod nunc non ita ~er illis liceat loqui* AC 8383; AM 496.

fraudulentus ~a ~um, *a*. Deceptive, fraudulent: *bona hypocritica, quae deceptoria et ~a* VI 9; AC 7360.

fraus fraudis, *f*. Deceit, deception, pretence: *utuntur... omni malitia, omni astu et fraude* AC 6666.2; CI 358; *mala...sicut fraudes, adulteria, odia* VI 24.

fregi: pf. of **frango**.

fremitus ~us, *m*. A low roar, grumbling, hum: *lamenta illorum audiuntur sicut ~us peculiaris soni* AM 510.3.

fremo ~ere ~ui, *intr*. To utter a deep roar, growl: *leo... ~it et apprehendit praedam* Isa. 5.29 (AE 278.11); *~imus sicut ursi* Isa. 59.11 (AE 781.18).

frendeo ~dere ~dui, *intr*. To gnash (with the teeth): *~debat dentibus* AC 820.

frendor ~oris, *m*. Gnashing (of the teeth): *sonus ~oris dentium...auditus* AC 820.

freno: see **fraeno**.

frenum: see **fraenum**.

frequens ~ntis, *a*. Often repeated, frequent: *a ~nte apostasia illorum* AC 8301.4; *~ns loquela ex memoria* AM 415.5.

frequentatio ~onis, *f*. The act of frequenting: *~o templi, auditio praedicationum* AC 7038.1.

frequenter, *adv*. Frequently, often: *Dominus ~er dixit, quod Pater Ipsum miserit* VR 92.1.

frequento ~are ~avi ~atum, *tr*. To attend frequently, frequent: *~are templum* AC 7038.1; *~asse Sacram Coenam* AE 231.2.

fretus ~a ~um, *a*. Relying upon promises, confident, reassured: *partim ~i* [*forte* J D Odhner] *remanserunt* ES 6012.2.

fricatio ~onis, *f*. The act of rubbing: DP 256.4; ES 4851.

frico ~are ~ui, *tr*. To rub: *piscis magnus...qui voluit ~ari* ES 442; ES 4851.

frigeo ~gere, *intr*. To experience cold, be chilled: *angeli ~gent toto corpore ad amorem incastum* AM 44.7; ES 721.

frigescentia ~ae, *f*. The process of growing cold, chilling: *~a haec facit ut pereat* [*amor conjugialis*] AM 147.

frigesco ~ere, *intr*. To become cold: *ut primum ~unt corporea interiora* AC 179; to become lacking in emotion, cool off: *quod...viri ~ant, et cupiant separationem* AM 167.2.

frigide, *adv*. Coldly: *vera...lucent ~e* CI 132.

frigidiusculus ~a ~um, *a*. Somewhat cold, cool: *afflatus est ~us* ES 3496; (neut. as sb.) ES 3629; lacking intensity, cool: *non erat gaudium angelicum...erat tam leve, quasi ~um* AC 543.

frigidus ~a ~um, *a*. (compar. *~ior*, superl. *~issimus*) **1** Lacking heat, cold: *in ~issimo...carcere* ES 271; (fem. as sb.) cold water: *poculum ~ae* Matt. 10.42 (AE 102.6). **2** Lacking emotional warmth, cold: *novi...quod neque ~us sis neque calidus* Rev. 3.15 (AR); *in tali ~a vita ...sunt* AC 34.1; *ab amore conjugiali spurio, falso et ~o* AM 224.

frigus ~oris, *neut*. **1** Lack of heat, cold: *per variationes...caloris et ~oris* AC 7381.3. **2** Lack of emotional warmth, coldness: *qui...erant in ~ore ad suas uxores* AM 55.5.

frivolus ~a ~um, *a.* Not to be taken seriously, frivolous: *opinio ~a ex phantasia* AM 500.3.

frondesco ~ere, *intr.* To become leafy, put forth foliage: *vitis... ~ens ab aquis multis* Ezek. 19.10 (AC 1069.4).

frondosus ~a ~um, *a.* Having much foliage, leafy: (neut. as sb.) *per fructifera et ~a* AC 2722.1.

frons[1] ~ndis, *f.* A leafy branch, foliage: *ab insitione ~ndium in arboribus* AC 7343.2; *successive ~ndes, folia, flores, fructus* AM 416; VR 41.2.

frons[2] ~ntis, *f.* The forehead: *pileus...depressus super ~ntem usque ad oculos* AM 263.1; *in ~nte*, in the face: *Dominus...videt angelos in ~nte* CI 145.

frontale ~is, *neut.* An ornament for the forehead: *sint in ~ia inter oculos tuos* Deut. 6.8 (AC 396.2).

frontispicium ~i, *neut.* The fore part of the skull, forehead: *in ~o occipitio, quod vocatur cerebellum...* VR 160.8; CI 251.

fructifer ~era ~erum, *a.* Fruit-bearing, fruitful: *arbor ~era* VI 46.

fructificatio ~onis, *f.* The production of fruit, fruiting: AM 92; (fig.) *~onem boni et multiplicationem veri* AE 163.4; VR 32.4.

fructifico ~are ~avi ~atum, *tr., intr.* **1** (tr.) To cause to be fruitful, propagate: *calor solis... ~at omnia telluris* CI 13; *~abo vos et multiplicabo vos* Lev. 26.9 (AC 6804.10); (fig., refl.) *bonum quod se ~at* AC 29.1; (pass.) *cum bonum... ~atur per multiplicationem verorum fidei* AC 6634. **2** (intr.) To be fruitful or fertile: *conatus ~andi* FI 16; (fig.) *quod tunc germinent, floreant et ~ent, sicut arbores* AM 201.

fructus ~us, *m.* **1** The fruit (of a tree or plant): *arbor...ex seminibus ~uum crescit in novas arbores* AC 8326; *arbores ~us*, fruit trees: VR 78.2. **2** The offspring, progeny (of animals): *quod ex nobilitatione hujus* [sc. *humanae*] *formae nascantur nobiles ~us* AM 201. **3** (transf.) That which is produced, product: *quod non sit fides nisi una cum ~u suo* AC 8311.1.

frugifer ~era ~erum, *a.* Fruitful: *mater tua sicut vitis... ~era* Ezek. 19.10 (AC 289).

fruitio ~onis, *f.* Enjoyment: *in ~one omnium bonorum* AC 1630; AM 3.5.

frumentum ~i, *neut.* The seed of edible plants, grain, corn: *messes ex varii generis ~is, ex triticis, miliis, hordeis et fabis* VR 78.2; FI 31.

fruor ~i ~ctus (*or* ~itus) sum, *intr.* (w. abl.) To have the use (of something pleasant or advantageous), enjoy: *quod illo* [sc. *jucundo vitae*] *~cturus sit* AC 7352; *~imini gaudiis caeli* AM 5.2; *illae, quae vita voluptatis ~itae sunt* ES 283.

frustatim, *adv.* In small pieces, piecemeal: *quasi ~im et minutim discissi* AC 829.2; ES 2746; *dantur mihi ~im quae possim scribere* 2AD 1065. (n.b. In every case the text has *frustratim* and has been corrected by editors; cf. **frustillatim**.)

frustillatim, *adv.* In tiny pieces: *quomodo* [*aves*] *...edunt grana, et panes ~im* ES 4176.

frustra, *adv.* To no purpose, in vain: *quid dies judicii, annon per saecula ~a exspectatus est* CI 312.3; AM 152.

frustraneus ~a ~um, *a.* Having no effect, vain: *conabatur idem...sed... ~o conatu* ES 1289; VR 500.1.

frustratim, *adv.* App. an error for **frustatim**: AC 829.2 (1st edn.); ES 2746 (Autograph); 2AD 1065 (Autograph).

frustro ~are ~avi ~atum, *tr.* **1** To render vain, frustrate (in quot. absol.): *pro iniquitate reputant fallere et ~are* VR 430. **2** (pass., w. abl.) To be cheated (of): *promissione et benedictione... ~arentur* 1AD 459.

frustulum ~i, *neut.* A tiny piece, morsel: *aliquid auri, quod in ~a, et haec in grana secant* AM 268.2; *nentes super ~is lineis* AM 218.2.

frustum ~i, *neut.* A small piece: *pro ~is panis* Ezek. 13.19 (AM 6767.3); *saccharum in ~a divisum* ES 645.

frutex ~icis, *f.* A shrub, bush: *per incrementa cujusvis arboris, ~icis et floris* VR 687.2.

frux frugis, *f.* The fruit of plants, produce: *duxi vos in terram frugis* Jer. 2.7 (AE 730.38); (pl.) crops: *primitias frugum tuarum* Exod. 22.28 (AE 28.3).

fuco ~are ~avi ~atum, *tr.* To paint with cosmetics, make up (the face): *meretrici, quae... ~at faciem purpura* VR 148.2; cf. *externum est, quasi ~atum, nihil vivum* ES 715.

fucus[1] ~i, *m.* **1** A red dyestuff used for cosmetic purposes, rouge: *ex purpura ~i apparuit sibi pulchra* VR 109.3; *ut pararent minia in ~os* AM 231.5. **2** A specious appearance: *quod possent res cujusvis quaestionis coloratis ~is illuminare* AM 231.2; *sinceritas et rectitudo illorum est modo larva, ~us, et astus* AE 972.2.

fucus[2] ~i, *m.* A drone: *inutiles ~i* AM 419; VR 12.7; *~us major*, a drone wasp or hornet: VR 335.4.

fuga ~ae, *f.* The act of running away, flight: *ne fiat ~a vestra in hyeme* Mark 13.18 (AC 34.2).

fugio ~gere ~gi, *intr., tr.* **1** To run away, flee: *deserit oves ~gitque* John 10.12 (AC 8002.5); *ad praesentiam unius hujus ~giunt mille* AC 6784.2. **b** (tr.) to run away from, shun: *angeli illos ~giunt* CI 10; *unum... ~git* *alterum* AC 6724.3. 2 (tr.) To abstain from, eschew, shun (actions): *~giunt mala ut peccata* VI 65. 3 (w. *ad*) To have recourse (to), take refuge (in): *ad suas formulas ~git et de gratia supplicat* ES 487.

fugo ~are ~avi ~atum, *tr*. To put to flight, drive away: *potentia...est ~are et a se ejicere infernalem turbam* AC 8304; AC 9332.

fulcimen ~inis, *neut*. A prop, support: *per costas, quia sunt ~ina pectoris, significantur vera sustentantia bonum* AC 10189.1.

fulcimentum ~i, *neut*. A basis, support: *'angularis tribuum', qui inserviret pro ~o illis quae sunt fidei* AC 1462.2.

fulcio ~cire ~civi ~tum, *tr*. To hold up, support, sustain: *ultimum in quo...interiora... ~ciuntur ne fiat divaricatio* AC 8005; *Jehovah...ex Zione ~ciet te* Ps. 20.3 (AC 923).

fulcrum ~i, *neut*. A prop, support: *cartilaginem ...quae est ~um musculorum diaphragmatis* ES 3245; (transf.) *justitia et judicium ~um throni Tui* Ps. 89.14 (VR 51); *ultima Verbi sunt ~a et sustentacula ejus* SS 35.4.

fulgens ~ntis, *a*. (pres. pple. of **fulgeo**) (superl. *~ntissimus*) Shining, gleaming: *ex ~nte auro* AM 15; *ex ~ntissimo auro* SA 68 (= i.[4]).

fulgeo ~gere ~si, *intr*. To emit a dazzling light, shine, gleam: *tanquam sol ~get in sua potentia* Rev. 1.16 (AE 74).

fulgor ~oris, *m*. Glitter, gleam: *splendor gladii et ~or hastae* Nahum 3.3 (AC 6978).

fulgur ~uris, *neut*. A flash of lightning: *~ur micans* VR 77.1; *vibratio lucis sicut ~uris* AM 415.1.

fulgurans ~ntis, *a*. (compar. *~ntior*) Resembling lightning, flashing: *splendor eo ~ntior, quo plus lux coeli intenebratur* AC 6971.2.

fulguratio ~onis, *f*. A flash of lightning: *universa athmosphaera ex talibus ~onibus constat* AC 1623.

fulguro ~are ~avi, *intr*. To shine out like lightning, flash: *obscurum...per quod ~ant radii solis* AC 1043; AC 1621; *pupilla oculi...quasi ~abat* AM 268.2.

fuliginarius ~i, *m*. A chimney sweep: *~us qui in furvo camini haeret* VR 61.2.

fuliginosus ~a ~um, *a*. Full of soot, sooty: *antra furva et sicut ~a* CI 429.

fuligo ~inis, *f*. Soot, lampblack: *~o qualis ex incenso camino* CI 585; *atrum sicut ~o* VR 12.10.

fullo ~onis, *m*. A fuller: *vestimenta...qualia non potest ~o in terra dealbare* Mark 9.3 (CI 129); *smegma ~onum* Mal. 3.2 (AC 8159.2).

fulmen ~inis, *neut*. Lightning that strikes, a thunderbolt: *apparuit ~en...quod rubuit* AM 316.5; *vidi Satanam sicut ~en e coelo cadentem* Luke 10.18 (DD 13); cf. VR 110.1; (fig.) a powerful weapon: *est in dextra mea ~en excommunicandi* AM 264.

fulminator ~oris, *m*. One who casts thunderbolts: (as translation of Hebr. *Shaddai*) *Ego Deus ~or* Gen. 35.11 (AC 1416.3).

fulmineus ~a ~um, *a*. Resembling a thunderbolt: *Jupiter cum continua vi quasi ~a* ES 440.

fulmino ~are ~avi, *intr*. To utter fierce imprecations, fulminate: *hi damnant omnes...et... ~ant super illos* AR 603.1.

fulsi: pf. of **fulgeo**.

fulvesco ~ere, *intr*. To become tawny: *amiciuntur vestibus...quae...pulchre ~unt* VR 537.

fulvus ~a ~um, *a*. Reddish-brown, tawny: *~is coloribus* VR 808.

fumarium ~i, *neut*. A place where smoke collects, curing house: Hos. 13.3 (AC 1861.6).

fumeus ~a ~um, *a*. Smoky: *vapor ~us* ES 1292.

fumigatio ~onis, *f*. The emission of smoke, smoking: AC 10177.3.

fumigo ~are ~avi, *intr*. To emit smoke, smoke: *linum ~ans non exstinguit* AC 25 (Matt. 12.20); Ps. 144.5 (AC 1311.3).

fumo ~are ~avi, *intr*. To emit smoke, smoke: *mons Sinai ~abat* Exod. 19.18 (AC).

fumosus ~a ~um, *a*. Smoky: (neut. as sb.) *~um ex fornace* AC 10188.2.

fumus ~i, *m*. Smoke: *ex ore eructabat ~um sicut furnus* AM 263.1; (pl.) plumes of smoke: *ascendunt quidem versus caelum, sed reflectunt se in via et decidunt, sicut ~i in aëre* VI 25.

functio ~onis, *f*. 1 The purpose which a thing is intended to serve, function: *~o cujusvis membri...se refert ad peculiare bonum* AC 8004; *~onem secretoriam in homine* ES 928. 2 The purpose served by a member of a society, office: *habitare et vestiri splendide secundum conditionem et ~onem* CI 359; *interrogavi satanam, quae ejus ~o, et ait, '~o mea est eruditio'* VR 80.2.

funda ~ae, *f*. The setting for a jewel, socket, bezel: *circumdatos ~is auri facies illos* Exod. 28.11 (AC).

fundamen ~inis, *neut*. A substructure for a building, foundation: *~en absque domo* AC 10276.8.

fundamentalis ~is ~e, *a.* Serving as a basis, fundamental: *amor ~is omnium amorum* AM 57; *~is error Ecclesiae* VR 114; (neut. as sb.) *~e est ut cogitatio et loquela...concordet* AC 5182.

fundamentaliter, *adv.* As a basis, fundamentally: *ut in floribus, pulchra...sistuntur, manentibus usque radicitus et ~er nigro et albo* AC 731.

fundamentum ~i, *neut.* The structure upon which a building is supported, foundation(s): *sicut qui construit domum, primum ponet ~um* AC 6937; *~a ex lapidibus pretiosis* CI 187.

fundatio ~onis, *f.* **1** The founding or creation (of the world): *ante mundi ~onem* DD 37.3. **2** The foundation (of a building): *plana quibus innitantur superiora sicut palatium super ~onibus suis* AM 447.1.

funditus, *adv.* From the bottom upwards, totally: *quod ~us eversa sint omnia Ecclesiae* AE 741.22.

fundo[1] ~are ~avi ~atum, *tr.* **1** To establish upon a firm basis, found: *oblivisceris Jehovae...qui extendit coelos et ~at terram* Isa. 51.13 (AC 82); *murum ~atum super lapidibus pretiosis* AM 3.5. **2** (pass.) To be based or founded (upon): (w. *in* + abl.) *in hoc spirituale ~atur jus primogenitorum* AC 8042.2; (w. *super*) *cogitationes ... ~ate sunt super tempore, spatio et materia* AE 23.1.

fundo[2] ~ere fudi fusum, *tr.* **1** To pour out (liquids): *ut ~erent aquam super holocaustum* SS 29 (1 Kgs. 18.34); to weep (tears): *ut lachrymas ~eret* CI 238; to cast (metal): *aurum...fusum in massam* VR 701.3. **2** To give forth abundantly, pour forth (prayers): *quotidie ~it preces* VI 25.

fundus ~i, *m.* **1** The lowest part, bottom: *faciebus ad ~um decidentibus* AC 7906.2; ES 867. **2** The fundamental part, basis: *primum et medium carent ~o, super quo subsistant* AM 151; AC 1843.3.

funeralia ~um, *neut. pl.* Funeral rites: *quod... ~a et exequiae eorum parentur ut sepeliantur* CI 312.4.

funestus ~a ~um, *a.* Deadly, death-dealing: *in tam ~is principiis sunt ut...* AC 775.2; *~as aves* AM 521.6.

fungor ~gi ~ctus sum, *intr.* (w. abl.) To perform, discharge (an office or duty): *qui ministrant et officio ~guntur* AC 7144; *mundanis ~gi* CI 359.

funiculus ~i, *m.* A line, string: *~os fere inconspicuos* CI 335; *facies...auratis ~is...ornata* ES 3732; *~us mensurae* Zech. 2.1 (DD 52).

funis ~is, *m.* **1** A rope: *~is nauticus* AM 328.1; *amor illorum est sicut vinculum aut sicut ~is* CI 479.3. **2** A piece of land measured out by a rope, portion, allotment: *portio Jehovae populus Ipsius, Jacob ~is haereditatis Ipsius* Deut. 32.9 (AC 2708.5).

funus ~eris, *neut.* Death: *idea sepulchri inest aliquid ~eris* AC 2299.

fur furis, *m.* A thief: *vociferans, fur, praedo, homicida* AM 512.1; VI 91.

furcifer ~eri, *m.* A criminal, villain: *omnis ~er, praedo, et latro* VR 672.2.

furfur ~uris, *m.* Bran (in quots. as a term of reproach): *cui responsum...quod ~ur et nequam sit* ES 4363; *si coloni fuerunt, agunt ~ures* [1st edn.; *fures* later edns.] DP 208.

furia ~ae, *f.* (n.b. used indifferently of males and females) **1** An evil spirit, fiend, fury: *quidem genii, seu potius ~ae* AC 814.1; *foeminae...fiunt sicut ~ae* AC 944. **2** (pl.) A state of frenzy, insane rage: *dum homo in ~as labitur* ES 225; VR 691.2.

furibundus ~a ~um, *a.* Frenzied, furious: *voce ~a clamando* AM 512.1.

furiosus ~a ~um, *a.* (compar. *~ior*) Demented, maddened, frenzied: *equo insidere ~o* ES 2708; *quod multo ~iores sint* [*homines*] *feris pessimis* ES 1063; *~a voce* AM 415.2.

furnus ~i, *m.* A furnace, oven: *eructabat fumum sicut ~us* AM 263.1.

furo ~ere, *intr.* To be mad, rave: *ubi corpus non ~it* ES 2420; ES 4397.

furor[1] ~oris, *m.* Fury, frenzy: *pugnabo vobiscum...et in ira, et in ~ore* Jer. 21.5 (AC 6997.3); *patet...ex cujusvis ~ore contra rivales* AM 106; FI 63.4.

furor[2] ~ari ~atus sum, *intr.* To commit theft, steal: *quod malum sit ~ari* VI 53; *praeceptum 'non ~aberis'* SS 67.2.

furtim, *adv.* Furtively, stealthily: *quae* [sc. *reliquiae*] *comparantur 'praedae' quia quasi ~im insinuantur* AC 576.3.

furtivus ~a ~um, *a.* Stealthy: *deflorare aliquam...vi ~a* ES 4741.

furtum ~i, *neut.* Theft, stealing: *astus et ~a* CI 462[a].2; (of things other than property) *virginitatum ~a* AC 828; *~o auferendo ablatus sum e terra Hebraeorum* Gen. 40.15 (AC).

furve, *adv.* In an obscure manner, darkly: *ignis sicut foci ~e transparuit* AM 264.1.

furvo ~are, *tr.* To make dark-coloured, darken: *lux... opacat se in vergentibus ad nigrum et ~at se* DP 292.2.

furvus ~a ~um, *a.* Dark-coloured, dusky, swarthy: *faciebus ~is* AM 232.2; *~a nubes* AC 6832.2; (neut. as sb.) *in ~o camini* VR 61.2.

fuscinula ~ae, *f.* A small fork: *crateres et ~as et forcipes* Exod. 38.3 (AC).

fuscus ~a ~um, *a.* Dark-hued, sombre: *color...in quibusdam vivus et lucidus, in quibusdam quasi mortuus et ~us* AC 6991; *nubes ~a* AM 233.7.

fuse, *adv.* (compar. *~ius*) Copiously, at length: *~e hic inferre illam [ideam] abstraheret mentes* AM 314.1; *~ius explicare* AC 5089.

fusilis ~is ~e, *a.* Made by means of a mould, cast: *deos ~es* AC 8301.5; *~e aeris* 1 Kgs. 7.16 (AE 219.5).

fusio ~onis, *f.* The casting (of metal): *artes sicut ~ones metallorum* ES 4663.

fustis ~is, *m.* A stick, rod: (used in winnowing) *quis non aristas e messe hordei excutit ~ibus triturae...?* VR 331.2; (used as a weapon) *~ibus illum...persequuntur* VR 122.

fusura ~ae, *f.* A melting, casting: *~a una, mensura una, proportio una omnibus illis* 1 Kgs. 7.37 (AC 10236.3).

fusus ~a ~um: pf. pple. of **fundo**[2].

futilis ~is ~e, *a.* Unprofitable, pointless, futile: *quam ~es scientiae hodiernae sunt* ES(M) 4578 titulus.

futurus ~a ~um, *a.* (fut. pple. of **sum**) **1** That is going to exist, future, to come: *nisi praeviderint... ~am rejectionem* AM 292.3; *hanc ~am damnationem Jehovah Deus...sustulit* VR 3.1. **2** (neut. as sb.) The future: *Deus...de praeterito et de ~o loquitur in praesenti* VR 30.3; *volentes scire quid de ~is scripseram* AC 6811.

G

galbanum ~i, *neut.* (prob. ultimately from Hebr. *chelbenah*) A gum extracted from oriental species of fennel, galbanum: *ex aromatibus fragrantibus, stacte, onyche, ~o et thure* AE 324.1.

galea ~ae, *f.* A helmet: *nisi circumdet corpus lorica et caput ~a* VR 124.1; AC 1788.1.

Galenianus ~a ~um, *a.* Of or typical of Galen, a celebrated physician of the 2nd century AD: *lingua Hippocratica et ~a* VR 665.6.

galerum ~i, *neut.* Wrong reading introduced by Worcester into VR 616.1, where *in navibus, galeres, vocatis* has been emended to *galeris*. The French word *galères* is intended.

galgal, *indecl.* (Hebr.) A Hebrew word for wheel: *rotae eorum vocabantur ~al* Ezek. 10.13-14 (AC 3901.5).

Gallice, *adv.* In the French language: [*pellex*] *~e vocatur maitress* AM 459.1.

gallicinium ~i, *neut.* (a word not used by Swedenborg but used by his editors) The time of cockcrow, the period of twilight before dawn: *~um seu diluculum* AE 187.2 (Worcester).

Gallicus ~a ~um, *a.* French: *loquitur...linguam... cum Gallo ~am* AM 326.4.

gallina ~ae, *f.* A hen: *'motitare' sicut solet ~a super ova* AC 19; AM 246.3.

gallinaceum ~i, *neut.* The time when cocks crow, cockcrow: *quod ~um et diluculum sit idem* AC 10134.13; VR 571.2; AE 9.2; AE 187.2. (n.b. Emended by some editors to *gallicinium*, but *gallinaceum* is correctly formed from the adjective, sc. *tempus*.)

gallinarium ~i, *neut.* A place where hens are kept, chicken-house, chicken run: *sicut vulpis in ~o* VR 383.2.

gallus ~i, *m.* A cock: *antequam ~us cecinerit* Matt. 26.34 (AE 9.2); VR 839.2.

ganea ~ae, *f.* and **ganeum** ~i, *neut.* A house of ill fame, brothel: *in lupanariis et ~is* VR 834; *~um in domo* AM 373; *~ae* AM 510.1.

ganeum: see **ganea**.

ganglio ~onis, *f.* = **ganglion**: CI 212.

ganglion ~i, *neut.* (Gk.) (anat.) A knot from which nerve fibres radiate, ganglion: *~is in corpore humano ac nodis in cerebro in quae influunt innumerabiles fibrae* ES 305; ES 3607.

gangraena ~ae, *f.* (Gk.) Gangrene: *~ae, quae serpit et putrefacit vicina* VR 120.2.

garrio ~rire ~rivi, *intr.* To talk idly, chatter: *stultus non* [*vult*] *nisi quam contra illa quae sapientiae sunt ~rire* VR 145.1; (w. *quod*) *~rientes quod salvari possent* AC 1063.2.

garrule, *adv.* Talkatively (in quot., of frogs): [*ranae*] *~e sonant et coaxant* AC 7352.

gastricus ~a ~um, *a.* (Gk.) Of the stomach, gastric: *regionem ~am* VR 119.1.

gaudeo ~dere gavisus sum, *intr.* **1** To experience pleasure, be glad, rejoice: *his auditis gavisi sunt* AM 44.6; *quod ~deat* [*Jehovah*] *ad perdendum...eos* AC 1874; (w. *quod*) *gavisi quod inter suos venirent* CI 35. **2** (w. abl.) To be endowed (with), rejoice (in an advantage): *quod spiritus...omni sensu ~deant* AC 1883; *unusquisque... ~det intellectu et voluntate* CI 369; (also, app. w. acc.) *prae iis* [*facultatibus*] *quae gavisi in vita corporis* ES 2252.

gaudium ~i, *neut.* Joy, pleasure: *cum ~o recipiunt illa* [sc. *vera*] FI 30; *privatio ~i* AC 7810; (w. pl.) an instance of this, a joy: *omne coeleste ~um producit cordis laetitiam* AC 418.1; *~a caeli* AM 10.7.

gaza ~ae, *f.* (Gk., prob from Persian) A treasure: *~ae apud regem Persiae* VR 245.2; AM 3.5.

gazophylacium ~i, *neut.* (Gk.) A repository for

treasure, treasure-chest: *domus occlusa, plena cimeliis et ~is* VR 701.2.

gehenna ~ae, *f.* (Hebr.) A name for hell: *obnoxius erit ~ae ignis* Matt. 5.22 (AC 1011); *de ~a seu inferno* AC 8481; a particular part of hell: AC 825.

gelatinum ~i, *neut.* (cf. French *gélatine*) (app.) A jelly: *iidem...non apparent sicut homines, nec ut monstra, sed sicut ~a* AM 510.3.

gelidus ~a ~um, *a.* (superl. *~issimus*) Ice-cold, icy: *correpti sunt a febri ~a* CI 572; chilling: *persuasione sua ~issima et pestiferissima* ES 3365.

gelu ~u, *neut.* Freezing cold, frost: *terrae constrictae ~u* VR 185.1; (transf.) lack of love, coldness: *aestus pro scortis ac ~u pro conjuge* AM 375.2.

gemellus ~i, *m.* A twin: *in Esavo et Jacobo, ~is* 2AD 59.

gemino ~are ~avi ~atum, *tr.* **1** To increase twofold, double: *~ata est eorum anxietas* ES 220. **2** To make twofold, duplicate: *reliquae viscera...~ata sunt* SA 77 (= iii.3.[3]).

geminus ~a ~um, *a.* Twofold: *cur lingua ~o muneri dicata sit* AC 4795; (masc. as sb.) a twin: *~i in utero ejus* Gen. 25.24 (AC).

gemitus ~us, *m.* A cry of pain or grief, groan: *te ad ~us et lachrymas...adiget* AM 499; *et audivit Deus ~um illorum* Exod. 2.24 (AC).

gemma ~ae, *f.* A precious stone, jewel, gem: *utensilia ...ex integris ~is* AM 12.1; AC 9847.

gemo ~ere ~ui, *intr.* To groan, moan: *~uit et dixit* VR 134.5; *~ente facie* CI 358; *auditum est sicut columba ~eret* AM 208.5.

gena ~ae, *f.* A cheek: *puella...volabat ad dextram ~am* AC 1872; *tenebant manus sub ~is* AM 8.3.

genealogia ~ae, *f.* (Gk.) A list of ancestors, genealogy: AC 339; AC 7231.1.

genealogicus ~a ~um, *a.* Relating to genealogy: (neut. pl. as sb.) *quod nomina haec nihil plus involvant quam ~a ex Esavo* AC 4642.3.

gener ~eri, *m.* A son-in-law: *liberos, nepotes, ~eros, nurus* AC 7368; AM 116.

general: modern word, not Latin, as military rank: ES 5981; ES 6047.

generalis ~is ~e, *a.* (compar. *~ior*) Of general (as opposed to specific) type, general, universal: *~is lex repraesentationis est* AC 1361.1; *tunc Domini adventus fuit ~is* ES 5202.2; DP 12; *in ~iore sensu* AC 9393.2.

generaliter, *adv.* In general: *in orbe Christiano ~er notum est* VR 343.

generatio ~onis, *f.* **1** (of living creatures) The act of reproducing, reproduction: *constat...ex ~one hominum* VR 92.1; *viscera ~onis* AC 1803.3; *membra ~onis* ES 499 1/2; *ut per ~ones, unius ab altera, perenniter renoventur* VR 78.3. **2** The act of producing: *~ones spirituales, quae sunt boni et veri* AE 28.1; *~ones fidei* VR 57.1. **3** A group of persons descended from ancestors by the same number of intermediaries, generation: *familiae et earum ~ones* AC 6690; *~o ista sibi videtur in urbe...vivere* ES 731; (esp. w. ref. to time) *in ~onem et ~onem* Ps. 89.4 (DD 44); *ad tertiam et quartam ~onem* Num. 14.18 (SS 51.2).

genericus ~a ~um, *a.* Relating to genus, generic: *differentias ~as et speciales perceptionum* AC 483.2.

genero ~are ~avi ~atum, *tr.* To give birth to, produce: *simul innovat spiritus seu mentes eorum, et ~at e novo* VR 16.1; (esp. pass.) to be born or produced: *quomodo potest homo ~ari cum senex est?...quod ~atum est ex spiritu spiritus est* John 3.4,6 (AC 8043.2); *affectio veri quae ~atur ex affectione boni* AC 1824.

generositas ~atis, *f.* Nobility of character: *virtutes... vocantur...liberalitas, ~as, strenuitas...* AM 164.

generosus ~a ~um, *a.* Of good stock, well bred: *~i equi* VR 328; ES 2275; (of wine) of a fine vineyard, vintage: *vino ~o inebriari* AM 461.2.

Genesis ~eos, *f.* (Gk.) Creation, the name of the first book of the Bible: *septem prima capita ~eos* SS 103.3.

genetrix ~icis, *f.* also **genitrix**. **1** A mother: *Mariam ...Dei ~icem* VR 111.11; (of animals) *usque dum [pullus] fiat avis in forma ~icis* VR 12.3. **2** (as adj.) Reproductive: *particulae ~ices* ES 884.

genialis ~is ~e, *a.* (prob.) Producing cheerfulness, cheering: *quod ille [amor] dum pertransiit pectus fiat amor ~is* AM 111; *quoad ~em suum amorem* VR 14.2.

genialiter, *adv.* In a cheerful fashion: *~er bibentes* AM 8.2; *papiliones...~er ludunt, et agunt connubia* VR 12.6; AM 183.6.

genimen ~inis, *neut.* That which is produced, produce: *~en vitis* Matt. 26.29 (VR 708); *omne ~en et germen e terra cognoscitur ex suo flore et semine* VR 96.2.

genitalis ~is ~e, *a.* Of or concerned with reproduction, reproductive, genital: *in regionem ~em* AM 183.2; *vesiculis ~ibus* ES 884; (neut. pl. as sb.) the genital organs: *lumbi cum ~ibus* AC 7045.

genitor ~oris, *m.* Male parent, begetter: *ut fiat avis...in forma ~oris* AM 416.2; a male ancestor: *benedictiones patris tui praevalebunt super benedictionibus ~orum meorum* Gen. 49.26 (AC).

genitrix: see **genetrix**.

genius ~i, *m.* **1** A person's inherent character, nature: *perspiciendi mores virorum ex ~is illorum* AM 299.1; *incolae unius telluris prorsus alio ~o sunt quam incolae alterius* AC 6701. **2** One's character regarded as needing to be indulged, predisposition, bent: *illa adblandiuntur sensibus externis et oblectant ~um* CI 87; *quisque depromit quod suo ~o favet* VR 154.2; *~o vivere* (and sim.), to enjoy a life of self-indulgence: *sunt quae vixerunt ~o, et solum studuerunt sibi et mundo* AC 831.1; *vixissent secundum ~um suum* AC 6963.2. **3** A member of one of the three classes of being in the other life, genius: *quod spiritus, ~i, angeli sint inter se prorsus separati* ES 161; *cum ~is interioris coeli* ES 224; (usu. confined to the class of evil spirits who act upon the will) *~i mali, ita vocari possunt hujus generis spiritus mali, qui incendunt eum* [sc. *hominem*] *suis cupiditatibus et foedis amoribus* AC 751.3; AC 5977.1; *infernales ~i* AC 8209.1; VR 395.2.

gens ~ntis, *f.* **1** A group of families, clan: *~ntes...constituerunt plures familiae* AC 1159.3; VR 103.2. **2** (in a wider sense) A people, nation: *nomina ~ntium et populorum* FI 49; *a ~nte Israelitica et Judaica* SS 11. **3** (pl.) Non-Christians, the heathen: *illi qui extra Ecclesiam nati sunt, qui ~ntes seu Gentiles vocantur* CI 318; *quales fuerunt ~ntes et hodie quoque sunt ~ntes* AC 410. **b** non-Jews, gentiles: *Ecclesia ~ntium...et Ecclesia Judaica* AC 367.2.

gentilis ~is, *m.* **1** A member of the same clan: *doctrina...tradita in ~es, quae non latius emanat, quam ad gentem* ES 523.3. **2** A non-Christian, heathen, gentile: *prisci ~es pro supremo Deo agnoverunt Jovem* VR 9.3; *~is fuit, et non ex Verbo aliquid novit* AE 31.3. **3** One who is not a member of a group, stranger, outsider: *stabant duo ~es juxta ostiarium in vestibulo* VR 390.3.

gentilismus ~i, *m.* **1** The area inhabited by heathens, heathendom: *Mahumedismus et ~us est in Asia, Indiis, Africa et America* DP 330.7. **2** *~us Christianus*, the Christian Church which permits the worship of saints: *in ~o Christiano, ubi permittitur adorare sanctos et eorum idola* AC 3447.1; AE 955.5.

genu ~u, *neut.* (dat. and abl. pl. *~ubus*) The knee: *usque ad lumbos et ~ua* CI 65; ES 3496; (as the part used in kneeling) *conjecit se super ~ua* AM 264.1; *caetum flectentem ~ua* VR 113.4; *super ~ubus Deo gratias agere* DP 251.5; (as the place where small children are seated) *super ~ubus delectabimini* Isa. 66.12 (AC 6745.5).

genuflexio ~onis, *f.* A bending of the knee as a sign of submission or adoration, genuflection: *sicut humiliatio cordis secum habet ~ones* ES 4099; *~ones coram simulachris* VR 831.

genuinus ~a ~um, *a.* **1** Not imitated or spurious, real: *arte parare similes [lapides pretiosos] ac phantasiam inducere quod ~i sint* VR 843. **2** Properly so called, authentic, proper: *innocentia sapientiae est ~a innocentia* CI 278.1; *quod bona et vera sint ~i cibi hominis* AC 680.1; *quid verba in ~o sensu involvunt* AC 201; *cognitiones ~i veri et boni* FI 29.

genus ~eris, *neut.* **1** Sort, type: *opiparae dapes multi ~eris* DP 254.4; *bina haec hominum ~era* AC 1079.2; *aves omnis ~eris* VR 44.1. **2** *Humanum ~us*, the human race, mankind: *misericordia erga omne ~us humanum* CI 522. **3** (as opposed to species) A generic class, genus: *~us est complexus eorum quae inde* AC 1068; *~era et horum aliquot species* AC 6706; *in ~ere*, in general, generally: *ubicunque bestiae nominantur in ~ere et in specie* AC 143; *quod...in ~ere omnia mundi correspondentiae sint* CI 103.

geometres ~ae, *m.* (Gk.) A geometrician: ES 3460.

geometria ~ae, *f.* (Gk.) Geometry: VR 387.5; ES 769.

geometricus ~a ~um, *a.* (Gk.) Of or proper to geometry: *a ~arum scientiarum studiis* ES 181; *ex punctis et...lineis ~is* VR 20.2; (neut. pl. as sb.) geometrical matters, geometry: *in ~is, stereometricis, arithmeticis, et physicis* VR 184.

gerah ~ae, *m.* Gerah, a Hebrew coin worth a twentieth of a shekel: *decem ~ae quae dimidium sicli* AC 2959.7.

Germanicus ~a ~um, *a.* German; *milliare ~um*, a German mile (= 7.4 kilometres): AC 10771.

germanus ~a ~um, *a.* Proper to one's nature, true: *amor conjugialis...potest etiam vocari nativus et ~us homini* AM 96; *caput...pictum coloribus ~is sicut facies humana* VR 381.3; VR 665.6; truly or properly related: *infantes ex amore conjugiali...nati fiunt proprii et ~i* AM 109.

germen ~inis, *neut.* **1** A shoot, sprout (of a plant): *omnis...arbor incipit a ~ine* VR 756; *suscitabo Davidi ~en justum* Jer. 23.5 (SS 85). **2** A plant: *flores in arbore et in reliquis ~inibus* AC 5116.6; AC 2452.

germinatio ~onis, *f.* The act of sprouting, germination: *memoria...est illarum humus, ac intellectus est ubi illarum ~o* VR 32.4; an instance of this: *subjecta regni vegetabilis ex influxu inde ducunt suas ~ones* CI 567.3.

germino ~are ~avi ~atum, *intr.* (of plants) To put forth shoots, sprout: *quod...quantum caloris...accedit luci, tantum crescant et ~ent omnia* AE 59; AM 60; (also pass. as dep.) *calorem ex quo ~antur horti* AC 8328.2; (transf.) *verum inde formatur et ~atur* AC 668.

gero ~rere ~ssi ~stum, *tr.* **1** To carry, bear: *in utero*

~rens Rev. 12.2 (AC 2584.2). **2 a** To carry on, wage (war): *qui bellum inter se ~sserunt* AE 31.4. **b** to hold, discharge (an office): *qui primatum in Ecclesia ~runt* VR 96.1; *tutelam ~ssimus* VR 17.1. **3** To hold (in the mind or heart): *continue ~rentes animo condemnare* AC 1079.2; *alia corde ~rerent et aliud ore ferrent* AC 8383; ES 2120. **4** (refl.) To behave (in a specified manner): *fiunt sicut ebrii, seque similiter ~runt* AC 1072.1; *se ~runt sicut qui in agone mortis sunt* AC 8265.1; CI 54.

gesta ~orum, *neut. pl.* (pf. pple. of **gero**) Deeds, exploits: *qui affectant immortalitatem famae per ~a* ES 2147.

gestatio ~onis, *f.* The act of carrying: *ex amaenitate ~onis illorum* [sc. *infantum*] *super ulnis* AM 396.2.

gesticulatio ~onis, *f.* The making of gestures, gesticulation: *tales mihi ex ~onibus illorum apparebant* VR 388.1.

gesticulator ~oris, *m.* One who gesticulates: AM 432.2.

gesticulatorius ~a ~um, *a.* Expressed by gestures: *amicitia... ~a et mimica* VR 455.3.

gesticulor ~ari ~atus sum, *intr.* To make gestures, gesticulate: ES 2283.

gestio ~tire, *intr.* To wish eagerly, long for: *quod nullus velit esse sui, sed singuli omnium ~tiant* ES 301.

gesto ~are ~avi ~atum, *tr.* To carry, bear: *quod se putent ~are homines a tergo* ES 380; (esp. of women) to carry (in the womb), be pregnant with: *Deus...non potuit aliter...quam concipi, ~ari in utero, nasci* VR 89; ES 283; (transf.) *illa recipere quasi utero, et sic concipere, ~are et parere* AM 115.5; CI 269.3.

gestus ~us, *m.* A sign given by a movement of the body, gesture: *elevatio manus ad Jehovam est ~us corporis correspondens mentis affectioni* AC 1745.1; *differunt etiam ~ibus et moribus* AM 33; *loquela per ~us* CI 244.

ghoim, *indecl. pl.* Reading of 1st edn., emended to **tziim** by Worcester (cf. VR 45.2): VR 611.2.

gibbosus ~a ~um, *a.* (superl. *~issimus*) Hunchbacked, humped: *homo non est homo, aliter quam sicut ~us* AM 269.3; ES 4626; *protuberant ~a pars erat tenuissima membrana...circumtecta* AS 432.

gibbus[1] ~a ~um, *a.* Protuberant: *in superiore ~a parte* AS 432.

gibbus[2] ~i, *m.* A protuberance on the body, hump: *corpora illorum sicut ~i* AM 432.2.

gigas ~antis, *m.* (Gk.) A giant: *~antes proceritatis duplae supra humanam communem* AM 77.1; VR 68.1.

gigno ~ere genui genitum, *tr.* **1** To become the father of, beget, procreate: *genuit filios et filias* Gen. 5.4 (AC); *ex illa ~eret filios* SS 79.7; also, to become the mother of, bear: *quod genuerit* [*Maria*] *Deum* VR 111.11. **2** To produce, engender: [*homo*] *ex bono illo ~it vera* AC 8042.2; AM 44.9; *perinde est, sive dicatur a Deo ~i sive procedere* VR 23.1.

gilvus ~a ~um, *a.* Yellowish, tawny: *topazius est ~us seu flavus splendescens* [*splendens* Tafel] 3AD 1844.

gingiva ~ae, *f.* The part of the mouth surrounding the teeth, gums: *~a erat talis, ut dentes ibi non essent firmi* ES 4419; AC 4791.1.

ginglymus ~i, *m.* (Gk.) (anat.) A hinge-like joint, ginglymus: *~i ossium cum suis ligamentis et membranis* VR 462.9.

gitthith, *indecl.* (Hebr.) The rendering of a Hebr. musical instruction in the title of Psalms 8, 81, and 84: *Psalmis pluribus Davidis...indicatum quomodo psallerentur, prout super neginoth, super nechiloth, super octava, schigajon, ~ith, muthlabben, scheminith, schoschannim, machalath* AC 8337.5.

glaber ~bra ~brum, *a.* Lacking hair, hairless, smooth: [*zelus*] *extrinsecus laevis, ~ber* VR 155.2.

glacialis ~is ~e, *a.* Icy: *aqua ~i operiuntur* VR 342.3.

glacies ~ei, *f.* **1** Ice: *feruntur curru aut rheda super tenui ~e* VR 342.3. **2** *~es Mariae*, Mary's ice, a name given to sheets of mica (German *Marienglas*): *lamellae sicut vitreae...quales sunt quae vocantur ~es Mariae* AM 380.2.

gladiolus ~i, *m.* A dagger: *quod circumcisio facta fuerit per ~os petrarum* AC 7044.

gladius ~i, *m.* A sword: *qui ~os veneno tingunt* VR 324; *visitabit Jehovah ~o Suo* Isa. 27.1 (DD 4); AR 836.2; *sub ~um mittere*, to put to the sword: VR 117.

glandula ~ae, *f.* (anat.) A gland: *~ae in glomeres dispositae* AC 7408.1; *~a pinealis* AM 315.4.

glandularis ~is ~e, *a.* Of glands, glandular: *quod cerebrum consistat ex binis substantiis, quarum una est ~is* VR 351.3.

glandulosus ~a ~um, *a.* Abounding in glands: *radix ~a* ES 1436; ES 2216.

glarea ~ae, *f.* Gravel: *quod deserta...non consistant nisi ex struibus lapidum, aut ex nuda ~a* VR 45.2.

glaucoma ~atis, *neut.* (Gk.) Glaucoma: *cum vitio oculi...quod vocatur ~a* VR 346.1.

gleba ~ae, *f.* **1** A clod of earth: *apparent modo calcare et terere unam ~am, et non progredi* AM 232.2;

VR 339.2. **2** A piece of land: *pars seu ~a agri, super quem non pluit* AC 382.2.

glis gliris, *m.* A dormouse: *oculi [felium] ex ardente appetitu glirium...apparent sicut candelae* AR 566.3; ES 377.

globulus ~i, *m.* A small sphere, round lump: *spiritus mali [apparent] instar ~orum ignis carbonarii* AC 1527; *~i chrystallini* ES 3237; a ball: *~us elasticus cadens in petram* AM 526; a musket-ball, bullet: DP 333.3.

globus ~i, *m.* **1** A sphere, esp. the earth regarded as a sphere, globe: *~us terraqueus* VR 33. **2** A round mass, crowd: *spiritus...cum congregati sunt, formant quasi ~um* AC 6926; *in ~o concurrerunt ad portas* AM 9.2.

glocito ~are ~avi, *intr.* (of animals) To utter a repeated cry, cluck, bleat: *bestia agri ~at ad Te* Joel 1.20 (AE 650.37; AE 730.13).

glomeratio ~onis, *f.* The act of coiling or an instance of this: *quidam mihi apparebat in anguium ~ones verti* ES 2395.

glomero ~are ~avi ~atum, *tr.* To form into a round mass, coil: *unaquaevis cohors se ~avit in orbem* AM 2.3; VR 79.3.

glomulus ~i, *m.* A small round mass, ball: *nubis ~i simul conglomerati* ES 2274; *credunt animam...esse caloris et lucis ~um aut micam* VR 695.3.

glomus ~eris, *m.* and **glomus** ~i, *m.* A roughly spherical mass, cluster, ball: *glandulae in ~eres dispositae* AC 7408.1; *~o serpentum* VR 361.3; *ipsum malum est harum* [sc. *concupiscentiarum*] *conglobata congeries seu ~us* AM 427; SE 56.

gloria ~ae, *f.* **1** Overwhelming brightness of light, splendour, glory: *lux solis supra nubes, quae lux in Verbo vocatur ~a* AC 8781; (as an attribute of the Risen Lord) *videbunt Filium Hominis venientem in nubibus caeli cum potentia et ~a multa* Matt. 24.30 (SS 14.1). **2** High status as exhibited by outward show, magnificence: *videt quod...mali in ~a et opulentia [sint]* DP 216.1; *est illis honor et ~a* CI 218. **3** High praise, renown, glory: *pro ~a sua occumbere...in praelio* ES 3188; *~a mundi* AC 6907.3; (as attributed to God) *Ipsi ~a et robur in saecula saeculorum* Rev. 1.6 (AR); *aequalis Divinitas, ~a et majestas* VR 170.1. **4** The glorified state of the Risen Lord, glory: *cum venturus [Dominus] in ~am* AC 900.

gloriabundus ~a ~um, *a.* Boasting (in quot. masc. as sb.): *dixi ~is, ne gloriemini* Ps. 75.4 (AE 316.22).

gloriatio ~onis, *f.* **1** The act of boasting or an instance of this: *quod non fastus sit, sed modo ~o* AC 6813; *exultatio et ~o falsi super destructionem veri* AE 323.13; *~onem inde captabat, quod...* ES 3618; DP 237. **2** A state of exaltation: *simul tunc eram in ~one visuali, illa ~o, quae venit ad auditum, erat auditus* ES 604.

gloriator ~oris, *m.* One who boasts, braggart: *piger ~or ex aliorum studiis et operis* DA 32 (= xii.[1]).

glorificatio ~onis, *f.* **1** The act of praising highly, glorifying: *perpetua ~o Dei* AM 3.6. **2** The process of making divine, glorification: *~o Domini est ~o Humani Ipsius* SS 99.

glorifico ~are ~avi ~atum, *tr.* **1** To ascribe high praise to, glorify: *Deus precibus et laudibus ab angelis ~atur in aeternum* AM 9.1; *[praedones] se inde laetificant et ~ant* VR 117. **2** To make divine, glorify: *Dominus totum Humanum Suum...~avit* CI 316; *cum plene ~atus est [Dominus]* AC 6716.3.

glorior ~ari ~atus sum, *intr.* To boast, brag: *de statu malorum, quod ~entur et exultent* AC 8164.2; (w. *de*) *~amur de hoc inter nos* AM 79.5; (w. *ex*) *cave... ne...~eris ex scortatione tua* AM 477.8; (w. *in* + abl.) *quod improbus laetetur et ~etur in mundo* AC 7007.2.

gloriosus ~a ~um, *a.* **1** Boastful: *[galli] sunt amatores ~i* AM 378. **2** Magnificent in appearance, glorious: *tota ~a filia regis intus* Ps. 45.13 (AC 490); of high renown, much praised: *Jehovah...in Israele ~um Se reddidit* Isa. 44.23 (AC 7090.2).

glottis ~idis, *f.* (Gk.) (anat.) The glottis: *agit pulmonem laryngem, ~idem, linguam* DP 181.1; AC 6057.1; ES 4610.

gluma ~ae, *f.* **1** Chaff: *erit sicut ~a e turbine abigitur ex area* Hos. 13.3 (AC 1861.6); Isa. 41.15 (AE 405.48); *cogitatio est modo sicut ~a* VR 160.3. **2** (pl.) Froth or scum (on the surface of water): *sicut ~ae quales in superficie marium* CJ 121.

gluten ~inis, *neut.* Glue: *talis persuasio...est sicut ~en, cui inviscantur bona et vera* AC 563; VR 11.3.

glutinosus ~a ~um, *a.* Glutinous, sticky: *fila... humectent aqua ~a* AC 10163.

gnarus ~a ~um, *a.* (superl. *~issimus*) Skilled, trained, expert: *interiora corporis...oculis non ~is exposita* ES 2462; (w. gen.) *qui ~i musices sunt* AC 8337.2; *qui ~issimi fuerunt linguae alicujus* ES 2040.

gnavus ~a ~um, *a.* Industrious: *quisque impiger, ~us, sedulus et diligens* DA 32 (= xii.[1]); (neut. as sb.) industriousness: CH 135 (= vi.2).

Goiim: see **Gojim**.

Gojim, *indecl.* also **Goiim**. Hebr. word for peoples, nations, or gentiles, which is used as a proper name: *Thidael rex ~im seu gentium* AC 1685.

gopher, *indecl.* (Hebr.) The wood of which Noah's ark was made: *fac tibi arcam lignorum ~r* Gen. 6.14 (AC).

Gordius ~a ~um, *a.* *Nodus ~us*, the Gordian knot, tied by King Gordias (it was prophesied that whoever untied it would become master of Asia): VR 74.2.

gorgon ~onis, *f.* (in Greek mythology) The gorgon Medusa who turned to stone all who looked upon her: *sicut caput ~onis seu Medusae clypeo Palladis insculptum* SE 66.2.

gossypium ~i, *neut.* Cotton: *auris erat obturata sicut ~o* VR 79.4.

gracilis ~is ~e, *a.* (compar. *~ior*) Slender, thin: *vir longus et ~is* AC 788.2; *homo...corpore ~ior quam nostrae telluris incolae* ES 3262; *septem aristae ~es* Gen. 41.6 (AC); *nubes ~is* ES 3275.

gradior ~diri (*or* ~di), *intr.* (4th conjugation forms sometimes corrected by editors, but *~diris* is retained in VR 80.5) To walk: *animalia...quae ~diuntur super terra* AE 282.8; *ungulae ~dientis equi* ES 1770; *quod postea non sciat ~diri* AM 133.1; *ut vix potuissem ~di* ES 153.

gradivi Prob. an error for *gradiri* (see **gradior**): ES 4502.

graduatim, *adv.* By stages, gradually: *cancer...partes integras...~im mortificat* CO 13.1.

graduor ~ari ~atus sum, *intr.* To vary in degree, be graduated: *~antur...* [*lux et calor*] *per illa quae transeunt* CC 16.4.

gradus ~us, *m.* **1** A step (of a staircase, etc.): *palatium in quod ascenditur per duodecim ~us* DP 36; AM 76.3; a rung (of a ladder): *~ibus scalae visae Jacobo* VR 24.2; ES 3656. **2** A degree of elevation: *sol...in ~u medio inter zenith et horizontem* VR 29.2; *in ~u caeli 45* AM 137.5. **3** A stage (in a process): *cum malum ad tantum ~um crevit* ES 2592; *hi ~us glorificationis Domini fuerunt* AC 7014; *~us continui vocantur decrementa...a crassiore ad tenuius* AS 184; *per ~us*, gradually: CI 3. **4** (philosophically) A discrete unit forming part of a series, degree: *de successivis ~ibus in quos coeli sunt distincti* AE 41; *quod tres ~us amoris et sapientiae sint* VR 24.1.

Graecus ~a ~um, *a.* Greek: *loquitur ejus linguam propriam...cum ~o ~am* AM 326.4; *error Ecclesiae ~ae* VR 153.3; (masc. as sb.) AC 8944.2.

gramen ~inis, *neut.* Grass: *in campo arenoso, ubi nec ~en* SS 96; *humus...impleta ~inibus et herbis* AM 134.1; (as the first stage in the growth of cereals) *primo ~en, dein spicam, dein frumentum in spica* Mark 4.28 (AC 5212.4).

gramineus ~a ~um, *a.* Grassy: *campi ~i* AM 78.3; *toris ~is* AC 8377.

graminosus ~a ~um, *a.* Grassy; (neut. pl. as sb.) grasses: *ubi campi super quibus aliqua arbusta...ac ~a* AE 411.32.

graminulum ~i, *neut.* A small grass plant: *ab oleis et palmis usque ad ~a* AM 222.3.

grammaticalis ~is ~e, *a.* Grammatical; (neut. as sb.) a grammatical element in language: *judicat...ex una voce, imo ex uno ~i* AC 241; ES 1951.

granarium ~i, *neut.* A building for storing threshed grain, granary: *putrefacta sunt grana sub glebis suis, devastata sunt horrea, destructa sunt ~a* Joel 1.17 (AC 5147.4).

grandinatus ~a ~um, *a.* (cf. **grandino**) Having white spots like hail, dappled: *equi ~i* Zech. 6.3 (AC 5321.8).

grandino ~are, *intr.* To hail: *~abit donec se demittet sylva* Isa. 32.19 (AR 399.3).

grandis ~is ~e, *a.* (compar. *~ior*) Of large size or amount, great, big: *exsurgeret hoc opusculum in ~e volumen* AM 209; *argentum multum et ~e* ES [3605] ½; *cervi ~iores* VR 815.1; (of abstract things) *signum ~is luctus* SS 35.2.

grandisonans ~ntis, *a.* Loud-sounding, noisy: *auditus tumultus quasi fluctuans et ~ns* AC 2128.1; ES 2382.

grandisonus ~a ~um, *a.* = **grandisonans**: ES 5113.

grando ~inis, *f.* Hail: *facta est ~o et ignis* Rev. 8.7 (AR); (pl.) hailstorms: *per ~ines, pluvias etiam* ES 196.

granulatus ~a ~um, *a.* Granulated: *~um salinum* ES 645.

granulum ~i, *neut.* A small particle, grain: *~a auri* AM 268.2.

granum ~i, *neut.* **1** A small seed, grain: *simile est regnum coelorum ~o sinapis* Matt. 13.31 (AC 54.3). **2** An extremely small amount, particle, grain: *quod ille ne quidem ~um intellectus possideat* AM 233.5; VR 71.3.

grassatio ~onis, *f.* The act of prowling in search of prey, preying: *per pestem* [*describitur*] *~o usque ad consumtionem* AC 2799.10.

grassor ~ari ~atus sum, *intr.* To roam about in search of prey, prowl: *multa pars talium libere ~abatur, et infestabat bonos* AC 6858; AC 8273.1.

grate, *adv.* In an agreeable manner, favourably: *quod...internum ~e aspiciat jucundum in externo*

DP 136.5; *simplices loquuntur valde simpliciter, sed usque ~e* ES 183.

gratia ~ae, *f.* **1** The showing of favour, indulgence, grace: *ut...captet amicitiam, benevolentiam ac ~am* CI 504; *quod Deus Pater exciderit ~a erga genus humanum* VR 161.1; *ex Divina ~a* AM 3.1. **2** The state of being favoured, grace: *salve, ~am consequuta* Luke 1.28 (DD 19.2); *in Deo et in ~a sunt* VI 4; *misericordia applicatur illis qui coelestes sunt, ~a autem illis qui spirituales* AC 598.2. **3** (pl., esp. w. *ago* and sim.) Thanks: *~arum actio* AC 8300; *Domino ~as egerunt* AM 25. **4** *~a* (w. gen.), for the sake of: *dum externum se tutandi ~a asperat* AM 365; *si bonum est sui ~a* AC 1088.2.

gratificor ~ari ~atus sum, *intr.* (w. dat.) To show kindness (to), treat kindly: *hospites...quibus... ~antur et benefaciunt angeli* AC 1631.

gratiose, *adv.* Graciously: *legem Tuam ~e largire mihi* Ps. 119.29 (AC 627.2); VR 159.3.

gratiosus ~a ~um, *a.* Showing favour, gracious: *~us est [Deus Pater]* VR 132.1; VR 160.6.

gratis, *adv.* Without payment or obligation, freely, for nothing: *~is salvamur* VR 567.1; *quod...Dominus mercedem det ~is ex misericordia* AC 735.

gratitudo ~inis, *f.* The state of being welcome, acceptableness: *cujus ~o describitur per odorem agri* AC 925.4; AM 243.

gratuitus ~a ~um, *a.* Given without payment, gratuitous, free: *suntne omnia salutis ~a?* VR 798.8; made as a sign of gratitude: *quae sacrificia eucharistica seu ~a vocabantur* AE 391.2.

gratus ~a ~um, *a.* (superl. *~issimus*) Pleasing, welcome, acceptable: *odores ~os et suaves* CI 569; *verba ...accepta, ~a et jucunda* AE 22.2; (neut. as sb.) *odor quietis est pacis seu ~um pacis* AC 925.3.

gravamen ~inis, *neut.* A burdensome task: *quod ...Divina Lex et doctrina non eximent illos a ~inibus* AC 7088; AC 7104.

gravedo ~inis, *f.* An oppressive sensation, pain, heaviness: *ambulant sicut ~ine obsessi* AM 267.3; *~ine ...ventris* ES(M) 4648.

graveolens ~ntis, *a.* Foul-smelling, stinking: *mortuus ~ns* VR 383.2; CI 569.

graveolenter, *adv.* With a foul smell: *~er olent* AC 7225.3.

graveolentia ~ae, *f.* Foul smell, stench: *~a cadaveris* AC 7319; AM 431.1.

graveolentus ~a ~um, *a.* (compar. *~ior*) Foul-smelling, stinking: *foetor ~us* AC 814.1; AM 253.2; (neut. as sb.) a stench: AM 431.2.

graveoleo ~lere, *intr.* To stink: AM 512.2.

gravida ~ae, *f. adj.* Pregnant: *quia tunc uxor ~a* ES 3922; (fem. as sb.) *~a et pariens simul* Jer. 31.8 (AE 721.10).

gravis ~is ~e, *a.* (compar. *~ior*, superl. *~issimus*) **1** Heavy: *materialia...sunt sicut ~ia quae...retardant* AC 6921; (neut. as sb.) a weight: *ut...delabatur [falsum] sicut ~e in mundo* AC 8279.1; also, heaviness: *quod...lapsi sint sicut ex ~i* AC 8272; *centrum ~ium*, centre of gravity: AE 159.3. **2** Burdensome, oppressive, serious: *~es tentationes* DD 15.2; *terrae motus sunt leviores et ~iores* AR 711; *post ~em somnum* ES 2342. **3** Weighed down, oppressed: *animi...ex se ~es mitescant* AM 56.4; *vae...po}dlo ~i iniquitate* Isa. 1.4 (SS 86). **4** Solemn, serious: *respondit tono ~i* VR 137.8.

gravitas ~atis, *f.* **1** Heaviness, weight: *globuli... differunt... ~ate, duritie, calore* ES 1038 1/2; AC 8279.2; DP 211.2; cf. *dimovit rotam curruum...et duxit illam in ~ate* Exod. 14.25 (AC). **b** gravity (as a physical force): *quod sit ~as in qualibet particula minima hominis* ES 3727. **2** Oppressiveness, seriousness, gravity: *haec...leniant ~atem adulterii* AM 488; *~ates et incrementa poenae* AC 395.2. **3** A feeling of being oppressed: *in somno sentiebam ~atem* AC 1270.2.

gravitatio ~onis, *f.* The tendency of heavy objects to move downwards, gravitation: *directio...quae vocatur centripetentia, et quoque ~o* CI 142; ES 3905.

graviter, *adv.* (compar. *~vius*, superl. *~vissime*) In an oppressive or burdensome manner, seriously, gravely: *quod...incipiat...pulmo ~viter anhelare* VR 119.2; *quod...nihil ~vius puteat* AC 7319; *~viter et misere puniuntur* AM 80.1; *sancta ~vissime prophanat* DP 232.

gravito ~are ~avi, *intr.* To move by gravity, gravitate: *caput meum ~aret antrorsum* ES 3905; ES 4063.

gravo ~are ~avi ~atum, *tr.* **1** To make heavy, weigh down: *somno ~ati dormiebant* ES 3231; ES 3905. **2** To oppress, burden: *id ~abat conscientiam ejus* ES 517 1/2; ES 4204.

gregarius ~a ~um, *a.* Of the common herd; *~us miles*, a common soldier: VR 424.

gremium ~i, *neut.* The area enclosed by the arms and chest as the place where objects are carried, bosom, lap: *matres quae delitiantur ex incubatione oris ...illorum [sc. infantum] super ~is* AM 396.2; *sicut ~o foveret serpentem* VR 582.2; (fig.) *continue osculatur naturam...sicut idololatra aureum sculptile in suo ~o* VR 508.3; *in ~o terrae* SS 66; VR 237.

gressus ~us, *m.* **1** The manner of walking, gait: *quod ~um illorum concernit, non ambulant erecti* AC 8371; *dum spiritus...intendit ~ui alicujus equi* ES 1770. **2** A pace, step: *in platea cum numeravi ~us* ES 4101; (as an indication of direction of movement) *datum est angelis movere meos ~us* CI 228; *direxit ~um ad me* AM 2.1.

grex ~egis, *f.* A flock (of sheep or goats): *~eges ovium cum agnis* VR 78.1; *~egem et armenta omnia* Ps. 8.7 (AC 776.2); (applied to people) *homines Ecclesiae in genere vocantur ~ex, et in specie oves* FI 61.

grisee, *adv.* Like grey: *~e alba* 'grey-white' ES 5464.3.

griseus ~a ~um, *a.* Grey: *barba visa ~a* ES 3275.

grossus ~i, *m.* An immature fig: *sicut ficus dejicit ~os suos* Rev. 6.13 (AR).

grumosus ~a ~um, *a.* Full of dust, dusty: *quod amor ita crassus et ~us existat* ES 3946.

grumus ~i, *m.* A particle of dust: *~um incidentem in oculum* VR 393.1; *sunt nomina...sicut ~i seu sicut squamae, quae decidunt* AC 1876.1; (collectively) dust: *sicut crassus et pungens ~us respective ad puram... auram* AC 545.2; *rarus ~us in athmosphaera* AC 7007.4.

gubernaculum ~i, *neut.* The tiller, helm (of a ship): *comparari potest navi, quae...non obsequitur ~o* VR 28.2; VR 620.2.

gubernatio ~onis, *f.* Government: *quod primum [princeps] introducatur in cognitiones quae ~onis sunt* VR 721.1.

gubernator ~oris, *m.* The steersman of a ship, helmsman: *navis...perit una cum ~ore, nauclero et nautis* VR 127; a governor, guider, controller: *de Deo Creatore et ~ore universi coeli* CI 324.

gubernatrix ~icis, *f.* A governor: *agnoscit... propriam prudentiam pro ~ice* AR 692.2.

guberno ~are ~avi ~atum, *tr.* To govern, control: *ut ~ent eos qui ibi* AC 1115; *quod Filius Dei...~et omnia in caelis et in terris* VR 111.10.

Gui: see **Guy**.

gula ~ae, *f.* The gullet (as the organ of gluttony): *qui... delicate vixerunt ac indulserunt ~ae et ventri* CI 488.5.

gummi, *indecl. neut.* Gum, resin: *ex corticis fibris ~i conglutinatis* ES 1547; AC 7485.

gurges ~itis, *m.* A whirlpool, vortex: *omnes ~ites aquae* VR 767.3; a gulf, chasm: *talis ~es est inter infernum et coelum* ES 1315.

gusto ~are ~avi, *intr.* To taste: *credunt...quod... lingua ~et ex se* AE 152.2; AM 8.3.

gustus ~us, *m.* **1** The sense of taste: *sensus hominis, nempe visus, auditus, olfactus, ~us et tactus* AE 349.4; AC 1516. **2** The flavour, taste (of food or drink): *non praeparant cibos secundum ~um* ES 596; AC 8378; *spiritus sciunt quinam ~us eorum quae edo et bibo* ES 3529; VR 328.

gutta ~ae, *f.* **1** A drop (of liquid): *sudor Ipsius ut ~ae sanguinis* Luke 22.44 (AC 1787.2); *in ~is aquae pluviae* AC 1042.1. **2** A small patch, spot: *alis...aureis, cum interspersis striis et ~is...argenteis* VR 71.1. **3** *~a serena*, the eye disease amaurosis: VR 346.2.

guttur ~uris, *neut.* The throat, neck: *torquem super ~ur tuum* Ezek. 16.11 (AE 126.3); *inferre escas in ~ura illorum* [sc. *pullorum*] VR 44.1; *halitus...retraxit clamorem retro in ~ur* VR 137.1; (pl.) the opening of the throat, jaws: *ejus ~ura diducebantur* ES 4500.

gutturalis ~is ~e, *a.* Of or belonging to the throat: *recondi...possunt vera...sicut semina...apud aviculas in ~i earum loculo* AC 3324.2.

Guy, *indecl. m.* also **Gui**, *indecl. m.* Saint Guy; *saltus S. Guy*, St Guy's dance, tarantism: *assimilari potest saltui S. Viti seu Guy, qui homini accidit ex ictu tarantulae* VR 367.7; VR 566.

gymnasiacus ~a ~um, *a.* (Gk.) *Ludus ~us*, a high school, college, 'gymnasium': AM 326.2.

gymnasista ~ae, *m.* A college student: VR 106.1.

gymnasium ~i, *neut.* (Gk.) A place of instruction for advanced students, high school, college, 'gymnasium': *~a in mundo spirituum sunt curiae, ubi conveniunt eruditi* VR 136.1; *~um ubi juvenes initiantur in varia quae sapientiae sunt* VR 697.1; *~a Olympiaca* AM 151[a].1.

gynaeceum ~i, *neut.* (Gk.) The women's apartments in a residence: *ingressae sunt ~um ubi etiam virgines ...erant* AM 22.

gypseus ~a ~um, *a.* Made of plaster: *paries quasi ~us cum sculpturis* AC 5393.2.

gypsum ~i, *neut.* (Gk.) Plaster: *sculpturis factis ex ~o* ES 943.

gyratio ~onis, *f.* Rotatory movement: *ex ~one telluris* VR 32.1; AC 4041.

gyro ~are ~avi, *intr.* To move in a circle, rotate: *sol ibi non ~at sicut in mundo* ES 4639.2.

gyrus ~i, *m.* **1** A circular course or track, ring, circle: *arbores hae in continua serie consitae erant, quae ...pergebat in perennes orbes seu ~os sicut perpetuae helicis* VR 741.2; *apparent in cerebro...circumvolutiones et ~i mirabiles* AC 4040; *vagati sumus per*

~os et ~os VR 737.3. **2** Movement of a circular or rotatory type, revolution: *~i erant lenes...operatio eorum...est communiter orbicularis* AC 5183; *veniebant chori angelici...ac suos ~os canoros...agebant* ES 553; *~us non est simplex ~us, sed volubilis circumcirca* ES 1036.

H

habena ~ae, *f.* (usu. pl.) Reins: *~ae quas tenebant manibus fulgebant* VR 386.1; (fig.) *furiis istis pauxillum relaxatae sunt ~ae* ES 225; (sg.) ES 2559 titulus.

habeo ~bere ~bui ~bitum, *tr.* **1** To hold, bear, have: *apparuit lagenam vini...~bens* ES 3801; *in utero ~bens clamavit parturiens* Rev. 12.2 (AR); *~bentes Nomen Patris Ipsius scriptum super frontibus suis* Rev. 14.1 (AR). **2** To have in one's possession, own: *et alias oves ~beo* John 10.16 (AC 7035); *concessum fuit... concubinam ~bere* AC 3246.3. **b** (w. preps.) to have in a specified place: *ostendebat mihi...fenestram...quam ~buit in palatio suo* ES 4418. **3** (of things) To be equipped with, possess, have: *quod planeta Saturnus... ~beat...cingulum magnum lunare* AC 6697; *haec lux in se ~bet calorem* AC 8328.2; *urbem...~bentem portas duodecim* Rev. 21.12 (AR). **4** To have given to one, receive: *ut credentes vitam ~beatis* John 20.31 (AC 6674.2); *ex Antiquissimae Ecclesiae posteris ~buit Moses haec de creatione* AC 66.1; *in hoc homo nullam partem ~bet* DP 120; (of things) *quod ille status finem ~buerit* AC 3256. **b** (w. *ab* or *ex*) to derive (from a source or origin): *quod homo sit homo, ~bet...a Domino* AC 272; *ex illo ~bet, ut scire aliquid possit* AC 3293.1. **5** To have at one's disposal, have available or accessible: *quod angeli...tantam potestatem...~beant* AC 6677; *~bent Mosen et Prophetas, audiunto illos* Luke 16.29 (DP 134[a]). **6** To have in one's mind, possess mentally: *prophanare vera quibus semel fidem ~buerant* AC 6963.2; *de Ente...cujus nullam ideam ~buissent* AC 6876.2; *fiduciam ~bere* VR 2.3; *quod frater tuus ~beat aliquid contra te* Matt. 5.23 (AE 746.17). **7** To exercise, apply, pay, have: *curam ejus ~buit* Luke 10.34 (AC 6708); *honorem ~be super me* Exod. 8.5 (AC); *nulla ratione ~bita ad personas* ES 448; *respectu ~bito ad statum* ES 2215; *Antiquissima Ecclesia cultum sanctum ~buerunt super montibus* AC 796. **8** To experience, undergo, have: *somnium triste ~bui* ES 4236. **b** *opus ~bere*, to need: *non magis opus ~bui quam cogitare de persona* ES 4558. **9** To regard, hold, reckon: (w. *pro*) *adulteria pro honesto ~bentur* AC 6666.3; (w. pred. adj.) *quod conjugia sint...sancta ~benda* AM 481; (w. *in* + abl.) *in qua idea illi ~bebant suum beatum* ES 4442. **b** *odio ~bere*, to look on with hatred, hate: *ut...odio ~berent Ipsum* DP 247; *qui odio ~buerunt proximum* AC 547. **10** *Se ~bere*, to behave, act, be: *Divinus Amor et...Divinum Verum se ~bent comparative sicut ignis solis et lux inde* CI 13; *quod ita se res ~beat* 'that this is the case' CI 342.1; (impers.) *Ecclesiae...succedentes...se habuerunt sicut se ~bet cum fructibus* AC 501. **b** (app., intr.) *sibi ~bere*, to pay attention: *sique non credere velint...~beant sibi, cum in alteram vitam veniunt* AC 322.1; ES 1719. **11** (w. pf. pple. to express perfectivity): *cum illis quos notos ~bui cum in corpore vixerunt* AC 1114; ES 4564.

habilis ~is ~e, *a.* (compar. *~ior*) Well-suited, apt: (w. gen.) *~iores intelligendi* ES 2252; ES 4350; (w. *ad*) *juvenis ad nuptias ~is* AM 316.3; (w. *ut*) *sic ut non evadant ~es ut impleantur* [*ideae*] ES 1826.

habilitas ~atis, *f.* An ability, potentiality: *alia quae sunt excitatoria ~atum in pueris latentium* AM 17.4.

habiliter, *adv.* (compar. *~lius*) Suitably, aptly: *amor ...qui interiora mentium fortius et ~lius aperit* AM 302.1; ES 3494.

habitabilis ~is ~e, *a.* Capable of being lived in, habitable: *in orbis ~is parte minima* DP 238; *terra ~is* DD 62.2.

habitaculum ~i, *neut.* A place to live in, dwelling place: *angeli habent sua ~a* ES 4292; AC 995.2; *in ~o serpentum cubile ejus* Isa. 35.7 (AC 7293.4); *locum Jehovae, ~a Forti Jacobi* Ps. 132.5 (DD 39); (transf.) *receptaculum vitae...et sic ~um Dei* AM 315.11; *~um amoris et sapientiae Ipsius* VR 13.4.

habitatio ~onis, *f.* **1** The act of living, dwelling: *Moschis ~o in Midiane* AC 7016; *religio ejus comparari potest ~oni in domo in qua non sunt fenestrae* FI 48; (transf.) *periret ~o hominis in Deo* VR 74.3. **2** A place to live in, residence, dwelling place, apartment: *necessitates vitae...ut ~onem* AC 6934; *pervagatus plateas fine inquirendi ~onem* AM 242.

habitator ~oris, *m.* One who lives in, inhabitant: *~oribus Chaldaeae* Jer. 51.24 (AC 8226.2); *urbem ex quo ~ores...aufugerunt* AM 79.11.

habitatrix ~icis, *f.* A female inhabitant: *~ix filia Aegypti* Jer. 46.19 (AC 6729).

habito ~are ~avi ~atum, *intr.* (*tr.*) **1** To have a residence: *nec plus ambiunt quam ut nutriantur et ~ent* AC 8380; to reside, dwell, live (in a place or circumstances): *quod antiquissimi...similiter ~averint* AC 8118.1; *quod... ~ent in palatiis magnificis* FI 63.2; VR 120.2. **2** (pass., of places) To be lived in, be inhabited: *desertum...significat parum ~atum et excultum* AC 6828; *urbes quae non ~antur* AC 8278.2. **3** (transf.) To be present, dwell: *innocentia ~at in sapientia* AC 7877.2; *quod in cerebello ~et amor voluntatis* VR 160.8.

habitus ~us, *m.* **1** State of being, condition: *quae naturalem ~um induunt* AC 7131; *ipsum hominem reputant ex amictu splendido...non ex interno ejus ~u* AM 478.1. **2** Habit, use, custom: *ex assuetudine et ~u* DP 117.1; *tandem ex ~u trahuntur usque illuc ut...* AC 7747; (w. gen.) *ex consuetudine contraxerunt ~um componendi interiora sua ad imitamen affectionum bonarum* CI 458. **3** Clothing, dress: *erat ~u coeruleo* ES 1158.

hac, *adv. Hac et illac*, in this way and that: *in gyros repugnantes hac et illac versus* ES 1259.

hactenus, *adv.* **1** Up to this time, until now: *quod sensus spiritualis Verbi ~us ignotus fuerit* SS 20.1; VR 776.1. **2** Up to this point in sequence, so far: *omnia quae ~us dicta sunt* VI 28.

haedus: see **hoedus**.

haemi-: see **hemi-**.

haemorrheus ~i, *m.* (ad. Gk.) = **haemorrhois**, sense 2: *angues, regulos, aspides, ~os* AC 251.1.

haemorrhois ~idis, *f.* (Gk.) **1** A pile, haemorrhoid: *percutiet te Jehovah ulcere Aegypti, et ~idibus* [*~idis* 3rd edn.] Deut. 28.27 (AC 8364.3); FI 52; VR 203.1. **2** A fabulous snake reputed to cause bleeding to death: *ululae, echidnae et ~ides* VR 531.

haereditarius ~a ~um, *a.* also **hered-**. **1** Inherited from ancestors, hereditary: *malum a parentibus quod vocatur ~um* VR 154.4. **2** (neut. as sb.) Heredity: *quale ~um habuerunt, dictum prius est* AC 788.1; *ex ~o* VR 621.2; *~o*, by inheritance, by heredity: *ut vitam aeternam ~o acciperet* Mark 10.17 (VI 66.1); AM 142.

haereditas ~atis, *f.* also **hered-**. **1** Acquisition by birth, inheritance: *similitudines... ~ate et simul educatione contractas* AM 246.2; *cesserunt primogenito binae partes ex ~ate* AE 28.2. **2** That which is acquired by descent, an inheritance: *affinem deprivavit ~ate sua* CI 462[a].6; VR 721.

haeredito ~are ~avi ~atum, *tr.* also **hered-**. **1** To be heir to, inherit from: *ecce filius domus meae ~ans me* Gen. 15.3 (AC); Zeph. 2.9 (VR 251). **2** To receive as an inheritance, inherit: *thronum gloriae ~are faciet eos* 1 Sam. 2.8 (AE 253.6); *quod nobilitas... ~etur et descendat* AM 110.

haerenter, *adv.* Tenaciously: *detentus sum ~er in eorum consortio* ES 1187.

haereo ~rere ~si, *intr.* **1** To hang on, cling: *fuliginarius qui in furvo camini ~ret* VR 61.1; (transf.) *vera quae... ~rent in superficie, et inde...sicut squamae decidunt* AC 7790; *~sit in mente idea* VR 786.2. **2** To act hesitantly: *nec ~ret manus in electione alicujus vocis* CI 262. **3** To be at a loss, be perplexed: *demum ~serint, et dixerint, crede si vis* AM 182.4; *angelus ...conticuit, ~sit enim in stupore* VR 134.3.

haeres ~edis, *m.* also **heres**. An heir: *omnes qui in regno Domini, sunt ~edes* AC 1799.1; AM 109.

haeresiarcha ~ae, *m.* (Gk.) The leader of a band of heretics: *phalanges ~arum Ecclesiam invaserunt* VR 378.2.

haeresis ~eos, *f.* (acc. sg. *~in*) An incorrect system of religious belief, heresy: *de doctrinis separatis ab Ecclesia seu ~ibus* AC 324; *mens...facilis ad ~es* SS 52; *~is Arii* VR 137.11.

haereticus ~a ~um, *a.* (Gk.) Heretical: *omnis Ecclesia usque ad summe ~am* VR 759.2; (masc. as sb.) a heretic: AC 6865.3; (neut. as sb.) a heretical belief: *inde... tam enormia ~a de Deo scaturiverunt* VR 23.1.

haesitatio ~onis, *f.* Hesitation: ES 4430.

haesito ~are ~avi, *intr.* To hesitate: *vidit illos adhuc ~antes* VR 335.6.

Haggai ~i, *m.* Haggai, a book of the Old Testament minor prophets: NH 266.

halelu-Jah: see **alleluja**.

halitus ~us, *m.* **1** The breath expelled from the lungs: *~us gemens retraxit clamorem retro in guttur* VR 137.1; *~us narium Jehovae* AE 419.3. **2** Any gentle movement of air, breath: *subtilis vitae ~us, sicut vapor* DP 233.12; *de ~u venti* AM 229. **3** A gaseous effluvium, emanation: *ex ~ibus in terra reconditis trahit aurum suum elementum, argentum suum* SS 66; *~us effluviosi e carne illorum assurgentes* AM 495.3.

halleluia: see **alleluja**.

halleluja: see **alleluja**.

hallelu-Jah: see **alleluja**.

halleluJah: see **alleluja**.

hallucinatio ~onis, *f.* A delusive vision, hallucination: *merae...phantasiae, seu ~ones sensuum* ES 426.

hallucinor ~ari ~atus sum, *intr.* To suffer from delusions, be deluded: *in hoc orbis Christianus ~atur* VR 102.1; *~antur in translatione Scripturae Sanctae* ES 1951.

halo ~are ~avi, *intr.* To exhale fragrance, smell: *ex consertione florum dulce ~antium* VR 353.2.

hamus ~i, *m.* A fish hook: *quasi ~os emittebant ut ad se attraherent eos, sicut piscatores* ES 3309; *num trahes Leviathanem ~o?* Job 41.1 (AE 455.18).

hariolatio ~onis, *f.* The act of playing the fool: VR 184.

hariolor ~ari ~atum sum, *intr.* To perform as a comic actor, play the fool: *hariolus non vult nisi ~ari* VR 145.1; VR 819.2.

hariolus ~i, *m.* also **ariolus**. **1** A soothsayer, fortune-teller: *animam quae respicit ad pythones et ad ~os* Lev. 20.6 (AE 141.14); (also app.) a telling of fortunes: *sunt [ea] similia ~is et praestigiis* ES 269. **2** A comic actor, mountebank, (court) fool: *apparent sicut ~i ambulantes super palmis manuum* VR 381.5; DP 121.2; *loquelae ~orum...qui per digitos loquuntur, et qui inversis vocibus* ES 3889; ES 4525.

harmonia ~ae, *f.* (Gk.) **1** Agreement, concord: *quod unum faciat per ~am* AC 8003; *ex pluribus consentientibus seu ~a plurium existit unum* ES 289; *influxus simultaneus...in corpus et...in animam, quem ~am praestabilitam nuncupant* VR 695.3. **2** A harmonious sound, chord: *auditui [jucundum] ex ~is* CI 402. **3** Visual harmony: *voluptatibus visus, seu pulchritudinem...ut...quae ex ~is jucunda sunt* AC 995.2. **4** A musical performance, concert: *his diebus sunt ~ae musicae et cantus in foris* AM 17.1; AC 8339.1.

harmonice, *adv.* Harmoniously: *affectio...amoris ~e profluens* AM 55.1.

harmonicus ~a ~um, *a.* (Gk.) Concordant, harmonious: *varietas omnium consentiens et ~a* AC 690; CI 405; (of sounds) *cantus ~us* ES 2090; *loquela angelica est ~a* AC 8261.3. **b** (neut. as sb.) a harmony: *cum ~um conveniens conspirat* AC 8337.2; *in ~o*, in tune: VR 61.1.

hasta ~ae, *f.* A spear: *aliquibus armis, ut ~is, clypeis, aut sclopetis* VR 84.

hastilis ~is ~e, *a.* Of or suitable for a spear: *lignum ~e* [i.e., sharpened to a point] VR 86.

haud, *particle.* Not: *si haud tu dimittis populum Meum* Exod. 8.17 (AC).

haudquaquam, *adv.* By no means, not at all: *illi ~am in aliqua illustratione possunt esse* AC 10551.3; VR 641.3.

haurio ~rire ~si ~stum, *tr.* **1** To draw up (liquids): *aquas obsidii ~ri tibi* Nahum 3.14 (AC 6669.2); (absol.) to draw water: *venerunt et ~serunt, et impleverunt canaliculos* Exod. 2.16 (AC). **2** To absorb (knowledge), learn, take in: *multa scientifica ~riri queunt* AC 6917.2; *intelligentiam et sapientiam ~serunt* CI 87; *nomina ...ex quibus nihil potest ~riri* SS 15.1; (w. inf.) *~serunt in mundo simulare bonas* ES 4573.

haustor ~oris, *m.* One who draws (water): *~ores aquarum* Josh. 9.27 (AC 1097.2).

haustrix ~icis, *f.* A woman who draws water: Gen. 24.11 (AC).

haustrum ~i, *neut.* A place where water is drawn, watering place: *cogentium greges inter ~a* 3AD 4736.

hebes ~etis, *a.* (compar. *~etior*) **1** (of the faculty of vision or perception) Dim, weak, feeble: *quod oculus hominis tam ~es et crassus sit ut ne quidem videat exstantiora* AC 5849; *homo ex hoc judicio parum discernit talia, quia est crassum et ~es* AM 57. **2** (of persons) Lacking in perception, dim-sighted, purblind: *est ~es acie videndi verum ut vix alius ~etior* AC 455.4; AC 6865.2.

hebesco ~ere, *intr.* (of light) To become faint, dim: *rutilum et coruscum, ex quo [sol] tantum splenduit, incipit ~ere* CI 159; (of other things) to become faint, pall: *post triduum coeperunt faustitates illae ~ere* AM 8.3.

hebetatio ~onis, *f.* A making dull or weak: *deprivatio perceptionis boni, ~o affectionis veri* AE 677.3.

hebeto ~are ~avi ~atum, *tr.* To make weak or faint, enfeeble, dull: *ut inciperet lumen oculorum meorum ~ari et obscurum fieri* AC 6925; *hoc intellectum rationalem ~at et opacat* SS 95; *turpia et faeda... ~antur apud angelos* AC 5981.

hebetudo ~inis, *f.* Lack of power of perception, dullness: *haec...vix audita sunt propter ~inem ex duorum dierum suspensione mentis* AM 9.3; AC 7298.1.

Hebraeus ~a ~um, *a.* (Gk.) Hebrew: *apud gentem ~am* AC 6917.2; *lingua ~a* CI 237; (masc. as sb.) AC 1343.1.

Hebraice, *adv.* In the Hebrew language: *nomen ei ~e Abaddon* Rev. 9.11 (AR).

Hebraicus ~a ~um, *a.* Hebrew: *vetustis literis ~is* SS 71; CI 260.

Hecateus ~a ~um, *a.* (Gk.) Of Hecate, a Greek

goddess of the underworld: *quod... Ulyssis comites... consperserit herbis ~is* AM 521.4.

hedad, *indecl.* (Hebr.) A shout (of exultation): Isa. 16.10 (AC 1071.4).

hei, *interj.* An expression of anguish, alas: *hei diei, quia propinquus dies Jehovae* Joel 1.15 (AC 1992.5).

heic: variant spelling of **hic**[2]: AC 2722.7; 1AD 61.

helix ~icis, *f.* (Gk.) **1** A spiral: *in spiralis seu ~icis formam* ES 1233; *~ix arborea* AM 13.2. **2** A device for lifting weights operating on the principle of the screw, jack: *pondus grave...subducere e terra per ~ices* DP 211.2.

helvus ~a ~um, *a.* Dull yellow, dun: *currus tracti a mannis coloris ~i* AM 103.2.

hemiplexia ~ae, *f.* (Gk.) also **haem-**. A stroke affecting one side of the body, hemiplegia: *paralysi unius lateris, quae vocatur ~a* VR 367.7.

hemisphaerium ~i, *neut.* (Gk.) also **haem-**, and **hemispherium**. A hemisphere: *cerebrum...in binas partes, quae vocantur ~a, divisum* AC 644; VR 376.1.

hemispherium: see **hemisphaerium**.

hepar ~atis, *neut.* (Gk.) (app. masc. acc. *~atem* AC 10031; ES 3581) (anat.) The liver: *jecur seu ~ar* ES 368; DP 174.1; VR 54.

hepaticus ~a ~um, *a.* (Gk.) Of or associated with the liver: *lienares sunt qui prophana sanctis commiscent ac separant, ~i qui moralia similiter* ES 1011.

hera ~ae, *f.* The mistress (of a servant): VR 106.1.

herba ~ae, *f.* **1** A small plant: *omnis ~a et omne gramen* AM 86; *quod...* [*apes*] *odorent flores et ~as, ex quibus colligant ceras* VR 12.7. **b** (as a stage in the growth of a plant): *primum ~am, dein spicam, deinde plenum frumentum in spica* Mark 4.28 (AC 29.2). **2** (collectively) The vegetative cover of the earth, plants: *sicut guttae super ~a* Mic. 5.7 (AE 278.5).

herbaceus ~a ~um, *a.* Of or resembling a plant, herbaceous: *viride quoddam ~um* AC 1625; ES 3229; (neut. as sb.) a herbaceous plant: VR 767.3.

herbosus ~a ~um, *a.* Abounding in grass, grassy: *quia ~a facta habitacula deserti* Joel 2.22 (AC 46.1).

hered-: see **haered-**.

heres: see **haeres**.

heri, *adv.* Yesterday: *~i et hodie* ES 2713; *ab ~i* Exod. 4.10 (AC).

hermaphroditus ~i, *m.* (Gk.) A hermaphrodite: *conjunctioni quasi conjugiali cum ~o* ES 5985.

hernia ~ae, *f.* Rupture, hernia: AM 253.2.

heroicus ~a ~um, *a.* (Gk.) Of or proper to a hero, heroic: *quod talia essent licita, et quasi ~a* ES 4634.

heros ~ois, *m.* (Gk.) **1** A man of outstanding bravery, hero: *ex ~oibus facti subito sicut mulieres* AC 950; *~oes et fortes in bello* DP 274.9; *vae ~oibus ad bibendum vinum* Isa. 5.22 (AC 1072.5). **2** (as an epithet of the Lord): *vocabitur nomen Ipsius, Mirabilis, Deus, ~os* Isa. 9.6 (VR 82.2).

herus ~i, *m.* The master (of a servant): [*status*] *famuli antequam fit ~us* VR 106.1; CI 219.

hesternus ~a ~um, *a.* Of yesterday: *ex sermone ~o* VR 73.1.

heterodoxon ~i, *neut.* (Gk.) A heterodox opinion, heterodoxy: *hoc sonat sicut ~on* VR 185.5; VR 639.2.

heterogeneitas ~atis, *f.* The fact of belonging to a different kind, heterogeneity: *plena ~as* VR 648.1; an instance of this: *quod...ibi sentiantur homogeneitates et ~ates* AM 273.1.

heterogeneus ~a ~um, *a.* (ad. Gk.) Of a different kind, alien: *absonae ac ~ae ideae de Deo* VR 163 (ix); (neut. as sb.) an alien element, foreign body: *nisi procellae forent in athmosphaera quae dissipant ~a* AC 842.3; ES 2357.

heu, *interj.* (as an expression of grief or dismay) Oh!, alas!: *praedestinatio heu quam pulchra apologia defectus* AM 105; *heu facinus* AR 655.7; (also, as expressing approval) *heu loquimini ex judicio* AM 521.2.

hexameter ~tri, *m.* A hexameter verse: 3AD 23 note.

hiatus ~us, *m.* A deep opening, gap, chasm: *hiabat solum, et per ~um ascendebant tres diaboli* AM 461.7; *inter quod* [sc. *infernum*] *et caelum...ingens ~us est* VR 56.2.

hic[1] haec hoc, *pron.*, *adj.* see also **hicce**. **1** (w. ref. to something present) This: **a** (as adj.): *adduc tibi natum hunc* Exod. 2.9 (AC); *in hac tellure* AC 6700. **b** (as pron.): *hi induti stolis albis quinam sunt* Rev. 7.13 (AR). **2** (w. ref. to something previously mentioned) This: **a** (as adj.): *quomodo Ipse lex Divina...factus est, hujus legis verum est quod intelligitur* AC 6717.3. **b** (as pron.): *inter spiritus infernales...hi circum volitant* AC 6724.2; *quomodo haec se habent, supra explicatum est* AC 6732. **3** *Hoc est*, that is to say, that is: *quod quantum angelus in innocentia est, tantum in coelo sit, hoc est, in Divino Bono et Divino Vero* CI 280; *ut Humanum Suum...glorificaret, hoc est, uniret Divino* VR 2.2. **4** (w. ref. to what follows): *in his locis...* AR 762.3; *causa legationis meae fuit haec, quod...* VR 731.2. **b** (w. rel. clause): *Mater Mea et fratres Mei hi sunt qui audiunt verbum Dei* Luke 8.21 (AC 8361.2). **5** (as pron., contrasted w. *ille*) The nearer of two, the latter: *vita est* *fugere mala et facere bona, ac homo haec facere et illa fugere non potest nisi ab ipso* SE 44. **6** (coupled w. *ille*) The one (or the other): **a** (as adj.): *hic et ille sensus...unum sunt* CI 307.3; AR 875.3. **b** (as pron.): *cur [revelatum est] per hunc aut per illum, et non per aliquem primatem Ecclesiae?* DP 264.1.

hic[2] *adv.* also **heic**. **1** In this place, here: *sum ibi diabolus at hic sum angelus lucis* VR 507.4. **b** to this place, hither, here: *hic ductus sum a duobus angelis* VR 48.2; *inde...projiciebantur, unus hic alter illuc* ES 3330. **2** (coupled w. *ibi*) In one place (or another): *ut sit hic aut ibi in caelo* DP 67; *hic et ibi*, in various places, here and there: VR 35.2. **3** In this case, under these circumstances: *ex repraesentatione 'Mosis' quod sit lex Divina...hic lex Divina in sua origine* AC 6725; at this point (in a narrative, book, etc.): *videatur hic infra* DD praef.

hicce haecce hocce, *pron., adj.* Emphatic variant of **hic**[1]: *spiritus hicce* ES 2081; *in formas hasce* AC 5881; *a corporeis hisce* ES 884.

hiem-: see **hyem-**.

hierarcha ~ae, *m.* (Gk.) A high priest, prelate: *ab omnibus episcopis, ~is, dynastis Ecclesiae et presbyteris* VR 633.1; VR 640.2.

hierarchia ~ae, *f.* **1** Rule by priests: *detexit ~am quam plures...affectant et quoque exercent* AR 716.3. **2** The successive orders of priests, hierarchy: *majores et minores ordinis in ~a eorum ecclesiastica* AR 759.1; AR 799.1.

hierarchicus ~a ~um, *a.* (Gk.) Of a priesthood: *de regimine aristocratico aut ~o* VR 133.2.

hieroglyphica ~orum, *neut. pl.* (Gk.) The earliest system of Egyptian writing, hieroglyphics: *a ~is Aegyptiorum, quibus etiam in sacris utebantur* AC 6692.1; SS 20.2; AM 76.1; (used of other writing systems) *lamellae cupreae, super quibus aliqua ~a exarata sunt* AM 182.8.

Hierosolymitanus ~a ~um, *a.* Of Jerusalem: *in medio templi ~i* VI 55.2.

higgaion: see **higgajon**.

higgajon, *indecl.* (Hebr.) also **higgaion**. Higgaion, a Hebr. musical term whose meaning has been lost: *super ~on in cithara* Ps. 92.3 (AR 276).

hilaris ~is ~e, *a.* Cheerful: *spiritus...tenebant faciem meam continue ~em et ridentem* AC 7807; *quod angeli ...non fiant moesti...sed ~es* AM 44.9.

hilaritas ~atis, *f.* Cheerfulness: *per ~atem mentis* CI 288.1; (w. pl.) an instance of this: *blandiloquia maritorum ac ~ates mentis illorum* AM 293.2; AE 323.2.

hilaritudo ~inis, *f.* Cheerfulness: *~o animi* ES 4644.

hilum, *indecl. neut.* (only after a negative) Anything at all, the smallest part: *tunc non potest ~um libidinis intrare* AM 75.6; *non ~um distat* 'there is not the slightest difference' VR 17.1; (esp.) *ne ~um*, nothing at all: *ut spiritus infernales ne ~um damni queant inferre* AC 6724.2; (adv.) *creditum est quod...abstersa fuerint illis peccata, cum tamen ne ~um* AE 71.3.

hin hinis, *m.* and *indecl.* (Hebr.) A Hebrew measure for liquids, hin: *per bathum et per hin mensurabantur liquida* AC 8540.1; *oleum olivae ~em* Exod. 30.24 (AC).

hinc, *adv.* **1** *~c et illinc*, on one side or the other, here and there: *postquam legit illa, et insuper aliquae ~c et illinc in Verbo* VR 484.1; Ezek. 47.12 (AC 57). **2** Consequently, as a result, hence: *haec est os de ossibus meis... ~c vocabitur Ischah* Gen. 2.23 (AM 32); AC 7236.1.

hinnio ~nire ~nivi, *intr.* (of horses) To neigh, whinny: *equus ~niens* Nahum 3.2 (AC 6978).

hinnitus ~us, *m.* (of a horse) The neighing, whinnying (in quot. transf.): *adulteria tua, ~us tui, scelus scortationis tuae* Jer. 13.27 (AE 141.7).

hio ~are ~avi, *intr.* (of surfaces) To display cracks, open up, gape: *terra ~abat sub pedibus ejus* AR 675.7; *in domo...quae...rimas ducit et ~at* CI 528; *osculis ibi ~antibus* DP 296.14.

Hippocraticus ~a ~um, *a.* Of or relating to Hippocrates, a Greek teacher of medicine in 5th-4th centuries BC: *loquimini lingua ~a* VR 665.6.

hircinus ~a ~um, *a.* Of a goat: *vestes ex pilis ~is* AR 456.2.

hircus ~i, *m.* A he-goat: *angus, ovis, ~us, vitulus, bos* SS 18.2; (w. ref. to Matt. 25) *statuet oves a dextris, et ~os a sinistris* DD 25; *malos a bonis et ~os ab ovibus separaverit* VR 95.

hirquus ~i, *m.* The corner of the eye; (abl. pl.) out of the corners of the eyes: *obliquant oculos et ex ~is tuentur* VR 332.4; *qui...obliquo oculo seu ~is intuetur* VR 362.3.

hirsutia ~ae, *f.* Hairiness: *quidam loco faciei solum ~a aut barba* ES 4626.

hirsutus ~a ~um, *a.* Covered with coarse hair, hairy, shaggy: *viri... ~i et pilosi* AC 1272; *pelle ~a* VR 797.3; (of hair) long, shaggy: *crinibus ~is* ES 1782.

hirundo ~inis, *f.* A swallow: ES 3340.

hisce: see **hicce**.

hisco ~ere, *intr.* **1** To gape open, yawn: *mons... diducebatur seu ~ebat in longum* ES 5231. **2** To make a slight move, raise a finger: *turba ea tenetur ita* *vincta ut nequaquam possint ~ere, minus infestare hominem* ES 225; ES 1778; ES 2322; *contra Divinum inferna non ~unt* AC 10367.7. **3** (w. inf.) To venture, dare (to): *nec ~unt minimum exsurgere* AC 581.1; AC 986.2; CI 48; VR 123.4.

hispidus ~a ~um, *a.* Bristly, rough: *excitat zelum, qui extrinsecus asper, ~us, ardens et ignivomus est* VR 155.2.

historia ~ae, *f.* (Gk.) An historical narrative, history: *patet ex ~is variarum gentium* AC 7249; AM 73.1; *naturalis ~a*, natural history: ES(M) [4730].

historice, *adv.* In the manner of an history: *ut ~e omnia cohaerere appareant* AC 295.

historicus ~a ~um, *a.* (Gk.) **1** Of or relating to history: *omnes scientiae...ut... ~a* AM 163; (neut. pl. as sb.) historical narratives: *nec expendunt quid ~a de illa gente memorant* AC 7051.3. **2** (of the Word) Written as history: *quoad Verbum ~um* AC 6723.3; *libros ~os* AC 6752.1; (of meaning, faith, etc.) regarded as history, historical: *sensus externus ~us* AC 6970; *quia est dictamen alterius in altero, est fides ~a* FI 1.

histrio ~onis, *m.* An actor: AM 7.3; VR 745.5; a clown, buffoon: *illi...apparent similes ~onibus, qui inverso corpore jacent super cubitis, et progrediuntur* AM 79.3; AM 17.5.

histrionicus ~a ~um, *a.* Of an actor, histrionic: *ex imitamine perfecte ~o* AM 512.1.

Ḥittaeus: see **Chittaeus**.

Ḥivaeus: see **Chivaeus**.

hodie, *adv.* **1** Today: *in Verbo cum nominatur heri, ~e, aut cras* AC 3998. **2** At the present time: *communis opinio ~e est* AC 6704.

hodiernus ~a ~um, *a.* Of the present time, present, modern: *in mundo ~o* AM 291.1; *ad ~um diem* VR 760; *~a fides* FI 1; (masc. pl. as sb.) men of today, modern people: *si de ~is dictum fuisset* AC 312.

hoedus ~i, *m.* also **haedus**. A young goat, kid: *pellis, ~i, ovis, arietis* AC 294; *agni, ~i, turtures* AM 430; VR 388.1.

Hollandicus ~a ~um, *a.* Of the Netherlands, Dutch: *urbs ~a* ES [6099.14].

holocaustum ~i, *neut.* (Gk.) A burnt offering (in which the victim is consumed whole): VR 203.2; VR 569.5.

holosericus ~a ~um, *a.* (Gk.) Made of pure silk: *panno ~o* VR 188.1; (neut. as sb.) *calcei ex ~o* AM 42.3.

ḥomer: see **chomer**.

homicida ~ae, *m.* A murderer, killer: *~a, adulter, fur et falsus testis* VI 91; (transf.) *spirituales ~ae* VR 380.4.

homicidium ~i, *neut.* The taking of human life, murder: *~a, furta et falsa testimonia* AM 528; VI chapter vii titulus.

homo ~inis, *m.* (derived from **humus** cf. VR 48.13) **1** A human being, person, man: *quod omnis ~o sit aeque proximus* AC 6704; (on other planets) *quod plures tellures sint et super illis ~ines* AC 6695; (as surviving death) *quod aliquot myriades ~inum per diem alluant* AC 6699. **b** (sg. as collective) human beings, man: *ut removeret [Dominus] infernum ab ~ine* VR 2.2; *~o...talis est, et quidem perplurima pars, ut nesciat...* AC 1083.3. **c** (dist. from **vir**): AC 915. **d** *Filius ~inis* (as a title of the Lord): CO 3; (also of Old Testament prophets) DD 28. **2** (w. defining epithet, to indicate a person in a particular character or relationship): *internus ~o* AC 986.2; *vetus ~o moriturus, antequam novus concipi potest* AC 18; *~o Ecclesiae non solum est ipsa Ecclesia, sed omne Ecclesiae* AC 768.1. **3** (coupled w. another sb. in apposition): *~o vir* 'husband' AM 172; *apud ~inem spiritum* CI 422; *~ines bestiae* VR 160.7; *~ini lupo* 'werewolf' VR 428. **4** *Maximus ~o*, the form of heaven, the Grand Man: *coelum Maximus ~o vocatur* AC 911.2.

homogeneitas ~atis, *f.* Likeness of type, homogeneity: *~ates et heterogeneitates* AM 273.1.

homogeneus ~a ~um, *a.* (Gk.) Belonging to the same type, similar in nature, homogeneous: *omnia sanguinis tam heterogenea quam ~a* AC 842.3; *bonum desiderat verum et recipit illud libenter, quia ~um est* AC 8313.4; (w. abl.) *exteriora eorum sunt ~a interioribus* CI 331; (neut. as sb.) *nisus ~orum et similium ad conjunctionem* VR 44.2.

homuncio ~onis, *m.* A diminutive person, mannikin, dwarf: *putabatur infans, sed perspectus et consideratus erat ~o seu homunculus* ES 3242; *estis quidem vos...sicut Enachim, et illi...sicut ~ones* VR 113.5; VR 162.2.

homunculus ~i, *m.* A person of very small stature, dwarf, mannikin: *quod ~i sint, parvi, vix ultra lumbos meos altitudo eorum pertingens* ES 1519; ES 3242.

honestas ~atis, *f.* Honourable action, honour: *civilem personam agere et ~atis officia exhibere* VR 443.1; *spectacula comaedorum...repraesentantium varias vitae moralis ~ates et virtutes* AM 17.5.

honeste, *adv.* Honourably: ES 1208.

honestus ~a ~um, *a.* (of persons) Honourable: *homo ~us* VR 145; (of actions, ideas, etc.) *ambire et rogare faeminas de conjugio est in se ~um et decorum viris* AM 297; (neut. as sb.) *ultra limites decori et ~i* CI 504; *hae [affectiones]...circumvelantur ~is quae sunt vitae moralis* DP 2774.

honor ~oris, *m.* also **honos** ~oris, *m.* **1** Respect paid to another, honour: *~orem habe super me* Exod. 8.5 (AC); *reges terrae afferent gloriam et ~orem suum in illam* Rev. 21.24 (AR). **2** Exalted rank or position, honour: *cogitatio de ~ore et de lucro* AC 6914.3; *accedit quod...velint...uxores nominari; hoc illis est nomen decoris et ~oris* AM 217; (pl.) *voluptates ~orum et officiorum in republica* AC 994.2.

honorabilis ~is ~e, *a.* Worthy of honour: *hic ~is in vestitu suo* Isa. 63.1 (VR 116.1); *locum pedum Meorum ~em reddam* Isa. 60.13 (AE 69.4).

honorarium ~i, *neut.* A gift as a token of honour: *reges Schebae et Sebae ~um adferent* Ps. 72.10 (AC 1171.1).

honoratio ~onis, *f.* The act of being honoured: *propter lucrationem et ~onem* AC 7640.

honorificus ~a ~um, *a.* Designed to convey honour, honorific: *~a habitatio* VR 152; *in ~o vestitu* VR 724.

honoro ~are ~avi ~atum, *tr.* (compar. of pf. pple. *~atior*) To pay respect to, honour, esteem: *quod parentes ~andi sint* VR 14.3; *qui ~ant et amant illum* [sc. *sensum literae*] SS 35.4.

honos: see **honor**.

hora ~ae, *f.* (Gk.) **1** A period of one twenty-fourth of a day, hour: *per unam ~am circiter* AC 8115; (as denoting a time of day) *circa ~am octavam* ES 5980. **2** An hour regarded as a point of time: *in ultima vitae ~a* AC 7127.2; *ex illa ~a* John 19.27 (AE 9.5); an appointed hour: *Pater, venit ~a* John 17.1 (DD 13).

horarius ~a ~um, *a.* Lasting an hour: *per tempus ~um* AC 3214; ES 2111.

hordeum ~i, *neut.* Barley: *e messe ~i* VR 331.2; (pl.) barley grains, barley: *semina...~a, tritica, et similia* AC 7112; VR 78.1. (n.b. In VR 524.3 for *in hordeis* read *in horreis.*)

horizon ~ntis, *m.* (Gk.) The horizon: *inter zenith et ~ntem* AM 137.5.

horizontalis ~is ~e, *a.* Horizontal: *in plano ~i, inque verticali* AC 1276.

horizontaliter, *adv.* In a horizontal plane, horizontally: *paena eorum est quod...sternantur ~er et circumrotentur* AC 829.1.

horologium ~i, *neut.* (Gk.) A clock: *cui non plus vitae inesset quam ~o* VR 364.1.

horrendus ~a ~um, *a.* To be shuddered at, horrible: *~a jucunda adulterii* AM 137.7; *monstra, ~a facie et ~o corpore* CI 131; (neut. as sb.) *ab ~is et abominabilibus* VR 110.7.

horreo ~rere ~rui, *intr., tr.* **1** (intr.) To feel horror, shudder: *incipiunt aversari, tum timere, et tandem ~rere ad praesentiam ejus* AC 7791; *exterius territus ~rui* AC 7803; *ad quod ipsa humana ratio ~ret* DP 157.5. **2** (tr. and w. inf.) To feel horror at: *qui ~ret aliquid, is fugit id* AC 6950; *~ret quicquam facere quod illum laedit* AC 1798.3; (impers.) *~ret...dicere quod...mactaverit cultro infantem* ES 4504. **3** (intr.) To cause horror, horrify: *fit timor qui ~ret* AM 368.3.

horrescentia ~ae, *f.* A shuddering: *ut...horror insinuatur, qui facit ut...redeat ~a illa* AC 7918.1; AC 8158.

horresco ~ere, *intr.* (*tr.*) To shudder, shiver: *~unt illi, qui ibi, sicut qui correpti sunt a febri gelida* CI 572; *si sciret homo...~eret* AC 803.2; (app. refl.) *se ~ebat, dicens...* ES 4289; (also tr.) to shudder at: *unusquisque eos ~it* AC 816.

horreum ~i, *neut.* A place for the storage of grain, granary, barn: *quis non zizania separat a messe tritici, antequam hoc infert in ~um...?* VR 331.2; FI 31.

horribilis ~is ~e, *a.* (compar. *~ior*) Causing shuddering, horrible: *inferna...eo pejora et ~iora quo remotiora ab oriente* CI 587.2.

horridus ~a ~um, *a.* **1** Having a rough surface, bristling, shaggy: *homo...cum inter latrones...est ~us quoad comas* AC 5246.4; *in statum turbulentum seu ~i maris* ES 2345. **2** Causing shuddering: *~us timor pro jactura illius amoris* AM 357; *post exactam ~am hyemem* VR 304; *ficus ~as* Jer. 29.17 (AC 1327.5).

horripilatio ~onis, *f.* Erection of the hairs on the skin, horripilation: *corrugatio et ~o* AC 4180.4; AR 56.

horror ~oris, *m.* **1** Trembling from cold, shuddering: *unde tale frigus et inde ~or* CI 572. **2** A feeling of horror: *incutit ~orem* CI 245; *post tentationes has et ~ores* AC 1863.

horsum, *adv.* In this direction, hitherwards: *ut...spargerent ignem ~um* Num. 16.37 (AE 324.6).

hortatio ~onis, *f.* Encouragement, urging: *per instructionem et ~onem ab intellectu* DP 282.

hortensis ~is ~e, *a.* Of a vegetable or fruit garden; *campus ~is*, the flat expanse of a garden: *oculus* [*eligit*] *ex campo ~i talia quae conducunt usibus vitae suae* AC 9035.

hortor ~ari ~atus sum, *tr.* To encourage, urge: *omnes et singulos ~atur ut resipiscant* 1AD 1527.

hortulanus ~a ~um, *a.* **1** Of or resembling a garden: *tractum...~um* ES 2072; CI 488.2; *domunculas ~as* 'summer houses' AM 8.2. **2** Concerned with gardening: *experientia naturalis sicut ~a* ES 772; (masc. as sb.) a gardener: *arbor...quam ~us exscindit* VI 46; ES 3349.

hortulus ~i, *m.* A small garden: *est... ~us, et in medio ejus domus* AM 316.1; ES 3624.

hortus ~i, *m.* A garden: *~i, luci, sylvae* SS 18.2; *Verbum est sicut ~us* VR 259.

horula ~ae, *f.* A short period of time, a few minutes: *post ~am apertae sunt fores* AM 14.1; VR 603.2.

hospes ~itis, *m.* **1** A visitor, guest: *ut ad illos novi ~ites angeli veniant* CI 71; AM 10.2; (unwelcome) *quod nihil conarer repellere ~ites illos* AC 1879.2. **2** One who provides entertainment, host: *dedit ~es nobis botrum* AM 76.8; (in an inn) Luke 10.35 (AE 444.14).

hospita ~ae, *f.* A female guest, lodger: *et petat mulier e vicina sua, et ex ~a domus suae* Exod. 3.22 (AC).

hospitale ~is, *neut.* A place of rest and retreat, esp. for the aged, hospice: *~ia, nosocomia, orphanotrophia et xenodochia* VR 459.8; DP 326.8; ES 5309.

hospitalitium ~i, *neut.* = **hospitale**: *impendat templis et ~is* VI 24.

hospitium ~i, *neut.* A lodging place, dwelling: *in ~o vilium* ES(M) [4747]; *in veris est ~um boni* AC 4205.2; AC 4269.

hospito: see **hospitor**.

hospitor ~ari ~atus sum, *intr.* also **hospito** ~are, *intr.* To be entertained, lodge, dwell: *in caelo non potest ~ari malum* AS 270; (act.) *qui in tertio coelo ~ant adhuc* ES 228.

hostia ~ae, *f.* (in a Roman Catholic mass) The Host: *cum monstratis... ~as* VR 111.11.

hostilis ~is ~e, *a.* Of enemies, enemy, hostile: *contra turmam ~em* AC 8282; *per invasionem ~em* AC 8295; proper to an enemy: *quod pleni sint ~i odio* CI 560.

hostilitas ~atis, *f.* A feeling of enmity, hostility: *plenum omni violentia et ~ate contra verum et bonum* AC 7047; (w. pl.) a hostile act: *erumpunt mala vel per artes vel per ~ates* AC 7437.2.

hostis ~is, *m.* **1** An enemy of the state, foreign enemy: *tradam vos in manum ~is* Lev. 26.25 (AC 7102.5); *tutari patriam...contra invasores ~es* DP 252.2. **2** A personal enemy: *habet...quisque alterum pro ~e, exterius autem pro amico* AC 7773; AM 271.

huc, *adv.* **1** To this place, hither: *nuper huc venisti* AM 477.2; *huc et illuc* (and sim.), hither and thither, in different directions: *et prospexit huc et illuc* Exod. 2.12 (AC); *vadit huc illuc* AM 2.1; ES 302. **2** (w. *usque*, sometimes written as one word) Up to this point in time or sequence, hitherto, so far: *ab illo tempore perstitit haec redemptio huc usque* VR 115.1; *in praecedentibus huc usque actum est de antiquissimis* AC 286; ES 2487.

hucusque: see **huc**.

hujuscemodi, *indecl.* = **hujusmodi**: ES 963.

hujusmodi, *indecl.* A thing of this sort: *~i et ludicriora adhuc sequuntur* VR 631.2.

humanitas ~atis, *f.* **1** The quality of being a man, humanity: *libertas et rationalitas in quibus consistit ipsa ~as* DP 281.3. **2** Humane conduct, civilization: *contra ~atis leges* VI 108.

humaniter, *adv.* In a humane manner, in kindly fashion: *quod...moneat ut angelos ~er excipiant* AC 8028.

humanus ~a ~um, *a.* **1** Of a human being, man's, human: *pro ~o genere* FI 38; *in corpore ~o* SS 20.1; *in forma ~a* AC 6700. **2** Typical of men as a class, human: *verba loquelae ~ae* AC 7088.2; *qui intellectum ~um habet* AC 477.1; *prudentiam politicam et oeconomicam ~am* VR 335.3. **3** (neut. as sb.) Human nature, humanity: *cum appercipiunt quod tale ~um iis sit sicut aliis* CI 326; *exuunt ~um et induunt ferinum* VR 13.4; (esp. of the Lord) *quod Dominus...in mundum venerit ut...glorificaret ~um Suum* VR 2.1. **4** Kindly, humane: *moneret ut ~i essent* ES Index s.v. 'loqui, loquela' (p. 18 Tafel), referring to ES 1648-56.

humecto ~are ~avi ~atum, *tr.* also **umecto**. To make wet, moisten: *quod fila... ~ent aqua glutinosa* AC 10163.

humeralia ~um, *neut. pl.* also **umeralia**. Shoulder-pieces: Exod. 39.4 (AC).

humerus ~i, *m.* also **umerus**. **1** The shoulder: *manus, brachia, ~i correspondent potentiae* AC 7296; (as the place on which burdens are carried) *recedet onus ejus desuper ~o tuo* Isa. 10.27 (SS 15.1); (as the part on which garments are worn) *vestem...posuerunt super ~o ...illi* Gen. 9.23 (AC); (fig.) *super cujus ~o principatus* Isa. 9.6 (DD 19.4). **2** The side (of a building): *juxta ~um domus a dextra* 1 Kgs. 7.39 (AE 600.21).

humi, *adv.* (locative of **humus**) On the ground: *formicas, quae repunt ~i* VR 35.1.

humidus ~a ~um, *a.* Wet, damp: *in ~a humo* CI 362.

humiliatio ~onis, *f.* **1** The act of making oneself humble, self-abasement: *~o [consistit] in sui agnitione quod apud se nihil vivum et nihil bonum* AC 1153.2; AC 7052. **2** The state of being humble, humility: *antiquissimi in ~one sua agnoverunt se pro feris* AC 840; *status est ~onis ejus coram parentibus* VR 106.1; *status ~onis [Domini] seu exinanitionis* DD 35.3.

humilio ~are ~avi ~atum, *tr.* **1** To make low, fell, raze: *quod Ego Jehovah ~em arborem altam* Ezek. 17.24 (AE 109.4); *omnis mons et collis ~abuntur* Isa. 40.4 (AC 1691.3); *urbem exaltatam, ~abit eam* Isa.

26.5 (AC 258). **2** To make humble: *quod Dominus continue ~et superbos* DP 183.4; *cum se coram Divino ~are debent* AC 7068.

humilis ~is ~e, *a.* (superl. *~imus*) **1** Of small height, low: *habitacula...sunt ~ia* AC 8379; *vallis est ~e quoddam inter montes* AC 1292.2. **2** (of sounds) Of low pitch, bass: *vocis altae et vocis ~is* AM 17.1. **3** Of low status, lowly, humble: *'terra Jordanis' pro illo quod est ~e, et sic quod distat a coelesti* AC 1585.3. **4** Lacking in pride, humble: *qui in charitate sunt ~es sunt* AC 8313.4.

humilitas ~atis, *f.* The quality of being humble, humility: *tametsi ore fassi ~atem, usque corde habuerint altitudinem* ES 2375.

humiliter, *adv.* (compar. *~lius*, superl. *~llime*) **1** At a low level, low: *ad idem latus, ~lius, est David* ES 463. **2** In humble fashion, humbly: *~liter se...gerere* AC 8253; *qui ~lius, hoc est, exterius cogitant* DP 48.1; ES 4560.

humor ~oris, *m.* **1** Moisture: *aqua non [datur] sine ~ore* DP 258.5. **2** A fluid in the body: *morbi...a nimia spissitudine...~orum* AM 253.2; *~ores... excrementitii, ut sunt plures salivales, tum biles, et similia* AC 1103.2; *induratio ~oris chrystallini* VR 346.1.

humus ~i, *f.* see also **humi**. **1** Ground, earth: *homini aedificanti domum super ~o sine fundamento* Luke 6.49 (VI 2); *~us ex miscela sulphuris, ramentorum ferri et argillae luti* VR 110.1; a piece of ground, plot: *in medio circi ~us elevata* AM 183.1. **2** Earth as the material in which plants grow, soil: *homo nullus ad colendum ~um* Gen. 2.5 (AC); *distinguitur ~us a terra* AC 566.1; SS 66; (fig.) *memoria...est illarum* [sc. *intelligentiae et sapientiae*] *~us* VR 32.4.

hyacinthinus ~a ~um, *a.* (Gk.) **1** Of blue colour: *tunica...coloris ~i* AM 15; *veste ~a* VR 386.1; (neut. as sb.) *~um est color coeruleus, etiam coelestis dictus* 3AD 1287. **2** (neut. as sb.) A blue material: *facient ephodum ex auro, ~o et purpura* Exod. 28.6 (AC); *vestitos ~o* Ezek. 23.6 (AC 1186.2).

hyacinthus ~i, *m.* (Gk.) **1** A precious stone of blue colour, jacinth: *~us, sapphirus, et alii lapides pretiosi* AC 1589.3. **2** A plant, perhaps hyacinth: *quod...non possit...~us vellicare sicut carduus* VR 653.

hydra ~ae, *f.* (Gk.) A poisonous snake, hydra: *desertum Arabiae, ubi serpentes, ~ae et presteres* VR 38.2; VR 124.1; AM 79.4.

hydria ~ae, *f.* (Gk.) A water jug, ewer: VR 350.1.

hydropicus ~a ~um, *a.* (Gk.) *Morbus ~us*, dropsy: AC 9086.2; (masc. as sb.) a sufferer from dropsy: *cum ~um in die sabbathi sanavit* AC 9086.2.

hyemalis ~is ~e, *a.* also **hiem-**. Of winter: *in luce ~i* DP 154.3; also, resembling winter, wintry: *ita nullius amoris sunt, sed sunt ~es* ES 3579.

hyems ~mis, *f.* also **hiems**. Winter: *ver, aestas, autumnus, et ~ms* CI 105; VR 12.7.

hymnicus ~i, *m.* (Gk.) A hymn-singer: *mihi auditi sunt ~i seu cantantes laudem Salvatoris nostri* ES 491.

hymnus ~i, *m.* (Gk.) A religious song of praise, hymn: *angelos...~um formantes* ES 489.

hypaethrum: see **hypethrum**.

hyperbola ~ae, *f.* (Gk.) (geom.) A hyperbola: ES 1003.

hyperbolice, *adv.* In an exaggerated manner, hyperbolically: *in scriptis prophanis talia ~e dici possunt* AC 776.2.

hyperbolicus ~a ~um, *a.* (Gk.) Exaggerated, hyperbolical: *in Verbo Domini nusquam ~a sunt* AC 776.2.

hyperboreus ~a ~um, *a.* (Gk.) Of the far north: *frigus mediae hyemis in regionibus ~is* AM 449.

hyperoum ~i, *neut.* (Gk.) An upper room, attic: *vae aedificanti...~a sua in non judicio* Jer. 22.13 (AC 655.2).

hypethrum ~i, *neut.* (Gk.) also **hypaethrum** (AM 208.1). An open courtyard: *introducebantur in ~um, ambulatorium palatii* AM 14.1.

hypochondriacus ~a ~um, *a.* (Gk.) Characterized by hypochondria: *morbus ~us* VR 665.5.

hypocrisis ~eos, *f.* (Gk.) (acc. sg. *~in*) Pretence of virtue, hypocrisy: *non sciunt quid ~is, et quid simulatio fraudulenta ac dolus* AC 7360; *~es scortatoriae* AM 477.1.

hypocrita ~ae, *m.* (Gk.) A hypocrite: *simulator, sycophanta, ~a* AM 267.3; VR 14.4.

hypocritice, *adv.* In a hypocritical manner: *licentiam simulate et ~e agendi* AC 8870.3.

hypocriticus ~a ~um, *a.* (Gk.) Hypocritical: *a simulationibus ~is* AM 279; *bonum meritorium et ~um* VR 162.4.

hypogastricus ~a ~um, *a.* (Gk.) Under the belly, hypogastric: *regiones...epigastricam et ~am* VR 665.5.

hypomochlium ~i, *neut.* (Gk.) The fulcrum (of a lever): *cum magna trabe posita super ~o suo* VR 478.2; ES 920.

hypostaticus ~a ~um, *a.* (Gk.) (neut. nom. and acc. sg. also *~on*) Relating to the person of the Divine: *quod Verbum ~on nec aliud sit quam Divinum Verum* CN De Deo Redemptore iii.6; *unio ~a*, hypostatic union (see quot.): *per unionem ~am intelligunt* *unionem sicut inter duos, quorum unus est supra et alter est infra* VR 94.2.

hypotheca ~ae, *f.* (Gk.) A safe deposit, repository: *cum...uxor...recondit suos nummos in crumenis, aut gazas in ~is* AM 287.

hypothesis ~eos, *f.* (Gk.) A hypothesis: *plena sunt ~ibus falsis* ES 249; *cum...ex doctrina et simul ex ~i cogitat* CI 456.2.

hypotheticus ~a ~um, *a.* (Gk.) Hypothetical: *veritas ~a* CC 2; (neut. as sb.) a hypothetical proposition: *qui excluserunt ~a, seu falsa* ES 1468; VR 371.3.

hyssopus ~i, *f.* (Gk.) An aromatic plant, hyssop: Exod. 12.22 (AC).

hystericus ~a ~um, *a.* (Gk.) Characterized by hysteria: *gravis morbus ~us* AM 252.

I

iaspis: see **jaspis**.

ibi, *adv*. In that place, there: AC 8384; in that passage: AM 41.3; (so, also) *ibi loci* AC 609; in that state: *perveni in statum tranquillum, ac ibi...permansi* ES 221.

ibidem, *adv*. (abbreviated *ibid.*) In the same place: AE 386.15; ES 2640.

ichorosus ~a ~um, *a*. (ad. Gk.) Ichorous: *peripneumonia...ex pituita lenta ac lympha ~a* VR 665.5.

icio ~cere, *tr*. To inflict a blow on, strike, smite: *vulnere lethali ~citur* VR 165.3.

ictus ~us, *m*. **1** A blow, stroke: *percipiebam tanquam ~um per cor* ES 1864; *ex ~u tarantulae* VR 367.7; (app.) *cultri...cum in ~u* [perh. read *actu*] *sunt percussionis adimuntur* ES 4049. **2** *Oculi ~us*, a glance: *percipiunt...innumera uno oculi ~u* ES 2822; *oculi ~u*, in the twinkling of an eye: *momento seu oculi ~u* ES 354.

idcirco, *particle*. As a consequence, for that reason, therefore: *quia nullus simili modo recipit Dominum ... ~o nec unus simili modo est proximus ac alter* AC 6706; CI 385.

idea ~ae, *f*. **1** A concept formed in the mind, idea: *omnes...ejus cogitationes, et cogitationum ~ae, imo voces et actiones, sunt apertae* AC 99; *indefinita...quae nusquam in hominis ~am venerunt* AC 969; *~am unius Dei* VR 8.2. **2** A form under which a thing may be conceptualized, pattern: *unicuique rei in universa natura...impressa est ~a regni Domini* AC 718; *ex lustrato mundo in universali hac ~a* VR 13.2; DP 34.

idealis ~is ~e, *a*. Existing only in the mind, conceptual: *amor et sapientia absque usu non sunt aliquid, sunt modo entia ~ia, nec fiunt realia priusquam sunt in usu* AR 875.6; VR 183.2.

idealista ~ae, *m*. One who denies the existence of objective reality, an idealist: *secundum visionarios, qui vocantur ~ae* DP 46.2; DP 309.3.

idealiter, *adv*. In the form of an idea, conceptually: *amor et sapientia non existunt nisi ~er, quia solum in affectione et cogitatione mentis* AM 16.3; AC 1808.2.

idem eadem idem, *pron.*, *adj*. **1** (as adj.) The same: *sugere hic est eadem vox cum lactari* AC 6745.2; *unus et idem*, one and the same: *nusquam datur apud duos bonum prorsus unum et idem* AC 6706. **b** (to call attention to an additional fact): *idem naturalis homo confirmat se contra Divinam Providentiam* 'the natural man also...' DP 238. **2** (as pron.) The same person or thing: (masc.) *iidem per surdos...significantur* AC 6989; (neut.) *sive dicatur malum sive diabolus, idem est* DP 233.3; *quod non detur idem, seu absoluta identitas duorum* AM 186.2.

identidem, *adv*. Time and time again, repeatedly: *~em visio urbis etiam perit* ES 848.

identitas ~atis, *f*. The fact of being the same, identity: *quod ~as trium Essentiarum Divinarum sit rationis scandalum* VR 23.2; AM 78.4.

ideo, *adv*. For that reason, therefore: *quod sit fides ex charitate, hic ~o verum et bonum* AC 1667.1; for the following reason: *imprimis dicunt ~o, quod dicam eos nihil esse* ES 3584.

idioma ~atis, *neut*. (Gk.) A form of speech, language: *Romano-Catholici missas suas Latino ~ate exclamant* VR 159.4; ES 400.

idololatra, ~ae, *m*. (Gk.) also **idololatres** ~ae, *m*. A worshipper of idols, idolater: *ipse Therachus...fuit ~a* AC 3778.1; *facti ~ae* CI 327; *etiam si vel immundissimus et corde suo ~es* AC 1361.4.

idololatres: see **idololatra**.

idololatria ~ae, *f*. (Gk.) The practice of worshipping idols, idolatry: *conjugium...externum, cui ~a... correspondet* AM 76.5; an instance of this, idolatrous act: *quod ~ae...ex scientia correspondentiarum traxerint originem* SS 23.1; AE 430.3.

idololatrice, *adv.* In an idolatrous manner: *illi Ipsum ~e colunt* AC 3732.2.

idololatricus ~a ~um, *a.* Concerned with idolatry, idolatrous: *cultus ~us* AC 639.2; *repraesentativa...versa sunt in ~a* SS 22; *quod [gens fuerit] corde ~a* AC 7051.3.

idolothytum ~i, *neut.* (Gk.) An offering of meat sacrificed to idols: *edere ~a et scortari* Rev. 2.14 (AR).

idolum ~i, *neut.* (Gk.) An image of a god, idol: *artifices qui conflant ~a* AC 424.

idoneus ~a ~um, *a.* Suitable, fit: *ego non ~us sum solvere corrigiam calceorum Ipsius* Luke 3.16 (AC 1748.5); *eligere tales, nempe qui ~i* AC 10329.1.

igitur, *conj.* (usu. second word in clause) Therefore, then: *hic ~ur agitur de Domino* AC 5078.2.

ignarus ~a ~um, *a.* Ignorant: *datum est loqui cum ~is, cum obscuris* FI 3; AC 1641.2.

ignavia ~ae, *f.* Sloth: *qui se ~ae et otio dedunt* AM 249.2.

ignavus ~a ~um, *a.* Slothful: *piger et ~us non admittitur in coelum* SA 134 (= xi.De Amore et Charitate.4).

ignesco ~ere, *intr.* To become ignited, catch fire: *per flammam, qua bucca eorum ~it* ES 1083; (transf.) to become excited with passion, be fired: *quod...velint ~ere per absolutas repugnantias* AM 511.

igneus ~a ~um, *a.* **1** Fiery: *sol...est...oceanus ~us* SS 95.2; *in fumum ~um* AC 814.2; *equi lucidi sicut ~i* AC 8029; (neut. as sb.) *quod ex ~o ejus* [sc. *solis*] *procedat calor* VR 41.1. **2** Productive of fire, inflammable: *bitumen et pix...in se ~a sunt* AC 6724.1.

igniculus ~i, *m.* A small fire, spark: *de apparentiis spiritibus sicut ~i et stellae* ES 2676; (fig.) *ex illorum oculis emicabat sicut ~us libidinis ad sexum* AM 44.2.

ignis ~is, *m.* **1** Fire: *~is solis et lux inde* CI 13; *arbor ...in ~em conjicitur* Matt. 7.19 (VI 2). **b** *~is fatuus*: see **fatuus**. **2** The heat of emotion, passion: *amor est ~is spiritualis* AM 235.1; *qui in ~e amorum sui et mundi sunt* AC 934.3; *aeque possunt usus praestare ...imo ex fortiori ~e* DP 250.3.

ignitim, *adv.* In a fiery manner, as in a fire: *apparet ille...facie ~im furva* VR 507.3.

ignitum ~i, *neut.* **1** (Bibl.) An offering consumed by fire, a burnt offering: *~um in odorem quietis Jehovae* AC 925.1; AC 7891. **2** A fiery mass: *circum quod apparuit furve ~um* VR 487.5.

ignitus ~a ~um, *a.* **1** Set on fire, burning, ablaze: *lux ex ~is carbonibus* CI 481.4; *jacula ~a arcus* Ps. 76.3 (AC 1664.7). **2** Appearing as if on fire, fiery: *lumbi ei erant plane ~i* AM 263.1; *~os diabolos* DP 33.3.

ignivomus ~a ~um, *a.* Vomiting forth fire: *ex montibus ~is* ME 11; *zelum, qui...ardens et ~us est* VR 155.2.

ignobilis ~is ~e, *a.* (compar. *~ior*) Of low esteem or value, lowly, ignoble: *Ecclesia...~is si non in genuinis veris* SS 77; *bestiae et aves, tam nobiles quam ~es* VR 48.2; *plumbum...reliquis metallis est ~ius* AC 8298.2.

ignominia ~ae, *f.* Low esteem, disrepute, ignominy: *in ~am aeternam* Dan. 12.2 (AC 8018.3); *ad evitandum ~am* VR 17.4.

ignominiose, *adv.* Without due esteem, disrespectfully: *qui nomen regis...~e enuntiat* VR 300.2.

ignominiosus ~a ~um, *a.* Involving disgrace, ignominious: *scandalosa et Deo ~a* VR 132.3; *quod abscindere barbam...esset ~um* AE 66.4.

ignorantia ~ae, *f.* The fact or condition of not knowing, ignorance: *ut homo in totali ~a nasceretur* VR 48.14; *qui in falsis ex ~a sunt* SS 15.2; (w. pl.) an instance of ignorance: *omnes ~ae veri etiam sunt 'nubes'* AC 1043.3.

ignoratio ~onis, *f.* Lack of knowledge, ignorance: *interpretans nemo illud significat ~onem quid inesset* AC 5250.

ignoro ~are ~avi ~atum, *tr.* To be unaware of, be ignorant of: *quod gentiles nequeunt facere quia ~ant illa* [sc. *bona et vera*] AC 6637.2; (w. *quod*) *quamdiu Ecclesia ~avit quod angeli et spiritus sint homines* SS 70; (pass.) *hoc hactenus ~atum fuit* FI 57.

ignosco ~ere, *intr.* To forgive an offence: *~ant* 'excuse this' AM 22; (impers. pass. w. dat. of person) *tunc ~itur iis* AC 1695.1; (w. pron. as subject) *hoc illis ~itur* AC 7250.

ignotus ~a ~um, *a.* (superl. *~issimus*) Not known, unknown: *artes...prorsus ~ae in mundo* AC 6832.9; *loqui cum illis sicut...~us cum ~o* CI 234; *hodierna fides est fides ~i* [i.e., in the unknown] FI 1; *~issimum plerisque est quid vita libertatis* AC 892.2.

iim: see **ijim**.

ijim, *indecl. pl.* (Hebr. *iyim* 'howlings') also **iim**, *indecl. pl.* (AC 1326.3), and **jim**, *indecl. pl.* (AC 7293.3). Hebr. word of doubtful meaning kept in transliterated form: Isa. 13.21 (AC 1326.3); Jer. 50.39 (AE 587.10); (understood as nocturnal birds) *dirae aves noctis, quae vocantur ochim et ijim* AM 264.4; cf. VR 133.1.

ilex ~icis, *f.* A holm oak: *sicut quercus et ~ex* Isa. 6.13 (AC 468.4).

iliacus ~a ~um, *a.* *Passio ~a*, a painful condition of the intestines, ileus: AM 470.

ilico: see **illico**.

illabor ~bi ~psus sum, *intr.* **1** To fall in, slip in: *sicut qui ~psus aquis in statu naufragii est* VR 31.2; *~buntur in infernum* AM 510.2; (of things) *sermo humanus ~bitur per aurem* AC 1635. **2** (transf.) To fall or slip (into a state or condition): *ideae eorum cogitationis ~buntur in voces quae sunt apud hominem* AC 1637.2; *influxus... ~batur in formas non correspondentes* VR 8.3.

illac, *adv. Hac et illac*, in this way and in that: see **hac**.

illaetus ~a ~um, *a.* Cheerless, unhappy: *illa laeta et haec jucunda faciunt ut illa appareant ~a et injucunda* AC 5116.5; ES 2294.

illapsus ~us, *m.* The action of falling upon, impact: *ad ~um lucis coeli* CI 132; *non sustinent ~um talis felicitatis* ES 4593.

illaqueatio ~onis, *f.* The action of being ensnared, entanglement: AE 171.

illaqueo ~are ~avi ~atum, *tr., intr.* To catch in a snare, trap (in quots. transf.): *ne forte ~eris illo* [sc. *auro*] Deut. 7.25 (AC 1551.5); (intr. w. dat.) *ita insinuat se infernum apud hominem, et ei ~at* AE 171.

illatio ~onis, *f.* A bringing in or into, an introducing: *per talem ~onem verorum in scientifica concordant ac unum faciunt interiora et exteriora quae alioquin discreparent* AC 6004.3.

illatus ~a ~um: pf. pple. of **infero**.

ille ~a ~ud, *pron.* and *adj.* **A** (as pron.) **1** That one, (according to gender) he, she or it, etc.: *non vocantur ~e et ~a, sed ~ud* DP 226; *~a duo* [sc. *Divinum Bonum et Divinum Verum*] *in Domino unum sunt* VI 32.1. **2** (w. ref. to a preceding sb.): *scrutari qualis hominis vita est, et secundum ~am charitatem exercere* AC 6704; (dist. from **hic**) the former: *datur ordo successivus et ordo simultaneus, et hic est ex ~o* AM 295.3; *ex ~is et his omnes doli* AC 1691.1. **3** (as antecedent of rel.) The one: *erga illos qui in una classe* AC 6705. **B** (as adj.) The aforesaid, that: *ex sole spirituali ...ita est ipse ~e Sol unica substantia* DP 6.1.

illecebra ~ae, *f.* An enticement, allurement: *~ae... amoris mali, quae in se sunt concupiscentiae, erumpunt* VR 41.3; AM 16.3.

illecebrosus ~a ~um, *a.* Enticing, alluring: *inquinat ultima...amoris ardore ~o* AM 304.2; AM 509.

illegitimus ~a ~um, *a.* Not sanctioned by law, illegitimate: *hae conjunctiones sunt ~ae in principio* AC 9182.2.

illibatus ~a ~um, *a.* Unimpaired, untouched: *quod Dominus binas illas facultates... ~as ac ut sanctas... custodiat* DP 96.1; *cui ratio ~a est* AM 419; ES 3441.

illibenter, *adv.* Unwillingly: *quod non ~er audiant nominari Patrem creatorem universi* AC 6197.2.

illibi: prob. erroneous for *illabi* (from **illabor**): *ne minimam cogitationem permittunt illibi, quam non momento arripiant* 4AD Jer. 5.15-16.

illic, *adv.* At that place, there: *neque dicent ecce hic aut ecce ~ic* Luke 17.21 (CI 33); *cum sphaera procreationis ~ic* [perh. read *illuc*] *vadit* AM 397.

illicitus ~a ~um, *a.* Not permitted, impermissible: *quod perceperint adhuc ~um esse* AC 205; *inde est quod homo...cogitet illa licita coram Deo, sed ~a coram mundo* VI 63.1.

illico, *adv.* also **ilico**. Without any delay, instantly, immediately: *quod ~o et momento percipitur* AC 582; *quod Deus... ~o percurrat terrarum orbem ad illos* VR 16.1; *~o ac*, as soon as: *~o ac a terrore redeunt, ad priorem animum...redeunt* ES 149; ES 3076.

illido ~dere ~si ~sum, *tr.* To cause to strike, hurl, drive: *~sum flumen domui isti* Luke 6.48 (AC 705.2); *conantes ~dere* [*phantasiam*]*...contra scopulos* ES 3798.

illigatus ~a ~um, *a.* Entangled: *cogitationes... talibus...immersae et ~ae seu irretitae* ES 591.

illimitatus ~a ~um, *a.* Unlimited, unbounded: *quod angelorum ideae sint absque tempore et spatio, et sic ~ae* CI 266.3; *de Divina potentia ~a* VR 74.1.

illinc, *adv. Hinc...illinc*, on one side...on the other: *juxta fluvium ascendit super ripam ejus hinc et ~c omnis arbor cibi* Ezek. 47.12 (AC 57); also, in one direction...in the other: *ad praesentiam illorum hinc ~c aufugiunt* AC 8200.2; *hinc et ~c*, at various places: *hinc et ~c in Verbo* VR 484.1.

illino ~linere ~livi ~litum, *tr.* (pf. act. also *~levi* VR 797.3) To smear on, paint: *parti...tabe infectae ~linere smegma* VI 112; *est sicut ~liverint fidem super omnia Verbi, quemadmodum qui minio ~linit scripturam* DP 153; VR 134.5; ES 853 (*~linire* Tafel).

illisio ~onis, *f.* A bruising: *~onem calcanei* 1AD Gen. 3.15 (Tafel, p. 20).

illotus ~a ~um, *a.* Unwashed: *est immundus ac ~us a capite ad volam pedis* DP 278[a].1; Mark 7.2 (VR 671.2).

illuc, *adv.* **1** To that place, thither: *qui ~c...veniunt* AC 6701; *omnes angeli se ~c vertunt* CI 142. **2** To that point in a sequence, to that extent: *historica vera Verbi inchoata sunt...capite praecedente xii; ~c fuerunt historica facta* AC 1540; *quod intellectus non potuerit penetrare ~c ut videret quod Deus unus sit* VR 24.1.

illuceo ~cere ~xi, *intr*. To dawn: *mane ~xit, quod significet statum illustrationis tunc constat ex significatione mane et ~cere* AC 5740; (fig.) to appear and begin to shine (upon someone): *peracta tentatione ~cet Dominus cum solatio* AC 5773.

illucesco ~lucescere ~luxi, *intr*. To become bright, shine forth, dawn: *nova lux seu mane ~luxit* AC 409; (impers.) *~luxit a latere dextro* AM 81.3; (fig.) *arcanum...quod nondum in alicujus intellectu ~luxit* VR 50.

illucido ~are ~avi ~atum, *tr*. To cast light upon, illuminate: *modo serviat [philosophia] ~andis iis qui nihil credunt* ES 650; to elucidate: *hoc coram iis ~are dabatur* ES 2545.

illudo ~dere ~si ~sum, *intr*. (*tr*.) **1** (w. dat.) To make fun (of), mock (at): *~serunt [pueri] Elisaeo vocantes illum calvum* 2 Kgs. 2.23 (AE 66.2); Gen. 39.14 (AC); ES 460. **2** To deceive by illusion, delude: *caveant itaque sibi...ne ~dantur* AC 4623.3.

illuminatio ~onis, *f*. Enlightenment: *ex qua ~one homo videt quid verum et bonum* AE 176.4.

illumino ~are ~avi ~atum, *tr*. **1** To cast light upon, make bright, illuminate: *angelus Dei... ~abat noctem* Exod. 14.20 (AC); *~avit filios Israelis* AC 8192.1; *~et Jehovah facies Suas super te* Num. 6.25 (AC 6674.8); (pass.) to shine: *surge, ~are, quia venit lux tua* Isa. 60.1 (AC 31.2). **b** to enable (the eye) to function, illumine: *sicut oculus ~atur a luce solis naturalis* VR 59. **2** To enlighten spiritually, make wise: *hi credunt se ~atos* AC 6865.3; *Dominus... ~at illum* [sc. *hominem*] *per bonum* AC 7078; *lux procedens ex sole mundi spiritualis...quod...sicut ~at, etiam vivificet intellectum hominis* VR 40.1. **3** To make clear, cast light upon: *res cujusvis quaestionis coloratis fucis ~are* AM 231.2.

illusio ~onis, *f*. A false appearance, illusion: *videte ~ones* Isa. 30.10 (AE 177.7); AC 1967.

illusivus ~a ~um, *a*. Causing illusion, delusive: *talis phantasia potest vocari phantasia ~a* ES 3797.

illusorius ~a ~um, *a*. Causing illusion, delusive, misleading: *didicerunt artes ~as per quas miracula magica fecerunt* AC 5223.2.

illustratio ~onis, *f*. **1** The act of making plain or clear, illustration: *pauca ~onis causa adducta* VR 73.3; (pred. dat.) *sit ~oni Verbum* AC 6789.2; AC 7753. **2** The state of being mentally enlightened, illumination: *in ~one esse non aliud est quam in perceptione esse* FI 5; *tempora diei...correspondent ~onibus quae sunt intelligentiae et sapientiae in altera vita* AC 8106.1.

illustrator ~oris, *m*. One who enlightens mentally, illuminator: *Unicus Creator, Salvator, et ~or a Se* AR 29.1; AE 1097.2.

illustris ~is ~e, *a*. (compar. *~ior*) **1** Illuminated, lit up: *universum aspectabile tot innumerabilibus astris ~e* AC 6698; CI 417; (of light) giving illumination, bright: *lux...est multo ~ior luce ex qua homo videt* CI 170. **2** Of noble rank, illustrious: *ex familia ~iore* AC 3974.2; *ab exercitu ~ium Ecclesiae* VR 137.8; typical of nobility, distinguished: *se exornant ~ibus togis et tunicis* VR 533.1. **3** Mentally enlightened: *quod dum exuitur homo corpore, multo ~iore intellectu polleat* AC 3957.2; *quod multae [cognitiones] fidem ~em [faciant]* FI 29.

illustrius, *compar. adv*. In a more enlightened manner: *ut viderer mihi...in perceptione plus interius ac ~us esse, quam alioquin prius* AM 293.1.

illustro ~are ~avi ~atum, *tr*. (compar. of pf. pple. *~atior*, superl. *~atissimus*) **1** To cast light upon, illuminate: *haec plana sunt quae ~antur a luce coeli* AC 6751; *haec lux simul ~at visum eorum internum* CI 266.1. **2** To make clear by examples or comparisons, illustrate: *haec quia arcana sunt non ~ari possunt quam per exempla* AC 4992.1; (impers. pass.) *~andum est quomodo cum hoc se habet* AC 8237. **3** To enlighten mentally, illuminate: *homo successive ~atur* AC 6766.2; *quod...non ~entur cum legunt Verbum* AC 7012; *vera...a viris doctis et ~atis tradita* AC 7055.2.

imaginarius ~a ~um, *a*. Existing only in the imagination, imaginary: *cum ita exspirata sunt ~a nostra gaudia* AM 8.3; AC 7441.2; (neut. pl. as sb.) *circum sensitiva et ~a illorum mentis est sicut aura* VR 80.3.

imaginatio ~onis, *f*. The faculty of forming mental images of things, imagination: *cogitatio...quae supra ~onem est requirit...res e materialibus abstractas* AC 681.4; *ex ideis ~onis, quae vocantur ideae materiales* AC 6987.3; (esp.) the forming of false images: *nimium indulgent suae ~oni* AM 267.4.

imaginative, *adv*. By forming images in the mind: ES 3581.

imaginativus ~a ~um, *a*. Existing only in the mind: *inclinationes ad conjugium ante illud sunt modo ~ae in mente* AM 190; ES 273; *si tales ~as opes possidere mihi liceat* ES 2449; (neut. as sb.) *~um cogitationis* AC 8630.2.

imago ~inis, *f*. **1** A physical object shaped so as to resemble something else, sculpture, image: *adorant... ~ines illorum* [sc. *sanctorum*] AC 7272.3; *gentiles qui adorarunt aliquem deum sub ~ine aut statua* CI 326; *antiqui...fecerunt sibi ~ines, quae caelestibus correspondebant* SS 23.1. **2** Any visible likeness, picture, image: *anima...continue vult externum...sibi simile et sui ~inem facere* AC 6716.2; *[pessimi] ~ines suae* *gloriae vident in liberis* ES(M) 4628. **3** A mental image, product of the imagination: *hic non amat nisi se et ~ines mentis suae* AM 77.4. **4** An analogue, model, likeness: *est quasi in quolibet sono vocis ~o doli* AC 1395; *regeneratio hominis est ~o glorificationis Humani Domini* AC 6716.4.

imbecillis ~is ~e, *a.* (compar. *~ior*) Weak, feeble: *quod [gestus] viris sit fortior et firmior, faeminis autem invalidior et ~ior* AM 218.1; *si aliquis etiam ~is* [*imbellis* 1st edn.] *ligatus foret* VR 478.1.

imbecillitas ~atis, *f.* Weakness, feebleness: *ex invaletudine ac ~ate* AC 8002.1; VI 111.

imber ~bris, *m.* A brief period of rain, shower: *subito tunc ~ber e caelo decidit* VR 110.8.

imbibo ~ere ~i, *tr.* To drink in, suck up, absorb: *tales ...recipiunt omne falsum, quod ~unt sicut spongia aquam* CI 354.2; DP 296.14.

imbuitio ~onis, *f.* The process of mentally absorbing, learning: *ab ~one talium ab infantia* AC 1679.3.

imbuo ~ere ~i ~tum, *tr.* **1** To absorb mentally, become steeped in: *~erunt principia falsi* AC 6971.2; *ex communi hoc favore tandem ~it persuasionem* VR 796.2. **2** To teach, indoctrinate, train: *finis propter quem, et inde habitus unumquemvis ~it* VR 563.2; (pass. w. abl.) *homo ~tus religione* VR 709.1; VR 746.1; (w. inf.) *ita ~itur pulmo producere varios sonos in trachea* DP 279.9.

imitamen ~inis, *neut.* The process of imitating, imitation: *gestus ad ~en illorum qui in vero cultu* AC 8873; *in me tali ~ine egerunt, ut...* ES 407; AM 512.1.

imitatio ~onis, *f.* = **imitamen**: *ad ~onem illius lymphae* AC 4050.3; *cum ~one boni et veri* AC 10286.2.

imitor ~ari ~atus sum, *tr.* To imitate, counterfeit: *ad ~andum affectiones, quales sunt spirituali homini* AE 401.35; *sibi impresserat voce... ~ari patrem meum* ES(M) [4793].

immaculatus ~a ~um, *a.* Without blemish, spotless: *ex significatione 'integrae' quod sit absque naevis, ita ~a* AC 7837; (transf.) undefiled, pure: *innocentiam ~am* AC 7837; *~i sunt coram throno Dei* Rev. 14.5 (AR).

immanis ~is ~e, *a.* (compar. *~ior*, superl. *~issimus*) **1** Savage, fierce: *~is leo* Hos. 13.8 (AE 388.9). **2** Frightful, barbarous: *quid... ~ius potest credi...?* SE 66.3. **3** Exceedingly great, monstrous: *quod aliter credere, sit ~is error* VR 26.1; *Domini tentationes...omnium ~issimae* AC 1787.3.

immanitas ~atis, *f.* A savage act: *~ates quae exercentur...per artes magicas* AC 6832.9.

immaniter, *adv.* In a savage fashion, monstrously: *passus Se suspendi cruce, et ~er occidi* FI 44.

immano ~are ~avi, *intr.* To flow in: *hoc in linguas humanas ~avit ex mundo spirituali* AE 14.1.

immansuetus ~a ~um, *a.* Not tamed, savage: *in iram apud mansuetos, et in vindictam apud ~os* AM 370.

immaterialis ~is ~e, *a.* Not composed of matter, non-material: *quod quia ~e, esset...tale obscurum ut nusquam capi aliqua idea posset* AC 1533; *memoriae rerum ~ium* AC 7253.

immaturus ~a ~um, *a.* Unripe: *animae...sunt similes ~is et tetris fructibus* ES 396; DP 98.6; immature: *cum aetas in bivio est inter maturam et ~am* AM 187.

immediate, *adv.* (compar. *~ius*) **1** With no space between, directly: *fructu...ex terra ~e pullulante* ES 1546. **2** With no intervening time, immediately: *quod aliqui post mortem ~e in coelum sublati sint* AC 317; AC 8199; VR 71.2. **3** Without any intervention, directly, immediately: *quae ~e ex luce sunt* AC 1620; *verum quod ~e procedit a Divino* AC 6982; *qui* [sc. *angeli*] *omnes ~e et ~ius ducuntur a Domino* ES 2573.

immediatus ~a ~um, *a.* (compar. *~ior*) Having nothing intervening, direct, immediate: *quod ~us sit influxus Domini* AC 7004.3; *prima seu ~a generatio* AC 8042.2; *quod hodie ~a talis revelatio existat* CI 1.

immedicabilis ~is ~e, *adj.* Incapable of being remedied, irremediable: *dicebant si ibi emergeret capite, quod jugiter praeferebat sicut serpens, quod tum ~e esset* ES 3221.

immense, *adv.* Immeasurably, immensely: *~e majus* ES 3310.

immensitas ~atis, *f.* The quality of being incapable of measurement, immensity: *~as Dei...se refert ad spatia* VR 27; AC 1610.2.

immensum, *adv.* Immeasurably, immensely: *omne quod in se...vitam habet, se fructificat et multiplicat ~um* AC 43; AC 1053; CI 576.

immensus ~a ~um, *a.* **1** Great beyond counting, immeasurable, immense: *~o numero* AC 6696; *a falsorum ~a copia* AC 8280; CI 415. **2** *In ~um*, immeasurably, immensely: *crescit bonum et verum in ~um* AC 55.3; AC 1610.2.

immergo ~gere ~si ~sum, *tr.* **1** To immerse, plunge (in a liquid): (w. *in* + acc.) *~si sunt in lutum pedes tui* Jer. 38.22 (AC 6669.2); *in voragines... ~guntur* CI 354; (w. dat.) *~sus undis* AC 6853. **2** (transf.) To immerse, swamp, drown: (w. *in* + acc.) *non altius in sua mala* *et falsa ~guntur* AC 6663.1; (w. dat.) *materialia...ferunt mentem deorsum et ~gunt terrestribus* AC 6921; (refl.) *phantasiae isti plus et plus se ~git* AM 374.

immerito, *adv.* Unjustifiably: *non ~o vocari potest ipsum frigus conjugiale* AM 247.

immeritus ~a ~um, *a.* (superl. *~issimus* 1AD 541) Undeserving: (masc. as sb.) *indignum et ~um evehere supra dignum et merentem* VR 57.1.

immersio ~onis, *f.* The act of immersing: *per ~onem in aquas Jordanis* NH 209.4; (transf.) swamping, drowning: *~ones in sua mala et falsa* AC 6663.1.

immigro ~are ~avi, *intr.* To move in, enter: *quod ...loco illorum mera falsa ~averint* AE 989.1.

immineo ~nere ~nui, *intr.* To overhang so as to threaten to fall, hang over, impend: *cum fluenta sicut cumulus consistunt, ~nent* AC 8287; (fig.) *inde totalis damnatio ante fores stetit et ~nuit* VR 3.1.

imminuo ~ere ~i ~tum, *tr.* To make fewer, diminish: *feram agri, quae orbabit vos... ~etque vos* Lev. 26.22 (AE 388.7).

immisceo ~scere ~scui ~xtum, *tr.* To combine by mixing, mix in: *loquebantur...de sapientiae initiis... quibus ~scuerunt varia de ejus successu* AM 18.1; *operationes quae se ~scebant et perceptionem variabant* ES 310.

immisericordia ~ae, *f.* Lack of pity, pitilessness: *'in saevitia' quod significet ~am constare potest* AC 6667; *ira, rabies et ~a* VR 155.2.

immisericors ~rdis, *a.* (compar. *~rdior*) Pitiless, remorseless: ES 377; ES 3421.

immissio ~onis, *f.* The act of sending in, admission, introduction: *~o in aliquam infernalem societatem* AC 699; *status ~onis inter mala et falsa* AC 6747.

immitis ~is, *a.* Savage, fierce: *bestiae mites et ~es* FI 63.3; *~es et paene ferini* AC 7246; *facie... ~i seu implacabili* ES 392.

immitto ~mittere ~misi ~missum, *tr.* **1** To send or put in, introduce, admit: *quid ~mitti potest in ignem solarem et non perire?* AC 6849.5; *paradisus...in quem ~mittuntur illi* AM 8.1; (refl.) *cum ~mittunt se ubi Dominus est praesens* AC 7926.2. **2** (w. *in* + acc.) To send against, set on: *Ego ~mitto in te...volatile noxium* Exod. 8.17 (AC); *canes quos ~mittunt in obvios* ES 762; *quod cultrum... ~mittere vellet in pectus* ES 1336. **3** (transf.) To bring into, introduce (into a state): *Dominus...Se in Divinam potentiam regendi omnia ... ~misit* AE 41; *qui Divina Vera statim ~mittunt in vitam* CI 348.

immo: see **imo**.

immoderatus ~a ~um, *a.* (compar. *~ior*) Uncontrolled, unrestrained: *quod viris sint [mores] ~iores* AM 218.1; *per fornicationes ~as et inordinatas* AM 456; AE 781.11.

immodeste, *adv.* Immodestly: *sic ut nuditas appareret ~e* ES 840.

immodicus ~a ~um, *a.* Unrestrained: *vermiculi ...qui ex appetitu ~o possunt generari* ES 397.

immolatio ~onis, *f.* The offering (of a victim) as a sacrifice: *haec quae de ~one Isaci dicuntur* AC 2775.

immoratio ~onis, *f.* The act of remaining long (in a state), tarrying: *~o in statu dubitationis* AC 5613.

immoriger ~era ~erum, *a.* Disobliging, inconsiderate: *si pater non castigat filium... ~erum et male facientem* ES 4421; AM 246.3.

immoror ~ari ~atus sum, *intr.* (w. dat.) To delay over, dwell upon: *quare iis non ~andum* AC 244; AC 1412.

immortalis ~is, *a.* Not subject to death, immortal: *spiritus... ~is est quoad omnia sua* CI 432.

immortalitas ~atis, *f.* Immortality: *de ~ate animae scripserunt* SS 115.3; AM 182.6.

immotus ~a ~um, *a.* Unmoving, motionless: *sol ~us stat* SS 95.2; AM 233.4.

immunditia ~ae, *f.* Uncleanness, filth, dirt: *aspicitur ...conjugium ut ~a* AM 247.

immundities ~ei, *f.* = **immunditia**: *per ~em significatur conspurcatio a malis* AC 10109.2.

immundus ~a ~um, *a.* (compar. *~ior*, superl. *~issimus*) **1** Unclean, dirty, filthy: *fons impurus et ~issimus* AC 874; *ex ~a aqua* AC 1688; AM 151ª.3. **2** Ceremonially unclean, impure, polluted: *si quis tangeret ...aliquem confossum gladio... ~us esset septem dies* Num. 19.16 (AC 6767.5); (neut. as sb.) *in Assyria ~um comedet* Hos. 9.3 (SS 79.3). **3** Unclean in thought or action: *quod egreditur ex ore, hoc ~um reddit hominem* Matt. 15.11 (AC 8910.2); *~orum spirituum copia qui ~iores reliquis* ES 4320; (neut. as sb.) uncleanness: *quod ~um in Ecclesia sit ex amore scortatorio* AM 431.2.

immunis ~is ~e, *a.* (compar. *~ior*) **1** (w. *ab*) Untouched (by), free (from): *ab omni damnatione ~es erunt* AC 7878; *amor... ~is ab omni idea lasciviae* AM 55.2. **2** Free from guilt, innocent: *~es seu mundae aut purae manus* AC 2526.

immunitas ~atis, *f.* Freedom from guilt, innocence: *in ~ate manuum mearum feci hoc* Gen. 20.5 (AC); AC 2526.

immurmuro ~are ~avi, *intr.* To murmur in: *juxta*

illum alius minister stat, et ~at auri ejus 'hoc recte dicis...' VR 141.

immutabilis ~is ~e, *a.* That cannot be changed, unchanging, immutable: *Divinum...est invariabile et ~e* AS 77.

immutatio ~onis, *f.* Change for the worse, corruption: *~o et perversio Ecclesiae* AE 400.3.

immuto ~are ~avi ~atum, *tr.* To change for the worse, corrupt: *exemplar Verbi...repositum est, ne illud... ~etur* SS 72; (w. *in* + acc.) *libertatem ~at in servitutem* AM 248.1; (of a devil becoming good) *usque non potui ~are me* VR 507.4.

imo, *particle* also **immo**. (to correct a previous statement) Or rather: *Divinum illud Verum...est ipsa vita quae implet coelum, ~o quae implet universum* AC 6685; *quod imago, ~o similitudo mariti sit in mente uxoris* ES 4408; *~o super cruce exclamavit, Deus mi* VR 104.

impacificus ~a ~um, *a.* Unpeaceful: *haec...sunt ...cum delabuntur versus inferiora, per gradus ~a* AC 8823; (neut. as sb.) lack of peace, disturbance: *'tollere pacem' significat ~um et intranquillum ex disjunctione eorum* [sc. *boni et veri*] AE 365.4.

impaenitentia ~ae, *f.* Reluctance or refusal to turn one's heart, mind, and life away from evil: *quod sola fides talem ~ae statum et tale cor induxerit* VR 567.7.

impaenitens ~ntis, *a.* Impenitent: *homo ~ns et impius* DD 18.3.

impar ~aris, *a.* Unequal: *cum bonum naturale spirituale conjungitur cum vero naturali non spirituali, sunt enim dissimilia et ~aria* AC 4997.1.

impartibilis ~is ~e, *a.* Incapable of being divided, indivisible: *haec* [sc. *Essentia Divina*]*...est ~is, quia una et individua* VR 17.3.

impatiens ~ntis, *a.* Impatient: ES 597.

impatientia ~ae, *f.* Reluctance to wait, impatience: *'et festinarunt' quod significet ~am* AC 5766.

impedimentum ~i, *neut.* **1** A hindrance, obstacle, impediment: *illis ut remoris et ~is...remotis* AC 1389; (as the title of a document) *in quadam Appendice Memoriali...quae vocatur ~a seu Offendicula Impaenitentium* DP 258.5. **2** *~o esse*, to be an obstacle: *quod iis multo ~o est* ES 2514.

impedio ~dire ~divi (*or* ~dii) ~ditum, *tr., intr.* To hinder, obstruct, prevent: **1** (tr.): *quamdiu malum est in cultu interno, ~diuntur illa quae bona et vera sunt* AC 1366.1; (w. inf.) *ut ~diant alios cogitare libere* ES 4310. **2** (intr.): *ibi* [sc. *in mundo*] *~diunt curae pro victu et amictu* AC 6648; (w. *quin*) *illa et haec sunt quae ~diunt quin possit ad coelestia pervenire* AC 1542.1.

impeditio ~onis, *f.* The act of hindering, obstruction: *'ducere illam in gravitate' est ~o per renisum* AC 8216.

impello ~pellere ~puli ~pulsum, *tr.* **1** To impart motion to, set in motion, disturb: *cum unus tantum reagit ac resistit quantum alter agit et ~pellit* CI 537.1; *impii sicut mare ~pulsum* Isa. 57.20 (AC 6669.1); (absol.) *sicut qui in caligine palpat, ac offendit et ~pellit ubivis* AC 7712. **2** (transf.) To distort, upset: *nihil solliciti de sensu, quem usque ~pellere potuerunt et vi urgere ut coincidat* ES 2040.

impendo ~dere ~di ~sum, *tr.* **1** To devote, spend (money, resources): *dicunt se velle bona sua et vitam suam pro illa* [sc. *patria*] *~dere* VR 441.2; (w. dat.) *donaria...quae...~dunt simulacris miraculosis* VR 453; (absol.) *homo...~dit templis* VI 9. **b** to pay (a salary): *quibus salaria et stipendia ex publico aerario ~denda sunt* VR 430. **2** To devote (thought, effort, etc.): (w. dat.) *ne* [*fuci*]*...escas suas, quibus nihil operae ~derunt, consumant* VR 12.7; (w. *ad* + acc.) *amor ~dit jugiter cogitationes suas ad conjungendum sibi virum* AM 173.

impenetrabilis ~is ~e, *a.* Impenetrable: *mihi erant ...subtilia et ~ia, nempe discrimina seu differentiae* ES 2235.

impense, *adv.* (compar. *~ius*) Earnestly, intently, insistently: *~e rogamus ut emittamur* AM 6.4; *~e flagitabant praefici aliis* CI 563; *quod ~e observetur, si aliqua...aspectet* AM 369.2; ES 1063.

impensus ~a ~um, *a.* Intense, earnest: *studium tam ~um* ES 3556.

imperator ~oris, *m.* An emperor: *Concilium Nicaenum ab Imperatore Constantino Magno convocatum est* VR 137.11; AM 7.4.

imperceptibilis ~is ~e, *a.* That cannot be perceived, imperceptible: *jucunda animae in se sunt beatitudines ~es* AM 16.2; *ex subtillissima et homini ~i seu sublimi imaginatione* ES 301.

imperceptibilitas ~atis, *f.* Inability to perceive: *totalis ignorantia et ~as jucundi amoris caelestis* VR 439.1.

imperceptibiliter, *adv.* Imperceptibly: *malum ... ~er cogitat* AC 8885.4.

imperfectio ~onis, *f.* The fact of being imperfect, imperfection: *quod ~o nativitatis hominis fiat ejus perfectio* AM 133.2; an instance of this: *nihil prorsus amiserunt...praeter ossa et carnem et... ~ones* AC 322.2.

imperfectus ~a ~um, *a.* (compar. *~ior*) Imperfect: *quod angeli caeli sint in perfecta forma homines, pariter spiritus inferni, sed in ~a* AM 27.

imperiose, *adv.* In a dictatorial manner: *uxores... ~e detinentur a colloquio cum viris* AM 375.1.

imperiosus ~a ~um, *a.* Dictatorial, domineering: (neut. as sb.) *sic ut vix apparuerit aliquid ~i et morosi* ES 2120.

imperitus ~a ~um, *a.* Unlearned, ignorant: *hoc mirabile omni ~o videri potest* ES 337.

imperium ~i, *neut.* **1** The dominion of a major king, empire: *~um, regnum, ducatus, respublica* VR 55; *quod non sub ~is sint, sed quod distincti in societates* AC 7363. **2** (transf.) Domination, control: *quare tentabat se removere quasi ab ~o voluntatis* ES 3026; *subordinationes...in inferno sunt ~i, et inde saevitiae* AC 7773.

impero ~are ~avi, *intr.* To exercise control, dominate, rule: *ex amore ~andi* FI 49; *sicut dicitur, divide et ~a* VR 133.2; (w. dat.) *...omnibus in suo regno ~are velint* AC 7375; (w. *super*) *quod ~are velint super omnia* AC 1675.7.

imperscrutabilis ~is ~e, *a.* Inscrutable: *perspicacia viris ~i* AM 208.4; *quod intimiora et intima sint ~ia* ES 2477; CO 33.1.

imperscrutabilitas ~atis, *f.* Inscrutability: ES 2477.

impertio: see **impertior**.

impertior ~tiri ~titus sum, *tr.* also **impertio** (AR Doc Ref.2). (w. dat.) To give a share of, impart (to): *~tiri intelligentiam et sapientiam illis qui in affectione veri ...sunt* AE 195.10; ES 1049; AS 128.

impete, *adv.* With violence, by force: *conjecit in mare dicens, sic ~e dejicietur Babylon* Rev. 18.21 (AC 9755.8).

impetuosus ~a ~um, *a.* (of winds) Gusty: *per ventos vehementes et ~os* AE 419.2.

impetus ~us, *m.* **1** A violent blow, assault: *~u dejicietur Babylon* Rev. 18.21 (AR). **2** An impulse: *animalia...feruntur ad fines sed quodam ~u naturali* 1AD 916; (w. gen.) *cum vi et ~u dominandi* AC 905.

impie, *adv.* Impiously: *sic communia, ut ~e vocarunt, conjugia sub specie sanctitatis habuerunt* AC 826; CI 291.

impietas ~atis, *f.* Impiety: *habitare in tentoriis ~atis* Ps. 84.10 (AE 220.7); AM 252.

impiger ~gra ~grum, *a.* (compar. *~grior*) Not slow or reluctant, energetic, quick: *quis ~grior et quis pigrior loquendo, agendo et percipiendo, et pro ~grioribus aliqua folia laurus* AM 17.4.

impigritas ~atis, *f.* Strenuousness, activity: AM 249.

impingo[1] ~pingere ~pegi ~pactum, *tr., intr.* **1** (tr.) To cause to hit, strike, dash (one thing upon another): *~pingit frontem in arborem* VR 90.2; *si quis caput in parietem ~pingat* ES 3037. **b** to deliver (a blow): *quod colaphos ~pegerint* DD 16.5. **2** (intr.) To stumble, trip: *caecus qui ubivis ~pingit* DP 259.2; (transf.) *~pegit in platea veritas* Isa. 59.14 (AC 8273.2).

impingo[2] ~gere ~xi ~ctum, *tr.* To paint on, write on in ink: *quod vir...tale quid ~xerit epistolae* VR 137.12.

impinguo ~are ~avi ~atum, *tr.* To make fat: *~a cor populi hujus* Isa. 6.10 (AC 897).

impius ~a ~um, *a.* Having no respect for religious sanctions, impious: *unumquemvis ~um momento purificare a peccatis* VR 58; CI 329; (masc. as sb.) *quod ~us vilipendat conjugem, notum est* AM 241; *~i seu mali* DP 250.3.

implacabilis ~is ~e, *a.* Implacable: *facie...immiti seu ~i, ut dicunt* ES 392.

implantatio ~onis, *f.* The act of implanting: *per ~onem fidei in amorem* AC 1737; *secundum ~onem Ecclesiae a Domino* AM 141.

implanto ~are ~avi ~atum, *tr.* To establish so as to grow, implant: *si non illa radix exstirparetur, et nova radix ~aretur* VI 93; *charitas ~ata per fidem* AC 436; (w. dat.) *quia amaverunt bonum et verum...et ~averunt illa vitae suae* CI 18; *vera...menti ~antur* VR 8.1.

impleo ~lere ~levi ~letum, *tr.* **1** To make full, fill: *hauserunt, et ~leverunt canaliculos* Exod. 21.6 (AC); (w. abl.) *quod Dominus...calore et luce ~leat universum coelum* AC 6645.3; *prata... ~lebant anguibus* AC 7071; *diabolus... ~leturus te omni iniquitate* BCP (VI 6). **b** to satisfy: *~lebitur illis anima mea* Exod. 15.9 (AC). **c** (Bibl., w. gen.) *manum ~lere*, to consecrate, inaugurate: Exod. 19.9 (AC). **d** to set (a precious stone in metal): *in sculptura lapidis ad ~lendum* Exod. 31.5 (AC). **2** To constitute the filling of, pervade, fill: *tranquillitas et jucunditas illa... ~lebat sensibiliter thoracem et cor* AC 8113; *ex multa experientia, quae...plures paginas ~leret* AC 6639.2; *Divinum... ~let coelum* CI 8. **3** To make complete, finish: *~le septimanam hanc* Gen. 29.27 (AC); *ut ~leatur bonum* AC 7836.5. **4** To make up (a deficiency): *providetur ...quod ut primum deest...quale aut quantum... illico...arcessantur qui ~leant* AC 6807; *haec mensura... ~letur in altera vita* AC 7984.3. **5** To fulfil (a prophecy, law, etc.): *ut ~leretur Scriptura* VR 85.2; *~le Legem* FI 44.

impletio ~onis, *f.* **1** The act of making full, filling:

anima est substantia spiritualis, cui non est extensio sed ~o AM 220.2; *loquela minus sapientium exterior et non cum ~one tali* CI 244. **b** the insertion, setting (of a precious stone): *~ones...fiebant in auro* AC 10333. **2** The act of making complete, completion: *~onem boni* AC 7829; *potentiae ~o* ES 1218. **3** Fulfilment: *per ~onem Legis* DD 18.1.

implexus ~a ~um, *a.* (pf. pple. of **implecto***) **1** Woven together, intertwined: *ex ramis ~is* AC 1443; (neut. as sb.) *Jehovah excidet ~a sylvae ferro* Isa. 10.34 (SS 15.1); (of a textile) *de ~is auri vestis ejus* Ps. 45.13 (AM 21.3). **2** Involved, complicated: *qui et quales status... significentur, prolixum foret exponere; praeter quod etiam sit ~um* AC 1332.

implicatus ~a ~um, *a.* Involved: (w. *in* + abl.) *~os in scientifico naturali* AC 2831.1; (w. dat.) *ita ~i sunt sensualibus* AC 6945.2.

implico ~are ~avi ~atum, *tr.* To entangle: *suos crines eis* [sc. *frondibus arboris*] *~at* VR 127.

imploratio ~onis, *f.* A calling for help, imploring: *'et clamabant' significat ~onem* AC 6797; AE 393.

imploro ~are ~avi ~atum, *tr.* **1** To ask insistently for, beg, implore: *quod homo...Domini opem ~et* DD 17.3; *illam* [sc. *misericordiam*] *~ant* CI 525. **2** To approach as suppliant, beg, implore: *qui clamant et ~ant Ipsum pro se solis* AC 6852.

impono ~nere ~sui ~situm, *tr., intr.* **1** To place on, put on: *per pulverem...quem olim ~suerunt capiti* AC 7418.3; *~suit digito ejus annulum aureum* AM 20.3. **2** To impose (a task, burden, etc.): *onera...quae filiis Israelis a Pharaone ~nebantur* AC 6757; *per damnationem Filio ~sitam* FI 45; cf. *super Te, Domine Jehovih, ~situs sum ab utero* Ps. 71.6 (AC 8043.4). **3** To give (a name): *Dominus ~suit Simoni nomen Petrus* Mark 3.16 (AE 9.1). **4** (intr., w. dat.) To impose upon, deceive: *vere ~nendo ~suisti populo isti* Jer. 4.10 (AC 2799.12).

impos ~otis, *a.* **1** (w. gen.) Not in control of, unable to restrain: *~otes sui erant* ES 2279; *~otes mentis* DP 294.3; *~os judicii* AM 488. **2** Incapable: (w. gen.) *sedent muti, ~otes loquendi* DP 231.4; (w. inf.) *ut ~os sit cogitare aliquid nisi una cum illis* ES 4601.

impositio ~onis, *f.* **1** A placing on, laying on: *per ~ones manuum* AM 396.3. **2** Imposition: *secundum ~onem tributorum* AC 6852.

impossibilis ~is ~e, *a.* Impossible: *dum ~e non obstat* AM 262.2; *quod angelis ~e sit enuntiare unam vocem linguae humanae* CI 237; *~e est ut recipi queant* ES 715.

impossibilitas ~atis, *f.* Impossibility: *qui in ~ate et impotentia sunt* AC 987.2.

impostor ~oris, *m.* An impostor, swindler: *comparari possunt cum ~oribus qui falsas monetas cudunt* VR 320.

impostura ~ae, *f.* Deceit, pretence, imposture: VR 320; CO 22.

impotens ~ntis, *a.* (w. gen.) Incapable (of): *sunt ~ntes intelligendi* ES 406; ES 620.

impotentia ~ae, *f.* **1** Lack of power, helplessness: *impeditio per renisum, et inde ~a* AC 821.6; *quod lex ordinis sit, quod homo...non stet in fide ~ae* VR 71.2. **2** Lack of sexual potency, impotence: *~a ante conjugium* AM 254; VI 111.

impraegnatio ~onis, *f.* also **impregnatio**. Impregnation: *~oni ovuli* AC 8847.2.

impraegno ~are ~avi ~atum, *tr.* also **impregno**. **1** To make pregnant, impregnate: *quod homo...uxorem ~et* DP 180.8. **2** To imbue, saturate, fill: *malignitas athmosphaerae quae ex halitibus virulentis... ~atur* AM 375.3; *minerae ~atae auro, argento, et ferro* SS 66.

impreg-: see **impraeg-**.

impressio ~onis, *f.* An idea impressed upon the mind: *quod ~ones captaverit quod nemo in coelum venire possit nisi per miserias* AC 892.1; ES 2090.

imprimis, *adv.* Especially, in particular: *magia... ~is est abusus correspondentiarum* AC 6692.2; *quod fit ~is apud eruditos* CI 183.2.

imprimo ~rimere ~ressi ~ressum, *tr.* **1** To make an impression, press: *ut ~rimat pes tuus in sanguinem* Ps. 68.23 (AC 7784.4); *typo ~ressus*, printed: VR 137.1. **b** to print: *cum tempus venit ~rimendi* 1AD 943. **2** (w. dat.) To impart (a form to), stamp (upon), impress (upon): *quod Deus...illi* [sc. *naturae*] *indiderit et ~resserit facultatem* VR 12.1; *quibus aliqua idea de vita aeterna ~ressa est* FI 46; *quod haec memoriis ejus... ~ressa sint* AC 7122.1. **3** *Sibi ~rimere quod*, to persuade oneself that, become convinced that: *sic ~rimunt sibi persuadentque quod falsum sit verum* AC 735; AC 6692.2.

improbitas ~atis, *f.* Dishonesty: *falsum doctrinae ex ~ate doctorum* AC 9272.7.

improbo ~are ~avi ~atum, *tr.* To disapprove: *sed contradixerunt et ~averunt* AR 675.1.

improbus ~a ~um, *a.* Wicked, dishonest: *quod probi felices in mundo essent prae ~is* AC 7007.1.

improles: see **improlis**.

improlis ~is ~e, *a.* also **improles**. Having no offspring, childless: *et ego ambulans ~is* Gen. 15.2 (AC); *~is mater* AC 1901.1.

improsper ~era ~erum, *a.* Unsuccessful: *~er et*

infelix [fit], si intellectum suum mittit sub obedientiam voluntatis CC 14.3.

improvise, *adv*. Without forethought: *arare sulcum, in quem ~e inseminavit naturalismum* VR 137.8.

improvisus ~a ~um, *a*. Unforeseen, unpremeditated: *~a infortunia non aliud sunt, quam perpetui conatus spirituum malorum* ES(M) [4784].

imprudentia ~ae, *a*. Lack of prudence, imprudence: AM 445.

impudens ~ntis, *a*. Shameless (in quot. neut. as sb.): *'frons' significat...malum amoris, et inde durum, obfirmatum, ~ns ac infernale* AE 427.9.

impudentia ~ae, *f*. Shameless arrogance, impudence: *mali...eo audaciae et ~ae sunt ut putent se posse ipsum coelum destruere* AC 8295.1.

impudicitia ~ae, *f*. Lack of modesty, immodest behaviour: *in lascivia et ~a* AC 8375; AM 252.

impudicus ~a ~um, *a*. Immodest: *~ae mulieres* AC 825.

impugnatio ~onis, *f*. Mental attack, assault: *quod subiturus ~ones et tentationes a falsis* AE 122.4; *cum ~one veri Ecclesiae a scientificis* AC 6639.2.

impugnator ~oris, *m*. One who attacks a person's ideas: *status incandescentiae contra ~orem* AM 358.

impugno ~are ~avi ~atum, *tr*. **1** To attack, assail (ideas, emotions, etc.): *quod ~entur naturales... amores* AC 847.2; *si malum... ~at bonum quod est amoris coelestis* AC 6677. **2** To attack the mind of, assail mentally (a person): *Dominus...tutatur illum cum ~atur ab infernis* AC 8273.1; CI 134.

impulcher ~chra ~chrum, *a*. (compar. *~chrior*) Not beautiful, unlovely, ugly: *lux...fit ~chra in ~chris* AC 7343.2; *aves immites, ~chras, et immundas* AC 866; *quod viri sint [facie]...barbata, ita ~chriore* AM 218.1.

impulsio ~onis, *f*. **1** The act of striking against, stumbling: *liberasti pedes meos ab ~one* Ps. 56.13 (AE 97). **2** A mental impulse: *attractio absque ~one non datur* AE 646.4.

impulsivus ~a ~um, *a*. Impelling: *ex hac causa ~a* AC 735.

impulsus ~us, *m*. A striking, blow: *sicut ~ibus malleorum* ES 1770.

impunis ~is ~e, *a*. Unpunished: *dicitur quod 'non relinquetur ~is qui nomen Dei prophanat'* AE 960.14.

impuritas ~atis, *f*. Impurity: *hic amor ab ~ate sua non separari potest* AS 419; AC 2053.1.

impurus ~a ~um, *a*. (compar. *~ior*, superl. *~issimus*) **1** Unclean, dirty, befouled: *sicut fons, cujus aqua est ~a ex vena* VI 25; *undae marium...sunt crassae et ~ae* AE 342.3. **2** Morally impure: *quod amor sexus...sit ~us et incastus* AM 48; *cultus... ~us* AC 7245[a].

imputabilis ~is ~e, *a*. Capable of being imputed: *meritum Christi non est ~e* VR 627.

imputatio ~onis, *f*. Attribution, imputation: *~onem meriti Filii* FI 39; *~o est illis qui norunt, et non illis qui ignorant* VR 107.3.

imputativus ~a ~um, *a*. Concerned with imputation: *de fide ~a* VR 487.4.

imputatorius ~a ~um, *a*. Attributed as a fault: *quod adulteria ab his facta ~a sint* AM 478.3.

imputo ~are ~avi ~atum, *tr*. To attribute, impute (faults, merit, etc.): *quod meritum Filii ~etur per illam fidem* FI 42; *quod dissidentiae mentium...sint in illorum culpa ac ~entur* AM 271; (w. dat.) *~avit illud ipsi in justitiam* Gen. 15.6 (AC); *non aliquid Domini potest ~ari homini* DD 18.2.

imus ~a ~um, *a*. **1** The lowest part of: *in ~is lateribus [montium]* AE 410.2. **2** (neut. as sb.) The lowest part, bottom: *a summo ad ~um* AC 7774; VR 187.2; *potest spiritus...visu penetrare in ~a* CI 586.

in, *prep. w. acc.* or *abl.* **A** (w. acc.) **1** (to denote motion) Into: *ejicitur...in ultimum finem caelorum* AS 25; *semen in gremium terrae illabitur* AS 61. **b** (w. destinations implying a state or condition): *transit e caligine in lucem* AS 69; *in mentem venit, quid significatum est* EA 3. **2** (to denote direction) Towards, on: *dum in solum Deum Messiam intuitum internum figerem* ES 256; *concentratio radiorum ejus [sc. solis] in focum arte optica* CC 9.3. **b** (to denote mental application) in: *credit in Deum* CC 13.5. **3** (To denote time) For: *Jehovah regnabit in saeculum et aeternitatem* Exod. 15.18 (AC); *in aeternum* CC 3.2. **4** (to denote progress to another stage) Up to and including, into: *Dominus...progressus est ad coelestia et in coelestia* AC 1554; *homo...non altius penetravit quam in interiora aut puriora naturae* AS 92; (in adverbial phr.) *in tantum* 'to such an extent' AS 70. **5** (to denote division) Into (parts): *tempora distincta in dies et annos* AS 104; *coeli angelici distincti sunt in tres gradus* CC 16.6. **6** Into (a state or condition): *cadit sicut in deliquium* AS 110; *[Dominus] redegit illud [sc. infernum] in ordinem* VR 2.2; *Jehovah Deus...sic rediit in Suum Divinum* VR 3.1. **7** To within the scope of, to become subject to: *ut hoc in intellectum cadat* AS 5; *[homo] nascitur in ultimum gradum naturalis mundi* AS 67; *qui in fidem suam non admittunt, quod...* AS 91; *quod omnia rationis humanae se conjungant et concentrent in id, quod Deus unus sit*

AS 23; *quod doctrina charitatis rejecta sit in scientiam quae vocatur theologia moralis* EA 8. **8** So as to act upon, towards, on: *amore in Dominum* AS 125; *ex operatione animae in musculos* AC 444; *influit amor...in interiora mentis* AS 138. **9** (to express identity) So as to be: *bonum...et verum...unita in unum* CC 8.5; *talia sunt illis...in gaudia* AM 6.5; (esp. Bibl.) *faciamus hominem in imaginem Nostram* Gen. 1.26 (AC); *viderunt oculi mei salutare Tuum, lucem in revelationem gentium* Luke 2.32 (VR 85.3); *Dominus...dedit illam* [sc. *Mariam*] *Johanni in matrem* VR 102.1. **10** (w. acc. + inf., in imitation of Bibl. Hebr.) For, because: *in audire Ipsum murmurationes vestras* Exod. 16.7 (AC). **B** (w. abl.) **1** (to denote position) In, at: *sicut pictura in pariete* CC 2.1; *multi finxerunt habitacula angelorum...in aethere* AS 92; *in propinquo* CC 5.4. **b** in (a book, document, etc.): *in Verbo* CC 6.1; *in opere De Coelo et Inferno* NH 229. **2** At (a point of time): *in die illo* Zech. 14.20 (EA 2); *in principio erat Verbum* John 1.1 (AR 256.1). **3** In the course of, during (a process): *Deus in perpetuo conatu est...salvandi hominem* VR 73.2; [*calor et lux*] *unum faciunt in exeundo a sole illo* AS 101; (Bibl.) *non cognovit in cubare ejus* Gen. 19.33 (AC). **4** At (a point in development): *non possunt aliter quam terminare ideas cogitationis suae in Epicuri atomis* CC 17.2. **5** Regarded from the point of view of, taken as, in: *in genere* AS 7; *in toto et in parte* AS 11; *omnia in complexu* AS 29; *haec tametsi ita distincta in se sunt usque unum faciunt* AS 83; *Verbum in sensu literae* EA 7. **6** Contained within, immanent in: *de infinitis in Deo* AS 17; *in illa* [sc. *idea naturali*] *est spatium* AS 111. **7** (to denote identity) Consisting in: *in eminentia et opulentia est felicitas mundana* AC 7007.3; *perfectio angelica consistit...in amore* CI 34; *is in causa sui damni est* ES 2018. **8** Actively present in, acting upon: *quia Deus universaliter et singulariter est in omnibus religionis* AS 13; *homo in quo est Ecclesia* AS 118. **9** Under the influence of, subject to: *quod...Deus non sit in spatio* AS 7; *qui in sensu literae sunt* AC 1025.4; *quoties homo est in corporeis suis* AC 933.3; *pictura...in luce stellarum noctu visa* CC 2.1. **10** (w. *sum*) In possession of, endowed with: *est...lingua universalis, in qua sunt omnes angeli* VR 19.2; *si spiritibus permitteretur esse in memoria corporea* ES 4125. **11** (Bibl.) Accompanied by: *exiverunt...mulieres post illam in tympanis et in choreis* Exod. 15.20 (AC). **12** According to, in (a particular form, order, etc.): *quae* [*muscae*] *in columna volant* CC 14.6; *cum sistitur Deus ut Homo in picturis* AS 94; *quod sit* [*sol*] *ignis in ipsa sua puritate* CC 9.3; *in suo ordine* AS 66; *angeli...in perfecta forma homines sunt* AS 11. **13** (to denote a group or category) Among: *quod rarum datur in spiritibus* ES 634; *non relictus est in illis usque ad unum* Exod. 14.28 (AC). **14** In the case of, with: *quod intellectus in homine possit elevari in lucem* CC 2.3; *delirat in sua idea de creatione universi* CC 4.3. **15** (Bibl., as translation of Gk. *en*) By means of, with: *caudae...similes serpentibus, habentes capita, et in his laedunt* Rev. 9.19 (AR); (also, non-Bibl.) *in cachinnis* AM 521.2.

inaccessibilis ~is ~e, *a*. Inaccessible: *quod Deus in luce ~i habitet* VR 59.

inaequalis ~is ~e, *a*. **1** Uneven: *charta longa ~is, a pluribus chartis conglutinata* AC 6930; *rupes ~is* ES 3911. **2** Not matching, unequal: *~es aetates* AM 250.

inaequalitas ~atis, *f*. Unevenness: *~ates in sphaera corporea* ES 2983; inequality: *~as status et conditionis* AM 234.

inaequaliter, *adv*. Irregularly, unevenly: *quod* [*cor*] *pulset lente vel celeriter,...aequaliter vel ~er* AS 378.1.

inamabilis ~is ~e, *a*. Unlovable, unattractive: *quod ...vir...sit torvus, austerus, siccus et ~is* AM 56.4.

inamaenus ~a ~um, *a*. also **inamoenus**. Unpleasant: *per vultus duros et ~os* AM 292.2; (neut. as sb.) *absque sensu cujusdam doloris aut ~i* ES 1042.

inamatus ~a ~um, *a*. Unloved: *cum viro ~o* AM 299.2.

inamoenus: see **inamaenus**.

inanimatus ~a ~um, *a*. Lifeless, inanimate: *homo ...staret sicut ~us, ore aperto et manibus remissis* VI 107; *moles nigra quasi ~a* ES 3219; (neut. as sb.) *nec solum animata...repraesentabant sed etiam ~a, sicut altare* AC 1361.3.

inanimis ~is ~e, *a*. Lifeless: *~e corpus* VR 10; CO 28.1.

inanis ~is ~e, *a*. (superl. *~issimus*) **1** Empty, unfilled: *divites dimisit ~es* Luke 1.53 (AE 118.5); (neut. as sb.) a void: *sicut de ~i aut nihilo* VR 20.2. **2** Meaningless, vain: *nusquam aliqua vocula est quae superflua et ~is* AC 734; *repetitio... ~is* AC 782. **3** Having no real existence: *nisi* [*lux solis*] *operaretur in homines...forent res ~es* VR 67.1; *~ia corpora* AC 6697.

inanitas ~atis, *f*. **1** Emptiness, void: *terra erat vacuitas et ~as* Gen. 1.2 (AC). **2** Lack of meaning, meaninglessness: *audivi quod tu ~atem in illa* [*fide*] *videas* VR 74.2; *~atem ideae* AM 148.1.

inaniter, *adv*. Without meaning, senselessly: *nihil ibi ~er dictum est* SS 13.1; *post subtilitates ~er agitatas* AM 111.

inapplicabilis ~is ~e, *a*. Not able to be applied, inapplicable: *piscis multus pro scientificorum applicabilium abundantia,...coenosa et paludes pro ~ibus et impuris* AC 2702.15.

inapplico ~are ~ui ~atum, *tr*. To fit onto, apply:

reliquae...affectiones ~ant se ei affectioni AC 7648; AE 357.12; ES 3635.

inaptabilis ~is ~e, *a.* Not suitable for fitting, unmatching: *[fallaciae] scientificum ~e reddunt* AC 6112.

inaptatio ~onis, *f.* The process of fitting on, application: *Divinum Bonum apud hominem influit in ejus rationale...ac ibi per ~onem format sibi vera* AC 3128.3; AC 5208.2.

inapto ~are ~avi ~atum, *tr.* (w. dat.) To fit on (to), apply (to): *spirituum...loquela...nulli voci ~ari potest in qua est aliquid sonans stridule* AC 1759.

inassuetus ~a ~um, *a.* Unaccustomed: *cogitatio ...quae tamen ~a est* ES 1030.

inauditus ~a ~um, *a.* Unheard of: *hoc novum prius ~um vobis refero* AM 329.2.

inauguratio ~onis, *f.* The act of formal introduction into an office or function, inauguration: *quod ~ones in sacerdotium...per impositiones manuum fiant* AM 396.3; VR 146; (transf.) the learning of a new skill: AC 1502.3.

inauguratorius ~a ~um, *a.* Of inauguration: *tum in [sacrificiis] purificatoriis et mundatoriis ut et in ~is* AC 2180.2.

inauguro ~are ~avi ~atum, *tr.* **1** To devote by a ritual to a religious purpose, dedicate, inaugurate: *ritus... ~andi et benedicendi* AC 878.7; *hoc* [sc. *templum*] *primum aedificandum est,...et postea ~andum est* VR 126.1. **2** To commence with due ceremony, inaugurate: *finem status... ~ati per desponsationem* AM 306. **3** To teach (a person) a new skill, train: *Dominus... ~atus a pueritia* AC 1502.3; (w. *ad*) *ut adsuescant et ~entur...ad resistendum falso et malo* CI 343; (w. *ut*) *sic ~atur magis magisque ut citius loquatur* ES 1014.

inauris ~is, *f.* A pendant worn on the ear, earring: *~es super aures tuas* Ezek. 16.12 (AE 195.7); Exod. 35.22 (AC); (including other ornaments) AC 4551.2.

inauro ~are ~avi ~atum, *tr.* To cover with a thin layer of gold, gild: *comparari possunt cum impostoribus qui falsas monetas cudunt, ~ant illas, aut illis colorem auri inducunt, et venditant pro puris* VR 320; *imaginibus ex coeno ~atis* AE 1058.2.

incaleo ~lere, *intr.* To become warm: *quantum in amore, tantum ~let* [perh. read *incalescit*] [*homo*] ES 4627.9.

incalescentia ~as, *f.* An increase in warmth, heating up: *fit primum ~a et postea flamma* VR 113.2; AE 481.3.

incalesco ~lescere ~lui, *intr.* **1** To become hot, warm up: *nulla pruna ad ~lescendum* Isa. 47.14 (AC 6832.8); *calor...sicut ex fornace ~lescente* CI 571. **2** To become excited by emotion, become heated: *quod...ex amore ~lescat homo, notum est* AC 7082; AM 358; VR 35.12.

incantamentum ~i, *neut.* An incantation: *per exorcismos, ~a, fascina et veneficia* CO 45.

incantatio ~onis, *f.* The use of a magic spell, incantation: *et fecerunt etiam illi, magi Aegypti, ~onibus suis ita* Exod. 7.11 (AC); *quod facta Isabelis una voce dicantur scortationes et ~ones* AE 161 (2 Kgs. 9.22).

incantator ~oris, *m.* One who uses magic spells, magician, sorcerer: *foris vero canes, et ~ores, et scortatores* Rev. 22.15 (AR); VR 324.

incanto ~are ~avi, *intr.* To use magic, practise sorcery: *quod per '~are' significetur persuadere falsum* AR 462.1.

incarceratio ~onis, *f.* Confinement in a prison, imprisonment: *captivitas et ~o* AM 79.5; ES 589.

incarcero ~are ~avi ~atum, *tr.* To commit to prison, imprison: *conjecti in cavernas, et ~ati* AM 231.5; ES 1460; (transf.) *mens in corpore quasi ~ata* DP 140; *ignis ~atus ligno* VR 146.

incarnatio ~onis, *f.* The endowment (of the Lord) with a human body, incarnation: *de assumtione Humani a Domino in mundo, quae vocatur ~o* DD 59.

incarno ~are ~avi ~atum, *tr.* To endow with a human body, make incarnate: *postquam Deus ~atus est* VR 170.1.

incassum, *adv.* **1** Without success, in vain: *expectavi reditum, sed ~um* AM 155[a].5; *volui pluribus evincere quod non ita sit, sed ~um* CI 246.3; *~um ire*, to come to nothing: *sic omnis operatio Divinae gratiae ~um iret* VR 633.3. **2** (quasi adj.): *cum hoc ~um fit* AC 7364; *~um est cum vobis de Filio Dei nato in mundo loqui* VR 159.7.

incaste, *adv.* Unchastely: *illi...qui ~e spectabant faeminas* AM 55.2.

incastitas ~atis, *f.* Lack of chastity, unchasteness: AM 139.

incastus ~a ~um, *a.* Unchaste: *si ~us est [amor sexus]* AM 44.4.

incavatio ~onis, *f.* A hollowing out: IM 23.

incavatus ~a ~um, *a.* Having a void within, hollowed out: *volumen apparebat sicut ~um in medio* AC 7077; *sculptile... ~um* CO 54.2.

incedo ~dere ~ssi, *intr.* **1** To walk, march, go: *is ~dens inter animalia* Ezek. 1.13 (AC 6832.3); (of things) to move, advance: *columna nubis...quae... ~ssit* *ante filios Israelis* AC 8192.1. **2** (w. pred.) To walk about, go (in a specified condition): *incolae...sub aequatore... nudi ~dunt* ES 566; *~dunt contracti a lumbis* AM 505.4; to behave, live (in a specified manner): *quod sic ~dat homo justificatus* AC 8313.1; *quod [homo] non opus habeat, ut ~dat devotus, tristi et gemente facie* CI 358.

incendium ~i, *neut.* **1** The destruction of a building or sim. by fire, a fire: *domus...facta est in ~um* Isa. 64.11 (AE 220.8). **2** A destructive emotion, fire: *eos qui in cupiditatum ~is vivunt* AC 757; *exteriora flagrarent ...simili ~o quo interiora* CI 506.3.

incendo ~dere ~di ~sum, *tr.* **1** To set on fire, kindle, light: *templo ibi ~so* VR 23.2; *clibanus ~sus a pistore* Hos. 7.4 (AC 7906.3). **2** To make inflamed: ES 3922. **3** To arouse to violent emotion, inflame: *quod mens... ~datur a sola cogitatione de sexu* AM 223.2; *~dunt eum suis cupiditatibus* AC 751.3. **4** To arouse violently (emotions and sim.): *quod...sentiant conjugiale ~di in cordibus suis* AM 44.6; AE 183.4.

incepto ~are ~avi, *intr.* To begin, commence: *inde est, quod hoc frigus ~et ibi* AM 236.

inceptum ~i, *neut.* A task begun, beginning: *en populus unus...et hoc ~um eorum ad faciendum* Gen. 11.6 (AC).

incertus ~a ~um, *a.* Undecided, uncertain: *quod mens eorum sit vaga et ~a, prona in errores* SS 52.

incessus ~us, *m.* The act of walking, journeying: *et Lubim...et Kuschim in ~ibus tuis* Dan. 11.43 (AC 1164.6).

inchoamentum ~i, *neut.* also **incohamentum**. A beginning, commencement: *tentationis ~um* AC 733; AM 333.2; *solum in ~is sunt ut possint fieri angeli* CI 330.

inchoatio ~onis, *f.* also **incohatio**. A beginning: *~o novae Ecclesiae* AE 386.29.

inchoo ~are ~avi ~atum, *intr.* also **incoho**. To begin, commence: *hic nunc ~at quintus status* AC 6772; (w. *ab*) *sic regeneratio ~at ab externo homine* AC 47; (also pass.) *~abatur ille status in fine deserti* AC 8104.

incidentia ~ae, *f.* The angle at which one line meets another, incidence: *calor variatur secundum radiorum solis ~am rectam et obliquam* AC 7177.

incido[1] ~ere ~i, *intr.* **1** To fall upon, strike, hit: *repellunt omne verum sicut elater osseus id quod ~it* CI 354; (w. *in* + acc.) *si [ignis]... ~eret in aliquem* AC 6834; *alioquin ~it mens humana sicut navis in scopulos* VR 127. **2** (of forces) To act violently (upon), strike: *vox Jehovae ~ens ut flamma ignis* Ps. 29.7 (SS 18.4); (w. *in* + acc.) *ne forte ~at [Jehovah] in nos peste et gladio* Exod. 5.3 (AC). **3** To come (upon) by accident, fall (among): *~it in latrones* Luke 10.30 (AC 6708); to fall (into a state): *~i in profundam meditationem* VR 25.1. **4** To happen, come about: *quando ~it afflictio* Matt. 13.21 (AE 47); (impers.) *loquutus sum cum angelo quodam, et ~ebat etiam de miraculis* ES 227.

incido[2] ~dere ~si ~sum, *tr.* To cut into, hew out: *~dens in petra habitaculum suum* Isa. 22.16 (AE 411.17).

incinctus[1] ~a ~um, *a.* (pf. pple. of **incingo**) Encircled, girt: *rosarium ~um parvis sapphiris* AM 315.3.

incinctus[2] ~us, *m.* That which serves as a girdle, girdling: *inservit [lux]...sapientiae et amori pro ~u et amictu* ME 17.

incingo ~gere ~xi ~ctum, *tr.* To surround as with clothing, encircle: *quod singula naturae sint sicut tunicae...quae ~gunt spiritualia* VR 695.6.

incipio ~cipere ~cepi ~ceptum, *intr.* (*tr.*) see also **inceptum**. To commence, begin: **a** (absol.): *postea in Syria ~cepit cultus quidam externus* AC 1238.2; *cum desiit Antiqua Ecclesia ~cepit Ecclesia Hebraea* AC 6738; *ad dextrum ubi ~cipiunt boni spiritus* ES 3660. **b** (w. *ab*): *~cipiendo a labiis* AC 8022; *omnis Ecclesia ~cipit a charitate* AE 104. **c** (w. inf.): *~cipiunt angi* AC 7042; *Verbum... ~cepit falsificari* SS 102.2; *~ceperunt...non scire quid amor* VR 37.1.

incircumcisio ~onis, *f.* Lack of circumcision, the state of being uncircumcised: *~o vocatur opprobrium Aegypti* 3AD 4484.

incircumcisus ~a ~um, *a.* Uncircumcised: *per '~um' seu 'praeputiatum' intelligitur qui...non purificatus* FI 54.

incisio ~onis, *f.* An incision, cut: *super omnibus manibus ~ones* Jer. 48.37 (AE 637.16).

incitae ~tarum, *f. pl.* A position in a game which allows no further move, checkmate (in quots. transf.): *vident se ad ~tas redactos* VR 802.2; CI 563; ES 4741; UJ(P) 24.

incitamentum ~i, *neut.* A thing which arouses, incitement: *ex fomitibus et inde ~is in adyto mentis et corporis ejus occultatis* AM 108.

incitatio ~onis, *f.* The state of being aroused, arousal, excitement: *hoc...apparet illis ex ~one masculina* AM 187.

incitatus ~a ~um, *a.* (compar. *~ior*) Aroused, excited: *qui ~iores sunt, et celerius erumpunt quasi cum indignatione* ES 3544.

incito ~are ~avi ~atum, *tr.* To arouse, excite: *quod si custoditur [uxor], ~etur* AM 376; (w. *ad*) *quod parentes eos ad talia ~ent* CI 344; (w. *in* + acc.) *quod... ~arentur* *in crudelitatem* ES 2417; (w. *contra*) *~avit Davidem contra eos* 2 Sam. 24.1 (AE 453.2).

inclamo ~are ~avi ~atum, *tr.* To implore, beg for: *~antes misericordiam Dei Messiae* ES 204.

inclemens ~ntis, *a.* Harsh, severe: *cum bonum amoris delabitur ad inferna, fit ~ns ac immite* AC 7679.1.

inclementia ~ae, *f.* Lack of mercy, cruelty: *summae ~ae et summae immisericordiae* AC 2447.3.

inclinatio ~onis, *f.* **1** *~o magnetica*, the dip of the needle of a compass, inclination: ES 222. **2** A desire, inclination, tendency: *quali amore et ~one inter se ad se mutuo fuerant* AM 48; *quod nascatur* [*homo*]... *~o ad amandum* VR 48.11.

inclinatus ~a ~um, *a.* (compar. *~ior*) Tending, prone, inclined (to): *in alia mala ~ior essem aliis* ES 2453.

inclino ~are ~avi ~atum, *tr., intr.* **1** (tr.) To set at an angle from the horizontal, make sloping, bend down: *Jehovah ~avit coelos et descendit* Ps. 18.9 (AC 2761.4); *~ate aurem vestram* Isa. 55.3 (AC 6804.3); *~atae sunt umbrae vesperae* Jer. 6.4 (AC 7844.6). **2** (w. parts of the body) To cause to rest, lay: *Filius Hominis non habet ubi caput ~et* Matt. 8.20 (DD 27); (refl.) to lean: *se ~ant versus tergum* AC 7803; *reginae...se ~antis ad brachium solii* ES 4458. **3** (intr.) To feel an attraction, incline: *intellectus non regit nisi voluntas ~et* AC 7342; (w. *ad*) *ut...duorum animae ~ent ad se mutuo* AM 301; *ad simile faciendum ~averunt* AC 8080.4.

includo ~dere ~si ~sum, *tr.* **1** To shut up, confine: *turbam...diabolicam in inferna conjicere, et ibi ~dere* AC 8273.1; *de leproso quod vel ~dendus, vel exiturus e communione* AC 6963.1; *aves quae ~derentur* ES 2550. **2** (of boundaries) To embrace, include: *ripa...est sicut continens, nam circuit et ~dit* AC 7308; (of concepts) *aeternum in se talia* [sc. *tempus, spatium et materiam*] *non ~dit* AE 23.1; *Divina...providentia ... ~dit illa quatuor* AE 278.1.

inclusio ~onis, *f.* A state of being surrounded or enclosed, confinement: *spatium temporis quod erat inter ~onem Draconis in abysso et ejus solutionem* AR 855; AC 9874.1.

inclusive, *adv.* Inclusively: *in Capitibus...a XXV ad XXXI ~e* AC 10396.1.

inclutus ~a ~um, *a.* Famous, renowned: *huc venient ~i fama sapientiae* AM 10.1.

incognito, *adv.* Without being recognized: *'venire sicut fur' est venire ~o et inexspectato* AC 9125.3; *~o dolose agunt* ES 3588; *~o regebat alia* ES 4467.

incognitus ~a ~um, *a.* Unknown: *cum lapidibus pretiosis, quos sibi per vias ~as comparant e caelo* VR 843.

incoh-: see **incho-**.

incola ~ae, *m.* An inhabitant: *~ae Martis* AC 7622.2; *omnium regnorum ~ae* SS 102.1; VR 117.

incolo ~colere ~colui ~cultum, *tr.* To dwell in, inhabit: *qui...ultimum coelum ~colunt* ES 223; *si ~coleretur una tellus* AC 6698.

incolumis ~is ~e, *a.* Unharmed: *per mediam damnationem ~es transibunt* AC 7889.

incolumitas ~atis, *f.* The state of being unharmed, safety: *coelum...continet omnia in nexu et ~ate* AC 5713; ES 4571.

incommodum ~i, *neut.* Disadvantage, inconvenience: *persuasiones falsi...spiritibus multum ~i inferunt* AC 1673.3; *sedare ex conscientia oboritura ~a* AM 271.

incommodus ~a ~um, *a.* Troublesome, awkward: *missus* [*spiritus*]...*ut serviret pro subjecto, quia erat ~us* ES(M) [4728].

incommunicabilis ~is ~e, *a.* Incapable of being shared or imparted: *proprietates...quas asserit ~es* VR 135.2.

incomparabilis ~is ~e, *a.* That does not admit comparison, incomparable: *~i prudentia et pietate* CI 335.

incompositus ~a ~um, *a.* Lacking an orderly arrangement, disorganized: *comparari possunt alicui congeriei indigestae et ~ae, et quasi cuidam chao* AC 3316.1.

incomprehensibilis ~is ~e, *a.* (compar. *~ior*) Incapable of being grasped with the mind, incomprehensible: *loquela* [*angelorum coelestium*]...*est multo ~ior...loquela angelorum spiritualium* AC 880.3; (neut. as sb.) *spiritualis homo cogitat ~ia et ineffabilia naturali homini* AM 326.5.

incomprehensibilitas ~atis, *f.* Incomprehensibility: AC 1972.

incomprehensibiliter, *adv.* Incomprehensibly: *Providentia Divina operatur...invisibiliter et ~er* AC 5508.2.

incomptus: see **incomtus**.

incomtus ~a ~um, *a.* also **incomptus**. Untidy: *chartam...non ita conglutinatam et ~am, verum decentem et nitidam* AC 6930.

inconcessus ~a ~um, *a.* Not permitted, impermissible: *aestuaverunt ~a libidine* AM 54.4.

inconcinnus ~a ~um, *a.* Not neatly arranged, inelegant: *quod Dominus sic regat ~a et inordinata, quae circumfluunt* ES 1176.

inconditus ~a ~um, *a.* (of sounds) Confused, inarticulate: *audiebam sicut ululatus, et...clamorem ~um sicut ex spectris in sylvis* VR 71.1.

incongrue, *adv.* Incongruously: *cum quo* [sc. *animali bruto*]...*tales non ~e se comparant* AC 8378.

incongruus ~a ~um, *a.* Not in keeping, incongruous: (neut. pl. as sb.) *vel ex fallaciis sensuum vel ex ~is capiuntur ideae* AC 9300.3.

inconjungibilis ~is ~e, *a.* Incapable of conjunction: *quia Ille* [sc. *Pater*] *est invisibilis, et inde inaccessibilis et ~is* VR 538.1.

inconnexus ~a ~um, *a.* Unconnected, disjointed: *quia sparsa forent et ~a si intersererentur illis quae in textu Verbi* AC 71; CI 304.3.

inconspicue, *adv.* Without being easily seen, inconspicuously: *~e agebat* ES 1158.

inconspicuitas ~atis, *f.* The quality of being inconspicuous: *ex ~ate et non apparentia coram oculis* SA 95 (= vii.1).

inconspicuus ~a ~um, *a.* Hard to see, inconspicuous, invisible: *funiculos fere ~os* CI 335; *se surripere...e conspectu et evadere ~ae* AC 831.2; VR 111.1; *ille...paene ~us factus est* AC 5060.2.

inconstans ~ntis, *a.* Not constant, changing: *quod inclinatio...sit constans et perpetua apud uxorem, sed ~ns et alterna apud virum* AM 156[a].3; ES 915.

inconstanter, *adv.* Inconstantly: AC 6493.

inconstantia ~ae, *f.* An instance of inconstancy, inconsistency: *quod...tot ~ae appercipiantur, quae fortunae adscribuntur* ES 213.

inconsultus ~a ~um, *a.* Not consulted: *si filia ex se, ~is parentibus...ad clientem procum consentit* AM 299.1.

inconsutus ~a ~um, *a.* Not sewn: *erat...tunica ~a a summo contexta tota* John 19.23 (AE 64.3).

incontaminatus ~a ~um, *a.* Not tainted by being mixed (with), free (from), uncontaminated (by): (w. *ab*) *qui zelus fuit pro doctrina ut ~a esset ab omni rationali et scientifico* AC 2543.

incontestabilis ~is ~e, *a.* That cannot be disputed, incontrovertible: *ex ipsa experientia ~i* 2AD 1483.

incontinenter, *adv.* Without a break, immediately: *quae ~er praecedunt* AC 1573.8; AC 3718.

inconvenientia ~ae, *f.* Unfitness or an instance of this: *haec aetas...perspicit conformitates et ~as* AM 298.

incorporo ~are ~avi ~atum, *tr.* To make members in, incorporate: (w. dat.) *ut illis* [*societatibus*] *~entur ut membra* AM 404; to make a part (of), embody (in): *charitas et fides, dum solum in mente sunt, non sunt ~atae homini* VR 375.2.

incrassatus ~a ~um, *a.* Made gross, lacking in feeling or perception: *qui habent cor ~um* AC 303.1; *patet quam ~a est mens illorum* AM 416.4.

increatus ~a ~um, *a.* Uncreated: *Pater est ~us, Filius est ~us* Sym. Ath. (DD 56).

increbesco ~bescere ~bui, *intr.* also **increbresco** ~brescere ~brui, *intr.* To become numerous or frequent, increase: *quod fluctuationes ejus ita ~buerint* [*~bruerint* 3rd edn.] AC 785; AC 1184; *prophanitas, quae... ~buit magis et magis* ES 4473.

increbresco: see **increbesco**.

incredibilis ~is ~e, *a.* Unbelievable, incredible: *loqueris ~ia* AM 355.2.

incredibiliter, *adv.* To an incredible extent, unbelievably: *talis est lux in coelo ut ~er superet lucem ...mundi solaris* AC 1521.

incredulitas ~atis, *f.* **1** A state of disbelief, incredulity: *quod...sint in tali ~ate ut putent se non victuros post mortem* AC 70; CI 1. **2** Untrustworthiness: *cum confirmare ~atem sensuum possint per scientifica* AC 232.

incredulus ~a ~um, *a.* Unbelieving: *non esto ~us sed credulus* John 20.27 (DD 35.9); *potuerunt spiritus ~i adduci ad credendum* AC 1378.2.

incrementum ~i, *neut.* An increase: *vera...quae ~a caperent* AC 980; *omnis...status suum principium habet, sua ~a, et suum maximum* AC 7715; *~a intelligentiae* AM 187.

increpatio ~onis, *f.* A reproach, rebuke, scolding: *quod sint verba ~onis, ita iracundiae* AC 6682; *per ~ones et alternas faventias* AM 292.2.

increpator ~oris, *m.* One who reproaches, rebuker, scolder: *hic spiritus erat spiritus ~or* AC 10382; ES 3463.

increpo ~are ~avi ~atum, *tr.* To reproach, rebuke, scold: *num argilla ~atura est figulum, quod ex se testam lotii faciat?* VR 72.1; *~asti gentes* Ps. 9.5 (AE 253.6); AM 352.

increscentia ~ae, *f.* Increase: *cum stabili mutatione, seu decrescentia et ~a* AM 108.

incresco ~rescere ~revi, *intr.* To become greater, increase: *successu temporis mala et inde falsa ~rescunt* AC 1835.1; AM 108.

incrustatio ~onis, *f.* A thin layer applied to a surface, plastering, incrustation: *ubi ~o qua incrustastis* Ezek. 13.12 (AE 237.5); ES 245.

incrustator ~oris, *m.* A plasterer: *~ores parietis* DP 318.8.

incrusto ~are ~avi ~atum, *tr.* To cover with a thin

layer, encrust, plaster: *parietem quem ~atis inepto* Ezek. 13.14 (AC 739.2); *hae [domus] constructae ex lateribus interjectis tignis, et ~atae* AM 78.3; *album sicut ~ati gypsi* ES 943; *~ant cerebrum* ES 3612.

incubatio ~onis, *f.* A sleeping upon: *delitiantur ex ~one oris et faciei illorum* [sc. *infantum*] *super gremiis* AM 396.2.

incubatus ~us, *m.* The act of sitting upon (eggs): *quod [aves]...tempus ~us sciant* VR 12.5.

incubo ~are ~avi, *intr.* (w. dat.) To sit on, hatch (eggs): *quod... [aves] ponant ova, ~ent illis* VR 12.5.

incubus ~i, *m.* A feeling of suffocation during sleep, incubus, nightmare: *cubans in lecto oppressus ~o* VR 367.7; AC 1270.2.

inculco ~are ~avi ~atum, *tr.* (w. dat.) To teach insistently, inculcate: *ii qui veritates coelestes...praedicarunt, et ardenter aliis ~arunt* ES 3105.

inculpatio ~onis, *f.* The attribution of blame, censure: *intentio...facit... ~ones et exculpationes* AM 452.3.

inculpatus ~a ~um, *a.* **1** Free from blame, blameless: *volunt insontes esse...utque ~os se praebeant, exuunt vestes* AC 821.1; AC 6705; ES 1259. **2** (as pf. pple. of **inculpo**) Blamed: *modo ii non ~i videantur* ES 1356.

inculpo ~are ~avi ~atum, *tr.* **1** (w. dat.) To attribute blame (to someone) for (an action): *angeli quibusdam ~abant illa ut mala peccati* AM 453. **2** To blame, censure (a person): *ne a sacerdotio...infamiae quod atheus sim ~er* VR 722.1.

incumbentia ~ae, *f.* The fact of pressing upon, weighing down, pressure: *dilatatio [pulmonum] fit media ~a aëris secundum columnam suam* VR 371.4; *etiam ~a et dolor perceptus supra caput ad cranium* ES 4559; ES 958.

incumbo ~mbere ~bui, *intr.* **1** To weigh heavily, exert pressure: *inferiora reagunt et resistunt, quantum superiora agunt et ~mbunt* CI 589.1. **2** To exert mental pressure, press: *satis valide ~mbebant spiritus* AC 1265. **b** (w. dat. and inf.) to be incumbent (on someone): *sunt duo debita, quae homini ~mbunt facere* VR 539.1; (impers.) *~mbit viris adblandiri faeminis* AM 297. **3** (w. dat. or w. *ut*) To apply oneself, devote oneself (to): (w. dat) *Aegyptii talibus ~mbebant* AC 7296; *doctrina...cui plerique...omni studio ~mbunt* VR 98.1; ES 4694; (w. *ut*) *~mbere animo et studio, ut ea sciantur* AE 102.1. **b** (w. *in* + acc.) to support, uphold: *ecce Servus Meus in quem ~mbo* Isa. 42.1 (AE 409.2).

incunabula ~orum, *neut. pl.* The bedding of an infant, swaddling clothes; (in quot. transf.) the earliest state, infancy: *Ecclesia Christiana ab ~is suis incepit a schismatibus...infestari* VR 378.1.

incurabilis ~is ~e, *a.* Incurable, irremediable: *plaga illa prorsus ~is* AE 785.3.

incuria ~ae, *f.* Lack of care, carelessness: *in ignorantia et ~a esse* AM 194.2.

incurro ~ere ~i, *intr.* (*tr.*) **1** (w. *in* + acc.) To become subject (to), run (into), incur: *quod...malus ~at in paenam malo respondentem* AC 1011; AC 7102.1; (also app. w. acc.) *ut... ~at illico discrimen vitae* ES 3963. **2** To be imposed, fall (upon): *Jehovah ~ere fecit in Ipsum iniquitates omnium nostrum* Isa. 53.6 (DD 15.1).

incurvatio ~onis, *f.* The act of bowing down: *humiliatio...producit ~onem secundum aestimationem* AE 77.

incurvo ~are ~avi ~atum, *tr.* (refl. and pass.) To bow down, bend: (refl.) *et inflexit se populus, et ~avit se* Exod. 12.27 (AC); *adorare solem mundi et lunam, ac ~are se illis* CI 122; (pass.) *incedunt contracti a lumbis, et sic ~ati* AM 505.4; to be curved: *literis inflexis et varie ~atis* VR 278.

incus ~udis, *f.* An anvil: *cum contusione ~udis* Isa. 41.7 (AC 3527.3).

incusatio ~onis, *f.* The bringing of an accusation, charging with wrongdoing: *~o post mortem, et inde judicatio* AM 489.

incuso ~are ~avi ~atum, *tr.* To bring an accusation against, charge: *spiritus...depromunt omnia male acta...quae apud hominem, et per illa ~ant eum et damnant* AC 8159.1; to make blameworthy: *circumstantiae...quae crimina...aggravant et ~ant* AM 530.1.

incutio ~tere ~ssi ~ssum, *tr.* To strike (fear, horror, etc.) into: *~tere timorem possunt mali spiritus* AC 7803; *ut terrorem cuivis ~teret* ES 243; *auditur sicut stridor dentium et ~tit horrorem* CI 245.

indagatio ~onis, *f.* The act of seeking out, investigation: *ex ~one causae* AS 40; *cognitio illius se abscondidit ac subterfugit ~ones* AM 83.

indagator ~oris, *m.* One who seeks out, investigator: *~or veritatum naturalium* CC 20.4.

indago[1] ~are ~avi ~atum, *tr.* To seek out, investigate: *causae inserviturae ~andis usibus* AC 6815; *non sciunt ubinam homines, quaerunt, sed non ~are possunt* ES(M) 4693; VR 48.9.

indago[2] ~inis, *f.* *Altioris ~inis*, requiring more profound investigation, of deeper study: *cum illis commercium sermonis habui de rebus altioris ~inis* VR 837; *per rationes altioris ~inis* DP 191.1; *alius ~inis,* requiring different investigation: *quomodo sic loqui possint...est res alius ~inis* ES 1662.

inde, *adv.* **1** From that place, thence: *apparuit unus ~e* [sc. *e caelo*] *sicut volans* VR 48.20. **2** From that source or origin: *recondunt* [*vera*] *in scientia et ~e depromunt illa* CI 271. **3** As a consequence, therefore: *potentia inferni valuit super potentiam caeli...et ~e totalis damnatio ante fores stetit* VR 3.1; *quoad conjugialem vitam, et ~e conjunctionem* AM 59.2; *~e est quod*, that is the reason why, thus it is that: *~e est quod per morbum...significetur malum* AC 8364.2; AM 457.

indebitus ~a ~um, *a.* Improper, unwarranted, undue: *qui de Deo ante mundum creatum absona et ~a cogitant* VR 31.4.

indecens ~ntis, *a.* Unfitting, unbecoming, improper: *audacia ~ns et temeraria* VR 162.1; *si prius exirent, hoc, quia ~ns est, futurum illis pudori* AM 6.4; (neut. pl. as sb.) *quod ~ntia occupent mentes* AC 8375.

indecorus ~a ~um, *a.* **1** Unsightly, ill-favoured: *vetulam faciei ~ae* AC 1774. **2** Contrary to good behaviour, ill-mannered: *apud illos ~um est ab aliis spectari quam a facie* AC 8371; AM 17.5. **3** Improper, unbecoming: *exortae sunt plures ~ae ideae de Deo, indignae Christiano orbe* VR 183.1.

indefessus ~a ~um, *a.* Unwearied, untiring: *mater ...cura ~a lactat, nutrit...et educat illos* AM 284.

indefinitas ~atis, *f.* The quality of being unlimited, infinity: *~as ~atum, ~atum, et adhuc ~atum* ES 2297.

indefinite, *adv.* Infinitely: *jucundum earum* [*voluptatum*] *~e excedit jucundum quod non inde* AC 995.3.

indefinities, *adv.* An unlimited number of times, infinitely: *calculum eorum infinitorum ~es transcendunt* ES 3482.

indefinitus ~a ~um, *a.* (compar. *~ior*) Limitless, unbounded, infinite: *cum varietate, quae ~a* AC 201; *adhuc formae sunt ~iores* ES 3607; *in ~um*, indefinitely: *incrementum in ~um* AC 6232.1; (dist. from **infinitus**) *~um coeli est imago Infiniti Domini* AC 1590; ES 226.

indelebilis ~is ~e, *a.* That cannot be wiped away, indelible: *tandem ut fiat persuasio ~is* AC 581.1; AM 409.

indemnificatio ~onis, *f.* The payment of an indemnity, compensation: *quod* [*'cessationem ejus dabit'*] *significet ~onem* AC 9030.

indemnifico ~are ~avi ~atum, *tr.* To bear the loss of, make good: *discerptum non adduxi ad te, ego ~avi id* Gen. 31.39 (AC).

indemnis ~is ~e, *a.* **1** Not liable to punishment, immune: *sic exempti inferno et inde ~es* VR 515. **2** Not to be condemned, not harmful: *damnabile genus primum describetur, ac postea alterum ~e* AM 463.3.

indemniso ~are ~avi ~atum, *tr.* To secure from harm, make safe: *ut possit ignem ex vestibus excutere, et corpus suum ~are* VR 630.

independens ~ntis, *a.* Independent: *quod inconnexum est et sic ~ns* AC 5377.1.

indesinenter, *adv.* Unceasingly: *Dominus...urget ~er sui receptionem* VR 498.1.

indeterminatus ~a ~um, *a.* Having no fixed limits, indeterminate: *multi qui de Deo Patre cogitant ideam ~am habent* AT 82; *cupiditate ~a* ES 3970.

indeterminabilis ~is ~e, *a.* Incapable of being limited, imprecise: *ut nihil distincte cogitet, ita mens ~is* ES 4150.

indevitatio, *adv.* Inevitably: *quod inde...effluat contemtus...~o sequitur* AM 247.

index ~icis, *m.* **1** A signpost: *quod doctrina vera sit...instar ~icis inviis* SS 54; *~ex venti*, a weathervane: VR 798.8. **2** An indicator, sign: *facies vocata est effigies et ~ex animi* AC 8249; *ille numerus est quasi ~ex rei de qua agitur* CI 263.

indicatio ~onis, *f.* The act of pointing out, indication: *reflexio et perceptio est ~o et dictatio interna* AC 2862; ES 3558.

indicium ~i, *neut.* An indication, sign: *~um praesentiae Domini* AC 1036; AC 7372; (esp. w. *quod*) *clarissimum ~um quod omnes in societates distincti sint* AC 1649; CI 354; VR 38.1.

indico[1] ~are ~avi ~atum, *tr.* **1** To announce, proclaim: *laudem Ipsius in insulis ~abunt* Isa. 42.12 (AC 1158.3); (w. dat.) *antequam...*[*nomen*] *Abrahami posteris per Moschen...~atum est* AC 7097.2; (w. *quod*) *quod Lex...sit de Domino, in primo articulo ~atum est* DD 19.9; (w. indir. qu.) *~atur quinam consociari possent* AC 7996. **2** To demonstrate without the use of words, make clear, show: *ut...iracundiam suam ~arent, dextrae parti capitis mei...inducebant speciem contractionis* AC 6811.

indico[2] ~cere ~xi ~ctum, *tr.* To order, impose: *dies festivitatis ~cti a principe* AM 17.1; AM 182.1; *contra leges ordinis cuivis homini ~ctas* VR 58.1.

Indicus ~a ~um, *a.* Indian: *volucres pulchrae ~ae* AM 380.4; *ad mare ~um* ES 4774.

indies, *adv.* (w. phrs. denoting increase or growth) Day by day, daily: *amor, qui ~es...crescit* AM 44.6; FI 31;

haec idea corroboratur ~es VR 8.2; (without such restriction) *quod status hominis mutentur ~es* ES 1928.

indifferens ~ntis, *a.* Making no difference, immaterial: *sine qua* [sc. *imputatione*] *~ns foret, sive malum sive bonum faceret* DP 176.1; *est...utrumque illis ~ns* AM 151; (neut. as sb.) indifference: *ipsum ~ns et jucundum quod ille habuit in eo, etiam mire communicabatur* ES 4494.

indifferenter, *adv.* Without showing concern, with indifference: *loqui cum aliis spiritibus, ut mecum, ~er* ES 2017.

indifferentia ~ae, *f.* Lack of concern, indifference: *cum uxores de hac prorsus frigida ~a virorum inciperent indolere* AM 161.2.

indigena ~ae, *m.* A person of a particular country or society, native: *distinctio...inter ~am terrae et peregrinum* AC 8013.3; *quod [homo] creatus sit ~a utriusque mundi* VR 14.1.

indigens ~ntis, *m.* A needy person: *dare pauperibus, opem ferre ~nti* AC 8120; VR 425.1.

indigentia ~ae, *f.* The condition of being needy, indigence, poverty: *secundum societatis...~am* CI 215; (transf.) the condition of needing: *~am boni pro vero* AC 5365.1.

indigeo ~gere, *intr.* (w. gen.) To have need (of): *nec aliud est quam misericordia, quia nullius ~get [Dominus]* AC 587.2; AC 6704; (also w. abl.) *omnibus iis non ~gent in altera vita* ES 2449.

indigestio ~onis, *f.* Indigestion: AC 5177; ES(M) 4574.

indigestus ~a ~um, *a.* Undigested: *cibus...manet ~us, ex quo fit nausea* AM 266.3; (neut. pl. as sb.) CI 299; (transf.) *confusum et ~um quid* VR 679.2.

indigito ~are ~avi ~atum, *tr.* To point out, indicate: *quod apparentiae distantiarum...in mundo spirituali sint secundum proximitates...amoris...saepius ~atum et confirmatum est* AM 158.1; AM 333.1.

indignatio ~onis, *f.* Indignation, annoyance: *abivit in ~one* AM 82.4; *effundam super eos ~onem Meam* Zeph. 3.8 (AC 6997.4).

indigne, *adv.* **1** In an unworthy manner, shamefully: *quod faeminae...~e repudiarentur* AM 297. **2** *~e ferre*, to be indignant: *~e ferre coeperunt viliorem se fratrem vocare* AC 6756.1.

indignitas ~atis, *f.* (Bibl., perh.) Unworthy treatment: *contabuit prae ~ate oculus meus* Ps. 31.9 (AE 622.7).

indignor ~ari ~atus sum, *intr.* (*tr.*) To be indignant, be annoyed: *valde ~ati sunt, et volebant...invehere in me* AC 6811; AM 199.2; (tr.) to be indignant at: *quod cum ~atus [sum]* ES 267.

indignus ~a ~um, *a.* (superl. *~issimus*) Unworthy: *quod...nusquam salvari possent, quia spurci et ~i* AC 7251; (neut. pl. as sb.) *quod...avertere ~a conetur* AC 8028.

indirecte, *adv.* By an indirect way, indirectly: *omnis actio...procedit ex regione inferiore mentis directe, et ex regione superiore ejus ~e* VR 420.1; AC 7081.

indirectus ~a ~um, *a.* Not direct or immediate, roundabout, indirect: *erga propinquum et amicum per beneficia directa, erga inimicum et malum autem per beneficia ~a* VR 407.

indiscriminatim, *adv.* Indiscriminately: *externae Ecclesiae homo... ~im facit* AC 6704.

indissolubilis ~is ~e, *a.* That cannot be dissolved, indissoluble: *opus continens finium, causarum, et effectuum in nexu ~i* VR 47.

indistincte, *adv.* Indistinctly: *amor conjugialis... non potest nisi ~e et sic obscure cognosci* AM 138.

indistinctus ~a ~um, *a.* Having no distinction, indistinguishable: *plagae coeli per id non ~ae fiunt* CI 146.

inditus: pf. pple. of **indo**.

individuatim, *adv.* As separate items, individually: *materialia ejus* [sc. *universi*] *~im spectata infinito numero sunt* VR 32.1.

individuus ~a ~um, *a.* **1** That cannot be separated, inseparable, indivisible: *si unus et ~us Deus, estne una persona...?* AM 82.2; *sunt scientia et amor ~i comites, nec possunt plus separari quam voluntas et intellectus* VR 48.12. **2** Regarded by itself, taken singly, individual: *interius...agit in singula ipsaque ~a exterioris* AC 6724.2; *proximus...est homo in composito et in ~o* FI 20.

indivisus ~a ~um, *a.* Undivided: *in ~a Persona* VR 137.9 (Book of Concord).

indivulse, *adv.* Inseparably: *quod status mentis ~e pendeat a statu corporis* VR 665.6.

indivulsus ~a ~um, *a.* Not pulled apart, unshattered: *est perpetuum quoddam conjugium et ~um cogitationis et voluntatis* AC 590; *haec ligatio...manet ~a* AM 377.1; (w. *ab*) *quae charitas...~a esset a fide* AC 393.

indo ~ere ~idi ~itum, *tr.* **1** To introduce, insert, apply, give: *conjunctivum illud a creatione ~itum est* AM 37; *nec potest Deus Pater ~ere animam ex se et deinde recedere* VR 110.3; (w. dat.) *Dominus...~it ei vitam coeli* CI 522. **2** To assign, give (a name): *singulis classibus ~ebant nomina* AC 7259.

indocilis ~is ~e, *a*. Unteachable: *qui supra [triginta annos] sunt dicuntur esse ~es* AC 8851; ES 546.

indocte, *adv*. In an untaught manner, uninstructedly: *inde videri potest quam ~e et inaniter illi cogitant* AC 5114.5.

indoctus ~a ~um, *a*. (superl. *~issimus*) (of persons) Untaught, unlearned, ignorant: *hos spectant ut simplices et ~os* AC 7749; *stupidus et prae aliis ~issimus* ES 767.

indolentia ~ae, *f*. A feeling of grief, grieving: *~a Domini, et quidem ~a inde quod destruerentur ita scientifica* AC 1492; AC 8344; AE 393.

indoleo ~lere ~lui, *intr*. To experience grief, grieve: *dicebant se peccavisse graviter, et ~luerunt* ES 3778; (w. *de*) *cum uxores de hac...indifferentia virorum inciperent ~lere* AM 161.2; (w. *quod*) *~lui spiritu quod conjugia...conversa sint in adulteria* AM 80.3. **b** (impers. w. dat.) it grieves (someone): *quod Ipsi ~luit* AC 1492.

indoles ~is, *f*. Innate character (of person or group of persons), nature: *alia prorsus ~es iis fuit quam usquam...hodie datur* AC 200; *quod nascantur [filii] in ~em patris* AC 6716.2; *infantes...ex ~e insita amant illas* CI 332; (as acquired during natural life) *unusquisque in alteram vitam secum trahit naturalem ~em quam acquisivit in vita corporis* ES 358.

indomitus ~a ~um, *a*. Untamed: *~us onager* CO 35.2; (fig.) *~us zelotypiae ignis* AM 375.2.

indormio ~mire ~mivi, *intr*. To go to sleep: *quia tutus et securus ~mivi* AC 1879.1; *secure ~miebam* AC 3891.2.

indubie, *adv*. Without doubt, indubitably: *inde satis manifeste et prorsus ~e concludere datur* ES 365; VR 364.1.

indubitanter, *adv*. Without doubt: *quae...a... Tridentina Synodo tradita et declarata sunt ~er recipio* Papal Bull in SE 106.1.

indubitato, *adv*. Indubitably: SE 109.

indubitatus ~a ~um, *a*. Undoubted: *~um est, quod Dominus universum regat* ES 1088.

indubius ~a ~um, *a*. Free from doubt: *nemo ita instrui potest ut fidem ~am habeat* AC 59.2.

induco ~cere ~xi ~ctum, *tr*. **1** (w. dat.) To apply as an outer layer: *~cendo iis* [sc. *spiritibus*] *quasi corpora* AC 959; *auro et argento ~cto scoriis* DP 14.2. **b** (pass., w. abl.) to cover with a layer (of), coat (with): *potest etiam lignum putidum... ~ci auro* VI 10. **2** To bring (a person or his mind) into (a state): (w. *in* + acc.) *cum regeneratur homo...in hos [status] ~citur* AC 1050.2; *quod in aliquem stuporem ~cant illos* SS 13.3; (w. *ad*) *~cebantur ad agnoscendum Jehovam* AC 6877; (w. inf.) *nusquam possunt ~ci credere* AC 6832.10. **3** To bring about (in someone or something), produce, induce, cause: *sciunt ~cere sensus exquisitos* AC 695; *apparet sicut Dominus etiam ~cat malum* AC 6991; *pulsavit solum, et ~xit* [perh. read *indixit*] *silentium* VR 137.1; (w. dat.) *ut aliis spiritibus...stuporem ~cant* AC 311; DP 112.2. **4** To infer, deduce: *ita quod fuerint ex gentium potius turba ~cere licet* ES 271. **5** To assume (another's personality): *sunt qui aliorum personas ~cant* ES 4277.

inductio ~onis, *f*. **1** The act of bringing in or inducing: *quod ~o unius boni in alterum impossibilis sit* SE 111. **2** An inference, deduction: *credidimus immortalitatem animarum hominum, ex ~onibus quas ratio nobis subministravit* AM 182.6.

induitio ~onis, *f*. **1** The act of putting on, assumption: *~ones variorum statuum a Domino* AC 2796.1; *per receptionem et ~onem justitiae Domini* AC 4007.2; *per ~onem speciosam, quod angeli sint* ES 1054. **2** That which is put on or serves as clothing: *anima prolis est a patre, et ~o ejus a matre* AM 184.

indulgentia ~ae, *f*. **1** The act of indulging or allowing scope to: *ex ~a imaginationis* ME 8. **2** Willingness to overlook faults, indulgence: *ob amorem Suum et ~am Suam* Isa. 63.9 (AC 7091 5). **3** *Canes ~arum*, dogs kept for one's amusement, pet dogs: *canes ~arum seu catuli delitiarum* AM 505.4.

indulgeo ~gere ~si, *intr*. (w. dat.) To give oneself up (to), indulge (in): *solum amarunt ~gere genio* AC 943; *non ita scientiis quibus hodie, ~serunt, sed cogitationibus profundis* AC 605; *qui multum ~serunt phantasiis* CI 249.

indumentum ~i, *neut*. A covering for the body, garment, clothing: *habent ~um factum ex libro...quo circumcingunt caput* AC 8245; *super omnes indutos ~o alienigenae* Zeph. 1.8 (DD 14.5); (anat.) the integument (of an organ): *praeter musculos qui faciunt ~um* DP 180.7; *hoc* [sc. *corpus*]*...est ~um ejus* [sc. *animae*] VR 103.1.

induo ~ere ~i ~tum, *tr*. **1** To cover with garments, clothe: *nudus fui et ~istis Me* Matt. 25.36 (VI 2); (w. abl.) *angelus... ~tus erat chlamyde* AM 2.1; (pf. pple. w. acc. of the thing worn) *~ti byssinum album et mundum* Rev. 19.14 (AC 5954.3). **2** To cover as with a garment, clothe: *quod... ~it illud intimum, quod corpus dicitur, est a matre* AC 6716.2; *corpore ~ti* AC 784.1. **3** To take to oneself, assume, put on: *exuunt humanum et ~unt ferinum* VR 13.4; *~unt vultum tristem* ES 233; *ille qui per vitam ~erat naturam mali* AC 8206.2.

induratio ~onis, *f.* A hardening, hardened area: *~o humoris chrystallini* VR 346.1; *quod similes ~ones apud me passim perciperet* ES 1018.

induresco ~rescere ~rui, *intr.* To become hard, harden: *interna faciei forma...contraxit se, ~ruit* AC 8250.1; *~rescere dicitur cerebrum* ES 1018; (transf.) *cavete vobis, ne mentes vestrae...intus ~rescant* AM 232.4.

induro ~are ~avi ~atum, *tr.* **1** To make hard, harden: *quod amor...substantias formae suae ~et* AM 361.2; (fig.) *et ~abo cor Pharaonis* Exod. 14.4 (AC); *cervicem vestram non ~ate amplius* Deut. 10.16 (FI 54). **2** (refl. and pass.) To be obstinate: *ex significatione '~are se' quod sit se obstinare* AC 8085; *obfirmatum ac ~atum cor esse* AC 7305; (so, absol.) *et erat quod ~averit Pharao ad dimittendum nos* Exod. 13.15 (AC).

indusium ~i, *neut.* A garment: *induti apparent ~o pulchro niveo* ES 1306; ES 3801; (transf.) *quod singula naturae sint sicut tunicae, vaginae et ~a, quae incingunt spiritualia* VR 695.6; *~um ferale*, a shroud: ES 6036.

industria ~ae, *f.* **1** The quality of being hard-working, industry: AM 164. **2** Activity, industry: *quae ab ~a humana...ad usum parantur* CI 104.

industrie, *adv.* With careful labour, industriously: *vidi quam ~e obvelarent injustum* AM 231.3; SE 79.

industriose, *adv.* = **industrie**: *spiritus...qui... converterat ~e omne bonum in malum* ES 477.

industriosus ~a ~um, *a.* = **industrius**: *~i latrones* ES 956.

industrius ~a ~um, *a.* Hard-working, industrious: *~i mercatores* ES 404.

indutus ~a ~um: pf. pple. of **induo**.

inebrians ~ntis, *a.* Intoxicating: *qui nimium indulserunt potui ~nti* ES 1842.

inebriatio ~onis, *f.* The act of being intoxicated, drunkenness: *per ~onem Noachi* AE 376.36.

inebrio ~are ~avi ~atum, *tr.* To intoxicate, make drunk: *~abo eos, ut dormiant somnum saeculi* Jer. 51.57 (AE 187.8); *bibere et vino generoso ~ari* AM 461.2; (transf.) *~ati paradoxis* VR 185.8.

inedia ~ae, *f.* Lack of food, hunger: *vultur in ~a devorans prosapiam suam* CO 40; *satiantes suas ~as* ES 1381.

ineffabilis ~is ~e, *a.* (compar. *~ior*) Incapable of being described, unspeakable, indescribable: *loquela coelesti...quae ~ior est quam loquela angelorum spiritualium* AC 202; *lux ~is* AC 6832.2; *quod...~em mercedem recipiant* ES 2420.

ineffabilitas ~atis, *f.* The quality of being indescribable: *ut ~atem in idea plenissima hominis sistere queant* ES 3097.

ineffigiatus ~a ~um, *a.* Lacking definite shape, shapeless: *quod homo post mortem sit...larva ~a* AE 988.3.

inemendabilis ~is ~e, *a.* Incapable of correction: *ut nulla sit fides, et sic paene ~is* 2AD 1076.

inenarrabilis ~is ~e, *a.* That cannot be fully described: *quod fuissent ~ia* ES 4826.

inenuntiabilis ~is ~e, *a.* Incapable of being spoken, ineffable: *illis sapientia talis est, ut describatur per ~ia et incomprehensibilia* AE 112.5; ES [4567] ½.

ineo inire inii (*or* inivi), *tr.* To enter upon, undertake, begin: *cum illis foedus iniit* AC 1197.2; *consilium inter se ineunt* AC 6681; *inclinationes ad ineundum conjugia* AM 246.2; *qui calculum init* CI 415; *quod... similem priori vitam ineant* VR 79.6.

ineptitudo ~inis, *f.* Lack of aptitude, incapacity, ineptitude: *quod inde sit impotentia, ~o, et stupiditas, qua homo ad omnia Divina seu spiritualia prorsus ineptus est* Book of Concord in VR 464.10.

ineptum ~i, *neut.* A plaster used on the surface of walls, perh. untempered mortar: *parietem, quem incrustatis ~o* Ezek. 13.14 (AC 739.2).

ineptus ~a ~um, *a.* (compar. *~ior*) Unfit, unsuited: *quo ~ior est homo...eo...pervertitur plus* ES 3254; *ad expiscandum talia... ~a est [filia]* AM 299.1.

inermis ~is ~e, *a.* Unarmed: *contra victos et ~es grassantur* AC 5393.1.

iners ~rtis, *a.* (compar. *~rtior*) Lacking in proper power or energy, inactive, inert: *quod non detur aliquid tale ~rs et mortuum, ut nihil efficientis sit in illo* AS 172; *quod [athmosphaerae] continue compressiores ac ~rtiores fiant* AS 302; (neut. as sb.) AC 6077.1.

inertia ~ae, *f.* Lack of energy, inactivity: *ex ~a cogitandi de spiritualibus* VR 185.1; an instance of this: *illi...apparent...sicut forent merae ~ae* DP 231.2.

ineruditus ~a ~um, *a.* (compar. *~ior*) Lacking in learning, unlearned: *notissimum est eruditis et sapientibus, at ignotum ~is et simplicibus* AM 184; ES 4628.

inescatus ~a ~um, *a.* **1** (w. abl.) Caught as with bait (by), ensnared, hooked (on) (in quots. fig.): *qui sui amore ~i sunt* AC 583; *pessimae...quae ambitu dominandi penitus ~ae sunt* AM 292.2; *virginem... quae malignis ~a* VR 331.3. **2** Swallowed as bait, (fig.) absorbed: *illi amores, ubi ~i sunt, se dilatant* VR 754.1.

inesco ~are ~avi ~atum, *a.* (pass.) To become embedded: *quae [delicta]...remanent et ~antur* VR 459.12.

inesse: see **insum**.

inevitabilis ~is ~e, *a.* That cannot be avoided, inevitable: *sequitur quod dissensiones... ~es sint* DP 259.2; ES 4601.

inevitabiliter, *adv.* Inevitably: *ideam...ex qua ~er fluit idea trium Deorum* VR 16.2.

inexcultus ~a ~um, *a.* Not cultivated, untilled: *terra ~a et arida* AC 7418.1; AC 8753.1.

inexhaustus ~a ~um, *a.* Not exhausted, inexhaustible: *pretiosa ibi sunt ~a, et supplentur continue* VR 701.2.

inexisto ~ere, *intr.* (w. dat.) To come into being in: *tales conatus nusquam ~ere potuissent singulis in regno vegetabili* AC 5116.2.

inexpectatus: see **inexspectatus**.

inexplicabilis ~is ~e, *a.* That cannot be undone, inextricable: *retia circumvoluta sicut in nodum ~ia* VR 74.2.

inexpressibilis ~is ~e, *a.* (compar. *~ior*) Inexpressible: *virginem pulchritudinis ~is* CI 382; AM 326.7; ES 2186; ES 2587.

inexspectato, *adv.* Unexpectedly: *'venire sicut fur' est venire incognito et ~o* AC 9125.3.

inexspectatus ~a ~um, *a.* also **inexpectatus**. Unexpected: *~a et subita mutatio* AC 5705.

inexstinguibilis ~is ~e, *a.* Inexstinguishable: *paleam...comburet igne ~i* Matt. 3.12 (AE 374.14); (fig.) *vindictam... ~em* ES(M) [4786.2].

inexstirpabilis ~is ~e, *a.* That cannot be totally removed, ineradicable: *id quod a creatione implantatum est animabus...indelebile et ~e est* AM 409.

inextricabilis ~is ~e, *a.* That cannot be disentangled, inextricable: *quam incomprehensibilis et ~is illa forma sit* CI 212; ES 4013.

infaecundus: see **infoecundus**.

infallibilis ~is ~e, *a.* Incapable of error, infallible: *sic ut putarent se ~es* ES 3583.

infallibiliter, *adv.* Inevitably: *quae omnia ~er sequuntur...naturales homines* ES 387.

infamia ~ae, *f.* Ill repute: *propter...evitationes ~ae* AM 288.

infamis ~is ~e, *a.* Infamous, disgraceful: *hoc...est ~e* ES 4270.

infandus ~a ~um, *a.* Not to be spoken of, unspeakable: *crudelitates exercent ~is modis* AC 824; *~um est illa addicare Deo* VR 132.2; (neut. as sb.) *ejulat, et clamat ~um* AM 512.1.

infans ~ntis, *m.* (gen. pl. *~ntum*) A young child: *timor... ~ntum erga parentes* AC 7280.1; *quod [Ipse Dominus] cum ~ns, perductus sit in Aegyptum* AE 50.1; *... ~ntem, 5 vel 6 annorum* ES 4354; (as adj.) *in omnium ~ntum puerorum manu* VI 64; *prima illa capita ex nostro Verbo...imprimis a pueris et puellis ~ntibus leguntur* SS(P) 34 (=14.6).

infantia ~ae, *f.* The earliest period of human life, infancy: *communes status vitae hominis vocantur ~a, pueritia, adolescentia, juventus et senectus* AM 185.1; *ab ~a ad ultimam senectam* VR 4.1; (transf.) *~a ejus [sc. Ecclesiae Christianae]* VR 4.1.

infantilis ~is ~e, *a.* Typical of a young child, childish: *quod ~e erat, funiculos...demittebant* AM 412; *similis illis [infantibus] ~is animus* CI 330; VR 16.1; (neut. as sb.) childishness: *percipi... ~e potuit* ES 3146.

infantiliter, *adv.* In a childish manner: *quod...non ~er sed sapienter ludendum sit* SS 26.3.

infantulus ~i, *m.* A very young child, baby: *possunt ...minima vi et per ~um abigi* ES 3528.

infatuatio ~onis, *f.* The act of being deprived of sense, foolishness: *fit...caligo, et inde ~o* CI 572.

infatuo ~are ~avi ~atum, *tr.* **1** To render foolish, deprive of sense: *quod talia fascinent oculos nostros, ac ~ent illos* AM 12.2; *fides illorum ~avit illos* VR 72.2; *ex quo ~atur intelligentia* DD 17.3. **2** To render tasteless: *si sal ~etur, per quid salietur?* Matt. 5.13 (AC 9207.2).

infaustitas ~atis, *f.* Unhappiness: *cum maxima molestia et ~ate eorum qui odio habuerunt* ES 2771; 1AD 952.

infaustus ~a ~um, *a.* Unhappy; (neut. as sb.) unhappiness: *laetitia...quae in altera vita vertitur in ~um infernale* AC 7007.2; AM 444.3.

infecto ~are ~avi ~atum, *tr.* To render morbid, infect: *omne malum contagiosum est, ac ~at sicut faex massam* AC 6666.3; *quidam genii...venenoso et pestifero halitu ~abant sphaeram* AC 814.1; *quod... persuasione ~et...illos* ES 4452.

infectus ~a ~um: pf. pple. of **inficio**.

infecundus: see **infoecundus**.

infelicitas ~atis, *f.* Unhappiness: *quod infernum sit ~as aeterna* VI 94; an instance of unhappiness: *quod talia in se ~ates et injucunditates etiam essent utilitati* ES 231.

infelix ~icis, *a.* (superl. *~icissimus*) Unhappy: *quod vivat homo post mortem, felix si bene vixit, et ~ix si male* AM 28; (masc. pl. as sb.) *inter ~ices sunt* AC 1103.1.

infensus ~a ~um, *a.* (superl. *~issimus*) (of enemies) Implacable, bitter: *si vel foret omnium pessimus et ~issimus hostis* AC 1683; AM 271.

inferior ~or ~us, *a.* (compar. of **inferus**) **1** Lower in position, deep: *terra ~or, ubi reservati sunt illi qui ab Ecclesia spirituali ad Adventum Domini, in Verbo aliquoties nominatur* AC 7089.2; (neut. as sb.) *jubilate ~ora terrae* Isa. 44.23 (AC 7089.2); *quod...vertantur ad centrum suum commune...in mundo ~ora* CI 142. **2** Lower in degree or status, inferior: *servi...sunt qui ~oris sortis sunt* AC 7396; *~ores spiritus* ES 3778; *vera ~ora* AE 219.1; (neut. as sb.) *quod e superiore videri queant ~ora* AC 8237.2; *occluditur mens ab ~ori* AM 203.

inferioritas ~atis, *f.* The fact of being inferior, inferiority: *quod...faeminis sit ~as* AM 291.1.

inferius, *adv.* (compar. of **infra**) Lower down: *Dagon ...qui superius fuit sicut homo, ~us sicut piscis* SS 23.2.

infermentatus ~a ~um, *a.* Unfermented, unleavened: *~um vinum* DP 284; (neut. as sb.) *azymum et ~um* AC 7906.1.

infernalis ~is ~e, *a.* **1** Of or belonging to hell, infernal: *spiritus ~es* AC 6724.2; *loquela ~is* CI 245; (masc. as sb.) *vexati a falsis, hoc est, ab ~ibus qui in falsis ex malo sunt* AC 7090.1. **2** Typical of hell, hellish: *cum cruciatu ~i* AC 301; *fugite adulteria ut ~ia* AM 356.

inferne, *adv.* Low down, at the base: *applicant se parti tergali ~e* ES 869.

infernum ~i, *neut.* **1** The abode of evil spirits, hell: *apud angelos caeli...apud spiritus ~i* AM 359.1; *quod homo, qui...vult malum, actualiter in ~o sit* AE 86. **2** Each of the separate societies or regions making up hell, a hell: *conjiciuntur versus ~a magicorum* AC 6692.2; *ut subjugaret ~a* FI 34. **3** Hell as a source of evil influence: *quod [Dominus] in mundum venerit, ut removeret ~um ab homine* VR 2.2; *malum et falsum est ~i* AC 6724.3.

infernus ~i, *m.* (as translation of Gk. *Hades*) The infernal one, Satan: *et Mors et ~us conjecti sunt in stagnum ignis* Rev. 20.14 (AR); cf. AR 870.

infero ~rre intuli illatum, *tr.* **1** To bring in, introduce: *Mea bona intulistis in templa vestra* Joel 3.5 (AC 1551.4); *loco ejus intulit imaginem...inferni* CI 202; *ut...ille amor in mentem et cor ejus...a Deo immediate ~ratur* VR 71.2. **2** (refl. and pass.) To betake oneself, move, go: *~rebant se quidam spiritus versus anteriorem partem capitis* AC 7745; *se ~rt in communionem cum satanis inferni* VR 14.2. **3** To introduce, bring into (a state): *homo...~rtur in liberum caeleste* DP 145.4; (refl., w. dat.) *quantum...se ~rt cultui, tantum recedit cultus internus* AC 1326.1; [*homo*] *~rret se ordini* DP 180.1. **4** To inflict, cause (harm, damage, etc.): *inferna paratissima sunt ad ~rendum malum* AC 7879; (w. dat.) *violentiam illatam charitati* AC 7326; *quod mali sibimetipsis ~rant vastationes* AC 7926.2. **5** To derive (a conclusion) by reasoning, infer: *quod contra Divinam Providentiam dubium possit ~rri ex eo, quod...* DP 264.1; (pass. impers.) *~rri potest quod... tunc consentiat* ES 1590.

inferus ~a ~um, *a.* (compar.: see **inferior**, superl.: see **infimus**) Lower: *ex ~a terra* AM 232.1; (masc. or neut. pl. as sb.) the lower regions, the underworld: *descensum Domini ad ~os* AC 6854.2; ES 235; *nimbus ex ~is ascendens* AM 7.2; *~a terrae* AC 247.

infestatio ~onis, *f.* A vexation, attack, assault: *de ~one verorum* AC 6635; *in statu non ~onis a falsis* AC 7093.2; *~onem Ecclesiae ab illis qui in fide separata a charitate* FI 59.

infestator ~oris, *m.* One who annoys or vexes, attacker: AC 7135.

infesto ~are ~avi ~atum, *tr.* To cause physical or mental discomfort to, annoy, vex, attack: *inferna...quae continue ~abant genus humanum* AC 1680.1; *Philisthaei...filios Israelis crebro ~arunt* FI 50; *verum fidei ~atum a falsis* AE 44; (absol.) *quia sic ~antes non a se amovere possent* AC 7087.

infestus ~a ~um, *a.* Actively hostile, inimical, vexing: *usque ut ~a fieret subjugationis intentio* AC 6650; *non sentientem aliquem odorem vitae suae ~um* VR 569.4; *nec faustum ex dominatione...sed ~um ex velitatione* AM 78.4.

inficio ~ficere ~feci ~fectum, *tr.* **1** To corrupt, spoil: *idea unius rei influit in ideam alterius et eam ~ficit* AC 1008.3; *ne...tale negativum... ~ficiat et corrumpat simplices corde* CI 1. **2** (of diseases) To seize upon, infect: *morticinium... ~ficit primum lumbos* VR 119.2; *parti...tabe ~fectae illinere smegma* VI 112.

inficior ~ari ~atus sum, *intr.* also **infitior**. To deny (a fact): *qui ~atus est quod Deus sit Homo* AE 1115.4.

infidelis ~is ~e, *a.* **1** Not keeping promises, unfaithful: *quod...sit insincerus, injustus, ~is et non rectus* VI 84.2. **2** Having no Christian faith, infidel: *damnatio ~ium* AC 7823; ES 227.

infidelitas ~atis, *f.* Lack of good faith, faithlessness: *per 'semen serpentis'* [*intelligitur*] *omnis ~as* AC 250; *si Ecclesia...perstat in ~ate* AC 69591; *inde est, quod in Verbo ~ates dicantur adulteria* ES 4406.

infidus ~a ~um, *a.* Unfaithful: *continue cogitant de uxoribus quod sint ~ae* AM 374; (masc. as sb.) Rev. 21.8 (AR).

infigo ~gere ~xi ~xum, *tr.* To fix in, implant: *ut ea ~gerentur* [sc. *in memoria*] ES 888.

infime, *adv.* In the lowest manner: *universa theologia a spirituali facta est ~e naturalis* VR 133.1.

infimus ~a ~um, *a.* (superl. of **inferus**) **1** Lowest in space: *quarum* [*athmosphaerarum*] *~a est aquea, superior est aërea* AM 188.3; CI 29. **2** Lowest in rank, humblest, lowliest: *cibus... ~us est stramen seu palea* AC 7112; *volatilia ~ae sortis* AC 7441; *scientifica ~a* AC 7106; (masc. as sb.) *'canis' significat omnium ~os seu viles in Ecclesia* AC 7784.3; (neut. as sb.) *quod per... valles intelligantur... ~a Ecclesiae* SS 18.3.

infinitas ~atis, *f.* Infinity (as an attribute of the Divine): *de Divina... ~ate et aeternitate* DD praef.; VR 27; *~as omnium beatitudinum in Domino est* AM 335.2.

infinite, *adv.* In an infinite degree, infinitely: *quod Deus sit ~e omne* VR 29.3; *loquela Divina quae ~e est supra loquelas in coelis* AC 6996.2.

infinities, *adv.* An infinite number of times: *varietas et correspondentia est ~es melior* ES 1931.

infinitus ~a ~um, *a.* **1** Unlimited, boundless, infinite: *quod licet innumera sciant usque tamen ~a sint quae non sciunt* AC 6813; *per ~am varietatem* AM 324.2; *substantialia... ~o numero sunt* VR 32.1. **b** *ad ~um* or *in ~um*, to an infinite extent: *quod unaquaevis mica cogitationis...sit dividua usque ad ~um* AM 329.2; *series in geometricis quae vadunt in ~um* VR 32.8. **2** (as an epithet of the Divine): *apud Dominum omne est ~um* AC 1590; *Deus, cui ~a sapientia est* SS 1.

infirmatio ~onis, *f.* The act of weakening: *~onem unius* [*veri*] AC 9025.1.

infirmitas ~atis, *f.* A weakness, infirmity: *Dominus ... ~ates habuit sicut alius homo* AC 1573.4; *permanens ~as ex apoplexiis* AM 253.2.

infirmitudo ~inis, *f.* Weakness, infirmity: *in ~ine animi* ES 1752.

infirmo ~are ~avi ~atum, *tr.* To make weak, weaken, enfeeble: *cornibus vestris feritis omnes oves ~atas* Ezek. 34.21 (AE 316.19); *qui per falsa ~are et destruere posse sibi videntur vera* AC 6655; DP 136.1.

infirmus ~a ~um, *a.* (superl. *~issimus*) Weak, feeble: *oves ~as non confirmastis* Ezek. 34.4 (AC 8364.4); *quod Simsoni esset robur in capillis, et quod illis abrasis factus sit ~us* AE 66.2; *propter carnem...quae ~a* AC 7090.4; (neut. as sb.) a weakness: *ira est... ~um quod non cadere potest in Deum* AC 6997.1; *~um retinuit* [*Dominus*] *quia alioquin tentari non potuisset* AT 192.

infitiae ~tiarum, *f. pl.* *~tias ire*, to deny: *quis ~tias ire potest, quin...* CO 40.

infitior: see **inficior**.

inflammo ~are ~avi ~atum, *tr.* **1** To set fire to, kindle, light: *ignis... ~abit fundamenta montium* Deut. 32.22 (AC 1691.4); *fax ~ata* VR 41.3; (transf.) *ignis inferni nec aliud est quam concupiscentia...quae ~at et cruciat* AC 8232. **2** To make inflamed: *quidam oculis ~ati* VR 72.2. **3** To arouse emotionally, excite, inflame: *~atus est facie et voce* AM 269.5; *tono ~ato alloquutus* AM 82.1; *inde est quod homo incendatur, incalescat et ~etur* VR 35.12.

inflatio ~onis, *f.* The act of inflating or the state of being inflated, a swelling with air: *loquela secundum ~onem follis istius et aperitionem meatus ejus exaltatur usque in clamorem, et secundum contractionem diminuitur* AS 382.

inflatorius ~a ~um, *a.* (of musical instruments) Played by blowing, wind: *per instrumenta ~a significantur coelestia* AE 323.1; (neut. as sb.) a wind instrument: AC 8337.2.

inflatus ~us, *m.* The act of blowing in: *sculptura ...sonora per ~um* CO 26.

inflecto ~ctere ~xi ~xum, *tr.* **1** To change the direction of, bend: *literae... ~xae vario modo* SS 71.1; CI 260; *in linea ~xa* AC 1272; *interiora...mentis... ~xa sunt in directionem obliquam* AM 153[a].2. **2** (refl.) To bend forwards, bow: *et ~xerunt se et incurvaverunt se* Exod. 4.31 (AC); (so, also) *corpus ~ctere*: *~ctunt parumper corpus* AC 7068.

inflexibilis ~is ~e, *a.* That cannot be bent, inflexible (in quot. transf.): *quia non se instrui patiuntur...sunt ~es* AC 8737.

inflexilis ~is ~e, *a.* = **inflexibilis**: ES 549.

inflexio ~onis, *f.* A curved part, bend: *quod illa* [sc. *arcana*] *insint ~onibus et curvaturis literarum* CI 260; ES 5579.

inflexus ~a ~um: pf. pple. of **inflecto**.

infligo ~gere ~xi ~ctum, *tr.* To inflict (harm, punishments, etc.): *et transibit Jehovah ad ~gendum plagam Aegypto* Exod. 12.23 (AC); *paenas ~gere et cruciare* CI 550; (w. dat.) *nulli aliquid mali ~gitur* ES 3038.

inflo ~are ~avi ~atum, *tr.* **1** To inject by blowing, blow in: *serpens...qui in cavernam ~abat venenum* AM 521.1. **2** To play by blowing (a wind instrument):

organum...est instrumentum medium inter chordaceum et quod ~atur AC 419. **3** To expand by blowing, blow up: *ut...ab eo quasi ~ati essent, ad aliud cogitandum* ES 1297.

influentia ~ae, *f.* (app.) An influence: *quod in una cogitatione humana concurrant myriadum myriades ~ae a coelis* ES 237.

influo ~ere ~xi ~xum, *intr.* **1** (of liquids, light, heat, etc.) To enter by flowing, flow in: *chylum qui crudus in sanguinem ~it* ES 1033; *lux ~ens in lapidem calcarium* VR 8.4; *calor a sole illo ~ens* AC 6849.1. **2** (of other things) To enter as if flowing, pour in, stream in: *quod [caeteri] in ingluviem magni draconis ~ant et absorbeantur* ES 508; *receptio boni et veri ~entis ab interno in naturale* AC 6675; *ut Ipsum Divinum ~ere posset in Humanum* AC 6720; *apud angelum ~it continue id quod loquitur* AE 8.1. **b** (of things which do not move) to run in: *gangliis...in quae ~unt innumerabiles fibrae* ES 305. **3** To extend one's effect (to), exert influence (upon): *interno homine ~ente et adjuvante* AC 1460.1; *ut...~at Dominus...in ejus intellectualia* AC 99; *quod objecta ~ant in interiora* AC 6948.3.

influus ~a ~um, *a.* Flowing in, incoming: *vir ab ~a sphaera meretricia refocillatur* AM 294.4; *non... reciperet aliquid ~um e caelo ad se* AM 438; *ex ~a perceptione* CC 19.1.

influxibilis ~is ~e, *a.* Capable of flowing in: *vita ...non creabilis est, sed summopere ~is in formas organicas* CC 11.4.

influxio ~onis *f.* = **influxus**: *influebat...sic ut vix differret quoad ~ones* ES 3496.

influxus ~us, *m.* **1** The process of flowing in, inflow: *~us in organa auditus interna est alius quam ~us sermonis* AC 1635; *~us a sole...in omnem arborem* VR 8.3. **2** (transf.) The process of entering as in a stream, influx: *ex ~u vitae a Divino* AC 6979; *hujus* [sc. *Divini Veri*] *~ui...nemo...potest resistere* VR 124.2; *homo... staret sicut inanimatus...exspectans ~um* VI 107. **3** That which flows in, received idea: *quod universalis ~us in animas hominum sit, quod Deus sit* VR 5.

infodio ~dere ~di ~ssum, *tr.* To bury in by digging: *tam ignota, sicut quae ~ssa terrae sunt* VR 362.1; *pecuniam quam...~diunt cellis* ES 384; (as a means of execution) *sicut vesta antiquorum...~ssa terrae* VR 137.4.

infoecundus ~a ~um, *a.* also **infaecundus**, and **infecundus**. Incapable of producing offspring, unfruitful, barren, sterile: *non erit in te ~us et ~a, et in bestia tua* Deut. 7.14 (AE 340.15); AC 9325.6.

informatio ~onis, *f.* The act of informing, information, instruction: *status...~onis a magistris et ministris* VR 106.1; *infantes...formantur in coelo...de qua formatione et ~one plura possunt dici* ES 168.

informo ~are ~avi ~atum, *tr.* **1** To impart information to, inform, tell: (w. *quod*) *~atus sum ab angelis quod...* AC 8249; *~avimus illos quod hodie nova Ecclesia...instauretur* VR 113.8; (w. indir. qu.) *non ~ati sunt quomodo se res habet* AC 995.1. **2** To instruct, teach: *ut spiritus ex mundo alluentes ~ent et doceant* AC 454; *~abantur de typis* AC 8385; *~andi in veris doctrinae* AE 391.23.

informis ~is ~e, *a.* Shapeless, formless: *ut minora naturae in quibus innumerabilia non aliter videant ac opacum quoddam et nigrum ~e* AC 1869.2.

infortunatum ~i, *neut.* A misfortune: *accidunt ~a* AC 6493.

infortunitas ~atis, *f.* Misfortune: *quia sic...illis eveniret ~as* UJ(P) 362.

infortunium ~i, *neut.* Misfortune: *absque tentatione, ~o, tristitia* AC 8; AC 7761; ES 4137.

infossus ~a ~um: pf. pple. of **infodio**.

infra, *prep.* and *adv.* (compar.: see **inferius**) **A** (as prep. w. acc.) **1** Underneath, below: *septentrio...~a terram est* CI 141. **2** At an inferior level or degree to, below: *ut...non reputent illas ut viles ~a ancillas* AM 292.3; *vera...menti implantantur, ita ~a animam* VR 8.1. **B** (as adv.) **1** Lower down, below: *~a est infernum et supra est caelum* VI 19; *vide ~a hac pagina* ES 3684. **2** At a lower level or degree, inferiorly: *in derivatis...quae ~a sunt, et inde sunt* VR 6.1.

infracaelestis: see **infracoelestis**.

infracoelestis ~is ~e, *a.* also **infracaelestis**. Lower than celestial, sub-celestial: *bonitates ~es, quae mediae sunt inter spirituales et naturales* 1AD 950.

infractio ~onis, *f.* A breaking down: *~o veri per falsa* AE 237.1.

infractus ~a ~um, *a.* (pf. pple. of **infringo**) Broken down, humbled: *sacrificia Dei spiritus ~us, cor ~um et contritum Deus non spernit* Ps. 51.17 (DD 49.2).

infraenis ~is ~e, *a.* also **infrenis**. Unbridled, unrestrained: *~is cupiditas vulgandi secreta domus* AM 252.

infralapsarii ~orum, *m. pl.* The Infralapsarians, those who believe that election to salvation occurred after the Fall of humankind: VR 486.2.

infraspiritualis ~is ~e, *a.* Less than spiritual, subspiritual: *non modo Divinorum coelestium et* *spiritualium sed etiam infracoelestium et ~ium, hoc est, rationalium et naturalium* AC 2571.

infrenis: see **infraenis**.

infrigero ~are ~avi ~atum, *tr*. To make cold, cool: *hoc frigus ~aret primum interiora mentis* AM 167.2; (pass.) to become cold: *quod vir...~etur ad extrema* AM 259.

infringo ~ringere ~regi ~ractum, *tr*. **1** To break open: *dixit se timere, ne tandem se ~ringat* ES 262. **2** (refl.) To introduce oneself by breaking, break in: *consultant quomodo semet in coelum possint ~ringere seu elevare* ES 576 ½. **3** (transf.) To damage as by breaking, break up: *ut influxum Divini ~ringant* [*nimbi*] AC 8265.1; *quod...vera...~ringantur* AE 163.4.

infrugifer ~era ~erum, *a*. Unfruitful, unproductive: *fraus divitiarum suffocat Verbum, ut ~erum fiat* Matt. 13.22 (DP 278[a].3); *quid terram ~eram reddet (ficus)?* Luke 13.7 (AE 109.6).

infucatio ~onis, *f*. The application of a dye, dyeing: *dabant illis...coccinum ad ~ones* VR 462.1.

infuco ~are ~avi ~atum, *tr*. To treat with dye, colour; (transf.) to disguise: *ipsum etiam malum ~ant, ut non videatur sicut malum* AC 8593.1; DP 278[a].4.

infula ~ae, *f*. A band or lappet worn by the higher clergy: *qui spectat...alium praesulem aut antistitem ex ~a ac mitra eorum* CO 51.3.

infulatus ~a ~um, *a*. Wearing bands: *in Ecclesia, primus* [read *primas*] *~us, antistites parochi, et flamines sub illis* CO 17.1.

infundibulum ~i, *neut*. **1** A funnel (for pouring in liquid): *septem...lucernae ejus...septena ~a lucernis* Zech. 4.2 (AE 62.2). **2** A funnel-shaped part of the brain, infundibulum: *pars in ventriculum tertium sub glandula pineali transit, et sic per ~um versus glandulam pituitariam* ES 831.

infundo ~ndere ~di ~sum, *tr*. **1** To pour on or in: *obligavit vulnera ejus et ~dit oleum et vinum* Luke 10.34 (AC 6708); to apply in a stream, pour a stream of: *cultros jugulo meo ~ndere conati* ES 3653 (Autograph reading unclear). **2** (transf.) To introduce, insert, pour in: (w. dat.) *est naturale...vas cui ~nditur spirituale* AC 880.2; *cogitationes...~ndunt et immergunt corporeis et terrestribus* AC 938; *verum...~ndunt phantasiis* AC 806; (w. *in* + acc.) *quod Deus...~derit Suum Divinum in illum* AM 135.2; *formas quae se ~ndunt in homines...quae tunc vocantur animae* VR 79.6. **3** To introduce (into the mind of a person), implant (ideas, etc.): *Dominus...non immediate nova* [*vera*] *~ndit* SS 26.2; *continue ~ndunt scandala contra vera fidei* AE 138; (w. dat.) *nefaria quae cultoribus suis ~derunt* CI 249; (w. *in* + acc.) *quod falsa...~ndantur in illos* AC 8146.2; (impers. pass.) *~ndebatur sicut essent anthropophagi* ES 3994.

infusco ~are ~avi ~atum, *tr*. To make dark or obscure, dim: *numne visus oculi ~atur ex solo albo, et vivificatur ex colore...?* VR 763.1.

infusio ~onis, *f*. The act of introducing, introduction: *est animorum...communicatio et...~o* AE 544.3; *insaniunt qui credunt quod in baculo aliqua potentia fuerit...per ~onem* AC 4876.3; the introduction of an idea into the mind: *ex qua ~one plures...cruciati sunt* ES 5731.2.

ingemisco ~miscere ~mui, *intr*. To groan: *~muerunt, et dixerunt, o quam siccum gaudium caeli* AM 44.3.

ingeneratio ~onis, *f*. Introduction by birth: *de ~one amoris mali a parentibus in proles* AS 269.2.

ingenero ~are ~avi ~atum, *tr*. To introduce by birth: *quomodo potest amor non creatus ~ari homini* AM 44.6; AS 269.1.

ingeniose, *adv*. In a clever manner, ingeniously: *confirmare doctrinalia...solerter et ~e* AC 7950.2; AM 231.3.

ingeniositas ~atis, *f*. Cleverness, ingeniousness, ingenuity: *sapientia tua, quae est ~as scribendi, seduxit te* VR 35.6; AM 152[a].1; ES 758.

ingeniosus ~a ~um, *a*. (compar. *~ior*, superl. *~issimus*) **1** (of persons) Possessing quickness of mind, clever: *quod illi illuminati et ~i sint in rebus mundi* AC 6865.2; *qui pro ~issimis habiti sunt* AC 10409.3. **2** (of things) Showing cleverness: *sermo eorum erat admodum ~us* AE 242.3; (neut. as sb.) *nunc astus pro ~o...habentur* AC 6666.3.

ingenitus ~a ~um, *a*. Inborn, innate: *quod naturali homini ~um est* AM 466.1.

ingenium ~i, *neut*. Mental powers, cleverness: *celebratissimos eruditione, perspicacissimos ~o* AM 2.1; *quia ~o pollet* CI 385.

ingens ~ntis, *a*. (abl. sg. *~nte* VR 35.1) **1** Of great size or extent, vast, huge: *profundum petierunt sicut plumbum in aquis ~ntibus* Exod. 15.10 (AC). **2** (w. nouns of number, size, etc.): *~ntem multitudinem piscium* AM 316.5 (John 21.6); *in mundo spirituum est ~ns numerus* CI 426; *~nti copia* AE 260.1.

ingenuus ~a ~um, *a*. Freeborn, noble: *reduc mihi gaudium salutis Tuae, et spiritus ~us sustentet me* Ps. 51.12 (AC 9818.5).

ingero ~rere ~ssi ~stum, *tr*. To thrust in, push in, insert: *ex cibis affatim ~stis* ES 1278; *spiritus...~sserunt incommoda* ES 3624; (w. *in* + acc.) *quidam...~ssit se* *in aliquam societatem* AC 1397; (w. dat.) *quod haec idea... ~sta sit fidei hodiernae* VR 133.2.

inglorius ~a ~um, *a.* Lacking fame, humble, obscure: *qui... ~i sunt, nauci pendentes nominis famam* AM 376.

inglutio ~tire ~tivi ~titum, *tr.* To swallow: *magni pisces...tentant ~tire [hominem] et evomunt* ES 1382; ES(M) 4700.

ingluvies ~ei, *f.* The gaping jaws (of a beast), maw: *terribiles canes...omnes horribili ~e* AM 79.2; *in ~em magni draconis* ES 508.

ingratiis, *adv.* In an unwelcome manner, offensively: *annon nobis ~is talia objecistis?* VR 162.4.

ingratus ~a ~um, *a.* Unwelcome, unpleasing: *sunt ...sphaerae concordes jucundae et gratae, ac discordes injucundae et ~ae* AM 171.1; *quae ~i odoris [erant]* AE 324.1.

ingravatus ~a ~um, *a.* Subject to disease, corrupted: *morbi ex quibus totum corpus ~um fit* AM 253.1; (Bibl.) hardened: *~um est cor Pharaonis* Exod. 7.14 (AC).

ingravescentia ~ae, *f.* The process of becoming more serious, increase in gravity: *~am falsi continue crescentem* AC 8161.

ingravesco ~ere, *intr.* To become more serious: *pugna, quae si ~it, vocatur tentatio* DP 145.2; *mortem ...ex ~ente fame* VR 710.

ingredior ~di ~ssus sum, *intr.* (*tr.*) **1** To go in, enter: *~ssi sunt in sanctam urbem* Matt. 27.53 (AC 8018.2); *ut homo...paret se...habitaculum in quod Deus... ~diatur* VR 105.1. **b** (w. acc.): *~ssae sunt gynaeceum* AM 22; *ea quae ~diuntur vesicam, sicut...musculi, nervi* ES 867. **2** To enter upon (a state): *orate ut non ~diamini in tentationem* Luke 22.40 (AC 1787.2); *nonne...oportebat...Christum... ~di in gloriam?* Luke 24.26 (DD 11). **3** (tr.) To make a start on: *Deus frustra aliquam redemptionem ~di potuit* VR 124.1; (w. inf.) to begin, start: *~ssus sum loqui cum illis* VR 135.1. **4** (tr.) To be a constituent of, compose, make up: *quod myriades concupiscentiarum sint, quae unumquodvis malum ~diuntur et componunt* DP 279.5; *cum omni bono et vero, quae hominem et Ecclesiam ~diuntur et faciunt* VR 43.3.

ingressio ~onis, *f.* Entrance: *~o in sanctam urbem* AC 8018.2.

ingressus ~us, *m.* **1** The act of entering, entrance: *mala sicut obstantia ~ui Domini* DP 33.3; *porta, per quam fit ~us in templum* VR 1. **2** Place for entering, entrance: *humile palatium, per quod patuit ~us in porticum* AM 7.1; *quidam...in ~u ad coelum indignati recesserunt* ES 339.

ingruo ~ere ~i, *intr.* To impend, threaten, come in with force: *cum tentatio ~it* AC 8162; AC 8217; *ne tela mea ~ente aëris vibratione diffluat* VR 335.3; *hoc tutatur ab ~ente malo damnum illaturo* AC 9629.

inguen ~inis, *neut.* The groin: *sub ~inibus* ES 5103.

inguinalis ~is ~e, *a.* Of the groin: *in glandulas ~ales* ES 3453.

ingurgito ~are ~avi ~atum, *tr.* To swallow, engulf: *infernum...exporrigebat ingluviem...et ~avit illos* ES 4573; (refl.) to plunge oneself (into), wallow (in): *qui... libris legendis se ~ant* ES 385.

ingyratio ~onis, *f.* An inward-running spiral motion: *~ones et egyrationes vorticillares* DP 319.2.

inhabilis ~is ~e, *a.* Unskilled, unprepared: *quod... [rex] eligat habilem functionis ac repudiet ~em* VR 410.1; ES 2500.

inhabitatio ~onis, *f.* A dwelling in, habitation: *de cujus ~one seu statu* VR 185.4.

inhabitatus ~a ~um, *a.* Uninhabited: *a significatione 'deserti' quod sit ~um et inexcultum* AC 6904.

inhabito ~are ~avi, *intr.* (*tr.*) (pf. pple. *~atus* VR 466) To dwell in, live in, inhabit: *urbem et ~antes in ea* Jer. 47.2 (FI 53); (w. dat.) *quod mens...patris ~et proli post prolem* VR 103.2. **b** (w. acc.): *Exaltatus Jehovah, quia ~at excelsum* Isa. 33.5 (AC 8153); *quamdiu malis spiritibus permissum est eam [sphaeram] ~are* ES 210; (pass.) AC 2712.1.

inhabituatus ~a ~um, *a.* (w. *in* + abl.) Accustomed (to), inured (to): *qui in sui et mundi amore sunt ~i* ES(M) 4677.

inhaereditatus: see **inhaeridatus**.

inhaerenter, *adv.* Inherently: *non sciunt aliter quam quod aliquid in ipsis sit ~er quod sic patitur* AC 751.1.

inhaereo ~rere ~si, *intr.* **1** (of things) To remain fixed, stick: *~ret dubium* VI 76; (w. *in* + abl.) *illa... ~rent...in interiore memoria* AC 7398; (w. dat.) *quod cordibus illorum ~serit cultus plurium deorum* AC 8301.5. **2** (of persons) To adhere mentally (to a view, belief, etc.), cling to: *dum instruuntur quomodo se habet, usque ~rent* AC 1072; (w. dat.) *~rent fidei suae* AM 182.5; *homo Antiquissimae Ecclesiae...ne hilum ~reret sensui literae* AC 1143; (w. inf.) *quod tam tenaciter ~rebant...me infestare* ES 4227.

inhaeridatus ~a ~um, *a.* also **inhaereditatus**, and **inheredatus**. Implanted by heredity: *quod habilitas ...illis...a nativitate ~a sit* AM 204.

inheredatus: see **inhaeridatus**.

inhibeo ~bere ~bui ~bitum, *tr.* **1** To put a stop to, prevent, block, inhibit: *~bebo flumina ejus* Ezek. 31.15 (AC 6693.5); *si...* [*Divinum*] *~beret et auferret mala* AC 8227.2; *haec* [*causa*] *prorsus ~bet influxum amoris conjugialis* AM 375.3. **b** (w. *ne*): *concupiscentiae malorum... ~bent ne aperiatur* [*mens spiritualis*] VI 86.4; CI 359. **2** To prevent (a person) from acting, restrain: *quod liceat homini...facere malum, quantum timores externi non ~bent* AC 7007.2; *occideret nisi ~berent leges* AE 137.1.

inhibitio ~onis, *f.* The act of stopping or restraining, restraint, inhibition: *~o et retractio jucundorum nostrorum* AM 461.8; *~o ne aliquid praeter panem ederent* AC 7810; AE 421.

inhio ~are ~avi, *intr.* (w. dat.) To regard covetously, long for: *qui...malitiose aliorum opibus ~averat* AC 939; *~ant illicitis et vetitis* AM 511; ES 585.

inhonestus ~a ~um, *a.* (superl. *~issimus*) Shameful, disgraceful: *ne aliquid oppositi, quod vocatur ~um et indecorum...exhibeant* AM 17.5; ES 3206.

inhumanus ~a ~um, *a.* Lacking in humanity, unkind: *ut...avertere conetur ea quae ~a sunt* ES 1656.

inibi, *adv.* Therein, inside, within: *urbem...et fana idolorum, quae ~i sunt* VR 84; *quae nusquam relata fuissent in Verbo...nisi arcana haec ~i recondita laterent* AC 1502.2; *quod quo interius aliquod objectum spectatur, ~i eo mirabiliora...conspiciantur* DP 6.1.

inimice, *adv.* (superl. *~issime*) In an unfriendly fashion: *agunt ex phantasiis ~issime contra alios* ES 374.

inimicitia ~ae, *f.* Hostility, enmity: *vivit...in contemtu aliorum, in ~a et odio* AC 7272.2; (w. pl.) a hostile act, quarrel: *si dissidentiae...in apertas ~as, rixas, et odii minas, erumperent* AM 286; CI 290.

inimico ~are ~avi ~atum, *tr.* To put enmity between, make into enemies, make hostile: *jucundum imperandi ...parit dissidia et ~at mentes* AC 10173.

inimicus ~a ~um, *a.* Unfriendly, hostile: *qui ~um illum habet si non sibi favet* AC 7370; *quod* [*volatile*] *cognoscat...quaenam earum* [sc. *avium*] *amicae, et quaenam ~ae sunt* VR 12.5; (esp. masc. as sb.) *bonum faciunt tam ~is quam amicis* AC 8223.2; *venit ~us et sevit zizania* Matt. 13.25 (AE 187.8); (dist. from **hostis**) SS 84.1.

inimitabilis ~is ~e, *a.* That cannot be imitated, inimitable: *decoramenta caelaturae ~is* AM 12.1.

inique, *adv.* Unfairly, unjustly: *confessionem quod nempe ~e fecerint* AC 5785.

iniquitas ~atis, *f.* Unfairness, injustice: *pleni estis hypocrisi et ~ate* Matt. 23.28 (AC 7046.2); an unjust act, injustice: *ex eo quod ~as haec tam levis videatur* AC 1093.2; *eos qui faciunt ~atem* Matt. 13.41 (CI 570.2).

iniquus ~a ~um, *a.* Unjust, unfair: *bona meritoria, quae in se sunt ~a* AE 789.9; (neut. as sb.) *'morbi' repraesentabant ~a et mala vitae spiritualis* AC 8364.6.

initialis ~is ~e, *a.* Of the beginning, initial: *subscribite ~em literam regni, e quo estis* AM 103.4; (neut. as sb.) an initial letter: *voces nominum non distinguuntur ~ibus majoribus* ES 2631.

initiamentum ~i, *neut.* An initial stage: *post aliqua ~a conjugii* AM 307; *non est rationale, solum quoddam ejus ~um* AC 1893.1.

initiatio ~onis, *f.* **1** The inauguration (of a building, etc.): *ad ~onem altaris* AE 430.9. **2** The process of introduction, initiation: *~o in cognitiones boni et veri* AC 6538; *in ~onibus fidelitatis* VR 297.1. **3** An initial stage, beginning: *actum est de ~one verorum quae sunt Ecclesiae* AC 6639.1; *~ones et progressiones amoris conjugialis* AM 301.

initiatus ~i, *m.* A trained follower, retainer: *expedivit ~os suos...et persequutus est usque Dan* Gen. 14.14 (AC).

initio ~are ~avi ~atum, *tr.* **1** To begin, start: *instructionem...coeptam seu ~atam* AC 401; *amorem conjugialem ~atum ante nuptias* AM 250. **2** (w. *in* + acc.) To introduce (into an office), inaugurate: *antequam in sacerdotium ~atus est* AC 6998. **3** (w. *in* or *ad* + acc.) To introduce (to any activity): *quod... illos in odia et vindictas ~ent* CI 344; *quod homo... ~etur ad recipiendum influxum boni et veri a Domino* AC 7831. **4** (pass.) To receive rudimentary instruction, be taught the principles: *ad portam...stant qui ~antur* CI 223; (w. *in* + acc.) *nemo...~ari potest in fidem et charitatem...nisi per cognitiones* AE 96; *quod infantes in religionem Christianam ~entur per illum* [sc. *Decalogum*] VI 64; (w. dat.) *~ari scientificis* AC 6638; ES 290.

initium ~i, *neut.* A beginning, initial stage: *nisi prudenter...obviam irent in ipsis ~is amori sui et amori mundi* AC 7364. **b** *ab ~o*, from the beginning: *ille homicida erat ab ~o* John 8.44 (AC 7051.3); *Domino fuit ab ~o Humanum ex matre* DD 35.3.

injectio ~onis, *f.* Insertion, introduction: *mali...qui per ~ones falsi et mali violentiam inferre bonis volunt* AC 8214.

injicio ~jicere ~jeci ~jectum, *tr.* **1** To throw, thrust or push in: *cur aquae illae ex ~jecto ligno dulces factae sunt* AC 8356; (w. *in* + acc.) *quod Jesus... ~jecerit digitum Suum in aures illius* AC 7430.1; *vidi...spiritum*

... *~jectum in tentorium* VR 110.1; (w. dat.) *semen quod ~jicitur terrae* AC 880.1. **2** To interpose, insert, introduce: *quod infestarent... ~jiciendo fallacia et fictitia falsa* AC 7087; AC 7111.2.

injucunditas ~atis, *f.* Unpleasantness: *quod talia in se infelicitates et ~ates etiam essent utilitati* ES 231.

injucundo ~are ~avi ~atum, *tr.* To deprive of pleasure, displease: *sapientia ~at illos* AM 498.

injucundus ~a ~um, *a.* Displeasing, unpleasant: [*objecta*] *vertunt receptam lucem in colores ~os et tetros* AC 681; (neut. as sb) unpleasantness: *num...amor illarum...sit in suo jucundo, aut in ~o...non... evulgatum est* AM 219; VR 61.1.

injunctum ~i, *neut.* That which is joined on, a predicate, qualification: *simile est cum vero, si id absque ~o auditur* AM 87.1.

injungo ~gere ~xi ~ctum, *tr.* **1** (w. dat.) To join on, link to: *haec se conjungunt cum communi ejus, et se ei ~gunt ita, ut simul unum faciant* VR 54; *dulcedo cantus ~gebatur mirabiliter ideis eorum* ES 2231. **2** To impose (commands, duties, etc.), enjoin: *statuta ...quae Dominus...per Mosen ~xit* AC 6804.5; *quod... potuerit talia stipulari, et illi ~gere* FI 46; (w. inf.) *posset intellectus... ~gere voluntati id facere* DP 259.2; (w. *ut*) *ei ~git, ut caveat* DP 109.1; VR 16.4; (w. *quod*) *haec... praecepta... ~gunt quod mala non facienda sint* VR 326.1.

injurgo ~are ~avi, *intr.* To utter reproaches, scold: *lacessendo alios, ~ando variis modis, et damnum iis inferendo* ES 1347.

injuria ~ae, *f.* An injury, harm: *~am vindicare* AC 1879.2; BCP (VI 6).

injuriosus ~a ~um, *a.* Inflicting insult, slighting: *~um est deducere originem amoris conjugialis a sanctis Ecclesiae* AM 79.10; *hoc vocant...merito Christi obvium, repugnabile, et ~um* VR 561.2.

injuste, *adv.* Unjustly: *prorsus insincere et ~e agerent* CI 530.2.

injustitia ~ae, *f.* Injustice: *capita faciunt illa quae amicitiae sunt, pectora illa quae ~ae* AM 231.4.

injustus ~a ~um, *a.* Unjust: *si tales quoad moralem et civilem vitam insinceri ac ~i sunt* AE 126.2; AM 231.3; (of things) characterized by injustice: *quod facerent sibi amicos ex ~o mammone* AE 141.13 (Luke 16.9); (neut. as sb.) an unjust act: *qui facit ~um propter lucrum* AC 8123.

innascor ~sci ~tus sum, *intr.* see also **innatus**. (w. dat.) To be born (in), arise, develop (in): *ei* [sc. *carni*] *~scuntur vermiculi* VR 367.5.

innaturalis ~is ~e, *a.* Unnatural: *quod...sic naturam ~em contraxerit* AC 2746; *quidam ~is spurcissimus* ES 4367 titulus.

innatus ~a ~um, *a.* Present at birth, innate: *ex ~a arrogantia* AC 940.1; *homo vivit tunc secundum malum ~um et acquisitum* AC 7327; *est cuilibet animali ~a scientia* CI 110.

innitor ~ti ~xus sum, *intr.* **1** To be supported, rest, lean: *super baculo argenteo ~xae magnifice ambulant* VR 80.1; *ut formentur plana, quibus ~tantur superiora sicut palatium super fundationibus suis* AM 447.1. **2** To trust (in): *super equis ~tuntur* Isa. 31.1 (VI 30.2).

innocens ~ntis, *a.* (compar. *~ntior*) Free from blame, blameless, innocent: *non ~ntem reddet Jehovah illum qui fert nomen Ipsius ad vanum* Exod. 20.7 (AC); *quo sapientiores angeli sunt, eo ~ntiores* AM 413; CI 281.

innocenter, *adv.* Innocently: ES 2119.

innocentia ~ae, *f.* Freedom from blame, innocence: *sphaera ~ae et pacis* AM 222.2; *de ~a infantiae* CI 276; *missus est ad eum quidam ex minoribus ~is* ES 291.

innocuus ~a ~um, *a.* Not causing harm, harmless: *percipit jucunda amoris conjugialis ut ~a et casta* AM 441; (masc. as sb.) *pelliciunt ~os in suas partes* ES 409.

innotesco ~tescere ~tui, *intr.* To become well known: *inde... ~tuit quali animo sunt* AC 941.2.

innovatio ~onis, *f.* A making new, renewal (esp. in regeneration): *reformatio et regeneratio, et secundum has ~o* VR 142.

innovator ~oris, *m.* One who introduces novelties, an innovator: *Antiqua Ecclesia...degenerata et ab ~oribus adulterata fuit* AC 1241.

innovo ~are ~avi ~atum, *tr.* **1** To make new, renew: *varietates...jugiter ~ant illa* [sc. *jucunda*] CI 489.4; (absol.) to introduce novelties, innovate: *cupidine...vel ~andi vel praeeminendi* AC 1188.1. **2** (especially in regeneration): *quod internus homo...purificandus et ~andus sit* DP 150.1; *simul ~at spiritus seu mentes eorum, et generat e novo* VR 16.1.

innoxius ~a ~um, *a.* Harmless: *bestiae sunt duplicis generis, malae quia noxiae, bonae quia ~ae* AC 143; *serpentes ~i* AR 455.1.

innumerabilis ~is ~e, *a.* (compar. *~ior*) That cannot be counted, countless, innumerable: *coelestia... dantur ~ium generum, et adhuc ~iorum specierum* AC 353.3; *universum aspectabile tot ~ibus astris illustre* AC 6698.

innumerabilitas ~atis, *f.* The quality of being

beyond counting: *~as horum significatur per chiliades chiliadum* AE 336.2.

innumerabiliter, *adv*. Beyond counting, innumerably: *multiplicare gentem Israeliticam et Judaicam ~er* AC 10445.

innumeralis ~is ~e, *a*. Countless: *repraesentativa quae ibi sunt innumerabilia, sicut paradisi, horti, sylvae...tum animalia et aves plurium generum, praeter ~ia* [*innumera alia* Autograph] AC 9457.2; *quod Deus sit omnipotens, omniscius, et omnipraesens homo se confirmare potest ex ~ibus* CN De Deo viii.3.

innumerus ~a ~um, *a*. Beyond counting, countless, innumerable: *societiates coeli, quae ~ae sunt* AE 256; AM 326.5; (w. collective sg.) *experientia ~a id mihi confirmavit* ES 635.

innuo ~ere ~i, *intr*. To hint: *ii melius intellexerunt quam ego, si modo ~erem, quid cogitarem* ES 584 1/2; *hic modo ~itur quomodo Dominus cogitavit de apparentiis* AC 1936.1.

innupta ~ae, *f. adj*. (of women) Unmarried: *adulterium...faeminae ~ae cum marito alterius* AM 478.3; ES 1071.

inobedientia ~ae, *f.* also **inoboedientia**. Disobedience: *ne respiciant ad ~am* AC 7697.

inobedio ~dire ~divi, *intr*. also **inoboedio**. Disobedient: *filii ~dientes et refractarii lapidabantur* AC 8899.2.

inoboedientia: see **inobedientia**.

inoboedio: see **inobedio**.

inobservabilis ~is ~e, *a*. Impossible to observe, unobservable: (w. dat.) *quod utrumque ~e sit homini, quia imperceptibile* AC 3884.3.

inobservatus ~a ~um, *a*. Unnoticed, unobserved: *quae alioquin ~a prorsus fuissent* ES 2901.

inoculatio ~onis, *f*. Engrafting: (fig.) *religio...est illius amoris initiamentum et ~o* AM 531.

inoculo ~are ~avi ~atum, *tr*. To implant (a bud in a growing plant), engraft: *si spina ~atur viti* VR 8.3; *succus...usque ad insitum aut ~atum ascendit* VR 584.2.

inopia ~ae, *f*. A state of neediness, want, destitution: *infirmitates et inde ~ae* AM 456.

inopinato, *adv*. Unexpectedly, suddenly: *quidam ...~o sublati sunt in coelum* AC 541; *angelus e caelo ~o stetit in medio illorum* AM 355.3; ES 2142.

inopinatus ~a ~um, *a*. Unexpected: *tempus ~um* AE 181.

inops ~opis, *a*. (w. gen.) Lacking (in), wanting (in): *~ops consilii* AM 325.1.

inordinate, *adv*. In a disorderly fashion: *ponunt unum supra alterum ~e* VR 281.8.

inordinatio ~onis, *f*. Lack of order, disorder: *dolorem cordis ob ~onem...omnium* AE 306; ES 3540.

inordinatus ~a ~um, *a*. (superl. *~issimus*) Lacking order, disordered, confused: *in sensu literali vix nisi ~um quoddam apparet* AC 1871; *~issima ordinate videre* ES 2178; *per fornicationes ~as et immoderatas* AM 444[a].

inormis: see **enormis**.

inquam (no inf.) ~ii, *intr*. (3rd. sg. pres. indic. *~it*, pple. *~iens*) To say: *sic ~it Jehovah* Ezek. 4.13 (DD 16.3); *prehenderunt me manu, ~ientes, sequere nos* AM 132.1; (w. *quod*) *~iit, quod possit utrumque confirmare* VR 35.5; (w. acc. + inf.) *~iit, mirum esse quod...* AC 1769.5.

inquieto ~are ~avi ~atum, *tr*. To make uneasy, disturb: *interiora iis vexant et ~ant* ES 744.

inquietudo ~inis, *f*. Something that causes uneasiness, disturbance: *longe ab indignatione, ira, ~inibus* AC 5725.2 (Autograph).

inquietus ~a ~um, *a*. Uneasy: *intellectus...versat varia, quae animum reddunt ~um* AM 285.1.

inquilinus ~i, *m*. One who resides in a place without being native, an alien, lodger, sojourner: *~us et mercenarius non comedet illud* Exod. 12.45 (AC); *statuta de alienigenis, servis, ~is, mercenariis et peregrinis* AC 8001; (in a heavenly community) *novos advenas, ex vestitu...apparentes ut ~i* AM 14.2.

inquinamentum ~i, *neut*. That which pollutes, pollution, defilement: *sunt...illa tenebrae et ~a quae cum luce et puritate coeli non concordant* AC 7090.3; AM 105.

inquino ~are ~avi ~atum, *tr*. To make dirty, pollute, defile: *noxiis quae...massam sanguinis ~ant* AC 1877; *nec vitam suam spiritualem ~averunt* CI 515; (pass.) to pollute oneself: *hi sunt, qui cum mulieribus non sunt ~ati* Rev. 14.4 (AR).

inquiro ~rere ~sivi ~situm, *intr., tr*. **1** (intr.) To make inquiry, search, investigate: (w. *in* + acc.) *~rere in fidei mysteria per sensualia et scientifica* AC 80; FI 42; (w. indir. qu.) *quod...nec ulterius ex Verbo ~rant num id ipsum verum sit* AC 7233.2; DP 179.2; (impers. pass.) *~situm est num fugerint mala ut peccata* VI 26. **2** (tr.) To search for, seek: *fine ~rendi habitationem* AM 242; *~runt vera ex Verbo* AE 115; also, to investigate, inquire into: *~siverunt illa quae in memoria mea essent* AC 6809.

inquisitio ~onis, *f*. **1** The process of inquiry,

investigation: *'quid hoc?' significat ~onem cur ita* AC 8071; *~o et pervestigatio veri* AE 282.5; AM 57. **2** The Roman Catholic organization for suppressing heresy, the Inquisition: *loquuti...quod ad ~onem ferar* ES 4101; UJ(P) 5.

inquisitor ~oris, *m.* An investigator, inquisitor: AM 451; VR 767.2.

inquisitorius ~a ~um, *a.* Investigative: *processus ~us et expurgatorius* AC 9262.3; ES 2845.

insalutifer ~era ~erum, *a.* Not bringing salvation: *quod haec moralitas...sit salvifica, at omnis alia ~era, quia meritoria* VR 459.3.

insane, *adv.* (compar. *~ius*) In an insane manner, madly: *qui...in malo fuit...is tunc insipide et ~e agit, imo ~ius quam in mundo* CI 505.

insania ~ae, *f.* **1** A state of madness, insanity: *error et ~a...in Verbo appellatur 'ebrietas'* AC 1072.1; an instance of this: *quod unusquisque...percipiat sicut ~am dicere quod plures sint [Dei]* VR 6.3; *tales ~as vidi pluries* DP 298.2. **2** An insane person, madman: *discurrentes sicut ~ae* AC 819; *quod ~ae essent si imperare suum a talibus quaerant* AC 5718.1; ES 2808.

insanio ~nire ~nivi, *intr.* To be mad, rave: *homo ...spiritualiter ~nit* SS 26.1; *obtenebratur visus eorum interior, usque ut ~niant* CI 481.4; (Bibl.) to behave in a crazy fashion: *ascendite equi, ~nite currus* Jer. 46.9 (AC 1195).

insanitio ~onis, *f.* Crazy behaviour, madness: *'titubare judicio' significat ~onem* AE 235.7.

insanus ~a ~um, *a.* (compar. *~ior*) Mad, crazy, insane: *ii apparent...tanquam ~i, nam absque ulla ratione agunt* ES 229; (masc. as sb.) *non...potest... sanum et ~um una esse* AM 463.2; (fem. as sb.) *vidi ~am in platea* ES 2808.

inscitia ~ae, *f.* Lack of knowledge, ignorance: *nasci in omnem ignorantiam et ~am* AC 7750.2; *ex communi ~a hodie de amore vere conjugiali* AM 239.

inscius ~a ~um, *a.* Unknowing, ignorant: *quod illa...inspiretur ab uxore, sed viro ~o* AM 225; (masc. as sb.) *coram ~is et coram malis* AE 318.

inscribo ~bere ~psi ~ptum, *tr.* **1** To write on, inscribe: *quod leges illae ~ptae fuerint binis tabulis lapideis digito Dei* VI 55.1; *arcana sapientiae chartae ~pta* VR 48.2. **2** To have a title or note written on: *aliquot Psalmi ~buntur per 'Jehovah regnabit'* AC 8331. **3** (w. dat.) To record irremovably (on), inscribe: *~bitur sensus internus Verbi...ejus intellectui* AC 9430.1; esp. pf. pple.: *leges charitatis... ~ptae cordibus* AC 8118.3; *amorem... cui insunt quasi ~pta singularia vitae* CI 269.2; *cui meritum Christi ~ptum est* VR 160.6. **4** To enrol, assign (to a position): *in hunc locum...quisque homo... ~bitur* DP 68.

inscriptio ~onis, *f.* The act of recording irremovably, inscription: *per ~onem ejus* [sc. *Justitiae Domini*] *apud hominem* VR 96.1.

inscrutabilis ~is ~e, *a.* Impossible to examine or understand, unfathomable, inscrutable: *quod loco imaginis Dei amissae in homine sit intima, pessima, profundissima, ~is, ineffabilis corruptio totius naturae* Book of Concord in VR 464.10.

insculpo ~ere ~si ~tum, *tr.* To carve (something) into (something else), engrave: (w. prep.) *super manus ~si te* Isa. 49.16 (AC 6419.2); (transf.) to record indelibly, engrave: (w. dat.) *qui praedestinationem per confirmationes cordi suo ~sit* VR 487.1.

insculptus ~a ~um, *a.* **1** Carved or engraved (upon): *bracteae ~us erat pullus aquilae* AM 20.2; AC 8369.3. **2** Covered with carving, engraved: *duodecim lapides pretiosi... ~i sunt auro* AC 6640.2.

insector ~ari ~atus sum, *tr.* **1** To pursue, chase: *super montibus ~ati sunt nos* Lam. 4.19 (AE 375.21); *eos...sicut feles ~antur et mordent* ES 392. **2** (as pass.) To be pursued: *antra...in quae fugiunt qui ~antur ab aliis* CI 586.

insectulum ~i, *neut.* A small insect: *in minimis...ut in maximis...in ~is sicut in alitibus* AM 416.2; ES 681.

insectum ~i, *neut.* An insect: *~a volantia in aëre* AC 7441.2; *vermiculi qui vocantur ~a* AM 133.2.

insecutus ~a ~um: pf. pple. of **insequor**.

inseminatio ~onis, *f.* The implanting of seed (in quot. fig.): *multiplicatio et ~o veri ex bono* AE 328.17.

insemino ~are ~avi ~atum, *tr.* To plant (seeds): (fig.) *arare sulcum, in quem improvise ~avit naturalismum* VR 137.8; (esp. transf.) to implant like seeds: (w. dat.) *omnia ~antur memoriae* AC 991.

insenesco ~ere, *intr.* To grow old (in): *vetulae quae solent ~ere in cupiditatibus* ES 893.

insensibilis ~is ~e, *a.* **1** Devoid of sensation, insensible: *totus homo fit ~is ad omnem amorem vitalem* AM 249.2; *~is fuit sensui interno Verbi* ES 4413. **2** Incapable of perception by the senses, imperceptible: *coeperunt faustitates illae hebescere...ac fieri ~es* AM 8.3; *dolorem...quasi ~em* ES 4419; *quae [perceptio] dici potest intellectualis, tametsi etiam ~is* ES 312.

insensibilitas ~atis, *f.* Lack of sensory perception, insensibility: *in statum ~atis quoad corporeos sensus perductus sum* AC 169; ES 3397.

insensibiliter, *adv*. Imperceptibly: *mirabiliter et ~er flectat cupiditates* ES 2194.

insensilis ~is ~e, *a*. Lacking sensation, non-sensory: *fibrillas... ~es in visceribus* ES 1941.

inseparabilis ~is ~e, *a*. Incapable of being separated, inseparable: *ita conjuncta ut ~ia* AC 1153.2.

inseparabiliter, *adv*. Inseparably: *alter hic usus Baptismi... ~er sequitur primum* VR 681.

inseparatus ~a ~um, *a*. Not separated: *una duplicitas est extensa et ~a* VR 629.

insepelio ~lire, *tr*. To bury in: [*avis*] *decidit in nivem, et ~litur* VR 385.3.

insequens ~ntis, *a*. Following, succeeding: *generationi ~nti* Ps. 48.13 (AE 453.10); *in transactionibus ~ntibus* AM 454; (neut. pl. as sb.) *conjugiale... implantatum est cujusvis animae, et quoque ~ntibus ab anima* AM 204.

insequor ~qui ~quutus (*or* ~cutus) sum, *intr*. **1** To pursue: *apparebat...quidam qui fugientes ~quutus* AC 5378.1. **2** To follow logically: *ex inductionibus, quae a principio in principiata necessario ~quutae sunt* SE 61.

insero[1] ~serere ~sivi ~situm, *tr*. see also **insitus**. To plant in: *humus...non recipit alia semina quam ~sita* VR 48.10; to graft on, engraft: *frons ~sita communi stirpi fert suum fructum* AC 7343.2; to implant like seeds: *corona ex auro cum ~sitis rubinis* AM 20.2.

insero[2] ~ere ~ui ~tum, *tr*. To introduce, insert: *herbae toxicatae...pulvinaribus ~tae* VR 511; *numeri in Verbo... ~ti modo ad concinnandam seriem* AC 813; *mala et falsa...removentur, ac bona et vera loco illorum ~untur* AC 6724.2.

insertio ~onis, *f*. **1** The act of introducing or inserting: *~o in societates angelicas* VR 140; *quasi ~o coeli...apud hominem* CI 246.2. **2** A part serving to introduce something, insertion: *~o nervorum acusticorum* ES 1090.

inserto ~are ~avi ~atum, *tr*. To introduce, insert: *accipiter...collum ~avit laqueo* VR 72.3; *ureteres qui a latere* [*vesicae*] *~antur* ES 870; *angelus ~abat illos consortiis* AM 14.1.

inservio ~vire ~vivi, *intr*. To be of use, serve: (w. dat.) *causae... ~viturae indagandis usibus* AC 6815; *relaxatio...ligamentorum motui ~vientium* AM 253.2; (w. *pro*) *illud pro signo repraesentativo ~vire potuit* AC 7049; (w. *ut*) *~viat hoc ut canon* VR 50; (w. *ad*) *qui* [*status*] *illi ~viverat ad introducendum ad bonum* AC 7857.1.

insideo ~sidere ~sedi ~sessum, *intr*. (*tr*.) (pf. act. also *~idi*) **1** (w. dat.) To sit (upon): *videntur sibi equo furioso ~sidere* AC 828; *Jehovah ~sidens cherubis* Ps. 99.1 (SS 97.4). **2** (transf.) To be firmly lodged, be fixed: [*illa vera*] *~sident memoriae interiori* AC 7935; *quod opinio illa de pluribus diis ~sederit mentibus Judaeorum* AC 8301.4; *hic nisus conjugialis ~sidens animabus est* AM 238.2. **b** (tr.) to be fixed in, grip: *talis cupido eos ~sedit* ES 1002.

insidiae ~diarum, *f. pl*. A treacherous attack, plot: *infestant omnes qui se non honorant, nectunt ~dias* CI 508.2; 3AD 4512.

insidiatio ~onis, *f*. The act of plotting, treachery: *~o ex sermone...elucebat* ES 727.

insidiator ~oris, *m*. One who attacks treacherously, plotter: *malum quod ~or facturus est* AC 9009.1.

insidiatrix ~icis, *f*. A treacherous woman: AC 4627.3.

insidior ~ari ~atus sum, *intr*. **1** To lie in ambush: *in deserto ~ati sunt nobis* Lam. 4.19 (AE 375.21). **2** To attack treacherously, plot: *quibus jucundum fuit clandestine ~ari* CI 488.2.

insidiose, *adv*. (compar. *~ius*) Treacherously: *qui in obscuro agunt ~e, et ~ius aliis* ES 3534.

insidiosus ~a ~um, *a*. Treacherous, insidious: (neut. pl. as sb.) *qui...in ~is posuerunt honorem prudentiae* AC 949.

insigne ~is, *neut*. A mark of rank, badge: *~e erat aquila...in vertice arboris cubans* AM 15; (pl.) insignia: *quintus...iisdem ~ibus ornatus* AM 315.9; (perh.) banners, ensigns: *quod rex...cum ~ibus equitaret super equo albo* AE 31.6.

insignio ~nire ~nivi ~nitum, *tr*. **1** To distinguish with a badge or other insignia: *quod reges, cum coronabantur, ~nirentur talibus* AE 31.6; *quisque ~nitus lauru* AM 10.1. **2** (transf.) To embellish, adorn, ennoble, make distinguished: *vegetabile...ramis, frondibus et foliis ~nitur* VR 106.2; *quod Deus injustum possit ...omnibus salutis donis... ~nire* VR 74.4; *Dominus variis nominibus ~nitur in Verbo Veteris Testamenti* DD 22.

insignis ~is ~e, *a*. (compar. *~ior*) **1** Embellished, distinguished: *comparari potest arbori ~i ramis, foliis et fructibus* DP 107. **2** Notable, remarkable, considerable: *~i distantia* CI 118; *quo ~ior usus...est, eo jucundum ejus est majus* AC 997.2; *per ~em futuram mutationem* AE 258.

insigniter, *adv*. In a notable manner, remarkably: *currus tracti a mannis... ~er phaleratis* AM 103.2.

insimul, *adv*. At the same time, simultaneously: *sequitur quod suprememoratae virtutes... ~l sint in Domino* VR 152; ES 1795.

insimulatio ~onis, *f.* An accusation: *quam horrendae fuerint ~ones et insidiae domus istius...contra Deum Messiam* 3AD 4512.

insimulo ~are ~avi ~atum, *tr.* (w. gen. of charge) To accuse (of a fault): *ne ~entur...incredulitatis* AC 8544; ES 1113.

insincere, *adv.* With dissimulation, insincerely: *prorsus ~e et injuste agerent* CI 530.2.

insinceritas ~atis, *f.* Deceitfulness, dishonesty: *quod injustitia, ~as, et scortatio cum aliorum uxoribus sint noxiae communi* DP 77.1.

insincerus ~a ~um, *a.* Dissembling, insincere: *~us, injustus, infidelis et non rectus* VI 84.2; AE 126.2.

insinuatio ~onis, *f.* **1** The act of introducing or instilling: *~o boni* AC 6740; *per ~onem in cogitationes* ES 327. **2** An indentation, alcove, recess: *ecce ibi octo ~ones sexangulares in quarum unaquavis erat librarium* AM 151[a].2; ES 5255.

insinuatorius ~a ~um, *a.* Prone to introduce oneself, insinuatory: *is ~us erat, nam permissum ei erat se insinuare in aliquas societates coeli* ES 1071.

insinuo ~are ~avi ~atum, *tr.* **1** To introduce subtly, instill: *nisi Dominus ~et affectionem amoris spiritualis* AC 7342; *amicitia quae tempore desponsationis... ~ata est* AM 214.3; (w. dat.) *quae bona jucundis...illis jugiter a Domino ~antur* CI 337; (w. *in* + acc.) *astus et dolus se ~ant...in spiritualem hominis mentem* VI 81. **2** To assign to an interior position: *angeli secundum perfectionem suam ascendunt...sive ~antur* ES 156.

insipiens ~ntis, *a.* Lacking in wisdom, foolish: *quod genus humanum tam ~ns est, ut id ne quidem intelligere possit* ES 1633.

insipide, *adv.* Unwisely: *is tunc ~e et insane agit* CI 505.

insipidus ~a ~um, *a.* Lacking in taste, tasteless, insipid: *cibi facti sunt nobis ~i* AM 6.4.

insipientia ~ae, *f.* Lack of wisdom, folly: *unum [principium] quod ducit ad omnem ~am et insaniam* AC 2568.4.

insisto ~ere institi, *intr.* **1** (w. dat.) To stand upon: *quod scire posset inde quod supra caput meum sit nec ~at telluri* AC 447; *ut vix potuissem ~ere plantis* ES 153. **2** (w. *in* + acc.) To persevere, persist (in): *institit in causam, quia juraverat in illam* AM 105. **3** (w. indir. qu.) To ask insistently, demand: *dolos suos insinuabat... ~ens...quomodo talis esse posset* ES 2876.

insitio ~onis, *f.* The act of engrafting: *illustrari etiam hoc potest ab ~one frondium in arboribus* AC 7343.2; DP 296.2; (transf.) *inde est ~o ejus [amoris], et quoque transplantatio ejus* AM 466.2.

insitus ~a ~um, *a.* (pf. pple. of **insero**[1]) (in senses of vb., esp. transf.) Implanted, entrenched: *timor ~us seu naturalis* AC 8381; *apud mere naturales radix mali manet ~a* VI 108; (w. dat.) *ex idea communi quae ~a cuivis* CI 74.2; (neut. as sb.) *patuit quod apud unumquemvis hominem...sit ~um de vita sua post mortem* CI 602; VR 584.2; *ex ~o*, by instinct: *infantes...sicut ex ~o amant illas tanquam suas matres* AM 410.

insolens ~ntis, *a.* Unaccustomed, unusual: *audivi ~ns murmur e longinquo* VR 72.1.

insolenter, *adv.* Insolently: *contra Jehovam ~er egit* Jer. 50.29 (AR 762.1).

insolentia ~ae, *f.* An insolent action: *inter jactationis ~as etiam effudit haec* AM 477.1.

insolitus ~a ~um, *a.* Unaccustomed, unusual: *audivi inde clamorem ~um* AM 207.1; VR 71.4.

insono ~are ~ui, *intr.* To utter a cry, make a noise: *~uerunt jubilo* Isa. 14.7 (AC 1066.4).

insons ~ntis, *a.* Free from guilt, guiltless, blameless: *quo magis ~ntia sunt interiora, eo magis ~ns est cultus externus* AC 1182; *ne ~ntes crederentur, omnia detecta sunt* CI 462[a].1; *fit reus dum...a malo agit, et ~ns dum...a bono* VR 154.4.

insopio ~pire ~pivi ~pitum, *tr.* To put to sleep, lull: *jucundum secum habet ut ~pat* ES(M) [4750]; esp. in pf. pple. *~pitus*, falling asleep: *mox ~pitus somnium triste habui* AC 959; ES 4236.

insorbeo ~bere ~psi ~ptum, *tr.* To absorb within oneself, take in, swallow: *illa quae in athmosphaeris ...sunt homo ~bet per pulmones* VR 470.2; (fig.) *vita...persuasionum talis est ut... ~beat omne falsum* AC 798; *percepi...bonos ~bentes jucunda malorum* VR 448.2.

inspectio ~onis, *f.* **1** The action of looking at, inspection: *serpentem aeneum...a cujus ~one...sanati sunt* AR 49.8. **2** Mental contemplation: *ex continuis mentium illorum ~onibus* VR 816.

inspecto ~are ~avi ~atum, *tr.* To examine, inspect: *angeli toties ~ant malos, quoties...* AC 4533.

inspectus ~a ~um: pf. pple. of **inspicio**.

inspergo ~gere ~si ~sum, *tr.* To sprinkle in; (transf.) to mix in at intervals: *causas...de uxore mentitas ~gunt* AM 474; *quia philosophicos terminos ~serim* ES 1602; (w. dat.) *huic callo ~sa quoque sunt vera et bona* ES 863.

inspicio ~picere ~pexi ~pectum, *tr.* (*intr.*) **1** To examine visually, look at, inspect: *homo...cum ~picitur e coelo* AC 18; *ex ~pectis fibris...veritas potest constare* AC 8247; *ut adstantes ~picerent se mutuo* AM 233.2. **2** To contemplate mentally, look into: *si penitius ~picis, videbis quod omnia interioris voluntatis hominis sint amoris ejus* AE 116; *haec conjunctio penitus ~pecta* SE 46. **b** (intr. w. *in* + acc.): *cum ~picerent in illa quae ego sciebam* AC 6811.

inspirabilis ~is ~e, *a.* Capable of being imparted by inspiration: [*amor*] *inspiratus primis parentibus, et ~is Christianis* AM 112.

inspiratio ~onis, *f.* Inspiration: *~o non est dictatio, sed est influxus ex Divino* AC 9094.4; *aspiratio erat signum repraesentativum externum Divinae ~onis* VR 140; AM 79.10.

inspiratus ~us, *m.* Inspiration: *per ~um Ipsius, quod acciperent Spiritum Sanctum* ES 4048.

inspiro ~are ~avi ~atum, *intr.*, *tr.* **1** (intr., w. *in* + acc.) To breathe on or into: *quod Jehovah ~averit in nares Adami* AE 130.6; *~a in occisos hos, ut vivant* Ezek. 37.9 (AC 9642.9). **b** (tr.) to breathe in: *~avit in nares ejus spiraculum vitarum* Gen. 2.7 (AC). **2** (tr.) To impart secretly, inspire: *jucunditas illa quae ab illis mihi ~abatur* AC 8113; *Abrahamus... ~avit plura ad impediendum ea quae scriberentur* ES 2873; (w. indir. qu.) *ut... ~ent quid cogitet* CI 228. **3** (tr.) To rouse by suggestion, egg on: *~ant alios ad faciendum malum clam* ES 4681; *aura phantasiae qua ~ati sunt* AM 7.2. **4** *~atus*, endowed with an internal sense, inspired: *quod Verbum quoad minimam jotham ~atum sit* AC 1756.4; SS 1.

instans ~ntis, *neut.* A moment of time, instant: *quod omnia haec essent Deo ~ns* VR 31.3; *nisi Deus...omni ~nti faceret* VR 74.5; (esp.) *in ~nti*, in an instant: *flectunt fere in ~nti affectionem boni...in affectionem mali* AC 751.3; AM 178.2.

instantaneus ~a ~um, *a.* Accomplished in an instant, instantaneous: *judicium eorum quasi ~um erat* AC 6923; SS 63.

instanter, *adv.* Urgently, insistently: *~er rogare* AC 8582.

instantia ~ae, *f.* An instant demand, insistence: *quod ad ~as rogationis virorum se sicut victas tradiderint* AM 297.

instar, *indecl. neut.* **1** (as sb.) A likeness, image: *in omnibus...quae in spirituali mundo... ~r conjugii est* AC 7022; *non corpus, sed candidum ~r corporis* ES 3429. **2** (w. gen.) Similar (to), like: *constat...quod ~r lignorum sint* ES 3758; *per illa quae sunt acuminata ~r ensium* AC 2799.21; *per odores foedos, ~r stagni ac ~r cadaveris* ES 201; *loquela...fluens ~r lenissimae athmosphaerae* AC 1759; *ferarum ~r vagantur* ES 1782.

instauratio ~onis, *f.* The act of establishing, establishment, foundation: *de ~one Ecclesiae* AC 6643; *a prima ~one conjugiorum* AM 332.1.

instaurator ~oris, *m.* One who establishes, founder: *Ecclesiae hodiernae ~oribus, Luthero, Calvino et Melanchthone* VR 64.1; AC 7233.1.

instauro ~are ~avi ~atum, *tr.* **1** To establish, found: *nova Ecclesia, quae a Domino ~anda est* SS 10; VR 4.1. **b** to establish (a person in an office): *postquam* [*sacerdos*] *~atus est, intrepide pergit* VR 563.2. **2** To establish as a theory, propose: *qui creationem universi ...per continuas mediationes a Primo ~ant* AS 303.

insterno ~sternere ~stravi ~stratum, *tr.* To saddle (a riding animal): *et ~stravit asinum suum* Gen. 22.3 (AC).

instigo ~are ~avi ~atum, *tr.* To incite, arouse, egg on: *in...phantasiis, quae cupiditates... ~ant* ES 387; *quomodo...se... ~arant spurcis ratiociniis* ES 3453.

instillo ~are ~avi ~atum, *tr.* To allow to fall in drops, drop in or on: *dum... ~at vinum linguae* CO 51.3.

instinctus ~us, *m.* Instinct: *scientia illa dicitur connata, et vocatur ~us* AC 7750.1; *ex coeco ~u* AC 8002.2; AM 208.3.

institor ~oris, *m.* A salesman, shopkeeper: *sunt similes ~oribus in cauponis, qui vendunt statuas idolorum* VR 617.2.

instituo ~ere ~i ~tum, *tr.* **1** To set up, establish, institute (an organization, practice, etc.): *cultus Divinus ... ~ebatur super montibus* AC 8153; *quod nova Ecclesia... ~enda sit* DD 61.1; *in recordationem eorum Sabbathum ~tum est* CI 287.3; (impers. pass.) *~tum est tradere doctrinam charitatis* AC 6703. **2** To start, open (a temporary state of affairs): *tunc ~ti sunt ludi* AM 6.2; *cum iis colloquium ~tum est* ES 226.

institutio ~onis, *f.* **1** The act of setting up, establishment: *de ~one sabbathi* AC 8891.2. **2** The order so established, institution: *~o conjugii monogamici* AM 332.1; *secundum ~onem a creatione* ES 1061.

institutor ~oris, *m.* One who sets up, founder: *Eberus fuit primus ejus ~or* AC 1238.2.

institutum ~i, *neut.* **1** An aim, intention, plan: *hanc* [*Doctrinam*] *dare, hujus operis ~um est* NH 7. **2** Precept, rule: AC 1896.

insto ~are ~iti, *intr.* **1** To be imminent, be at hand, impend: *hoc tempus...vident non evenire nec ~are* AC 1850.1; *cum ~abat passio crucis* DD 13. **2** To be insistent, urge: *ex significatione 'urgere' quod sit ~are*

AC 7132; *dicebatur ei...quod non posset...sed usque ~abat* AC 5058; (w. inf.) *si usque ~at penetrare in illa* VR 31.2; (w. *ut*) *quod contumaciter ~iterint ut essent Ecclesia* AC 7041.2; (w. *quod*) *~abant, quod illi ament* AM 161.2.

instructio ~onis, *f.* The process of teaching, instruction: *pro veris...quae ad ~onem generis humani... inserviunt* AC 885.1; *post aliquam colloquutionem, ~onem et admonitionem de vita morali* AM 406.

instructivus ~a ~um, *a.* Instructive: (neut. as sb.) *loquutus quoque est cum iis ~a vitae* ES 2681.

instructor ~oris, *m.* One who teaches, teacher, instructor: *habent quendam ~orem apud se...qui eas castigat* AC 1113.

instructus ~a ~um, *a.* (compar. *~ior*, superl. *~issimus*) (in senses of vb., esp.) Well-taught, learned: *se credebant ~iores aliis* CI 404; *ex tot annorum experientia ~issimus sum de mundo spirituum* AC 59.2.

instrumentalis ~is ~e, *a.* **1** Serving as an instrument, instrumental: *visus eorum erat solum ~e quid* AC 241; *causae ~es* AC 6815. **b** (neut. as sb.) an instrument, means: *natura est modo ~e per quod* AC 7352; *~ia per quae agunt sunt vera* AC 8168. **2** (of music) Performed by instruments: *ex audita musica ~i* ES 2112.

instrumentum ~i, *neut.* **1** A tool, instrument, means: *dicitur...de ~o quod agat, moveat aut feriat* CI 432; [*artifex*] *emit ~a* VI 39. **2** A musical instrument: *tympanum non est ~um chordaceum* AC 8337.3; *~is non concordibus* ES 887.

instruo ~ere ~xi ~ctum, *tr.* **1** To teach, instruct: *qui ita...credunt, in altera vita ~untur illico* AC 716.3; (w. *in* + abl.) *cum ~itur in veris* AC 1101; (w. *quod*) *~ebar ab angelis quod essent spiritus ex tellure Martis* AC 7745; (w. indir. qu.) *sensus internus ~it quid... intelligitur* AC 8281.2. **2** (w. abl.) To equip or provide (with): *haec significant quod Dominus ~xerit eos bono spirituali* AC 292; (esp. in pf. pple.) *visi pileo ~cti acuto* AC 546; *candelabrum ~ctum septem calamis* AM 20.1. **3** To draw up in military formation (in quot. fig.): *ipsa vera et ipsa falsa ~cta ad pugnas* AC 8215.1. **4** To order, arrange: *discit ex illis...quomodo ~ere debeat vitam* AC 3310.3.

insudo ~are ~avi ~atum, *intr.* (w. dat.) To sweat (over); (transf.) to labour hard, toil (at): *qui linguis ac grammaticalibus multum ~arunt* ES 1952.

insuetus ~a ~um, *a.* Unaccustomed, unwonted: *anxietate ~a prius affectae sunt* [*meae cogitationes*] ES 969.

insufficiens ~ntis, *a.* Insufficient: *hoc medium ~ns fuit* ES 4394.

insufflatio ~onis, *f.* The act of secretly suggesting, inspiring: *per pravarum affectionum ~ones* AC 8593.2; ES 3110.

insufflo ~are ~avi ~atum, *tr.* **1** To introduce by blowing, blow in: *serpentem... ~antem venenum* AM 521.6; (fig.) *nec possibile fuit ~are aliam vitam* DP 338.7. **2** To suggest secretly, inspire: *separationem quasi ~antibus quibusdam* ES 3110; ES 4041. **3** To make proud, puff up (in quot. absol.): *visus sibi quod solus gubernaret universum, nam in tantum amor sui ~at* AC 1506.

insugo ~gere ~xi ~ctum, *tr.* To suck in: *nutritioni ejus* [sc. *arboris*] *ex variis succis et essentiis... ~ctis* SS(P) 53 (= 19.5).

insula ~ae, *f.* An island: *quidam...in ~a seu scopulo erant* ES 243; *orbem...Asiaticum cum ~is circum* AM 342.3; (app. in pl.) the East Indies: *populos in ~is natos* SS 116.1; cf. SS 117.

insulanus ~a ~um, *a.* Living in islands: *aves sylvestres, seu ~ae* 4IB s.v. 'Iim'.

insulcatus ~a ~um, *a.* Furrowed: *pars* [sc. *faciei*] *foede ~a cum foedo vulnere* ES(M) [4732.2].

insulsus ~a ~um, *a.* Lacking in serious content, vapid: *absque hoc timore est amor ~us et cutaneus* DP 140; *redegit omnia illa quae dicta sunt in ~am farraginem* IM 12; ES 4054.

insultatio ~onis, *f.* Aggressive behaviour: ES 4634.

insulto ~are ~avi, *intr.* To behave aggressively: *~arunt absque ulla causa, sed non ita...ut...damnum inferre vellent corpori, sed ~abant verbis* ES 4634; *si quis inimicum ~antem repellit* VR 407.

insultus ~us, *m.* Assault, aggression, attack: *murus est verum quod ab ~u falsorum...tutatur* CI 73; *regnum...tutum a similium ~u reddit* VR 117.

insum inesse infui, *intr.* To be present or contained within: *idem sanctum Divinum intus inerat* AC 10453.4; (w. dat.) *uni ideae insunt perplura* AC 6987.2; (w. *in* + abl.) *quia in vero ex bono nihil falsi inesset* AC 7971.

insumo ~ere ~(p)si ~(p)tum, *tr.* To spend upon: *quodcunque insuper ~seris* Luke 10.35 (AE 444.14).

insuo ~ere ~i ~tum, *tr.* To sew in: *vestibus...quibus aurum et argentum eorum ~tum esset* ES 471.

insuper, *adv.* In addition, besides: *Africani...et quoque Asiatici...et ~r Judaei* VR 9.2; AC 6697.

insurgo ~gere ~rexi, *intr.* **1** To rise up, ascend:

~gebant et intendebant lora super jubis equorum AM 103.1; *apparet spiritibus quod vincent, et tunc ~gunt* AC 6657.2. **2** To take hostile action, rise up: *ut non hiscant ~gere contra bonos* AC 7788; *post Apostolorum tempora ~rexerunt plures alii* [*haeretici*] VR 378.2; (masc. of pres. pple. as sb.) *persequutores, ~gentes* AE 734.10.

insurrectio ~onis, *f.* An uprising, insurrection: *si non reageret bonum contra malum, ac ~onem ejus jugiter coerceret* CI 592; FI 67.

insusurro ~are ~avi ~atum, *tr.* To whisper to: *quaedam* [*simulachra*] *fovebant gremiis...ac ~abant petitiones* CO 43.

intamino ~are ~avi ~atum, *tr.* To pollute, defile: *ut ...conjugiale amoris ~ent* AM 304.2.

integer ~gra ~grum, *a.* **1** Whole, complete, total: *~ger status a principio ad finem* AC 7715; *per ~gram horam* ES 2289; *hoc foret ~gri operis* 'this would take up a whole book' VR 115.1. **2** Intact, unblemished, whole: *ex significatione '~grae' quod sit absque naevis, ita immaculata* AC 7837; *illa... ~grae chartae* [i.e., a clean sheet of paper] *mandabant* VR 161.1. **3** Upright, honest: *qui ambulat ~ger et facit justitiam* Ps. 15.2 (VI 84.1).

intego ~gere ~xi ~ctum, *tr.* To cover over, overlay: *Divinum... ~gitur per talia, quae accommodata sunt perceptionibus angelorum et hominum* VR 6.2; AC 9515.

integralis ~is ~e, *a.* Of or relating to the whole: *partes ~es* ES 2216.

integratio ~onis, *f.* The process of making whole, development: *pro...refocillatione sensualium corporis, et status eorum ~one* VR 434.1; AM 187.

integre, *adv.* With wholeness, fully, unimpairedly, perfectly: *est jactura visus et tamen oculus apparet sicut ~e videns* VR 346.2.

integritas ~atis, *f.* **1** The quality of being whole or unimpaired, wholeness, soundness: *a vola pedis usque ad caput non in eo ~as* Isa. 1.6 (AC 8364.4); *qualis ille amor est in ipsa sua essentia et ~ate* AM 57. **2** Moral uprightness, integrity: *per sinceritatem...intelligitur ~as, justitia, fidelitas et rectitudo* VI 83; SS 44.3.

integro ~are ~avi ~atum, *tr.* To make whole, develop: *apud utrosque* [sc. *viros et faeminas*]... *~atur forma externa quae est corporis* AM 187; CO 29.2.

integumentum ~i, *neut.* **1** (anat.) The covering of the body or an organ, integument: *corpus humanum absque ~is quae vocantur cutes* SS 33; *provinciam durae matris, quae est ~um...cerebri* AC 4046.1. **2** Any outer covering, clothing: *Divinum caeleste, spirituale et naturale, quae non aliud sunt quam ~a Dei* VR 6.1; AC 6275.2.

intellectualis ~is ~e, *a.* **1** Relating to the faculty of understanding, intellectual: *vita ~is* AC 7021.1; *fides hominis mali est fides ~is, cui nihil boni ex voluntate inest* VI 46; (often dist. from **voluntarius**) *solum quoad partem ~em, non autem quoad partem voluntariam* AC 6854.2; AC 863; AC 7021.1; (neut. sg. and pl. as sb.) the part or parts of man relating to the intellect: *lux caeli ...hominis ~e, quod vocatur rationale, illuminat* SS 41; *sunt tres gradus ~ium in homine* AC 657. **2** Perceived or apprehensible by means of the understanding, intellectual: *~e verum* AC 1495.1; *rationes ~es* AC 7130; (neut. as sb.) that which is so apprehensible: *~e Ecclesiae est omne ex doctrina boni et veri e Verbo* AR 360.2; *de ~i seu vero fidei* AC 863. **3** (of persons) Able to understand, thinking, intelligent: *spiritus etiam satis ~es usque non persuaderi possunt* ES 891[a]; *hypocritae...qui extus loquuntur bene, et apparent sicut ~es* ES(M) 4654.

intellectualiter, *adv.* With the use of the understanding, intellectually: *ut ea ~er comprehendantur* SS 30.

intellectus ~us, *m.* **1** The process of understanding, comprehension: *quod 'equus albus' sit ~us Verbi* AC 2761.1; *ignoti... ~us* ES 2420. **2** The ability to understand, power of comprehension: *misericordia Domini...infinite transcendit omnem ~um hominis* AC 588.1; *cogita de hoc etiam ex aliquo ~u* DP 114.3; CI 128. **3** The faculty of understanding, intellect: *~us hominis potest elevari in lucem caeli* VI 15; *ponunt ~um sub obedientia hujus fidei* FI 39; (esp. dist. from **voluntas**) *~us est audire Verbum, et voluntatis est facere* AC 44; AC 6717.2; SS 3.2. **4** That which is to be understood, a meaning: *quod spiritualis ~us sit in omnibus...quae Dominus loquutus est* AM 41.3.

intelligens ~ntis, *a.* (compar. *~ntior*, superl. *~ntissimus*) **1** Possessing intelligence, intelligent: *tales ...credunt se ~ntissimos omnium esse* AC 8313.4; *quod omnia...se referant ad bonum et verum, ab omni homine ~nte agnoscitur* AM 60; (masc. as sb.) *haec ~nti sint dicta* AC 7270.4; AC 10711. **2** Characterized by intelligence: *sunt quasi in statu seu...aura ~ntiori* ES 1840.

intelligenter, *adv.* With the use of intelligence, intelligently: *ut simplices illud simpliciter possint intelligere, et intelligentes ~er* SS 91.

intelligentia ~ae, *f.* The ability to understand, intelligence: *'hortus'...significat ~am seu intellectum veri* AC 305; *cum discrimine, ita cum ~a* AC 6704; *qualis est homini fides...talis est ei ~a* FI 29.

intelligere, *indecl. neut.* (inf. of **intelligo**) = **intelligentia**: *inde...est posse, velle, et ~ere illorum* VR 74.3.

intelligibilis ~is ~e, *a.* (compar. *~ior*) Capable of being understood, intelligible: *ideas aliis non ~es* AC 7745; *haec loquela mihi ~ior priore erat* AC 8023.

intelligo ~ligere ~lexi ~lectum, *tr.* **1** To grasp by means of the understanding, understand: *quod ~ligat verum et velit bonum* AC 7929; *non sensum internum ...Verbi ~lexerunt* AE 1. **b** (w. *quod*): *~lexerunt...quod non dixisset ut caverent a fermento panis* AC 7906.1. **c** (w. indir. qu.): *non ~ligebant quid innocentia* AC 7073. **2** To understand the words of (a language): *loquelam eorum ~lexi* AC 7359. **3** To understand (words in a specified manner), take: *a sordibus spiritualiter ~lectis* AC 6730; *quomodo haec ~ligenda sunt, constare potest* AC 7270.2. **4** To interpret as meaning, understand (as): *pro quod honorandi parentes ~ligunt quod colendus Dominus* AC 7089.1; (esp. pass.) to be meant: *dicitur doctrina...ac ~ligitur doctrina pro Nova Ecclesia, qua...instauranda est* DD praef.; (w. *per*) *per Verbum ibi ~ligitur Dominus* SS 2.3; *hoc per credere in Ipsum ~ligitur* VR 2.3.

intemperantia ~ae, *f.* Lack of restraint, intemperateness: *incuria infantum, ~a, luxuria, nimia prodigalitas* AM 252; *ex ~a variorum vitiorum* ES 4592; *interiora...plena sunt rapina et ~a* Matt. 23.25 (VI 30.1).

intempestive, *adv.* At the wrong time, unseasonably: *ut ~e misericordes evadant* ES 3596.

intempestivus ~a ~um, *a.* Untimely, unseasonable: *~a misericordia* ES 3593.

intempestus ~a ~um, *a.* Stormy, violent: *motus ~i naturalis hominis sedantur a Domino* AE 514.22.

intendo ~dere ~di ~tum, *tr.* **1** To stretch out, extend: *insurgebant et ~debant lora super jubis equorum* AM 103.1. **b** to extend in time, stretch out, prolong: *si in infinitum possent dolores...augere et ~dere* AC 695. **2** (w. dat.) To direct (against), aim (at): *malum ~dunt proximo* AC 6655. **3** To direct (the mind, thought, attention, etc., in a specified direction): (w. *ad*) *~debant mentes ad indagandum...causas* VR 48.9; (w. indir. qu.) *dum mentem ~di, quid lux intellectualis* ES 564. **4** To direct one's mind to, attend to, aim at: *in singulis quae homo ~dit et cogitat* AC 6692.2; *quia Deus... ~dit unum finem* VR 13.1; (pass.) *unio...quae per haec verba Abrami ~ditur* AC 1577.4. **5** (intr.) To form an intention: *spiritus est qui cogitat et ~dit* AE 121; to direct one's thoughts (in a specified direction): (w. dat.) *cogitatio...dum alicui rei ~dit* AC 362; *dum spiritus aliquis ~dit gressui alicujus equi* ES 1770; (w. adv.) *illuc quo homo ~dit* CI 532.1. **b** (w. inf.) to intend (to): *quod ~derent destruere* AC 6679; (of things) to intend (to): *instar ensis qui ~dit caput intrare* ES(M) 4594. **c** (w. indir. qu.) to seek: *oculi quasi ~dunt... quomodo nocere possint* ES 957.

intenebro ~are ~avi ~atum, *tr.* To make dark, darken: *quo plus lux coeli ~atur* AC 6971.2.

intense, *adv.* (compar. *~ius*, superl. *~issime*) With great effort or concentration, intently, hard: *cum ibi cogitatur de aliquo ~e, sistitur is praesens* AC 6893; *~ius oravit* Luke 22.44 (AC 1573.5); *Deus... ~issime ac intime ardet amore* ES 300.

intensio ~onis, *f.* Concentration (of the mind): *~o animi* AM 207.3; *omnis qui in ~one mentis cogitat, potest clare videre* DP 4.2; intensity: *sunt perplures gradus jucunditatum...tam quoad differentias, quam ~onem* ES 428.

intensus ~a ~um, *a.* (compar. *~ior*, superl. *~issimus*) In a high degree, strong, intense: *talis lux, et adhuc ~ior* AC 1117; *in statu ~i amoris* AE 278.8; *in ~um frigus* CI 572; *~is oculis*, with intense visual effort, with deep scrutiny: *pictas ibi irides ~is oculis intuemur* AM 76.7.

intente, *adv.* (compar. *~ius*) = **intense**: *tunc potui lustrare ~ius* AM 42.4; AC 10329.2.

intentio ~onis, *f.* The direction of the mind towards a specified aim, intention: *in singularissimis ejus conatus et ~onis seu voluntatis* AC 1040.2; *~o fuit ad illa* AC 3199; *effectuationes ab ~onibus* AM 190; (w. gen.) *subjugationis ~o* AC 6670; *cum plena ~one faciendi* AC 7119.

intento ~are ~avi ~atum, *tr., intr.* **1** (tr.) To direct (against): *quod illi...sibi mutuo mala multa ~ent* AC 5061. **2** (intr., w. inf.) To aim, attempt (to): *~ant omni modo perdere illum* AC 6724.2.

intentus ~a ~um, *a.* (superl. *~issimus*) (of eyes) Keenly fixed, intent: *~issimos oculos habent, et illico ea capiunt seu rapiunt ad primum nutum* ES 1768.

inter, *prep. w. acc.* **1** In the intervening space of, between: *altera urbs est ~r Gehennam et stagnum* ES 751; *lucus ~r cujus arbores humus...formabat... theatrum* VR 48.1; *ab ~r*, from between: *quatuor currus exeuntes ab ~r duos montes aeris* Zech. 6.1 (SS 12.2). **2** In the intervening time of, between: *aetatis ~r pueritiam et infantiam* AC 1616.5; *~r loquendum cum angelis* VR 12.1; (repeated) *~r judicium a Domino... factum et ~r judicium quod nunc factum* UJ(P) 133; *~r hominem et ~r bestiam* VI 15. **3** In the surroundings of, among: *~r Christianos vivunt* AC 408; *nec viverent nisi ~r feras sylvae* ES 3765; *~r jactationis insolentias etiam effudit haec* AM 477.1. **4** Belonging with, out of, in (a group): *non ~r illa sunt quae saepe memorantur* AC 1234; *vix quinque ~r centum...hoc norunt* VR 98.1. **5** Between (members of a group, opposites, etc.): *conjugium ~r fidem et amorem* AC 476; *consilium ~r se ineunt* AC 6681; *fluctuationes ~r verum et falsum* AC 847.1.

intercalaris ~is ~e, *a.* Inserted in a regular sequence, intercalated: *vix in die intercedit horula ~is* AM 293.3.

intercapedo ~inis, *f.* A dividing void, gap: *inter nos et illos erat hians ~o, quae non transiri potuit* VR 159.2.

intercedo ~dere ~ssi, *intr.* **1** To be between (points in space or time), intervene: *nullo ~dente spatio aut tempore* AC 1382; *a quibus* [*temporibus*] *~sserunt aliquot millia annorum* CI 415; *equites ~dentes desuper inter bina illa inferna* ES [4632] ½. **2** (of connections or differences) To exist between: *quod non aliud foedus ~dere possit inter Dominum et hominem* AC 665; *tanta similitudo ~dit inter cor et charitatem* FI 19.2; *cum tamen multa ~dit differentia* AC 85.1; *adeo ut nullum ~dat discrimen* ES 621. **3** To make intercession, plead: *quod salventur illi pro quibus ~dit* AE 328.3; AC 7946.

interceptio ~onis, *f.* A breaking of continuity, interruption: *per successivas ~ones et occlusiones interiorum mentis* AM 509.

intercessio ~onis, *f.* Intercession, pleading: *Deum Patrem credunt per ~onem Filii commoveri* CI 526.1; AC 7379.

intercessor ~oris, *m.* One who intercedes: *quod absque ~ore Deo nusquam salvari possint* ES 1449; ES 1601.

intercipio ~cipere ~cepi ~ceptum, *tr.* To interrupt, cut off, break (a connection): *haec communicatio ~cipitur* AC 8349; to cut off the supply of: *quod caelestes nuptiales ludi...plus et plus ~cepti cessent* AM 183.8; *si non a Domino ~ciperetur sensatio...foret cruciatus ineffabilis* ES 661.

intercludo ~dere ~si ~sum, *tr.* To block (a path): *persuasiones falsi...~debant viam pro reliquiis ne operari possent* AC 660; to block the way to, cut off: *quod haec sedes ~di possit* AM 466.2; to prevent: (impers. pass.) *~sum ne loquerentur* ES 2987.

interclusio ~onis, *f.* A cutting off, blocking: *per apparentem ~onem interiorum mentis et sic communicationis cum coelo* NH 196; *cum amplius non ~o et interceptio, influit bonum* AC 3603.1.

interdico ~cere ~xi ~ctum, *tr.* (w. dat.) To forbid: *utrique...~citur scortatio promiscua* AM 54; (impers. pass.) *dicere illis...mihi ~ctum erat* AC 1880.2; (w. *ut*) *caetera ~citur ut scribam* ES 420.

interdictio ~onis, *f.* A forbidding of (some activity), a prohibition: AC 10362.2.

interdiu, *adv.* During the daytime, by day: *supra illud fuit nubes ~u, et ignis noctu* VI 55.2; ES 1450.

interea, *adv.* In the intervening period, in the meanwhile, meantime: *nec prius potuerunt elevari in coelum, quapropter ~a tenebantur in terra inferiore* AC 6854.2; *quod homo non vivat homo nisi quam die ultimi judicii, et quod ~a sit anima absque corpore* AM 182.5.

intereo ~rire ~rii, *intr.* **1** (of living creatures) To die, perish: *non conveniens est prophetam ~rire extra Hierosolymam* Luke 13.33 (DD 15.3). **2** (of other things) To be destroyed, pass away: *quod novum coelum et nova terra creanda,...ac ita quod omnia ~ritura* AC 1850.1

interest: see **intersum**.

interficio ~ficere ~feci ~fectum, *tr.* To kill: *~fecit Jehovah omne primogenitum in terra Aegypti* Exod. 13.15 (AC); *de Goliatho...a Davide ~fecto* FI 52.

interim, *adv.* For the time being, for the present: *~m alii...adhuc libertate fruuntur* ES 218; *~m hic observandum est* 3AD 4467.

interimo ~rimere ~remi ~rem(p)tum, *tr.* To put to death, kill: *projiciunt homines...in aquas, ac eo modo ~rimunt* AC 7248; AM 481.

interior ~oris, *a.* see also **interius**[1]. **1** Of the inside, inner, interior: *cum totum cerebrum sit organicum sensuum ~orum* AC 444. **2** Not externally visible or apparent, interior: *os...correspondet loquelae ~ori, quae est cogitationis* AC 6987.1; *in sensu proxime ~ore* AC 65. **3** (of persons) More concerned with underlying truth, interior: *~or homo est medius inter internum et externum...~or homo est qui dicitur rationalis homo* AC 1702.2; *idcirco ~ores homines fuerunt, et quia ~ores, fuerunt sapientiores* AC 6629; (of angels) *angeli qui regnum coeleste constituunt...vocantur angeli ~ores* CI 22. **4** Typical of such persons, interior: *elevationem ad ~orem et magis spiritualem vitam* AC 7013; *non in veris ~oribus sunt* AC 6775.

interiora: see **interius**[1].

interitus ~us, *m.* Death: *de ~u Aegyptiorum* AC 7704; destruction: *de ~u coeli et terrae* AE 304.3.

interius[1] ~oris, *neut.* (pl. *~ora ~orum*) **1** The inward part, interior, inside: *purgatis exterius poculi et patinae, ~ora vero plena sunt rapina...purga prius ~us poculi* Matt. 23.25, 26 (VI 30.1); *comparari potest ~oribus illorum fructuum* VR 109.3. **2** The hidden or invisible part, interior: *cum per microscopium eadem* [sc. *minora naturae*] *spectantur, sistuntur videnda ~ora* AC 1869.2; *~ora Verbi scire* AC 908.3. **3** (usu.

pl.) The interior parts of the human mind or spirit: *~ora mentis et spiritus mei aperuit [Dominus]* AM 1; *sunt... apud unumquemvis hominem ~ora et exteriora* AC 1029; (sg.) *quod sonus cantus illarum se sicut inspiret et animet ex ~ori* AM 17.2.

interius[2], *adv.* Inwardly, interiorly: *Verbum ~us est spirituale et caeleste* SS 8; *qui ~us cogitat* CI 576; *ut ~us mali separarentur [separentur* Worcester] *ab ~us bonis* AE 258.

interjicio ~jicere ~jeci ~jectum, *tr.* To interpose, insert: *post epulas ludi ac choreae... ~jectis cantibus odarum* AM 3.3; *cum loquebatur, etiam ~jiciebat aliquid terroris* AC 8021.

interloquor ~i ~utus sum, *intr.* To interpose a remark, interject: *spiritus...quandoque ~ebatur... monens ut...modeste agerem* AC 8027; ES 1654.

intermedians ~ntis, *a.* Intermediate: *quaeritur modus ~ns* AM 459.1; (neut. as sb.) *quod Humanum sit ~ns* IM 19.

intermediatio ~onis, *f.* The act of mediating, mediation: *cum ~one quam 'Moscheh' nunc repraesentat* AC 9419.2.

intermedie, *adv.* Intermediately: *intra societatem aut extra aut ~e* ES 2341.

intermedius ~a ~um, *a.* **1** Situated midway between first and last, intervening, intermediate: (in space) *apparet sicut mons ~us* AC 311; (in time) *qualis fuit [Ecclesia Jared dicta] constare potest ab Ecclesia...quae praecedit, et ab Ecclesia...quae sequitur, quarum ~a est* AC 514; (in sequence) *primum arboris est fructus...et ultimum ejus est fructus...ac ~a ejus sunt rami seu folia* AC 7690. **2** Acting as intermediary: *loquebantur mecum sed per spiritus ~os* AC 6923.

intermeo ~are ~avi, *intr.* To pass between, go through: *si aëri non daretur copia ~andi* VR 524.3.

interminate, *adv.* Without limits, indeterminately: *si quis absque idea Divini Hominis cogitat de Ipso Divino, cogitat ~e* AC 8705.4.

interminatus ~a ~um, *a.* Having no limits, unbounded, indeterminate: *internum absque externo foret ~um quoddam* AC 1083.3.

interminor ~ari ~atus sum, *intr.* To utter threats meantime: *similis apparuit prope me... ~atus, si quisquam adesset, quem sic torqueret* ES 726.

intermisceo ~scere ~scui ~xtum, *tr.* To mix among, intermingle: *ubicunque datur occasio, se ~scent [Judaei]* ES 2260; *deserta...ex nuda glarea, ~xtis paludibus* VR 45.2.

intermissio ~onis, *f.* The periodic remission of debts: *proclamata ~o Jehovae* Deut. 15.2 (AC 2360.2).

intermitto ~mittere ~misi ~missum, *tr.* (*intr.*) **1** To leave off, intermit: *si tentationes ~mitterentur* AC 8179.3; *illico ac donum hoc ~mittitur* ES 662. **b** to leave (land) untilled: *et septimo [anno] ~mittes eam* [sc. *terram*] Exod. 23.11 (AC). **2** (intr.): *mirabar...quod non ~mittere possent* ES 217; (w. inf.) *si similia facere non ~mitterent* AC 7810.

intermixtim, *adv.* In an intermingled way: *non conseres vineam tuam ~im, non arabis bove et asino simul, non indues vestem mixtam lana et lino simul* Deut. 22.9 (AC 10669.5).

intermixtus ~a ~um: pf. pple. of **intermisceo**.

interne, *adv.* Inwardly: *externa forma repraesentant angelos, sed ~e [interna* Tafel] *sunt lupi* ES 2602.

internecinus ~a ~um, *a.* (of hatred or evil) Murderous, deadly: *tale ~um odium regnat in mundo spirituum* AC 59.2; CI 249; *quod duo propria illa sint mala ~a viro* AM 194.2.

internecio ~onis, *f.* Murder, slaughter: *cum diaboli intendunt malum et ~onem hominis, societatis, generis humani* ES 802; destruction: *ne fines oppositi...creationis opus labefactent usque ad ~onem* CN De Deo vii[a].14.

internodium ~i, *neut.* A joint (in a limb): *brachia ...vibrantur sicut expertia virium in ~is* CI 3.

internosco ~noscere ~novi ~notum, *tr.* To recognize as distinct, know apart, distinguish: *unaquaevis societas...spirituum ~nosci potest a loquela* AC 1758; CI 2; ES 2100.

internum ~i, *neut.* **1** The inward part, interior: *'purgare ~um poculi'* SS 40.2; *ea quae crescunt ab ~o incipiunt* ES 252. **2** The spiritual part of a person, soul, internal: *~um hominis est ex quo homo est homo* AC 1999.3; *Divinum Bonum quod est amor...fuit ~um Domini* AC 2063.2. **3** (esp. pl.) The things of the spirit, internals: *delectabantur solum ~is* AC 54; *in ~is est sanctum* AC 1327.3; *in externis fuerunt absque ~is* AC 4459.2; (sg.) *quod illis modo naturale seu externum fidei esset, et non spirituale seu ~um ejus* VI 49.

internuntius ~a ~um, *a.* Serving as messenger, intermediary: *per voces ~as angelorum* 3AD 356; (masc. as sb.) *quod...Jehovah loquatur per ~um ad populum* AC 8778.2.

internus ~a ~um, *a.* **1** Not outwardly perceptible, internal: *qui ad ~am quandam faciei provinciam pertinent* AC 1525; *respondent tono ~o paene tacito* VR 35.1. **2** Of or relating to the spirit or interior of persons, internal: *vitam ~am* AC 6832.10; *tam externus quam ~us motus systolicus* SA 100 (= vii.3.[2]); *status ~i Ecclesiae* AC 6645.1; *cognitiones rerum ~arum* AC 7245[a]; *quod causae frigorum...sint plures, quaedam ~ae, quaedam externae* AM 234. **b** *sensus ~us*, the internal sense (of the Word): *in litera, quae absque sensu ~o mortua est* AC 755.5; *revelatus mihi est a Domino sensus ~us Verbi* SS 4. **3** *~us homo*, a person regarded as his spirit: *homo qui...externus est et ~us... ~us homo est ejus anima* AC 3. **4** (of faculties or actions) Operating in the mind, internal, inward: *loquutus...tam clara voce, sed ~a, sicut cum amicis in mundo* AC 448.1; *respirationem habuit ~am* AC 607.2; *perceptio ~a* AC 6640.2; *visum... ~um, qui est mentis* CI 266.1. **5** Characterized by attention to spiritual matters, internally guided: *~i homines, hoc est, qui conscientiam habent* AC 2842.9; *~ae Ecclesiae homo* AC 6704; (dist. from **interior**) *spiritus constituunt externum hominem, spiritus angelici interiorem, angeli ~um* AC 911.2; AC 1799.2.

interpolo ~are ~avi ~atum, *tr.* To interrupt: *voluerunt Armageddoni passim ~are sermonem nostrum* VR 113.9; *nec ~antur [cogitationes] ab aliquibus curis* CI 266.3; (absol.) *nunc quia incepi loqui...dixi, ~abo, si licet, adhuc aliqua interrogatione* VR 137.9.

interpono ~nere ~sui ~situm, *tr.* To place between, insert: *quod columna illa ~neret se inter castra Israelis et inter castra Aegyptiorum* AC 7989; *inde est quod in Verbo toties ~natur vocula 'et'* CI 241; *per ~sitam nubem* VR 780.

interpositio ~onis, *f.* The placing between, insertion, interposition: *obscurationes illorum* [sc. *solis et lunae*] *ex ~onibus, quae vocantur eclipses* DP 190.1; CI 241.

interpres ~etis, *m.* One who interprets or translates: *dictum mihi ab ~ete angelico* ES 3785; AE 388.22; *~etes 'Schaddai' reddunt 'omnipotentem'* AC 1992.5.

interpretatio ~onis, *f.* An explanation in other terms, interpretation: *nisi [vera] falsificentur, quod fit per ~ones sinistras* AC 8149; *~ones Verbi* AM 44.10; (of dreams) Gen. 40.5 (AC).

interpretator ~oris, *m.* An interpreter (of dreams): *et ~or nullus illi* Gen. 40.8 (AC).

interpretor ~ari ~atus sum, *tr.* To explain in other terms, interpret: *~atus est...quae ad Ipsum pertinerent* Luke 24.27 (AC 6752.6); (w. manner specified) *quod... talia ~entur in bonum* AC 975; *ex factis...quae...sinistre ~abatur* AC 7803; *sensum...aliter ~ando* DD 50.2.

interpunctio ~onis, *f.* Punctuation: *continuant gyrum absque ~onis cujusdam nota* ES 579.

interrogatio ~onis, *f.* A question: *ad ~onem quid conjugiale illud, dixit...* AM 80.2; *ex ~one Pilati, quid est veritas* AE 31.3.

interrogativus ~a ~um, *a.* Used to form a question, interrogative: *quapropter...est vox ~a* AC 5754.

interrogo ~are ~avi ~atum, *intr., tr.* **1** (intr.) To put a question, ask: *ut...non...~antibus opposita objicerent* AC 7074; (w. indir. qu.) *responsum ad discipulos Johannis, ~antis num Ille esset qui venturus* SS 17.4; (w. internal acc.) *~abat plura* 'he put many questions' AC 7744. **2** (tr.) To question, ask (a person): *~avi illum de statu suo* AC 7744; *~a doctores Ecclesiae* DP 262.3; (w. indir. qu.) *~atus est num esset rex* AE 27.4.

interrumpo ~rumpere ~rupi ~ruptum, *tr.* To break into, interrupt: *communicatio... ~rumperetur et nulla fieret* AC 7893; *inclinatio...non ~rupta* VR 521.3; ES 357.

interruptio ~onis, *f.* A break in continuity, interruption: *quod multiplicatio illa a creatione mundi absque ~one huc usque perstiterit* VR 32.3; AC 7933.3.

intersero ~ere ~ui ~tum, *tr.* To insert between, intersperse: *si ~erentur illis quae in textu Verbi* AC 71; *consortio aliorum ~untur* ES 484.

interspersus ~a ~um, *a.* (pf. pple. of **interspergo***) Scattered between, interspersed: *hic et ibi erant ~a conchilia nitentia* VR 35.2; *loquebantur varia amabilia... ~is facetiis* AM 5.1.

interstinguo ~guere ~xi ~ctum, *tr.* To tell apart, distinguish: *ex quodam differenti murmuratione... ~guuntur* ES 187.

interstitialis ~is ~e, *a.* Forming a gap or interval: *per ideas adhuc minus discretas, adeo ut vix aliquid ~e perciperetur* AC 8023; *per filum longum ~e* ES 3379.

interstitiolum ~i, *neut.* A small interval of time, slight respite: *erat adactio in reciprocas vibrationes ...semper cum renisu ejus in quovis ~o et momento* ES 1073.

interstitium ~i, *neut.* **1** An interval of space, gap: *cum ad magnum illud ~um venerunt* AC 9583; *sic evacuatur omne ~um quod est a cogitatione ad os* VR 110.7. **2** An interval of time, respite: *usque sua ~a habent* AC 825; *~um inter duos illos status* AM 306.

intersum ~resse ~rfui, *intr.* **1** To be between, be present: *tunc fere nihil corporis ~rerat* AC 1883; *quando mutuus amor ~resset in vita corporis* ES 290; (w. dat.) to be among: *datum ~resse spiritibus* AC 816. **2** (impers.) It is of interest, it is important: (w. inf.) *~rest scire qualis forma coeli est* CI 201; (w. *ut*) *~rest ut sciatur* AM 42.1; (w. dat.) *nihil plus ~rest homini quam scire quid verum* AC 794.2; *prudentiae Christianae ~rest bene* *scrutari* AC 6704; (w. gen. of person) *nisi eorum ~resse pro lucris...conscientia parum...operatur hodie* ES 2801.

intertextus ~a ~um, *a.* (pf. pple. of **intertexo***) Woven in or among: *in togis...quibus ~i erant flores* AM 15; AM 137.7; *in amictu coeruleo...cum ~is miculis auri* AC 7801.

interturbo ~are ~avi ~atum, *tr.* To introduce a disturbance into, upset: *~ant quietem* ES 4294; (absol.) *quod falsitates adhuc ~arent* AC 864.

intervallum ~i, *neut.* **1** An intervening space, interval: *principium...distabat ab arbore...insigni ~o* AM 13.2. **2** An intervening period of time, interval: *in minimis ~is* AC 482.1; *per ~a*, at intervals: CI 249.

intervenio ~nire ~ni, *intr.* To come between, intervene: *si apud illos* [sc. *angelos*] *~nit idea ex tempore et spatio* AC 8918.1; *dum...alia ~niunt, adhuc ea recusant* ES 1125.

intervolvo ~vere ~vi ~utum, *tr.* To rotate between: *unus iste iterum ~ebatur* ES 1763.

intestina ~orum, *neut. pl.* The intestines: AM 329.1; AC 7859.

intestinalis ~is ~e, *a.* Of or relating to the intestines: *~ia faeda* AC 5559; *formae ~es conglutinatae* ES 2762.

intestinus ~a ~um, *a.* **1** Contained within, internal: [*statuae*] *accensae igne ~o diffluebant* VR 110.8; *dolorem...sicut parturientis, seu ~um* ES 487; *~us amor* AM 281.1; *ex ~a vecordia* AM 339.3. **b** of the intestines: *~um colon* AC 5393.1; ES 1062. **2** (of hatred, conflicts, etc.) Confined within a particular group, internal, civil: *non curantes...sive odia ~a foveant* AC 1844; *in bellis ~is* AC 7046.1; *~ae pugnae contra omne spirituale* AM 240.

intexo ~ere ~ui ~tum, *tr.* To weave in: *ex...lino, cui ~ta erant fila ex argento* AM 42.3; (fig.) *loco signi Christi, cujus nomen tamen aureis staminibus in Baptismo ~tum est* VR 683.1.

intime, *adv.* (compar. *~ius*) In an inward manner, intimately, deeply: *plura ~e recondita habent* AC 155.1; *~e in omnibus mediis est finis* VR 13.3; *facies ejus ~e sicut radiabat* AM 42.3; *non praeparati ~ius intrare* ES 307; AC 202.

intimum ~i, *neut.* **1** The inmost part: *aurum quod ab ~o aurum* VI 10. **2** The most spiritual part: *quod ad intimiora et ~a Verbi Domini attinet...* ES 2462; *in ~is ejus non aliud est quam Deus* VR 6.1.

intimus ~a ~um, *a.* (compar. *~ior*) **1** Inmost: *communicationem habet cum interiore et ~o coelo* AC 1399; *in ~o seu tertio coelo* AC 6701; (of the senses of the Word) *in sensu ~o, qui etiam est sensus universalis* AC 99. **2** (of man or his faculties) Inwardly operating or disposed: *reliquiae interioris et ~ioris hominis* ES 1504; *aperitur visus ~us* VR 66; *memoria ~ior* ES 295; *ex affectione ~a* AC 6823. (n.b. In ES *~ior* is used to denote a degree intermediate between *interior* and *intimus*.)

intingo ~gere ~xi ~ctum, *tr.* To immerse (in a liquid), dip: *~get sacerdos digitum suum in sanguine* Lev. 4.6 (AC 716.3); *quod stragulam ~xerit aquis* ES 2791.

intitulatio ~onis, *f.* The giving of a heading, titling: *sub ~one Voluptates Insaniae* AM 138.

intolerabilis ~is ~e, *a.* (compar. *~ior*) That cannot be borne, intolerable: *quod durius et ~ius est* DP 294.3.

intolerantia ~ae, *f.* Lack of tolerance, impatience: AM 473.

intono ~are ~ui, *intr.* To sound like thunder, thunder: *~a voce tua, filia Gallim* Isa. 10.30 (AC 1888.2); *quod vox eorum ex abdomine ad instar eructationis emissa ita ~aret* TE 111.

intonsus ~a ~um, *a.* Uncut, untrimmed: *nigram ~am plane barbam* ES 1157.

intorqueo ~quere ~si ~tum, *tr.* (refl.) To twist: *ii qui ~quent se undulando crassiuscule per speciem terebrationis* ES 3218.

intorsio ~onis, *f.* A twisting: *per ~onem inferiorum* AS 23.

intra, *prep. w. acc.* and *adv.* **A** (prep.) **1** Within the space of, inside: *juxta aut ~a corpus* AC 1640.1; *~a terminos mundi hujus solis* AC 6697; *erat subjectum quoddam ~a me* ES 3755. **2** Within the time of, during: *~a horam temporis* AC 1641.1; *~a aliquot annos* SE 1. **3** Not going outside, restricted to, inside (a group or category): *~a domos et familias vixerunt* AC 230; *antiqua haec Ecclesia...non ~a paucos fuit* AC 1238.2; *plura sunt ~a naturam quae contra fallacias sensuum sunt* AC 1378.2. **4** Withdrawn from, untouched by: *quomodo...angeli teneantur quasi supra malum, aut ~a illud* ES 3085. **B** (adv.) Inside: *contra illa quae ~a* VR 62; *infinitatem Dei...ab ~a cognoscere* VR 28.2.

intraho ~here ~xi ~ctum, *tr.* To draw in, withdraw: *uxor...tantum ex amore suo conjugiali celat ac ~hit in pectus* AM 294.3; *postquam lux illa ~cta est* VR 335.2.

intranquillitas ~atis, *f.* Lack of peace: *ex timore jurgiorum...et inde ~atis vitae* VI 111; AM 153.2.

intranquillus ~a ~um, *a.* Lacking in peace, restless: *status ~us est, nam tunc pugnae tentationum* AC 4393; (neut. as sb.) *sollicitudines...quae ~um et injucundum inducunt* AC 8113; ES 920.

intremisco ~miscere ~mui, *intr*. To tremble: *et ~muerunt vir ad fratrem suum* Gen. 42.28 (AC).

intrepide, *adv*. Fearlessly: *postquam [sacerdos] instauratus est, ~e pergit* VR 563.2.

intrepiditas ~atis, *f*. Fearlessness, intrepidity: *aliter in ~ate quam in timore* AS 378; AM 164.

intricatus ~a ~um, *a*. (pf. pple. of **intrico**) (compar. *~ior*) Entangled, knotted: *utcunque abstrusum, ~um ...usque in ordinem...redigi potest* ES 155; *cogitationem non ideis talibus ~am et conspurcatam* ES 4628; involved: *is ~iora quam haec intueri amat* AC 4096.3.

intrico ~are ~avi ~atum, *tr*. To entangle: *~at crines ramis ejus* [sc. *arboris*] VR 90.2; (transf.) *~a ideas quousque potes, at usque non extricaberis quod...* AR 490.3.

intrinsecus[1], *adv*. Within the mind, internally: *videntur sibi ~us angi* AC 1033.3; *extrinsecus sicut oves apparent, ac ~us sicut lupi sunt* VR 120.1; *ut simplices teneantur ~us in vinculo per ejus* [sc. *religionis*] *leges* AM 151[a].5.

intrinsecus[2] ~a ~um, *a*. Internal: *afflatum ~um pulmonicum* ES 3279; felt or experienced deep within: *~um odium* AM 240; *~o cruciatu* CJ 61.

intro ~are ~avi, *intr*., *tr*. **1** (of living beings) To go in, enter: **a** (intr.): *comitati sunt angelum, et ~averunt* AM 23; *~abo ad illum, et coenabo cum illo* Rev. 3.20 (AE); *postquam ~abant filii Dei ad filias hominis* Gen. 6.4 (AC); *cum ~ant in coelum* AC 1876.1. **b** (tr.): *non potest sponsus ~are thalamum virginis non desponsatae* VR 73.2. **2** (intr.) To come into, enter (a state): *quod quisque homo...binos status subeat et quod per primum ~et in alterum* VR 105.2. **3** (intr., w. *in* + acc.) To come into possession of, acquire: *~are volunt in mysteria fidei* AC 42.2; *ne...aliquis in sensum spiritualem Verbi ~et* SS 26.2. **4** (of material things) To go in, enter: *afflatus...defluebat...ad labia, ~abat per os* AC 7359; *hae [meninges cerebri] per fila...in omnes substratas glandulas ~ant* VR 60.2. **5** (of immaterial things) To enter, become absorbed: **a** (intr.): *fallaciae sensuum tales sunt ut non possint non ~are* AC 735; *verum...~at in voluntatem hominis* AC 7056.3; *ratiocinia ~abunt in jucunda cupiditatum* AC 7356.1. **b** (tr.): *ad talia quae intellectum propius ~ant* VR 53; *omnes illi amores ~ant amorem communem* ES(M) 4589; *quod nomina...non ~are possint coelum* AE 8.2.

introduco ~cere ~xi ~ctum, *tr*. **1** To lead in, bring in (living beings): *~cti in terram Canaanem* AC 6639.3; *tunc eximitur ex inferno et ~citur in caelum* SS 49.1. **2** To introduce, bring (into a new state or contact): *ut Essentia Ipsius Humana...~ceretur ad Essentiam Divinam* AC 1661.5; *~cuntur ad bonum charitatis per verum fidei* AC 7836.1; *vera ~centia* CI 307.2. **3** To bring about, introduce (a new situation or sim.): *Divinum Verum...illum ordinem ~cit* AC 7396; *non potuissent...~ci idololatriae* FI 8.

introductio ~onis, *f*. **1** The act of bringing in, introduction: *~onem in terram Canaanem* AC 6658. **2** The act of bringing into a new state or condition: *~o ac introitus in statum novum* AM 306; *~o in mundum spiritualem* CI 447.

introductor ~oris, *m*. One who introduces, esp. an official who admits visitors to a high dignitary: *quis...adit immediate aliquem Caesarem, Regem aut Principem, annon procurator et ~or erit* VR 161.3; *angelus ~or* AM 11; (of things) *hi amores fuerunt primi ~ores* AC 5270.2.

introeo ~roire ~roivi, *intr*. To go inside, enter (into): *non potest ~roire in Regnum Dei* John 3.5 (AE 183.6); Matt. 19.24 (CI 365.3).

introitus ~us, *m*. **1** The act of going in, admission, entrance: *~us...filiorum Israelis* AC 1443; *cum ostium clauditur, negatur ~us* AE 208.1. **2** An entrance passage, gate: *prope ad ~um in coelum* AC 7042; *'cherubos' qui...ad ~um ejus* [sc. *horti Edenis*] *positi sunt* SS 97.2.

intromissio ~onis, *f*. The act of sending in, admission: *~o in coelum* AC 7051.4.

intromitto ~mittere ~misi ~missum, *tr*. To send in, admit: *cum filii Jacobi ~missi in terram* AC 1167; *a Domino ~missus sum in vestrum mundum* VR 76.2.

introrsum, *adv*. In an inward direction, inwards: *non ...sursum seu ~um, hoc est, in coelum et ad Dominum* AC 6952.1; CI 586.

introspectio ~onis, *f*. Careful examination: *~o, quae est intromissio visus* AE 260[a].

introspicio ~picere ~pexi ~pectum, *tr*. To look inside: *angelus duxit me ad unam aedem, ac ~peximus* AM 77.2; to examine carefully, look into: *quod... confirmatur a numeris annorum, dum ~piciuntur et evolvuntur* AC 1331; *opus Jehovae non ~piciunt* Isa. 5.12 (AC 1460.2).

intrudo ~dere ~si ~sum, *tr*. To push in: *camelum ~dere per foramen acus netoriae* AM 240; *quidam ex illis ~sit se in cohortem* VR 72.2; ES 688.

intueor ~tueri ~tuitus sum, *tr*. **1** To look at, gaze on: *dum intense ~tuetur solem* AM 233.3; *cum in speculo me ~tuerer* ES 2205. **2** To examine mentally, contemplate: *illa suo intellectu ~tuentur* CI 74.2; *iis data est copia semet ~tuendi* ES 229. **3** To have regard to, fix one's mind upon: *qui ~tuiti sunt Ipsum, servati sunt* AC 197; *non ~tuetur proximum...minus Dominum* AC 7367.

intuitio ~onis, *f.* **1** The act of looking at, inspection: *per ~ones in varias partes capitis* ES(M) 4703; the direction of looking, gaze: *derivat omnium ~ones in se* AC 4997.2. **b** *panes ~onis*, the shewbread (cf. Exod. 25.30): *non recondere illos* [sc. *cibos*] *liceat ad mane, hoc est...quod panes ~onis* [*in tentorio* Rogers] *quovis die novi apponerentur* UJ(P) 345 (Tafel, p. 108). **2** Mental contemplation, consideration: *ex...rerum ~one in sensu interno* AC 1412; *per ~onem Ejus passionis super cruce* FI 45; *quamdiu haec sub ~one sunt* AE 122.1.

intuitive, *adv.* By intuition or contemplation, intuitively: *usque ut videat aut ~e agnoscat Dominum* AM 432.1.

intuitivus ~a ~um, *a.* **1** (w. gen.) Having regard (to), concerned (with): *quae* [*sphaera*] *fuit ~a sui* AC 1506. **2** Presenting ideas directly to the interior sight, intuitive: *cogitatio ~a* AM 293.3; *per similem ~am loquelam* ES 4128. **3** Resulting from contemplation or intuition: *fides absque bonis operibus...quae fides ~a est* ES 4021.

intuitus ~us, *m.* The act of looking at, sight, gaze: *primo ~u* 'at first sight' AC 774; *sub ~u continuo angelorum...fuerunt* AC 6914.2; *ex mutuo ~u* AM 384; *~um vestrum figite in charta* AR 566.5; *~us internus*, mental contemplation: ES 256.

intuli: pf. of **infero**.

intumesco ~mescere ~mui, *intr.* To swell up: *~mescente pectore* DP 215.9; ES 995 1/2.

intumulo ~are ~avi ~atum, *tr.* To cover with a mound, bury: *dicentes quod... ~ent id quod inserviverat illis in mundo* CI 452.

intus, *adv.* **1** Inside, within: *quod ~us in arca lex Divina posita fuerit* AC 6723.3; *unum palatium splendidius quam alterum; ~us similiter* CI 185; *in omni fructu...nuclei ~us latent* ES 251. **2** Not apparently, inwardly, interiorly: *angeli percipiunt quid ~us in idea* AC 1391; *blanda voce in qua ~us erat astus* VR 71.3.

inumbro ~are ~avi ~atum, *tr.* To cast shade on, overshadow: *nubes lucida ~avit eos* Matt. 17.5 (AE 64.2); (transf.) to make unclear, obscure: *in bono et vero apparente quod ~at* AC 1712.1; *confirmatio per haec plus ~aret quam illustraret* AM 223.2; AC 6924.

inundatio ~onis, *f.* A covering with water, inundation, flood: *cum spiritus mali* [*influunt*], *tunc est quasi ~o in sinistram cerebri partem* AC 641; *~onibus ab aquis* DP 112.2; *qui scit...qualis ejus* [sc. *inferni*] *altitudo et ~o super universum mundum spirituum* VR 123.1; (Bibl.) *in ~one irae* Isa. 54.8 (AC 6997.4).

inundo ~are ~avi ~atum, *tr.* To cover with water, flood, submerge: *cum transieris...per flumina, non ~abunt te* Isa. 43.2 (AC 739.3); *quod...urbes...diluvio ~averit* VR 124.3; to cover as with a flood: *quomodo mali spiritus...influxerunt et ~arunt* AC 751.3; AM 267.4.

inungo ~gere ~xi ~ctum, *tr.* To smear (with ointment and sim.), anoint: *quod Dominus fecerit lutum... et ~xerit super oculos coeci* AC 6669.6; *meretrici, quae ~it se balsamo* VR 148.2; (as a mark of royalty) *Ego ~xi regem Meum super Zionem* Ps. 2.6 (DD 6).

inurgeo ~gere, *tr.* To thrust in: *sic putantes se ~gere posse, ut possiderent* ES 3718.

inutilis ~is ~e, *a.* (compar. *~ior*) Not good for service, useless: *servum... ~em* Matt. 25.30 (AC 7770.2); *~es fuci* AM 419; serving no purpose: *ad functiones in republica ~es* AC 1509.

invado ~dere ~si ~sum, *tr.* **1** To enter with hostile intent, break in, invade: *malorum...conatus continuus est ~dendi loca ubi boni* AC 8054.3; *ne Aegyptii ~derent* AC 8194.1; [*ferae*] *quae ~dunt greges et armenta* VR 117. **2** (transf.) To take possession of, take over: *cum animum ~sit cupiditas dominandi* AC 8118.3; *~sit mentem meam stupor* AM 10.4; *fides separata a veritate... ~sit Ecclesiam cum dominio Papali* FI 8.

invaleo ~lere, *intr.* To increase in power and effectiveness, grow strong: *quod quantum charitas recedit, tantum ~leat religio de sola fide* UJ 39; *ne itaque ~leat opinio quae apud plures regnat* AE 102.3.

invalesco ~lescere ~lui, *intr.* To become strong or powerful: *quod talis religio in Ecclesia ~luit* AC 1173; *apud quosdam ~luit opinio quod...* CI 545; (w. *super*) to prevail (over): *Jehovah...super hostes Suos ~lescet* Isa. 42.13 (AC 8273.3).

invaletudo ~inis, *f.* also **invalitudo**. Poor health, sickness: *'morbus' et 'aegritudo' significant ~inem interni hominis* AC 9031.3.

invalidus ~a ~um, *a.* (compar. *~ior*) Lacking strength, weak, feeble: *cum coelum ~um factum est* AE 151.3; *quod viris sit* [*gestus*] *fortior et firmior, faeminis autem ~ior et imbecillior* AM 218.1.

invalitudo: see **invaletudo**.

invariabilis ~is ~e, *a.* Not liable to variation, unvarying: *Divinum...est ~e et immutabile* AS 77.

invasio ~onis, *f.* An invasion: *velle destruere coelum...non fit per ~onem hostilem* AC 8295.2; *~onem Ecclesiae ab illis* FI 67.

invasor ~oris, *m*. An invader: *tutari suam patriam ...contra ~ores hostes* DP 252.2.

invectio ~onis, *f*. The act of inveighing: *~onem ab illis qui putant...* AE 119.1.

invectivus ~a ~um, *a*. Reproachful, abusive; (neut. as sb.) a verbal assault, denunciatory speech, inveighing: *in ~is et injuriis erant* TE 102.

inveho ~here ~xi, *intr*. also **invehor** ~hi ~ctus sum, *intr*. (w. *in* + acc.) To inveigh (against): *volebant... ~here in me, dicentes quod pessimus essem* AC 6811; ES 3256; (in pass. form) *unus ~hitur in alterum* CI 354.

invehor: see **inveho**.

invenio ~nire ~ni ~ntum, *tr*. **1** To discover, find (a person or thing): *qui [amici] utplurimum se ~niunt* [i.e., find one another] AC 1114; *quem scripsit Moses in Lege, ~nimus Jesum* John 1.45 (AC 6752.6); *verba libri foederis ~nti in domo Jehovae* 2 Kgs. 23.2 (AC 6804.7). **2** To have given to one, encounter, find: *quantum gratiae ~nies* Jer. 22.23 (AC 8313.2). **3** To become aware of, discover (a fact): *~nta...urbe proxima* [i.e., which city was nearest] Deut. 21.3 (AC 6767.5); *ego nullam causam ~nio in eo* John 19.4 (AE 31.3). **4** To think up, invent: *plura confirmantia pro sua sententia... ~nit* AC 6663.2; *antequam literae ~ntae sunt* CI 260. **5** (w. pred.) To find (to be): *si quis occisus ~niretur...super agro* Deut. 21.1 (AC 6767.5); *non... ~ni tua opera plena coram Deo* Rev. 3.2 (AR); *omnis qui ~nietur scriptus in libro* Dan. 12.1 (DD 4). **6** (pass.) To be in existence, be found: *talis indoles...non hodie existit et ~nitur* AC 201; *septem diebus fermentum non ~nietur in domibus vestris* Exod. 12.19 (AC) *et non locus ~ntus eorum amplius in caelo* Rev. 12.8 (AR).

inventio ~onis, *f*. An invention, device: *hoc arripiunt, et in foedas ~ones ac machinationes vertunt* ES 2577.

inventum ~i, *neut*. An invention: *assevero in veritate, quod non sint ~a, sed vere facta et visa* AM 1; AM 82.1.

invenustus ~a ~um, *a*. Lacking in charm, unbeautiful: *facie non ~a* AC 9233; ES 3242.

inverse, *adv*. In the opposite way, contrariwise: *talium affectiones erant...inverse ac penes nos* ES 3378.

inversio ~onis, *f*. A change to the opposite, inversion: *totalis ~o status* AC 6977; *abusus et ~ones ordinis Divini* AC 7297.3.

inversum, *prep. w. acc*. In the opposite way to, contrary to: *~um ordinem vivunt homines, ferae autem secundum ordinem* ES 2026.

inversus ~a ~um, *a*. (pf. pple. of **inverto**) (in senses of vb., esp.) Opposite: *in ~o ordine* CI 510; (neut. as sb.) *quod est ~um prioris* AC 1175.1.

inverto ~tere ~ti ~sum, *tr*. **1** To turn upside down, invert: *homo ~sus corpore, pedibus sursum et capite deorsum* DP 217.3; *in speculo ~so seu a tergo* VR 11.3. **2** To change into its opposite, invert: *~tebant totum ordinem Ecclesiae* AC 7779.4; *influxus ille ~titur* VR 8.3.

investigatio ~onis, *f*. An investigation: *'et aperuit et vidit illum natum' significat ~onem quale esset* AC 6728; AM 183.2.

investigo ~are ~avi ~atum, *tr*. **1** To go in search of, seek out: *ne abite nec ~ate* Luke 17.23 (AE 63.4); *examen...evolat ad ~andum sibi domicilium* VR 12.7. **2** To inquire into, examine, investigate: *quod ~are voluerit illa quae sunt fidei* AC 1071.1; *qui ~ant causas* AM 461.3; (w. indir. qu.) *~are quale esset* AC 6735.

investimentum ~i, *neut*. A garment worn as a symbol of office, uniform: *ex horum* [sc. *aulicorum*] *magnificis ~is* AM 7.4.

investio ~tire ~tivi ~titum, *tr*. **1** To clothe, cover: *calceus est qui ~tit plantam pedis et calcaneum* AC 1748.1. **2** To serve as a covering for: *exterius naturale est quod ~tit interiora* AC 7601.5; *Divina Vera...quae nuda sunt in se, sed in Verbi sensu literae ~tita* DP 220.6.

investitio ~onis, *f*. A clothing, dressing: *quod ~o illa* [sc. *naturalium*] *a Deo provisa sit* IM 11.

investitura ~ae, *f*. The putting on of clothes, dressing: *omnis cinctura et ~a significat statum paratum ad recipiendum* AC 7863.

inveteratus ~a ~um, *a*. Long-standing, chronic: *non sanant illa* [sc. *vulnera*], *quia ~a* VR 134.5.

invetero ~are ~avi ~atum, *tr*. To make accustomed, accustom: *desuetudo ~at hominem* VR 561.1.

invicem, *adv*. In respect to one another, mutually: *a se ~em recedunt* AM 54; *prospiciunt sibi [partes] ~em* CI 64.1; *ab ~em*, from one another: *solum corpore ab ~em distincti* AC 1013.2.

invictus ~a ~um, *a*. That cannot be defeated, invincible: (masc. as sb.) *~us Israelis non mentitur, et non Ipsum poenitebit, quia non homo Ille, ut Ipsum paeniteat* 1 Sam. 15.29 (AC 587.1).

invideo ~dere ~di ~sum, *tr*. (w. acc. and dat.) To begrudge or envy (something to someone): *~dent aliis sua bona et concupiscunt illa* AC 7374; CI 364; (absol.) *dolent et ~dent, si aliqui thesauri latent reconditi* AM 267.3.

invidia ~ae, *f*. Envy: *inde indignatio apud eos orta est, postmodum per gradus ~a* ES 166; CI 562.

invidiosus ~a ~um, *a*. Envious: *intus regnat ~um quid et inimicum* ES 4942.

invidus ~a ~um, *a.* Envious: *quia sunt ~i et tales ut possidere ea cupiant* ES 3184.

invigilo ~are ~avi, *intr.* **1** (w. dat.) To stay awake to work (on): *qui continuo studiis ~ant* ES 302. **2** (w. dat.) To keep a watch (for), look out (for): *tales sunt...ut animo ~ent aliorum malis* ES 3290.

invincibilis ~is ~e, *a.* That cannot be overcome, invincible: *dicentes...quod illis ignorantia ~is sit* DP 325.1.

inviolabilis ~is ~e, *a.* (of a law) That cannot be broken, inviolable: *lex Divina ~is est quod homo erit in libero* AC 5854.2.

inviolatus ~a ~um, *a.* Unharmed: *ut...tuti et ~i possent transire* AC 8311.2.

invisco ~are ~avi ~atum, *tr.* To cover with viscous matter, make slimy: *tunc [pituita] ~aret esculenta* ES 939; ES 1272; to ensnare with sticky surfaces, catch, trap: *sicut gluten, cui ~antur bona et vera* AC 563.

invisibilis ~is ~e, *a.* Invisible: *quod Deus non ~is sit, sed visibilis sub humana forma* CI 514; (neut as sb.) *in ~ibus sicut in visibilibus* AM 416.2; *credere in ~e* AE 52.1.

invisibiliter, *adv.* In such a way as not to be seen, invisibly: *noxia animalcula et insecta...in aquis foetidis, vinis acetosis, et in aëre pestifero ~er natant et volant* AS 342; *Providentia Divina operatur...~er et incomprehensibiliter* AC 5508.2.

inviso ~ere ~i, *tr.* To visit: *benedictus Dominus Deus Israelis, quod ~erit et redemerit populum Suum* Luke 1.68 (AE 316.11).

invitatio ~onis, *f.* An invitation: *~ones ad percipiendum ea quae extra eos sunt* ES 203; VR 727.1.

invitator ~oris, *m.* One who issues an invitation: VR 727.1.

invitatus ~i, *m.* One who is invited, guest: *dederunt cuivis ~o suum panem* AM 20.3.

invite, *adv.* Unwillingly: *operas ibi faciunt...~e* [app. *invito* in Autograph] *ex necessitate* DA 45 (= xv.[2]).

invito[1] ~are ~avi ~atum, *tr.* To invite: *~abantur iterum ad epulas* AM 6.2; *omnes ~ati sunt ut venirent* SS 9; *~abant nos ad solia adhuc vacua* VR 48.2.

invito[2], *adv.* Unwillingly: *non potest id nisi ~o et cum lucta* VI 93; *alliciuntur in societatem talium, et quandoque ~o seu iis nolentibus* ES 2740.

invitus ~a ~um, *a.* Unwilling: *ne [filia] ~a feratur ad copulam cum viro inamato* AM 299.2.

invocatio ~onis, *f.* The act of calling upon, summoning, invocation: *~o nominis Jehovae* AC 441; DP 257.2.

invoco ~are ~avi ~atum, *tr.* To call upon, invoke: *cum ~avit Patrem Suum sicut a Se separatum* AC 7058.3; *alioquin non potuissent...sancti eorum ~ari* FI 8; to cry out: *filiis corvi qui ~ant [Illum]* Ps. 147.9 (AE 650.13).

involo ~are ~avi, *intr.* To fly into: *vidi cygnos ~are in palatium per fenestras apertas* AM 270.2; ES 4500; (transf.) to swoop upon: *~abunt in humerum Philisthaeorum* Isa. 11.14 (AE 433.7).

involucrum ~i, *neut.* (anat. and in botany) A wrapping, envelope, involucre: *cuticulae seu ~a in quae fructus aut semina desinunt* AC 501; *~um cujusvis musculi* VR 60.2.

involuntarius ~a ~um, *a.* Not subject to the will, involuntary: *quae cordis et cerebelli sunt, vocantur ~a* AC 9670.2; (neut. as sb.) AC 3603.5; ES 4085.

involutio ~onis, *f.* The act of wrapping up or enveloping: *~o ista iterabatur aliquoties* ES 3298; AE 934.1; a rolling or spiraling: *per quasi ~onem in formam helicis* AC 5989.

involvo ~vere ~vi ~utum, *tr.* **1** (w. dat.) To roll (in): *bis ~vebatur atrae scrobi quam effodit* AC 817; to wrap up (in): *~vebatur subtili reti* ES 745; (transf.) *~vunt id ratiociniis, sicut aranea capturas filis* AM 231.4. **2** To put inside, include (in): (w. *in* + abl.) *in una idea cogitationis plura ~vunt [spiritus] quam in mille cum cogitarunt in vita corporis* AC 322.2; (w. dat.) *ut ~verentur omnia typis* AC 605. **3** To form the wrapping of, envelop: *in toto homine...communia ~vunt particularia* VR 60.1. **4** To bring as a necessary consequence, involve: *misericordia Domini ~vit et spectat salvationem totius generis humani* AC 598.1; *talem contradictionem ~vit fides vestra* VR 74.4; (w. *ut*) *in religioso quod ~vit ut colantur sicut numina* DP 139.8. **5** To have as an additional or hidden factor, include: *singula verba ~vunt peculiarem statum ejus* [sc. *Ecclesiae*] AC 782; *quod omnia prophetica ~verent coelestia* AC 8261.3; *bella in Verbo descripta in sensu spirituali ~vunt et significant bella spiritualia* FI 50; *Divinum ab aeterno...non ~vit dies, annos et saecula* VR 31.3; (w. *quod*) *~vunt...omnes hi versus...quod sensuale se averterit a coelesti* AC 279; VI 2.

iota: see **jotha**.

ipse ~a ~um, *pron.* and *adj.* (gen. sg. *~ius*, dat. sg. *~i*) see also **ipsemet**, and **ipsissimus**. **A** (as pron.) **1** (to emphasize identity) Himself, herself, itself (also, myself, yourself, themselves, etc.): *non sciverunt [spiritus] aliter quam quod ~e spiritus essem* CI 436; *quod haec facienda sint ab homine ut a ~o* VR 3.2. **2** (used esp. referring to the Lord): *est...Dominus in bono praesens quia id ~ius est* AC 6707. **B** (as pron. adj.) **1** (to emphasize identity) Himself, herself, itself, etc.: *loquutus non sum cum ~is incolis tellurum sed cum spiritibus* AC 6695; *~i Judaei nec prophanant id sanctum* DP 228.1. **2** (to emphasize reality) True, actual, real: *eadem lux fit caligo apud malos, etiamsi in ~a luce sunt* AC 8197.2; *~a causa est, quia...* AM 200. **3** Regarded in itself, essential, very: *quod Jehovah Deus sit ~e Amor et ~a Sapientia* VR 3.1; *hi [angeli] ideo sunt ~ae innocentiae coeli* CI 280; (neut. as sb.) the essence: *quod charitas...sit ipsa fides quia est ~um fidei* AC 2442.

ipsemet ipsamet ipsummet, *a.* (reinforced form of **ipse**) **1** The very, himself (herself, itself, themselves, etc.): *quod mihi ostensum per ipsammet respirationem* ES 3318. **2** True, actual, real: *nec potest bonum nisi ex ipsomet fonte venire* AC 39.1. **3** Essential, very: *in quibus [phantasiis] ipsamet eorum vita consistit* AC 695.

ipsissimus ~a ~um, *a.* (quasi-superl. of **ipse**) In the truest sense, veriest: *ad Dominum, Qui est ~a vita* AC 2; *amor sui...est... ~um infernale* AC 1304.

ir, *indecl.* (Hebr.) Transliteration of Hebr. word for city: *ir...est urbs* AE 391.13.

ira ~ae, *f.* Anger, wrath: *~a est affectio communis resultans ex omni quod contrariatur amori proprio* AC 357.

iracundia ~ae, *f.* The state of being angry: *cum in statu ~ae essem* ES 3604; AC 6682; (pl.) *quod ~ae ac dissimulationes illae pro fine habeant sapientiam* AM 294.6.

iracundus ~a ~um, *a.* Characterized by anger, angry: *ex ~a quadam invidia* ES 825.

irascor ~sci ~tus sum, *intr.* To be angry: *credebant quod Jehovah ~sceretur et puniret* AC 6997.3; (w. dat.) *~sci fratri* VI 73; (w. *contra*) *Deus Pater ~tus contra genus humanum* FI 44.

ire: see **eo**[1].

irideus ~a ~um, *a.* Of or resembling the rainbow: *arcum ~um* AM 294.1; (neut as sb.) *ut athmosphaerae, paradisiaca, ~a, palatia et habitacula* AC 1620.

iris ~idis, *f.* (Gk.) **1** A rainbow: *~is signum foederis facta est* AC 868.2; any similar effect: *~is circuitus throni similis aspectu smaragdo* Rev. 4.3 (AR); AM 269.3. **2** The iris (of the eye): *apparet ~is et pupilla nunc dilatata, nunc contracta* AE 37.

irradicatio ~onis, *f.* The act of forming roots, rooting in: (transf.) *inseminatio et ~o fidei* AC 2875.

irradico ~are ~avi ~atum, *tr.* To establish with roots; (transf.) to implant deeply: *coactum non reformat, quia nihil ~at* AC 7007.2; *hoc flagitium...manet ~atum* AM 504.2; *si non cognitiones ~atae sunt vitae ejus* AE 242.3.

irradio ~are ~avi ~atum, *tr.* To cast rays upon: *ex flammea luce, quae sicut aurum coruscat, ~at, et stringit aulaea* AM 75.7.

irrationalis ~is ~e, *a.* Not subject to reason, irrational: *mali spiritus qui ~es facti sunt* CI 455.1; (of things) *quod nihil tam ~e sit, quod non in rationale reducatur* ES 241.1.

irrefraenatus ~a ~um, *a.* also **irrefrenatus**. Unrestrained, unbridled: *ex licentia... ~a illarum* AM 456.

irrefragabilis ~is ~e, *a.* (of promises) That cannot be broken: *quod sint sponsiones Dei ~es* AM 3.5; (of facts or statements) irrefutable: *veritas ~is est...quod nemo hominum ex sepulchris suis excitari...possit* ES 300.

irrefrenatus: see **irrefraenatus**.

irregenitus ~a ~um, *a.* Not reborn, unregenerate: VR 509.

irregularis ~is ~e, *a.* Irregular: *plateae ~es* AM 78.3.

irremediabilis ~is ~e, *a.* Irremediable: *nullus datur morbus seu malum ~e* ES 2299.

irremissibilis ~is ~e, *a.* That cannot be forgiven, unpardonable: *peccatum ~e* VR 138 (Matt. 12.31).

irrepo ~ere ~si, *intr.* To creep in, insinuate itself: *ne cupiditas dominii et cupiditas lucri ~ant* AC 7364; VR 52.

irrequies ~ei, *f.* Lack of peace or respite, disturbance: *cessante pugna, seu ~e a cupiditatibus* AC 92; *quod magna ~e essent [spiritus]* ES 2343.

irrequiete, *adv.* Uneasily, restlessly: *cogitat ~e* AC 5725.1.

irrequieto ~are ~avi ~atum, *tr.* To make uneasy, disturb: *cum alii vellent ~are* ES 4284.

irrequietudo ~inis, *f.* Unpeacefulness, unrestfulness: *longe ab indignatione, ira, ~ine [inquietudinibus* Autograph] AC 5725.2.

irrequietus ~a ~um, *a.* (superl. *~issimus*) Lacking tranquillity, restless, uneasy: *cupiditates sunt quae hominem ~um reddunt* ES 742; *me in statum ~issimum suum redigere* ES 2343.

irresistibilis ~is ~e, *a.* Irresistible: *artes... ~es* ES 4949.

irretio ~tire ~tivi ~titum, *tr.* To catch in a net, ensnare: *ut si musca involat, ~tiatur illa* VR 335.3; (transf.) *cogitatio a suis quasi pedicis quibus ~tita ...liberata* AC 1757.

irrevocabilis ~is ~e, *a.* That cannot be recalled, irrevocable: *confirmatio a Divino ~is* AC 8055.

irrideo ~dere ~si ~sum, *tr.* To laugh at, deride: *~dent* *eos qui nominant conscientiam* AC 831.1; (absol.) *cachinnati sunt, ~serunt, et cavillati* AM 79.7.

irrigo ~are ~avi ~atum, *tr.* To water (ground): *~avit [vapor] omnes facies humi* Gen. 2.6 (AC); (transf.) *tranquillitas...est instar vaporis, quo ~atur et perfunditur externus ejus ab interno* AC 91.

irriguus ~a ~um, *a.* Well-watered: *vidit omnem planitiem Jardenis, quod tota ea ~a* Gen. 13.10 (AC); *sicut hortus ~us* Isa. 58.11 (AE 71.2).

irrisio ~onis, *f.* The act of laughing at, mockery, derision: *pro formulis nugarum aut ~onis* AC 961; *~o et blasphematio sanctorum* CI 570.1.

irrisor ~oris, *m.* One who mocks or laughs to scorn, mocker: *desinet violentus et consumetur ~or* Isa. 29.20 (AC 6353.4).

irrisus ~us, *m.* = **irrisio**: *quod Jacobus per ~um fecit* 2AD 87.

irritatio ~onis, *f.* The act of arousing or provoking, arousal: *per ~ones in corporeo* AM 513.

irrito ~are ~avi ~atum, *tr.* To provoke, arouse: *excitantur et ~antur ad scelesta* ES 3781; to anger, annoy: *cognoscetis quod ~averint viri hi Jehovam* Num. 16.30 (AC 8306).

irritus ~a ~um, *a.* Of no effect, ineffectual, unavailing: *cum ~us factus eorum conatus* AC 1879.2; *consilium ~um factum est* AC 6681; VR 31.3. **b** *in ~um cedere*, to prove ineffectual, fail: *inde facta conspiratio, quae in ~um cessit* ES 458.

irrogo ~are ~avi ~atum, *tr.* (w. dat.) To impose, inflict (penalties, punishments on): *Dominus non ~at illis punitiones* AC 6997.6; *ut paenas illis ~arent* AM 500.4.

irrumpo ~mpere ~pi ~ptum, *tr.* To invade forcibly, break in: *oceanum cum fluctibus suis ~mpentem in regiones et urbes* VR 123.5; (transf.) *quod falsa in cogitationes eorum ~mpant* AE 121.

irruo ~ere ~i, *intr.* To rush in or against: *spiritus malus ipse ~it* [sc. *in infernum*] AC 696; *nisi Divinum ageret contra illa* [sc. *inferna*], *~erent sicut maximus oceanus* AC 8175; *vidi hircos...cum furore ~entes in oves* FI 63.4.

irruptio ~onis, *f.* The act of breaking in: *perversio veri ac ~o falsi* AE 400.11.

is ea id, *pron.* and *adj.* (dat. and abl. pl. *eis* AC 6756.6, *iis* AC 6677) **A** (pron.) **1** (referring to a person or thing previously mentioned) He, she, it, etc.: *quia sensus internus, et is coelestis..., inest* AC 2310.4; *defendit sententiam suam contra alios qui eam impugnant* AC 6663.2. **b** (in gen. serving as pron. adj.) his, her, its, etc.: *ex homine naturali ejusque infirmo* AC 6876.2. **2** (resumptive after a preceding rel.): *qui alicui pauperi ...malefico opem fert, is per illum malefacit proximo* AC 8120; *quod 'vocem audire' attinet, significat id proprie obedientiam* AC 8361.1. **3** *Is qui*, the one who, he (she, etc.) who: *iis qui in illis sunt* AC 6677; *id quod*, the fact that: *miracula...Divina...distinguuntur per id quod illa involvant...status Ecclesiae* AC 8364.6. **b** (w. gen.): *inter eos sui temporis* ES 3904; (w. pple. in imitation of Gk.) *et eos in caelo habitantes* Rev. 13.6 (AR). **4** (used where the reflexive would be expected): *quidam boni spiritus coeperunt me increpare quod eos infestaverim* AC 1983.2; AC 2303; *sumunt ex affectione quod iis prodesse putant* ES 4373. **B** (adj.) The previously mentioned, that: *de eo statu* AC 2682.3; *eo tempore* AC 6692.1; *in fine Ecclesiae regnant ea falsa* AE 783.2.

isch, *indecl.* (Hebr.) Transliteration of a Hebr. word for man: *huic vocabitur nomen ischah, quia de isch, viro, sumta est haec* Gen. 2.23 (AM 156[a].1); AM 193.1.

ischah, *indecl.* (Hebr.) Transliteration of a Hebr. word for woman: *huic vocabitur nomen ischah, quia de isch, viro, sumta est haec* Gen. 2.23 (AM 156[a].1); AM 32; AM 193.1.

Israeliticus ~a ~um, *a.* Of Israel, Israelitish: *populus ~us* AC 730.4; *a gente ~a et Judaica* SS 11; *in Ecclesia ~a* AE 28.2.

Israelitis ~idis, *f. adj.* Of Israel, Israelitish: *filius mulieris ~idis* AC 7456.6.

iste ~a ~ud, *pron.* and *pron. adj.* (gen. sg. *~ius*, dat. sg. *~i*) **A** (as pron.) The one previously mentioned, he, she, it, etc.: *dic nobis quando ~a fient* Matt. 24.3 (AC 6895.1). **B** (adj., almost always used in a derogatory sense) That: *nescientes quod bona ~a sint mala* AC 20; *loco solis ~ius caliginosum quid* CI 151; *quantum fraena amoribus ~is relaxantur* AM 264.4; *quod genti ~i permissum sit crucifigere Dominum* DP 236; (app. without derogatory implication) *infantes qui nusquam ad aetatem ~am venerunt ut loqui adhuc potuerint* ES 2309; *indicabis filio tuo in die ~o* Exod. 13.8 (AC).

isthinc, *adv.* also **istinc**. From or on your side: *~inc transire ad nos* Luke 16.26 (NH 239).

isthmus ~i, *m.* (Gk.) (anat.) The narrow segment of the brain between the cerebrum and the cerebellum, isthmus: ES 3837.

istinc: see **isthinc**.

ita, *adv.* **1** In the manner specified, as stated, thus: *omnia quaecunque Domini sunt, comparantur 'diei' ...ita pluries in Verbo* AC 21; *dicunt ita esse, vel non ita esse* AC 1384; *ita fui per 4 nunc annos* ES 4228; (ellipt.) *non ita, ite quaeso juvenes* Exod. 10.11 (AC);

sermo vester erit Ita ita, non non Matt. 5.37 (CI 271). **b** *ita vocatus* or *dictus*, so-called: *ex orbe ita vocato Christiano* AC 826; *contra Christianos ita dictos* ES 4401. **c** *ita...ita*: in one way...in another way, so...so: *dicere quod ita vel ita sit* ES 1902; *est ita vel ita, aut est sic vel aliter* ES 2557; *societates...quae ex proprio conjecturant, una ita, altera ita* ES 4154. **2** To such an extent, so much: *omne quod...vitam habet se fructificat et multiplicat immensum; quamdiu homo in corpore vivit, non ita, sed in altera vita stupende* AC 43; *sunt corda adamantina, ita dura* VR 536.2. **3** As a consequence, thus, so: *lex me non damnat, ita nec malum* DP 258.2; *quod mala una cum inferno, ita post creationem exstiterint* VR 53. **b** *ita est quod*, this is the reason, this is why: *ita est quod illi scandunt* [*et quod illi scandant* Rogers] *supra quod permissum* UJ(P) 359 (Tafel, p. 95).

Italicus ~a ~um, *a.* Of Italy, Italian: *praeter gentem ~am* ES 5043.

itaque, *adv.* Consequently, therefore: *qui ~que alios amant sicut se...ii omnes originem proximi ducunt a Domino* AC 6711; CI 86.

item, *adv.* Likewise, similarly: *caetera...a voluntate pendent...at facies non ~m* ES 3861; *Abrahamus et Jacobus, quorum filios se nominant* [*Judaei*], *non ~m Isaci* 3AD 4494.

iter ~ineris, *neut.* A journey, march: *~er continuandum ad mare Suph* AC 8181; *~inera ab uno loco in alterum* AC 8103.

iteratio ~onis, *f.* Verbal repetition, reiteration: *~o seu repetitio* AC 8933.

iterato, *adv.* A second time, again: *cum ~o dicitur* AC 8016; *quin matrimonium ~o contrahant* AM 317.

itero ~are ~avi ~atum, *tr.* To do or use again, repeat: *vicibus ~atis* AM 54; *involutio ista ~abatur aliquoties* ES 3298; *~etur gladius tertio* Ezek. 21.14 (AE 131.5); (also absol.) *~a, circumcide filios Israelis secundo* Josh. 5.2 (AC 2799.6).

iterum, *adv.* A second time, again: *post aliquam temporis moram ~um nesciverunt* AC 1387; *inde ~um patet, cur...* CI 65; *bis et ~um* 'twice and again' ES 512.

itio ~onis, *f.* The act of going, movement: *~ones et ambulationes spirituum super illis* [sc. *viis*] CI 590.

iturus ~a ~um: fut. pple. of **eo**[1].

itus ~us, *m.* The act of going: *facilis...~us ab una tellure ad alteram* ES 1513.

ivi: pf. of **eo**[1].

J

jaceo ~cere ~cui, *intr.* **1** (of persons or animals) To be recumbent, recline, lie: *~centes in aqua calida balnei* AM 339.3; *~cebis super latere tuo dextro* Ezek. 4.6 (DD 16.2); *equus ~cens mortuus* SS 26.3. **2** (of things) To be situated, rest, lie: *civitas ~cet quadrangularis* Rev. 21.16 (AC 648.1); *sinum...qui in cerebro inter bina ejus hemisphaeria ~cet* AC 7744; *arbor ubi cadit, ibi ~cet* DP 277[a]. **3** To lie dormant or hidden: *tunc prodeunt...falsa quae apud illos recondita ~cuerunt* AC 7778.3; *malum...circumvelatum et obvolutum ~cuit externa probitate* CI 577.2.

jacio ~cere jeci ~ctum, *tr.* To cast, throw: *ex seminulo ~cto in terram* VR 12.2; to cast (lots): *quod...super tunicam jecerint sortem* VR 130.1.

jactabundus ~a ~um, *a.* Characterized by boasting, boastful: *~a verba* ES 169; ES 291.

jactantia ~ae, *f.* Boastfulness: *ex ~a et elatione animi* AE 405.37; ES 3750.

jactatio ~onis, *f.* The act of boasting: *arrogantiae et ~onis variae species* AC 6203.

jactito ~are ~avi ~atum, *intr.* To keep boasting: *~ant quod...justificati sunt* 3AD 6465.

jacto ~are ~avi ~atum, *tr.* **1** To throw repeatedly, toss about: *~abat...ulnas quemadmodum infans recens natus* CI 203.3; *afflicta, turbine ~ata* Isa. 54.11 (AC 655.1). **2** (refl.) To boast, brag: *spiritum... ~antem se ex scortationibus* AM 477.1; *~abant se de meritis* ES 4349.

jactura ~ae, *f.* The act of being deprived, loss (of something): *timor... ~ae vitae, opum, lucri* AC 81.3; *varios dolores et varias ~as subeunt* AC 8164.2; *propter ~am conjugis et infantum* ES 743.

jactus ~us, *m.* A throw (as a measure of distance): *abstractus est ab illis quasi ad ~um lapidis* Luke 22.41 (AC 1787.2); *~us arcus*, a bowshot: Gen. 21.16 (AC).

jaculator ~oris, *m.* One who shoots, marksman: *~ores arcus* Ps. 78.9 (SS 79.2).

jaculor ~ari ~atus sum, *tr.* To discharge, shoot (missiles): *quod Jonathan... ~aretur tres sagittas* SS 29 (1 Sam. 20.20); (absol.) *et exacerbant eum, et ~antur* Gen. 49.23 (AC).

jaculum ~i, *neut.* A missile, dart, esp. an arrow: *fregit ~a ignita arcus* Ps. 76.3 (AC 1664.7); *sagittae, ~a et tela* AE 357.1.

jaculus ~i, *m.* The name of a kind of snake which strikes like a dart: *serpens ~us super semita* Gen. 49.17 (AC).

Jah, *indecl. m.* (Hebr.) An abbreviated form of Jehovah, Jah: *Jah est ex Jehovah* AC 8267.2.

jam, *adv.* see also **jamjam**. **1** At this time, now: *jam vero dicitis quod videtis* John 9.41 (AM 348); *qui...jam in caelo* VR 695.2. **2** *Jam...jam*, at one time...at another, now...now: *quod hoc ambiguum ferat mentem jam sursum jam deorsum* VR 35.10; ES 4413. **3** Already: *qui...non credit, jam judicatus est* John 3.18 (AC 6674.7).

jamdudum, *adv.* Already a while ago: *cum sol ~um occubuerat* AC 4527.1.

jamdum, *adv.* Already: *qui...cupit, ~um in malo est* AC 139; *bestia est sicut humus ~um sata* AM 134.1.

jamjam, *adv.* also spelled as two words **jam jam**. **1** Already: *jamjam securis ad radicem arborum jacet* Luke 3.9 (DD 18.4). **2** In the near future, very soon: *jamjam venturi sunt aulici* AM 7.2; AM 263.1.

janitor ~oris, *m.* One who keeps a door, doorkeeper, porter: *~or aperuit fores* AM 20.1; ES 4675.

janua ~ae, *f.* A door, gate: *aperiebatur ~a e conclavi* AM 20.2; *pulsare ~am* Luke 13.25 (VI 2); (transf.) *quod Filius solus sit ~a* ES 1601; *custodi ~as oris tui* Mic. 7.5 (AC 6960.2).

Januarius ~i, *m.* The month of January: ES 4550.

Jaschar, *indecl.* The name of a prophetic book of the Ancient Word: *liber propheticus Verbi Vetusti, vocatus Liber Jaschar, seu Liber Recti* SS 103.3 (2 Sam. 1.18, Josh. 10.13).

jaspis ~idis, *f.* (Gk.) also **iaspis**. A precious stone, jasper: *domus ex ~ide et sapphiro* AM 355.1; Rev. 4.3 (AR).

jecur ~oris, *neut.* The liver: *per pinguedinem super ~ore, seu reticulum* AC 353.1.

Jehovah ~ae, *m.* (a Christian representation of the tetragrammaton, the four-letter Hebr. name YHWH) (acc. *~am*, abl. *~ah*) The divine name of God, Jehovah: *Dominus ab aeterno, Qui est ~ah* VR 2.1; *~ah ...significat supremum et unicum Ens* VR 9.3; *nemini ~am nominare licuit, nisi cui verae fidei cognitio, et Deum cuicunque* AC 624.

Jehovi: see **Jehovih**.

Jehovih, *indecl. m.* (an alternate Christian representation of the tetragrammaton, the four-letter Hebr. name YHWH) (gen. also *Jehovi* 4IB s.v. 'Jehovah', p. 271 Kahl) *Dominus ~ih*, the Lord Jehovih: *quoties Jehovah Dominus dicitur, appellatur non Dominus Jehovah, sed Dominus ~ih* AC 1793.1.

jejunatio ~onis, *f.* The act of fasting: AE 730.41.

jejunium ~i, *neut.* A period of abstinence from food, fast: *~a erunt domui Jehudae in gaudium* Zech. 8.19 (AC 7093.5).

jejuno ~are ~avi, *intr.* To abstain from food, fast: *quod ~aret bis in septimana* Luke 18.12 (VI 30.3).

jejunus ~a ~um, *a.* Fasting: *quando evigilat, ~a est anima ejus* Isa. 29.8 (AC 9050.7).

Jesuiticus ~a ~um, *a.* Of the Jesuits: *ex ordine ~o* AR 578.2.

jim: see **ijim**.

Jirah, *indecl.* (Hebr.) 'Jireh', a rendering of a Hebr. word meaning 'will see (to it)' that was added to Jehovah to form a place name: *solenne...antiquis fuit aliquid adjicere nomini Jehovae...ut...Jehovah Jirah, hoc est, videbit* AC 2724.3 (Gen. 22.14).

jobel, *indecl.* (Hebr.) Jobel, a rendering of a Hebr. word meaning a sound of a horn or trumpet (see quot.): *in trahendo ~el, seu quod idem, in audiendo sonum buccinae* AC 8802.1 (Exod. 19.13).

jocor ~ari ~atus sum, *intr.* To joke: *~ando dixit* AM 56.2; AM 294.2.

jocularis ~is ~e, *a.* Full of jokes, jocular: *loquela ~is* AM 461.2; (neut. as sb.) a joke: *illa ~ia decora* CH 189 (= xi).

joculator ~oris, *m.* One who makes jokes, jester: DP 231.1.

joculor ~ari ~atus sum, *intr.* To speak jestingly, joke: *rogavimus illum...num ~etur* AM 233.5; ES 1997.

jocus ~i, *m.* A joke, jest: *quod sit ['ludere'] esse quasi ~us, fabula, nugae* AC 2403.

jota: see **jotha**.

jotha ~ae, *f.* and *indecl. neut.* also **iota**, and **jota**. **1** The Greek letter corresponding to *i* and the Hebrew corresponding to *y*, iota, yodh: *~a unum ac unum corniculum non praeteribit de Lege* Matt. 5.18 (AC 6752.2). **2** (as the type of the smallest part) A jot: *usque ad minimam ~am* AC 2; *in singulis dictis et ~is* ES 4331.

Jovialis ~is ~e, *a.* Of or belonging to the planet Jupiter: *spiritus ~es* AC 7809; *coelum ~e* ES 3030.

juba ~ae, *f.* The mane (of a horse): *intendebant lora super ~is equorum* AM 103.1.

jubar ~aris, *neut.* A ray of light, beam: *intervallum coruscabat ~are lucis* AM 13.2; *~ar flammeum* CI 121; effulgence, radiance: *vidi orientem solem in suo ~are* VR 112.1; *omnia...aurei splendoris seu ~aris erant* ES 1183.

jubeo ~bere ~ssi ~ssum, *tr.* **1** To order, command: (w. inf.) *propheta ~ssus est ire in domum figuli* AC 6669.5; (w. *ut*) *quod Elias ~sserit, ut funderent aquam* SS 29 (1 Kgs. 18.34). **2** (w. dat.) To impose (commands upon): *omnia quae illi spiritibus castigatoribus... ~bent et praecipiunt* AC 7811.

jubilaeus ~a ~um, *a.* Of jubilee: *~us ille [annus quinquagesimus] erit vobis* Lev. 25.10 (AC 2252.3); (neut. as sb.) the jubilee, a festival of the Jewish church held in the fiftieth year: *quod ~um quovis quadragesimo nono anno proclamaretur, et quinquagesimo celebraretur* AC 493.

jubilatio ~onis, *f.* Shouting in triumph: AE 376.13.

jubilo ~are ~avi, *intr.* To shout in triumph: *laetabuntur et ~abunt gentes* Ps. 67.4 (SS 86).

jubilum ~i, *neut.* A shout of triumph: *quod arca introducta sit in Zionem...cum sacrificiis et cum ~o* VI 59 (2 Sam. 6.15).

jucundatio ~onis, *f.* Gratification, pleasing: *ex mentis jucundo oritur ~o corporis* DP 38.

jucunde, *adv.* Pleasantly: *quod sonus cantus... ~e exaltet* AM 17.2.

jucunditas ~atis, *f.* The quality of being pleasant, agreeableness, delight: *ipsa vitae eorum ~as in eo consistit* AC 741; (w. pl.) a feeling of pleasure: *conflictio ~atum seu affectionum* AC 8352.2.

jucundo ~are ~avi ~atum, *tr.* **1** To make pleasant: *crediderunt quod ~anda sit vita omni voluptate* AC 6971.2; (refl. and pass., w. *in* + abl.) to take one's pleasure in: *[crabro] in ejus* [sc. *sterquilinii*] *nidore se ~at*

VR 69.2; *in aprico solis ~ari* VR 57.1. **2** To give pleasure to, delight: *consortia quae angelorum...pectora ~ant* AM 5.4.

jucundus ~a ~um, *a.* (compar. *~ior*, superl. *~issimus*) Pleasant, agreeable, delightful: *haec...in ~o ordine ita percipiuntur ab angelis ut...* AC 855; *Divina Vera...dicuntur verba gratiae...quia accepta, grata et ~a* AE 22.2; *quod...fruantur consortiis similibus...sed ~ioribus et beatioribus* AM 45; *quam ~i sunt...pedes evangelizantis* Isa. 52.7 (AC 8331). **b** (neut. as sb.) A pleasant thing or act, pleasure, delight: *~issimum suum ponunt in eo ut alios laedant* AC 592.2; *ex ~o faciendi malum* AC 7032.1; *num...amor illarum...sit in suo ~o aut in injucundo...* AM 219.

Judaicus ~a ~um, *a.* Jewish: *de Ecclesia Israelitica et ~a* VI 79.2; *gens ~a* CI 365.2.

Judaismus ~i, *m.* The Jewish religion: *qui a ~o ad Christianismum convertuntur* AC 4868.6; VR 94.1.

judaizo ~are ~avi ~atum, *tr.* (Gk.) To make (others) follow Jewish religious practices, Judaize: *Paulus per opera legis intellexit opera legis Mosaicae quae pro Judaeis, quod etiam vidimus clare ex ejus verbis ad Petrum, quem increpavit quod ~aret* AR 417.2.

judex ~icis, *m.* A judge: *qui...judicatur a rege vel ~ice et punitur* AC 8282; AM 252; (as a senior magistrate of the Israelites) *sedere super asino...erat insigne summi ~icis et regis* AE 31.7; (pl., as title of a book of the Word) AC 10325.

judicatio ~onis, *f.* Judgment: *quod angeli...speciem ~onis habeant super hominem* AC 7811; AM 489.

judicialis ~is ~e, *a.* Of or concerned with the administration of justice, judicial: *~is hic caetus* AM 77.4; *per legitimas causas hic non intelliguntur ~es* AM 252.

judiciarius ~a ~um, *a.* Of or concerned with lawsuits, legal: (neut. pl. as sb.) CO 40.

judicium ~i, *neut.* **1** The power of judging, judgment: *altius non vadit ~um in pueritia* AC 1434; AC 6814; *ex ~o*, judiciously: AM 521.2; *sui ~i*, able to judge for oneself, endowed with discretion: AM 202.2. **2** An instance of judging, judgment: *audire Legis statuta et ~a* AC 6752.8. **b** *ultimum ~um*, the Last Judgment: *quod Dominus ad ultimum ~um venturus sit in nubibus* AE 36.2; cf. *ultimum ~um unicuique est, cum Dominus venit* AC 900. **3** An assembly of judges, law court: *mandavit nos ad ~um* AM 77.3; AM 207.3.

judico ~are ~avi ~atum, *tr., intr.* **1** (tr.) To submit to judicial process, judge, condemn: *de iis qui ~antur ad mortem* AC 900; *~abunt populum judicio justitiae* Deut. 16.18 (AC 7111.3); *homo secundum facta ~abitur* CI 358. **2** (intr.) To sit in judgment: *quoties disponit et ~at [magistratus]* VI 72; (w. *de*) *illi ~ant de aliis* AC 7747. **3** (tr.) To deliver as a judgment: *loquebantur ad populum quae ~abantur* AC 7111.3. **4** (intr.) To form an opinion, judge: (impers. pass., w. *de*) *non ~andum est de colore corvi* AM 233.4; (w. *quod*) *a fluminis magnitudine...~are potui quod aliquot myriades hominum per diem alluant* AC 6699.

jugalis ~is ~e, *a.* **1** Bearing the yoke; (masc. as sb.) a team (of draught animals): *agricolam et ~em ejus* Jer. 51.23 (AC 1565). **2** United in marriage, mating: *papiliones ~es volantes in horto* CO 22.

jugerum ~i, *neut.* A measure of land, about two thirds of an acre: *decem ~a vineae* Isa. 5.10 (AC 576.1).

jugi, *adv.* Constantly: *sphaera quae ~i exundat* AM 171.2; ES 1637.

jugis ~is ~e, *a.* Constant, unvarying: *ex ~i influxu recentium virium* AM 44.9; *holocaustum ~e* Num. 28.10 (AE 314.10); (so, also) *~e*, regular offering: Dan. 8.11 (FI 64).

jugiter, *adv.* Constantly, continually: *~er ad vitam juventutis...tendunt* AC 1854.2; *sunt...spiritus et angeli apud hominem ~er* DD 37.2.

jugularis ~is ~e, *a.* (anat.) *Vena ~is*, the jugular vein: ES 831.

jugulo ~are ~avi ~atum, *tr.* To cut the throat of: *quod cultris ~arent me* ES 3653.

jugulum ~i, *neut.* The throat: *cultros ~o meo infundere conati* ES 3653.

jugum ~i, *neut.* **1** A yoke: *disrumpes ~um illius desuper collo tuo* Gen. 27.40 (AC). **2** (fig.) A means of subjection, yoke: *~um enim Meum facile est* Matt. 11.30 (CI 359); *cum Dominus liberat hominem a dominio et ~o eorum* [sc. *malorum spirituum*] AC 905; *sub ~o legis*, subject to the law: DP 42; FI 39.

Julius ~i, *m.* The name of the seventh month, July: ES 2471.

jumentum ~i, *neut.* An animal used for riding or traction: *sustulit super proprium ~um* Luke 10.34 (AC 6708); *~um ante plaustrum* DP 176.2; ES 3531.

junctim, *adv.* Jointly: *tres illi nominantur ~im hic* AC 4844.5.

junctura ~ae, *f.* A joint (in a structure): *apparebant ~ae asserum paulum* ES 846.

juncus ~i, *m.* A rush: *gramen pro calamo et ~o* Isa. 35.7 (AC 6723.2); (as a material for wicker work) *capsam ~i* Exod. 2.3 (AC); *macerias...ex ~is* AM 477.5.

jungo ~gere ~xi ~ctum, *tr.* **1** To put together, join; *~cto oculo*, on a combined view: AM 298. **2** To make by joining, enter into (a marriage): *quod...conjugia potuissent ~gere* ES 3537; *quod...connubia ~gant* [*aves*] VR 12.5.

junior ~oris: compar. of **juvenis**.

Junius ~i, *m.* The name of the sixth month, June: ES 2170.

juramentum ~i, *neut.* A sworn statement, oath: *hoc voluerunt... ~o confirmare* AC 1770.

jurator ~oris, *m.* One who swears an oath: VR 297.1.

jure, *adv.* (abl. of **jus**) Correctly, rightly, fairly: *credere quod homo...non salvetur...potest ~e arguere Deum immisericordiae* VR 341.1.

jurgatio ~onis, *f.* Quarreling, wrangling: *invidere in lingua originali etiam significat aemulari et jurgari, et quia aemulatio et ~o est effectus odii, per eandem quoque significatur aversio* AC 4702.

jurgium ~i, *neut.* A complaint, wrangle, nagging: *ex timore ~orum domi ab uxore* AM 153.2; ES 431.

jurgor ~ari ~atus sum, *intr.* To complain bitterly, wrangle: *et ~atus populus cum Mosche* Exod. 17.2 (AC).

juridicus ~a ~um, *a.* Concerned with legal disputes, juridical: *scientiae...ut... ~a* AM 163.

jurisprudentia ~ae, *f.* The practice of the legal profession, jurisprudence: *quia...fraudes...non contra ~am aestimat* CI 531.2.

juro ~are ~avi ~atum, *intr.*, *tr.* **1** (intr.) To swear an oath: (w. dat.) *~avi Davidi servo Meo* Ps. 89.3 (AC 6804.9); (w. *per*) *Dominus non per alium ~at quam per Se* AC 8281.5; (w. *in* + acc.) swear by: *qui ~ant in nomen Jehovae* Isa. 48.1 (DD 39); swear to: *institit in causam, quia ~averat in illam* AM 105; (w. *quod*) *scio etiam quod ~aturae sint quod...* AM 44.7. **2** (tr.) To swear to give, promise on oath: *ad terram quam ~avit Abrahamo* Gen. 50.24 (AC).

jus juris, *neut.* see also **jure**. **1** Law as a system of justice: *juris civilis* ES(M) 4657; *ex legibus juris* AE 182.2; *singula num juris vel non juris essent, percepi* AM 231.3; *de principiis juris naturalis* ES [1770 ½]. **2** Legal action, law: *si quis velit te in jus trahere* Matt. 5.40 (AC 9049.4). **3** The power conferred by law, right: *quod tunc dictum sit illis jus regis* AC 8770.4 (1 Sam. 8.11); (w. *in* + acc.) *putant sic jus in eum habere* ES 3710; (w. *super*) *quibus...suum jus est super milites* VR 10. **4** *Sui juris*, under one's own control, responsible for oneself: *cum adolescit* [*homo*] *ac sui juris fit* AC 987.2; *cum sui juris esse possunt* [*pulli*] CI 108.3.

jussus[1] ~a ~um: pf. pple. of **jubeo**.

jussus[2] ~us, *m.* The act of ordering, order, command: *ex ~u principis* AM 16.1; AE 475.18; *~u Jehu* AE 160.1.

juste, *adv.* Correctly, truly, properly: *si ~e cogitat* AC 7779.3; *licet judicare, at ~e* SS 51.5; *quae* [*instrumenta*] *concordant ~e et bene* ES 887.

justificatio ~onis, *f.* Justification: FI 39; AE 226.

justificator ~oris, *m.* One who justifies: *a ~oribus et sanctificatoribus per solam fidem* VR 181.

justificatorius ~i, *m.* One who believes in the doctrine of justification by faith alone: *Divina Vera...a ~is* [*Justificatariis* 1st edn.] *non lectu digna censerentur* SE 81.

justifico ~are ~avi ~atum, *tr.* **1** To make correct: *tunc enim ~abitur sanctum* Dan. 8.14 (AC 7844.4); *~antes multos* Dan. 12.3 (AC 7988.4). **2** To endow with righteousness in the sight of God, justify: *fides per quam ~ari possunt* AC 7318.2; *quod non malum vitae... condemnet ~atos per solam fidem* VI 4; *quod Deus Pater cum Suo Filio jugiter de ~andis colloquatur* VR 16.1.

justitia ~ae, *f.* The quality of being just, righteousness, justice: *si non in operibus ponunt ~am* AC 989; *Dominus...factus est ~a per pugnas tentationum* AC 1813.1; *ex ~a* FI 44; (Bibl.) *sacrificia ~ae* Deut. 33.19 (AC 6745.2).

justus ~a ~um, *a.* (superl. *~issimus*) **1** (of persons) Practising justice, just, righteous: *quisque... ~us et verus...vult in mundo videri* AC 6907.2; (masc. as sb.) *in tentoriis ~orum* Ps. 118.15 (AC 8281.4). **2** (of actions, decisions, etc.) Characterized by justice, just, fair: *~um judicium judicate* John 7.24 (SS 51.5); *si sententia super lance aequilibris et ~a apparet* VR 48.2; (neut. as sb.) justice: *qui in sincero est, in ~o, et in bono* AC 7046.2. **3** Properly so called, real, true: *quia est* [*amor vere conjugialis*] *~um seminarium generis humani* AM 143.

juvenca ~ae, *f.* A heifer: *~as quadraginta et juvencos decem* Gen. 32.15 (AC).

juvencus ~i, *m.* A bull calf: *boves et ~i* CI 110.

juvenesco ~ere, *intr.* To become youthful: *senescere in coelo est ~ere* CI 414; *in ~ente aetate* AM 450.

juvenilis ~is ~e, *a.* Youthful: *uxores... ~es et venustae* AC 829.2.

juvenis ~is, *m.* and *adj.* (compar. *junior*) **1** A young man, youth: *deficient virgines...et ~es siti* Amos 8.13 (DD 4); AM 183.1. **2** (as adj.) Young: *leoni gentium ~i similis factus es* Ezek. 32.2 (AC 7293.2); *cum esses junior* John 21.18 (AE 9.3).

juventus ~utis, *f.* The prime of life, youth: *infantia, pueritia, adolescentia, ~us et senectus* AM 185.1; *ad vitam ~utis et adolescentiae tendunt* AC 1854.2.

juvo ~are ~avi ~atum, *tr.*, *intr.* **1** (tr.) To help, assist: *et ~abit te* [*Deus*] Gen. 49.25 (AC); *quod ne quidem semet in minimis ~are possint* ES 2802. **2** (intr.) To be of assistance, help: *haec ~ant, quia confirmant bona* AC 8179.2; *desponsationis status...vix ad aliud ~at quam...* AM 304.2.

juxta, *prep. w. acc.* and *adv.* **1** Close to, near, next to: *habitacula contigua sunt, unum ~a alterum* CI 184; *homo cum tentatur etiam ~a infernum est* AC 8131; VR 69.2. **2** In a similar way to, like: *conflabo eos ~a conflare argentum* Zech. 13.9 (AC 720); *excitabit Jehovah...flagellum, ~a plagam Midianis* Isa. 10.26 (SS 15.1). **3** In accordance with, after: *habitare faciam vos ~a antiquitates vestras* Ezek. 36.11 (AC 55.1); *verum Ecclesiae ~a religiosum ibi* AC 6728. **4** (adv.) Near by, close: *omnes tam praesentes, ut ~a sint, si vel forent in ultimo universi* ES 4016.

K

kesia ~ae, *f.* (Hebr.) = **casia**: Ps. 45.8 (AE 195.19).

kesitah: see **kesithah**.

kesithah ~ae, *f.* (Hebr.) also **kesitah**. Transliteration of a Hebr. word for a silver coin: *per ~as, quae nummi erant* AC 4400.

korus ~i, *m.* (Hebr.) A Hebrew measure equal to ten baths: Ezek. 45.14 (AC 576.1); AC 10262.4.

L

labefactatio ~onis, *f.* The act of causing to totter or collapse: (transf.) *~o Ecclesiae* AE 400.11; *per extremam ~onem hominis* AT 122.

labefacto ~are ~avi ~atum, *tr.* To cause to totter, shake to the foundations, ruin: *ut tandem [vitia] totam membranam ~ent* AC 5188.1; (transf.) *omnes caeli ~arentur* AM 352; VR 321; AE 413.2.

labes ~is, *f.* A fault, failing, defect: *quod...pulmo ...laboret, et si ~es ingravescit moriatur homo* DP 180.3; *homo ex ~e haereditaria nascitur in mala omnis generis* AS 432.4; SA 79 (= iii.4.[2]).

labium ~i, *neut.* **1** (usu. pl.) The lips: *os cum ~is* AC 6987.1; AM 316.4. **2** (Bibl.) A language: (sg.) *et fuit tota terra ~um unum, et verba una* Gen. 11.1 (AC); (pl.) *quique civitates...loquentes ~a Canaanis* Isa. 19.18 (DD 4).

labor[1] ~oris, *m.* **1** A piece of work to be done, task: *opera erant ~ores* AC 7104; *duae manus [faciunt] unum ~orem* AM 316.4. **2** Hard labour, toil, distress: *vidit afflictionem nostram, et ~orem nostrum* Deut. 26.7 (AC 1846.2); *ex ~ore animae Suae* Isa. 53.11 (DD 15.1); (w. gen.) a struggle (to): *angeli in ~ore sunt avertendi mala et falsa* AC 227.

labor[2] ~bi ~psus sum, *intr.* **1** To come down from above, fall, slip: *vidi stellam e coelo ~psam in terram* Rev. 9.1 (AC 8278.2); (fig.) *dum ~buntur [ideae angelicae] in mundum spirituum* AC 730.5. **2** To move gently or imperceptibly, glide: *loquela est soni articulati ~bentis versus membranam auris externam* AC 7359; cf. AC 1648; AC 6923. **3** (w. *in* + acc.) To change gently (to another state or mode of being): *ut ~berentur...in somnum* ES 3618; *quicquid...homo vult, ~bitur... sponte in actum* CI 212; ES 3278. **4** (w. *in* + acc.) To fall (into error and sim.): *in errores ~psus* AC 1071.1; *in falsitates ~bitur* AC 1212. **5** To fall apart, collapse: *frustra allaborat reparare ~psa et laesa* ES 2716; *quod Dominus...rem ~psam restituerit* AC 8273.2; (of persons) to fall from grace: *tunc homo non ultra sustinet, sed ~bitur* AC 8165.2.

laboriosus ~a ~um, *a.* Hard-working, industrious: *solent inspicere eos...qui ~i, qui probi* ES 2501.

laboro ~are ~avi ~atum, *intr., tr.* **1** To work, labour: *illi qui pro mercede ~abant* AC 8002.4. **b** (tr.) to till, work (the ground): *pulli asinini ~antes humum* Isa. 30.24 (AC 566.5). **2** To exert oneself, labour, toil: (w. *in* + abl.) *in quibus [praestigiis] ~asti a juventute tua* Isa. 47.12 (AC 7297.2); (w. inf.) *a se discutere falsa ~ant* AC 7320; ES 461; (w. *ut*) *omni arte ~abat ut se inferret* ES 602. **3** To experience difficulty, suffer: *~abunt Aegyptii ad bibendum aquas e fluvio* Exod. 7.18 (AC); *vita illorum...a praesentia Divina ~at* AC 8265.1; *~at pectore et anhelitu* AM 50. **b** (w. abl.) to suffer (from a disease or malady): *mulier profluvio sanguinis ~ans* Luke 8.43 (AE 79.3); *~avit mortifero malo* ES 1260; *quod in vita corporis phantasia ea ~averit* AC 444.

labrum[1] ~i, *neut.* The lip: *regionem circum ~a prominentem* AC 7807; ES 529; (sg.) AM 182.8; (transf.) a border (on a garment): *~um erit ori ejus* [sc. *ephodi*] Exod. 28.32 (AC).

labrum[2] ~i, *neut.* A large basin, bowl: *sub decem ~is circa templum Salomonis* AC 8215.5.

labrusca ~ae, *f.* A wild grape: *cur...apportastis uvas malas seu ~as* AM 294.7; Isa. 5.2 (AC 1069.2); also, a wild vine: *pro hordeo ~a* Job 31.40 (AE 374.8).

labyrintheus ~a ~um, *a.* Labyrinthine: *mille ~is nexibus* AC 179; *per quasi vias ~as circumferri* ES 308.

labyrinthus ~i, *m.* A maze, labyrinth: *spatiosus ~us, qui talis est, ut qui vult exire, penitius intret* AM 8.3; ES 1020.

lac ~ctis, *neut.* (pl. *~ctes* AC 1002) Milk: *ad terram fluentem ~cte et melle* Exod. 3.8 (AC): *quod infantes ament ~c* ES 2084; (pl.) kinds of milk: *~ctes et quae ex ~ctibus, ut butyra* AC 1002.

lacer ~era ~erum, *a.* Tattered, ragged: *sunt illis ~erae vestes* AM 510.3; AE 195.5.

laceratio ~onis, *f.* A tearing, lacerating: *paena ~onis* AC 956; ES 4087.

lacero ~are ~avi ~atum, *tr.* To tear, wound: *ne* [*porci*] *...versi ~ent vos* Matt. 7.6 (AC 7784.4); (transf.) *zelum pro...vero, quod sic ~atum* AC 2576.16.

lacertus ~i, *m.* A lizard: *quidam illam* [sc. *praedestinationem*] *abjiciunt sicut anguem* [*vel*] *~um* VR 803 (n.b. 1st edn. reads *anguem lacertum*, but perh. *anguem laceratum* is intended).

lacessitio ~onis, *f.* Harassment, annoyance: *~o et continua voluntas malefaciendi* ES 4648.1.

lacesso ~ere ~ii ~itum, *tr.* To harass, annoy, attack: *natura mali est ut unumquemvis ~ere velit* AC 1683; CI 508.2; VR 300.2; ES 4420.

lachryma ~ae, *f.* also **lacrima**. A tear: *ad ~am meam ne taceas* Ps. 39.12 (AC 8002.3); (usu. pl.) *ut ~as funderet* CI 238; (Bibl.) *in lingua originali dicitur ... ~a vini... ~ae sunt quae stillantur* AC 9223.2.

lachrymatio ~onis, *f.* also **lacrimatio**, and **lacrymatio**. The shedding of tears, crying: *luctus et ~o* SS 84.1; AM 8.3.

lachrymo ~are ~avi, *intr.* also **lacrimo**. To shed tears, weep, cry: *cum...inciperent indolere, et... ~are* AM 161.2.

lacinia ~ae, *f.* An openwork fabric, lace: *contextus pulcher ex spiris mirabiliter consertis ad modum ~arum* AC 5559; ES 231.

lacrim-: see **lachrym-**.

lacrymatio: see **lachrymatio**.

lactans ~ntis, *f. adj.* Giving suck; (as sb.) a ewe: *a post ~ntes adduxit eum* Ps. 78.70 (AE 409.5).

lactatio ~onis, *f.* The act of suckling: [*natus*] *crevit per ~onem* AC 6749; AM 176.

lactatrix ~icis, *f.* One who gives suck, wet nurse: *erunt reges nutritii tui, et principes mulieres ~ices tuae* Isa. 49.23 (AE 31.5).

lactens ~ntis, *m.* An unweaned infant, suckling: *adhaesit lingua ~ntis palato ejus ob sitim* Lam. 4.4 (AC 6745.6); *~ntes, infantes et puerulos* AC 430.1.

lacteo ~tere, *intr.* (of infants) To suck milk: *quod praeter ~tere et respirare nihil possint* [*infantes*] VR 335.7.

lacteus ~a ~um, *a.* Of or concerned with milk: (in the body) *vasa ~a* DP 164.6; *via ~a*, the Milky Way: AC 10589.

lacticinium ~i, *neut.* The supply of milk (to infants): *ex suctione uberum et ~o* AM 396.2; (transf.) nourishment: *auferre illis* [sc. *infantibus*] *omne ~um spirituale* VR 23.2.

lactisugium ~i, *neut.* The sucking of milk: 3AD 1175.

lacto ~are ~avi ~atum, *tr.* **1** (of women and female animals) To give suck to: *~a illum mihi* Exod. 2.9 (AC); *lactentes et ~antes aliquoties in Verbo memorantur* AC 3183.1; *etiam balaenae praebent mammam, ~ant foetus suos* Lam. 4.3 (AC 6745.6). **2** (transf.) To nourish as with milk, nurture, encourage: *uxores... ex hac...cogitatione continue ~ant amorem suum* AM 216[a]; AM 254; (pass.) *~or spe quod...* AM 78.8; AM 167.2.

lacuna ~ae, *f.* An opening, hole: *facies...qualis cadaverum, cum ~is horrendis* AC 949; *~as... excrementitias sudoris* ES 3720.

lacunar ~aris, *neut.* **1** A vaulted roof, arch: *sicut e templo auferrentur parietes et ~aria* VR 55. **2** A space roofed with arches, vault: *in quoddam ~ar divisum in cellulas* AR 484.4; *pervasit longum ~ar, et venit in antrum* ES 6036; *quod advenas...in ~ar suum non admittat* UJ(C) 47.

lacunatus ~a ~um, *a.* Covered with an arched roof, vaulted: [*inferna*] *similia ~is cavernis et cryptis quales sunt in fodinis* CI 586; *mapalia ~a sicut ex lateribus* AR 421.2; *in camera saxea ~a* UJ(C) 47.

lacus ~us, *m.* **1** A lake, pool: *terrae et ~us, montes et colles* AM 182.3; *portare aquas ex ~ubus seu mari* ES 363. **2** A wine vat: *plenum est torcular, exundarunt ~us* Joel 3.13 = Hebr. Bible 4.13 (AE 922.3).

laedo ~dere ~si ~sum, *tr.* To cause injury to, hurt, harm: *perplures sunt qui...neminem ~serant* AC 1835.3; *ne ~derentur a praesentia Ipsius Divini* AC 6838; *haec dira inceperunt ~dere aures nostras* VR 78.5; (transf.) *conscientia ~ditur* AC 8159.1.

laesio ~onis, *f.* The act of injuring, damaging, harm: *ex ~one vitae naturalis* AC 8164.1; *propter ~onem boni* AC 8313.3; *ne utar aliqua voce ~onis* [i.e., wounding remark] ES 1116.

laete, *adv.* (superl. *~issime*) **1** Luxuriantly: *floretum ... ~issime exsplendescebat* AC 2296. **2** In a cheerful manner, gladly: *flamma...flagrans ~e* AC 6922.

laetificatio ~onis, *f.* The act of making cheerful, gladdening: AC 7857.2; a joyful occasion: *festivitatibus et ~onibus* VR 361.2.

laetifico ~are ~avi ~atum, *tr.* To make cheerful, gladden: *vinum ~at cor hominis* Ps. 104.15 (AE 375.23); *cum volui ~are animum meum* AM 10.4; *dum homo*

~at vultum ES 2181; (refl.) [*praedones*] *qui...dividunt praedam inter se, et se inde ~ant et glorificant* VR 117.

laetitia ~ae, *f.* A feeling of cheerfulness, gladness: *quod omne coeleste gaudium producit cordis ~am* AC 418.1; *appercepi teneritudinem ~ae...talem ut exprimeret lachrymas ex oculis meis* AC 7251; (dist. from **gaudium**) SS 84.1; ES 904.

laetor ~ari ~atus sum, *intr.* To be glad, rejoice: *ex praeda ~ati* AC 7248; (w. *in* + abl.) *exsultemus et ~emur in salute Ipsius* Isa. 25.9 (AC 1736.2); (w. abl.) *contenti paucis... ~antur illis* CI 277.2; (w. *quod*) *~ati sunt, quod...visuri sint nuptias* AM 19.

laetus ~a ~um, *a.* (compar. *~ior*, superl. *~issimus*) **1** (of crops) Luxuriant, rich: *seges et sementis ~a* ES 231. **2** (of persons or their minds) Cheerful, glad: *quisque ex corde ~us erat* AC 8118.2; *ex ~o animo* AC 7088; (neut. as sb.) cheerfulness, gladness: *hoc oleum significabat ~um et faustum* AE 375.24. **3** Giving gladness, cheering: *~issima consortia cum angelis* AM 3.2; *flamma...perquam ~a* ES 687; (neut. as sb.) *in amaenis et ~is sunt* CI 168.3.

laevigo ~are ~avi ~atum, *tr.* also **lev-**. To rub smooth, polish: *~antem malleum* Isa. 41.7 (AC 3527.3); *super caudicibus ~atis* AM 77.6; *aeris ~ati* Ezek. 1.7 (AC 425).

laevis ~is ~e, *a.* also **levis**[2]. Smooth: [*zelus*] *extrinsecus ~is, glaber, tonans et flagrans* VR 155.2; *~is serpentis* ES 461.

laevitas ~atis, *f.* also **lev-**. Smoothness: *super ~atem collorum illius* Gen. 27.16 (AC).

laganum ~i, *neut.* (Gk.) A thin, flat cake, wafer: *~a azymorum uncta oleo* Exod. 29.2 (AC).

lagena ~ae, *f.* (ad. Gk.) A bottle, flask, flagon: *eme ~am figuli* Jer. 19.1 (AE 177.9); *~am vini rubri* ES 3801.

laicus ~i, *m.* (Gk.) A layman (as opposed to a cleric): *quod vocari possit...atheus ex clericis, et quod vir non sanae rationis a ~is* AM 380.5; VR 16.1.

lambo ~ere ~i, *tr.* **1** To touch with the tongue, lick: *vidi quod...* [*testudo*] *~eret manus eorum* AR 463.1; (transf., of flames) *hoc flammeum... ~ebat manum circumcirca* AC 7620. **2** To lick up, lap: *~ent pulverem sicut serpens* Mic. 7.17 (AC 249).

lamella ~ae, *f.* A small plate, plaque: *insignia quae erant ~ae cupreae* AM 182.8; *~is sicut vitreis* VR 35.2.

lamentabilis ~is ~e, *a.* (compar. *~ior*) Deserving of tears, lamentable: *de...statu ~i infidelium* AC 5; *quod nihil ~ius foret, quam nasci homo* AM 29.

lamentabiliter, *adv.* In a lamentable fashion: ES 4600.

lamentatio ~onis, *f.* A noisy expression of grief, wailing, lamentation: *tolle ~onem super Pharaonem* Ezek. 32.2 (AC 7293.2); AC 7782.

lamentatrix ~icis, *f.* A wailing woman: Jer. 9.17 (AE 484.4).

lamentor ~ari ~atus sum, *tr.* To grieve noisily, wail, lament: *~atus est David...super Schaule* 2 Sam. 1.17 (SS 103.3); *ex periclitatione ~antur...nauclerus et nautae* CO 57.

lamentum ~i, *neut.* A wailing, lament: *convertam ...cantica vestra in ~um* Amos 8.10 (AC 7093.5); *~a illorum audiuntur sicut fremitus peculiaris soni* AM 510.3.

lamina ~ae, *f.* A flat piece, sheet, plate: *tectum ex ~is auri* AM 12.1; ES 3807; (anat.) *~a cribrosa*, a sieve-like plate of bone in the nose: ES 1239; ES 1793.

lampas ~adis, *f.* (Gk.) **1** A lamp: *hortum plenum ~adibus et lucernis* AC 7072; *cum argenteis nunc accensis ~adibus in manibus* AM 20.3. **2** A fixed light for navigation, lighthouse: *~ades super petris in mari* VR 379.5.

lana ~ae, *f.* **1** The wool (of sheep): *crinis...sicut ~a munda* Dan. 7.9 (AC 6832.5); *tunica ex ~a candida* AM 75.4. **2** Similar material from other animals or plants: *ex ~is an ex ~is sylvestribus* ES 1547; *~a caprina*, goat's wool (as a type of non-existent object): *ratiocinatio vestra est de ~a caprina* VR 72.2; VR 335.2.

lanatus ~a ~um, *a.* Covered with wool, woolly: *hirci ~i* CI 325.

lancea ~ae, *f.* A light spear, lance, javelin: *cum Josua extenderet ~am* AC 878.6 (Josh. 8.18).

lanceola ~ae, *f.* A small pointed weapon, lance: *solebant se gladiolis, ~is, aut cultris...pungere* AC 2799.23.

laneus ~a ~um, *a.* Made of wool, woollen: *toga ~a* AM 266.1; *panno seu velo ~o* ES 1371.

langueo ~guere ~gui, *intr.* To be weak, droop, languish: *ficus ~guet* Joel 1.12 (AC 8369.2).

languesco ~ere, *intr.* To become weak, fail, languish: *expandentes rete... ~ent* Isa. 19.8 (AC 6693.2); *portae ejus ~entes factae sunt* Jer. 14.2 (AE 208.11).

languiditas ~atis, *f.* Feebleness: *lipothymia quae est totalis ~as corporis* AM 253.2.

languidus ~a ~um, *a.* Feeble, languid: *quamdiu cor integrum est...viscera possunt vivere; at cum illud ~um, tabes occupat omnia* AC 468.2; *totum cor ~um* Isa. 1.5 (AC 8364.4).

languor ~oris, *m.* Physical weakness, debility, languor: *omnes ~ores Aegypti malos* Deut. 7.15 (AC 8364.3).

laniena ~ae, *f.* Savage slaughter, butchery, massacre: *~ae forent crudeliores quam usque ferarum ferocissimarum* ES 374; *per ~am Hispanorum in America* ES 3867.

laniger ~era ~erum, *a.* Wool-producing, woolly: *~erae oves* ES 4663.

lanio[1] ~are ~avi ~atum, *tr.* To tear the flesh of, scarify: *ita ~antur, ut quasi frustatim...discissi...sibi videantur* AC 829.2; *~ando faciem* AM 512.1.

lanio[2] ~onis, *m.* A slaughterer, butcher: *~ones, qui credunt se peritos anatomiae, quia lustrarunt viscera boum et ovium* CC 16.7.

lanuginosus ~a ~um, *a.* Resembling wool, woolly: *~um quid* ES 1866; ES 4357.

lanx ~ncis, *f.* Either of the pans of a pair of scales: (fig.) *si sententia super ~nce aequilibris et justa apparet* AM 132.2; (pl.) scales: *~nces justitiae* Ezek. 45.10 (AC 576.1); AE 373.1.

Laodicensis ~is ~e, *a.* Of Laodicea: *[Ecclesiae] ~i* AE 108.1; (masc pl. as sb.) *angelo Ecclesiae ~ium scribe* Rev. 3.14 (AR).

lapidatio ~onis, *f.* Execution by stoning: AE 315.8.

lapideus ~a ~um, *a.* Made of stone: *bonum non vivum [percipitur] sicut quoddam...~um* AC 671; *decem praecepta tabulis ~is...inscripta* AC 6752.1; *avis ...facta...sicut ~a* AC 7622.2; *aedificium ~um* ES 4575.

lapido ~are ~avi ~atum, *tr.* To execute by stoning, stone: *alium ~arunt* Matt. 21.35 (AE 122.3); John 8.5 (DD 9).

lapillus ~i, *m.* A small stone, pebble: *planum ~is varie coloratis stratum* AM 132.1; VR 639.

lapis ~idis, *m.* **1** Stone as a material: *~is ex quo arena est* AC 6762; *in ~idem calcarium* VR 8.4; *~is lydius*, touchstone: see **Lydius**. **2** A piece of stone, rock: *ponam Hierosolymam ~idem oneris* Zech. 12.3 (DD 4); *super ~ide altaris* Josh. 8.32 (AC 6752.6); (also app.) a lump of other materials: *~idem plumbi* Zech. 5.8 (AC 8540.4). **b** (regarded as valuable): *~ides pretiosi* AC 6640.2; *opus ~idis sapphiri* Exod. 24.10 (AC); *columnae ...ex ~ide lazuli* AM 12.1. **3** An object made of stone: *servire ligno et ~idi pro sculptilibus ex ligno et lapide* AC 643.3; *et erit sanguis in omni terra Aegypti, et in lignis et in ~idibus* Exod. 7.19 (AC).

lapsarius: see **infralapsarii** and **supralapsarius**.

lapsus[1] ~a ~um: pf. pple. of **labor**[2].

lapsus[2] ~us, *m.* **1** A falling down, fall: *proni ad ~um* AM 505.4; *in...naufragiis, ~ibus, incendiis* DP 140. **2** A falling away from the proper state, fall: *causa ~us Antiquissimae Ecclesiae* AC 127; *~us ad omne falsum* AC 977.2.

laqueare ~is, *neut.* A vaulted roof, vault: *sonus qualis resilit ex arboribus sylvae seu ~ibus* VR 683.1; *arcuatum seu ~e erat sicut solet esse Hollandiae sub eorum pontibus* ES 2380; *~ia et cellaria* ES(M) [4823].

laqueus ~i, *m.* A noose, snare (in quots. fig.): *praevenerunt Me ~i mortis* Ps. 18.5 (DD 14.6); *quod theologica sint speciosi ~i ad captandum columbas* VR 147.

large, *adv.* Copiously, in abundance: *~e bibebat cum eo* Gen. 43.34 (AC).

largior ~giri ~gitus sum, *tr.* To bestow in abundance, lavish: *nati quos gratiose ~gitus Deus servo tuo* Gen. 33.5 (AC); Ps. 119.29 (AC 627.2).

largus ~a ~um, *a.* (compar. *~ior*) Copious, large: *barba...totum mentum occupans, ~a, et usque comta* ES 5126.

larva ~ae, *f.* The apparition of a dead person, an insubstantial figure, ghost: *circum alios sicut ~ae volitare* CI 578; *visus illorum est sicut videntis ~as in umbra* SS 60; *assimilari possunt homini aëreo, qui dicitur ~a* VR 375.2.

larynx ~ngis, *m.* (Gk.) (anat.) The larynx: DP 180.3.

lascive, *adv.* Wantonly, lasciviously: *cogitant...de hoc ex carne ~e* AM 178.1.

lascivia ~ae, *f.* Wantonness, lasciviousness: *quantum quis fugit ~am adulterii* VI 75; *meretrix inspiravit viro ~am* VR 80.1.

lascivio ~vire ~vivi, *intr.* To behave wantonly: *internum non potest ~vire* AM 148.2; ES 386.

lasciviosus ~a ~um, *a.* Prone to wantonness: *ii qui amarunt vitam ~am* ES 386; AM 148.2.

lascivus ~a ~um, *a.* Sexually unrestrained, wanton, lascivious: *~a meretrix* VR 7; *ille amor est ~us* AM 345.1; (neut. pl. as sb.) *~a loqui* VI 74.

lassitudo ~inis, *f.* Weariness, tiredness: *inducebant ~inem animi* ES(M) 4599.

lassus ~a ~um, *a.* Weary, tired: *~os spiritu ex taedio* AM 9.2; *aves... ~ae volatu* VR 67.1.

late, *adv.* (compar. *~ius*) To a wide extent, widely: *quod infernum hoc...extendat se satis ~e versus sinistrum* AC 8099.2; AM 189.

latebra ~ae, *f.* A hiding place: *occultas opes ~arum* Isa. 45.3 (AC 7091.3).

latenter, *adv.* Stealthily, secretly: *qui non ita ~er agit* ES 641.

lateo ~tere ~tui, *intr., tr.* **1** (intr.) To lie hidden, be concealed: *interiora...patent ibi in facie...nec minimum ~tet* CI 131; (w. *in* + abl.) *quod sanctum sit quod in sensu illo ~tet* AC 6745.3; *quod in illis* [sc. *ovis*] *~teat pullus* VR 12.3. **2** (tr.) To escape the notice of, be hidden from: *non me ~tet quod plures dicturi...* AC 68; *talia ...non ~tent angelos* AC 1701; *causa ~tuit eos* ES 2359.

later ~eris, *m.* A brick (in antiquity usu. made from mud): *dare paleam...ad laterificandum ~eres* Exod. 5.7 (AC); *quod sumeret ~erem et sculperet super eo Hierosolymam* DD 15.7 (Ezek. 4.1); *domus constructae ex ~eribus* AM 78.3.

lateralis ~is ~e, *a.* Of or belonging to a side, lateral: *a parte postica et ~i dextra* CO 52.

Lateranensis ~is ~e, *a.* Of the Lateran, a district in Rome that gave its name to the cathedral church and to councils held there, esp. the fourth in 1215: AR 776.2.

latericius: see **lateritius**.

laterifico ~are ~avi ~atum, *tr.* To mould (bricks): *~emus lateres* Gen. 11.3 (AC).

lateritius ~a ~um, *a.* also **latericius**. Of or for bricks: *repara fornacem ~am* Nahum 3.14 (AC 6669.2); *color ...paene ~us* ES 844; brick-shaped: *arcuatum...ex ~is lapidibus* ES 2380.

latex ~icis, *m.* (pl.) Moisture: *terra modo suggerit et ~ices et elementa* VR 491.2.

latibulum ~i, *neut.* A hiding place: *tu ~um mihi* Ps. 32.7 (AC 739.3); (fig.) *ut amor vitae...e ~is suis in lucem...prodeat* DP 281.4.

Latinus ~a ~um, *a.* Latin: *in ~o sermone* VI 6; *Romano-Catholici Missas suas ~o idiomate exclamant* VR 159.4; *~ae literae*, the Latin alphabet: *scriptura similis scripturae in mundo, ~is literis* ES 5561.

latitudo ~inis, *f.* **1** Measurement in a transverse direction, width: *longitudo et ~o et altitudo ejus aequalia erant* Rev. 21.16 (AR); *apparent...lata facie, cujus ~o aequat quatuor...facies aliorum* AC 830; a point so measured, latitude: *omnia mala...~inem et altitudinem sortiuntur* AM 478.3. **2** The quality of being wide (in quot. fig.): *in angustia invocavi Jah, respondit mihi in ~ine* Ps. 118.5 (AC 8267.2).

lator ~oris, *m.* One who carries or proposes (a law); *~ores legum* 'legislators' AM 500.2.

latratus ~us, *m.* The barking of a dog: *aliquid ~us auditur in sonis loquelae illorum* AM 505.4.

latria ~ae, *f.* Honour, service, and worship aimed at God alone: *quod invocatio Sanctorum non sit idololatrica nec adversetur honori unius Mediatoris Dei et hominum; vocatur ~a* AR Doc RC.8.

latrina ~ae, *f.* A latrine: *delectantur...morari in ~is* AC 954; CI 488.5.

latro[1] ~onis, *m.* A robber, highwayman, brigand: *incidit in ~ones* Luke 10.30 (AC 6708); *cum amore ~onum* VR 45.1; (transf.) *tales sunt violatores conjugii ...et sic ~ones spirituales* AM 504.3.

latro[2] ~are ~avi, *intr.* (of dogs) To bark: *omnes sunt canes muti, non possunt ~are* Isa. 56.10 (AC 7784.4); ES 4997.

latrocinium ~i, *neut.* A robbery: *omnia mala, facinora, ~a, artes, doli* CI 462ᵃ.8; ES 723.

latrocinor ~ari ~atus sum, *tr., intr.* **1** (tr) To steal: *ut...praedas ~entur* VR 45.1; ES 727. **2** (intr.) To commit robbery: *furari et ~ari* VI 80.

latronicus ~a ~um, *a.* Of a robber, highwayman, brigand; (neut. as sb.) robbery, brigandage: *potest... omnis furcifer, praedo, et latro se lavare usque ad nitorem, num sic furciferum, praedonicum, et ~um abstergitur?* VR 672.2.

latus[1] ~eris, *neut.* **1** The side (of the body): *quod cubaret super ~ere suo sinistro* SS 16 (Ezek. 4.4); *per militem qui transfixit ~us Ipsius* AE 38 (John 19.34). **2** The side (as opposed to the middle of anything): *conclavia...quae ad ~era ibi exteriora sunt* AC 7353. **3** The place next (to something), the side: *puellae ejus euntes ad ~us fluminis* [i.e., alongside the river] Exod. 2.5 (AC); *a ~ere*, beside: *dum aliquod deforme a ~ere est* VR 61.1; *adstitit mihi a ~ere angelus* VR 35.2; *consiliarii a ~ere* 'privy councillors' AM 14.1. **4** The side (as an indication of direction): *mensae, quindecim ab uno ~ere, et quindecim ab altero* AM 6.1; *ad ~us quod spectabat meridiem* CI 185.

latus[2] ~a ~um, *a.* (pf. pple. of **fero**) (compar. *~ior*, superl. *~issimus*) **1** Broad, wide: *in ~um campum* AC 6811; *secures ~as* AC 824; *per unam [forem] ~iorem* AM 14.1. **b** *in ~um*, in width, sideways: *haec [sphaera] se extendit...in longum et in ~um* CI 49. **2** (of speech, perh.) With broad vowels, broad: *erat sonus loquelae ~us, qui se vibrabat sicut solet vibratile aëreum* ES 3750. **3** Broadly understood or interpreted (opposed to strict): *'terra'...in ~o sensu significat amorem* AC 636; *in stricto sensu...in minus stricto...in ~iori...in ~issimo* AC 10451.

laudabilis ~is ~e, *a.* Worthy of approbation, praiseworthy: *simulationes conjugiales, quae ~es* AM 271; ES 1056.

laudatio ~onis, *f.* An exaltation in words, praising: *lauda Ipsum cum cymbalis vociferationis...pro bonis et veris fidei propter quae ~o* AC 420.4.

laudo ~are ~avi ~atum, *tr.* To exalt in words, praise:

~abo nomen Dei cantico Ps. 69.30 (AC 8261.6); *ut ~arent et celebrarent Deum* CI 404.

laurea ~ae, *f.* **1** A laurel tree: [*viae*] *ornatae vineis et ~is* CI 520. **2** A laurel wreath (given as a reward and mark of honour): *haec tibi ~a datur* AM 461.8; *~as in quibus rubini et sapphiri* VR 48.20; a wreath of other foliage: *~a ex foliis aesculi ligata* VR 815.2.

laureatus ~i, *m.* A person wearing a laurel wreath: AM 10.1.

laureus ~a ~um, *a.* Made of laurel: *in horto...ex transtris quasi ~is...ornatissimo* CI 337; ES 166.

laurus ~us, *f.* A laurel or bay tree: *lucus ex palmis et ~ibus* AM 183.1; a branch or wreath of laurel: *unus cui non pallium, tiara, et ~us* VR 137.2.

laus laudis, *f.* **1** An enunciation of another's merit, praise: *Tu...venerandus laudibus* Exod. 15.11 (AC); *susurrabant laudem votivam ad Dominum* AM 16.1. **2** An object of praise: *Tu laus mea jugiter* Ps. 71.6 (AC 8043.4); *dabo vos in nomen et in laudem* Zeph. 3.20 (DD 4).

laute, *adv.* Luxuriously: *~e epulando* AM 453.

lautitia ~ae, *f.* Luxurious living, sumptuousness: *indulgendo genio, in ~a et otio* ES 592; (pl.) delicacies: *opimae dapes, cupediae et ~ae* AM 6.5; ES 397.

lautus ~a ~um, *a.* (compar. *~ior*) Sumptuous, extravagant: *~a vita* ES 3514; *ut voluntas non sentiat aliquid ~ius et cupidius* AM 495.3.

lavacrum ~i, *neut.* **1** A bowl for washing, basin: *~a eorum fuerunt ex aere* AC 2162.12 (cf. Exod. 30.18). **2** The act of washing, bath: *ut inducerent speciem ~i a capite ad pedes* ES 403; *quod Baptismus...vocetur ~um regenerationis* VR 685.2.

lavatio ~onis, *f.* The act of washing, ablution (esp. as a ritual): *per sacrificia, per ~ones, per aspersionem sanguinis* AC 7272.1; *per 'baptisma' intelligitur ~o spiritualis* DD 18.5.

lavo ~are ~i ~atum, *tr.* (pf. act. also *~avi* Lev. 17.16 (AC 3147.10, AC 4171.2), pf. pple. also *lotus* AC 10243) To wash, cleanse: *faciem suam multum ~ant et mundant* AC 8245; (spiritually) *ab illis* [*immunditiis*] *~ati sunt* AM 430.

laxatio ~onis, *f.* The act of slackening, relaxation: *secundum ~onem vinculi* ES 2171.

laxo ~are ~avi ~atum, *tr.* To slacken, relax: *ut primum ~atur vinculum* ES 2171; (fig.) *hi bini amores crescunt quantum illis ~antur fraena* AC 7375; CI 559; cf. *quando iis malis licentia ~atur* ES 2577.

laxus ~a ~um, *a.* Not tightly fitting, loose: *ambulant ...cum operculo ~o* [J D Odhner; *cano* Tafel] *superinduti* ES 559.

lazureus ~a ~um, *a.* Of lapis lazuli, azure: *ex pretioso lapide coloris sapphirini et ~i* AM 76.3.

leaena ~ae, *f.* (Gk.) A lioness: *mater tua ~a* Ezek. 19.2 (AE 280.11); AM 392.2.

lebes ~etis, *m.* (Gk.) A cauldron, tub: *et facies ~etes ad decinerandum* Exod. 27.3 (AC).

lechytus ~i, *m.* (Gk. *lekythos*) also **lecythus**, and **lecytus**. A vessel for oil, bottle, pot: Zech. 4.3 (AC 886.2, AE 375.39).

lectica ~ae, *f.* *Feralis ~a*, a bier: AC 817; so *~a* alone: ES 4564; *~a infantis*, a baby carriage, perambulator: ES 4500.

lectio ~onis, *f.* **1** The act of reading: *per ~onem Verbi* AC 8078.4; ES(M) 4573. **2** A particular text, reading: *variantes ~ones autorum classicorum* ES 805.

lector ~oris, *m.* **1** One who reads, reader: *in tam amplum codicem, ut defatigaret ~orem* AM 209; VR 142. **2** A lecturer: *cum...constituti ~ores in gymnasiis* VR 815.2.

lectus ~i, *m.* A bed, couch: *cubant in ~o* AC 8376; *cum in ~um ivi* ES 2711; *dum jacet in ~o moribundus* AM 28; *in mortis ~o* ES 1235.

lecythus: see **lechytus**.

lecytus: see **lechytus**.

legatio ~onis, *f.* **1** The sending of an ambassador, embassy: *causa ~onis meae fuit haec* AM 2.2. **2** A bequest, legacy: *quid ~o et testamentum absque obsignatione?* VR 730.2.

legatus ~i, *m.* An envoy, ambassador: *ite ~i...ad gentem...conculcatam* Isa. 18.2 (AE 304.22); *cum quodam ~o regni disceptantes* DP 197.2.

legio ~onis, *f.* A vast number, legion: *duodecim ~ones angelorum* Matt. 26.53 (AE 430. 16); *~onum ~ones* ES 2020; ES 4683.

legislator ~oris, *m.* One who makes laws, lawgiver, legislator: *en testem populis dedi Ipsum, ducem et ~orem populis* Isa. 55.4 (AC 666.2).

legisperitus ~i, *m.* One who is learned in law, a legal expert, lawyer: *~us volens seipsum justificare* Luke 10.29 (AE 444.12); DP 296.11.

legitimus ~a ~um, *a.* **1** Sanctioned by law, legal: *~um et amabile consortium cum una* AM 49; *conjugia ~a* ES 230. **2** Prescribed by natural rules, regular, proper: *omnia...in suos gyros ~os fluunt* ES 1026.

lego ~gere ~gi ~ctum, *tr.* **1** To gather, collect, pick:

~gentes ex arboribus fructus AM 8.2; *sciunt apes ~gere mella ex floribus* CI 108.1. **2** To read aloud, recite (a book or its contents): *cum ~gerem in Verbo aliquid de passione Salvatoris nostri* AC 8383; *ex oratione, quae... ~gitur coram populo* VI 4. **3** To grasp by reading, read: *~gat quaeso illa quae...supra allata sunt* DD 21; *hominem qui illud* [sc. *Verbum*] *a Domino, et non a semet solo, ~git* SS 3.2. **b** (impers. pass.) it is to be read, it is written: *sicut ~gitur de Alexandro* VR 74.2; (w. *quod*) *~giturne in Verbo, quod in caelo non dentur nuptiae...?* AM 44.10.

legumen ~inis, *neut.* A vegetable: *omne arbustum, virgultum et ~en* VR 54; ES 1521.

Leibnitzianus ~a ~um, *a.* Of the philosopher Leibnitz; (masc. as sb.) a follower of Leibnitz: *tres Aristotelici, tres Cartesiani, et tres ~i* VR 696.1.

lemma ~atis, *neut.* (Gk.) A section of a book smaller than a chapter: *in ~ate hujus capitis de creatione* VR 29.2; SE 23.

lenio ~nire ~nivi ~nitum, *tr.* **1** To make soft or gentle, soften: *qui callus vel ~niendus est, sed non frangendus* ES 862. **2** To make mild or light, lessen, mitigate: *angeli...dolores miserabilium ~niunt* AC 967; *quod haec... ~niant gravitatem adulterii* AM 488.

lenis ~is ~e, *a.* (compar. *~ior*, superl. *~issimus*) **1** Lacking intensity, gentle, mild: *sicut oculus laesus non* [*suffert*] *radios etiam ~es solis* AC 7768; *instar ~is fluvii* CI 241. **2** Not stiff, yielding, soft, delicate: *ex ~ibus filis serici* DP 296.3; *tanquam volutio nubis ~is incumbentis* ES 255. **3** (of sounds) Soft, gentle: *~e murmur* AM 316.5.

lenitas ~atis, *f.* Gentleness, mildness: *per ~atem eorum loquelae* ES 578.

leniter, *adv.* Gently, mildly: *influebant satis ~er* AC 4049; *redarguunt etiam, sed ~er* AC 7804.

lenitudo ~inis, *f.* Gentleness, mildness: *probitas per ~inem et suavitatem...se manifestat* AC 8111; ES 578; ES 3109.

leno ~onis, *m.* A brothel-keeper, pimp: *hi non absimiles sunt uxoratis ~onibus* AM 376.

lenocinium ~i, *neut.* A gratifying sensation, charm, allurement, enticement: *indulgent gustui et ~is tactilium corporis* CI 462.2; *totus dissolutus eram in delitiosa ~a, sicut thermarum dulcium* ES 379.

lens ~ntis, *f.* **1** A lentil: *tritica, hordea, ~ntes, milium et zeas* DD 15 (Ezek. 4.9). **2** A lens (in the eye): *in ~nte chrystallina sunt striae* ES 1075.

lente, *adv.* Slowly, gradually: *acclivitas ~e surgens* AM 76.1.

lenticula ~ae, *f.* A flask: *~a olei* 1 Kgs. 17.14 (AC 4844.12).

lentor ~oris, *m.* Slowness: *ut me cum ~ore deportarent* AM 10.4; sluggishness: *materialia...sunt sicut gravia quae ~orem inducunt* AC 6921.

lentus ~a ~um, *a.* (compar. *~ior*) **1** Moving or happening slowly, slow: *variationes ~ae fuerunt, et subitae* ES 215; *per quod...sanguis fiat viscosus, tenax, spissus, ~us, acer* AM 374. **2** (transf.) Sluggish, slow: *sunt... ~i ac ingenii hebetis* ES 920.

leo ~onis, *m.* (Gk.) A lion: *~ones, tigrides, ursos* AM 378; (fig.) *ecce vicit ~o, qui est ex tribu Jehudae* Rev. 5.5 (AR).

leoparda ~ae, *f.* A female leopard, leopardess: *apud leones et leaenas, ursos et ursas, leopardos et ~as* AM 392.

leopardus ~i, *m.* A leopard: AM 78.2.

lepidus ~a ~um, *a.* *aquas ~as* ES 1002 (Tafel; the author prob. intended to write *tepidas*).

lepra ~ae, *f.* (Gk.) **1** Leprosy: *propter ~am ut morbum* AC 6963.1; *corporis...exulceratio, scabies, ~a, pediculi et similia* ES 654; (w. pl.) a case of leprosy: *sapientia moralis fugit mala et falsa, ut ~as* AM 102. **2** Any contagious disease: *quae* [*meretrix*]*...inficit illos sua ~a* VR 148.2.

leprosus ~a ~um, *a.* Affected by leprosy, leprous: *et ecce manus ejus ~a sicut nix* Exod. 4.6 (AC); *facies ei erat ~a a fronte ad mentum* AM 264.1; (masc. as sb.) a leper: *~i mundantur* Matt. 11.5 (SS 17.4).

Lernaeus ~a ~um, *a.* (Gk.) Of Lerna, a town in southern Greece, reputed in mythology to be the home of a monster: *echidnas ~as* CO 38.2.

letalis: see **lethalis**.

Lethaeus ~a ~um, *a.* (Gk.) also **Letheus**. *Aquae ~ae*, the waters of the river Lethe, reputed in mythology to induce forgetfulness: ES 1773.

lethalis ~is ~e, *a.* also **letalis**. Causing death, deadly, lethal: *persuasio illa ~is* AC 586.1; (neut. as sb.) *ut ~e ex contagio inducatur* AM 253.1.

lethargia ~ae, *f.* (Gk.) **1** Sluggishness, lethargy: *quae* [*haeresis*]*...de vita aeterna ~am induxit* VR 497.1.

Letheus: see **Lethaeus**.

lethifer ~era ~erum, *a.* also **letifer**. Bringing death, fatal: *quod talis persuasio ~era et suffocativa non existet* AC 1031.

lethus ~i, *m.* (variant form of **let(h)um*** ~i, *neut.*) Death: DP 112.2; (fig.) extinction: *hic status est ~us gaudiorum vestrorum* AM 5.3 (repeated VR 734.3).

letifer: see **lethifer**.

leviathan ~anis, *m*. (Hebr.) Leviathan: *super ~anem serpentem oblongum* Isa. 27.1 (AC 42.2); VR 74.2.

leviculus ~a ~um, *a*. Very light, slight: *apparuit aliquo ~o indusio quasi cinctus* ES 4863.

levidensis ~is ~e, *a*. Of slight importance, trivial: *Praeter plura ~ia* VR Errores Typographici (1st edn.).

levigo see **laevigo**.

levir, *indecl*. The husband's brother who was obligated to marry the husband's wife after the husband died: *non intravit Jehudah ad illam ut ~ir ad uxorem sed ut scortator ad meretricem* AC 4911.3; AC 4835.2.

leviratus ~us, *m*. The custom of remarriage of a widow to her husband's brother, levirate: Deut. 25.5 (AC 1748.4).

levis[1] ~is ~e, *a*. (compar. *~ior*, superl. *~issimus*) **1** Lacking in weight, light: *jugum enim Meum facile est, et onus Meum ~e* Matt. 11.30 (CI 359); (neut. as sb.) *ut [verum] ad superiora ascendat sicut ~e in mundo* AC 8279.1. **2** Rapidly moving, quick: *~es sunt prae pardis equi* Hab. 1.8 (AE 281.11). **3** Lacking strength, slight: *terrae motus sunt ~iores et graviores* AR 711; *venti ~issimi* ES 3861. **4** (transf.) Having little force, not serious, slight: *tentatio quoad intellectualia ~is est* AC 734; *~e argumentum* DP 133; *per... ~em reflexionem* ES 1438. **5** Of little importance, minor: *naevi corporis ~iores* AM 288.2.

levis[2]: see **laevis**.

levitas: see **laevitas**.

leviter, *adv*. To a small extent, slightly: *non prophanant verum nisi ~er* AC 6959.2; *quod [loquela]... influat in linguam, et illam ~er vibret* CI 248; *post se januam ~er occludunt* 'push the door to behind them' AM 512.1.

Leviticus ~i, *m*. The name of a book of the Word: AC 7102.4.

leviuscule, *adv*. Very slightly: *quidam me laesit ~e* ES 2849.

levo ~are ~avi ~atum, *tr*. To relieve, lessen (suffering): *spes...quae ~aret dolorem* ES 170; *ut ~etur [conscientia]* VR 539.2.

lex legis, *f*. **1** A law as part of a judicial system: *ex timore legis* AM 267.3; *praefecti administrant omnia secundum leges* CI 215. **2** The laws prescribed for the Israelites, the law of Moses: *jotha unum aut corniculum unum non praeteribit de Lege* Matt. 5.18 (CI 260); *Lex et Prophetae* AC 36; *omnis lex veri et recti, principaliter lex conjugiorum* AC 162.1. **b** *Lex Divina*, the divine law: *agitur in supremo sensu de Domino quomodo Ipse Lex Divina quoad Humanum factus est* AC 6717.3. **3** A necessary condition of existence, law: *generalis lex repraesentationis est* AC 1361.1; *ex lege ordinis* AC 6724.3; *lex est, quod nihil usquam absque usu* ES 3144.

lexicon ~i, *neut*. (Gk.) A dictionary, lexicon: *qui ~a concinnarunt* ES 2040.

libamen ~inis, *neut*. **1** An offering of liquid, libation: *de holocaustis, sacrificiis, minchis et ~inibus* SS 16. **2** The use or enjoyment of anything for the first time: *post ~en rejiciunt ac libidinantur ad alias* AM 508.

libellus ~i, *m*. A small book, tract: *quod Decalogus... sit ~us, qui...rejectibilis sit* VR 14.3; (esp. Bibl.) *~us repudii*, a document constituting a statement of divorce: *si vir...scribat ei* [sc. *uxori*] *~um repudii* Deut. 24.1 (AC 213).

libenter, *adv*. also **lubenter**. (compar. *~ius*, superl. *~issime* ES 273) Willingly: *quod homo amat, non modo ~er facit sed etiam ~er cogitat* VI 1; *malum appetit falsum, et id ~er arripit pro vero* AC 10648.3; ES 2480.

liber[1] ~bri, *m*. **1** The bark (of a tree): *naturale circumcingit illud* [sc. *spirituale*] *sicut ~ber lignum, ac sicut vagina ensem* AM 449; VR 78.4; *indumentum ...capitis, factum ex ~bro* ES 547. **2** A book: *quod... tenerent ~bros in manibus, ac legerent* AM 512.2; (esp.) a book of the Bible: *~ber Legis pro ~bris Mosis* AC 6752.4; *~ber creationis*, the Book of Genesis: VR 20.1. **3** *~ber vitae*, the book of life: *~ber...qui est vitae* Rev. 20.12. (AR); *~ber vitae hominis* CI 236.4.

liber[2] ~era ~erum, *a*. (compar. *~erior*, superl. *~errimus*) see also **liberi**. **1** Legally free (as opposed to slave): (masc. as sb.) *carnes omnium ~erorum et servorum* Rev. 19.18 (AR). **2** Unrestricted, uncontrolled, free: *forma...coelestis est ~errima et nullius resistentiae* AC 7068; *homini est ~erum arbitrium comparandi sibi cognitiones* VR 24.2. **3** (neut. as sb.) Freedom: *in septimo [anno] exibit [servus] ad ~erum gratis* Exod. 21.2 (AC); *omne ~erum est ex bono fidei* AC 891; *quod ~erum amoris vere conjugialis sit ~errimum* AM 257.2; *in [suo] ~ero esse*, to be in a state of freedom: *ut...appareat sibi in ~ero esse* AC 6663.1; CI 44; *ex [suo] ~ero*, from freedom, freely: *ut homo ex ~ero secundum rationem agat* VI 101; VR 110.6. **4** (w. *ab*) Not subject (to), free (from): *a laceratione se dicebant liberos esse* ES 2747.

liberalitas ~atis, *f*. Freedom in giving, liberality: AM 164.

liberatio ~onis, *f*. The act of setting free, liberation: *in memoriam ~onis a servitute in Aegypto* AC 7093.2; (transf.) *~onem a malis* AE 278.7.

liberator ~oris, *m*. One who sets free, deliverer, liberator: *ideo toties in Verbo...~or et Redemptor dicitur* AC 2025.5.

libere, *adv*. Without restriction, freely: *nec amplius potest cogitatio eorum ~e extendi* AC 5089.2; *multa pars talium ~e grassabatur* AC 6858.

liberi ~orum, *m. pl*. Children: *consurgent ~i contra parentes* Mark 13.12 (AC 6767.4); *vir qui amavit conjugem, ac suos infantes et ~os* AM 28; *puerulos ~os* 'young children' CI 344.

libero ~are ~avi ~atum, *tr*. **1** To set (a person) free, deliver: *vir Aegyptius ~avit nos e manu pastorum* Exod. 2.19 (AC). **2** (transf.) To set free (from troubles, adversity, etc.): *qui...~atur a falsis et ab angustia* AC 7093.2; *fideles ab impugnationibus...~aturus* AC 8261.2; *omnes in sua inferna detrusi sunt, et regio illa ~ata est* AC 6858.

libertas ~atis, *f*. Freedom, liberty: *ad praedicandum captivis ~atem* Isa. 61.1 (AC 6854.5); ES 218; (transf.) *quando homo regeneratus est, tunc primum in statum ~atis venit; antea in statu servitutis fuit* AC 892.1; (w. gen.) *~atem dimittendi uxores ex quacunque causa* AM 276.1; ES 530.

libertinus ~i, *m*. A person of unrestrained sexual habits, libertine: AM 307.

libet ~uit ~itum, *impers. vb*. also **lubet**. It pleases; *si ~et*, if you please, if you will: *expende, si ~et...annon ...unum expungit alterum* VR 4.2; AM 23; (w. rel. words) *quod homo se convertere possit ad quam sphaeram ~et* AM 438; *sicut placuit et...sicut ~uit* VR 504.1; *sume quodcunque ~et* VR 714.

libidinor ~ari, *intr*. To indulge one's lusts, behave lustfully: *~antur ad alias* AM 508.

libidinose, *adv*. Lustfully: *~e amavit eos* Ezek. 23.16 (AC 1368.3).

libidinosus ~a ~um, *a*. Lustful: *pro illecebris amoris ~i* AM 75.6.

libido ~inis, *f*. Immoderate desire, lust: *propter ~inem imperandi* AC 7293.5; *igniculus ~inis ad sexum* AM 44.2.

libitum ~i, *neut*. That which pleases one, one's pleasure: *voluntas...est...aliquod placitum, ~um et volupe, quod facit velle* AM 461.6.

libo ~are ~avi ~atum, *tr*., *intr*. **1** To pour out (a liquid offering), make a libation of: *non ~abunt Jehovae vinum* Hos. 9.4 (AE 376.17); *~avit mustum daemonibus* VR 151. **2** To taste (food): *cibi facti sunt nobis insipidi...non sustinemus ~are illos* AM 6.4; (absol.) *cum ~avit de favo mellis* AC 212 (1 Sam. 14.27). **3** To touch lightly, brush: *quaedam [objecta] ~abant osculis* CO 43. **4** To enjoy for the first time, be the first to use: *maritus postquam ~averat pulchritudinem naturalem uxoris, non videt illam amplius* AM 330.3.

libra ~ae, *f*. **1** (pl.) A pair of scales: *staterae, lances seu ~ae* AE 373.1. **2** **a** *ad ~am*, on the scales, to the last ounce: *hoc fit exactitudine sicut ad ~am* AC 6663.1. **b** *in ~a*, in the balance, undecided: *quod mens in ~a teneatur* AM 318.3.

librarium ~i, *neut*. A place for storing books, bookcase: *octo insinuationes...in quarum unaquavis erat ~um, et quoque mensa* AM 151[a].2; [*bibliotheca*] *distincta...in ~a minora* AM 207.5; VR 797.2.

libratio ~onis, *f*. A weighing in the balance: *exploratio est exquisitissima ~o ne minimum falsi conjungatur bono* AC 3116.2; ES 193.

libro ~are ~avi, *intr*. **1** To weigh one thing against another, balance: *bona...~antur sicut pondera in scalis bilancis* VR 659. **2** To incline, tip: *detrahit occipitium ...adeo ut ~et quasi deorsum* ES 1748.

licentia ~ae, *f*. The act of giving free rein to one's desires, licence, freedom: *quod...vivendum...ex arbitrio et in ~a* AC 7812; AR 449; *quod...potentia cum conjuge sit ex aliqua ~a cum sexu* AM 106; *cervi...percurrunt campos...in plena ~a* VR 815; (pl.) *ad eum* [sc. *amorem conjugialem*] *flectendum in ~as* ES 230; (w. gen.) *in ~a cupiditatum* AC 1017.

licentiose, *adv*. Licentiously: ES 3714.

licentiosus ~a ~um, *a*. Characterized by lack of restraint, licentious: *vitam ~am* ES 570.

licet ~ere ~uit, *impers. intr. vb*. **1** (w. inf.) It is permitted, it is allowable: *quia hodie nescitur...~et breviter tradere* AC 811; (w. dat.) *quod ~eat homini cogitare malum* AC 7007.2; *ut ~eret mihi...loqui cum uxoribus* AM 155[a].2. **2** (as conj.) *Licet*, although: (w. indic.) *at spirituales tale ~et sciunt, non tamen agnoscunt* AC 981.3; ES 598; ES 635; ES 2432; (w. subj.) *tametsi ...putarent quod populosa esset terra, ~et Cain primogenitus esset Adami* AC 403; ES 154; (w. ellipse of vb.) *tales...~et in linguis peritissimi...usque tamen... hallucinantur* ES 1951. (n.b. Indic. is sometimes altered to subj. by editors.)

licitus ~a ~um, *a*. (cf. **licet**) Permitted, permissible, allowable: *quod homo...cogitet illa ~a coram Deo* VI 63.1; *quod non ~um sit marito dicere uxori, quod...* AM 219.

lien ~enis, *m*. (anat.) The spleen: *de suo hepate, ~ene et pancreate* AS 22; *provinciam ~enis* ES 1005.

lienaris ~is ~e, *a*. Of or belonging to the spleen: ES 1011.

liga ~ae, *f.* A league, confederation: *multitudo nihil valet contra illos, nihil artes, astutiae, et ~ae* CI 229; *~a malorum* ES 857; ES 4552.

ligaculum ~i, *neut.* A binding, tie: *sicut fascia ablato ~o, quae diffluit* AM 320.1.

ligamentum ~i, *neut.* (anat.) A ligament: *~orum motui inservientium* AM 253.2; ES 867; (transf.) a bond: *referunt ~a inter angelos et homines* ES 985.

ligatio ~onis, *f.* The act of binding: *volunt uxores esse, et hoc fit per ~onem arctiorem...cum maritis* AM 217.

lignarius ~i, *m.* One who cuts and supplies wood, woodcutter: *quod ~i et aquarii essent* ES 151; ES 3079; *faber ~ius*, a carpenter: AT 99.

ligneus ~a ~um, *a.* Made of wood, wooden: *canalis ~us* AC 6777; *machina ~a* ES 897; *per ~um quoddam fere expers vitae* CI 341.3.

lignum ~i, *neut.* **1** Wood (as the constituent matter of trees): *ne a ~o virente faciat illum siccum stipitem* AM 294.6; *athmosphaerae ambientes priores illas, sicut ...philyrae ~a* VR 76.3. **b** (Bibl.) a tree: *suspendet te super ~o* Gen. 40.19 (AC); Eccles. 11.3 (ES 2805). **2** Wood (as a constructional material): *vasa ex ~o* AC 7920; *templa...ex ~o* CI 223. **3** (esp. pl.) Wood (as fuel): *per... ~i sectiones* ES 271; (pl.) *caesores ~orum et haustores aquarum* Josh. 9.23 (AC 6860); *accendet super eo* [sc. *altari*] *~a* Lev. 6.12 (AC 6832.7). **4** A piece of wood, a wooden object: *servire ~o et lapidi* AC 643.3; *sicut...violina et similia, nisi habeant ~um, cui...chordae alligatae sint, non sonare possint* ES 4482; (used as a weapon) a stick, club: *exivit turba...cum gladiis et ~is* Matt. 26.47 (AE 1145.9).

ligo[1] ~are ~avi ~atum, *tr.* **1** To bind, tie: *desumpsit ex arbore aliquot termites, et ~avit in fasciculum* AM 77.7; *qui ~abit ad vitem asininum pullum suum* Gen. 49.11 (AE 31.7). **2** To form (an attachment or society): *ut cum iis consortium ~are queant* ES 481; ES 2774. **3** To place under restraint, hamper, tie: *tyrannus, cujus potestas ~ata est* VR 57.2; *hoc non licere, vocabant ~ari quoad ipsam vitam* DP 294.3.

ligo[2] ~onis, *m.* An agricultural implement, mattock: *contundent gladios in ~ones* Isa. 2.4 (AC 1664.3).

lilium ~i, *neut.* A lily: *odores amaeni, sicut florum, ~orum, aromatum* AC 1519; AM 137.1; ES 252.

lima ~ae, *f.* A file: ES 2640.

limatus ~a ~um, *a.* Sharpened by filing; (transf.) sharp, acute: *qui... ~a ratione et acuta acie sunt* AM 103.2; VR 697.7.

limbus ~i, *m.* **1** An edge, rim, border: *pileos, quorum ~os ornabant fasciae ex auro* VR 48.20; *vidi...sub ~o ejus* [sc. *solis*] *ascendentem nubem* VR 112.1; *in ultimis ~is linguae* ES 4589. **2** Limbo, the place where, according to the Fathers of the early Church, the souls of the righteous had dwelt prior to the Lord's coming: *si homo post mortem...reservaretur...cum Patribus in ~o* AM 29.

limen ~inis, *neut.* A threshold: *custodes ~inis* AC 372; *intra ~en recepti* AM 20.1; *ad primum ~en coeli elevari* CI 83.

limes ~itis, *m.* A boundary, limit: *cupiunt dominari super universum, imo extendere ejus ~ites illuc* AM 267.3; ES 277; (transf.) *ne mali spiritus extra ~ites ...vagentur* AC 741; *omnes ~ites amoris sexus spernit et rumpit* AM 511.

limitatio ~onis, *f.* A limitation: *patet...quae sunt ~ones spatii* AC 4482.4.

limito ~are ~avi ~atum, *tr.* To restrict, limit: *determinatio cogitationis...ad aliquam personam ~at et finit ideas* AC 6653; *~atus*, restricted: *pro tam parvo et ~ato fine* AC 6698; AM 49.

limpidus ~a ~um, *a.* (superl. *~issimus*) (of water) Transparent, clear: *parvulus lacus aquae ~ae* AM 294.1; VR 122.

linea ~ae, *f.* **1** A cord used to mark a straight line: *extendet super eam ~am inanitatis et perpendicula vastitatis* Isa. 34.11 (AC 5044.7). **2** (geom.) A line: *ex punctis et dein ~is geometricis* VR 20.2; *non...est ~a aliquid nisi fiat area* AR 875.7. **3** A line of sight, direction: *ad sinistrum ~a obliquata paulum retrorsum* ES 4642; a line of descent or derivation: *qui intra Ecclesiam in bono et vero sunt, non in ~a collaterali sunt, sed in ~a directa* AC 4189.3. **4** A visible line, esp. in writing: *quod... ~as vario ductu, curvatura et flexione scripserint* ES 4848; *in notis sub ~a* CI 305; a line of writing: *quod per binas ~as exponere possit eandem rem clare* ES 3960.

lineamentum ~i, *neut.* A feature (of the face), lineament: *tunc sisti solet homo cum omnibus suis ~is* ES 889.

linearis ~is ~e, *a.* Extending in a straight line, linear: *reciprocationes quasi ~es* AC 1761; *literae quae hodie quoad aliquam partem ~es sunt* SS 90.1.

lineola ~ae, *f.* A small line, dash: *percepi...sicut ~as albas* ES 2299; SS(P) 33 (= 14.4).

lineus ~a ~um, *a.* Made of linen: *fila...quae instar ~orum* AC 7601.3; *puellae...nentes super frustulis ~is* AM 218.2; (neut. pl. as sb.) linen cloths: *cadavera induta suis ~is* ES 4641.

lingo ~gere ~xi ~ctum, *tr.* To lick: *per canes qui ~gebant ulcera Lazari* AC 7784.3 (Luke 16.21); *pulverem pedum tuorum ~gent* Isa. 49.23 (AE 433.29).

lingua ~ae, *f.* **1** (anat.) The tongue: *laryngem, glottidem, ~am, labra* DP 181.1; *cum gustu absque ~a* AM 186.1. **b** (esp. as the organ of speech): *quod is cogitat, id loquitur os et ~a* CI 228. **2** A language: *in ~a originali* AC 6742; *in ~is humanis* AE 14.1; a group of people speaking a language: *omnes populi, gentes et ~ae Ipsum colent* Dan. 7.14 (DD 6). **3** Anything shaped like a tongue: *devovebit Jehovah ~am maris Aegypti* Isa. 11.15 (SS 15.2); *~a auri* 'an ingot of gold' Josh. 7.21 (AC 5135.6).

linteum ~i, *neut.* A piece of linen: *~a, quae quidem alba, sed maculata* ES 5144; *~a appensa in aliquo horto* VR 61.2; (as a garment) *cursor amictus ~o* AM 19; (as a towel) *ecce ibi aqua, sapo et ~um* SE 52.

linum ~i, *neut.* (Gk.) **1** Flax: *~um et hordeum percussum est* Exod. 9.31 (AC). **2** Linen: *tibialia ex splendente ~o* AM 42.3; *~um sericorum*, silk thread: Isa. 19.9 (AE 654.50). **3** The wick (of a lamp): *~um fumigans non exstinguet* Isa. 42.3 (AR 671.2).

lipothamia ~ae, *f.* (Gk.) also **lipothymia**. Unconsciousness, fainting: *~a, quae est totalis languiditas corporis et defectus virium* AM 253.2; AM 470.2; VR 665.4.

lipothymia: see **lipothamia**.

Lipsiensis ~is ~e, *a.* Of Leipzig, Leipzig: *ex Formula Concordiae, editionis ~is, anno 1756* VR 463.

liquefacio ~facere ~feci ~factum, *tr.* To make liquid, melt: *mittit verbum Suum, et ~facit illa* Ps. 147.17 (AC 8286.4); *~facta est Philisthaea* Isa. 15.4 (AE 208.10).

liquefio ~eri, *tr.* (in pf., pass. of **liquefacio** is used) To become liquid, melt: *montes sicut cera ~ent* Ps. 97.4 (DD 14.7); (transf.) *ut ~at cor* Ezek. 21.15 (AC 309); *tantus terror ut corde ~ant* AC 878.8.

liquesco ~ere, *intr.* To become fluid, melt: *obvelatio ...incipit attenuari, dein quasi ~ere* AM 148.1; (fig.) *ut ~at omne cor* Ezek. 21.7 (DD 48.4).

liquet ~it, *impers. vb.* It is clear or plain: *ut ~et apud Esaiam* AC 6723.1; (w. indir. qu.) *sic ~et, quomodo intelligendum...* AC 8223.2.

liquido, *adv.* Clearly, plainly: *sicut mihi ostensum est ~o aliquoties* ES 153.

liquidus ~a ~um, *a.* Fluid, liquid: (neut. pl. as sb.) AC 8540.1.

liquor ~oris, *m.* A liquid, fluid: *lignum spongiosum ...quod imbibit... ~ores* CI 479.5; ES 645.

lis litis, *f.* A dispute, quarrel: *et fuit lis inter pastores* Gen. 13.7 (AC); *ex lite...de circulatione sanguinis* AC 6948.4; *ut lis hujus arcani dirimeretur* AM 161.2; *in litem venire*, to be disputed: *res judicii nusquam ibi in litem veniunt* CI 214.

litamen ~inis, *neut.* (w. gen.) Indulgence (in): *~ina jucunditatum corporis* VR 434.2.

liteo ~tere, *tr.* see also **lito**². To debate, dispute: *exorta est lis inter spiritus..., ~tebatur num aliquis possit [sumere quicquam] nisi adeat immediate Dominum* AR 566.1; VR 162.1 (1st edn.).

litera ~ae, *f.* also **littera**. **1** A letter of the alphabet: *unaquaevis ~a in alphabeto* AM 326.5; VR 19.2; *chartula...scripta ~is Hebraicis* ES 4671. **2** The literal sense: *animus detinetur in ~a* AC 755.4; *omnia... abstracte a ~a intelligenda* AC 1405; (so, also) *sensus ~ae*: *ex ~a seu sensu ~ae* AC 1; AC 4279. **3** (pl.) An epistolary communication, letter: *accepi ~as quod non plura exemplaria...vendita sunt quam quatuor* ES 4422; also, any written document, writing: *ut Arium...ex sacris ~is convincerent et damnarent* VR 637.

literalis ~is ~e, *a.* also **litter-**. According to the letter, literal: *de sensu externo seu ~i* AC 1771.3.

literarius ~a ~um, *a.* also **litter-**. Concerned with literature, literary: *ludi... ~i* AM 207.6; *quod...historiae ~ae...dediti sint [Germani]* VR 814.

literatus ~a ~um, *a.* also **litter-**. Educated: *quod cuivis ~o potest notum esse* AC 1756.2; *scitur in ~o orbe* VR 67.2; (masc. as sb.) *quod...ablegentur studiosi ad ~os ex Christianis* AM 151ª.2.

literula ~ae, *f.* also **litterula**. A small or mere letter: *quoad singulas ~as cujusvis vocis* AC 1870.2; ES 2270.

litigatio ~onis, *f.* A dispute, quarrel: *'~o virorum' significat contentionem de veris* AC 9024.1.

litigiosus ~a ~um, *a.* Given to disputes, quarrelsome: *~us aut ~a* AM 246.3.

litigo ~are ~avi, *intr.* To dispute, quarrel: *vae ~anti cum formatore suo* Isa. 45.9 (AE 177.6); (w. cognate acc.) *Jehovah ~et litem meam* Mic. 7.9 (SS 85); (w. indir. qu.) *~ant quid substantia* AC 446.

lito¹ ~are ~avi, *intr.* (w. dat.) To indulge (in): *postquam... ~avit voluptatibus suis* VR 151; AR 458; AE 827.7.

lito² ~ere, *intr.* (app. formed from **lis**, unless misprint) see also **liteo**. To dispute: *exorta est lis...quapropter ~ebatur [litigebatur* Worcester*] num aliquis possit* VR 162.1.

litter- see **liter-**.

littus: see **litus**.

litura ~ae, *f.* An erasure, blot: *Verbum est illis sicut ~is maculatum* VR 7.

litus ~oris, *neut.* also **littus**. The bank (of a river), shore (of the sea): *et vidit Israel Aegyptios mortuos super ~ore maris* Exod. 14.30 (AC); ES 243.

livens ~ntis, *a.* Livid: *apparent* [*interiora*]...*apud quosdam ~ntia* DA 50 (= xvii.[4]).

livesco ~ere, *intr.* To become livid: *incipiunt... cruciari, ~ere facie* CI 48.

lividus ~a ~um, *a.* Livid: *apparuit sicut velamen... ~um sicut cadaveris* AM 421; VR 12.10.

livor ~oris, *m.* A livid mark on the body, bruise: *virum occidi in vulnus meum, et parvulum in ~orem meum* Gen. 4.23 (AC).

lixa ~ae, *m.* A camp follower, attendant: *calones et ~ae* VR 388.4. (n.b. Poss. fem. in view of following *quae*, but this is prob. to be emended to *qui*, both here and in AR 655.4.)

lixivium ~i, *neut.* A lye: *per varia ex illis* [sc. *vegetabilibus*] *facta ~a* AE 1214.2.

lixo ~are ~avi ~atum, *tr.* To cook by boiling: *in culinis ubi ~antur* [perh. read *elixantur*] *carnes* VR 834.

lobulus ~i, *m.* A small lobe: DP 319.2.

lobus ~i, *m.* (Gk.) Either of the two lobes (of the lungs): *duo ~i pulmonis* AM 316.4.

loco ~are ~avi ~atum, *tr.* **1** To put in (a specified) position, locate, place: *is...Abrahamum pone me ~avit* ES 461; (pass. and refl.) to be located or placed: *binae statuae... ~atae in termino universi* AC 8325.3; *mumia...in cippo argenteo ~ata* VR 595.1; *se ~ant infra* AC 7812. **2** To sell the use of, let out, rent: *vineam suam ~abit aliis agricolis* Matt. 21.41 (VI 65); *similes virgini, quae...post nuptias cum uno ~at noctes* VR 7.

locomotivus ~a ~um, *a.* Of or concerned with movement from place to place: *~a potentia* Book of Concord in SE 15(e); *per mutationes quasdam, correspondentes ~is* ES 354.

loculamentum ~i, *neut.* A small compartment for storage, pigeonhole: *chartaphylacium cum ~is* VR 797.2.

loculus ~i, *m.* **1** A coffin: *Jesus accessit et tetigit ~um defuncti* Luke 7.14 (AE 79.3); AC 4622.4; ES 4564. **2** Any sort of container: *apud aviculas in gutturali earum ~o* [sc. the crop] AC 3324.2.

locuples ~etis, *a.* Well-endowed, rich: (transf.) *fides fit ~es et plena* FI 28.

locupletatio ~onis, *f.* The act of making rich, enrichment: *desiderium veri erat, ex quo ~o* AC 1485.

locupleto ~are ~avi ~atum, *tr.* To make rich: *ad ~andum memoriam* AC 7078; (pass. w. abl.) *~ari omni bono* AC 981.1.

locus ~i, *m.* (pl. uses *~a ~orum* neut. endings) **1** A position in space, location, place: *interrogabam cur praeterirent magnifica ~orum* AC 6809; *in mundo ...spirituali sunt ~a sicut in mundo naturali* AM 10.7; *progressio e ~o in ~um* VR 25.3. **b** (w. defining adj.): *erit aridus ~us in stagnum* Isa. 35.7 (AC 6723.2). **c** *hic ~i*, here: AC 552; ES 530; *ibi ~i*, there: AC 1180; (so w. *alibi*) ES 1879; (w. *ubicunque*) ES 2651. **2** The correct or appropriate place: *quod...animae...appareant constanter in suis ~is* AC 1377; *unicuivis est suus ~us* VR 32.6. **b** *~o* (w. gen.), in place of, instead of: *recedit charitas...et ~o ejus succedit amor sui* AC 1304; *antiqui... ~o fidei dixerunt veritatem* FI 6; (so w. *quod*) *~o quod Dominum...intueretur, semet intueatur* AC 7643.1; ES 741. **3** A place in a series: *mundus spirituum ...est ~us medius* CI 428; *hoc* [sc. *bonum coeli*] *primo ~o est* AE 28.1. **b** *~um cedere*, to yield place, give way: *pugna quae perstat usque dum unum alteri cedit ~um* DP 100.1. **4** A passage in a book, place: *si haec ~a conferantur cum aliis pluribus* AC 6788; *hujus ~i*, appropriate to this place: *hoc hujus ~i non est* DP 78.2; VR 33. **5** (w. gen.) Space or room (for): *ut vix vestigii ~us daretur inter duos* VR 160.2; (transf.) *nec dant ~um explorandi convenientias affectionum* AM 274; (so w. inf.) *quae...non ita describere ~us adhuc est* ES 1761. **6** Space regarded as a quality of matter, place: *cum idea ~i obvenit* AC 1008.2; *Divinum est supra illa quae ~i et temporis sunt* AC 6843.

locusta ~ae, *f.* A locust: *Johannes Baptista...comedit ~am et mel agreste* DD 15.8 (Matt. 3.4); *~as ascendentes ex abysso* AM 26; *quod...* [*homo*] *valeat...multo minus quam ~a contra elephantem* VR 68.2.

locut-: see **loquut-**.

logicus ~a ~um, *a.* (Gk.) Of or concerned with logic: (neut. pl. as sb.) *quod vocent illa metaphysica et ~a* AC 3348; (masc. as sb.) a logician: *dicentes quod fuerint ~i et metaphysici* AC 4658.1.

logos ~i, *m.* (Gk.) A fiction, story, fairy tale: *fructus fidei est loquutio inanis et ~os* SE 49; AM 151.

longaevitas ~atis, *f.* Length of life, longevity: *'prolongare dies' non significat ~atem* AC 488.2.

longaevus ~a ~um, *a.* Long-lived: *credit quod ~us fiat* AE 375.3; (of life) long-lasting, lengthy: *vitam in mundo ~am* AC 5159.2.

longanimis ~is ~e, *a.* Long-suffering: *quia gratiosus et misericors Ipse, ~is* Joel 2.13 (AC 588.3).

longe, *adv.* (compar. *~ius*, superl. *~issime*) **1** To or at a great distance, remotely, far: *planeta Saturnus... ~issime a sole distat* AC 6697; *quod hi... ~e aufugerint* CI 479.5. **2** (transf.) To a great extent, far: *~e supra cogitationem humanam* AC 6804.2; *ponunt dignitates ~e supra usus* AM 262.3.

longinque, *adv.* (compar. *~ius*) At a great distance, remotely: *cum discederent aliquantum ~e* ES 2256.

longinquitas ~atis, *f.* Remoteness, distance: *spectabunt terram ~atum* Isa. 33.17 (AE 304.31).

longinquus ~a ~um, *a.* (superl. *~issimus*) **1** Situated at a great distance, remote, far: *~um [est] quod non desiderat* AE 25.1; *ex gentibus ~is* ES 402; *in ~issima planeta* ES 2332. **b** *e ~o*, from a distance, afar off: *stabat soror ejus e ~o* Exod. 2.4 (AC); *quod e ~o [apes] odorent flores* VR 12.7; (transf.) *stant...e ~o ab intelligentia* CI 38.3. **2** Remote in time, far off: *in tempora ~a ille prophetans* Ezek. 12.27 (DD 4).

longitudinalis ~is ~e, *a.* (anat.) *Sinus ~is*, the longitudinal sinus: AC 7744; ES 3879.

longitudinarius ~a ~um, *a.* = **longitudinalis**: ES 1727.

longitudo ~inis, *f.* Length: *quod...~o, latitudo et altitudo essent aequales* SS 10 (Rev. 21.16); *stagnum... ~ine majore quam latitudine* ES 1380.

longus ~a ~um, *a.* (compar. *~ior*, superl. *~issimus*) **1** Long: *charta ~a...a pluribus chartis conglutinata* AC 6930; ES 3541. **b** (of persons) tall: *vir ~us et gracilis* AC 788.2. **2** *In ~um*, lengthwise, longitudinally: *tentoria...protensa in ~um* AC 8379; *in ~um et latum* ES 435; *ad ~issimum*, to a very great distance: ES 4583. **3** (of time) Long-lasting, lengthy: *tempora quibus ibi manent, sunt ~iora et breviora* AC 1106.

loquax ~acis, *a.* Conveying speech, expressive: *quod ~aces sint [ideae rationales]* ES [1558 1/3].

loquela ~ae, *f.* **1** The act of speaking, conversation, speech: *per ~am cum angelis* AC 1378.1; *unus est [Deus] in oris ~a* VR 4.2. **2** A particular manner of speaking, speech: *talis eorum erat ~a* AC 108; *~a angelica* AC 6804.2. **3** A thing said, utterance, expression: *animadvertit se offendisse...aut ~a aut facto* BCP (VI 6).

loquor ~qui ~quutus (*or* ~cutus) sum, *intr.* (*tr.*) **1** To utter words, speak: *facultas ~quendi* AC 6982; *~quere et dic* Ezek. 29.3 (AC 7293.2); *cogitatio activa ...vocari potest cogitatio ~quens* AC 6987.1; CI 2. **2** To speak (in a specified manner): *ut comparative ~quar* AC 6849.5; *~quebatur ille per ideas angelicas* AC 7077; *an Deus...ita ~qui potest?* SS 1. **3** To hold converse, talk, speak: (w. *cum*) *Dominus cum unoquovis homine ~quitur* AC 904.1; *cum tali homine non potest angelus caeli ~qui* FI 48; (w. *ad*) *~quimini ad omnem coetum Israelis* Exod. 12.3 (AC); (w. *inter*) *spiritus...inter se ~quentes* AC 6996.2. **4** (w. acc.) To utter, speak, say: *ut non aliud quam verum ~querentur* AC 7074; *Verbum quod ~quutus sum* John 12.48 (DD 25); *dum os ~quitur unum* VR 4.2; (as pass.) *quid cogitatur et quid ~quitur* ES 2376; (impers.) *~quutum cum eo...plura* ES 3437.

loquutio ~onis, *f.* also **locutio**. A manner of speaking, expression: *talis ~o apud eos familiaris fuit* AC 144; AC 755.5.

loramentum ~i, *neut.* A strap, loop: *et facies ~a hyacinthini super ora aulaei* Exod. 26.4 (AC).

lorica ~ae, *f.* A corslet, breastplate: *induit justitiam sicut ~am* Isa. 59.17 (AC 8273.2); *nisi circumdet corpus ~a* VR 124.1.

lorum ~i, *neut.* A thong; (esp. pl.) reins: *quod... fregero ~a jugi eorum* Ezek. 34.27 (AC 93); *intendebant ~a super jubis equorum* AM 103.1.

lotio ~onis, *f.* The act of washing: *Moabus pelvis ~onis Meae* Ps. 60.8 (AC 2468.10).

lotium ~i, *neut.* Urine: *num argilla increpatura est figulum, quod ex se testam ~i faciat* VR 72.1; ES 870.

lotteria ~ae, *f.* A lottery: *in ludis...sicut in ~a* ES 4008.

lotus ~a ~um, *a.* (pf. pple. of **lavo**) Washed, clean: *qui ~us est, non opus habet, nisi ut quoad pedes lavetur, et mundus est totus* John 13.10 (DP 151.2); *credit se post confessiones mundum et ~um* DP 278[a].1.

lubens ~ntis, *a.* Pleasing: *non aliter sentiebatur quam sicut volupe et ~ns* DP 215.9.

lubenter: see **libenter**.

lubet: see **libet**.

lubitus ~us, *m.* Free choice, pleasure: *qui potest ex ~u facere quicquid vult* VR 57.1; *millia...ad nutum et ~um eorum sponte ruunt* CI 137.3.

lubrice, *adv.* In a slippery manner: *erat quasi ~e* [Autograph reading unclear] *hebetatum* ES 1085.

lubricus ~a ~um, *a.* Slippery, deceitful, shifty: *maxime ~us est [draco], quando in poenis et terrore spondet omnia* ES 505.

lucanus ~a ~um, *a.* (app.) Of a copse: *in locis delitiosis, ~is* [perh. read *lacunis*], *amoenis pratis* ES 161.

luceo ~cere, *intr.* **1** To emit light, shine: *Divinum quod ~cet ut sol in coelo* AC 6700. **2** (transf.) To appear clear or bright: *veritates quae ~cent a bono* AC 7072; *apud quos Verbum ~cet et translucet* SS 57.

lucerna ~ae, *f.* An oil lamp: *non opus habent ~a* Rev. 22.5 (AR); (fig.) *sola doctrina est ~a* SS 52; also, a candle: *cera...inservit humano generi pro ~is* CI 108.1.

lucide, *adv.* (compar. *~ius*) Transparently, clearly, plainly: *ut discernat...hoc ~ius quo melius aperitur communicatio* AC 9103.3.

lucidus ~a ~um, *a.* (compar. *~ior*, superl. *~issimus*) **1** Emitting light, shining, bright: *color...vivus et ~us* AC 6991; *equi ~i sicut ignei* AC 8029; *vidi...diabolum cum circulo albo ~o circum caput* AM 269.4; (neut. as sb.) *vidi... ~um circum circa illum* VR 110.1. **2** Intellectually illuminated, enlightened: *in statum ~um quoad interiora* AC 1456; *cultus non coactus...est cultus spiritualis, vivus, ~us, et laetus* DP 137.

Lucifer ~eri, *m.* The morning star, used as a name of the Devil: *quomodo cecidisti de coelo, ~er, fili aurorae* Isa. 14.12 (AC 3387.5); *in Verbo nominatur Diabolus et Satanas, et quoque ~er* CI 544; (of evil spirits) *illi qui exercuerunt id dominium...sunt ~eri* AE 1188.2.

lucratio ~onis, *f.* The obtaining of an advantage, profit, gain: *propter ~ones, hoc est, propter aucupandos honores et opes* AC 8148.2; VR 98.1.

lucror ~ari, atus sum, *tr.* To obtain (an advantage), gain: *si totum mundum ~atus fuerit* Matt. 16.26 (AC 7021.2); *ut... ~entur opes* AM 266.5; (absol.) *propter libidinem imperandi et ~andi* AC 7293.5.

lucrum ~i, *neut.* The obtaining of an advantage, gain: *si amantes sui, vel amantes ~i...sunt* CI 295; *inserviunt famae, ex qua ei honor aut ~um* VI 35.

lucta ~ae, *f.* A struggle: *invito, et cum ~a, ita cum pugna* VI 93; *respirare cum ~a* AR 611.2.

luctatio ~onis, *f.* The act of struggling: *Naphtali a ~onibus dictus* AE 295.10.

luctor ~ari ~atus sum, *intr.* To struggle: *Deus...non ducit illum* [sc. *hominem*], *sed ~atur cum illo* VR 61.1; *qui ~antur cum morte* AE 131.5.

luctus ~us, *m.* Grief, mourning: *convertam festa vestra in ~um* Amos 8.10 (AC 7093.5); *haec causa est maestitiae, ~us et lachrymationis* AM 8.3.

lucubratio ~onis, *f.* The study of a subject, discussion: *articuli, in quos haec ~o distinguitur* AM 295.3.

lucubratiuncula ~ae, *f.* A short study, treatise: *ne... ~a haec...manca sit* CC 18.3.

lucubro ~are ~avi ~atum, *tr.* To produce by lamplight or by prolonged study: *quaesivi, quid nunc ~atur* IM 52.

luculenter, *adv.* With utmost clarity, transparently: *sicut ~er constat a Judaeis* AC 1205; AC 8250.2.

lucus ~i, *m.* **1** A plantation of trees, copse, grove: *inde eorum cultus super montibus, inque ~is* AC 920.4; *~us cujus arbores...formabant sicut theatrum* AM 132.1; (in a town) a park: *spectabant...aliquid de urbe, domos et ~um* ES 3306. **2** A carved representation of a tree or trees as an object of worship, Asherah: *Menascheh... fecit ~um...et posuit sculptile ~i, quod fecerat, in domo Dei* 2 Kgs. 21.3, 7 (AC 2722.3).

ludibrium ~i, *neut.* **1** An imposture, sham, pretence: *luserunt ~a vobiscum* AM 7.3; AM 16.3. **2** Mockery, derision: *cum illa quae Verbi sunt...~o habentur* AC 8882.4.

ludicer ~cra ~crum, *a.* (compar. *~crior*) Absurd, ridiculous: *narrabam quod videam tam ~crum equitatum* AR 839.1; AM 249.2; *quid ~crius potest audiri...?* VR 82.3.

ludicrum ~i, *neut.* A theatrical entertainment, show: *de varii generis spiritibus, et eorum ~is* ES 180 titulus.

ludificatio ~onis, *f.* An illusion: *visiones phantasticae, quae sunt ~ones mentis abstractae* DP 134.1.

ludio ~onis, *m.* An actor, stage player: *sicut duo ~ones dimicantes pugnis* AM 55.6; AM 326.1.

ludo ~dere ~si, *intr.* (*tr.*) **1** To engage in play, sport: *amant...infantes socios cum quibus in innocentia ~dunt* CI 277; (impers. pass.) *quod cum illis non infantiliter... ~dendum sit* SS 26.3. **b** (tr.) to play (a game): *quondam ~si ludum fortunae cum quodam* ES 4567. **2** (of animals) To behave playfully: [*nymphae*] *~dunt...inter se ponuntque ova* ES 877. **b** (tr.) to engage in playfully: *quod* [*papiliones*]... *~dant sua conjugia, ponant ova* ES 2475. **3** (of things) To behave as if playing, move like children at play: *nubeculae apparebant quasi inter se dimicarent, sed ~debant* AM 315.1; *ex meteoris quae ~dunt coram oculis plurium* VR 80.2.

Ludius ~a ~um, *a.* see also **Ludim**. Of Lud; (masc. as sb.) a descendant of Lud: AC 1195.

ludus ~i, *m.* **1** A game, sport: *~i ac choreae virginum et juvenum saltantium* AM 3.3; *hic ~us usque est auctoramentum justitiae* VR 72.3; (in the theatre) a play: DP 217.7. **2** A school: *nostine aliquid de ~is sapientiae...?* AM 132.1.

lues ~is, *f.* An infectious or contagious disease, plague: *~es venereae* AM 253.1; *alios...infecerunt contagione sua et ~e* ES 1787.

lugeo ~gere ~xi, *intr.* To feel grief, grieve: *non ideo ~gebunt piscatores* Isa. 19.8 (AC 6693.2); *callo ablato ~get* ES 807.

lugubris ~is ~e, *a.* Gloomy, ill-boding: *quod super*

mapalia illorum volent aves ~es VR 45.2; (neut. as sb.) *veniunt...in altera vita ad ~ia* ES 4911.

lumbi ~orum, *m. pl.* The loins: *corpus a cervice ad ~os* AM 231.5.

lumen ~inis, *neut.* **1** Light, illumination: *~en candidum pulchre flavescens* AC 186; *~en solis* AC 6697; (pl.) *spiritus...certa ~ina solent quoque ostendere* ES 1689. **2** Illumination of relatively low power, (feeble) light: *luna non dabit ~en suum* Matt. 24.29 (AC 1839.2); *~en solis* AC 6697; *~ini ex igne carbonario* AC 7870.2; *~en...nocturnum* ES 1518; (dist. from **lux**) *lux coeli...ad lucem mundi se habet respective sicut ~en solis meridiani ad ~en candelae* AC 1053.2. **3** *~en oculorum*, the power of sight: *ut inciperet ~en oculorum meorum hebetari* AC 6925. **4** The power of mental perception, illumination of the mind: *hi credunt se illuminatos...sed est ~en sensuale* AC 6865.3; *contra genuinum ~en rationis* AM 481; *dum ratio humana ex Verbo et inde ~ine convincitur* VR 4.3.

luminare ~is, *neut.* A source of illumination, light: *sit* [sic] *~ia in expanso coelorum* Gen. 1.14 (AC); *~ia coeli, ut sol, luna, ac stellae* AC 7988.2; *quod...apes suppeditarent ceras pro ~ibus* AM 420.

luminosus ~a ~um, *a.* Illuminated, lit up: *conclave est ~um* ES 879; (neut. as sb.) illumination: *fenestrae ...per quas ~um...influxit* VR 134.5.

luna ~ae, *f.* The earth's satellite, the moon: *sol, ~a, et stellae* AM 342.2; a satellite of another planet: *quod aliqui eorum* [sc. *planetarum*] *habeant ~as* AC 6697.

lunaris ~is ~e, *a.* Of or belonging to the moon, lunar: *in nocturna illa luce ~i* AM 380.4; also, resembling a moon: *quod planeta Saturnus...habeat quoque cingulum magnum ~e* AC 6697.

lunaticus ~i, *m.* A lunatic: *quis ~us non credit fatuitatem suam esse sapientiam...?* VR 759.3.

lunula ~ae, *f.* A small moon: *vidi lunam splendentem, quae erat pluribus ~is minoribus cincta* AC 1531; ES 4219.

luo ~ere ~i ~itum, *tr.* To pay (a penalty): *in altera vita ~it paenam* CI 342.3; (also, absol.) to pay a penalty: *quod quisque secundum qualitatem suam ~at in altera vita* ES 4363.

lupa ~ae, *f.* A she-wolf: AM 392.2.

lupanar ~aris, *neut.* also **lupinar**. A brothel: *quod... ~aria tolerentur* AM 444[a]; VR 381.4.

lupanaris ~is ~e, *a.* Of or appropriate to a brothel: *certamina ~ia* AM 512.2.

lupanarium ~i, *neut.* Variant form of **lupanar**: VR 834.

luparius ~i, *m.* (perh.) A brothel-keeper: *a sirenibus ...et quoque a ~is ibi, e longinquo audivi* AM 433 (possibly to be emended to *lupanariis*, from **lupanarius*** ~i, *m.*, with the same meaning given in this entry).

lupercus ~i, *m.* (app.) A lascivious man: *meretrici... quae nudat se coram ~is* VR 148.2.

lupinar ~aris, *neut.* Variant spelling or misreading of **lupanar**: ES 1663.

lupinus ~a ~um, *a.* Resembling a wolf, wolfish: *satyros ~os* AM 521.3.

lupus ~i, *m.* A wolf, esp. as a type of rapacity: *apud bestias immites...ut apud...~os et lupas* AM 392.2; *intus sunt ~i rapaces* Matt. 7.15 (AE 195.13); *fiunt...vulpes quoad astutiam, ~i quoad ferociam* VR 13.4; (as a devil in hell) *dicere quod ~us voluisset eos auferre* ES 699.

luridus ~a ~um, *a.* Sickly yellow: *quae* [sc. *facies*] *a candida primum facta est ~a, et mox atra* VR 71.4; AM 514.3; ES 4213.

luscus ~a ~um, *a.* Having only a single eye, one-eyed: *~us intrare in vitam* Matt. 5.29 (AE 152.12).

lusilis ~is ~e, *a.* Relating to games, sportive: *serius, quod ~e et jucundum quoque recusans* ES 3432. (n.b. At 3AD 7651 Tafel reads *lusilae*, from **lusilus*** ~a ~um, *a.*, 'playful'; but Autograph app. reads *lusilis*.)

lusorie, *adv.* With pretence, in play: *cum hac* [*voluntate uxor*] *non conjungit se nisi simulatorie aut ~e* AM 195.

lusorius ~a ~um, *a.* **1** Of or suitable for games: *chartae* or *chartulae ~ae*, playing cards: DP 212.1; AM 231.5; (neut. pl. as sb.) games, play: *cum in suis ~is sunt* [*infantes*] CI 338; also, places of amusement: *~ia frequentare* CI 358. **2** Performed only in play, pretended: *hi* [*favores*] *pro fine spectant famam utriusque, et si non hanc, sunt ~i* AM 282.2.

lustratio ~onis, *f.* Mental examination, consideration: *numerare involvit ~onem* AC 10217.1; AE 700.16.

lustratorium ~i, *neut.* The circulatory function: *pulmones...agunt...~um aëris* DA 12 (= v.[2]).

lustro ~are ~avi ~atum, *tr.* **1** To examine visually: *datum...est videre angelum...~avi eum* CI 75. **2** To examine with the mind, consider, reflect upon: *singulos versus ~are* DD 37.1; *sume...aliquod objectum...et id ex aliqua sapientia ~a* DP 3.2; *quo intimius ~antur, eo sunt pulchriora* ES 252.

lustrum ~i, *neut.* The den (of a wild animal): *quaedam inferna apparuerunt...similia ~is et speluncis, quales sunt feris in sylvis* CI 586.

lusus ~us, *m.* Play, sport: *~us sicut infantiae* CI 281; ES 379; a play (in a theatre): *~us super theatris* AC 4581.2.

luteus ~a ~um, *a.* Containing mud, muddy: *delectantur...quidam in...graveolentibus stagnis, quidam in ~is* AC 954; ES 1384; also, made of mud or clay: *tuguriola ~a* ES 392.

Lutheranus ~a ~um, *a.* Of Luther or his followers, Lutheran: *Ecclesia ~a* AE 885.3; *religionem ~am* ES 5928; (masc. pl. as sb.) AC 1799.4.

lutulentus ~a ~um, *a.* Muddy: *inundatur aquis ~is* VR 617.1.

lutum ~i, *neut.* Mud, clay: *ferrum mixtum cum argilla ~i* Dan. 2.41 (AM 79.1); *e ~o ac e tenebris inferni ascendere* VR 77.1; (as a building material) *domus erant structae ex ramis arborum... ~o conglutinatis* AM 79.4.

lux lucis, *f.* **1** Light (as opposed to darkness): *quod 'tenebrae' ibi opponantur 'luci'* AC 7711.2; *quod planeta Saturnus...habeat...cingulum...quod multam lucem...telluri illi dat* AC 6697. **b** (w. pl.) a manifestation of light: *in coelo...ubi vera et bona...per luces... manifestantur* AC 6640.1. **2** Spiritual illumination: *quod Ipse sit lux quae illustrat* SS 2.1; *sensus spiritualis, in quo Divinum Verum est in luce* VR 85.2. **b** a state of being mentally illuminated: *erant tunc in luce intellectus* FI 3; *in luce fatua sunt* VR 42.2. **c** an instance of illumination, glimpse: *Spiritus Dei...dedit primam lucem quod Dominus sit* AC 24.1.

luxatio ~onis, *f.* A dislocating (of a joint), disjointing: *luctatio viri cum Jacobo et femoris ejus ~o et emotio* AC 4279.3.

luxatus ~a ~um, *a.* (of bones or joints) Dislocated: *cum ~a aut cum distorta* [*ossa*], *forma corporis inde variatur* AC 8005; *~a vola femoris Jacobi* Gen. 32.25 (AC); applied to the sinew of a dislocated joint: *nervus femoris ~us* ES 2617 (Gen. 32.32).

luxo ~are ~avi, *intr.* (app.) To make convulsive movements: *sicut laborantes cum morte torquerentur, ~ando pedibus* VR 641.3.

luxuria ~ae, *f.* Indulgence in extravagance, luxury: AM 252; AE 617.32.

luxurians ~ntis, *a.* Growing profusely, luxuriant: *arbores...fructibus opimis ~ntes* AM 13.2.

luxuries ~ei, *f.* = **luxuria**: *insania quod in ~e et voluptate ponatur omne vitae jucundum* AC 8378; *protraximus aliquot dies et noctes in ~e illa* AM 6.4.

luxurior ~ari ~atus sum, *intr.* To be luxuriant: *arbor quae...apparet ~ari ramis, foliis, et fructibus* SS(P) 50 (= 19.2).

luxuriosus ~a ~um, *a.* Devoted to extravagant living: (masc. as sb.) ES 777 titulus.

luxus ~us, *m.* Extravagance, luxury: ES 2422.

Lybius ~a ~um, *a.* An inhabitant of Lybia, Lybian: AC 117.1.

lyceum ~i, *neut.* (Gk.) A senior school, high school: *doctores didascali in ~is illorum...student mysticis fidei* VR 803; SE 59.

lychnare ~is, *neut.* A lamp-stand, sconce: *ad parietes pendebant ~ia ex argento* AM 20.1; VR 353.2.

lychnuchus ~i, *m.* (Gk.) A lamp-holder: VR 505.3.

lychnus ~i, *m.* (Gk.) A lamp: *exstincto ~o* AR 484.6.

Lydius ~a ~um, *a.* Lydian; *lapis ~us*, touchstone: *lapis ~us, per quem exploratur aurum et argentum* VR 163; VR 379.5.

lympha ~ae, *f.* A watery fluid in the body, lymph: *ex vitiata ~a* AM 253.2; *serum seu ~a* ES 830.

lymphaticus ~a ~um, *a.* Carrying lymph, lymphatic: *in vasa ~a* ES 1015 ½.

lymphatus ~a ~um, *a.* Frenzied, maniac: *tam ~o delirio* CO 38.1; (masc. as sb.) DA 43 (= xv.[1]).

Lynceus ~a ~um, *a.* (Gk.) Resembling Lynceus in keenness of sight, sharp-sighted: *qui coeci fuerunt... aeque ac qui ~i fuerunt* AC 9944.

lyra ~ae, *f.* (Gk.) A lyre: *sonus ~ae* UJ(P) 316.

M

maccus ~a ~um, *a.* Foolish: *quod ~a* [*macra* J D Odhner] *sint et illico terminata quae ab homine ex proprio conatu* ES 1982 (Tafel).

macer ~cra ~crum, *a.* Thin, lean: *quod tam macilentus et ~cer factus sit* [*Hiobus*] AE 556.11; (fig.) *hic* [*amor*] *vocari potest...carneus ~cer et siccus* AM 312.

maceria ~ae, *f.* A wall: *ad aedificandum ~as* Mic. 7.11 (DD 4); *~as...ex juncis* AM 477.5.

maceries ~ei, *f.* = **maceria**: AR 484.7; AE 237.1.

macero ~are ~avi ~atum, *tr.* To pound up, mash: *injiciendo in tonnam homines et sic percutiendo, sicut solent olera quae ~anda* ES 2615.

machaera ~ae, *f.* (Gk.) A single-edged sword: Rev. 6.4 (AR).

machalath, *indecl.* (Hebr.) The rendering of a Hebr. musical instruction in the title of Pss. 53 and 88: *Psalmis pluribus Davidis inscriptum ac indicatum quomodo psallerentur, prout super neginoth, super nechiloth, super octava, schigajon, gitthith, muthlabben, scheminith, schoschannim, ~ath* AC 8337.5.

Machiavellisticus ~a ~um, *a.* Machiavellian: *progenies...insana, impia et ~a* SE 67.

machina ~ae, *f.* (ad. Gk.) A machine, engine: *quod stent sicut ~ae muti* AM 233.6; *~a lignea* ES 897; (of a water-wheel) VR 328.

machinamentum ~i, *neut.* Machination: *dolos et ~a sua contra ea quae vera et bona sunt exercere* ES 439; ES 2922 titulus.

machinatio ~onis, *f.* A machination: *quod nihili fecerint...astus, nihili ~ones dolosas* AE 231.2; ES 2577.

machinator ~oris, *m.* One who devises, planner: *~ores iniquitatis* Job 4.8 (AE 419.10).

machinatrix ~icis, *f.* One who devises: *coeperunt ad naturam suam redire, quae erat ~ix dolorum* ES 2045.

machinor ~ari ~atus sum, *tr.* To devise, plot, plan: *quicquid contra alterum cogitaverunt et ~ati sunt* AC 1395; *ad ~anda mala prompti* AC 8031.

macies ~ei, *f.* Leanness, thinness: *desolatio veri et ~es theologica* VR 391.1.

macilentus ~a ~um, *a.* Emaciated: *apparent ~i sicut constantes ossibus sola cute obductis* AM 512.2.

macrocosmus ~i, *m.* (Gk.) The macrocosm: VR 71.2.

macrouranus ~i, *m.* (Gk.) A major heaven (see quot.): *sicut Deus ex suo ~o seu mundo spirituali regit macrocosmum seu mundum naturalem* VR 71.2.

mactatio ~onis, *f.* The act of killing, slaughter: *quid...sacrificium quam ~o bestiae?* AC 922.1; *gladius exacutus...ut mactet ~onem exacutus est* Ezek. 21.10 (AE 131.5).

macto ~are ~avi ~atum, *tr.* To kill (esp. in a sacrifice), slaughter: *~are boves et pecudes* AC 921.2; *in sanguinem avis ~atae* Lev. 14.6 (AC 7918.2); *quod nempe velint socios... ~are, securi dividere* ES 377.

mactra ~ae, *f.* (Gk.) A kneading trough (used in the making of bread): *~ae sunt vasa in quibus massa pro pane praeparatur* AC 7356.1.

macula ~ae, *f.* A spot, stain: *~as retinebit iniquitas tua* Jer. 2.22 (AE 475.15); a blemish (on a sacrificial animal): AR 625 (Lev. 22.19-25); a patch, mass: *sicut densae ~ae nubis* AC 865.1; *~ae errantes circum solem* VR 80.4.

macularis ~is ~e, *a.* Covered with spots or blemishes: *qui in tenebris ~es strias videt in pariete* AC 4156.3.

maculatus ~a ~um, *a.* Covered with spots, blotched: *Verbum illis est sicut lituris ~um* VR 7; ES 583.

maculosus ~a ~um, *a.* = **maculatus**: *vestes... ~ae* AE 476.

madefacio ~facere ~feci ~factum, *tr.* To make damp, moisten, wet: *~facere cubile* AE 484.4.

maeander ~dri, *m.* (Gk., name of a river) A tortuous passage, winding, meander: *transeunt...illa per mirabiles ~dros* AM 189; DP 164.6.

maecha ~ae, *f.* (Gk.) also **moecha**. An adulterous woman: SE 59.

maechatio ~onis, *f.* also **moechatio**. An act of adultery: *~ones cum uxoribus* AM 459.5.

maechor ~ari ~atus sum, *intr.* also **moechor**. To commit adultery: *praecepta nosti, non ~aberis* Mark 10.19 (VI 66.1); AM 79.5; (transf.) *~ata est* [sc. by idolatry] *cum lapide et ligno* Jer. 3.9 (AE 141.5).

maechus ~i, *m.* (Gk.) also **moechus**. An adulterer: *non sum amplius maritus, sed ~us* AM 216.3.

maenia ~um, *neut. pl.* also **maenia** ~orum, *neut. pl.* also **moen-**. Fortification walls: *falsa comparantur ~bus circum urbem* AC 7437.2.

maereo ~rere, *intr.* also **moereo**. To be sad, mourn: *~rebunt piscatores* Isa. 19.8 (AC 991).

maeror ~oris, *m.* also **moeror**. Grief, sorrow: *descendere facietis canitiem meam in ~ore sepulchrum* Gen. 42.38 (AC); *~orem, formidinem, et terrorem* VR 561.1; ES 1909.

maestitia ~ae, *f.* also **moestitia**. Sadness, sorrow: *haec causa est ~ae, luctus, et lachrymationis* AM 8.3; AE 992.3.

maestus ~a ~um, *a.* also **moestus**. Sad, gloomy: *inde est quod angeli post delitias non fiant ~i...sed hilares* AM 44.9.

maga ~ae, *f.* A sorceress, witch: *~ae seu praestigiatrices* AC 831.2.

Magdalena, *f. adj.* Of Magdala: *Maria ~a* Matt. 28.1 (AE 400.14).

magia ~ae, *f.* The practice of witchcraft, sorcery, magic: *illi...ad ~am pronissimi sunt* AC 6692.2; *~a naturalis Aegyptiorum* ES 263; (w. pl.) an instance of this: *praestigiae et ~ae* AC 7296.

magice, *adv.* By magic, by sorcery: *qui... ~e exercent potentiam* AC 8200.2; ES 4940.

magicus ~a ~um, *a.* (Gk.) Of or concerned with sorcery, magic: *a miraculis diabolicis seu ~is* AC 6988.3; *potentiam ~am* AC 7296; (masc. as sb.) a sorcerer: *versus inferna ~orum* AC 6692.2; (fem. as sb.) a witch: ES 3924; (neut. as sb.) magic: *apud tales ~um non potest existere* AC 6692.3; AM 252.

magis, *compar. adv.* (superl.: see **maxime**) **1** To a greater extent, more: **a** (w. adj. or adv. to form compar.): *tunc amor ~is purus fit* AC 548.2; AM 255; (redundantly w. compar.) *qui ~is remotiores sunt* ES 3529. **b** (w. vb.): *dilexerunt homines ~is tenebras quam lucem* John 3.19 (VI 2); (repeated) *sunt qui prophanant exterius ~is ~is* AC 10287.3. **2** (to introduce a new clause) Even more: *qui...alios amant sicut se, et ~is qui...alios plus quam se* AC 6711; *evidenter patet spiritibus probis, ~is angelis* ES 1824. **3** *~is aut minus* (also *minusve, minusque*), more or less: *hoc perstare solet per horae spatium, ~is aut minus* AC 963; *in statu somni ~is minusve* ES 2046; *serpentes... ~is minusque venenatos* ES 4470. **4** (w. neg.) Any longer, any more: *quod falsa illa non ~is apparerent* AC 7600; ES 3614.

magister ~tri, *m.* **1** A schoolmaster, teacher: *quod decalogus...a parentibus et ~tris doceatur* DP 258.4; *illam scripturam sciunt angeli absque arte et ~tro* CI 260. **2** (Bibl.) A master, lord: *unus est vester ~ter, Christus* Matt. 23.8 (AC 6756.5).

magisterium ~i, *neut.* Teaching, instruction: *quoniam e societate, ubi ~a sunt, advenis, dic mihi quid credis* VR 80.2.

magistra ~ae, *f.* A female teacher: *scorti... ~ae praestigiarum* Nahum 3.4 (AC 6978).

magistratus ~us, *m.* **1** A magistracy: *persona ~us*, a magistrate: AM 163; VI 72. **2** A magistrate: *praefecti... super...civilia vocantur ~us* AC 10793.

magnalia ~um, *neut. pl.* The mighty works, wonders: *quidam viderunt ~a Dei* HE 4.3.

magnanimitas ~atis, *f.* Magnanimity: ES(M) 4589.

magnanimus ~a ~um, *a.* Ready to forgive, magnanimous: ES(M) 4589.

magnas ~atis, *m.* A person of high rank, grandee, magnate: *venient ~ates ex Aegypto* Ps. 68.31 (AC 1164.6); *nullum discrimen habetur regum et ~atum* ES 1512.

magnes ~etis, *m.* (Gk.) A magnet: *sphaera attractionis a ~ete circum illum* AM 386.1; ES 222.

magneticus ~a ~um, *a.* (Gk.) Of a magnet, magnetic: *inclinationes ~as* ES 222.

magnetismus ~i, *m.* Magnetism: *aether medius... ex quo ~us* UJ(P) 320.

magnifacio ~facere ~feci ~factum, *tr.* To make larger, enlarge: *erant granula auri quae per... phantasiam ita ~fecerunt* AM 268.2.

magnifice, *adv.* In a magnificent manner, splendidly, majestically: *quod...bombyces...~e ornarent et faeminas et viros* AM 420; *super baculo argenteo innixae ~e ambulant* VR 80.1.

magnificens ~ntis, *a.* (compar. *~ntior*, superl. *~ntissimus*) Magnificent: *palatiis ~ntissimis* AC 10514; *quod angeli sint ~ntissimi* ES 4427.

magnificentia ~ae, *f.* Magnificence: *~am caeli* AM 3.5; *omnis ~a Salomonis ne minimo lilio aequiparari potest* ES 252.

magnifico ~are ~avi ~atum, *tr.* **1** To make large: *~ant fimbrias palliorum suorum* Matt. 23.5 (AE 395.11); *dextra Tua, Jehovah, ~ata in robore* Exod. 15.6 (AC); (transf.) *illi ~asti laetitiam* Isa. 9.3 (AC 1259.2). **2** To praise exceedingly, magnify: *~at anima mea Dominum* Luke 1.46 (DD 34.2).

magnificus ~a ~um, *a.* Of imposing appearance, majestic, magnificent: *quis sicut Tu ~us in sanctitate?* Exod. 15.11 (AC); *quod...habitent in palatiis ~is* FI 63.2; *quod omnia in societate illa sint ~a ex palatiis et paradisis* AM 266.2; (neut. as sb.) *cur praeterirent ~a locorum* AC 6809.

magnifio ~eri, *intr.* To be made great, be exalted: *quod velint [viri] ~eri ex illo* [sc. *honore*] AM 373.

magniloquus ~a ~um, *a.* Given to boasting, boastful: 3AD 4632.

magnipendo ~ere ~i, *tr.* To regard as valuable, esteem: *aspiratio ad honores...ut ~antur* AM 274.

magnitudo ~inis, *f.* **1** Size, magnitude: [*stella*] *instar nostri solis, in varia ~ine* CI 417. **2** Greatness, largeness, abundance: *a fluminis ~ine...judicare potui quod aliquot myriades hominum...alluant* AC 6699.

magnus ~a ~um, *a.* (compar.: see **major**, superl.: see **maximus**) **1** Large in size, great, big: *balaena ~a* Ezek. 29.3 (AC 6693.4); *homo ~us ut gigas* AS 79; *ad distantiam satis ~am* ES 4709. **2** (of sounds) Loud: *clamavit voce ~a* Rev. 19.17 (AR). **3** (of persons) Of high rank, powerful, mighty: *omnes ~os populos* Ps. 89.50 (AC 6960.2); *qui ~i in orbe volunt esse* ES 277; (masc. as sb.) *quod sint...vincula, quibus ~os et parvos ...captent* AM 499. **4** Of great significance, important, great: *dies Jehovae ~us et terribilis* Joel 2.31 (DD 4); *videbo visionem ~am hanc, quare non comburitur rubus* Exod. 3.3 (AC). **5** (of words) Proud, boastful: (neut. as sb.) *genium ~a loquentem* ES 169; *os loquens ~a et blasphemias* Rev. 13.5 (AR).

magus ~i, *m.* (Gk.) A practitioner of the occult sciences, magician, sorcerer: *miracula ~orum in Aegypto* AC 6988.3; *illi, qui correspondentias...noverunt, vocati sunt sapientes et intelligentes, at postea divinatores et ~i* SS 102.1; (of the Wise Men, Matt. 2.1): *a ~is, qui ab orientalibus venerunt* AC 52234.

Mahumedanus ~a ~um, *a.* Of or belonging to Mohammed, Mohammedan, Muslim: *~ae religioni* CI 514; (masc. as sb.) *quod hodie ~is permissum sit plures uxores ducere* AM 332.2.

Mahumedismus ~i, *m.* The Mohammedan religion, Islam: *cogitavi, quod nova tua doctrina sapiat ~um* VR 137.12.

maitress, *indecl.* (French) also **maîtresse**. A woman having an ongoing sexual relationship with a man who is not her husband but who provides her financial support, mistress: *non aliud apparet refugium...quam addicatio pellicis, quae gallice vocatur ~ess* AM 459; ES 6054.

maîtresse: see **maitress**.

majestas ~atis, *f.* The dignity which befits a king, majesty: *praesentiam Jehovae cum tanta ~ate* AC 8301.5; DD 55.2.

major ~or ~us, *a.* (compar. of **magnus**) **1** Greater in size or quantity, larger, bigger: *si coelum foret millies ... ~us* AC 6232.2; *in ~ore aut minore copia* FI 26. **2** Greater in degree, deeper: *aversationem ~orem* AC 6650; *progressio boni ad ~us et minus bonum* AM 444.3. **3** (of persons) Of higher rank or importance, greater: *~or velle esse aliis, non est coelum sed est infernum* AC 450. **4** More significant, more serious, greater: *est adhuc ~us mysterium* AC 6854.2; *in ~ore gradu* AC 7326; *bella minora et ~ora* DP 251.2.

majorennis ~is ~e, *a.* Of greater age, elder: *quia ~es ex vobis futuri sunt reges* AM 7.1.

Majus ~i, *m.* The month of May: ES 5762.

majusculus ~a ~um, *a.* Fairly large, considerable: *per fluctuationes ~as* ES 1802.

malacia ~ae, *f.* (Gk.) A calm: *et facta est ~a* Luke 8.24 (AE 419.24).

male, *adv.* (compar.: see **pejus**) In an evil fashion, wickedly: *qui... ~e vivunt* AC 7635; CI 470; injuriously, badly: *~e tractare eum* ES 3797.

maledico ~cere ~xi ~ctum, *intr.*, *tr.* **1** (act., w. dat.) To utter imprecations (against), curse: *vetitum fuit ... ~cere surdo* AC 6989 (Lev. 19.14); *benedicite ~centibus vobis* Matt. 5.44 (AC 8223.2). **2** (pass.) To be cursed: *cum...Adamus propter illam fidem ~ctus est* VR 48.18.

maledictio ~onis, *f.* **1** The act of cursing: *post ~onem* [*Adami*] AM 132.4. **2** The consequence of cursing, curse: *benedictiones, si fecerint praecepta, et ~ones si non fecerint* VI 2; *mittet Jehovah in te ~onem* Deut. 28.20 (AC 8364.3).

malefacio ~facere ~feci ~factum, *intr.* To do evil, do wrong: *nihil aliud cupiunt quam ~facere* AC 6914.4; *abstinet a ~faciendo* CI 319.2; (w. dat.) to wrong, offend: *mali... ~faciunt proximo* AC 6703.

malefactor ~oris, *m.* A wrongdoer, malefactor: *~ores, qui inhiant illicitis* AM 511; CI 550.

maleficium ~i, *neut.* An evil deed: *quod cedat bono ...liberis dum a parentibus propter ~a castigantur* VR 459.15.

maleficus ~a ~um, *a.* Doing evil: *qui...indigenti ~o opem fert* AC 8120; (masc. as sb.) a wrongdoer: *judex cum videt ~um puniri* AC 8223.3.

malefio ~fieri, *intr.* (pass. of **malefacio**) For evil to be done: (w. dat.) *praecavetur ne ~fiat bonis per eos* AC 5008.3.

maleolens ~ntis, *a.* Foul-smelling: *odores ~ntes* VR 108.

maleolentia ~ae, *f.* The quality of having a foul smell, stench: *discernit ignem stercoris...ex ~a ejus* AM 439.

maleoleo ~lere, *intr.* To have a foul smell, stink: AM 505.4.

malevelle, *indecl.* (inf. of **malevolo***) Ill will, malevolence: *ex ~elle malefaciunt* AC 4776.2.

malevolentia ~ae, *f.* Ill will, malevolence: *falsa ~ae occupabunt omnia mentis naturalis* AC 7433; BCP (VI 6).

malevolus ~a ~um, *a.* Willing evil, malevolent: *falsum ~um* AC 7433.

malignitas ~atis, *f.* The quality of being harmful, noxiousness, malignity: *~as athmosphaerae* AM 375.3; *omne creatum...vilipenditur ex ~ate interna* VR 595.1; *qui impleverunt ~atem suam dolis* CI 491.

malignus ~a ~um, *a.* (compar. *~ior*, superl. *~issimus*) Causing harm, noxious, malignant: *febres ~ae et pestilentiales* AM 253.1; *arbores...cum fructibus ~is* AE 109.2; (of persons) *illis praeficiuntur ~iores* CI 220; (neut. pl. as sb.) a malign condition (of the body): *nisi... auferuntur ~a, homo moritur* VR 524.1.

malitia ~ae, *f.* Ill will, malice: *status mali et falsi, seu ~ae et phantasiae* AC 561; CI 506.2.

malitiose, *adv.* Maliciously: *hoc mali spiritus tam solerter et ~e facere possunt ut...* AC 751.1; CI 491.

malitiosus ~a ~um, *a.* (compar. *~ior*, superl. *~issimus*) Activated by ill will, malicious: *qui...interius ~i fuerunt* CI 491; AE 66.5; ES 6040; (of actions) *~a desertio* AM 468.

malleatus ~a ~um, *a.* Hammered: *ex ferro ~o* ES 2691.

malleus ~i, *m.* **1** A hammer: *habent...~um in manu* AC 821.2; (fig.) *~us Tu mihi* Jer. 51.20 (AC 8226.2). **2** (anat.) One of the bones in the ear, malleus: AC 4653.

malo ~lle ~lui, *intr.* To prefer: *quaeratur...an hoc coeleste est...aut si mavis, an hoc humanum* ES 1064; ES 4618.

malogranata: see **malogranatum**.

malogranatum ~i, *neut.* also **malogranata** ~ae, *f.* **1** The pomegranate tree: *arbores fructus...vites, ficus, ~a* VR 78.1. **2** The fruit of this tree, a pomegranate: *rediit cum ~o, in quo fuit copia seminum ex auro* AM 75.9; also, a decoration in the form of a pomegranate: Exod. 25.31 (AC); *et facies super fimbrias ejus ~a hyacinthini* Exod. 28.33 (AC).

malua (app.) A word of the angelic language (see quot.): *congeriem [paradoxorum]...vident angeli apud hominem, et hi illam vocant MALUA, hoc est, confusionem et caliginem* SE 56.

malum ~i, *neut.* **1** Evil (as a positive force): *potentia ~i [valuit] super potentiam boni* VR 3.1; *~um quod est amoris sui et mundi* AC 6677; *~um falsi* AE 504.27. **2** An evil quality possessed by a person: *is...immittitur in sua ~a et falsa* AC 6724.2; *ex ~is vitae* SS 12; *qui in ~o [sunt]* AC 6708. **3** An evil action: *quod non facienda sint ~a, quia sunt diaboli et a diabolo* VR 3.2. **4** An injurious event or circumstance, misfortune: *delectatur ~is quae fiunt aliis* CI 424.

malus[1] ~a ~um, *a.* (compar.: see **pejor**, superl.: see **pessimus**) **1** Morally bad, wicked, evil (of persons): *~us spiritus* CI 232; (masc. as sb.) *amare proximum... potest etiam ~us* FI 21. **b** (of desires, affections, intentions, etc.): *cupiditates illorum ~as* AC 7868; *finis ~us* AC 6935; *jucunda ~arum affectionum* AC 7967. **c** (of actions): *erant...opera eorum ~a* John 3.19 (VI 2). **2** Harmful, dangerous: *fera ~a* AC 7102.2; *arbores quae ferunt ~os fructus* DP 160. **3** In poor condition, unsatisfactory: *partes ~ae in corpore* ES 1711; *~a sanguinis...temperie* AC 847.2. **4** Concerned with evil: *in utroque sensu...tam in ~o quam in bono* AC 1163. **5** (of pain) Severe, bad: *dolorem creant satis ~um et gravem* ES 4348.

malus[2] ~i, *f.* **1** An apple tree: *~us punica etiamque palma et ~us, omnes arbores agri exsiccatae sunt* Joel 1.12 (AE 109.4); *~us punica*, a pomegranate tree: Joel 1.12 (AE 109.4). **2** An upright pole, flagstaff: *donec reliqui sitis sicut ~us super capite montis* Isa. 30.17 (AC 649); the mast (of a ship): VR 32.8.

malva ~ae, *f.* Mallow: *carpentes ~am super frutice* Job 30.4 (AC 2682.1).

mamilla ~ae, *f.* The breast: *praecinctum ad ~as zona aurea* Rev. 1.13 (AR).

mamillaris: see **mammillaris**.

mamma ~ae, *f.* A teat: *etiam balaenae praebent ~am* Lam. 4.3 (AC 6745.6).

mammillaris ~is ~e, *a*. also **mamillaris**. Mamillary: *processus ~es* ES 939.

Mammon ~nis, *m*. (Gk. from Aramaic) also **Mammonas** ~nae, *m*. Mammon, wealth: *ex injusto ~ne* Luke 16.9 (AE 141.13); *Deo servire et ~nae* Matt. 6.24 (VI 28); (as a name given to certain people) *hi ab antiquis in Ecclesia dicti sunt ~nes* VR 404.2.

Mammonas: see **Mammon**.

man, *indecl. neut.* (Hebr.) (abl. also *manne* AC 8487.4) = **manna**: *patres vestri comederunt man in deserto* John 6.49 (AC 680.2).

mancipium ~i, *neut*. A slave: *qui in mundo dominati sunt...illi post vitam...sunt...vilia ~a* NH 564.3; AM 125; ES 3786.

mancipo ~are ~avi ~atum, *tr*. To sell (someone to someone else) as a slave: (w. dat.) *cum muliere quae ancilla ~ata viro, non redemta, nec manumissa* AC 3400.2.

mancus ~a ~um, *a*. **1** Having a useless limb, crippled, maimed: *pauperes, ~os, claudos et coecos introduc huc* Luke 14.21 (AE 223.22); AC 7260. **2** Lacking an essential part, defective: *ne itaque lucubratiuncula haec propter ignorantiam illorum ~a sit* CC 18; *ut si unum [componens] deesset, ~um foret* ES 2213.

mandatum ~i, *neut*. An order, command: *accurrit unus ex curia cum ~o* AM 10.2; *ex ~o Domini* DD praef.

mando[1] ~are ~avi ~atum, *tr., intr.* **1** (w. dat.) To entrust, assign, commit: *quod enim vitae ~atur, taliter inest* CI 271; CI 348; (intr.) *~abo super vobis terrori* Lev. 26.16 (AC 8364.4). **2** (intr.) To give an order, command: *non opus habemus, quam ut ~emus, ac caelum et infernum...obediunt* AM 264.2; (w. *ut*) *cum... ~averit ut iret* AC 7041.1; (w. *quod*) *~atum fuit Mosi, quod percuteret baculo super aquas* AC 6693.6; **3** (tr.) To give (an order) *quae a duce ~abantur* AC 7111.3; (w. dat.) *statuta quae Dominus... ~avit populo Israelitico* AC 6804.7. **4** (pass., w. inf.) To be ordered (to): *ad illa [festa] omnis masculus... ~atus est ire* DD 64.1; *contradicens ~atur exire* VR 110.1.

mando[2] ~dere ~di ~sum, *tr*. To chew, bite: *et ~debant linguas suas prae molestia* Rev. 16.10 (AR).

mandragoras ~ae, *m*. (Gk.) The plant mandrake: 1AD 733.

manducatio ~onis, *f*. The act of eating: *fibrarum series...quae non ad ~onem et ad loquelam...solum creatae sunt* AC 8247; ES 4221; *quod [Sancta Caena] sit ~o spiritualis* VR 716.2.

manduco ~are ~avi ~atum, *tr*. To eat: *qui ~at hunc panem, vivet in aeternum* John 6.58 (AC 276.1); VR 699.

mane, *adv*. and *indecl. neut.* **1** (adv.) In the morning: *sicut ros ~e cadens* Hos. 6.4 (SS 79.3); Isa. 26.9 (DD 49). **2** (as sb.) Morning: (nom. or acc.) *cum ~e factum* ES 3086; *inde faciant dies et horum tempora, nempe ~e, meridiem, vesperam, et noctem* AC 6697; (gen.) *status ~e et meridiei* AC 7218; (abl.) *quodam ~e* AM 270.1. **b** the corresponding period of life: *senex ...reducitur in ~e suae aetatis* VR 766.

maneh, *indecl.* (Hebr.) A fairly large unit of weight or money, mina: *viginti sicli, quinque et viginti sicli, quindecim sicli, maneh...erit vobis* Ezek. 45.12 (AC 2959.6).

maneo ~nere ~nsi ~nsum, *intr., tr.* **1** (intr.) To be left in the same place, remain: *qui ~nserit in urbe hac morietur gladio* Jer. 21.9 (AC 7102.7); *si eum volo ~nere donec veniam* John 21.22 (AE 9.3); *quod sicut arbor cadit, ~neat* ES(M) 4645. **2** (intr.) To continue, remain (in a specified condition): *qui legunt Verbum et ~nent in sensu literali* AC 6789.2; *hoc flagitium... ~net irradicatum* AM 504.2; *homo post vitam... ~net qualis in mundo vixerat* SS 17.2. **3** (intr.) To continue in existence, endure, last: *nos audivimus...quod Christus ~neat in aeternum* John 12.34 (DD 10); *abstinet... ~nente usque cupiditate faciendi malum* AC 6977. **4** (tr.) To be in store for, await: *talis sors ~net illos* AC 1506; SE 110.1.

mania ~ae, *f*. (Gk.) Madness: AM 252; *ex ~a spirituali* VR 566.1.

maniacus ~i, *m*. A madman, maniac: *daemones, qui cum a Domino ejicerentur ex ~o...rogabant...* AC 1742.3 (Mark 5.10); VR 503.3.

manicae ~carum, *f. pl.* Fetters for the hands, handcuffs: *nisi Dominus...illud monstrum ~cis et pedicis vinctum teneret* VR 123.6.

manifestatio ~onis, *f*. The act of making plain, demonstration: *~onem potentiae Divinae* AC 7433; *~o quod Verbum de Ipso solo scriptum sit* DD 26.1.

manifeste, *adv*. (compar. *~ius*, superl. *~issime*) Plainly, clearly: *quod interiora talia sint, patet adhuc ~ius a malis* AC 7046.1; *quid...disponitur...non influit ~e in perceptionem* CI 435; *sicut expertus sum apud me ~issime* ES 295.

manifesto ~are ~avi ~atum, *tr*. **1** To render plainly visible, display, show: *cum Dominus ~atus est Petro, Jacobo et Johanni* AC 1530; *sicut stellae quae lucibus suis ~ant...illam* [sc. *fidem*] VR 137.5; (refl.) *placuit... Domino Se Ipsum mihi ~are* AM 1. **2** To make apprehensible, make plain, show forth: *~are Divinum in Humano* AC 8264; *liberatio illorum... ~ata est per exsuscitationem mortuorum* AC 8018.2; *quod sint [nuptiae] inter essentialia, quae solenniter ~anda sint* AM 306; (refl.) *ne aliquid affectionis se ~et* AC 7745.

3 To explain, demonstrate (a fact): *quod ita sit... ~atur in altera vita* AC 7778.3; *opuscula...in quibus ~ata sunt plura, quae...ignota fuerunt* DD praef.; *a plurimis locis apud evangelistas, ubi Dominus id ~at* AE 83.

manifestus ~a ~um, *a.* (compar. *~ior*) 1 Clearly apprehensible by the senses, plain, manifest: *per experientiam ~am* AC 7298.2; *alii ponunt operationem ~am* FI 39; *reflexio ~ior* ES 3842. 2 Plain to the mind, obvious: *quod influxus sit a Deo in hominem ~um est ab omnium confessione* VR 8.1; AC 1059.1.

manipulatim, *adv.* In bundles: *vera ~im disposita sunt* AC 9295.2.

manipulatio ~onis, *f.* A bundle, sheaf: *fecit autem terra in septem annis saturitatis juxta ~onem* Gen. 41.47 (2AD 681).

manipulo ~are ~avi ~atum, *tr.* To tie into bundles, bind (sheaves): *et ecce nos ~antes manipulos in medio agri* Gen. 37.7 (AC).

manipulus ~i, *m.* A bundle: *quod quatuor illa ...faciant simul sicut unum ~um* DP 111.2; a sheaf (of hay and sim.): *sicut facem ignis in ~o* Zech. 12.6 (AE 433.18).

manna ~ae, *f.* (ad. Hebr.) (abl. sg. also *~e* AC 8487.4) see also **man**. Manna: *~a est bonum spirituale* AC 8395; VR 810.

mannus ~i, *m.* A pony: *currus tractus a ~is albis* AM 76.8; CO 35.2.

mano ~are ~avi, *intr.* To flow, pour: *lachrymae ~abant mihi ex oculis* 3AD 5396.

mansio ~onis, *f.* 1 A dwelling place, abode, residence: *~onem apud illum faciemus* John 14.23 (AC 8269); *circumferuntur ad plures ~ones* AC 1273; AM 261.1; (for doves) a cote: *variae ~ones columbarum* ES 4142. 2 (in a building) A storey, floor: *ad fenestram primae ~onis* VR 24.2; *in...tertia ~one* ES 1579.

mansuete, *adv.* In a gentle fashion, mildly: *respondebat ~e, quod non opus habeant* ES 521.

mansuetudo ~inis, *f.* Gentleness: *equita super verbo veritatis, ~inis et justitiae* Ps. 45.4 (AE 298.7).

mansuetus ~a ~um, *a.* (compar. *~ior*) Gentle, mild: *mirari quam mites et ~i sunt spiritus incolarum Jovis* ES 708; ES 2643; AM 370.

mantelium ~i, *neut.* A towel: *cum ~is circumcirca lumbos ex tunica...pendentibus* AM 78.4.

mantica ~ae, *f.* 1 A wallet: *et ecce illud in ore ~ae illius* Gen. 42.27 (AC); cf. *~a...erat anterior pars sacci* AC 5497.1. 2 The sleeve (of a garment): [*vestis*] *cum ~is longis* ES 4133.

manualis ~is ~e, *a.* *Liber ~is*, a manual: *in libro ~i...Formula Concordiae appellato* VR 137.9.

manuarius ~a ~um, *a.* Performed with the hand, manual: *operae ~ae* SA 105 (= vii.5.[3]).

manubrium ~i, *neut.* A handle: *sculptura...mobilis per ~um* CO 26.

manuduco ~cere ~xi ~ctum, *tr.* To lead by the hand, guide: *dum...fit sui juris, ut semet posset ex sua mente ~cere* ES 2821.

manuductio ~onis, *f.* Guidance: *ex ~one patris novit tunc quid aget* AC 6492; ES 2821.

manumissio ~onis, *f.* The act of setting free, liberation, manumission: (fig.) *pro expansione animi, et ~one cogitationum inclusarum* VR 434.1.

manumitto ~mittere ~misi ~missum, *tr.* To release from slavery, set free, manumit: *nos eripimus e servitute, et ~mittimus* AM 79.5.

manus ~us, *f.* 1 The hand: *brachia et ~us sunt ultima hominis* CI 65; *tangere ~u* AM 241. 2 The hand as the part used in actions, esp. in making something: *si non ~u, usque animo...occidit* AC 374.1; *opus ~us Tuae omnes nos* Isa. 64.8 (AC 6669.4). 3 The hand as symbolizing power or control: *habitatores eorum breves ~u* Isa. 37.27 (AC 878.2); *liberavit nos e ~u pastorum* Exod. 2.19 (AC); *anima cujusvis in ~u Domini est* DP 94; *Deo tenente illum in ~u et ducente* VR 24.2. 4 The left or right direction: *juxta duas ~us throni* AE 278.11. 5 A signpost, fingerpost: *lapides aut ~us in viis, qui monstrant viam ad templum* VR 379.5. 6 (in carpentry) A projection to fit a socket, tenon: *duae ~us asseri combinatae* Exod. 26.17 (AC). 7 Some part of a wheel, perh. an axle pin: *~us illarum* [*rotarum*] 1 Kgs. 7.33 (AC 8215.5).

mapale ~is, *neut.* A wretched dwelling, hut: *quod super ~ia illorum volent aves lugubres et ululent* VR 45.2; FI 63.2.

mappa ~ae, *f.* A map: *absque cysti nautica et ~is* VR 620.2.

marcesco ~ere, *intr.* To wither, wilt: *calamus et alga ~ent* Isa. 19.6 (AC 6726); *ut homo dum ad senectutem vergit, tunc corpus ex se ~at* ES 2665.

mare ~is, *neut.* 1 An extensive area of water, sea, lake: *vidi ex ~i bestiam ascendentem* Rev. 13.1 (AR); (pl.) *sicut balaenae in ~ibus* Ezek. 32.2 (AC 7293.2); (w. proper name) *in ~i Suph* Exod. 15.4 (AC). 2 *~e aeneum*, the bronze sea, the name given to a large vessel in Solomon's temple: 1 Kgs. 7.23 (AC 5291.10).

margarita ~ae, *f.* (Gk.) A pearl: *ne projicite ~as vestras ante porcos* Matt. 7.6 (AC 7784.4); *sicut ~a* *alligaretur naribus porci* AM 525.4; *duodecim portae duodecim ~ae* Rev. 21.21 (AR).

margaritice, *adv*. (Gk.) With pearl-like smoothness: *influebat leniter, sicut ~e* ES Index s.v. 'oculus' (p. 127 Tafel), referring to ES 3496.

margariticus ~a ~um, *a*. (Gk.) Of or resembling pearl, pearly: *in aura lucis...splendentis ~ae* AC 1116; AC 7620; ES 3213.

margo ~inis, *f*. A margin (of a page): *aliquid in ~ine annotare licuit* ES 29 (Bath fragment).

marinus ~a ~um, *a*. Of the sea, marine: *monstrum ~um* CO 54.

maritalis ~is ~e, *a*. Of a husband, marital: *quod... mutetur...juvenile in ~e apud viros* AM 199.1.

maritimus ~a ~um, *a*. Adjacent to the sea, coastal, maritime: *e locis ~is* SS 21; *in Kapernaum ~a* Matt. 4.13 (AE 447.5).

maritatus ~a ~um, *a*. Married; (fem. as sb.) a married woman: AM 460.1.

marito ~are ~avi ~atum, *tr*. To provide with a husband, marry (a woman): *ut puellae eorum virgines sint, et sic ~entur* ES 3769; (fig.) *terra tua ~abitur* Isa. 62.4 (AC 55.2).

maritus ~i, *m*. A husband: *uxores et ~i* AE 25.1; (w. ref. to the Lord) *quare Dominus in Verbo vocatur sponsus et ~us* CI 180.

marmor ~oris, *neut*. Marble: *simulachrum ex ~ore* VI 109; (w. pl.) a kind of marble: *mirabatur quam multa ~ora* ES 339.

marmoreus ~a ~um, *a*. Of or resembling marble: *basis ~a* ES 392; *sphaera sicut ~a brunea colorata* ES 4196.

Martius ~i, *m*. The month of March: ES 1123.

martyr ~yris, *m*. (Gk.) A witness: *Antipas ~yr Meus fidelis qui occisus apud vos* Rev. 2.13 (AR); one who suffers for his faith, a martyr: *~yres et qui persecutiones passi* ES 1325.

martyrisatio ~onis, *f*. The making of a martyr, martyrdom: *quot non exstant pictae ~ones...?* ES 3187.

martyrium ~i, *neut*. (Gk.) A martyrdom: *quia nullae tales persecutiones...sic non ~a* ES 1326.

mas maris, *m*. A male, man: *quod mas et faemina creati sint* AM 83; *tales visi sunt...tam mares quam foeminae* ES 4696.

maschal, *indecl*. also **mashal**, *indecl*. (sg. of **moschalim** q.v.) A transliteration of a Hebr. word meaning a proverb or prophecy: *quod Bileamus ediderit enuntiatum suum, quod fuit propheticum...enuntiatum ejus vocatur ~al in singulari* VR 265.2.

masculinus ~a ~um, *a*. Male, masculine: *sexus ~us* AC 568.2; AM 32.

masculus ~a ~um, *a*. Of the male sex: *peperit filium ~um* Rev. 12.5 (AR); *pecus integra, ~a* Exod. 12.5 (AC); (masc. as sb.) *quod tunc ~us sit ~us, et quod faemina sit faemina* AM 32.

mashal: see **maschal**.

maskil, *indecl*. (Hebr.) A psalm: *canite ~l* Ps. 47.7 (AE 326.12).

massa ~ae, *f*. **1** A quantity of dough prepared for making bread: Exod. 12.34 (AC); *~a pro pane* AC 7356.1; also, a similar preparation made from other substances: *~am ficuum* 2 Kgs. 20.7 (AE 403.17). **2** A substantial body, mass, lump: *aurum...fusum in ~am* VR 701.3; CI 212. **3** The major bulk of a substance, mass: [*vitiosa*] *pervadunt venas...ac ~am sanguinis inquinant* AC 1877; ES 914.

mater ~tris, *f*. **1** A mother: *corpus...est a ~tre* AC 6716.2; *Domini verba...ad Mariam ~trem* AE 9.5; (fig.) *sicut in pomis...superficies seu cortex est ~ter fructus interiorum* ES 396; *quod loquela angelorum...sit quasi ~ter loquelae spirituum* ES 2139. **2** (anat.) Any of the integuments of the brain: *sicut...~tres et meninges* [*investiunt*] *cerebra* VR 78.4; *provinciam durae ~tris* ES 1691.

materia ~ae, *f*. **1** The constituent substance of a thing: *quod corpora* [sc. *tellures*] *terrestris ~ae sint* AC 6697; matter (in abstract): *cogitationes...fundatae sunt super tempore, spatio, et ~a* AE 23.1. **2** The subject matter (of a book): *non licet a ~a hic proposita abire* AM 156[a].3.

materialis ~is ~e, *a*. **1** Composed of matter, material: *credant quod corpori ~i iterum conjungenda sit* [*anima*] AC 6929; *homo naturalis seu ~is* AM 31; (neut. as sb.) *quod producta ex ~ibus ament* AC 6816; *si ideae temporis, spatii et ~ium auferrentur* CI 169. **2** Of or concerned with matter, material: *ideae ~es, mundanae et corporeae* AC 1025.2; *cogitationem...vocant ~em* AE 30.1.

materialiter, *adv*. In a material fashion, materially: *cogitant sensualiter et ~er* VR 12.3.

materiatus ~a ~um, *a*. Composed of matter: (neut. as sb.) *substantia et ~a illa momento conciderent* VR 30.2.

maternus ~a ~um, *a*. Of a mother, maternal: *in haereditario ~o* AC 6866; *ex teneritudine ~a* AM 410; (neut. as sb.) that which is derived from the mother: *~um, hoc est, illud quod a matre traxit* AC 1793.1.

matertera ~ae, *f.* A maternal aunt: ES 5979.

mathematicus ~a ~um, *a.* (Gk.) Concerned with numbers, mathematical: *scientiae utiles sunt...~a* ES(M) 4578.

mathesis ~eos, *f.* (Gk.) Mathematics: ES 5141.

matrimonialis ~is ~e, *a.* Of or concerned with marriage: *faedere ~i* AM 282.1; (neut. as sb.) *cum ~e intelligitur* AC 3914.

matrimonium ~i, *neut.* Marriage: *~a cum pluribus* AC 865.2; AM 49.

matrix ~icis, *f.* **1** The womb: *in fractura ~icis filiorum* Hos. 13.13 (AC 264); *ad...os ~icis venire* ES 261; (fig.) *quod [orbis terraqueus]...sit sicut ~ix, ex qua effectus...producuntur* AS 165. **2** The rock surrounding a precious stone, matrix: *sicut gemma in sua ~ice* AM 83; VR 192.

matrona ~ae, *f.* A married woman of rank, matron: *in conjugiis, ut...~ae illustris cum famulo* AM 250.

matula ~ae, *f.* A chamber pot: *missus in urinae ~am* ES 4490; ES 3466.

maturatio ~onis, *f.* The process of ripening: *per... fructuum progressivas ~ones* VR 687.2.

maturesco ~rescere ~rui, *intr.* To become ripe, ripen: *usque dum ~ruerit fructus* ES 251.

maturitio ~onis, *f.* Ripening: *~o botrorum in uvas* AC 5117.1.

maturo ~are ~avi ~atum, *tr.* To ripen; (fig.) to develop: *exscindentur omnes ~antes iniquitatem* Isa. 29.20 (AC 6353.4).

maturus ~a ~um, *a.* **1** Ripe: *in arborum fructibus...in ~is* AC 5117.1. **2** (of age) Mature: *ab aetate infantili ad ~am* AM 187. **3** Advanced to a satisfactory condition, mature, ripe: *cognitiones... implantatae ab infantia, et nondum ~ae* AE 403.1; *dictum...quod nondum ~a* [sc. for admission to a hell] ES 4515.

matuta ~ae, *f.* The early part of the day, morning: *status diei sunt sicut vesperae, noctis, ~ae et meridiei* AC 1458.1.

matutinus ~a ~um, *a.* Of the morning: *in custodia ~a* Exod. 14.24 (AC); *Ego sum...stella splendida et ~a* Rev. 22.16 (AR); *~o tempore* ES 217; (neut. as sb.) the morning: *in ~o* Exod. 7.15 (AC).

maurus: see **morus**.

mausolaeum ~i, *neut.* (Gk.) also **mausoleum**. A mausoleum: VR 676.

mausoleum: see **mausolaeum**.

maxilla ~ae, *f.* A jawbone: *dolor sinistram ~am... invasit* AC 5720; (pl.) the jaws: *dabo hamos in ~as tuas* Ezek. 38.4 (AC 1151.2).

maxime, *adv.* (superl. of **magis**) To the greatest extent, most: *illa quae ~e conveniunt* AC 6690; *cavent quam ~e* ES 3882; (used to form superlative of adjs. and advs.) *objecta ~e dissita* AC 10181.2; *~e sollicite inquisiverunt* ES 3630.

maximopere, *adv.* To the greatest extent, very much: *~e mirati* AC 70; *~e fallitur* AC 7950.2; *~e conati* ES 3843.

maximum ~i, *neut.* The highest point of development, maximum: *omnis...status suum principium habet, sua incrementa, et suum ~um* AC 7715.

maximus ~a ~um, *a.* (superl. of **magnus**) **1** Largest, greatest: *aquae ~i oceani* AC 7077; *quoad ~am partem* AC 7131. **2** On the major scale, very great: *in receptaculis minimis...in receptaculo ~o* AM 220.2; esp. *~us Homo*, the Grand Man: (as a description of the Heavens) *coelum vocant ~um et Divinum Hominem* CI 59. **3** Of the highest importance, supreme, greatest: *Dominum...ut ~um Prophetam* DD 15.8. **b** *~i esse*, to be of the hightest importance: *scire veritates ~i est* ES 737. **4** Highest in degree, most: *~am felicitatem* AC 452; *damnatio omnium ~a et dirissima* AC 8169.

me: see **ego**.

meatus ~us, *m.* A bodily opening or passage: *et si ~us obstipatur, cessat loquela* AS 382; *per varios ~us, canales, et sinus...feruntur* ES 831.

mechanice ~es, *f.* (Gk.) The science of mechanics, engineering: *arcana ~es* AC 6057.1; SS(P) 51 (= 19.3).

mechanicus ~a ~um, *a.* (Gk.) Concerned with machines: *scientiae...ut...~a* AM 163; *~ae praxi* ES 768; (masc. as sb.) an engineer: *~us ille...continuo meditatus est construere machinas mobiles* ES 4722.

mecum, *pron.* = *me* (see **ego**) combined with *cum* (see **cum**[1]). With me: ES 1501. (n.b. *cum me* for *mecum*: AM 326.4.)

medela ~ae, *f.* Curative treatment, a remedy: *facti sumus...proni ad deliquium, si non subito ~a affertur* VR 73.1; ES 151.

medeor ~deri, *intr.* (w. dat.) To apply remedies (to), cure: *dicunt...~dere nobis* VR 459.12; *ad ~dendum iis quae inordinata sunt* ES 1758.

mediastinum ~i, *neut.* (anat.) The partition between the two pleural cavities, mediastinum: ES 983; ES 1766.

mediastinus ~i, *m.* A servant who performs humble tasks, drudge: *servi et ancillae cum ~is aliis* CO 29.2; *~i sacerdotum* VR 178.2.

mediate, *adv.* Through the intervention of others, indirectly: *percipitur quod vox...immediate non possit audiri...sed ~e per spiritus* AC 6985; *Dominus... praesens fuit apud homines Ecclesiae, sed ~e per angelos* VR 109.1.

mediatio ~onis, *f.* The intervention of another, mediation: *erit ~o, quae ~o fit per coelum* AC 6996.1; *quod continuae sint ~ones incomprehensibili modo distributae a Deo Messia* ES 194.

mediator ~oris, *m.* One who mediates, mediator: *quod...crediderint in quendam summum creatorem, absque ~ore* AC 7251; ES 408.

mediatrix ~icis, *f. adj.* Serving to mediate: *causa... ~ix* ES 341.

mediatus ~a ~um, *a.* Arising through the intervention of another, indirect: *facta est communicatio ~a per repraesentativa* AC 1850.3.

medicamen ~inis, *neut.* = **medicamentum**: ES(M) 4650.

medicamentum ~i, *neut.* A healing substance, medicament: Ezek. 47.12 (AE 109.5).

medicina ~ae, *f.* **1** The science of healing, medicine: *quod medici, ~a ac medicamenta...significent praeservationes a malis et falsis* AC 6502.2. **2** A remedy, medicine: *quibus [morbis] nisi applicantur ~ae... homo moritur* VR 524.1.

medicus ~a ~um, *a.* Of healing, medical: *scientiae utiles...ut... ~a* ES(M) 4657; (masc. as sb.) a physician, doctor: *non opus habent valentes ~o* Matt. 9.12 (AC 8365); AM 163.

medio ~are ~avi ~atum, *intr.* (but cf. **mediatus**) To act as intermediary, mediate: *alter qui redemit nos, et hic quoque ~at* VR 135.2; *absque mediis seu ~antibus non datur communicatio* AC 4154.

mediocris ~is ~e, *a.* Neither great nor small, middling: *vir staturae ~is* ES 2645.

mediocriter, *adv.* To an average extent, fairly: *hominem ~er doctum* AS 239.

meditabundus ~a ~um, *a.* Deep in thought, meditating: *vadunt... ~i, obmutescunt* CI 438.

meditatio ~onis, *f.* A matter considered mentally, reflection, meditation: *haec ~o elucebat ex oculis meis* AM 316.1; *ut...vacarent piis ~onibus* CI 360.1.

meditato, *adv.* With forethought, deliberately: *qui ~o et ex voluntate malum fecerunt* AE 316.28 (1 Kgs. 2.28-31).

Mediterraneus ~a ~um, *a. Mare ~um*, the Mediterranean Sea: ES 4777.

meditor ~ari ~atus sum, *intr., tr.* To meditate, reflect: (w. *in* + abl.) *in Lege Ipsius ~atur diu et nocte* Ps. 1.2 (AC 6752.4); (w. *de*) *dum ~atur de eo* AM 34. **b** (tr.) to reflect upon: *cum perceperunt quod arcana sapientiae de amore ~arer* VR 48.1.

meditullium ~i, *neut.* The central or inmost region, middle: *in medio seu ~o terrae* AC 468.2; *in omnia ejus* [sc. *arboris*] *~a ac centra* ES 251.

medium ~i, *neut.* **1** The middle, centre: *ille amor in ~o est, et circum se ordinat singula* AC 6690; *convertite faciem...ad ~um sylvae* AM 521.6. **2** *In ~um afferre*, to make public, divulge: *si omnia in ~um afferrem* CI 229. **3** (usu. pl.) That which serves as a means: *~a potentiae* AC 7027; *usus amat ~a* FI 14; (sg.) *haec est via et hoc est ~um, ut...* BCP (VI 6).

medius ~a ~um, *a.* **1** Situated in between, middle: *in infima serie...in ~a serie...in suprema serie* AM 270.2; *secundum seu ~um caelum* SS 6. **2** Intermediate in order or quality: *fines ~i conjungunt se cum fine ultimo* AC 7017; *lux ~a, qualis est cum incipit immisceri umbrae vesperae* VR 136.1; *in statu inter vigiliam et somnum ~o* ES 3975. **3** The middle of: *in ~a nocte* Exod. 12.29 (AC); *per ~am damnationem incolumes transibunt* AC 7889; *in ~a via* VR 4.2; *~o corpore* ES 4687. **4** Serving as means; (usu. w. sb. in abl.) by means of: *quod...spiritus... ~a respiratione interna junctus fuerit coelo* AC 1121; *~is luce et calore* VR 76.3; *per ~os spiritus* ES 2285.

medulla ~ae, *f.* **1** The marrow (of the bones): *veneno...quod ad ipsas ~as penetrat* AC 8625.2. **b** *~a spinalis*, the spinal cord: AS 366. **2** Any interior part, the vitals: *gaudium...penetrabat...ut ajunt, intimas ~as* ES 293; *quod amor conjugialis...exurat ~as* AM 312. **b** *~a oblongata*, the rearmost segment of the brain: AS 366. **3** The pith (of a plant): *arbores qui absque ~a sunt* AM 232.1.

medullaris ~is ~e, *a.* Medullary: *una [substantia cerebri] corticalis, et altera ~is* AC 7408.1; AM 315.5; ES 939.

medullatus ~a ~um, *a.* Full of marrow: (neut. as sb.) *convivium...pinguium ~orum* Isa. 25.6 (AC 2341.2).

medullosus ~a ~um, *a.* Containing or resembling marrow, medullary: *instar substantiae ~ae, qualis in cerebro humano* CI 466; ES 862.

mel mellis, *neut.* Honey: *terram fluentem lacte et melle* Exod. 13.5 (AC); *quod sciant [apes]...exsugere mel* AM 419; (w. pl.) a particular kind of honey: *mel agreste* Matt. 3.4 (DD 15.8); *sciunt apes legere mella* CI 108.1.

melancholia ~ae, *f.* (Gk.) A state of mental depression, melancholy: *dolor animi ac tristitia interior quae ~a vocatur* CI 299; ES 1336.

melancholicus ~a ~um, *a.* (Gk.) Of or caused by melancholy: *anxietas ~a* AC 8164.2; subject to melancholy: *simplices et ~os* ES 2779.

melecheth, *indecl. f.* (Hebr.) A Hebr. word for queen: Jer. 7.18 (AC 9993.6); AE 324.23.

meles ~is, *f.* A badger: *pellibus ~ium* Exod. 26.14 (AC); a badger skin: *calceavi te ~i* Ezek. 16.10 (AC 297).

melior ~or ~us, *a.* (used as compar. of **bonus**) (in senses of **bonus**) Better: *non...quia aliis gentibus ~ores essent* AC 7439.2; *in ~orem statum redactus est* AC 8028.

melioratio ~onis, *f.* Improvement: *ad sui ~onem* ES 1069.

melioratus ~a ~um, *a.* Made better, improved: ES 524.

melioresco ~ere, *intr.* To become better, improve: *sed usque angeli ~ere possunt* ES 883; ES 4741.

melius, *adv.* (used as compar. of **bene**) Better: *ut veritas... ~us appareat* AC 7075; *ut sic ~us dolos nectant* ES 2408.

melodia ~ae, *f.* (Gk.) A tune, melody: *aves edoctae canere ~am hymni sancti* VR 452.

melolontha ~ae, *f.* (Gk.) The grub of a beetle: *residuum locustae comedit ~a* Joel 1.4 (AC 7643.7).

melos ~us, *neut.* (Gk.) (abl. sg. *~o* VR 694.8) A song: *auditum est suavissimum ~os* AM 55.1.

membrana ~ae, *f.* **1** A membrane: *~am auris externam* AC 7359; *influxu lucis...in ~am transparentem* VR 34.3. **2** A thin skin prepared for use as a material, parchment: *libri illorum fuerant ~ae* AR 335; ES [6109.3]. **3** A thin skin or vellum used as a binding material for a book; (transf.) a tome, volume: *viri... incluti ex ~is typo impressis* VR 137.1; *implere ~am/~as*, to fill a volume/volumes: *implerent, sicut dicitur, ~as* CI 436; AR 285; VR 462.10; *opus ~ae/~arum*, a task requiring a volume/volumes to complete: *confirmare illa ad captum plurium ~arum opus foret, sed usque confirmata quoad partem sunt in Sapientia Angelica de Divino Amore et Divina Sapientia nuper Amstelodami edita* AR 29.1; AM 492; VR 371.8.

membranaceus ~a ~um, *a.* Of or resembling a membrane: *naturam ~am illorum* [sc. *fructuum aut seminum*] AC 505; (neut. pl. as sb.) *organica seu ~a corporis* ES 3419.

membranula ~ae, *f.* A small membrane: AC 184.

membrum ~i, *neut.* **1** A major part of the body, limb, member: *cuivis ~o, organo et visceri* AC 6698; ES 270. **2** A member of a corporate body: *Ecclesiae capita et ~a* VR 133.1. **3** A section (of a written work): *hoc ~um hujus capitis...in sequentes articulos dispescetur* VR 36.

memet: acc. of *egomet* (s.v. **ego**).

memini ~isse, *intr.* (pf. form w. pres. sense; fut. imperative sg. *memento* and pl. *mementote* w. pres. sense) **1** (w. gen.) To remember: *mementote Legis Mosis* Mal. 4.4 (AC 6752.10); *indignatus, quod non ~isset eorum quae in vita corporis* ES 4410; (w. acc.) *responsa non ~i* ES 379; (w. *quod*) *interrogavi num usquam ~erint quod adulterium esset contra sextum praeceptum* AM 521.5; (absol.) *quantum ~i* AC 7359. **2** To remember in writing, mention: *de iis videntur veteres ~isse* ES 1773.

memor ~oris, *a.* Remembering, mindful: *~or esto... unde excideris* Rev. 2.5 (AR).

memorabilis ~is ~e, *a.* Worthy of being remembered, noteworthy, memorable: *~e est quod Dominus... convocaverit...Suos discipulos* VR 4.1; (neut. as sb.) a memorable event, noteworthy occurrence: *loca... significant res, et res...sunt...a ~i quod ibi factum est* AE 50.1; (esp. as title of sections of works) *~ia post capita* AM 1.

memorandum ~i, *neut.* A memorandum, note: VR 791; (pl.) noteworthy occurrences: *sensus...internus ~a et historica...nihil curat* AC 4864.

memoratio ~onis, *f.* A mention: *~o Canaanitae* AC 1573.2.

memoria ~ae, *f.* **1** The faculty of remembering, memory: *spiritus qui in Maximo Homine referunt ~am* AC 6696; *vera solum in ~a habent* AE 6; (pl) *omnia inseminantur ~ae seu potius ~is* AC 991; AC 7122.1. **2** *E* or *ex ~a*, from memory: *decalogo e ~a lecto* DP 258.4; *pro ~a*, a memorandum: PM titulus.

memorialis ~is ~e, *a.* **1** Of or belonging to the memory: *ipsi eorum libri ~es...aperti sunt* CI 462[a].3; serving as a reminder, memorial: *in quadam Appendice ~i* DP 258.5. **2** (neut. as sb.) A memorial, reminder: *mactare boves et pecudes, et quidem in ~e* AC 921.2; *hoc ~e Meum in generationem, generationem* Exod. 3.15 (AC); *hoc ~e dabitur* VR 224.4.

memoriter, *adv.* From memory: *sciverunt ~er doctrinalia* ES 5829.

memoro ~are ~avi ~atum, *tr.* To place on record, record, mention: *quatuor genera vastationum... ~antur* AC 7102.2; *nec expendunt quid historica... ~ant* AC 7051.3; *~atu dignus*, worthy of being recorded, worth mentioning: AM 269.1; (w. *quod*) *in antecessum ~are licet, quod homo possit divitias acquirere* CI 358.

mendaciter, *adv*. Untruthfully: ES 1622.

mendacium ~i, *neut*. A deliberately untrue statement, lie: *pro falso, quod in Verbo vocatur ~um* AC 6952.5; *tam multa ~a narrarent* ES 1622; (Bibl.) a pretence, sham: *fusile... ~um est* Jer. 51.17 (DD 47.2).

mendax ~acis, *a*. Speaking falsehoods, lying: *ex... simulatoribus et ~acibus* AM 48[a].2; (masc. as sb.) a liar: *gladie, contra ~aces* Jer. 50.36 (AR 52.2); (of things) pretended, deceptive: *planum istud falsum et ~ax* ES 250.

mendico ~are ~avi ~atum, *intr.* To ask for alms, beg: *tales qui in plateis ~ant* AC 3688.3; ES 431.

mendicus ~i, *m*. A beggar: *~is qui se prae aliis pauperes vocant* AC 9209.2.

mene, *indecl.* Mene, to assess the number or value of (see quot.): *~e seu numeravit* AC 3104.4; *per ~e seu numerare* AR 313.

meningeus ~a ~um, *a*. Of a membrane, meningeal: *~a cerebri* VR 665.5.

meninx ~ngis, *f.* (Gk.) (anat.) A membrane, meninx: *involucra... communia quae vocantur ~nges* AC 501; VR 60.2; ES 1725.

Menius ~i, *m*. (?) (Hebr. *meni*) Meni, or Destiny, the name of a god: *impletis ~o libamen* Isa. 65.11 (AC 4581.7).

mens ~ntis, *f.* **1** The mental faculties of a person, mind: *quisque consulere debet ~nti suae victu* AC 6936; *~ns quae in veris est* AE 47; (w. gen.) the mental ability (to): *nemo cui aliqua ~ns vere cogitandi* AC 878.5. **2** The mind as composed of will and understanding: *~ns hominis consistit ex intellectu et voluntate* VR 151; *~ntem intellectualem* AC 398; (dist. from **animus** or **anima**) *~ns, animus, indoles, inclinatio et affectio amoris* VR 103.2; *facies...est index animi, imo ~ntis* ES 574; *vera... ~nti implantantur, ita infra animam* VR 8.1. **3** The mind as possessing several levels: *~ns naturalis* AC 6690; *~ns rationalis* AC 7130; *~ns spiritualis* FI 32. **4** The concentration of the mind on a particular subject, attention: *dum ~ns tenetur solum in historicis literae* AC 878.6; *sed ~ns est de illis qui nihili faciunt amorem conjugialem* AM 230; *ludificationes ~ntis abstractae* DP 134.1. **5** Mental view, opinion, mind: *interrogavimus, quae ejus ~ns* VR 35.7.

mensa ~ae, *f.* **1** A table: *est in medio... ~a, dum super illa...charta...ponitur...* AR 566.5; *ad ~am sedere et ibi scribere* ES 4910; (used for the display of the bread of the Presence) Exod. 25.23 (AC). **2** A dining table: *quod Johannes ad pectus Domini ad ~am accubuerit* AC 7038 3; *quum loquor cum sociis in consortio, ut super ~am* ES 159. **3** The food served at table, a meal: *ei ~a subministrata opipara* ES 777. **4** *~a feralis*, a bier: CI 433; ES 1357.

mensalis ~is ~e, *a*. Of or for a dining table: *decoramenta ~ia* ES 6088.7.

mensarius ~i, *m*. A banker: *oportebat te exponere argentum meum ~is* Matt. 25.27 (AE 193.10).

mensis ~is, *m*. A month: *non per diem aut septimanam sed per plures ~es* AC 6695; *ante aliquot ~es* VR 4.1.

menstrua ~ae, *f.* (app.) A cloth soiled with menses: *ideo in ~am facta [Hierosolyma]* Lam. 1.8 (AC 5433.5).

menstruatus ~a ~um, *intr*. Menstruous: *ad mulierem ~am non accedit* AE 555.21; (neut. as sb.) a menstrual cloth: *disperges ea sicut ~um* Isa. 30.22 (AC 9424.7).

menstruum ~i, *neut*. A fluid which breaks down complex molecules, solvent, menstruum: *quod ventriculus cibos...per ~a aperiat et separet, hoc est, digerat* DP 296.14; AE 1214.2; *~a dissolventia* ES 2129.

mensura ~ae, *f.* **1** The process or method of measuring, measurement: *~a hominis, quae est angeli* Rev. 21.17 (AR); *juxta ~am* 'in measured quantities' DD 15.7; *non ex ~a dedit [Pater] Illi Spiritum* John 3.34 (SE 120.10). **2** The correctly measured quantity, full measure: *~a bona, pressa...dabitur* Luke 6.38 (AC 6960.3); (fig.) *de iis qui...peccatorum ~am implent* AC 488.1.

mensurabilis ~is ~e, *a*. Capable of being measured, measurable: *quia tempora non ~ia sunt* AE 194.2.

mensuratio ~onis, *f.* Measurement: *ideae spatii existunt ex ~one per tempora* AC 7381.3; *ut cuncta referrent ad ~ones* ES 181.

mensuro ~are ~avi ~atum, *tr*. To measure, count: *non ~atur arena maris* Jer. 33.22 (AC 1025.10); *cum... spatia ~at [sol]* AC 7381.4; *sphaera... ~ata per fasciam perpendicularem* ES 3395.

mentalis ~is ~e, *a*. Existing only in the mind, imagined: *quod charitas et fides sint modo res ~es et caducae* VR 375.1; *persuasio ~is* VR 633.1.

mentio ~onis, *f.* A mention: *cujus rei ~o aliquoties ...facta est* AM 314.3; (Bibl.) a calling to mind, remembrance: *non fiet ~o contra eum* Ezek. 33.16 (SS 85).

mentiono ~are ~avi ~atum, *tr*. To make mention of: *non alibi ~atur [stacte]* AC 10292.3 (Autograph and 1st edn.).

mentior ~tiri ~titus sum, *tr., intr*. **1** (intr.) To speak falsehood, tell lies: *per 'false testari'...intelligitur...etiam ~tiri et diffamare* VI 87. **2** (intr., of things) To display a misleading appearance, lie: *silente vel etiam simul ~tiente facie* AC 8250.1; *cujus non ~tientur aquae* Isa.

58.11 (AC 108). 3 (tr.) To pretend falsely to be, counterfeit: *non bonum, solum tale quod ~titur bonum* AC 1096.3; *Jacobus ~titus Esavum* AC 3539.3; *caligo ~tiens lucem* SS 60. 4 (tr.) To pretend to have: *docti sunt ~tiri affectiones coelestes* CI 347.3.

mentitus ~a ~um, *a.* (pf. pple. of **mentior**) (in senses of vb., esp. as pass.) Falsely alleged, trumped up: *causas... de uxore ~as inspergunt* AM 474; counterfeit, pretended: *didici quod ea omnia ficta ac ~a essent* ES 399.

mentum ~i, *neut.* The chin: *~o barbato* AM 33.

mercator ~oris, *m.* A merchant: VR 106.1; ES 404.

mercatorius ~a ~um, *a.* Of a merchant: *in... officinis ~is* ES 457.

mercatrix ~icis, *f.* A female merchant: *Tharschisch [erat] ~ix tua* Ezek. 27.12 (AC 4453.2).

mercatura ~ae, *f.* The business of a merchant, trade: *qui negotiationibus et ~is operam...dederunt* CI 360.3; ES 3523.

mercatus ~us, *m.* Trafficking, trading: *turmae tuae in ~u tuo* Ezek. 27.25 (AE 514.2).

mercenarius ~a ~um, *a.* Hired: *per novaculam ~am* Isa. 7.20 (AC 3301.7); (masc. as sb.) one who works for hire, hired servant: *inquilinus et ~us non comedet illud* Exod. 12.45 (AC); Isa. 16.14 (AC 482.2).

merces[1] ~edis, *f.* Payment for work, wages, hire: *lacta illum mihi, et ego dabo ~edem tuam* Exod. 2.9 (AC); *ideam ~edis seu remunerationis* AC 8002.7; (transf.) *quod ~edem in altera vita accipiat* AC 735.

merces[2] ~ium, *f. pl.* Commodities for sale, merchandise, wares: *currus onerati varii generis ~ibus* AC 8215.2; AM 287.

mercor ~ari ~atus sum, *intr.* To deal in merchandise, trade: *negotiari et ~ari* AE 355.12.

mere, *adv.* Without admixture, purely, solely: *~e materialia* AC 6811; *notum est quod omnis homo, dum nascitur, sit ~e corporeus* AM 59.1.

mereo ~rere ~rui ~ritum, *intr.* (*tr.*) also **mereor** mereri meritus sum, *intr.* 1 To be deserving: *credentes se ~ruisse* CI 360.1; SS 61.3; (dep.) *qui per opera mereri volunt* AC 8002.4; (impers.) it is worth while: *~retur... memorare quod...* VR 158. 2 (tr.) To perform, undertake (duties): *ubi officia diu ~renda sunt* AM 450.

mereor: see **mereo**.

meretricatio ~onis, *f.* Prostitution: *vitam agunt ~onis* ES 230; (transf.) *spiritualis ~o et scortatio* VR 41.3.

meretricatus ~us, *m.* An act of prostitution, whoredom: *adulteria, scortationes et ~us* AM 428; ES 3922.

meretricius ~a ~um, *a.* Of a prostitute: *in vitam ~am* AC 828; *sphaera... ~a* AM 225.

meretricor ~ari ~atus sum, *intr.* To prostitute oneself: AR 719.

meretrix ~icis, *f.* A prostitute, whore: *pulchra ~ix... ornata purpura et auro* VI 46; *similes mulieri, cui plures mariti sunt, quae non est uxor, sed lasciva ~ix* VR 7.

mergus ~i, *m.* A seabird, gull: VR 165.3.

meridianus ~a ~um, *a.* Of midday: *lux est millies illustrior luce ~a mundi* AC 8197.2.

meridies ~ei, *f.* 1 Midday, noon: *tempora diei, ut mane, ~es* CI 105; ES 293. 2 The south: *quatuor plagae, oriens, ~es, occidens, et septentrio* CI 141.

meridionalis ~is ~e, *a.* Of the south, southern: *in plaga ~i* AM 380.2; VR 48.12.

meritorius ~a ~um, *a.* Performed to acquire merit, merit-seeking: *bonum...est vel ~um, vel simulatorium, vel hypocriticum* AM 444.4; *exercitia pietatis... ~a* VI 25.

meritum ~i, *neut.* Merit: *per ~um Domini* AC 7762; *possunt ~a quasi transcribi* AM 526.

merula ~ae, *f.* A blackbird: VR 383.1.

merum ~i, *neut.* Wine unmixed with water: *bibet ex vino irae Dei mixto ~o in poculo excandescentiae Ipsius* Rev. 14.10 (AR).

merus ~a ~um, *a.* Unmixed, unadulterated, unrelieved, pure, nothing but: *quod lumen...vertatur in ~am caliginem* AC 6948.5; *ratiocinia ex ~is falsis* AC 7295.3; *societas composita ex ~is angelis* AM 266.4; *ut constaret [oceanus] ex ~is piscibus* VR 32.3.

merx: see **merces**[2].

mesentericus ~a ~um, *a.* (Gk.) (anat.) Of the mesentery: CI 212.

mesenterium ~i, *neut.* (Gk.) (anat.) The mesentery: *chylus [fertur] per ~um et vasa lactea ibi in cisternam* DP 164.6; ES 1020.

meshalim: see **moschalim**.

mesocolon ~i, *neut.* (Gk.) (anat.) The mesocolon: VR 679.1.

messatio ~onis, *f.* The gathering of the harvest, harvest-time: *in aratione et in ~one quiesces* Exod. 34.21 (AC).

Messias ~ae, *m.* The Messiah: *sciunt etiam Judaei quod venturus ~as* AC 250; *Deus ~as*, God the Messiah (used in AD and early part of ES in place of *Dominus*): ES 154; 1AD 1515.

messis ~is, *f.* A harvest: *victus ex ~ibus agri* VR 12.9.

messor ~oris, *m.* A harvester: Matt. 13.30 (AE 374.15).

-met: emphatic particle suffixed to pronouns as *memet* (see **ego**), *ipsemet*, etc.

meta ~ae, *f.* A terminal marker, goal: *sic [amor] a sua origine ad ~am progreditur* AM 111; CO 21.10.

metallicus ~a ~um, *a.* Of or concerned with metals: *partes lapideae et ~ae* AS 192; *scientiae utiles... botanica, ~a* ES(M) 4578.

metallum ~i, *neut.* (Gk., = English 'mine') A metal: *plumbum...reliquis ~is est ignobilius* AC 8298.2.

metamorphosis ~eos, *f.* (Gk.) A change of shape, transformation: *quod talem ~in subeat* DP 298.2; (spec.) the metamorphosis of insects: AM 418; (as the title of a work by the Roman poet Ovid) SS(P) 18 (= 7.3).

metaphoricus ~a ~um, *a.* (Gk.) Metaphorical: *loquutio ~a seu comparatio* AC 8989.11.

metaphysice, *adv.* In a metaphysical manner: AT 108.

metaphysicus: see **methaphysicus**.

metempsychosis ~eos, *f.* (Gk.) The transmigration of souls: VR 79.6.

meteoron ~i, *neut.* (Gk.) An atmospheric phenomenon, a meteor: *sicut ~on in aëre quod evanescit* DP 35; VR 110.1.

methaphysicus ~a ~um, *a.* (Gk.) also **metaphysicus**. Metaphysical: *terminos commodatos ex arte ~a* VR 17.4; *a talibus...quae vocant logica et ~a* ES 4446; (masc. as sb.) a student of metaphysics: *quod fuerint logici et ~i* AC 4658.1.

methodus ~i, *f.* (Gk.) A manner of proceeding, method: *ex ~o castigandi homines* ES [628].

metior ~tiri mensus sum, *tr.* **1** To measure: *quod angelus mensus sit superliminaria novi...templi* AC 7847.4; *angelum ~tientem illa* DD 52. **2** (refl.) To lie down full length, prostrate oneself: *quod Elias se mensus sit super filium viduae* SS 29 (1 Kgs. 17.21).

meto ~ere messui messum, *tr.* To reap, harvest: *messuerunt spinas* Jer. 12.13 (AE 304.10); (absol.) AR 643.

metor ~ari ~atus sum, *tr.* see also **castrametor**. To measure out, pitch (camp): *si mali ~abuntur contra me castra* Ps. 27.3 (AC 4236.4).

metrice, *adv.* Rhythmically: *~e loquuntur spiritus et angeli* ES 3423.

metricus ~a ~um, *a.* (Gk.) Rhythmical: *~a loquela* ES 3423.

metropolis ~eos, *f.* A capital city: *Hierosolyma fuit ~is in Terra Canaane* VR 782.1; AE 1088.1.

metuo ~ere ~i, *tr.* (*intr.*) To be afraid of, fear: *niger spiritus quem ~unt* AC 942; (intr., w. *ab*) *~ite ab Ipso* Ps. 22.24 (AC 1025.11).

metus ~us, *m.* Fear, fright: *illis tantum ~um et terrorem incutiunt ut...* AC 842.2; *prae ~u* Luke 21.26 (AE 304.47).

meus ~a ~um, *pron. adj.* (voc. *mi*) My, mine: *hoc scire desiderium ~um fuit* AC 6695; *quod...cogitent, juvenis, quod haec ~a sit, et virgo, quod hic ~us sit* AM 229; *mi lector* VR 634.2.

mi: voc. of **meus**.

mica ~ae, *f.* A tiny particle, scrap, crumb: *catelli etiam edunt de ~is quae cadunt de mensa* Matt. 15.27 (AC 7784.3); CI 365.2; (of light) a gleam: *~ae lucis e sole... delapsae sunt* VR 76.5; (transf. of immaterial things) *in omni ~a affectionis ejus* AM 33.

micatio ~onis, *f.* Rapid oscillatory movement, beating: *angelis...aeque ac hominibus est respiratio et ~o cordis* DD 51.3.

mico ~are ~ui, *intr.* **1** To glitter, sparkle: *oculi ejus ~abant ex luce caeli sui* AM 42.4; *lamellae sicut vitreae ex auro et argento quasi ~antes* AM 380.2. **2** To throb, beat: *~at...tunc cor eorum* DA 58 (= xx.[2]).

microcosmus ~i, *m.* (Gk.) A small-scale world, microcosm: *homo ab antiquis vocatus est microuranos et ~us* VR 71.2.

microscopium ~i, *neut.* (Gk.) A microscope: AC 1869.2; CI 269.2; ES 2298.

micro-uranos ~i, *m.* (Gk.) A small-scale heaven (see quot.): *homo ab antiquis vocatus est ~os et microcosmus* VR 71.2.

micula ~ae, *f.* A flash or gleam: *in amictu coeruleo ...cum intertextis ~is auri* AC 7801.

middim: see **middin**.

Middin, *indecl.* (Hebr.) also **Middim** (AC 2709.2 and AE 355.33 1st edns., although the final letter may be a typographical error). Transliteration of a Hebr. word meaning places of judgment: *sedere super ~in significatur perceptio* AE 355.33 (Judg. 5.10).

migratio ~onis, *f.* The removal of people from one place to another, migration: *~o Jacobi...in Aegyptum* AC 1462.6; *post ~onem seu translationem e mundo naturali in hunc spiritualem* AM 207.2; *vasa ~onis*, baggage for a journey: Jer. 46.19 (AC 6729).

migro ~are ~avi, *intr.* To transfer one's abode to another place, remove, migrate: *~avimus e mundo in mundum* AM 44.2.

miles ~itis, *m.* A soldier: *vestimentum purpureum*

a ~itibus impositum DD 16.7 (John 19.2); *gregarius ~es* VR 424.

milia: see **mille**.

miliare: see **milliare**.

militia ~ae, *f.* Military service, soldiering: *ii in ~a qui nihil amant nisi caedes et spolia* ES 1397; (transf.) *ministerium Levitarum vocabatur ~a* AR 500.6.

milito ~are ~avi, *intr.* To serve as a soldier, fight: *Jehovah ~abit pro vobis* Exod. 14.14 (AC); *qui...pro Domino ~arent* AE 38.

milium ~i, *neut.* Millet: *placentam ex triticis, hordeis, ~is, et zeis* SS 16 (Ezek. 4.9); VR 78.1.

mille, *indecl. adj.* (pl. *millia*; in some edns. pl. is *milia*) A thousand: *contrarium scio a ~e et ~e experientiis* AC 322.1; (pl. as sb.) *ad stadiorum duodecim ~ia* Rev. 21.16 (CI 197.3).

millenarii ~ae ~a, *pl. adj.* Numbering a thousand: *anni ~i* AC 482.2 (Rev. 20.2).

millenaris: VR 563 1st edn. has *carpere viam millenaris*, app. meaning 'to run a mile'. Tafel, followed by Worcester, emended to *milliaris*.

milleni ~ae ~a, *pl. adj.* Numbering a thousand: *per aliquot ~as vices* SS 64; ES 2709.

millesimus ~a ~um, *a.* Thousandth: *quoad ~am partem* AC 6632.

millia: see **mille**.

milliare ~is, *neut.* also **miliare**. A mile: *aliquot millia ~ium* AC 1274; VR 64.1.

millies, *adv.* A thousand times: *paene ~es mille* AC 969; AM 220.2.

millio ~onis, *f.* A million: *300,000,000 seu 300 ~ones* AC 9441; CI 415.

milvus ~i, *m.* A bird of prey, kite: VR 165.3.

mimicus ~a ~um, *a.* (Gk.) Of or resembling a farce, farcical: [*amicitia*] *gesticulatoria et ~a* VR 455.3; (neut. as sb.) CO 57.2.

mimus ~i, *m.* (Gk.) An actor in farces, comedian: *sicut personati, harioli et ~i super theatris* DP 121.2; ES 5076.

mina ~ae, *f.* (Gk. *mna*) The one-sixtieth part of a talent, either as a weight or a sum of money, mina: *tollite ab illo ~am, et date ei qui decem ~as habet* Luke 19.24 (AC 7984.4); cf. DP 210.2.

minae ~narum, *f. pl.* Threats: *exhortationes et ~nae nihil prorsus faciunt* AC 7032.2; CI 553.1.

minax ~acis, *a.* Threatening: *me vultu ~aci aspexit* AM 82.1; VR 123.4.

minchah ~ae, *f.* (Hebr.) also **minḥah**. An offering of a biscuit made from flour and oil: *ex ~a...quae constabat ex similagine mixta oleo et facta in placentas* AC 2177.1.

minera ~ae, *f.* An ore: *~ae impregnatae auro, argento, et ferro* SS 66; VR 54.

mineralis ~is ~e, *a.* Of minerals, esp. as the designation of one of the three kingdoms into which all natural things are classified: *ex tribus regnis naturae, quae vocantur animale, vegetabile et ~e* SS 66; (neut. pl. as sb.) AM 397.

mingo ~gere ~xi, *intr.* To pass water, urinate: ES 4489.

minḥah: see **minchah**.

minime, *superl. adv.* To the smallest extent, least: *omnium ~e sapientes sunt* AM 18.2; far from it: *creditis quod Deus...possit convertere hircum illum in ovem... ~e, est enim contra leges ordinis Ipsius* VR 72.3; not at all: *distincte percipiendi sunt, ac ~e confundendi* AS 199.

minimum ~i, *neut.* The smallest part, the least: *unumquodvis ~um ejus* [sc. *mutationis*] AC 7077; *ut homo ne ~um cogitare possit* CI 302; *ad ~um*, at least: *ad ~um bini spiritus* AC 50.1; ES 1499.

minimus ~a ~um, *a.* (used as superl. of **parvus**) **1** Smallest, least: *in ~a forma* AC 10303.4; *in receptaculis ~is, quae sunt semina* AM 220.2. **2** Youngest: *an hic frater vester ~us...?* Gen. 43.29 (AC). **3** Of least importance, slightest, meanest: *uni ex fratribus Suis ~is* Matt. 25.40 (AC 6711); *singula usque ad omnium ~a* AC 7933.3.

minister ~tri, *m.* **1** A servant, attendant: *ne...judex tradat te ~tro, et in carcerem conjiciaris* Matt. 5.25 (VI 73); *ex numero aulicorum, ~trorum, et satellitum* AM 7.4. **2** A minister of state: *induite vestes ~trorum politicorum* DP 197.2. **3** A minister of religion, clergyman: *~tri docentes* AC 6822; *Verbum, ex quo ~tri sonant Deum* VR 14.3.

ministerium ~i, *neut.* **1** The act of ministering, ministration: *Dominus ~o angelorum utitur* AC 1925.3. **2** The office of a servant, function: [*regimina*] *differunt...secundum ~a* CI 213; the office of clergyman, diaconate: *gymnasistae qui initiatur in ~um antequam fit sacerdos* VR 106.1. **3** A ministry of state: *de aulis, de ~is, de statu politico* AM 5.1. **4** That which acts as servant, minister: *intellectus...non est nisi quam ~um et famulitium voluntatis* AM 196.

ministra ~ae, *f. adj.* Acting as a servant, serving: *patina...auferebatur...a foemina ~a alia* ES 3016.

ministratio ~onis, *f.* The performance of religious rites: *loca ubi ~o* AC 1437.

ministrator ~oris, *m.* One who administers, administrator: *servi ~ores quibus dominus dedit talenta* DP 309.2.

ministro ~are ~avi, *intr.* (*tr.*) **1** (intr.) To act as a servant, minister: *angeli quidem ducunt, sed solum ~ant* AC 50.3; (w. dat.) *quod homo naturalis dicatur 'servus' est quia factus est ad ~andum spirituali* AC 7998; (esp.) to be a servant of God, minister: *separavit Jehovah Levitas,...ut ~arent et benedicerent* Deut. 10.8 (AE 102.4). **2** (tr.) To administer: *quia... ~aret sancta ad usus animarum illorum* AM 266.2; (pass.) to be ministered to, be attended: *ut ~entur cum non bene valent* CI 381.

minium ~i, *neut.* Vermilion: *ut pararent ~a in fucos* AM 231.5; *~o illinit scripturam* DP 153.

minnith Hebr., see quot.: *mercatores tui, in triticis minnith et pannag* Ezek. 27.17 (AC 3941.7; AE 375.35).

minor[1] ~oris, *a.* (used as compar. of **parvus**) **1** Smaller in size or quantity, less: *volucres majores et ~ores* AC 7072; *super terram, quae ~or stellis est* AM 182.6. **2** Less in age, younger: *Jacobum filium suum ~orem* Gen. 27.15 (AC). **3** Of less worth or importance, humbler: *aequalis Patre quoad Divinum, et ~or Patre quoad Humanum* DD 35.1; *mala et falsa...quae sunt ~oris gradus* AC 1682; (neut. as sb.) *quod tales nihili facerent cultum Divinum, ~oris Dominum* ES 3745.

minor[2] ~ari ~atus sum, *tr., intr.* To threaten: (tr.) *quod iis ~arentur interitum* ES 1175; (intr., w. inf.) *ut ~ati sint me punire* ES 1369; (w. *quod*) *gravi tono ~atur [scortum] quod...molitura sit perniciem ejus* AM 512.1.

minorennis ~is, *m.* A young man, boy: *majorennes ex vobis futuri sunt reges, ac ~es futuri principes* AM 7.1.

minorennitas ~atis, *f.* The state or condition of being younger or the youngest, youth: *consedere secundum primogenituram, et secundum ~atem* AC 5704.1.

minuo ~ere ~i ~tum, *tr.* To make smaller, diminish: *donum Domini, quod ~itur et augetur ad beneplacitum Ipsius* ES 2267.

minus, *compar. adv.* **1** To a smaller extent, less: *nebulosum magis ~usve furvum* AC 6853; *quo ~us durus est homo...eo est perfectior* ES 2250. **2** *Nihil ~us quam*, anything rather than, as different as possible from: *Judaei, qui nihil ~us fuerunt quam coelestes homines* AC 1097.3; *nihil ~us quam sapientes sunt* AM 18.2. **3** Not to speak of, much less: *non possunt rationaliter, ~us spiritualiter de illis cogitare* VR 12.3; *ita nullus facit, ~us Filius Dei* VR 110.2.

minute, *adv.* (superl. *~issime*) To a very small extent, slightly: *si [telum] ex collimatione ~issime declinaret a scopo* DP 202.3.

minutiae ~tiarum, *f. pl.* Tiny details, trivialities: *quod ...delectatus fuerim ~tiis* ES 2169.

minutim, *adv.* In small pieces, in bits: *quasi frustatim et ~im discissi* AC 829.2; *ossa mea ~im contundere* CI 231.

minutulum ~i, *neut.* A very short period of time, moment: *ut ne quidem ~um [vitae] desit* AC 9333.3; *per ~um* ES 914; ES 4268.

minutum ~i, *neut.* A minute of time: *ne ~um temporis vivere potest* AC 687.2; *intra ~um* CI 240; (so in full) *~um primum*: *intra 4 aut 6 ~a prima* ES 906. **b** *~um secundum*, a second: ES 579.

minutus ~a ~um, *a.* (compar. *~ior*, superl. *~issimus*) Extremely small, minute, tiny: *potuit explorare ea quae ~iora erant* ES 1675; (neut. as sb.) *ut ~issima appercipiant* CI 462.1.

mirabilis ~is ~e, *a.* (compar. *~ior*, superl. *~issimus*) To be wondered at, wonderful, remarkable: *tam ~e ut nihil ~ius* AC 10634.3; *quod ~e est* SS 67.6; (as a divine title) *et vocabit nomen Ipsius, ~is, Consiliarius* Isa. 9.6 (DD 6); (neut. as sb.) a remarkable act or event, wonder: *unumquodvis ~e seu miraculum* AC 6910.

mirabiliter, *adv.* In a remarkable manner, wonderfully: *quod duo sint...quae agunt in se ~er ut sistant unum* AM 316.4; ES 266.

mirabundus ~a ~um, *a.* Wondering: *sed quisque ~us stetisset, quid illud* AC 4210.2.

miraculose, *adv.* In a miraculous manner: *Dominus...adaptat illa ~e per charitatem* AC 1832.3; AC 10602.

miraculosus ~a ~um, *a.* Of or concerned with miracles, miraculous: *qui in fide ~a fuerunt* AC 7317.2; AE 405.53; *credunt talia vim ~am habere* ES 269.

miraculum ~i, *neut.* An event apparently contrary to the laws of natural order, miracle: *distinguuntur ~a Divina a ~is diabolicis seu magicis* AC 6988.3; *eaedem leges...super monte Sinai cum stupendo ~o promulgatae sunt* AM 351.2.

mire, *adv.* In a wonderful fashion: *cadunt verba tam ~e, ut...* 3AD 6962.

mirifice, *adv.* In a wonderful manner: *ad modum... inflexarum helicum...~e confasciatarum* DP 319.2.

mirificus ~a ~um, *a.* (superl. *~issimus*) Wonderful: *~o modo* ES 295; (neut. as sb.) AM 21.1.

miror ~ari ~atus sum, *intr.* To feel surprise, be amazed, wonder: *clamaverunt '~amur, ~amur'* VR

721; (w. *quod*) *~abar quod talis loquela dari posset* AC 7745; (w. indir. qu.) *~atus sum...quid et cur hoc* AM 42.1.

mirus ~a ~um, *a.* Strange, remarkable, wonderful: *~um est, quod...agnoscant* VI 4; (neut. as sb.) *de diris... persuasionibus, quae, ~um, tales sunt ut...* AC 570.

miscela ~ae, *f.* Something compounded of several different things, a mixture: *humus ex ~a sulphuris, ramentorum ferri, et argillae luti* VR 110.1.

misceo ~cere ~cui mixtum (*or* mistum), *tr.* see also **mixtus**. To mix, combine: (w. abl.) *bona mixta malis et falsis* AC 6724.3; *indignationem mistam invidia* ES 2113; (w. *cum*) *quod bonum ~ceri possit cum malis* AC 6724.3.

miser ~era ~erum, *a.* (superl. *~errimus*) Wretched, pitiable: *~eros et afflictos* AC 7260; *sors post mortem ~era* AM 506.

miserabilis ~is ~e, *a.* (compar. *~ior*) Wretched, pitiable: *sors... ~is* AC 1878; *in statu ~i* CI 327; of poor quality, mean, sorry: *quaedam ~is rota acta ab aquis* ES 3790.

miserabiliter, *adv.* Wretchedly: *~er ejulantes* ES 750.

miserabundus ~a ~um, *a.* Prone to pity, pitying: *qui a nativitate ~i sunt* VR 428.

miseratio ~onis, *f.* The act of pitying, compassion: *ferre misericordiae opem seu ~o* AC 6862; *quod... nullius ~onis fuisset* ES 4351.

miserator ~oris, *m.* One who takes pity: *~or tuus Jehovah* Isa. 54.10 (AC 6804.10).

misere, *adv.* Wretchedly: *degunt extra societatem, admodum ~e* AC 7364; *~e puniuntur* AM 80.1.

misereor ~sereri ~sertus sum, *intr.* To show pity, have mercy: *rogandus est Ipse Dominus ut ~sereatur* AE 26.2; (w. gen.) *~sereatur nostri* AC 699; *despexerunt angeli, et ~serti illorum* AM 7.3; (w. *super*) *~serta super illum* Exod. 2.6 (AC).

miseresco ~ere, *intr.* To feel pity: *~ens eorum* Isa. 49.10 (AE 386.27).

miseria ~ae, *f.* A state of mental or physical distress, wretchedness, misery: *cum quis ex charitate videt aliquem in ~a* AC 6737; *ex ~a visa in Illo super ligno crucis* VR 134.2; (pl.) *nisi...se in ~as redigat* AC 7318.1.

misericordia ~ae, *f.* **1** The disposition to pity, mercy, mercifulness: *ex Divina Domini ~a* AC 6708; *sphaera ~ae et gratiae* AM 222.2. **2** An act of mercy: *qui... ~as suas naturales non faciunt spirituales* VR 428.

misericorditer, *adv.* Mercifully: *operantur semper ~er* AC 224.

misericors ~rdis, *a.* Prone to pity, merciful: *quod Dominus etiam ~rs sit illis qui malefaciunt* SS 90.1.

miseror ~ari ~atus sum, *intr.* To feel pity, be merciful: *crudelis ille nec ~antur* Jer. 6.23 (AC 8313.3); (w. gen. of person pitied) *afflictorum Suorum ~abitur* Isa. 49.13 (AC 8261.4); *persuadere quod ~andum earum* ES 4344.

missa ~ae, *f.* The Mass: *Romano-Catholici ~as suas latino idiomate exclamant* VR 159.4.

missio ~onis, *f.* The act of sending, despatch: *per ~onem Spiritus Sancti* VR 146; the act of putting forth: *in omni ~one manus tuae* Deut. 28.20 (AC 8364.3).

missionarius ~i, *m.* A person charged with the conversion of pagans, missionary: *monachi peregrinatores seu ~i* AC 10812.

mite, *adv.* (compar. *~ius*) Mildly: *quod duo episcopi adeundi sint, ac ~e arguendi* AR 675.2; *talia quae intellectum... ~ius afficiunt* VR 53.

mitesco ~ere, *intr.* To become mild or gentle, soften: *hoc falsum ~it apud illos qui in bono vitae sunt* AC 831.11; *ut...animi illorum ex se graves ~ant* AM 56.4.

mitigo ~are ~avi ~atum, *tr.* To make mild or gentle, soften: *ex ardore proprio corporis nondum per amorem spiritus ~ato* AM 145.1.

mitis ~is ~e, *a.* (compar. *~ior*) **1** (of persons or animals) Mild in character, gentle, pacific: *beati ~es* Matt. 5.5 (AE 304.44); *sunt qui ~es et humani* AC 7246; *bestias ~es et immites* AM 392.1. **2** (of things) Not distressing, gentle: *quod...in lumen ~ius veniat* AC 6844.3; *falsa... ~ia fiunt* AC 8311.1.

mitra ~ae, *f.* (Gk.) A ceremonial headdress, bonnet: *sicut qui spectat...praesulem aut antistitem ex infula ac ~a eorum* CO 51.3.

mitratus ~a ~um, *a.* Wearing a bonnet: *doctores ~os et magistros laureatos* CO 59.4.

mitto mittere misi missum, *tr.* **1** To cause to go, send: *Ego mitto angelum ante te* Exod. 23.20 (AC); *mali... mittuntur in infernum* AC 7795.2; *per angelum significatur missus* AC 6280.1; (absol.) to send a message: *significavit, mittens per angelum Suum servo Suo Johanni* Rev. 1.1 (AR). **2** To cause to be given, send (things): *ad me mittebant aliam chartam* AC 6930; *vestes...quas princeps...ad vos miserat* AM 19. **3** To cause to move, put forth (parts of the body): *nunc forte mittet manum suam* Gen. 3.22 (AC); [*manus*] *missa in sinum* AC 6973. **4** To cause to come (into a state or condition): *in hunc statum mittitur omnis qui reformatur* AC 6724.2; *sed haec mittentur in clariorem lucem per explicationes* DP 220.1; *hoc in seriam* *ventilationem missum est* VR 111.4; *vermes...mittunt se in uterum, ut renascantur* VR 12.6. **b** *in usum mittere*, to put into use, apply: AC 8337.2; *in actum mittere*, to put into action, effect: VR 125; *in vitam mittere*, to apply to life: *angeli...statim ut audiunt illa* [sc. *Divina Vera*]*...mittunt in vitam* CI 271.

mixtim, *adv.* In a random mixture, indiscriminately: *sunt qui pro principio habent omnium communionem, sic etiam uxorum, ita ~im coeunt* ES 2867.

mixtio ~onis, *f.* A mixture, blending: *illico agnoscunt, quae ~o* ES 3334.

mixtura ~ae, *f.* A mixing, mixture: *rubor et candor, et horum amabilis ~a inter se* AM 384.

mixtus ~a ~um, *a.* (pf. pple. of **misceo**) (in senses of vb., esp.) (of songs) Performed by a group of singers, choral: AM 17.1; (neut. as sb.) a mixture: *impudicitiam immiscent pudicitiae, et ex ~o insaniunt* AM 507.

Moabiticus ~a ~um, *a.* Moabite: *populi ~i* AE 401.33.

mobilis ~is ~e, *a.* Capable of motion, moving: *stellae ~es* AC 7803; ES 998; (of a machine) capable of working, running: *horologio, quod ~e est ex pendulo* VR 364.1; capable of being moved, movable: *statua...cum articulis ~ibus* VR 23.2.

mobilitas ~atis, *f.* The power of movement: *in omni re, quae in aliqua activitate et ~ate est* VR 577.2.

moderamen ~inis, *neut.* Control, direction: *cum vita motrice naturali, quae a ~ine cerebelli fluit* DA 12 (= v.[2]); self-control, moderation: *auscultate primum cum ~ine, quid ordo* VR 74.3.

moderate, *adv.* In a controlled manner: *nisi redigeretur* [*homo*] *in ordinem ~e, et per gradus... exspiraret* AC 5854.3.

moderatio ~onis, *f.* An act of self-control: *per ~ones ex prudentia* AM 108.

moderator ~oris, *m.* A controller, foreman: *praecepit Pharao...exactoribus in populo et ~oribus ejus* Exod. 5.6 (AC); *cum magnatibus et ~oribus, qui...praestolabantur principem* AM 14.1.

moderatus ~a ~um, *a.* (compar. *~ior*) Restrained, moderate: *ut ~iores sint in querimonia* AC 8566.

moderor ~ari ~atus sum, *tr.*, *intr.* **1** To prevent from being excessive, keep in check, restrain: *per nubem, quae...calorem e sole... ~atur* AC 6849.5. **2** To control, regulate: *~ari ne sit* [*vita*] *malis contaminata* VR 443.1.

modeste, *adv.* In a restrained manner: *cum illis ~e et caste loquutus est* AM 477.8.

modestia ~ae, *f.* The quality of self-restraint, modesty: AM 164.

modestus ~a ~um, *a.* (superl. *~issimus*) Restrained, modest: *virgines ~ae cum uxore casta* SS 26.3; *quod intelligentia faeminarum in se sit ~a* AM 209; (neut. as sb.) *eluxit ex illis* [sc. *faciebus*] *sincerum et ~um* AC 8242.

modicus ~a ~um, *a.* Of small size or importance, minor: *quia in ~o fidelis fuisti* Luke 19.17 (AE 112.5).

modificatio ~onis, *f.* The process of modifying, modification: *ex ~one radiorum lucis, in guttis aquae pluviae* AC 1042.1; the result of modifying, variation: *~ones...suam formam accipiunt a formis quae sunt substantiae* AC 7408.2; *quod sint* [*colores*] *ejus* [sc. *lucis*] *~ones* AE 269.

modifico ~are ~avi ~atum, *tr.* To change to a limited extent, modify: *patet...quod amor voluntatis ~et illam* [sc. *vitam*] VR 39; (w. *in* + acc.) *illa lux... ~atur in varios colores* AE 431.3.

modius ~i, *m.* A measuring vessel, peck: *nec accendunt lucernam et ponunt illam subter ~um* Matt. 5.15 (AE 223.18).

modo, *adv.* and *conj.* **1** Shortly before, just now: *ex illis quae ~o dicta sunt* AC 1500. **2** Not more than, only, merely: *in hunc statum ~o ter aut quater immissus sum* AC 1883; *non est spatium, sed ~o apparentia spatii* VR 64.1; *non ~o...sed etiam*, not only ...but also: *quod in Verbo non modo sit sensus naturalis sed etiam spiritualis* DD 2.2. **b** *~o quod*, apart from the fact that, only that: *regnum spirituale...erat unum cum coelesti, ~o quod externum ejus esset* AC 6372. **3** (as conj.) So long as, provided: **a** (w. subj.): *quisque scit... ~o intendat animum* AM 174; *~o gustus sit* ES 3998; (negative *~o ne*) *vitam agunt...contentam, ~o ne infestentur* ES 392. **b** (w. indic.): *si possunt, ~o timor abest, auferunt* [*bona*] ES 1353.

modulamen ~inis, *neut.* An effect produced by variation, modulation: *voces loquelae et ~ina cantus* DP 279.8; VR 79.5.

modulatio ~onis, *f.* A variation, modulation (of sound): *per modificationes vocis canorae seu ~ones* AM 17.2.

modulor ~ari ~atus sum, *intr.* To play a tune: *qui ~antur super nablio* Amos 6.5 (AE 448.12).

modulus ~i, *m.* (pl.) The intervals of musical notes, tune, melody: *sicut auris discernit ~os cantus* AM 155[a].4.

modus ~i, *m.* **1** A manner, way: *multis ~is* AC 6650; *omnes ~i occidendi* VI 67; *~us intermedians* AM 459.1. **2** (in philosophy) An attribute of a substance: *quod spiritus sit substantia, quibus non ~i adscribendi* ES 2264. **3** A rhythm, measure (of music): *choreae virginum et juvenum saltantium ad ~os symphoniarum* AM 3.3. **4** *Ultra ~um*, beyond measure, excessively: AC 7375.

moech-: see **maech-**.

moenia: see **maenia**.

moereo: see **maereo**.

moeror: see **maeror**.

moestitia: see **maestitia**.

moestus: see **maestus**.

mola ~ae, *f.* A mill for grinding grain: *quidam... sedens ad ~am, et quasi molens farinam* AC 1510.3; a windmill: *ad alas ~ae* VR 364.3.

molaris ~is, *m.* **1** A millstone: *non in pignus accipiet molas et ~em* Deut. 24.6 (AC 4335.4). **2** A molar tooth: *~es leonum juvenum everte* Ps. 58.6 (AC 9052.4).

molecula ~ae, *f.* A small mass, particle: *nubes candida distincta in ~as* AC 6614; ES 680.

moles ~is, *f.* A mass, lump: *instar ~is nigrae cui nihil vitale* AC 18; *quod...planetae...non sint ~es vacuae* AC 6697.

molestia ~ae, *f.* Mental distress, worry: *ut...non modo summam ~am causaretur, sed et intimiorem dolorem* ES 166; distress caused to others, mischief: *~a labiorum eorum contegit eos* Ps. 140.9 (AE 455.16); *esse contemtui, ~ae, et aversationi* AR 509.

molestus ~a ~um, *a.* (superl. *~issimus*) Troublesome, disturbing: (neut. as sb.) *cum una [uxore]...foret ... ~um ex paritate* AM 78.4; (of sleep) troubled, vexed: *post somnum ~um* ES 166.

molimen ~inis, *neut.* Exertion, effort: *ad singula cogitata, ~ina, et phantasias hominis* ES 152; ES 3680.

molior ~liri ~litus sum, *tr.* **1** To accomplish with effort, labour at: *~liri sibi viam videbantur...per quasi rupis cavernas* AC 1270.1. **2** To devote mental effort to, strive after: *angelus non volvit et ~litur nisi caelestia* VR 145; *quod...similia clandestine ~lirentur* CI 506.3.

molitio ~onis, *f.* The process of milling: AR 794.1.

molle, *adv.* Softly, gently: *qui...fluide et ~e agunt* ES 3311.

mollesco ~ere, *intr.* **1** To become soft or flexible, soften: *rigidum illud incipit ~ere* AC 7068; *videbis cristam dorsi ~ere* AR 438.1; *ut ~at [cibus] sola puriori saliva* ES 1742. **2** (transf.) To become mild or gentle: *cor tuum ne ~at* Isa. 7.4 (AC 6952.6); *ut viri ex se duri ~ant* AM 56.4.

molliculus ~a ~um, *a.* Somewhat soft or flexible: *~os funiculos* ES 235.

mollio ~lire ~livi ~litum, *tr.* To make soft or gentle: *quod coelestes...quasdam consonantes ~liant* ES 1645; (transf.) *in tantum ~liebantur ut quasi in ecstasin laberentur* ES 2231.

mollis ~is ~e, *a.* (compar. *~ior*, superl. *~issimus*) **1** Soft or flexible to the touch: *illi sunt quasi ~es, et...se incurvant usque ad terram* AC 7068; *massa ~is continua* CI 212. **2** Gentle, mild, soft: *[loquela] erat sicut ~issima aura* AC 7359; *charitas cum fide est cedens et ~is* AC 8321.2.

molliter, *adv.* In a gentle fashion, mildly, delicately: *quod non exprimerent aliquas literas consonantes aspere, sed ~er* SS 90.2; *infantes... ~er repraesentabant Messiam in sepulchrum missum* ES 233.

mollities ~ei, *f.* Softness: *~es carnis* VR 16.1; (transf.) *~em cordis* AC 1033.3.

molliusculus ~a ~um, *a.* Somewhat soft or gentle: *loquela erat quoad fluxum ~a* AC 7359; *funiculos... ~os* CI 335; *simplicitas ~a* ES 1048.

molo ~ere ~ui ~itum, *intr.*, *tr.* **1** (intr.) To grind grain, mill: *duae ~entes in mola* Matt. 24.41 (AC 7780); *apparent sibi ~ere* ES(M) 4673. **2** (tr.) To make (flour) by grinding: *quasi ~ens farinam* AC 1510.3; ES 4305. **3** (tr.) To reduce to dust, grind up: *~e nigrum lapidem ...in tenuem pulverem* AM 233.4; (transf.) *contudi illum ~endo probe* Deut. 9.21 (AC 7418.4).

momentaneus ~a ~um, *a.* Happening in a moment, instantaneous: *cogitatio...liberata, fit ~a magis* AC 1757; *creatio ~a* VR 78.4.

momentum ~i, *neut.* **1** A very short period of time, moment, instant: *in...morbis, ~is mortis* AC 268; *parum ~i*, (Bibl.) for a short while: *occulta te sicut parum ~i* Isa. 26.20 (AC 7353); *ad ~a*, from moment to moment: Ezek. 32.10 (AE 131.5). **b** *~o*, in a moment: *si recederent ...angeli, [homo] ~o periret* AC 50.1; VR 30.2. **c** the period between repetitions of a frequent event, rate: *~a spiritualis pulsus ad ~a coelestis sunt ut 2 1/2 ad 1* ES 4136. **2** A short stage in development, step: *homo non scit aliquod ~um progressionis cum regeneratur* CI 269.3; *tot falsitates...in Ecclesiam influxerunt, quot sunt ~a, articulationes et generationes fidei ibi* VR 57.1. **3** A small item which causes a shift in balance: *secundum omnia et singula ~a eorum inclinationis ducuntur* CI 336; *magni ~i*, of great importance: *velim hanc rem, quia magni ~i est, in lucem sistere* CI 191; *nullius ~i*, of no consequence: AC 2342.5.

monachalis ~is ~e, *a.* Resembling a monk, monkish: *spiritus ~es* AC 10812.

monachus ~i, *m.* (Gk.) A monk: AM 500.3.

monarcha ~ae, *m.* (Gk.) A sole ruler, monarch: *inter duos ~as, quorum unus est rex...et alter tyrannus* VR 57.2.

monarchia ~ae, *f.* (Gk.) Monarchy, kingdom, empire: *ex Imperatore Constantino Magno, et ejus ~a* VR 636.1.

monarchicus ~a ~um, *a.* (Gk.) Relating to the rule of a single person, monarchical: *de potestatibus ~is* AC 1066.3; *imperia ~a* VR 9.2.

monas ~adis, *f.* (Gk.) An ultimate unit of being, monad: *dixit [Leibnitzius] quod ~ades quidem pro unitatibus agnoverit, sed quod in illis essent substantiae simpliciores* UJ(P) 287; AC 5084.4.

monasterialis ~is ~e, *a.* Of or belonging to a monastery, monastic: *post exactam vitam ~em* AM 54.4.

monasterium ~i, *neut.* (Gk.) A monastery or convent: *qui... ~is inclusi sunt, tam virgines quam viri* AM 54.4.

moneo ~nere ~nui ~nitum, *tr.*, *intr.* (w. *ut* or *ne*) To warn: *~nens ut etiam ego illos...bene excipiam* AC 8021; *~net ne colamus idola* AM 78.7; (pass.) *~nentur ut faciant illa quae ibi* DP 258.4.

moneta ~ae, *f.* A coin: *~ae ex auro et argento* VR 78.2.

moneticus ~a ~um, *a.* In the form of coins, coined: *aurum non ~um* ES 4543.

monile ~is, *neut.* A ring worn on the nose as jewellery, nose-ring: *accepit vir ~e auri* Gen. 24.22 (AC); *~e auri ponebatur super nasum* AC 3103.1.

monitum ~i, *neut.* A warning: *his addiderunt hoc ~um* AM 292.3.

monoceros ~otis, *m.* (Gk.) A unicorn: *equos... quosdam...sicut ~otes* AM 76.2; (used as translation of Hebr. *re'em*) Deut. 33.17 (AC 2832.4).

monogamicus ~a ~um, *a.* (Gk.) Monogamous: *conjugia ~a* AM 70.

monogamus ~i, *m.* (Gk.) A person with a single wife or husband: *quod zelotypia detur spiritualis apud ~os* AM 357.

monosyllaba ~ae, *f.* (Gk.) A word of one syllable: *dixerunt...quod terminatio debeat esse in ~am* 3AD 23.

monosyllabicus ~a ~um, *a.* (Gk.) Monosyllabic: (neut. as sb.) *concentus...qui...desinit in ~um* AC 7191.2.

mons ~ntis, *m.* A mountain or hill: *e ~nte Sinai* AC 6723.3; *super ~nte Olivarum* Zech. 14.4 (AE 638.16); AC 795.1.

monstro ~are ~avi ~atum, *tr.* **1** To render visible, point out, show, display: *~a nobis Patrem* John 14.8 (AC 1602); *~avit illi Jehovah lignum* Exod. 25.25 (AC). **2** To render apprehensible by the mind, demonstrate: *intellectus modo docet et ~at viam* VI 15; (w. indir. qu.) *~abo vobis cui similis es* Luke 6.47 (AC 8361).

monstrositas ~atis, *f.* The quality of being monstrous, monstrosity: *~as remanebat* UJ(P) 365.

monstrosus ~a ~um, *a.* (superl. *~issimus*) Horribly abnormal, monstrous: *virgines...apparent in sua deformitate, ~ae et furvae* AM 505.2; *hominem cum tribus capitibus...quae forma ~a est* VR 15.2; (neut as sb) *~a in variis formis visa sunt* VR 797.4.

monstrum ~i, *neut.* An abnormal specimen, monster: *inter se apparent ut homines, sed in luce coeli ut ~a* CI 131.

montanus ~a ~um, *a.* Of or belonging to mountains, mountainous: *eminentiam sicut ~am* AM 76.1; as large as a mountain: *infestari a muribus quasi ~is et magnis* ES 384; (masc. as sb.) a mountain-dweller AM 75.3; (neut. as sb.) a mountainous region: *in amplo monte, et ~o circum circa* ES 5347.

monumentum ~i, *neut.* **1** A sepulchral monument, tomb: *per exsuscitationem mortuorum e ~is* AC 8018.2 (Matt. 27.53); *angelus dixit ad mulieres venientes ad ~um* DD 24 (Luke 24.5). **2** A record, memorial: *ut patet etiam a gentilium antiquissimis libris et ~is* AC 9293.3.

mora ~ae, *f.* **1** Delay, interval: *haec ~a etiam fit ob illam causam, ut...* AE 413.1; *removentur successive... per ~as temporis* ES 4452. **2** A lapse of time: *post aliquam ~am apparebant...mensae* AM 6.2; (w. *temporis*) *principia falsa nusquam aliquis potest exuere...nisi per ~am temporis* AC 1107. **3** The fact of staying in a place, lingering, stay: *per...~am illorum* [sc. *filiorum Israelis*] *in deserto* AC 8096.1.

moralis ~is ~e, *a.* Of or concerned with correct behaviour, moral: *verum ~e* AC 7977; *notum est quod gentiles ~em vitam vivant* CI 319.1; *qui in externis fuerunt ~es* FI 64.1; (neut. as sb.) *cultus, doctrinalia et ~ia* AC 1832.3.

moralista ~ae, *m.* One who teaches correct behaviour, moralist: *naturales ~ae, qui credunt civilem et moralem vitam...producere omnia* DP 117.2.

moralitas ~atis, *f.* Correct behaviour, morality: *per ~atem agit hypocritam* VR 14.4; VI 68.

moraliter, *adv.* In a moral fashion, correctly: *sic ~er contra illa* [sc. *adulteria*] *loquuntur* AM 153.2; VR 148.1.

morate, *adv.* With good behaviour, correctly: *qui ~e vixerunt* ES 5353.

moratus ~a ~um, *a.* (compar. *~ior*) Possessing or characterized by correct behaviour, well-behaved: *extus ~iores...propter legis paenas* AC 822; *qui ~am egerunt vitam* CI 321; *a spiritibus ~is* ES 3167.

Moravianus ~a ~um, *a.* Of Moravia, esp. of the

Moravian Church: *ab Ecclesia ~a* ES 3492; (masc. as sb.) *cum ~is, qui etiam Herrenhuteri vocantur* UJ(C) 86.

morbosus ~a ~um, *a.* Suffering from disease, diseased: *non absimiles foeminis quae...intus ~ae* AC 2468.2.

morbus ~i, *m.* **1** A disease: *omnem ~um et omnem plagam...mittet Jehovah super te* Deut. 28.61 (AC 6752.4); *ex timore ~orum* VI 111. **2** A sickness, illness: *per infortunia, ~os, et similia* AC 7761; (Bibl.) any instance of suffering, distress: *~os nostros Ipse tulit* Isa. 53.4 (AC 1846.3).

mordeo ~dere momordi ~sum, *tr.* To bite: *~debant linguas volentes acuere illas in dicteria* VR 74.3; (of wild beasts, insects, etc.) *serpentes...qui momorderunt populum* Num. 21.6 (AE 70.5); *sicut feles... ~dent* ES 392; (transf.) *nonne subito surgent ~dentes te?* Hab. 2.7 (AC 6669.2).

moribundus ~a ~um, *a.* Close to death, dying, moribund: *dum jacet in lecto ~us* AM 28.

morior mori mortuus sum, *intr.* **1** (of living things) To die: *quod moriturus sit totus homo cum moritur is quoad corpus* AC 6929; *non potestis mori in aeternum* AM 315.11; (w. abl. of manner) *qui...gladio morientur* Ezek. 33.27 (AC 7102.3); (in a specified condition) *quae... senio confectae mortuae sunt* CI 414; *qui in Domino moriuntur* Rev. 14.13 (VI 2). **2** (of things) To cease to be active, fail: *faciunt* [*tentationes* etc.] *ut ea quae sunt corporis et mundi...quiescant et quasi moriantur* AC 8; *facultas vegetandi illico moreretur* FI 16.

moror ~ari ~atus sum, *intr.* (*tr.*) **1** To put off action, delay: *tunc ~abantur et detinebantur* AC 7072; *tunc paulum ~ata dixit* VR 102.3. **2** To stay (in a place), wait, abide: *spiritus...non ~antur in uno loco* AC 6925; *~antur ibi quidam...per mensem* AR 866.2. **3** (w. neg.) To be concerned, bother (about): (w. *circa*) *quia non ~ati sunt circa talia* AC 681.1; (w. acc.) *haec nihil ~or, nam vidi, audivi, sensi* AC 68; ES 1532.

morosus ~a ~um, *a.* Of a carping nature, critical, fault-finding: *vir ~us, nihil patiens, contra omnes... illico increpans* AC 1949.2; *ut...ita ~i fuerint, ut vivere non potuerint quin increparent* ES 2120.

mors ~rtis, *f.* **1** The fact of dying, death: *in agone ~rtis* AC 6677; (as a punishment inflicted) *cubare cum nuru erat ~rtis* AC 4818.2; *~rti date* AC 7248. **2** The time of dying, the moment of death: *post ~rtem* AC 6756.2; *circa ultimam ~rtis horam* FI 39. **3** Death regarded as an active force: *non timebis tibi...a ~rte* [*quae*] *vastat in meridie* Ps. 91.6 (AC 7102.10); *notum est...quod Dominus vicerit ~rtem* DD 12. **4** The death of the spirit, spiritual death: *vitam contrariam vitae spirituali, quae in Verbo appellatur '~rs'* AC 6685; CI 297; VR 48.19.

morsio ~onis, *f.* The act of biting: *conatum ~onis linguae* ES 4582.

morsus ~us, *m.* **1** A nip or bite: *quod...filii Israelis ...quoque patientur similes ~us* [*pediculorum*] 2AD 1991. **2** (transf.) Mental pain, remorse: *haec pugna... causatur conscientiae ~um et cruciatum* AC 751.1; CI 566.

mortalis ~is ~e, *a.* Subject to death, mortal: *aufertur id quod est ~e apud illum* DP 324.3; (esp. masc. pl. as sb.) people in this world, mortals: *quod Verbum... contineat arcana coeli...nemo ~ium ex litera capit* AC 1; VR 2.1; (as translation of Hebr. *methim*) *~es famis* Isa. 5.13 (AC 1460.2).

mortarium ~i, *neut.* A mortar: Num. 11.8 (AC 10303.5).

morticinium ~i, *neut.* Necrosis: *cum... ~um progressive scandit* VR 119.2.

morticinus ~a ~um, *a.* Affected by necrosis, necrotic, mortified: *caro ~a* VR 119.2; (transf.) causing spiritual death, fatal: *obfirmatissima et ~a phantasia* AC 586.1.

mortifer ~era ~erum, *a.* Causing death, lethal: *apostemata ~era* ES 1766; (neut. as sb.) *~erum facere* AC 794.2.

mortificans ~ntis, *a.* Death-dealing, fatal: *vis argumenti...quae facit persuasiones eorum tam ~ntes* ES 3374.

mortificatio ~onis, *f.* The process of rendering dead, mortification (in quot. transf.): *~o vitae cum uxore* AM 500.2.

mortifico ~are ~avi ~atum, *tr.* To make dead: *gelu quod ~at membra hominis* ES 3375; (transf.) to deaden, numb: *ex otio collabitur mens...seu ~atur homo et non vivificatur* AM 207.3.

mortuus ~a ~um, *a.* (pf. pple. of **morior**) In senses of vb., esp. **1** Lifeless, dead: *qui homines ~os ut sanctos supplicatione adeunt* AC 7272.3; *homo...caderet ~us* CI 302; (masc. pl. as sb.) the dead: *si quis ex ~is resurrexerit* Luke 16.31 (AC 6752.6). **2** Spiritually dead: *homo est ~us ex se* AC 39.1; *quod ~i homines raro talem miseriam...sentiant* AC 270; VR 48.20. **3** (of things) Lacking proper force or activity, inactive, lifeless, dead: *Verbum non foret Verbum Domini, sed ~a quaedam litera* AC 639.2; *quando quasi ~a sunt* [*corporea*] AC 1408.2; *eo possunt uti ut mero instrumento ~o* ES 3786; *pondera quasi ~a* ES 4593.

morus ~i, *m.* also **maurus**. A Moor, negro: *ex nigro seu ~o* DP 277.3; ES 432.

mos moris, *m.* **1** A custom, habit: *contra morem solitum* AC 6811; *pro more habent ut...* AC 7076; *ex recepto more loquendi* AE 260.2. **2** (pl.) The behaviour or manners (of a person): *differunt animis et moribus* AC 8031; *amamus virgines ex illarum pulchritudine et elegantia morum* AM 22.

Mosaicus ~a ~um, *a.* Of or belonging to Moses: *in historia creationis ~a* 1AD 23.

moschalim, *indecl. pl.* also **meshalim** (SS 103.2 Worcester). (pl. of **maschal** q.v.) A transliteration of a Hebr. word meaning proverbs or prophecies: *ex significatione vocis ~im in lingua Hebraea, quod non modo sint proverbia sed etiam enuntiata prophetica* VR 265.2.

motio ~onis, *f.* **1** A moving, motion: *~onem capitis* 'a shaking of the head' Ps. 44.14 (SS 86); *conveniente ~one* [*faciei*] AC 8024. **2** An emotion, feeling: *percipere ...misericordiae ~onem...potui* ES 220.

motitatio ~onis, *f.* A to and fro movement, wavering, swaying: *reciproca ~o* AC 7077; ES 3238; *panis ~onis* Lev. 23.17 (AC 7906.3).

motito ~are ~avi ~atum, *tr.* (refl. and pass.) To move to and fro, sway: *Spiritus Dei se ~ans super facies aquarum* Gen. 1.2 (AC); *circumaguntur et ~antur sicut ebrius* Ps. 107.27 (AC 1072.4).

motiuncula ~ae, *f.* A small movement: *per labiorum ~as* AC 1118; *ne minimam corporis ~am* ES 2464.

motivus ~a ~um, *a.* Characterized by movement: *vitam sensitivam et ~am* AM 87.3.

motorius ~a ~um, *a.* Concerned with movement, motor: *ex...organis sensoriis et ~is* VR 10; (neut. as sb.) SA 70 (= ii.[1]).

motrix ~icis, *f. adj.* Concerned with movement, motor: *per fibras nerveas et ~ices* CI 95; VR 60.2.

motus ~us, *m.* **1** Movement, motion: *currus ~um suum...habet per rotas* AC 8215.3; *~us cordis* DD 47.1; *apparentem solis ~um* SS 95.2; *organa ~uum, quae sunt musculi* VR 12.3. **b** *terrae ~us*, an earthquake: CI 229; VR 31.2. **2** An impulse of the mind, emotion: *primus ~us, qui est misericordia Domini* AC 7; *quod conatus sit ipsa essentia ~us* AM 215; *a nullis non ~ibus animi agitantur* ES 742.

moveo ~vere ~vi ~tum, *tr.* **1** To take to another place, remove: *~vebo candelabrum tuum e loco suo* Rev. 2.5 (AR); (refl.) *cum avi coelorum et se ~vente humi* Hos. 2.18 (AC 40.3). **2** To set in motion, set working: *non ~vebit canis linguam suam* Exod. 11.7 (AC); *loquela angeli... ~vet illud* [sc. *organum auditus*] *ab interiore* CI 248. **3** To cause a change in the emotions of, move emotionally: *ut corda auditorum ad pietatem ~veant* AC 6914.3; *ad misericordiam ~veri* FI 45; *non ~veri se patiuntur a cupiditatibus aliorum* ES 742. **4** To make active, arouse, move: *nec illud singularia cogitationis ~vet, sed communia ejus* AC 8159.3; *cum his solifidiani timent ~vere lites* VR 812; *ut nusquam aliquid dubium inde ~veri queat* ES 319.

mox, *adv.* At a short remove in time, shortly (before or after): *pensitarunt aliquantum, et mox dixerunt* AC 6700; *fit intellectus nihil, et mox etiam voluntas* VR 367.2; (w. *prius* or *supra*) *ex eo quod mox prius dicatur* AC 484; *quae mox supra dicta sunt* AC 1047; (w. *postquam*, *sequens*, etc.) *mox postquam venit* [*Dominus*] *ex deserto* AC 1690.1; *in mox sequentibus* AC 6752.4. **b** *mox ut*, as soon as: *mox ut extra timorem sunt, redeunt ad malitiam* ES 2919.

mucidus ~a ~um, *a.* Full of viscous fluid, squashy: *fructibus...qui intus ~i vel putidi sunt* AC 2468.2.

mucilentus ~a ~um, *a.* Wet from decomposition, mouldy: *cum frumentis...quae ~a et rancida et sic inutilia redderentur* VR 524.3.

mucor ~oris, *m.* A viscid or slimy substance: *excrescentiis arborum, quae sicut spongiae vel alius ~or* [*muci* J D Odhner] *sunt* ES(M) [4739] (Tafel).

mucosus ~a ~um, *a.* Producing mucus: *glandulae ... ~ae et salivales* AC 5386.

mucro ~onis, *m.* The point of a sword or other weapon: *cultrum, ~onem aut sicam* ES 4494; *radii nunc visi sunt acuti sicut ~ones, nunc obtusi sicut enses fracti* AM 315.1.

mucus ~i, *m.* Mucus: *~us narium* ES 939; ES 4030.

mufti, *indecl. m.* (Arabic) A Muslim religious leader and expert on law, mufti: ES 4723; (of the Ottoman Empire) Grand Mufti: ES 4658.

mula ~ae, *f.* A female mule: 1 Kgs. 1.33 (AE 31.7).

mulceo ~cere ~si, *tr.* To stroke, caress: *mulier... volens genam meam ~cere* ES 3952.

mulcimen ~inis, *neut.* A caress: *delectat...pulchritudo oculos... ~ina cutem* VR 394; a soothing influence: *laetificamur sicut ex ~ine aurae odoriferae* VR 159.4.

mulcimentum ~i, *neut.* A caress: *cutis...se per ~a externa patitur decipi* ES 3704.

mulcio ~cire, *tr.* (= **mulceo**) To soothe: *dulces odas quibus ~ciebant praesentium auditus* AM 8.2; ES 2231.

mulcta ~ae, *f.* also **multa** (ES 658 Tafel). A monetary penalty, fine: *minimum ~ae...fuit quinta pars* AC 649; AM 268.3; ES 658 (J D Odhner).

mulcto ~are ~avi ~atum, *tr.* To punish: *miserabiliter ... ~antur per colluxationes* AC 829.2; *quod...faemina ~etur plagis* AM 369.2.

muliebris ~is ~e, *a.* Of women: *varia quae operarum ~ium sunt* AM 370; ES 2494.

mulier ~eris, *f.* A woman: *~eres Aegyptiae* Exod. 1.19 (AC); *quod ~er sit pro viro, ac vir pro ~ere* CI 366; (as a type of timidity) *ex heroibus facti subito sicut ~eres* AC 950.

mulsum ~i, *neut.* A drink of honey and wine, a sweet potion: *~a ex aconitis* VR 380.4.

multa: see **mulcta**.

multicolor ~oris, *a.* Many-coloured, variegated: *decoramenta... ~oria, non sicut iridis, sed tamen iridea* ES 1087.

multifariam, *adv.* In a large number of ways: *quod una vis... ~am variari possit* AC 5189.3.

multifarius ~a ~um, *a.* Of many kinds, multifarious: *quia scientiae sunt cuivis peculiares...ideo sunt ~ae* AM 163.

multiloquium ~i, *neut.* Garrulity: Matt. 6.7 (AE 325.6).

multiloquus ~a ~um, *a.* Speaking much, garrulous: *orantes ne sitis ~i, sicut ethnici* Matt. 6.7 (AE 325.6).

multiplex ~icis, *a.* (compar. *~icior*) Composed of many parts, complex, manifold: *ex ~ici et diutina experientia* AC 691; *ex sensu interno...qui ~icior est quam usquam aliquis credere possit* AC 618; *innumerabilia vera et ~icia bona* AC 6917.1; *amores sunt ~ices* DP 106.1.

multiplicabilis ~is ~e, *a.* Capable of being multiplied: *quod omne sit divisibile in infinitum...quod similiter sit ~e* AM 185.3.

multiplicabilitas ~atis, *f.* The quality of admitting multiplication: *~as Divini Veri in infinitum* VR 350.1.

multiplicatio ~onis, *f.* The act of making more numerous, multiplying: *'Ponam semen tuum sicut pulverem terrae' significat ~onem in immensum* AC 1609; (in arithmetic) multiplication: *ex ~one trium cum septem* AC 7842.

multipliciter, *adv.* In manifold ways, multifariously: *variatur hic odor... ~er* ES 1046.

multiplico ~are ~avi ~atum, *tr.* **1** To make more numerous, multiply: *fructificate et ~ate vos* Gen. 1.22 (AC); *bonum ~at vera et fructificat illa* FI 31; to make greater, increase: *cum facultate ~andi sapientiam* AM 355.8; *etiam si ~atis orationem, non Ego audiens* Isa. 1.15 (VI 30.1). **2** (in mathematics) To multiply (numbers): *numerus...duplicatus et in se ~atus* [i.e., squared] AC 4177; AC 7973.2; AE 39.3.

multiprolis ~is ~e, *a.* Having much offspring, having many children: *~is autem defecit* 1 Sam. 2.5 (AE 257.3).

multis, *adv.* By much: *ubi perceptio ~is excedit apperceptionem talem* AC 1640.3; ES 4293; on many occasions: *quod ~is expertus* ES 241.

multitudo ~inis, *f.* **1** Greatness of number, multitude: *quod appareant sicut flumen ob ~inem* AC 6699; a great number: *ingentem ~inem piscium ceperunt* AM 316.5 (John 21.6). **2** Exceeding size or quantity, greatness: *~ine excellentiae Tuae* Exod. 15.7 (AC); *incedens in ~ine roboris sui* Isa. 63.1 (VR 116.1).

multo, *adv.* = **multum**: *~o perfectius* CI 47.

multoties, *adv.* On many occasions, many times: *~es alibi* AC 115; *apparent ~es currus* AC 8215.2.

multum, *adv.* To a great extent, much, far: *~um fallitur* AC 803.1; *doctrina... ~um a vero abalienata* AC 6633.

multus ~a ~um, *a.* (compar.: see **plus**[1], superl.: see **plurimus**) **1** Great in amount or quantity, much: *ex ~a experientia* AC 6639.2; *ad ~am distantiam* AC 6692.2; *~o pretio* ES 252; (neut. as sb.) a great part: *per ~um noctis* ES 356. **2** (pl.) Many: *~i...homines mortui sunt ex aquis* AC 7854 (Rev. 8.11); (masc. as sb.) *~i ab oriente et occidente venient* Matt. 8.11 (AC 6804.2); (neut. as sb.) *quae explicare ~is opus* AC 487.2.

mulus ~i, *m.* A mule: AM 246.3.

mumi, *neut.* (pl. *~ia*) also **mumi**, *m. pl.*, and **mumia** ~ae, *f.* A corpse embalmed in the Egyptian manner, mummy: *factus niger sicut Aegyptiorum ~i* AC 817; *~i Aegyptiacum* AE 1059.2; *Aegyptii ~i* ES 1262; ES 5669; *cum ~ia inaurata* VR 595.1.

mumia: see **mumi**.

mundane, *adv.* In a worldly fashion: *Paulus...nihil cogitavit de altera vita quam ~e* ES(M) 4561.

mundanus ~a ~um, *a.* Of or belonging to this world, worldly: *homo factus est ~us et corporeus* AC 6631; *amores... ~i* AC 7918.1; (neut. pl. as sb.) *est...in ~is, ita in externis* CI 309.

mundatio ~onis, *f.* The act of cleansing: *in ~one leprae* AC 643.4 (Lev. 14.2).

mundatorius ~a ~um, *a.* Of cleansing: *in sacrificiis...purificatoriis et ~is* AC 2180.2.

munditia ~ae, *f.* = **mundities**: AC 2526.

mundities ~ei, *f.* Cleanliness: *sicut substantia coeli quoad ~em* Exod. 24.10 (AC); (transf.) purity: *~em amoris conjugialis* AM 424.

mundo ~are ~avi ~atum, *tr.* **1** To make clean: *faciem suam multum lavant et ~ant* AC 8245; *tentoria ... ~are* AC 8379. **2** To free from disease, pollution, etc., cleanse: *pro ~ando leproso* AC 7918.2 (Lev. 14.2); *~ata* *est terra a feris illis* VR 71.4; ES 397; to purify from sin: *in die quo ~avero vos ab omnibus iniquitatibus vestris* Ezek. 36.33 (DD 4).

mundulus ~i, *m.* A small world: *in tali ~o* [sc. a moon of Jupiter] ES 1670; *ex suo micro-urano seu ~o spirituali* VR 71.2.

mundus[1] ~i, *m.* **1** The physical universe as visible to people on earth, the world: *res quae sunt in ~o aut super tellure* AC 1361.1; *a fundatione ~i* Matt. 25.34; (VI 2); *juxta polos ~i* ES 222. **2** A particular solar system, family of planets: *licet illis extra hujus solis ~um transire in alios* AC 6696; *in ~um nostri solis* VR 160.1; *in nostro ~o* ES 4673. **3** The world as the place where this life is lived, as opposed to the next world: *nisi Dominus in ~um veniret* VR 2.2; *in luce ~i* AC 6686; *cuivis homini est...mens naturalis pro ~o, et mens spiritualis pro caelo* FI 32; (more fully) *~us naturalis*, the natural world: AM 1. **4** The world standing for the people in it, people: *non sicut ~us dat, Ego do vobis* John 14.27 (CI 287.1); (w. pl. vb.) *quod ~us talia agnoscere potius velint* ES 676; ES 4426. **5** The world as composed of the objects in it: *in ~o inanimato et animato* ES 3575. **b** this world as the object of love: *qui in vita corporis vixerunt ~o et genio* ES 2683. **6** *~us spiritualis*, the spiritual (as opposed to the natural) world: *in ~o spirituali cum angelis esse* AM 1; AE 8.1. **b** *~us spirituum*, the intermediate state into which people come after death: *convoca sapientissimos in ~o spirituum* AM 2.2.

mundus[2] ~a ~um, *a.* **1** Free from dirt, clean: *loca ~a et sordium expertia* CI 488.5; *ut candida et ~a sit* [*facies*] ES 547. **2** Ceremonially pure, acceptable for religious purposes: *bestiarum ~arum et utilium* AC 1823.2. **3** Morally clean, pure credit: *se post confessiones ~um et lotum* DP 278[a].1; *fit ille amor ~us et purus* AM 64.1.

munia, *neut. pl.* (abl. *~is* VR 351.3) Functions, duties: *concupiverunt redire...quidam ad sua ~a* AM 6.4; *quod in Domino sint duo ~a, sacerdotale et regium* VR 114.

munificentia ~ae, *f.* Generous provision, munificence: *propter Divinam ~am beatitudinis illorum* AM 3.6.

munimentum ~i, *neut.* A fortification: *confirma ~a tua* Nahum 3.14 (AC 6669.2); [*hostis*] *intra sua ~a ...se reciperet* DP 233.2; (transf.) *~um maris* Isa. 23.4 (AC 1201.3).

munio ~nire ~nivi ~nitum, *tr.* To fortify: *coeperunt se ~nire per turres, aggeres et muros* DP 215.3; (transf.) *pro damnatione mali quod per falsum se ~nit* AC 7102.3.

munitio ~onis, *f.* A fortified place, fortification: *ascendent...carduus et sentis in ~ones ejus* Isa. 34.13 (AC 7293.4).

munitus ~a ~um, *a.* (pf. pple. of **munio**) Fortified: *arx ~a mea* Ps. 144.2 (AC 1788.2); (app. of a wood) defended against intruders, impenetrable: *quia descendit sylva ~a* Zech. 11.2 (AC 1585.5).

munus ~eris, *neut.* see also **munia**. **1** A gift, offering: *si obtuleris ~us tuum super altare* Matt. 5.21 (VI 73); *haec...sunt...~eri* [i.e., as a gift] *data principi nostro* AM 12.2. **b** a corrupt gift, bribe: *non accipies ~us* Deut. 16.19 (AE 152.10); *fuerunt qui ~era acceperunt et quaestus ex judicio fecerunt* CI 462[a].3. **2** A function, office, duty: *hi praedicatorum ~ere funguntur* CI 393.1; *hoc est vestrum ~us* AM 9.5; ES 925.

murmur ~uris, *neut.* A low, indistinct sound, murmur: *sonorum ~ur* AM 5.2.

murmuratio ~onis, *f.* A murmuring: *ex quodam differenti ~one...interstinguuntur* ES 187; a murmuring in complaint: *per ~ones filiorum Israelis in deserto* AC 8351.1.

murmuro ~are ~avi, *intr.* To make a complaint, murmur: *~arunt et contenderunt* AC 1678.3; *~abant hoc, en novum hospitem non indutum veste caeli* AM 10.2; (also, of things) to make an indistinct sound, hum: *auditur confusum murmur aut ~ans strepitus* ES 1316.

murrhinus ~a ~um, *a.* (Gk.) Of the colour of myrrh, reddish-brown: AC 5056.1; AC 8847.1; cf. ES 874.

murus ~i, *m.* A fortification wall, town wall: *urbem... habentem ~um magnum et altum* Rev. 21.12 (AR); *~us aheneus* AC 699; *~us Chinensis*, the Great Wall of China: UJ(P) 132; also, anything resembling a wall: *aquae... ~us* Exod. 14.22 (AC); *~us ignis* Zech. 2.5 (AE 504.12).

mus muris, *m.* (gen. pl. *murium* or *murum*) A rat or mouse: *ex foetore murium* AC 940.1; *mures majores et minores* VR 78.5.

musaeum ~i, *neut.* (Gk.) A place set apart for study, research institute (probably not 'museum'): *deducti sunt ad ~a, gymnasia, et collegia* AM 207.6.

musca ~ae, *f.* A fly: *sibilabit Jehovah ~ae quae in extremitate fluviorum Aegypti* Isa. 7.18 (AC 7441.2).

muscularis ~is ~e, *a.* Muscular: *~ium fibrarum... series* AC 607.2.

musculus ~i, *m.* A muscle: *organa motuum, quae sunt ~i* VR 12.3; CI 212.

musica ~ae, *f.* (Gk.) Music: *~a veteris Ecclesiae* ES 904; *~a chordacea* ES 2090.

musicalis ~is ~e, *a.* Musical: *~e instrumentum* ES 1143; (neut. pl. as sb.) musical performances: *sunt ~ia et cantica* AM 6.5.

musice ~es, *f.* (Gk.) The art of music: *qui gnari ~es sunt* AC 8337.2.

musicus ~a ~um, *a.* (Gk.) Musical: *instrumenta ~a* AC 8261.3; *licuit cantibus et harmoniis ~is adjungere choreas* AC 8339.1; (masc. as sb.) a musician: *sedent ~i cum instrumentis chordae* AM 17.1.

mussitatio ~onis, *f.* The making of an indistinct noise, mumbling: *per tacitam ~onem* AR 462.3; *artificem peritum ~onis* [sc. an obscurantist], *qui potest dealbare nigrum et denigrare album* AR 655.4.

mussito ~are ~avi, *intr.* To speak indistinctly, mumble, mutter: *~antes inter se, quid nobis cum illis deliriis* VR 72.2.

mustela ~ae, *f.* A weasel: *apparent e longinquo sicut ~ae* AM 514.3.

mustum ~i, *neut.* New wine: *ex ~is delicatissimis uvarum laetificari* AM 8.1; *~a vinorum concreta* AM 14.2; *vinum et ~um* Hos. 4.11 (AE 141.12); the juice of other plants: *quod... [papiliones] se adplicent suis rosis, ~um earum edant* ES 2475.

mutabilis ~is ~e, *a.* Liable to change, changeable: *quod omne varium et ~e sit in recipiente* VR 25.3.

mutatio ~onis, *f.* A change, transformation, alteration: *post status ~ones plures* AC 6797; *insignem ~onem per cruciatum subire* ES 269.

mutatorius ~a ~um, *a.* (of clothes) Worn in substitution for ordinary ones, festal: *~as vestes* Isa. 3.22 (AC 2576.11); AC 5954.

mute, *adv.* Inarticulately, dumbly: *loquela...tarda et ~e sonans* AC 4658.1; *obstipatio ~e dolorosa* ES 1273.

mutesco ~ere, *intr.* To become dumb: *lingua ~eret, et manus obtorpesceret* VR 497.1.

muthlabben, *indecl.* (Hebr.) The rendering of a Hebr. musical instruction in the title of Ps. 9: *Psalmis pluribus Davidis inscriptum ac indicatum quomodo psallerentur, prout super neginoth, super nechiloth, super octava, schigajon, gitthith, ~en, scheminith, schoschannim, machalath* AC 8337.5.

muticus ~a ~um, *a.* (of plants) Lacking an awn or beard, muticous: *hic dicuntur ~i seu barbati sicut linum* 2AD 2070.

mutilo ~are ~avi ~atum, *tr.* To render incomplete, mutilate: *non ~are...corpus* VR 309; *quod Verbum quoad sensum literae...non ~atum sit* AE 1085.2.

mutilus ~a ~um, *a.* Maimed: (masc. as sb.) *quod... ~i et quoque leprosi sanarentur* AC 7337.1.

mutio ~tire ~tivi, *intr, tr.* To speak indistinctly, mutter: *quod possit solum ~tire* DP 231.4; (w. acc.) *num ~tiret aliquid cogitationis* AM 152ª.1.

muto ~are ~avi ~atum, *tr.* **1** To make different, alter, change: *status ~atus est* AC 8118.3; [*vita*] *manet ...eadem...et non ~atur* VI 8; *satanas ille ~atus est quoad faciem* VR 71.4. **b** (w. *in* + acc.) to change (into): *per avem... ~atam in lapideam* AC 7743; *quod conjugium actualiter ~et virginem in uxorem* AM 306. **2** To take in substitution, change: *num ~avit gens deos...?* Jer. 2.11 (AC 8301.5); *quod ~entur vestes* CI 181; *spiritus et angeli ~ant societates* ES 2091.

mutuo[1] *adv.* see also **mutuum**. Reciprocally, mutually: *ita sibi ~o subordinata sunt* AC 1486; *qui se ~o aversati sunt* AC 2732; *inter conjuges, qui se ~o intime amant* AM 158.2; (so, also) *a ~o*: *dissimilia quae se a ~o distrahunt* AC 4997.1; AC 7078 (emended to *a* [*se*] *~o* Tafel).

mutuo[2] ~are ~avi ~atum, *tr.* To borrow: *plumas ex alis pavonum ~atas* VR 487.2.

mutus ~a ~um, *a.* **1** Incapable of speech, dumb: *quod stent sicut machinae ~i* AM 233.6; (masc. as sb.) *cantabit lingua ~i* Isa. 35.6 (AE 455.20). **2** (of pain) Incapable of accurate definition, dull: *oritur...dolor ~us* AC 1668.2; ES 4419.

mutuum ~i, *neut.* A loan: *cupientem ~um accipere a te* Matt. 5.42 (AC 9049.4); *~o petitus*, borrowed: DP 205; *~o dare*, to lend: AC 9174.3.

mutuus ~a ~um, *a.* Reciprocal, mutual: *in... ~a charitate inter se vivunt* AC 7975.2; *regimen amoris ~i* CI 213; (neut. as sb.) AC 4725.

myops ~opis, *m.* (Gk.) A short-sighted person: DP 189.2.

myriadies, *adv.* Ten thousand times: *millies, imo ~es* AC 8918.1.

myrias ~adis, *f.* (Gk.) A group of ten thousand: *si ~ades ~adum multiplicarentur in aeternum* AC 7236.2; *excedit...sapientia angelorum superioris coeli sapientiam angelorum inferioris, sicut ~as unum* CI 209; (pl. as numeral) *amor vere conjugialis, cujus delitiae sunt ~ades* AM 293.6; *pars ~dis*, a ten thousandth part: AC 937.

myrica ~ae, *f.* (app. not the classical word, but perh. corrupted from Gk. *murmex*) An ant or poss. an anthill: *potentia illa comparari potest ~ae contra ~am, pulici contra pulicem* AE 783.4; ES 4662; *quod cruciarentur sicut serpentes in ~is* CJ 61.

myrotheca ~ae, *f.* (Gk.) A perfume container, pomander: AM 300.2.

myrothecidium ~i, *neut.* (Gk.) = **myrotheca**: CO 43.2; Isa. 3.19 (AC 10540.4).

myrrha ~ae, *f.* (Gk.) The perfume myrrh: *significabat... ~a bonum naturale* SS 23.3.

myrrhatus ~a ~um, *a.* Flavoured with myrrh: *quod dederint Domino 'acetum felle mixtum', quod etiam vocatur '~um vinum'* AE 519.2.

myrtus ~i, *f.* (Gk.) A myrtle tree: *cum vidit [Sacharias] virum equitantem inter ~os* DP 134.2 (Zech. 1.8).

mysterium ~i, *neut.* (Gk.) A secret, mystery: *dicemus tibi ~um* AM 415.5; (esp. of faith) *intrare volunt in ~a fidei* AC 42.2.

mysticus ~a ~um, *a.* (Gk.) Secret, mystic: *hoc unum est unio illa ~a de qua aliqui cogitant* AC 1013.3; *arcana, quae ~a vocantur* SS 23.4.

N

nablium ~i, *neut.* (Gk.) A stringed musical instrument, lute, psaltery: *in ~o decachordo psallite Illi* Ps. 33.2 (AC 420.1); AE 323.2.

naevus ~i, *m.* **1** A blemish on the skin, birthmark, mole: *ex significatione integrae quod sit absque ~is, ita immaculata* AC 7837. **2** A blot on a person's character, defect: *possunt ~os suos exculpare* AC 6813; *quod quaereret continue aliorum ~os et vitia* ES(M) 4676.

nam, *conj.* (to introduce a reason or explanation of the preceding statement) For, because: *spectant in specie voluntatem, nam a voluntate scaturiebant mala eorum* AC 209.

namque, *conj.* (usu. second word in clause) = **nam**: *vos vocatis Me Magister et Dominus, et recte dicitis, sum ~que* John 13.13 (AC 9167.2); AM 457.

nanciscor ~i nactus sum, *tr.* To get possession of, obtain, acquire: *bonum illud suum quale ~itur a vero* AC 7759; *unaquaevis persona Divina partem suam nacta est* VR 17.1; ES 891[a].

nardus ~i, *f.* An ointment of antiquity, spikenard: *venit mulier habens alabastrum unguenti ~i potabilis* [*potatilis* 1st edn.] *multum pretiosae* Mark 14.3 (AC 10011.2).

naris ~is, *f.* A nostril: *conjunctio...odoris et ~is* VR 371.8; (usu. pl.) *vento ~ium Tuarum coacervatae sunt aquae* Exod. 15.8 (AC); *spernunt et contrahunt ~es ad libidines vagas* AM 49; (as the organ of smell) *captant ~ibus sphaeras vitae transeuntium* AM 78.2.

narratio ~onis, *f.* A telling, narration: *perceptio...est quasi ~o interna* AC 3209.1.

narro ~are ~avi ~atum, *tr.* To relate, tell: *hoc mihi spiritus illorum ~abant* AC 8376; *~avi plura ignota de mundo spirituali* VR 12.1; (absol.) *quis inde venit et ~avit?* AC 6971.2; (w. *quod*) *~avi illis, quod homines ...in...ignorantia sint* CI 74.1; (w. indir. qu.) *ut ~ent quid...cogitant* AM 151[a].2.

nascentia ~ae, *f.* The time or act of being born, birth (in quot. fig.): *verum Ecclesiae in sua ~a deperditum* AE 376.31.

nascor ~i natus sum, *intr.* **1** (of persons or animals) To be born: *quod Dominus natus sit sicut alius homo* AC 6716.1. **b** (in a specified place or condition): *qui intra Ecclesiam nati sunt* FI 3; *se credunt natos in coelo* CI 345. **c** (w. *ad* or *in* + acc.) to be destined by birth (to): *quod quidam...~erentur ad salutem* AC 7051.4; *quisque...~itur in religionem parentum suorum* SS 92. **2** (of vegetable products) To be produced, grow: *quod planta...ex semine suo ~atur* ES 251; (fig.) *ex nobilitatione hujus formae ~untur nobiles fructus* AM 201. **3** (of immaterial things) To be produced, come about, arise: *tertius* [*stylus*] *est propheticus, qui natus a stylo Antiquissimae Ecclesiae* AC 66.2; *~ituram per fidem charitatem* AC 432.

nasus ~i, *m.* The nose: *versus septum ~i* CI 450; *in os sub ~um* AM 182.8.

natalis ~is ~e, *a.* Of or relating to birth: *de...~i solo* AC 2491.

natatilis ~is ~e, *a.* Water-borne, floating: *ideam urbis ~is* CI 325.

natator ~oris, *m.* A swimmer: *sicut ~ores in aquis progressum adjuvare manibus* AC 8374.

nates ~ium, *m. pl.* The buttocks: *sub ~ibus est infernum horrendum* AC 818.

natio ~onis, *f.* A nation: *~ones liberae sunt sicut cervi grandiores* VR 815.1; *quod talis ~o sit* [*Judaei*], *quae prorsus ab aliis ~onibus diversa* ES 2260.

nativitas ~atis, *f.* **1** The act or fact of being born, birth, nativity: *hic liber ~atum Hominis* Gen. 5.1 (AC); *~ates in sensu externo...sunt generationes unius ab altero* AC 1145; *quod imperfectio ~atis hominis fiat ejus perfectio* VR 48.9. **b** the time of birth: *quod Humanum Ipsius non fuerit Divinum a ~ate* AC 6716.2.

2 (transf.) The creation or production (of other things): *hae ~ates coelorum et terrae, cum creavit illos* Gen. 2.4 (AC); *per colores et eorum ~ates* AC 1043.1; *nova ~as seu regeneratio* AC 6756.2.

nativus ~a ~um, *a.* **1** Born in or peculiar to a place, native: *ex arbore ~a seu propria nostri caeli* AM 77.7; *fuit Germanus, ~us ex Saxonia* VR 112.2. **2** Acquired by birth, natural: *virgini ex purpura ~a formosae* VR 109.3; *in capillis ~is* VR 137.1.

nato ~are ~avi, *intr.* To swim, float: *quasi ~ant supra* ES 214; ES 3370; (fig.) *in his [jucundis] ~at cogitatio ejus* DP 296.9.

natu, *adv.* By order of birth, by birth; *major ~u*, the older: AC 9375.1; *minor ~u*, the younger: *ex significatione minoris ~u, quod sit altero loco esse* AC 6270; *minimus ~u*, the youngest: *frater eorum minimus, hoc est, natus post omnes seu ~u minimus* AC 5688.1.

natura ~ae, *f.* **1** The sensible universe, the world, Nature: *hoc...ab illis quae in ~a illustrari potest* AC 7343.2; *homo, qui ~am pro Deo...colit* SS 1; *quod ~a sit creatrix universi* VR 178.1. **2** The inherent qualities of a person or thing, nature: *unaquaevis affectio hominis trahit suam existentiam et ~am ex ejus intellectualibus et...voluntariis* AC 803.1; *deploret vitiosam suam ~am* BCP (VI 6); *[Deus] est prorsus unus, sed non ita, quod binae ~ae sint commixtae* Sym. Ath. (AE 10.2).

naturalis ~is ~e, *a.* **1** Of or belonging to the physical universe, natural: *imagines rerum ~ium* AC 7926.1; *secundum ordinem ~em* CI 296; *experientia ~is sicut hortulana ac similia* ES 772; (neut. as sb.) *praeter fallacias in ~ibus* AC 6948.3. **2** (as distinct from **spiritualis, coelestis**) Natural: *Verbum in litera est ~e, at in sinu suo est spirituale* AE 1; *vocatur id Divinum coeleste, spirituale et ~e* VR 6.1; (neut. as sb.) *sunt tria apud hominem quae concurrunt...nempe ~e, spirituale et coeleste* AC 880.2; VR 103.1. **3** (of a person or his mind) Restricted to natural matters, natural: *mens ~is* AC 4973.1; *homo ~is...non persuaderi potest* SS 3.1; (neut. as sb.) the natural component of the personality: *~e ubi vera scientifica* AC 6681. **b** typical of such a person, natural: *in charitate ~i vixerunt* AC 845.1; *vera ~ia* FI 3. **4** Derived from birth, inherited, inborn: *omne malum actuale...cum saepe recurrit, fit ~e et additur haereditario* AC 494.1; *quod illi tolerare eos nequeant, est inimicitia ~is* ES 3329; (neut. as sb.) *hoc ~e est cum ab esu ejus* [sc. *carnis*]*...homo detinetur* AC 999.2.

naturalismus ~i, *m.* The worship of Nature in place of God: *~us hodie regnans* VR 4.2; VR 75.7.

naturalista ~ae, *m.* One who worships Nature in place of God, Nature-worshipper: *quod vocari possit ~a, et sic atheus* AM 380.5; AE 242.6.

naturaliter, *adv.* In a natural fashion, naturally: *angeli...omnia spiritualiter intelligunt quae homo ~er* AC 7112; AM 320.2.

naturatus ~a ~um, *a.* Belonging to the natural universe, created: (neut. pl. as sb.) *de influxu naturae in ~a* VR 695.2.

natus ~i, *m.* (pf. pple. of **nascor**) A son: *vocavit matrem ~i* Exod. 2.8 (AC); *de ~is Hebraeorum hic* Exod. 2.6 (AC).

nauci, *indecl.* (gen. of obsolete sb.) Of no value, worthless: *quae in se ~i sunt* AC 1103.2; *spectat alios...ut viles ac ut ~i* DP 259.1; *gaudia...primum fiunt adiaphora, deinde sicut ~i* AM 5.4.

nauclerus ~i, *m.* (Gk.) A ship's captain: *[navis] perit una cum gubernatore, ~o et nautis* VR 127; ES 2243.

naufragium ~i, *neut.* Shipwreck: *in statu ~i* VR 31.2.

naufragus ~a ~um, *a.* Shipwrecked: (fig.) *immergeris et peribis ~us* VR 185.6; (of a ship) wrecked: *navis ~a cujus mali summitas solum exstat* NE 40; VR 378.1.

nausea ~ae, *f.* A nauseous condition, nausea: *farciverant ventres cibariis usque ad ~as* AM 6.4; VR 42.2; *~am pro vino* ES 2458.

nauseabundus ~a ~um, *a.* Causing nausea, nauseating: *sentit illa ut injucunda, tetra, et ~a* AM 441; *nidor... ~us* ES 1045.

nauseo ~are ~avi ~atum, *tr.* To feel nausea at, be sickened by: *quod...eam [vitam] fastidirent et ~arent* AC 454; *ritus prorsus rejecerunt, imo ~arunt et odio habuerunt* AC 1195; ES 4092.

nauta ~ae, *m.* A sailor: AM 163; ES 1328.

nauticus ~a ~um, *a.* (Gk.) Of a ship, ship's: *funis ~us* AM 328.1; *in suo opere...quod est ~um* CH 171.

navale ~is, *neut.* A harbour: AR 463.1; VR 462.1.

navarcha ~ae, *m.* (Gk.) also **navarchus** ~i, *m.* (VR 533.2), and **naviarchus** ~i, *m.* (VR 422). A commander of a ship or fleet, admiral, captain: *~is et naucleris* VR 619.6; CO 57.3; *aliqui ~ae praeternavigantes* VR 803.

navarchus: see **navarcha**.

naviarchus: see **navarcha**.

navicula ~ae, *f.* A small boat, esp. a ship's boat, lifeboat: *nisi per quandam ~am...saluti suae possit consulere* VR 119.2; VR 342.3.

navicularis ~is ~e, *a.* Of a sailor, sailor's: *pilei ~es crispati* 'sailors' cocked hats' AM 78.4.

navigatio ~onis, *f.* The act of sailing, navigation: *~o circum globum telluris* AC 1378.2.

navigium ~i, *neut.* A boat: *ut emitterent rete in dextram partem ~i* AM 316.5 (John 21.6); ES 243.

navigo ~are ~avi, *intr.* To travel by ship, sail: *ex Anglia ... ~are ad Plejades* SE 98; ES 2545.

navis ~is, *f.* (acc. sg. *~im* AC 1378.2) A ship: *fert...sicut secunda vena ~em* AM 207.7.

Nazarenus ~a ~um, *a.* Of Nazareth, Nazarene: *a Jesu ~o* 3AD 4521.

ne[1], *adv.* Not so much as, not even: **1** (alone): *homo ne momentum temporis vivere potest nisi...angeli apud eum sint* AC 1266; *infinita quorum ne unum ad ejus cognitionem venit* DP 120; *sic ut ne sciant aliter* ES 2895. **2** (followed by *quidem*): *ne tunc quidem acquiescerent* AC 695; *ne quidem scire potest* AC 657. **3** *Ne hilum*, nothing at all, not a jot: *ut spiritus...ne hilum damni queant inferre* AC 6724.2; not at all: *quod...ne hilum possent infestare* AC 8280.

ne[2], *conj.* **1** In order that not, lest: *hoc facit amor...ne extinguatur* AM 359.2; (after a verb of ordering) that...not: *ut dicerent ad me ne hoc propalarem* AC 8544. **2** *Ne dicam*, not to speak of: *spirituum...bonorum, ne dicam angelorum* ES 1487.

-ne[3], *interrogative particle.* (To ask a question expecting an affirmative reply): *nostine quod mens humana sit elevabilis...?* 'do you not know...' VR 35.6; *estne omnipotens* [*Deus*]? VR 72.1.

Neapolitanus ~a ~um, *a.* Of Naples, Neapolitan: *nationes...~ae* VR 521.1; (masc. as sb.) the inhabitants of a city called Naples in the spiritual world: ES 5652; ES 5847.

nebula ~ae, *f.* A mist: *in ~a nubis* [i.e., a thick cloud] Exod. 19.9 (AC 6752.8); *ubi nec visi, nisi sicut ~a* ES [5765] 1/4.

nebulo ~onis, *m.* A worthless person, scoundrel: *a quodam ~one...sublata est illis idea aeterni* AM 216.2; CO 59.4.

nebulosus ~a ~um, *a.* Cloudy, misty: *in inferno sub ~a et densa quasi petra* AC 581.1; AC 6849.2.

nec, *conj.* and *particle.* **1** (as conj.) And not, nor: *quod supra caput meum sit nec insistat telluri* AC 447; *modo non pangatur* [*pellicatus*] *cum pluribus, nec cum virgine* AM 444[a]; *nec...nec*, neither...nor, nor...nor: *quod nemo possit videre Patrem, nec cognoscere Ipsum, nec venire ad Ipsum* VR 94.2. **2** (as particle) Not either, neither: *per Adamum...percipiunt Antiquissimam Ecclesiam, et nec Ecclesiam, sed...fidem* AC 64; *si non oculi, quod nec objecta* CI 170; *quam* [sc. *prolem*] *si haberent, nec amant* ES 3899. **3** (as negative with words meaning 'some', 'any' etc.): *nec aliquid memoratur* 'nothing is mentioned' AC 514; *nec aliter* 'in no other way' AC 1735.1; *nec unus* AC 7236.2; *nec quisquam* VR 3.1; *nec usquam* ES 1700; *nec ullus* ES 4403.

necativus ~a ~um, *a.* Murderous: *talis persuasionis natura...est ~a seu suffocativa* AC 562; AC 1673.3.

necdum, *adv.* Not yet: *quinam...per Debirim urbem ...intelliguntur, necdum constat* 3AD 4572.

necessario, *adv.* Of necessity, necessarily: *ubi Ecclesia, ibi ~o erit internum et externum* AC 1083.1.

necessarius ~a ~um, *a.* **1** That cannot be dispensed with, necessary: *hoc promptuarium maxime ~um est, quoniam absque illo non formari potest fides* FI 28; AM 271; (w. *ad*) *talium quae non ~a sunt ad usus vitae* CI 278.2; (neut. pl. as sb.) necessities: *~is vitae* CI 361. **2** *A ~is*, an intimate servant or courtier (of royalty): *a secretis et ~is regum...ambiverant esse* ES 1804.

necessis ~is ~e, *a.* Necessary; (neut. as sb.) a necessity: *per prope significatur necessum,...et propinquum status est ~e* AR 947.1.

necessitas ~atis, *f.* **1** A compulsion, necessity: *remotionis ~as* AC 7980; *quaedam ~as, cui opponi amplius nequit* ES 244. **2** A thing necessarily required, necessity: *curis de ~atibus vitae* CI 266.3.

necessum, *neut. adj.* (usu. in the phr.) *~um est*, it is necessary: *quod etiam ~um est* AE 71.1; (w. *ut*) *~um est ut mala...revelentur* AC 7122.2; VR 5; *quod ~um fuerit ut revelatio exstiterit* ES 3676.

nechiloth, *indecl.* (Hebr.) The rendering of a Hebr. musical instruction in the title of Ps. 5: *Psalmis pluribus Davidis inscriptum ac indicatum quomodo psallerentur, prout super neginoth, super ~oth, super octava, schigajon, gitthith, muthlabben, scheminith, schoschannim, machalath* AC 8337.5.

neco ~are ~avi ~atum, *tr.* **1** To put to death, kill, murder (a person): *quod... ~are voluerint infantes* AC 6639.1; *vicinum clandestine ~avit veneno* CI 462[a].7. **2** To destroy (other things): *~ant omne rationale spirituum praesentium* AC 570; *~are omnem cogitationis...potentiam* AC 1673.2; *~are animam hominis* SS 67.4.

necromanticus ~a ~um, *a.* (Gk.) Used in necromancy: [*baculi*] *quidam tincti succis ~is* CO 45.

nectar ~aris, *m.* (Gk.) The supposed drink of the Greek gods, nectar: *cibum vocabant ambrosiam et potum ~arem* AC 4966.2.

nectareus ~a ~um, *a.* Resembling nectar: *vino ~o* AM 14.2.

necto ~ctere ~xui ~xum, *tr.* **1** To make by interweaving, plait: *serta ~ctunt* CI 176; (transf.) to make by joining, establish (marriages, contact, etc.): *connubia quae ~ctuntur et dirimuntur* AM 192; *cum iis non facile commercium ~cti potest* ES 1739. **2** To conspire to produce, plot: *tales dolos simul ~ctunt contra Dominum* ES 480; *dolos nexuit* ES 4461; *dolosum hoc consilium ~ctebant* ES 2922.

nefandus ~a ~um, *a.* Unspeakably horrible, atrocious: *~ae gentes* AC 1673.2; *detinentur a ~is suis dolis* AC 6914.2; *quod adulteria sint ~a* CI 385; *~is insectis* ES 4466.

nefarius ~a ~um, *a.* Morally wrong, wicked: *~as artes et astutias* AR 800; *quod Paulus... ~us sit* ES 4321; (neut. as sb.) *erumpunt in ~a* CI 506.2.

nefas, *indecl. neut.* That which is morally wrong, a crime, wicked act: *nihil curantes num per fas aut ~s* AC 953; *si potestatem suam ultra fas in ~s extendunt* AM 291.2; *ut alter in se suscipiat alterius ~s* VR 134.4.

negatio ~onis, *f.* **1** The refusing of a request, refusal, denial: *'non ita', quod significet ~onem, constat absque explicatione* AC 7667; *suntne qui pro faemina ...rogata in sponsam, ex ~one amentes facti sunt?* AM 333.1. **2** The refusal of belief, denial of a fact or the existence of a thing: *quod qui...scientifica consulunt de credendis, non solum in dubitationem sed etiam in ~onem...se praecipitent* AC 233.3; (w. gen.) *~o Dei* VR 14.1; (w. *quod*) *ex ~one quod nihil salutis...in illis sit* FI 68.

negativus ~a ~um, *a.* Tending to or expressive of refusal, negative: *~a dubitatio* AM 243; *sententiae affirmativae...et ~ae* AR 147; (neut. as sb.) a negative principle: *cum ~um regnat* AC 6729; CI 1; also, a contradiction: *ex meris falsis, hoc est, ex prorsus ~is veri* AC 7392.2.

negator ~oris, *m.* One who denies: *confirmator falsi est ~or veri* DP 98.5.

neginoth, *indecl.* (Hebr.) The rendering of a Hebr. musical instruction in the title of Pss. 4, 6, 54, 55, 67, and 76: *Psalmis pluribus Davidis inscriptum ac indicatum quomodo psallerentur, prout super ~oth, super nechiloth, super octava, schigajon, gitthith, muthlabben, scheminith, schoschannim, machalath* AC 8337.5.

neglectus ~us, *m.* Lack of care, neglect: *frigus pro conjugio ac ~us cum fastidio pro conjuge* AM 305.2; AE 275.5.

negligenter, *adv.* Through neglect, negligently: *et si modo negligenter* [*malum* Rogers] *faciunt, severe puniuntur* UJ(P) 227 (Tafel, p. 74).

negligo ~ligere ~lexi ~lectum, *tr.* To treat without respect, neglect: *non intelligitur quod crucifixus sit...sed quod ~lectus in Ecclesia* AR 59.

nego ~are ~avi ~atum, *tr.* (*intr.*) **1** To deny (a fact, statement, etc.): *notum est...quod Deus unus sit, nec ullus homo...id ~at* DD 45.1; (w. *quod*) *~at quod verum sit* VI 45. **b** (intr., of arguments) to be negative: *plura confirmantia pro sua sententia...ut et plura ~antia pro opposita* AC 6663.2. **2** To refuse to recognize, deny the truth or existence of: *prorsus etiam fidem ~avit* AC 409; *plerique ~abant resurrectionem* AC 1200; *qui corde ~ant vera et bona fidei* AC 7293.5; *omnes satanae ~ant Deum* VR 14.2. **3** To refuse to give or allow, deny: *quod nusquam mihi ~atae sint...voluptates corporis* ES 3623; (w. *ut*) *qui ~at ut quis colat Deum* AC 6907.1.

negotiatio ~onis, *f.* Business dealings, trade: *qui ~onibus et mercaturis operam...dederunt* CI 360.3.

negotiator ~oris, *m.* A businessman, trader: VI 39.

negotiatrix ~icis, *f.* A female trader (in quots., of places): *Tharschisch ~ix tua* Ezek. 27.12 (AC 426.1); Ezek. 27.20 (AC 1172).

negotior ~ari ~atus sum, *intr.* To engage in business, trade: *de talentis...cum quibus ~arentur* VI 2 (Matt. 25.16); *cum faenore... ~ando* AM 453.

negotium ~i, *neut.* **1** A business dealing, trading venture: *si...agat...sinceritatem in ~is* VI 24; CI 359. **2** Any sort of occupation, affair: *tametsi in ideis et in ~is de aliis rebus est* AC 8067; *distracti a ~is mundi* SS 59; *in justificationis ~o* VR 72.2. **3** Trouble, bother: *omnis...ambitus facillime et nullo ~o regitur* ES 2234.

negro ~onis, *m.* A negro: *mori seu negrones* [*Mauri et Nigritae* Tafel] ES 432.

nemesis ~eos, *f.* (Gk.) Retribution (regarded as a personification), Nemesis: *patet quod ~is Divina illos persequatur* AM 504.3.

nemo ~inis, *m.* No one: *Divinum... ~inem vastat* AC 7796; *nisi Verbum foret, ~o sciret Deum* SS 114 titulus; *~ine sciente* ES 2688; (w. gen.) *quod absque eo ~o mortalium salvari potuerit* VR 2.1.

nempe, *particle.* (to give a more precise definition of a preceding phrase) To be precise, that is to say: *'accipere illam' ~e capsam* AC 6734; *similia... ~e omnia vera et bona* SS 10; *simile aliud, ~e, quod aliquoties audiverim...* AM 444.8.

nemus ~oris, *neut.* A stretch of woodland, wood: *~ora plena castaneis, palmis, tiliis* VR 78.1.

neo nere nevi netum, *tr.*, *intr.* **1** To spin: *ut praeparem me ad nendum sericum* VR 335.4; (absol.) *omnis mulier ...manibus suis neverunt* Exod. 35.24 (AC). **2** To sew: (intr.) *quaedam nentes super frustulis lineis* AM 218.2.

neotericus ~a ~um, *a.* (Gk.) Of recent origin, new: *cum spiritibus ~is* ME 8; (masc. pl. as sb.) modern writers: *quod vanum a ~is inventum fuerit* AM 315.8.

nepos ~otis, *m.* A grandson: *quod nascantur... ~otes et pronepotes in indolem avi et atavi* AC 6716.2; CI 556.

neptis ~is, *f.* (gen. pl. *~um*) A granddaughter: *nativitates filiorum ac filiarum...et postmodum nepotum et ~um* AC 8042.2; AM 402.

nequaquam, *adv.* In no way, by no means, not at all: *absque communicatione...cum coelo... ~am vivere potest [homo]* AC 50.1; *quod ~am fieri potest, nisi in libero sit* CI 293; *constat quod ~am ex Domino, sed ex diabolo procedant* ES 3774.

neque, *conj.* And not: *non videt illum, neque cognoscit illum* John 14.17 (AC 6788); *neque...neque*, neither...nor: *quae neque arte neque voce exprimi possunt* AM 355.1.

nequeo ~quire ~quivi, *intr.*, *tr.* **1** (w. inf.) To be unable: *cum quibus amor...concordare ~quit* AC 1547; *quod prius tentationes subire ~quiverint* AC 8159.2. **2** To be unable to do or act: (w. acc.) *haec Deus... ~quit* VR 58; (w. *contra*) *quod contra illas [leges Providentiae] ~queat* VR 73.3.

nequicquam, *adv.* To no extent, not at all: *haec...ad intellectum ~am explicari possunt* AC 1870.2; VR 22.1.

nequidem, *adv.* Not so much as, not even: *illi prorsus nihil sciunt quid est literae, ~em unam vocem quid proxime significat* AC 64; *~em aliquid vitae* AC 6266.

Nero ~onis, *m.* The Roman Emperor Nero: VR 73.1; (as a type of tyranny) *quod crudeles sint, prorsus ut ~ones* ES 2572.

Neronicus ~a ~um, *a.* Of or relating to the Roman Emperor Nero, Neronic: *in ~a Babyloniae seu Romae persecutione* 2AD 1536.

nerveus ~a ~um, *a.* (anat.) Of or concerned with nerves: *per fibras ~as et motrices* CI 95; SS 66.

nervulus ~i, *m.* A small nerve: ES 1730.

nervus ~i, *m.* **1** (anat.) A nerve: *a magno illo nervo in femore qui ramos suos emittit...per pedes ad plantas* AC 5051.1; *quod dolores mihi inferrent... ~is dorsalibus* ES 153; (as stretched in excitement) *inde flaccescunt ~i et cadunt vires, sic ut nihil ausint* AC 8316; AM 44.7; also, a tendon: *luxatum ~um Jacobi* ES 2617 (Gen. 32.32). **2** A bowstring: *praeparant telum suum super ~o* Ps. 11.2 (AE 357.12).

nescie, *adv.* In ignorance, without knowledge: *pervertebat ~e [nescienter* Tafel*] et non praemeditato... meas cogitationes* ES 927.

nescio ~cire ~civi ~citum, *tr.* (pf. act. also *~cii* Jer. 8.12 (AC 217)) To be unaware of, be ignorant of: *haec tunc ~cit* VI 25; *vitam...aliam ~ciunt* ES 2102; (w. *quod*) *quod mali spiritus inducant tentationes, homo ~cit* DD 33.1; (absol.) *illo ~ciente* AC 6789.3; (pass.) *hoc quidem non negatum est, sed ~citum* DP 172.2; (impers. pass.) *hodie ~citur quid coelestis homo* AC 81.1.

nescius ~a ~um, *a.* Not knowing, ignorant: *tunc me de eo ~um alloquuti angeli* AM 242; (w. indir. qu.) *~i quonam alluunt* ES 1013.

netio ~onis, *f.* Sewing: *in aliquo opere spirituali, quod correspondet ~oni* ES 6087.

netorius ~a ~um, *a.* Of or for sewing: *per foramen acus ~ae* AM 240.

netus ~a ~um, *a.* (pf. pple. of **neo**) Sewn: *opera manuum...vocantur ~a, acupicta* AM 91; (neut. as sb.) a piece of sewing: *virgo...cum ~o in manu* ES 6009.

neuter ~tra ~trum, *a.* Not one nor the other, neither: *quod est ~trum non est alicujus denominationis* AM 151; AR 875.6.

neutiquam, *adv.* By no means, not at all: *sensus... ~am patet, nisi sciatur...* AC 6745.3; AS 184; ES 295.

neve, *conj.* Or not, nor: *non credetis ex miraculis... neve plus quam illi crediderunt, dum...viderunt miracula ab Ipso Domino...facta* AM 535.

Newtonianus ~a ~um, *a.* Of Newton: *in causa ~a* UJ(P) 291.

nex necis, *f.* (nom. sg. not in use) Violent death, murder: *cum primogeniti ibi neci dati sunt* AC 7844.1; *bella, depraedationes, ac neces* AC 8117; *tanto percitus est odio...ut flagraret necem ejus* CI 562.

nexus ~us, *m.* **1** The connection or link between different things, bond: *ex his conspici potest ~us rerum* AC 146; *~us verorum rationalium* AC 1495.1; *separant spiritum suum paene a ~u cum corpore* AM 267.4. **2** The state of being connected, connection: *omnia hominis in tali ~u sunt...ut...sicut unum agant* DP 124.1.

ni, *conj.* (= **nisi**) Unless; (usu. in phrase) *ni fallor*, if I am not mistaken: ES 417; ES 1912.

Nicaenus ~a ~um, *a.* also **Nicenus**. Of Nicaea: *concilium ~um* VR 94.2; VR 136.3.

Nicenus: see **Nicaenus**.

nicto ~are ~avi, *intr.* To blink: *ad lucem diei ~ant oculis et parum vident* AE 342.12; (as a sign) to wink: *~abant palpebris ut dicerent, quod bene loquantur* AR 417.5.

nictus ~us, *m*. A blinking or winking (of the eyes): *~us oculi* ES 2057.

nidifico ~are ~avi, *intr*. also **nidificor** ~ari ~atus sum, *intr*. (SE 96). (of birds) To build nests: *cedri Libani ...ubi volucres ~ant* Ps. 104.17 (AC 776.4).

nidificor: see **nidifico**.

nidor ~oris, *m*. A foul smell, stench: *~or vomitalis* AC 1514; *ex foedo sulphureo ~ore* AC 1688; *~or in bestiariis* VR 57.1; *~or purulenti ex pulmone* AE 237.8; *in stercoris humani ~orem* ES 2624; (of a strong and sickly smell) *~or...dulcis seu vinosus* ES 1047.

nidorosus ~a ~um, *a*. Stinking: *excrementitia, stercorea, ~a et urinosa* DP 38.2.

nidulor ~ari ~atus sum, *intr*. (of birds) To roost: Matt. 13.32 (AC 55.3).

nidus ~i, *m*. A (bird's) nest: *vulpes foveas habent, et volucres ~os* Matt. 8.20 (DD 27); *quod...[aves] arte struant ~os* AM 417.

nigella ~ae, *f*. Black cummin: *dispergit ~am* Isa. 28.25 (AE 374.9).

niger ~gra ~grum, *a*. (compar. *~grior*, superl. *~gerrimus*) Black: *unum genus...apparet obscurum, paene ~grum* AC 7801; *equus ~ger* Rev. 6.5 (AR); (neut. as sb.) *se habet fere sicut ~grum et album* AC 731; also, a black pigment, ink: *dum pusillum ~gri in aquam mittitur* AC 1008.3.

nigre, *adv*. In a black manner: *obscurum quid barbatum ~e* ES 1157.

nigredo ~inis, *f*. A black appearance, blackness: *~o illa in qua apparuerunt interiora eorum* CI 354; *~inem corporis detestantur [Africani]* ES 453.

nigresco ~ere, *intr*. To turn black, become dark: *tunc ~it cingulum* AM 269.5; *~it super iis dies* Mic. 3.6 (AE 372.2).

nigricor ~ari ~atus sum, *intr*. To be black: *apparebant coram oculis eorum ~ari* UJ(P) 365; (esp. in pres. pple.) *nubes ~ans* AC 10314.

nigritae ~tarum, *m. pl*. Negroes: *Mauri seu ~tae* [Tafel for *negrones*] ES 432.

nigrities ~ei, *f*. Darkness, blackness: *inducitur forma monstrosa faciei, tum ~es* UJ(P) 241.

nigritudo ~inis, *f*. Darkness, blackness: *scientificum per mare significatur secundum aquarum ejus densitatem et ~inem, et vice versa secundum illarum tenuitatem et pelluciditatem* AC 9755.16.

nigror ~oris, *m*. A dark colour or appearance, darkness: *angeli [apparent] in candore et pulchritudine ineffabili, infernales autem in ~ore et deformitate inexpressibili* AC 5377.3.

nihil ~li, *neut*. also **nihilum** ~li, *neut*. **1** Nothing: *ut ~l credatur nisi falsum* AC 6729; *voluntas ~l producit ex se absque intellectu* FI 15; (w. gen.) *quod ... ~l Ecclesiae cohaereat* VR 5. **b** (form *~lum*): *at post ~lum illud exsurgit aliquid* AM 150; *de inani aut ~lo* VR 20.2; *ex ~lo ~l fit* VR 76.4. **c** *~l non*, everything: *~l non in homine...vivit et sentit* CI 433; ES 4121. **2** (as adv.) To no extent, not at all: *disposuit Dominus...ut mihi ~l nocere possent* AC 1270.1; ES 2040; *~l minus quam*, as far as possible from: *~l minus quam sapientes estis* AM 79.11. **3** A thing of no value: *inde...concludi potest...quam ~l sit philosophia* ES 226; *quid...existeret, nisi mere confusio et ~lum* ES 2101; (esp. gen.) of no value, worthless: *ut lux mundi respective ~li sit* AC 1053.2; *mala ut peccata ~li facit* VI 24.

nihilominus, *adv*. Nonetheless: *sed ~us valet veritas* AM 337; VR 56.1.

nihilum: see **nihil**.

nimbosus ~a ~um, *a*. Misty: *circumdati sunt quasi ~a petra* AC 1673.2; *apparet coelum illorum sicut ~um* CI 209; (neut. as sb.) a mistiness: *dum ~um illud usque ad illum pertingit* VR 119.2.

nimbus ~i, *m*. **1** A vaporous atmosphere, mist: *per ~os, nubes, seu aquas* AC 8137.2; *stant in denso ~o, et ex eo non possunt videre num homines sint* VR 22.2. **2** A rain cloud: *Jehovah faciet ~os, et pluviam imbris dabit illis* Zech. 10.1 (AC 7571.3); (contrasted with **nubes**) *sub specie crassi et atri ~i* AS 292. **3** (app.) The supposed emanation from objects which renders them visible, nimbus: *atmosphaera...quae producit visum...per reflexiones ~i omnium objectorum* ES 222.

nimirum, *particle*. To be sure, of course: *hujus rei eadem est causa, ~um, quia omnes...avertunt se a Domino* AM 444.8; VR 72.2.

nimis, *adv*. Too much, too: *prolixum ~is foret exponere* AC 1370; *dicendo hoc ~is eleganter* AC 6924; *acuitis et sublimatis ~is hanc rem* AM 79.8; *vita... ~is contraria est quam ut possint regenerari* ES 4383.

nimium, *adv*. = **nimis**: *~um indulgent suae imaginationi* AM 267.4.

nimius ~a ~um, *a*. Excessive: *in statu ~i frigoris* AC 3755.2; *~a sanctitas* IM 28.

nisi, *conj*. **1** If...not, unless: *quod nullus...salvari potuerit, nisi Dominus in mundum venerit* VR 2.2. **2** (following a neg.) Except: *ut nihil credatur nisi falsum* AC 6729; *fiduciam habere non potest nisi qui bene vivit* VR 2.3; (so, also) *nisi quam*: *hoc non potest nisi quam sapiens* VR 12.9. **3** *Nisi quod*, apart from the fact that, except that: *fluens lacte et melle illa [terra] ...nisi quod fortis populus habitans in terra* Num. 13.28 (AC 1444.3).

Nissi, *indecl.* A title of Jehovah (see quots.): *et vocavit nomen ejus Jehovah Nissi* Exod. 17.15 (AC); *Jehovah Nissi in lingua originali significat Jehovah vexillum seu signum meum* AC 8624.1.

nisus ~us, *m.* A striving, effort, activity: *est sicut ~us ad centrum gravium* AC 6952.6; *per ~um voluntatis* CI 229; (w. *ad*) *amor...non aliud est quam ~us ad conjunctionem* VR 43.3; (w. gen. of gerund) *in ~u illabendi sunt* AC 8287.

nitens ~ntis, *a.* (compar. *~ntior*) Shining, brilliant: *is [angelus] ~ntiori et splendentiore facie erat* CI 75; *in stolis albis ~ntibus* AE 475.1.

niteo ~tere ~tui, *intr.* To be bright, shine: *columba... cujus alae ~tebant sicut ex argento* AM 155[a].4.

nitide, *adv.* Neatly, elegantly: *Verbum ~e scriptum* VR 842.

nitidus ~a ~um, *a.* (compar. *~ior*, superl. *~issimus*) **1** Bright, shining: *athmosphaerae...radiatae coloribus ~issimis* AC 1621; *candidum [lumen] cum ~is bullis* ES 2436. **2** In good condition, clean, smart: *chartam... non ita conglutinatam et incomptam, verum decentem et ~am* AC 6930; *vasi exterius ~o et polito* CI 505.

nitor[1] ~oris, *m.* **1** Brilliance, brightness: *colores qui ex ~ore et splendore...superant pulchritudinem colorum...in terra videntur* AC 1053.1; *trahit...uxor a viro splendentem ~orem sapientiae ejus* AM 192. **2** Smartness, elegance: *qui solum ~ori styli student* ES 2993.

nitor[2] ~ti (~sus sum?), *intr.* **1** To make efforts, strive, tend: *omnis determinatio illuc vergit et ~titur* CI 151; *[homo] totus... ~titur in id* AE 105.2; (w. inf.) *~tebaturque summo studio...ascendere* ES 272. **2** (w. *super*) To lean (upon), rely (upon): *super Deo Israelis ~tuntur* Isa. 48.2 (DD 39).

nitrosus ~a ~um, *a.* Nitrous: *sphaera... ~a circum nitrum* VR 499.2.

nitrum ~i, *neut.* (Gk.) Soda, natron: *si laveris te ~o* Jer. 2.22 (AE 475.15); VR 673.

niveus ~a ~um, *a.* Snow-white: *ut color existat, debet esse quoddam obscurum et ~um* AC 1042.2; AE 107.2; (neut. as sb.) *quod id...appareat...solum ut ~um in coelo* AC 8952.

nix nivis, *f.* Snow: *sicut desertum et terra nive obtecta* AC 7626; (esp. as a type of whiteness) *vestimenta... coruscantia et candida ut nix* Mark 9.3 (CI 129); *ex luce caeli, quae erat candida sicut nix* AM 10.4.

Noachicus ~a ~um, *a.* Of or belonging to Noah: *diluvium ~um* AE 650.20.

nobilis ~is ~e, *a.* (compar. *~ior*, superl. *~issimus*) **1** Of high birth, noble: *de ~i gente Anglica* UJ(C) 39; *multi ex ~i stemmate* AM 505.3. **2** Possessing outstanding natural qualities, excellent, fine, noble: *metalla ~iora et ignobiliora* CI 104; *~e vinum* SS 40.1; *fructus ~is* DP 215.13.

nobilitas ~atis, *f.* **1** High birth, nobility: *virorum qui ex prima ~ate fuerunt* CJ 10. **2** High quality, excellence: *secundum ~ates fructuum* AM 13.2.

nobilitatio ~onis, *f.* The process of making more excellent, ennobling: *ex ~one hujus formae nascuntur nobiles fructus* AM 201.

nobilito ~are ~avi ~atum, *tr.* To render more excellent, improve, ennoble: *[amor] ~atur* AM 161.3; AM 184.

nobiscum, *pron.* = *nobis* (see **nos**) combined with *cum* (see **cum**[1]). With us: TE 157.

noceo ~cere ~cui ~citum, *intr.*, *tr.* To do an injury, harm, hurt: **1** (intr.): *quid hoc ~cet ibi?* AM 483; (w. dat.) *talia nihil ~cuerunt mihi* AC 6811. **2** (tr.): *illi spiritus non ~cent homines* CI 249; *phantasiae de similibus quae mihi [me Autograph] ~cerent* ES 2171; *ut ~ceri a nullo putaret* ES 3089.

nocivus ~a ~um, *a.* Harmful: *similes...insectis... quae ~a foedaque sunt* ES 2506.

noctambulo ~onis, *m.* also **noctambulus** ~i, *m.* A sleepwalker: *~ones, qui ex caeca scientia...faciunt quae faciunt* AM 134.4; *~i* VR 48.13.

noctambulus: see **noctambulo**.

noctilucus ~a ~um, *a.* Shining by night; *vermis ~us*, a glow-worm: VR 339.2.

noctu, *adv.* By night: *supra illud fuit nubes interdiu, et ignis ~u* VI 55.2; VR 109.3; ES 1450.

noctua ~ae, *f.* An owl: *nonne ~a videt caliginem noctis ut lucem diei...?* AM 233.3; VR 7.

nocturnus ~a ~um, *a.* Of or by night, nocturnal: *lumen ~um a luna* AC 7233.2; AM 380.4.

nocumentum ~i, *neut.* A source of harm, harmful thing: *quod si bona opera commiscentur negotio salutis per fidem...sint ~a* SE 59; (pred. dat.) *omnes cognitiones non sunt ~o* ES 773.

nodosus ~a ~um, *a.* Abounding in knots, lumpy: *[diabolus] flavo ~oque corpore* ES 453.

nodulus ~i, *m.* A small or tight knot: *referunt ~os fibrarum in cerebro* AC 4051.1; (fig.) *in vinculo seu* *filo fidei et charitatis sunt plures ~i quos nos sacerdotes solum solvere possumus* VR 506.5.

nodus ~i, *m*. 1 A knot: *retia circum voluta sicut in ~um inexplicabilia* VR 74.2; *~um ligationis* ES 3298. b (anat.) an enlargment on a nerve, knot: *a ~is qui ganglіones vocantur* CI 212; *~is in cerebro* ES 305. 2 A rhythmic beat, pulse: *sic ut sonus sit quasi quadrupes, sic cum distinctis ~is* ES 1031. 3 A difficult question, knotty problem: *nec potest extricari e ~o isto* AC 8325.2; *ut...hunc ~um quaestionis solverent* VR 79.5.

nolo ~lle ~lui, *intr*. 1 To be unwilling, not to wish: (w. inf.) *~lunt loqui de personis* AC 7002; (w. *ut*) *unus eorum ~lebat ut id dicerem* ES 1794. 2 (imperative w. inf.) Do not: *~li timere* Judg. 6.23 (AC 6849.2); *~lite vocari doctor* Matt. 23.8 (SS 51.6).

noluntas ~atis, *f*. Unwillingness: *desuetudo inveterat hominem, ac inducit ~atem* VR 561.1.

nomen ~inis, *neut*. 1 The peculiar appellation of a person, place or thing, name: *vocavit ~en illius Moscheh* Exod. 2.10 (AC); *quod omnia ~ina, quae in Verbo, non significent personas* AE 8.2. b (Bibl., as a periphrasis for a person): *habes pauca ~ina etiam in Sardibus* Rev. 3.4 (AR). 2 The name (of God as symbolizing His essence): *benedicite ~ini Ipsius* Ps. 96.2 (AC 8261.5); *in ~ine Tuo multas virtutes fecimus* Matt. 7.22 (VI 2). 3 The appropriate word for anything, appellation, name: *unamquamvis classem nominaverunt secundum ~ina eorum qui apparent...opitulandi* AC 6705; AC 6742; (as opposed to reality) *castae uxores non ~ine tenus, sed actualiter volunt uxores esse* AM 217. 4 A reputation, name (for something): *ad convocandum... eminentissimos ~ine sapientiae* AM 2.1; (Bibl.) fame: *dabo vos in ~en et in laudem* Zeph. 3.20 (DD 4).

nominatio ~onis, *f*. 1 The act of giving a name, naming: *~o fit per linguam spiritualem* DP 230.1. 2 The utterance of a name, naming: *coelum...horret ad solam ~onem prophani* AC 6963.3; *ad ~onem amoris vere conjugialis forte cachinnaturi* AM 240.2.

nominativus ~i, *m*. The nominative case: *in ~o dicitur* AC 6880.

nomino ~are ~avi ~atum, *tr*. 1 To give a name to, name, call: *filii Jacobi, ut quoque tribus ab illis ~atae* AC 6640.1; *quod Divinum procedens a Domino... ~etur caeleste, spirituale et naturale* SS 6. 2 To mention by name, speak of, name: *cum Sion et Hierosolyma una ~antur* AC 6745.4; *cum plures [arbores] ex conjectura ~arem* AC 8377.

non, *negative adv*. 1 (with vbs.) Not: *si fiat hic et ibi, non concludit* AM 469; (following *ut*) *provisum ut non se praecipitarent in...mortem* ES 3008. b (w. ellipse of vb.): *veni et non vir* Isa. 50.2 (AC 40.1); *quaesivi num etiam sic facere vellent suis infantibus, dicebant Non* ES 2284; *quaesivi...num...sint...vel non* VR 798.10. 2 (repeated or combined with another negative): a *non possum non*, I cannot but, I must: *quod humanum genus non posset non perire* AC 629; CI 191. b *non... nisi [quam]*, not...except, only: *non potuit amor ille amare nisi progressionem* AM 401.1; *ligati et non nisi quam ope Divina...extricandi* AC 8383; CI 52. c *non alius* [etc.]...*quam*, no other than: *non alii...elevantur, quam qui abdicant pellices* VR 832; *quod non aliquis salvari possit, quam qui Christianus natus est* VR 833.1. 3 (to negate a sb. or other phrase): *quod...de statu non Ecclesiae agatur* AC 624; *amicitia inter non bonos* VR 44.2; *..punitionibus non ex justo* AC 8164. b *non aliquis*, not any, no: *non aliquis scit...* DP 174.1; *non aliquem locum invenit* VR 759.3. c (app. redundant): *quando prorsus erat non nihil* [i.e., nothing at all] *visum* ES 4250. 4 a *Non solum* [or *non modo*]...*sed etiam...*, not only...but also...: VR 795; VR 771.1. b *modo non*, so long as...not: *beatus homo cui non imputat Jehovah iniquitatem, modo non in spiritu ejus dolus* Ps. 32.2 (AC 9013.9). 5 *Non quod* (w. subj.), not that: *non quod ex...dolo id faciant* ES 1423; *non quod ii id vellent* ES 2372.

non-agentia ~ae, *f*. Unwillingness to act: *talis... sphaera fuit ut...induceret torporem et ~am animo, tandem et corpori* ES(M) 4677 (Tafel).

nonaginta, *indecl. adj*. Ninety: *dies mille ducenti ~a* Dan. 12.11 (DD 4).

nondum, *adv*. 1 Not yet: *arcanum e caelo, quod ~dum...illuxit* VR 50; CI 35. 2 No longer: *forte de aliquo tertio loquutus cum iis, sed ~um tertii memini* ES 3489.

nongenti ~ae ~a, *pl. adj*. Nine hundred: Gen. 5.11 (AC).

nonna ~ae, *f*. A nun: ES [5469] ½ (Tafel).

nonne, *particle*. (to ask a question expecting an affirmative answer) Is it not the case that...?: *~ne subito surgent mordentes te?* Hab. 2.7 (AC 6669.2); *~ne per nomen Tuum prophetavimus...?* Matt. 7.22 (CI 471); AM 333.2.

nonnullus ~a ~um, *a*. Some: *quia ~am habes potentiam* Rev. 3.8 (AE).

nonus ~a ~um, *a*. Ninth: *~a Ecclesia* AC 465; *~a hora*, the ninth hour (of the day, i.e., mid-afternoon): Matt. 20.5 (AE 194.2).

norma ~ae, *f*. A standard (by which things are judged), rule: *faciebant doctrinam ut serviret pro ~a* AC 519.1; *secundum ~am praeceptorum Dei* BCP (VI 6); *statuta, leges et ~ae, quae vinciunt homines* AM 130.2.

norunt: see **nosco**.

nos, *pron.* (gen. pl. forms *nostri, nostrum, nostrorum*; dat. and abl. pl. *nobis*) We: AM 208.2; (gen.) *cum respectu nostri capita eorum* [sc. *antipodum*] *deorsum tendunt* ES 859.

noscibilis ~is ~e, *a.* Capable of being known, knowable: *nec differentiae ~es sunt* ES 851.

nosco ~ere novi notum, *tr.* (contracted forms of pf. *nosti, norunt, nosse*, etc.) **1** (pres.) To become acquainted with, get to know: *nisi hic ejus status... ~atur* AM 57; *pusillum cogitationis ~ere mihi dabatur* ES 1911; (impers. pass., w. indir. qu.) *inde ~itur quid faciendum* AC 6989. **2** (pf.) To be aware of, know (a fact): *qui non novit verum* AC 6652; *si...novissent interna Verbi* AC 6963.2; *nostine aliquid de ludis sapientiae...?* AM 132.1; (w. *quod*) *nostine quod mens humana sit elevabilis...?* VR 35.6; (w. indir. qu.) *si quis occisus inveniretur...nec notus quis occiderit...* Deut. 21.1 (AC 6767.5). **b** (dist. from **scio**): *ex perceptione nosse et scire quid bonum et verum* AC 125; AC 1555.2. **3** (pf.) To be familiar with, know (a person): *cum illis quos notos habui cum in corpore vixerunt* AC 1114; *Aegyptii...noverunt Jehovam* AC 7097.1; *non novi vos, discedite a Me* Matt. 7.23 (VI 2).

nosocomium ~i, *neut.* (Gk.) A place for the care of the sick, hospital: *hospitalia, ~a, xenodochia* VR 425.1; VR 459.8.

nosse = *novisse* (see **nosco**).

noster ~tra ~trum, *a.* **1** Of us, our: *adjunget se...ad inimicos ~tros* Exod. 1.10 (AC); *domos ~tras* Exod. 12.27 (AC); AM 208.2. **2** Belonging to our experience, familiar to us: *~tra tellus* AC 6697; *Verbum ~trum* SS 42; *~tro die* ES 879.

nostine = *novisti* (see **nosco**) combined with *–ne* (see **-ne**[3]).

nostras ~atis, *a.* (gen. pl. *~atium*) (masc. as sb.) A person of our country or society: *certe non es in statu vitae ~atium* AM 326.1; VR 80.2; a person of our time: *qui ab Ecclesia Antiqua fuerunt...multo sapientiores fuerunt ~atibus* AC 6876.2.

nostri: see **nos, noster**.

nota ~ae, *f.* **1** A mark, sign: *usque manet... ~a quod tales sint* AC 939; *jucundum absque ulla horroris ~a* ES 4494. **2** A note (in a book): *in ~is sub linea* CI 305; AE 304.9.

nothus ~a ~um, *a.* (Gk.) Not genuine, pseudo-: *peripneumonia ~a ex pituita lenta* VR 665.5.

notifico ~are ~avi ~atum, *tr.* To make known, indicate: *quomodo ~antur tetri amores* ES 1080 titulus.

notio ~onis, *f.* A general mental concept, rough idea, notion: *cum temporis ~o removetur* AC 488.3; *ex communi ~one de Divino* AC 7032.1; *~o et idea spatii* CI 195; *supra ideas vocum et supra ~ones artis* AM 477.5.

notitia ~ae, *f.* Awareness, knowledge: *quod ne quidem ad ~am communium pervenire queant* AC 6813; *absque ~a de correspondentiis* VR 698.

noto ~are ~avi ~atum, *tr.* To apply a mark to, mark: *illi ~ati, et mox inde ejecti* ES 5254; to notice, remark: *illico animadvertunt et ~ant societatem cum qua communicatio fit* SS 64.

notula ~ae, *f.* A minor mark or characteristic: *coarctatio...ad singulas ~as loquelae* ES 805.

notus ~a ~um, *a.* (pf. pple. of **nosco**) (compar. *~ior*, superl. *~issimus*) (in senses of vb., esp.) Well known, familiar: *quod plures tellures sint... ~issimum est in altera vita* AC 6695; *in antiquissimis temporibus ~issima fuit* [*correspondentia*] SS 20.1; (masc. as sb.) *agnoscunt...pro ~o omnem qui recipit ideas suas* ES 4716; (neut. pl. as sb.) *haec inter ~a familiaria sunt* AM 170.

novacula ~ae, *f.* A razor: *quod ~am tonsorum traduceret super caput suum* DD 15.5 (Ezek. 5.1); *sume acum seu ~am, et aperi plumas...corvi* AM 233.4.

novale ~is, *neut.* Newly ploughed and sown land: *prata, ~ia, hortos* AC 7071; *novate vobis ~e* Jer. 4.3 (AC 9144.8); *vidi ex arvo illo enascens ~e circumcinctum arbustis* AM 522; *pluvia tempestiva quae ~ia agri refocillat* CO 20.

novalista ~ae, *m.* (perh. to be spelled **novellista**) One who collects and disseminates news, newsmonger, journalist: *~ae...sciscitant nova ubivis et narrant aliis* ES [6109.5].

novator ~oris, *m.* An innovator: *utinam daretur loqui cum ~ore, qui pomum Eridis inter antistites Ecclesiae projecit* VR 112.1.

novella ~ae, *f.* **1** A young plant, seedling: *cum laetificatione ex ~is in agris* VR 304. **2** (pl.) Fresh information, news: *loquebantur ~as de aulis* AM 5.1. **3** (pl.) Publications containing news, newspapers: *diversoria utilia...lectiones in libris...tum nova in ~is* CH 189 (= xi); *illi qui ex ~is sciunt quod tantae gazae ibi sint* VR 245.2.

novellista: see **novalista**.

novem, *indecl. a.* Nine: AM 10.1.

November ~bris, *m.* The month of November: ES 4059.

novendecim, *indecl. a.* Nineteen: Gen. 11.25 (AC).

noverca ~ae, *f.* A stepmother: *matris seu ~ae* AE 237.9.

novi: pf. of **nosco**.

novilunium ~i, *neut.* A feast of the new moon: *suffitus abominatio Mihi est, ~um et sabbathum* Isa. 1.13 (VI 30.1).

noviter, *adv.* Newly, recently: *omnes qui e mundo ~er adveniunt* AM 261.1.

novitius ~a ~um, *a.* Of recent origin, newly established: *~os spiritus qui sunt qui recentes e mundo veniunt* CI 391; (esp. masc. as sb.) *instruere ~os et ignaros* AC 1641.2; VR 12.1.

novo ~are ~avi ~atum, *tr.* **1** To make as new, renew: *hae* [sc. *vires*]...*continue ~antur* AM 355.5. **2** To plough (land) for the first time: *~ate vobis novale* Jer. 4.3 (AC 9144.8).

novus ~a ~um, *a.* (superl. *~issimus*) **1** Newly made, new, fresh: *vinum ~um* Matt. 9.17 (VR 784.1); *vestimenti ~i* Luke 5.36 (AC 9212.7). **2** Not previously used, new: *haec inscripserunt ~ae chartae* AM 136. **3** Not previously experienced, new: *~is semper cognitionibus implentur* CI 489.4. **4** Replacing a previous one, new: *absque ~a instructione* AC 895.2; *quod...perducantur successive in ~os status* AC 6645.3; *ubi agitur de ~o Templo* AC 7091.3; *~am voluntatem* AC 7342. **b** (in names): *~a Hierosolyma* Rev. 3.12 (AR); *~a Ecclesia* AM 1; *~um Testamentum* DD 22. **5** (of persons) Made new (by regeneration): *tunc incipit* [*homo*] *~us fieri et regenerari* AC 728.1. **6** (neut. as sb.) A new thing, news: *his adjiciam hoc ~um* VR 102.3; *quid ~i e terra?* AM 182.3; (pl.) *~a in novellis* CH 189 (= xi). **b** a new state, newness: *quod ~um vitae ejus pereat* AC 8891.3; *~um Ecclesiae quoad amorem et fidem* SS 14. **c** *e ~o*, anew, afresh: *homo...tunc e ~o nascitur* AC 16; *ut evangelium e ~o ibi praedicarent* VR 4.1. **7** (superl.) Latest, last: *non videbit ~issimum nostrum* Jer. 12.4 (AC 776.4).

nox noctis, *f.* **1** The night: *mane, meridiem, vesperam et noctem* AC 6697; *media...nocte* Matt. 25.6 (SS 17.1); *caliginem noctis* AM 233.3. **2** The night as the time for evil actions: *opera enormia, quae vocantur opera noctis* ES 4657; cf. *similes virgini, quae...post nuptias cum uno locat noctes* VR 7. **3** (fig.) Night as a time of obscurity: *Divina Trinitas divisa in personas intulit... noctem in Ecclesiam* VR 23.1.

noxa ~ae, *f.* Harm, hurt, injury: *ne calor et lux... inferant illis aliquam ~am* AM 11; *in arbores ~ae, ut in spinas et sentes* VR 38.2.

noxius ~a ~um, *a.* Harmful, injurious: *effluvia detrimentosa et vapores ~i* AM 253.1; *bestiae ~ae* AE 388.21; (neut. as sb.) *volatile ~um* Exod. 8.17 (AC); *comparantur illi vitiosis et ~is quae influunt in sanguinem* AC 1877.

nubecula ~ae, *f.* A small cloud: *vidi nubem divisam in ~as* AM 315.1; *~am objectam soli* ES 565.

nubes ~is, *f.* A cloud: *~es fusca obvelavit illos* AM 233.7; (Bibl.) *videbunt Filium Hominis venientem in ~ibus coeli* Matt. 24.30 (AC 4056); (fig.) *causa est quod tanta ~es in parte eorum intellectuali non sit* AC 1059.2; (contrasted with **nimbus**, a rain cloud) AS 292.

nubilis ~is ~e, *a.* (of a woman) Ready for marriage: *virgo ~is* AM 229; (also, of a state) *dum in statum ~em venerunt* AM 502.1.

nubilus ~a ~um, *a.* Cloudy: *si...flammeum, apparet hoc multo longinquius quam ~um et fuscum* AC 6601.2.

nubo ~bere ~psi ~ptum, *intr.* To enter into marriage, marry, wed: *~bentes et nuptui dantes* Matt. 24.38 (AC 4332); (transf.) *cum Ecclesia se desponsat suo Domino, ac ~bit* AM 293.6; (w. dat.) *qui in malo est et ~bit falso* AM 428.

nuclearis ~is ~e, *a.* Of the kernel: (neut. pl. as sb.) *sicut squama et palea respective ad ~ia* AC 4557.

nucleatus ~a ~um, *a.* Having a kernel: *hic* [*amor*] *vocari potest crustaceus non ~us* AM 312.

nucleus ~i, *m.* **1** The kernel (of a nut): *crustae circum amygdalas absque ~o* AM 232.1; *tres athmosphaerae ambientes priores illas, sicut putamina ~os* VR 76.3. **2** A hard lump, nodule: *tales sinistrae parti capitis mei dolorem incutiunt, quasi ibi ~os duros formantes* ES 3612. **3** (transf.) A nucleus: *semper aliquis ~us Ecclesiae manet* AC 407; ES 250.

nudatio ~onis, *f.* The act of making bare, stripping: *~onem interni* AC 7040.

nude, *adv.* Without other attributes, by itself: *dic alicui ~e bonum, et non hoc aut illud est bonum, num bonum est aliquid?* DP 11.2; *non aliquis ibi est ~e imperator* AM 263.2.

nuditas ~atis, *f.* **1** Nakedness, nudity: *~as quam non erubescunt* AC 165 (Gen. 2.25); *~as correspondet innocentiae* CI 280; *~ates inhonestas* ES 3447; (transf.) *sistam illam* [sc. *fidem separatam a charitate*] *in sua ~ate* FI 44. **2** Lack of vegetation, bareness (of land): *ad videndum ~atem terrae venistis* Gen. 42.9 (AC).

nudius tertius, *adv.* The day before yesterday, two days ago: *etiam ab heri, etiam a nudius tertius* Exod. 4.10 (AC).

nudo ~are ~avi ~atum, *tr.* **1** To make bare, strip of covering: *quod ~andum sit caput* FI 47; (pass., w. abl.) *vidi illos ~atos vestibus* SS 52; ES 1696; (w. *ab*) *res a vagina sua ~atas* AC 6816; to unsheathe, draw (a sword): *quod ~averit ensem* VR 74.2. **2** (transf.) To lay bare, reveal: *interna ~antur* AC 7046.1; *calor...se ~at tunc* AM 75.7.

nudus ~a ~um, *a.* (compar. *~ior*) **1** (of persons or parts of the body) Not covered by garments, naked: *qui in zonis...callidis vivunt ~i vadunt* AC 8375; *ex palpatione ~i corporis* AM 396.2; *si homo in calceis accederet, vel si ~is plantis* AC 6844.1. **b** (of the eye or vision) unassisted, naked: *arcana quae nusquam ad oculum ~um patent* AC 578; *coram visu ~o* AC 7408.1. **2** (of other things) Lacking equipment or adornment, bare: *ex ~a glarea* VR 45; *equos ~os rubentes* ES 3718; *~us arcus* [sc. without arrows] VR 86; *si ~um Jehovam adiret [homo]* VR 135.5. **3** (of immaterial things) Plain, unadorned: *~ae cognitiones* AC 6814; *~a spiritualia* AC 6943; AS 204; *ex ~a voce 'Deus'* VR 4.2; *veritates ~as* ES(M) 4579; (neut. as sb.) *ubi ipsum verum in suo ~o est* AC 8186.

nugae ~garum, *f. pl.* Meaningless words, nonsense, rubbish: *pro formulis ~garum aut irrisionis* AC 961; *forte dicent, quod sint ~gae, aut quod sint mystica quae transcendunt* AM 58; VR 57.1.

nugator ~oris, *m.* One who talks nonsense, blatherer: (app. of false prophets) *gladius ad ~ores, et insanient* Jer. 50.36 (AC 2799.13).

nugor ~ari ~atus sum, *intr.* To talk nonsense: *sic putantes quod ~entur aut irrideant eleganter* AC 961.

nullatenus, *adv.* To no extent, not at all: *quod fuerit [cultus] internus, et ~us externus* AC 920.3; *mali... ~us ...sustinere possunt praesentiam Divinam* AC 8265.1.

nullibi, *adv.* Nowhere: *illo tempore ~i erat Ecclesia* AC 8006; *inquisiverunt...per aliquot dies, et ~i invenerunt* CI 6; *quod in Verbo Veteris Testamenti ~i nominetur Spiritus Sanctus* VR 158.

nullus ~a ~um, *a.* (gen. sg. *~ius*, dat. sg. *~i*) **1** Not any, no: *~i spiritui apparet sol mundi* AC 7247; *de re evidente et ~ius dubii* CI 98; *apud hos est conjugium corporis, et ~um spiritus* AM 304.2. **b** (masc. as sb.) no one: *Dominus...vult...~ius mortem* AC 6639.3; *~us mortalium* VR 2.2. **c** (neut. as sb.) nothing: *cadit idea in ~um* AC 6876.3. **d** *~us non*, some: *ex ~is non locis in Verbo* AC 308.1; also, everyone: *~us non natus in mundo in alteram vitam transit* ES 4471. **2** Lacking reality or importance, of no consequence: *percipiunt quam ~a et quam tristis...vita sit illorum* AC 2363.2; *dixit... nihil sum, ~us sum* ES 910.

num, *interrog. particle.* **1** (to put a direct question): *num ibo et vocabo tibi mulierem?* Exod. 2.7 (AC): *num hi duo plus cohaerent quam ferrum et argilla?* AM 79.11. **2** (in indirect questions) Whether: *cum non in quaestionem...mittunt, num ita sit* CI 183.2; *num recens e mundo venerint non scio* ES 2206.

numen ~inis, *neut.* A supernatural power, heathen deity: *coeperunt imagines et simulachra...colere ut sancta, et tandem ut ~ina* SS 23.1; AM 78.3.

numeralis ~is ~e, *a.* Of or concerned with number, numeral: *~is illa scriptura* CI 263.

numeratio ~onis, *f.* The act of numbering, counting: *propter ~onem populi a Davide* AC 7879 (2 Sam. 24).

numericus ~a ~um, *a.* Of or concerned with numbers: *idea Trium in Deo uno ~a* ES(M) 4609.

numero ~are ~avi ~atum, *tr.* **1** To ascertain the number of, count: *~a stellas, si poteris ~are illas* Gen. 15.5 (AC); *ut singula in illis [libris] usque ad literas ~ata essent* SS 13.4. **2** To count, reckon (as a member of a group): *cum praevaricatoribus ~atus est* Isa. 53.12 (DD 15.1); *ab angelis non plus inter Christianos ~atur* AM 464.

numerosus ~a ~um, *a.* (compar. *~ior*) Having large numbers, numerous: *regnum Domini, quod tam vastum est et ~um ut nusquam aliquis credere possit* AC 1810; *'pulvis' in Verbo...significat sepulchrum, tum humile, ut et ~um* AC 7418.4.

numerus ~i, *m.* **1** A numeral, figure: *~us 'quadraginta'* AC 6828; *illius ~i significatio* AC 7284. **2** The number of a group, total, count: *audivi ~um signatorum; centum quadraginta quatuor millia signati* Rev. 7.4 (AR); *qui...faciebant ~um* ES 3469; *~o*, in number: *tellures...immenso ~o* AC 6696; *erant ~o 8* ES 4688. **3** (as a grammatical category) Number: *Deus in lingua originali pluralis ~i est* AC 8192.2. **4** (pl., as the title of a book of the Word) Numbers: AC 10225.8. **5** (pl.) Rhythmical patterns, measures: *loquela...cadens in ~os* AC 8261.3; *saltantes hic in ~os et ibi in orbes* AM 8.2.

nummulus ~i, *m.* A small coin: *divites qui...vehuntur non possunt advertere oculos ad sedentes ad latera juxta parietes et ~os porrigere* VR 459.8.

nummus ~i, *m.* A coin: *copia ~orum aureorum* AM 268.2; *is ~us, quia erat omnium minimus* AE 374.1.

numne, *interrog. particle.* **1** (to ask a question expecting an affirmative answer): *~ne nulla sepulchra in Aegypto?* Exod. 14.11 (AC); *postea dixerunt, ~ne conveniens est, ut aliquis sacerdos adsit...?* AM 21.4. **2** (in indirect questions) Whether: *appello ad sapientes, ut expendant...~ne sit contradictio* SE 69; ES 3223.

numquid, *interrog. adv.* (introducing a question that anticipates a negative answer) Is it really possible that?: *~id est Ecclesia ubi trinum adoratur unum separatim ab altero...?* AC 4766.2.

numularius ~i, *m.* A money changer: *mensas ~orum* Matt. 21.12. (AE 840.4).

nunc, *adv.* perh. also **nunce** (ES 594). **1** At this point in time, now: *quomodo hi status apud angelos mutantur, hic ~c dicetur* CI 154; *Suos discipulos, ~c angelos* VR 4.1; *per 4 ~c annos* ES 4228. **b** (w. impf. vb.) in the immediate past, just now: *erant ~c spiritus... qui...* ES 2987; *~c permulti boni glorificabant Dominum* ES 3029. **2** *~c... ~c*, at one time...at another, now... now: *~c in sensu genuino, ~c in sensu opposito* AC 1142; *~c sursum et ~c deorsum* VR 383.1. **3** (to introduce a conclusion) So, then: *~c quia Deus descendit ...non potuit aliter...quam concipi* VR 89; *hoc ~c est quod Deus Messias dicit* ES 252.

nunce: see **nunc**.

nuncupo ~are ~avi ~atum, *tr.* To give a name to, name: *aetas...quae a ferro ~atur* AM 78.1; (w. pred.) to call (something) a name: *qui* [sc. *Pharao*] *cum rex Aegypti ~atur* AC 8142; *in ultimo capite operis Vera Christiana Religio ~ati* CO 1; VR 394.

nundinae ~narum, *f. pl.* A fair, market: *in ~nis tuis* Ezek. 27.19 (AC 3923.5); *vidi... ~nas cum omnis generis utensilibus pro infantibus pueris* ES 4437.

nundinatio ~onis, *f.* An exchanging of goods or the goods exchanged, a trading, trade: *in argento, in ferro, in stanno et plumbo, dederunt ~ones tuas* Ezek. 27.12 (AC 4453.2); *in exire ~ones tuas e maribus satiasti populos multos* Ezek. 27.33 (AC 2967.4).

nunquam, *adv.* Never: *hoc faciunt mali... ~am boni* AC 8223.2; ES 866.

nuntio ~are ~avi ~atum, *tr., intr.* To bring a message, announce, report: (w. acc.) *~antes...quae contingunt* ES 917; (imperf. pass.) *~atum est Jesu a dicentibus...* Luke 8.20 (DD 35.4); (w. *quod*) *famulus... ~avit quod octo sapientes...adsint* AM 18.1.

nuntius ~i, *m.* A messenger: *venit ~us a principe* AM 14.1; *per ~os dicebant* ES 288.

nuper, *adv.* Recently: *in mundo naturali, e quo ~r venistis* VR 16.1.

nuptiae ~tiarum, *f. pl.* A wedding: *ingressae sunt cum ipso ad ~tias* Matt. 25.10 (SS 17.1); *non indutus veste ~tiarum* CI 180; AM 3.1.

nuptialis ~is ~e, *a.* Of or appropriate to a wedding: *absque veste ~i* AM 10.2; (neut. pl. as sb.) a wedding: *de saltatione in ~ibus* ES 2083.

nuptus ~us, *m.* The state of being married, marriage: *quod...non dentur ~ui* AM 27.

nurus ~us, *f.* A daughter-in-law: *cum...filio, filia, genero, ~u* AC 6653.

nusquam, *adv.* Never: *qui* [sc. *angeli*] *cum adsunt, ~am mali spiritus possunt adesse* AC 87; *~am datur apud duos bonum prorsus unum et idem* AC 6706; VR 102.1.

nuto ~are ~avi ~atum, *intr.* **1** To move to and fro, sway, rock: *~ando emota est terra* Isa. 24.19 (AC 1066.1); *quoddam aëreum ~ans* ES 3748; (of the head) to nod: *capite ~ante* CI 358; *cum moriturus est, ~at capite* ES 4687; (of the feet) to stumble: *in tempus ~abit pes eorum* Deut. 32.35 (AC 7051.3). **2** To incline from the vertical, lean: *vitibus...quarum vertices... ~abant versus arborem vitae in medio* AM 13.1; *iis caput apparet antrorsum ~ans* ES 3179; *quod ~arent antrorsum, sic ut se cogerent recte stare* ES 3434.

nutricio: see **nutritio**.

nutricius: see **nutritius**.

nutrimentum ~i, *neut.* An agent that promotes growth or development, nutriment: *vegetabile...spontanee recipiat sua ~a* VR 496.1.

nutrio ~rire ~rivi ~ritum, *tr.* **1** To provide with food, feed, nourish: *cibus et potus ~riunt corpus* AC 8352.3; *victu amaeno et dulci ex floribus se ~riunt* [*papiliones*] VR 12.6. **2** (transf.) To feed, nurture: *ita ~riebatur mens et quoque corpus* AC 7996; *vera ex quibus jucundum amoris... ~ritur et formatur* VI 39; *~riverat... odium contra eos* ES 760.

nutritio ~onis, *f.* also **nutricio**. Nourishment: *~o corporis* AC 7996; *intelligentia et sapientia est ipsa ~o spiritualis* AM 411.

nutritius ~a ~um, *a.* also **nutricius**. Of or concerned with nursing; (masc. as sb.) a foster-father: *erunt reges ~i tui* Isa. 49.23 (AC 3183.3); (fem. as sb.) a foster-mother: *matrem suam ~am vocari voluit* ES 3302.

nutritivus ~a ~um, *a.* Nourishing, nutricious: *cibi... in quibus amarum...parum ~um* AC 5175.

nutrix ~icis, *f.* A woman who rears another's child, nurse: *infantes quandoque a ~icibus amantur plusquam a matribus* AM 393.2.

nutus ~us, *m.* A gesture indicating one's wishes, whim: *saevit in illos qui non omni suo ~ui favent* AC 7773; *millia ibi simul ad ~um et lubitum eorum sponte ruunt* CI 137.3; *apud illos qui ut mancipia pendent a ~ibus suarum uxorum* AM 125.

nux nucis, *f.* A fruit with a hard shell, nut: *nuces terebinthinas* Gen. 43.11 (AC); (as a plaything) *augurando vana spargunt nuces* AM 79.10.

nyctalopia ~ae, *f.* (Gk.) A condition in which the eye is unable to see in bright light, day-blindness, nyctalopia: *~a, quae est visio ex luce fatua in tenebris* VR 346.2.

nympha ~ae, *f.* (Gk.) **1** A bride: *sicut ~ae ante nuptias* AE 1203.2. **2** An insect undergoing metamorphosis, pupa, nymph: CI 108.2; AM 418.

O

o, *interj.* see also **oh**. (to express surprise, wonder, etc.) Oh: *o quam siccum gaudium caeli* AM 44.3; *o quantum mysterium* VR 105.3.

ob, *prep. w. acc.* On account of, because of: *ob nullum alium finem* AC 831.1; *quod scientifica solum forent ob intellectualem hominem* AC 1495.1.

obbruteo ~tere ~tui, *intr.* To become senseless or speechless, become brutish: *scientificum illud hic intelligitur infatuatum, nam dicitur stulti facti principes Zoanis, consilium ~tuit* AC 6015.1 (Isa. 19.11).

obdormio ~mire ~mivi (*or* ~mii), *intr.* To fall asleep: *dormitarunt omnes et ~mierunt* Matt. 25.5 (SS 17.1); AM 194.1.

obdormitio ~onis, *f.* The act of falling asleep: *per somnum et ~onem viri* AM 194.1.

obduco ~cere ~xi ~ctum, *tr.* **1** (w. abl.) To cover with a layer (of), overlay, coat (with): *sculpsit sculpturas cheruborum...et ~xit auro* 1 Kgs. 6.32 (AC 8369.3); *mensa... ~cta auro* VI 55.1; AM 75.7; (fig.) *quasi callo quodam ~citur ejus cogitatio* ES 807. **2** To bring over as a cover, spread over: *a mundanis...quae tenebras ~cunt* AC 5816.2.

obductio ~onis, *f.* The act of overlaying: AC 9722.

obduro ~are ~avi ~atum, *tr.* To make hard, harden: (neut. pl. of pf. pple. as sb.) *ex ~atis* ES 1623; (usu. fig.) *~abo cor Pharaonis* Exod. 7.3 (AC); *forte ad illa ~aturi estis corda vestra* AM 535.

obedienter, *adv.* also **oboedienter**. Obediently: VR 119.2.

obedientia ~ae, *f.* also **oboedientia**. Obedience: *'auditus' correspondet et perceptioni et ~ae* AC 6989; *sub ~a fidei* FI 4; an obedient thing: *corpus est modo ~a* DP 103.

obedio ~dire ~divi ~ditum, *intr.* also **oboedio**. To be obedient: *quod illi auscultarent et ~dirent* SS 17.4; (w. dat. of person) to obey: *~diunt Deo* AE 6; (w. acc. of commands) *~diunt quae spiritus ejus ibi dictat* AC 4658.1.

obeo obire obivi (*or* obii), *tr., intr.* **1** (tr.) To discharge, undertake, perform (duties, functions, etc.): *ut quisque... functionem suam rite obeat* AC 7038.1; *ministeria quae societates obeunt* CI 217; ES 962. **2** (tr.) To present oneself for, attend (a sacrament): *obire sacramentum coenae* AC 8253; VI 4. **3** (intr.) To die: *cum obeunt et fiunt spiritus* AC 7248; *fuistis in mundo naturali, et obivistis ibi* VR 77.3; *quod e mundo priori...obiverint* AM 44.1; (fig.) *quod illa inclinatio non possit...obire cum corpore* AM 46.

oberro ~are ~avi, *intr.* To go astray, stray: *~ant oves Meae in omnibus montibus* Ezek. 34.6 (AE 405.51).

obesitas ~atis, *f.* Lack of intellectual ability, dullness, stupidity: *~as in talibus quae cogitationis et judicii sunt* AC 8378; *oh, qualis et quanta ~as saeculi* AM 478.2.

obesus ~a ~um, *a.* Lacking intellectual ability, dull, stupid: *sunt crassae et ~ae mentis* AC 7419; *qui tantum ~i et stupidi sunt quoad vera spiritualia* CI 462.2; DP 98.2.

obex ~icis, *m.* A bolt: *nos hic ~icem hujus carceris effringimus* AM 79.5; CO 28.

obf-: see also **off-**.

obfirmatio ~onis, *f.* Obstinacy: *vidi ~onem horrendam* Jer. 23.14 (VI 79.2).

obfirmatus ~a ~um, *a.* (pf. pple. of **obfirmo**) (compar. *~ior*, superl. *~issimus*) (in senses of vb., esp.) Obstinate: *tota domus Israelis ~i fronte, et duri corde* Ezek. 3.7 (AC 1286.3); *~issima et morticina phantasia* AC 586.1.

obfirmo ~are ~avi ~atum, *tr.* To render obstinate, harden: *quo magis quis se amat, eo magis ~at se* AC 570; *Ego ~abo cor illius* Exod. 4.21 (AC).

obfundo ~ndere ~di ~sum, *tr.* also **offundo**. To overwhelm, swamp: *quod...aestus libidinis ~ndat* *spiritum illecebra* AM 488; (absol.) *quia historica ~ndunt et obtenebrant* AC 1502.3.

obfuscatio ~onis, *f.* The act of making (light) dim: *~o veri luminis* ES 2263.

obfusco ~are ~avi ~atum, *tr.* To make dark, obscure, dim: *memoria particularium... ~at interiorem* AC 1639; *mundana ~ant coelestia* AC 4099.2.

obitus ~us, *m.* Death, decease: *quod homo post ~um...fiat angelus* CI 304.1.

objectio ~onis, *f.* An objection: *potest fieri ~o, quod...* AM 245.

objectivus ~a ~um, *a.* Observable, objective: *quod non videri potest, et non audiri... ~um accommodatum erit, quod fide et amore comprehendendum* AC 10267.

objectum ~i, *neut.* **1** A person or thing regarded as that on which a sense or force acts, object: *percipiuntur [affectionis singula] secundum capacitatem ejus qui est ~um* AC 545.2; *memoria...propius subministrat cogitationi ~a sua* AC 6814; *amori cognoscendi ~a...est sensus tactus* AM 210; *~a odorum* 'things which give off odours' ES 2051. **2** A subject (of discussion): *alterum ~um ventilationis assumserunt* VR 48.8; *quod in Domino Divina Trinitas conjuncta sit, est hujus operis principale ~um* VR 108.

objicio ~jicere ~jeci ~jectum, *tr.* **1** (w. dat.) To put in the way (of), expose (to): *rerum visui ~jectarum* 3AD 5190. **2** To raise as an objection: *ut...non... interrogantibus opposita ~jicerent* AC 7074; to make an accusation of, confront with: *~jicit ignominiam, si non* AM 488; *ejus dolos ei saepe ~jiciens* ES 538.

objurgatio ~onis, *f.* A noisy quarrel, battle of words: *hoc evadit in jucundum ~onum, et quantum licet vituperationum* AM 374; *contentio et ~o cum spiritibus* ES 216.

objurgo ~are ~avi, *intr.* To protest noisily, quarrel, scold: *valde indignatus est et ~avit* VR 796.3.

oblatio ~onis, *f.* The making of an offering: *~o primogenitorum* AC 349.1; *~o thuris* AE 340.26; a thing offered: *primitiae erant ~ones et munera* AC 9223.3.

oblatus ~a ~um: pf. pple. of **offero**.

oblectamentum ~i, *neut.* Pleasure, enjoyment: *in omnibus laetitiis et ~is illorum* AM 5.4.

oblectatio ~onis, *f.* A feeling of pleasure, delight: SS 40.3.

oblecto ~are ~avi ~atum, *tr.* To give pleasure to, delight, please: *chori illi... ~abant spiritus Joviales* AC 8115; *illa adblandiuntur sensibus externis, et ~ant genium* CI 87; *consortia quae angelorum mentes exhilarant, animos ~ant* AM 5.4; (refl.) *ex quorum aspectu...se quotidie ~at* CO 30; to indulge (one's fantasies): *ibi ~ant ita phantasias suas* ES 2643.

obligatio ~onis, *f.* An obligation: *quod amare conjugem sit solum ~o ex pacto* ES(M) 4612.

obligatorius ~a ~um, *a.* (neut. as sb.) An obligation: *a significatione 'servire gratis' quod sit absque ~o* AC 3816.1.

obligo ~are ~avi ~atum, *tr.* **1** To bind up, bandage (a wound or the injured): *Samarita... ~avit vulnera ejus* Luke 10.34 (AC 6708); *oves infirmas non confirmastis... fractam non ~astis* Ezek. 34.4 (AC 8364.4); *misit me ad ~andum fractos corde* Isa. 61.1 (AE 375.17). **2** (w. *ut*) To put under obligation, oblige, compel: *~antur, ut vera...cogitent* AC 8054.2.

oblimo ~are ~avi ~atum, *tr.* To cover with slime, beslime: *[mucus] ~at poros* ES 1272; ES 4592; (fig.) *per adulterium ~atur et operitur amor conjugialis* AM 480.

oblino ~linere, *tr.* (n.b. *oblinirent* in VR 332.5 is prob. an error for *oblinerent*; cf. AM 231.5.) To smear, paint: *fucos quibus ~linerent facies* AM 231.5; *oculos ejus ~line, ne forte videat oculis suis* Isa. 6.10 (AC 897.1).

oblique, *adv.* (compar. *~ius*) At an angle, obliquely: *~e ferit et...praeterlabitur* AC 6911; *antra...tendentia ~e deorsum* CI 429; *pectorale ~e cinctum fascia* VR 110.8; (fig.) *unus [usus] proximius et directius, alter remotius et ~ius spectat regnum Domini* AC 997.2.

obliquitas ~atis, *f.* Obliquity: *quidam apparent supra caput ad variam altitudinem, et ad variam ~atem* AC 7111.2.

obliquo ~are ~avi ~atum, *tr.* To divert from a straight line, twist: *ad omne id quod contra illum* [sc. *amicum*] *est, ~ant oculos* VR 332.4; (fig.) *ii...quae bona sunt ~ant quasi in id quod convenit eorum naturae* ES 933.

obliquus ~a ~um, *a.* **1** Departing from a straight line, slanting, oblique: *in aspectu ~o minus* AM 42.4; *per ~as semitas* ES 1120; *~o oculo*, out of the corner of the eye (i.e., with sidelong glance): VR 362.3. **2** (of ideas) Crooked, askew: *quod vertantur in contraria, seu ~a alia* ES 4003.

obliteratio ~onis, *f.* The act of wiping out, obliteration: *ex allectamentis...ad incasta fit ~o ejus* [sc. *faederis pacti*] AM 307.

oblitero ~are ~avi ~atum, *tr.* also **oblitt-**. To remove from sight, wipe out, blot out: *~atur sensus literae sicut nullus foret* AC 1783.2; *postquam scientia correspondentiarum... ~ata fuit* CI 306; *malum ~at verum* VR 77.3.

oblittero: see **oblitero**.

oblivio ~onis, *f.* **1** The act of forgetting, forgetfulness: *~o faederis pacti* AM 307; *~o expulit reminiscentiam* VR 80.4. **2** The state of being forgotten, oblivion: *talia illis nota fuerunt...sed ~oni data cum venerunt in coelum* AC 7112; *~oni traditur* ES 333.

obliviscor ~sci ~tus sum, *intr.* (w. gen.) To fail to remember, forget: *quod... ~ti fuerint nominis Jehovae* AC 6877; *num ~ti estis verborum Domini...?* AM 7.3; (Bibl.) to be forgotten: *~sci fecit illam Deus sapientiam* Job 39.17 (AE 355.10).

oblongatus ~a ~um, *a. Medulla ~a*, the rearmost segment of the brain: *medulla ~a, ubi conjungitur fibra cerebelli cum fibra cerebri* AC 9670.2.

oblongus ~a ~um, *a.* **1** Of greater length than width, oblong: *post tabulatum ~um* AM 113; *vas ~um in quo quasi lac* ES 4018. **2** (Bibl. in doubtful sense, perh., of a snake) Uncoiled: *Leviathanem serpentem ~um* Isa. 27.1 (AC 7293.3; cf. VR 74.2).

obloquor ~qui ~quutus (*or* ~cutus) sum, *tr.* To say by way of insult: *praeter alia quae ii ex phantasia ~quuti sunt* ES 408; 2AD 1558.

obmutesco ~tescere ~tui, *intr.* To fall silent, cease to speak: *vadunt...meditabundi, ~tescunt* CI 438; *sicut ovis coram tonsoribus suis, ~tescit* Isa. 53.7 (DD 12); *~tescebant et nihil dicere poterant* ES 2460.

obnitor ~ti ~xus sum, *intr.* To exert a contrary influence, strive against: *non potuit enuntiare scortationem, quia castitas caeli illorum ~tebatur* AM 75.6.

obnixe, *adv.* (compar. *~ius*) Resolutely, steadfastly: *qui oculos ~e figunt in sole* DP 115; *qui ~ius perstant eniti* AC 1267.

obnixitas ~atis, *f.* Stubbornness: *summa ~as non obtemperandi justo et aequo* AM 252.

obnixus ~a ~um, *a.* (pf. pple. of **obnitor**) (compar. *~ior*) (in senses of vb., esp.) Resolute, stubborn: *quod viri sint [facie] duriore, ~iore* AM 218.1.

obnoxius ~a ~um, *a.* Liable, exposed (to injury or loss): (w. dat.) *quod...multis infirmitatibus ~us fuerit* 2AD 1860; (w. *ut*) *magis sunt [parte] frangibiles et ~ae ut disperdantur* ES 242.

obnubilatio ~onis, *f.* A covering with cloud, clouding over: *dies nubis et ~onis* Zeph. 1.15 (DD 4); AC 1047.

obnubilo ~are ~avi ~atum, *tr.* To cover with cloud: *et erit in ~ando Me nube super terram, et videtur arcus in nube* Gen. 9.14 (AC).

oboed-: see **obed-**.

obolus ~i, *m.* (Gk.) also **obulus**. A small coin: *laborare...pro aliquibus ~is* AM 268.3; (as translation of Hebr. *gerah*) *viginti ~i siclus* Exod. 30.13 (AC).

oborior oboriri obortus sum, *intr.* (of obstacles) To come into existence, arise: *quod...oboriantur tenebrae* AC 3793.3; SS 24; *nunc incipit pectus contrahi, et oboriri anxietas* AM 5.2.

obruo ~ere ~i ~tum, *tr.* To submerge, overwhelm: *fluctus ~it me* Ps. 69.2 (AC 6669.3); *in...coenum, ut eo ~antur* ES 751; (transf.) *[homo] ~itur a sensualibus* ES 1983; *~tae erant ideae naturalibus* ES 3314 ½.

obryzus ~a ~um, *a.* (Gk.) (of gold) Unalloyed, fine, pure: *aurum quod ab intimo aurum, et vocatur ~um, hoc bonum aurum est* VI 10; *parietes fulgent sicut ex ~o auro* AM 443; (neut. as sb.) fine gold: Lam. 4.1 (AE 242.14).

obsaepio: see **obsepio**.

obscaenitas ~atis, *f.* also **obscen-**, and **obscoen-**. An obscene act, obscenity: *manifestae ~ates, quae solvunt pudorem* AM 468.

obscaenus ~a ~um, *a.* also **obscen-**, and **obscoen-**. (compar. *~ior*, superl. *~issimus*) Sexually impure, obscene: *~us amor scortatorius* AM 430; (neut. as sb.) *~a facere, lasciva loqui, et spurca cogitare* VI 74.

obscen-: see **obscaen-**.

obscoen-: see **obscaen-**.

obscuratio ~onis, *f.* The cutting off of light, obscuration: *~o solis et lunae* SS 14.3.

obscure, *adv.* (compar. *~ius*, superl. *~issime*) In an obscure way, dimly: *quia remotius et ~ius...in amore... sunt* AC 6832.2; *amor conjugialis...non potest nisi indistincte et sic ~e cognosci* AM 138; *myriades radiorum simul oculus modo percipit, et quidem ~e* ES 682; ES 3434.

obscuresco ~rescere ~rui, *intr.* To become dim: *visum est cingulum ~rescere magis* CI 159; *igneum lumen eorum ~rescit* ES 3539; (transf.) to see dimly: *~rescunt, ut postea in ipsa veritate coecutiant* ES 1937.

obscuritas ~atis, *f.* Lack of illumination, obscurity: *dies nubis et ~atis* Joel 2.2 (AC 7711.2); (transf.) *~ate intellectus* AC 1188.1.

obscuro ~are ~avi ~atum, *tr.* **1** To take away the illumination of, darken: *sol ~abitur, et luna non dabit lumen suum* Matt. 24.29 (AC 1839.2); *prata et novalia ~abant* AC 7071. **2** (transf.) To make dim or obscure: *falsum...et malum... ~ant et paene auferunt influxum veri et boni* AC 6828; *~ati et hebetes in rebus coeli* AC 6865.2.

obscurus ~a ~um, *a.* (compar. *~ior*, superl. *~issimus*)

1 Lacking illumination, dark: *camera ~a* AC 949; *ut color existat, debet esse quoddam ~um et niveum* AC 1042.2; of a dark colour: *pileus turritus ~us* ES 588; (neut. as sb.) *indutus ~o* AC 1510.3. **2** (transf.) Lacking clarity, obscure, dim: *homo...tunc in ~issima vita est, fere nihil novit* AC 848.3; *falsa quae... ~iora sunt* AC 7441.2; *in perceptione ~a* CI 148; *in ~o*, without mental illumination, in the dark: *in ~o de omni veritate* SS 52. **3** Of lowly status, low-born: *datum est loqui cum ignaris, cum ~is, cum stupidis* FI 3.

obsecratio ~onis, *f.* **1** A sacred entreaty or request: *eris immunis ab ~one mea significat quod tunc nulla culpa naturali homini* AC 3154. **2** A curse: *erit mulier in ~onem in medio populi sui* Num. 5.27 (AC 3021.2).

obsecro ~are ~avi ~atum, *tr.* (as the formulaic beginning of a prayer or communication to God) *~o*, O God I pray, I beseech You O God: *~o, peccavit populus hic peccatum magnum* Exod. 32.31 (AC).

obsecundo ~are ~avi, *intr.* (w. dat.) To comply (with), fall in (with): *incipiunt vasa illa fieri cedentia, et ~antia vitae amoris Domini* AC 3318.3; *~ando eorum licentiae* ES 2194.

obsepio ~pire ~psi ~ptum, *tr.* also **obsaepio**. **1** To block with a hedge: *ecce Ego ~piens viam tuam per spinas* Hos. 2.6 (AE 237.6). **2** To fill up holes in, plug: *erigam tabernaculum Davidis collapsum, ~piamque rupturas eorum* Amos 9.11 (AC 414.2).

obsequiose, *adv.* In an obedient manner: *corpus... agitur prorsus ~e ad nutus intellectus et voluntatis* CI 60.

obsequiosus ~a ~um, *a.* (superl. *~issimus*) Obedient: (w. dat.) *ut externa hominis domentur et sic ~a reddantur internis* AC 857.2; *haec omnia... ~issima sunt animae* ES 1053.

obsequium ~i, *neut.* An act of obedience, service: *nondum externus homo ~a praestare vult et servire interno* AC 91; *patet quod totum corpus formatum sit ad ~a boni et veri* CI 137.3; AM 250.

obsequor ~qui ~quutus (*or* ~cutus) sum, *intr.* (w. dat.) To be subservient (to), comply (with), obey: *nutibus illarum ~qui* AM 292.1; (of a ship) *navi quae...non ~quitur gubernaculo* VR 28.2.

observabilis ~is ~e, *a.* Capable of being observed, observable: *vices pulsus cordis erant ita ~es, ut singula numerare possem* ES 1615.

observabiliter, adv. In a manner capable of being observed, manifestly: *quod...fit successive, et ~er multum* ES(M) 4703.

observantia ~ae, *f.* The observance (of a law): *per solam ~am Legis in externis* 3AD 1398; 3AD 4454.

observatio ~onis, *f.* Watching, observation: *non venit regnum Dei cum ~one* Luke 17.20 (AC 29.2); noticing, remarking: AC 5494.

observo ~are ~avi ~atum, *tr.* **1** To keep under observation, watch: *~ate vos per spiritum vestrum* Mal. 2.16 (DD 48.5). **2** To notice, remark, observe: *~avimus mutationes inclinationum* AM 208.4; *loquelam ~abam, quod esset...dulcis* ES 2172; (w. *quod*) *~abam ...quod labia apud me moverentur* AC 7359. **3** To remark in speech or writing, comment on, observe: *id solum ~atu memorandum nunc occurrit* ES 761 ½; (w. *quod*) *solum hic ~andum quod omnia se respective habeant ad statum Ecclesiae* AC 509; *quod ita sit, scriptores...in libris suis... ~arunt* VR 64.2. **4** To act in accordance with, keep, observe (a rule, custom, etc.): *qui ordo nisi ~etur, nusquam aliqua sapientia* AC 1475; *omnia statuta et omnes leges stricte ~are* AC 8006. **5** To use in accordance with a rule, treat strictly: *~abitis azyma* Exod. 12.17 (AC); *apud Prophetas accurate voces ~antur, nec usquam una loco alterius sumitur* AC 519.3.

observator ~oris, *m.* An observer: *~ores caelorum, spectantes stellas, divinantes in menses* Isa. 47.13 (AR 800).

obsessio ~onis, *f.* Hostile pressure, attack: *~o a falsis* AC 6829; obsession by spirits: CI 257.

obsessor ~oris, *m.* A spirit who takes possession of a man's mind, obsessor: *sunt plura genera ~orum* ES 5981.

obsideo ~sidere ~sedi ~sessum, *tr.* (pf. act. also *~sidi* AC 2356.3; DP 145.2 1st edn.; UJ(C) 83 1st edn.) **1** To besiege, invest (a city): *cum ~sideretur aliqua urbs* AE 109.6; CO 57; to make dangerous, beset (a road): *quod... viae ad caelum... ~sessae sint furibus et latronibus* VR 133.1. **2** (transf.) To subject to hostile pressure, attack: *usque dum illa doctrina omne punctum mentis eorum... ~sideat* VR 98. **3** (of spirits) To take possession of a person's mind, possess, obsess: *illi sunt spiritus qui ~sident hominem* CI 257; *spiritus...quasi ~sident cerebrum et caput* ES 542; (pf. pple.) *adductus est ad Jesum daemonio ~sessus* Matt. 12.22 (AC 6988.2); ES 3766.

obsidio ~onis, *f.* The act of besieging: *da eam parietem ferri...ut sit in ~onem* Ezek. 4.3 (AE 706.20).

obsidium ~i, *neut.* A siege: *aquas ~i hauri tibi* Nahum 3.14 (AC 6669.2).

obsignatio ~onis, *f.* The marking as with a seal, designation: *quod Sancta Caena sit illis...sicut ~o et sigillum quod filii Dei sint* VR 728; VR 730.2.

obsigno ~are ~avi ~atum, *tr.* **1** To place a seal upon (to keep closed or secret), seal up: *nonne istud absconditum apud Me, ~atum in thesauris Meis?* Deut. 32.34

(AC 7051.3); *librum... ~atum sigillis septem* Rev. 5.1 (AR); cf. *ad ~andum peccata* Dan. 9.24 (AC 728.2). **2** To mark as with a seal, designate: *quod centum quadraginta quatuor millia ~ati essent* Rev. 7.4 (SS 11); *~at frontes eorum signo crucis* VR 16.1.

obsitus ~a ~um, *a.* (w. abl.) Densely covered (with): *scrinium... ~um lapidibus pretiosis* VR 137.4; *campestria ~a arbustis* AM 231.1; *sic ut tota facies barba nigra esset ~a* ES 470.

obsoleo ~lere *intr.* To be degraded by age or use, be worn out, rot, decay: *utraque ~leret, aqua in putorem, et spongia in mucum* CO 28.

obsolesco ~lescere ~levi, *intr.* To become worn out, decay: *tunc amor conjugialis...contaminatur, et ~lescit, et sic perit* AM 476.

obsoletus ~a ~um, *a.* Worn-out, broken down: *parieti ex lapillis ~is conglutinato* VR 639; *venusta facies meretricis ~ae* VR 657; (transf.) *~ae veneris libidines* AM 433; (neut. as sb.) *[sanguinis] purificatio ab ~is* VR 687.2.

obsopio ~pire ~pivi ~pitum, *tr.* To put to sleep; (transf.) to lull: *qui... ~piverunt intellectum ex inertia cogitandi de spiritualibus* VR 185.1.

obstaculum ~i, *neut.* An obstacle: *quod sic removere studuerit ~a, ut potuisset venire in tales domos* ES 4082; (as the title of a book) *~a Impoenitentium* AE 885.5.

obstetricatus ~us, *m.* The function of a midwife, midwifery: AC 4921.

obstetricor ~ari ~atus sum, *a.* To act as midwife: *naturale recipit id quod ab interno influit, et sic quasi ~atur* AC 6673.

obstetrix ~icis, *f.* A midwife: *et vocavit rex Aegypti ~ices* Exod. 1.18 (AC).

obstinate, *adv.* Obstinately: *~e agere, sed incassum* ES 217.

obstinatio ~onis, *f.* Obstinacy: *quantum in jucundo illo sunt, tantum in ~one sunt* AC 7032.2.

obstinatus ~a ~um, *a.* (pf. pple. of **obstino**) Obstinate: *sunt ~i, ac ore et corde fidem renuunt* ES 214; (neut. as sb.) *ex ~o non liberare velle* AC 7032.1.

obstino ~are ~avi ~atum, *tr.* (refl.) To be determined, behave obstinately: *'obfirmare cor' quod sit ~are se* AC 7632; *per id quod ~et se contra verum Divinum* AC 7796; (w. inf.) *quod ~averint se non relinquere illos* AC 7305.

obstipatio ~onis, *f.* A blockage, obstruction: *circa orificium...ventriculi erat ~o mute dolorosa* ES 1273; (transf.) a state of being hemmed in, obstruction: *immersionem illorum qui in falsis ex malo in infernum, et ~onem ibi a falsis sicut ab aquis* AC 8138.

obstipo ~are ~avi ~atum, *tr.* **1** To hem in, surround: *quod... ~ati sint falsis* AC 8297; *~antur columna angelica* AE 78. **2** To obstruct, block: *concupiscentiae malorum ~ant interiora mentis* VI 86.4; *interiora rationis suae... ~averunt mundanis et corporeis* VR 9.1.

obsto ~are ~eti, *intr.* (fut. pple. *~iturus* AC 10504) **1** To stand in the way, form an obstruction: *permanente usque sole in continuo conatu dissipandi ~antes nubes* CI 549. **2** To form an obstacle, hinder, block: *mala... ~ant et inhibent* AC 8307; (w. dat.) *falsis ibi ~at Divinum Domini* AC 8288; (w. *quin*) *quod illa nihil ~ent, quin homo in coelum veniat* CI 358.

obstrepo ~ere ~ui, *intr.* To make a noise in opposition, shout disapproval: *sed ad haec caetus ~uit* VR 112.3.

obstrictio ~onis, *f.* Restriction: *'et adjuravit Joseph filios Israelis...' significat ~onem* AC 6586.

obstringo ~ngere ~nxi ~ctum, *tr.* To place under restraint, constrain, bind: *quod Deus ~ctus sit ad suas leges* VR 73.1.

obstructio ~onis, *f.* An obstruction, blockage: *tot ~ones vitae intimae* AM 313.3.

obstruo ~ere ~xi ~ctum, *tr.* To obstruct, block: *sic vena ejus in corpus ~itur* AM 482; *~ere viam per spinas* AE 237.6; (transf.) *vera et bona fidei destruuntur et sic ~untur* ES 201.

obstupefacio ~facere ~feci ~factum, *tr.* To make astonished, amaze: *contigit...quod aliqui amicos suos... per me viderint...et ~facti* AC 1880.2.

obstupescentia ~ae, *f.* Amazement, astonishment: AC 8461.

obstupesco ~pescere ~pui, *intr.* To feel astonishment, be amazed: *~pescunt angeli, cum audiunt* CI 102; *haec [lux] visum meum hebetavit; quare modo ~pui* AM 42.4.

obsum obesse obfui, *intr.* (w. dat.) To be a hindrance: *his non obest polygamia* AM. 340.2; (impers., w. inf.) *obest uxoribus amorem suum disperdere apud viros* AM 379.1; (w. *quin*) *quod illis...nihil obstet et obsit, quin matrimonium iterato contrahant* AM 317.

obtectio ~onis, *f.* Protection: *~onem a malis*: AE 407.

obtego ~gere ~xi ~ctum, *tr.* **1** To cover up, hide, obscure: *et ~xit Moscheh facies suas* Exod. 3.6 (AC); *reversae sunt aquae, et ~xerunt currus et equites* Exod. 14.28 (AC); *nubes atra... ~xit aperturam* VR 134.1; (fig.) *Verbum illis est sicut...quoad unitatem Dei ~ctum* VR 7. **2** To form a covering over, cover: *turma* *camelorum ~get te* Isa. 60.6 (AC 1171.3); *in speculo inverso...quod argentum vivum... ~git* VR 11.3.

obtegumentum ~i, *neut.* A covering: *super omni gloria ~um* Isa. 4.5 (SS 33).

obtemperanter, *adv.* With deference, submissively: *quod...quibusdam suis petitis ~er auscultent* AM 292.1.

obtempero ~are ~avi, *intr.* (w. dat.) To obey the commands (of), defer (to): *summa obnixitas non ~andi justo et aequo* AM 252; *~ando carni* AM 312; (w. no dat.) VR 604.

obtenebratio ~onis, *f.* An overshadowing, darkening: *mera ~o luminis* ES 2264; AC 4406.

obtenebresco ~ere, *intr.* To become dark: *lux ~et in ruinis* Isa. 5.30 (DD 4); (impers.) *antequam ~ere facit [Jehovah]* Jer. 13.16 (AC 1458.4).

obtenebro ~are ~avi ~atum, *tr.* To deprive of light, darken: *~atus sol* Isa. 13.10 (AC 31.1); *~abo terram in die lucis* Amos 8.9 (DD 4); (transf.) *pro Ecclesia quae per ratiocinia ex scientificis se ~at* AC 6723.1; *~are intellectum ne intelligat* AE 152.3.

obtestor ~ari ~atus sum, *tr.* To call on, implore: *descende, ~are populum ne forte perrumpant ad Jehovam* Exod. 19.21 (AC).

obtineo ~nere ~nui obtentum, *tr.* (*intr.*) **1** To acquire for oneself, gain: *viri qui...imperium ~nent* AM 291.2; *ut ~neat prae aliis omnia* AE 182.2. **2** To achieve, bring about (a result): *communicatio illa non obtenta fuisset* AC 7893; *hic finis ~netur* AC 8165.2. **b** (impers., intr.) it comes about, it happens: *inde ~nuit quod per 'Aegyptum' significata sint...scientifica* AC 5223.1.

obtingo ~ngere ~gi, *intr.* To fall to one's lot: *ex illis quae proviso ~gerunt* AC 4262.1.

obtorpesco ~pescere ~pui, *intr.* To become numb or paralysed: *lingua mutesceret, et manus ~pesceret* VR 497.1.

obtrectator ~oris, *m.* One who disparages, critic: *omnes illi refractarii refractariorum, ~ores* Jer. 6.28 (AC 8298.2); *~or aut sugillator Verbi Ipsius* BCP (VI 6).

obtrudo ~dere ~si ~sum, *tr.* To superimpose aggressively on, to thrust or force upon: *qui potest removere intellectum a fide, potest...cuivis religioso ~dere mille visionaria* AR 451.3.

obtuli: pf. of **offero**.

obtundo ~ndere ~si ~sum, *tr.* To beat the ears of repeatedly, wear out with repetition, assail: *annon amor ille, qui est diabolus, ~nderet loquentem anathematibus?* AR 802.3.

obturo ~are ~avi ~atum, *tr.* **1** To close off, block (a passage): *~ati sunt fontes abyssi* Gen. 8.2 (AC); *si...viam ~aret ne operari possent [reliquiae]* AC 661.2; *sicut aspis venenata surda ~at aurem suam* Ps. 58.4 (AC 195.2); *dextra ejus auris erat ~ata sicut gossypio* VR 79.4. **2** To shut in, confine: *sicut ulcus ~atum* DP 113; *aquae impurae ~atae* DP 117.1; (fig.) *apud hos interiora...plus et plus occluduntur, et in corpore ~antur* AM 240.

obtusus ~a ~um, *a.* (pf. pple. of **obtundo**) (compar. *~ior*) Blunted: *radii... ~i sicut enses fracti* AM 315.1; (of pain) not acute, dull: *qui ~o seu muto dolore afficerentur* ES 1623.

obulus: see **obolus**.

obumbro ~are ~avi ~atum, *tr.* To cast shade upon, overshadow: *nubes densae, quam ~ant et obtenebrant ...lucem* ES 556; (transf.) *mali incipiunt ~ari a falsis* AC 8211.1; *virtus Altissimi ~abit te* Luke 1.35 (VR 92.2).

obvelatio ~onis, *f.* The interposition of a veil, veiling: *absque ~one nubis* AC 6849.3; *~o inter externum et internum* AM 148.1.

obvelo ~are ~avi ~atum, *tr.* **1** To cover as with a veil: *qui [nimbus]... ~are incepit spiritus* AC 1507; *~avit illos nubes candida* AM 7.4. **2** (transf.) To conceal from view, hide: *sciunt...exstinguere vel ~are vera per fallacia* AC 6949; *haereditarium malum...post mortem ...rumpit tegmen quo in mundo ~atum fuit* VI 110.

obvenio ~nire ~ni, *intr.* **1** To come about, take place, occur: *erit quod ~niant bella* Exod. 1.10 (AC); (w. dat.) *intelligere quid ~niet populo tuo* Dan. 10.14 (DD 4). **2** To come into the mind, occur: *cum...cogitat de fide et charitate...illico tunc ~nit fides* AC 8094.1; (w. dat.) *~niebat mihi cogitatio de Johanne Baptista* AC 8028; (impers.) *vidi equos, et dicebant, quod illico iis ~niret de intellectualibus* ES 4296; (w. *quod*) *~niebat, quod concinnus ordo esset* ES 278. **3** (w. pred.) To make an impression of being, strike one as: *hoc non potest non unicuique ~nire ut paradoxon* ES 242; *contigit quod id quod bene saperet mihi ~niret tanquam tetrum* ES 645.

obversor ~ari ~atus sum, *intr.* **1** (of things) To present themselves, appear: *sunt quasi tenebrae quae ~antur* ES 157; (impers.) *quod ~aretur oculo, quod moverem manum* ES 2000. **2** (of persons, w. *in* + abl.) To be affected (by), be under the influence (of): *quidam dubitant, ex eo quod multitudo tam ingens in eorum ideis ~etur* ES 2234.

obverto ~tere ~ti ~sum, *tr.* To turn away, avert: *caligo totalis ~ebat oculos* ES(M) 4670; (esp. in pf. pple.) turned away: *quod duo conjuges...in toro jaceant ~si, tergo ad tergum* AM 171.2; (w. dat.) *in aliquo speculo oculis ~so* VR 11.3.

obviam, *adv*. In the opposite direction, so as to meet: *cum prope petram istam eram, ~am factum est frigus* AC 1268; (w. dat.) *ecce ille exit ~am tibi* Exod. 4.14 (AC); *~am venerunt virgines* AM 42.5; *cognitiones per quas hominem oportet Deo ~am ascendere* VR 24.1; *~am ire* (w. dat.), to take action (against): *nisi prudenter et severe ~am irent...amori sui* AC 7364..

obvio ~are ~avi, *intr*. (*tr*.) (w. dat.) To go to meet, encounter: *facie civili sibi ~ant* AM 376; (tr., w. dat.) to present (oneself) to: *~at...se amor amori* AM 44.6.

obvius ~a ~um, *a*. **1** Standing in the way, encountered: *interrogavimus ~os* AM 8.3; *reflexio super ~a dum ambulat* ES 4226; (w. dat.) *si non advertit ad illa quae ei ~a sunt* CI 493; (as an obstacle) *hoc vocant ...merito Christi ~um, repugnabile et injuriosum* VR 561.2. **2** Proceeding towards oneself, coming to meet one: (in quot. fig.) *quomodo potest dari amor sexus, nisi sit ita ~us et reciprocus, ut spiret aeternam unionem* AM 44.7.

obvolutio ~onis, *f*. Wrapping up, shrouding: *Jehovah ...absorbebit...facies ~onis* Isa. 25.7 (AC 795.3).

obvolvo ~vere ~vi ~utum, *tr*. To wrap around as a cover, wrap up: [*innocentia*] *recepta ab illis ~v itur circum amorem illorum proprium* AM 405.2; *malum ... ~utum jacuit externa probitate* CI 577.2.

occaecatio ~onis, *f*. also **occoecatio**. The act of making blind, blinding: (transf.) *~onis intellectus* DP 138; ES 250.

occaeco ~are ~avi ~atum, *tr*. also **occoeco**. **1** To make blind, blind: *minimus pulvisculus ante pupillam oculi ~at* ES 3667. **2** To deprive of perception, render unseeing: *~avit illorum oculos* John 12.40 (DP 260.2); *munus ~at oculos sapientum* Deut. 16.19 (AE 152.10). **3** To make intellectually blind: *quo magis ex iis* [sc. *sensualibus*] *sapere vult, eo magis se ~at* AC 128; *nihil aliud ~at hominem quam proprium ejus* SS 60. **4** To render (truths) incapable of enlightening: *quomodo... spirituales veritates... ~entur ut sint sicut nullae* ES 2314.

occalesco ~ere, *intr*. (Neo-Latin spelling of **occallesco***) **1** To become covered with callus: *manet plaga ut cicatrix quae ~it* AC 9103.2. **2** To become insensitive, be hardened: *heu quis potest in tantum ~ere ad audiendum aliquid de caelo...?* AR 716.3.

occasio ~onis, *f*. An opportunity, chance: *defraudant alios cum datur ~o* CI 364; *quoties ~o se praebet* VI 92.

occasionalis ~is ~e, *a*. Acting as a secondary or incidental cause, occasional: *quod affectiones amoris sint mutationes status ~es ex influxu radiorum solis* VR 178.2; *influxus...animae in corpus, quem vocant ~em* VR 695.3.

occasus ~us, *m*. **1** The setting (of a heavenly body): *ab ortu solis ad ~um ejus* AC 8615.1. **2** *~us solis*, the quarter where the sun sets, the west: *plagae determinantur secundum solis ortum et ~um* CI 123; (pl.) *ab ~ibus portae tres* Rev. 21.13 (AR); so *~us* alone: *timebunt ab ~u nomen Jehovae* Isa. 59.19 (AC 6674.7).

occento ~are ~avi ~atum, *tr*. To sing an accompaniment to, descant upon (in quot. fig.): *causas...mentitas inspergunt quae...a civibus amicis assentiuntur et ~antur* AM 474.

occidens ~ntis, *m*. The west: *quatuor plagae, oriens, meridies, ~ns, et septentrio* CI 141.

occidentalis ~is ~e, *a*. Of the west, western: *venti ~is* AC 7702; *ab angelis caeli orientalis et ~is* AM 81.1; (masc. as sb.) *postea ~es loquuti sunt* VR 48.11.

occido[1] ~ere ~i, *intr*. **1** (of the sun) To set: *nondum sol ~it* AC 1837; AM 152[a]; (fig. of the Lord) *Dominus est sol... ~it apud unumquemvis qui non recipit* AC 5097.2. **2** (of other things) To come down, fall: *inopinato ~it flammeum ingens ante oculum meum* ES 3629.

occido[2] ~dere ~si ~sum, *tr*. To kill, slay: *flagellabunt Ipsum...et ~dent Ipsum* Mark 10.34 (DD 24); (absol.) *praeceptum 'non ~des'* SS 67.4.

occiduus ~a ~um, *a*. (of the sun) Setting: (neut. as sb.) *non in sole est ~um, sed in remotione incolae telluris a luce ejus* AC 5097.2.

occipitium ~i, *neut*. The rear part of the head: *quod nusquam liceat alicui...stare a tergo alterius, et spectare ad ~um ejus* CI 144; *non...in fronte, sed in ~o* VR 12.2.

occiput ~itis, *neut*. = **occipitium**: *in plano ~itis* AC 6922; ES 1745.

occisio ~onis, *f*. The act of killing, murder: *~o hominis* AC 1010.2; CI 570.1.

occisor ~oris, *m*. One who kills, killer, murderer: *effusor sanguinis seu ~or* AC 1011.

occisus ~a ~um: pf. pple. of **occido**[2].

occludo ~dere ~si ~sum, *tr*. **1** To close, shut (a door, window, etc.): *~sit januam* Luke 13.25 (AC 6806.2); *~si fenestram* VR 80.1. **b** (the eyes or mouth): *oculos suos ~serunt, ne forte videant* Matt. 13.15 (VR 7); *iis os illico ~ditur* ES 263. **2** To render inaccessible, close off: *~de verba, et obsigna librum* Dan. 12.4 (DD 4); *qui non ~serunt viam e caelo in intellectum* AM 126; *sic etiam ~sissent sibi caelum* SS 24; *apud eos... interiora quae mentis ~sa sunt* CI 377. **3** To keep confined, hold in, shut in: *~dentur aquae magnae* Ezek. 31.15 (AC 6693.5); *a Domino stricte ~sa* [*inferna*] *tenentur* AC 7879.

occlusio ~onis, *f.* A shutting: *~o portarum* AE 86; *per... ~ones interiorum mentis* AM 509.

occo ~are ~avi ~atum, *tr.* To harrow (ground): *aperiet et ~abit terram suam* Isa. 28.24 (AE 374.9).

occoecatio: see **occaecatio**.

occoeco: see **occaeco**.

occultatio ~onis, *f.* A concealment, hiding: *unde quasi ~o facierum ab Ipso* Isa. 53.3 (AC 1846.3); *~onem mali* AE 283.7.

occulte, *adv.* (compar. *~ius*) In a secret manner, secretly: *conatum ad bonum qui ~e operatur* FI 39; *quam oppugnant quidam apertius, quidam ~ius* ES 2080.

occulto[1] ~are ~avi ~atum, *tr.* **1** To conceal from view, hide: *~abo facies Meas ab iis* Deut. 32.20 (AC 7051.3); *[mala] ~antur in interioribus* AC 7437.2. **2** To keep secret, conceal: *interior homo hodie a plerisque ~atur* AC 7372; *rem, qualis in se est, ~ant* CI 265; *ars...quam...summopere cupiunt ~andam* AM 292.1.

occulto[2], *adv.* Perh. an error for **occulte**: ES 3849.

occultus ~a ~um, *a.* (compar. *~ior*, superl. *~issimus*) **1** Concealed from view, hidden: *~as opes latebrarum* Isa. 45.3 (AC 7091.3); *quod nihil tam ~um sit in mundo, quod non fit manifestum post mortem* CI 462[a].9. **2** Not generally known, secret: *artibus ~is et apertis* AC 6832.9; *hoc hactenus ignoratum fuit, et quoque ~um ex non cognitione sensus spiritualis Verbi* FI 57. **b** *in ~o*, in secret, secretly: *quaerite in ~o, quid cogitant de Deo* AM 497; *in ~issimo volunt dolis fallere* ES 3664.

occumbo ~mbere ~bui, *intr.* To fall dead: *momento [homo] ~mberet mortuus* AC 3884.2; (w. dat.) *interior illorum vita quasi letho ~mberet* AM 285.1.

occupatio ~onis, *f.* A thing which occupies one's mind, occupation: *nisi usus sit ejus affectio vel ~o* DA 43 (= xv titulus).

occupo ~are ~avi ~atum, *tr.* **1** To be in possession of, occupy (a place): *angeli...qui ~abant cordis provinciam* AC 170; *quod, ut primum aliquis locus a spiritibus bonis relinquitur, ~etur a malis* AC 6858; *montes qui ~ati fuerunt a malis* CI 229. **2** (of things) To exercise a preponderating influence on, seize, grip: *frigus quod inferiorem tergi regionem ~abat* AC 1268; *nihil aliud cogitationes eorum ~at* AC 6666.2; *qui ~atus a mundanis* AC 6839; *cum jucundum mali ~at mentes nostras* VR 77.4.

occurro ~rere ~ri ~sum, *intr.* **1** (w. dat.) To come to meet, come up against: *et fuit in via in diversorio, et ~rit illi Jehovah* Exod. 4.24 (AC); *quod charitas ~rat fidei* AC 2435.2; (w. *in* + acc. of the person met, in imitation of Bibl. Hebr.) *~rerunt in eum angeli Dei* Gen. 32.1 (AC). **2** (of events, situations, etc.) To present themselves, happen, occur: *quod nusquam esse potuisset nisi coelestia... ~rerent* AC 1495.2; *quoties similia ~runt* AC 6812. **3** (of words, expressions, etc.) To be used, occur: *quoties in Verbo ~rit profectio* AC 1463.1; *hic sola nomina ~runt* SS 15; (impers., w. *quod*) it is said that, the expression occurs: *saepius ~rit quod mortui sint* AC 1854.1.

occursus ~us, *m.* **1** An encounter, meeting: *virginibus quae...exiverunt in ~um sponsi* Matt. 25.1 (SS 17.1). **2** A coming up against, meeting with (obstacles): *se cavere ab ~u dum ambulat* ES 4221; cf. *torrens ~uum* 3AD 4796.

oceanus ~i, *m.* (Gk.) **1** The whole of the salt water on the face of the globe, the seas, the ocean: *pisces maris... intra 20 aut 50 annos implerent ~um* VR 32.3. **2** Any of the large bodies of sea, ocean: *aquae maximi ~i* AC 7077; *irruerunt [inferna] sicut maximus ~us* AC 8175. **3** A vast mass (of other things), ocean: *sol...est...~us igneus* SS 95.2; VR 79.3; *ii ex ~o isto malorum... depromunt malum* ES 2486.

ocellatura ~ae, *f.* A decorative motif resembling an eye on a dress, perh. rosette: *ex ~is auri vestis ejus* Ps. 45.13 (AC 490).

ocellus ~i, *m.* An eye: *jucunditates...ex oppositis seu intellectualibus ~is potuissent percipere* ES 231.

ochim, *indecl. pl.* (Hebr.) Howling creatures: *implentur domus eorum ~im* Isa. 13.21 (AC 1326.3); *dirae aves noctis, quae vocantur ~im et ijim* AM 264.4.

ociter, *adv.* (compar. *ocius*) Quickly, swiftly: *quod imperceptibiliter seu ~er disponerent vasa memoriae* ES 4042; *abi ocius in plateas* Luke 14.21 (AE 223.22); ES 1073.

octava ~ae, *f.* The rendering of a Hebr. term in the title of Ps. 6: AC 8337.5.

octavus ~a ~um, *a.* Eighth: *initium ~i status* AC 1353.

octennium ~i, *neut.* A period of eight years: *in Arcanis Coelestibus...per ~um elucubratis* CO 23.

octimestris ~is ~e, *a.* Lasting eight months: *per ~e spatium* 1AD 943.

octingenti ~ae ~a, *pl. a.* Eight hundred: Gen. 5.17 (AC).

octo, *indecl. a.* Eight: *sunt ~o viae* CI 520.

October ~bris, *m.* The month of October: ES 3789.

octodecim, *indecl. a.* Eighteen: *juvenes ~im annorum* AM 444.8.

octoginta, *indecl. a.* Eighty: Exod. 7.7 (AC).

octogonus ~a ~um, *a.* (Gk.) Octagonal: *palatium ~um* AM 151ª.2.

ocularis ~is ~e, *a.* **1** Of or performed by the eye, ocular, visible: *quid opus est alia confirmatione, quam ~i illa?* DP 279.6; *~es testes mutui amoris* AM 300.2; *lux ~is* VR 620.2. **2** Endowed with eyes: *credit se...plus ~em quam Argus* VR 165.3.

ocularlter, *adv.* With one's own eyes: *fac mihi videre illa ~er, aut demonstra scientifice quod ita sit, et tunc credam* AC 6015.3.

oculatus ~a ~um, *a.* Provided with eyes, sighted: (masc. as sb.) *ambulationi caeci in die, aut ~i in nocte* VR 177.4.

oculus ~i, *m.* **1** The eye as the organ of vision: *planetae qui coram ~is nostris visibiles sunt* AC 6697; *ante dextrum ~um* AC 7078; *aperientur ~i coecorum* Isa. 35.5 (AC 6989); *ad ~um*, visibly: AC 8249; VR 385.1. **2** The eye as indicating the direction of looking: *attolle ~os tuos circumcirca* Isa. 60.4 (AC 6740); *cum...illuc ~um misi* ES 5254. **3** The eye as indicating the thoughts: [*sensus spiritualis*] *est intus in illo* [sc. *sensu literae*]...*sicut cogitatio in ~is* SS 5; *ex illorum ~is emicabat sicut igniculus libidinis ad sexum* AM 44.2. **4** The eye as indicating a certain way of observing or considering: *lustra illam* [sc. *pleuram*] *~o anatomico* DP 180.3; *non vident talia ~is rationis in fronte, sed in occipitio* VR 12.2. **5** The intellect's power of perception, the inner eye: *cujus ~i aperti sunt super omnes vias hominum* Jer. 32.19 (VI 2); *intellectualis ~us* ES 231.

ode ~es, *f.* (Gk.) (acc. sg. *~en*, gen. pl. *~arum*, acc. pl. *~as*) A song: *interjectis cantibus ~arum suavissimis* AM 3.3.

odi ~isse, *tr.* (pf. w. pres. sense) (gerund *~endus*, pres. pple. *~ens* Ezek. 16.27 (AC 3024.3) and *~iens* Exod. 18.21 (AC)) To hate, loathe: *qui facit injustum...is ~it proximum* AC 8123; *~isti opera Nicolaitarum* Rev. 2.6 (AR); (of things) *malum vitae...interius ~it vera* FI 30.

odium ~i, *neut.* **1** Hatred, loathing: *misericordiam* [*vertunt*] *in ~um et in crudelitatem* AC 7343.1; (w. pl.) an instance or kind of hatred: *in ~is et vindictis inter se* AC 6963.2; *fraudes, adulteria, ~a* VI 24. **2** *~o habere*, to hate: *qui maximo ~o habent omne quod bonum et verum* AC 59.1; *ut ~o internecino habeant hominem* CI 249.

odor ~oris, *m.* A smell, odour: *sicut ~or malus qui ferit nares* CI 245; *sphaera ~oris a virgulto circum illud* AM 386.1; *~or volans in athmosphaera* VR 30.2; (in sacrifices) *qui fecerit ignitum ~oris quietationis Jehovae* Num. 15.14 (AC 8013.3).

odoratio ~onis, *f.* The act of smelling: *perceptio est principium ~onis* ES(M) [4730].

odoratum ~i, *neut.* A scent, smell: *jucunda ex unoquovis exhalant, sicut ~a ex omni vegetabili* AM 524.4.

odoratus ~us, *m.* The sense of smell: *ex visu, auditu, gustu, ~u, tactu* AC 7038.2; VR 12.3.

odorifer ~era ~erum, *a.* Emitting odours, smelling: *eorum sphaera cum vertitur in ~eram, est quasi odor panis usti* AC 1514; *fragrantias ex...~eris foliis exhalatas* AM 8.2; (neut. as sb.) CI 402.

odoro ~are ~avi ~atum, *tr.* and **odoror** ~ari ~atus sum, *tr.* To perceive by the sense of smell, smell: **1** (act.): *quod e longinquo* [*apes*] *~ent flores* VR 12.7; *si...jucunda sentirentur nare seu ~arentur* AM 272. **2** (dep.): *~atus est odorem vestium illius* Gen. 27.27 (AC); *quod ~ari significet percipere* AE 324.1.

odoror: see **odoro**.

oeconomia ~ae, *f.* (Gk.) Economic affairs: *leges tam justitiae quam ~ae* CH 83 (= iv.3).

oeconomicus ~a ~um, *a.* (Gk.) Concerned with economic affairs: *regimina...~a, civilia, et ecclesiastica* AE 1120.1; CH 78 (= iv.2).

oeconomus ~i, *m.* (Gk.) A person in charge of a household or estate, steward: *laudavit Dominus ~um injustitiae* Luke 16.8 (DP 250.5); *minister ~us* AS 333.

oecumenicus ~a ~um, *a.* also **aec-**. Applicable to the worldwide Christian Church, worldwide, ecumenical: *hoc symbolum ut ~um seu universale a tota Ecclesia Christiana receptum est* VR 172.1; *numne omnis Ecclesia usque ad summe haereticam...clamore implet regiones et urbes quod sola sit orthodoxa et ~a* VR 759.2.

oesophagus ~i, *m.* (Gk.) also **aesophagus**. (anat.) The tube which conveys food from the mouth to the stomach, oesophagus: AC 5175; AS 408.

oestrum: see **oestrus**.

oestrus ~i, *m.* (Gk., literally 'gadfly') also **aestrum** ~i, *neut.*, **aestrus** ~i, *m.*, and **oestrum** ~i, *neut.* Intense stimulation, goading: *in igneae suae libidinis ~o sunt* AC 825; *ex ~o lasciviae* AM 79.11; *qui ex ~o amoris sui dominati sunt* AR 755; *quod...flagraverit ~o venereo* ES 4496.

offa ~ae, *f.* A small piece of food, morsel: *sicut Deus...quosdam sicut ~as diabolo traderet* VR 629.

offendiculum ~i, *neut.* **1** An obstruction: *coram coeco dare ~um* Lev. 19.14 (AC 6989). **2** (transf.) Anything which gives offence, a stumbling block, impediment: *mittet...angelos suos, qui colligent...omnia ~a* Matt. 13.41 (CI 570.2); *quod in horto...positae fuerint binae arbores...haec in ~um* DP 241.2; DP 258.5.

offendo ~dere ~di ~sum, *tr.*, *intr.* **1** (tr.) To encounter, meet, come across: *quoscunque desiderant, possunt ~dere* AC 1114; *quaesivi ubinam ~derem... illos* VR 17.1. **b** (intr., w. dat., of things) to be presented, occur (to): *quae objecta tunc memoriae meae ~derunt* ES 3671. **2** (intr.) To meet with obstructions, stumble: *~dimus in meridie* Isa. 59.10 (AC 7711.2). **3** (intr.) To give offence, offend: *in quibuscunque animadvertit se ~disse voluntate aut loquela aut facto* BCP (VI 6); (pass.) to take offence, be offended: *~duntur et spirant usque necem omnium* AE 137.3.

offensa ~ae, *f.* A sin, offence: *si animadvertit ~as tales esse* BCP (VI 6).

offero ~rre obtuli oblatum, *tr.* **1** To present, confer (a favour): *quod potiora ~rant illis* CI 406; *benevolentias oblatas ab uxoribus* AM 285.2. **2** To present to a deity, offer (sacrifices, etc.): *quod nusquam num oblatum sit pro altero* AC 1823.1; *si...obtuleris munus tuum super altare* Matt. 5.23 (VI 73). **3** (refl. or pass.) To present oneself, appear: *~runt se falsa loco verorum* AC 7012; *si...verum ~rtur* AC 8087.

officiarius ~i, *m.* A person charged with an official function, official, officer: *omnis functio...* [*dilabitur*], *nisi* [*pendet*] *ab uno ~o* VR 10; ES 4363.

officina ~ae, *f.* A shop: *in...~is mercatoriis* ES 457; *eram in quadam ~a ad emendum costum* ES 2954.

officiose, *adv.* Solicitously: *~e rogavi* AM 155ª.4; AM 297.

officiositas ~atis, *f.* The quality of being attentive to one's obligations, solicitude: AM 164.

officiosus ~a ~um, *a.* Attentive to one's obligations, solicitous: *boni, mites, ~i* ES 4574.

officium ~i, *neut.* **1** A service performed for another, friendly act: *affectatione ~orum* AC 1509; *ut...~a praestet* AC 7038.1. **2** That which one ought to do, one's duty: *quod uxor non possit intrare in ~a propria viri* AM 156ª.3. **3** A particular function, office: *voluptatibus honorum et ~orum in republica* AC 995.2; *ita nominantur ex ~o qualicunque sunt* AC 1705.

offula ~ae, *f.* A small scrap of food, morsel: *sicut ~ae datae Cerbero* VR 453.

offundo: see **obfundo**.

oggannio ~nire ~nivi, *intr.* To speak in a snarling fashion, growl: *~niunt ad nomen Ipsius* VR 683.2.

oh, *interj.* (expressing astonishment) Oh!: *oh qualia nunc in terris tempora* AM 152ª.1; *oh quam simplices estis!* VR 77.2.

ohalim, *indecl. pl.* (Hebr.) Transliteration of a Hebr. word for tabernacles or tents: AC 4391.1.

olea ~ae, *f.* An olive tree: *viti, ~ae, cedro* CI 111; AM 183.1; *arborem ~ae* Hag. 2.19 (AE 403.9).

oleo ~lere ~lui, *intr.* To emit a smell, stink: *falsum... non ~let nisi appositum sit vero* AC 7319; *libidinosum quod ~luit sicut caenum* AM 78.5.

oleosus ~a ~um, *a.* Resembling or rich in oil, oily: *panis, proventus humi, erit pinguis et ~us* Isa. 30.23 (AC 415.2).

oleum ~i, *neut.* **1** Olive oil: *Samarita...obligavit vulnera ejus et infudit ~um et vinum* Luke 10.34 (AC 6708); (used for anointing kings) *quod rex ~o ungeretur* AE 31.6; (as fuel for lamps) *vidi quosdam habere lampades et non ~um* VI 26. **2** The oil of any plant: *~um olivae* AC 886.1; *arbores ~i* AM 13.2; *postes ex ligno ~i* AM 103.3; *seminula* [*fici*]*...circumfusa dulci quasi ~o* ES 2187.

olfacio ~facere ~feci ~factum, *tr.* To perceive by the sense of smell, scent: AC 4624.

olfactus ~us, *m.* The sense of smell: *quod visum habeat* [*spiritus*], *quod auditum, quod ~um* AC 444; CI 402; an instance of smelling, whiff: *illi ad primum ~um amoris conjugialis aufugiunt in cavernas* AM 212.

olidus ~a ~um, *a.* Foul-smelling, rank: *ructus tetri, graveolenti, ~i* AM 253.

olim, *adv.* In former time, of old, once: *tentationes spirituales parum hodie notae sunt, nec permittuntur ita ut ~im* AC 762; *quidam qui ~im inter sapientiores fuit* CI 322.1.

oliva ~ae, *f.* The fruit of the olive tree, olive: *arboribus ~ae, aurantii, et citri* AM 8.3; *mons ~arum*, the Mount of Olives: Zech. 14.4 (DD 4); an olive tree: *~am virentem* Jer. 11.16 (AC 886.1).

olivetum ~i, *neut.* A plantation of olive trees, olive grove: AE 638.16.

olla ~ae, *f.* An earthenware vessel, pot: *omnis ~a in Hierosolyma* Zech. 14.21 (AC 7857.2).

olor ~oris, *m.* A swan: *columba, avis pulchra et ~or* DP 292.2; AM 155ª.5.

olus ~eris, *neut.* A green vegetable: *sicut ~us herbae dedi vobis id omne* Gen. 9.3 (AC); *vasa...trituratoria sicut quae sunt ~erum* AC 824.

olympiacus ~a ~um, *a.* (Gk.) Olympic (w. ref. to contests or sports): *Gymnasia ~a* AM 151ª.1.

omega: see **omegah**.

omegah ~ae, *f.* and *indecl.* (Gk., = English 'big O') also **omega**. Omega, the last letter of the Greek alphabet: *alphah est prima et ~ah est ultima syllaba in* *alphabeto Graeco* VR 19.2; (as a type of what is last) *Ego sum Alpha et ~a, Principium et Finis* Rev. 1.8 (AR).

omen ~inis, *neut.* An omen; *primis ~inibus*, with the first omens of marriage, i.e., for the first time, neither previously having been married (perh. with ref. to Vergil, *Aeneid* 1.346): *desponsati et pacti sumus, et juncti primis ~inibus* AM 444.2.

omentum ~i, *neut.* (anat.) The membrane which covers the intestines, omentum: *sanguinem...tradunt ~i venis* ES 1007.

omer ~eris, *m.* A Hebrew dry measure of approximately 5 pints or 2.3 litres: AC 10262.4; AE 373.1.

ominor ~ari ~atus sum, *tr., intr.* To conclude as from omens, guess: *spiritus...plura ~ati, quid visio haec dicere vellet* ES 2691; (w. *quod*) *Ecclesia primitiva... nusquam potuit ~ari, quod successura sit Ecclesia quae...* VR 638.

omissio ~onis, *f.* Failure to perform, omission: *ex ~one charitatis* FI 62.

omitto omittere omisi omissum, *tr.* **1** To release, let go: *homines...tertio aetatis anno amissos aut omissos in sylvis* AM 151ª.3; *ut...oraret, ut is eum omitteret* ES 291. **2** To leave undone, give up: *qui...ex doctrina cogitant..., illi omittunt bona* AE 233.2; FI 39; (w. inf.) to fail (to): *solum omittit facere illa propter mundum* VI 63.2. **3** To leave out (from a series), omit: *ut ne quidem vocula...omissa esse potuerit* AC 7933.3.

omnimode, *adv.* In all ways, in every respect: *unius amor regnans non est ~e similis alterius* CI 486; AM 143; VR 57.2.

omnimodus ~a ~um, *a.* Operating in all respects, total, absolute: *potentia ~a* AC 9720; *est...communicatio affectionum...~a* CI 552.2; *~a requies a laboribus* AM 207.1.

omnino, *adv.* **1** In all respects, completely, utterly: *novi Ephraimum...quod ~o scortatus sit* Hos. 5.3 (SS 79.6); *dicitur...ad communicantes ut ~o...paenitentiam agant* AR 531.8; *~o cavete vobis, ne aliud... cogitetis* AM 9.1. **2** To be sure, certainly: *dicebant quod ~o facies habeant, et nunc quod pulchras* ES 1672 ½. **3** As a general observation, in general: *discrimina proximi, quae homo Ecclesiae ~o scire debet* AC 6706; *quod universum sit opus continens Divini Amoris...et sic ~o opus cohaerens a primis ad ultima* VR 47; VR 75.7.

omnipotens ~ntis, *a.* Having all power, omnipotent: *coelum ~ntis Dei* AC 6927; *Dominus Deus ~ns [dicitur] pro Jehovah Zebaoth* Isa. 6.3 (AC 2921.5).

omnipotenter, *adv.* With exercise of all power, omnipotently: *non est contradictio ~er agere secundum leges justitiae* VR 74.4.

omnipotentia ~ae, *f.* Omnipotence: *~a praedicatur ex quantitate* AC 3934.1.

omnipraesens ~ntis, *a.* Present at every place, omnipresent: *Divinum procedens a Domino ~ns est ac ubivis videt ubinam aliquid nutat* CI 593.

omnipraesentia ~ae, *f.* The quality of being omnipresent: *de Ipsius ~a absque spatio* AM 328.2; VR 63.

omniprovidens ~ntis, *a.* All-providing: *quomodo Deus potest...omnisciens et ~ns esse* AS 21.

omnis ~is ~e, *a.* **1** (sg.) Each single, every: *intentant ~i modo perdere illum* AC 6724.2; *videbit Ipsum ~is oculus* Rev. 1.7 (AR). **2** (w. pl.) All: *~es hae cognitiones* FI 27; *~ia discrimina* AC 6706; (masc. pl. as sb.) all people, everyone: *Dominus...~ium salutem vult* AC 6639.3; (neut. pl. as sb.) everything: *~ia quae in caelo* VR 3.1. **b** *~es et singuli*, each and every person: *putantes sic quod vita Domini non influat in ~es et singulos* ES 3666; *~ia et singula*, each and every thing: *[Dominus] ~ia et singula novit* AC 1049; *in ~ibus et singulis Verbi* SS 9. **3** The whole quantity of, all: *~e bonum procedit a Domino* AC 6706; *quod ex amore conjugiali sit ~is pulchritudo angelis* CI 382; *~i ardore* ES 4843. **4** The whole of, all: *~is plenitudo Divinitatis* VR 11.1 (Col. 2.9); *quod ~is religio sit vitae* VI 1 titulus; *experientia...~em paginam impleret* ES 2150. **5** (neut. as sb.) The sum total, the only thing that matters: *ad Dominum, Qui iis erat ~e* AC 54; *memoria particularium...~e facit* AC 1639; (w. gen.) *Deus est ~e Ecclesiae* VR 14.1; so, *~e in ~ibus*: *Dominum, Qui est ~e in ~ibus Sui regni* AC 1585.1. **6** All that can exist, any: *quod...[angeli] loqui possint cum illo ad ~em distantiam* CI 255.2; *coram ~i illo qui statum mentis suae formavit a Deo* VR 6.2; (in neg. sentence) *qui... cupiunt...deflorare virgines...absque ~i fine conjugii* AC 828.

omnisciens ~ntis, *a.* Knowing everything, omniscient: *quomodo Deus potest omnipraesens, ~ns, et omniprovidens esse* AS 21.

omniscientia ~ae, *f.* Knowledge of everything, omniscience: *esse in ~a omnium Divinorum* AC 2572.1.

omniscius ~a ~um, *a.* Knowing everything, omniscient: *quod Deus ~us sit, hoc est, percipiat, videat, et sciat omnia* VR 59.

onager ~gri, *m.* A wild ass, onager: *~ger est...mulus deserti seu asinus sylvestris* AC 1949.1; *cum ~gris habitatio ejus* Dan. 5.21 (AE 376.23).

onero ~are ~avi ~atum, *tr.* To load, burden: *currus ~ati varii generis mercibus* AC 8215.2; (fig.) *vae multiplicanti non suum...et ~anti super se lutum* Hab. 2.6 (AC 6669.2).

onerosus ~a ~um, *a*. Burdensome: *verbo sunt ~i, seu solum onera reipublicae* ES 2501.

onus ~eris, *neut*. **1** A heavy object to be carried, burden: *asini portantes ~era* AM 232.5; *affligere illum* [sc. *populum*] *~eribus* Exod. 1.11 (AC). **2** A burdensome task: *non impono super vos aliud onus* Rev. 2.24 (AR). **3** Anything which constitutes a source of trouble, nuisance: *sunt onerosi, seu solum ~era reipublicae* ES 2501.

onustus ~a ~um, *a*. (w. abl.) Laden (with): *cum navi mercibus... ~a* VR 378.1.

onyche ~es, *f*. (ad. Gk. *onyx*) A kind of aromatic substance, onycha: *accipe tibi aromata fragrantia, stacten, et ~en, et galbanum* Exod. 30.34 (AC); AE 324.1.

opacitas ~atis, *f*. Lack of light, gloom: *dies nubis et ~atis* Zeph. 1.15 (AC 1839.5).

opaco ~are ~avi ~atum, *tr*. To make dark or gloomy, darken: *lux...pellucet in hoc, et ~atur in illo* VR 8.4; (transf.) *hoc intellectum rationalem hebetat et ~at* SS 95.3.

opacus ~a ~um, *a*. Poorly lit, dark, gloomy: *noctua videt...ipsum solem ut globum ~um et furvum* AM 233.3; *~a sylva* ES(M) 4655; (neut. pl. as sb.) *influxu lucis in ~a terrae* VR 34.3.

opalinus ~a ~um, *a*. Having an iridescent appearance, opalescent: *tunicae...ex serico coloris ~i* AM 15; *nubem ~i coloris* VR 112.7.

opera ~ae, *f*. **1** Work performed, labour: *admetiar pretium ~ae illorum* Isa. 65.7 (AC 6960.5). **2** Work allocated, a task: *imponit illis ~as, quas quotidie facturi sint* UJ(P) 227. **3** Handicraft, skill: *varia quae ~arum muliebrium sunt* AM 370; *~ae manuariae* SA 105 (= vii.5.[3]). **4** Industry, effort: *cavent angeli summa ~a, ne...* CI 450; *quod mandatum...omni zelo et ~a obeunt* VR 108; *~am dare* (w. dat.), to devote one's time (to), attend (to): ES 1950.

operarius ~i, *m*. A workman, worker: *parabolae Domini de ~is in vineis* AC 1069.5; *~i iniquitatis* Matt. 7.23 (CI 471).

operatio ~onis, *f*. The act of working, functioning, operation: *tempus pugnae est tempus ~onis Domini* AC 63; *activitates interiores inservientes ejus* [sc. *hominis*] *animi ~onibus* CI 418; (pl.) processings, workings: *~ones Domini...quae sunt reformatio, regeneratio, innovatio, vivificatio, sanctificatio, justificatio, purificatio, remissio peccatorum, et demum salvatio...influunt* VR 146.

operator ~oris, *m*. One who performs work, executor: *de Spiritu Sancto ~ore* VR 4.3.

operculum ~i, *neut*. A covering, cover: *quod teneant faciem suam versus anteriora porrectam cum ~o cano* [Tafel; *laxo* J D Odhner] *superinduti* ES 559.

operimentum ~i, *neut*. A covering: *quod spiritus corpus habeat sicut quoddam ~um* ES 2355.

operio ~rire ~rui ~rtum, *tr*. **1** To cover up, hide: *per aquas quae hos ~ruerunt* AC 8125; *nihil ~rtum est quod non retegendum est* Luke 12.2 (CI 507). **2** (transf.) To overwhelm, cover: *quod falsitates... ~ruerint illos* AC 8272; (w. abl.) *~riretur ille contumeliis tectis in caetibus virorum* AM 469.

operor ~ari ~atus sum, *tr*., *intr*. **1** (tr.) To produce by work, work, perform, make: *discedite a Me, ~antes iniquitatem* Matt. 7.23 (AC 7778.4); *in ~ando usus* FI 17; *quomodo natura ~ata est universum* VR 79.2. **2** (tr.) To obtain by work, work for: *~amini cibum, non qui perit* John 6.27 (DD 27). **3** (intr.) To operate, act: *angeli ~antur per vera et bona fidei* AC 8002.2; (w. *in* + acc.) *nusquam coeleste potest ~ari in naturale* AC 1702.2.

opertura ~ae, *f*. That which covers, a covering: *potest ...angelus...lustrare qualia sunt, non obstantibus ~is* CI 586.

opes: see **ops**.

opifex ~icis, *m*. A craftsman: *opere ~icis lapidis* Exod. 28.11 (AC); *haec...sunt condita ab ~ice universi* AM 12.2.

opificium ~i, *neut*. The product of a craftsman, manufacture: *quod universum sit ~um unius Dei* VR 13.3.

opimitas ~atis, *f*. Richness: *secundum cujus* [sc. *praedae*] *~atem et copiam dispensat jura* VR 428.

opimo ~are ~avi ~atum, *tr*. To endow with riches: (transf.) *felicitas...facit ut gaudia sint gaudia, ~at illa* AM 6.5.

opimus ~a ~um, *a*. (compar. *~ior*) (of food) Rich, sumptuous: *~ae dapes, cupediae et lautitiae* AM 6.5; (of a land) rich in resources, prosperous: *Jehovah Deus tuus introducturus est te in terram ~am* Deut. 8.7 (AE 70.3).

opinio ~onis, *f*. A particular belief, opinion: *communis ~o hodie est quod omnis homo sit aeque proximus* AC 6704; *quae...ad favorem cujuscunque ~onis trahi queunt* AC 7127.2.

opinor ~ari ~atus sum, *intr*. To hold a belief, have an opinion: (w. *de*) *illi non aliter de Deo ~ari possunt* AC 6877; (w. *quod*) *quidam ~antur quod pauperes recipiantur* CI 357; (w. acc. and inf.) *quod ~entur et dicant se credere* FI 31; (w. pred.) to regard as, think: *spiritus quos ~atus sum bonos* ES 1110.

opipare, *adv*. Sumptuously, richly: *qui...pro fine habuerunt solum ~e vivere* AC 1509; ES 2500.

opiparus ~a ~um, *a.* (of food) Luxurious, sumptuous, rich: *super...mensis erunt edulia delicata et ~a* AM 3.3; ES 777; (neut. as sb.) ES 2513.

opitulatio ~onis, *f.* The bringing of aid, help: *clamando ad scorta consocia ut ad famulas pro ~one* AM 512.1.

opitulor ~ari ~atus sum, *intr.* To bring aid, help: (w. dat.) *homo dat pauperibus, ~atur egenis* VI 9; (pass. in gerundive) *qui apparent...~andi* AC 6705.

opobalsamum ~i, *neut.* The gold-coloured oleoresin from a balsam tree, balm of Gilead, opobalsam: AC 4453.3.

oportet ~ere ~uit, *impers. intr. vb.* (w. inf.) There is an obligation, there ought, it is proper: *~et avertere faciem* CI 223; *quae ~et fieri cito* Rev. 1.1 (AR); (w. acc. and inf.) *dicebant quod ~eat quemcunque...secum ferre aliquid auri* AM 268.2; (also w. subject) *quod illarum* [sc. *tellorum*] *usus insignior...~eat esse* AC 6697.

oppeto ~ere ~ii, *intr.* To encounter, meet with (death): *quod pro amoribus mundi etiam mortem ~ant* ES Index s.v. 'martyres' (p. 63 Tafel), referring to ES 3188.

oppidulum ~i, *neut.* A small town, village: 3AD 4578.

oppidum ~i, *neut.* A town: *ex Bethleem, ~o ubi David erat* John 7:42 (AC 3008.1).

oppignero ~are ~avi ~atum, *tr.* To take as a pledge: *si ~ando ~averis vestem socii tui* Exod. 22.25 (AC).

oppignoratus ~a ~um, *a.* Bound by mutual pledges, pledged: *firmaverunt sponsiones per munera, quod sint ~i* AM 300.1.

oppleo ~lere ~levi ~letum, *tr.* **1** To fill up, cover: *quod falsis...~leta sit* [*mens naturalis*] AC 7387; *cum... illud involucrum, quod est pleura...ulceribus ~letur* DP 180.3. **2** To set (with precious stones): *et ~lebis illud* [sc. *pectorale*] *oppletura lapidis* Exod. 28.17 (AC).

oppletura ~ae, *f.* A setting (of precious stones): *et opplebis illud* [sc. *pectorale*] *~a lapidis* Exod. 28.17 (AC).

oppletus ~a ~um, *a.* (pf. pple. of **oppleo**) (superl. *~issimus*) Filled up, full: *mundi illi spirituum ~issimi sunt copia alluentium* AC 2121.

oppono ~nere ~sui ~situm, *tr.* **1** (refl.) To set oneself against, be opposed: *quod falsum se ~siturum* AC 6889; (w. dat.) *qui se ~nunt doctrinae charitatis* AC 6779. **2** (pass. w. dat., of a term) To be used in distinction (from), be used as opposite (to): *quod 'tenebrae' ibi ~nantur 'luci'* AC 7711.2; FI 61.

opportunus ~a ~um, *a.* (of times) Suitable, opportune: *~a tempora observando* ES 2764; ES 5864.

oppositio ~onis, *f.* **1** Activity directed against a person or thing, opposition: *quod ~o sit contra Divinum* AC 7042. **2** The fact of being opposites: *de ~one amoris scortatorii et amoris conjugialis* AM 423 titulus.

oppositus ~a ~um, *a.* (pf. pple. of **oppono**) **1** Set in an inverted or contrary position, opposite: *in* or *ex ~o*, in the opposite position: *crederent et navim et nautas, cum in ~o sint, delabi* AC 1378.2; *ex ~o ad Solem coeli* AC 10809. **2** Acting against, opposing: *quando binae vires sibi ~ae agunt* AC 8168; *conatus...~os* AC 8209.2; (w. dat.) *in malis prorsus ~is bono* AC 8313.3; *falsitas...~a veritati* FI 29. **3** Utterly contrasting, reversed, opposite: *in ~o sensu* AC 1071.2; (neut. as sb.) [*conjugiale*] *in via mutatur...multis modis, et quandoque in ~um* AM 203; *de Domini adventu... redemptione et salvatione...et simul de ~is* DD 37.1.

oppressio ~onis, *f.* Harsh treatment, oppression: *vidi ~onem qua Aegyptii opprimunt illos* Exod. 3.9 (AC); *posuisti ~onem super lumbos nostros* Ps. 66.11 (AE 355.35).

oppressor ~oris, *m.* An oppressor: *conficiam ~ores tuos* Zeph. 3.19 (DD 4); ES 391.

opprimo ~rimere ~ressi ~ressum, *tr.* To treat harshly, oppress: *quod filii Israelis...~ressi fuerint ab Aegyptiis* AC 6657.3; ES 217.

opprobrium ~i, *neut.* Contemptuous treatment, insult, contumely: *memento, Domine, ~i servorum Tuorum* Ps. 89.50 (AC 6960.2); *~um populorum non portabis amplius* Ezek. 36.15 (SS 86); *~a mihi dixerunt* ES 1141; a cause of insult, reproach: *ne id ~um illi fuisset* AM 481.

oppugnantia ~ae, *f.* Contrary action, repugnance: *quia 'ira' est aversio, est etiam ~a contra bonum et verum* AC 5798.1.

oppugnatio ~onis, *f.* A hostile action, attack: *per ~ones urbis illius describuntur ~ones veri a falsis* AC 6419.2.

oppugnator ~oris, *m.* An attacker: ES 1737.

oppugno ~are ~avi ~atum, *tr.* To take hostile action against, attack: *~ari portas* Judg. 5.8 (AC 2851.11); *ut ~ent te, et non praevaleant tibi* Jer. 15.20 (AE 70.3); (fig.) *vera sunt quae ~ari possunt* AC 6677.

ops opis, *f.* also **opes** opum, *f. pl.* **1** (sg.) Assistance, help, aid (of a person): *quod...nihil opis ferre possint* AC 940.4; *Dominus solus vicit inferna, cum nulla ope alicujus angeli* DD 14.9; (of a thing) *ex quibus* [*nominibus*] *nihil potest hauriri nisi ope sensus spiritualis* SS 15.1; AS 93. **2** (pl.) Means, resources, wealth: *et sumserunt omnes opes Sodomae et Amorae* Gen. 14.11 (AC); *thesauraria sunt ubi opes reponuntur* AC 6661.2; *opes medicae*, the resources of medicine: ES 4571.

optatum ~i, *neut.* (neut. pf. pple. of **opto**) That which is desired, one's wish: *~o suo potiuntur* AC 8244; AM 10.3.

optatus ~a ~um, *a.* (pf. pple. of **opto**) (compar. *~ior*) Desirable, to be wished for: *malis spiritibus nihil ~ius est quam...* AE 783.5.

optice[1] ~es, *f.* (Gk.) The science of optics: *consule gnaros scientiae ~es* AM 233.4; VR 64.2.

optice[2], *adv.* In an optical manner, to the sight, optically: *cylindrus politus, in quo ~e repraesentatur imago* ES 2164; ES 4214.

opticus ~a ~um, *a.* (Gk.) Of or concerned with sight, optic: *cylindros ~os* AC 1871; *ex obstructione nervi ~i* VR 346.2; *scientiae utiles sunt physica, ~a...* ES(M) 4578; *vitrum ~um*, a magnifying glass: CI 76; *tuba ~a*, a telescope: VR 22.3.

optimas ~atis, *m.* A person of excellent character, good fellow: *quod [eum] agnoscat pro ~ate* AC 724.

optime, *adv.* (used as superl. of **bene**) Extremely well: *quod ~e novi* ES 1150.

optimus ~a ~um, *a.* (used as superl. of **bonus**) Best, most excellent: *tertium genus, quod ~um* AC 7801; (w. gen.) *angelorum ~i* CI 50.

optio ~onis, *f.* A choice, option: *nonne despiceret ~onem* AM 333.2.

opto ~are ~avi ~atum, *tr.* To wish for (something desirable), hope for, long for: *is coelum...alteri ~at et vult* AC 6822; *quod obtinuerint...quicquid ~assent* ES 2236; to express in words a wish for, wish: *~abam felicem adventum* VR 12.1.

opulentia ~ae, *f.* The quality of possessing much wealth, wealthiness: *propter dignitatem aut ~am sibi acquirendam* AC 1774; AM 250.

opulentus ~a ~um, *a.* (compar. *~ior*, superl. *~issimus*) **1** Possessing much wealth, wealthy: *dives et ~us* AE 238.1; *inter ~iores numeratus* ES 777. **2** Characteristic of wealth, rich: *in supereminentibus dominiis, ac ~issimis gazis* AM 7.1.

opus ~eris, *neut.* **1** A deed, act: *propter malitiam ~erum vestrorum* Jer. 21.12 (AC 6997.4); (esp. in theology) *fidem...salvificam dicunt absque ~eribus* AC 4683.1; *~era Legis*, the acts prescribed by the Law: AR 571; *in ~ere conjugii* 'in the marital act' ES 3768. **2** (w. ref. to the maker) A product, work: *~us digitorum Dei* AC 63; *~ere pistoris* Gen. 40.17 (AC); a written work, book: *in ~ere De Coelo et Inferno* EA 11; *ut sit sicut facies ante ~us quod sequitur* VR 1. **3** A prescribed piece of work, task: *quare...abstrahitis populum ab ~eribus ejus?* Exod. 5.4 (AC); *illa singulatim exponere...magni voluminis ~us foret* VR 75.7. **b** *maximi* (and sim.) *~eris est*, it is a mighty task: *maximi ~eris est reducere ideas Christianorum ad unum Deum* ES(M) 4623; *hoc prolixi ~eris foret* 3AD 5016. **4** *~us est* (w. abl.), there is need (of): *quid ~us tunc nisi Sola Fide...?* SE 114.1; *longiori tempore ~us est* ES 4308; (w. inf.) *non ~us fuisset idem dicere* AC 435; (w. *ut*) *non ~us fuisset ut hic diceretur quod esset frater* AC 1222. **5** (in neg. sentences) *~us habere*, to need: (w. abl.) *haec non ~us habent confirmatione* AC 367.1; (w. gen.) *Dominus... nullius ~us habet* ES 1870; (w. inf.) *ita ut non ~us haberem attrahere animam* ES 1614; ES 3549; (w. *ut*) *non ~us habet ut videat* AC 626.

opusculum ~i, *neut.* A short written work, publication: *in ~o De Equo Albo* SS 9.

ora ~ae, *f.* **1** An edge, border: *folia ex argento, et horum ~as exornatas smaragdis* AM 13.1. **2** *~a maritima*, the shore of the sea, coast: *prospexi ad ~am maritimam,...et vidi ibi magnificum navale* AR 463.1.

oraculum ~i, *neut.* An oracular response, oracle: *~um Divinum* AC 1574.3; also, a source of prophecies, oracle: *sumus per scientiam mysteriorium illius fidei ~a* VR 182.3.

oralis ~is ~e, *a.* Expressed in speech, oral: *pugna ~is sicut inter...litigantes* VR 124.2; *in pietate ~i* AE 325.3.

orantius: see **aurantius**.

oratio ~onis, *f.* **1** The act of praying: *quid ~o oris, si non ei inest mens...?* AC 1094; *non fidendum ~oni* AC 8179.3. **2** A specific prayer: *ex ~one, quae in templis ...legitur coram populo* VI 4; *~o Domini* or *Dominica*, the Lord's Prayer: AC 1875; AE 48.3.

orator ~oris, *m.* An orator, speaker: *quod fuerint in mundo ~ores...et quod operam dederint facundiae* AM 381.

oratorius ~a ~um, *a.* Characterized by oratory, rhetorical: *praedicationes ~ae* VR 798.8; *paenitentiam... oralem et ~am* SE 52.

orbatio ~onis, *f.* Deprivation of children: *cum... orbitas seu ~o dicitur* AC 5536.2; (fig., of other things) *'fames' pro ~one cognitionum* AC 1460.3.

orbicularis ~is ~e, *a.* Running in loops, curving: *operatio eorum [gyrorum] est diversa, sed est communiter ~is* AC 5183.

orbiculus ~i, *m.* A small globe, ball: *~us super basin pyramidalem* AC 947; *fasciae colligatae ad fines adamantinis ~is* AM 7.2.

orbis ~is, *m.* **1** A globe, sphere: *quod aliqui eorum [sc. planetarum] habeant lunas quae...circum ~em suum...vagantur* AC 6697; *in...planetario ~e* VR 22.3.

2 *~is terrarum*, the Earth: *idololatriae, quae impleverunt totum terrarum ~em* AM 342.3. 3 The world as composed of the people in it: *qui magni in ~e voluerint esse* AC 953; *~i ignotum* AC 425; (esp. w. defining adj.) the people of a particular section of the world: *nondum ~i erudito notum* AC 1756.4; *in Christiano ~e* CI 311.1; *in toto Europaeo ~e* VR 159.3. 4 A circular curve, loop, ring: *cohors se glomeravit in ~em, faciebus ad facies conversis* AM 2.3; *arbores hae in continua serie consitae erant, quae...pergebat in perennes ~es seu gyros, sicut perpetuae helicis* AM 13.2.

orbita ~ae, *f.* A circular track, orbit: *~a primum plana* AC 5188.2; ES(M) 4660.

orbitas ~atis, *f.* The fact of being without children: *venient tibi duo illa momento in die uno, ~as et viduitas* Isa. 47.9 (AC 7297.2).

orbo ~are ~avi ~atum, *tr.* 1 To deprive of children, make childless: *consumens hominem tu, et ~ans populos tuos fuisti* Ezek. 36.13 (AE 280.10); (absol.) *foris ~abit gladius* Deut. 32.25 (AC 7353). 2 (w. abl.) To deprive (of): *sic ~arentur omni vita* AC 1387; *~are faciem rubore* VR 41.3.

orbus ~a ~um, *a.* Having no children, childless: *~am faciam te* Ezek. 5.17 (AC 7102.2).

orchestra ~ae, *f.* (Gk.) A gallery in a theatre or the like, balcony: *in foris tunc sunt elevatae ~ae* AM 17.1; AM 315.2.

orcus ~i, *m.* (Gk.) The underworld of the ancient Greeks: *sequuntur serpentem in ~um, et cohabitant* VR 380.4.

ordinarie, *adv.* Regularly, as a rule: *Dominus super illo monte ~e commoratus est* AE 638.16.

ordinarius ~a ~um, *a.* Regular, ordinary: *visa ~a* AC 1885; *remissus sum in sphaeram ~am* ES 258; *miles ~us* ES 3191.

ordinate, *adv.* (superl. *~issime*) In an ordered fashion: *omnia genera...ita ~issime distincta sunt ut ne quidem omnium minimum sit quod non distinctum* AC 644; *in serie ~issime disposita* ES 2316.

ordinatio ~onis, *f.* 1 A reducing to order, ordering: *haec ~o facit quod mali...devastentur* AC 7710; (w. pl.) an instance of this: *~ones veri et boni a Domino* AC 8155. 2 The result of ordering, orderly arrangement: *differt ~o totius coeli ab ~one societatis* CI 149. 3 A prescription, ordinance: *secundum ~onem ecclesiasticam* ES(M) 4573.

ordinatus ~a ~um, *a.* (compar. *~ior*, superl. *~issimus*) 1 Set in order, arranged: *instructionis loca... ~a et distincta secundum...genera et species* CI 513. 2 Well-arranged, orderly: *in pellicatu, qui est ~ior et sanior fornicatio* AM 459.5; *in ~issima forma* AC 545.2.

ordino ~are ~avi ~atum, *tr.* 1 To set in order, arrange, dispose: *ille amor in medio est et cirum se ~at singula* AC 6690; *universum ita ~are et formare non potest nisi Deus* VR 12.9; to draw up (troops for battle): *~averunt cum iis praelium* Gen. 14.8 (AC). 2 To issue orders, command, ordain: *facere statutum seu ~are quod prorsus ita doceatur* AE 827.1.

ordior ~diri orsus sum, *intr.*, *tr.* (intr.) To arise, begin: *quia ratiocinia perplurium non ~diuntur nisi quam ex effectibus* AM 385; *post haec...alia vita ~ditur* ES 1117; (tr.) to begin: *vitam propriam ~ditur* AM 446.1; AC 186.

ordo ~inis, *m.* 1 A physical arrangement of objects in a line, row: *pones illas [placentas] in duos ~ines, senos ~ine* Lev. 24.6 (AC 7978.2); *in triplici ~ine pensiles lampades* VR 16.1. 2 The sequence in which things follow, order: *haec bona sequuntur in hoc ~ine; bonum spirituale est supremum, bonum morale est medium, et bonum civile est ultimum* VI 12; *si viro plures uxores fuerint conjungit se cum illis ~ine* AM 47[a]; *in suo ~ine*, in their proper sequence: VR 4.3. 3 The correct order or arrangement of everything in the universe, regarded as ordained by the Lord: **a** (in general): *quod Dominus in mundum venerit, ut omnia...in ~inem redigeret* DD 14.1; [*Dominus*] *redegit illud* [sc. *infernum*] *in ~inem, et sub suam obedientiam* VR 2.2; *quod ~o sit qualitas dispositionis, determinationis et activitatis partium, substantiarum aut entium...* VR 52. **b** (in particular instances): *fides vult dominari ei* [sc. *charitati*], *quod est contra ~inem* AC 365; *magia non aliud est quam perversio ~inis* AC 6692.2; cf. *cum homines inversi ~ines vitae facti sunt* AC 301. 4 An organization of persons serving a particular function, class: *qui ex ~ine civili erant* VR 74.1; *in domo comitis equestris ~inis* ES 4151; esp., a religious order: *ex ~ine Jesuitico* DP 222.2; *omnes e sacro ~ine* VR 138.

oretenus, *adv.* By direct personal contact, face to face: *quod...dictarent id ~us, dicendo etiam quod vellicarent aures nostras* VR 113.5; ES 443; *fides solum ~us* ES 2474.

organice, *adv.* Organically: *annon omnia et singula ibi* [sc. *in corpore humano*] *~e formata sunt ad producendum illa quae amor vult ac intellectus cogitat?* AM 380.6.

organicus ~a ~um, *a.* (Gk.) 1 Of or concerned with bodily organs: *oculus est forma ~a ex qua et per quam visus* AC 4223.1; *ad vitam ~am carnis* AC 6959.2. 2 (of substances) Suitable for the reception of life, organic: *cum substantiis ~is quae interius recipiunt* *influxum coeli* CI 418; (neut. pl. as sb.) *in ipsis ~is hominis compositis et simplicibus...est passivum et activum* AC 718.

organismus ~i, *m.* (Gk.) Organic structure: *in mente humana, cujus ~us spiritualis est talis* VR 147; *hominis ~us talis est ut correspondeat coelis* ES 354.

organista ~ae, *m.* An organist: ES 5990.

organizatio ~onis, *f.* The organized nature, structure (of a thing): *quod si mutaretur [vita], discerperetur ~o* AM 524.3.

organizatus ~a ~um, *a.* **1** (w. *ad*) Organically designed (to): *corpora hominum...non sunt nisi formae mentium exterius ~ae ad efficiendum nutus animae* AM 310.1; *unumquodvis [insectulum] ~um est ad sentiendum et ad se movendum* VR 12.4. **2** Structured, organized: *vita... ~a est secundum amorem ejus* AM 524.3.

organulum ~i, *neut.* A small organ (in the body): *mediis ~is, membranis, et fibris, quae intus in aure* AC 7359; *a minimo vitae ~o quod est seminis* ES 2479.

organum ~i, *neut.* (Gk.) **1** An instrument serving a specified purpose: *nam [proprium] est solum ~um vitae* AC 149.2; *quod homo sit ~um recipiens Dei* VR 34.1. **2** An organic form, organism: *quod homo a parentibus nascatur ~um* AM 134.2. **3** (anat.) An organ of the body: *in unoquovis viscere, membro, ~o* CI 212; *fibrillas...sensiles in ~is* ES 1941; *os...est ~um vocis* AC 6985. **4** A musical instrument operated by air contained in a reservoir, bagpipe, organ: *pater omnis pulsantis citharam et ~um* Gen. 4.21 (AC); *~um...est instrumentum medium inter chordaceum et quod inflatur* AC 419; *fistulas, tibias, tubas, buccinas, et ~a* AM 86; ES 4281.

orgia ~orum, *neut. pl.* (Gk.) Orgies: *ut daemones ibi repraesentent ~a Bacchi* CO 33.

oriens ~ntis, *m.* The point of rising (of the sun): *versus ~ntem solis* AC 2441.7; the east: *quod...verterint faciem...ad solem in ~nte* CI 119; *in plaga septentrionali superiore prope ad ~ntem* AM 261.1; (w. gen.) *ab ~nte Hierosolymae* AE 638.16.

orientalis ~is ~e, *a.* **1** Of the east, eastern: *ventum ~em* Exod. 10.13 (AC); *sub caelo ~i* AM 2.1; (masc. as sb.) *ultimo loquuti sunt ~es* VR 48.14. **2** Eastern from the point of view of Europe, oriental: *vocibus linguarum ... ~ium* AC 10217.1; (masc. as sb.) DP 255.4.

orientaliter, *adv.* Eastwards: *is [fluvius] vadit ~er versus Aschur* Gen. 2.14 (AC).

orificium ~i, *neut.* **1** The opening, mouth (of a jar, pipe, etc.): *e cado ~i minoris* ES 2691; *ad ~um venae* VR 814. **2** (anat.) The aperture of a bodily organ: *in glottide per varias aperturas ejus ~i* DP 279.8; *~um superius ventriculi* ES 1273.

originalis ~is ~e, *a.* **1** Serving as origin or source: *hae repraesentationes sunt quasi ~es eorum quae sunt in mundo* ES 4215. **2** Existing from the beginning, original: *lingua ~is* (of the Old Testament), Hebrew: AC 7293.1; *peccatum ~e*, original sin: AR praef. 6.

originarius ~a ~um, *a.* Originating: *ipsa ~a causa illius amoris* AM 399; (w. gen.) *per ideas ~as vocum, quales sunt cogitationis* AC 1757; (neut. pl. as sb.) *cum ~is repraesentativorum* AC 1876.2.

originitus, *adv.* By way of origin: *quod omnis fructificatio...sit ~us ex influxu amoris* AM 183.5; *nec hi receperunt aliquid a se, sed ~us a Deo* VR 48.13.

origo ~inis, *f.* A starting point, source, origin: *spirituale in sua prima ~ine est Divinum Verum* AC 6685; *sunt binae ~ines mali* AC 6859; (pl. w. no ref. to more than one origin) *quod gens illa talis fuerit a primis ~inibus* AC 7041.2; *~inem ducere*, to trace the origin: *ii qui naturam colunt, et ex ea ducunt rerum ~ines* AC 775.2; *~inem trahere*, to take one's origin: *quod idololatriae gentium...ex scientia correspondentiarum traxerint ~inem* SS 23.1.

Orion ~onis, *m.* The constellation Orion: *stella nostra, quae lucet sicut ~on in noctibus* VR 137.2; (Bibl. after Hebr., app.) a constellation: *stellae coelorum et ~ones eorum* Isa. 13.10 (AC 31.1).

orior oriri ortus sum, *intr.* **1** (of the sun or other heavenly bodies) To appear to view, rise: *dicitur quod sol oriatur et occidat...cum tamen sol immotus stat* SS 95.2. **2** To come into existence, spring up, arise: *ideo oritur pugna* AE 164; (w. *ab*) *ideas, quae oriuntur a sensibus externis* ES [1558 1/3]; (w. *ex*) *quod hoc oriatur ex lege ordinis Divini* AC 8223.1.

oriundus ~a ~um, *a.* Coming into existence, arising (from a specified source or cause): *delitias inde ~as* AM 76.6; (w. *ab*) *crustae a phantasiis ~ae* ES 1742; (w. *ex*) *fallacia ~a ex idea spatii* DP 6.1; *animus pugnandi ... ~us ex amore dominandi* VR 113.4.

ornamentum ~i, *neut.* An adornment, decoration: *~a ineffabilis decoris* AM 12.1.

ornatus[1] ~a ~um, *a.* (pf. pple. of **orno**) (superl. *~issimus*) Highly adorned, ornate: *lecti apparent ibi ~issimi* AC 10360.9; *~issimum palatium* DP 36.

ornatus[2] ~us, *m.* Adornment, decoration: *in sua vita et in suo ~u* AM 42.3.

orno ~are ~avi ~atum, *tr.* To embellish, beautify, adorn: *sicut sponsam ~atam marito suo* Rev. 21.2 (AR); *pileos, quorum limbos ~abant fasciae ex auro et* *margaritis* VR 48.20; (w. abl.) *meretrix... ~ata purpura et auro* VI 46.

oro ~are ~avi ~atum, *tr.*, *intr.* **1** To make supplication, pray: **a** (intr.): *in templo stans ~abat, dicens...* Luke 18.11 (VI 30.3). **b** (w. acc. of person addressed): *~avit [Dominus] Patrem sicut alium a Se* DD 35.3. **c** (w. *ad*): *~avit devote ad Deum, ut instrueretur* AM 461.1. **d** (w. acc. of thing sought) to pray for: *~ans auditionem submittit Domino* AC 8179.3. **e** (w. cognate acc.): *cum Orationem Domini ~arem* CI 336. **2** To make a speech, speak: *surrexit unus ~aturus de origine pulchritudinis sexus faeminini* AM 381.

orphanotrophium ~i, *neut.* (Gk.) An orphanage: *hospitalia, nosocomia, ~a et xenodochia aedificare* VR 459.8.

orphanus ~a ~um, *a.* (Gk.) Orphaned: *non relinquam vos ~os* John 14.18 (DD 51.1).

orthodoxe, *adv.* In an orthodox manner: *nos loquuti sumus ex orthodoxis ~e* VR 503.7.

orthodoxia ~ae, *f.* (Gk.) A system of correct belief, orthodoxy: *secundum fidem Evangelicorum in capite librorum ~ae illorum, quod vocatur Formula Concordiae* VR 101.1; *~a hodierna in orbe Christiano a Romano-Catholicis separato* VR 356.

orthodoxus ~a ~um, *a.* (Gk.) (superl. *~issimus*) Holding a correct theological belief, orthodox: *quod nemini liceat...vocari ~us, nisi qui agnoscit doctrinam illam* AR 606.1; (masc. as sb.) *quid plus hodie libros ~orum implet...?* VR 132.1; (neut. as sb.) *nos loquuti sumus ex ~is orthodoxe* VR 503.7.

ortivus ~a ~um, *a.* Of arising; (neut. as sb.) rising: *quia Dominus est sol...et Ipse semper est in ~o* AC 5097.2.

ortus[1] ~a ~um: pf. pple. of **orior**.

ortus[2] ~us, *m.* **1** The rising (of the sun): *prima ejus* [sc. *Ecclesiae*] *aetas* [*comparatur*] *~ui solis seu aurorae* AC 1837. **2** The quarter where the sun rises, the east: *versus meridiem et versus ~um* Dan. 8.9 (AC 7988.1); CI 69. **3** The coming into existence of anything, rise, origin: *de omnium ~u a Domino* AC 1807.2; *a primo ~u hujus telluris* CI 415; *ex horum ~u et flore perpetuo* AM 3.4. **b** *~um ducere* or *trahere* (w. *ab* or *ex*), to trace one's origin (to), be derived (from): *haec conjugia ducunt principium et ~um suum a conjugio coelesti* AC 718; *illud religiosum...trahit suum ~um ex amore imperandi* FI 49.

os[1] oris, *neut.* **1** The mouth (as a part of the body): *ejecit serpens...ex ore suo aquam tanquam flumen* Rev. 12.15 (AR). **b** (esp. as the organ of speech): *ex abundantia cordis os loquitur* Matt. 12.34 (VI 28); *dicebant ore semipleno* AM 115.4; *in oris loquela* VR 4.2; *aperire os ad enuntiandum* VR 6.3; *in ore est*, it is said: *in omnium ore est, quod Verbum sit a Deo* SS 1; *in ore ferre*, to have a saying: AC 6816; *ore ad os*, face to face (in conversation): *cum quibus Dominus loquutus ore ad os* AC 49.1; VR 107.1; (Bibl.) *super os* (w. gen.), on the command (of): Num. 13.3 (AC 2714.4). **c** (as used in laughter): *tenentur...ora totius consortii in risibus* AM 3.2. **d** (as the organ of eating): *et amabat Jischak Esavum, quia venatio in ore ejus* Gen. 25.28 (AC). **2** The aperture, opening, mouth (of other things): *juxta os fluminis* Isa. 19.7 (AC 6693.2); *in ore manticae illius* Gen. 42.27 (AC); *os vestium* Ps. 133.2 (AE 375.26); *cum foetus venit ad matricis os* ES 244. **b** the edge (of a sword): *cadent ore gladii* Luke 21.24 (AE 131.6); *gladius orium* 'a two-edged sword' Ps. 149.6 (AE 131.5).

os[2] ossis, *neut.* A bone: *os non confringetis Ipsius* John 19.36 (DD 11); *corpus humanum...absque sustentaculis quae vocantur ossa* SS 33; (esp. pl., of the dead) *intus... plena sunt ossibus mortuorum* Matt. 23.27 (AC 7046.2); *ut cadavera, ossa et sepulchra illorum sancta crederentur* FI 8.

osanna, *interj.* (Hebr.) Hosanna: *~a Filio Davidis* Matt. 21.9 (AC 6674.5).

oscinis ~is, *m.*(?) A songbird: *corvus volens canere sicut ~is* VR 173.3; *quod ~es in prima matuta dulciter canant* VR 308.

oscitatio ~onis, *f.* Yawning (as a sign of boredom): *in hebetudine et ~one de omnibus quae vitae ibi* ES 5396.

oscito ~are ~avi, *intr.* To yawn: *viderunt plerosque dormientes, et qui evigilati sunt, ~antes* AM 9.2; *ad illud* [sc. *verum*] *~ant, et se avertunt* AR 421.1.

osculatio ~onis, *f.* The act of kissing: *ex amplexibus et ~onibus* AM 396.2.

osculor ~ari ~atus sum, *tr.* **1** To kiss: *dum illa accepit [pignora], ~atus est illam* AM 20.3; *~amini Filium ne irascatur* Ps. 2.12 (DD 6). **2** (of things) To come into light contact, brush: *audivi...vocem alarum illorum, ~antium se unius ad alterum* Ezek. 1.24 (AE 283.13). **3** (transf.) To pay respect to, salute warmly: *naturam ut creatricem universi ~antur* VR 37.3.

osculum ~i, *neut.* **1** A small mouth: [*avis cogitat*] *per ~a inferre escas in guttura illorum* [sc. *pullorum*] VR 44.1. **2** A small opening, aperture, orifice: *insorbent [arbuscula] illa libere per ~a, poros et meatus* VR 491.2; *quod ventriculus cibos receptos...digerat...~is ibi hiantibus* DP 296.14; ES 1090.

osor ~oris, *m.* One who hates: *hostes, inimici, et ~ores vocantur...quia illi ~ores et hostes sunt contra Divinum* AC 8282.

osseus ~a ~um, *a.* Of or resembling bone, bony:

proprium hominis...apparet prorsus ut ~um inanimatum...quid AC 149.2; *membranam... ~am factam* AC 7748; *sceleton ~um* AM 182.5.

ossificatus ~a ~um, *a.* Turned to bone, ossified: *quod interiora eorum... ~a sint* CI 354.

ostendo ~dere ~di ~sum, *tr.* **1** To give a visual demonstration of, display, show: *~debat mihi...punitionum genera* AC 7810; *binae facies ~sae sunt* AC 8242; (Bibl.) *qui ~disti mihi angustias multas* Ps. 71.20 (AC 8278.3). **2** To demonstrate by argument, prove, show: *quae prius ...dicta et ~sa sunt* AC 7007.4; (w. *quod*) *antequam ~di potest quod 'Moses' repraesentet legem Divinam* AC 6752.1; VI 44.

ostensio ~onis, *f.* A demonstration, show: *~o potentiae* AC 7298.1.

ostentatio ~onis, *f.* Pretentious display, showing off, ostentation: *non curat opes ~onis causa* AC 4751.2.

ostento ~are ~avi, *intr.* To show off: *inde gloriantur, ac ~are cupiunt* ES 358.

ostiarius ~i, *m.* A doorkeeper: *qui pastor ovium est, huic ~us aperit* John 10.3 (AC 9926.3).

ostiatim, *adv.* From door to door: *~im ambulant, quaeruntque ubi recipi queant* ES 692.

ostium ~i, *neut.* **1** The door of a house or other building: *non exibitis quisquam ex ~o domus suae* Exod. 12.22 (AC); *ingressae sunt...et ~um clausum est* Matt. 25.10 (SS 17.1). **2** The entrance (to anything): *portae ac ~a inferni et coeli* CI 428; *ut primum tangit ~um auditus nostri* VR 159.4.

ostrea ~ae, *f.* (ad. Gk.) An oyster: *crustis ~ae* ES 3611.

otiosus ~a ~um, *a.* Characterized by leisure, idle: *in vita ~a* AC 454; (masc. as sb.) *quod sedulis sit copia, et non ~is* AM 220.3.

otium ~i, *neut.* The state of having no occupation, idleness, leisure: *in faedo ~o et inertia vixerunt* AC 5723; *quod ~um ejus vitae sit modo recreationis causa* CI 403.

ovalis ~is ~e, *a.* Oval: *lucem...in forma ~i* VR 25.1; *rotundam fenestram, seu ~em* ES 4418.

ovarium ~i, *neut.* **1** (anat.) An ovary: *in [provincia] cervicis uteri et ~orum* AC 5054. **2** A clutch of eggs laid at one time: *continuum quoddam ~um ex ovis multiplicatis rubentibus flave* ES 2242.

ovatio ~onis, *f.* Exultation: *producit...laetitia animi... cantum et ~onem* AC 4215.2.

oviformis ~is ~e, *a.* Having the form of an egg, egg-shaped, egg-like: *ex nulla materia ~i* AS 342.

ovile ~is, *neut.* A sheepfold: *et alias oves habeo quae non sunt ex ~i hoc* John 10.16 (AC 7035); AM 129.

ovinus ~a ~um, *a.* Made of sheepskin: *tunicas ~as* ES 633.

ovis ~is, *f.* A sheep: *loquutus sum cum illis de ~ibus et agnis* AC 7073; (w. ref. to the good) *dicet ~ibus a dextris* Matt. 25.34 (VI 2); *quod Deus...hominem hircum posset convertere in hominem ~em* VR 58.

ovo ~are ~avi, *intr.* To exult: *laetabuntur et ~abunt gentes* Ps. 67.4 (AC 1259.5); *intus in se non ~at ex strage hostium* CH 164 (= vii.[5]).

ovulum ~i, *neut.* A small egg: *stagnum ex ~is ranarum viridescens* VR 120.1; (in human beings) an ovum: AC 1815.1.

ovum ~i, *neut.* An egg: *ex ~o excluduntur* AM 350.1; (fig.) *aetas infantiae est quasi ~um aetati, pueritiae* AC 4378.2.

P

pabulum ~i, *neut.* Food for animals, fodder: *~um... est cibus quo pascuntur asini, et sunt stramen et palea* AC 5495.

pacifice, *adv.* Peacefully: *ex pacifico agit [Dominus], sic ~e* ES 1176.

pacificus ~a ~um, *a.* **1** Bringing about peace, peacemaking: *sacrificaverunt sacrificia ~a Jehovae juvencos* Exod. 24.5 (AC). **2** Peaceful: *fera agri ~a erit tibi* Job 5.23 (AC 46.2); *status ~us* AC 7744; *in prima vigilia, quae interna, ~a et dulcis est* AM 155[a].1; (neut. as sb.) *'pax' significat ~um mentis* AE 365.4.

paciscor pacisci pactus sum, *tr.* To promise to give, pledge: *nisi [faemina] paciscatur se voto illorum* AM 333.1.

paco ~are ~avi ~atum, *tr.* To restore calm to, establish peace in, make peaceful: *Dominus...Schiloh vocatur ex eo quod ~averit et tranquilla reddiderit omnia* AC 6373; *~atus erat Moabus* Jer. 48.11 (AC 2468.11).

pactum ~i, *neut.* An agreement, contract: *constipulationes illae seu ~a etiam vocantur foedus* AC 6804.5; *cum faedere, quod post ~a conventa pangitur* VR 730.1.

paelex: see **pellex**.

paena ~ae, *f.* (Gk.) also **poena**. A punishment, penalty: *mala ac ~ae in altera vita conjuncta sunt* AC 6997.6; *ex timore legis et ejus ~ae* AM 267.3; (w. gen. of punishment) *sub ~a mortis vetitum* 'on pain of death' AC 7893.

paene, *adv.* also **poene**. Almost: *~e semper* AC 81.3; *falsa...qualitatem falsi ~e exuunt* AC 8311.1; *~e simile* AM 59.2.

paenitens ~ntis, *a.* also **poen-**. Showing regret, regretful: *quia gratiosus et misericors Ipse...et ~ns super malum* Joel 2.13 (AC 588.3); *sed ~ns Jehovah ipsius mali* 2 Sam. 24.16 (CI 229).

paenitentia ~ae, *f.* also **poen-**. **1** A feeling of sorrow for evil actions, regret: *~a et dolor* AC 588.1; AC 6563; AC 10441.1. **2** The process of turning away from an evil life and beginning a new religious and moral life, repentance: *actus ~ae sunt omnes illi qui efficiunt quod mala quae peccata contra Deum sunt non velit et inde non faciat* VR 510.1; DP 114.2; *agere ~am*, to take the actions involved in such a process, undertake repentance: AR 224.6; AR 937; (w. *ab* + abl.) *~am a malis operibus in mundo egerunt* AR praef.; AR 69; BCP (VI 6); *actualis ~a*, the practice of repentance: VR 567.5; VR 528.

paenitentialis ~is ~e, *a.* also **poen-**. Of or relating to repentance; (neut. as sb.) a penance: *cum... ~ia imposita absolvit* AC 3993.10.

paeniteo ~tere ~tui, *intr.* also **poen-**. **1** (impers., w. acc.) It is a cause of regret (to), it grieves: *~teat vos* Matt. 4.17 (DD 18.4); (w. *quod*) *~tuit Jehovam, quod fecerit hominem in terra* Gen. 6.6 (AC). **2** (personally) To feel regret, be sorry: *coeperunt ~tere quod non voluissent credere* ES 2055.

paenitudo ~inis, *f.* also **poen-**. Regret, sorrow: *simul aestuarunt ~ines Meae* Hos. 11.8 (AC 588.3).

Paesach, *indecl. neut.* (transliteration of Hebr.) = **Pascha**: Exod. 12.11 (AC); AC 7860.

paganice, *adv.* In a pagan manner: *~e vivunt* VR 484.1.

paganismus ~i, *m.* A pagan system of belief: *statim imbuuntur ~o* ES 347; AE 1029.8.

paganus ~i, *m.* A pagan: *homo ex ~o fit Christianus* VR 525; AM 351.3.

pagina ~ae, *f.* A page (of a book): *quae [experientia] omnis si adduceretur, plures ~as impleret* AC 6639.2; *quae scripta sunt pluribus ~is* CI 240.

pagus ~i, *m.* A village: *[urbs] vertitur in ~os* AC 941.1; ES 751; *eduxit eum extra ~um* Mark 8.23 (AE 239.20).

pala ~ae, *f.* A shovel: *facies lebetes ejus ad decinerandum illud, et ~as et crateres ejus* Exod. 27.3 (AC).

palaestra ~ae, *f.* (Gk.) **1** An arena in which public spectacles are held, stage: *ubi erat planum sicut ~a* *elevatum* AR 839.5; AM 6.3. **2** A contest of argument, debate: *dixistis quod nobis in nostris ~is non sit aliquod verum* AR 566.4; *solitum est...instituere quasdam ~as de rebus sacris* ES 233; cf. *credit ea ex ipsius sapientiae ~a desumta esse* AC 4741.3.

palaestricus ~a ~um, *a.* (Gk.) (of contests) Performed in a public arena, staged: *certamina ~a inter pueros* AM 17.4.

palam, *adv.* Without concealment, openly: (used as pred.) *voluerunt ut omnia quae cogitant ~am essent* CI 489.6; *ob...causas, quae hic nondum ~am fieri possunt* 1AD 1646.

palatiolum ~i, *neut.* A small palace: *porticus tendens ad ~um* AM 316.1.

palatium ~i, *neut.* A large and magnificent residence, palace: *templa, ~a, domos* AC 6809; *~um absque fundamento* SS 33.

palatum ~i, *neut.* (anat.) The palate (of the mouth): *adhaesit lingua lactentis ~o ejus ob sitim* Lam. 4.4 (AC 6745.6); *in lingua per varias ejus applicationes ad ~um et dentes* DP 279.8; *circa regionem ~i interioris* ES 1177.

palea ~ae, *f.* The external integument and straw of grain, chaff: *quod hic distinctus sit ab illo, sicut triticum a ~a* AM 44.6; *separantur ~ae a tritico ex ventilabro agitato* VR 26.2; (for making mud bricks) *non addetis dare ~am populo ad laterificandum lateres* Exod. 5.7 (AC); (as a type of worthlessness) *cum...horum sermo...est sicut squama et ~a respective ad nuclearia* AC 4957; (as a type of instability) *alioquin foret homo sicut ~a in vento* VI 107.

palla ~ae, *f.* A robe worn as outer garment, cloak: *~am equestrem* ES [5461] ½.

Palladium ~i, *neut.* (Gk.) **1** (in ancient Greece) A statue of Athena Pallas: *sicut Graeci [osculati sunt] ~um in templo Minervae* VR 759.2. **2** A temple of wisdom: *ecce super clivo palatium octogonum, quod vocaverunt ~um* AM 151ª.2. **3** An object of supreme veneration: *hanc [sc. praedestinationem] ut ~um religionis ante templa Ecclesiae suae appenderunt* VR 177.4.

Pallas ~adis, *f.* (Gk.) **1** A title of the Greek goddess Athena: *caput gorgonis...clypeo ~adis insculptum* SE 66.2. **2** A name given to certain female spirits: *dicebant quod tales [mulieres] priscis quandoque visae fuerint et ab illis vocatae ~ades* AC 4658.5; ES 3952.

pallens ~ntis, *a.* Of pale colour: *equus ~ns* Rev. 6.8 (AE 186.5).

pallesco ~ere, *intr.* To become pale: *non jam facies ejus ~ent* Isa. 29.22 (AC 489.2).

palliative, *adv.* By palliative treatment: *vulnus ~e curatum* VR 435.2.

palliativus ~a ~um, *a.* (of medical treatment) Designed to remove symptoms rather than cause, palliative: *sanatio ~a* DP 282; AE 1152.2.

pallide, *adv.* Palely: *faciei indecorae sed usque ~e niveae* AC 1774.

pallidus ~a ~um, *a.* Of pale colour: *equus ~us* Rev. 6.8 (AR); (as indicating sickness or death) *facie ~a sicut mortui* AM 269.3.

palliolum ~i, *neut.* A veil: Isa. 3.23 (AC 2576.11).

pallium ~i, *neut.* A loose outer garment, cloak: *sponsus indutus erat ~o ex purpura lucente* AM 20.2; ES 4151; (esp. as the distinctive garment of a priest) *vestes sanctitatis Aharonis...tunicam, ~um* SS 16; *sub ~o monachi* VR 108; VR 137.2.

pallor ~oris, *m.* Paleness, pallor: AS 379; AE 381.2.

palma ~ae, *f.* **1** The palm of the hand: *cum gradiuntur, adjuvant se ~is* AC 8371; *sustuli ~am, rogans* VR 136.3. **2** A palm tree: *porticus ex ~is et lauribus* AM 56.1; also, a palm frond: *et ~ae in manibus illorum* Rev. 7.9 (AR). **3** An award, prize: *~am seu praemium* AM 103.3.

palmes ~itis, *m.* A branch or shoot of a tree: *Ego sum vitis, vos ~ites* John 15.5 (DD 32.6); VR 193.

palmo ~are ~avi ~atum, *tr.* To measure with the palm of the hand: *dextra mea ~avit coelum* Isa. 48.13 (AC 10044.6).

palmus ~i, *m.* The palm of the hand: *dextra Mea ~o mensa est coelos* Isa. 48.13 (AC 878.3).

palor ~ari ~atus sum, *intr.* To wander about: *spectat ad habitantes et ~antes extra urbem* VR 808.

palpatio ~onis, *f.* The act of touching or feeling: *ex ~one nudi corporis illorum [sc. infantum]* AM 396.2.

palpebra ~ae, *f.* The eyelid: *illi ad Divina...effata claudunt ~as* VR 83; *quasi dum homo in prima vigilia per ~as spectat* [i.e., through half-closed eyes] CI 450.

palpitatio ~onis, *f.* A palpitation: *per ~ones [praecipitationes* Tafel] *cordis sensibiles* ES 327 (J D Odhner, Autograph).

palpito ~are ~avi, *intr.* **1** To feel tentatively, grope: *~ant circum parietes* VR 7. **2** (of the heart) To beat rapidly, palpitate: *cor in timore ~at* AC 5501.

palpo ~are ~avi ~atum, *tr.* To perceive by the sense of touch, feel: *~ate Me, et videte* Luke 24.39 (AC 1729.2); *~amus sicut coeci parietem* Isa. 59.10 (AC 7711.2); *amicus...illum [sc. amicum] osculatur, ~at et* *conjungit manus* VR 44.2; (absol.) to grope: *extende manum tuam...et ~abit caligine* Exod. 10.21 (AC). (n.b. *palpavit mihi cor* AM 10.4 should be emended to *palpitavit*; the word is divided between two lines in the 1st edn.)

paludinosus ~a ~um, *a.* Swampy, marshy: *nidore ~o* AE 659.5; *palus...seu liquidum prorsus ~um, stagnum* ES 4788.

palus[1] ~udis, *f.* A swamp, marsh: *in voragines, quae apparent sicut ~udes* CI 354; *absorbetur sicut adamas injectus ~udi* AM 526.

palus[2] ~i, *m.* A pole, stake: *ne quid...subintret, quod convellit ejus funes et ~os, per quos systematicum suum sicut tentorium firmum aedificavit* VR 758.2; ES 3006.

paluster (or perh. **palustris**) ~tris ~tre, *a.* Marshy, swampy: *ex locis ~tribus* VR 385.3; (of plants) *cannae ~tres* VR 375.2; VR 94.2.

palustris: see **paluster**.

pampineus ~a ~um, *a.* Of the grapevine: *arbores ...circumligatas vitibus ~is* AM 13.1.

pancreas ~atis, *m.* (Gk.) (anat.) The pancreas: VR 54; VR 60.2.

pancreaticus ~a ~um, *a.* Of the pancreas: *ductum ~um* AC 5185.

pando ~dere ~si ~sum, *tr.* **1** To open up (a road): *sibi ~dere conabatur viam ut inde elaberetur* ES 3221; (fig.) ES 205. **2** (w. indir. qu.) To display, set forth: *quales sunt formae...non potest ~di, quia sunt formae spirituales* SA 70 (= ii.[1]).

panegyricus ~i, *m.* (Gk.) The speaker of a laudatory oration, panegyricist: *quis ~us, qui super mortuos lamentatur, non illos in caelum evehit...?* DP 274.2.

pango ~ere pepigi pactum, *tr.* To conclude, make (a covenant or treaty): *Dominus novum foedus cum iis ~it* AC 40.3; *pepigi foedus electo Meo* Ps. 89.3 (AC 6804.9); *faedus conjugiale pactum in mundo* AM 45; (also absol.) *affectionem sponsi et sponsae cum ~unt* AM 55.1.

panicus ~a ~um, *a.* (Gk.) (of fear) Panic: *inde illis terror ~us* ES 5294.

panis ~is, *m.* (gen. pl. *~um*) **1** Bread: *pro frustis ~is* Ezek. 13.19 (AC 6767.3); (used in the Lord's Supper) AC 1798.5. **2** A loaf of bread: *mensas, super quibus... repositi erant ~es* AM 20.1; *fractio ~is amygdali* ES 2464; (esp. as used in Hebr. ritual) *mensa aurea cum ~ibus* AC 6723.4; *~es propositionis* AC 6804.11; *~es facierum* SS 16. **3** Food of any kind: *qui comedit Mecum ~em* John 13.18 (DD 11); *homo non ex solo ~e vivit* Matt. 4.4 (SS 69).

pannag, *indecl.* (Hebr.) Pannag, a transliteration of a Hebr. word of uncertain meaning for a substance (perh. edible) that was traded: *merces eorum, ut argentum, ferrum, stannum,...tritica, minnith, ~ag, mel* AC 4453.3 (Ezek. 27.17).

panniculetum ~i, *neut.* A cloth patch used as a blindfold: *pueris ludentibus, qui ~um ligant ante oculos* VR 165.2.

panniculus ~i, *m.* A patch (on a garment): *nemo ~um novi vestimenti indit in vestimentum vetus* Luke 5.36 (AE 195.15); (also app.) a cord worn to carry a seal: Gen. 38.18 (AC); *~us...erat...ex filiis contortis* AC 4875.

pannus ~i, *m.* A piece of cloth, drape: *feralis lectica, nigris ~is circumtecta* AC 817; *brachia apparent sicut ~i* AC 956; *sermo eorum* [sc. *Africanorum*] *est conjunctus cum quodam collisu, quasi ~i* ES 453.

Pantheon ~i, *neut.* A religious building in Rome dating from pagan times, the Pantheon: *in quodam templo rotundo simili templo Romae, quod vocatur ~on* VR 503.1.

panthera ~ae, *f.* (Gk.) A panther: *~ae indutae pellibus ovis* VR 148.1; AM 512.2; ES 3191.

pantherinus ~a ~um, *a.* Resembling a panther: *satyros ~os* AM 521.3.

pantherus ~i, *m.* = **panthera**: AE 388.21.

Papa ~ae, *m.* The Pope (of Rome): *quod dictamen ~ae sit nullius rei* SS 24; AM 265.

papaei ~orum, *m. pl.* Papists: *quaedam* [*objecta*]... *exornabant et decorabant...sicut ~i sua simulachra* CO 43.

papalis ~is ~e, *a.* Of the Pope, papal: *cum dominio ~i* FI 8; *per bullam ~em* VR 90.2; (masc. pl. as sb.) the followers of the Pope, papists: *sicut mos est paparum et ~ium hodie* ES 3934.

papatus ~us, *m.* The dominion of the Pope, papacy: *sicut multi in ~u* VR 426.1.

papilio ~onis, *m.* A butterfly: *sicut ~ones qui in aëre volant* AM 380.1; VR 12.6.

papilla ~ae, *f.* (anat.) A nipple: *praesunt sinistrae pectoris ~ae* ES 3655.

Papismus ~i, *m.* The papist religion: *transitus a ~o ad Christianismum* VR 821.1; the area where this holds sway: *in toto ~o* NE 52.2.

papista ~ae, *m.* A papist: ES 5347.

Papisticus ~a ~um, *a.* Of or typical of the papist religion: *caligo ~a* ES 5450.

papula ~ae, *f.* A pustule, pimple: *tumor, abscessus, ~a* AC 7524.3.

papyrus ~i, *f.* (Gk.) **1** A papyrus plant: *~i juxta flumen* Isa. 19.7 (AC 6693.2). **2** A sheet of paper: *in...mansione ...cujus fenestrae sunt ex ~is conglutinatis* VR 839.2.

par[1] paris, *a.* **1** Equally matched, like: (w. *cum*) *quomodo parem te praestabis cum equis?* Jer. 12.5 (AC 1585.4); (w. dat.) *omnis arbor in horto Dei non par fuit illi in pulchritudine* Ezek. 31.8 (AE 110.2). **2** Of equal standard, matching: *quae [intelligentia]...in pari gradu est cum amore usus* CI 393.2; *pari passu*, in step: *innocentia et pax pari passu ambulant* CI 288.2. **3** (of persons) Of equal status: *in coelo sunt omnes sicut pares* AC 7773; *conjugia cum paribus* AM 246.2.

par[2] paris, *neut.* A group of two, pair: *par turturum* Luke 2.24 (DD 9); *par conjugum* AM 42.1; *paria et paria*, two by two, in pairs: *apud aves quae se amant paria et paria* AM 79.10; *virgulta et flores erant paria et paria* AM 316.2.

parabola ~ae, *f.* (Gk.) **1** A story told to convey a moral lesson, parable: *quod Dominus per ~as cum iis loquutus* AC 302; *in ~a de divite in inferno* AM 41.1; *quod...perceperim loquelam angelorum...in ~as cecidisse* ES 3916. **2** A derisive utterance, reproach: *ut enunties hanc ~am de rege Babelis* Isa. 14.4 (AC 6852). **3** (in geometry) A parabola: *formant...paene ~am* AC 5380; *inter asymptotas ~ae* [but app. a hyperbola is intended] ES 883.

parabolicus ~a ~um, *a.* (Gk.) Of or typical of a parable: *ex una ~a idea innumerabilia sequuntur applicabilia* ES 4006; ES 4095.

parabolizo ~are ~avi ~atum, *tr.* (Gk.) To speak derisively: *~a contra domum rebellionis parabolam* Ezek. 24.3 (AC 3812.5).

paracletus ~i, *m.* (Gk.) An advocate, intercessor, paraclete: *Ego rogabo Patrem, ut alium ~um det vobis* John 14.16 (AC 6788); *quod Dominus per ~um seu Spiritum Sanctum intellexerit Se Ipsum* VR 139.4.

paradisiacus ~a ~um, *a.* (Gk.) **1** Of an ornamental park, park-like: *in horto ~o* CI 337; (neut. pl. as sb.) *feruntur primum ad ~a* AC 540. **2** Of paradise, paradisiac: *somnia quae illis erant delitiosissima et ~a* AC 125; *~am vitam* ES 3097. **b** *avis ~a*, a bird of paradise: AC 1594.4; AM 270.2.

paradisus ~i, *m.* or *f.* (Gk. from Persian) (gender: masc. VR 461.1; fem. AC 1588) **1** An ornamental park or garden (on earth): *calorem ex quo germinantur horti et fiunt sicut ~i* AC 8328.2; (in the spiritual world) *sistuntur visibiles ~i quae omnem imaginationis humanae ideam...pulchritudine excedunt* AC 1588; *~i et horti, et in illis arbores omnis generis* FI 63.1. **2** (Bibl.) The Garden of Eden or the Garden of the Lord: *serpens... qui seduxit...Evam in ~o ex arbore scientiae* AC 6952.4; *~us, hortus Jehovae* VR 38.2; *de arbore vitae, quae in medio ~i Dei* Rev. 2.7 (AR). **3** The heavenly paradise: *introducitur in coelum seu in ~um coelestem* AC 63.

paradoxon ~i, *neut.* (Gk.) A statement apparently contrary to reason, paradox: *~on potest videri sed usque est verissimum* AC 1776; *nonne illa ~a sicut contradictoria dissipantur a seipsis?* AM 182.6.

paradoxus ~a ~um, *a.* (Gk.) (compar. *~ior*) Paradoxical: *quid ~ius credi potest...?* AM 182.6.

paragraphus ~i, *f.* (Gk.) A section of a book, paragraph: *post ~os seu capita hujus operis* AM 39; ES 3437.

paralele, *adv.* In a parallel plane: *antrorsum inferius paulo seu ~e cum inferiori pede* ES 4402.

paralelismus ~i, *m.* (Gk.) also **parallelismus**. The fact or quality of being parallel, a parallel: *haec dicta sunt ut per ~um illustretur qualis status illorum est* AC 8118.3; *plenus etiam ~us est inter vivificationem hominis et vegetationem arboris* FI 32.

paralelus ~a ~um, *a.* (Gk.) **1** (in geometry) Parallel: *bestia...stat super pedibus in situ ~o cum terra* VR 69.1. **2** Similar in all respects, parallel: *ex multis ~is locis e Verbo* VR 520.2; ES 4133.

parallelismus: see **paralelismus**.

paralysis ~eos, *f.* (Gk.) Paralysis: *~is, quae est resolutio et relaxatio membranarum et ligamentorum motui inservientium* AM 253.2; VR 367.7.

paralyticus ~a ~um, *a.* (Gk.) Suffering from paralysis: *faetus ~us* VR 165.2; (masc. as sb.) *lectum super quo ~us jacebat* Mark 2.4 (AE 163.7).

parasanga ~ae, *f.* (Gk. from Persian) A Persian measure of distance, parasang, used in expressions denoting extreme superiority: *quod talia beneficia...sint publica, et multis ~is excedant privata* VR 459.8; *talis lux est...ut superet ~is indefinitis etiam lucem solarem* ES 712; ES 4674.

paratus[1] ~a ~um, *a.* (pf. pple. of **paro**) (superl. *~issimus*) In senses of vb., esp. **1** Made ready, prepared: *Hierosolymam Novam... ~am sicut sponsam ornatam marito suo* Rev. 21.2 (AR); AC 3142.1. **2** (w. *ad*) In a suitable condition (for), ready (for): *~us ut vir ad bellum* Jer. 6.23 (AC 8313.3); *inferna ~issima sunt ad inferendum malum* AC 7879.

paratus[2] ~us, *m.* The action of preparing, preparation: (of food) *cogitat...de ~u hoc* AC 2176.

parcimonia ~ae, *f.* also **parsimonia**. Frugality, niggardliness: *per ~as congerunt et cumulant* *pecunias* ES 908; (transf.) restraint, economizing: *quod dogmata...non possint...nisi cum multa ~a et cautela ...praedicari et doceri* SE 58.

parco ~ere peperci, *intr.* (*tr.*) To behave with compassion, spare: *occidisti in die irae Tuae, non pepercisti* Lam. 2.21 (AE 315.9); (w. dat.) *non ~es loco propter quinquaginta justos...?* Gen. 18.24 (AC); *oculis et auribus... ~ere velim, ea referendo* ES 247; (personal pass.) *quod propter bonum quod egerunt ~erentur* ES(M) 4630.

parcus ~a ~um, *a.* Restricted, restrained: *quibus tam parcus amor sexus est* AM 450.

pardus ~i, *m.* (Gk.) A leopard: *~us cum hoedo cubabit* Isa. 11.6 (AC 430.1); *fiunt... ~i quoad dolum* VR 13.4.

parenchyma ~atis, *neut.* (Gk.) (anat.) The substance of the internal organs of the body: *~a cordis* VR 665.5.

parens ~ntis, *m.* (*f.*) **1** A parent: *consurgent liberi contra ~ntes* Mark 13.12 (AC 6767.4); *quisque...nascitur in religionem ~ntum suorum* SS 92. **2** Any direct ancestor, forefather: *primi eorum ~ntes, qui Antiquissimam Ecclesiam constituerunt* AC 310; (fig.) *de Ecclesia Antiquissima, principali et ~nte reliquarum et succedentium* AC 491.

parentator ~oris, *m.* A writer of funerary eulogies: *ita quoque scribunt ~ores super defunctis* UJ(C) 6.

parentela ~ae, *f.* A relationship: *si ~ae et clientelae sint uxori ab agnatis et cognatis* AM 469.

parenthesis ~eos, *f.* (Gk.) An incidental phrase or remark, parenthesis: *adjiciuntur quoque haec verba... sed in ~i* AR 95.

parento ~are ~avi, *intr.* or perh. **parentor** ~ari, *intr.* (UJ(P) 90 Rogers) To write a funerary eulogy: *illi qui de illis ~ant, aperte scribunt quod sint inter angelos* UJ(P) 90 (Tafel, p. 28).

parentor: see **parento**.

pareo ~rere ~rui, *intr.* (w. dat.) To be subject (to), obey: *hic* [sc. *amor*] *filiarum, in prima illarum nubili aetate,... ~ret concupitis ex sensibus* AM 299.1.

paries ~etis, *m.* The wall of a house, room, etc., esp. as viewed from inside, internal wall: *Salomo omnes ~etes domus...sculpsit* 1 Kgs. 6.29 (AC 8369.3); *quod...exiret... per effossum ~etem* DD 15.5 (Ezek. 12.5); *intrant cameras...et palpitant cirum ~etes* VR 7; (of other things) *non volebant ut converterem me versus ~etem lecti* ES 587; *fodinae quarum... ~etes splendent mineris* VR 534.2.

parilis ~is ~e, *a.* Of the same sort, similar: *ex his et ~ibus causis* AM 494.2; *~ia attributa...assignaverunt suis diis* VR 17.2.

pario ~rere peperi ~rtum, *tr.*, *intr.* **1** (tr.) To give birth to, bear: *mulierem ~rientem filium masculum* AM 26 (Rev. 12.5). **2** (intr.) To give birth, produce offspring: *antequam venit ad eas obstetrix, et pepererunt* Exod. 1.19 (AC); *sub ramis ejus pepererunt omnis fera agri* Ezek. 31.6 (AC 3384). **3** (tr., transf.) To bring into existence, bring about, cause: *quod deprivatio veri et boni...anxietatem... ~riat* AC 7217; *talia et similia possunt illi...concipere et ~rere* VR 90.1.

paritas ~atis, *f.* Equality: *cum una* [*uxore*]*...non foret...blandum ex obedientia, sed molestum ex ~ate* AM 78.4.

pariter, *adv.* To an equal extent, equally: *quod homines...finiti sint, ~er angeli et spiritus* VR 29.3; *~er in hoc psalmo agitur de Domino* DD 14.7.

parlamentum ~i, *m.* (the only two citations appear to read **parlementum** in Autograph) **1** A provincial assembly, *parlement*: (of the *Parlement de Paris* in France) ES 5980.2. **2** A legislative assembly, parliament: (of the Parliament in England) *omnibus Lords reformatis in ~o* ES [6101.2].

parlementum: see **parlamentum**.

parma ~ae, *f.* A small, round shield: *aliud significat clypeus, aliud scutum, aliud ~a* AC 1788.1.

Parnassis ~idis, *f.* (Gk.) A maiden of Parnassus, i.e., a Muse: *vocabant...aliquos ludos ~idum* AM 207.6; [*sirenes*] *figurant...decorem oris sicut esset ~is* VR 80.1.

paro ~are ~avi ~atum, *tr.* **1** To make ready, prepare: *homo per veritates ex Verbo ~at intellectum suum* VR 110.5; *sic etiam ~atur via ad sequentia* CI 88. **2** To prepare for oneself, acquire, get: *ut dicerent ad populum ut ~arent viaticum* AC 7111.3 (Josh. 1.11); *ad societatem cum qua communicationem sibi ~ant* AC 7137. **3** (app.) To make equal, measure: *coelos palmo ~avit* [perh. to be emended to *pariavit*] Isa. 40.12 (AC 3104.3).

parochus ~i, *m.* (prob. corrupted from Gk. *paroikos*) A parish priest: *antistites ~i* CO 17.

paropsis ~idis, *f.* (Gk.) A small dish, saucer: *ut mitterent in ~ide nova salem* 2 Kgs. 2.20 (AC 9325.9); *~ides et patinae mundatae a Judaeis* VR 673; AE 960.2.

paroxysmus ~i, *m.* (Gk.) A paroxysm: *~os febris gelidae* ES 4572.1; (fig.) *quod per 'terrae motum' hic significentur omnium Ecclesiae concussiones, ~i, inversiones* AR 711.

pars ~rtis, *f.* **1** A fraction, part: *quoad unam myriadis ~rtem* 'one ten thousandth' AC 1573.4; *millesimam ~rtem* AC 6632; *plurima ~rte* 'for the most part' ES 4236. **2** A particular part of a whole, member: *haec* [sc. *mens*] *se gerit secundum statum ~rtium recipientium* *quae sunt corporis* AC 8378; *dextrae ~rti capitis* AC 6811; *~rtis intellectualis hominis* AC 8215.1. **b** any part, a piece: *illi...dederunt Ipsi piscis assi ~rtem* Luke 24.42 (DD 35.10). **3** A part of the world, region: *in duabus ~rtibus orbis, Asia et Africa* VR 107.3; *feruntur in eorum ~rtes* ES 4311. **4** *In ~rte*, partially, in part (as opposed to wholly): *quod facit coelum in communi et in ~rte* CI 7; *in specie et in ~rte* CI 20. **5** (pl.) A part played by a character, role: (fig.) *intellectus agit primas ~rtes et voluntas secundas* VR 105.2. **b** *a ~rte* (w. gen.), on the part (of): *universale fidei...a ~rte hominis est...* FI 36; *leges ordinis tunc a ~rte Dei sunt* VR 73.2. **6** (pl.) *In suas ~rtes*, to agree with oneself, to one's side: *trahit illa [affectio] verum in suas ~rtes* AC 7342; *machinationibus insitis pelliciunt innocuos in suas ~rtes* ES 409; (sg.) *reliquas [leges]...traherent in ~rtem* [i.e., put a partial interpretation on] AM 231.3. **b** *a ~rtibus* (w. gen.), on the side (of): *putabant totum coelum spirituum ab eorum ~rtibus esse* ES 458.

parsimonia: see **parcimonia**.

partialis ~is ~e, *a*. Of or corresponding to a part, partial: *unumquodvis sculptile repraesentat aliquod ~e virtutis aut veritatis* AM 76.1; (neut. as sb.) a detail: *cum...innumerabiliora adhuc specierum ~ia dentur* AC 483.1.

partibilis ~is ~e, *a*. Capable of being reduced to parts, divisible: *quod Divina Essentia non sit ~is* IM 1.

particeps ~ipis, *a*. Taking part, participating: *ut quis fiat dignus ~eps Sanctae Caenae* BCP (VI 6).

participatio ~onis, *f*. The act of participating in or sharing: *per honoris... ~onem* AC 4769.2.

participo ~are ~avi, *intr*. To take part, participate, share (in): (w. *ab*) *ut omnis eorum cultus ~et ab interno* AC 1083.4; VI 72; (w. *de*) [*homo*] *magis ~at de mundo, corpore et terra* AC 1153.3; SS 84.2; (w. *ex*) *quae [voluptates]...ex felicitate coelesti ~ant et vivunt* AC 997.2; AM 55.7.

particula ~ae, *f*. A small part: *absque illis non ~am corporis movere potest* CI 228; ES 667.

particularis ~is ~e, *a*. **1** Peculiar to oneself, individual: *'insulae' sunt ~es tractus* AC 1157; *sunt sphaerae ~es circum unumquemvis hominem* AC 6657.1; *si aliquis finem spectat ~em, sicut semet* ES 802. **2** (neut. as sb.) A single part of a whole, detail: *differt ordinatio totius coeli ab ordinatione societatis ut commune a ~i* CI 149; (pl.) *abductus sum ab ideis ~ium seu corporis* AC 1526; *~ia doctrinae et fidei* AC 6751. **b** *in ~i*, in detail, in particular: *Divinum Verum...facit coelum in communi, et apud unumquemvis angelum ibi in ~i* AE 27.1.

particulariter, *adv*. (compar. *~larius*) In detail: *quae si traderentur ~lariter* AM 209; VR 6.3.

particulatim, *adv*. In small pieces: *sic ut ~im lacerarentur* ES 4236.

partim, *adv*. In part, partially: *binae statuae ~im carneae, et ~im lapideae* AC 8325.3; AM 277.2.

partior ~tiri ~titus sum, *tr*. To cut into pieces, divide, split: *et ~titus est illa [animalia] in medium* Gen. 15.10 (AC); (fig.) *Divinam Trinitatem in tres personas... ~titi sunt* VR 4.1.

partitim, *adv*. In pieces, piecemeal: *truncus securi... discinditur et tunc tota [arbor] ~im conjicitur in ignem* CO 7.

partitio ~onis, *f*. Division into separate pieces, splitting, partition: *~o et divisio non cadit in illam* [sc. *Essentiam Divinam*] VR 17.2.

parturiens ~ntis, *f*. A woman in labour: *dolor qualis est ~ntium* AC 8313.2; ES 244.

parturio ~rire ~rivi, *intr*. (*tr*.) (intr.) To be in labour, give birth: *vox Jehovae ~rire facit cervas* Ps. 29.9 (AC 6971.4); *a coram Domino ~ris, terra* Ps. 114.7 (DD 39); (tr., fig.) to give birth to: *concipiunt chimaeras, et ~riunt larvas* VR 37.3.

partus ~us, *m*. **1** Childbirth: *a ~u ad senectam* AM 107; *cum tempus ~us instat* VR 12.7. **2** Offspring: *filios et filias qui sunt conceptus et ~us talis Ecclesiae* AC 533; AC 6794.

parum, *adv*. and *indecl. neut*. **1** (adv.) To a small extent, a little: *si ~um elevat ratiocinium mentis suae* VR 32.7; only a little, hardly: *preces illorum... ~um audiuntur* AC 8179.3; *per fidem in plures deos, quae ~um discriminatur a fide in nullum deum* VR 8.4. **2** (sb.) A small amount, a little: *quia ~um Ecclesiae remansit* AC 628; *pro Divino quod Infinitum, cui ~um et vix aliquid essent millia...tellurum* AC 6698. **3** *~um est ut*, it is a small thing that: *tu Bethlechem Ephrataea, ~um est ut sis inter millenas Jehudae* Mic. 5.2 (DD 6).

parumper, *adv*. To a small extent: *solum inflectunt ~er corpus* AC 7068; for a short time: *moremur hic ~er* VR 160.3.

parvifacio ~facere ~feci ~factum, *tr*. To regard as of little importance, belittle: *qui ~fecerunt cultum reliquorum* VR 841.

parvitas ~atis, *f*. The quality of being small, smallness: *de ~ate coeli* CI 420.

parvulus ~a ~um, *a*. Rather small, tiny: *~us lacus aquae limpidae* AM 294.1; *cum ~o sono sibili* ES 2864; (masc. as sb.) a young person, child: *virum occidi in vulnus meum, et ~um in livorem meum* Gen. 4.23

(AC); CI 280; (neut. as sb.) a very short period (of time): *inter ~um temporis* ES 2105.

parvus ~a ~um, *a.* (compar.: see **minor**[1], superl.: see **minimus**) **1** Small in size: *imagines ~ae sicut fusae ex argento* AM 766; (of time) short: (neut. as sb.) *post ~um temporis a morte* ES 2568. **2** Of small importance, petty: *pro tam ~o et limitato fine* AC 6698; (masc. pl. as sb.) humble people: *carnes... ~orum et magnorum* Rev. 19.18 (AR).

Pascha ~atis, *neut.* (Hebr.) also **Pascha** ~ae, *f.* The feast of the Passover: *diebus ~atis* AC 2342.3; *nullus praeputiatus comedet ~a* Exod. 12.48 (FI 54).

Paschalis ~is ~e, *a.* Of or proper to the Passover, Paschal: *pecus ~is* AC 7831; *in coena ~i* AC 7850.2.

pasco ~ere pavi pastum, *tr.* (alt. pres. pple. **pavens** q.v.) **1** To give food to, feed (animals): *et Moscheh fuit ~ens gregem Jethronis* Exod. 3.1 (AC); *quomodo vos ~itis illos* AM 9.4; (fig., w. abl. of manner) *ut ~at eas* [sc. *gentes*] *virga ferrea* Rev. 2.27 (AC 426.3). **2** (of animals) To graze: *super viis ~ent* Isa. 49.9 (AC 6854.4).

pascuum ~i, *neut.* A place where animals may graze, pasture: *in ~is herbae cubare facis me* Ps. 23.2 (AC 57); Isa. 49.9 (AC 8261.4); *per Me si quis introiverit... ~um inveniet* John 10.9 (AE 208.2).

passer ~eris, *m.* A sparrow: *conjunctionibus diversarum specierum animalium...sicut... ~erum et avium nobilium* AM 246.3.

passim, *adv.* On many occasions, frequently: *somnium habui e quo ~im expergefactus* ES 228; *animae recentes...circumferuntur ad plures mansiones...et ~im recipiuntur* AC 1273; *status...describitur etiam ~im in Verbo* CI 271.

passio ~onis, *f.* **1** The act of suffering, esp. the Lord's passion on the Cross: *~o crucis* FI 35; *de ~one Domini* DD 16.4. **2** A violent emotion, passion: *quod ipsae ~ones et cupiditates...ex principio coelesti...influant* ES 331. **3** *~o iliaca*, a painful condition of the intestines, ileus: AM 470.

passive, *adv.* Without any spontaneous action, passively: *ut ~e exspectarent* ES 1628.

passivus ~a ~um, *a.* Acted upon rather than active, passive: *cogitatio ~a* AC 6987.1; *in vi ~a seu mortua* AM 489; *quod homo ex se mere ~us sit* VR 110.6; (neut. as sb.) *in ipsis organicis hominis...est ~um et activum* AC 718.

passus ~us, *m.* **1** A pace, step: *in gradiendo quovis tertio ~u...spectant ad latus* AC 8371; *in primo ~u* AM 232.4; *~um movere*, to take a step: *non potest equus movere ~um* AC 187; CI 228. **2** *Pari ~u*, in step: see **par**[1].

pasta ~ae, *f.* (Gk.) A mixture of flour and water, paste: (fig.) *ex diversis bonis* [*facit*] *unam ~am* AM 444[a].

pastor ~oris, *m.* A shepherd: *et venerunt ~ores, et depulerunt illas* Exod. 2.17 (AC); (fig.) *qui ducit et docet, appellatur ~or* AC 343; *Dominus...in Verbo vocatur ~or* FI 61.

pastoritius ~a ~um, *a.* Of a shepherd: *baculos ~os* AC 10754; *dicit quid velint cum puella ~a* [i.e., with a shepherd girl] UJ(P) 64.

patefacio ~facere ~feci ~factum, *tr.* To throw open: *Jehovah...ostia coelorum ~fecit* Ps. 78.23 (AE 146.4).

patefio ~eri, *intr.* To be opened: *percipere quomodo animi eorum tunc ~unt* ES 927.

patella ~ae, *f.* A small dish, saucer: *patinae et ~ae cibis omnis generis refertae* AM 14.2.

pateo ~tere ~tui, *intr.* **1** (of doors and sim.) To be unobstructed, lie open: *ostia, quae ~tebant in floreta* AM 13.2; CI 430; (of other things) to be approached by a clear passage, lie open: *tunc clausa sunt interiora quae ~tuerunt in coelum* CI 252; *cogitationes...sunt apertae ...et ~tent usque a Domino* AC 99. **2** To be clearly visible, be exposed to view: *interiora cujusvis ~tent ibi in facie* CI 131. **3** To be apparent to the mind, be apprehensible: *quae causa nusquam alicui ~tere potest nisi ex sensu interno* AC 7093.3; *non ~tet* [*fides*] *coram intellectu* FI 1. **4** (impers.) It is clear, it is plain: (w. *quod*) *quod ultimum sit damnatio... ~tebit a sequentibus* AC 7766; *ex his ~tet, quod...nullus salvari potuerit* VR 3.1; (w. indir. qu.) *ut... ~teat cuivis manifeste quid cogitant* AC 6655.

pater ~tris, *m.* **1** A father: *intimum vitae...quod anima vocatur, est a ~tre* AC 6716.2. **2** (as the title by which the Lord in His incarnation addressed God): *~ter, venit hora* John 17.1 (DD 13); (as one person of the Trinity) *hodierna fides...ponit Deum ~trem et Deum Filium* FI 39; (w. gen. as divine title) *~ter Aeternitatis* Isa. 9.6 (CI 287.1). **3** (usu. pl.) Ancestors, forefathers: *Deus ~trum vestrorum* Exod. 3.13 (AC); (sg.) *quod plures familiae...a suo primo ~tre cognoscantur* VR 103.2. **4** Any aged and respected man, esp. a founder of the Christian Church: *discubuerunt viri cum ~tribus illis* AM 6.2; *stabilitur, tam ex Scriptura Sacra, quam ex ~tribus,...quod...* VR 101.1; *~tres Apostolici* VR 137.1.

paterfamilias patrisfamilias, *m.* The head of a household: *Dominus Se comparat patrifamilias qui plantavit vineam* AC 124; AC 829.2; VR 727.2.

paternus ~a ~um, *a.* Of one's father, paternal: *separati a domo ~a* ES 1520.

patesco ~ere, *intr.* **1** To become clear, be revealed: *quod hoc ~at ex substantiis compositis* AM 316.4; *quare* *non ~unt* [*miracula*] ES 2434. **2** (impers.) It becomes clear: *ut mox ~et* AC 1752.1; (w. *quod*) AC 7038.3; (w. indir. qu.) AC 7069.

patheticus ~a ~um, *a.* (Gk.) Arousing the emotions, impassioned: *praedicator et scriptor valde ~us fuit* AC 10735; *libros ~os* ES 5814; (neut. as sb.) the power of arousing emotions: *~um illud fuerat arte acquisitum* AC 10755.

pathologia ~ae, *f.* (Gk.) The study of diseases, pathology: *hos* [*morbos*] *~a docet* AM 253.1.

patiens ~ntis, *a.* (pres. pple. of **patior**) **1** Patient, long-suffering: *consocius in afflictione...et ~nte exspectatione Jesu Christi* Rev. 1.9 (AR); *bonum amoris est...clemens, ~ns et pudicum* AE 427.9. **2** Passive: *agens et ~ns* ES 2722.

patientia ~ae, *f.* Perseverance in the face of difficulties or affliction, patience: *fructum faciunt in ~a* Luke 8.15 (AC 8361); *quod voluerit pati...quod vocabat ~am Christianam* AC 952.

patina ~ae, *f.* (ad. Gk.) A plate, dish: *purgatis exterius poculi et ~ae* Matt. 23.25 (AC 7046.2); *~a argentea* SS 40.1; *parva ~a panum...plena* ES 2626.

patior ~ti ~ssus sum, *tr.*, *intr.* **1** (tr.) To undergo, suffer (unpleasant things): *quod ab his ~tiantur dura* AC 6893; *postquam extrema ~ssi sunt* AC 7251. **2** (intr.) To allow something to happen to oneself, be acted upon: *instar conjugii est ubi agens et ~tiens* AC 7022; *ut... sequamur permittendo et ~tiendo* AM 208.2. **b** *se ~ti* (w. pass. inf.), to allow oneself (to): *Dominus Se ~ssus tentari a diabolo* AC 730.5; [*infantes*] *se ~tiuntur duci* CI 277.2. **3** (intr.) To be ill-treated, suffer: *ejus miseretur, cum ~titur* AC 351; *inde ~titur mens* ES 596; (esp. of the Lord's crucifixion) *quia ~ssus pro illo Dominus* AC 6639.3.

patratio ~onis, *f.* The act of performing, commission: *~o mali in abscondito* AC 9125.1.

patria ~ae, *f.* One's native land, fatherland, country: *inserviendo ~ae, societatibus, et proximo* AC 7038.1; *in mundo spirituali est ipsa habitatio ejus, ac ut dicitur, ~a ejus* AE 1094.2.

patriarcha ~ae, *m.* (Gk.) A patriarch (among the Jews): *aliqui suum ~am quaerunt* ES 475.

patrinus ~i, *m.* A sponsor at baptism, godparent: *facit illa quae ~i pro illo spoponderunt* AR 224.11; VR 685.2.

patrius ~a ~um, *a.* Of one's native land, native: *quod lingua qua...loquuntur, sit eorum propria et ~a* AC 1637.

patro ~are ~avi ~atum, *tr.* To carry out, commit (a crime): *crimina et flagitia, quae ~averunt in mundo* CI 462[a].1; *ad scelestissima talia ~anda* ES 3594.

patrocinatio ~onis, *f.* Support, encouragement: AE 654.44; an instance of this: *timet...~ones ejus* [sc. *meretricis*] *a judicibus* AM 469.

patrocinium ~i, *neut.* Patronage, support: *mali spiritus...abutuntur hac communicatione ad comparandum sibi ~um e coelis* AE 832.2.

patrocinor ~ari ~atus sum, *intr.* (w. dat.) To give support or encouragement (to), favour: *cupiditates, quibus sensus literae ~ari posset* AC 1879.1; *~antur* [*ratiocinia*]*...jucundis carnis contra jucunda spiritus* AM 481; (gerundive) *ad ~anda falsa* AC 7039.2.

patronus ~i, *m.* A superior giving support to an inferior, patron: *ei instituunt cultum, vocando illum suum ~um* ES 5655.

patruelis ~is, *m.* The child of a father's brother, paternal cousin: AC 1153.3.

patruus ~i, *m.* A father's brother, uncle: *contra ~um seu Esavum* 2AD 1605.

patulus ~a ~um, *a.* Laid open, bare: *cum interiora hominis usque ab anima... ~a sunt* AM 355.4.

paucitas ~atis, *f.* Fewness, paucity: *de ~ate generis humani respective ad infinitatem Creatoris* AC 9441.2.

paucius, *compar. adv.* To a smaller extent, more sparingly: *sic implentur communia, quae vocata sunt vasa... ~us et plenius secundum beneplacitum Domini* ES 1958.

pauculus ~a ~um, *a.* Rather few: *haec quae memorata sunt modo ~a sunt* AC 4180.7; (neut. as sb.) a small amount, a little: *vita...intra ~um temporis perit* AC 726; *~um exspectati visi sunt* AM 6.2.

paucus ~a ~um, *a.* (compar. *~ior*, superl. *~issimus*) **1** (pl.) Few, scarce: *~i sunt qui regenerantur, et adhuc ~iores qui reflectunt* AC 4245.2; *haec sunt ~a illustrationis causa adducta* VR 73.3; (neut. as sb.) *contenti ~is et pusillis* CI 277.2. **b** *~is*, in a few words, briefly: *licet adhuc ~is exponere quid sit* AC 6685; *quomodo haec fiunt, non ~is dici potest* SS 32. **2** (sg.) Small in quantity, little: *tam ~am vitam residuam habent* AC 6959.2; (neut. as sb.) *milvo, qui videt ~um tergi a pisci magno super aquas* VR 165.3. **b** (of time) short: *ante ~um tempus* AC 443.

paulatim: see **paullatim**.

Paulinus ~a ~um, *a.* Of the apostle Paul, Pauline: *in dicto ~o* VR 338.2.

paulisper, *adv.* To a small extent, slightly: *sub planta pedis, ~er antrorsum* AC 8099.2; for a short while: *moremini hic ~er* VR 160.7.

paullatim, *adv.* also **paulatim**. Little by little, by degrees: *quod ~im et successu temporum decrescant* [*Ecclesiae*] AC 497; AC 7359; CI 533.

paullo: see **paulo**.

paulo, *adv.* also **paullo**. **1** To a small extent, a little: *ad dextram ~o versus anteriora* AC 6692.2; *~o obscuriores* CI 181. **2** At a short distance: *~o ante oculos* ES 3840.

paululum, *adv.* To a fairly small extent, a little: *carere quidem Ipsum fecisti ~um prae angelis* Ps. 8.5 (DD 6); *quod nec timeant mortem, nisi ~um* AC 8113.

paulum, *adv.* To a small extent, a little: *facies...circum labra ~um prominebant* AC 8246; *loquela angelorum spiritualium est ~um vibratoria* CI 241.

pauper ~eris, *a.* (nom. fem. sg. *~era* 2AD 1434, gen. pl. *~erum*, superl. *~errimus*) **1** Lacking in riches, poor: *quod intrare in coelum nemo possit nisi qui miser sit et ~er* AC 7318.1; ES 4427; (masc. as sb.) *homo dat ~eribus* VI 9; spiritually poor: *qui spiritualiter miseri sunt et ~eres* ES 1327 1/2. **2** (transf.) Impoverished: *sapientia ejus nunc erat ~era* 2AD 1434.

paupertas ~atis, *f.* The fact of being poor, poverty: *pauperes non in coelum propter ~atem veniunt, sed propter vitam* CI 364.

pauxillum ~i, *neut.* A very small amount: *~um frigoris* ES 1858; (acc. as adv.) *quod ~um apparere inciperent [bona et vera]* AC 879.

pavens ~ntis, *a.* (alt. pres. pple. of **pasco**; cf. AC 6277) To give food to, feed: *Deus ~ns [pascens* 3rd edn.] *me* Gen. 48.15 (AC).

paveo ~vere, *intr.* To tremble with extreme fear: *~vebunt sicut avis ex Aegypto et sicut columba e terra Aschuris* Hos.11.11 (AC 1186.6).

pavidus ~a ~um, *a.* Fearful, terrified, trembling: *propter teneras et ~as conscientias* Book of Concord in VR 516.

pavimentum ~i, *neut.* A paved floor, paving: *humiliant se paene ad ~um* VR 452; VR 797.3.

pavo ~onis, *m.* A peacock: *plumas ex alis ~onum mutuatas* VR 487.2; CO 30.2.

pavor ~oris, *m.* Intense fear, terror, dread: *non timebis tibi a ~ore noctis* Ps. 91.5 (AC 7102.10); AC 4180.1.

pax pacis, *f.* **1** A state of freedom from war, peace: *pangam illis foedus pacis* Ezek. 37.26 (AC 6804.9). **2** Freedom from discord or disturbance, tranquillity: *sphaera innocentiae et pacis* AM 222.2; *pax totius corporis delitiosa et perceptibilis* ES 370. **3** (in greetings or benedictions): *pax tibi, noli timere* Judg. 6.23 (AC 6849.2); *gratia vobis et pax* Rev. 1.4 (AR); a blessing: *surrexit princeps...ac pacem dixit* AM 16.3.

paxillus ~i, *m.* A pin or bolt for fixing anything, peg: *per ~um vel clavum* AC 8990.5; *nisi compressi tenerentur [serpentes] ~is* VR 524.2.

peccator ~oris, *m.* A sinner: *Filius Hominis tradetur in manus ~orum* Matt. 26.45 (DD 24).

peccatrix ~icis, *f. adj.* Sinning, sinful: *vae genti ~ici* Isa. 1.4 (AC 254).

peccatum ~i, *neut.* **1** An offence against divine law, sin: *quod remittere possint ex lubitu ~a* CI 508.3; *omnis qui...fugit mala ut ~a* AM 266.5. **2** (Bibl.) A sin-offering: *in lingua...originali per '~um', ubi agitur de sacrificiis, intelligitur sacrificium pro ~o* AC 10039 (Exod. 29.14).

pecco ~are ~avi, *intr.* To commit an offence against divine law, sin: *ex significatione '~are', quod sit facere contra ordinem Divinum* AC 7696; (w. dat.) *~avi Jehovae Deo vestro, et vobis* Exod. 10.16 (AC); also, to commit other offences: *qui contra leges ~at* AC 8282.

pectino ~are ~avi ~atum, *tr.* To comb (hair): *~avit comas* AC 5246.4.

pecto ~ere, *tr.* To comb (hair): *~ere comas* AC 5570; ES 1228; to groom by combing: *visi pueri...quos ~erent tam crudeliter quasi securibus ut sanguis a capite flueret* ES 3992; AC 2125.

pectorale ~is, *neut.* A garment worn about the chest: *~e oblique cinctum fascia ex lapidibus pretiosis* VR 110.8; (worn by a woman) a stomacher: ES 3017; (of the breastplate of Aaron) *facies ~e judicii* Exod. 28.15 (AC).

pectoralis ~is ~e, *a.* **1** Of or for the chest: *amicta erat...veste ~i purpurea* AM 42.4; *respirationem... ~em* ES 3805. **2** Of the heart as seat of emotions, cordial: *amor ~is qui...est plenus amicitia et plenus confidentia* AM 111.

pectus ~oris, *neut.* The chest, breast, bosom: *quae... ~oris sunt correspondent amori* AC 6960.1; *haec [tunica] erat circa ~us aperta* AM 15; (as the seat of the emotions) *religionem a ~ore in tergum rejecerunt* VR 9.1; VR 503.1; (of an animal) AC 10090.2.

pecuarius ~i, *m.* A sheep farmer, sheep breeder: AC 3995.3.

peculiaris ~is ~e, *a.* **1** Not shared with others, peculiar to oneself, individual: *singula verba involvunt ~em statum ejus* AC 782; *quae repetitio supervacanea foret...si non aliquid ~e distinctum a priore significaretur* AC 1015.1. **2** Set aside for the purpose, individually designed, special: *de quibus in ~i opusculo actum est* CI 309; AM 334.

peculiariter, *adv.* In an individually appropriate manner, specially: *si non regenerati essent, et tunc ~er illustrati* AC 7233.2.

peculium ~i, *neut.* A special possession, personal

property: *ut sint Mihi...in ~um* Mal. 3.17 (DD 4); cf. AC 6804.10.

pecunia ~ae, *f.* Money: *negotiatio est amor finalis eorum, et ~a amor medius inserviens* UJ(C) 48.3; (usu. pl.) *curas pro conquirendis ~is et opibus* AC 3957.4; AC 4751.2.

pecus[1] ~udis, *f.* A small domesticated animal, esp. a sheep or goat: *per opes, armenta, ~udes, domos* AC 6917.3; (specifically) a sheep: *ecce Ego judicans inter ~udem et ~udem, inter arietes et inter hircos* Ezek. 34.17 (FI 68); a goat: *~udes cornibus...praeditas solum habent* ES 1451; (contrasted with human beings) *vocantur ~udes rationales* DP 168.5.

pecus[2] ~oris, *neut.* (sg. collectively) Domesticated animals, cattle: *et etiam ~us nostrum ibit cum nobis* Exod. 10.26 (AC); (pl.) *quae sunt eorum terrae et eorum ~orum* AC 7249; (distinguished from oxen) *sic facies bovi tuo et ~ori tuo* Exod. 22.30 (AE 28.3).

pedes ~itis, *m.* A person who travels on foot, walker, marcher: *sexcenta millia ~itum virorum* Exod. 12.37 (AC).

pedetentim, *adv.* Little by little, gradually: *mens... spiritualis... ~im aperitur* CO 29.2.

pedicae ~carum, *f. pl.* Chains to secure the feet, fetters: *cogitatio a suis quasi ~cis quibus irretita...liberata* AC 1757; *monstrum manicis et ~cis vinctum* VR 123.6; (app.) a snare for the feet, mantrap: *in medio ejus* [sc. *agri*] *abscondit ~cas* CO 33.2.

pediculus ~i, *m.* **1** A louse: *~i in extrema cute sunt* AC 7419; *nidorem ~orum parietis tetrum* ES 1150; so, *~us domesticus*: AC 1514; ES 3424. **2** A maggot: *folia illorum* [sc. *virgultorum*] *implentur ~is et consumuntur* VR 41.3.

pedissequus ~a ~um, *a.* Attendant: *bestia cum omnibus ideis ~is amoris naturalis sui* VR 480; (fem. as sb.) *quod charitas sequatur fidem sicut ~a dominam* VR 459.2.

pejero ~are ~avi ~atum, *intr.* **1** To swear falsely, perjure oneself: Zech. 5.3 (AC 5135.5). **2** (app.) To invoke curses: *~avi contra me illum* 'I invoked curses against myself in that capacity' AM 269.4.

pejor ~or ~us, *a.* (used as compar. of **malus**[1]) Worse (in senses of **malus**[1]): *facies...~or mortuo* AC 949; *~ores fiunt in altera vita* AC 6655; *loquutus sum de genere humano, quod ~ores feris sint* ES 2026.

pejus, *adv.* (used as compar. of **male**) In a worse fashion: *quod noverint Christianos ~us vivere quam illi* CI 325; *insaniunt ~us quam ferae* AM 498.

Pelagianus ~a ~um, *a.* Of Pelagius, a British monk condemned as heretical in AD 416; (masc. as sb.) a Pelagian, a follower of Pelagius: AR Doc Ref.11.

pelagus ~i, *m.* (Gk.) A sea: *suffocati aquis ~i* VR 342.3; *ut quasi instar ~i sit* ES 4203.

pelecanus ~i, *m.* (Gk.) A pelican: *homo cui est religio, est in spiritualibus sicut ~us* [Worcester; *phoenix* Nordenskjold] *alens pullos sanguine suo* CO 40.

pellacia ~ae, *f.* Seductiveness, allurement: *eludimus et circumvenimus...hos alia politica arte et ~a* VR 665.3.

pellax ~acis, *a.* Seductive: *fallaces testificationes amoris mutui, ~aces insinuationes in favores* VR 434.2.

pellectio ~onis, *f.* Enticement: *sunt variae ~ones et concupiscentiae* AM 274.

pellecto ~are ~avi ~atum, *tr.* To entice: *~ant* [*pelliciunt* Tafel] *innocuos in suas partes* ES 409; *~ant* [*pelliciunt* Tafel] *eas* [sc. *virgines*] *ad scortandum* ES 1070.

pellex ~icis, *f.* also **paelex**. **1** A concubine: *qui abdicant ~ices et vivunt cum una uxore* AM 342.1. **2** A mistress: *non aliud apparet refugium...quam addicatio ~icis, quae gallice vocatur maitress* AM 459.1.

pellicatus ~us, *m.* The taking of a mistress: *quod ~us libidini vagae praestet* AM 460.1.

pellicio ~licere ~lexi ~lectum, *tr.* To entice: *impudicae mulieres quae...innocentes...ad talia ~lexerunt* AC 825; *fuerunt qui ~lexerunt virgines ad stupra* CI 462[a].4.

pellicula ~ae, *f.* The skin (in a derogatory sense): *qui solis sibi indulgent, et solam ~am curant* AC 4054; AC 4459.6.

pellis ~is, *f.* The flayed skin of an animal, hide: *sculptilia...vestita ~ibus pardi* AM 231.5; *apparuit indutus ~e hirsuta* VR 797.3.

pellucens ~ntis, *a.* Translucent: *cyathi...ex gemmis ~ntibus* AM 14.2; ES 1058; (fig.) *vera ~ntia ex bono* SS 44.3.

pellucentia ~ae, *f.* The quality of being translucent: *ex significatione vitrei, quod sit ~a* AE 275.1.

pelluceo ~cere, *intr.* To shine through: *lux influens ...in adamantem...~cet* VR 8.4; *igneum...quod ~cebat* ES 1680; (fig.) *~cet doctrina* CI 307.2.

pelluciditas ~atis, *f.* Translucence: *scientificum per mare significatur secundum aquarum ejus densitatem et nigritudinem, et vice versa secundum illarum tenuitatem et ~atem* AC 9755.16.

pellucidus ~a ~um, *a.* (superl. *~issimus*) Translucent: *de humore vitreo oculi, ubi est substantia ~a*

ES 3213; (fig.) *formae illae* [sc. *mentium*] *fiunt ~ae...per fidem* VR 8.4.

pelvis ~is, *f.* A small bowl, basin: *in sanguine qui in ~i* Exod. 12.22 (AC); (for washing) *Moabus ~is lotionis Meae* Ps. 60.8 (AC 1441); (anat.) a receptacle in the body for blood and other humours: *quod vasa seu ~es magnitudine crescant* ES 999.

penarium ~i, *neut.* (variant of **penuarium**) A container for grain and sim.: *omnia illa...quae...sunt cognitiones veri et boni, sunt modo ~a* AE 1154.3.

penates ~ium, *m. pl.* The household gods of the ancient Romans: *ex quibusdam* [*correspondentiis*] *fecerunt ~es* CO 43.

pendeo ~dere pependi, *intr.* **1** To be suspended, hang: *accipiter...collum insertavit laqueo, et pependit* VR 72.3; (w. *ex*) *sapphiri e collo ex aureo torque ~dentes* AM 15; (w. *ab*) *membra quae ~dent a pectore* VR 379.1. **2** To hang free, lack direction, waver: *brachia eorum ~dent et vibrantur* CI 3; (fig.) *ne... ~deant inter coelum et infernum* AC 7039.2; *pependerunt utrinque, et inclinaverunt illuc ubi favor* ES 4564. **3** (w. *ab* or *ex* or *in* + abl.) To be dependent (upon), hang (on): *ut omnes domus et familiae ~derent a parente* AC 471; *quod omne divisum nisi ~deat ab uno, ex se dilabatur* VR 10; *...ex his duobus mandatis Lex et Prophetae ~dent* Matt. 22.40 (DD 9); *in his duobus mandatis Lex et Prophetae ~dent* Matt. 22.40 (AC 6752.3). **b** *ex* or *ab ore* (+ gen.) *~dere*, to hang on the lips (of), be obedient (to): *mariti non ~debunt ex tuo ore* AM 208.5; AE 163.1; *~dent ab ore cujusvis magistri* VR 137.13.

pendo ~dere ~si ~sum, *tr.* **1** To weigh; (transf.) to estimate, reckon: *nihili ~dunt opes* AM 333.1. **2** To pay: *usuras ~dere* VR 432.

pendulum ~i, *neut.* A pendulum: *horologis, quod mobile est ex ~o et simul pondere aut elatere* VR 364.1; ES 3912.

pendulus ~a ~um, *a.* Suspended, hanging down: *tiaras ~as* Ezek. 23.15 (AC 1368.3); *~a vestis mulierum* ES 1386; *tenebatur ~us in illa flamma* ES 4453.

penes, *prep. w. acc.* **1** In the presence of, face to face with: *agnoverunt tandem cum ~es me, quod spiritus essent* AC 941.2; *ii qui ~es gehennam* ES 3086. **2** In, with, among: *quod... ~es externum Ipsius hominem... fuerit penuria cognitionum* AC 1460.1; *sciunt...quod ...omne malum* [*sit*] *a se, hoc est, ~es se ab inferno* AC 5069; *~es eos vetitum...vulgare ea quae spiritus loquuntur* ES 572; *mutationem status in malum ~es illos qui in falsis a malo* AC 8143.

penetralia ~um, *neut. pl.* The inward parts, inmost recesses: [*faemina*] *retrahit internas* [*affectiones*] *in ~a mantis suae* AM 274.

penetranter, *adv.* (compar. *~ius*) In a penetrating manner: *quod sensus literae pateat multo ~ius* ES 2056; *illi tam malitiose et quoque ~er insidiantur contra amorem conjugialem* ES 4638.

penetratio ~onis, *f.* Penetration (with the mind): *ex acumine ingenii et ~one rerum...judicare nemo potest* ES 956.

penetro ~are ~avi ~atum, *tr.*, *intr.* **1** (tr.) To reach the inside of, penetrate: *nubes ~ans tectum intravit* AM 315.12; *imber... ~avit utramque statuam* VR 110.8; (transf.) to penetrate mentally: *putaverunt se omnia potuisse ~are et intelligere* AC 1387. **2** (intr.) To proceed deep inside, penetrate, reach: *quod nomina nusquam ~ent in coelum* AC 6804.1; *verum et bonum versus interiora ~ant* AC 6829.

penibilis ~is ~e, *a.* Painful, distressing: *~es cruciatus inferre* ES 376; 3AD 3892.

peniculamentum ~i, *neut.* A fringe: *cum illis qui velant oculos ~o* VR 378.3; *ut facerent sibi ~um super alis vestium suarum* VI 2 (Num. 15.38).

penis ~is, *m.* (anat.) The penis: *in bulbum ~is* ES 3922.

penitior ~or ~us, *compar. a.* (superl. *~ssimus*) Deeply felt, intimate: *~ores cruciatus* ES 958; *dolor ~ssimus* 3AD 4536.

penitus, *adv.* (compar. *~ius*) Towards the centre or interior, inwardly, intimately, deeply: *labyrinthus, qui talis est, ut qui vult exire, ~ius intret* AM 8.3; (fig.) *affectiones meas intueri ~us* AC 1769.5; *dolus intrat ~ius cogitationes* CI 578; *haec conjunctio ~us inspecta non est conjunctio* SE 46.

penna ~ae, *f.* **1** A feather: *aperi plumas seu ~as corvi* AM 233.4. **2** A quill pen: ES 2248.

pennatus ~a ~um, *a.* Feathered: (neut. as sb.) *cum avibus et ~is omnis generis* VR 335.5.

pensilis ~is ~e, *a.* Hanging, pendent: *~es vites* AM 183.1; *~es lampades* VR 16.1.

pensito ~are ~avi, *intr.* To think to oneself, ponder, reflect: *~arunt aliquantum, et mox dixerunt...* AC 6700; AM 82.4; (w. indir. qu.) *~ant quid dicunt* AC 8384; ES 164.

pensum ~i, *neut.* **1** A carefully calculated amount, ration: *quod quisque...trahat suum ~um secundum suum situm* DP 164.3; *viscera inde hauriunt* [*sanguinem*], *quodlibet suum ~um secundum quale usus, quod praestat* VR 154.3. **2** A sum of money given as payment for work, wage: *~a solvere operariis* VR 432; *~a* [*data*] *Charonti, ut in campos Elysios transferantur* VR 453.

penu ~u, *neut.* **1** A store of provisions: *cum horreo, cujus ~u nusquam diminuitur* AM 148.3; VR 364.3. **2** Resources of any kind: *minores...quibus non tale est ~u* VR 459.8.

penuarium ~i, *neut.* see also **penarium**. A container for storing grain or other foodstuffs, bin: *~um in horreo, quod non nutrit hominem, nisi...inde frumentum desumit* FI 31; *~um ubi poma, citrea et similia talia* ES 3898.

penultimus ~a ~um, *a.* Next before the last, penultimate: *~us gradus* AE 1125.2.

penuria ~ae, *f.* Scarcity, shortage: *'fuit fames in terra' significat ~am cognitionum* AC 1459; AE 223.5.

peplum ~i, *neut.* (Gk.) A headdress used to cover the face, veil: *et accepit ~um et obtexit se* Gen. 24.65 (AC); *sponsae...obtegebant se ~o* AC 4859.1.

per, *prep. w. acc.* **1** Through, along (a space, path, etc.): *janua...per quam...advenae...introducti sunt* VR 692.3; *per medium auditorii deducti sunt* VR 694.2. **b** all through, throughout: *mirati...quod vulgari talia possent per tellurem* ES 554. **2** Through, for (a period of time): *per aliquantum temporis* AC 1106; *per noctem* ES 3755. **b** *per tempus*, for a short time, for a while: *aberant per tempus* AC 6198. **3** Through the instrumentality of, by means of, by: *Verbum est per coelum a Domino* AC 1619; *a Pharaone per quem repraesentatur scientificum* AC 6692.1; *quod infans nascatur niger ex nigro...per faeminam albam* DP 277.3; *liber per me scriptus* VR 461.8. **4** Through the causality of, as a result of: *Ecclesiae per Reformationem...separatae* SE 18; *haec...per continuum aspectum...solita...facta sunt* VR 695.5; *raro moriuntur per morbos* ES 580. **5** (w. distributive force) In each, by: *per diem* 'daily' AC 6699; *regnum sacerdotale per omnes tribus dispersa fuit* 3AD 4563. **6** *Per se*, taken by himself (herself, itself, etc.), individually: *quod omnia...ut per se subsistant, in suos ordines creata sint* VR 54; *Paulo...data habitatio per se* ES(M) 4562.

pera ~ae, *f.* A bag carried by travellers, pack: *nunc qui habet crumenam tollat, similiter ~am* Luke 22.36 (AE 131.3).

peraeque, *adv.* Altogether equally, every bit as well: (w. *ac*) *vident illi ~e ac alii, et quandoque ad apparentiam perspicacius* AC 5464.1.

perago ~ragere ~regi ~ractum, *tr.* **1** To be engaged in, conduct, pass: *quod...similem...vitam ineant et ~ragant* VR 79.6; *in tentoriis suis cultum sanctum ~regerunt* AC 414.3. **2** (pass.) To be accomplished, take place, happen: *quicquid ~ragitur in inferno* VR 61.1; *nondum...Ultimum Judicium fuit ~ractum* DD 61.2; *tentationes...priusquam plene ~ractae sunt* AC 8179.3.

peragro ~are ~avi ~atum, *tr.* To wander over, traverse: *ad ~andum terram* Zech. 6.7 (AE 355.9).

perambulo ~are ~avi ~atum, *tr.* To walk through: *quando...spiritus immundus exit ab homine, ~at loca arentia* Matt. 12.43 (DD 48.6).

peramo ~are ~avi ~atum, *tr.* To love deeply, be in love with: *mariti qui ~ant suas uxores* AM 224.

percello ~cellere ~cellui ~culsum, *tr.* To affect violently, strike, hit: *quando aliquid subitum contingit quod interiora...~cellit vel mutat* ES 1357; *ex quo [cruciatu] ~culsi* CI 525; *quae tantopere ~cellebat eos ...quos autem ~celluit* 3AD 4171; (w. abl.) *stupore ~culsi sunt* AC 7077; *malis conscientia ~cellitur* AC 8162.

perceptibilis ~is ~e, *a.* (compar. *~ior*) **1** Capable of being perceived, perceptible: *idea quadam apud me ~i* AC 1875; *in jucundum coeli, quod omnibus modis ~e et sensibile fit* CI 401; *pulchritudinem, quae excedit omnem pulchritudinis ideam usquam visu ~em* CI 414; (neut. as sb.) *visibilia in mundo, et...~ia in Verbo* VR 28.1. **2** (w. gen.) Capable of containing perceptions: *communia quae non ~ia sunt singularium* AC 6686; *ideae...~iores rerum* ES 1559.

perceptibilitas ~atis, *f.* The quality of being perceptible: *quae de ~ate interiorum spiritus...dicta sunt* AC 1520; AM 359.2.

perceptibiliter, *adv.* In a perceptible manner, perceptibly: *animadverti...~er et sensibiliter influxum illum nunc per 25 annos* AM 419.

perceptio ~onis, *f.* **1** The act of perceiving, perception: *de difficili ~one originis amoris conjugialis* AM 183.2; *~onem quod insinuandum ei bonum* AC 6728. **2** The faculty of perceiving, the ability to perceive, grasp: *solum ex laetitiis...mundanis ~onem capiunt* AC 540; *quam exquisita ~o angelorum sit num...* AC 228; *~o est videre quod verum sit verum et bonum bonum* AC 7680; *qui...in ~one boni sunt* SS 13.3. **3** A thing grasped by perception, perceived idea: *doctrinalia...fuerunt...ex Antiquissimae Ecclesiae revelationibus et ~onibus* AC 1068; *arbores...correspondent ~onibus* CI 111.

perceptiuncula ~ae, *f.* A small perception: *unaquaevis idea et unaquaevis ~a...in suo ordine est* ES 2268.

perceptive, *adv.* By means of perception: *percipitur ...vel ~e vel intellectualiter* ES 2186.

perceptivus ~a ~um, *a.* Endowed with powers of perception, perceptive: *Ecclesia ~a fuit qualis hodie nulla datur* AC 495; (esp. neut. as sb.) power of perception, perceptivity: *~um hoc proprium erat Antiquissimae Ecclesiae* AC 371; *~um fidei* AC 6751.

percipio ~cipere ~cepi ~ceptum, *tr.* **1** To become

aware of, perceive (a feeling, sensation): *loquela spirituum mecum tam distincte audita et ~cepta est sicut loquela cum homine* AC 1635; *nec fatigatio ulla ~cipitur* AC 1884; *quod post obitum ~cepturi sint ignem* AC 8244; *non ~cipiunt aliquam lucem ibi* VR 7. **2** To become intellectually aware of, perceive, grasp (a fact, the existence of a thing, etc.): *quod...per 'Deum patrum vestrorum' non ~cipiant Deum Abrahami* AC 6884; *alii quidem possunt audire illa quae e coelo, sed non ~cipere* AE 8.2. **b** (in a specified manner): *~cipitur ab angelis praedicate ad subjectum* AC 6985; *quia ea illis ~cepta sunt ut terrestria* AC 7073; *inde est quod unusquisque ... ~cipiat sicut insaniam dicere quod plures sint [dei]* VR 6.3. **c** (w. *quod* or acc. + inf.): *quod ratio humana ... ~cipere aut concludere possit...quod Deus sit* VR 5; *quod... ~cipiat se in cerebro cogitare* SA 365.1. **d** (w. indir. qu.): *cum ~cipit qualis externus homo est* AC 1584; *cum... ~ciperent quid scriberem* AC 6929.

percitus ~a ~um, *a.* Deeply moved, stirred, impelled: (w. *ex*) *ex...suavitate penitus affecti et ~i* AM 19; (w. abl.) *odio ~us internecino* ES 225; *~i ira* ES 2119.

perclare, *adv.* Very clearly: *illae [sc. lenitudo et suavitas] distingui ~e potuerunt a lenitudine et suavitate spirituum bonorum nostrae telluris* AC 8111.

percolo ~are ~avi ~atum, *tr.* To filter: *glandulae ~ant [sanguinem]* VR 496.4.

percontor ~ari ~atus sum, *tr.* To enquire of, question: *~ati sunt eruditos, quid sciunt de conscientia* IM 69.

percurro ~rere ~ri ~sum, *tr.* **1** To go rapidly through, run through: *quod Deus Spiritus Sanctus... illico ~rat terrarum orbem ad illos* VR 16.1; *cervi...qui ~runt campos* VR 815.1; (w. *per*) *lumen solis, quod... sicut per formas ~rit, seu in iis influit* ES 1709. **2** To pass rapidly through (states): *unusquisque angelus tales mutationes status subit et ~rit* CI 157. **3** To pass in rapid mental review, run through, run over: *illico ~rebant illa quae in memoria mea erant* AC 6922; *quod mihi datum sit omnes Prophetas et Davidis Psalmos ~rere* DD 37.1; DP 259.2.

percussio ~onis, *f.* The act of striking: *culter iis...in ictu ~onis adimitur* AC 818.

percussor ~oris, *m.* One who strikes, smiter: *non permittet ~ori venire ad domos vestras ad percutiendum* Exod. 12.23 (AE 329.1); 3AD 4596.

percutio ~tere ~ssi ~ssum, *tr.* **1** To strike, hit: *Jehovah ~tiet terram virga* Isa. 11.4 (AC 1286.2); *quod... ~ssus baculo Aharonis fluvius* AC 7346; (w. *in* + acc.) *~tiet eum [sc. fluvium] in septem rivos* Isa. 11.15 (SS 15.2). **2** To strike fatally, smite, kill: *non addam amplius ~tere omne vivum sicut feci* Gen. 8.21 (AC); *quod... ~ssi sint Bethschemitae ad plura millia* VI 55.3. **3** (w. abl.) To affect, strike (with something detrimental): *de haemorrhoidibus et muribus quibus ... ~ssi et infestati sunt* FI 52; *~tiam omnem equum stupore* Zech. 12.4 (DD 4).

perdite, *adv.* In an abandoned fashion, without restraint: *indolui...quod conjugia...tam ~e conversa sint in adulteria* AM 80.3; ES 4117.

perditio ~onis, *f.* Destruction, ruin: *crediturus quod inde veniat ei ~o cum tamen ab ipso* AC 8282; *filius ~onis* John 17.12 (DD 11).

perditor ~oris, *m.* A destroyer: *omnes illi ~ores* Jer. 6.28 (AC 8298.2); *~or gentium* Jer. 4.7 (AE 304.9).

perditus ~a ~um, *a.* (pf. pple. of **perdo**) (in senses of vb., esp.) No longer known, lost to memory: *qualis eorum...computus fuerit, inter res ~as est* AC 575; beyond redemption, lost: *gens ~a consiliis illi* Deut. 32.28 (AC 7051.3).

perdix ~icis, *m.* A partridge: Jer. 17.11 (AE 236.7).

perdo ~ere ~idi ~itum, *tr.* **1** To annihilate, destroy: *fur non venit nisi ut furetur, occidat, et ~at* John 10.10 (AC 6767.4); *angelus extendit manum suam contra Hierosolymam ad ~endum illam* 2 Sam. 24.15 (CI 229). **2** To render non-existent, destroy (spiritually): *in malis quae omne bonum... ~erent* AC 7378; *ne amor conjugialis... ~atur* AM 444[a]. **3** To render spiritually dead, ruin (a person): *Ecclesia se tunc prorsus ~idit* AC 234; *intentant omni modo ~ere illum* AC 6724.2. **4** To have taken away, lose: *non ~et mercedem* Mark 9.41 (AC 6674.5); *quod non sciant quod aliquid ~iderint* CI 312.4; *ut ~ere sibi videantur suos pedes* ES 3852. **5** To waste, squander: *quod [ebrietas] ~at id in luxu quod multis potest esse in usum* ES 2422.

perdomatio ~onis, *f.* Thorough taming, complete subjugation: *quod finis omnium tentationum spiritualium sit ~o mali et falsi* CN De Redemptione vii.5.

perduco ~cere ~xi ~ctum, *tr.* **1** To lead through, conduct, take: *a Domino ~ctus sum in coelos* CI 192; *quando... ~cerer per mansiones aliquas* ES 277. **2** To bring (into a specified state), reduce, introduce: *quod... ~cantur successive in novos status* AC 6645.3; *si... ~citur in aliquid desperationis* AC 7090.4; *~cere animos illorum ad sapiendum* AM 294.2; (of things) *haec... ~cunt illam vitam ad mortem* AC 8364.2; *cum malum ad summum ~ctum est* AC 1311.2. **b** to bring into the appropriate state, change: *cum iis de hac tellure ita loqui licet...sunt spiritus intermedii, qui momento ~cunt loquelam* ES 1513.

perduro ~are ~avi, *intr.* To persist, last: *zelus amoris mali ~at* AM 365; *ut...homo fiat constans et ~ans in aeternum* VR 14.1; ES 153.

peregre, *adv.* Abroad: *de homine qui ~e abiit* AC 2967.2 (Matt. 25.14).

peregrinatio ~onis, *f.* The act of going abroad, travel: *per filiorum Israelis ~ones in deserto* AC 8098; AM 475.2.

peregrinator ~oris, *m.* A traveller: *monachi ~ores seu missionarii* AC 10812.

peregrinor ~ari ~atus sum, *intr.* **1** (Bibl.) To stay among foreigners, live as a stranger: *lex una erit indigenae et peregrino ~anti in medio vestrum* Exod. 12.49 (AC); *in Aegyptum descendit populus Meus ad ~andum ibi* Isa. 52.4 (AE 328.16). **2** To move from one place of residence to another, travel: *cum ita ~antur* AC 6925.

peregrinus ~a ~um, *a.* **1** Not native, foreign: *'~um' significat quod non natum in terra* AC 1843.1; (esp. masc. as sb.) a foreigner, stranger: *de alienigenis... inquilinis...et ~is* AC 8001; *~us fui et collegistis Me* Matt. 25.35 (VI 2). **2** Unfamiliar, strange: *quod ita se habeant, non potest non ~um apparere* AC 755.4; *Verbum in litera apparet sicut scriptum vulgare, stylo ~o* SS 1; AM 161.2.

perennatio ~onis, *f.* Endurance over a long time, permanence: *communicationes tales dantur in hac tellure, et ~ones* [J Chadwick's reading of Autograph; *peregrinationes* Tafel] ES 4781.

perennis ~is ~e, *a.* Permanent, everlasting: *quod ignem sacrum ~em instituerint* AC 6832.7; *exspectatione ~i et ~i frustra* VR 160.5.

perennitas ~atis, *f.* The quality of lasting for ever, permanence: *quod sapientia...vitam intellectualem... beet ~ate* AM 433.

perenniter, *adv.* Everlastingly, permanently: *quod ita ~er succedere possint variationes* AC 1627; VR 78.3.

perenno ~are ~avi ~atum, *intr.* To last for ever, endure: *quod sit perpetuum...proinde ~aturum, et sic futurum ut prius* AC 7140; *festum ~ans in aeternum* AM 3.6; ES 711.

pereo ~rire ~rii, *intr.* **1** To die, perish: *quod dein ~rierint in mari Suph* AC 7039.2. **b** to suffer spiritual death: *ne a malis quae ipsi faciunt ~reant* AC 6997.2. **2** To cease to exist, pass away, be lost: *etiam hoc arcanum ~riit* AC 54; *hoc jucundum... ~riturum foret* AC 7364; *nexus rumperetur et copula ~riret* SS 13.4. **b** to be lost to view: *turris...media sui altitudine ~riit in coelo, sic ut videri non posset* ES(M) 4601.

perez, *indecl.* (Hebr.) see also **perizin**. Peres, to divide: *per ~ez seu dividere* AR 313 (Dan. 5.28).

perezin: see **perizin**.

perfacile, *adv.* Very easily: *hoc faciunt angeli per influxum ~e* AC 7807.

perfecte, *adv.* (compar. *~ius*) Perfectly: *quod homo post mortem sit ~e homo, imo ~ius homo quam prius* AM 182.3; VR 89.

perfectio ~onis, *f.* The state of being perfect, perfection: *ut...sic ~o sit omnium* AC 1598; *crescit...omnis ~o in coelis secundum pluralitatem* CI 418.

perfectus ~a ~um, *a.* (pf. pple. of **perficio**) (compar. *~ior*, superl. *~issimus*) Perfect: *in aliquibus statibus potest homo ~ior dici* AC 894; *distinctae formae...quae simul sumtae formam ~issimam coeli constituent* AC 8004; *millia objecti visa ~o microscopio* CI 269.2.

perfero ~ferre ~tuli ~latum, *tr.* **1** To cause to go, take, transmit: *~latus sum ad alios* AC 10808; *voce ad me ~lata* ES 241. **2** To impel (to a course of action): *in quod [malum]...ex coeco jucundo ~lati sunt* CI 509.

perficio ~ficere ~feci ~fectum, *tr.* **1** To finish making, complete: *fenestram facies arcae, et ad cubitum ~ficies illam superne* Gen. 6.16 (AC); *qui fundaturus domum Dei, et ~fecturus illam* AE 62.2. **2** To put into effect, accomplish, fulfil (orders, prophecies, etc.): *ubi ~ficientur omnia quae scripta sunt per Prophetas* Luke 18.31 (AC 7933.2); *quantum hoc ~fecit, tantum Se univit Patri* VR 73.3. **3** To render closer to an ideal, make perfect: *angeli ~ficiuntur continue* AC 6648; *[artifex] per talia quae sunt scientiae ejus, ~ficit se* VI 39; (w. abl.) *homo potest ~fici scientia, intelligentia et sapientia in aeternum* AM 134.2.

perfide, *adv.* Treacherously: *nec agite ~e* Mal. 2.16 (DD 48.5).

perfidia ~ae, *f.* Treachery: Isa. 24.16 (AC 390).

perfidus ~a ~um, *a.* Treacherous, perfidious: *~i perfide agunt* Isa. 24.16 (AC 390); Jer. 3.8 (AE 141.5).

perflo ~are ~avi, *tr.*, *intr.* Occurs only as a doubtful reading *perflarent* at ES [5792] 1/3; J D Odhner gives *perstarent*, but perh. it should be emended to *praestarent*.

perfluo ~ere ~xi, *intr.* To flow through: *bonum quod influit, ~it* ES 4561.

perfodio ~dere ~di ~ssum, *tr.* To penetrate by digging, dig through: *non sineret ~dere domum suam* Matt. 24.43 (AE 193.5); (absol.) *ubi fures ~diunt et furantur* Matt. 6.19 (DP 217.6); also, to pierce: *~disti illis omnem humerum* Ezek. 29.7 (AC 9836.4).

perforatio ~onis, *f.* The action of boring through, perforating, piercing (of an ear): *quod ~o auris fieret per subulam* AC 8990.5; AC 8989.2.

perforatorius ~a ~um, *a.* Relating to the action of boring holes, perforatory: *undulatio ~a* ES 3218.

performo ~are ~avi ~atum, *tr.* To form completely:

in ea opinione erant, quod ii suomet studio [candelabrum] ~averint ES 2647.

perforo ~are ~avi ~atum, *tr.* To bore through, perforate: *tria canistra ~ata* Gen. 40.16 (AC); *~abit dominus ejus aurem ejus subula* Exod. 21.6 (AC).

perfossio ~onis, *f.* The act of digging through a wall, breaking in: Jer. 2.34 (AE 329.26).

perfringo ~ringere ~regi ~ractum, *tr.* To break through, break down: *fores, quas ~ringere difficilius est* 3AD 2280.

perfundo ~ndere ~di ~sum, *tr.* To drench: *instar vaporis, quo irrigatur et ~nditur externus ejus [homo] ab interno* AC 91; to fill as with a liquid: *cum...aspiciebant lunam, similiter quadam sancta veneratione ~ndebantur* AC 4288.3.

pergo ~gere ~rexi, *intr.* **1** To continue to move, proceed, go on: *sed ~gite, et appropinquate* AM 13.1; AM 75.3. **2** To extend, spread, proceed: *punitio... ~gebat circum me ad cohortes plures* AC 959; *influxus... ~git usque ad illa quae...ultima sunt* AC 6845. **3** To continue (in a course of action), go on (to): *~rexit in malitia* ES 260; (w. inf.) *et exspectavit adhuc septem dies alios, et ~rexit emittere columbam de arca* Gen. 8.10 (AC).

pergraecatio ~onis, *f.* An orgy: *tales fornicationes sunt ~ones* AM 456.

perhibeo ~bere ~bui, *tr.* To relate, tell, say: *hoc novum est, quod quidam ~beat se loqui cum angelis* AM 182.3; *illa quae de Spiritu Sancto ~bentur* VR 16.2; (impers. pass.) *~betur quod nemo possit implere legem* VR 523.1.

perhorresco ~rescere ~rui, *tr.* To shudder violently at, loathe: *~ruerunt amatoria scortorum* AM 433.

pericardium ~i, *neut.* (Gk.) (anat.) The pericardium: VR 60; ES 983.

periclitatio ~onis, *f.* The act of being endangered, peril: *ex ~one lamentantur...nautae* CO 57.

periclitor ~ari ~atus sum, *intr.* To be endangered, be in peril: *percipiunt suam vitam...aut suum lucrum ~ari* AC 1033.3; *si...fama non ~atur* SS 52.

pericranium ~i, *neut.* (Gk.) (anat.) The pericranium: *membranam...cui adjungitur ~um extus* ES 3888.

periculosus ~a ~um, *a.* (superl. *~issimus*) Dangerous, perilous: *si declinant [posteri] a vero et bono, ~issimum est* AC 310.1; *loqui cum spiritibus... ~um est* CI 249; *ii spiritus... ~issimi sunt* ES 647.

periculum ~i, *neut.* A dangerous event or situation, peril: *quod pro amicis ~a subeant* CI 406; *cum ~o animarum nostrarum* 'at the risk of our lives' Lam. 5.9 (AE 131.11); *ascendere conabar...cum ~is, ne delaberer* ES 1579.

perinde, *adv.* *~e est*, it is equally significant, it is all the same: *sive dicatur cultus internus et externus, sive Ecclesia interna et externa, ~e est* AC 1227; *illis ~e est, sive doctrinalia illa sint vera vel falsa* AC 8148.2; *quod ~e esset si morerentur aliquot annos prius quam serius* ES 1282.

periodicus ~a ~um, *a.* (Gk.) Recurring at regular intervals, periodic: *omnia haec sunt consummationes alternae, quae...temporariae, sed usque ~ae* VR 756.

periodus ~i, *f.* (Gk.) **1** The proper time during which any event is completed, period: *omnes status...suas ~os habent* AC 3845; *integra ~us a principio ad finem* AC 6721; *absolvamus ~um aetatum* AM 78.1. **2** A sentence: *videatur expositio praemissa n. 4272, in nova ~o* AC 4279.3.

periosteum ~i, *neut.* (Gk.) The membrane which envelops the bone, periosteum: *ex ~is, quae sensu acuto gaudent* AM 511; *in ~a dentium* ES 4348.

peripheria ~ae, *f.* (Gk.) A circumferential region, periphery: *opus cohaerens cum ~is a centro ad superficiem* SS 38.1; *recedebat lux ad latera, et intrabat in ~as* VR 25.1.

peripneumonia ~ae, *f.* Inflammation of the lungs, pneumonia: *~a notha ex pituita lenta* VR 665.5.

periscelida ~lidae, *f.* (Gk. *periskelis*) also **periscelis** ~lidis, *f.* An ornament worn on the leg, anklet: *quaedam [objecta]...decorabant torquibus, myrothecidiis, et ~lidis* CO 43.

periscelis: see **periscelida**.

peritia ~ae, *f.* Knowledge of a craft, skill: *nisi nauclerus tunc ex sua ~a sciat avertere illam* [sc. *navem*] CO 59.4.

peritonaeum ~i, *neut.* (Gk.) also **peritoneum**. (anat.) The peritoneum: VR 60.2; ES 983.

peritoneum: see **peritonaeum**.

peritus ~a ~um, *a.* (superl. *~issimus*) Skilled, expert: (w. gen.) *~i artis musicae* AE 326.13; (w. *in* + abl.) *in linguis ~issimi* ES 1951.

perizin, *indecl.* (Hebr.) also **perezin**, *indecl.* (AE 373.3), and **upharsin**, *indecl.* (AC 3104.4). see also **perez**. Upharsin or perezin, a word in the handwriting on the wall meaning 'and divided' or 'divided': *mene, mene, thekel, ~in, hoc est, numeratus, numeratus, appensus, divisus* Dan. 5.25 (AR 313); AE 373.3.

perla ~ae, *f.* A pearl: [*charitas*] *apparet...sicut ~a similis oculo piscis cocti* VR 459.13; *loquela labente quasi in ~as* ES 3925.

perlatus ~a ~um: pf. pple. of **perfero**.

perlego ~gere ~gi ~ctum, *tr*. To read through: *dum ~gi Verbum a primo capite Esaiae usque ad ultimum Malachiae* SS 113.

perlustro ~are ~avi ~atum, *tr*. To look over, survey: *in ~ando urbem, vidimus...consortes* AM 76.4; to consider: *quod ita sit, perspicitur a quovis, qui ~at mores, animos et facies liberorum* VR 469.2.

permagnus ~a ~um, *a*. Very great: *talium numerus est ~us* ES 230.

permanentia ~ae, *f*. Persistence: *absque ~a jucundi non est illis voluntas* AM 461.6; perseverance: *~am in veris ad finem* AE 111.

permaneo ~nere ~nsi ~nsum, *intr*. **1** To remain, stay (in a place): *in desertum ubi per quadraginta annos ~nserunt* AC 8099.1; AM 5.2. **2** To remain (in a state): *~nebunt in bono* AC 7911; *qui ~net in genuina affectione veri* AE 111; (w. pred.) *naturales ~nserunt* VR 11.2; ES 4421. **3** To remain in existence, persist, endure: *fides caeca etiam ~nsit postea apud plures Reformatos* FI 9; *ex communi facierum ex patre in posteritate etiam sera ~nentium* AM 238.1.

permansio ~onis, *f*. Continuance or persistence (in a state of mind): *sessiones significant ~ones in statu interiorum* AC 9422.2.

permaximus ~a ~um, *a*. By far the greatest: *~a pars...non credunt* ES 4661.

permeabilitas ~atis, *f*. The ability to pass through or be transferred: *ex ~ate illius amoris...a mente in corpus* AM 110.

permiror ~ari ~atus sum, *intr*. To feel astonishment, wonder: *ipsi viri ~ati sunt, unde tale antipathicum ...obortum est* AM 292.2.

permisceo ~scere ~scui ~xtum (*or* ~stum), *tr*. To mix thoroughly: *insania varie ~xta* ES 231; *lumen est lumini solari... ~stum* 2AD 143.

permissibilis ~is ~e, *a*. Permissible: *quod...polygamica conjugia...in se etiam forent ~ia Christianis* AM 340.1.

permissio ~onis, *f*. The granting of permission, esp. divine permission: *Dominus...providet ac disponit omnia et singula, sed quaedam ex ~one, quaedam ex admissione* AC 1755; *non est a Domino ~o qualis est volentis sed qualis est non volentis* AC 7877.5.

permissive, *adv*. By (divine) permission: *~e etiam calorem effingere iis datur* ES 324; ES 399.

permitto ~mittere ~misi ~missum, *tr., intr*. **1** To give permission for, permit, allow: *quo...non significent quod mandata sint, sed quod ~missa* AC 6914.5; *hae causae non obstant, quin... ~mittantur separationes* AM 276.2; (w. dat. of person) *indignati sunt, quod ea iis ~mitterentur* ES 195. **2** (intr.) To allow, permit (to): (w. inf.) *Moses ~misit libellum repudii scribere* Mark 10.4 (AC 6752.7); *cum res memoriae naturalis non reproduci amplius ~mittitur* CI 563; (impers. pass.) *quondam etiam ~mittebatur spiritibus malis nostrae telluris...infestare spiritus Joviales* AC 8383; (w. *ut*) *~missum ut repraesentarent* AC 7040.

permulceo ~cere ~si ~sum, *tr*. To soothe: (absol.) *jucundum est gratum ac ~cet* AE 920.2.

permultoties, *adv*. Very many times: *quod ~es fassi sunt* ES 1720.

permultus ~a ~um, *a*. (superl.: see **perplurimus**) **1** (pl.) Very numerous, very many: *ex ~is locis apud Prophetas* AC 489.1; *~i ex eruditis...obstupescunt* CI 313. **2** (neut. sg. as sb.) An excessive thing, too much: *sed omnia exponere foret ~um* ES 4095.

permutatio ~onis, *f*. A changing, exchange: *sicut cambium, in quo fit ~o* VR 11.3.

permuto ~are ~avi ~atum, *tr*. To change completely: *omnia ~are in nova* ES 277; *incolae regionum illarum ~antur* AC 8054.3; to give in exchange: *num...populus Meus ~avit gloriam suam cum eo quod non prodest?* Jer. 2.11 (AC 8301.5).

pernicies ~ei, *f*. Ruin, perdition: *si non obstarent illa, ruerent in ~em omnium qui sibi non favent* AC 7032.3; AM 283.

perniciosus ~a ~um, *a*. (superl. *~issimus*) Causing destruction, ruinous, pernicious: *opes apud illos qui in malo sunt ~ae sunt* AC 6917.1; *vita ~a* CI 361; *tales sunt ~issimi, obstinati ut nusquam desistant* ES 4572.3.

pernicitas ~atis, *f*. Quickness of movement, rapidity, speed: *mirabili ~ate involabant in oculum sinistrum* AC 1977.1.

perniciter, *adv*. Rapidly, quickly: [*currus*] *~er ferebantur ad spatiosam domum* AM 103.2.

pernoctatio ~onis, *f*. The spending of a night, overnight stay: *~o in uno loco significabat quod nulla amplius hostilitas* AC 4213.

pernocto ~are ~avi, *intr*. To pass the night: *tam platea quam chippod in malogranatis ejus ~abunt* Zeph. 2.14 (AC 655.2); *justitia ~abat* Isa. 1.21 (SS 85).

perobscure, *adv*. In a very obscure manner, dimly: *non intellecta mihi loquela, modo ~e* [*per obscura* Autograph and Tafel] *in idea* ES 2632 (J D Odhner).

perparum, *adv*. and *indecl. neut*. **1** (adv.) To a very small extent, very little: *~um attendebant ad illa*

AC 10712; ES 2570. **2** (sb.): *quod id quod per mediatum influxum fit...sit ~um respective* AC 7004.3; *~um aliquid...cogitant* AM 293.3.

perpauci ~ae ~a, *pl. adj.* Very few: *apud ~os in Christiano orbe* AM 369.1; *ibi ~a sunt quae descripta* UJ 27.4.

perpaulo, *adv.* By a very little, slightly: *~o antrorsum ad multam distantiam* ES 4546.

perpendicularis ~is ~e, *a.* Perpendicular: *in linea ~i* ES 3110.

perpendiculariter, *adv.* Perpendicularly: ES 2831.

perpendiculum ~i, *neut.* A plumb line: *Deus... tenet digito ~um supra libram* VR 504.5; *in ~o* or *ad ~um*, perpendicularly: *stabimus in ~o sub vobis* VR 665.1; ES 1701.

perpendo ~dere ~di ~sum, *tr.* To consider carefully: *quod usque cum ~dunt, undenam eorum cogitatio boni...* ES 2161.

perpetim Tafel's reading of a possibly incomplete or faulty form in ES 3807 Autograph.

perpetro ~are ~avi ~atum, *tr.* To carry into effect: *ut ~arent intentiones suas* ES 5857.

perpetuitas ~atis, *f.* Perpetuity: *~as absque mutatione* AC 9502; ES 241.

perpetuo[1], *adv.* Perpetually: [*crescunt vera*] *in immensum, et hoc ~o in aeternum* AC 6648; AM 37.

perpetuo[2] ~are ~avi ~atum, *tr.* To make everlasting, perpetuate: *quod homo ~etur quoad vitam* 3AD 6795.

perpetuus ~a ~um, *a.* Constantly in existence, perpetual: *ut ignis ~us esset super altari* AC 6832.7; *quod ~a varietas sit* AC 7236.2; *inclinatio...constans et ~a* AM 156[a].3; (neut. as sb.) perpetuity: *quercus...significabat ~um* AC 4552.1; *in ~um*, perpetually, for ever: *ne hoc lateret in ~um* SS 70; AM 64.1.

perplaceo ~cere ~cui, *intr.* To be highly pleasing: *quod talis sit* [*scientia*] *ut sibi ~ceat* AC 1478.

perplexitas ~atis, *f.* Confusion: *dies tumultus, et conculcationis et ~atis Domino* Isa. 22.5 (AC 1292.3).

perplexum ~i, *neut.* An entanglement, thicket: *aries post detentus in ~o cornibus suis* Gen. 22.13 (AC); (fig.) *in tali ~o sunt* AC 6945.2.

perplexus ~a ~um, *a.* Confused, perplexed: *~i illi in terra* Exod. 14.3 (AC); *intuitionem inferiorem...ita ~am* AC 6865.3; (of things) muddled, unclear: *quid inde nisi ~um et non cohaerens...resultat?* VR 15.2.

perplures ~es ~a, *pl. adj.* Very many: *ex ~ibus illis locis* AC 6729; AM 314.2.

perpluries, *adv.* Very many times: AC 8286.4.

perplurimus ~a ~um, *a.* (superl. of **permultus**) (sg.) Very much: *~um habet* AC 1043.3; (pl.) very many: *ex his et ~is aliis locis Verbi* AC 589; *~i hodie credunt quod...* AE 126.2.

perpulcher ~chra ~chrum, *a.* Very beautiful: *decoramentis ~chris* ES 2160; ES 3636.

perpurgo ~are ~avi ~atum, *tr.* To clean thoroughly: *~abit aream Suam* Matt. 3.12 (AE 374.14).

perquam, *adv.* To a great extent, very much, exceedingly: (w. adj. or adv.) *~am constanter occurrunt binae expressiones* AC 100; *~am notum est* AM 284; (w. vbs.) very much, exceedingly: *~am cruciantur* ES 2774; ES 3347.

perquiro ~rere ~sivi ~situm, *tr.* To search for, seek out: *viri...alias et alias ~runt* AM 504.1; *discurrunt... ~rendo ea* ES 276.

perrimor ~ari ~atus sum, *tr.* To investigate thoroughly, probe: *ut status hujus Ecclesiae ~emur* CO 46.

perrumpo ~mpere ~pi ~ptum, *tr.* To break through, break open: *si ~mperetur agger rima* AC 1692.2; *quod ~ptus sit* [*fons*] *ab ungula equi Pegasi* AM 182.2.

persaepe, *adv.* (compar. *~ius*) Very often: *distinguuntur ~e sono* AC 793; *ut Matth. 10.40; 15.24...et ~ius alibi* VR 92.1.

perscrutor ~ari ~atus sum, *tr.* To examine diligently, search: *in tempore illo ~abor Hierosolymam lucernis* Zeph. 1.12 (DD 4); *quod non ~anda sint intellectu* AE 242.5; ES 3607.

persecutio: see **persequutio**.

persecutor: see **persequutor**.

persentio ~tire ~si ~sum, *tr.* To feel deeply or intimately: *~simus illum suavitate excedentem omnem alium amorem* AM 55.3; *claudebatur...mundus interior, quod ~tire potui per silentium subitum* ES 2855.

persentisco ~ere, *tr.* To begin to feel: *~ere mihi etiam dabatur species laetitae* ES 231; AE 618.1.

persequor ~qui ~quutus (*or* ~cutus) sum, *tr.*, *intr.* **1** To pursue, chase: *~quebantur filios Israelis* AC 8212; *~quar hostes meos, et comprehendam eos* Ps. 18.37 (DD 14.6); (absol.) *et ~quuti Aegyptii post illos* Exod. 14.9 (AC). **2** (w. abl.) To ply (with attention), follow: *aliquo cultu illum* [sc. *Mahumedem*] *~quuntur* AM 342.1. **3** To treat with hostility, attack, persecute: *eos... dicteriis laedunt et ~quuntur* AC 1844; *quod continue ~quantur fideles* ES 2018.

persequutio ~onis, *f.* also **persecutio**. A persecution: *qui patiuntur ~ones, et subeunt tentationes* AC 1851.

persequutor ~oris, *m.* also **persecutor**. A persecutor: *veloces fuerunt ~ores nostri* Lam. 4.19 (AE 281.11); *spiritus ~ores* ES 1460.

perseveratio ~onis, *f.* Continued existence, perseverance: *ex qua* [sc. *potentia*] *~o amoris illius sequitur* AM 334; persistence: *~onem in amore* AE 149; ES 3526.

perseverantia ~ae, *f.* Continuance: *de origine et ~a virtutis seu potentiae conjugialis* AM 108.

persevero ~are ~avi, *intr.* To continue, persist: *~abat cantus* AM 55.2; (w. *in* + abl.) to persist (in): *qui in malo ~ant* AC 7102.2.

persisto ~ere perstiti, *intr.* **1** To continue in existence, last, endure: *haec delectatio ~ebat per menses* AC 1880.3; *quod multiplicatio illa a creatione mundi...huc usque perstiterit* VR 32.3. **2** (w. abl. or *in* + abl.) To continue or persist (in a course of conduct): *~unt jugiter in infestatione* AC 6907.2; *~ere in affectione veri* AE 130.1. **b** (w. inf.) to continue (to): *usque perstiti dicere quod...* ES 890; ES 4579.

persolvo ~vere ~vi ~utum, *tr.* To pay off: *donec ~veris ultimum dodrantem* Matt. 5.26 (VI 73).

persona ~ae, *f.* (sometimes followed by masc. relative in accordance with sense) **1** A specific human being, a particular person: *tales ~ae nusquam fuerunt* AC 1140; [*angeli*] *nolunt loqui de ~is* AC 7002; *~a quidem quae* [*qui* 1st edn.] *in dignitate ibi est* DP 217.5. **2** Human form: *quod societas sit homo seu ~a composita* ES 2324; *in ~a*, in person: *quod Dominus toties venerit, quoties Ecclesia vastata fuit, non quod in ~a, sicut cum assumsit Humanum* AC 4060.5. **3** The individuality of a person, personality, character: *in sensu a ~a abstracto* AC 8314.1; *rex qui credit quod regium sit in sua ~a...non sapit* AC 10801; *quis...amat hominem solum ut ~am?* FI 20. **4** A person regarded as discharging a function or playing a part: *nullum discrimen habetur regum et magnatum, sic nullus respectus ~arum* ES 1512; (w. gen.) *~a magistratus... quoties...judicat, bonum opus facit* VI 72. **5** Each of the three aspects of the Divinity, person: *quod Filius Dei sit altera ~a Divinitatis, distincta a ~a Patris* DD 19.1; *universale fidei est quod Deus sit unus essentia et ~a* VR 2.2; *modo loco trinitatis ~arum intelligatur trinitas ~ae* DD 55.6. **6** An actor, player: *sicut ~a theatri in regia veste* DP 217.7. **7** A part played by a person, role: *agnoscebant quidam suas ~as quas agerent* ES 1882; *quod homo possit mentiri ~as non suas in externis* DP 224.1; *sub piorum ~is agere dolum volens* ES 2374.

personalis ~is ~e, *a.* Of or relating to a person, personal: *unio ~is, sicut est animae et corporis* VR 137.10 (Book of Concord).

personalitas ~atis, *f.* The individuality of a person, personality: *tres Personae Divinae...quarum cuique ~as, existentia et subsistentia...esset* VR 174.2.

personaliter, *adv.* Regarded as persons, in person: *Pater, Filius et Spiritus Sanctus, qui essentialiter Unus Deus sunt, sed ~er Tres* VR 185.3.

personatus ~a ~um, *a.* Portrayed by actors, staged: *~i harioli et mimi super theatris* DP 121.2; *~i illi reges et principes descenderunt e thronis et soliis* AM 7.4; (masc. as sb.) AM 3.3.

persono ~are ~avi, *intr.* (w. abl. or *ex*) To be filled (with sound), ring (with): *montes et colles ~abunt coram vobis cantu* Isa. 55.12 (AC 368); *suavissimi cantus ...ex quibus tota urbs ~at* AM 17.2.

perspectio ~onis, *f.* Scrutiny, inspection: *apparentiam Divinae custodiae et providentiae...quoad ~onem undequaque* AE 281.1.

perspecto ~are ~avi ~atum, *tr.* To see thoroughly: *quisque ex communi perceptione ~at* AM 449.

perspicacia ~ae, *f.* The ability to perceive acutely, sagacity, perspicacity: *~a rationis* AC 118; *~a viris imperscrutabili* AM 208.4.

perspicacitas ~atis, *f.* = **perspicacia**: ES(M) [4749].

perspicaciter, *adv.* (compar. *~cius*) With acuteness of perception, perspicaciously: [*spiritus*] *loquuntur de rebus ita acute et ~citer* AC 1641; AM 285.2.

perspicax ~acis, *a.* (superl. *~acissimus*) Acute in perception, clear-sighted, sagacious, perspicacious: *ad convocandum celebratissimos eruditione, ~acissimos ingenio* AM 2.1; *spiritus... ~aces in aliis et susceptibiles percipiendi* ES 898.

perspicilla ~orum, *neut. pl.* Eyeglasses, spectacles: *stant sicut in caverna cum ~is super naribus* VR 176.1; *quosque oculus ~is penetrat, usque plura detegit mirabilia* ES 1825; CO 30.

perspicio ~picere ~pexi ~pectum, *tr.*, *intr.* **1** To scan, look keenly: *avis volans ex alto ~picit undequaque* AE 282.1. **2** To grasp mentally, see with the mind's eye: *haec a verbis manifeste ~piciuntur* AC 84; (w. *quod*) *quod gaudia caeli...illa sint, ~peximus ex illis...qui potiti sunt illis* AM 3.5; (w. indir. qu.) *~pice num quis homicida...possit fidem habere* VI 91.

perspicue, *adv.* Clearly, manifestly: *tandem ~e deprehendes quod ita sit* VR 16.2; VR 61.2.

perspicuitas ~atis, *f.* The ability to comprehend mentally, clear-sightedness: *quod ~as rationis a Domino veniat* AC 118.

perspicuus ~a ~um, *a.* (compar. *~ior*) Clearly grasped, manifest: *in rationis lucem ~am magis* *veniunt* AM 255.1; *ex ~is his effatis evidens est* VR 371.2; ES 168.

perspiratio ~onis, *f.* The exudation of moisture or other fluids, perspiration: *a ~one insensibili* ES 977; ES 1738.

perstrepo ~ere ~ui, *intr.* To make a great noise, resound everywhere: *per quod mare et salum resonabit ...significatum est...quod haereses et controversiae...ita ~ent* AC 2120.

persto ~are ~iti, *intr.* **1** To continue in existence, last: *fluctuationes...non cessant ita sed diu ~ant* AC 851; *ex lite quae adhuc ~at de anima* AC 6948.4; *repraesentatio haec modo ~at hodie* AM 21.1. **2** (of persons, w. *in* + abl.) To persist in: *~a in incantationibus tuis* Isa. 47.12 (AC 7297.2); (w. *quod*) to insist (that): *adhuc ~abant... quod vellent adire Jehovam Parentem* 2AD 1426.

perstringo ~ngere ~nxi ~ctum, *tr.* **1** To affect violently, seize upon: *cum vento qui ~nxit faciem* ES 479; *quale obscurum quod a fulgure radiorum ~ngitur, talis color* AC 1043.1. **b** To dazzle (the eyes): *decidit flammeum intensum ante oculum, quem valde ~nxit* AC 1524; ES 3629. **2** To examine cursorily, go over (with the eye): *illa quae leviter oculo ~nxi* ES(M) 4556. **3** (transf. of emotions) To seize upon, grip: *usque ut pudor ~ngat intima* AC 956; cf. ES 946.

persuadeo ~dere ~si ~sum, *tr., intr.* **1** (tr.) To persuade, convince (a person): *me ad discenda similia ~dere cupiebant* ES 269; (usu. pass.) *quod nemo ~deri momento de vero debeat* AC 7298.2; (w. *quod*) *~sus sum quod etiam tu...illis fidem adjungas* VR 16.1. **2** (intr., w. dat. of person) To persuade: *~dere ex fallaciis sensuum* AE 175.9; *ex falso sibi ~sit...quod mala non sint* AC 7272.2. **3** (tr., w. acc. of thing) To persuade belief in or induce practice of: *spiritus etiam coeperunt ~dere mala* CI 249; (w. dat. of person) *per omnia quae sibi ~det* AC 303.1.

persuasibilis ~is ~e, *a.* Capable of being persuaded, suggestible: *in caeteris erat ~is prae aliis* ES 3431.

persuasio ~onis, *f.* **1** A state of being persuaded, conviction, firm belief: (w. gen.) *~o falsi omne spirituale et coeleste exstinguit* AC 806; (w. *quod*) *nec fides est fides, sed modo scientia talium quae fidei sunt, et quandoque ~o quod ita sit* AC 7757. **2** A belief supported only by natural ideas, false or insufficient belief, persuasion: *~ones seu principia falsi radicata* AC 635; *ibi naturalis fides, quae modo est ~o, fit spiritualis* VR 11.3; VR 73.2.

persuasive, *adv.* (compar. *~ius*) As the result of incorrect belief, falsely: *cum tamen ~e crediderint vera fidei* AC 4802.3; (compar.) with more conviction: *quis ~ius loquitur de certitudine suae phantasiae...?* VR 759.3.

persuasivus ~a ~um, *a.* **1** Successful in persuading, persuasive: *natura earum* [sc. *sirenum*] *tam ~a est ut...* AC 831.3. **2** Derived from incorrect belief: *lux ~a* AC 2682.2; *fides naturalis, quae etiam fides ~a dicenda est* AE 232.1; *qui in fide ~a fuerunt, ac in vita mali* AC 7317.1; CI 482. **3** (neut. as sb.) False belief: *sciunt etiam ~um injicere, et sic hebetare apperceptionem veri* AC 7298.1; *quod...in forti ~o sint de falsis* AC 6907.3.

persuasor ~oris, *m.* A persuasive person, persuader: *quod [Zinzendorfius] maxime ~or fuerit* UJ(P) 38 (Rogers).

persuasorius ~a ~um, *a.* Concerned with persuasion: *per alios ~os modos* AC 4214.2.

persuasus ~a ~um, *a.* (pf. pple. of **persuadeo**) (compar. *~ior*, superl. *~issimus*) Based upon incorrect belief: *inde quoque ~issima sua principia confirmarunt* AC 570.

persufflo ~are ~avi, *intr.* To blow through: *perseverabat in ~ando* ES 5976.

perterebro ~are ~avi ~atum, *tr.* To bore through: (absol.) *sic columnatim ~ans* ES 3218.

perterrefacio ~facere ~feci ~factum, *tr.* To frighten thoroughly, terrify: *[tonitrua] ~faciunt et occoecant malos* AE 273.5; ES 991.

perterreo ~rere ~rui ~ritum, *tr.* To frighten: *omne cor hominis liquescit, et ~riti sunt* Isa. 13.8 (AC 8313.2); Matt. 27.54 (AE 400.14).

pertinacia ~ae, *f.* Stubbornness, obstinacy: *ostensum mihi est, quod ne hilum ~ae debeat esse in homine* ES 2994.

pertinaciter, *adv.* Stubbornly: *praeter quod cogitationem ~er teneant in una re* AC 1820.4.

pertinax ~acis, *a.* Stubborn, obstinate: *per resistentias ~aces contra maritos* AM 292.2; ES 3024 1/2.

pertineo ~nere ~nui, *intr.* **1** (w. *ad*) To be connected or concerned (with): *illa quae ad rem ~nent* AC 6653; *omnia quae ad vitam hominis... ~nent* SS 55. **2** (of words or utterances) To refer (to), point (to): *interpretatus est in omnibus scripturis, quae ad Ipsum ~nerent* Luke 24.27 (AC 6752.6). **3** To be assigned (to), belong (to): *unusquisque spiritus ad aliquam societatem ~net* CI 294; *dixit...quod terra sit Domini, sed urbs ad eos ~neret* ES 728.

pertingo ~ngere ~gi, *intr.* To extend, reach: *quod nostrae telluris incolae modo ad umbilicum eorum ~ngant* AC 7249; *montem, cujus altitudo ~git ultra regionem nubium* AM 75.2; (transf.) *sic...colitur Ipsum Divinum ad quod nulla cogitatio alioquin ~ngit* AC

6674.4; *ad quae scientiae humanae nusquam ~ngunt* CI 269.1.

pertranseo ~sire ~sii (*or* ~sivi) ~situm, *tr.*, *intr.* **1** To pass through, cross: *Jehovah...cum ~siit coelum* AC 6831; *quam* [*viam*] *omnes... ~seunt* VR 160.2; (intr.) *quod amicitiae societates ~siverint super caput* ES(M) [4716]. **2** To go through (states): *quod delitiae...in via ~seant jucunda amorum caelestium* AM 144; (intr.) to pass: *quum mutationes plurium statuum ~seunt* ES 309.

pertuli: pf. of **perfero**.

perturbatio ~onis, *f.* Disturbance of the mind, perturbation: *inde illis ~o* AC 8214; *~onem mentis* AE 376.35; *confusio seu ~o* ES 155.

perturbo ~are ~avi ~atum, *tr.* To set in disorder, confuse, upset: *Jehovah... ~avit castra Aegyptiorum* Exod. 14.24 (AC); (transf.) *ne...illi...amplius ~ent et seducant simplices fide et corde* CI 312.4; *haec forma... ~atur, quando contrario ordine degit homo* ES 155.

pervado ~dere ~si ~sum, *tr.* To pass through: *quae* [*noxia*]... *~dunt venas et arterias* AC 1877; *illi in tali potentia inde sunt ut inferna absque ullo discrimine ~dere possint* AC 8200.2; to pervade, fill: *quae* [*calor et lux*] *~dunt universum a primis ad ultima ejus* VR 63.

pervagor ~ari ~atus sum, *tr.* To wander through: *licet illis ~ari universum* AC 7078; *~atus plateas fine inquirendi habitationem* AM 242; (transf.) to spread through: *primaeva revelatio ~ata est universum orbem* VR 11.1.

pervehor ~hi ~ctus sum, *intr.* To be transported, travel: *quo magis homo in exteriora ~ctus est* ES 539.

pervenio ~nire ~ni ~ntum, *intr.* **1** To come (to a specified place), reach, arrive: *cum afflatus illuc ~nit, tunc loquelam eorum intellexi* AC 7359. **2** To reach (a goal, end, etc.): *malis mediis utuntur ad finem quemcunque ~niendi* AC 5188; *vetus...Ecclesia ad finem suum ~nit* DD praef. **3** To come (into), arrive (at a state): *quod...in gravem anxietatem... ~nerint* AC 8130; *~ni in statum tranquillum* ES 221. **4** To develop (up to a specified point): *harmoniae quae distincte non ~niunt ad perceptionem* AC 545.1; *quod* [*cognitiones*] *ne quidem ad notitiam communium ~nire queant* AC 6813.

perverse, *adv.* In a manner contrary to natural order, wrongly: *internus* [*visus*] *non potest...videre nisi ~e* AC 9061.2.

perversio ~onis, *f.* An upsetting, perversion: *magia non aliud est quam ~o ordinis* AC 6692.2; *omnis ~o Ecclesiae existit ex binis amoribus* AE 159.1.

perversitas ~atis, *f.* Incorrect judgment, perversity: *Jehovah commiscuit in medio ejus spiritum ~atum* Isa. 19.14 (DD 48.5).

perversor ~oris, *m.* One who upsets or perverts: *omnes quotcunque a sinistra sunt perversi et ~ores* ES 439.

perversus ~a ~um, *a.* (pf. pple. of **perverto**) (in senses of vb., esp.) Contrary to natural order, perverted: *ex... ~is et falsificatis veris* AC 6661.1; *intellectuale ~um* AC 8156; *status ~us eorum qui credunt illustrari a semet* AE 376.37.

perverto ~tere ~ti ~sum, *tr.* To upset, destroy (order): *ordinem Divinum ~terunt* AC 6692.1; *~tendo fines ordinis* AC 7297.1; to make wrong, pervert, distort: *omnia vera Ecclesiae ~tunt et falsificant* AC 6661.1; *judicia justitiae possunt ~ti* AM 471.

pervestigatio ~onis, *f.* The action of tracking down, searching out: *~onem veri* AC 7303; AE 282.5.

pervestigo ~are ~avi ~atum, *tr.* To track down, search out: *quod 'fodere' sit ~are* AC 7343.3.

pervicax ~acis, *a.* (superl. *~acissimus*) Stubbornly held, obstinate: *per persuasionum ~acissimarum suarum influxum* AC 562.

pervideo ~dere ~di ~sum, *tr.* To scan thoroughly, scrutinize: *ut ~deret regnum coeleste* AC 1611.

pervolo ~are ~avi, *intr.* To fly through: *alius qui inter pedes magni istius ab anteriori ~abat* AC 5378.1; ES 995.

pes pedis, *m.* **1** The foot: *quod non manus agant et pedes ambulent ex se* AM 310.1; (as the lowest part of the body) *a capite ad plantam pedis* CI 433; *luna sub pedibus ejus* Rev. 12.1 (AR). **2** The lowest part (of anything), foot: *ad pedem collis* VR 48.1.

pessime, *adv.* Very badly or very little: *quod esset ~e contentus* [i.e., far from content] ES 2513.

pessimus ~a ~um, *a.* (used as superl. of **malus**[1]) **1** (of persons) Very or most wicked, worst: *sacerdotes mali, imo etiam ~i* AC 6914.3; *~ae* [*uxores*] *hujus farinae* AM 292.2. **2** Very or most unpleasant, worst: *quod sors prophanatorum omnium ~a sit* AC 6959.3.

pessum, *indecl. neut.* see also **pessumdo**. *In ~um ire*, to be ruined or destroyed: *ad prospiciendum sibi et simul domui...ne in ~um eant* AM 283.

pessumdo ~are ~edi ~atum, *tr.* To ruin, destroy: *adulteria, quae ~ant animas* AM 105; *in luxuriam, qua corporis sanitas ~atur* ES 590.

pestifer ~era ~erum, *a.* (superl. *~erissimus*) Causing death, pestiferous, plaguy: *halitus...est venenatus et ~er* ES 1279; *persuasione... ~erissima* ES 3365.

pestilentialis ~is ~e, *a*. Pestilential: *febres malignae et ~es* AM 253.1.

pestilentus ~a ~um, *a*. Causing plague, pestilent: *fumus ~us* SE 114.1.

pestis ~is *f*. **1** A plague: *ne forte incidat in nos ~e et gladio* Exod. 5.3 (AC); CI 229. **2** A cause of severe distress, trouble, curse: *quod fugiat malum adulterii ut ~em animae* AM 130.4; *sunt quasi ~es in societatibus bonorum spirituum* ES 2081.

petitio ~onis, *f*. The act of asking, petition: *si non ipsa ~o foret a Domino* AR 376.

petitum ~i, *neut*. A request: *quod...quibusdam suis ~is obtemperanter auscultent* AM 292.1.

peto ~ere ~ii (*or* ~ivi) ~itum, *tr*. **1** To ask for, request: (w. acc.) *si quid ~ieritis in nomine Meo* John 14.13 (AC 6674.3); *haec quae mulieres...ab Aegyptiis mutuo ~ierunt* AC 6917.3; (w. double acc.) *quodcunque ~ieritis Patrem in nomine Meo* John 15.16 (AC 6674.3). **b** (w. *ut*): *qui ~it ut alius pro se supplicet* AC 7391; *~ebant ut soli essent* ES 3793. **c** (w. inf.): *qui ~iit a Domino videre Patrem* AT 160. **2** *~ere mutuo*, to borrow: *haec sunt modo vestes mutuo ~itae* DP 205. **3** To look for, seek (from a specified source): *inde quoque ~enda est...significatio* AC 7284; ES 594. **4** To move towards, be attracted to: *profundum ~ierunt sicut plumbum in aquis ingentibus* Exod. 15.10 (AC).

petra ~ae, *f*. (Gk.) **1** Rock, stone (as a firm surface or foundation): *constituit super ~a pedes meos* Ps. 40.2 (AC 6669.3); *aedificavit domum suam super ~a* Matt. 7.24 (VI 2); *globulus elasticus cadens in ~am* AM 526; (Bibl., w. ref. to the Lord) *~a eorum vendidit illos* Deut. 32.30 (AC 5886.3). **2** A large rock on the surface of the earth, boulder: *et dicebant montibus et ~is, cadite super nos* Rev. 6.16 (AR); *vallis inter montes et ~as* CI 429; *putabat ~as e loco movere* ES 282. **3** A stone implement, flint: *et accepit Zippora ~am, et abscidit praeputium filii sui* Exod. 4.25 (AC); AC 7044.

petrosus ~a ~um, *a*. Rocky, stony: *qui super ~a [terra] seminantur* Mark 4.16 (AC 1846.4); *tellus... perquam ~a* AC 10712; (neut. as sb.) CI 488.3.

petulans ~ntis, *a*. Insolent, self-assertive: *~ntes cupiunt ...expiscari aliorum cogitata* AC 5180; *es tu qui circumscripsisti Deum legibus...? Hoc quam ~ns est* VR 74.2.

petulanter, *adv*. Insolently: *qui ~er mali* ES 4681.

petulantia ~ae, *f*. Wantonness: *instructorem...qui eas castigat quoties...in tales ~as erumpunt* AC 1113.

phaenomenon ~i, *neut*. (Gk.) A strange event, phenomenon: *ex tam multis ~is et effectibus* AC 6948.4; *de causis naturalibus ~orum* ES 249.

phalanx ~ngis, *f*. (Gk.) A formation of armed men, battle array: *praetore ~ngum ab exercitu illustrium Ecclesiae* VR 137.8; (of spirits) *erat ~nx spirituum exsurgens a latere Gehennae* AC 950.

phaleratus ~a ~um, *a*. (ad. Gk.) (of horses) Wearing metal discs as ornaments on the harness: *equi pulchre ~i* VR 815; AM 76.2.

phantasia ~ae, *f*. (Gk.) **1** The power of creating mental images, imagination: *spiritualia et coelestia nec oculis videt nec ~a capit* AC 129; *illis...loco perceptionis est ~a, quae facit apparentiam perceptionis* AC 7680. **2** A false appearance (or belief) arising from the imagination, an imaginary event or state: *eorum principia falsi vertuntur...in ~as, quod videantur sibi scindere ligna* AC 1110; *videsne quod ex ~a supereminentiae insanias?* AM 263.2; *si...secundum ~as exercere crudelitates potuissent* ES 374.

phantasma ~atis, *neut*. (Gk.) An unreal apparition, ghost: *si ipsissima miracula Divina videret...illa...sicut ~ata rejiceret* AC 7290.4; *quia internum non illis [veris] inest, sunt ~ata* AC 4335.5.

phantasta ~ae, *m*. (Gk.) One who causes delusions: *vovant illos ~as* ES 5172.

phantasticus ~a ~um, *a*. (Gk.) Resulting from imaginary causes: *putabant quod hoc ~um esset* ES 2325; (neut. as sb.) belief in imaginary events: *naturalis homo non potest non in ~um de Divino labi* AC 8325.2.

Pharao ~onis, *m*. also **Pharaoh**. The ruler of Egypt in antiquity, Pharaoh: *~o, rex Aegypti* AC 42.1; *et praecepit ~o omni populo suo* Exod. 1.22 (AC).

Pharaoh: see **Pharao**.

pharetra ~ae, *f*. (Gk.) A quiver: *venationis arma... ~a, arcus et facula* AC 3309.2; *in ~a Sua occultavit me* Isa. 49.2 (AE 357.9).

Pharisaicus ~a ~um, *a*. Typical of the Pharisees, hypocritical: *fides hypocritica seu ~a, quae est oris et non cordis* VR 345; *cum bono ~o* VI 10.

pharmaceuticus ~a ~um, *a*. (Gk.) Concerned with the preparation of drugs, pharmaceutical: ES(M) 4578.

pharmacopola ~ae, *m*. (Gk.) A vendor of drugs or medicines, apothecary, chemist: *inter quos [medicos] etiam erant chirurgi et ~ae* VR 665.5.

pharmacum ~i, *neut*. (Gk.) A drug, medicine: *quod corpora...per varia...lixivia, menstrua et ~a sanentur* AE 1214.2; AM 79.10.

pharmaticus ~a ~um, *a*. (Gk.) Of or concerned with drugs, pharmaceutical: *periti artis... ~ae* AE 1214.2.

pharynx ~ngis, *f.*(?) (Gk.) (anat.) The pharynx: *in ~ngem et laryngem* ES 1723.

phasma ~atis, *neut.* (Gk.) A ghost: *qui videt ~ata in nocte, et credit esse homines* VR 606.1.

phiala ~ae, *f.* (Gk.) A shallow dish, bowl: *ite et effundite ~as irae Dei in terram* Rev. 16.1 (AR); (also app.) a bottle: *qui vendunt...viperas in ~is* VR 617.2.

Philadelphiensis ~is ~e, *a.* Of Philadelphia: *~is Ecclesiae* AE 90.2.

philautia ~ae, *f.* (Gk.) Self-love: *ex ~a, hoc est, amore sui seu proprio* AC 1326.1.

Philistaea: see **Philisthaea**.

Philistaeus: see **Philisthaeus**.

Philisthaea ~ae, *f.* also **Philistaea**. The country of the Philistines: DP 264.2; CI 327; (as representing a spiritual state) *omnis Ecclesia...progressu temporis...fit vel Babylonia vel ~a* AE 1029.18.

Philisthaeus ~i, *m.* also **Philistaeus**. A Philistine: *Dagon deus ~orum* VI 55.3; (with ref. to spiritual state) *~i, qui sunt qui solam fidem profitentur* AR 812.3.

philosophia ~ae, *f.* (Gk.) Philosophy: *hae sunt regulae, quas ~a novit* ES 210; *de ~a, seu artificiali humano, per quod discet distincte cogitare* ES(M) 4655.

philosophice, *adv.* According to the rules of philosophy: *nihil credunt nisi quod ~e verum* ES 650.

philosophicus ~a ~um, *a.* (Gk.) Of philosophy, philosophical: *non intelliguntur scientifica ~a, sed scientifica Ecclesiae* AC 6750.2; (neut. as sb.) a philosophical argument or tenet: *qui ex sensualibus scientificis et ~is concludunt de coelestibus* AC 196.1; *inde est hoc ~um veterum, quod omne sit divisibile in infinitum* AM 185.3.

philosophor ~ari ~atus sum, *intr.* To engage in philosophical argument, philosophize: *quomodo [spiritus] ~antur hic loci* ES 591.

philosophus ~i, *m.* (Gk.) A philosopher: *antiqui... agnoverunt sapientiam rationis pro sapientia, et hi vocati sunt ~i* AM 130.1; VR 79.1.

philyra ~ae, *f.* (Gk.) The inner bark (of a tree), bast: *athmosphaerae ambientes priores illas, sicut... ~ae ligna* VR 76.3; (also, anat.) the coating of a nerve fibre: *sicut... ~ae [investiunt] illorum* [sc. *nervorum*] *fibras* VR 78.3.

phlegma ~atis, *neut.* (Gk.) Phlegm: *qui... ~ati viscoso minus vitali correspondent* AC 5724.

phoenix ~icis, *m.* (Gk.) The mythical bird reputed to rise again from its ashes, the phoenix (in quot. app. an error for pelican): *sicut ~ix alens pullos sanguine suo* CO 40 (Nordenskjold).

phosphorus ~a ~um, *a.* (Gk.) Phosphorescent: *lignis putribus lucentibus et ~is* VR 590.2.

Photinianus ~a ~um, *a.* Of Photinus, Bishop of Sirmium, whose doctrines were condemned between AD 336-51, Photinian; (masc. as sb.) a Photinian, a follower of Photinus: VR 378.2.

phrasis ~is, *f.* An expression, saying: *rejicitur et damnatur ~is, quod bona opera necessaria sint ad salutem* Book of Concord in SE 12(i); AR Doc Ref.3.5; *quod ~es de bonis operibus ad salutem necessariis... explodendae et rejiciendae* Book of Concord in SE 12(k).

phrenesis ~eos, *f.* (Gk.) Disturbance of the mind, insanity, frenzy: *quod...emanaverit sicut ~is in universam theologiam* VR 4.2.

phrenitis ~is, *f.* Inflammation of the brain, phrenitis: AM 252.

phthisis: see **phtisis**.

phtisis ~eos, *f.* (Gk.) also **phthisis**. A wasting away, phthisis: *~is scorbutica* AM 253.1; ES 1812.

phylacterium ~i, *neut.* (Gk.) A thing worn by Jews about the person to ward off evil, phylactery (cf. Deut. 6.8): *dilatant ~a sua* Matt. 23.5 (AE 395.11).

physica ~ae, *f.* = **physice**: ES 2299.

physicalis ~is ~e, *a.* (neut. pl. as sb.) The science of physics: *in Divina mysteria per philosophiam naturalem seu ~ia intrare* ES 2299 titulus.

physice ~es, *f.* (Gk.) The science of physics: AC 6057.1; SS(P) 51 (= 19.3).

physicus ~a ~um, *a.* (Gk.) Of or concerned with nature, physical, material: *scientiae...ut philosophica, ~a* AM 163; *influxus ~us* AE 349.6.

pica ~ae, *f.* A species of bird, jay or magpie: VR 42.2; VR 58.

piceus ~a ~um, *a.* Made of or of the colour of pitch, tarry: *hoc constructum erat ex lapidibus ~is* AM 380.2; *quod ~us esset...sic quod ater esset* ES 3210.

pictor ~oris, *m.* A painter, artist: *pulchritudo...quae talis ut illam aemulari...non possit ullus ~or* AM 42.4; CI 459.

pictura ~ae, *f.* A painting: *homo foret sculptura aut ~a* AM 383; ES 252.

picturatus ~a ~um, *a.* Represented in painting, painted: *imagines ~as avium* AM 231.2.

picus ~i, *m.* A woodpecker: AE 1100.22.

pie, *adv*. In a pious manner: *loquitur ~e et devote* AC 9; *narravit ~e quod mortuus sit* AC 817.

pietas ~atis, *f*. Respect for divine law, piety: *~atem vitae* AC 1679.3; *~atis libros* 'religious books' VI 25.

pietista ~ae, *m*. A member of the devotional reform movement in 17th- and 18th-century Lutheranism known as Pietism, a Pietist: ES 4740.2.

piger ~gra ~grum, *a*. (compar. *~grior*) Slow or reluctant to act, lazy: *quis impigrior et quis ~grior loquendo* AM 17.4; *ultima quae apud hominem...sunt ~gra respective et inde frigida* AC 7270.3.

pigmentarius ~i, *m*. One who makes drugs, apothecary, druggist, pharmacist: *pigmentum, opus ~i* Exod. 30.35 (AR 777.2).

pigmentum ~i, *neut*. A drug, medicament: *cinnamomum, et suffimenta, et ~um et thus* Rev. 18.13 (AR). (n.b. AE here has *unguentum*; so too AC has *unguentum* at Exod. 30.35, where AR 777.2 has *pigmentum*.)

pignoro ~are ~avi ~atum, *tr*. To give an object as security or an assurance for a loan or an obligation, give as a pledge: *non in pignus accipiet molas et molarem, quia anima illa ~antis* [*est*] Deut. 24.6 (AC 4335.4).

pignus ~oris, *neut*. An object given as an assurance, token, pledge: *dixit, accipe haec ~ora* AM 20.3.

pigresco ~ere, *intr*. To become more and more inert or inactive, become sluggish, grow lazy: *dormitare in sensu interno est ex mora ~ere in illis quae sunt Ecclesiae* AC 4638.4.

pigritia ~ae, *f*. Laziness, sloth: *in vitae ~a* AC 6078.1.

pila ~ae, *f*. A ball (for play): *quod...ita ludi* [*possit*] *cum vero per falsum sicut cum ~a* AE 837.10; AM 17.4.

pilamen ~inis, *neut*. A ball (for the game of rackets): *ludi cum ~inibus repercussis* AM 17.4.

pileus ~i, *m*. A headdress, hat, cap: *~i naviculares crispati* 'sailors' cocked hats' AM 78.4; *ostendebatur etiam mihi tegumentum capitis...est ~us turritus obscurus* ES 588.

pilosus ~a ~um, *a*. Covered in hair, hairy: *viri... hirsuti et ~i* AC 1272; *tunica ~a* AE 66.2 (2 Kgs. 1.8).

pilus ~i, *m*. (usu. pl.) Hair, bristles (of animals, as a material): *~os auferunt aqua calida* ES 1292; *~is camelarum* Mark 1.6 (AE 66.2); (sg.) *tunicam ~i* Zech. 13.4 (DD 15.8).

pincerna ~ae, *m*. A servant in charge of wine, butler: *et loquutus princeps ~arum cum Pharaone* Gen. 41.9 (AC).

pinealis ~is ~e, *a*. (anat.) *Glandula ~is*, the pineal gland: AM 315.4; ES 831.

pingo ~ngere ~nxi ~ctum, *tr*. To represent in colours, paint: *ita deformia ut deformius nusquam ~ngi possit* AC 154; *angeli in templis, sive sculpti sive ~cti* CI 74.3.

pinguedo ~inis, *f*. A fatty substance: *convivium ~inum* Isa. 25.6 (AE 252.7); *adipes seu ~ines* AE 167.6.

pinguefacio ~facere ~feci ~factum, *tr*. To make fatty: *~facies oleo caput meum* Ps. 23.5 (AE 375.34).

pinguefio ~eri, *intr*. To become fatty: *gladius Jehovae implebitur sanguine, ~et adipe* Isa. 34.6 (AE 314.8).

pinguis ~is ~e, *a*. Containing fat, fatty: *ostrea mollis et ~is* ES 3611; (neut. as sb.) *pacificum ~ium vestrorum non aspiciam* Amos 5.22 (AC 922.3); *quod '~e' sit coelestie...nec modo ~e quod in animali, sed etiam ~e quod aliunde, sicut butyrum, oleum* AC 5943.1.

pinna ~ae, *f*. **1** The fin of a fish: *pisces qui habent ~am et squamam* 3AD 5535; a similar pointed structure on a human face: *nasus...qui aetate decrevit, ut vix aliquid nasi superesset, nisi aliqua ~a* ES 1376. **2** A pinnacle or parapet on a building: *a diabolo ductus super ~as templi* AC 1663.2 (Matt. 4.5).

pinnula ~ae, *f*. = **pinna**, sense 2: Matt. 4.5 (AC 1691.5).

pinso ~ere ~ui ~itum, *tr*. To knead (dough): *quod ~itur ita, putatur esse farina* ES(M) [4720]; Gen. 18.6 (AC).

pinus ~i, *f*. A pine tree: *folia abietis, populi, quercus, ~i* AR 936.3.

pipio ~onis, *m*. A fledgling: Gen. 15.9 (1AD 183).

pirata ~ae, *m*. (Gk.) A pirate: *latrones et ~ae* AM 511.

piraticus ~a ~um, *a*. Piratical; (fem. sg. or neut. pl. as sb.) piracy: *qui...exercet ~am* ES 2953; *...qui latrocinia ...exercuerunt et qui ~a* AC 820.

pirum: see **pyrum**.

piscatio ~onis, *f*. The catching of fish, fishing: *per ~onem...significatur instructio* AE 600.7.

piscator ~oris, *m*. A fisherman: *inferioris conditionis homines, ut ~ores* ES 1216.

piscatorius ~a ~um, *a*. Used for fishing: *retibus quasi ~is* VR 462.11.

piscatura ~ae, *f*. The catching of fish, fishing: *reformatio repraesentabatur per ~am illam* AE 513.16 (John 21).

pisciculus ~i, *m*. A small fish: John 21.9 (AC 7852.2).

piscina ~ae, *f*. A pool for bathing, swimming pool: *ad ~am Bethesdae* AE 163.7 (John 5.2). (n.b. Hindmarsh mistakenly reads *Bethsaidae*.)

piscis ~is, *m*. A fish: *~is assi partem* Luke 24.42 (DD 35.10); *pecudes et aves...tum ~es et reliqua* SS 23.1.

piscor ~ari ~atus sum, *tr.* To catch (fish): *qui ~abuntur eos* Jer. 16.15 (AC 10583.6); AE 820.3.

pistillum ~i, *neut.* A pestle: *occlusio apparebat sicut ~um injectum siphoni magno* ES 4952.

pistor ~oris, *m.* A baker: *sicut clibanus accensus a ~ore* Hos. 7.4 (AC 7356.2); *panis e ~ore* VR 71.2.

pistrix ~icis, *f.* A female baker: *filias vestras sumet...in coquas et in ~ices* 1 Sam. 8.13 (AC 2567.9).

pisum: see **pisus**.

pisus ~i, *m.* also **pisum** ~i, *neut.* A pea: *patina...in qua ~i* [*~a* Tafel] *cum pisce* ES Index s.v. 'edere' (vol. 5, p. 278 J D Odhner), referring to ES 3016.

pituita ~ae, *f.* Mucus, lymph: *processus mammillares sunt qui imbibunt ~am interioris...substantiae cerebri* ES 939; AC 5718.1.

pituitarius ~a ~um, *a.* (anat.) Pituitary: *versus glandulam ~am* ES 831; (of membranes) mucous: *membranae...~ae oris* ES 1725.

pituitosus ~a ~um, *a.* Mucous: *in ventriculos magnos, ubi ~a* ES 1239; AC 5386.

pius ~a ~um, *a.* **1** (of persons or their actions) Motivated by respect for divine law, pious: *quod scelesti possint aeque in coelum recipi ac ~i et probi* AC 7051.1; *~am egerunt vitam* AC 1110; *quod ~ae preces...influerent in coelum* ES 3254; (neut. as sb.) *cogitare et loqui ~a* VI 25. **2** (anat.) *~a mater* or *meninx*, the pia mater: *ad provinciam ~ae matris, quae est integumentum alterum et propius investit cerebrum et cerebellum* AC 4047; ES 1239.

pix picis, *f.* Pitch: *bituminavit illam* [sc. *capsam*] *bitumine et pice* Exod. 2.3 (AC); *erit terra in picem ardentem* Isa. 34.9 (CI 570.2).

placenta ~ae, *f.* (ad. Gk. *plakous*) A loaf, cake: *~am ex miliis* CI 325; *~am hordeorum* DD 15.7 (Ezek. 4.12); *amygdalinas ~as* ES 3858.

placentia ~ae, *f.* An act of giving pleasure, a pleasing: *facere odorem, quod sit ad placendum,...affectiones veri et boni sunt hae quae per ~am significantur* AC 10309.1.

placeo ~cere ~cui ~citum, *intr.* **1** (w. dat.) To be pleasing (to): *ad faciendum quod Ipsi ~cet* AC 6840; *~cent illa Domino* AE 126.2. **2** (impers., w. dat. and inf.) It pleases (someone to): *Divino ~cuit Humanum assumere* AC 8273.1; *~cuit Domino nunc sensum spiritualem revelare* SS 18.1; (w. *ut*) *~cuit Domino, ut talis conjunctio...sit apud hominem* CI 246.2.

placitum ~i, *neut.* That which pleases one, choice: *~i libertatem* AM 248.1.

placo ~are ~avi ~atum, *tr.* To appease, conciliate: *per odorem quietis ~abor vobis* Ezek. 20.41 (AE 324.27).

plaga ~ae, *f.* (Gk.) **1** The striking of a blow, stroke, blow: *licet faciat digna ~is, percutietur paucis* Luke 12.48 (AC 7790); *quod...faemina mulctetur ~is* AM 369.2. **2** A grievous infliction, plague: *percussit Jehovah Pharaonem ~is magnis* Gen. 12.17 (AC); *angelos septem habentes ~as septem* Rev. 15.1 (AR). **3** A point of the compass, direction: *ad dextram...ad sinistram...ad alias ~as* AC 1274; *quod* [*apes*]*...revolent secundum ~am ad suum alveare* VR 12.7. **4** A region, quarter: *stabam super colle in ~a meridionali* AM 2.1; *e quatuor ~is mundi* VR 90.1.

plagatus ~a ~um, *a.* Hurt by blows, struck, beaten: *reputavimus Ipsum ~um, percussum Dei, et afflictum* Isa. 53.4 (AC 1846.3).

planctus ~us, *m.* Wailing, lamentation: *in die illo crescet ~us in Hierosolyma* Zech. 12.11 (DD 4); *in mediis doloribus et ~ibus* ES 170.

plane, *adv.* Utterly, completely, quite: *scientia correspondentiarum hodie ~e deperdita est* CI 110; *quod ~e dissimilia sint* AM 148.2.

planeta ~ae, *m.* (Gk.) A planet: *ex ~a Mercurii* AC 6696; *in ~is hujus mundi* VR 64.

planetarius ~a ~um, *a.* Of a planet, planetary: *in aliquo ~o orbe* VR 22.3.

plango ~gere ~xi ~ctum, *tr.*, *intr.* **1** (tr.) To strike, beat: *~gimus pectora nostra* VR 159.4. **2** (intr.) To utter cries of woe, wail, lament: *et tunc ~gent omnes tribus terrae* Matt. 24.30 (AC 6895.1); *cum violator in accinctu est, ~git* [*scortum*] *et lachrymatur* AM 512.1.

planities ~ei, *f.* A large flat stretch of country, plain: *quod ibi sint...montes et colles, ~es et valles* AM 182.3.

planta ~ae, *f.* **1** The sole (of the foot): *a ~a pedis usque ad caput* Isa. 1.6 (AC 431); *in plano sub ~is* AC 6692.2. **2** A young plant, cutting: *in die ~am tuam crescere facies* Isa. 17.11 (AC 8211.3); *quod ~a vel arbor ex semine suo nascatur* ES 251.

plantatio ~onis, *f.* **1** The act of planting: *regeneratio se habet sicut ~o* AC 8326. **2** That which is planted, a young plant: *omnis ~o, quam non plantavit Pater Coelestis, eradicatur* Matt. 15.13 (AE 254.3).

planto ~are ~avi ~atum, *tr.* To set (seeds, plants, etc.) in the ground to make them grow, plant: *~avit Jehovah Deus hortum in Eden* Gen. 2.8 (AC); *arbor...cum ~atur, crescit in ramos* AC 8326; *quae* [*semina*] *si totidem...~arentur* VR 32.3; (fig.) *~abis illos in monte haereditatis Tuae* Exod. 15.17 (AC).

planum ~i, *neut.* **1** A flat area, stage: *theatrum,* *intra quod erat ~um lapillis...stratum* VR 48.1; *super ~o quodam, quale aedificatur hariolis* ES 3771. **b** a flat surface: *pupilla oculi in ~o viridi quasi fulgurabat* AM 268.2. **2** (in geometry) A plane, level: *in ~o horizontali* AC 1276; *in ~o sub plantis* AC 6692.2; *sicut columna graduum subsidens fit corpus cohaerens in ~o* SS 38.1. **3** The field of activity of anything, esp. regarded as one of a series of stages, level: *ipsa conscientia est ~um illarum [tentationum], in quod operantur* AC 762; *quod innocentia infantum sit ~um omnium affectionum boni et veri* CI 341.1; *...ultimum ~um potest assimilari humo* AM 447.1; *primum ~um est intimum rationalis* ES(M) 4545.

planus ~a ~um, *a.* **1** Flat: *per pileos, qui...sunt... quadratae formae, supra ~i* ES 1084. **2** Plain, obvious: *in sensu ~o literae* AE 95.

plasticus ~a ~um, *a.* (Gk.) Formative, shaping: *vis haec propagativa seu ~a in seminibus* AM 238.2.

platanus ~i, *f.* (Gk.) A plane tree: *populus, corylus, ~us* AC 4013.3.

platea[1] ~ae, *f.* (Gk.) A street in a town: *in ~is nostris docuisti* Luke 13.26 (AC 6806.2); *habitacula...disposita in formam civitatis cum ~is* CI 184; AM 3.5; (of passages in a beehive) VR 12.7.

platea[2] ~ae, *f.* A bird, prob. a spoonbill: *tam ~a quam chippod* Zeph. 2.14 (AC 655.2); AE 1100.22.

plaudo ~dere ~si, *intr.* To clap (with the hands): *flumina ~dant manu* Ps. 98.8 (AE 326.11).

plausibilis ~is ~e, *a.* Plausible: *argumentis ~ibus, probabilibus, et verosimilibus* DP 213.

plaustrum ~i, *neut.* A waggon, cart: *vidimus equos et currus...et quoque...aliqua ~a* AM 76.2.

plausus ~us, *m.* A clapping, beat: *complosi ~us robustorum* [sc. *equorum*] *ejus* Judg. 5.22 (AE 355.33).

plebeius: see **plebejus**.

plebejus ~a ~um, *a.* also **plebeius**. Of the lower classes, plebeian: *communio ~a* VR 159.5; *~a idea in Christianismo* AS 12.

plebs ~bis, *f.* The common people, lower classes: *ex infima ~be permulti* AC 822; *quis nisi ~bs et vulgus agnoscit...?* VR 77.2; (in ancient Rome, in the title of a magistrate) *tribunus ~bis*, the tribune of the plebs: VR 141.

plecto[1] ~ere, *tr.* To punish corporally, beat: *si aliquis... ita faceret, ~eretur* AC 7074; DP 278ª.5; ES 1124 ½.

plecto[2] ~ctere ~xi ~xum, *tr.* To weave, plait: in AM 8.2 *flectentes serta* may be an error for *plectentes*.

plenarie, *adv.* Completely, fully: *internum apud illos ~e occlusum est* AC 10492.3.

plenarius ~a ~um, *a.* Complete, total: *rediguntur in ignorantiam ~am* AC 1109; *unitio ~a* DD 35.8; *~a requies a laboribus* AM 8.1; (neut. as sb.) AC 9437.1.

plene, *adv.* (compar. *~ius*) Completely, totally, fully: *cum ~e glorificatus est* AC 6716.3; *pugna per quam ~e vicit inferna* DD 34.1; *ejus forma est ~e et perfecte forma humana* AM 315.11; *~ius expergefactus* ES 243.

plenitudo ~inis, *f.* The quality of being full or complete, fullness: *~o [frumenti] est messis matura* AC 9223.2; *quod multae [cognitiones] fidem [faciant] illustrem secundum ~inem* FI 29; *quod Scriptura sacra sit ~o Dei* VR 6.2; *in ~ine temporum*, at the completion of an age, in the fullness of time: DD 3.1.

plenus ~a ~um, *a.* (compar. *~ior*, superl. *~issimus*) **1** (w. abl.) Abounding (in), full (of): *verum... ~um spirituali* AC 671; *myriades tellurum, et omnes ~ae incolis* AC 6698; *inferna hodie ~issima talibus sunt* ES 4566. **2** Complete, total, full: *in ~o statu veri et boni* AC 7849; *haec contiguitas fit proprior et ~ior* AR 55; *quod solus Dominus...sit ~us homo* VR 109.1; cf. *percipio quod non ~us sis in hoc mundo* AM 151ª.1. **b** *~is oculis*, with complete vision: *possunt quidem conformia videre, sed usque non ~is oculis* SE 20; *~o ore*, with full power of speech, at the top of one's voice: *dicimus ~o ore quod Deus unus sit* VR 135.1. **c** (neut. as sb.) *~um temporis*, a complete period of time: *'et abscondit illum tribus mensibus' significat ~um temporis quo non apparuit* AC 6715; *ad ~um*, fully: *hoc non fieri potest ad ~um* AM 39; *in suo ~o*, at its full development: *quando [Divinum] est in suo ultimo gradu, est in suo ~o* SS 6.

plerique ~raeque ~raque, *pl. a.* Most: *~rique... patres...recordantur suorum liberorum* AM 406; (esp. masc. as sb.) most people: *~rique in mundo non aliam notionem...habent* CI 38.1.

plerumque, *adv.* For the most part, most often: *transmutant ea in alia et ~que in contraria* AC 7070; *~que, et fere semper* ES 468.

pleura ~ae, *f.* (Gk.) (anat.) The covering of the lung, pleura: *involucrum pulmonis, quod ~a vocatur* VR 60.2; ES 1723.

pleuritis ~idis, *f.* Inflammation of the pleura, pleurisy: DP 180.5.

plexus ~us, *m.* (anat.) A group of interconnected nerves or vessels, plexus: *~us cardiaci et pulmonares* AC 9670.2; CI 212; ES 831.

plica ~ae, *f.* A fold, wrinkle: *contorserunt labia in ~as usque ad indignationem* VR 111.6; ES 3961.

plicabilis ~is ~e, *a.* Capable of being bent or folded, pliable: *[corpus] ita ~e ostensum, ut non...laedi sic posset* ES 3393.

plicatio ~onis, *f.* The act of bending or folding: *per ~ones frangebantur et lacerabantur* ES 3927.

plicatura ~ae, *f.* The act of folding, fold: *per ~as vestium et chartarum* VR 184.

plico ~are ~avi ~atum, *tr.* To bend back, fold: *sicut... sumerent chartam, ac ~arent, volverent et revolverent illam digitis* AM 533; *~averunt labia in plures sinus* VR 111.2; ES 4614.

ploratus ~us, *m.* An expression of grief or pain, wailing: *ibi erit ~us et stridor dentium* Matt. 13.42 (AR 422).

ploro ~are ~avi, *intr.* To weep: *ut* [*ut iis* Tafel] *persuasive induxerint Dominum ~antem* [*placantem* Tafel] *super eos* ES 3593 (J D Odhner).

pluma ~ae, *f.* A short, downy feather: *sicut ~ae in vento* AC 7761; *aperi ~as seu pennas corvi* AM 233.4; *quod* [*aves*] *congressus sub ~is sciant* VR 12.5.

plumatus ~a ~um, *a.* Covered in feathers, feathered, downy: *videbam...aliquid ~um* ES 3680.

plumbum ~i, *neut.* The metal lead: *sicut ~um in aquis ingentibus* Exod. 15.10 (AC); *argentum, cuprum, ferrum, stannum, ~um* VI 10.

plumula ~ae, *f.* A small feather: *quod ne ~am quidem motitare queat* 3AD 7567.

pluo ~ere ~i, *intr.* **1** (impers.) To rain: *non ~ere fecit Jehovah Deus super terra* Gen. 2.5 (AC). **2** To fall like rain: *et Jehovah ~ere fecit...sulphur et ignem* Gen. 19.24 (AC); *ecce Ego ~ere faciens vobis panem e coelo* Exod. 16.4 (AC).

pluralis ~is ~e, *a.* (in grammar) Plural: *Deus in lingua originali ~is numeri est* AC 8192.2; (neut. as sb.) *dicitur in ~i 'faciamus hominem'* AC 50.3.

pluralitas ~atis, *f.* The quality of being more than one, plurality: *~as deorum* AC 8301.4; *de ~ate mundorum* CI 417; *quod haec forma in aeternum perficiatur secundum ~atem* DP 62.

pluries, *adv.* Several times, a number of times: *ita ~es in Verbo* AC 21; *~es conati sunt* ES 1659.

plurifariam, *adv.* In several ways: *quod...res sint sparsae et ~am divisae* AC 9022.

pluriformis ~is ~e, *a.* Of several forms: *in ~ibus consertionibus* ES 3607.

plurimum, *adv.* **1** To the greatest extent, most: *'et multiplicabantur...' significat quod ~um crescerent quoad vera a bono* AC 6644; *quod sibi fideret ~um* ES 1414. **2** For the most part, most often: *ubi nominatur 'Israel', significatur ~um Ecclesia spiritualis* AC 768.2; (freq.) *ut ~um*: *angeli...habitant ut ~um in editioribus locis* CI 188.

plurimus ~a ~um, *a.* (as superl. of **multus**) **1** Largest in amount, most: *quoad ~am partem* AC 7130; *~a cum Ipso redemptio* Ps. 130.7 (DD 34.2). **2** (pl.) Very numerous: *ex ~is locis in Verbo* AC 6828; (so, in sg.) *verum...datur ex ~a alia origine* AC 612.2; *quarum ~a mentio fit* AC 1106.

plus[1] pluris, *a.* (no nom. masc. or fem. sg. in use) **1** (as compar. of **multus**) More, greater: *et ultima plura prioribus* Rev. 2.19 (AR); *cruciarentur cum multo pluri cruciatu ac in corpore suo* ES 1720; *quoad plurem partem* AC 7249. **2** Very much, a great deal of: *quod a pluri experientia scire datum* AC 842.2. **3** (pl.) Very many: *plurium gentium religiosa* AC 6729; (masc. as sb.) *possunt plures ibi in uno loco esse* CI 144; (neut. as sb.) *discit plura quae illi usui erunt* FI 25. **b** (sg. in same sense): *draco potest vocari biceps pluri modo* ES 634.

plus[2], *adv.* To a greater extent, more: *quo ~s se dissolvere cupiunt...eo arctius ligantur* AC 960; *si...abstinent ab uno malo...abstinent a pluribus, et ~s adhuc si abstinent ab omnibus, et adhuc si abstinent a pluribus* AM 529; *~s et ~s*, more and more: AM 190; VR 14.2.

plusquam, *adv.* = **plus**[2] and **quam**: AM 393.2.

Pluto ~onis, *m.* **1** The Greek and Roman god of the underworld: *Saturno, Jovi, Neptuno, ~oni, Apollini* VR 17.2; (pl.) the gods of the underworld: *dii infernales quos antiqui vocabant ~ones* AR 752.2; DP 139.6. **2** A kind of evil spirit (see quot.): *quidam qui dixit se ~onem esse, ex illis qui vocantur plutonici, qui phantasiam illam habent, quod videant thesauros immensos auri* ES 4428.

plutonicus ~a ~um, *a.* The name given to certain evil spirits (see quot. under **Pluto**, sense 2): ES 4428.

pluvia ~ae, *f.* Rain: *nubes, nimbi, ~ae* CI 105; *influxus sentiebatur instar tenuis ~ae striatae* AC 7747; (of other things) *apparuit sicut ~a aurea* AM 155[a].1; ES 4175.

pluvialis ~is ~e, *a.* Of or consisting in rain: *aqua ~is* AE 644.4.

pluvius ~a ~um, *a.* *Aqua ~a*, rainwater, rain: *in guttis aquae ~ae* AC 1042.1.

pneuma ~atis, *neut.* (Gk.) A breath of air, puff of wind: *de anima et spiritu fovent ideam sicut de tenui aethere seu ~ate* AM 27; CI 77; *qualem ideam habuit* [*Aristoteles*] *de anima aut spiritu, quem vocabat ~a* ES 3954.

pneumaticus ~a ~um, *a.* (Gk.) Operated by or on air, pneumatic: *siphoni ~o* VR 28.2.

poculum ~i, *neut.* also **poculus** ~i, *m.* (AR 794). **1** A drinking vessel, cup, glass: *purgatis exterius ~i et patinae* Matt. 23.25 (VI 30.1); *quemadmodum ~um* *chrystallinum includit nobile vinum* SS 40.1. **2** (w. gen.) A cupful: *quisquis potaverit vos ~o aquae* Mark 9.41 (AC 6674.5).

poculus: see **poculum**.

podex ~icis, *m.* The buttocks, fundament: Isa. 3.17 (AE 240.7).

poena: see **paena**.

poene: see **paene**.

poenit-: see **paenit-**.

poesis ~eos, *f.* (Gk.) Poetry: *qui...operam dederunt ~i simulatoriae, in qua nihil nisi fictiones* ES 1045; ES 1224.

poeta ~ae, *m.* (Gk.) A poet: ES 2522.

polio ~lire ~livi ~litum, *tr.* To polish: *quod ebur significet verum naturale, est quia est album, et ~liri potest* AR 774.3.

politicus ~a ~um, *a.* (Gk.) Of or concerned with the administration of the state, political: *bona...civilia et ~a* AR 417.7; *induite vestes ministrorum ~orum* DP 197.2; *leges ~ae* VR 55; (masc. as sb.) a politician: *unus sacerdos, alter ~us, et tertius philosophus* AM 182.1; VR 160.6; (neut. pl. as sb.) political matters, politics: *in ~is et naturalibus* VR 482.1.

polities ~ei, *f.* Glossy surface, polish: *rubuerunt ossa prae margaritis, sapphirus ~es eorum* Lam. 4.7 (AC 9873.6).

politus ~a ~um, *a.* (pf. pple. of **polio**) **1** Polished, burnished: *visi sunt quoad faciem sicut ex ~o chalybe* VR 332.5; *ex aere ~o* 1 Kgs. 7.45 (AE 70.4). **2** Elegantly finished, smart: *mirati sunt quod tam nitidae et ~ae essent* [*scripturae*] AM 207.5. **3** (of persons) Civilized, elegant, polite: *dissimilitudines morum, ut...barbarus seu barbara cum ~a aut ~o* AM 246.3.

pollen ~inis, *m.* A fine dust, powder: *unio dilapsa in ~inem* VR 362.1; VR 585.4; AS 65.

polleo ~lere ~lui, *intr.* (w. abl.) To be well endowed (with), be strong (in): *antequam intellectu et judicio ~let* AC 1661.2; *qui genio confirmandi ~lent* SS 91; *quod rationalitate ~leant* [*homines*] VR 12.3.

pollex ~icis, *m.* The thumb (of the hand): *quod sanguis mitteretur super ~icem* AC 7430.2; the big toe (of the foot): *super ~icem pedis eorum dextri* Exod. 29.20 (AC).

polliceor ~ceri ~citus sum, *tr.* To promise (a thing): *per illam* [sc. *fidem*] *~centur coelum* AC 6779; *~cetur officia usus* VR 44.2.

pollicitum ~i, *neut.* A promise: *benedictionibus ac ~is praemiorum* VR 483.1.

polluo ~ere ~i ~tum, *tr.* **1** To make dirty, befoul: *non ~erunt vestimenta sua* Rev. 3.4 (AC 6674.6). **2** To make ritually or morally impure, pollute: *quia ~it Dinam sororem illorum* Gen. 34.13 (AC); *~ebantur qui tetigerunt immundum* AE 79; *cupiditatibus corporeis ~ti* ES 1435.

pollutio ~onis, *f.* The act of making unclean, pollution: AC 4439.

polus ~i, *m.* (Gk.) Either end of the axis about which the earth rotates, pole: *quod excentricum ejus* [sc. *telluris*] *in ~is faciat* VR 32.1; *juxta ~os mundi* ES 222.

polygamia ~ae, *f.* (Gk.) Marriage to more than one wife or husband at the same time, polygamy: *num conjugia iterata aliquid commune obtineant cum ~a* AM 317; AM 340.2.

polygamicus ~a ~um, *a.* (Gk.) (of marriages) Polygamous: AM 77.3.

polygamus ~i, *m.* (Gk.) A polygamous person: AM 79.5.

pomarium ~i, *neut.* A plantation of apple trees, orchard: AM 147.

pomifer ~era ~erum, *a.* Apple-bearing: *quod arbor ~era producat poma* AR 417.7.

pompa ~ae, *f.* (Gk.) Ostentatious luxury, display, pomp: *cum processionibus ~ae* AM 3.6; ES 1684.

pomum ~i, *neut.* An apple: CC 12.3; *~um Eridis*, the apple of strife in Greek mythology: VR 112.1; *~um Africanum*, a pomegranate: VR 403.2; *~um aurantium*, an orange: AM 42.5.

ponderatio ~onis, *f.* The act of weighing: *mensurae et ~ones* AE 373.1.

pondero ~are ~avi ~atum, *tr.* **1** To weigh: *bilanx in manu ~antis* VR 72.1; to add weight to: (in fig. phr.) *lanx qua inclinationes ad conjugia iterata ~antur* AM 318.1. **2** To review carefully, weigh (words): *verba ~ant* ES 454.

ponderosus ~a ~um, *a.* (compar. *~ior*) Weighing heavily, ponderous: *ambulatio...~a, audita sicut ambulatio ursi* ES 6040; *haereditarium...cum accedit actuale, fit crassius et ~ius* ES 4523.

pondo, *indecl. neut.* Weight: *per ~o significatur grave ex malo* AE 1026.1; *talenti ~o*, the weight of a talent: *quod dicatur talenti ~o, est quia talentum erat maximum pondus argenti et...auri* AR 714.

pondus ~eris, *neut.* **1** An object used to exert the force of gravity, weight: *sicut ~era delabuntur* AC 8279.1; *horologio, quod mobile est ex pendulo et simul ~ere* VR 364.1; *~era lancium* AE 373.1. **2** Heaviness, weight:

malum...correspondet gravi...quod ex ~ere suo delabitur AC 8279.2; cf. *comedent panem ~ere* Ezek. 4.16 (AE 71.2). **3** (transf.) Importance, influence: *falsum ex se nihil ~eris habet* AC 8298.1.

pone, *prep. w. acc.* Behind: *Abrahamum ~e me locavit* ES 461; ES 2974.

pono ~nere ~sui ~situm, *tr.* **1** To place, put, set (in a specified position): *arcula in qua ~situs fuit infans* AC 6724.3; *sibi proxime ~nit illa quae maxime conveniunt* AC 6690; *ut emeret sibi cingulum, et ~neret super lumbis* SS 16 (Jer. 13.1); (fig.) *et ~nas verba in ore illius* Exod. 4.15 (AC). **b** to direct, turn (parts of the body): *~ne facies tuas versus Gogum* Ezek. 38.2 (AC 1151.2); *qui ex falsis cogitat, non ~nit cor ad Divinum* AC 7341. **2** To put on the ground, set down: *et ~nens genua oravit* Luke 22.41 (AC 1787.2). **b** (of birds) to lay (eggs): VR 12.5. **3** To set up, erect, establish: *in planitiem...super qua ~sitae erant mensae* AM 6.1; *~sui ibi locum arcae* 1 Kgs. 8.21 (AC 6804.6). **b** to lay (foundations): *primum ~net fundamentum* AC 6937. **c** (transf.) to bring into existence, establish: *regnum ibi suum voluerunt ~nere* 3AD 4641. **4** (w. *super*) To put (a person in authority over): *et ~suerunt super illum principes tributorum* Exod. 1.11 (AC). **5** (Bibl., w. *in* + acc. or w. predicate) To cause to be, make: *~nam te in magnificentiam aeternitatis* Isa. 60.15 (AC 6745.3); *~nam ea in sylvam* Hos. 2.12 (AE 388.5); *...dum ~suero inimicos Tuos scabellum pedum Tuorum* Ps. 110.1 (AC 8281.2); *Jehovah ~nit nubes currum Suum* Ps. 104.3 (AE 36.3). **6** (w. dat.) To confer (on), assign (to): *et ~nat [Jehovah] tibi pacem* Num. 6.26 (AC 6674.8). **b** (w. *super*) to impose (a task on): *demensum laterum... ~netis super illos* Exod. 5.8 (AC). **7** (w. *in* + abl.) To regard as consisting (in), find (in): *jucundissimum suum ~nunt in eo ut alios laedant* AC 592.2; *quod [homo] possit delicate edere et bibere, modo non ~nat in eo vitam* CI 358. **b** (w. *inter*) to regard as belonging (among): *quis...non illos in caelum evehit, ~nit inter angelos...?* DP 274.2; (w. *supra*) to regard (as superior to): *~nunt dignitates longe supra usus* AM 262.3. **8** To lay down, prescribe: *velim adducere... varia, quae ~nit [illa fides]* FI 39; *~sita significatione vocis* ES 2041; (w. *ut*) *sunt...omnia sub ejus* [sc. *solis*] *intuitu, quia ~suit ut sint* AS 152. **9** To set up as a hypothesis, suppose: *~natur quod in mundo sit societas composita ex meris diabolis* AM 266.4. **10** To presuppose the existence of, involve: *omnis affectio ~nit usum* AE 1214.2; *hoc 'ex se' ~nit prius et sic tempus* VR 21.1.

pons ~ntis, *m.* A bridge: *inter hanc urbem et Gehennam apparet sicut ~ns* AC 942; ES 853.

ponticulus ~i, *m.* A small bridge: *erat ~us qui distinxit, et ibi porta a parte luci, et porta a parte horti* AM 183.1.

pontifex ~icis, *m.* **1** A high priest: *~ice maximo praeeunte* AM 3.6; (among the Jews) *~ices et Pharisaei* AE 400.14. **2** The head of the Roman Catholic Church, the Pope: *raro aliquis Papa in mundo agit ibi* [sc. *in mundo spirituali*] *~icem* UJ(C) 59; (pl., app.) Roman Catholic priests: *apud Quakeros...et apud ~ices* ES(M) 4664.

pontificalis ~is ~e, *a.* Of a priest, priestly: *amictu ~i indutus* AC 1361.4; (esp.) of the Pope, papal: *functus est ~i munere* UJ(C) 59.

Pontificius ~a ~um, *a.* Of the Roman pontiff, papal, Roman Catholic: *ex religione ~a* CI 508.3; *ex gente ~a* DP 136.4; (masc. pl. as sb.) papists, Roman Catholics: *per 'bestiam' intelliguntur ~i* SS 25 (Rev. 19.19).

popina ~ae, *f.* A shop selling hot food, cookshop: *calor in ~is, ubi esculenta faetida veno exstant* VR 834.

poples ~itis, *m.* The wrist (of the hand): *versationes ~itum manus* DP 212.1; AM 20.3; also, the hollow behind the knee, hough: *dictum ei quod maledictionem attraxerit usque ad genua, et...quod superius crescat ad ~ites et ultra* ES(M) [4775].

popularis ~is, *m.* A representative of a people: AM 103.4.

populor ~ari ~atus sum, *tr.* To carry off as booty, loot: *humanum genus, et quae ad eos pertinent, ita perdere et ~ari cupiunt* ES 1063.

populosus ~a ~um, *a.* (compar. *~ior*) Containing many inhabitants, well populated, populous: *quod ~a esset terra* AC 403; *urbs ~a* AM 179.

populus[1] ~i, *m.* **1** The inhabitants of a particular country, people: *et praecepit Pharao omni ~o suo* Exod. 1.22 (AC); *de gentibus seu ~is extra Ecclesiam* CI 318 titulus. **2** The common people (as opposed to its rulers): *quod tolerentur [lupanaria]...a ~o...notum est* AM 451; (as opposed to the clergy) *ex oratione quae in templis...legitur coram ~o* VI 4.

populus[2] ~i, *f.* The poplar tree: *olea, vitis, cedrus, ~us, quercus* SS 18.2; (as timber) *ex asseribus ~i* AM 103.3.

porcellinus ~a ~um, *a.* Of porcelain: *vas chrystallinum seu ~um* SS(P) 6 (= 3.4); (neut. pl.) *~a indica*, china ware, china: UJ(P) 77.

porcus ~i, *m.* A pig: *ne projicite margaritas vestras ante ~os* Matt. 7.6 (AC 7784.4); CI 429; ES(M) 4566.

porosus ~a ~um, *a.* Porous: *lignum spongiosum ac ~um* CI 479.5.

porphyrites ~is, *m.* (Gk.) Porphyry: *palatium... structum ex ~e* AM 12.1.

porrigo[1] ~rigere ~rexi ~rectum, *tr.* To hold out,

present, offer: *veneficus... ~rexit poculum* CI 462[a].7; *~rexit mihi chartam* VR 508.6; [*aves*] *escas ~rigunt* VR 12.5.

porrigo[2] ~inis, *f.* Scurf: *papula, ustio, ~o, vitiligo* AC 7524.4.

porro, *adv.* Furthermore, in addition: *~o a spiritibus ...informatus sum* AC 8371; *haec intelliguntur per hoc...et ~o per hoc...* VR 3.1; *et sic ~o*, and so forth, and so on: CI 38.2; AM 220.1.

porrum ~i, *neut.* A leek: Num. 11.5 (AE 513.6).

porta ~ae, *f.* **1** A door (in a building): *super postem ~ae atrii interioris* Ezek. 45.19 (AC 7847.3). **2** A gate (in a wall or sim.): *urbem...habentem ~as duodecim* Rev. 21.12 (AR); *erat ponticulus...et ibi ~a a parte luci, et ~a a parte horti* AM 183.1. **3** (fig.) A means of entry, gateway: *quibus ~a in coelum aperta est* ES 203.

portatilis ~is ~e, *a.* Capable of being carried, portable: *altare...erat ~e* AC 9714.10.

portatio ~onis, *f.* **1** A carrying: *describitur per aquilam,...ejus motitationem super pullis, et ~onem eorum super alis* AE 281.6. **2** A taking upon oneself, a bearing of a burden: *ex... ~one iniquitatum seu peccatorum a Domino* AC 9937.2.

portentum ~i, *neut.* A strange or abnormal happening regarded as a sign, portent, omen: *vide omnia ~a quae posui in manu tua* Exod. 4.21 (AC); *quid hoc ~um, quomodo huc venit avis noctis?* AM 10.3; VR 16.4.

porticus ~us, *m.* An arcade, portico: *habitacula... habent ~us seu atria longa* AC 1629; an avenue (of trees): *in horto...ex transtris quasi laureis, et sic ~ibus, ornatissimo* CI 337; *ad pedem collis ~us ex palmis* AM 132.1.

portio ~onis, *f.* A share, allotment: *tunc Jehovah haereditatem Sibi faciet Jehudam, ~onem Suam super terra sanctitatis* Zech. 2.12 (AE 119.5); *omnia sunt plena Deo, et quisque...accipit suam ~onem* VR 364.3.

porto ~are ~avi ~atum, *tr.* **1** To carry (a burden): *asini ~antes onera* AM 232.5; *illa quae religionis sunt ~ant sicut in sacco super tergo* VR 22.3. **b** to carry (persons, often fig.): *infantes amant...amplectendo, ~ando* AM 405.2; *assumsit illos et ~avit illos omnibus diebus aeternitatis* Isa. 63.9 (AC 7091.5). **2** To transport, carry off: *~atus ab angelis in coelum* CI 365.2. **3** To carry upon the person, wear: *et ~abit Aharon nomina filiorum Israelis in pectorali judicii* Exod. 28.29 (AC); *quod ~aret* [*rex*] *coronam ex auro* AE 31.6. **4** To take upon oneself, bear the burden of (sin, grief, etc.): *filius non ~abit iniquitatem patris* Deut. 24.16 (AC 1093.2); *dolores nostros ~avit* Isa. 53.4 (DD 6); ES 3435. **5** *Secum ~are*, to involve as a necessary concomitant, bring with it: *inauguratio...illas* [sc. *illustrationem et instructionem*] *secum ~at* VR 146; ES 4464.

portus ~us, *m.* A harbour, haven: *Sebulun ad ~um marium habitabit* Gen. 49.13 (AC).

porus ~i, *m.* (Gk.) A small orifice in the skin, pore: *vapor exundans e ~is corporis* ES 397; *per ~os cutis* ES 3124; also, in bone: *per ~os ossis cranii* ES 3718 1/2.

posco ~ere poposci, *tr.* To call for, demand: *~ebant demonstrationem* VR 12.1; AM 319.

positio ~onis, *f.* **1** The act of laying, fall, deposit: *fuit ~o roris circum castra* Exod. 16.13 (AC). **2** An attitude of mind, position in an argument: *est talis ~o damnosa* AC 3394.3; ES 3617.

positus ~us, *m.* Position with respect to the vertical, attitude: *brachium...in vario ~u* ES 1754; *in ~u directo* 'the right way up' ES(M) 4683.

posse, *indecl. neut.* (inf. of **possum** used as sb.) The fact of being able, potentiality: *sic ex Domino adoratio, nam Dominus dat omne ~e et omne esse in adoratione* AC 1150; *Ipsius ~e et velle unum sunt* VR 56; VR 74.3.

possessio ~onis, *f.* **1** The fact of possessing, ownership, possession: *quibus regio illa coeli in ~onem data est* AC 6914.4; *'haereditas terrae' non significat ~onem terrae* AE 304.44. **2** A thing (esp. a piece of land) possessed, possession: *amoris mundi sunt imprimis opes et ~ones* AM 49; *quod per thesauros significentur ~ones cognitionum* AE 236.4.

possessionatus ~a ~um, *a.* Possessing a large estate in goods or land, wealthy in possessions: *credunt se divites...aut ~os ab aliorum praediis, domibus, et mercibus* VR 245.2; (neut. pl. as sb.) objects possessed, possessions: *illa non aliter aspiciunt, quam sicut alius sua famulitia et ~a* VR 533.2.

possessor ~oris, *m.* One who possesses, owner: *oves ...quas ~ores earum occidunt* Zech. 11.5 (AC 6767.3); (fig.) *hic amor est ~or illius arboris* AM 135.3.

possessus ~a ~um, *a.* (pf. pple. of **possideo**) Subject to the power (of), possessed (by): *ut ~us potuerim esse a spiritibus* ES 3963.

possibilis ~is ~e, *a.* Possible: *ut...detineantur a malo quantum ~e est* CI 295; (neut. as sb.) *illos secundum omne ~e infestant* AC 6907.2.

possibilitas ~atis, *f.* Possibility: *crescendo ad quemvis gradum datae ~atis* AC 8678.1.

possideo ~sidere ~sedi ~sessum, *tr.* (pf. act. also *~sidi* AC 1675, AR 676) **1** To have under one's control, own, possess: *cupiditas dominandi et ~sidendi aliorum bona* AC 8118.3; *quod...daret decimas omnium quae ~sidebat* VI 30 (Luke 18.12). **2** To have as part of one's mental equipment, possess: *quod ille ne quidem granum intellectus ~sideat* AM 233.5; *quod spiritus* *omnem linguam hominis ut vernaculam ~sideant* ES 433.

possum posse potui, *intr.* **1** (of persons, w. inf.) To be able (to): *qui...destruere posse sibi videntur vera* AC 6655; *quid haec significant, nemo videre potest* SS 9. **b** (elliptically, w. no inf.): *ad magiam pronissimi sunt, et quantum possunt, etiam imbuunt* AC 6692.2; *ipse Athanasius non potuit aliter* DP 262.1; *ut non possit homo quin credat* ES 1622. **c** (w. acc.) to be able to do: *quia omnia potest [Deus]* AC 300; *hoc non potest nisi quam sapiens* VR 12.9. **2** (of things, w. inf.) To be capable (of), be able (to): *hoc quoque constare potest a hieroglyphicis Aegyptiorum* AC 6692.1; *secundum pretium auri quod abradi potest* VI 10.

post, *prep. w. acc.* and *adv.* **1** (prep.) **a** (of space) At the back of, behind: *janua post pulpitum a sinistro* AM 23; *non revertatur ad post se* Luke 17.31 (CI 208). **b** (of time) after: *post mortem* CI 421; *post breve tempus* CI 427. **c** (of succession) after: *quod mens...patris inhabitet proli post prolem* VR 103.2; *unus post alterum* ES 3618. **2** (adv.) **a** At the rear, behind: *voluntaria sistuntur a tergo seu post* AC 8194.1. **b** afterwards, subsequently: *surrexerunt, et suspexerunt ad Dominum, et post remiserunt se super solia* VR 48.5.

postdiluvianus ~a ~um, *a.* Of the period after the Flood, post-diluvian: *homo ~us* ES 2348; (masc. as sb.) AC 310.2.

postea, *adv.* Afterwards, subsequently: *primum qui sedebant ad septentrionem, dein illi qui ad occidentem, ~a qui ad meridiem* VR 48.2.

posterior ~or ~us, *compar. a.* **1** Situated to the rear, hinder, back: *ad mare ~us* Zech. 14.8 (AC 935.3); (neut. pl. as sb.) the hinder parts, back: *et videbis ~ora Mea* Exod. 33.23 (AC); *per equi ~ora* AC 1644; *super ~ora habitaculi* Exod. 26.12 (AC). **2** Later in time, subsequent: *opera tua ~ora plura primis* Rev. 2.19 (VI 2); *credent voci signi ~oris* Exod. 4.8 (AC). **3** Subsequent in order, latter: *duo priora sunt fidei, duo ~ora sunt charitatis* VR 3.2; AM 16.2; *sicut prius, ~us et postremum* SS 7. **4** Logically subordinated, posterior: *praefertur semper prior seu superior gradus ~ori seu inferiori* AC 6824; (neut. as sb.) AC 5116.3.

posterioritas ~atis, *f.* A later point in time, the future: *in ~ate annorum venies super terram reversam a gladio* Ezek. 38.8 (AC 1151.2).

posteritas ~atis, *f.* Descendants regarded collectively, posterity: *'generationes' sunt ~ates* AC 1041; *~ati ex Jacobo* AC 6832.1; *[papiliones] prospiciunt sibi ~atem* VR 12.6; (Bibl.) *~as dierum*, time to come, the future: *fiet in ~ate dierum, stabilis erit mons Jehovae* Isa. 2.2 (DD 4).

posterius, *compar. adv.* Further back: *habitant ~us* AM 492.

posterus ~a ~um, *a.* **1** Next, following: *~o mane* ES 3029; (neut. as sb.) *in ~um*, for the future: ES 2176. **2** (masc. pl. as sb.) Descendants, successors: *~i ex Jacobo* AC 6832.2; *quod ~i...in...vitas parentum similes ferantur* AM 202.2.

posthac, *adv.* From now on, henceforward: *Ecclesiam quae ~c instauranda* CI 187; *omnis...homo...qui non credit in Dominum, ~c nec exauditur* VR 108.

posthaec, *adv.* Hereafter, subsequently: *~c vidi quod vocarent judices* AM 500.4.

posthumus ~a ~um, *a.* (of offspring) Born after the death of the father, posthumous: *Symbolum, quod vocatur Athanasium, ut faetus ~us, prodiit* VR 172.1; (in general) living after death: *spiritus seu ~us homo post excessum ejus e materiali corpore vivens* VR 816.

posticus ~a ~um, *a.* Rear, back: *a...parte ~a* CO 52.

postis ~is, *m.* An upright post framing a door or window, doorpost: *et accipient de sanguine, et dabunt super binos ~es et super superliminare* Exod. 12.7 (AC); *fenestrae altae...harum ~es etiam ex auro* AM 12.1.

postliminio, *adv.* With reversion to a previous proposition, going back: *si ~o dicitur quod bona opera usque sponte sequantur fidem* SE 46.

postmodum, *adv.* Afterwards, later: *is nondum habet vitam verae fidei quam tamen ~um recipere potest* AC 29.1.

postnuptialis ~is ~e, *a.* Contracted after marriage: *pactum antenuptiale...et ~e* AM 462.

postpono ~nere ~sui ~situm, *tr.* To place behind, give second place to: *charitatem quidem non rejiciunt sed ~nunt* AC 3447.1.

postquam, *conj.* (w. indic.) After: *~am desiit conjunctio immediata* CI 365.3; AM 463.2.

postremitas ~atis, *f.* The final stage, end: *in ~ate dierum fiet stultus* Jer. 17.11 (AE 236.7).

postremo, *adv.* In the last place, finally: *ad sensuale...quod ~o recipit influxum* AC 7270.2.

postremus ~a ~um, *a.* Last in series, final: *~o tempore, quod vocatur Ultimum Judicium* CI 1; *in hac Trinitate nullus est primus et ~us* Sym. Ath. (DD 56); (neut. as sb.) *nam ~um viro pax* Ps. 37.37 (AE 365.15).

postridie, *adv.* On the following day, next day: *~e venit ad me angelus prior* AM 76.1.

postulo ~are ~avi ~atum, *tr.*, *intr.* **1** (w. acc.) To ask insistently for, demand: *deos fusiles, quos adorarent,* *sibi ~abant* AC 8301.5; (of things) to necessitate, call for: *unaquaevis* [*operatio*] *suam analysin... ~at* VR 142. **2** (intr.) To demand, require: *sicut usus ~at* AE 124; (w. inf.) *~at salvari ex se* AC 8172; (w. *ut*) *necessitas ~at, ut dominus et domina concordent* AM 283.

potabilis: see **potatilis**.

potatilis ~is ~e, *a.* also **potabilis**. Suitable for drinking, liquid: *alabastrum unguenti nardi ~is* [*potabilis* Autograph and 3rd edn.] *multum pretiosae* Mark 14.3 (AC 10011.2).

potatio ~onis, *f.* A drinking bout: *~o et bibitio* AC 5165.1.

potatorium ~i, *neut.* A drinking trough: *constituit baculos...in ~is aquae, quo veniebant greges ad bibendum* Gen. 30.38 (AC); a drinking bout, party: *~a, epularia, saltatoria ac histrionica* CO 57.

potatum ~i, *neut.* A liquid for drinking, drink: *percepi quod liquor ~i in se salinum haberet* ES 645.

potens ~ntis, *a.* (gen. pl. *~ntium* and *~ntum*) (compar. *~ntior*, superl. *~ntissimus*) Powerful, mighty: *angeli ~ntissimi robore* Ps. 103.20 (CI 229); *angeli... sunt...tantum ~ntes, quantum a Domino accipiunt* AE 43; *falsa ~ntiora* AC 8185.2; (masc. as sb.) *~ntes Moabi* Exod. 15.15 (AC); *quendam inter ~ntissimos* ES 4158.

potenter, *adv.* With power, effectively, powerfully: *quod tunc detineantur ~er a malis* AC 2406.1; *qui ~er possunt adulterare et falsificare vera Verbi,...quibus potentia accedit secundum facultatem ratiocinandi* AE 782.1.

potentia ~ae, *f.* **1** Strength, vigour, energy, powers: *quod ~a ejus* [sc. *Simsonis*] *constaret in crinibus ejus* SS 49.2; *~a naturalis* AC 7011; *promptus erit ad restitutionem...omni ~a sua* BCP (VI 6); (of the Lord) *quod Ipse illud* [sc. *humanum*] *ex propria ~a Divinum fecerit* AC 6716.2; *fugere mala sicut a se ipso ex ~a Domini* VI 31. **2** A specific capacity or power: *facultates seu ~ae recipiendi verum* AC 5623.1; AC 6343.1; *quod homo...in ~a contra mala et falsa...sit* VR 68; *apparet... sicut Petro data sit illa ~a* AE 9.2. **b** sexual potency: *quid vita amoris illius nisi ex vena ~ae?* AM 44.8; *in supereminente ~a sunt* AM 55.7. **3** Control over others, authority, power: *perplures qui in ~a, dignitate et opulentia vixerunt* AC 995.4; *quod sensualia... apparerent illis sicut in ~a super omnia* SS 13. **4** (of things) The ability to exert influence, capacity, power: *verum scientificum...valuit supra ~am doctrinae falsi ex malo* AC 6770; *Divino Vero inest ~a in se* CI 137.3; *~a amori est per sapientiam* AM 21.2. **5** Latent capacity, potentiality: *inde illis non rationalitas in facultate seu in ~a est amplius* DP 227.5; *quod in Domino...fuerint bini gradus priores actualiter, et tertius gradus in ~a* AS 233. **6** (in mathematics) The power (of a number): *in ~a subtriplicata* VR 168. **7** A person or thing capable of exerting influence, power: *cum baculis...qui illis... inserviunt pro ~is* AC 7026; *quod angeli...sint ~ae... notum est* AC 9410.5; *quod humanae mentes...sint merae ~ae* 1AD 943.

potentialiter, *adv.* Potentially: *bina corpora ~er ita unita sunt ut non sint duo amplius* AE 1004.3.

potestas ~atis, *f.* The ability to exercise control, power (over): *quod angeli...tantam ~atem super infernales spiritus habeant* AC 6677; *qui Divinam Domini ~atem sibi arrogant* VI 79.1; *usque dum suae ~atis fiunt* [*pueri*] 'become their own masters' AM 176.

potior[1] ~tiri ~titus sum, *tr.*, *intr.* To gain possession of, acquire, realize: **a** (tr.): *quia non ~tiri potuerunt quae cupiverunt* CI 6. **b** (intr., w. abl.): *optato... ~titus sum* AM 10.3; *ut votis ~tiamur* AM 44.10.

potior[2] ~or ~us, *a.* (compar. of **potis**) **1** More powerful, stronger: *denominatio fit a ~ore* AC 8314.1. **2** Preferable, more desirable: *quod ~ora offerant illis* CI 406; ES 1234.

potis, *a.* (only used as nom.) (compar.: see **potior**[2]) Able: *quis ~is est videre...?* AM 22.

potissimum: superl. of **potius**.

potius, *compar. adv.* (superl. *~tissimum*) As a preferable alternative, rather: *ut sentiant in se ~tius infernum quam coelum* CI 400.2; more correctly: *distinctus...sicut triticum a palea, aut ~tius sicut humanum a ferino* AM 44.6; (superl.) especially: *in eo ~tissimum vitam consistere putans* ES 3430.

poto ~are ~avi ~atum, *tr.* To give drink to, water: *quisquis ~averit vos poculo aquae* Mark 9.41 (AC 6674.5); *~avit gregem* Exod. 2.17 (AC); VR 122.

potulenta ~orum, *neut. pl.* Drinkable liquids, drinks: *ex cibis et ~is* AC 994.2.

potus ~us, *m.* A drink: *recipit verum sicut sitiens ~um* AC 6829; *sanguis Meus est vere ~us* John 6.55 (AC 7850.2); ES 2084.

practice, *adv.* In practice: *~e mali sunt, qui nihili faciunt praecepta Divina* VR 382.

practicus ~a ~um, *a.* (Gk.) Put into practice, applied: *sunt etiam vera fidei theoretica, et sunt ~a* AC 9297.4; *illam viam vocant religionem ~am* AE 250.5.

prae, *prep. w. abl.* **1** In comparison with: *illi qui alios prae se contemnunt* AC 2219.5. **2** In excess of, above, more than: *Ecclesia Antiquissima...prae sequentibus erat Domini sabbathum* AC 85.1; *qui apparent ...prae aliis opitulandi* AC 6705; *mortui...qui myriades* *sunt prae iis qui vivunt* ES 2878. **3** Through excess of, for: *non potuerunt bibere aquas prae amaritudine* Exod. 15.23 (AC); *quae [turma] prae luce reliquis non visa est* AM 2.3.

praeabundantia ~ae, *f.* Over-abundance, surplus: *timentes...quod ~a esset spirituum...in coelo* ES 699.

praeabundo ~are ~avi, *intr.* To be over-abundant, be too many: *num sic ~arent equi* ES 561.

praeadamita ~ae, *m.* A person of the time before Adam, preadamite: *argumenta de ~is ex computis et chronologiis* VR 466; ES 3390.

praeamo ~are ~avi ~atum, *tr.* To love better: *apud illos qui praeferunt et ~ant statum conjugialem* AM 452.3.

praebeo ~bere ~bui ~bitum, *tr.* **1** To offer, provide: *etiam balaenae ~bent mammam* Lam. 4.3 (AC 6745.6); *quod ~buerint Ipsi acetum ad bibendum* DD 16.6; *~bere aures*, to lend an ear: *rogans ut ~beant aures ad pauca quae...loqui desidero* VR 136.3. **2** (transf.) To offer the chance of, provide (an opportunity): (refl.) *quoties occasio se ~bet* VI 92; (w. gerundive) *videndum ~bent coelum stelliferum* ES 998.

praecaveo ~cavere ~cavi ~cautum, *intr., tr.* **1** (intr.) To take precautions, guard: *sed Dominus ~cavit, et curam hominis habet* ES 3781; (w. *ne*) *~cavent ne cupiditas dominii et cupiditas lucri irrepant* AC 7364; (impers. pass.) *~cavetur quam maxime, ne aliquis angelus...despiciat in societatem inferioris [coeli]* CI 208. **2** (tr.) To take precautions against: *per illum* [sc. *pellicatum*] *~caventur adulteria* AM 459.5; *sed Dominus id ~cavet* ES 1590. **b** (pass.) To be the object of precautions, be guarded: *ita ~cavetur...homo, ne mali spiritus influant* ES 3085.

praecedaneus ~a ~um, *a.* Preceding in order, preliminary: *ex oratione ~a ante Communionem* VR 526.

praecedens ~ntis, *a.* (pres. pple. of **praecedo**) Preceding: *ad caput ~ns* AC 6818; (neut. pl. as sb.) the preceding passage: *ut patet a mox ~ntibus* AC 6674.1; CI 431.

praecedo ~dere ~ssi, *intr.* (*tr.*) **1** To go in front: *~sserunt cantantes* Ps. 68.25 (AC 6742). **2** To come before in sequence, precede: *~dunt pisces et aves...et sequuntur bestiae* AC 52; *patet ab illis quae ~dunt* AC 6684; *nisi ~sserit cognitio* AM 127. **3** (tr.) To go before, precede: *timor ~dit amorem* AC 6997.2.

praecellentia ~ae, *f.* The quality of excelling, superiority: *ex ~a sui prae aliis* ES 437.

praecello ~ere ~ui, *intr., tr.* To be superior (to), excel: (w. dat.) *laetitiae quae reliquis ~uerunt* AC 8339.1; *~uerunt aliis doctrina et praedicatione* CI 346; (w. acc.) *cupiditas ~endi alios intellectu* ES 437.

praeceps ~ipitis, *a.* (compar. *~ipitior*) **1** Head first, headlong: *dejiciunt se ~ipites inde* CI 400.2; *quin in damnationem ~eps cadat* 3AD 7529. **2** Impetuous, headstrong: *gentem amaram et ~ipitem* Hab. 1.6 (AE 355.24).

praeceptor ~oris, *m.* An instructor, teacher: *ex ore ~oris* CC 10.4.

praeceptum ~i, *neut.* A commandment, order, instruction, esp. given by God: *qui Deum timent custodiunt ~a* AC 6678; *per vitam secundum ~a Ipsius* AM 29.

praeceptus ~a ~um, *a.* (compar. *~ior*) Formed in advance, preconceived: *cadunt ideae nostrae ~ae [praeconceptae* Tafel] *de omnipotentia* VR 74.1; *~o judicio congruunt* ES 2202; (app.) sensitive to commands: *si ~iores aures haberet* 3AD 117.

praecido ~dere ~si ~sum, *tr.* To cut back, trim: *abradendi [sunt] capilli capitis ejus, ~dendi ungues* Deut. 21.12 (AC 3301.8).

praecingo ~gere ~xi ~ctum, *tr.* To surround with a belt, girdle: *~ctum ad mamillas zona aurea* Rev. 1.13 (AR).

praecipio ~cipere ~cepi ~ceptum, *intr., tr.* **1** (intr.) To issue commands, give orders: *quemadmodum ~cipit Jehovah* Exod. 7.20 (AC); (w. dat.) *~cepit Pharao omni populo suo* Exod. 1.22 (AC). **2** (w. acc.) To impose (a command), give (orders): *judicia quae Ego ~cipiens tibi hodie* Deut. 7.11 (AC 8364.3); (impers. pass.) *ita ~ceptum est in Verbo* CI 472.3. **b** (w. inf.): *Moses... ~cepit tales lapidare* John 8.5 (DD 9); *quod...Moses ~ceperit dare libellum repudii* Matt. 19.7 (AM 276.1).

praecipitanter, *adv.* With undue haste: *ne hoc ~er fiat* AC 3755.2.

praecipitatio ~onis, *f.* An instance of rapid movement, fast beating (of the heart): *per ~ones cordis sensibiles* ES 327.

praecipitium ~i, *neut.* A precipice: *repsi usque ad ~um, et per id me dejeci* AM 10.5.

praecipito ~are ~avi ~atum, *tr.* **1** (refl.) To hurl oneself down, plunge: *ut...cupiat...in infernum se ~are* AC 1049; *sicut feces, quae se ad fundum... ~ant* AM 272. **2** To bring about speedily, hasten: *quod corpori damnum inferat, sic ~et mortem* ES 2422. **b** (refl.) to act hastily, be rash: *cor ~antium se intelliget ad sciendum* Isa. 32.4 (AE 455.19).

praecipue, *adv.* Especially, above all: *hi usus sunt ~e exercitia charitatis* AC 7038.1; AM 246.2.

praecipuus ~a ~um, *a.* Outstanding, leading, chief: *~um tutamen religionis istius fuit ignorantia veri* FI 8; *de ~o essentiali Ecclesiae* AE 151.6; (neut. as sb.) the leading characteristic, chief feature: *~a sapientiae* AC 7052; *id scire...est ~um intelligentiae angelorum ibi* CI 59.

praecise, *adv.* Outright: *terra [non] vendetur ~e, Mea enim est terra sed peregrini et inquilini vos Mecum* Lev. 25.23 (AC 8002.3).

praecisus ~a ~um, *a.* Precise: *sicut libratio quaedam est ~a et exacta* ES 193.

praeclarus ~a ~um, *a.* Famous, renowned: *strenui et ~i duces* AM 292.1.

praecludo ~dere ~si ~sum, *tr.* also **precludo**. To block off, close, shut: *~serunt sibi coelum* CI 183.2; *aditus ad Divinum ~sus* AE 52.2.

praeco ~onis, *m.* One who makes public announcements, crier, herald: *a quodam ~one acclamatum est* AM 7.2; (transf.) *capis hoc evangelium, ~o 'peccati et paenitentiae'?* AR 531.2.

praecogitatio ~onis, *f.* Forethought: *ut iis talis memoria et talis ~o detur* ES 2190.

praeconceptus ~a ~um, *a.* (of ideas) Preconceived: *cadunt ideae nostrae ~ae [praeceptae* 1st edn.] *de omnipotentia* VR 74.1; ES 2369.

praecordia ~orum, *neut. pl.* The parts of the body below the heart, the vitals: *usque ut dolerent quasi eorum ~a, ut dicitur* ES 166.

praecox ~ocis, *a.* Too early, hurried on: *ex conjunctionibus ~ocibus* AM 305.2.

praecursor ~oris, *m.* One who runs before a carriage, runner: *~ori cum baculo et in mollibus calceis* VR 563.1.

praeda ~ae, *f.* **1** Booty captured in war, spoil: *de ~a Hadad-Eseris* 2 Sam. 8.12 (AC 6917.3); *~a facti sunt fortes corde* Ps. 76.5 (AE 187.8). **2** The prey (of wild animals): *quod...sit...feris furor, si...aufertur ~a, notum est* AM 358.

praedatio ~onis, *f.* Highway robbery, theft: *in plateis et vicis sunt latrocinia et ~ones* CI 586.

praedator ~oris, *m.* One who seizes booty, despoiler: (in quot. fig.) *faemina...fit meretrix, in cujus causa etiam ~or ille est* AM 504.2.

praedatum ~i, *neut.* A thing seized by force, booty: *latrones et piratae, qui delectantur raptis et ~is* AM 511.

praedestinatianus ~i, *m.* One who believes in predestination: VR 72.1.

praedestinatio ~onis, *f.* Predestination: AM 105.

praedestino ~are ~avi ~atum, *tr.* To ordain beforehand, predestinate: *effectus...quos Dominus in creatione ~avit* AM 386.1; (w. *ad*) *alicujus animam ~are ad mortem aeternam* VR 56.

praedicabilis ~is ~e, *a.* Capable of being predicated: *de substantia, nisi sit forma, non est aliquid ~e* VR 21.2.

praedicabiliter, *adv.* With reference to predication: *nomina...significant res ~er ad suum subjectum* AC 4502.1.

praedicamentum ~i, *neut.* That which is predicated, quality, (in Aristotelian philosophy) category: *terminis scholasticis, ut...~is, entitatibus et similibus* ES 3960.

praedicate, *adv.* (w. *ad*) With reference (to): *se habent omnia ~e ad rem de qua agitur* AC 1686; AC 6985.

praedicatio ~onis, *f.* **1** (in philosophy) The assignment of attributes, predication: *ex subjecto fit ~o* AC 386; *res cui aufertur sua ~o, quae non est aliquid* AM 55.5; *ex punctis...geometricis, quae quia nullius ~onis, ita in se non aliquid sunt* VR 20.2. **2** Public instruction (esp. on religious matters), preaching: *per Verbum et ~onem Verbi* AC 1043.2; *~o fidei in Ipsum* AC 6988.1; *~ones devote auscultare* AC 8253.

praedicator ~oris, *m.* A preacher: *~ores, non dissimiles illis qui se...Jesuitas vocant* AC 8383; VR 374.4; *~ores publici* ES 594.

praedicatum ~i, *neut.* That which is predicated of a thing, attribute: *quale subjectum, tale ~um* AC 103; *subjectum absque ~is est quoque ens nullius rationis* AM 66.

praedico[1] ~are ~avi ~atum, *tr.* also **predico**. **1** To speak aloud, proclaim: *quod in aurem loquuti fueritis in cubiculis, ~abitur super tectis* Luke 12.3 (AC 7795.2). **2** To proclaim (a doctrine), preach: *novam doctrinam quam ~abant* AC 7418.2; *qui solam fidem...~averunt* VI 7; *ut evangelium e novo ibi ~arent* VR 4.1; (absol.) *de illis qui pie loquuntur et ~ant* CI 291. **3** (in philosophy, pass., of a term, w. *de*) To be predicated (of): *quod 'populus' ~etur de veris* AC 6688; *quia de amore et sapientia non ~ari possunt spatia et tempora* AM 380.11.

praedico[2] ~cere ~xi ~ctum, *tr.* To foretell, predict: *universa Scriptura Sacra de Ipso prophetavit, et Ipsum ~xit* SS 23.4; *per 'Novam Hierosolymam', quae in Apocalypsi...~citur ventura* DD praef.; (w. *quod*) *~co tibi quod futurus sis imbecillis* AM 477.8; (w. indir. qu.) *cum a Jehovah ~citur quid fiet* AC 7793.

praedictio ~onis, *f.* A statement of a future event,

prediction: *ad finem ~onum de successivis statibus* CI 1; *si...eventum ex Divina ~one sciret* DP 178.1.

praeditus ~a ~um, *a.* **1** (w. abl.) Equipped, furnished (with): *quod ~um sit [insectulum] fibris et vasis* VR 12.4; *tribulae... ~ae aculeis* Isa. 41.15 (AE 405.48). **2** (w. abl.) Endowed (with qualities): *quicunque sunt ~i bono charitatis* AC 294; *acutissima acie intellectus ~i* AM 231.4.

praedium ~i, *neut.* A piece of real estate, property: *qui credunt se...possessionatos ab aliorum ~is, domibus et mercibus* VR 245; DP 251.2.

praedo ~onis, *m.* A looter, plunderer, thief: *amor ~onum inter se* CI 560; *cum exercitu ~onum aut rebellium* VR 117; AM 501.

praedoctus ~a ~um, *a.* Pre-eminently learned, superiorly erudite: *quod se... ~um aestimet* AR 426.

praedominium ~i, *neut.* A leading role, predominance: *lux mundi apud illos ~um habet* AC 6865.2; *in conjugiis...in coelis non est aliquod ~um* CI 369; *in quibus* [sc. *mulieribus*] *cupiditates ~um solent habere* ES 436.

praedominor ~ari ~atus sum, *intr.* To exercise dominion, predominate: *ut primum malum ~ari... incipit* AC 8356; *gloria...sui ~atur* CI 347.2.

praedonicus ~a ~um, *a.* Of a looter, plunderer, thief; (neut. as sb.) looting, plundering, thievery: *potest...omnis furcifer, praedo, et latro se lavare usque ad nitorem, num sic furciferum, ~um, et latronicum abstergitur?* VR 672.2.

praedor ~ari ~atus sum, *intr., tr.* **1** (intr.) To take away the property of others without permission, steal, plunder: *quod certis temporibus exirent reges, et ~arentur, sic laetarentur ex rapinis* ES 3346; *ut dum alii de aliis loquuntur et cogitant, is solum ea, quomodo...noceat, ~etur, aut malum infligat* ES 3290. **2** (tr.) To rob (someone): *lucri causa quemcunque ~ari* AC 4751.2. **3** (tr.) To steal (something): *est...similis furi in turri qui...ut primum videt infra objectum rapinae, accelerat cursum deorsum et id ~atur* CC 14.

praeeminentia ~ae, *f.* Pre-eminence: *quod in gaudio coelesti nusquam sit aliquid ~ae prae altero* AC 1936.4.

praeemineo ~nere ~nui, *intr.* To be outstanding, be pre-eminent: *cupidine...vel innovandi vel ~nendi* AC 1188.1.

praeeo praeire praeivi, *intr.* To go in advance, go before: *liberos qui praeibant* AC 1272; *pontifice maximo praeeunte* AM 3.6.

praeexcello ~ere ~ui, *intr.* To surpass in excellence: *quod alii ~ere velint...in gloria mundana* ES 710.

praeexisto ~xistere ~xstiti, *intr.* To come into being beforehand: *est...Esse Dei universalius quam Essentia Dei ...non quod Esse Dei ~xistat, sed quia...* VR 36; ES 3574.

praefatio ~onis, *f.* An introductory section of a book, preface: *videatur ~o ad Gen. xviii* AC 6752.8; SS 32.

praefectura ~ae, *f.* Governance, rule: *et ponam ~am tuam pacem* Isa. 60.17 (AE 70.2).

praefectus ~i, *m.* A person put in charge, governor: *urbis ~us* ES 751 1/2; (esp. in an army) an officer: *~is militum* AM 373; [*status*] *cujusvis militis antequam fit ~us* VR 106.1.

praeferentia ~ae, *f.* A liking for or estimation of something above something else, preferring, preference: *in statu ~ae veri prae bono* AC 4537; *in ~am sui prae aliis* AC 2380.4.

praefero ~ferre ~tuli ~latum, *tr.* **1** To carry before: *si...emergeret capite, quod jugiter ~ferebat sicut serpens* ES 3221. **2** To put on an appearance of, make a show of: *nusquam potuerunt alium vultum ~ferre quam secundum illa quae cogitabant* AC 7361.2; *non licet alium amorem ad apparentiam ~ferre* CI 479.3; *amicitiam, benevolentiam et sinceritatem ~ferre* CI 492; *ore ~ferunt misericordiam* ES 247 titulus. **3** To give precedence to, exalt, prefer: *quantum spectat ad amorem conjugialem, et hunc ~fert* AM 444[a]; (w. dat.) *quisque suum deum ~tulit deo alterius* AC 7401; *quod ...velint... ~ferri omnibus aliis* AC 1877; (w. *quam*) *quod ~tulerint mortem quam ut laederetur conjux* CI 406.

praeficio ~ficere ~feci ~fectum, *tr.* **1** (w. dat.) To put in charge (of): *quod ~fectus sit [Josephus] domui Pharaonis* AC 6643; *in totidem deos, quibus ~fecerunt supremum, quem vocaverunt Jovem* SS 117. **2** (w. dat.) To place (before): *Dominus Deus... ~fecit omnibus praeceptis religionis illorum hoc* VR 9.2; *~ficitur sic descriptioni cuivis Ecclesiae Divinum characteristicon* AE 96.

praefigo ~gere ~xi ~xum, *tr.* (w. dat.) To attach at the beginning (of): *principia organica cerebri, quae fibrillis ~xa sunt* ES 1970.

praefinitio ~onis, *f.* Predetermination: *'et posuit Jehovah tempus statum', quod significet ~onem, constat absque explicatione* AC 7508.

praefinio ~nire ~nivi ~nitum, *tr.* To lay down in advance, preordain: *quod hoc tempus ~nitum sit* CI 420.

praefor ~ari ~atus sum, *tr.* To say by way of introduction, preface: *in limine hujus transactionis aliquid ... ~abor* AM 48; (gerundive as pass.) *aliquid de eo ~andum est* AM 184.

praejudicium ~i, *neut.* A judgment made beforehand, prejudice: *omnia judicia illorum sunt ~a* AM 231.4; ES 921.

praejudico ~are ~avi, *intr.* To anticipate judgment, judge beforehand: *forte ~ant de illis* ES 1406.

praelatus ~i, *m.* A dignitary of the Church, prelate: *tales qui ~i dicti, ambierunt pontifices esse* ES 3999.

praelectio ~onis, *f.* **1** A lecture: *in ~onibus in Gymnasiis* AR 143. **2** An instance of reading out loud: *praelegi coram illo quae in libro...Formula Concordiae appellato...scripta sunt,...post ~onem quaesivi illum...* VR 798.10.

praelego ~gere ~gi ~ctum, *tr.* To read aloud, recite: *cum ~gerem illi aliquid ex Propheticis* CI 322.2; *haec a sacerdote alta voce ~guntur* DP 114.1.

praelibo ~are ~avi ~atum, *tr.* To treat in preliminary fashion, touch upon: *quod amor conjugialis...sit talis, mox supra paucis confirmatum est, sed ibi solum ~atum* AM 64.1.

praeliminaris ~is ~e, *a.* Preliminary: *ut aliqua ~is idea sit de eo* AM 61; (neut. pl. as sb.) *coelestis...homo non in ~ibus illis haeret* AC 2718.4.

praeliminariter, *adv.* As a preliminary: *hoc ~er hic dicitur* AM 84.

praelior ~ari ~atus sum, *intr.* To do battle, fight: *et ~abuntur quia Jehovah cum illis* Zech. 10.5 (AE 355.28).

praelium ~i, *neut.* also **proelium**. A battle: *in die ~i* Zech. 14.3 (DD 14.5); *cum ~um gesserunt contra Midianitas* Num. 31.7 (AE 55.2); *si homo...moritur...in ~o* ES 1099.

praelongus ~a ~um, *a.* Unduly long, tedious: *per seriem...quam ~um foret describere* ES 269.1; ES 3214.

praeluceo ~cere, *intr.* To cast light before, illuminate the way: *sensus literae Verbi, nisi genuina doctrina ~ceat, distrahit mentes in varia* CI 311.3; *qui...sibi fidunt, et sic omnibus ~cere se putant* ES 1402.

praeludium ~i, *neut.* An introductory section, prelude: *primordia quidem sicut ~a ex Verbo depromunt* VR 810.

praemeditate, *adv.* Prob. false reading for *praemeditato*: ES 927 (Tafel).

praemeditatio ~onis, *f.* Premeditation: *momento... absque ulla ~one* AC 1638.

praemeditatum ~i, *neut.* Premeditation: *absque... cogitatione, et praevio consilio, seu ~o* [*praemeditate* Tafel] ES 927; *~o* or *ex ~o*, with premeditation: *sunt ii qui ex ~o dolos exercent* AC 830; ES 2848.

praemeditor ~ari ~atus sum, *tr.* To plan beforehand, premeditate: *non ~antur dolos* ES 2849.

praememoratus ~a ~um, *a.* Previously mentioned, aforesaid: *novus ille ~us status* AM 306.

praemissa ~orum, *neut. pl.* Things set before, preface, introduction: *in ~is hujus capitis* AC 790.1; antecedent propositions, premises: *quae in hoc versu continentur sunt ~a sequentium* AC 1063.1.

praemitto ~mittere ~misi ~missum, *tr.* **1** To send in front or beforehand: *quod ~mittatur spiritus qui praeparet viam* AC 8028; *vidi...navem...circumagi, et quasi tunc essent ei equi ~missi* ES 2240. **2** To place (statements) before, preface: *ante capita...~mittenda sunt doctrinalia* AC 6627; *fides in forma universali et singulari ~mittitur* VR 1.

praemium ~i, *neut.* A reward, prize: *leges...in quibus honores et lucra erant ~a* AC 8118.3; *vita aeterna victoriae ~um* SS 12.1.

praemoneo ~nere ~nui ~nitum, *tr.* To advise in advance, forewarn: *~nentur omnes ut...paenitentiam agant* VR 530.

praemunio ~nire ~nivi ~nitum, *intr.* To take strong action ahead of time; (w. *ne*) to guard against, prevent: *sic...* [*judex*] *~nit ne ille* [sc. *maleficus*] *ulterius malefaciat...ac ne tale judicium scandalo sit* VR 459.15.

praenuntio ~are ~avi ~atum, *tr.* To announce in advance, foretell: *futura quae per illa* [sc. *somnia*] *~antur* AC 5091; *~atum*, a prediction: *quod fidem haberent ~ato ex Verbo* AC 6969.

praenuntium ~i, *neut.* A harbinger, forerunner: *postquam plura exitia et quasi judicia, quae erant ~a exitii et judicii generalis* UJ(P) 139.

praeopto ~are ~avi ~atum, *tr.* To choose in preference, prefer: *cum* [*ephebus*] *ex sexu sibi ~at unam* AM 111.

praeordino ~are ~avi ~atum, *tr.* To arrange in advance, preordain: *quod antequam aliqua mutatio existit, omnia ~entur et ad futurum eventum praeparentur* AE 258.

praeparatio ~onis, *f.* The act of making ready, preparation: *quod ibi agatur de ~one Noachi* AC 709; (w. *ad*) *status...~onis ad recipiendum boni et veri influxum* AC 7831.

praeparatorius ~a ~um, *a.* Preparatory: *judicia... quae vocari potuerunt ~a* UJ(P) 133; (neut. as sb.) DA 12 (= v.[2]).

praeparo ~are ~avi ~atum, *tr.* To make ready, prepare: *vasa in quibus massa pro pane ~atur* AC 7356.1; *quod praemittatur spiritus qui ~et viam* AC 8028; (w. *ad*) *quod homo ad coelum ~andus sit* AC 7439.3.

praepollens ~ntis, *a.* Very highly developed, extremely effective: *quod spiritus...gaudeant...tactu ~nte* AC 1883; *in ~nte potentia* AM 55.4; (w. abl.) *quidam... sapientia ~ns* AR 675.2.

praepolleo ~lere ~lui, *intr.* To be highly developed, act strongly: *quae [voluptates] tantum obscurant... intellectum, quantum ~lent* CI 462.2; (w. abl.) to be strong (in): *ea quibus ~lere videtur homo, sicut propria prudentia* ES 269.

praepondero ~are ~avi, *intr.* To exert the force of gravity, force down: *homo se deorsum agit, sic ut ejus vis ~et* ES 4423.

praepondium ~i, *neut.* A superior weight: *ita ~um erat intus, sic malum exterius quasi nihil sensit* ES 3397.

praepono ~nere ~sui ~situm, *tr.* **1** To set in first place, place before: *in scriptura illa... ~nitur semper numerus* CI 263; (w. dat.) *quod in hoc versu primum ~natur coelum terrae* AC 89. **2** (w. dat.) To regard as superior (to): *nec ~nunt dignitatem praestantiae usus* AM 250.

praepostere, *adv.* In inverted order, back to front, upside down: *homo potest...loqui sicut rationaliter, sed ~e* AM 295.

praeposterus ~a ~um, *a.* Contrary to order, inverted: *cum scientificum intrat in illa quae fidei sunt via ~a* AC 4588.2; *fides visionaria et ~a, quae est apparentia falsi sicut veri* VR 346.2.

praeprimis, *adv.* Above all else, most especially: *officia per quae uxores ~is se cum maritis conjungunt* AM 174; *tali colore ~is delectantur* ES 1172.

praeputiatus ~a ~um, *a.* Uncircumcised: *non addet ut veniat in te amplius ~us et immundus* Isa. 52.1 (DD 64.4); (fig.) *et dixit Moscheh... 'Ecce ego ~us labiis'* Exod. 6.30 (AC).

praeputio ~are ~avi ~atum, *tr.* To treat as unclean: *fructus arboris inserviens esui ~abitur* Lev. 19.23 (AE 109.6).

praeputium ~i, *neut.* **1** (anat.) The foreskin, prepuce: *et circumcidetis carnem ~i vestri* Gen. 17.11 (AC); *proprie significat ~um invidiam propter felicitatem aliorum* ES 2113; (fig.) *removete ~a cordis vestri* Jer. 4.4 (FI 54). **2** (collectively) The uncircumcised: *distinxit ...inter Judaeos et Gentes, seu circumcisionem et ~um* VR 506.2.

praeripio ~ripere ~ripui ~reptum, *tr.* To take away hastily or by force, snatch: *absque faedere conjugii ~ripere illam* [sc. *virginitatem*] AM 460.2; *quod omnibus et singulis cuperent eorum gaudium et felicitatem ~ripere* ES 2509.

praerogativa ~ae, *f.* A privileged position, privilege: *leges in Ecclesia Judaica...de ~a viri et obedientia uxoris* AC 568.2; *inde tot ~ae spirituum prae homine* ES 1077.

praerogativus ~a ~um, *a.* Of privilege or priority: *fidei primogeniturae eminentiam et jus ~um attribuerunt* VR 336.1.

praerupta ~orum, *neut. pl.* Steep places, precipices: ES 4895.

praesaepe: see **praesepe**.

praescientia ~ae, *f.* Foreknowledge, prescience: *~a futurorum tollit ipsum humanum* DP 179.1; VR 631.1.

praescio ~cire ~civi ~citum, *tr., intr.* To have foreknowledge, know in advance: (w. indir. qu.) *~cire qualis est* AC 145; *conjuges optant ~cire, num post mortem separentur* AM 45.

praescribo ~bere ~psi ~ptum, *tr.* To lay down in advance, ordain, prescribe: *quod Christiana doctrina... amorem et charitatem ~bat* CI 325; *cultus ~bitur in doctrina* DD 64.1.

praescriptio ~onis, *f.* A rule laid down in advance, ordinance: *~o de rege apud Mosen loco citato* AC 2015.11 (Deut. 17.14-18).

praesens ~ntis, *a.* (compar. *~ntior*) **1** Spatially present: *se sistere ~ntem coram alio* AC 7124; *mittuntur illuc angeli, ac ~ntes moderantur illas* [sc. *turbas*] CI 543; (masc. pl. as sb.) the audience: *odas quibus mulciebant ~ntium auditus* AM 8.2; (neut. pl. as sb.) *concludit...a ~ntibus quae videt* AC 7007.3. **2** (of time) Present: *nec modo pro tempore ~nti, sed etiam pro venturo* AC 6934; *in ~nti*, for the present: *haec plura arcana continent quam ut in ~nti dici queant* AC 37. **3** Present so as to exert an influence, actively operating: *usque ~nti erant animo* ES 805; *quod omnes facultates in altera vita...increscant et fiant ~ntiores* ES 4359; (esp. of the Lord) *quantum ~ntior est Dominus, tantum liberior est homo* AC 905; *quod Dominus in illo sensu sit maxime ~ns* SS 50; *quod Deus ~ns sit in spatio absque spatio et in tempore absque tempore* VR 30.2.

praesenter, *adv.* (compar. *~ius*, superl. *~issime*) With immediate presence, effectively present: *momento adsunt et ~issime* AC 1114; *influit...bonum illud ~ius ad malos* AC 7710; *mirati quod tam solerter, ~er et cito inveniant...tales artes* ES 4359.

praesentia ~ae, *f.* **1** Presence in space: *quia illa non legere vellem in ~a illorum* AC 6811; *in ~a testium* AM 295.3. **2** Active or effective presence: *ad ~am boni consistere nequeunt [infernales]* AC 6677; (of the Lord) *~a Domini in Verbo* SS 14.2; *~a Ipsius cum angelis* AM 431; *quod ~a Domini sit idem cum ultimo tempore quod judicium vocatur* AC 2441.2.

praesento ~are ~avi, *tr.* (refl.) To present oneself: *hae [uxores] non adjungunt se maritis, modo se ~ant*

AM 47[a]; (in a specified manner) *quidam putant se esse [deos] et sic se ~ant* ES 440.

praesepe ~is, *neut.* also **praesaepe**. A stall for cattle: *~e in stabulo* SS 26.4; VR 277.

praesertim, *adv.* Above all, first and foremost, especially: *in Ecclesia repraesentativa, ~im Judaica et Israelitica* AC 8995.5.

praeservatio ~onis, *f.* Preservation: *medelam et ~onem ab illis* [sc. *malis*] AC 8365.

praeservator ~oris, *m.* One who preserves, preserver: *pro ~ore a malis* AC 6502.3.

praeservo ~are ~avi ~atum, *tr.* To keep safe, preserve: *quod Dominus solus ~et a malis* AC 8344.

praeses ~idis, *m.* A presiding officer, president, chairman: *voluit ~es oratione finire synedrium* VR 137.12.

praesidium ~i, *neut.* A body of men to keep a gate or the like, guard: *~a ad portas collocata erant, ne cuiquam...liceret exire* AM 9.2.

praestabilitus ~a ~um, *a.* Pre-established: *influxus simultaneus...in corpus et simul in animam, quem harmoniam ~am nuncupant* VR 695.3; CC 1.3.

praestans ~ntis, *a.* (compar. *~ntior*, superl. *~ntissimus*) Of high quality, excellent, outstanding: *gens Israelitica...prae omni alia gente electa, et inde reliquis ~ntior* AC 7051.1; *jucundum conjugiale...~ntius est omnibus illis* CI 402; *Ecclesia...~ns et pretiosa* SS 79.8; *primae arbores erant omnium ~ntissimae* AM 13.2.

praestanter, *adv.* (compar. *~ius*) Excellently: *quod sentiant* [*spiritus*]...*~ius quam illi* [sc. *homines*] AC 1881.

praestantia ~ae, *f.* High quality, excellence: *secundum ~am dotum suorum judiciorum decernebant* AM 103.4.

praestatio ~onis, *f.* The act of performing or serving: *verus cultus consistit in ~one usuum* AC 7038.1.

praester: see **prester**.

praestigiae ~giarum, *f. pl.* **1** Trickery, deceit: *subtraxerunt se a ~giis mundi* AM 155.3; *si aliqua uxor meretrix callet ~gias* AM 488. **2** Black magic, sorcery: *de ~giis seu truldom in altera vita* ES 2740 titulus.

praestigiator ~oris, *m.* One who works magic, magician, sorcerer: *et vocavit etiam Pharao sapientes et ~ores* Exod. 7.11 (AC); *baculos ~orum, per quos magi...fecerunt miracula* VR 137.4.

praestigiatrix ~icis, *f.* A female magician, witch: *filii ~icis* Isa. 57.3 (AC 254); *~ices seu sirenes* AC 831.3; ES 2741; (as fem. adj.) *per ~ices artes* ES 2905.

praestitutus ~a ~um, *a.* Appointed ahead of time, foreordained, pre-established, predetermined: *si...divellerentur ante tempus ~um, pateretur coelum* UJ 70; SE 63.

praesto[1] ~are ~iti ~itum, *tr.*, *intr.* **1** (tr.) To bring about, provide, offer: *salutem ~itit Mihi brachium meum* Isa. 63.5 (DD 14.2); *absque ~andis bonis charitatis* AC 456. **2** (tr.) To perform, offer (service, duty, etc.): *obsequia ~are* AC 95; *illi ei omnia officia ~abant* AC 318; *opera charitatis ~ant* AC 1062; *per obedientiam quam Deo Patri...~itit* [*Dominus*] VR 35. **3** (tr.) To serve, effect (a purpose): *secundum usum quem ~at* AM 6.6. **4** (intr.) To be superior, excel: *sicut ~at intelligentia* AC 7773; *qui ~ant bono* CI 43; (w. dat.) *quid...cogitatio hominis ~at rationi avis...?* VR 57.1. **5** (impers., w. *ut*) It is preferable, it is better (that): *~at...ut homo studeat Verbo* SS 56; *~at...ut spiritus prorsus pravus sit quam ita dissidens* ES 1124 ½.

praesto[2], *adv.* *~o esse*, to be near or ready, be at hand: *hoc dixi quia ~o erat sacerdos* VR 79.4; (transf.) *malum quod ~o est et intrare vult* AC 364.

praestolor ~ari ~atus sum, *tr.* To await: *qui...~abantur principem* AM 14.1.

praestruo ~ere ~xi ~ctum, *tr.* To shut off, block: *janua...obice chalybeio ~cta* CO 28; *~it...vias* ES 507.

praesul ~lis, *m.* A person in charge, president, chief: *~les mensarum* AM 6.2; *~l congregationis* VR 136.4; *quae* [sc. *Ecclesia*], *qualescunque sint ~les, usque apud subditam gentem permanet* DP 257.4.

praesum praeesse praefui, *intr.* To be in control, govern: *principes...qui praeerant in Israele* AC 8314.3; (w. dat.) *Diabolus...qui infernis praeest* CI 544; *regnum cui praeest* [*rex*] AE 373.3; *tales...praesunt vesicae urinariae* ES 1154.

praesumo ~ere ~psi ~(p)tum, *tr.* To be presumptuous, presume, dare: (w. inf.) *ne ~ite dicere in vobis ipsis, Patrem habemus Abrahamum* Matt. 3.9 (AC 3703.4).

praesum(p)tus ~a ~um, *a.* (pf. pple. of **praesumo**) Taken on oneself, assumed: *non ex ~a dignitate, et praerogativa prae aliis* ES 2516.

praetego ~gere ~xi ~ctum, *tr.* To use as a means of concealment, make a show of: *innocentia quam ~xit ad tam abominabilia producenda* ES 4583.

praetendo ~dere ~di ~tum, *tr.*, *intr.* To lay claim to: *~dunt dominium super quemlibet hominem* ES 824; (w. inf.) *quod...~dant dominari* ES 824; (w. *quod*) to claim (that): *~derunt...quod ideo aliis praedominarentur* ES 3187.

praeter, *prep. w. acc.* see also **praeterquam**. **1** Alongside, beside: *cum praeterivi ~r te* Ezek. 16.8 (AC 6804.9).

2 In addition to, besides: *~r plura* AM 295.2; *voluntas... quae...a suis cupiditatibus refraenatur ~r a lege civili* ES 326. 3 Except: *apud omnes homines ~r apud Dominum* AC 1557.2; *~r Me non Deus* Isa. 44.6 (DD 45.2). 4 *~r quod,* apart from the fact that: (w. subj.) *continuus labor, ~r quod delectentur in literis* ES 2391; (w. indic.) *ideam coeli multo pleniorem habeat, quam qui nihil ~r quod vidit sidera et solem, habet* ES(M) 4619. 5 *~r quod,* in such a way as not to, without: (w. subj.) *disponitur ad usum...~r quod sciat* AC 1399; *quae audiverunt, ~r quod quicquam dicerent* ES 581; *inde illis, ~r quod sciant unde, mores decentes* CI 277.3.

praeterea, *adv.* In addition to this, besides: *et ~ea in naturali non sunt ipsa bona et vera* AC 6686; *~ea... audiuntur suavissimi cantus* AM 17.2.

praetereo ~rire ~rivi (*or* ~rii) ~ritum, *tr.* 1 To go past, pass by: *quem semimortuum sacerdos ~rivit* AC 6708 (Luke 10.31); *interrogabam cur ~rirent magnifica locorum* AC 6809; *ut nihil usquam ~rire queant [fibrae sensibiles], quin percipiant* ES 1758. 2 To go out of existence, pass away: *usque dum ~reat coelum et terra, jota unum ac unum corniculum non ~ribit de Lege* Matt. 5.18 (AC 6752.2). 3 To avoid mention of, pass over: *quae hic ~reuntur* CI 132; *obscura et discordantia...non videt et ~rit* SS 54; *quod hoc sit causa... ~ritur absque commentatione* AM 259. 4 (w. inf.) To omit (to): *quare ~reo ea memorare* ES 3526.

praetergredior ~di ~ssus sum, *tr.* To walk past: *vulnerato...quem sacerdos et Levita videntes ~ssi sunt* VR 410.3.

praeteritus ~a ~um, *a.* (pf. pple. of **praetereo**) Situated in past time, past: *per nexum rerum ~arum et simul futurarum* DP 252.1; *idem status vitae sequens cum ~o* AM 186; (of time) *pro antea seu pro tempore ~o* AC 6983.2; (neut. as sb.) a past tense: *quod 'genuit tres filios' in ~o dicatur* AC 618.

praeterlabor ~bi ~psus sum, *intr.* 1 To slip past: *caetera...modo superficiem tangunt et ~buntur* AC 6812; *percipiebant omnes ideas cogitationis meae...sic ut nihil ~beretur* ES(M) [4749]. 2 (of time) To go past, slip away: *post tot inde saecula ~psa* AC 1850.1; *tempus... ~psum est sicut somnus* VR 160.7; *hac nocte et ~psa* ES 449.

praetermitto ~mittere ~misi ~missum, *tr.* To leave out (of a written text), omit to mention, pass over: *quia Dani non cecidit sors inter haereditates reliquarum tribuum... ~missa est illa tribus...in Apoc. 7.5-8* AC 3923.9.

praeternavigo ~are ~avi, *intr.* To sail past: *navarchae ~antes demittunt velum mali* VR 803.

praeterquam, *adv.* also spelled as two words **praeter quam**. Apart from, except: *~am quod malum id resciret* AC 10808; *ne hilum ejus ex homine est, praeter quam* [spelled as one word in 2nd and 3rd edns.] *facultas recipiendi illa* AM 353; (w. *ut*) *omnes affectiones ...possunt cognosci, ~am ut explorentur* [i.e., without being investigated] ES 2046.

praetervolo ~are ~avi, *intr.* To fly past: *columba viso accipitre ~avit* VR 72.3; SE 96.

praetexo ~ere ~ui ~tum, *tr.* To make a show of, allege, pretend: *dominando...per...sancta quae ~unt* AC 5120.13; ES 2618; (w. *quod*) *~endo quod honestum* ES 3700; *~entes quod propter me* ES 4370.

praetexta ~ae, *f.* A garment with a purple border: *senes et juvenes in ~is et palliis* AM 231.3.

praetextus ~us, *m.* A pretended reason, pretext: *affinem deprivavit haereditate sua sub ~u doloso* CI 462ª.6; ES 4098.

praetor ~oris *m.* A person invested with authority, presiding official, leader, commander: *~ore phalangum ab exercitu illustrium Ecclesiae* VR 137.8; VR 730.2.

praetorium ~i, *neut.* A headquarters, administrative centre: *vidi domunculas...et...unam quae erat sicut ~um reliquarum* AM 380.2.

praevalens ~ntis, *a.* Having superior strength, stronger: *multus ei timor est pro judice, quia ~ns* ES 6040.

praevalentia ~ae, *f.* Superiority in strength, mastery: *significatur in pugnis illis ~a* AC 6656.

praevaleo ~lere ~lui, *intr.* 1 To be superior in strength, prevail, win: *et draco pugnavit et angeli ejus; et non ~luerunt* Rev. 12.7-8 (AR); (w. dat.) *potentia inferni ~luit potentiae caeli* DD 65.1. 2 (transf.) To be superior in other ways, prevail: *hujus sententia ~luit* AM 153ª.2; *talis idea...inter Christianos incepit ~lere* VR 94.2; (w. dat.) *tunc minimus scrupulus ~let mille veritatibus* AC 215; (w. *super*) *hoc immensum ~let super id quod exterius agit* AC 6724.2; (w. *contra*) *novum voluntarium... ~let contra proprium voluntarium* AC 8209.2.

praevaricatio ~onis, *f.* The commission of a fault, sinning: *gravis erit super eo ~o ejus* Isa. 24.20 (AC 390); *visitaturus ~ones Israelis super illum* Amos 3.14 (DD 4).

praevaricator ~oris, *m.* A sinner, transgressor: *cum ~oribus numeratus est* Isa. 53.12 (DD 15.1).

praevaricor ~ari ~atus sum, *intr.* To commit a fault, sin: *num ~ati sint contra proximum* CI 325; *qui ~atur contra unum praeceptum decalogi* AM 528.

praeveniens ~ntis, *a.* (of grace) Prevenient: *si gratia illa, quae vocatur ~ns, foret universalis* VR 631.2.

praevenio ~nire ~ni ~ntum, *tr., intr.* **1** (tr.) To come to meet, approach: *num ~niam Jehovam holocaustis* Mic. 6.6 (AC 922.3); *cum pane ejus ~nite vagantem* Isa. 21.14 (AC 1664.4); (of things) *~nerunt Me laquei mortis* Ps. 18.5 (DD 14.6). **2** (intr.) To prevent: (w. *ne*) *modus...quo ~nire possit ne amor conjugialis... pereat* AM 459.1.

praeventio ~onis, *f.* Prevention: *torrens ~onum* 3AD 4796.

praevidentia ~ae, *f.* The power or act of foreseeing, foresight: *Divina intelligentia, seu ~a* AC 8215.4; *~a est malorum, providentia est dispositio eorum ad fines bonos* ES 1088.

praevideo ~dere ~di ~sum, *tr.* To foresee: *damnationem ~sam aut destinatam* DD 18.2; *nativitatem Ipsius ab aeterno ~sam* VR 26.1; (w. *quod*) *~deo quod multi...credituri sint* AM 1; AE 250.10.

praevisio ~onis, *f.* The power to foresee: *non habent ~onem futuri* ES 2188.

praevius ~a ~um, *a.* Going beforehand, preceding: *haec absque ~a cognitione plurium...nequicquam explicare possunt* AC 1870.2; *ex ~a cogitatione et voluntate* ES 4457.

prandium ~i, *neut.* A midday meal, lunch: *convivia, tam ~a quam coenae* AC 7996; *in media die, circa ~um* ES 397.

prasinus ~a ~um, *a.* (Gk.) Bright green: *intimum [circulum] ~i seu nitentis viridis coloris* AM 294.1.

pratum ~i, *neut.* A meadow: *~a, novalia, hortos* AC 7071; *pascent greges tui...in ~o lato* Isa. 30.23 (AE 482.3).

pravitas ~atis, *f.* Moral obliquity, wickedness: *non ita ex malo vitae, quam ex ~ate naturali* AC 5185.

pravus ~a ~um, *a.* Morally wrong, wicked: *ex cupiditate et ~a voluntate* DD 17.3; *~ae inclinationes* AM 79.3; *praestat...ut spiritus prorsus ~us sit quam ita dissidens* ES 1124 1/2.

praxis ~eos, *f.* (Gk.) Activity: *quando indulget quis nimium mechanicae ~i* ES 768.

precario, *adv.* By permission, on sufferance: *comedunt cum illis ~o, sed hoc non diu perstat* ES 6088.3.

precatio ~onis, *f.* The act of praying, prayer: *~o mea super sinum meum relabitur* Ps. 35.13 (AC 6960.2); AE 182.4.

preces ~um, *f. pl.* Prayers: *Dominus pro ~ibus contra finem...non agit* AC 8179.3; *quotidie fundit ~es* VI 25.

precludo: see **praecludo**.

precor ~ari ~atus sum, *tr., intr.* **1** (intr.) To say a prayer, pray: *audire... praedicationem, et ~ari* AC 7038.1; AE 325.3. **2** (tr.) To address in prayer, pray to: *~are quaeso facies Jehovae* 1 Kgs. 13.6 (AC 878.8). **3** (tr.) To utter, say (a prayer): *quoties Orationem Domini nostri ~arer* ES 258 titulus. **4** (intr.) To beg, implore: *rogo et ~or, ut aeternum hoc arcanum vos ipsi aperiatis* AM 315.9.

predico: see **praedico**[1].

prehendo ~dere ~di ~sum, *tr.* To take hold of, grasp: *~de caudam ejus* [sc. *serpentis*] Exod. 4.4. (AC); *arcum et hastam ~dunt* Jer. 6.23 (AC 8313.3); *~dit me manu* AM 380.2.

premo ~mere ~ssi ~ssum, *tr.* **1** To exert physical pressure on, press down: *mensura bona, ~ssa, agitata et superfluens* Luke 6.38 (CI 349); *quod... ~mam pennam* [sc. in writing] ES 2248. **2** *Silentio ~mere*, to keep silent about: *naevi, qui propter infamiam...silentio ~muntur* AM 288. **3** To treat strictly, press: *qui literam ~mit, is non aliud capit* AC 277; AC 8581.4. **4** To exert mental pressure on, oppress: *ubi ille, quem ~mebant* AC 7745; *a falsis ignorantiae ~ssi* AE 357.26.

presbyter ~eri, *m.* (Gk.) An elder of the Church, minister: *datum est interrogare aliquos ~eros Angliae* VI 7; AM 500.3.

presbyterium ~i, *neut.* (Gk.) A council of presbyters or elders: *nos...ad sacerdotium et ~um nostrum consensu unanimiter accedimus* VR 159.5.

presse, *adv.* Closely, tightly: *incumbunt capiti ~e* ES 1089; (transf.) *sequuntur ~e ejus cogitationem* ES 2201; ES 3966.

pressio ~onis, *f.* Pressure: *tunc percipit calorem, frigus, ~onem* ES 733; AC 6057.1.

pressus ~a ~um: pf. pple. of **premo**.

prester ~eris, *m.* (Gk.) also **praester**. A kind of snake, serpent: *~eres seu serpentes ignitos* AC 251.1; *~er volans* Isa. 14.29 (FI 53); cf. *quod...momentanea salvatio...sit hodie ~er volans in Ecclesia* SE 65; *desertum Arabiae, ubi serpentes, hydrae et ~eres* VR 38.2.

pretiositas ~atis, *f.* A precious object or material, gem: *aula ex auro et ~atibus splendens* AM 3.5; VR 44.2; (fig.) *tres illae ~ates fidei* VR 379.4.

pretiosus ~a ~um, *a.* (compar. *~ior*, superl. *~issimus*) Of high value, precious: *Ephraim vocatur 'filius ~us'* SS 79.2 (Jer. 31.20); *lapides ~i*, precious stones, gems: AC 6640.2; AM 182.3; cf. *lumen ejus simile lapidi ~ssimo* Rev. 21.11 (AR).

pretium ~i, *neut.* **1** A sum of money paid in exchange for something, value, price: *quod dabit homo ~um sufficiens redemtionis animae suae?* Matt. 16.26

(AC 7021.2); *~um auri* VI 10. **2** (in general) Value, worth: *doctrina charitatis, quae tanti ~i fuerat apud antiquos* AC 6632; *operis ~um censui fore* 'I judged it worth the effort' AM 317.

prex: see **preces**.

pridem, *adv*. Long since, long ago: *quidam qui non ita ~em e vita corporis excessit* ES 288.

primae ~marum, *f. pl*. *~mas agere*, to play the leading part: *sapientia quae tunc ~mas agit* AC 1555.3; *apud hos corpus ~mas agit* AM 191.2; also, *~mas tenere*: AC 1103.1.

primaevus ~a ~um, *a*. Of an early age: *qualis fuit* [*amor ille*] *in ~o suo statu* AM 57; *~a revelatio* VR 11.1.

primario, *adv*. Principally, primarily: *inde ~o per 'vesperam' significatur Adventus Domini* AC 7844.3; *quod finis... ~o spectetur a Domino* AM 146.

primarius ~a ~um, *a*. Principal, chief, primary: *haec ~a causa est* AC 494.2; *finem...qui est omnium ~us et ultimus* AC 7081; (masc. as sb.) *praeibant illum...consiliarii a cameris, et post hos ~i ex aula* AM 14.1; (neut. as sb.) *~um est, ut exploret suae vitae facta* BCP (VI 6).

primas ~atis, *m*. A person holding a chief office, chieftain, prince: *una gens erat circum suum ~atem collecta* ES 402; (esp. in the Church) a bishop or other high dignitary, primate: *pontifice maximo praeeunte...sequentibus illum ~atibus* AM 3.6; *~ates Ecclesiae* SS 61.2.

primatus ~us, *m*. High office, esp. in the Church: *nostrates qui ~um in Ecclesia gerunt* VR 96.1.

primitiae ~tiarum, *f. pl*. **1** The earliest crop, first fruits: *~tias frumenti tui, et ~tias vini tui non tardabis* Exod. 22.28 (AC); *festum ~tiarum* SS 20.2. **2** The initial phase, beginning: *illae leges...fuerunt ~tiae Verbi* VI 54; *in ~tiis conjugii* AM 199.2.

primitius ~a ~um, *a*. Newly made or arisen: *sponsus et ~us maritus* AM 224.

primitivus ~a ~um, *a*. **1** Existing at an early stage, early: *Ecclesia ~a* AC 393; *in ~um statum in quem Adamus et ejus uxor creati sunt reduci* AM 3.4; *inveni Israelem, sicut ~um in ficu* Hos. 9.10 (AC 1071.2). **2** Fundamental, original, undeveloped: *loquela eorum* [sc. *spirituum*] *est...per ideas ~as vocum* AC 1641.1; *omnia vera et bona derivativa...trahunt suam essentiam a ~is* AC 8042.2; (neut. as sb.) an origin, starting point: *~um hominis...connititur ad formationem totius hominis* AC 3633; *est...substantiale ~um materialis* VR 79.7.

primitus, *adv*. In the first stage, originally: *de decem tribubus, quae dispersae erant... ~us in septentrionales plagas Europae* 2AD 1605.

primo, *adv*. Firstly, first: *subeunt ~o eam poenam* ES 1763.

primogenitura ~ae, *f*. The rights of the firstborn son, primogeniture: *adempta est ei ~a* AE 237.10 (1 Chron. 5.1); *lis de ~a* AC 367.1.

primogenitus ~a ~um, *a*. Earliest born, firstborn: *ecce Ego occido filium tuum, ~um tuum* Exod. 4.23 (AC); *usque dum peperit filium suum ~um* Matt. 1.25 (DD 21); (neut. as sb.) *antequam ~a exstincta sunt* AC 7273.2.

primordium ~i, *neut*. An initial stage, first beginning: *quomodo...a ~o suo progressio creationis facta est* VR 76.3; VR 798.1; (pl.) *quod haec duo sint illius amoris ~a* AM 337.

primoris ~is, *m*. A leading person, headman, chief: *~ores populi* Num. 21.18 (AC 7343.3); *~ores illi quos vidistis ad capita mensarum* AM 6.3; *nuntius ex ~ore urbis* AM 79.6.

primum, *adv*. **1** First: *~um dicendum est quid proximus* AC 6703; CI 279. **2** *Ut ~um*, as soon as: *ut ~um cor moritur, omnia...moriuntur* AC 637.1; VR 42.2.

primus ~a ~um, *a*. **1** First in time, earliest: *in sua ~a origine* AC 6685; *in aetate... ~ae juventutis* AC 6766.2; *~o tempore Ecclesiae* AE 9.4; *ad ~am praesentiam* ES 3573; (neut. as sb.) the earliest stage: *'et concepit mulier' significat ~um ortus* AC 6715. **2** First in order or sequence: *vocales tres ~ae* AC 793; *duo ~i gradus vastationis* AC 7378; (neut. as sb.) the first point: *~um erit scire quis Deus coeli est* CI 2. **3** Typical of the first stage, earliest, first: *esse in ~is veris* AC 6751; *instructionem ~am* AC 6873; (neut. as sb.) [*Deus*] *est...in purissimis et ~is* VR 124.1. **4** *Minutum ~um*, a sixtieth part of an hour, minute: ES 906. **5** First in rank or importance: *hi sunt inter illos qui ~i esse volunt* AC 2027.3 (Matt. 19.30); *vera falsificata fidei quae ~o loco* AC 7779.1.

princeps ~ipis, *m*. (or *f*.) A chieftain, male (or female) leader: *~ipes tributorum* Exod. 1.11 (AC); *Dominus vocatur ~eps pacis* CI 287.1 (Isa. 9.6); *~ipes Sodomae* Isa. 1.10 (VI 30.1); (fem.) *erunt... ~ipes foeminae lactatrices tuae* Isa. 49.23 (AE 175.4).

principalis ~is ~e, *a*. Most important, principal, chief: [*status*] *~is omnium statuum* AC 7824; *in ~i idea* AM 322; (neut. as sb.) *quod amor...et charitas...sint ~ia et essentialia Ecclesiae* AC 7233.3; *num haec possunt unum esse quam sicut ~e et instrumentale?* VR 35.6; *~e agere*, to play the leading part: AC 63.

principaliter, *adv*. Especially, chiefly: *usus...per quos Dominus ~er colitur* AC 7038.3; AM 306.

principatus ~us, *m*. **1** The office of prince,

chieftaincy, government: *super cujus humero ~us* Isa. 9.6 (DD 6); AR 341.2. **2** The region governed by a prince, principality: *coeli...distincti sunt in ~us* AC 5044.3. **3** The holder of a princely office, prince: *~us isti dicunt se adorare Jehovam* 4AD Isa. 14.10; *angeli 'potentiae' nominati sunt, et quoque ~us* AC 3858.15.

principiata ~orum, *neut. pl.* Derivatives of first principles: *~a faciunt principia...et sic resupinant omnia* VR 37.3.

principio ~are ~avi ~atum, *tr.* To form the first principle of: *lex...coelestis quae legem hanc ~at* 3AD 5978.

principium ~i, *neut.* **1** A point of origin, beginning: *sunt hi status ~a regenerationis* AC 1050.2; *integra periodus a ~o ad finem* AC 6721; *sequutus sum tramitem soni, et...cum ad ~um ejus veni* VR 72.1. **b** *in ~o*, at the beginning: *in ~o creavit Deus coelum et terram* Gen. 1.1 (AC); at first (as opposed to later): *in ~o miratus sum* CI 126; so, *~o* alone: AC 7809. **2** An elementary substance: *in ~is...organicis quae in cerebro sunt* AC 6872.3; *in ~is corticalibus* ES 914. **3** A basic idea, principle: *~a falsa* AC 6723.1; *ex ~o quod homo salvetur ex sola fide* DD 18.2.

prior ~or ~us, *compar. a.* **1** Earlier in time, antecedent: *status ~or tunc inservit pro plano statui sequenti* AC 6645.2; *habeo contra te, quod charitatem ~orem reliqueris* Rev. 2.4 (VI 2). **2** Earlier in sequence, former: *in ~ori loco apud Johannem* AC 6674.3; *duo [singularia] ~ora sunt fidei, duo posteriora sunt charitatis* VR 3.2. **3** Logically prior: *quod nihil existere possit a se, sed a ~ori se* CI 9.1; SS 28.

prioritas ~atis, *f.* Priority: *intelligitur non modo ~as temporis, sed etiam ~as gradus* AC 3325.2.

priscus ~a ~um, *a.* Of former times, ancient: *~i gentiles...agnoverunt Jovem* VR 9.3; (masc. as sb.) *saeculum in quo vixerant a ~is vocatum est a cupro* AM 77.2.

prisma ~atis, *neut.* (Gk.) A prism: *~a chrystallinum* VR 808.

pristinus ~a ~um, *a.* Of former times, previous: *ut primum...redit ad ~um statum* AC 857.2.

prius, *compar. adv.* **1** At an earlier time, previously: *quod ~us nusquam lachrymaverit* CI 238; (w. *quam*) before (see also **priusquam**): *nec ~us aliquis in inferno dejicitur, quam cum in falsis...est* CI 539. **2** Nearer the front, ahead: *columna nubis...quae ~us incessit ante filios Israelis* AC 8192.1. **3** More particularly, more vehemently: *nihil... ~us et potius amant quam verum fidei* AC 1033.2; ES 2743.

priusquam, *conj.* (w. indic.) Before: *amor sexus non potest fieri spiritualis, ~am fit conjugialis* AM 447.2; (ellipt.) *haec vocantur fidei tametsi non sunt fidei ~am charitati conjuncta* AC 1832.1.

privatim, *adv.* In private: *dicitur in domo, quia ~im inter illos* AM 275.

privatio ~onis, *f.* The act of taking away, deprivation: *~o cultus interni* AC 1328; *~one honoris et famae* CI 577.4.

privativum ~i, *neut.* A negation, opposite: *quod ~um ejus* [sc. *amoris*]*...occludat...externa corporis* AM 260.

privatus ~a ~um, *a.* (pf. pple. of **privo**) **1** (of citizens) Acting in a personal capacity, private: *ut praestent usus publico et ~is* VR 405.1. **2** Relating to private citizens, private: *quod pacis publicae et ~ae sit, ut promiscua libido...restringatur* AM 349; *debita charitatis ~a* VR 432.

privilegium ~i, *neut.* A special right granted to a person, privilege: *per donationes ~orum* AR 799.2.

privo ~are ~avi ~atum, *tr.* (w. abl.) To deprive (of): *si ~antur gaudio* AC 8037; *~are...proximum suis bonis* AC 8318.3.

pro, *prep. w. abl.* **1** In place of, for: *simulachra pro diis colunt* VR 9.1; *pro gaudio coelesti modo angustiam habebant* ES 2258. **2** As equivalent to, as: *'filia Aegypti' pro affectione ratiocinandi de veris fidei* AC 6729; *in Symbolo Athanasii, quod...pro Doctrina de Deo receptum est* VR 98.2; *pro feris et tyrannis...haberi* ES 1066; (w. clause) *'Ambulabo in medio...' pro ut viverent secundum doctrinam legis* AC 519.3. **b** *pro exemplo*, as an example: AM 47; *pro certo*, as a certain fact, for sure: *quod dabilis sit, pro certo asseverare possum* AM 444.8. **3** For the making of, for: *vasa in quibus massa pro pane praeparatur* AC 7356.1. **4** For the use of, to benefit: *reliquiae apud hominem sunt pro angelis apud eum* AC 737.1; *de spiritualibus...quae erunt pro vita aeterna* VR 94.2; *pro plano inservit id quod in memoria est* AM 446. **5** For protection from, against: *faciunt sibi tecta pro imbre et pro aestu solis* AC 10161; *ut omnes...pro una musca fugerent* ES 2921ª. **6** In favour of, in support of: *confirmationes pro Divino* CI 356.1; VR 83; *militant pro illa [fide] sicut pro ipso coelo* AC 8148.3. **7** Caused by, of: *timor pro paenis infernalibus* DP 139.4; *in afflictione pro hostibus* ES 2363.

proavus ~i, *m.* A great-grandfather: *a parente unoquovis, ab ejus avo, ~o, atavo et antecedentibus ordine* AC 313.

probabilis ~is ~e, *a.* Capable of proof, demonstrable: *scribe libros, et imple illos argumentis plausibilibus, ~ibus et verosimilibus* DP 213.

probatio ~onis, *f.* A testing, trial: *~o quoque talis est, quod ducant spiritum in loquelam* ES 482; *lapidem ~onis* Isa. 28.16 (AE 417.12).

probatorium ~i, *neut.* A means of testing, criterion: *est ~um num ex coelo, num ex inferno sunt* CJ 72.

probe, *adv.* Thoroughly, well: *contudi illum molendo ~e* Deut. 9.21 (AC 7418.4); *qui [spiritus] tam ~e animadvertunt et percipiunt quid homo cogitat* AC 784.2; *~e sciendum est quod charitas et fides...arcte conjunctae sint* VR 442.1; (esp. with vbs. of distinguishing) *homines post obitum...a Domino ~e distinguuntur* CI 427; *internoscuntur tam ~e, sicut columbae a bubonibus* VR 564.2.

probitas ~atis, *f.* Uprightness, honesty: *~as per lenitudinem...in altera vita se manifestat* AC 8111; AM 164.

problema ~atis, *neut.* (Gk.) A subject for debate, topic: *pro juvenibus qui ad ~a...propondendum responderunt* AM 315.2; *conclusio fiet ex his duobus ~atibus* VR 382.

probo ~are ~avi ~atum, *tr.* **1** To put to the trial, test: *intelligentes... ~abuntur ad purgandum et mundandum* Dan. 11.35 (DD 4); *sermo Jehovae ~avit eum* Ps. 105.19 (AE 448.16). **2** To approve of, recommend: *quod Augustana Confessio illum cultum maxime ~et* VR 137.7.

probrum ~i, *neut.* A reproach, insult: *illos ~is affecturi* AE 122.2; (pred. dat.) *nuditas est ~o et scandalo* AC 213.

probus ~a ~um, *a.* (compar. *~ior*) (of persons) Morally good, upright, honest: *quod ~i felices in mundo essent prae improbis* AC 7007.1; *constabat quod ~iores sint spiritibus...aliarum tellurum* AC 8111; *apud gentes ~as* AE 52.2.

procedens ~ntis, *neut.* That which is emitted or emanates, a proceeding: *quod Divina Trinitas sit, et quod haec sit in Domino...sicut anima, corpus et ~ns in homine* VR 4.3.

procedo ~dere ~ssi, *intr.* **1** (w. *ab* or *ex*) To be emitted (by), radiate, emanate (from): *ex luce quae ~dit ex sole mundi naturalis* VR 40; *ex causticitate ejus* [sc. *ignis*] *~dit calor* VR 39; *in veris...quae a Domino ~dunt* AC 6685; *sunt duo quae ~dunt a Domino, Divinus Amor et Divina Sapientia* SS 3.2. **2** To develop, advance, proceed: *quod omnia et singula momenta regenerationis ~dant a vespera ad mane* AC 24.3; *~dit dominium ejus [hominis] ab externo homine ad internum* AC 52; *si spina inoculatur viti, influxus ille invertitur et ~dit secundum spinae formam* VR 8.3; *ut in medio...sint pessimi...qui inde ~dunt versus ambitum* ES 197. **3** (w. *cum*) To take action, proceed in dealing with: (impers. pass.) *quomodo ~dendum cum illis* AC 7267.

procella ~ae, *f.* A storm, squall: *nisi ~ae forent in athmosphaera* AC 842.3; *Jehovae via cum nube et ~a* Nahum 1.3 (AE 36.4); (fig.) *cavebit sibi a ~a e naturali homine exsurgente* VR 32.9.

procellosus ~a ~um, *a.* Stormy: *per ventum ~um* AE 419.22.

proceres ~um, *m. pl.* Leading people, leaders: *quod congregationem ibi viderint, sed sub variis figuris, nunc ut homines ~es, et nunc...ut statuas* AR 839.4; but perhaps *proceros* should be read here and in VR 113.4.

proceritas ~atis, *f.* The quality of being tall, height: *exscindam ~atem cedrorum ejus* Isa. 37.24 (AE 405.29); *gigantes ~atis duplae supra humanam* AM 77.1.

procerus ~a ~um, *a.* (compar. *~ior*) Tall: *postea sicut infantes...et demum ~iores* AM 137.2; *arbores ~ae* ES 1681.

processio ~onis, *f.* A procession: *cum ~onibus pompae* AM 3.6.

processualis ~is ~e, *a.* Having to do with a sequence of actions, procedural; (neut. as sb.) procedure, process: *quod in ritualibus et ~ibus sacrificiorum continentur arcana coeli* NH 221.

processus ~us, *m.* **1** An action proceeding by stages or over a period of time, process: *totum ~um regenerationis* AC 937; *quod homo statim...damnetur... et quod hoc fiat absque omni ~u* AC 7795.2; (in legal proceedings) *non opus habuissent ulla inquisitione, ~u inquisitorio* ES 2845. **2** A procession: *ducentes foeminas in ~u* ES 5453; ES(M) [4773].

procidentia ~ae, *f.* The act of falling on one's face: *quia humiliatio quae ex corde venit pro Divino, illam ~am producit* AE 77.1.

procido ~dere ~di, *intr.* To fall forwards, fall on one's face: *~debant et adorabant Ipsum* Matt. 2.11 (AC 1171.5); AR 926.4.

procinctus ~us, *m.* *In ~u*, in a state of readiness: *in ~u se separandi fuit* AC 4073.1.

proclama ~?, *neut.* (= **proclamatio**) A proclamation: *~a appositum ante dogmata Ecclesiae* SE 59.

proclamatio ~onis, *f.* A proclamation: *in diluculo audiverunt ~onem 'Hodie Sabbathum'* AM 23.

proclamo ~are ~avi ~atum, *tr.* To announce in a loud voice, proclaim: *ad ~andum annum beneplaciti Jehovae* Isa. 61.2 (AC 6854.5); *en super montibus pedes evangelizantis, ~antis pacem* Nahum 1.15 (AC 7093.5); *ad cultum Dei, qui...a sacerdotibus ~atur* AM 23.

proclivis ~is ~e, *a.* (compar. *~ior*) **1** (neut. as sb.) An incline, slope: *tunc quasi in ~i sunt, seu quasi in lapsu ad infernum* AC 8165.2. **2** Mentally inclined, prone: *inde voluntas ~ior ad mala et falsa* AC 2910.4; *~es sunt ad recipiendum verum* AC 10302.

proclivitas ~atis, *f.* Proneness, proclivity: *~ate ad mala inhaerente* VR 512.

procrastinor ~ari ~atus sum, *intr.* To put off acting till tomorrow, delay: *quia veniendo veniet, nec ~abitur* Hab. 2.3 (DD 4).

procreatio ~onis, *f.* The procreation (of offspring): *finis conjugii est ~o sobolis* AM 254; the propagation (of other things): *~onem veri et boni* AE 374.4; CI 315.

procreo ~are ~avi ~atum, *tr.* **1** To beget, engender, procreate: *~are sobolem* AC 1123; ES 546. **2** (transf.) To give rise to, generate: *verum conjunctum bono quod ~at* CI 382[a].

procul, *adv.* At a distance, far off: *in monte...non ~l a vertice ejus* AM 75.3; *~l dubio*, with little room for doubt, certainly: ES 339; ES 2109.

proculcatio ~onis, *f.* A trampling or crushing under foot: *per dejectionem e fenestra, aspersionem sanguinis ad parietem, et ~onem ab equis* AR 132.2.

proculco ~are ~avi ~atum, *tr.* To tread underfoot, trample on: *quem pedibus ~at* CI 558[a]; (fig.) *illa quae justitiae...supplantant et ~ant* AM 231.4.

procumbentia ~ae, *f.* A falling forward, kneeling: *flexionem genuum, ~am super genubus* AC 5323.1.

procumbo ~mbere ~bui, *intr.* To fall forward: *talis timor eos occupavit, ut ~mberent in genua* ES 229; *~buerunt in facies suas* ES 339.

procuratio ~onis, *f.* The office of steward, stewardship, administrative office: *omnis... ~o pertinet ad externum Ecclesiae, sicut administratio ritualium* AC 1795.1.

procurator ~oris, *m.* One who takes charge, steward: *filius ~or domus meae, is Damascenus Eliezer* Gen. 15.2 (AC).

procuro ~are ~avi ~atum, *tr.* To bring about, cause: *ad ~andum amaenitatem visus* VR 62.

procurro ~rere ~ri ~sum, *intr.* To run forward: *feles, qui...dimicant, ~runt, et ejulant* AM 512.1; *spiritus qui cis et retro quasi ~runt* ES 986; *ad supplicationis speciem ~runt* ES 3678.

procus ~i, *m.* A suitor: *faeminis est arbitrium electionis unius ex ~is* AM 296.1; VR 7.

prodeo ~dire ~dii, *intr.* **1** To go forward or into view, advance, come forth: *et ~diisti cum fluminibus tuis* Ezek. 32.2 (AC 7293.2); *sphaerae ab angelis ~deuntes* CI 17; *ex ore... ~dibat romphaea acuta* Rev. 19.15 (AR). **2** (transf.) To be revealed, come into action: *non ~deunt* [*bona et vera*] *nisi cum externus quasi moritur* AC 268; *quae ratiocinia ~deunt ex illis qui corde negant vera et bona fidei* AC 7293.5.

prodesse: inf. of **prosum**.

prodigalitas ~atis, *f.* Lavish expenditure, prodigality: AM 252.

prodigiosus ~a ~um, *a.* Portentous, miraculous: *quod a multa et ~a experientia mihi datum nosse* AC 968.

prodigium ~i, *neut.* An event regarded as a sign from heaven, portent: *dabo ~a in coelis et in terra, sanguinem, et ignem, et columnas fumi* Joel 2.30 (AC 1861.3); *per quod...iret nudus et discalceatus tres annos, in signum et ~um* DD 15.3 (Isa. 20.3); *si veritas est, sane est ~um* AM 4.1.

prodigo ~digere ~degi, *tr.* To spend lavishly without forethought, squander: *qui...nihili pendunt opes...et quoque qui ~digunt illas* AM 333.1; AE 279.6.

prodigus ~a ~um, *a.* Prodigal: *de filio ~o* AE 279.6 (Luke 15).

prodire: inf. of **prodeo**.

proditor ~oris, *m.* A betrayer, traitor: *de Jehuda ~ore* 2AD 1479.

prodo ~ere ~idi ~itum, *tr.* To betray: *quod a Juda ~itus fuerit* DD 16.5; (transf.) to give evidence of: *fines...non possunt prodire et ~ere se antequam...* AM 401; *ut terrorem manifeste ~erent* ES 225.

produco ~cere ~xi ~ctum, *tr.* **1** To draw out, elongate, extend: *domus humiles...in longum ~ctae* AC 10769. **2** To cause to appear, make visible or audible: *Spiritus Dei... ~xit in diem cognitiones veri et boni* AC 24.1; *non potuerunt se coercere quin voces spurcas... ~cerent* ES 2206. **3** To bring forth, produce (offspring, shoots, fruit, etc.): *et filii Israelis fructificabantur et ~cebantur* Exod. 1.7 (AC); *fit succus frondis aptus ~cendi ejus folia et fructus* AC 7343.2. **4** (transf.) To cause to exist, bring about: *falsum... ~citur a malo* AC 8311.2; *Divina Ipsius Sapientia non potest ~cere aliud quam usus medios ad illum finem* VR 13.2.

producta ~orum, *neut. pl.* Products: *quod ~a ex materialibus ament* AC 6816.

productio ~onis, *f.* **1** The act of bringing forth, production: *in ~onibus tam vegetabilium quam animalium* VR 12.2; (transf.) *~ones veri* AC 263. **2** The act of drawing out or enlarging: *non...exsumptio partis, sed... ~o totius* AM 220.2; (in mathematics) multiplication: *ducendo ~onem unius continue in 20 aut 30* VR 32.3.

proelium: see **praelium**.

profan-: see **prophan-**.

profectio ~onis, *f.* The act of setting out, start of a journey: *de ~one filiorum Jacobi ad Aegyptum* AC 6638.

profecto, *adv.* Undoubtedly, surely: *~o Tu Deus occultus* Isa. 45.15 (DD 34.2).

profectus ~us, *m.* Advancement, development, progress: *instrui in veris fidei sed absque ~u* AC 9272.5.

profero ~ferre ~tuli ~latum, *tr.* **1** To bring forth, bring out, produce: *bonus homo ex bono thesauro cordis sui ~fert bonum* Luke 6.45 (VI 51); *qui ~fert ex memoria mandata alterius* AE 8.1; *humus quae... potest... ~ferre et fructificare illa* [sc. *semina*] VR 48.10. **2** To make known, disclose, reveal: *angelus... ~tulit arcana...ad centena* CI 269.3; *causas...non licet... ~ferre* AM 258. **3** To reveal in words, pronounce: *dum spiritus aliquem locum secundum sensum literae ~ferunt* AE 816.3; *spirituales non aliquid naturaliter ferre possunt* CI 246.2.

professio ~onis, *f.* The act of professing: *~o veri* AC 7790.

professor ~oris, *m.* A university teacher, professor: *~ores Theologiae* AR 677.

professus ~a ~um, *a.* (pf. pple. of **profiteor**) *Ex ~o*, overtly, explicitly: *de quo influxu alibi ex ~o dicetur* AM 187; ES 3320.

proficio ~ficere ~feci, *intr.* To make progress, advance, develop: *Jesus ~fecit sapientia, aetate et gratia* Luke 2.52 (DD 32.1).

proficiscor ~ficisci ~fectus sum, *intr.* To start on a journey, begin to move, set out: *et ~fecti filii Israelis de Raamses ad Succoth* Exod. 12.37 (AC); AM 351.2.

proficuus ~a ~um, *a.* Advantageous, efficacious: *quod inde nihil ~um* AC 4751.1.

profiteor ~fiteri ~fessus sum, *tr.* **1** To claim to believe in, make profession of: *qui ~fitentur fidem absque charitate* AC 381; *omnes qui Divinum Humanum Domini ~fitentur* AE 129. **2** To practise as one's business, occupy oneself in: *quae ~fessae magicas artes* ES(M) [4753].

profligatio ~onis, *f.* The act of putting to flight, rout: *per internecionem et ~onem ferarum illarum* VR 17.

profligo ~are ~avi ~atum, *tr.* To put to flight, rout: *hirci ~ati sunt* AE 817.13; (transf.) *ipsam veritatem ~are ab Ecclesia* VR 323.

profluentia ~ae, *f.* Fluency: *angeli ex modulationis symmetria et ~a percipiunt rem affectionis* AM 55.1.

profluo ~ere ~xi, *intr.* To be derived, proceed, flow: *nusquam aliquod gaudium nisi quod ~it ex amore* AC 33; *loquela et actio, quae ~unt ex cogitatione* AM 36.

profluvium ~i, *neut.* A discharge (of a fluid); *~um sanguinis*, a haemorrhage: Luke 8.43 (AE 79.3).

profugo ~are ~avi ~atum, *tr.* To put to flight, chase away: *unicum quod diabolum...a janua ~at* AC 364; AE 392.3.

profugus ~i, *m.* An outcast, exile: *vagus et ~us eris in terra* Gen. 4.12 (AC).

profunde, *adv.* (compar. *~ius*) **1** At a great depth, deeply: *dejiciuntur ~e in infernum* AC 6677. **2** (transf.) Not superficially, deeply: *in...damnationem adhuc ~ius infernalem* AC 270; *vae illis qui ~e sapiunt* Isa. 29.15 (VI 30.2).

profunditas ~atis, *f.* **1** A deep place, depth: *~ates maris* AC 18; *in ~atem terrae* ES 292. **2** Seriousness, depth: *altitudo et ~as...cum praedicatur de sapientia* AC 1613.3; *populum ~atum labii* Isa. 33.19 (AE 455.13).

profundo ~are ~avi ~atum, *tr.* To immerse deeply, plunge: (in quot. fig.) *~avit se cogitatio mea in aliqua arcana amoris conjugialis* AM 270.1.

profundus ~a ~um, *a.* (compar. *~ior*, superl. *~issimus*) **1** Extending far downwards, deep: *in luto ~o* Ps. 69.2 (AC 6669.3); *in arena ~a* ES 2391. **b** (neut. as sb.) a deep place, depth: *illos transferunt nunc in altum, nunc in ~um* AC 7337.3; *~um infernale* AC 904.2. **2** (of thought, understanding, etc.) Serious, profound, deep: *doctrinae separatae...fuerunt multo ~ioris cogitationis quam hodie* AC 442; *incidi in ~am meditationem* VR 25.1. **3** Requiring profound thought, deep: *talis est illa Lex...in sensu interno, imo est adhuc ~ior* AC 7089.2.

progenitus ~a ~um: pf. pple. of **progigno**.

progenies ~ei, *f.* Offspring, progeny: *~es viperarum* Matt. 3.7 (AC 6997.6); *est communis imago in singulis faciebus ~ei* VR 103.2.

progerminatio ~onis, *f.* The product of germination, shoot: *flores sunt ~ones* AC 9553.1.

progermino ~are ~avi, *intr.* To send forth shoots, germinate: *~are faciat terra herbam teneram* Gen. 1.11 (AC).

progigno progignere progenui progenitum, *tr.* To be the parent or ancestor of; (pass.) to be descended (from): *ex quo [semine] proles et familiae...progignuntur* VR 178.1; *omnes a se progenitos* VR 629.

prognatus ~a ~um, *a.* Born, descended, originated: *nova haeresis ex binis prioribus... ~a* SE 67; (masc. as sb.) a descendant: *quod tot angelis quot ~is locupletaverint caelum* AM 404; *benedictionem Meam super ~os a te* Isa. 44.3 (AC 255).

progredior ~di ~ssus sum, *intr.* **1** To go forward, advance: *~ssus paululum, cecidit super terram* Mark 14.35 (AC 1787.2); *visum est candidum illud ~di ad sinistrum* CI 159. **2** To proceed in speaking or writing, go on: *antequam ulterius ~di licet...* AC 560; *sed in hoc arcanum ulterius ~di nondum vacat* AE 23.1. **3** To advance in development, develop, proceed: *Dominus ~ssus est secundum ordinem Divinum* AC 6716.3; *vastatio... ~ditur ab externis ad interna* AC 7795.3; *ut possit* [*homo*]*... ~di in intelligentiam* VR 48.15.

progressio ~onis, *f.* **1** Motion forwards, progress: *currus motum suum et ~onem habet per rotas* AC 8215.3; *~o e loco in locum* VR 25.3. **2** Advancement to a different state, development, progress: *~o ab amore boni ad fidem* VI 36; *initiationes et ~ones amoris conjugialis* AM 301; *~o in infinitum* VR 32.8.

progressive, *adv.* Progressively: *in...statu anxio...et ~e in anxiori* AM 29.

progressivus ~a ~um, *a.* Progressive: *quod...* [*transitiones*] *~ae sint a momentis in momenta* AM 185.1; *de ~is gradibus justificationis* AE 239.2; (neut. as sb.) progressive influence: *~um ejus* [sc. *solis spiritualis*] *vadit usque ad ultima* VR 29.3.

progressus ~us, *m.* **1** Motion forwards, progress: *videntur...sicut natatores... ~um adjuvare manibus* AC 8374; extension: *plateae...in principiis angustae, sed in ~u dilatatae* AM 79.4. **2** The progress, advancement (of time): *~us temporis* AC 346. **3** Advancement in state, development, progress: *de ~u Divini Veri apud hominem* AC 6766.2; *accendunt sibi lucernam ad ulteriorem ~um* SS 59; (pl.) *ut hoc possit, ~us ulteriores faciet* AC 6766.2.

proh, *interj.* (to express grief) Oh!: *proh dolor, capillitia nostra* VR 185.6.

prohibeo ~bere ~bui ~bitum, *tr.* **1** To hold back, restrain: *non ~buit a morte animam illorum* Ps. 78.50 (AC 7102.10); *sinite infantes venire ad Me, ne ~bete eos* Mark 10.14 (AM 414). **2** To forbid, prohibit (an action): *vera fidei talia ~bent* AC 7327; *gradibus ~bitis* AM 519; (w. inf.) *non apud eos ~betur quod cogitant facere* AC 1318; (w. *ut*) *conversationes terrestres ~bent ut coelestia spectent* ES 294.

prohibitio ~onis, *f.* Prohibition: AE 840.1.

proinde, *adv.* Accordingly, so: *nunc est...amor paene nullus, ~e nec fides* AC 32; *faciunt bonum quia verum dictat quod faciendum, ~e ex obedientia* AC 8234.

projectio ~onis, *f.* **1** The act of throwing in front, putting out: *ex ~one baculi Moschis super terram* AC 6973. **2** That which is thrown ahead, a projection: *illa...apparent nullius formae...sed modo ~ones confusae* AC 1871.

projectus ~us, *m.* A casting in front, projection: ES 1411.

projicio ~jicere ~jeci ~jectum, *tr.* **1** To throw, cast: *in flumen ~jicietis illum* Exod. 1.22 (AC); *~jiciunt homines...in aquas* AC 7248; *ne ~jicite margaritas vestras ante porcos* Matt. 7.6 (AC 7784.4); *per divitem qui... ~jectus est in infernum* CI 365.2. **2** To throw or place before one, cast: *et ~jecerunt quisque baculum suum* Exod. 7.12 (AC); *videns fui usque dum throni ~jecti fuerunt* Dan. 7.9 (AC 6832.5); *repraesentantur imagines pulchrae ab illis quae circum circa ruditer ~jecta sunt* AC 1871. **3** To throw away, reject: *inanime corpus quod... ~jiceretur et sepeliretur* VR 10; (transf.) *~jectus est amor sexus...ac loco ejus amor unius e sexu...insidet* AM 58.

prolabor ~bi ~psus sum, *intr.* To fall (in quot. transf.): *~psi sunt in idololatriam* 4AD Isa. 47.10.

prolatus ~a ~um: pf. pple. of **profero**.

proles ~is, *f.* Offspring: *sciunt* [*vermiculi*]*...excludere ~em sui generis* CI 103.2; (pl.) *fames...eos non vetat quin procreare ~es debeant* ES 546; (transf.) *a charitate, quae est ~es amoris* AC 362.

prolicio ~licere ~lexi ~lectum, *tr.* To lure forward, induce to flow: *sanguinem in se ~lectum* [*protectum* 1st edn.; *projectum* Tafel] *explorant* [*renes*] AC 5381; (transf.) *protrahunt aliorum cogitationes...tunc ~liciunt plura quam alioquin* ES 3966.

prolificatio ~onis, *f.* The production of offspring, reproduction: *in omnia quae amoris sexus et ~onis sunt* VR 48.9; (transf.) *~o spiritualis* AM 45.

prolificum ~i, *neut.* Reproductive power: *semen injectum arenae, quod non excrescit, sed cum ~o suo perit* CI 475; *~um mariti foret in continuo vere* AM 115.5.

prolixitas ~atis, *f.* A tedious discussion: *ad evitandas ~ates inanes* AM 209.

prolixus ~a ~um, *a.* (compar. *~ior*) Wearisome by reason of length, tedious: *quid singula involvunt ~um foret exponere* AC 771; *de quadam re admodum ~a* ES 894.

prologus ~i, *m.* (Gk.) An introduction, foreword: *in hoc ~o aliquid de communi fide...dicetur* DP 191.1.

prolongatio ~onis, *f.* The act of making longer, prolongation: *~o temporis per plures adhuc annos* AE 706.16.

prolongo ~are ~avi ~atum, *tr.* To make long: *ut ~entur dies tui super terra* Deut. 25.15 (AE 304.42).

proloquor ~qui ~quutus sum, *tr.* To express in words, speak of: *iterum odia sua ~quutus* ES 3216.

promano ~are ~avi, *intr.* To flow out (as or like a liquid), pour forth: *caput omnium peccatorum, e quo ut radice et scaturigine omnes transgressiones ~ant* VR 464.10 (Book of Concord); *de haeresibus, paradoxis, et contradictionibus ~antibus ex hodierna fide* VR 485.

promereo: see **promereor**.

promereor ~mereri ~meritus sum, *tr., intr.* also **promereo** ~merere ~merui ~meritum, *tr.* **1** (tr.) To become deserving of (a future reward), earn in advance, deserve: *vitam aeternam... ~meruisse* Council of Trent in SE 5(e); AR Doc RC.5.2; *gratiam Dei... ~mereri* Book of Concord in SE 14(g). **2** (intr.) To be deserving of future reward, be meritorious: *quod opera ~mereantur* SE 8.

prominentia ~ae, *f.* A projecting part, projection: *super quatuor angulos ~ae altaris* Ezek. 45.19 (AC 7847.3); *facies...monstrosa ex ~is et tuberibus* ES 5925.

promineo ~nere ~nui, *intr.* To project, stand out: *facies...quae circum labra paulum ~nebant* AC 9246.

promiscue, *adv.* Without distinction, indiscriminately: AM 448.

promiscuus ~a ~um, *a.* Indiscriminate, promiscuous: *scortatio ~a* AM 54.

promissio ~onis, *f.* A promise: *quod sit ~o in Verbo* AC 7933.1.

promitto ~mittere ~misi ~missum, *tr.* To promise: *aperitio Verbi... ~missa est in Apocalypsi* SS 25.

promo ~ere ~psi ~ptum, *tr.* To bring out of store, prepare for use: *secures et instrumenta mortis per phantasias quasi ~unt* ES 374.

promotio ~onis, *f.* **1** The act of being moved, movement: *sicut ~ones e loco in locum* AC 10734. **2** The advancement (of an end): *in omni sapientia est ~o finis per causas medias* VR 47; promotion (to an office): *~o ad aliquod officium* VR 730.2.

promotrix ~icis, *f. adj.* Advancing, promoting: *ad hunc finem quae causa media ~ix et effectrix alia quam religio?* CO 40.

promoveo ~vere ~vi ~tum, *tr.* **1** To move forward, advance: *dum ~vent gradus, se adjuvant modo per manus* ES 559. **2** To advance to a further stage, promote: *quod omnipotentia Divina nequaquam possit...id* [sc. *malum*] *~vere a se* VR 56.2; *ut...divitiae mundi nihil prohibeant hominem a vita aeterna, nec...paupertas ~vet* ES 766.

prompte, *adv.* (compar. *~ius*) Without delay, promptly: *loquebantur volumatim et tamen usque tam ~e et cito* AC 6923.

promptitudo ~inis, *f.* Speed in execution, promptitude: *quae observabant, non appercipere potui ob ~inem illorum* AC 6922; *populus Tuus ~inum* Ps. 110.3 (AC 1725.3).

promptuarium ~i, *neut.* A storehouse, granary: *~a...sunt ubi annona colligitur* AC 6661.2; (transf.) *omnes hae cognitiones...modo sunt ~um ex quo fides charitatis formari potest* FI 27.

promptus[1] ~a ~um, *a.* (compar. *~ior*) Prepared for rapid action, prompt: *aliis spiritibus in pervidendo... ~iores et citiores sunt* AC 6921; (w. *ad*) *steterunt... ~i ad fandum* AM 381.

promptus[2] ~us, *m.* *In ~u*, ready to hand, exposed to view: *causae...in ~u sunt* 3AD 87.

promulgatio ~onis, *f.* The announcement (of a law), promulgation: *leges illae, per ~onem e Monte Sinae a Jehovah, factae sunt leges religionis* VI 53.

promulgo ~are ~avi ~atum, *tr.* To announce publicly, promulgate (a law): *Dominus ex Monte Sinae ~avit Legem* AC 795.5; AM 351.2.

promurale ~is, *neut.* A defensive structure in front of a wall, outwork, bastion: *lugere facit ~e, ac murum* Lam. 2.8 (AC 402.4).

promus ~i, *m.*? (app.) A store: (in quot. fig.) *ex meo ~o et condo aperiam mentem de hoc* AM 315.9.

prone, *adv.* (compar. *~ius*) In a headlong fashion: *videri potest...quam ~e antistites Ecclesiae arripiunt quod talis potestas data sit Petro* AC 8581.4; AE 52.1.

pronepos ~otis, *m.* A great-grandson: *si non in filiis, usque in nepotibus et ~otibus* AM 206.

proneptis ~is, *f.* A great-granddaughter: AC 8042.2.

pronitas ~atis, *f.* The quality of being disposed, proneness: (w. *in* + acc.) *~as in omne malum* AC 977.2; (w. *ad*) *~as ad iracundiam* ES 2351.

pronuntiatio ~onis, *f.* Pronunciation: *vocum ~onem* ES 412.

pronuntiatum ~i, *neut.* An utterance: *et ~um labiorum Meorum non mutabo* Ps. 89.34 (AE 205.5).

pronuntio ~are ~avi ~atum, *tr.* **1** To utter, speak, pronounce (words, sentences, etc.): *dicebant quod non ~are potuerint, quia voces illae crassius materiales* AC 1876.2. **2** To express in words, assert, state (facts or ideas): *ex igne amoris sui...illa* [sc. *scientifica*] *~ant* AE 763.2; (w. indir. qu.) *possunt ~are quomodo se habet cum veris* AC 5464.1. **3** (w. pred.) To pronounce formally to be: *tunc mundam ~abit plagam* Lev. 13.13 (AC 6963.4).

pronus ~a ~um, *a.* (superl. *~issimus*) **1** In horizontal position, headlong: *~us [angelus] volabat* AM

2.1; *supino seu ~o corpore, facie sursum* ES 753; (fig.) *labatur ~us in naturalismum* VR 75.7. **2** Particularly liable, inclined, prone (to): (w. *ad*) *ad flagitia et adulteria ~issimae* AC 831.1; *~i ad deliquium* VR 73.1; (w. *in* + acc.) *mens... ~a in errores* SS 52; (w. gen.) *~issimi sunt omnes divinandi* ES 2189; (w. inf.) *~issimi sunt credere* ES 4353.

propagatio ~onis, *f.* Propagation (by reproduction): *~o generis humani* AC 7038.2; transmission, propagation (of light): *~o lucis coeli* AE 97.1.

propagativus ~a ~um, *a.* Propagative: *ex facultate ~a animabus insita a creatione* AM 238.1.

propagator ~oris, *m.* One who spreads or propagates (doctrines): *acerrimus ~or et defensor suorum dogmatum fuit* [*Lutherus*] VR 796.1.

propagatrix ~icis, *f. adj.* Propagative: *vis ~ix* AE 1201.3.

propago[1] ~are ~avi ~atum, *tr.* **1** To propagate by reproduction: *~are sobolem* AC 7750.1; (fig.) *prolificum mariti foret...in nisu... ~andi suum verum* AM 115.5. **2** To spread abroad, diffuse, propagate: *luci, quae e medio ~atur* CI 308; *quod Chanoch...scientiam illarum* [sc. *correspondentiarum*] *~averit ad posteros* SS 21.

propago[2] ~inis, *f.* **1** An offshoot (of a plant): *et in vite tres ~ines* Gen. 40.10 (AC); *portam ex ramis et ~inibus...arborum compaginatis exstructam* AM 8.1. **2** Anything derived like a shoot from a plant, offshoot: *est...in semine cujusvis...tradux seu ~o animae patris* VR 103.2; *janua ad illam fidem et ejus ~ines* VR 178.2. **3** Offspring, a generation (of persons or animals): *habitaverunt...plerique sub terris ibi, una ~o sub altera* UJ 58.6; *foemella eorum* [sc. *apum*] *ponit ova...ut inde nova ~o nascatur* CI 108.1.

propalatio ~onis, *f.* The act of making public, publication: *~o errorum* AC 1080.

propalo ~are ~avi ~atum, *tr.* To make public, publicize: *~antur quae in abscondito egerunt* CI 507; *pudoris est... ~are illas* [*ideas*] VR 17.4.

propatulum ~i, *neut.* The public domain, full view: *qualis status...est...apud me in ~um venit* AM 216.2; *omnia quae cogitaverunt et fecerunt, tam in ~o quam in abscondito* CI 469.

prope, *prep. w. acc.* and *adv.* (compar. *~ius*, superl.: see **proxime**) **1** (prep.) Close to, near: *cum me viderunt ~e se* VR 74.2; ES 476. **2** (adv.) Close by, near: *cum* [*angelus*] *~e erat* AM 2; *~e illuc missi* ES 4435; (compar.) *quod...perducantur... ~ius ad Dominum* AC 6645.3. **3** (adv.) Close in time, at hand: *quia tempus ~e* Rev. 1.3 (AR). **4** (adv.) *~e esse ut...*, to be on the point of...: *cum* [*quoddam oblitum*]... *~e esset ut revocaretur* ES 3573. **5** (adv.) In a close relationship, nearly: *consanguinei, affines, ~ius et remotius* ES 3795; *ad talia quae intellectum ~ius intrant* VR 53.

propello ~pellere ~puli ~pulsum, *tr.* To drive forth, expel: *accipiuntur, sed...inde ~pelluntur* ES 404.

propemodum, *adv.* Very nearly, almost: *quia ~um saliunt, se elevando frequenter in lapsu* ES 559.

propendeo ~dere ~di, *intr.* To hang forward, hang out: *superiore parte ~dente antrorsum sicut proni ad lapsum* AM 505.4.

propensio ~onis, *f.* An inclination, propensity: AC 3127.

propensus ~a ~um, *a.* Favourably disposed: *~o animo esse erga superiores* AE 412.24.

propere, *adv.* In haste, quickly: *exivi domo, et ~e accessi* AM 293.1; VR 459.1.

propero ~are ~avi, *intr.* **1** To go hastily, hurry: *quod... ~arent ad exeundum* AM 5.2. **2** (of things) To be imminent, come quickly, hasten: *~ant futura illis* Deut. 39.35 (AC 7051.3).

prophanatio ~onis, *f.* also **profanatio**. Desecration, profanation: *~ones Verbi* AC 571; *~o boni et veri* AM 339.1.

prophanator ~oris, *m.* also **profanator**. One who desecrates or profanes: *quod sors ~orum omnium pessima sit* AC 6959.3.

prophane, *adv.* In an irreligious manner: ES(M) 4570.

prophano ~are ~avi ~atum, *tr.* also **profano**. To treat (what is sacred) without respect, desecrate, profane: *~asti Me apud populum Meum* Ezek. 13.19 (AC 6767.3); *Dominus... ~avit regnum et principes* Lam. 2.2 (AE 316.14); *is ~at qui vera fidei novit...et tamen in odiis...vivit* AC 1008.1; *quod totum Verbum destruxerint et ~averint* DD 16.6; *quod... ~etur conjugium Domini et Ecclesiae* AM 339.1.

prophanus ~a ~um, *a.* also **profanus**. (compar. *~ior*, superl. *~issimus*) **1** Not religious, secular: *apud aliquem ~um scriptorem* AC 755.5; *quod illa urbs ...nullatenus sancta fuerit, sed potius ~a* AE 223.11. **2** Contrary to religious precept, irreligious, blasphemous, profane: *adulteria...spectantur...ut ~a* CI 384; *inventiones...tam ~ae et foedae* ES 2577; *alii, qui impii sunt et summe ~i* ES 218; (neut. as sb.) *conspurcare sanctum ~is* DD 18.3.

propheta ~ae, *m.* (Gk.) A prophet: *Eliam ~am* Mal. 4.5 (AC 6752.10); *quae visa sunt ~is* CI 171; (esp. w. ref. to the prophetic books of the Old Testament) *quod ex illis mandatis Lex et ~ae pendeant* Matt. 22.40 (AC 36); *si non creditis Mosen et ~as, hoc est, Verbum Domini* AM 535.

prophetia ~ae, *f.* A prophecy: *prima ~a de Adventu Domini* AC 250; *testimonium Jesu est spiritus ~ae* Rev. 19.10 (AR).

prophetice, *adv.* In the manner of a prophecy: *tentationes Domini... ~e ita describuntur* AC 1691.5.

propheticus ~a ~um, *a.* (Gk.) Of or concerned with prophecy, prophetic: *formula ~a* AC 1585.4; *Libri ~i* AC 6752.4; *sermo ~us* AC 7343.3; (neut. as sb.) a prophecy: *~um de Domino venturo* VR 101.2; also, a prophetical book of the Word: *ex ~is Verbi* FI 53.

prophetissa ~ae, *f.* A female prophet, prophetess: *Mirjam ~a* Exod. 15.20 (AC); Rev. 2.20 (AR).

propheto ~are ~avi ~atum, *intr.* (*tr.*) To make a prophecy, prophesy: *nonne per nomen Tuum ~avimus?* Matt. 7.22 (CI 471); *universa Scriptura Sacra de Ipso ~avit* SS 23.4; (tr., pass.) *quod haec a Daniele ~ata sint* VR 788.

propinatio ~onis, *f.* The act of drinking: *et reduxit principem pincernarum super ~onem suam* Gen. 40.21 (AC).

propino ~are ~avi ~atum, *tr.* To consume as a drink: *omne quod potui inservit, seu quod ~atur, sicut vinum, lac, aqua* AC 5077.5.

propinque, *adv.* (compar. *~ius*) At a short distance, closely: *ubinam tunc essent... remotius aut ~ius* AC 1640.1.

propinquatio ~onis, *f.* The action of coming close, approaching: *distantiae... a Domino et ~ones ad Ipsum* AC 9378.3 (Autograph).

propinquitas ~atis, *f.* **1** The state of being close, proximity: *solem cujus lucis radii tales sunt ex ~ate* AC 7058.2. **2** Close association, propinquity: *secundum affinitates et ~ates amoris* AM 50.

propinquo ~are ~avi, *intr.* To come near, approach: *illi ad distantiam, sicut ~abant, facti sunt sicut furiae* AM 71.3.

propinquus ~a ~um, *a.* (compar. *~ior*, superl. *~issimus*) **1** Physically close, near at hand: *vicinus... ~us* Exod. 12.4 (AC); (w. dat.) *in terra inferiore, quae ~a infernis* AC 7240. **b** *in ~o*, nearby, close: *quod in ~o sint qui in simili statu* CI 193; VR 13.2. **2** Close in time: *~us est dies tumultus* Ezek. 7.7 (DD 4). **3** Closely associated, related: (w. dat.) *qui ~i Deo sunt* AM 113; (masc. as sb.) a relative: *voluerunt... ut dicerem illa ad ~os eorum* AC 4527.3.

propior ~or ~us, *compar. a.* (see also **proximus**) Nearer, closer: *~ores sunt Domino* AC 1802.2; *ex ejus* [sc. *innocentiae*] *~ore receptione* AM 405.1.

propitiatio ~onis, *f.* Propitiation: *absque illa expiatione, satisfactione et ~one* DD 18.1.

propitiator ~oris, *m.* One who propitiates: *Dominus est ~or* AE 392.7.

propitiatorium ~i, *neut.* A place of propitiation, mercy-seat, a structure above the Ark of the Covenant: Exod. 25.17 (AC).

propitio ~are ~avi ~atum, *tr.* **1** To render favourable, propitiate: *quod Filius sic ~averit Patrem* VR 134.2; DP 326.12. **2** To find acceptable: *non Ego ~abo illa* [sc. *holocausta*] Jer. 14.12 (AC 2799.9).

propitius ~a ~um, *a.* Favourably inclined, propitious: *et ~us sis ad iniquitatem nostram* Exod. 34.9 (AC); *bone Deus, sis mihi ~us* DP 278[a].1.

propono ~nere ~sui ~situm, *tr.* **1** To set before, present: *cum quis sibi ~nit aliquid, percipit id sicut praesens* AC 7017; *Ego ~no vobis viam vitae et viam mortis* Jer. 21.8 (AE 186.4). **2** To set out in words, propose: *illa tria ~sita fuerunt Davidi* AC 7102.8; *illi qui evestigaret secretum mox ~nendum* AM 103.3; ES 477.

proportio ~onis, *f.* A proportion: *rationes decimarum seu ~ones* AC 2276.4; AC 5291.10.

proportionate, *adv.* Proportionately: *charitas... decrescit secundum remotionem, hoc est... ~e* AC 2973.3.

propositio ~onis, *f.* **1** The act of setting on view, display: *panes ~onis* AC 4292.5 (Lev. 24.5-9). **2** The act of putting forward (an idea): *ex significatione 'ponere coram illis verba', quod sit ~o* AC 8774. **3** A statement put forward for discussion, proposition: *sume falsissimum, et da illud in ~onem* AS 267.3; AC 4727.1.

propositum ~i, *neut.* An aim, purpose: *cum pleno ~o emendandi vitam* BCP (VI 6); *~um seu intentio voluntatis* AM 146; *ex ~o*, of set purpose, deliberately: *qui omnia fraena concupiscentiis laxaverunt et ex ~o illis indulserunt* VI 97.

proprie, *adv.* As correctly understood, properly: *vox 'creare' ~e spectat hominem cum e novo creatur* AC 472; *per Spiritum Sanctum ~e significatur Divinum Verum* VR 139.1.

proprietarius ~i, *m.* Self-made: *illi qui prudentiae propriae addixerunt omnia, qui etiam vocari possunt ~i in imagine sua* DP 309.1.

proprietas ~atis, *f.* **1** An attribute, property: *totidem ~ates, qualitates et attributa unius Dei* VR 9.3. **2** A piece of property, possession: *vult possidere illam* [sc. *virginem*] *ut ~atem supra omnia amabilem* AM 106.

proprium ~i, *neut.* **1** A peculiar distinguishing quality, property, characteristic: *spectare supra se est ~um hominis* AC 7821; *~um... amoris est ut velit quod omne suum ex se in aliis sit* AC 9310.1; *sunt duo ~a mundi naturalis... unum est spatium, et alterum est* *tempus* VR 27. **2** The quality that distinguishes an individual, personality, self: *~um Domini est vita* AC 149.2; *ex ~o coelesti et angelico* AC 253; *patet quod Divinum Domini faciat coelum, et non angeli ex aliquo ~o suo* CI 8. **3** The self of human beings regarded as essentially evil, the ego: *ex se et suo ~o, et non e caelo a Domino, cogitat* SS 1; *ex cupiditate et prava voluntate, quae sunt ~um hominis* DD 17.3. **4** Each part making up the self: *Dominus miraculose separavit ~um ejus intellectuale a ~o isto corrupto voluntario* AC 1023.2; *~um voluntatis et ~um intellectus* AM 194.2; (pl.) *quantum tunc non ~a impediunt, tantum est [homo] Domini* AC 1745.3.

proprius ~a ~um, *a.* (compar. *~or*) **1** Belonging to oneself, one's own: *hic ~as oves vocat nomine tenus* John 10.3 (AC 6674.6); *in ~a venit, sed ~i Ipsum non receperunt* John 1.11 (DD 18.5); *bona...non dari queunt homini nec angelo ut sint ~a* AC 8497. **2** Characteristic, peculiar, special: *hic amor est hominis ~us per quem distinguitur a bestiis* AC 7750.2; *quod ~us sensus amoris conjugialis sit sensus tactus* AM 209; *hi termites sunt ex arbore nativa seu ~a nostri caeli* AM 77.7. **3** Arising from the self, personal, own: *quod Ipse illud ex ~a potentia Divinum fecerit* AC 6716.2; (esp. as being fundamentally evil) *quicquid ~um est hominis, hoc nullam in se vitam habet* AC 41; *apparent tales in ~a luce* AM 232.2; *non ex libero interiori, quod est ejus ~um liberum* DP 89. **4** Properly so called, real: *absque cooperatione intellectus et voluntatis non est homini aliqua vita ~a* SA 82 (= iii.5). **5** *In ~o sensu*, in the correct sense, properly understood: *unaquaevis terra significat aliquod certum in communi, et hoc in sensu ~o et opposito* AC 1662; *quid charitas in ~o sensu* FI 23.

propter, *prep. w. acc.* On account of, because of: *~er varias causas* AM 153; *bonum...est vel ~er se vel ~er mundum* AM 444.4; *~er finem, ut...* VR 3.1.

propterea, *adv.* On account of this, for this reason, therefore: *subtraxerunt se...a concupiscentiis carnis, et ~ea perpetuam virginitatem voverant* AM 155.3; (correlated w. *quia*) *omnes...salvari possunt, modo... vivant secundum praecepta...ne occidant... ~ea quia facere talia est contra religionem* DP 253.

propugnaculum ~i, *neut.* A defensive structure, bulwark: *Jehovah... ~um meum* Ps. 18.2 (AE 316.10); AC 8261.2.

propugno ~are ~avi, *intr.* To contend strongly, defend the view: (w. acc. and inf.) *qui ~ant fidem salvare absque bonis operibus* ES 4021.

propullulo ~are ~avi, *intr.* (of plants) To exhibit new growth, shoot: *autumo quod talia ex intimiori coelo ~ent* ES 710 1/2; *mali radix continuo ~at* ES 3547.

prorepo ~ere ~si, *intr.* To crawl forth: *~ere faciant aquae reptile* Gen. 1.20 (AC); *~ere faciet fluvius ranas* Exod. 7.28 (AC).

prorepto ~are ~avi, *intr.* To creep forward: *omnis anima vivens quae ~abit ad quodcunque ubi venit aqua fluviorum vivet* Ezek. 47.9 (AC 40.2).

proripio ~ripere ~ripui ~reptum, *tr.* (refl.) To move violently, hurl oneself: *in foramina petrarum se ~ripiunt* CI 488.1; VR 111.1; *se ~ripere ex societate* ES 3012.

prorogo ~are ~avi ~atum, *tr.* To keep going, prolong: *sunt animalium species...quae absque alio cibo ~ant vitam* SA 121 (= x.3).

prorsus, *adv.* Completely, totally, utterly: *vita ejus pendet ~us a conjunctione illa* AC 50.1; *agitur ~us obsequiose ad nutus intellectus* CI 60; *malum et bonum sunt duo opposita ~us sicut infernum et caelum* VI 70; (also) directly, immediately: *in zenith seu ~us super caput* ES 461.

prorumpo ~mpere ~pi, *intr.* To burst or gush forth: *falsitates quae ex cupiditatibus ~mpunt* AC 1666.2.

prosapia ~ae, *f.* **1** A group of people connected by descent from a common ancestor, stock, family: *ex ~a et semine antiquissimorum fuerunt* AC 788.2; *cum talibus ex nobili ~a* AM 483. **2** A type, genus: *~ae piscium* DP 56.3; *sive major numerus sive minor, modo ejusdem ~ae* AC 1856; *quod bona unius ~ae se in fasciculos ligent* VR 38.3.

proscribo ~bere ~psi ~ptum, *tr.* To denounce, proscribe: *imputatio hodierna ~bit potentiam ad ita faciendum sicut internecinum fidei* VR 630.

proselyta ~ae, *m.* (Gk.) also **proselytus** ~i, *m.* A proselyte: *~ae qui ad religionem Christianam convertuntur* VR 677.3.

proselytus: see **proselyta**.

prosemino ~are ~avi ~atum, *tr.* (refl.) To reproduce by means of seed, seed itself: *Dominus primum progerminare facit tenerum quoddam...tum aliquid utilius, quod rursus se ~at* AC 29.1.

prosequor ~qui ~quutus sum, *tr.* **1** To go in search of, seek: *siceram ~quuntur* Isa. 5.11 (AE 323.14). **2** (w. abl.) To accompany, attend (with): *deos...quos...Divino cultu ~quebantur per festum* AC 8301.5; *non solum omnes alios prae se contemnunt, sed etiam vituperiis ~quuntur* AC 8318.2.

prospectio ~onis, *f.* The act of providing, provision: *cum ~one naturalis ita se habet* AC 5286.

prospectus ~us, *m.* **1** The direction in which a structure faces, outlook: *~us laterum [domus] ad plagas* AM 103.3; *~us ejus* [sc. *arboris*] *usque ad finem...*

terrae Dan. 4.11 (AE 650.29). 2 The appearance of anything end on, section: *ea* [sc. wooden beams] *facta sunt quadrata ~u* AC 7847.4 (Ezek. 41.21).

prosper ~era ~erum, *a.* (compar. *~erior*) Successful, prosperous: *ut ~er sit in mundo* CC 14.3; *de statu ejus ~eriori* AM 287.

prospere, *adv.* Successfully, prosperously: *omnia quae ~e sibi eveniunt sibi tribuunt* AC 8717.3.

prosperitas ~atis, *f.* Prosperity: AC 1300.

prospero ~are ~avi ~atum, *tr.* 1 To grant success to, prosper: *Jehovah ~avit viam meam* Gen. 24.55 (AC). 2 (pass.) To enjoy success, prosper: *qui regnet Rex et ~etur* Jer. 23.5 (DD 6); *et ~ata es usque ad regnum* Ezek. 16.13 (AE 195.7).

prospicio ~picere ~pexi ~pectum, *tr.*, *intr.* 1 (intr.) To direct one's gaze outwards, look out: *et ~pexit huc et illuc, et vidit quod nullus vir* Exod. 2.12 (AC); *~pice e coelo* Isa. 63.15 (AC 8309.2). 2 (tr.) To make available, provide: *ut...haereditatem ~piciat illis* AC 1865.3; *~piciuntur...omnia illa bona* AM 279; [*papiliones*] *~piciunt sibi posteritatem* VR 12.6. b (w. abl.) to provide (someone with something): *quisque... ~picere se talibus potest* AC 6938. 3 (intr.) To make provision, provide: (w. dat.) *qui propter se male sibi ~picit* AC 6938; *~picere saluti animarum* VI 39; (w. *ut* or *ne*) *quisque primum sibi ~piciet ut habeat necessitates vitae* AC 6934; (impers. pass.) *~picitur ne illa* [sc. *janua*] *stet aperta* AM 146.

prostata ~ae, *f.* (Gk.) (anat.) The prostate gland: *membris quae generationi dicata sunt, sicut testes, ~ae* ES 1138.

prosterno ~sternere ~stravi ~stratum, *tr.* (refl. and pass.) To cast oneself down, prostrate oneself: *se ~sternunt super genua* AM 333.1; *illi ~sternuntur ad pedem Tuum* Deut. 33.3 (AE 204.7).

prostibulum ~i, *neut.* A prostitute: AM 296.2; ES 3899.

prostituo ~stituere ~stitui ~stutum, *tr.* 1 To sell for immoral purposes, prostitute: *eas* [*foeminas*] *postea relinquunt... ~stituunt* AC 828; *quod faeminae... pudicitiam suam ~stituerent* AM 297. 2 (transf.) To put to improper use, prostitute: *absque pudore et timore sancta externa et interna ~stituere* AC 9960.10.

prostitutio ~onis, *f.* Prostitution (in quot. fig.): *timet ... ~onem nominis sui* AM 469.

prostitutor ~oris, *m.* One who puts (something) to an unworthy use, a prostitutor: *violatores et ~ores sanctitatum Ecclesiae* VR 310.

prosto ~are ~iti, *intr.* To be exposed, be on view: *sic adytum, ara et pulpitum sub diu variis exposita violentiis ~arent* VR 55; *in repraesentationes obscoenas ...quae ~ant coram aliis spiritibus* ES 1695.

prostratio ~onis, *f.* 1 The act of casting oneself on the ground, prostration: *adoratio vera... ~onem ad terram super facies coram Domino...secum habet* AC 1999.1. 2 The act of casting down (other things), overthrow: *~o infernorum ac falsorum* AE 922.5.

prosum prodesse profui, *intr.* To be of use or profit, be advantageous: *vita carnis, quae non prodest quicquam* VI 99; (impers.) *quid prodest homini, si totum mundum lucratus fuerit...?* Matt. 16.26 (AC 7021.2); (w. *ut*) *prodest ad evitandum ignominiam ut unum Deum ore confiteamini* VR 17.4.

protectio ~onis, *f.* Protection: *~o aeterna coeli per Divinam sphaeram boni et veri* AC 9502.

protego ~gere ~xi ~ctum, *tr.* To protect, guard: *~get Jehovah habitatores Hierosolymae* Zech. 12.8 (DD 4); *vera illa tegunt et ~gunt illum* [*amorem*] AE 208.10.

protendo ~dere ~di ~sum, *tr.*, *intr.* 1 (tr.) To cause to stretch forth, extend: *ex substantia hac medullari ~duntur fibrae conspicuae* AE 775.2; SA 77 (= iii.3.[3]); SA 86 (= v.[3]). 2 (intr., of a scale pan) To tend: *scala... nutat et ~dit ad alteram partem* AM 318.1.

protensus ~a ~um, *a.* (pf. pple. of **protendo**) Extended, elongated: *tentoria...superne rotundata, ac ~a in longum* AC 8379; *fissurae rupium... ~ae in latum* CI 584; *pileo rotundo nigro satis ~o* ES 3589.

protervitas ~atis, *f.* Impudence: *dico tibi...quod sit ~as scandere ad Deum Patrem* VR 161.3.

protervus ~a ~um, *a.* Impudent, shameless: *~a expostulatio debiti conjugialis* AM 472.

protoplastus ~a ~um, *a.* (Gk.) First formed: *quod per illa quae de Adamo memorantur non intelligantur aliqui status hominis ~i* CO 33.

prototypon ~i, *neut.* An original thing of which something else is a representation, prototype: *quod honor, qui illis* [sc. *Sanctis*] *exhibetur, referatur ad ~a quae illae repraesentant* AR Doc RC.8.

protractio ~onis, *f.* A drawing out of time, delay: *ex nimia ~one...temporis desponsationum* AM 305.2.

protraho ~here ~xi ~ctum, *tr.* 1 To draw forth, take out: *~hite et accipite vobis pecudem gregis* Exod. 12.21 (AC); (fig.) *dum per explicationem correspondentiarum in lucem intellectus ~huntur* VR 123.2. 2 To make longer, draw out: *ipsa via ~hitur et decurtatur secundum desiderium* CI 195. 3 To make longer in time, prolong: *dies ejus non ~hentur* Isa. 13.22 (AC 23); to make to appear long, draw out: *~ximus aliquot dies et noctes in luxurie illa* AM 6.4; AM 18.3.

protrudo ~dere ~si ~sum, *tr.*, *intr.* (tr.) To push out, put forth: *termites... ~serunt uvas* IM 48; (intr.) to put forth shoots: *spectate ficum et omnes arbores, quando ~serint jam...cognoscetis* Luke 21.30 (AE 403.15).

protrusio ~onis, *f.* A thrusting out: *loquebatur... coacte, tanquam per ~ones vocis* ES 622.

protuli: pf. of **profero**.

prout, *adv.* and *conj.* **1** (adv.) As for example, such as: *qui...se non amant prae aliis, ~ut omnes qui a regno Domini sunt* AC 6711; *illa cultus... ~ut confessiones, adorationes, preces et similia* AC 9475.1. **2** (adv. correlated with word expressing likeness) As: *infernum similiter in societates distinctum est ~ut coelum* CI 541. **3** (conj. w. indic.) In proportion as, as: *ad distantiam secundum gradus ~ut diminuitur perfectio* CI 43; *et ~ut adolescunt, genialiter conjungunt se* AM 183.6.

provectus ~a ~um, *a.* (pf. pple. of **provehor**) (compar. *~ior*) (of age) Advanced: *homo... ~ioris aetatis* AC 6766.2; *in aetate ~a* AM 298.

provehor ~hi ~ctus sum, *intr.* To progress in development, advance: *nondum in vera Ecclesiae tantum ~ctus* AC 6754; *cum haec* [sc. *soboles apium*] *ad aetatem suam ~cta est* VR 12.7.

provenio ~nire ~ni, *intr.* To be derived, come (from a source): *nihil mali ab Ipso ~nit* AC 7877.3; *verba ex Domino immediate ~niebant* CI 254.

proventus ~us, *m.* Produce, fruits (of the earth): *terra dabit ~um suum* Ezek. 34.27 (AC 93); *'triginta' pro parvo ~u* AC 9276.6.

proverbium ~i, *neut.* A proverb, saying: *loquutus est [Salomo] tria millia ~orum* 1 Kgs. 4.32 (AC 5223.2); a byword: *ponis nos ~um inter gentes* Ps. 44.14 (SS 86).

providenter, *adv.* By providence, providentially: *Dominus...Divino auspicio ~er ab imputatione reatus abducit illos* AM 350.2.

providentia ~ae, *f.* Providence: *per ~am Divinam* AC 7007.3; *sapientia angelica de Divina ~a* DP titulus; AM 87.4.

provideo ~dere ~di ~sum, *tr.* (pf. act. also *~si* VI 69) **1** To make available, supply, provide: *Dominus... praevidet malum, at ~det bonum* AC 6951; *nisi Dominus ~serit media reformationis* VI 69. **2** (w. *ut* or *ne*) To make provision, see to it (that): *Dominus... ~det ut omnia...cedant ei ad bonum* AC 6303; *~dere ne intrare possit* AC 306; (w. *quod*) *~sum fuit quod Moses repraesentaret Dominum* AC 6723.3.

providus ~a ~um, *a.* Providing for future needs or events, provident: *mala...praevidentur et bona providentur, et mala quae praevidentur per dispositionem ~am Domini continue flectuntur versus bonum* AC 6489.

provincia ~ae, *f.* An administrative district, province: *incolae...regni divisi in plures ~as* VR 813; (fig.) *Divinus Amor...distinguitur porro in minor regna, quae vocari possunt ~ae* DA 24 (= x.[1]); (esp. in the Grand Man) *angeli ...qui occupabant cordis ~am* AC 170; AC 7358; SS 107.

proviso, *adv.* Providentially: *ex illis quae ~o obtigerunt, ita quae ex Divina Providentia* AC 4262.1.

provoco ~are ~avi ~atum, *tr.*, *intr.* **1** To rouse to anger, provoke: *~arunt Sanctum Israelis* Isa. 1.4 (DD 40); Isa. 65.3 (AE 324.19). **2** To summon (before a court of law): *~are proximum ad judicia* AC 819. **3** (intr.) To call for judgment, appeal: *~o ad eruditos... ~o ad sapientes...* AM 315.7.

proxime, *adv.* (superl. of **prope**) (compar. *~ius*) **1** Most closely in space: *sibi ~e ponit illa* AC 6690; *infernum...quod est ~e ultra desertum latronum* ES 4496. **2** Most closely in time, shortly: *~e ante diluvium* AC 276.2. **3** Most closely in order, most nearly: *angeli... nihil sciunt...nequidem unam vocem quid ~e significat* AC 65; *in quod Divinum Domini primum aut ~e influit* CI 435; (compar.) *quorum* [*usuum*] *unus ~ius et directius, alter remotius et obliquius, spectat...Dominum* AC 997.2.

proximitas ~atis, *f.* **1** Closeness, proximity: *ex ~ate ad solem* ES 1425. **2** Closeness in relationship: *secundum ~ates, propinquitates et affinitates amoris* AM 158.1.

proximus ~xima ~ximum, *a.* (compar. *~ximior*, superl. *~xissimus*) Close in space, near: *inventa sic urbe ~xima* Deut. 21.3 (AC 6767.5); *regiones ~ximae ad hominem occupantur a malis* AC 8054.3; *per viam ~ximiorem et remotiorem* ES 2784. **2** Closely associated, near: *cogitationem ~ximam loquelae* CI 502; *non est vita, sed est ~ximum receptaculum vitae a Deo* AM 315.11. **3** (masc. as sb.) The neighbour, the next person: *amor erga ~ximum* CI 238; *~ximo auferre sua bona* SS 67.2.

prudens ~ntis, *a.* (compar. *~ntior*) **1** (of persons) Taking thought for the future, prudent: *omnis qui audit Mea verba et facit illa, comparo viro ~nti* Matt. 7.24 (AC 7317.2); *quinque ex illis* [*virginibus*] *erant ~ntes* Matt. 25.2 (SS 17.1). **2** (of things) Displaying prudence: *spiritus Jovis...habent...sermonem ~ntem* AC 8384.

prudenter, *adv.* (compar. *~ius*, superl. *~issime*) Prudently, circumspectly: *interrogabat plura, et haec tali prudentia ut vigil non ~ius* AC 7744; *admittebant ~er in sepulchrum quoddam athmosphaericum* CI 335.

prudentia ~ae, *f.* Prudence: *~ae Christianae interest bene scrutari qualis hominis vita est* AC 6704; *~a ex proprio* CI 277.2.

pruina ~ae, *f.* Hoar frost: *minutum sicut ~a super terra* Exod. 16.14 (AC).

pruna ~ae, *f.* A piece of burning fuel, red-hot ember: *imple volas tuas ~is ignis* Ezek. 10.2 (AC 308.2); *coxi super ~is ejus panem* Isa. 44.19 (AC 7852.3); *lux ex ~is seu ignitis carbonibus* AS 254.

prunosus ~a ~um, *a.* Of or typical of embers; *apparebant sicut inesset iis ignis ~us* ES 1680.

prurigo ~inis, *f.* **1** Itching: *percutiet te Jehovah ...scabie et ~ine* Deut. 28.27 (AC 8364.3); (fig.) *~o falsitatum* AC 6110.6. **2** Sexual excitement: *initia amoris scortatorii sunt modo carnis oestra et ~ines* AM 440.

pruritus ~us, *m.* Itching: *~um scabiei intulerunt corpori meo* ES 5839; (fig.) an intense desire, itch: *injiciebant ~um mordendi linguam* ES 4589; *in ~u loquendi* ES 5143; a sexual itch or craving: *sunt...juvenes, qui ex vesania aetatis et ~u conceperunt principia nefanda, quod uxores...non debeat esse marito, sed sibi* AC 829.2.

psallo ~ere ~i, *tr.* To accompany (singing) on musical instrument, play: *Psalmis pluribus...indicatum quomodo ~erentur* AC 8337.5; *Psalmi Davidis... ~ebantur ...ac canebantur* AR 279.2; (absol.) *quod tunc quoque ~ant* AC 8633; *~ite Domino* Ps. 68.32 (AC 219).

psalmodia ~ae, *f.* (Gk.) A book containing psalms: *habent Verbum scriptum, et ~as* ES 5666.

psalmus ~i, *m.* (Gk.) A sacred song, psalm: *aliquos ~os Davidis* AC 1771.1; ES 5947.

pseudopropheta ~ae, *m.* (Gk.) A false prophet: *ex ore ~ae* Rev. 16.13 (AR).

psittacus ~i, *m.* (Gk.) A parrot: VR 22.3.

psychologia ~ae, *f.* (Gk.) Psychology: ES 4698.

psychologicus ~a ~um, *a.* (Gk.) Of or concerned with psychology: *experimentalia... ~a* CI 353.1.

-pte, *emphatic particle.* : *suapte essentia* 3AD 2478.

Pu, *indecl.* (Gk., = English 'where?') A place in which souls were believed to live after death: *suntne illi interea animae, quae sunt pneumata, et in quodam pu seu ubi* AM 28; VR 29.2; ES 4616.

pubes ~is, *f.* (anat.) The pubes: *in ~em membri genitalis* ES 3752; ES 3900.

publicanus ~i, *m.* One who is contracted to collect taxes for the Roman Empire, tax-gatherer: AE 617.22 (Mark 2.15).

publicus ~a ~um, *a.* **1** Of the people at large, public: *pro bono ~o* VI 7; (esp. neut. as sb.) the public: *non intuetur proximum, ita non ~um* AC 7367; *quod talia vellem ~o dare* AC 7809; *edere in ~um*, to publish: AM 73.2. **2** Available to all, public: *vetor...conjugia illa in lucem ~am sistere* AM 292.1.

pudefacio ~facere ~feci, *tr.* To put to shame: *~facient equitantes super equis* Zech. 10.5 (AE 355.28); AC 4236.4.

pudefio ~fieri ~factus sum, *intr.* To become ashamed, be put to shame: *tantum non ~fiunt, ut se jactent de malo* AC 217; *~facti sunt agricolae* Jer. 14.4 (AC 566.2).

pudenda ~orum, *neut. pl.* The private parts: *non sciret velare ~a* DP 281.3; ES(M) 4643.

pudeo ~dere ~dui, *intr.* To be ashamed: (w. inf.) *non ~dent...talia scribere* ES 3934; (usu. impers. w. acc.) *~deat te* VR 111.11; (w. gen. of thing) *~duit me cogitationum priorum* AM 182.7; (w. *quod*) *non ~debat eum quod talis factus* ES 3456.

pudice, *adv.* With propriety, modestly: *incipiebant modeste loqui et ~e agere* AM 521.3.

pudicitia ~ae, *f.* Sexual purity, chastity: *quod faeminae... ~am suam prostituerent* AM 297.

pudicus ~a ~um, *a.* Chaste, modest: *in ~is et castis jucundis amoris conjugialis* AM 431.1; AE 427.9.

pudor ~oris, *m.* A feeling of embarrassment, shame: *quod spiritus...non afficiantur ~ore* AC 7746; (w. gen. of cause) *~orem nuditatis* ES 355; (pred. dat.) *quod nuditas non ~ori sit* AC 8375.

puella ~ae, *f.* **1** A female child, girl: *cum [Verbum] legitur...ab infante puerulo seu ~a* AC 1871; *educationes... ~arum usque ad aetatem, qua dantur nuptui* AM 174. **2** A serving girl, maidservant: *et ~ae ejus euntes ad latus fluminis* Exod. 2.5 (AC).

puellaris ~is ~e, *a.* Of a girl, maidenly: *floridum ~e decus* AM 505.2; ES 1190.

puellus ~i, *m.* A small boy: *qui recipit unum ~um talem in nomine Meo, Me recipit* Matt. 18.5 (AC 6674.5).

puer ~eri, *m.* **1** A boy or young man (between his fifth and twentieth year AC 10225): *et ecce ~er flens* Exod. 2.6 (AC); AM 218.2; (in pl. including both sexes) children or youths: *ut Verbum...legatur, etiam a ~eris* AC 3982.3. **2** A servant, boy: *et accepit duos ~eros secum* Gen. 22.3 (AC); cf. AC 2782.

pueresco ~ere, *intr.* To become a boy: *infans...sicut ~it seu adolescit* DP 277.4.

puerilis ~is ~e, *a.* **1** Of a boy or young man: *in aetate ~i* AC 1050.1; *Domini status... ~is* AC 1557.1. **2** Childish: *quid nobis viris cum ~i illo codicillo?* AM 521.5.

pueritia ~ae, *f.* A period covering both childhood and

adolescence (from the fifth to the twentieth year AC 10225), youth: *in ~a adsunt spiritus* CI 295; *ex prima ~a* FI 25; *de scientia...quam Dominus in ~a primum arripuit* AC 1482.

puerpera ~ae, *f.* A woman who has just given birth: *quod ~a...in holocaustum offerret agnum* AC 3994.7.

puerulus ~i, *m.* A small boy: *vidi ~os inter se dimicantes* AC 2309; AM 293.6; (in pl. including both sexes) little children: *lactentes, infantes et ~i* AC 430.1.

pugil ~lis, *m.* A boxer: *striae illae nunc excurrebant obviam, nunc retrahebant se in se, plane sicut ~les* AM 315.1.

pugillo ~are ~avi ~atum, *intr., tr.* (intr.) To fight with the fists, box: *duo viri ratiociniis et rationciniis inter se ~ant sicut duo athletae* AM 55.6; (tr., app.) to measure with the hand: *manus Mea fundavit terram, et dextra Mea ~avit caelos* Isa. 48.13 (VR 136.4).

pugillus ~i, *m.* A handful: *pro ~is hordeorum* Ezek. 13.19 (AC 6767.3).

pugio ~onis, *m.* A dagger: *dimicantes ~onibus* AM 248.1; ES 1283.

pugna ~ae, *f.* **1** A fight, battle: *quod...parentes excitent puerulos liberos ad tales ~as* CI 344. **2** A spiritual fight, struggle: *spiritualis homo in ~a est* AC 81.3; *~ae Domini cum inferno* SS 103.1.

pugnator ~oris, *m.* A fight: *~ores contra mala et falsa* AE 357.11.

pugnax ~acis, *a.* Prone to fighting, pugnacious: *fit rationale...morosum, ~ax* AC 1964.2.

pugno ~are ~avi ~atum, *intr.* **1** To engage in physical combat, fight: *currus...fuerunt per quos ~abant* AC 8215.1; *pueri...colludebant...vociferando, ~ando, verberando* AM 218.2; (w. *cum*) *~abo Ego Ipse vobiscum* Jer. 21.5 (AC 6997.4); (w. *contra*) *ut ~et vir contra fratrem* Isa. 19.2 (AC 6756.3). **2** To engage in spiritual combat, fight: *Ecclesia Domini dicitur '~ans'* AC 59.1; *ex Domino, qui solus ~avit et vicit inferna* DD 18.2; (w. *contra*) *quod non ~averit contra concupiscentias* VI 66.2. **3** (of things) To be opposed, struggle: *~at vita unius contra vitam alterius* AC 6677; *varietates...quae disponuntur...ne quicquam ~et, sed concordent* ES 2086.

pugnotenus, *adv.* also written as two words **pugno tenus**. With the fist (exact meaning unclear): *nisi ~us laverint manus* Mark 7.3 (VR 671.2 1st edn.).

pugnus ~i, *m.* The clenched hand, fist: (as used in fighting) *lacessunt ~o* AC 822; *pueri ~is dimicantes* ES 3620; (as used in measuring) *accipiet...plenitudinem ~orum suorum suffimentum aromatum* Lev. 16.12 (AE 324.4).

pulcher ~chra ~chrum, *a.* (compar. *~chrior*, superl. *~cherrimus*) Pleasing to the eye, beautiful: *similes... sepulchris dealbatis, quae foris quidem apparent ~chra, intus vero plena sunt ossibus* Matt. 23.27 (AC 7046.2); *repraesentativa ~cherrima* AC 10194.

pulchre, *adv.* (compar. *~chrius*, superl. *~cherrime*) Beautifully: *per flammeum colorum variegationibus ~chre coruscum* AC 7743.

pulchritudo ~inis, *f.* Beauty: *confisa es ~ini tuae* Ezek. 16.15 (VI 79.3); (w. pl.) an instance or example of beauty: *quod faeminae [sint facie]...teneriore, candidiore, et inde ~ines* AM 218.1.

pulex ~icis, *m.* A flea: *sicut factum cum ~icibus* ES 4353; (prov.) *quod...non plus valeat...quam ~ex contra balaenam* VR 68.2.

pullulo ~are ~avi, *intr.* To send out shoots, sprout: *semen... ~at e terra* VR 374.3; (fig.) *vera et bona quae ex radicali medulloso corpore ~ant* ES 863.

pullus ~i, *m.* **1** The young of a bird, chick: *aquila super ~is...cubans* AM 15; *cum exclusit [avis] ~os ex ovis* VR 44.1. **2** The young of any animal: *cur Dominus ...sederit super ~o asinae* AE 31.7; *ita facere non potest ...fera contra catulos et ~os suos* VR 134.3.

pulmentum ~i, *neut.* A broth, soup: *ex diversis facit unum ~um* AM 444[a]; ES 3607.

pulmo ~onis, *m.* (anat.) The lungs (regarded as a single organ): *respiratio ~onis* DD 47.1; VR 37.2.

pulmonalis ~is ~e, *a.* = **pulmonaris**: AM 329.1.

pulmonaris ~is ~e, *a.* Of or relating to the lungs, pulmonary: *respiratio ~is* FI 19.2; *fides oralis et simul fiducia ~is* SE 65.

pulmonarius ~a ~um, *a.* = **pulmonaris**: ES 494.

pulmonicus ~a ~um, *a.* Of the lungs: *spiritus ~us* 'the breathing of the lungs' AE 251; *fistulis ~is* AM 416.4.

pulpitum ~i, *neut.* A raised platform for a speaker: *steterunt post quoddam ~um, prompti ad fandum* AM 381; (esp. in a church or similar building, for the preacher) a pulpit: *ascendit sacerdos ~um* AM 24; *vox sonans ex ~is* VR 14.3.

puls ~ltis, *f.* Porridge: *et coxit Jacob ~ltem* Gen. 25.29 (AC); *cerebrum, quod ~ltis instar sit* ES 3581.

pulsatilis ~is ~e, *a.* Characterized by rhythmic beats, throbbing, hammering: *quod...gressus ejus audiantur ~es, sicut qui ferreis calceis induti...incedunt* VR 797.6; (neut. as sb.) *audivi sicut stridorem dentium, et quoque sicut ~e* VR 460.1; (anat.) *fons ~is*, the anterior fontanelle: ES 4631.

pulsatio ~onis, *f.* Rhythmic movement, throbbing,

pulsation: *ut pulsaret, sicut cor...quae ~o mihi sensa* ES 3673.

pulsativus ~a ~um, *a.* Rhythmic, pulsating: *mihi nunc novam actionem monstrabit...molliter ~am* ES 884.

pulsatorius ~a ~um, *a.* = **pulsativus**: ES 1203.

pulsitivus ~a ~um, *a.* Possibly an alternative spelling, or else a misspelling, of **pulsativus**: ES 1556.

pulso ~are ~avi ~atum, *tr.* To hit repeatedly, keep striking: *quod non... ~averit in quoddam quod vocatur tympanum auris* AC 7361.1. **b** to knock on (a door): *~are januam* Luke 13.25 (AC 6806.2); (esp. absol.) to knock: *contulimus nos ad hanc portam, et ~avimus* AM 5.2. **c** to strike, play (a musical instrument): *pater omnis ~antis citharam et organum* Gen. 4.21 (AC); (absol.) *praecesserunt cantantes, post ~antes* Ps. 68.25 (AC 6742).

pulsus ~us, *m.* The rhythmical beat of the heart: *micatio cordis seu pulsus* DD 51.3; (as felt in other parts of the body) the pulse: *~us tunc, sicut digito sentiebam, erat aequalis* ES 1101; (as a very short period of time) a heartbeat: *minuto secundo seu minuto ~us pronuntiant omnia quae sentiunt* ES(M) 4557.

pulto ~are, *tr.* (app. nonce word formed to translate Hebrew *zid*) To cook (broth): *in lingua...originali est vox propria pultis, quasi diceres '~avit pultem'* AC 3316.1 (Gen. 25.29).

pulvillus ~i, *m.* A small cushion used as an amulet: *vae consuentibus ~os subter omnes axillas manuum Mearum* Ezek. 13.18 (AE 750.5).

pulvinar ~aris, *neut.* A pillow: *cum aurem dextram ponerem ad ~ar* ES 3957; (fig.) *ab experientia notum factum est, quod otium sit ~ar diaboli* ES 6072.

pulvis ~eris, *m.* **1** Finely divided matter, dust: *sceleton osseum...dilapsum in ~erem* AM 182.5; *cera colorata, in qua intus est ~is aut bitumen* DP 215.13. **b** a single particle of dust: *usque ad unumquemvis ~erem terrae* VR 54. **2** Dust as the covering layer of the ground: *percute ~erem terrae* Exod. 8.12 (AC); *praecipitantur homines in ~erem ut elevari nequeant* ES 676. **b** (as the surface on which one walks): *nubes ~is pedum Ipsius* Nahum 1.3 (AE 36.4). **3** Dust as the scene of combat (in quot. fig.): *apud eos qui in ~ere scholastico haerent* AC 521. **4** Dust as the type of the worthless or insignificant: *quis credere potest quod Dominus...irascatur ~eri tam miserabili, hoc est, hominibus...?* AC 1093.1.

pulvisculus ~i, *m.* A speck of dust: *sicut ~us qui adpositus pupillae oculi facit ut universum...non videat* AC 215; ES 3667.

punctatio ~onis, *f.* **1** Penetration with a sharp point, pricking: *per quosdam quasi lenes ~ones in facie* ES 541. **2** A diacritical mark or point in writing: *sunt ~ones super literis* SS 71.1.

punctatus ~a ~um, *a.* Covered with small points, starred, speckled: *induti coeruleo ~o aureis stellulis* AC 8030; (of Hebrew letters) written with a dot, dotted: *quod literae quaedam Hebraicae intus ~ae sint* SS 90.2.

punctio ~onis, *f.* A puncturing, pricking: *crabrones ...alati sunt et praediti aculeis quibus ~ones venenatas inferunt* AC 9331.1.

puncto ~are ~avi ~atum, *tr.* To write by means of dots or points: *literae vocales nec scribuntur, sed ~antur* SA 105 (= vii.5.[3]).

punctorius ~a ~um, *a.* Causing pricking, pungent: *quasi quoddam liquidum ~um seu urinosum* ES 1159; (neut. as sb.) a prickle: *dum...intrarent ea quae acuta essent, ~a et similia* ES 208; AC 5981.

punctulum ~i, *neut.* **1** A small point: *cum ~is flavidioribus sicut stellulis* ES 3636. **2** A brief moment, instant: *voluntas...ne quidem ~um fertur, nisi a jucundo* AM 461.6; ES 2878.

punctum ~i, *neut.* **1** A position in space, point: *ex ~is et dein lineis geometricis* VR 20.2; (as the smallest unit of space) *sunt... [calor et lux] in minimo ~o unum* SA 65 (= i.[1]). **2** A small mark, spot: *idea clausa apparuit instar ~i nigri* AC 6620; (in writing) a dot, point: *ne illud* [sc. *Verbum*] *quoad aliquod ~um alibi immutetur* SS 72; ES 2414. **b** a minute amount, jot: *quod ne quidem ~um justificationis sit a semet* VR 71.3. **3** A point in time, instant: *in ~o mortis* ES 1102; ES 3509. **4** A point in an argument or theory: [*dogmata*] *non in uno ~o aut momento conveniunt* SE 96; *non...est aliquod stabile ~um...ad quod...illa se referant* AM 57; *omne ~um ferre*, to occupy the whole position, be of supreme importance: *usque dum illa doctrina omne ~um mentis eorum hodie ferat* VR 98.1; *quod...doctrina justificationis...in Ecclesiis Christianis omne ~um ferat* VR 181.

pungens ~ntis, *a.* Causing pricking, pungent, prickly: *~ns grumus* CI 413; *vinula...fiunt...ex titillantibus ~ntia* DP 296.3; (neut. as sb.) AC 5981.

pungo ~gere ~xi ~ctum, *tr.* **1** To penetrate with a sharp point, prick: *solebant se gladiolis...usque ad sanguinem ~gere et lacerare* AC 2799.23. **2** (transf.) To inflict pain or distress, hurt: *vera...usque clam et tacite pugnant...atque ita ~gunt* AC 7320; *quod tunc jucunda...sint injucunda et ~gant* UJ(P) 242.

punicus ~a ~um, *a. Malus ~a*, the pomegranate tree: *vitis exaruit et ficus languet, malus ~a* Joel 1.12 (AC 8369.2).

punio ~nire ~nivi ~nitum, *tr.* To punish (a malefactor): *quod Deus ~niat hominem* CI 545; *sicut judex cum videt maleficum ~niri* AC 8223.3; also, to punish (a crime): *hoc severe ~nitur* ES 543.

punitio ~onis, *f.* The act of punishing, punishment: *angelici spiritus moderantur ~onem* AC 7808; (of a wicked act) *quod sit destructio et ~o conatuum apud illos* AC 8284.

punitor ~oris, *m.* One who punishes: *spiritus ~ores* AC 959.

pupa ~ae, *f.* A doll: *puellae...quaedam amicientes ~as* AM 218.2; CO 43; ES 4598.

pupilla ~ae, *f.* The pupil of the eye: *sicut homo [custodit] ~am oculi sui* DP 97; AE 37.

pupillus ~i, *m.* A child looked after by a guardian, ward: AC 7260; ES 1328; (fig.) *nos fuimus...tutores...ac ~us cujus tutelam gessimus, fuit fides nostra* VR 17.1.

puppis ~is, *f.* The stern of a ship, poop: *a procella... quae navem...a ~i...submerget* VR 32.9; VR 434.2.

pure, *adv.* (compar. *~ius*) **1** Without admixture, purely, wholly: *imaginum ~e materialium* AC 6814; *opus ~e Divinum* VR 123 titulus. **2** (transf.) In a pure manner: *quod...sancta Ecclesiae non plus occupent mentes...tametsi ~ius et interius* VR 695.1.

purgatio ~onis, *f.* Purification: *post partum die ~onis* Lev. 12.6 (AE 314.10); *~ones perstant continuo* ES 5509.

purgator ~oris, *m.* One who cleans; *caminorum ~or*, a chimney sweep: *sunt etiam spiritus inter Joviales, quos caminorum ~ores vocant quia in veste illis simili apparent et quoque facie fuliginosa* TE 79.

purgatorium ~i, *neut.* A medieval term used by Roman Catholics in the 18th century to denote the place where spirits are prepared for heaven after death: *e loco cruciatus quem vocant ~um* AR 784.1.

purgo ~are ~avi ~atum, *tr.* To make clean, cleanse: *~a prius interius poculi* Matt. 23.26 (AC 7046.2); *quod... ~averit caminos* ES 874; to purify (metals): *conflans et ~ans argentum* Mal. 3.3 (AC 8159.2); cf. *~are et defaecare illos sicut aurum et argentum* AC 8159.2.

purificatio ~onis, *f.* **1** The act of making clean, cleansing: *~ones fiunt per ignem* AC 7861. **2** A spiritual cleansing, purification: *~onem ab amoribus spurcis* AC 6804.11; *dies ~onis juxta Legem Mosis* Luke 2.22 (DD 9).

purificatorius ~a ~um, *a.* Of or for purification: *in ~is [sacrificiis]* AC 1823.1; (neut. as sb.) a means of purification: *quod cogitatio sit ~um et excretorium malorum* VR 659.

purifico ~are ~avi ~atum, *tr.* To make spiritually clean, purify: *status non adhuc ~atus* AC 7906.2; *~are bonum separando malum* AE 167.3; (w. *ab*) *homo... ~andus est a talibus* AC 6635.2; VI 30.1.

puritas ~atis, *f.* **1** Freedom from adulteration, purity: *sicut substantia coeli quoad ~atem* Exod. 24.10 (AC). **2** Freedom from evil, purity: *vitae ~as et integritas* AM 73.1.

purpura ~ae, *f.* (Gk.) **1** A deep red dye, purple: *~a... est color rubeus seu roseus permistus coeruleo* 3AD 1289. **2** Purple-dyed cloth: *divitem qui induebatur ~a et bysso* CI 365.2; *cum aulaeis...ex bysso, ~a et coccino* VI 55.1; *vidi duos angelos in ~a et coccino* AM 183.1. **3** A red cosmetic, rouge: *meretrici quae...fucat faciem ~a* VR 148.2; cf. *virgini ex ~a nativa* [sc. her natural high colour] *formosae* VR 109.3.

purpuraceus ~a ~um, *a.* Of purple colour: (neut. as sb.) *quod viderint...cogitationes per varie colorata, per ~a qualia in aulaeis pictis* AC 4627.2.

purpuratus ~a ~um, *a.* Dressed in purple: *sumus doctores ~i* AR 463.6.

purpureus ~a ~um, *a.* Of purple colour: *vestimentum ~um* DD 16.7 (John 19.5); *lux ~a, qualis est in nubibus ante solis ortum* VR 136.1.

purulentus ~a ~um, *a.* Purulent: (neut. as sb.) *graveolentia...est sicut nidor ~i ex pulmone* AE 237.8.

purus ~a ~um, *a.* (compar. *~ior*, superl. *~issimus*) **1** Composed of fine particles, lacking substance, pure: *[angeli] sunt...tam ~i et tenues ut ne quidem videri possint oculis* CI 228; *quod haec* [sc. the internal organs of insects] *contexta sint a ~issimis in natura* VR 12.4; *nubes ~ior et densior* AE 36.1; cf. *prius, quia est in se ~ius, non apparere potest posteriori quod in se est crassius* AM 31. **2** (of physical things) Unadulterated, unmixed, pure: *ex ~o auro* AC 6832.6; *sol, qui est ~us ignis* VR 12.2. **3** (of immaterial things) Unmixed, pure: *~us amor* AC 1690.3; *usque dum ~a justitia factus* AC 1813.1; *homo ~um verum et ~um bonum non sustinet* AC 7854; *a ~a ignorantia* ES 260. **4** Free from evil, morally pure: *altera [mulier]...ex castitate aut ex genuino amore conjugiali tota quanta intus ~a est* AC 7337.3; *quod ~is sint omnia ~a* AC 7343.2.

pusillanimus ~a ~um, *a.* Small-minded, pusillanimous: *congregatio simplicium, ad credendum facilium, et ~orum* VR 14.3; ES 915.

pusillulum ~i, *neut.* A very small amount, grain: *per experientiae ~um* ES 557.

pusillus ~a ~um, *a.* Very small in size or amount, tiny: *sicut aquae maximi oceani ad aquas ~i fontis* AC 7077; *fides fit ~a et egena* FI 28; ES 4695; (masc. as sb.) *ne contemnatis ullum ex ~is his* Matt. 18.10 (AC 254.4). **b** (neut. as sb.) a very small amount, grain, particle: *relictus erit homo ~um* Isa. 24.6 (AC 477.4); *dum ~um nigri in aquam mittitur* AC 1008.3; *~um cogitationis* ES 1911.

pustula ~ae, *f.* A pustule (on the skin), spot: *ex ~is, varicis et ulceribus* CI 553.2; *maculati...facie rubris ~is* ES 583.

pustulatus ~a ~um, *a.* Covered in pustules, spotty: *facies...verrucosae et ~ae* AC 8246.

putamen ~inis, *neut.* The peel or shell (of a seed or nut): *quod semina custodiantur ~inibus sicut fasciis* AM 399.2; *ambientes...sicut ~ina nucleos* VR 76.3; ES 269.

putatio ~onis, *f.* A pruning: *ramos earum* [*arborum*] *a teneris aptant et parant per sectiones et ~ones* AC 10514.

putatorius ~a ~um, *a.* Of or for pruning: *contundent...hastas suas in cultros ~os* Isa. 2.4 (AE 734.2).

puteo ~tere ~tui, *intr.* To emit a rotten smell, stink: *et ~tuit fluvius* Exod. 7.21 (AC); *quod...nihil gravius ~teat quam prophanatum verum* AC 7319; *ubi cavernae ~tent ex stercoribus* AM 477.8.

puteus ~i, *m.* **1** A well: *habitavit juxta ~um* Exod. 2.15 (AC); (containing substances other than water) *et vallis Siddim ~i ~i bituminis* Gen. 14.10 (AC); (fig.) *ex quibus...alii amores, ut ex suis ~is scaturiunt* ES 2910. **2** A pit: *et data ei clavis ~i abyssi* Rev. 9.1 (AR).

putidus ~a ~um, *a.* Foul-smelling from rottenness, stinking: *lignum ~um* VI 10; AM 182.5; (of persons) *~a meretrix* AC 876; AC 7337.3.

puto ~are ~avi ~atum, *tr., intr.* **1** To cut branches from (a tree), prune: *omnem...palmitem fructum ferentem, ~abit illum ut plus fructus ferat* John 15.2 (VI 2); ES 1681. **2** (intr.) To hold an erroneous opinion, think: (w. pred.) *mera cupiditas quam ~ant...voluntatem* AC 568.1; (w. acc. and inf.) *~at se credere sed fallitur* AC 7950.3; (pass. w. inf.) *hoc persuasivum...~atur esse fides* AC 7778.4; (w. *quod*) *~ant quod angeli sint formae aethereae* CI 183.1.

putor ~oris, *m.* A smell of rottenness, stink: *calor... educit nidores graveolentes et ~ores* CI 569; a thing or place full of such smells: *cum jucunditatibus...ranarum in stagnis, ut et serpentum in ~oribus* DP 40; *obsoleret aqua in ~orem et spongia in mucum* CO 28.

putredo ~inis, *f.* Putrefaction: *corpora a vermibus exesa, ~ine consumta* CI 312.2.

putrefacio ~facere ~feci ~factum, *tr.* To make to putrefy: *gangraenae quae...~facit vicina* VR 120.2.

putrefactio ~onis, *f.* Putrefaction: ES 5459.

putresco ~rescere ~rui, *intr.* To become rotten, putrefy: *corpus...frigescit et ~rescit* CI 446; *humus acescens aut ~rescens* VR 41.3.

putridus ~a ~um, *a.* Decaying, rotten: *quod moverent linguam versus dentem ~um* ES 4035.

putris ~is ~e, *a.* (compar. *~ior*) Decayed, rotten: *arbor ~is* VI 93; *corpus ~e* AM 240; ES 3764.

pygmeus ~i, *m.* (Gk.) A pygmy: *~i seu homunciones* AR 424.1.

pyra ~ae, *f.* (Gk.) A funeral pyre: *in conatu illum... super ~am conjiciendi* VR 510.1.

pyramidalis ~is ~e, *a.* Shaped like a pyramid, pyramidal: *orbiculus super basin ~em* AC 947; ES 4361.

pyramis ~idis, *f.* (Gk.) A pyramid: *spatiola...ornata parvis ~idibus cum condituris* AM 6.2.

pyrius ~a ~um, *a.* (Gk.) *Pulvis ~us*, gunpowder: *cum pulvere ~o accenso* VR 159.1; ES 3506.

pyropus ~i, *m.* (Gk.) A vague term for a fiery red gem such as a carbuncle, garnet, or ruby (but dist. from **rubinus** CI 382): *ponam ~um soles* [*fenestras*] *tuos* Isa. 54.12 (AC 655.1); *quatuor ordines lapis; ~us, topazius et smaragdus, primus ordo* Exod. 28.17 (SS 44.2); *nubem quae ~i instar, a flamma solis coruscabat* VR 112.1.

pyrum ~i, *neut.* also **pirum**. A pear: VR 109.3; ES 3858.

Pythagoreus ~a ~um, *a.* Of or belonging to Pythagoras: AM 153[a].2.

python ~onis, *m.* (Gk.) A sorcerer who foretells the future, soothsayer: *divinatores, auguratores, praestigiatores, ~ones* AC 3698.2; *illi qui falsa loquuntur ex dolo...ab antiquis dicti sunt... ~ones et serpentes arboris scientiae boni et mali* VR 324; *~onem agere* ES 3683.

pythonicus ~a ~um, *a.* (Gk.) Concerned with soothsaying or false prophecy: *ne appareant* [*oracula*] *aenigmatica, vel sicut ~a* SE 79; *idea ~a* ES 3683; (masc. as sb.) ES 3004.

pyxis ~idis, *m.* (Gk.) A box: *habebat...~idem tabaci* [*tabaki* Autograph] ES 5008; *~is magnetica*, a compass: *qui absque ~ide magnetica navigant* VR 165.3.

Q

qua, *indefinite adv.* In whichever direction, wherever: *super quatuor quadraturis illarum* [sc. *rotarum*] *~a ibant, ibant* Ezek. 1.17 (AC 8215.4).

quadragesimus ~a ~um, *a.* Fortieth: *quod jubilaeum quovis ~o nono anno proclamaretur* AC 493.

quadraginta, *indecl. adj.* Forty: *murus...centum ~ta quatuor cubitorum* Rev. 21.17 (AR).

quadrangularis ~is ~e, *a.* Of square shape: *urbs ~is sita est* Rev. 21.16 (AC); *magna apertura ~is* ES 4590.

quadrans ~ntis, *m.* A quarter: *per ~ntem horae* ES 660; ES 3161.

quadratura ~ae, *f.* (Bibl., app.) A course directed towards a point of the compass, quartering: *super quatuor ~is illarum* [sc. *rotarum*] *qua ibant, ibant* Ezek. 1.17 (AC 8215.4).

quadratus ~a ~um, *a.* Square: *vidi quod* [*domus*] *esset ~a* AM 103.3; VR 48.1.

quadrijugis ~is ~e, *a.* Yoked in a group of four: *cum aurigis qui ~es equos alligant post currum* CC 9.4.

quadrimestre ~is, *neut.* A period of four months: *quod adhuc ~e sit, donec messis veniat* John 4.35 (AR 645.2).

quadringenti ~ae ~a, *pl. adj.* Four hundred: *et affligent illos ~is annis* Gen. 15.13 (AC).

quadro ~are ~avi, *intr.* **1** To reduce to a square: *de ~ando circulo* DP 335.3. **2** (transf.) To fit neatly, square: *rationalia...~ant cum luce mundi spiritualis* CI 355; *nullus spiritus ~at ad meum corpus quam meus* ES 3158.

quadrupedus ~a ~um, *a.* Typical of four-footed animals: *internoscuntur per id quod modo ~o, ut ita dicatur, agant* AC 4227.3; ES 1819.

quadrupes ~edis, *a.* **1** Four-footed: *animalia terrestria seu ~edia* ES 567; (masc. as sb.) a four-footed creature, quadruped: *reperet sicut ~es* DP 275. **2** Typical of a quadruped: *ut sonus sit quasi ~es* ES 1031; *spiritus qui loquuntur modo ~ede quasi pulsatorio* ES 1203.

quadruplex ~icis, *a.* Fourfold, quadruple: *per atmosphaeras triplices vel ~ices* ES 418.

quadruplicatim, *adv.* In a quadruple manner, in a fourfold rhythm: *spiritus...qui...agunt ~im* ES 1127.

quadruplicato, *adv.* With a fourfold rhythm: *loquela quorundam spirituum quae terminatur ~o* AC 1763.1.

quadruplicatus ~a ~um, *a.* Fourfold, quadruple: *cum terminis ~is* ES 1036; ES 1127.

quaero ~rere ~sivi ~situm, *tr., intr.* **1** To try to find or obtain, look for, seek: *Dominus quem vos ~ritis* Mal. 3.1 (AC 6804.3); *regnum Domini non ~runt sed mundum* AC 7012; *Jehovam non ~runt* Isa. 31.1 (VI 30.2). **b** (intr., w. indir. qu.): *palpitant circum parietes, et ~runt ubi victus* VR 7. **2** (intr., w. inf.) To attempt, seek (to do something): *~sivit occidere Moschen* Exod. 2.15 (AC); *fratres tui foris stant, ~rentes tibi loqui* Matt. 12.47 (AE 46). **3** (tr.) To ask (someone) a question: (w. dir. qu.) *alloquutus illum ~sivi, quid rei nunc?* AM 2.1; (w. indir. qu.) *~sivimus illum, quid nunc scribit* VR 35.5; ES 729; (impers. pass.) *~ritur...quomodo paenitentia agenda est* VR 530. **b** (intr., w. indir. qu.): *~rebant an tales possunt angeli fieri* AC 6929; *~sivit cur ita* FI 42.

quaeso, *interj.* Pray, please, I beg of you: *legat ~o illa quae...supra allata sunt* DD 21; *intrate, ~o, penitius in cogitationem meam* VR 26.1.

quaestio ~onis, *f.* An inquiry, investigation: *quod possent res cujusvis ~onis...illuminare* AM 231.2; (generally) a question: *ex more illorum est ut non directe ad ~ones respondeant* AC 7172.

quaestus ~us, *m.* **1** The making of money, gain, reward: *redibit* [*Tyrus*] *ad ~um meretricium suum* Isa. 23.17 (AC 2466.5); (pl.) *~us ex judicio fecerunt* CI 462[a].3; AM 376. **2** Money earned by services, hire: *devovi ~um eorum Jehovae* Mic. 4.13 (AC 7770.5); *~um argenti non ceperunt* Judg. 5.19 (AE 447.4).

Quakerianus: see **Quaquerianus**.

quale ~is, *neut.* Quality, nature: *spectant...omnes ex ipsa qualitate seu ex eorum ~i* AC 1258; *hoc, quia non habet ~e, est in se nihil* VR 21.2; *facit...fides formam, pulchram secundum ~e ejus* FI 31.

qualificatio ~onis, *f.* The endowment (of something) with qualities: *~o rei in spiritualibus fit per ordinationem...a Domino* AC 10217.6.

qualifico ~are ~avi ~atum, *tr.* To endow with qualities: *bonum ut sit bonum, erunt vera quae ~abunt* AC 6916; *~atum statum* AM 291.2; ES 767 titulus.

qualis ~is ~e, *a.* see also **quale**. **1** (interrog. with indir. qu.) Of what sort, what kind of: *scrutari ~is hominis vita est* AC 6704; *describitur... ~is fides futura est* AE 9.4. **2** (rel.) Of the sort which: *tantae moles ~es sunt planetae* AC 6697; *loculus in ~i corpora mortua reponuntur* ES 4658. **b** (correlated w. *talis*): *[Verbum] in sensu ultimo scriptum est tali stylo, ~i apud Prophetas* SS 8.

qualiscumque: see **qualiscunque**.

qualiscunque qualiscunque qualecunque, *rel. adj.* also **qualiscumque**. Of whatever kind: *homo qui esset Ecclesiae, quicunque et qualiscunque* AC 288; *inde ...trahit vitam moralem...in externis, qualiscunque sit in internis* CI 492.

qualitas ~atis, *f.* **1** The essential nature of anything, quality: *[angeli] spectant...omnes ex ipsa ~ate, seu ex eorum quali* AC 1258; *ipsam ~atem...trahunt ex sua origine* AS 310. **2** A distinguishing feature, characteristic, quality: *proprietates, ~ates et attributa unius Dei* VR 9.3; *ex hac ~ate ordinis in universo* VR 60.1.

qualiter, *adv.* **1** (interrog.) In what way, how: *non refert ~er apparent* AC 7372. **2** (rel.) In the way in which: *alios vultus praeferre quam ~er cogitant* ES 2456.

qualitercumque: see **qualitercunque**.

qualitercunque, *adv.* also **qualitercumque**. In whatsoever manner, however: *credit quod salvetur... ~que...vixerat* AC 7272.2; AC 10265.

quam, *adv.* **1** (in exclamations) How...!: *oh quam felix status est angelorum* AM 356. **2** (in indir. qu.) To what extent, how: *patet quam elegans...est loquela illorum* CI 238. **3** (after compar.) Than: *plures quam mille advenas* DP 265.2; *quam ut*, than so as to: *plura sunt quam ut dici possint* AC 50.1; ES 4466. **4** (after *alius*, *aliter*, etc.) Than: *prorsus aliud est ex perceptione nosse quam ex doctrina discere* AC 521; *homo vix aliter de Deo cogitat...quam ex nuda voce Deus* VR 4.2. **5** (after negs.) Other or otherwise than, except: *nemo novit quam Dominus solus* AC 1505; *quae [incredulitas] non dissipatur quam per media a Domino provisa* AC 1771.1; *hi gradus aperiuntur...non perceptibiliter... quam post ejus excessum e mundo* DP 32.3; *is non potest non credere, quam quod homines sint* TE 3.1. **6** (w. superl.) As much as possible: *in altera vita sunt quam inimicissimi* ES 3775. **7** *tam...quam*, as much... as, both...and: see **tam**.

quamdiu, *adv.* For as long as, so long as: *a quibus ~u est pugna separari nequeunt* AC 1580; VR 69.3; (correlated w. *tamdiu*) *~u hoc manet, tamdiu homo est mortuus* AC 731.

quammaxime, *adv.* As much as possible: *tale eos ~e [quam maxime Tafel] movet* ES 2503 (J D Odhner).

quammulti: see **quamulti**.

quamobrem, *rel. adv.* (i.e., *quam ob rem*) For which reason: *~em etiam preces illorum...parum audiuntur* AC 8179.3; AM 6.6.

quamoptime, *adv.* As well as possible: *~e id datur percipere* AC 3404.2.

quamplures ~es ~a, *pl. adj.* Very many: *similiter se habet cum ~ibus aliis* AC 6917.2; ES 4389.

quampluries, *adv.* Very many times: *opprobria mihi dixerunt ~es* ES 1141.

quamplurimus ~a ~um, *a.* = **quam** (sense 6), and **plurimus**. In very large amounts or numbers: ES 1165; 3AD 5406.

quamquam, *rel. adv. w. indic.* Although: *~am nemo potest justus esse nisi cui merita passionis Domini... communicantur, id tamen in justificatione fit* Council of Trent in SE 5(b).

quamsaepe, *adv.* Very often: ES 1141.

quamulti ~orum, *m. pl.* (perh. an error for *quammulti* or *quam multi*) Very many: ES 318 (J D Odhner).

quamvis, *rel. adv. w. indic.* Although: *quod angeli non sciant quid tempus, ~is omnia apud illos successive progrediuntur* CI 163.

quando, *rel. adv.* **1** At the time at which, when: *de statu Ecclesiae, ~o omnes cognitiones veri...deperditae sunt* SS 13.1; *~o...in lucem spiritualem venitis... inquirite* AR 875.3. **2** In such circumstances that, when: *~o unus amat alterum sicut se...* AC 1013.2. **3** Seeing that, since: *~o in stupore...eram, adstitit mihi...angelus* VR 35.2. **4** = **quandoque**: *quod...spiritus transportari videantur... ~o sicut fulminis velocitate* ES 354 titulus; ES 1641.

quandocunque, *rel. adv.* Whenever: *~que Domino beneplacet* ES 3413.

quandoque, *adv.* **1** At times, on occasion: *brachium*

...~*que in conspectum venit* AC 878.8; CI 52; ~*que*... ~*que*, at one time...at another: *loquutus...sum cum illis* ...~*que cum uno*, ~*que cum pluribus in consortio* CI 74.1. **2** = **quandoquidem**: Judg. 6.22 (AC 1925.3).

quandoquidem, *rel. adv.* Seeing that (in quot. ellipt.): *dixit Gideon, Domine Jehovih*, ~*em vidi angelum Jehovae, faciem ad faciem* Judg. 6.22 (AC 4299.4).

quantillum, *rel. adv.* To however little extent: *ut*... ~*um ejicit* [*digitum*]...*torquetur et cruciatur* CI 400.4.

quantitas ~atis, *f.* Size in respect of magnitude or multitude, quantity: *ex* ~*ate quae est magnitudinis et*... *ex* ~*ate quae est multitudinis* AC 3934.1; *secundum malorum...qualitates et* ~*ates* AC 8306.

quantopere, *rel. adv.* (i.e., *quanto opere*) To how great an extent, how much: *ex his constare potest* ~*e interest colere Ipsum Dominum* AC 10642.3.

quantuluscunque ~lacunque ~lumcunque, *rel. adj.* However small: *haec ipsa*, ~*lacunque sunt...veneno infecta sunt* Book of Concord in VR 464.8.

quantum, *rel. adv.* To the extent that, in so far as: *tenet illos in libero*, ~*um in bono* CI 45; ~*um scio* 'so far as I know' ES 2047. **b** (correlated w. *tantum*): *annon* ~*um frigescit affectio...tantum frigescat cogitatio...?* AM 34.

quantumvis, *rel. adv.* For all that, although: ~*vis omnia succedunt...in coelo sicut in mundo, usque tamen angelis nulla notio...temporis...est* CI 162; DP 251.3.

quantus ~a ~um, *interr.* and *rel. adj.* **1** How great: (in indir. qu.) *inde* ~*us Domini amor sit, constare potest* AC 6645.3; (pl.) how many: *constare potest* ~*a arcana latent in Verbo* AE 9.6; (neut. as sb.) how much: *ostensum...est* ~*um vere humani apud tales sit* ES 1764. **b** (in exclamations): *oh, qualis et* ~*a obesitas saeculi* AM 478.2. **2** As large as: *magna multitudo hominum*... ~*am tellus posset nutrire* AC 8116; (correlated w. *tantus*) *vita...quae tanti aestimanda* ~*i sunt vera* AC 7935. **3** *Totus* ~*us*, in all respects, completely: *una* [*mulier*]...*tota* ~*a putida* AC 7337.3; VR 23.1.

quapropter, *adv.* For which reason: ~*er illi... formaverunt sibi simulacra* VR 11.2; (in qu.) for what reason: *et dixit illis* ~*er facitis verbum istud...?* Exod. 1.18 (AC).

quaquaversum, *adv.* In all directions: *angeli... vertunt et flectunt suas facies*... ~*um* CI 143; AM 105.

Quaquerianus ~a ~um, *a.* also **Quakerianus**. Of or belonging to the Quakers: *animae* ~*ae* ES 423.

quare, *rel.* and *interr. adv.* **1** For which reason, wherefore: *inde est quod homo Ecclesiae...sit...angelus caeli*, ~*re etiam post mortem in caelum venit* VR 1. **b** *quia*... ~*re*, because...therefore: *quia ignoratur*... ~*re paucis hic dicetur* AM 32. **2** For what reason, why: *disquirebatur* ... ~*re inferioris conditionis homines...eligerentur* ES 1216.

quartanus ~a ~um, *a.* Of or belonging to the fourth; (masc. as sb.) the people of the fourth generation: *visitare iniquitatem super tertianos et* ~*os* Num. 14.18 (AR 322.2).

quartus ~a ~um, *a.* Fourth: *de* ~*o et quinto gradu* AC 7378; ~*o* (as adv.), fourthly: DP 157.7.

quartusdecimus ~tadecima ~tumdecimum, *adj.* also spelled as two words **quartus decimus**. Fourteenth: *ex significatione 'diei* ~*tidecimi'* AC 7842; *ad* ~*tum decimum diem mensis* Exod. 12.6 (AC).

quasi, *adv.*, *conj.* **1** (adv., to apologize for or tone down an expression) As it were, so to speak: *plagae...sunt angelo*... ~*si inscriptae* AS 134; *spiritus*... ~*si detrahit occipitium* ES 1748; (postponed) *cum ad eos per pontem* ~*si venirem* ES 1579. **2** (adv.) As good as, practically, nearly: *putantes se* ~*si deos esse* AC 562; *hoc nesciunt* ~*si* ES 3715; (w. numerals) about: ~*si 2000 viri... ascendent* Josh. 7.3 (AC 4539.3). **3** (conj.) As if: *interior homo percipit, sicut foret* ~*si quis indicaret* AC 1701.

quasso ~are ~avi ~atum, *tr.* To shake up, shatter: ~*ata sunt omnia ossa mea* Jer. 23.9 (AE 313.11); *apparuerunt...quaedam* [*loca*] ~*ari et tremere sicut a terrae motu magno* AE 400.2; CO 57.3.

quatenus, *adv.* To the extent that, in so far as: *ut objecta nihil curent nisi* ~*us ea influunt in ejus ideam communem* AC 920.2; (w. ellipse of verb) *quod assimilarem illos cum aquilis*, ~*us aves rapaces* ES 4673.

quater, *adv.* Four times: *in hunc statum modo ter aut quater immissus sum* AC 1883.

quaternus ~a ~um, *a.* Divisible into four segments, fourfold: *per duodecim* [*lapides ephodi*] *in* ~*o ordine* VR 218.

quattuor: see **quatuor**.

quattuordecim: see **quatuordecim**.

quatuor, *indecl. a.* also **quattuor**. Four: *e* ~*or plagis mundi* VR 90.1.

quatuordecim, *indecl. a.* also **quatt-**. Fourteen: AC 1670.

quaversum, *adv.* = **quaquaversum** (perh. error). In all directions: *si* ~*um disquirat* AM 333.2.

-que, *conj.* (added as suffix to the word it connects). And: *nec novit quid vita aeterna...sique scit, non credit* AC 81.2; ES 406.

quemadmodum, *rel. adv.* **1** In the way in which, as: ~*um scriptum est in Lege Domini* Luke 2.23 (DD 9); VR 8.3; *jactabat...ulnas* ~*um infans recens natus*

CI 203.3. **2** As it were, as if: *universum infernum...est non modo ~um nihilum, sed est prorsus nihilum* DP 19.2.

queo, *intr.* (only used in pres. indic. and subj.) To be able: (usu. in neg. or quasi-neg. sentences) *plura arcana ...quam...dici queant* AC 37; *nusquam intelligi queunt aliae familiae* AC 1254; *non quimus cogitare de Deo universi* AM 78.6; (in positive sentences) *quod ab homine credi queat* AC 6698; CI 153.

quercetum ~i, *neut.* A plantation of oaks: *usque ad ~um Moreh* Gen. 12.6 (AC).

quercus ~us, *f.* An oak tree: *olea, vitis, cedrus, populus, ~us* SS 18.3; *in sylva ex fagis, aesculis et ~ubus constante* AM 78.2.

querela ~ae, *f.* A complaint: *ex eorum lamentatione et ~a* ES 318.

querimonia ~ae, *f.* A complaint: *ex significatione 'jurgari' quod sit gravis ~a* AC 8566.

queror queri questus sum, *intr.* To complain: *tentatio haec in eo consistit quod querantur* AC 8352.1; *amarissime questi sunt de injuria ista* ES 220.

qui quae quod, *rel. adj.* (nom. and acc. neut. pl. *qua* ES 208, ES 2178; abl. pl. *queis* ES 1277) see also **quo**. Which: *a hieroglyphicis Aegyptiorum, quibus... utebantur* AC 6692.1; *puella cui non perceptio* AC 6740; (w. inclusion of antecedent) *loquela cum mortuis similem effectum ederet quem miracula* DP 134[a].

quia, *conj.* **1** Because: *quod moralis vita...sit charitatis vita, est quia exercitia moralis vitae et charitatis sunt eadem* VR 444.1. **2** (app. introducing indic. speech) That: *respondit Jesus, tu dicis quia* [Gk. *hoti*] *Rex sum Ego* John 18.37 (AC 3009).

quicumque: see **quicunque**.

quicunque quaecunque quodcunque, *rel. adj.* and *pron.* also **quicumque**. **1** (as rel.) Whoever, whatever: *omnes...quicunque in coelis sunt* AC 6706; *infernales delectat...malum facere, quocunque modo id fieri potest* AC 7392.2. **2** (adj.) Any whatever: *sacrificia quaecunque...vocantur munera* AC 349.1; *quod doctrinalia fidei conjunxerint cum cupiditatibus, et quidem cum quibuscunque* AC 569; *privantur... facultate cogitandi verum de quacunque re* CI 3. **3** (pron.) Anyone or anything whatever: *in...odio contra quemcunque qui non illum colit* AC 7272.2; *absque ulla misericordia occiderent quoscunque* AC 7032.3.

quid: see **quis**.

quidam quaedam quoddam, *adj.* and *pron.* (nom. and acc. neut. sg. also *quiddam*) **1** (as adj.) Some or other (i.e., not further defined): *super foliis cujusdam arboris* AC 8377; *fit similis cuidam animali* VR 34.3. **2** (as adj.) Of a certain kind, a sort of: *non perfectio quaedam est nisi conjuncta sint* AC 1203; *nesciunt quod naturalis quaedam mens datur* ES 1827. **3** (pl., as adj.) Some (but not all): *quaedam societates tales ad resipiscentiam...tentant cogere* AC 7364. **4** (as pron.) Some one (or thing): *quod...is appareat in quoddam simile inanimato verti* AC 6849.3; AM 315.6; *quiddam horroris aspectus ejus incutiebat* ES 1080; ES 1084. **5** (pl., as pron.) Some (but not all): *conscientiam hodie quibusdam notam* AC 608; *vidi...quosdam illorum* AC 7251; *quidam...quidam*, some...others: *talis inde color fit, in quibusdam...lucidus, in quibusdam ...fuscus* AC 6991; CI 179.

quidem, *particle.* **1** (to contrast a clause w. a following one) Indeed, to be sure, admittedly: *potes ~em loqui ex apparentia...sed non potes id cogitare* AM 233.4; *rictus, qui instar ~em leonis latus, sed coloris tetri* ES 1687; *quae nisi demonstrentur, ~em agnosci possunt sed usque non comprehendi* DP 279.1. **2** (to add a fresh point) *Et ~em*, and what is more, and in fact: *executio judicii, quae fit per spiritus, et ~em per malos* AC 1320; VR 827; ES 4049. **3** *Ne ~em*, not even: see **ne[1]**.

quies ~etis, *f.* Rest, repose: *in die quo ~etem daturus est Jehovah tibi* Isa. 14.3 (AC 6852); *ad aquas ~etum deducet me* Ps. 23.2 (AE 71.2); *quia in utroque latere ~etis causa decumbere debeam* ES 587.

quiescentia ~ae, *f.* The process of becoming inactive, quiescence: *sciendum quod non sit separatio [malorum] sed quod sit ~a* AC 1581.

quiesco quiescere quievi, *intr.* **1** (of persons) To cease from activity, rest: *et quievit [Deus] in die septimo ab omni opere Suo* Gen. 2.2 (AC); *vidi eos sic quievisse per semihorium* CI 411; *non possunt quiescere, sed quadam animi cupiditate auferuntur ut ea nuntient aliis* ES 986. **2** (of things) To cease moving, come to rest: *et quievit arca...super montibus Ararat* Gen. 8.4 (AC); *quando [mare] quiescere non potest* Isa. 57.20 (AC 6669.1). **3** (of immaterial things) To cease from activity, become inactive, stop: *desinit...spirituale in naturali, et ibi quiescit* AC 8106.4; *non potest amor quiescere nisi faciat* AM 183.3; (neut. pl. of pres. pple. as sb.) *totidem [gradus] in quiescentibus, ex quibus globus terraqueus consistit* VR 33.

quietatio ~onis, *f.* Repose, tranquillity: *qui fecerit ignitum odoris ~onis Jehovae* Num. 15.14 (AC 8013.3).

quiete, *adv.* (compar. *~ius*, superl. *~issime*) Quietly: AC 4330.3.

quietudo ~inis, *f.* Repose, tranquillity: *ubi tanta amoenitas seu amoena ~o esset* ES 2612.

quietus ~a ~um, *a.* Quiet, tranquil: *cave tibi, et ~us esto* Isa. 7.4 (AC 6952.6); *in statu ~o* AC 7721.

quilibet quaelibet quodlibet, *adj.* and *pron.* also spelled as two words **qui libet** (AM 423). **1** Any you like to name, whatever: **a** (adj.): *ad quemlibet minimum apicem* AC 7933.3; *quaelibet eorum species* VR 12.5. **b** (pron.): *potestas intromittendi quoslibet in coelum* AC 7318.2. **2** (pron.) Each one severally: *viginti quatuor seniores...habentes quilibet citharas* Rev. 5.8 (AC 420.5); *ante quemlibet erat mensa* AM 268.2.

quilibetcumque: see **quilibetcunque**.

quilibetcunque quaelibetcunque quodlibetcunque, *adj.* also **quilibetcumque**. Any whatever: *ad credendum falsa quaelibetcunque* AC 8315.

quin, *adv.* and *conj. w. subj.* **1** (adv., to reject a previous suggestion) Rather: *invenit Josephus gratiam in oculis ejus ut ministraret ipsi; quin praefecit eum domui suae* Gen. 39.4 (2AD 410); (w. *imo*) *alterum [bonum]...usque potest esse non bonum, quin imo malum* AC 3408. **2** (conj.) In such a way that...not, so as to prevent: *homo...non potest illustrari, quin credat quod malum sit ab ipso* AC 761; *hos nihil retardat quin ferantur* CI 270.4; *non potui amplius retinere risum quin erumperet* VR 80.5; (so, also) *quin ut*: *non potuisset aliter, quin ut homo...incideret* VR 123.6. **b** (ellipt.) *non quin*, not that...not: *non quin perfici queat qui in bono* ES(M) 4645. **3** (conj., w. neg.) But that, without: *ut ne quidem ad primum limen atrii coelorum approximare possint, quin retro fugiant* AC 34.1; *prope accessit [hic status] ad pacem, sed quin pax esset* ES 221. **b** *non posse quin*, to be unable not to: *ex eo quod non potuissent quin aliquid repraesentarent* AC 870.2; VR 23.2. **4** (conj., w. expressions of denial) That...not: *non...negari potest, quin unum et alterum sit liberum* DP 43; *id non tollit apud eos, quin Dominus sit Messias promissus* ES 3537.

quinam quaenam quodnam, *rel. adj.* **1** (in dir. qu.) Which, who?: *quinam magis se apertos habere oculos... credunt...?* AC 206.1. **2** (in indir. qu.) Which in particular: *significant...aliquid doctrinale; sed quodnam nemo scire potest* AC 402.2; *circumspexi, quinam angeli tunc adessent* AM 232.1.

quindecim, *indecl. a.* Fifteen: *mensae ~im ab uno latere* AM 6.1.

quindecimus ~a ~um, *a.* Fifteenth: *usque ad ~um diem* AM 6.2.

quingenarius ~a ~um, *a.* Of five hundred: *numerus ~us* 'a number in the five hundreds' ES 906.

quingenti ~ae ~a, *pl. a.* Five hundred: Ezek. 48.16 (AE 417.3).

quinquageni ~ae ~a, *pl. a.* Forming a group of fifty: *principes ~orum* Exod. 18.21 (AC); *ingressae ibi sunt [sirenes] turmatim, ~ae, centenae* ES 4573.

quinquagesimus ~a ~um, *a.* Fiftieth: *die ~o* AC 2252.3.

quinquaginta, *indecl. a.* Fifty: AM 5.1.

quinque, *indecl. a.* Five: *cum ~que corporis sensibus* CI 402.

quinquies, *adv.* Five times: *quater vel ~es* ES 653.

quinto ~are ~avi ~atum, *tr.* To take a fifth part of: *et ~et [Pharao] terram Aegypti* Gen. 41.34 (AC).

quintuplicatus ~a ~um, *a.* Fivefold, quintuple: ES 579.

quintuplus ~a ~um, *a.* Five times as large, quintuple: *quod multiplicaret portionem Benjaminis prae portione omnium ~um* AC 4592.5 (Gen. 43.34).

quintus ~a ~um, *a.* Fifth: *~us status progressionis* AC 6772. **b** *~o*, fifthly: DP 157.8. **c** *~a essentia*, quintessence: *tunc fit illa [virtus] nobilis sicut ~a essentia abstractis inquinamentis* AM 105.

quintusdecimus ~tadecima ~tumdecimum, *a.* also spelled as two words **quintus decimus**. Fifteenth: *~todecimo die* Num. 33.3 (AC 8017); *per ~tum decimum* AC 8400.

quinus ~a ~um, *a.* Five: *unum mille coram increpatione unius, coram increpatione ~orum fugientes* Isa. 30.17 (AC 5291.8).

quippe, *adv.* To be sure, indeed: *~pe haec spectant Dominum* AC 1568.2; *~pe omne malum contagiosum est* AC 6666.3; *neque eriges tibi statuam, ~pe quam odit Jehovah* Deut. 16.22 (AC 10643.4).

quis[1] quae quid, *interr. pron.* and *adj.* **1** (pron., in dir. qu.) Who, what: *hic cum me vidit, dixit, 'Quis es?'* AM 326.1; *quid meditaris?* AM 380.2. **b** *quid* (w. dat.)... *cum* (w. abl.)..., what has...to do with...?: *quid mihi juveni cum tam sublimi theoremate?* VR 697.6. **2** (in rhetorical qu.) **a** Is there anyone who...?: *quis amat personam nisi ex qualitate voluntatis...ejus...?* VR 418. **b** (neut.) is...anything?: *quid Deus nisi natura?* AM 380.1. **3** (neut.) **a** What is the meaning of...?: *respondit, 'Quid uxor, hoc nescio'* VR 80.1; AR 962.4. **b** what is this, that...?: *quid loquimini?* AR 675.3. **c** (ellipt.)...?, what use is it?: *sed quid talia memorare, non crederentur* ES 4639. **d** (in indignant qu.) *quid...?*, ...indeed!: *quid schismaticum, est haereticum* VR 112.1. **4** *Quid*, in what way, how: *haec in mundo spirituum, adhuc perfectius in coelo; quid non coram Domino...?* AC 1274; *cum sphaera procreationis illic vadit, quid tunc non...usque ad vermes* AM 397; *quid tunc usquam reformari possit homo...?* ES 2292. **5** (pron., in indir. qu.) Who, what: *sciebant quis esset* ES(M) 4558;

quid amare proximum dicetur VR 407. **6** (adj., in dir. qu.) Which, what: *dixit, 'Quid discrimen?'* AM 326.3; *quae...faemina potest unire amorem suum frigori...?* AM 331.2; *quis pius et sapiens non vult scire sortem vitae suae post mortem?* VR 568.1. **b** (in exclamations): *oh quae enormitas!* VR 135.1.

quis[2] quid, *indefinite pron.* **1** (w. neg. or conditional or sim. clause) Anyone, anything, any: *sicut non quis operari potest nisi ei sit brachium* VR 84; *quod nusquam possint quid efficere* ES 229; *...si quis bonum illis tribuit* CI 9.3; *apud liberos, si quos gigneret* DP 281.4; *quantum quis semet amat tantum odit proximum* AC 1047. **2** Someone, something: *'fera' quid dignius...involvit* AC 774; *potest...quis amice loqui...et tamen inimicus esse* DP 104.1; (neut. w. gen.) *per affectionis quid* AC 4186.2.

quisnam quaenam quidnam, *interr. pron.* **1** Who, which: *disceptabatur quisnam eorum major esset* AC 8301.4. **2** Is there anyone...who...?: *quisnam qui aliquem amat, non timet ei malefacere?* DP 140.

quispiam quaepiam quippiam (*or* quidpiam), *a.* Anyone or anything at all: *audies illum plus rationalem zeloten, quam quempiam alium* AM 499; *non enim amat quempiam extra se* VR 45.1.

quisquam quisquam quicquam, *pron.* and *adj.* (nom. and acc. neut. sg. also *quidquam*) **1** (in neg. or virtually neg. clauses) Anyone, anything: *num quisquam ...potest cogitare...?* DP 100.1; *nisi Dominus iterum... veniat...nec quisquam potest salvari* VR 3.1; (neut. as adv.) *nec quicquam differens ab homine* CI 74.1. **2** (in positive clause, as adj.) Any: *dum quisquam spiritus aut aliqui angeli comparent aut quicquam existit* ES 1699.

quisque quaeque quodque, *pron.* Each: *Dominus apparet cuique secundum quale ejus* AC 6832.2; *sumite quisque patellam* AM 16.1.

quisquiliae ~liarum, *f. pl.* Rubbish, garbage: *in conclavibus...sunt sordes et ~liae omnis generis* AM 443; ES 2773.

quisquis quisquis quicquid, *pron.* Whoever, whatever: *quisquis...fecerit voluntatem Patris Mei* Matt. 12.50 (AC 6756.5); *quicquid procedit a Domino* AM 389.

quivis quaevis quodvis, *a.* **1** Any: *ut...fit a quovis haeretico* SS 26.2. **2** Each: *dedit quamvis partem suam obviam alteri* Gen. 15.10 (AC); *campana quavis hora sonabat* ES 2248.

quo, *interr.* and *rel. adv.* **1** (interr.) To what place, whither: *nec sciunt quo illi vadunt* ES 4681; (also. app.) whence: *ventus flat, et homo nescit quo venit* ES 4273; (also) where: *nescientes quo habitent* ES 2288. **2** (rel.) To which place, whither: *quo vertit interiora, etiam vertit faciem* CI 272. **3** *Quo...eo...* (w. compar.), by as much...by so much..., the...the...: *quod quo sapientiores angeli sunt, eo clarius percipiant hoc* CI 79.

quoad, *prep. w. acc.* **1** In respect of, with regard to: *diversitates...~ad amorem* AM 317; *fiunt...vulpes ~ad astutiam* VR 13.4; *ex auditis illis ~ad nomina* VR 16.1. **2** *~ad tempus*, for a time: *separari ~ad tempus a naturali* AC 6100; *possunt ~ad tempus in mundo spirituum esse* ES 4579.

quocunque, *adv.* Whithersoever, to whatever place: *~que vertimus acies oculorum nostrorum* AM 13.3.

quod, *conj. w. subj.* (or *indic.*) **1** (to introduce indir. speech) That: *dixi quod universa natura sit a Deo* VR 79.4. **b** (after sbs.): *fugiebat cum clamore, quod nollet talis amoris simulachrum habere* ES 1082. **2** (after vbs. of knowing, perceiving, etc.) That: *percipimus quod cogites de creatione* VR 79.1; *ut pateat quod religio illis insit* VR 282. **b** (after sbs.) to the effect that: *doctrina... quod fides separari possit* AC 355. **3** (after expressions of willing, causing, etc.) That: *quod angeli prorsus non velint...quod illis aliquid veri et boni tribuatur* AC 8192.2; *quod Jehovah Deus in mundum...descenderit, erat causa ut redemptionem ageret* VR 86. **4** The fact that: *quod usque mali sint mali...est in ipsis subjectis* VR 43.2; *quod Jehovah Deus factus sit homo...sequitur ut conclusum* VR 101.1. **5** (w. indic.) As for what: *quod redemptionem concernit* VR 114. **b** *quod ad*, as for: *quod ad gentem Anglicam* VR 807. **6** (w. indic.) Because: *quia extrema sunt [sensualia]...et quod iis non altius se elevare permittendum* AC 746; (app. w. subj.) *eo stupidiores...nempe quod scientias applicuerint ad indagationem spiritualium* ES 250.

quodammodo, *adv.* In a certain manner, to some extent: *quod ita sit, ~o etiam constare potest ex eo...* AC 6884; *per haec...potest omnipraesentia Divina ~o illustrari* VR 64.2.

quomodo, *interr. adv.* In what manner, how: **a** (in dir. qu.): *~o potest homo vivere in aeternum...?* VR 48.6. **b** (in indir. qu.): *patebit ~o se res habet* AC 1061; VR 76.1.

quomodocumque: see **quomodocunque**.

quomodocunque, *adv.* also **quomodocumque**. In whatsoever manner, however: *nec desistere potuit, ~que persuadebatur quod non ita loquendum* AC 1513; ES 795.

quondam, *adv.* At some unspecified earlier time, once: *~am venerunt ad me* AC 6809; *cogitabam ~am de aeterno* CI 167.

quoniam, *conj. w. indic.* Seeing that, since, because: *~am...Dominus est vera lux...ideo ad discipulos*

...*dixit*... VR 761.2; [*verum*] *non fit bonum...nec appropriatur homini, ~am homo est homo ex voluntate* CI 26.

quoque, *adv*. (placed after the word or expr. it qualifies) Also, too: *hoc ~que constare potest* AC 6692.1; *inde ~que est, quod*... CI 95; *et ~que*, and also: *quae* [*virgo*]...*cum uno locat noctes, et ~que cum reliquis* VR 7.

quorsum, *adv*. In what direction: *qui ambulat in tenebris, non scit ~um abit* John 12.35 (AC 51); ES 2053.

quot, *interr.* and *rel. adj*. **1** (interr.) How many?: *in monasteriis..., quot non exstant pictae martyrisationes* ES 3187. **2** (correlated w. *tot*) As many...as...: *quot vera firmantur, tot augentur* AC 6664; *quot capita, tot animi* VR 32.2; *interiora...distincta sunt in totidem gradus, in quot sunt caeli angelici* AS 186.

quotannis, *adv*. Each year, annually: *festa...quae fuerunt tria ~is* AC 7093.2; SS 95.2.

quotcumque: see **quotcunque**.

quotcunque, *adv*. also **quotcumque**. However many: *omnes ~que in mundo vixerunt, in altera vita sunt* CI 456.3.

quotidianus ~a ~um, *a*. also **cotidianus**, and **cottidianus**. Of every day, daily: *da nobis panem ~um* Matt. 6.11 (AC 680.1); *per ~am plurium annorum experientiam* CI 456.1.

quotidie, *adv*. also **cotidie**, and **cottidie**. Every day, daily: *apparentia est, quod sol ~ie circum tellurem feratur* AS 108; AM 79.11.

quoties, *conj*. As many times as, as often as: *illorum reminiscuntur ~es similia occurrunt* AC 6812; (correlated w. *toties*) *toties in Verbo adhibetur* [*ille numerus*], *~es tale designatur* SS 29.

quotiescumque: see **quotiescunque**.

quotiescunque, *rel. adv*. also **quotiescumque**. As often as: *~que audiunt aliquem...apud se subsannant* AC 6907.2.

quotquot, *indecl. adj*. As many as: *~ot receperunt, dedit illis potestatem* John 1.12 (AC 51); *infantes inter brachia, ~ot usque portare queant* ES 419.

quousque, *interr.* and *rel. adv*. **1** (interr.) Up to what point in time, how long: *~que, Jehovah, occultas facies tuas a me?* Ps. 13.1 (AC 10579.8); (in indir. qu.) *cogitaverunt ~que hoc* AM 533. **2** (rel.) For as long as, while: *~que lucem habetis, credite in lucem* John 12.36 (DD 1). **3** (interr., in indir. qu.) Up to what point, how far: *percipere...datum quando venirent et quando abirent, quo et ~que* AC 1640.2; *judicare...a corpore, ejus nuditate, ~que patet* ES 1229. **4** (rel.) Up to which point in space, as far as: *erat...Euphrates terminus ad Aschur ~que dominium Israelis* AC 120; also, to what extent: *inde est quod...sensus externus Verbi...flectatur ~que libet* AC 9409.4.

quo versus, *adv*. = **quorsum**: ES 4572.

quum: see **cum**[2].

R

rabbi, *indecl.* (Hebr.) The Hebr. term for 'master': *nolite vocari ~i, unus est vester magister, Christus* Matt. 23.8 (AC 6756.5).

rabbinus ~i, *m.* (ad. Hebr.) A (Jewish) Rabbi: *dicebat quod ~us Judaeus esset* AC 943.3; ES 731.

rabidus ~a ~um, *a.* Affected with rabies, mad: *a canibus ~is* [*rapidis* Autograph, but cf. ES Index s.v. 'examinare, explorare' (p. 282 Tafel)] ES 2305; (of persons) frenzied: *posuerunt ~um quendam* ES 5043.

rabies ~ei, *f.* Frenzy, rage: *ira, ~es et immisericordia* VR 155.2.

racematio ~onis, *f.* **1** (pl.) Grapes left on the vine after the vintage: *sicut ~ones quando consummata est vindemia* Isa. 24.13 (AE 313.12). **2** A clustering as of grapes: *prima substantia, quae est glandularis, disposita est in racemos, sicut uvae in vite, ~ones illae sunt ejus series* VR 351.3.

racemosus ~a ~um, *a.* Clustering, racemose: *vesiculis ~is bronchiorum* AS 415.

racemus ~i, *m.* **1** A bunch of grapes or similar fruit: *~us uvarum rubrarum magnarum super patella* ES 3135; AE 918.9. **2** (anat.) A cluster resembling a bunch of grapes: *substantia...disposita est in ~os, sicut uvae in vite* VR 351.3.

rachets A misspelling of English 'rackets', as the name of a game: AM 17.4.

radiatio ~onis, *f.* The emission of rays: *~ones lucis in coelo* AC 1458.1; the act of shining: *~o facierum* AC 6752.9.

radiatus ~a ~um, *a.* Emitting rays of light, sparkling, shining, radiant: *sunt athmosphaerae... ~ae coloribus nitidissimis* AC 1621; AC 1623.

radicalis ~is ~e, *a.* Having firm roots, radical: *~e malum ex haereditate* ES 317.

radicatio ~onis, *f.* The act of striking root (in quot. fig.): *~o nusquam incipit nisi cum homo bonum charitatis accipit* AC 880.1.

radicitus, *adv.* From the roots up, (fig.) basically, fundamentally: *manentibus usque ~us et fundamentaliter nigro et albo* AC 731; ES 198.

radicor ~ari ~atus sum, *intr.* **1** (of plants) To strike root: *sicut successive ~atur et crescit arbor e semine* AM 525.4; (fig.) *non ~atur in terra truncus illorum* Isa. 40.24 (AC 8286.4). **2** (transf.) To become firmly established, take root: *non possunt vera fidei, utcunque inseminata, ~ari* AC 875.2; *quia illa cogitatio non fuit ~ata in agnitione* VR 111.6.

radio ~are ~avi, *intr.* also **radior** ~ari. To emit rays of light, shine, sparkle: *cum descendit de monte Sinai, ~abat cutis facierum ejus* AC 6752.9 (Exod. 34.29); *ex qua luce facies ejus intime sicut ~abat* AM 42.3; (pass.) *internus homo non ~atur facie* 3AD 3543.

radior: see **radio**.

radiosus ~a ~um, *a.* Emitting rays of light, sparkling: *cingula ~a ex flammeo quae circumdant Solem* AC 7270.2; *quidam...circum caput cinctus circulo quodam ~o* ES 3951.

radius ~i, *m.* **1** The emission of light in a single direction, beam, ray: *per nubem quae ~os et calorem e sole illo temperat* AC 6849.5; *mille hostes non sustinent ibi unum ~um lucis coeli* CI 137.2. **2** The direction of the eye to one object, a glance: *ejus* [sc. *oculi*] *minimus ~us potest inordinatissima ordinate videre* ES 2178; a perceptive effort of the mind, grasp, stretch: *consummatissima sapientia ne quidem aliquo ~o intellectus potest illum amorem...attingere* AM 111.

radix ~icis, *f.* **1** The root (of a plant): *arbor cum trunco ...stat super ~ice sua* SS 66; *quod ex seminulo jacto in terram exeat ~ix* AM 416.1. **2** The lowest and concealed portion of any structure: (of a tooth) *dentium stridor et dolor in ~icibus et in periosteis gravis* ES 4348. **3** (transf.) Any point of origin, base, stem: *~icem Jischaji...gentes* *quaerent* Isa. 11.10 (DD 4); *sunt [Abramus, Nachor et Lotus]...gentium stirpes seu ~ices* AC 1362; *inclinatio ad idem malum in ~ice, haereditario, recondita jacet* ES 2453.

rado ~dere ~si ~sum, *tr.* To shave: *statutum etiam fuit pro sacerdote magno, quod non ~deret caput* SS 35.3 (Lev. 21.10); *tabula ~sa*, a writing tablet with all trace of previous writing removed, 'a clean slate': *tabula secunda Decalogi...est sicut tabula ~sa, in qua non apparet aliquid scriptum* AR 461.

raeda: see **rheda**.

raka, *indecl.* (?) Foreign word of uncertain meaning, perh. 'fool', in Matt. 5.22 (AC 374.1): *dicere raka significat pro vacuo habere, ita pro vili* AE 746.18.

ramentum ~i, *neut.* A small piece scraped off, scraping, filing, chip: *ex miscela sulphuris, ~orum ferri, et argillae luti* VR 110.1; *~a lignea* ES 4053.

ramificatio ~onis, *f.* A ramification: *~ones bronchiorum pulmonis* AS 405.2.

ramifico ~are ~avi ~atum, *tr.* (refl. and pass.) To spread into branches, branch out: *sunt pulmoni bronchia, quae ~antur* AS 405.2; *qui [nervi] mirabiliter fluunt...seque ~ant* ES 2561.

ramosus ~a ~um, *a.* Abounding in branches: *mater tua, sicut vitis...juxta aquas plantata, frugifera, et ~a facta ab aquis multis* Ezek. 19.10 (AC 5113.6).

ramoth, *indecl.* (Hebr.) Hebr. word of uncertain meaning, perh. black coral, in Ezek. 27.16 (AC 1232).

ramulus ~i, *m.* A small branch, twig: *ex ~is desumptis ex arbore vitae* DP 332.4.

ramus ~i, *m.* **1** A branch of a tree, bough: *arbor... crescit in ~os, folia et fructus* AC 8326; *portam ex ~is ...arborum compaginatis exstructam* AM 8.1. **2** Any similar structure, especially in anatomy: *per ~os in viscera totius corporis* DP 296.14.

ramusculus ~i, *m.* A small branch: *super ~um alicujus arboris* VR 375.1; *et accepit ~um cedri* Ezek. 17.3 (AE 281.2).

rana ~ae, *f.* A frog: *et prorepere faciet fluvius ~as* Exod. 7.28 (AC); VR 120.1; (as the name given to certain unclean spirits) 2AD 1956.

rancidus ~a ~um, *a.* Rotten, putrid: *cum frumentis ...quae mucilenta et ~a...redderentur* VR 524.3; *nidores foedi, ~i* SA 124 (= x.6.[2]); (fig.) *calori...inerat sicut ~um, austerum et urens ex zelotypia* VR 834.

rapax ~acis, *a.* **1** (of wild animals) Predatory, savage: *avibus et feris ~acibus, ut corvis, lupis, porcis* CI 429. **2** (of persons) Greedy, rapacious: *dicens quod non esset sicut reliqui homines, ~ax, injustus, maechus* Luke 18.11 (VI 30.3).

rapidus ~a ~um, *a.* Fast, rapid: *ad flumen ~um* Deut. 21.4 (AC 6767.5). (n.b. In ES 2305 for *rapidis* read *rabidis.*)

rapina ~ae, *f.* **1** The forcible seizure of others' property, plundering, looting: *aquilae...significant homines ~ae* DP 20; *ad evitandum...caedes, violationes et ~as* AM 107. **2** The prey (of a wild animal): *quemadmodum rugit leo...super ~a sua* Isa. 31.4 (AC 1664.9).

rapio ~pere ~pui ~ptum, *tr.* **1** To seize violently, pounce on: *et lupus ~pit illas* [sc. *oves*] John 10.12 (AC 8002.5); (absol.) *Ego ero ut leo Ephraimo...~piam et ibo* Hos. 5.14 (SS 79.3). **2** To carry off by force, snatch: *ut viderentur sibi quasi in coelum ~pti* AC 8115; *cum scortis et faeminis ~ptis* AM 107; *puella...quae me ~pere vi vellet* ES [3605] 1/2. **3** To take away by violence, steal, seize: *timentium ne opes eorum ~perentur* ES 910; *venit malus, et ~pit quod seminatum est* Matt. 13.19 (AE 48.2); (neut. pl. of pf. pple. as sb.) loot, booty: *piratae qui delectantur ~ptis et praedatis* AM 511.

rare, *adv.* In a rarefied manner, thinly: *sphaera vitae unumquemque...circumstipat, dense a pectore, et ~e a tergo* AM 224.

rarefio ~fieri ~factus sum, *intr.* To become rarefied: *obscuriora...quae densantur et ~fiunt* ES 2186.

raro, *adv.* (superl. *~issime*) Infrequently, rarely: *qui status ~o hodie existit* AC 8; *~o in Verbo* AC 1066.5; *quam ~issime super interiora...reflectunt* VR 535.2.

rarum, *adv.* = **raro**: *quod ~um datur in spiritibus* ES 634.

rarus ~a ~um, *a.* (compar. *~ior*) **1** At a low concentration, not dense: *~us grumus in athmosphaera* AC 7007.4. **2** Infrequently found, scarce, rare: *~um reddam hominem prae auro puro* Isa. 13.12 (AE 131.7); *amor vere conjugialis, qui hodie tam rarus est ut...* AM 57.

rastrum ~i, *neut.* A tool for breaking up the soil, hoe: *rutra, ~a, et plura instrumenta manus pro elaboranda terra* AE 1154.2.

rasus ~a ~um: pf. pple. of **rado**.

ratio ~onis, *f.* **1** The power of drawing logical inferences, reason: *intellectus, ~o et scientia* AC 658; *quisnam cui aliqua ~o illustrata est...non videt...?* FI 45; *gens cui religio et sana ~o* VR 5; (distinct from **ratiocinatio**) *hominis intellectuale, sive sit ~o sive ratiocinatio, hoc est, visus ejus internus* AC 655.1; AC 238. **2** A piece of reasoning, argument, inference: *stabilitur...ex Scriptura Sacra...et quoque per ~ones quod...* VR 101.1; *~ones confirmantes* AE 260.1; *ens* *nullius ~onis* AM 66. **3** A relationship, proportion (between two things): *in ~one quadam opposita sunt* AC 7601.8; *ad justam ~onem aequilibrii redigitur* CI 594; *~o infiniti et finiti nulla datur* DP 32.3. **b** *in ~one* (w. gen.), in proportion (to): *quo plures sunt...eo major felicitas, nam in ~one plurium augescit* AC 549; ES 359; *in inversa ~one*, in inverse proportion: AC 8413.3. **4** An account (in bookkeeping): *de...rege qui conferebat ~onem cum servo* AC 4314.2 (Matt. 18.23); (fig.) *ut ~o constet* 'to balance the account' AC 6807; *homo reddet ~onem operum suorum* VI 105.

ratiocinatio ~onis, *f.* **1** The process of drawing false inferences, false reasoning: *ut non amplius ratio manserit, sed ~o* AC 238; *per rationem et rationalia intelliguntur proprie illa quae vera sunt, per ~onem autem et ratiocinia ea quae falsa* AC 1186.1. **2** A false inference or deduction: *~ones ex meris falsis* AC 7378; *ejus* [sc. *mentis naturalis*] *operationes interiores dum perversae sunt,* [*vocantur*] *~ones, dum secundum ordinem, simpliciter ratio* ES 222.

ratiocinator ~oris, *m.* One who relies on his own powers of reasoning, a (false) reasoner: *ex illis qui in mundo fuerant ~ores* AM 231.1; ES 3703.

ratiocinium ~i, *neut.* A false use of reasoning, false inference or deduction: *spiritus mali qui ~a hominis excitant* AC 653; *intellectualia, rationalia et scientifica, et...opposita, quae sunt ~a et falsa* AC 866; *per ~a ex naturali homine* SS 92.

ratiocinor ~ari ~atus sum, *intr.* To draw inferences, reason, think: [*influxus*] *facit ut homo possit ~ari* AC 657; *angeli...de veris Divinis nusquam ~antur* CI 270.2; *qui... ~antur, num sit vel non sit* AM 232.1; (w. *ex*) *ex meris falsis ~antur* AC 7352.

rationale ~is, *neut.* **1** The faculty of drawing correct inferences, reason: *~e...est intelligentiae aemulum* AC 265; *nisi sciat...quod sit ~e quod correspondet coelo spirituum angelicorum* AC 978.2. **2** (pl.) Sound inferences, correct reasoning: *per rationem et ~ia intelliguntur proprie illa quae vera sunt* AC 1106.1; *si quis per ~ia ponit illos in aliqua cogitatione* AC 6971.2; CI 455.3.

rationalis ~is ~e, *a.* **1** (of persons or their minds) Guided by sound reason, reasoning, rational: *homo ~is est medius inter utrumque* AC 978.3; *mens... ~is est mens hominis interni* AC 7130; *anima ~is* VR 4.3. **2** (of truth, actions, qualities, etc.) Consonant with sound reason, rational: *progressio...a scientificis ad vera ~ia* AC 1495.1; *ex lege ~i* VI 12; *sapientia ~is et sapientia moralis* AM 195.

rationalitas ~atis, *f.* The power of correct reasoning: *~ate orbantur* AC 948; *quod ~ate polleant* [*homines*] AM 416.3.

rationaliter, *adv.* By the correct use of reason, rationally: *quod homo qui non spiritualis est usque possit ~er cogitare* VI 15.

ratus ~a ~um, *a.* (pf. pple. of **reor**) Having legal validity, valid: *quid judicatio absque sententia subscripta, ut judicium ~um sit?* VR 730.2.

rauce *adv.* Hoarsely: *respondit ~e, sum ex inferis* AM 263.2.

raucus ~a ~um, *a.* Hoarse: *audiebant illum sicut discordem et ~um* AM 55.2.

reactio ~onis, *f.* A reciprocal movement or action, reaction: *inter duo opposita...ex quorum actione et ~one resultat aequilibrium* CI 536; *per cordis actionem in pulmone...et per pulmonis ~onem ex se a corde* VR 154.3.

reactivus ~a ~um, *a.* Reacting: (in quots. neut. as sb.) *non* [*dabilis est*] *conjunctio activi cum passivo absque ~o* CC 14.4; AE 616.1.

reaedificatio ~onis, *f.* Rebuilding, reconstruction: *per... ~onem templi* AC 728.4.

reaedifico ~are ~avi ~atum, *tr.* To build again, rebuild: *solitum erat urbes quas destruxerunt, ne ~arentur, conserere sale* AC 1666.4.

reagentia ~ae, *f.* Reciprocal action, reaction: *quies ex simili agentia et ~a vocatur aequilibrium* CI 589.1.

reago reagere reegi reactum, *intr.* To act in response, react: *aequilibrium est inter binas vires, quarum una agit et altera reagit* CI 589.1; (pres. pple. as sb.) *status sapientiae maritorum est...reagens seu reactio* AM 293.5; ES 360.

realis ~is ~e, *a.* (compar. *~ior*) Having an existence in fact (as opposed to in appearance), real, actual: *~is correspondentia est baculi cum potentia* AC 7026; *apparentiae ~es...apparentiae non ~es* CI 175; *in mundo naturali...non repraesentativae sed ~es bestiae dantur* AM 133.2; *quod interiora hominis sint ~es substantiae, et ~iores quam exteriora ejus* ES 4609. **b** (neut. as sb.) a really existing thing: *dicebant quod illis nulla delectatio sit spectare materialia...sed solum ~ia* AC 6809; *Divinum Verum procedens a Domino est ipsissimum ~e* AC 6880.

realiter, *adv.* In a real manner, actually: *cum usus est productus, amor et sapientia ~er existunt* VR 67.2.

reascendo ~dere ~di ~sum, *intr.* To go up again: *in societatem suam ~dit* [*angelus*] VR 76.5.

reassumo ~mere ~m(p)si ~m(p)tum, *tr.* **1** To put on (clothes) again: *quod vestes...quae non in usu conservent, et dum in usu ~mant* CI 181. **2** To take up again (a topic), revert to: *eadem res aliis et aliis vocibus* *exprimitur; et quandoque etiam ~mitur et iterum describitur* AC 707; *illa, quae nunc dicta sunt ut nota, ~menda sunt* DP 136.1.

reatus ~us, *m.* The fact of being guilty of an offence, guilt: *sic homo, [potest] a ~u inde liberari* AC 6959.2; *terra plena est ~u* Jer. 51.5 (DD 40); (w. pl.) an instance of this: *omnes... ~us a parentibus haereditati* AM 448.

rebellio ~onis, *f.* A rebellion, revolt: ES 408.

rebellis ~is, *m.* One who opposes government by force of arms, rebel, terrorist: *si aliter velit imperare, ~is est* AC 451; *cum exercitu praedonum aut ~ium* VR 117.

rebello ~are ~avi, *intr.* To revolt, rebel: *tertio decimo anno ~arunt* Gen. 14.4 (AC); AE 324.6.

recalcitratio ~onis, *f.* A kicking back: AC 6212.3; ES 2276.

recalcitro ~are ~avi, *intr.* (of a horse) To kick back: *equus qui rejecit insidentem et ~avit* AC 6212.3; ES 2275; (fig.) *cum pinguis factus est Jeschurun, ~avit* Deut. 32.15 (CO 2.3).

recapitulatio ~onis, *f.* A summary repetition, recapitulation: *in his versibus...est ~o* AC 286.

recapitulo ~are ~avi ~atum, *tr.* To repeat in summary form, recapitulate: *ut exinde ~entur universalia* CO 23.1.

recedo ~dere ~ssi, *intr.* **1** To go away, withdraw, depart: *montes ~dent, et colles dimovebuntur* Isa. 54.10 (AC 6804.10); *cum narrabant, paulum a me ~debant* AC 8382; *~ssit ab illis nimbus* AM 7.4. **2** (of persons) To depart (from a course of action), give up: *ut non ~dant a Me* Jer. 32.40 (AC 6804.8); *quod plures hodie incipiant ~dere a coelesti illo amore* AC 7743. **3** (of things) To cease to operate, be withdrawn: *quod ~sserit charitas* AC 357; *ab omnipotentia omne absolutum ~dit* VR 73.1.

recens[1], *adv.* Shortly before, recently: *ex spiritibus qui ~s e mundo...veniunt* AC 449; *plerique ex ~s mortuis* CI 312.5; *~s natus* VI 69.

recens[2] ~ntis, *a.* Recently arrived or provided, newly come: *spiritus...cumprimis ~ntes in altera vita* AC 6928; *ex jugi influxu ~ntium virium* AM 44.9.

recenseo ~sere ~sui ~situm, *tr.* To make a list of, enumerate: *angelus... ~sebat modo genera universalissima gaudiorum* AC 457; *quae mox supra ~sita sunt* CI 355; (w. *inter*) *Ecclesia 'Kenan' dicta non ~senda ita est inter perfectiores illas tres* AC 507.

recensio ~onis, *f.* **1** The making of a list, enumeration: *~o eorum qui fuerunt ab Ecclesia Antiquissima* AC 469; VR 52. **2** A review (of a book): *opera...tam faede rejecta...ut ne quidem digna habita sint inter libros ~onis nominari* AR 716.3.

recensitio ~onis, *f.* Enumeration: AC 10727; ES 5493.

receptaculum ~i, *neut.* A thing which serves to hold something, container, receptacle: *ex significatione 'sacci' quod sit ~um* AC 5489.1; (fig.) *pro ~is veri vilissimis* AC 6723.1; *homo, sicut est ~um, est imago et similitudo Dei* AM 132.3.

receptibilis ~is ~e, *a.* **1** (w. gen.) Capable of receiving: *Dominus...facit ut [homo] ~is sit gaudii coelestis* CI 526.1; *in statum ~em amoris* AM 321.2. **2** Capable of being received: *Dominus...creavit successivum, per quod Divinum Verum...quoad aliquam partem ~e esset* AC 7270.2.

receptibilitas ~atis, *f.* The ability to receive: *quae ~atem amoris et sapientiae apud illum exaltant* AM 199.1.

receptio ~onis, *f.* **1** The act of taking or receiving, acceptance, reception: *~o Sanctae Communionis* BCP (VI 6); *omnia discrimina proximi, quae se habent secundum ~onem Domini* AC 6706; *de ~one doctrinae* FI 59. **2** That which receives, a receiver: *faeminae natae sunt amores, at viri...sunt ~ones* AM 160; *angeli et homines sunt modo ~ones* AE 23.2.

receptivus ~a ~um, *a.* Receiving; (neut. as sb.) a receiver: *quod subjectum sit quasi nihil...modo ~um cogitationis* AC 5985.

receptrix ~icis, *f. adj.* Receiving: *gratia illa ~ix fidei* VR 631.1.

recessio ~onis, *f.* The act of going away or withdrawing, departure, withdrawal: *~onem a charitate* AC 357.

recessus ~us, *m.* An interior part, recess (in quot. fig.): *Verbum...Domini in sinu et ~u suo...nusquam agit de aliis rebus* AC 1194.

recido ~ere ~i, *intr.* **1** To fall back: *~et ad dextram et esuriet* Isa. 9.20 (AC 574.2). **2** To revert (to a lower state), backslide: *hoc, si ascendit per elevationem cogitationum...attamen ~it ad concupiscentias* AM 304.2; *si forte ~issent aliqui, ii exterminantur a societate* ES 623. **3** *Eodem* or *in idem ~it* it comes to the same thing: *sive dicas esse in forma coeli, sive in ordine coeli, eodem ~it* CI 201; *Divinum Verum, seu quod in idem ~it, Divina Sapientia* VR 50.

recipiens ~ntis, *a.* (pres. pple. of **recipio**) (w. gen.) Receptive (of), holding, containing: *formae ~ntes vitae* AC 6872.3; *quod homo sit organum ~ns Dei* VR 34.1.

recipio ~cipere ~cepi ~ceptum, *tr.* **1** To have given to one, receive: *~cipere tabulas Legis* AC 6752.8; *nisi per exercitium charitatis... ~ceperat illam facultatem* AC 8206.2; *quod caeci ~ceperint visum* SS 17.4. **2** To take to oneself, accept: *cum homo bonum charitatis* *accipit et ~cipit* AC 880.1; *nullus simili modo ~cipit Dominum* AC 6706; *agnoscunt vera et cum gaudio ~cipiunt illa* FI 30; (w. *pro*) *quod... ~ciperetur circumcisio pro signo repraesentativo purificationis* AC 7040. **3** To receive (a person into one's house), entertain: *urbs quae non ~ceptura esset discipulos* AC 7418.2; (w. *in* + acc.) *quod scelesti possint...in coelum ~cipi* AC 7051.1. **4** (w. *quod*) To accept the fact (that): *dum prius instructi sint et ~ceperint quod Dominus sit solus Deus* AC 7251. **b** *~ceptus*, generally accepted as valid: *nisi Verbum tale fuisset...non ~ceptum fuisset* AC 6839; *quod ~ceptum sit dicere...* CI 134; *~ceptae consuetudines* AM 295.2. **5** (refl.) To take oneself off, withdraw: *haec dimicatio...recedit ab externis, at ~cipit se in mentis interna* AM 248.2; *facies...quae mox se ~cepit intus* ES 913.

reciprocatio ~onis, *f.* **1** An alternate action in two directions, reciprocal movement: *sunt spiritus qui... influunt...per vibrationes et ~ones quasi lineares* AC 1761. **2** Mutual influence in either direction, reciprocation: *de ~one boni et veri...ab intellectu...in voluntatem, et a voluntate...in intellectum* AC 9300.2.

reciproce, *adv.* In a reciprocal manner, mutually: *~e influit ita unum in alterum* AC 802; *quod vir ~e conjungat se uxori* AM 198.

reciproco ~are ~avi ~atum, *tr.* (refl.) To act mutually in either direction, reciprocate: *spurcae illecebrae quae sicut ascendunt et descendunt et se ~ant, ita excitent* AM 440.

reciprocus ~a ~um, *a.* **1** Moving to and fro, reciprocating: *~a...motitatio* AC 7077; *per fluxiones quasi lineares et ~as* ES 1057. **2** Operating in both directions, mutual, reciprocal: *amari a Domino est quoque amare Dominum, nam amor est ~us* CI 350; *conjunctio ~a* FI 22; *habitatio ~a hominis in Deo* VR 74.3; (neut. as sb.) *amare aliquem et conjungi illi, cui non est ~um, non datur* VI 102.

recito ~are ~avi ~atum, *tr.* To say aloud, repeat, recite: *~ant...aliquot dicta ex sensu literae Verbi* SS 64; *ad aedes ubi concionata ~arentur* AM 9.3.

recludo ~dere ~si ~sum, *tr.* **1** To open the way to, unstop, unblock: *aperi oculos et ~de aures* FI 46; *nec aliud quam cognitiones illud* [sc. *Verbum*] *~dunt* CO 1. **2** To close off, shut away: *viderunt...quosdam...sicut facies ~sas a corpore* AM 9.2.

reclusio ~onis, *f.* **1** An opening up, exposure: *sicut ~o interiorum increvit, ita ordo...inversus est* UJ(C) 24. **2** A shutting away: *~onem et separationem amoris conjugialis ab amore sexus* AM 109.

recogito ~are ~avi ~atum, *tr.* To think about again, think over: *dum ~aretur* [*loquela*], *inexpressibilis erat* 3AD 1660.

recognosco ~noscere ~novi ~nitum, *tr.* To recognize, know again: *quod intus ~noscant* [*uxores*] *illa... quae...audiverant ex maritis* AM 165; *contigit quod animae... ~noscerent omnia ea quae iis in vita corporis nota fuerunt* ES 1932; ES 5601.

recolligo ~ligere ~legi ~lectum, *tr.* **1** To gather together again: *quod dispersi ab hostibus ~ligerentur* AC 1228.2. **2** To recall from the memory, recollect: *~ligere volui quae audivi* CI 239.2; *~legimus illa quae in caelis vidimus* VR 78.5.

recommendo ~are ~avi ~atum, *tr.* To speak approvingly of, recommend (a course of action): *Lutherus ...aliquo tempore cavit, et opera ~avit* ES 6042.

reconciliatio ~onis, *f.* Reconciliation: *per ~onem cum proximo* VI 73.

reconcilio ~are ~avi ~atum, *tr.* To bring back into friendship, reconcile: *quod apparentes amicitiae ~ent* [*conjuges*] AM 289; (refl.) *~abit se illi* BCP (VI 6).

recondite, *adv.* Secretly, privately: *qui...se conferunt ad Judaismum, sive aperte sive ~e apud se* ES 2097.

reconditio ~onis, *f.* The act of keeping secret, hiding: *~o et absconditio perceptionis* AM 167.1.

reconditorium ~i, *neut.* A place for keeping safe or secret, hiding place: *conjugiale unius viri cum una uxore est... ~um religionis Christianae* AM 444[a].

reconditus ~a ~um, *a.* (pf. pple. of **recondo**) (in senses of vb., esp.) Deeply hidden, recondite: *~am sapientiam in se habuerunt* CI 354; (neut. as sb.) a hidden treasure: *dominabitur in ~a auri et argenti* Dan. 11.43 (AC 117.1).

recondo ~ere ~idi ~itum, *tr.* (superl. of pf. pple. *~itissimus*) **1** To put away for safe keeping, store, lay up: *armamentaria...sunt ubi ~untur arma belli* AC 6661.2; *stellam... ~ere in bursa togae* VR 137.3; (fig.) *illa quae Dominus apud hominem ~it* AC 19; *prodit falsum mali quod ~itum in illis jacuerat* AC 7790. **2** To keep hidden, conceal: *non potest quisquam ibi vultu ~ere interiora* CI 48; (refl.) *~unt se in antris* CI 481.4.

recordatio ~onis, *f.* A calling to mind, remembrance: *de perpetua ~one quod ab Ipso liberati sint* AC 8038; *quod quandoque obvenerit eis quasi ~o rerum, quas tamen nusquam viderunt* CI 256; AM 300.2.

recordor ~ari ~atus sum, *tr.* (*intr.*) (w. gen. or *quod*) To have in remembrance, call to mind: (w. gen.) *et ~atus est Deus Noachi* Gen. 8.1 (AC); *~atus sum istius rei* ES 4516; (w. *quod*) *~ati sunt quod Deus esset petra eorum* Ps. 78.35 (DD 34.2); AM 208.1.

recreatio ~onis, *f.* The renewal of mental or physical powers, refreshment: *jucundum odoratus...modo* *inservit ~oni, ac ita quoque sanitati* AC 7038.2; *quod otium ejus vitae sit modo ~onis causa* CI 403.

recrementosus ~a ~um, *a.* Of waste matter, faecal: *humor ~us cerebri* ES 1793.

recrementum ~i, *neut.* Waste matter, recrement: *ventriculus, hepar, pancreas, lien...quod...suas sordes et sua ~a conjiciant in intestina* AC 10030.1.

recreo ~are ~avi ~atum, *tr.* To renew the powers of, refresh: *laetissima consortia, quae angelorum mentes exhilarant...et corpora ~ant* AM 5.4; ES 751.

recta, *adv.* In a straight line, directly: *quod rueret ~a versus infernum* ES 1118.

recte, *adv.* Correctly, properly, rightly: *~e loquutus es* Exod. 10.29 (AC); *cogitare juste et ~e* CI 364; AM 269.4.

rectificatio ~onis, *f.* (in chemistry) Rectification: AM 145.2.

rectifico ~are ~avi ~atum, *tr.* **1** (in chemistry) To rectify: *cum alcohole, quod est spiritus summe ~atus* AM 145.2; (fig.) *quod amor conjugialis...purificetur et ~etur* AM 147. **2** To amend, correct, rectify: *ut pravae inclinationes possint ~ari* AM 202.2.

rectitudo ~inis, *f.* Morality, uprightness: *si...agat... ~inem in operis* VI 24; *in judicium, a quo officiorum ~o interius dependet* AM 175.2.

rector ~oris, *m.* A ruler, officer: 3AD 4471.

rectum ~i, *neut.* (anat.) The rectum: *in inferno coli et ~i* AC 5393.2.

rectus ~a ~um, *a.* **1** Straight: *pes ~us eorum* Ezek. 1.7 (AE 279.2); *in intestinum ~um* 'the rectum' ES 1062; (neut. as sb.) *ut ~um appareat curvum* AE 1019.2. **2** (of persons) Upright, honest: *nisi quis interius sit sincerus, justus, fidelis et ~us* VI 84.2; AM 286. **3** (of actions) Morally correct, right: *quemadmodum ~um fuit in oculis figuli facere* Jer. 18.4 (AC 6669.5); *facere justum et ~um in omni opere* CI 364. **4** (app.) Right (as opposed to left): *ad angulum ~i oculi* ES 3097.

recubo ~are ~avi, *intr.* To take one's ease, recline: *in habitaculis suis ~ant* Ps. 104.22 (AE 278.8); ES 154.

recumbo ~mbere ~bui, *intr.* To lie back, recline: *usque dum fatigati ~mbant* ES 435.

recuperatio ~onis, *f.* The act of getting back, recovery: *quod ~onem salutis Deo adscribant* ES 4572.3.

recupero ~are ~avi ~atum, *tr.* To get back again, recover: *ubi iterum vitam suam ~ant* AC 6677; AC 9213.2.

recurro ~ere ~i, *intr.* **1** To become present again, recur: *cum saepe ~it [malum], fit naturale* AC 494.1; VR 79.8. **2** (impers.) It comes back to mind: *~it...quod homines ibi noctu interficiantur* ES 3729.

recursus ~us, *m.* Repetition, recurrence: *haec...per ...perennem ~um solita...facta sunt* VR 695.6.

recuso ~are ~avi ~atum, *tr.* To decline, reject: *dum ...alia interveniunt, adhuc ea ~ant* ES 1125.

reda: see **rheda**.

redamatio ~onis, *f.* A loving in return: *quod desit ~o a marito* AM 200.

redamo ~are ~avi ~atum, *tr.* To love in return: *ut ~et Dominum et amet proximum sicut se* AC 1038.1; *quod bonum non possit amare aliud verum quam suum, nec verum ~are aliud bonum quam suum* AM 76.5.

redarguitio ~onis, *f.* also **redargutio** (AC 219 and AC 6997.4 3rd edns.; cf. **redarguitor**). Reproof, criticism: *ubi 'vox Jehovae' accipitur...pro conscientia...etiam pro omni ~one [redargutione* 3rd edn.] *inde* AC 219; AC 2546; AC 6997.4.

redarguitor ~oris, *m.* One who reproves: *spiritui punitori et ~ori* ES 627.

redarguo ~ere ~i ~tum, *tr.* To reprove, criticize: *ut non amplius potuissent ~i seu scire quid malum* AC 573; *incepit me ~ere ex factis et cogitatis, quae deprompsit ex memoria mea* AC 7803.

redargutio: see **redarguitio**.

reddo ~ere ~idi ~itum, *tr.* **1** To give back, repay: *~et...unicuique secundum facta ejus* Matt. 16.27 (AC 8256). **b** to perform (a promise), pay (a vow): *~e vota tua* Nahum 1.15 (AC 7093.5). **c** to pay (a penalty): *~ere poenam malefactis correspondentem* AE 1114.1. **2** (w. pred.) To cause to be, make, render: *illum...tutum ~unt* AC 6724.2; *ut ex plurium ore certi ~amur* AM 2.2. **3** (w. pred.) To translate as, render: *interpretes 'Schaddai' ~unt 'omnipotentem'* AC 1992.5.

redemptio ~onis, *f.* also **redemtio**. **1** The act of buying back, redeeming: *lex de ~one primogenitorum* AC 8080.4. **b** the price of redeeming, ransom: *ut...det animam suam ~onem pro multis* Matt. 20.28 (AC 1419). **2** Redemption (as the Lord's act): *quod ~onem attinet, est illa idem ac reformatio et regeneratio* AC 2954.1; *quod ipsa ~o fuerit subjugatio infernorum et ordinatio caelorum* VR 115.1.

Redemptor ~oris, *m.* (as a title of the Lord) Redeemer: *~or noster Jehovah Zebaoth* Isa. 47.4 (AC 7091.4); *de Domino ~ore* VR 4.3.

redemtio: see **redemptio**.

redeo ~dire ~dii, *intr.* (pf. also *~divi*) **1** To come back, return (to a place): *~dierunt aquae Jordanis in locum suum* Josh. 4.18 (AC 6983.2); *post caenam ~dierunt* AM 19; *~divimus supra terram* VR 389.7. **2** (fig., of things) To be returned, come back: *quod quis cupit alteri ~dit in ipsum* AC 391; *in falso, quod ~dit ad illum qui in falso est* AC 696. **3** To return, revert (to a state): *a statu ultimo ~deunt iterum ad primum* CI 155; *Jehovah Deus...sic ~diit in Suum Divinum* VR 3.1; *coeperunt ad naturam suam ~dire* ES 2045; *ad se ~dire*, to come to oneself, recover one's senses: AC 948. **4** (of things) To be repeated, recur, come back: *omnes... vitae status ~deunt in altera vita* AC 1618; *~dit facies atavi in nepote* DP 277.2; *quod omnia...constanter in annis ~deant* VR 78.4.

redigo ~digere ~degi ~dactum, *tr*. **1** To bring forcibly, compel, drive, reduce (to a state): *ad ultimum desperationis ~diguntur* AC 7250; *nisi quis...se in miserias ~digat* AC 7318.1; *ut externus homo ~digatur ad obedientiam interni* AC 7990; *cum in meliorem statum ~dactus est* AC 8028; (w. inf.) *~digebantur fateri quod scirent id verum esse* ES 325. **2** (w. *in* + acc.) To arrange, put: *~digere vera in doctrinam, et sic praepare ad usum vitae* AC 10105.3; *antiqui proximum ~degerunt in classes* AC 6705; *in ordinem ~digere*, to arrange in orderly fashion, put in order: *sic ~digebant doctrinam charitatis in ordinem* AC 7259; [*Dominus*] *~degit illud* [sc. *infernum*] *in ordinem* VR 2.2.

redimo ~dimere ~demi ~dem(p)tum, *tr*. **1** To release by payment of a price, ransom, redeem: *~demit Jehovah Jacobum* Isa. 44.23 (AC 7090.2); *annus ~demptorum Meorum venit* Isa. 63.4 (DD 4); *~dimere ...in proprio sensu significat sibi restituere et appropriare quod suum fuerat* AC 6281.1. **2** (of the Lord) To redeem: *sic* [*Deus*] *angelos et homines ~demit* VR 3.1; VR 118.

redintegratio ~onis, *f.* A making whole again, restitution: *ut non locus ~onis superesset apud illum* DP 281.4.

redintegro ~are ~avi ~atum, *tr*. To make whole again, restore to integrity: *placuit Domino...implere Verbum, et per id ~are et restituere illud* SS 111; *dum aliquid elabitur ex ordine,* [*Deus*] *reducit illud et ~at* VR 74.4.

reditio ~onis, *f.* A going back, return: *recessio a bono et ~o ad malum* DP 233.4.

reditus ~us, *m*. **1** A coming back, return: *expectavi ~um, sed incassum* AM 155[a].5; AE 279.6. **2** Income, resources: *ex suo censu et ~u sustentare domum* AM 287.

redivivus ~a ~um, *a*. Restored to life: *bini testes occisi et ~i* AE 674.2.

redolentia ~ae, *f.* A scent, fragrance: *~ae ex fructibus et fragrantiae ex floribus* AM 430.

reducibilis ~is ~e, *a*. Capable of being brought back: *ostensum quod ~is in statum pristinum* ES 3394.

reduco ~cere ~xi ~ctum, *tr*. **1** To bring back, return: *~c manum tuam ad sinum tuum* Exod. 4.7 (AC); *quod gens illa...~cetur in terram Canaanem* AC 7051.2; *Jehovah...~cet captivitatem illorum* Zeph. 2.7 (AC 7844.5). **2** To bring back (to a state): *homo ~citur in statum...qui medius est inter somnum et vigiliam* AC 1883; *illa in ordinem concordem universali...~cere* VR 56.1.

reductio ~onis, *f.* A bringing back, returning: *per ~onem populi ex captivitate* AE 405.19; *spes ~onis ejus in...antiquam suam sanctitatem* AM 74; the reduction (of a number to its factors): *ex ~one numeri hujus in suos simplices* AC 7285.

redundatio ~onis, *f.* A flowing back, reverse influence: *~onem falsorum ex malo ad illos* AC 8220; AC 8226.1.

redundo ~are ~avi, *intr*. **1** To flow back, extend backwards: *dimidium aulaei superflui ~are facies super posteriora habitaculi* Exod. 26.12 (AC). **2** (transf.) To flow back, redound, recoil: *quod falsa ex malo ~arent ad illos* AC 8223.1; *ex quibus non aliud ~at quam aestus* AM 375.2; *nisi aliquid sensus inde ad reliqua ~et* VR 60.1.

redux ~ucis, *a*. Brought back, returned: *hos vidi ~uces inde* AM 354.2; *nunc ~ux super caput meum est* ES 1389; (masc. as sb.) *Zion in justitia redimetur, et ~uces ejus in judicio* Isa. 1.27 (SS 85).

refectorium ~i, *m*. A restorative, refresher: *pulmones quoad sanguinem agunt colatorium, emunctorium, ~um* DA 12 (= v.[2]).

refello ~ere ~i, *tr*. To refute, rebut: *falsa illa per influxum e coelo...~untur* AC 7474.3; to refute the arguments of (a person): *erat contra omnes quos ~ere et vituperare...potuerat* AC 5567.

refero ~ferre ~tuli ~latum, *tr*. **1** (w. *inter*) To place (in a group): *cognitiones...in memoria ejus reconduntur et inter scientifica ~feruntur* AC 27. **2** (refl., w. *ad*) To have reference (to), be connected (with): *omnis cultus se ~ferebat ad sacrificia* AC 6905; *omnia...se ~ferunt ad bonum et verum* VI 43.1. **3** To present an image of, resemble: *omnis idea seu imago minima hominis ~fert prorsus hominem in effigie* ES 378; *quod coelum in toto complexu ~ferat unum hominem* CI 418. **4** To be associated with by correspondence, correspond to, stand for: *sunt spiritus qui in Maximo Homine ~ferunt memoriam* AC 6696; *unde est quod affinitates in terris dicantur propinquitates, quia*

~ferunt affinitates spirituales AE 16; *Ecclesia repraesentativa... ~tulit ejus corpus* ES 2259. **5** To relate, tell: *licet illa ad finem capitum sequentium ~ferre* AC 6695; (impers. pass.) *~latum est de pulchra ave* AC 7742; (w. *quod*) *quod aliqui... ~tulerint quod ne quidem unus... sciat* AM 2.2; (w. indir. qu.) *angelus quidam...aliis angelis ~ferebat quot genera felicitatum dentur* ES 906. **6** To make a reply, rejoin: *ad quae ~tuli 'Ita non est...'* VR 17.3; FI 41.

refert, *impers. vb.* It is of importance, it concerns: *nihil ~rt quod bonum illud...differat* CI 51; (w. *mea*, etc.) it concerns me (etc.): *quid mea ~rt, si credam...?* VR 160.4.

refertus ~a ~um, *a.* (pf. pple. of **refercio***) (w. abl.) Filled completely, crammed, stuffed (with): *patellae cibis ... ~ae* AM 14.2; *quod illis* [sc. *ceris et mellibus*] *~ae revolent* [*apes*] VR 12.7; ES 475.

reficio ~ficere ~feci ~fectum, *tr.* To restore to full powers or effectiveness, repair, replace, refresh: *id quod exsumitur* [*ex horreo*], *e novo ~ficitur* AM 148.3; [*angeli*] *cupiunt et desiderant ~fici* ES 178.

reflecto ~ctere ~xi ~xum, *tr.*, *intr.* **1** (tr.) To turn around: *ascendunt...sed ~ctunt se in via et decidunt* VI 25; (esp.) to reflect (light, images, etc.): *lumen solis ~ctunt* AC 6697; *in speculo...quod...imaginem non ~ctit* VR 11.3; (fig.) *ut externa illis nihil essent, modo ut aliquid possent ab iis ~ctere ad interna* AC 54. **2** (intr.) To cogitate, reflect, think: *homo spiritus...cogitat, ~ctit, afficitur* CI 461.2; (w. *super*) *raro ~ctit super bono* AM 123; (impers. pass.) *nihil ~ctitur super personam* AC 665; (w. *ad*) *si ~ctit ad respirationem* ES 733.

reflexio ~onis, *f.* **1** A reflection (of light): *per ~ones mirabiles omnium objectorum* ES 222. **2** A consideration, reflection: *quae ~o abstraheret mentem ab idea universali* AC 6653; (w. gen.) *nullam ~onem magis habet corporis sui* ES 2542; (w. *ad*) *per ~onem ad experientiam* AC 933.2; (w. *super*) *~onem super revelatione hac* AC 6826; (w. indir. qu.) *nondum illis* [sc. *infantibus*] *est ~o...quid inanimatum* CI 338.

reflexus ~a ~um: pf. pple. of **reflecto**.

refluo ~ere ~xi, *intr.* To move back as if liquid, flow back, return insensibly: *vidimus...quod hic color ~eret per hyacinthinum in purpureum* AM 76.6; *amorem conjugialem mariti ~entem ad uxorem* AM 76.7; *quomodo...* [*animae*] *iterum in captivitatem ~ebant* ES 218.

refocillatio ~onis, *f.* The act of refreshing, refreshment: *de spirituum eorum sancta ~one* CO 54.1; ES 351.

refocillo ~are ~avi ~atum, *tr.* To renew the strength of, refresh: *qui infestantur a mere falsis, et non ~antur per vera* AC 7218; AM 5.4; *pluvia tempestiva quae novalia agri ~at* CO 20.2.

refodio ~dere ~di ~ssum, *tr.* To reopen by digging, dig again: *redibat Jischak et ~dit puteos* Gen. 26.18 (AC).

reformabilis ~is ~e, *a.* Capable of being reformed: *homo non foret ~is, neque foret culpabilis* VR 154.4; VR 611.1.

reformatio ~onis, *f.* The act of reforming, reform: (of a person) *ab omni homine, de quo aliqua spes ~onis est* CI 579; (of a church) *descriptio ~onis seu regenerationis novae Ecclesiae* AC 610; (esp. of the Christian Church) the Reformation: *si dominium papale non fractum fuisset tempore ~onis* AR 759.2; SE 18.

reformator ~oris, *m.* A reformer: (used of the Lord) *Dominus qui est Ipse ~or et Regenerator* VI 112; (of the Church) *~ores antesignani, Lutherus, Melanchthon et Calvinus* SE 21.

reformatus ~i, *m.* A member of the Reformed Church: *~i, qui in falsis doctrinae sunt* SS 25; FI 42; *sicut hodie somniant et Romano-Catholici et ~i* VR 82.3.

reformo ~are ~avi ~atum, *tr.* **1** To give a new form to, reshape: *a vermiculis, qui dum ~antur et alatae fiunt, tunc nanciscuntur aliam corporis formam* ES 2917. **b** to reform (the church): *quando Ecclesia ~ata est* DP 262.8. **2** To make (people) spiritual, reform: *nisi homo in libero sit, nusquam potest ~ari* AC 7007.2; *quod homo possit ~ari et spiritualis fieri* VI 15.

refractarie, *adv.* In a refractory manner: *~e negant quod Deus...sit una Persona* VR 173.1.

refractarius ~a ~um, *a.* Rebellious, defiant, refractory: *dederunt humerum ~um* Zech. 7.11 (AC 1085.3); *justiam...inferre in aliquem ~um* VR 72.3; (of penitence) hard to accomplish, intractable: *illis est paenitentia actualis summe ~a* VR 561.1.

refractio ~onis, *f.* The refraction (of light): *sistuntur irides secundum incidentias, ~ones et sic receptiones lucis* CC 13.6.

refraenatio ~onis, *f.* also **refrenatio**. The act of holding back, restraint: *per ~ones libidinum* AM 108.

refraeno ~are ~avi ~atum, *tr.* also **refreno**. To hold back, restrain: *ad ~andas concupiscentias* AM 105; *per paenas...coerciti et ~ati sunt* VR 79.8; (absol.) *si ille timor non ~aret...* CI 358.

refrenatio: see **refraenatio**.

refreno: see **refraeno**.

refrigero ~are ~avi ~atum, *tr.* To make cold, cool: *ut intingat extremum digiti in aquam, et ~et linguam* Luke 16.24 (AC 1861.11).

refrigesco ~ere, *intr*. To grow cold: *~et charitas multorum* Matt. 24.12 (AC 3488.6).

refugium ~i, *neut*. **1** A place of safety, refuge: *Deus meus... ~um meum* Ps. 18.2 (AC 8261.6); *urbes ~i* Isa. 17.9 (DD 4). **2** A means of achieving safety, expedient: *non aliud apparet ~um et quasi azylum* AM 459.1; *unicum ~um, ne quis pereat* VR 120.3.

refundo ~ndere ~di ~sum, *tr*. To pour back, return (a fluid): *pulmo ~ndit illum* [sc. *sanguinem*] *in sinistrum thalamum cordis* VR 371.5.

refuto ~are ~avi ~atum, *tr*. To disprove, refute (a theory): *fallacia... ~ata per antipodes* ES 3727; to refute the arguments of (a person): *jucundum vitae ejus fuit omnes ~are* ES 5995.

regeneratio ~onis, *f*. **1** Reproduction: *in vegetatione et ~one arborum* DP 332.4. **2** The process of spiritual rebirth, regeneration: *omnis ~o ideo est ut homo novam vitam accipiat* AC 848.1.

regenerator ~oris, *m*. One who gives a second, spiritual birth, regenerator: *Dominus qui est Ipse Reformator et ~or* VI 112.

regeneratorium ~i, *neut*. A means of regeneration: AC 10275.

regenero ~are ~avi ~atum, *tr*. To bring to a second, spiritual birth, regenerate: *quod homo per reliquias ~etur* AC 7831; *Dominus ~at hominem, hoc est, illum spiritualem facit* VR 105.1; (also, with truths as object) *quod vera non ~ari queant nisi per bona* AC 671.

regenitus ~a ~um: pf. pple. of **regigno**.

regero ~rere ~ssi ~stum, *intr*. **1** To reply, retort: (w. dir. speech) *ad quae viri ~sserunt, estisne faeminae sicut prius?* AM 199.2; (w. *quod*) *cum legatus ~rebat quod sic nec aliquid cogitationis* [*sit*] DP 197.2. **2** To refuse to accept, reject: *cum indignati, hoc ~sserunt... quod dictum eos nihil esse* ES 2418.

regicida ~ae, *m*. A killer of a king, regicide: *rebelles et ~ae* VR 683.2.

regigno regignere regenui regenitum, *tr*. = **regenero**: *qui...a semine coelesti regeniti* ES 1475.

regimen ~inis, *neut*. **1** The exercise of control, government: *~en Domini in regno spirituali vocatur judicium* SS 85; *~en Ipsius, quod vocatur Providentia* VR 73.3. **2** A form of government: *quale ~en hoc foret, cum plures tales* [*domini*] *sunt* AC 1594.3; *nec scit regna et ~ina* ES 1400. **3** Any form of control or restraint, restriction: *gentium ibi statuta, leges, ~ina* AC 6810; *omne ~en justitiae* VR 50.

regina ~ae, *f*. A queen: [*uxor*] *induta chlamyde sicut ~a* AM 21.1.

regio ~onis, *f*. **1** A district, region: *de partibus, ~onibus et regnis hujus telluris* CI 415; (distinguished vertically) *mundus* [*distinctus*] *est in ~ones quoad athmosphaeras* AM 188.3; VR 403.1; (in heaven or the Grand Man) *sunt... ~ones coeli aliquae a talibus occupatae* AC 8054.2; *in plano ~onis infra umbilicum* AC 7077. **2** A region, level (of the mind): *mens humana ...in tres ~ones...formata est* VR 34.1. **3** *E ~one*, opposite, over against: *cum partita et sibi e ~one posita* AC 1830; *solium quod e ~one candelabri positum erat* AM 20.2.

regium ~i, *neut*. Kingship, royalty: *per eos repraesentabatur ~um et Sanctum Domini* AC 1097.3; VR 114.

regius ~a ~um, *a*. Of or relating to a king, royal: *potentia ~a* AC 7026; *curia ~a* AM 179; *quod in Domino sint duo munia, sacerdotale et ~um* VR 114.

regnans ~ntis, *a*. Dominant, ruling, principal: *amor ~ns* CI 143; *naturalismus hodie ~ns* VR 4.2; *haec... perceptio ~ns est in coelo* AE 14.2.

regno ~are ~avi, *intr*. **1** To be king, reign: *Jehovah ~abit in saeculum et aeternitatem* Exod. 15.18 (AC). **2** To play the leading part, be dominant: *usque dum amor ~at* AC 12; *ut...cupiditas ~et prae intellectu* AC 568.2; *etiam tunc ~abat innocentia* AC 8118.1.

regnum ~i, *neut*. **1** A kingdom, country: *ex foederibus inter ~a* AC 6804.5; *inter ~orum monarchas* DP 251.2. **2** A division of anything: *infernum in duo ~a...distinctum est* AR 387.1; (w. gen.) an area controlled (by): *per ~um voluntatis et per ~um intellectus* AC 3888. **3** Each of the three divisions (animal, vegetable and mineral) of the natural world, kingdom: *in omnibus subjectis trium ~orum naturae* VR 8.3. **4** The Lord's Kingdom or Kingdom of Heaven: *omnes qui a ~o Domini sunt* AC 6711; *coelum distinguitur in duo ~a, quorum unum vocatur ~um coeleste, alterum ~um spirituale* CI 21; *dabo tibi claves ~i coelorum* Matt. 16.19 (AE 9.2).

rego ~gere ~xi ~ctum, *tr*. To control, rule: *homo nescit prorsus quod ~gatur a Domino* AC 50.1; *quod voluntas sit quae ~git hominem* AC 7342; *cor sanguine suo ~git et corpus et caput* AM 315.7.

regula ~ae, *f*. A regulating principle, rule: *a ~a communi, quod puris sint omnia pura* AC 7343.2; *omnes hujus artis* [sc. *architectonicae*] *~ae* AM 12.2.

regularis ~is ~e, *a*. (superl. *~issimus*) Having an ordered structure, regular: *respiratio... ~is* ES 3662; *quod ~issimum foret* ES 3666.

regulariter, *adv*. In a regular manner: *visa foramina ...regulariter sicut favi apum* ES 4027.

regulator ~oris, *m*. One who controls, regulator: [*Ecclesia*] *nullum alium ~orem habet quam intellectum* AC 4672.2.

regulatrix ~icis, *f. adj.* Regulating: *absque doctrina ~ice et ductrice* AC 9409.4.

regulus ~i, *m.* **1** A minor ruler, prince, duke: *primates et antistites ~i nostri* VR 185.6. **2** A poisonous kind of snake, basilisk: *per serpentum genera, ut per angues, ~os, aspides, haemorrheos* AC 251.1.

regurgito ~are ~avi ~atum, *tr.* To bring up from the stomach, regurgitate: *usque ut... ~arem ventriculi tetram aciditatem* ES 1272.

reinduo ~ere ~i ~tum, *tr.* To put on again as clothing: *quod [homo] tunc ~iturus pulverem rejectum* AC 5078.5; VR 770; (pass. w. abl.) to be clothed again (with): *quod anima possit ~i suo corpore* AM 182.5.

reinfluo ~ere ~i, *intr.* To flow back in: *falsa et mala... limitata ne ~ant et perdant* AE 435.21.

reintro ~are ~avi, *intr.* To go back in again, to re-enter: *oblectamentum...facit ut per vices ~emus* AM 268.3.

reipsa, *adv.* In fact, really: *~a etiam ita se habet, quod nempe corpus non sit quod videt...sed spiritus ejus* AC 4622.3.

rejectaneus ~a ~um, *a.* To be discarded as useless: *corpus...est ~um et immundum* 3AD 5921.

rejectibilis ~is ~e, *a.* That may be rejected, dispensable: *quod decalogus...sit libellus qui... ~is sit* VR 14.3.

rejectio ~onis, *f.* **1** A throwing off: *~o ab equo* ES 2276. **2** A throwing away, rejection: *quod sepultus [Dominus] significabat ~onem humani residui a matre* DD 16.6; AC 1875.

rejicio ~jicere ~jeci ~jectum, *tr.* **1** To throw or push back: *fumus...qui a procella... ~jicitur in oculos ejus* VR 108; (fig.) *religionem a pectore in tergum ~jecerunt* VR 9.1; *culpam mali ~jiciunt in Dominum* ES 4432. **2** To dispose of, get rid of: *quod homo talis sit cum suum corpus... ~jecerit* AC 6945.2; *in die illo ~jicient vir idola argenti* Isa. 31.7 (DD 4). **3** To send away, banish, reject: *~jicitur [homo] inter infernales* AC 1680.3; *vera et bona non genuina... ~jiciuntur ad latera* AC 7975.1; *quod Deus Pater... ~jecerit illud* [sc. *genus humanum*] *a Se* FI 44. **4** To be unwilling to accept, reject, refuse: *recipere bonum et ~jicere malum* CI 298; *si illis caelestia...detecta fuissent, non modo ~jecissent illa, sed etiam prophanavissent* SS 23.4.

relabor ~bi ~psus sum, *intr.* **1** To fall or slip back: *hiabat solum sub illis, et ~psi sunt ad suos* AM 415.6; (esp. transf.) *precatio mea super sinum meum ~bitur* Ps. 35.13 (AC 6960.2); *quod falsa et mala quae intendunt inferre ~bantur in illos* AC 8214. **2** To return (to a lower state), slip back: *statim ~buntur ad statum vitae prioris* AC 6971.2; *~psos in exteriora* CI 411; *~psus sum a consortio spirituum* ES 185.

relapsus ~us, *m.* **1** A falling back: *~us falsorum... super illos* AC 8214; AC 8226.1. **2** A return to a lower state, relapse: *ex nullo ~u illarum* [sc. *cogitationum*] *in corpus* AM 9.2.

relatio ~onis, *f.* **1** The reference (of a thing) to a standard of comparison: *bonum...non cognoscitur quale est, nisi per ~onem ad minus bonum* DP 24; *ex modulamine [toni], quod variatur per ~ones* VR 763.1. **2** A description in words, recital, narration: *de his plura videantur in ~one de Babylonia destructa* CI 229.

relative, *adv.* In a relative manner: *omnis veritas apparet ~e ad opposita* AC 7075.

relativus ~a ~um, *a.* Relative: *secundum reflexionem ~am ad discrimina* AC 7812; (neut. as sb.) *~a ...sunt dispositionis plurium...in ordinem* VR 62.

relatus ~a ~um: pf. pple. of **refero**.

relaxatio ~onis, *f.* The act of making slack, relaxation: *resolutio et ~o membranarum et ligamentorum* AM 253.2.

relaxo ~are ~avi ~atum, *tr.* **1** To make slack, relax: (fig.) *si... ~aretur vinculum* AC 257; *~antes sic omnia fraena suis cogitationibus* AE 233.4. **2** To allow to recover, give relaxation to: *ut animi ~entur a defatigatios* AM 17.1.

relegatio ~onis, *f.* The act of banishing, relegation: *per ~onem inter falsa* AC 6762.

relego[1] ~are ~avi ~atum, *tr.* To banish, relegate (to a less desirable place): *~antur dein in inferna* AC 6762; *aliqui ~antur in septentrionem* AM 273.3.

relego[2] ~ere ~i, *tr.* To read over, reread: *postquam scripsit et reliquit illa super mensa, et ~it, non videt illa* UJ(P) 29 (Rogers).

religio ~onis, *f.* **1** A system of religious belief and worship, religion: *quod ~o non aliud sit quam ut simplices teneantur in vinculis* AC 7352; *quod omnis ~o sit vitae* VI 1 titulus. **2** A particular organization for religious purposes, religious sect: *quisque...nascitur in ~onem parentum suorum* SS 92; *ex ~one Pontificia* AE 26.2. **3** A particular religious practice or belief: *unde talis ~o...orta de barbis* AC 1124; *invaluit ~o quod nemo possit implere legem* VI 63.1.

religiose, *adv.* With careful attention to detail, scrupulously: *quendam externum cultum habuerunt quem ~e observarunt* AC 1158.1.

religiosus ~a ~um, *a.* (superl. *~issimus*) **1** Given to religious belief, religious: *omnis ratio sana, tametsi non ~a, videt...* VR 10. **2** (neut. as sb.) A system of religious belief: *Dominus...iis conscientiam recti et boni secundum ~um eorum donat* AC 1032.3; *varia ~a* *per gentes* FI 49; (pl.) religious matters in general: *qui multum de ~is cogitant* CI 249.

religo ~are ~avi ~atum, *tr*. To fasten, hold together: *cum*... [*Verbum*] *sancte legitur ab homine, tunc ~antur ...interiora ejus* SS(P) 27 (= 11).

relinquo ~nquere ~qui ~ctum, *tr*. **1** To go away without taking, leave behind: *~nquam in deserto te* Ezek. 29.5 (AC 6693.4); *pecus nostrum ibit cum nobis, non ~nquetur ungula* Exod. 10.26 (AC); *quod* [*Dominus*] *nihil de corpore Suo ~querit in sepulchro* AE 41. **2** To give up having or using, abandon, leave: *omnis qui ~querit domos aut fratres* Matt. 19.29 (AC 6674.5); *cum non amplius inserviunt* [*vera*], *~nquuntur* AC 7778.4; *quod charitatem tuam primam ~queris* Rev. 2.4 (AR). **3** (w. dat.) To leave exposed or available (to): *~cti vesanis cupiditatibus* AC 307; *quod Dominus unicuique ~nquat suum liberum* AC 7007.2; *domi sibi ~ctus* VR 14.3; *~nquamus consociis nostris...dicere...* VR 48.4. **b** (impers. pass. w. inf.) there is left available the possibility (of): *nec voluptates...rejiciendae...sed iis ~nquitur frui ad usum* ES 2523. **4** To leave untouched, leave alone: *~nquendi ut colant Dominum* AC 7720; *et non ~nquetis de illo usque ad mane* Exod. 12.10 (AC); *non ~ctus est in illis usque ad unum* Exod. 14.28 (AC). **b** (w. *solus* as pred.): *non ~quit Me solum* John 8.29 (DD 32.2). **5** To leave (doubt): *ut non sit ~cta aliqua dubitatio* AC 7293.2; SS 64. **6** To leave undecided, leave aside: *~nquo usque num talis sit* ES 3732.

reliquiae ~quiarum, *f. pl.* **1** That which is left over, remainder, remnant: *Dominus...requiret ~quias populi Sui* Isa. 11.11 (DD 4); *Ecclesia...in tantum consummata est, ut vix aliquae ~quiae ejus supersint* VR 4.1. **2** The remains of good and truth which serve as the means of salvation: *nisi apud unumquemvis a Domino conservarentur ~quiae, non potuisset non perire aeterna morte* AC 468.2; *~quias veri et boni* AC 6959.2.

reliquus ~a ~um, *a*. **1** (sg.) What is left, the remainder of: *in ejus pueritia, sive in ~a ejus aetate* AC 1667.3. **2** (pl.) Not previously counted, remaining, other: *angeli qui ex tellure illa sunt simul cum angelis ~arum tellurum sunt* AC 7801; *cur Dominus dilexit Johannem prae ~is discipulis* AE 9.5; (neut. as sb.) *haec et ~a in toto illo psalmo agunt de pugnis* DD 14.6.

reloquor ~qui ~quutus sum, *intr*. To speak again, speak further: *angeli sapienter cum illis de ea re ~quuti sunt, sed incassum* UJ(P) 168.

reluctatio ~onis, *f*. Struggling in reaction, contrariety: *ex perpetua illa ~one, renitentia...et reactione mali et falsi* VR 61.1; ES 3682.

relucto ~are ~avi, *intr*. also **reluctor** ~ari ~atus sum, *intr*. To struggle in reaction, fight back: *dum contra illa* [sc. *bonum et verum*] *~ant malum et falsum* VR 61.1; (deponent) *per horulae tempus ~atus* ES 3682.

reluctor: see **relucto**.

reluxatio ~onis, *f*. The reduction of a dislocated joint: *mulctantur per colluxationes et ~ones* AC 829.2.

remanentiae ~tiarum, *f. pl.* Remains, relics: *~tiae non erant perceptionis, sed integritatis* AC 530.2.

remaneo ~nere ~nsi, *intr*. (fut. pple. *~nsurus*) **1** To remain in place, not to move: *quod illi...relegarentur versus suum orbem, reliquis ~nentibus* AC 7077. **2** To be left as the result of a process, be over, remain: *vita quae ~net est vita quae vocatur 'mors'* AC 6707.1; *apud Aegyptios ~nserunt plura ex repraesentativis Ecclesiae Antiquae* AC 6917.2. **3** To continue in existence, remain unchanged: *ea quasi sponte sua influunt et ~nent* AC 6812; *quod...in spiritu hominis est...hoc ~net post mortem* CI 395.

remedium ~i, *neut*. A means of effecting a cure, remedy: *sanationes, medelae, ~a et medicamenta* AC 6502.4; ES 2874.

remex ~igis, *m*. A rower, oarsman: *habitatores Zidonis ...fuerunt ~iges tui* Ezek. 27.8 (AC 1201.3).

reminiscentia ~ae, *f*. **1** The act or power of remembering, remembrance: *ut in ~am revocarent sancta cultus* AM 342.3; *in plenum quasi intellectum et ~am redibat* ES 306. **2** An instance of remembering, memory: *loquelae, cogitationes, ~ae, reflexiones variae* AC 7935.

reminiscor ~i, *intr*. To recall to mind, remember: (w. gen.) *~untur eorum quae in vita corporis cogitarunt* AC 1108; *ut ~antur malorum* AC 7721; (w. indir. qu.) *ut...~erer quomodo resuscitatio fit* CI 449.3.

remissio ~onis, *f*. **1** The act of letting go, release, relaxation: *ad evangelizandum vinctis ~onem* Luke 4.18 (DD 11); *per ~onem conatus eorum* ES 1944. **2** The forgiveness or remission (of sins): *paenitentia et ~o peccatorum* VI 27.

remissus ~a ~um, *a*. (pf. pple. of **remitto**) (superl. *~issimus*) (in senses of vb., esp.) Lacking in energy, feeble, slack: *quia ~i illi* Exod. 5.8 (AC); *influxum ~um et lenem* AE 425; *cum ~issima respiratione* ES 3138.

remitto ~mittere ~misi ~missum, *tr*., *intr*. **1** To send or put back, replace: *~miserunt se super solia* VR 48.5; *in coelum spirituum ~mittuntur* ES 1321; to reflect (light): *similes objectis quae radios lucis non ~mittunt, sed absorbent* AC 6388.2. **b** to send to consult, refer: *~mittitur lector ad illa quae...sequuntur* VR 142. **2** To put back, return (to a state): *~mittuntur...in statum exteriorum suorum* CI 506.3; AC 2116.2. **3** To allow to slacken, relax: *si externa...vincula...illis ~mitterentur*

AE 107.4; (impers. pass.) *~mittebatur iis aliquantisper dum memoraretur Deus* ES 2507; (pass.) to become feeble, slacken: *quod... ~mittatur omnis actio pulmonis et moriatur homo* DP 180.3. **b** *manum ~mittere*, to stay one's hand, remain inactive: *jam ~mitte manum tuam* 2 Sam. 24.16 (CI 229); *talis est ordo ut homo... non ~mittere debeat manum* AC 1712.2; *sicut qui staret ~missis manibus, aperto ore* DP 210.1. **c** (intr.) to relax one's efforts, slacken: *vertunt eum in ferum animal...et ligant...et trahunt, si ~mittit* ES 4381; *si Dominus vel tantillum ~mitteret ut homo ex voluntate propria ageret* AC 875.4. **4** To forgive, remit (sins or offences): *potestas ~mittendi peccata* AC 7318.2; *promptus erit ad ~mittendum aliis offensas* BCP (VI 6).

remonstro ~are ~avi ~atum, *tr*. To show again: (impers. pass.) *usque dum iis ~aretur quod nusquam possint quid efficere* ES 229.

remora ~ae, *f*. A thing which causes delay, hindrance: *~is et impedimentis...remotis* AC 1389; *fluit sermo absque ~a* ES 1109.

remoratio ~onis, *f*. Hindrance, delay: *cogitatio abstracta pervadere potest universum coelum absque ~one ullibi* AC 8985.2.

remoror ~ari ~atus sum, *tr*., *intr*. To hinder, delay: *plures consonantes non admittuntur, quia fluvium ~antur* ES 1147; (intr.) *obstantia...quae continue assurgunt et ~antur* AE 98.5.

remote, *adv*. (compar. *~ius*, superl. *~issime*) **1** At a distance, distantly: *qui se amat, ~issime abest ab amore ...coelesti* AC 760; *propius ad aequatorem... ~ius ab illo* AC 10200. **2** (transf.) At a remove, not closely: *unus proximius et directius, alter ~ius et obliquius, spectat regnum Domini* AC 997.2; *~e a re...loqui* AC 10709; *correspondentiis quae ~e significabant caelestia* SS 102.2.

remotio ~onis, *f*. **1** The act of removing, removal: *~onem malorum e coelo* AC 6997.1. **2** (transf.) The placing of distance between, making remote: *quo significabant, etiam per ~onem decentem, vitam spiritualem* AM 412.

remotive, *adv*. Without close connection: *loquuntur ...de coelo... ~e a doctrinali de Ultimo Judicio* AC 10758.2.

remotus ~a ~um, *a*. (pf. pple. of **removeo**) (compar. *~ior*, superl. *~issimus*) **1** At a distance, remote: *tantum ...Dominus ~ior* AC 981.1. **2** (transf.) Distanced, remote: *in statu prorsus ~o a falsis* AC 7088; *sensus internus... qui... ~us apparet a sensu literae* AC 7112; (neut. pl. as sb.) *in inferno...ubi omnes sunt in ultimis et crassissimis, et sic in ~issimis* VR 124.1. **3** Far removed from the obvious, far-fetched: *aliud Verbum per correspondentias non ita ~as conscriptum* SS 102.2; *apparet ~um intelligere vera a Domino loco sanguinis Ipsius* AE 30.1.

removeo ~vere ~vi ~tum, *tr*. **1** To move from its place, take away, remove: *et ~vebuntur ranae a te* Exod. 8.7 (AC); *~vebo candelabrum tuum e loco suo* Rev. 2.5 (AE 62.2). **2** To remove (a person from a state): *quantum...genus humanum a bono amoris...se ~vit* AC 6630; *si...homo non ~veretur a sensualibus* AC 6845. **3** To take away, banish, get rid of (immaterial objects): *omne spirituale a se ~verunt* AC 7090.1; *~vebo iniquitatem terrae* Zech. 3.9 (DD 4); *ut [Dominus] ~veret infernum ab homine* VR 2.2. **4** To leave out of account, set aside: *amor vere conjugialis...est solum modo cum una... ~tis omnibus aliis* AM 44.5; *si a cogitatione ~veas affectionem* FI 15.

remuneratio ~onis, *f*. **1** The payment of a reward: *jucundum...sentit in benefaciendo, non autem in ~one* AC 8002.8. **2** A reward, payment: *bona secum habent ~ones* AC 6997.5.

remunero ~are ~avi ~atum, *tr*. To give reward to, pay: *ex nullo fine propter se ut ~etur, sed ex amore* CI 408; ES 3171.

remus ~i, *m*. An oar: *e quercubus...fecerunt remos* Ezek. 27.6 (AC 6385.2) *navis ~i* Isa. 33.21 (AE 514.10).

renalis ~is ~e, *a*. Of the kidneys, renal: *capsulae ~es* ES 968.

renascentia ~ae, *f*. A second birth, rebirth: *regeneratio est ~a quoad spiritualem hominem* CI 279.

renascor ~nasci ~natus sum, *intr*. **1** (of natural products) To grow again: *[fructus] in menses ejus ~nascitur* Ezek. 47.12 (AC 57); *cuncta quae existunt, nascuntur et ~nascuntur super tellure* VR 12.1. **2** (of persons) To be born again: *antequam [homo] ~nascitur novus seu fit spiritualis et coelestis* AC 730.1.

renes ~um, *m. pl*. The kidneys: *qui probas corda et ~es* Ps.7.9 (AC 1788.4); *quod...intus in homine...duo ~es* AM 316.4; (as a province of the Grand Man) CI 96; (Bibl.) *veritatem desideras in ~ibus* Ps. 51.6 (AE 196.2).

renisus ~us, *m*. Struggling against a force, resistance: *~us inditur et simul dolor* AC 829.1; (transf.) *non potuerunt propter ~um internae [cogitationis] eloqui 'Divinum Humanum'* VR 111.8.

renitens ~ntis, *a*. Resisting: *inde ille* [sc. *intellectus*] *...tam obtusus et ~ns factus est* DP 70.2.

renitentia ~ae, *f*. Struggling against a force: *ex perpetua illa reluctatione, ~a, resistentia, repugnantia et reactione mali* VR 61.1.

renitor ~ti ~xus sum, *intr*. (fut. pple. *~surus*) To offer resistance, struggle in response: *ardor violandi faeminas...quae...violenter ~tuntur* AM 511; *si voluntas ~titur* AC 7342.

renovatio ~onis, *f.* A making new, renewal: *~o vitae* AM 525.2; ES 251.

renovo ~are ~avi ~atum, *tr.* **1** To make anew, renew: *~as facies humi* Ps. 104.30 (AC 16); *sicut semen sciret...processum quo se ~aturum sit* VR 12.2. **2** To reinvigorate, refresh: *animi continue ~ati* AM 3.4; *ut ~eris sicut aquila* Ps. 103.5 (AE 281.4).

renuentia ~ae, *f.* Refusal, reluctance: *nulla est ~a et repugnantia a parte uxorum* AM 258.

renuntio ~are ~avi ~atum, *tr., intr.* **1** To bring back (a message), report back: *~avit populo omnia verba Jehovae* Exod. 24.3 (AC); (w. *quod*) *~a illis quod adventus illorum mihi sit acceptus* AM 11. **2** (intr., w. dat.) To withdraw from, forsake, give up: *avertunt se et amicitiae ~ant* VR 441.1.

renuo ~ere ~i, *tr., intr.* **1** To refuse, reject: *ut ~ant et respuant omne verum* AC 845.2; *~unt omnem gratiarum actionem* CI 9.2; (intr.) *quod internum ita ~at coactum ab externo* DP 136.3. **2** (Bibl., w. inf.) To refuse (to): *~erunt auscultare* Zech. 7.11 (AC 1085.3); *si ~is tu dimittere populum Meum* Exod. 10.4 (AC).

reor reri ratus sum, *intr.* To hold a belief, think (as opposed to knowing): *quae...nusquam, ut reor, fidem adjicerent* ES 244; (w. *quod*) *reor quod multi tales* ES(M) 4597.

repagulum ~i, *neut.* A door-bar; (in quots. fig.) restraint, barrier: *alioquin malum...rumperet ~a, ac disperderet externa* AM 510.1; *ex vesano amore erumpente et relaxante ~a* AS 259; VR 501.3.

reparatio ~onis, *f.* The act of making good, repair: *quod non sit ulla pars intus in homine...quae se non renovat, quod fit per solutiones et ~ones* AM 171.2; revival, restoration: *qui* [*calor*] *nisi inesset...non foret ~o* AM 257.1.

reparo ~are ~avi ~atum, *tr.* To make good (something damaged), repair: *~a fornacem lateritiam* Nahum 3.14 (AC 6669.2); to revive, restore (a person): *tantum vir...refocillatur et ~atur* AM 294.4.

repello ~pellere ~puli ~pulsum, *tr.* To refuse admittance to, drive away, repel: *percepimus aliquid quod ~pulit et retroduxit nos* AM 22; *eorum...preces intus in se habent tale quod ~pellit coelum a se* AE 126.2; *lignum...quod imbibit tales liquores...ac caeteros ~pellit* CI 479.5.

rependo ~dere ~di ~sum, *tr.* (*intr.*) **1** To give in return or as compensation: *quinque boves ~det pro bove* Exod. 22.1 (AC); (intr.) to pay compensation: *dominus foveae ~det* Exod. 21.34 (AC). **2** To make return for, requite, repay: *cogitare coepit quomodo tantam gratiam ~dere posset* ES 2038.

repente, *adv.* Suddenly, quickly: *infectunt corpus, quod fit ~e* AC 8371; CI 48.

repercussio ~onis, *f.* The action of throwing back, reflection: *ex ~one soni e valvis* VR 577.3.

repercutio ~tere ~ssi ~ssum, *tr.* (pass.) To rebound, bounce: *ludi cum pilaminibus ~ssis* AM 17.4; (of light) to be reflected: *lux...visa est sicut ~ti* VR 137.13; cf. *bonum... ~titur et resilit, sicut globulus elasticus* SE 112.

reperio ~rire repperi ~rtum, *tr.* To find out, discover: *cupiunt...causas habere et sollicite quaerunt ubicunque eas ~rire possint* ES 959; *quae ~rta sunt per experientiam* ES 999 ½ (J D Odhner).

repetitio ~onis, *f.* **1** The saying of a thing more than once, repetition: *si caligo non aliud significaret quam tenebrae, foret ~o inanis* AC 7711.3; SS 81. **2** The repetition of an action: *sustinent...gravissimas poenas, et hoc in serie satis longa...per ~ones plures* ES(M) [4791].

repetito, *adv.* With repetition: *ex eo quod ~o dicatur 'fecerunt'* AC 7945; ES 994.

repeto ~ere ~ivi (*or* ~ii) ~itum, *tr.* **1** To say again, repeat: *quod una vox ~atur* AC 683; AC 8146.3. **2** To do again, repeat: *quod mane ~ere vellent...id quod prius* ES 4227; *~itis vicibus* 'repeatedly' ES 220.

repleo ~lere ~levi ~letum, *tr.* To fill to or beyond capacity, fill: *ille mundus ita ~letus est malitiosis, prout stagnum ex ovulis ranarum viridescens* VR 120.1; AC 7648.

replico ~are ~ui, *tr., intr.* (tr.) To turn back: *invertit oculos, agnovit et ~uit illos* ME 3; (intr.) to turn oneself round: *circumspexit...et tunc ~uit dicens...* VR 79.4.

repo ~ere ~si, *intr.* To walk on all fours, crawl: [*homo*] *primum ~eret sicut quadrupes* DP 275; (of worms, snakes, etc.) to move without the use of feet, crawl: *vermes qui... ~unt in loca* VR 12.6; ES 2475.

repono ~nere ~sui ~situm (*or* ~stum), *tr.* **1** To return to its place, put back: *illam* [sc. *chartam*] *~nite super hac mensa* VR 48.2. **2** To put away for safe keeping, store: *thesauraria sunt ubi opes ~nunur* AC 6661.2; *tabulae lapideae... ~sitae sunt in arca* AC 6804.6; *lapidem fundi sub quo Verbum erat ~stum* VR 187.3; (in the memory) *volunt et faciunt illa, nec ~nunt in memoria* CI 26. **3** (refl.) To place oneself, sit down: *erant ibi cespites...super illis se ~nebant* VR 113.5; *accurrebant...et amiciverunt se et ~suerunt se* AM 7.2.

reporto ~are ~avi ~atum, *tr.* To bring home, acquire for oneself: *irascuntur Deo, quia non ~ant praemia* VR 441.4.

reposco ~ere ~i, *tr.* To ask to be returned, demand back: *dum...mutuo alicui dat, nec ~it* ES 2964.

repositorium ~i, *neut.* A storehouse, granary: *~a ubi frumentum* AC 5370.

repostus ~a ~um, *a.* (alternative form of pf. pple. of **repono**) Stored away: *illa* [sc. *origo*] *in sacrariis mentis latet intime ~a* AM 111; *haec illis tam ignota et ~a sunt, sicut illa quae in fundo oceani* VR 391.1.

repotium ~i, *neut.* A drinks party: *festiva ~a celebrare* AM 8.1.

repraesentatio ~onis, *f.* **1** A natural object or action used to symbolize a spiritual idea: *quae existunt a spiritualibus in naturalibus sunt ~ones* AC 2987; *ipsi gestus et actiones, quae sunt corporis, repraesentant illa quae sunt mentis et sunt ~ones* AC 2988. **2** The spiritual idea represented by a natural object or action: *ex ~one 'Pharaonis', quod sint scientifica falsa in communi* AC 6683; *quod illa urbs absque illa ~one et inde significatione nullatenus sancta fuerit* AE 223.11. **3** The presentation of an idea in a visible form in the spiritual world: *repraesentabatur tunc in coelo prophanatio...quae ~o...non potuit aliter...quam horrorem angelis incutere* AC 1001.1.

repraesentative, *adv.* In the form of a representation, representatively: *quod sistantur* [*ideae angelicae*] *~e* AC 730.5; *ei circumdabatur ~e veritas* ES 260.

repraesentativus ~a ~um, *a.* also **representativus**. Serving to denote something else, symbolic, representative: *historica vera...quae omnia ~a sunt* AC 1401; *in sensu ~o* AC 6756.5; *omnes Ecclesiae...~ae fuerunt* VR 109.1; (w. gen.) *quod sensus literalis...sit significativus et ~us rerum quae in sensu spirituali* AC 6996.3; (neut. as sb.) *per ~a et significativa Ecclesiae ...fuit communicatio cum coelo* AC 8692.1.

repraesentator ~oris, *m.* One who represents: *~or Ipsius Salomo* DP 245.

repraesento ~are ~avi ~atum, *tr.* also **represento**. **1** To display in visible form, make a picture of: *dum illa concentrantur versus cylindrum, ~ant ibi imaginem venustam* AC 1871; *~abam illis volucres...quales in nostra tellure sunt* AC 7072; *~ata mihi quondam est via* CI 534.1. **2** To be the representative of (a person): *Dominus...praesens fuit...mediate per angelos qui ~abant Ipsum* VR 109.1. **3** To make known in words, represent: *qui solum per voces...hoc est, per loquelam, ~ant res aliis* ES 1050; ES 597. **4** (of persons, things, events, actions, etc.) To stand as a symbol for, represent (spiritual ideas): *Moses ~at Dominum quoad legem Divinam* AC 6714; *talis ereptio...nusquam...mandata fuisset nisi talia in spirituali mundo ~avisset* AC 7770.3.

reprehendo ~dere ~di ~sum, *tr.* To criticize, find fault with: *deprompsit solum talia quae posset ~dere* AC 10381; *datum est...~dere illos* AE 1147.3.

representativus: see **repraesentativus**.

represento: see **repraesento**.

repressio ~onis, *f.* The act of keeping in check, suppression: AC 9072.

reprimo ~rimere ~ressi ~ressum, *tr.* To keep in check, suppress: *quod Jehovah...~resserit Aegyptios per plagas* AC 6657.3; *inferna...~rimuntur a solo Domino* AC 8273.4; *homo qui novit quod malum sit, et non ~rimit illud* AC 9075.

reprobatio ~onis, *f.* Disapproval, rejection: *desolatio et vastatio significant ~onem et rejectionem Divini Veri* AE 83.3.

reprobo ~are ~avi ~atum, *tr.* To discard as unsuitable, disapprove of, reject: *odi, ~avi festa vestra* Amos 5.21 (AC 925.4); *lapis quem ~averunt aedificantes* Matt. 21.42 (CI 534.3); *prius oportet Filium Hominis pati et ~ari a generatione hac* Luke 17.25 (AE 63.10); *sequitur quod qui ~ant Verbum etiam ~ent Dominum* VR 384.1.

reprobus ~a ~um, *a.* Subject to disapproval, wrong: *ut quicquid iis apparet disconveniens et coram iis ~um, hoc culpant* ES 1221.

reproduco ~cere ~xi ~ctum, *tr.* To create anew, reproduce: *cum ~citur verum, etiam affectio cui verum adjunctum fuit ~citur* AC 7835; *objecta naturalia quae insunt memoriae,...non ~ci possunt in spirituali mundo* CI 461.3.

reproductio ~onis, *f.* Recreation, reproduction: SA 86 (= v.[3]).

reptatus ~us, *m.* A crawling movement, creeping: *quod similis esset* [*agitatio*] *~ui undulatorio substantiarum corticalium in cerebro* 3AD 2361.

reptile ~is, *neut.* Any creature, whether animal or insect, which crawls, creeping thing: *prorepere faciant aquae ~e, animam viventem* Gen. 1.20 (AC); *animalia terrae, volucres caeli, ~ia, pisces, vermiculi qui vocantur insecta* AM 133.2.

repto ~are ~avi, *intr.* To crawl, creep: *omnis anima vivens quae ~at* Ezek. 47.9 (AE 179.7); *vermes et anguiculi, qui quasi ~arent et ederent* ES 2897.

repudio ~are ~avi ~atum, *tr.* **1** To refuse to accept, reject: *qui sancta Verbi...in obfirmatione ~averunt* VI 97; *oretenus id ~ant* ES 443. **2** To reject (a suitor): *quod faeminae...indigne ~arentur* AM 297; to divorce (a wife): *mulierem ~atam a viro suo* Lev. 21.7 (AE 141.15).

repudium ~i, *neut.* The divorcing (of a wife): *ubi est libellus ~i matris vestrae?* AC 289.

repugnabilis ~is ~e, *a.* Repugnant: *hoc vocant... merito Christi obvium, ~e et injuriosum* VR 561.2.

repugnans ~ntis, *a.* (compar. *~ntior*) Repugnant: *sphaera eorum... ~ntior est sphaera aliorum* ES 3515.

repugnantia ~ae, *f.* A feeling of distaste, repugnance: *~a quaedam apud eos percepta est* CI 325; (w. pl.) an instance of this: *uxores...non faciunt licitum per varias ~as* AM 256.

repugno ~are ~avi, *intr.* **1** To struggle, resist: *cum appercipiunt...tunc ~ant quantum possunt* AC 5660.2. **2** To be distasteful, be repugnant: *bonum facere prorsus non possunt quia ~at* AC 6666.2; (w. dat.) *quod non concordat, hoc ~at ipsi eorum vitae* CI 237.

repurgatio ~onis, *f.* A purification, cleansing: *de ~onibus societatum* ES 5511.

repurgo ~are ~avi ~atum, *tr.* To make clean, purify: *nec a naturali faece sanguis ~atur* ES 1189; *ab illis plene ~are Ecclesiam* AE 257.1.

reputatio ~onis, *f.* A calculation, reckoning: *~o immunitatis, meriti, justitiae* AR 451.2.

reputo ~are ~avi ~atum, *tr.* **1** (w. pred.) To value, esteem, regard (as): *prae reliquis ~ati sapientes* VR 79.1; (w. *pro*) *qui...adulteria pro nihilo ~avit* AC 539; (w. *ut*) *~at illos ut viles servos* VR 45; (w. *sicut*) *mundana sicut nihili ~at* AM 182.1. **2** To hold in high esteem, regard: *contemtus ut non ~averimus Ipsum* Isa. 53.3 (AC 8364.5).

requies ~ei (*or* ~etis), *f.* Rest, pause: *plenaria ~es a laboribus* AM 8.1; *status ~ei* AC 8506; *locus ~etis* AC 5495; *in animi ~e* AM 316.1; *~em non habebant die et nocte* Rev. 4.8 (AR).

requiesco ~quiescere ~quievi, *intr.* **1** To be idle, rest: *ut ~quiescant ex laboribus suis* Rev. 14.13 (AR); (fig.) *amor et sapientia...sedem sibi faciunt, et sicut in sua domo ~quiescunt* VR 67.2. **2** (Bibl., w. *super*) To alight, rest (upon): *~quiescet super illo pax vestra* Luke 10.6 (CI 287.2).

requiro ~rere ~sivi ~situm, *tr.* **1** To seek after, search out: *Dominus... ~ret reliquias populi Sui* Isa. 11.11 (DD 4); *est illis omnis scientia ~sita* AC 7750.1. **2** To demand, require: *nec Dominus plus ab homine Ecclesiae ~rit quam ut vivat secundum id quod scit* AC 6706.

requisitum ~i, *neut.* That which is needed, a necessity: *quod talia inscripta sint amori conjugiali, ut ejus ~a* AM 295.2; *quod in illis* [sc. *ovis*] *lateat pullus...cum omni ~o ad formationem* VR 12.3.

res rei, *f.* **1** A physical object, thing: *cognitiones rerum quae in universo* AC 6696; *rerum natura*, the natural universe, Nature: *non...datur aliquid in rerum natura quod non existit...ex aliis* AC 4345.2. **b** property, goods: *rei familiaris amplificatio* AM 274. **2** A thing as opposed to a person: *nihil reflectitur super personam, sed super rem quae repraesentatur* AC 665; AE 8.2. **3** Any thing, either physical or abstract, which has a separate entity: *forma cujusvis rei est ex ordine* CI 201; *bonum est ipsum esse rei* VI 43.2; *unaquaevis litera...significat aliquam rem* VR 19.2. **4** Any activity or practice, deed: *rem foedam fecit virgo Israelis* Jer. 18.13 (AE 411.28); *'numerus hominis' significat rem et statum illius Ecclesiae* AC 10217.8; *dicentes quod nullam rem habere velint cum viris* ES 3896; (pl.) affairs, things: *cum res feliciter succedunt* AC 8717.3; *omnes res quae civiles, morales et spirituales vocantur* AS 209. **5** A matter under discussion, subject: *quod ipsam rem attinet* AC 6724.2; *de communi fide hujus rei* DP 191.1; *sed ad rem* 'but to return to the subject' VR 113.5. **6** (w. gen.) A matter (of or concerned with), thing: *cognitiones fidei facere res memoriae* AC 1197.1; *rebus intellectus* AC 6750.1; *haurit illa quae rei negotii sunt* FI 25. **b** *res communis*, the interests of everyone, the common weal: *nihil...est quod non aliquid facit ad rem communem* CI 64.1; ES 3446. **7** That which is real, reality: *quia non ita discernere res potest* AC 6704; *quod sit* [*Deus*] *omne rei ab Alphah ad Omegah* VR 159.7. **b** *re ipsa*, in very truth, in fact: *re ipsa etiam mali...consilium inter se ineunt* AC 6681. **c** *res se habet*, the matter is, the truth is: *aliter...res se habet cum angelis ultimi coeli* CI 271. **8** A matter of importance, substance: *quod dictamen Papae sit nullius rei* SS 24; *voces inanes quibus nihil rei...inest* DP 278[a].2; *quid rei?* 'What is the matter?' VR 112.2.

resaluto ~are ~avi, *intr.* To return a greeting: *mariti ...salutati cum favore ~abant* AM 209.1.

resarcio ~cire, *tr.* **1** To make whole again, mend, repair: *ut discerptum ~ciatur* VR 4.3; *si probi...facile... ~ciuntur* ES 4384. **2** To heal, make up (a quarrel): *dissidium inter illos cito ~citur* AC 8112; ES 614.

rescio ~cire ~civi ~citum, *tr.*, *intr.* To get to know, become aware of: *tam clandestine...ut alter nihil de eo ~ciat* CI 579; *hoc ita ~ciunt sicut memoria optima pollerent* ES 4168; (w. *quod*) *quod Deus sit...Primum... naturalis homo ex sua ratione nequicquam potest ~cire* VR 22.1.

reseco ~are ~ui ~tum, *tr.* To cut back: [*gramen*] *sub auroram florebit...sub vesperam ~abit* [*~abis* 1st edn. and in Swedenborg's rough draft] Ps. 90.6 (AC 7844.6); *~tum erat* 3AD 4483.

reservatio ~onis, *f.* The act of holding in store, safe keeping: *~o boni et veri apud hominem a Domino* AC 7556.

reservo ~are ~avi ~atum, *tr.* To maintain in safe keeping, store, keep: *ubi... ~ati sunt illi qui ab Ecclesia spirituali* AC 7090.1; *~aretur in quodam pu* AM 29; *adhuc exemplaria...apud typographum ~ata sunt* VR 123.1.

resideo ~sidere ~sedi, *intr.* To reside, dwell (in quots. fig.): *in tertio gradu ~sidet ejus sapientia* CI 208; *quod amor...in hac* [sc. *sapientia*] *~sideat sicut rex in suo regno, aut sicut herus in sua domo* VR 50.

resido ~sidere ~sedi, *intr.* To become less violent, abate: *usque dum tandem ardor talis ~sedit* AC 8232; *cum ~sedit tunc cupido, datur aliquid requiei* ES(M) 4698.

residuus ~a ~um, *a.* Still existing after a process, left over, residual: *tam paucam vitam ~am habent, qualis est ossium* AC 6959.2; *rejectionem humani ~i a matre* DD 16.6. **b** (neut. as sb.) that which is left, residue: *de ~o olei* Lev. 14.17 (AC 7430.2); *sicut ~um non esset aliquid* VR 29.3.

resignatus ~a ~um, *a.* (w. dat.) Handed over (to), consigned (to): *mens...est morti aeternae ~a* 3AD 3683.

resilio ~lire ~livi, *intr.* **1** To jump up, bounce: *quin rejiciatur et ~liat sicut globus elasticus conjectus in parietem* VR 642; *omnia quae loquuti estis... ~liunt in aërem* VR 136.3. **2** To spring back, rebound: *quod... cum ad orientem* [*se vertant*], *usque ~liant ad occidentem* ES [5535] ½; (fig.) *si non est* [*amor*] *reciprocus, numne ~lit, et fit nihil?* AM 444.1.

resina ~ae, *f.* Resin: *ex lignis arborum ~ae* AM 77.2; AC 5620.1.

resipiscentia ~ae, *f.* A recovery of wisdom, coming to one's senses: *quaedam societates tales ad ~am... tentant cogere* AC 7364; *quod malum non possit ablui ...per saponem et aquam, sed per ~am* AM 525.2.

resipisco ~piscere ~pui, *intr.* To become wise again, come to one's senses, recover: *se gerens tanquam ~puerit* AC 1513; ES 3412; (w. *ab*) *potest...videre insanias suas, et ab illis ~piscere* AM 48ª.3.

resistentia ~ae, *f.* **1** A contrary force, reaction, resistance: *da modo superpondium ab una parte, et nihil ~ae ab altera* CI 592; *ex...renitentia, ~a...et reactione mali* VR 61.1. **2** Opposition (on the part of persons), resistance: *per ~as pertinaces contra maritos* AM 292.2; *~am contra illos qui impugnant vera fidei* AE 101.

resistibilis ~is ~e, *a.* Capable of withstanding or opposing, resistant: *non dura et ~ia sed...mollia et cedentia* AC 3986.4.

resisto ~ere restiti, *intr.* To offer resistance, oppose: *qui credit quod Dominus solus ~at in tentationibus, is vincit* AC 8172; *fides absque charitate est dura et ~ens* AC 8321.2; (w. dat.) *quod viri...nequaquam possint obnixitatibus suarum uxorum ~ere* AM 292.2; (impers. pass.) *ei malum, quantum non ~i potest, infertur* AC 6657.1.

resolutio ~onis, *f.* **1** A relaxed state, unfastening: *paralysis quae est ~o et relaxatio membranarum et ligamentorum motui inservientium* AM 253.2. **2** A firm decision, resolve: *nam remanebat ~o seu voluntas* ES 4751.

resolvo ~vere ~ui ~utum, *tr.* **1** To undo the fastenings of, unfasten, unshackle, set free: *media quibus ~vuntur et discutiuntur mala et falsa* AC 1692.1; *sicut interiora essent plane aperta et ~uta ad recipiendum jucundum* CI 409. **2** To dissolve (a bond, structure, etc.): *textus interiores omnes* [*fibrarum*] *~verentur* AS 260.2.

resono ~are ~ui, *intr.* To make a loud noise, roar: *~ante mari et salo* Luke 21.25 (AC 1808.7); *vox eorum sicut mare ~at* Jer. 6.23 (AC 8313.3).

respective, *adv.* In comparison, relatively: *patuit mihi quanta illis sapientia et ~e quanta ignorantia homini* CI 269.3; SS 24.

respectivus ~a ~um, *a.* Determined by other factors, relative: *dextrum et sinistrum est nihil aliud quam ~um quoddam* AC 1582; *ex statu spiritus hominis ~o* VR 447; *in sensu ~o* AC 6714; AE 102.1; (neut. as sb.) relative nature: *~um status Domini* AC 2157.1.

respectus ~us, *m.* **1** The paying of attention, respect, regard: *nullo prorsus ~u habito ad parentes* AC 685; *omnium ~us ibi est quoad amorem et fidem in Dominum* AC 1159.3; *~um pro vero Divino* AC 7764. **2** The situation of one thing relative to another, point of view, mutual relationship: *talis est ~us coeli ad infernum...sicut inter duo opposita* CI 536; VR 27; *~u* (w. gen.) with respect to, from the point of view of: *quod artificialia nauci sint ~u naturalium* ES 251 titulus; *a sinistra ejus ~u mei* ES 462.

respicio ~picere ~pexi ~pectum, *intr.* (*tr.*) **1** (intr.) To turn one's gaze away, look back: *et ~pexit Pharao* Exod. 7.23 (AC); *quod ~pexerit post se* [*uxor Lothi*] AC 7857.1. **2** (intr.) To look towards, pay attention: *Jehovah, ~pice e coelis* Ps. 80.14 (AC 8281.4); (w. *ad*) *~piciam ad vos, et fructificabo vos* Lev. 26.9 (AC 6804.10). **3** (tr.) To look at, pay attention to: *~picit post se seu infra se officia quae pertransierat* AM 99; *nequaquam reliqua genera...affectionum existere possunt, et se mutuo ~picere* ES 486; (w. pred.) *~piciunt eos tanquam longe infra se* ES 2504.

respiratio ~onis, *f.* **1** The act of breathing, respiration: *media ~one edunt voces* CI 235; *~o pulmonaris* VI 46; VR 37.2; (distinguished into internal and external) *Antiquissimae Ecclesiae homo ~onem habuit internam, nec externam nisi tacitam* AC 607.2; AC 1118. **2** An intermission, pause, rest: *quasi ~o a captivitate* ES 218.

respiratorius ~a ~um, *a.* Of or concerned with breathing, respiratory: *motus ~i pulmonum* CI 445.

respiratus ~us, *m.* Breathing: ES 3353.

respiro ~are ~avi, *intr., tr.* **1** (intr.) To draw breath, breathe: *jucundum facit homini ~are libere et plene* AC 7411; *~ant etiam angeli in sua athmosphaera* CI 235. **2** (tr., fig.) To draw in with one's breath, breathe in: *~antes in otio gaudium aeternum* AC 454; *ad quae...populus cadit super genua, et ~at sanctum* VR 159.4; ES 3985.

respondeo ~dere ~di ~sum, *intr.* (*tr.*) **1** To speak in reply, answer: *Jesus ~dens dixit illis* Mark 10.3 (AC 6752.73); (impers. pass.) *si ~detur, Hoc non comprehendo* FI 1; (w. *quod*) *~derunt quod delectentur cognitionibus* AC 6815; (w. *ad*) *ad illas [res]... ~dent, Ita ita, vel, Non non* AE 14.2. **b** (w. acc.) to utter in reply: *si testis mendacii mendacium ~derit contra fratrem suam* Deut. 19.18 (AC 8223.1). **2** To make a noise in reply, answer: *~debunt jim in palatiis ejus* Isa. 13.22 (AC 7293.4); *~dete illi, Vinea meri* Isa. 27.2 (DD 4). **3** (w. *pro*) To be called to account (for), answer (for): *quod ~dendum pro singulis vocibus in altera vita* ES 2661 titulus. **4** (w. dat.) To be equivalent (to), answer (to): *in fine sexti diei, qui ~det vesperae Sabbathi* AC 480; *quod intima felicitas hominis...ne quidem ~deat minimae felicitati angelorum* ES 314 titulus. **5** (w. dat.) To be proportionate (to), correspond (to): *paena est cum intensiori cruciatu quia ~det eorum dolis absconditioribus* AC 960; *quod respiratio communis coeli ~deret meae respirationi sicut 3 ad unum* ES 605.

responsio ~onis, *f.* A responding, reply, answer: *in perceptione quacunque est tam propositio quam ~o* AC 2080; *post aliquas interrogationes et ~ones* VR 796.3; *quod [spiritus] non solum inducant cogitationes et loquelam homini, sed etiam ~onem, sic ut homo nihil aliud sciret, quam quod is respondeat, responsum nempe ad eorum favorem* ES 1795.

responsorius ~a ~um, *a.* Of or making a reply, answering: *formula ~a annuentiae* AC 2920.

responsum ~i, *neut.* A reply, answer: *sit commercium sermonis per interrogationes et ~a* AM 183.2; *~um* or *~a ferre*, to receive a reply: *per effulgurationes varias lucis tulerunt ~a* AC 6640.2; *~um tulit* FI 44.

respublica reipublicae, *f.* (declined in both parts) The political organization of a country, state: *voluptates honorum et officiorum in republica* AC 994.2; *illa quae reipublicae sunt, et vocantur civilia* AM 130.2.

respuo ~ere ~i, *tr.* To reject contemptuously, spurn: *qui omne verum ~unt* AC 806; *ut ~ant omnem doctrinam sapientium* CI 487.1.

restauratio ~onis, *f.* Re-establishment, restoration: *agitur ibi de ~one Ecclesiae* AE 239.6.

restauro ~are ~avi ~atum, *tr.* To establish again, restore: *cultus...qualis postea ~atus apud Jacobi posteros* AC 1343.1; *ut... ~etur imago seu forma coeli* CI 202.

restituo ~ere ~i ~tum, *tr.* **1** To give back, return: *porrexit mihi chartam, sed... ~i* VR 508.6. **2** To place upright again, restore to former situation: *quod Dominus ...rem lapsam ~erit* AC 8273.2; *ad ~endum et ad aedificandum Hierosolymam* Dan. 9.25 (DD 6); *tetigit illum et ~it super stationem suam* AE 79.3 (Dan. 10.10). **3** To establish again, restore to full vigour: *ita ordo... ~tus est* AC 99; *implere Verbum et per id redintegrare et ~ere illud* SS 111; *sphaera amoris...quae... ablata fuit, ~ta est* AM 161.2; (w. *in* + acc.) *dum in statum pristinum ~untur* ES 662; (w. dat.) *bono... privari potest et ~i statibus pristinis* ES Index s.v. 'bonum' (p. 76 Tafel), referring to ES 662.

restitutio ~onis, *f.* **1** Re-establishment, restoration: *agitur ibi de Ecclesiae ~one* AE 219.3. **2** Paying back, compensation, restitution: *promptus erit ad ~onem et satisfactionem* BCP (VI 6).

resto ~are, *intr.* To be left, remain: *ita ut...ne scintilla quidem spiritualium virium manserit aut ~et* VR 356 (Book of Concord).

restrictio ~onis, *f.* Limitation, restriction: *volebant quod totum coelum nihil absque ~one esset* ES 3443; *qui simpliciter absque ulla ~one credit* ES 4121.

restrictorius ~a ~um, *a.* Restricting, repressive: *motum constrictorium et ~um* AC 958.

restringo ~ngere ~nxi ~ctum, *tr.* To set limits to, restrain: *ut promiscua libido in communi ~ngatur* AM 349; *duplicitas... ~cta et separata* VR 629.

resulto ~are ~avi, *intr.* To be produced as a consequence, come about as a result: *potest inde ~are amicitia* AM 290; (w. *ab*) *ille sensus...qui a pluribus locis sensus literae inter se rite collatis ~at* AC 7233.3; (w. *ex*) *ex quorum actione et reactione ~at aequilibrium* CI 536. **b** (impers., w. *quod*) the result is (that): *ex quo dissidio ~at quod nullus Deus sit* VR 4.2.

resumo ~ere ~psi ~ptum, *tr.* **1** To take back, reclaim: *si beneplaceat Deo Messiae donum Ipsius ~ere* ES 333. **2** To take up again mentally, go over in the mind: *~it et quasi ruminat illa quae prius didicerat* AC 5135.2.

resupino ~are ~avi ~atum, *tr.* To turn upside down: (in quot. fig.) *principiata faciunt principia...et sic ~ant omnia* VR 37.3.

resupinus ~a ~um, *a.* Lying on one's back, supine: *bestiae quae ~ae incumbunt dorsis* AM 79.3.

resurgo ~gere ~rexi ~rectum, *intr.* **1** To rise again: *de eorum inferno, a quo non amplius ~gent* AC 581.2. **2** To rise again from the dead, be resurrected: **a** (of the Lord): *solus est [Dominus] qui ~rexit in coelum etiam corpore* AC 1729.2; *quod Jesus tertio die ~rexerit* SS 29. **b** (of persons): *nec si quis ex mortuis ~rexerit, persuadebuntur* Luke 16.31 (AC 6752.6); *Dominus docet quod omnes mortui ~gant* AM 28.

resurrectio ~onis, *f.* **1** The resurrection (of the Lord): *~o Domini quoad Humanum Suum* AC 7828. **2** The resurrection (of people): *exibunt qui bona fecerunt in ~onem vitae* John 5.29 (VI 2); cf. *Jesus dixit, Ego sum ~o et vita* John 11.25 (DD 32.6).

resuscitabilis ~is ~e, *a.* Capable of being revived: *lactor spe quod ille amor...resuscitetur, quia ~is est* AM 78.8; AM 466.2.

resuscitatio ~onis, *f.* Restoration to life, resuscitation: *per ~onem intelligitur eductio spiritus hominis a corpore, et introductio in mundum spiritualem* CI 447; SA 110 (= viii.2.[6]); (of a state) *rejectio status prioris et ~o novi* AC 4593.1.

resuscito ~are ~avi ~atum, *tr.* **1** To restore to life after death, revive: *cum ~atur [homo] seu...intrat in vitam aeternitatis* AC 70; *cum jacent in ferali mensa, antequam ~ati sunt* CI 433. **2** To bring into activity again, revive: *quod ~anda, nempe Ecclesia* AC 6516.1; *dum imperandi animum apud semet ~ant* ES 2812.

retalio ~are ~avi, *tr.* To wreak by way of revenge: *insulis retributionem ~abit* Isa. 59.18 (AE 406.19).

retardatio ~onis, *f.* A delaying, retardation: *num id quod dicunt fluat libere absque aliqua ~one* ES 1569; ES 3423.

retardo ~are ~avi ~atum, *tr.* To exercise a delaying influence, impede, hinder, hold back: *talia quae lenta sunt...et... ~ant visum internum* AC 6811; *hos nihil ~at quin...progrediantur absque limite* CI 270.4.

rete ~is, *neut.* **1** A net: *vir fratrem suum venantur ~i* Mic. 7.2 (AC 1178.3); *ut emitterent ~e in dextram partem navigii* AM 316.5 (John 21.6); (of a spider's web) ES 4735. **2** Anything constructed like a net, grid: *et facies ei cribrum, opus ~is* Exod. 27.4 (AC).

retectio ~onis, *f.* The act of uncovering: ES 5009.

retego ~gere ~xi ~ctum, *tr.* To remove the coverings of, uncover: *nec adhuc interiora ejus ~cta sunt* CI 457; (transf.) to disclose, reveal: *quia caro et sanguis haec tibi non ~xit* Matt. 16.17 (AE 206.3).

retentio ~onis, *f.* A holding back, restraint: *per ~onem quatuor ventorum terrae* AE 418.1; *ex...suspensione mentis et ~one a domesticis et forensibus* AM 9.3.

reticeo ~cere ~cui ~citum, *tr.* To pass over in silence, keep secret: *ad alium cujus nomen hic ~cetur* ES 948; 3AD 5661.

reticularis ~is ~e, *a.* Resembling a net, lattice-type: *opus ~e quod ex aere* AC 4489.2; *in extremis corporis sunt ~es formae et quasi cribra* AC 9726.

reticulum ~i, *neut.* (anat.) An enveloping membrane, caul: *~um super jecore* Exod. 29.13 (AC); AC 353.1.

retiformis ~is ~e, *a.* Net-like, reticular: *fila ~ia araneae* DP 107; *aves vesperae, quibus alae ~es sunt* AM 380.4.

retineo ~nere ~nui retentum, *tr.* **1** To hold back, check, restrain: *angelos... ~nentes quatuor ventos terrae* Rev. 7.1 (AR); *duo spiritus...illis occurrebant et ~nebant* AM 44.2. **2** To place under restraint, prevent from acting: *quod quantum ~nemus usus in nobis, et non communicamus, tantum pereat beatitudo* AM 266.3; (refl.) *spiritus...non potuerunt se ~nere quin eos ducerent ad loquendum* CI 343. **3** To keep in mind, preserve mentally: *quod quae spiritus audiunt... ~neant* AC 6812; *nunc ~nebo hoc narraturus sociis meis* VR 80.5. **4** To keep in use or in force, retain: *postea... eadem festa retenta fuerunt* AC 7893; *quod Adamus ~nuerit similitudinem Dei, postquam amiserat imaginem Dei* VR 48.4.

retorqueo ~quere ~si ~tum, *tr.* To twist back, reverse: *~serunt illa quae illuc spectare possent* CI 353.2; *cum id [sc. caput] elevat ad caelum, ~quet musculos* VR 404.2; (transf.) *quod...in malo sit tale, ut ~queatur in eum* ES 2913; ES(M) 4548.

retorsio ~onis, *f.* A twisting back, reversal: *mulctantur per...contorsiones et ~ones* AC 829.2; AS 254.2; ES 3918.

retorta ~ae, *f.* A vessel with a long and downward-pointing neck, retort: *sicut ignis in ~is acuit, clarificat et sublimat materias* VR 141.

retractio ~onis, *f.* **1** A drawing back, retraction: *appercepi ~onem anterioris partis capitis versus occiput* AC 7481. **2** Withdrawal, removal: *hoc animadvertimus ex ~one sensus ex oculis, auribus et corpore illorum* AM 203.4.

retracto ~are, *tr.* To undo, reverse: *ego Deus...facio et quis ~abit illud?* Isa. 43.13 (AC 4402.10).

retractus ~a ~um, *a.* (pf. pple. of **retraho**) **1** Drawn back, retracted: *monstrum...cum ~o naso* AS 254.2; averted: *quod...acie ~a adspectent* AM 224. **2** Held back, repressed: *~o spiritu* DP 210.1; *voce soni ~i* AM 241.

retraho ~here ~xi ~ctum, *tr.* **1** To pull in the reverse direction, draw back: *quando binae vires sibi oppositae agunt, quod una trahat et altera ~hat* AC 8168; (refl.) *striae illae nunc excurrebant obviam, nunc ~hebant se in se* AM 315.1. **2** (transf.) To inhibit, prevent, withdraw: *mali... ~hebant a bono et vero* AC 8321.1; *cogitatio ejus ~xit linguam ejus* VR 16.4; cf. *et stellae ~hent splendorem suum* Joel 2.10 (AC 31.1).

retribuo ~ere ~i ~tum, *tr.*, *intr.* **1** To repay, requite: *Jehovah... ~ens iniquitatem patrum in sinum filiorum eorum* Jer. 32.18 (AC 6960.5); *~am Babeli...omne malum illorum* Jer. 51.24 (AC 8226.2). **2** (intr.) To make a return, reward: *~e illis juxta opus illorum* Jer. 25.14 (VI 2); *ut vir gratias agat Domino...et ~at per receptionem sapientiae ab Ipso* AM 56.5; (impers. pass.) *dicitur...quod ei secundum opera ~etur* CI 358.

retributio ~onis, *f.* Repayment for an action, recompense: *affectio inserviendi aliis absque aliquo fine ~onis* AC 3419.3; (for a wicked action) retribution: *Mihi vindicta et ~o* Deut. 32.35 (AC 7051.3).

retributor ~oris, *m.* One who executes retribution, punisher: AC 6559.1.

retributorius ~a ~um, *a.* Of or concerned with repayment: *sacrificia eucharistica et ~a* AC 3880.8.

retro, *adv.* **1** Back in space, behind: *planeta Veneris... apparet ad sinistrum paulo ~o* AC 7247. **b** backwards, away: *se vertunt constanter ~o a Domino* CI 17. **2** Back in time, in the past: *multis a saeculis ~o* DP 135; *a pluribus annis ~o* ES 219. **3** In return: *quaeram ~o [ex] vobis* VR 850.

retroago ~roagere ~roegi ~roactum, *tr.* To drive back, repel: *cum Divinum Verum influit, et conatur ~roagere interiora quae mentis eorum* AE 411.2.

retrocedo ~dere ~ssi, *intr.* To go backwards, retreat, recoil: *ii ne ad primum quidem limen venire possunt, sed ~dunt* ES 2519.

retroduco ~cere ~xi ~ctum, *tr.* To make to retreat: *percepimus aliquid quod repulit et ~xit nos* AM 22; (refl.) to reintroduce: *in vita corporis, quo ~xit se, ibi manet* ES 3920.

retrogradus ~a ~um, *a.* Operating in reverse order, retrograde: *series...amoris infantum a maximo ad minimum ejus...est ~a* AM 401.2.

retrogredior ~di ~ssus sum, *intr.* To move backwards, retreat: *illae... ~ssae per cavernas retrorsum versus stagnum* ES 4453.

retrorsum, *adv.* Backwards: *indutus...chlamyde, quae ex volatu fluebat ~um* AM 2.1; *circumcursitare in orbem ~um seu a dextro ad sinistrum* ES 436.

retrospicio ~picere ~pexi, *intr.* To look back: *non licet et amplius ~picere* AC 8505.3.

retuli: pf. of **refero**.

reunio[1] ~nire ~nivi ~nitum, *tr.* To make one again, reunite: *mutua inclinatio ad ~niendum se* AM 89; *qui sanguis solvitur et ~nitur* ES 1033.

reunio[2] ~onis, *f.* Reunion: (of soul and body at Judgment Day) *quod homo non fiat homo quam die Ultimi Judicii, et quod interea moretur alicubi, et exspectet ~onem* AS 386.

reunitio ~onis, *f.* Reconstitution, reunion: *de ~one corporis* CI 183.3.

reus ~a ~um, *a.* Bearing responsibility for a misdeed, guilty: *fit ~us dum ex se a malo agit* VR 154.4; (w. gen.) *quod magni facinoris ~us esset* ES 2787.

revelatio ~onis, *f.* The revealing of knowledge from a heavenly source, revelation: *est sicut quis nihil discere vellet nisi ei ~o* AC 1712.3; *quod non talis immediata ~o fuerit* CI 300; *quod cognitio de Deo...non dabilis sit absque ~one* VR 11.1; an instance of this: *cognitiones verae fidei habebant per ~ones* AC 125; as the name of the last book in the Bible: *in Libro ~onis* UJ 44.

revelator ~oris, *m.* One who reveals: *~orem occultorum* AC 5331.

revello ~vellere ~velli ~vulsum, *tr.* To tear (something) loose from its attachment, tear away: *illi non possunt quin hypotheses fractas et ~vulsas a suis causis condant* AS 303.

revelo ~are ~avi ~atum, *tr.* **1** To make visible, disclose: *~ata sunt fundamenta orbis* Ps. 18.15 (AC 8286.4); *intimum hominis...prodit et se ~at in progenie postea* AM 206. **2** To make known, reveal (secrets): *~atus mihi est a Domino sensus internus Verbi* SS 4; *Deus providit Verbum, in quo...Semet Ipsum ~avit* VR 22.1; (as title of book) *Apocalypsis ~ata* AR titulus; (neut. of pf. pple. as sb.) *conscientia formatur ex ~atis* AC 371.

revera, *adv.* In truth, really: *lux quae illuminat mentem...est ~a lux* AC 6032.2.

reverberatio ~onis, *f.* A violent throwing back, bouncing: *ex quibus ~onibus...laniantur* AC 829.2.

reverbero ~are ~avi ~atum, *tr.* To throw back violently, echo: *haec et similia...in templis sonant et ~antur e parietibus* VR 132.2.

reverenter, *adv.* Respectfully, politely: *angelus... ~er adduxit illos* AM 14.2.

reverentia ~ae, *f.* A feeling of awe, respect, reverence: *nec ~a pro aliqua sanctitate Ecclesiae* AM 530.1; ES 1051.

revereor ~vereri ~veritus sum, *tr.* **1** To have respect for, revere: *angelus noster, quem ~veremur* AM 78.7. **2** To show partiality towards: *pauperem non ~vereberis in lite ejus* Exod. 23.3 (AC).

reversio ~onis, *f.* The act of returning (to a course of action): *~o ad mala priora* DP 231.8.

reversus ~us, *m.* A turning back, recoil: *redeunt post breves ~us* AC 822; ES 1349.

revertor ~ti ~sus sum, *intr.* **1** To go back, return: *~tar ad fratres meos* Exod. 4.18 (AC); *ne ~tatur retro ad tollendum vestimenta sua* Matt. 24.18 (AC 7857.1); (of things) *~sae sunt aquae, et obtexerunt currus et equites* Exod. 14.28 (AC); AM 394 (Matt. 10.13). **2** To return to a former state, recover: *et eduxit illam* [sc. *manum*] *e sinu suo, et ecce ~sa sicut caro illius* Exod. 4.7 (AC).

revideo ~dere ~di ~sum, *tr.* To look at again: ES(M) 4562.

revisio ~onis, *f.* A court of appeal: *in legendis actis senatus et ~onis* ES 5479.

revivisco ~viscere ~vixi, *intr.* To come to life again, revive: *quod nova Ecclesia ~visceret* AC 1778; *et venit in eos spiritus, et ~vixerunt* Ezek. 37.10 (AC 8286.2).

revivo ~vere ~xi, *intr.* To come to life again, revive: *quando defuncti sunt et quoad spiritum ~vunt* AR 153.1; (fig., of things) *ut Ecclesia Christiana...iterum ~vat* AM 532.2.

revocatio ~onis, *f.* Summoning to mind, recall: *percipitur solum per ~onem talium in memoriam* AC 751.2; AC 7398.

revoco ~are ~avi ~atum, *tr.* **1** To summon back, recall: *nec quod Israel... ~ari potuerit* AE 433.16. **2** To recall (to mind): *cum ~antur in memoriam quae cogitaverunt* CI 313; AM 307. **3** To bring back into use, reinstate: *ut cultus repraesentativus...restauraretur, eadem ~ata sunt* AC 4449.3.

revolo ~are ~avi, *intr.* To fly back: *quod illis refertae* [*apes*] *~ent...ad suum alveare* AM 419.

revolutio ~onis, *f.* **1** The progress of a cycle to the same point, revolution, turn: *vices et ~ones coelestes se habent secundum ordinem repraesentatum in mundo per annos...tum per dies* ES 2680. **2** A change, upset: *post aliquas ~ones status ejus vitae* AC 5058; *erat species cujusdem ~onis spirituum* ES 220.

revolvo ~vere ~vi ~utum, *tr.* To turn round, rotate, revolve: *apparebat sicut aliqui sumerent chartam...et ~verent illam digitis* AM 533; (in reading an ancient book in roll form) *et ~vit librum et invenit locum* Luke 4.17 (AE 375.17); to churn: *~vebantur ea quae in ventriculo, sic ut evomere dapes coactus sim* ES 1278.

rex regis, *m.* **1** An absolute monarch, king: *idcirco... regibus est sceptrum* AC 7026; *tyrannus cujus potestas ligata est, unde non rex dicendus est* VR 57.2. **2** *Liber Regum*, either of the Books of Kings: FI 50. **3** (as a title of the Lord): *Rex gloriae* Ps. 24.7 (DD 33.5); *Rex regum et Dominus dominorum* Rev. 19.16 (AR); *quod Dominus sit rex universi* ES 2664. **4** (transf., among animals): *bombyx...evolat ut rex papilionum* VR 80.3.

rhamnos: see **rhamnus**.

rhamnus ~i, *f.* (Gk.) also **rhamnos**. A thorny shrub, bramble: *dixerunt omnes arbores ad ~um, Ito tu, regnato super nos* Judg. 9.14 (AC 9277.4).

rheda ~ae, *f.* (Celtic) also **raeda**, and **reda**. A wheeled vehicle, wagon: *super ~is cameratis* Isa. 66.20 (AC 6756.4); *curribus aut ~is vehi* ES 297.

rheubismus ~i, *m.* Prob. error for **rheumatismus**: CO 51.3.

rheumatismus ~i, *m.* (Gk.) A cold in the head: *qui sonore loqui non poterant, sed sicut illi qui in ~o sunt* AC 1763.2; ES 3966.

rhombus ~i, *m.* (Gk.) **1** Anything of lozenge shape, rhomb: *trahunt filum ex ~is* ES 4828; *pectus tumens in ~um* AM 263.1. **2** A flat fish, prob. turbot: *projeci rete in lacum et captavi ~os et conchas* VR 381.3.

rhoncus ~i, *m.* (Gk.) The noise made by heavy breathing, snort: *auditus est ~us equorum ejus* Jer. 8.16 (AE 355.31).

rhythmicus ~a ~um, *a.* (Gk.) Rhythmical: *est loquela...plurium...labens sicut ~a* AC 1648.

rhythmus ~i, *m.* (Gk.) A rhythm: *species cantici, tametsi non cum ~is* 3AD 23.

rictus ~us, *m.* The open jaws, gape: *crocodili...suis latis et dentatis ~ibus in nos hiabant* AM 79.2; *magnus canis cum ~u horrendo* ES 2614.

rideo ~dere ~si ~sum, *intr., tr.* **1** (intr.) To express amusement, laugh, smile: (w. *ad*) *ad illa* [sc. *vera*] *~dent* SS 93; *ad quae ~debant amaene* AM 137.2; (of the face) *faciem...continue hilarem et ~dentem* AC 7807. **2** (tr.) To greet with amusement, smile or laugh at: *~dentur qui aliter sentiunt* AC 6666.3; *quod Chamus ~serit nuditatem patris sui* Gen. 9.22 (AE 240.9); *~dent eos corde suo, contemnunt* ES 4083. **3** (intr., of things) To present a cheerful appearance, smile: *omnia quae audit et videt, apparent ei sicut laeta et ~dentia* AC 920.2; *omnia coram oculis illorum quasi ~dent* CI 489.3.

ridiculosus ~a ~um, *a.* Likely to provoke amusement, laughable, ridiculous: *dictum... ~um appareret* ES 4650.

ridiculus ~a ~um, *a.* Likely to provoke amusement, laughable, ridiculous: *quis...non illa ut absona et ~a exsibilaturus est?* VR 356.

rigiditas ~atis, *f.* Inability to yield, rigidity: *perit fibrarum illarum tensibilitas et elasticitas, unde illarum obnixitas et ~as* VR 665.4.

rigidus ~a ~um, *a.* Unable to bend, unyielding, rigid: *qui in vero sunt, sunt quasi ~i* AC 7068; *in linguam quam... ~am faciunt* ES 4614; (fig.) *verum...absque bono prorsus ~um est* AC 7068.

rigo ~are ~avi ~atum, *tr.* To make wet: *~abo te lachryma mea* Isa. 16.9 (AC 2608).

rigor ~oris, *m.* Inflexibility, severity: *nunc substitit legis ~or* 3AD 3521.

rima ~ae, *f.* A narrow opening, crack, chink: *per ~as superne aliquid lucis...influit* CI 430; *~as ducere*, to develop cracks, split open: *quod illud chaos ~as duxerit, et per has ignis eruperit* VR 79.3.

rimator ~oris, *m.* One who examines a problem, researcher: *a ~oribus audiverunt* AM 133.1.

rimor ~ari ~atus sum, *tr.* To explore the nature of, examine, research into: *qui vult ~ari illam* [sc. *animam*] AM 315.8; *~ando quid pudor* ES 1051; (pf. pple. or gerundive in pass. sense) *per formam...a sagaci...lustratam et ~atam* CI 212; VR 368.

rimosus ~a ~um, *a.* Full of cracks: *domus structa ex calamis, sic ~a* AM 268.2.

ripa ~ae, *f.* The edge of land abutting on a piece of water or hole, a bank (of a river, lake, cave, etc.): *circa anteriorem ejus* [sc. *stagni*] *~am* AC 819; *ad ~am fluminis* Exod. 2.3 (AC); *evocant illos ex magna illa caverna...et ad ~as ejus...consistunt* ES 4681.

risus ~us, *m.* An expression of amusement, laugh, smile: *si...apud non bonos est hilaritas et ~us in faciebus, est in cute externa* AC 8247; (of other things) a cheerful appearance: *in statu pacis omnia coelestia...in suo quasi aurorae aut verno flore et ~u sunt* AC 1726.

rite, *adv.* In the correct manner, duly, properly: *ut quisque...functionem suam ~e obeat* AC 7038.1; *qui ~e expendit* CI 417.4; *a...rebus naturalibus ~e connexis* ES 155.

rituale ~is, *neut.* A symbolic act which was performed for a religious reason, ceremony, ritual: *per hoc ~e repraesentabatur fidei voluntas* AC 3869.10; (usu. pl.) *qui cognitiones, scientifica et ~ia coluerunt* AC 1132; *~ia...et statuta quae mandata fuerunt posteris Jacobi* AC 6846; *in ~ibus Ecclesiae Israeliticae* AM 14.11.

ritus ~us, *m.* A religious ceremony, rite: *si non externos ~us sancte observat* AC 1098; *in singulis Ecclesiae eorum ~ibus* AC 6846.

rivalis ~is, *m.* A rival: *ex...furore contra ~es* AM 106.

rivulus ~i, *m.* A stream, brook: *effundam... ~os super aridam* Isa. 44.3 (AC 8185.3).

rivus ~i, *m.* **1** A stream, brook: *pulverem...projeci in ~um descendentem a monte* (Deut. 9.21) AC 7418.4. **2** (fig.) A derivative, offshoot: *quod vita hominis sit ~us inde* CI 9.1; *ex variis causis...quae omnes ex dissimilitudine...trahunt ~os* AM 275.

rixa ~ae, *f.* A violent dispute, quarrel: *in... ~is, in ebrietate* CI 325; *qui...vixerunt continuo in ~is et furtis* ES 1347.

rixatio ~onis, *f.* A quarrel: *quod inter conjuges...sint alternae... ~ones et compositiones* AM 289.

rixator ~oris, *m.* A quarrelsome man: *Lutherus... quod nempe ~or* ES 5105.

rixor ~ari ~atus sum, *intr.* To quarrel: *vidi aliquos ~antes inter se de charitate et fide* FI 63.4; AM 294.6.

roboro ~are ~avi ~atum, *tr.* To endow with strength, make strong: *et ~antur brachia manuum ejus* Gen. 49.24 (AC).

robur ~oris, *neut.* **1** Physical strength, might: *extolle in ~ore vocem tuam* Isa. 40.9 (AC 795.4); *quia Ipsi a malis et falsis eorum nullum ~ur* AC 1658; (transf., of love) *quia* [*amor*] *etiam nobilitatur,* [*quod*] *maneat in suo ~ore* AM 161.3. **2** The name of a tree of doubtful identification: *sub quercu, populo et ~ore* Hos. 4.13 (AC 2466.10).

robustus ~a ~um, *a.* (compar. *~ior*, superl. *~issimus*) Strong, powerful: *manu ~a eduxit te Jehovah ex Aegypto* Exod. 13.9 (AC); *equi...satis ~i et alti* AC 8381.

rodo ~dere ~si ~sum, *tr.* To eat away, corrode: *humor acris qui fibras...mordet et ~dit* VR 665.4.

rogatio ~onis, *f.* The act of asking, request: AM 297.

rogo ~are ~avi ~atum, *tr.*, *intr.* To ask, beg, request: *Ego ~abo Patrem ut alium Paracletum det vobis* John 14.16 (AC 6788); (w. no acc.) *angelus... ~avit ut cohortes ...expromerent suam sapientiam* AM 2.3.

rogus ~i, *m.* A funeral pyre: *ligna...ad ~um adhibita* AC 643.4; Isa. 30.33 (AE 419.10).

Romanus ~a ~um, *a.* Of Rome, esp. in ancient times: *regimini ~o ante Caesarum tempora* VR 141; (masc. as sb.) ES 3394; *Catholicus ~us*, Roman Catholic: *Ecclesia Catholica ~a* AR 718.

romphaea ~ae, *f.* (Gk.) A broad sword: *et ex ore Ipsius prodibat ~a acuta* Rev. 19.15 (AR).

ros roris, *m.* Dew: *ex rore qui e coelo descendit* CI 289; *ros matutinus* AM 155[a].1.

rosa ~ae, *f.* A rose: *super ~is ambulare* AM 8.1; VR 12.7.

rosaceus ~a ~um, *a.* Decorated with rose pattern: *exornaverunt conclave ejus decoramentis et tapetibus ~is* VR 797.6.

rosarium ~i, *neut.* **1** A rose garden: AM 294.1. **2** A rosary: *~um ex chrysolithis* AM 42.4; (also, app.) an ornament resembling a rosary: *pileum, super cujus vertice erat ~um incinctum parvis sapphiris* AM 315.3.

rosetum ~i, *neut.* A flower bed or garden filled with roses, rose bed: *sedentes super ~is* AM 8.2; AE 411.32.

rostrum ~i, *neut.* **1** The beak (of a bird): [*mergus*] *infigit ei ~um* VR 165.3. **2** The trunk (of an elephant): *ab elephantis ~o dejici* ES 5896.

rota ~ae, *f.* A wheel: *dimovit ~am curruum illius* Exod. 14.25 (AC); ES 276; (of a mill) VR 576.2; (of a wheel-like structure) *conati sunt attrahere in suam ~am...alios* AC 5188.2.

rotatilis ~is ~e, *a.* Capable of being rotated, swivelling: *caput...externum quod est ~e circum internum* VR 381.3.

rotatio ~onis, *f.* A rotatory movement, rotation: *quod tellus circum axem suum rotet, et quod ~ones illae ...secundum zodiacum pergant* VR 29.1.

roto ~are ~avi ~atum, *tr.*, *intr.* **1** (tr.) To cause to turn about an axis, rotate: *extensis quasi brachiis ~atur* ES 946; (pass.) to spin, rotate: *quod circum axem suum ... ~entur* [*planetae*] AC 6697. **2** (intr.) To spin, rotate: VR 29.1.

rotularis ~is ~e, *a.* Capable of being rotated: *orbiculum ~em circum cylindrum* ES(M) [4819].

rotundatus ~a ~um, *a.* Rounded: *tentoria... superne ~a* AC 8379.

rotundus ~a ~um, *a.* **1** Roughly circular, round: *quod...facies suae majores futurae sint et... ~ae* AC 8243; (neut. as sb.) *et ecce super facies deserti minutum ~um* Exod. 16.14 (AC); *in ~um*, to make a circle: *sedilia continua...in ~um circumducta* AM 23. **2** (of numbers, measurements, etc.) Approximated to a convenient figure, round: *numerus ~us quadraginta pro non ~o quadraginta duo assumtus est* AC 730.3; *unitas ultima fit ~a per sequentem* ES 3423.

rubedo ~inis, *f.* Redness: *per sanguinem et ejus ~inem* AC 3527.2.

rubens ~ntis, *a.* (pres. pple. of **rubeo**) (compar. *~ntior*) Fiery red, ruddy: *igneum Gehennae quod ~ntius est* AC 826.

rubeo ~bere ~bui, *intr.* To be fiery red: *fulmen...quod ~buit* AM 316.5.

ruber ~bra ~brum, *a.* Red, ruddy: *si* [*peccata vestra*] *~bra fuerint sicut purpura* Isa. 1.18 (AE 67.2); *serpentes ~bri* AM 265; *lagenam vini ~bri* ES 3801; *mare ~brum*, the Red Sea: AC 4601.2.

rubesco ~ere, *intr.* To become red: *rubes a candido ~ens* CI 69; to blush: *a quo...verecunde ~it superior* AM 250.

rubeus ~a ~um, *a.* Of a red colour: *qualis sanguis, seu candidus seu ~us* ES 1059; ES 1306.

rubicundus ~a ~um, *a.* Reddish: *quare ~us quoad vestem Tuam...?* Isa. 63.2 (DD 14.2).

rubigo ~inis, *f.* A rust-coloured blight on plants, rust: *percussi uredine et ~ine plurimos hortos vestros* Amos 4.9 (AE 638.20).

rubinus ~i, *m.* A precious stone of red colour, ruby: *corona ex auro cum insitis ~is* AM 20.2; AE 364.7.

rubor ~oris, *m.* A red colour, redness: *calor sanguinis, et quoque ~or ejus, non aliunde sunt* AM 34; *orbare faciem ~ore* VR 41.3.

rubus ~i, *m.* A bramble bush: *et ecce ~us ardebat igne* Exod. 3.2 (AC); *neque ex ~o vindemiant uvam* Luke 6.44 (VI 28).

ructus ~us, *m.* An emission of wind from the throat, belch: *ex ventriculo ~us tetri, graveolenti* AM 253.2.

rudera ~um, *neut. pl.* Broken stones and masonry, rubble: *~a domuum ac urbium post incendia* CI 586; *~a templorum* ES 3931.

rudimentum ~i, *neut.* An initial stage, rudiment: *~a doctrinae Ecclesiae* AC 6751.

rudis[1] ~is ~e, *a.* (compar. *~ior*, superl. *~issimus*) **1** Coarsely or badly constructed, crude, rough: *~es casae* CI 586; *incedit* [*agricola*] *veste nova ex ~i lana* DP 254.4; *amictus nunc ~ior erat* ES 884; *~issima vascula* ES 2423. **2** (of persons) Uneducated, coarse: *apud uxores ~es* AM 292.2. **3** (of things) Not well worked, crude: *tametsi appareat* [*Verbum*] *in sensu literae ut ~e historicum* AC 855; AC 7780.

rudis[2] ~is, *f.* A wooden sword presented to gladiators on their discharge: (in quot. fig., as a token of the end of slavery) *quod illa fides donet renatos seu adeptos ~e libertatis, ut non sub lege sint* SE 79.

ruditas ~atis, *f.* Coarseness, crudity: *sic ipsae ~ates falsi absterguntur* AC 8149.

ruditer, *adv.* (superl. *~issime*) In a poorly constructed or organized manner, crudely: *repraesentantur imagines pulchrae ab illis quae... ~iter projecta sunt* AC 1871; *appercipere quidem ~issime* ES 2194.

rufus ~a ~um, *a.* (of hair, horses' coats, etc.) Reddish, ruddy: *alius equus, ~us* Rev. 6.4 (AR); VR 113.1; *draco magnus ~us* Rev. 12.3 (AR).

ruga ~ae, *f.* A fold in the skin, wrinkle: *facies...circa oculos ~is obsita* ES 1376.

rugio ~gire ~givi (*or* ~gii), *intr.* (of lions) To roar: *sicut leo ~git* Rev. 10.3 (AR); *leo ~giit, quis non timeat?* Amos 3.8 (AE 601.8); (transf.) *~givi, prae rugitu cordis mei* Ps. 38.8 (AR 471.2).

rugitus ~us, *m.* The noise made by a lion or similar beast, roaring: *vox ~us leonum juvenum* Zech. 11.3 (AC 1585.5).

ruina ~ae, *f.* A ruin: *lux obtenebrescet in ~is* Isa. 5.30 (DD 4).

rumen ~inis, *neut.* The first stomach of ruminant animals (in quot. fig.): *hoc iterum demonstrare foret ~en superfluum* VR 167.

ruminatorius ~a ~um, *a.* Used for ruminating, ruminatory: *ventriculum ~um* VR 146; *cum alvo ~o* DP 233.8.

rumino ~are ~avi ~atum, *tr.* To chew over again; (in quot. fig.) to ponder in the mind: *tunc resumit et quasi ~at illa quae...didicerat* AC 5135.2.

ruminor ~ari ~atus sum, *intr.* To ponder in the mind, chew (over): *meditatus et ~atus sum de hoc discrimine* AM 326.4; *~antur...super ea quae prius dicta* ES 829.

rumor ~oris, *m.* A noise: *audituri...estis bella et ~ores bellorum* Matt. 24.6 (AC 3353.2).

rumpo ~mpere ~pi ~ptum, *tr.* **1** To break apart (bonds or restraints): *illico vincula illa ~mpit* AC 7090.4; *~mperet repagula* AM 510.1; to break in pieces, shatter: *si...ei licuisset...evolare, non dubito quin ~mperetur* ES 198; *quod prius idea ~mperetur quam ut pervenire posset...in coelum* ES 2184. **2** To dissolve (an immaterial bond, friendship, pact, etc.): *cum amicitia ~pta* AC 1044.3; *communicatio ~pta est* CI 204; *si vocula auferretur, nexus ~mperetur et copula periret* SS 13.4. **3** To break into, interrupt: *voluerunt...interpolare sermonem nostrum; et tandem ~perunt illum* VR 113.9.

ruo ~ere ~i, *intr.* **1** To move rapidly, rush: *~unt tales ubi sphaera eorum* ES 4571; (esp. w. hostile intent) *unus ~it in alterum* AC 1322; cf. *dicent montibus et petris, ~ite super nos* Rev. 6.16 (AC 6849.4). **2** To proceed hurriedly, rush (into a course of action): *~erent in perniciem omnium* AC 7032.3; *~erent in omne nefas* AE 107.4. **3** To fall to ruin, perish: *alioquin universum ~eret* AM 391.1.

rupes ~is, *f.* A rocky cliff, crag: *scabrae ~es in quibus cavernae* CI 586; *~es satis altae* ES 4895.

rupetum ~i, *neut.* A place full of cliffs: *non vidi virgultum...sed arenaria et ~a* UJ(P) 217.

ruptio ~onis, *f.* A breaking or tearing apart: *~o aut discissio vestium* AC 4763.6.

ruptura ~ae, *f.* A break, crack: *obsepiamque ~as eorum* Amos 9.11 (AC 414.2); *per ~as murorum et domuum, usque ut cadant* AE 237.1.

rursum, *adv.* = **rursus**: John 12.28 (AC 6887.2).

rursus, *adv.* Again: *et glorificavi, et ~us glorificabo* John 12.28 (AC 1603.2); *prior angelus...~us aderat* AM 79.1.

Russicus ~a ~um, *a.* Russian: *gentem Italicam, et ~am* ES 5043.

rusticalis ~is ~e, *a.* Typical of a countryman or peasant: *haec responsa sunt ~ia et non forensia* AM 461.3; ME 4.

rustice, *adv.* In a countrified manner: *tu [loquutus es] ex rusticis ~e* VR 503.7.

rusticus ~a ~um, *a.* Typical of the countryside, countrified: *qui ex ~a gente et ex plebe erant* CI 364; (masc. as sb.) a countryman, peasant: *quod influxus sit secundum cujusvis formam, etiam a ~o potest videri* AM 86.

rutilans ~ntis, *a.* (compar. *~ntior*) Having a red tinge, glowing: *[lux] sicut adamantinum ~ns erat* AC 1526; *lux...quo magis in falso ex malo, eo ~ntior* AC 6907.3.

rutilatio ~onis, *f.* A reddening (of light): *tunc apparuit ~o viva lucis adamantinae* AC 1526.

rutilo ~are ~avi, *intr.* To become red, redden: *lux mundi non ~at, sed obscura est* AC 6907.3; *facie rotunda, quae ~abat sicut squama cochleae* AM 268.2; (fig.) *visus oculi ejus ~at ex igne lasciviae* DP 199.1.

rutilus ~a ~um, *a.* (superl. *~issimus*) Having a red tinge, reddish, ruddy: *ut sol, primum ~us et coruscans* CI 159; (neut. as sb.) *~um inde illustravit quorundam tempora* VR 73.4; ES 4639.

rutrum ~i, *neut.* A digging implement, spade: *sicut homo hortulanus...comparat sibi ~a, rastra, et plura instrumenta manus pro elaboranda terra* AE 1154.2.

S

sabbatarius: see **sabbatharius**.

Sabbath: see **Sabbathum**.

sabbatharius ~a ~um, *a.* (Hebr.) also **sabbatarius**. (of years) Sabbatical: *septimo anno qui est annus ~us* AE 388.24 (Exod. 23.11).

Sabbathum ~i, *neut.* (Hebr.) also **Sabbath**, *indecl.*, and **Sabbatum**. **1** The name given to the seventh day of the week, the Sabbath: *septimus dies sanctificatus est, et dictus ~um a quiete* AC 84; *quod nullum opus in festis et ~is facerent* AC 7893; *dies Dominica est dies ~i* AE 54. **2** A period of rest or tranquillity: *quod homo coelestis sit...dictus ~um a quiete* AC 85.1; *perpetuum ~um*, the perpetual Sabbath enjoyed by angels in heaven: *apud illos* [sc. *angelos*] *est perpetuum ~um* AC 1618; *vita caeli...vocatur perpetuum ~um* AM 9.1.

Sabbatum: see **Sabbathum**.

saccharinus ~a ~um, *a.* also **sach-**. Of sugar: *veneno ~i saporis* VR 595.2; *panis ~us*, a sugared loaf: AM 14.2.

saccharum ~i, *neut.* (Gk. from eastern origin) Sugar: *contigit...quod ~um [mihi obveniret] paene ut salinum* ES 645; VR 455.3.

saccus ~i, *m.* (Gk.) A bag made of coarse cloth, sack: *illa quae religionis sunt portant sicut in ~o super tergo* VR 22.3; a pocket (in clothing): *argentum magnum quod in vestis meae ~um illatum* ES 4045. **2** A sack used as clothing, sackcloth: *cinxerunt se ~is* Lam. 2.10 (AC 7418.3); *induti ~is nigris* AM 232.2.

sacer ~cra ~crum, *a.* see also **sacrum**. Dedicated to religious purposes, sacred, holy: *quod ignem ~crum perennem instituerint* AC 6832.7; *in cultu suo ~cro* AC 7097.1. **b** *~cra Caena*, the Holy Supper: VI 4; *Scriptura ~cra*, the Holy Scripture: AC 6632.

sacerdos ~otis, *m.* A person devoted to the service of God, minister of religion, priest: *cum rege...cum principe ...cum ~ote* AC 6653; VI 39; (in antiquity) *semimortuum ~os praeterivit* AC 6708 (Luke 10.31); *tu ~os in aeternum juxta modum Malkizedechi* Ps. 110.4 (AC 6148.4).

sacerdotalis ~is ~e, *a.* Of a priest, priestly: *regnum ~e Domini* CI 24; *quod in Domino sint duo munia, ~e et regium* VR 114; (neut. as sb.) priestly function, priesthood: *reges...repraesentabant regium Domini... sacerdotes ~e Domini* AC 1409.4.

sacerdotium ~i, *neut.* **1** The office of priest, priesthood: *si in bono ~i est* VI 39; *~um Aharonis et Levitarum* SS 20.2. **2** A priestly order: *quod tribus Levi...facta ~um* AC 352 (Num. 3.40-45).

sacharinus: see **saccharinus**.

sacramentalis ~is ~e, *a.* Brought about by the sacrament of the Holy Supper, sacramental: *quod...corpus et sanguis Christi...ratione ~is unionis cum pane et vino sumantur* AR Doc Ref.8.

sacramentaliter, *adv.* By involvement in a sacrament, sacramentally: *quod si populus non ~er communicat, sed solus minister, tunc populus spiritualiter communicet* AR Doc RC.3.

sacramentum ~i, *neut.* **1** A sacrament: *obire ~um coenae* AC 8253; *~um baptismi* AC 3670.2. **2** An agreement ratified by oath, sworn compact: *sit quaeso ~um inter nos* Gen. 26.28 (AC).

sacrarium ~i, *m.* A place for keeping holy objects, sacristy: *exemplar Verbi...in ~o...repositum est* SS 72; (fig.) *in ~is mentis* AM 111.

sacrificatio ~onis, *f.* The act of sacrificing: *per omnem processum ~onis* AC 5943.5; AC 8080.4.

sacrificium ~i, *neut.* The offering to God of a living creature, sacrifice: *tabernaculum, vestes Aharonis, ~a* AM 342.2.

sacrifico ~are ~avi ~atum, *tr.* To offer (an animal) to God by ceremonial killing, sacrifice: *ut agnus aut hoedus... ~aretur* AC 7839; cf. *ne ~arent filios suos* AC 8080.4; (w. cognate acc.) *~abunt sacrificia justitiae*

Deut. 33.19 (AC 6745.2). **b** (absol., w. dat.): *ad ~andum Jehovae Deo* AC 6907.1.

sacrilegium ~i, *neut.* Sacrilege: *si fieret* [*conjugium*] *cum pluribus...vocaremus illud ~um* AM 76.5.

sacrimonium ~i, *neut.* A sacred pledge, sacrament: *conjugium cum una uxore vocamus ~um* AM 76.5.

sacro ~are ~avi ~atum, *tr. Bellum ~are*, to conduct a holy war: *~ate contra illam bellum* Jer. 6.4 (AC 1664.4).

sacrosanctus ~a ~um, *a.* **1** Forbidden under pain of divine displeasure: *quod violare fidem... ~um esset* AC 395.1. **2** Protected by divine favour, sacred, inviolable: *tria et septem...sunt ~a* AC 900.

sacrum ~i, *neut.* A religious rite: *a hieroglyphicis Aegyptiorum, quibus etiam in ~is utebantur* AC 6692.1.

saecularis ~is ~e, *a.* **1** Of the conventional period of time, calendar: *qui in sensu literae sunt, ii putant annos esse ~es* AC 482. **2** Non-clerical, lay, civil: *in veste ~i* AR 341.2; *in ~i potestate* AR 716.4; (masc. as sb.) AR 784.1.

saeculum ~i, *neut.* **1** Any of the successive periods of historical time, esp. in antiquity of the four Ages: *apud antiquos, qui in ~o aureo...vixerant* AM 57; CI 115; *in ~is obscuris* 'in the Dark Ages' ES 5957. **2** A period of a hundred years, century: *quod quidam ibi jam per 20 ~a manserint* AC 947; [*pisces*] *intra ~um implerent spatia totius orbis* DP 56.3; (of the Christian era) *~o tertio, quando surrexerunt Ariani* VR 94.2. **3** (Bibl.) A period of ten years: *quae* [sc. *captivitas Babylonica*] *erat septem ~orum, seu septuaginta annorum* AC 395.2; *~um in Verbo est decem annorum* AC 433. **4** The present age as composed of people now living, the time: *sicut...sunt scripta ~i* SS 1; *error ~i est quod credatur...* DP 279.1. **b** *consummatio ~i*, the consummation of the age: Matt. 24.3 (AC 6895.1). **5** (Bibl.) *In ~um*, for ever: *non addetis videre illos amplius usque in ~um* Exod. 14.13 (AC); cf. AC 8174; *in ~a ~orum*, for ever and ever: *Viventi in ~a ~orum* Rev. 4.9 (AR).

saepe, *adv.* (compar. *~ius*, superl. *~issime*) Frequently, often: *prius ~e ostensum est* AC 6647; *Dominus ...Se ~ius vocat Filium Hominis seu Hominem* AC 49.4; *Dominus...in Monte Olivarum ~issime fuit* AC 10261.10.

saepenumero, *adv.* On many occasions, often: *quod homo ~o vertat illa quae dicuntur...in talia* AC 6884.

saepiuscule, *adv.* Rather often: *quandoque, imo ~e contigit* ES 645; ES 720.

saeve, *adv.* (compar. *~ius*) Savagely: *duriter et ~e afflixit filios Israelis* AC 6652.

saevio ~vire ~vivi, *intr.* To act savagely, rage: (w. *in* + acc.) *~vit in illos qui non omni suo nutui favent* AC 7773; (w. *contra*) *amant ~vire contra proximum* AC 7370.

saevitia ~ae, *f.* Savagery, ferocity: *fiunt...tigrides quoad ~am* VR 13.4; a savage act: *in rapinis, in ~is et similibus* AC 7272.1.

saevus ~a ~um, *a.* Of unrestrained ferocity, savage: *attraxerunt naturam ~am et crudelem* CI 488.6; cf. *dies Jehovae ~us* Isa. 13.9 (SS 14.3).

saga ~ae, *f.* A sorceress, witch: *satyri et priapi cum scortis et ~is* CO 57.2.

sagacitas ~atis, *f.* Acuteness of mind due to experience, sagacity: *rationalitas, judicium, ingenium, eruditio, ~as* AM 163; VR 35.13.

sagaciter, *adv.* With keen discernment and quick wit, sagaciously: *spiritus boni, angelici, et angeli...loquuntur inter se...acute, subtiliter, ~er, et distincte* AC 322.

sagax ~acis, *a.* (compar. *~acior*, superl. *~acissimus*) **1** (of animals) Keen-scented: *quae sphaera...sentitur odoratu a bestiis ~acibus* AC 7454.1. **2** Wise through experience, sagacious: *per formam omnium in corpore humano a ~aci et sapiente lustratam* CI 212; VR 699; ES 2252.

sagena ~ae, *f.* (Gk.) A dragnet for fishing: *~a jacta in mare* Matt. 13.47 (AC 2449.2); AE 513.17.

saginarius ~a ~um, *a.* (of animals) Fattened for slaughter: *vituli ~i* Jer. 46.21 (AC 8002.5).

saginatus ~a ~um, *a.* = **saginarius**: *boves ~i* 1 Kgs. 4.23 (AC 2165.1).

sagitta ~ae, *f.* An arrow: *quod Jonathan...jacularetur tres ~as* SS 29 (1 Sam. 20.20); *sicut ~ae ex arcu* AE 273.2.

sagittarius ~i, *m.* An archer: *prae voce equitis et ~orum* Jer. 4.29 (AE 223.7); *jaculator arcus seu ~us* AC 6422.

sal ~lis, *m.* **1** Common salt: *ne mentes vestrae...fiant statuae ~lis* AM 232.4; also, salt of other kinds: *copia ~lium varii generis* AS 420.2. **2** A sharp remark, witticism: *absque repugnantiis convenientibus nullum est ~l* ES 2362; *~les maximopere noxii* ES 2246.

salacia ~ae, *f.* Sexual fervour, lust: *qui...propter ~am non possunt inhibere libidines* AM 444[a].

salarium ~i, *neut.* A salary: *quibus ~a et stipendia ex publico aerario impendenda sunt* VR 430.

salax ~acis, *a.* Lustful: AM 459.1.

salinus ~a ~um, *a.* Tasting of salt: *contigit...quod saccharum* [*mihi obveniret*] *paene ut ~um* ES 645.

salio[1] ~lire ~livi, *intr.* **1** To jump, leap: *tunc ~liet sicut cervus claudus* Isa. 35.6 (AC 6988.1); *locustae* *quae super gramine humi ~liebant* VR 71.1. **2** (of liquids) To rise into the air, spring up, spurt: *fons aquae ~lientis* John 4.14 (SS 2.2); *ad fontes et aquas ~lientes* AM 8.2.

salio[2] ~lire ~livi ~litum, *tr.* To make salty: *cibus ~litus* AC 3718; *si sal infatuetur, per quid ~lietur?* Matt. 5.13 (AC 9207.2).

saliva ~ae, *f.* Saliva, spittle: ES 1742; ES 3096.

salivalis ~is ~e, *a.* Of or associated with the saliva: *humores... ~es* AC 1103.2; *ductus ~es* ES 3556.

salix ~icis, *f.* A willow tree: *~ices torrentis* Lev. 23.40 (AC 7093.2).

salsedo ~inis, *f.* The quality of being salt, saltiness: *sal dum ~inem suam amittit* CH 190 (= xi).

salsugineus ~a ~um, *a.* = **salsuginosus**: AC 10300.5 (Autograph).

salsuginosus ~a ~um, *a.* (of land) Abounding in salt, salty: *terra ~a* Jer. 17.6 (AC 1666.3).

salsugo ~inis, *f.* A piece of ground impregnated with salt, salt marsh: *ponit...terram fructus in ~inem* Ps. 107.34 (AE 730.17).

salsus ~a ~um, *a.* Salty: *terra ~a* Jer. 17.6 (AC 2455.3).

saltatio ~onis, *f.* Dancing: *de ~one in nuptialibus* ES 2083; (as an entertainment) a dance: *voluptates, ludi, ~ones, comessationes* AC 943.

saltator ~oris, *m.* A dancer: ES 3950.

saltatorius ~a ~um, *a.* Of dancing; (neut. pl. as sb.) dances: *potatoria, epularia, ~a ac histrionica et mimica* CO 57.2.

saltem, *adv.* At least: *ut ~em tangerent fimbriam indumenti Ipsius* Mark 6.56 (AC 10130.7).

saltito ~are ~avi, *intr.* To leap repeatedly, keep jumping: *currus ~ans* Nahum 3.2 (AC 6978).

salto ~are ~avi, *intr.* **1** To dance: *choreae virginum et juvenum ~antium ad modos symphoniarum* AM 3.3; ES 3212; (of things) *confringit Jehovah cedros Libani, et ~are facit eos* Ps. 29.6 (SS 18.4). **2** (of animals) To jump, hop: *cui crura super pedes ejus ad ~andum illis super terra* Lev. 11.21 (AE 543.15).

saltus ~us, *m.* **1** A jump, leap: *locustae sequebantur illos ~ibus* VR 71.4. **2** *~us S. Viti*, St Vitus's dance, tarantism: VR 367.7; VR 566.

salubris ~is ~e, *a.* Conducive to good health, salubrious: *non alia edunt quam...quae iis ~ia sunt* ES 3998; [*victus*] *~is et conveniens* AC 1516.

salum ~i, *neut.* The rough sea: *resonante mari et ~o* Luke 21.25 (AC 1808.7); *num insistant terrae aut ~o* ES 352.

salus ~utis, *f.* **1** Maintenance in a good condition, safety, health, welfare: *quorum cor est in ~ute publica* AM 7.4; *~us corporis* AE 744.2. **2** The preservation in good condition of the soul, salvation: *ut serviant... ~uti animarum* AC 8148.2; *absque Domino nulla ~us* CI 318; FI 42; (pl.) means of salvation: *quod Dominus illas ~utes continuo operetur* VR 142.

salutaris ~is ~e, *a.* **1** Conducive to health, wholesome: *per cibos bonos et ~es* ES 3565. **2** Conducive to salvation, saving: *bonum ~e* VR 564.1; (neut. as sb.) a means of salvation: *viderunt oculi mei ~e Tuum* Luke 2.30 (SS 86); *~ia generi humano sic praevisa et provisa* ES 224.

salutatio ~onis, *f.* A greeting: *cogitavit quanta esset ~o illa* Luke 1.29 (DD 19.2); CI 287.2.

salutifer ~era ~erum, *a.* **1** Health-giving: *virgulta boni usus seu ~era* DP 292.1; *cibus...plus ~er* ES 4117. **2** Bringing about salvation, saving: *fides ~era* FI 24; (neut. as sb.) *confusa idea de ~eris* SE 42.

saluto ~are ~avi ~atum, *tr.* **1** To express good wishes to, greet: *qui venientes suscipiebant, ~abant* AM 9.1; *ingredientes in domum ~ate eam* Matt. 10.12 (AE 365.8). **2** (pass., w. predicate) To be hailed as: *pro intellectualibus angelis volunt se ~ari* ES 157; ES 1238.

salvatio ~onis, *f.* The raising (of a human soul) to heaven, salvation: *propter ~onem generis humani* AC 6700; *de ~one et de condemnatione hominis* CI 471.

salvator ~oris, *m.* One who saves, saviour; esp. as title of the Lord: *de passione ~oris nostri* AC 8383; *Dominus Deus ~or Jesus Christus* VR 2.2.

salve, *interj.* Greeting: *angelus...dixit, ~e, gratiam consequuta* Luke 1.28 (DD 19.2).

salvifico ~are ~avi, *intr.* To produce salvation, save: *fides...est quae ~at* ES 1244.

salvificus ~a ~um, *a.* (of faith) Producing salvation, saving: *per fidem corde, quae est fides amoris seu ~a* AC 30.2; *quod fides ~a sit credere in Ipsum* VR 3.2; (neut. as sb.) *~um fidei* AC 4683.2.

salvo ~are ~avi ~atum, *tr.*, *intr.* **1** To make safe, rescue, save: *quod...* [*Lothus*] *~atus per angelos* AC 1428; ES 243. **2** To save from damnation: *quod Messias venturus ut ~aret animas in aeternum* AC 6963.2; *dicunt ~ari hominem, utcunque vixerat* AC 7127.2. **b** (intr.) to effect salvation, save: *bonum naturale nullum ~at* AC 7761; *fiduciam habere quod Ille ~et* VR 2.3.

salvus ~a ~um, *a.* Protected from harm, safe: *fides tua te ~am facit* Luke 7.50 (VI 51); *in ~o*, in safety: *in ripa seu litore, seu in ~o* ES 4155.

Samaritanus ~a ~um, *a.* (Gk. from Hebr.) Samaritan:

a Simone, qui fuit gente ~us VR 378.2; (masc. as sb.) a person from Samaria, Samaritan: *Jesus dixit ad duodecim,...In urbem ~orum ne ingredimini* Matt. 10.5 (AC 4169.2).

Samaritis ~idis, *f. adj.* Of Samaria: *mulier ~is* AE 483.12 (John 4.7).

sanatio ~onis, *f.* The act of healing: *~ones morborum* AC 8364.6; *~ones coecorum* AE 152.13.

sanator ~oris, *m.* One who heals, healer: *Ego Jehovah ~or tuus* Exod. 15.26 (AC).

sancio ~cire ~civi (*or* ~xi) ~citum, *intr.* To specify as an order, command, prescribe: *religio quae ~cit, quod non liceat plures uxores ducere* DP 256.1; *quod...Pater ... ~civerit, quod condonaturus sit...* VR 134.2; (impers. pass.) *lege ~citum est ne aliquid oppositi...exhibeant* AM 17.5.

sancitum ~i, *neut.* That which is commanded, prescription: *faedus antenuptiale manifestat ~a amoris vere conjugialis* AM 307.

sancte, *adv.* (compar. *~ius*) With due reverence, in a holy manner: *ritus Ecclesiae ~e observant* AC 1062; *qui id* [sc. *Verbum*] *~e legunt* SS 19.

sanctificatio ~onis, *f.* **1** Dedication to religious purposes: *per ~onem intelligere coeperunt sacrificationem* AC 8080.4. **2** The act of making holy, hallowing: *cum illo dogmate quod justificatio sit realis ~o* AR 758.

sanctificator ~oris, *m.* One who sanctifies: *a justificatoribus et ~oribus per solam fidem* VR 181.

sanctifico ~are ~avi ~atum, *tr.* **1** To set apart as a religious offering, dedicate: *cum argento et auro, quod ~averat ex omnibus gentibus quas subegit* 2 Sam. 8.11 (AC 6917.3); *~a Mihi omne primogenitum* Exod. 13.2 (AC); *ideo fontes ~abant* DP 255.2; *totidem a nobis ~atae aedes* AM 9.1. **2** To make holy, hallow: *opera per charitatem a Domino ~ata* AC 349.2; *~etur nomen Tuum* Matt. 6.9 (AC 6674.8); *quod populus...se praeparaverit et ~averit per tres dies* VI 59 (Exod. 19.10). **b** (of Roman Catholics) to treat as a saint, canonize: *Romano-Catholici Mariam matrem super reliquos ~averunt* VR 94.1.

sanctimonium ~i, *neut.* A religiously ordained institution, sacrament: *num illa* [sc. *conjugia*], *apud vos...sint ~a, vel non* AM 79.8.

sanctitas ~atis, *f.* **1** The quality of being holy, holiness: *de Verbi Divinitate et ~ate* SS 4; *Judaei non ausi sunt nominare Jehovam propter ~atem* VR 81.1; *~as ~atum*, the holy of holies: AC 7978.2 (Lev. 24.9); also, the height of holiness: *sabbathum...fuit ~as ~atum* VR 301. **2** A holy act, piety: *facile se per ~es externas abduci patiuntur* AC 3900.4.

sanctuarium ~i, *neut.* **1** A place of especial holiness, sanctuary: *nullus praeputiatus...intrabit in ~um* Ezek. 44.9 (FI 54); *~um, ubi in arca jacet Verbum* AM 77.2; cf. *causae quae in arcano et ~o Domini* ES 2393. **2** (Bibl.) A place of refuge, sanctuary: *factus est Jehudah in ~um Ipsius* Ps. 114.2 (AC 3654.6).

sanctus ~a ~um, *a.* (compar. *~ior*, superl. *~issimus*) **1** Inspired by or proceeding from God, holy: *timor ~us* AC 6678; *sphaera...quae ~a est in origine sua* AM 225; *~a Communio*, Holy Communion: BCP (VI 6); *~a Coena*, the Holy Supper: AC 6804.11. **b** (neut. as sb.) holiness: *status ~i procedentis a Divino Humano Domini* AC 6845; *qui ~um Verbo...derogant* VR 148.2; (pl.) *de ~is amoris et bonis inde* AC 412. **2** To be treated with awe, deserving reverence, holy: *tentoria ~iora habita sunt quam templum* AC 414.4; *terra inde appellata fuit 'Terra ~a', tametsi nihil minus quam ~a fuit* AC 1437; *inde arca ~issima fuit quia repraesentabat Divinum Humanum Domini* AC 6723.4; (neut. as sb.) *Sacerdos Maximus, cui ~issima Ecclesiae commissa erant* AC 10401. **b** (neut. as sb.) that which is holy, holiness: *in ~o quo afficitur homo* AC 5466. **c** (neut. as sb.) a holy place, shrine: *~a ~orum*, the holy of holies: *et distinguat velum vobis inter ~um et ~um ~orum* Exod. 26.33 (AC); (also, Bibl.) a very holy thing: *~um ~orum illa* Lev. 6.17 (AC 2177.5). **3** (masc. as sb.) A person who is redeemed, saint: *multa corpora dormientium ~orum suscitata sunt* Matt. 27.52 (AC 8018.2); *ille in communione ~orum in terris est* VR 15.1; ES 326. **b** a dead person honoured as a mediator by certain Churches, saint: *qui homines mortuos ut ~os supplicatione adeunt* AC 7272.3; FI 8.

sane, *adv.* **1** In a sane manner, rationally: *sanitati corporis, secundum quam mens ~e agat* AC 7038.2; *loquebantur ex interiori judicio ~e* AR 675.1; ES 3949. **2** To be sure, really, actually: *si veritas est, ~e est prodigium* AM 4.1; *si tunc scivisset... ~e discerpsisset illam* [sc. *epistolam*] *digitis* VR 137.12.

sanguificatio ~onis, *f.* The making of blood: *ad usus chylificationis et ~onis* SA 127 (= x.7.[3]).

sanguifico ~are ~avi, *intr.* To make blood: *hepar ~at* VR 496.4.

sanguineus ~a ~um, *a.* **1** Of or concerned with the blood: *vasis ~is* AM 329.1. **2** Blood-coloured, bloodstained: *~a sphaera* ES 2691; (of persons) ES 391.

sanguinolentus ~a ~um, *a.* Bloodthirsty: *qui ~i fuerunt, ii delectantur cruciare spiritus* AC 954; ES 377.

sanguis ~inis, *m.* The red fluid circulating in the bodies of men and animals, blood: *mala ~inis et fluidorum corporis temperie* AC 847.2; *cor regnat per ~inem* AM 179; *status mutationes in ~ine utroque* [i.e., venous and arterial blood] ES 167. **b** (fig.) *~is uvarum*, the 'blood' (i.e., juice) of grapes: Gen. 49.11 (AC); *vinum appellatur '~is uvarum'* AC 5117.9 (Deut. 32.14); cf. *exivit ~is e torculari* Rev. 14.20 (AR). **2** Spilt blood, gore: *ecce ~is foederis quod pepigit Jehovah* Exod. 24.8 (AC); *Te vidi super cruce, et tunc ~inem Tuum* FI 44. **3** (pl., Bibl.) Blood as standing for bloodshed, violence: *qui non ex ~inibus...sed ex Deo nati sunt* John 1.13 (AC 5823.6); *obturat aures suas ne audiant ~ines* Isa. 33.15 (VI 84.1); *sponsus ~inum* Exod. 4.25 (AC).

sanguisuga ~ae, *f.* A leech: *occidere ut ~a* ES 2974.

sanies ~ei, *f.* Corrupt blood or other bodily humours, pus: *sicut ~es per ulcus modo exterius sanatum* VI 110; AM 149; *sanguis...separatus a carne est cruor et fit ~es* VR 367.5.

sanitas ~atis, *f.* The good condition of the body or mind, health: *inservit... ~ati corporis* AC 7038.2; *nec cogitat de ~ate mentis* AC 6936; (fig.) *folia arboris ad ~atem gentium* Rev. 22.2 (AE 109.5).

sano ~are ~avi ~atum, *tr.* **1** To restore to health, heal, cure (the sick): *quod...leprosi ~arentur* AC 7337.1; (w. *ab*) *a plagis tuis ~abo te* Jer. 30.17 (AC 8365). **2** To heal, cure (a disease, wound, etc.): *quod Dominus omnem morbum... ~averit* AC 8364.6; *ulcus modo exterius ~atum* VI 110. **3** To make wholesome: *per quod aquae amarae ~atae sint per lignum illis injectum* AC 8349.

santalus ~i, *f.* (etymology obscure) The sandalwood tree: *sicut ~os plantavit Jehovah* Num. 24.6 (AC 108).

Santorianus ~a ~um, *a.* Prob. error for *Santorinianus* 'discovered by the Italian anatomist G D Santorini [1681-1737]': *a perspiratione ~a* ES 1738.

sanus ~a ~um, *a.* (compar. *~ior*) **1** In good physical health, healthy: *et statim factus est ~us homo* John 5.9 (AE 163.7); cf. w. sense 2: *ut mens sana sit in corpore ~o* AC 6936. **2** (of mental powers, attitudes, etc.) Soundly based, sound, sensible: *gens cui religio et ~a ratio* VR 5; *contra ~am rationem* AM 182.5; *absque permissione malorum, quae ~o sensu intelligenda est* ES 398.

saphir: see **sapphirus**.

sapidus ~a ~um, *a.* (compar. *~ior*) (of food) Having an agreeable taste, tasty: *addebant quod cibus utilis illis ~us sit* AC 8378; ES 596; (neut. as sb.) *gustui [jucundum] ex ~is* CI 402.

sapiens ~ntis, *a.* (compar. *~ntior*, superl. *~ntissimus*) (gen. pl. *~ntum* AC 7296; *~ntium* VI 30.2) **1** Possessing wisdom, wise: *homines...quia interiores, fuerunt ~ntiores* AC 6629; AE 14.2; (masc. as sb.) a wise man: *quod anima sit a patre, a nullo ~nte in dubium vocatur* AM 206. **2** (masc. as sb.) One skilled in magical arts, sorcerer: *et vocavit etiam Pharao ~ntes et praestigiatores* Exod. 7.11 (AC); *~ntes ab oriente* Matt. 2.1 (AC 1171.5). **3** (masc. as sb.) One skilled in a craft, craftsman: *vestis...opus ~ntum tota* Jer. 10.9 (AC 9466.5).

sapienter, *adv.* (compar. *~ius*) In a wise manner, wisely: *quod simplices simpliciter intelligerent... Verbum, et sapientes ~er* AC 7263; *illi qui in coelo sunt ... ~ius cogitant, quam cum fuerunt in mundo* CI 462.1.

sapientia ~ae, *f.* **1** Soundness of understanding, wisdom: *~a seu intelligentia humana* AC 42.1; *Deus, cui infinita ~a est* SS 1; (dist. from **intelligentia**) *quod dein creverit scientia, tum intelligentia et ~a* AC 6716.1. **2** Wisdom regarded as a kind of knowledge, wise teaching: *Aegyptii scientias rerum vocabant ~am* AC 7296; *~a Angelica de Divino Amore* AS titulus; *recipiunt omnem suam ~am per auditum* AE 14.2.

sapio ~pere ~pui, *intr.*, *tr.* **1** (intr.) To be wise: *qui supra alios se credunt ~pere* SS 91; *alternis ~pimus et insanimus* AM 268.3; *homo vult ex corporeis... ~pere* ES 4121; (w. *de*) *quid...intellexerant et ~puerant de gaudio caelesti* AM 2.1. **2** (w. acc.) To be wise about, be skilled in: *sciunt et ~piunt talia quae nusquam prius noverant* AC 7750.3; *qui multa e mundo ~piunt* CI 1. **3** (tr., of things) To possess a taste of, smack of: *quod in linguis humanis 'sapor et' ~pere etiam praedicetur de perceptione rei* AE 617.33; (esp. fig.) *quod nova tua doctrina ~piat Mahumedismum* VR 137.12; *regis nomen mundanum ~pit* ES 531; (intr., w. *ex*) *idea...quae ~pit ex amore* CI 450.

sapo ~onis, *m.* Soap: *abstergi sicut sordes per ~onem et aquam* AM 525.2.

sapor ~oris, *m.* Pleasant taste, flavour: *fructibus ~oris delicati* AM 3.4; *~or ejus sicut placentae in melle* Exod. 16.31 (AC).

sapphirinus ~a ~um, *a.* (Gk.) Of sapphire or lapis lazuli: *coloris ~i et lazurei* AM 76.3.

sapphirus ~i, *f.* (Gk. from Hebr.) also **saphir**, *indecl.* (AC 114). A precious stone, prob. lapis lazuli: *sicut opus lapidis ~i* Exod. 24.10 (AC); perh. also sapphire: *fascia ex pyropis et ~is* AM 2.1; VR 48.20.

sarcina ~ae, *f.* A packet made up for transport, load, bundle: *quod...adigantur ad portandum ~as* AM 232.5.

sarculum ~i, *neut.* A hoe: *omnes montes qui ~o sarrientur* Isa. 7.25 (AE 304.12).

Sardensis ~is ~e, *a.* Of Sardis: *unicuivis Ecclesiae (hic Ephesinae... ~i...)* AE 108.1.

sardinus ~i, *f.*? = **sardius**: Rev. 4.3 (DD 41).

sardius ~i, *f.*? A precious stone of red colour, cornelian: *lapidi jaspidi et ~o* Rev. 4.3 (AR).

sardonychus ~i, *m.* = **sardonyx**: 3AD 1733.

sardonyx ~ychis (*or* ~ycis), *m.*? (Gk.) A precious stone, sardonyx: Rev. 21.20 (AR); *de ~yche, qui est lapis coloris carnei, pellucidus* 3AD 1303; (pl.) *~yces* VR 192.

sarrio ~rire ~rui ~tum, *tr.* To hoe (land): *omnes montes qui sarculo ~rientur* Isa. 7.25 (AE 304.12).

sartago ~inis, *f.* A griddle: *accipe tibi ~inem ferri* Ezek. 4.3 (AC 426.3).

sarte, *adv.* Unbrokenly indissolubly: *omnium...quae inter se ~e conjuncta sunt* VR 99.2.

sartus ~a ~um, *a.* (pf. pple. of **sarcio***) Tightly held together, indissoluble: *ut conjunctio ~a teneatur* AC 6804.5; *aequilibria...quae a Domino jugiter ~a conservantur* CI 596; *stata et ~a societas et civitas* AM 130.2; UJ(C) 26.

sat: see **satis**.

sata ~orum, *neut. pl.* Growing plants, crops: *agri, ~a, novalia et quoque messes* AC 9272.2; ES 1422.

satago ~tagere ~tegi, *intr.* To make strenuous efforts, work hard: *homo qui ultra ~tagit* VR 28.2; ES 449; (w. inf.) *homo ~tagit venire in aliquam justam cognitionem de Deo* VR 362.1; UJ(C) 46.

Satan: see **Satanas**.

Satanas ~ae, *m.* (Gk. from Hebr.) also **Satan**, *indecl.* (AR Doc Ref.6). **1** A name of the evil one, Satan: *abi post Me, ~a* Matt. 4.10 (AC 1690.4); *creditur...quod Diabolus seu ~as fuerit lucis angelus* CI 311.1; *dum negatur Deus et colitur ~as* VR 34.4. **2** A name given to a class of evil spirits, satan: *vocantur... ~ae qui confirmaverunt se pro natura, et inde negaverunt Deum* AM 380.2; VR 14.2; VR 35.2.

Satanicus ~a ~um, *a.* Of or belonging to Satan, satanical: *spiritus ~i* AR 110.3; *~o vultu* VR 487.2.

satelles ~itis, *m.* **1** One who guards or attends upon a monarch, henchman, attendant: *servus principi ~itum* Gen. 41.12 (AC); *venit ~es e curia cum mandato* AM 10.4; (in a beehive) *vadit [regina] in comitatu a ~itibus, qui vocantur fuci* VR 12.7. **2** A smaller body orbiting around a celestial body, satellite: *quod...habeant lunas, quae vocantur ~ites* AC 6697; CI 417.6.

satellitium ~i, *neut.* An escort: *jamjam venturi sunt aulici cum ~is* AM 7.2; (in a beehive) *[apes] quasi aulam...struunt cum ~is circum* VR 12.7.

satietas ~atis, *f.* The condition of having had enough, satiety: *comedetis adipem ad ~atem* Ezek. 39.19 (SS 15.3); *post mediam ~atem* AM 16.2; *cum ~as tibi nulla, cum quibus scortata es* Ezek. 16.28 (VI 79.3).

satio ~are ~avi ~atum, *tr.* To provide enough for, satisfy, glut (an appetite): *sic ~antes suas inedias* ES 1381; (pass.) to satisfy one's appetite, glut oneself: *~abimini super mensa Mea* Ezek. 39.20 (SS 15.3).

satis, *adv.* and *indecl. sb.* also **sat**. **1** (adv.) To a sufficient extent, adequately, enough: *sicut ~is ostensum est* AC 277; *~is superque*, enough and more than enough: AC 1673.1. **2** (adv.) To a reasonably large extent, fairly, pretty: *in multa ~is dignitate fuerunt* AC 949; *lapis ~is magnus* CI 534.1; *ascensus ~is diu perdurabat* ES 259; *frigus quod...pedes meos... ~is afficiebat* ES 1909. **3** (as sb.) A sufficiently large amount: *per ~is temporis* ES 379; *~is est*, it is enough: *~is est ut inde sciatur* SS 10; (and w. ellipse of vb.) *sed dixit, ~is hac vice* AM 270.6.

satisfacio ~facere ~feci, *intr.* **1** To be adequate, satisfy: *etiam voces naturales non possunt ~facere* ES 241.3. **2** To give satisfaction, please: (w. dat.) *quod Dominus per passionem crucis... ~fecerit Patri* DD 15.1; *mens per hoc tranquillat se, et ~facit sibi* AM 6.6; (w. *pro*) *ut [Filius] ~faceret pro humano genere* FI 38.

satisfactio ~onis, *f.* The act of giving satisfaction: *promptus erit ad restitutionem et ~onem* BCP (VI 6); (esp. of the act of redemption) *hodierna fides...ponit ~onem a Filio* FI 39.

satisfactorius ~a ~um, *a.* Serving to make satisfaction or atonement for sin: *satisfactio...fiat per paenas ~as a ministro ex arbitrio pro mensura delicti imponendas* AR Doc RC.4.

satisfio ~fieri ~factus sum, *intr.* (impers.) Satisfaction is given: (w. dat.) *ut rationi humanae... ~fiat* VR 33.

satius, *compar. adv.* and *sb.* (adv.) More adequately, preferably: *sed de his ~ius in prophetis* 3AD 5541; (as sb.) a preferable thing: *~ius foret nasci asinus quam homo* AM 182.5.

satrapa ~ae, *m.* (Gk. from Persian) A prince or lord among eastern peoples: *quod Philisthaei propterea convocaverint ~as et divinatores* VR 203.1 (1 Sam. 5.8); VR 627.

satum ~i, *neut.* (Gk. from Hebr.) A measure of volume: *in farinae ~is tribus* Matt. 13.33 (DP 25).

satur ~ura ~urum, *a.* Replete, full: *mortuus est Abraham...senex et ~ur* Gen. 25.8 (AC); (w. gen.) *senex et ~ur dierum* Gen. 35.29 (AC); (w. abl.) *Naphtali ~ur beneplacito* Deut. 33.23 (AE 439.3).

saturitas ~atis, *f.* Satiety, fullness: *~as panis* Ezek. 16.49 (AC 2220.3); *et comedetis pinguedinem ad ~atem* Ezek. 39.19 (AE 329.10).

Saturninus ~a ~um, *a.* **1** Of the Roman god Saturn; *aevum ~um* or *tempora ~a*, a name for the mythical golden age: *haec tempora...appellata aurea, et quoque*

~*a* AC 8118.1; AM 153[a].2. **2** Of the planet Saturn: *de incolis ~is* ES 460.

saturo ~are ~avi ~atum, *tr*. To fill to repletion, satiate: *si animam afflictam ~averis* Isa. 58.10 (AC 7711.4); *desiderans ~ari micis cadentibus de mensa divitis* Luke 16.21 (AC 9231.3); *~antur arbores Jehovae* Ps. 104.16 (AE 109.5).

satyriacus ~a ~um, *a*. Of a satyr: *quod ~a haec forma esset forma adulterii dissoluti* AM 521.4.

satyriasis ~eos, *f*. (Gk.) Excessive sexual desire in men, satyriasis: AM 459.3; *amat ex ~i spirituali* VR 566.1.

satyrus ~i, *m*. (Gk.) (in antiquity) A demigod of half-human, half-bestial form: *cum veterum ~is et Priapis, qui vagabantur in sylvis* VR 316; cf. *~i saltant ibi* Isa. 13.21 (AC 1326.3); a class of lustful evil spirits: *~i erant quoad pectora hirsuti et quoad pedes...sicut vituli* AM 521.1.

saucio ~are ~avi ~atum, *tr*. To wound, injure: *obligavit vulnera ~ati a latronibus* VI 2; *si propter aurum ~asset, imo occidisset hominem* ES 4543.

saucius ~a ~um, *a*. Wounded, injured: *eructationes ex pulmone ~o* VR 108; (neut. as sb.) *mens eorum naturalis tale ~um nunc est* AC 7768.

saxeus ~a ~um, *a*. Made of stone, stone: *inter congeries ~as habitant* CI 488.3; *domum ~am* DP 189.2.

saxosus ~a ~um, *a*. Abounding in stones, stony: *sunt paludinosa, ~a et sterilia omnia* AE 417.1.

saxum ~i, *neut*. A stone: *petrae ex ~is* CI 188; *non sumus ~a et stipites* AM 44.4.

scabellum ~i, *neut*. (diminutive of **scamnum**) A footstool: *usque dum posuero inimicos tuos ~um pedum tuorum* Ps. 110.1 (DD 6); VR 121.3.

scaber ~bra ~brum, *a*. **1** Having a rough surface, rugged: *portae ad inferna...sicut fissurae rupium... pleraeque ~brae* CI 584. **2** (of speech) Rough, coarse: *loquelae illorum sunt ~brae, et gestus scenici* AM 432.2.

scabies ~ei, *f*. A disease of the skin causing itching, scabies: *~es virulenta* AM 253.1; *per ~em pestilentem, quae caput ejus occupabat* ES 4466.

scabiosus ~a ~um, *a*. Having scabies or skin disease causing itching: [*vir*] *gibbosus, contusus, confusus oculo, ~us, verrucosus, aut contusus teste* Lev. 21.20 (AC 10109.5).

scala ~ae, *f*. **1** A flight of steps, staircase, ladder: *sicut gradus ~ae in cujus vertice est Dominus* AC 6819; *gradibus ~ae visae Jacobo* VR 24.2; *struit ~as a mansione in mansionem* VR 152. **2** A scale pan of a balance: *sicut pondera in ~is bilancis* VR 659; (fig.) *~a superpondii...ut plurimum attollit se* AM 318.1.

scalprum ~i, *neut*. An engraving tool: *peccatum Jehudae scriptum est stylo ferri, ~o adamantis* Jer. 17.1 (AE 391.24).

scamnum ~i, *neut*. A long seat, bench: *non sedent super sellis aut ~is* AC 8377; *~a seu sedilia continua* AM 23; ES 4024.

scandalizatio ~onis, *f*. The act of giving offence: *'petra offendiculi' pro ~one* AC 9348.10; AE 600.8.

scandalizo ~are ~avi ~atum, *tr*. To cause to stumble, give offence: *si dexter oculus ~averit te* Matt. 5.29 (AM 316.5); (pass.) to take offence, be scandalized: *quando afflictio...oritur...statim ~antur* Mark 4.17 (AC 1846.4); *hodie si Jehovah appareret in Ecclesia sicut homo, ~arentur* AC 6876.3.

scandalose, *adv*. In a scandalous manner: *unus ex iis ~e contra Dominum loquutus* AC 950.

scandalosus ~a ~um, *a*. Giving offence, scandalous: *plura adhuc ~a et Deo ignominiosa* VR 132.3; ES(M) 4564.

scandalum ~i, *neut*. **1** A stumbling block: *qui docebat Balacum objicere ~um coram filiis Israelis* Rev. 2.14 (AR). **2** A statement or action which gives offence, scandal: *spiritus quidam...inferebant dira ~a* AC 8383; *quod identitas trium essentiarum Divinarum sit rationis ~um* VR 23.2; *magnum ~um auditum a Papa* AE 114.9; *~a alicui facere* ES 4378. **b** *~o esse*, to be a cause of offence: *nuditas est probro et ~o* AC 213; AM 342.1.

scando ~ere ~i, *intr*. **1** To ascend to a higher level, climb: *ut... ~ere velint in thronum Dei* AC 7375; *omnes volunt ~ere in altum* ES 5876. **2** (of things) To extend upwards, reach a higher level: *cum...morticinium... progressive ~it* VR 119.2. **3** To rise to a higher degree: *in quo gradu amor sui ~it* DP 250.3; *dum quis ~it ab officio per officia ad quoddam supereminens* AM 99.

scapula ~ae, *f*. (anat.) One of the shoulder blades: (usu. pl.) *volas tenentes in alterius ~is* AC 822; *a ~is ad lumbos* AM 137.1; (sg.) Job 31.22 (AE 627.11).

scapuleja See quot.: *scapuleja in lingua spirituali significat ut ejiciat foras* UJ(P) 332; ES 6090.

scapus ~i, *m*. The upright member, shaft (of a lampstand): *solidum fiet candelabrum, ~us ejus, et calamus ejus* Exod. 25.31 (AC).

scatebra ~ae, *f*. (fig.) A prolific source: *quod jucunditates carnis...non sint nisi quam libidinum effervescentiae, quae...fiunt ~ae impudicitiarum* AM 440.

scateo ~tere ~tui, *intr*. (w. abl. or *ex*) To be prolific (in), teem (with): *quod...omnia corporis...incastis ~teant* AM 140; *...corpus ~tens ex ulceribus* AE 126.2.

scaturigo ~inis, *f.* A prolific spring, fountain: *erit aridus locus in stagnum, et siticulosus in ~ines aquarum* Isa. 35.7 (AC 6723.2); (fig.) *inde ~o illius amoris clauditur* AM 242; DP 38.1.

scaturio ~rire ~rivi, *intr.* To come forth in large numbers or amount, pour forth: *~rivit sicut fons saliens cum vino nectareo* AM 14.2; *fibrae...quae ~riunt a vasis sanguineis* ES 1075; (fig., w. *ab*) *a voluntate ~riebant mala eorum* AC 209; (w. *ex*) *falsa quae ex malo ~riunt* AC 7711.1.

sceleratus ~a ~um, *a.* Criminal, sinful, atrocious: *modo non vita illis manifeste ~a sit* AC 4311.3; (masc. as sb.) a malefactor, criminal: *in his doloribus sunt quandoque ~i* AC 8164.1; AE 1012.3.

scelestus ~a ~um, *a.* (superl. ~issimus) Wicked, evildoing, criminal: *quod ~i possint...in coelum recipi* AC 7051.1; *quod ~issimus salvetur per fidem* AC 8094.2; (of actions) wicked, criminal: *~a sua inceperunt moliri* ES 3682.

sceleton ~i, *neut.* (Gk.) A skeleton: *isti novo corpori induci ~on osseum* AM 182.5; *quod homo...foret... quoad ossa merum ~on* VR 364.1.

scelus ~eris, *neut.* A crime: *~us scortationis tuae* Jer. 13.27 (AE 141.7).

scena ~ae, *f.* (Gk.) A representation in a theatre, scene: *vertuntur tales ~ae theatrales in diras infernales* AR 655.2; *mutatur ~a, palatia sensim dissipantur* AC 1631; *sic conjugia verterentur in ~as tragicas* AM 297.

scenicus ~a ~um, *a.* (Gk.) Theatrical: *gestus ~i* AM 432.2.

scepticus ~a ~um, *a.* (Gk.) Sceptical: *vulgo dicuntur ii in mundo ~i, quia nihil credunt* ES 3335.

sceptrum ~i, *neut.* (Gk.) The ceremonial staff of a king, sceptre: *regibus est ~um, quod est curtus baculus* AC 7026; (Bibl., as a symbol of royalty) *surget ~um ex Israele* Num. 24.17 (AC 1675.5).

Schaddai, *indecl.* (Hebr.) also **Shaddai**. A title of God, usually rendered 'Almighty' but see first quot.: *interpretes ~ai reddunt omnipotentem, alii fulminatorem; sed proprie significat tentatorem, et post tentationes benefactorem* AC 1992.5; *sicut devastatio a ~ai veniet* Isa. 13.6 (DD 4); *Deus ~ai* VR 17.2.

schalom, *indecl.* (Hebr.) also **shalom**. Shalom, the Hebr. word for peace: *aedificabat Gideon altare Jehovae, et vocavit Jehovae ~om, hoc est, pacis* Judg. 6.24 (AC 2724.3).

schaon, *indecl.* (Hebr.) A Hebr. word meaning tumult, app. taken by Swedenborg at Jer. 48.45 to be a proper name: *ignis exivit ex Chesbone, et flamma ab inter Sichonem, quae comedit angulum Moabi, et verticem filiorum ~on* Jer. 48.45 (VR 265.3).

schedula ~ae, *f.* A small sheet of paper, document, slip: *epistolae et ~ae quae...lectae sunt* CI 462[a].6; VR 161.1.

schema ~atis, *neut.* (Gk.) A summary description, sketch: *in sequentibus dabitur aliquod ejus* [sc. *progressus creationis*] *~a* VR 33.

scheminith, *indecl.* (Hebr.) The rendering of a Hebr. musical instruction in the title of Pss. 6 and 12: *Psalmis pluribus Davidis inscriptum ac indicatum quomodo psallerentur, prout super neginoth, super nechiloth, super octava, schigajon, gitthith, muthlabben, ~ith, schoschannim, machalath* AC 8337.5.

schigajon, *indecl.* (Hebr.) The rendering of a Hebr. musical instruction in the title of Ps. 7: *Psalmis pluribus Davidis inscriptum ac indicatum quomodo psallerentur, prout super neginoth, super nechiloth, super octava, ~on, gitthith, muthlabben, scheminith, schoschannim, machalath* AC 8337.5.

schisma ~atis, *neut.* (Gk.) A doctrinal division in a church, schism: *'humus'* [*significat*] *~a seu haeresin* AC 373; VR 11.1.

schismaticus ~a ~um, *a.* (Gk.) Of or relating to schism, schismatic: *codicillum...est sane ~um* VR 112.1.

schittah ~ae, *m.*? The shittah tree: *cedrum ~ae* Isa. 41.19 (AC 9472).

schittim, *indecl.* (Hebr.) also **shittim**. The wood of the shittah, regarded by Swedenborg as a kind of cedar: *lignum ~im erat lignum cedri praestantissimae* AC 9472.

schoham, *indecl.* (Hebr.) A precious stone, onyx: *et accipies duos lapides ~am* Exod. 28.9 (AC).

schola ~ae, *f.* (Gk.) **1** A place of instruction, esp. in higher education, school: *scientiae in quas adolescentes initiantur in ~is* AM 163; *illi qui haec dogmata alte impresserunt mentibus suis in ~is et gymnasiis* AR 500.2. **2** A group of philosophers, school: *illi qui e ~a Socratica erant* AM 182.8.

scholaris ~is, *m.* A pupil, esp. in a philosophical school: *Diogenes cum suis ~ibus* AM 182.1.

scholasticus ~a ~um, *a.* Of the school of philosophy started by Aristotle and continued through the Middle Ages, scholastic: *apud eos qui in pulvere ~o haerent* AC 521; *terminos ~os* ES(M) 4578. **b** (masc. pl. as sb.) the followers of Aristotle in the Middle Ages, schoolmen: *metaphysici et ~i* AR 421.2. **c** (neut. as sb.) a scholastic argument: *qui hypothesibus confundit et ~is* ES 2736.

schoschannim, *indecl.* (Hebr.) The rendering of a Hebr. musical instruction in the title of Pss. 45, 69, and 80: *Psalmis pluribus Davidis inscriptum ac indicatum* *quomodo psallerentur, prout super neginoth, super nechiloth, super octava, schigajon, gitthith, muthlabben, scheminith, ~im, machalath* AC 8337.5.

schyphus ~i, *m.* (Gk.) also **scyphus**. **1** A large drinking vessel, goblet: *et bibunt ex ~is vini* Amos 6.6 (AE 163.4). **2** A bowl or cup on a candleholder to catch melted wax: *magnificum candelabrum instructum septem calamis et ~is ex auro* AM 20.1; AC 9551.

sciagraphia ~ae, *f.* (Gk.) **1** An outline drawing; (transf.) a summary description, sketch: *~a Doctrinalium Novae Ecclesiae* SE 16 titulus; VR 54.

scibilis ~is ~e, *a.* Capable of being known: *quod regeneratio non sit ~is in Ecclesia hodierna* VR 591.2; (neut. as sb.) *absque idea ex ~ibus et sensibilibus* AC 9300.3.

sciens ~ntis, *a.* (pres. pple. of **scio**) (superl. *~ntissimus*) Equipped with knowledge, knowing: *illi...vocant sapientem qui modo intelligens est, imo qui modo ~ns* AC 10331.2; (w. gen.) skilled (in): *et fuit Esau vir ~ns venationis* Gen. 25.27 (AC).

scienter, *adv.* With knowledge: *sciens [est] qui ~er facit* AC 10331.2.

scientia ~ae, *f.* **1** Cognizance, knowledge (of facts, ideas, etc.): *qui ~am cognitionum fidei habent* AC 1162; *hoc non cadit in ~am* AC 7877.2; *testari ex ~a, seu ex memoria et cogitatione* AE 10.3; (dist. from **cognitio**) *fides nusquam est...cognitio credendorum; hoc solum est ~a* AC 654; (dist. from **sapientia**) *quod nempe non sint in aliqua sapientia, sed solum in ~a* CI 267. **2** A capacity for knowing, faculty of knowledge: *tres illi gradus...intellectualium hominis, nempe intellectus, ratio et ~a* AC 658; *quod homo non nascatur ~a sicut bestia* VR 48.11. **3** An organized body of knowledge on a particular subject, science: *antiquis illis temporibus non ita ~is...indulserunt* AC 605; *Aegyptii ~as rerum vocabant sapientiam* AC 7296; *~a correspondentiarum docet* SS 9.

scientifice, *adv.* As a matter of factual knowledge: *quod...putent...quod non capiunt sensualiter et ~e, hoc nihil esse* AC 210; *agnoscebant oretenus et ~e quod Dominus regat universum* ES 3493.

scientificus ~a ~um, *a.* **1** Known as a fact, factual: *per fidem memoriae, quae est fides ~a* AC 30.2; *vera rationalia et ~a* AC 671. **b** (neut. as sb.) an item of memory knowledge, fact: *quicquid...memoriae externi hominis insinuatur...ibi manet ut ~um* AC 27; *sunt... triplicis generis ~a, intellectualia, rationalia et sensualia* AC 991; *quod cognitiones apud hos sint ~a* AC 1193. **2** (of persons) Relying upon factual knowledge: *qui ~us est seu ex scientiis concludit* AC 196.2; *quod spiritus rationales non possint simul esse cum spiritibus ~is* ES 4143. **b** (neut. as sb.) the faculty of factual knowledge: *quod rationale ejus sit a ~o distinctum* AC 657.

scilicet, *particle.* To be precise, more exactly: *pro salute, ne ~et pereant quoad animas* AC 7280.1; *quando...inversum est, ~et dum naturale est intus in spirituali* VR 361.3.

scindo ~ere scidi scissum, *tr.* **1** To cut in pieces, chop up: *~ere ligna* AC 1110; *patina panum scissorum in quadratas tesseras plena* ES 2626. **2** (Bibl.) To rend (a garment as a sign of mourning): *scidit togam suam* Job 1.20 (AE 395.9). **3** (fig.) To break up, split apart: *nihil jucundius illis est quam ~ere conjugia* CI 488.6; *modo non defluat [idea], et ~at unitatem Dei in ore* VR 135.1.

scintilla ~ae, *f.* **1** A small flame, spark (in quot. transf., of arrows): *ibi fregit ~as arcus* Ps. 76.3 (AE 365.38). **2** A minute amount, spark (of other things): *hoc latet in unaquavis ~a amoris sui* AC 257; AM 161.2; *~a vitae* CC 11.7.

scintillatio ~onis, *f.* The twinkling (of a star): *ex ipsa rutilatione et ~one stellarum constare potest... qualia sunt* AC 1808.2.

scintillo ~are ~avi, *intr.* To sparkle: *percipiebam... universalia sicut aliquantum quasi ~antia* ES 448; (of the eyes) *apparet ex oculis, quod ~ent* AM 359.2; AE 37.

scintillula ~ae, *f.* A small spark: *singulae...particulae fumi fiunt ~ae* VR 159.1.

scio scire scivi scitum, *tr.*, *intr.* (superl. of pres. pple. *scientissimus*) **1** To be aware of, know (facts): *ut vivat [homo] secundum id quod scit* AC 6706; *hoc arcanum nisi sciatur* AC 6724.3; (dist. from **agnosco**) *aliud est veritates scire, et veritates agnoscere* AC 896.1. **b** (w. *quod*): *sciebant quod coelum non esset in alto* AC 8153; (impers. pass.) *sciendum porro quod bonum misceri possit cum malis* AC 6724.3. **c** (w. indir. qu.): *non scio num verum sit* FI 2; (impers. pass.) *nisi...scitur qui sunt proximus* AC 6703. **d** (absol.): *ad sapientiam... introducitur per scire et nosse* AC 1555.2. **2** To have knowledge of, know about: *[Aegyptii] sciverunt correspondentias* AC 7926.1; *quod qualibet...species sciat sua alimenta* VR 12.5. **b** (w. inf.) to know (how to): *sciunt apes legere mella* CI 108.1.

scipio ~onis, *m.* A walking stick, staff: *judex...cum ~one in manu* VR 137.1; *removens...ex Jehudah baculum et ~onem* Isa. 3.1 (AE 433.33).

scirpus ~i, *m.* (app.) A tangle (of threads): *foretne illud...sicut...filum ex inextricabili ~o evolvere?* CO 35.2. (n.b. This sense may have arisen through misinterpretation of the proverbial phrase *nodum in ~o quaerere* 'to look for a knot in a bulrush', i.e., to waste one's labour.)

sciscito ~are ~avi, *intr.* To enquire, ask: *angeli... ~abant, Quid in mundo...sciunt...?* VR 695.2; AM 44.1.

scissio ~onis, *f.* The act of cutting: *per ~onem graminis per serram* ES 575 titulus.

scissura ~ae, *f.* A narrow opening, cleft: *ad intrandum in ~as petrarum et in fissuras rupium* Isa. 2.21 (AC 10582.5); *~as petrae* AE 410.5.

scite, *adv.* Cleverly, neatly: *dicendo...hoc nimis ~e* AC 6924; ES 1426.

scitu, supine of **scio**. For knowing: *inter ~u necessaria est quoque caelum angelicum* DP 60; *haec... ~u et relatu digna sunt* AM 73.2.

scitus ~a ~um, *a.* Skilled, clever: *dum ~us quidam evolvit sensum inde* ES 3960.

scius ~a ~um, *a.* Possessing knowledge, knowing: *docti...eruditi et modo ~i vocantur sapientes* AM 130.1; (neut. as sb.) knowledge: *quod...sit gnavum, ~um, probum apud illos* CH 130 (= vi.1).

scleroticus ~a ~um, *a.* (Gk.) (anat.) *Tunica ~a*, the sclerotic coat (of the eye): VR 346.2.

sclopetarius ~i, *m.* A musketeer: *si jaculator aut ~us collimaret ad scopum* DP 333.3.

sclopetum ~i, *neut.* A musket, carbine: *qui enses faciunt, ~a, pulverem pyrium* ES 3506; VR 84.

scomma ~atis, *neut.* (Gk.) A joke, jest: *dicunt talia ~ata* [*sonantia* Rogers] *Verbi* UJ(P) 224 (Tafel, p. 72).

scopae ~parum, *f. pl.* A broom: *comae...sicut ~pae cingunt caput* ES 1347; *domum... ~pis purgatam* Matt. 12.44 (DP 231.8).

scopula ~ae, *f.* A small brush or broom: Exod. 25.29 (AC 9544).

scopulus ~i, *m.* A rock projecting from water, reef: *navi quae...fertur in ~os et syrtes* VR 28.2; *quidam etiam in insula seu ~o erant qui salvati* ES 243.

scopus ~i, *m.* (Gk.) A target, mark: *si...sclopetarius collimaret ad ~um* DP 333.3; (fig.) *assumsimus has duas* [*causas*], *quia collimant et spectant ad unum ~um, qui est bonum publicum* AM 109.

scorbuticus ~a ~um, *a.* Of or caused by scurvy: *phtisis ~a* AM 253.1.

scoria ~ae, *f.* (Gk.) The waste material produced by smelting, dross, slag: *potest etiam lignum putidum et ~a...induci auro* VI 10; *~ae argenti* Ezek. 22.18 (AC 8298.2); (fig.) *rejectis essentialibus caetera sunt ~ae* AE 888.4; (app.) any dust: *sicut ~ae librae reputantur* Isa. 40.15 (AE 406.19).

scorpio ~onis, *m.* A scorpion: ES 2748.

scorpius ~i, *m.* A scorpion: *habebant caudas similes ~is* Rev. 9.10 (AR); *venenosa animalia, sicut ~i* ES 2743.

scortatio ~onis, *f.* Promiscuous sexual behaviour, fornication: *erant praecipue adulteria et ~ones* CI 462[a].1; *in caelo prorsus non sciunt quid ~o* AM 44.7; (of spiritual fornication) *spiritualis meretricatio et ~o, quae sunt falsificatio veri et adulteratio boni* VR 41.3; *de ~one Ecclesiae posterorum Jacobi* ES 246.

scortator ~oris, *m.* A fornicator: *is usque tamen interius adulter et ~or est* VI 111.

scortatorius ~a ~um, *a.* Of or concerned with promiscuous sexual behaviour, fornicatory (see quot.): *per amorem ~um...hic intelligitur amor adulterii, dum talis est ut non reputetur pro peccato* AM 423.1; *dantur etiam conjugia ~a* AM 376.

scortor ~ari ~atus sum, *intr.* To engage in fornication, live promiscuously: *per 'adulterari'...non modo intelligitur ~ari, sed etiam obscaena facere* VI 74; (Bibl.) *Hierosolyma ~ata es cum filiis Aegypti* Ezek. 16.26 (AC 1186.3); *cum qua* [sc. *meretrice magna*] *~ati sunt reges terrae* Rev. 17.2 (AR).

scortum ~i, *neut.* A common prostitute, whore: *omnes nervi cadunt ad aspectum ~i* AM 44.7; (fig.) *intellectus, qui tunc est ~um voluntatis* DP 144.2.

scriba ~ae, *m.* A professional writer, scribe: *ad Schaphanem ~am* 2 Kgs. 22.8 (DD 9); AM 207.5; (esp. as the title of a class in Judaea in our Lord's time) *vae vobis, ~ae et Pharisaei* Matt. 23.25 (AC 7046.2).

scribo ~bere ~psi ~ptum, *tr.* **1** To commit to writing, write down: *cum absolvisset Moses ~bere verba legis hujus super librum* Deut. 31.24 (AC 6752.4); *possunt per aliquot voces sistere quae ~pta sunt pluribus paginis* CI 240. **2** To compose in writing, write (a book, narrative, etc.): *cum ~berem aliquid de venturis* AC 6811; *quod universa Scriptura Sacra de solo Domino ~pta sit* DD 7; *simili stylo, quo Prophetica... ~pta sunt* AE 1; (absol.) *qui de sola fide... ~pserunt* AE 236.2; (also) to write a letter: *angelo Ephesinae Ecclesiae ~be* Rev. 2.1 (AR). **3** To mention in writing, write about: *quem ~psit Moses in Lege, invenimus, Jesum* John 1.45 (AC 6752.6).

scrinium ~i, *neut.* A receptacle for valuable objects, case: *in ~o recondere opes* CC 18.2; *idolum...inclusum ~o* VR 7; *ut cultrum meum in ~o absconderem* ES 4530.

scriptio ~onis, *f.* The act of writing: *~o est ultimus actus cogitationis* AE 898; also, an instance of writing: *quod ~onum inflexiones sint secundum formam coeli* ES 5583.

scriptor ~oris, *m.* A writer, author: *haec tempora etiam ~oribus antiquis fuerunt nota* AC 8118.1; *~ores theologiae naturalis* SS 115.3.

scriptum ~i, *neut.* A piece of writing, written composition, book: *antiqui in suis ~is* AC 7026; *Verbum in litera apparet sicut ~um vulgare* SS 1.

scriptura ~ae, *f.* **1** The act of writing: *per... ~am plurium membranarum* ES 1051. **2** A method of writing, script: *ex hac origine est loquela spiritualis...et quoque ~a ibi* VR 19.2; ES 5583. **3** A piece of writing, written document: *qui noctu in luce lunae...legit ~am* VR 109.3; *apparuit ~a in pariete* AE 373.3 (Dan. 5.5). **4** *~a Sacra*, the Holy Scripture, the Word: *tota ~a Sacra non aliud est quam doctrina amoris et charitatis* AC 6632; SS titulus. **5** A passage of Holy Scripture: *Jesus... interpretatus est in omnibus ~is quae ad Ipsum pertinerent* Luke 24.27 (AC 6752.6); *quae Dominus... dicit de impletione legis seu ~ae* AC 7933.3; *secundum omnem rationem et ~am* VR 161.1.

scrobis ~is, *f.* A hole dug in the ground, trench: *sub pedibus visus est ~em effodere* CI 462[a].7; *in tenebrosissimis ~ibus* ES 1493; (app.) earth removed in digging, soil: *ibi ~em coepit ejicere, tanquam ii qui pro mortuis qui sepeliendi* AC 817; ES 1260.

scrotum ~i, *neut.* (anat.) The scrotum: *sub provincia ~i* ES(M) 4582.

scrupetum ~i, *neut.* A heap of rocks: *ipsi colles, super quibus habitabant,* [*versi sunt*] *in ~a* UJ(C) 23.

scrupulus ~i, *m.* A very small weight, grain (in quot. fig.): *in qua abysso cum sunt, tunc minimus ~us praevalet mille veritatibus* AC 215; *~um movere*, to raise an objection: *movent contra illa omnes ~os* AC 1072.2; *quod possint uniri, hoc nullum movet ~um* AM 157; also, without *movere*: *inciderat... ~us...quod...* ES 2591.

scrupus ~i, *m.* A grain (of sand): *et esset sicut arena semen tuum, et egressi viscerum tuorum sicut ~i ejus* Isa. 48.19 (AC 1803.2).

scrutatio ~onis, *f.* Careful study, perusal: *absque ~one scripturae* AC 8993.4.

scrutator ~oris, *m.* One who examines carefully, student: *~ores coeli* Isa. 47.13 (AC 9188.3).

scrutinium ~i, *neut.* An investigation, study: *sunt modo ~a ex intellectu philosophica* AM 186.2; VR 46.1.

scrutor ~ari ~atus sum, *tr.* To submit to careful investigation, study: *~amini Scripturas* John 5.39 (DD 11); *quando quis ~atur et explicat Verbum* SS 5; (w. indir. qu.) *bene ~ari qualis hominis vita est* AC 6704; *nec ~abantur quis essem* ES 4575.

sculpo ~ere ~si ~tum, *tr.* **1** To decorate in relief, carve: *Salomo omnes parietes domus... ~sit aperturis sculpturarum* AC 8369.3 (1 Kgs. 6); *~ti sapphiri* AM 15. **2** To represent by carving, sculpt: *angeli in templis, sive ~ti sive picti* CI 74.3; *per quod sumeret laterem, et ~eret super eo Hierosolymam* Ezek. 4.1 (DD 15.7).

sculptilis ~is ~e, *a.* Carved, sculpted: *~es equos, boves, vitulos, agnos...fecerunt* DP 255.2; *sunt hi vix aliter quam sicut formae ~es, sed usque receptibiles vitae a Domino* AM 396.1; (neut. as sb.) a carved image, sculpture: *quid prodest ~e, quia sculpsit illud fictor ejus...?* Hab. 2.18 (AC 586.2); *sicut ~ia e saxo vestita pellibus pardi* AM 231.5.

sculptura ~ae, *f.* **1** The act of carving: *~a sigilli* Exod. 28.36 (AC). **2** A carved image, sculpture: *mutati sunt... in ~as hominum* AM 79.3.

scutella ~ae, *f.* A small dish: *viderunt...pyramidem ex auro cum centum ~is in triplici ordine* AM 14.2; AM 16.1.

scutica ~ae, *f.* A whip, strap: *vox ~ae* Nahum 3.2 (AC 6971.3).

scutiformis ~is ~e, *a.* Shield-shaped, scutiform: *cartilaginem ~em seu xiphoiden* AC 9236.

scutula ~ae, *f.* A dish, plate: *12 ~as argenti* Num. 7.84 (AE 430.9).

scutum ~i, *neut.* A heavy shield: *aliud significat clypeus, aliud ~um, aliud parma* AC 1788.1; AE 734.7.

scyphus: see **schyphus**.

se sui, *refl. pron.* (gen. sg. and pl. *sui*, acc. and abl. sg. and pl. *se*, dat. sg. and pl. *sibi*) **1** Himself, herself, itself, themselves: *ex...amore sui* AC 1326.1; *quod Humanum in Se etiam Divinum fecerit* AC 4687.3; *se habere*, to be (in a specified condition): see **habeo**; *secum*, with himself (etc.): *scio quod plures secum dicturi sint* [i.e., will say to themselves] DP 49; similarly, *intra se*: *intra se de coelo...reflectendo* AC 3747.3. **2** *In se*, essentially, basically, in itself: *omnis...conjunctio boni et veri in se gaudium habet* AC 4572.2; *intellectuale in se spectatum* AC 4574.2; *naturalis homo in se spectatus est oppositus spirituali homini* AM 426. **3** (w. pl. vb.) Each other, one another: *cum amicis qui utplurimum se inveniunt* AC 1114; *quaedam se osculantes* AM 218.2. **4** (as a sb. with a modifier) A self: *si sciret, non amplius cogitaret ex interiore se...sed solum ab exteriore se* DP 179.1.

sea: see **seah**.

seah ~ae, *f.* also **sea**. A Hebrew dry measure, one third of an ephah: AE 373.5.

sebaceus ~a ~um, *a.* Of tallow: *lumina potius cerea...quam ~a* ES 3410.

secedo ~dere ~ssi, *intr.* **1** To go apart: *et dixit Moscheh, ~dam* Exod. 3.3 (AC); *ille ad unum latus ~ssit* AC 7745; *~sserunt ab invicem* AM 19. **2** To depart (from a state): *videbatur...non ita pridem vita corporis ~ssisse* ES 1915.

secerno ~cernere ~crevi ~cretum, *tr.* **1** To concentrate by separation, separate out: *quod fluidiora se ex his ~creverint* VR 79.2; ES 830; (fig.) *in vero lustrante, ~cernente et castigante* CI 96. **2** To secrete (from the body): *ab homine ~cernitur stercus et urina* DP 164.7.

secessus ~us, *m.* A privy: *omne quod ingreditur in os in ventrem abit et in ~um ejicitur* Matt. 15.17 (AC 8910.2).

secludo ~dere ~si ~sum, *tr.* To shut out, cut off: *quod principia falsi...incluserint et ~serint...reliquias* AC 798; (w. *ab*) *tunc ~si sunt ab omni communicatione cum coelo* AC 8210.2.

seclusio ~onis, *f.* The state of being shut out: *~o ab intellectu ejus* AE 811.5.

seco ~are ~ui ~tum, *tr.* **1** To cut: *~are gramen* AC 1111; *quemadmodum artifex ~at adamantem* VR 110.5. **2** To divide, cut: *sylva... ~ta in plures tramites angustos* AM 75.2.

secretio ~onis, *f.* A secretion: *integra series ~onum ...serositatum sanguinis* ES 999.

secretorius ~a ~um, *a.* Of or concerned with secretion: *viscus...quod...munere ~o fungitur* ES 925; (neut. pl. as sb.) secretory organs: *provinciam ~orum* ES 924.

secretus ~a ~um, *a.* **1** Secret: *e ~is consiliis* AM 5.1; *~i doli genus* ES 3780; (neut. as sb.) a secret: *ut... solvant ~um de amoris conjugialis origine* AM 103.2; *a ~is*, a privy counsellor: *a ~is et necessariis regum... ambiverant esse* ES 1804. **2** (neut. as sb.) A secret council: *in ~um eorum ne veniat anima mea* Gen. 49.6 (AC).

secta ~ae, *f.* A division of a church, sect: *de haeresibus et ~is* AC 337.1; AM 5.1.

sectarius ~i, *m.* An adherent of a sect, sectary: *quarum [haeresium] unaquaevis a ~is confirmatur ex sensu literali Verbi* AC 6222.2; (pl.) the Protestant Dissenters in England, Sectaries: *cum loquuti sumus... cum ~is* VR 621.2.

sectator ~oris, *m.* A follower (of a leading figure), adherent: *~ores Cartesii* VR 696.1; *qui ~ores et cultores sunt hominum* ES 1558.

sectio ~onis, *f.* The act of cutting: *per...ligni ~ones* ES 271; AE 279.7.

secto: see **sector**[1].

sector[1] ~ari ~atus sum, *tr.* also **secto** ~are ~avi ~atum, *tr.* To aim at, pursue (an end): *quod mala vitae non ~anda* AC 9319; *attendite ad Me ~antes justitiam* Isa. 51.1 (AE 411.6); *honesta ~avimus* VR 568.1.

sector[2] ~oris, *m.* One who cuts; *~or lignorum*, one who cuts or splits wood, a woodcutter: AC 1110; AC 2784.

secum, *pron.* = **se** combined with *cum* (see **cum**[1]). With himself (herself, itself, themselves): *ex perceptione ... ~um communicata* CI 489.5; *~um dicere*, to say to oneself: AM 461.2. **b** *~um habere*, to have as a concomitant circumstance, involve: *amor sui id ~um habet, quod non duci velint a Domino* AC 205.

secundanae ~narum, *f. pl.* A second storey: *infimas, ~nas et tertianas facies illam* [sc. *arcam*] Gen. 6.16 (AC).

secundario, *adv.* At one remove, secondarily: *quod mundus naturalis per hunc solem a Jehovah Deo ~o creatus sit* CC 9.1.

secundarius ~a ~um, *a.* Occupying second place or rank, secondary: *bonum...est primarium...verum... est ~um* AC 1613.1; *in curru ~o qui sibi* Gen. 41.43 (AC); (neut. as sb.) AC 8149.

secundinae ~narum, *f. pl.* The afterbirth: *uterinis e matre post partum elapsis tunicis, seu ~nis* SE 67.

secundo[1], *adv.* A second time: *hoc ~o, et hoc tertio* AC 1787.2 (Mark 14.39, 41).

secundo[2] ~are ~avi, *intr.* To be favourable: *ex voluntate spontanea et ~ante solvunt illa [debita]* VR 430.

secundum[1], *prep. w. acc.* **1** In agreement with, in keeping with, according to: *est gaudium cum facit ~um conscientiam et est anxietas cum cogitur quid facere... contra conscientiam* AC 977.1; *~um Domini verba* AC 6686; *statuta, ~um quae institutus fuit cultus* SS 20.2. **2** Depending on the nature of, in proportion to, in accordance with: *in subjectis variatur [vita] ~um formam* AC 6685; *homo ~um facta et opera judicabitur* CI 470; *mens humana, ex qua et ~um quam homo est homo* VR 34.1.

secundum[2], *adv.* A second time: Ezek. 4.6 (VR 130.1).

secundus ~a ~um, *a.* **1** Second: *in primo capite... in ~o* AC 6825; *~um seu medium caelum* SS 6; *~a vice*, the second time: VI 55.1; (neut. as sb.) the second item: *charitas est primum Ecclesiae...fides est ~um* AC 1091. **b** *minuta ~a* or *minutum ~um*, a second (of time): ES 914; ES 579. **2** Moving in the same direction, favouring, following: *jucundum usus fert illum sicut ~a vena navem* AM 207.7; *~o fluvio*, with the current, downstream: ES 2384.

secure, *adv.* Without anxiety, confidently: *illis qui... ~e de uxore [cogitant]* AM 256; *Israel habitabit ~e* Jer. 23.6 (DD 4).

securis ~is, *f.* (acc. sg. *~im*) An axe: *habent ~im et malleum in manu* AC 821.2; *jamjam ~is ad radicem arborum jacet* Luke 3.9 (DD 18.4).

securitas ~atis, *f.* **1** Freedom from anxiety, confidence: *~as vitae oritur...ex fide impii quod non sit vita post mortem* DP 340.4. **2** Safety, security: *inde...pendet ~as publica* NH 325; *in tutela contra inferna, quae est ~as spiritualis* AR 306.

securus ~a ~um, *a.* **1** Free from anxiety, confident, careless: *~i se confirmant in sua securitate quod tale nihii sit* AC 1850.1; *ex...consortiis tranquillis, ~is, amabilibus* AM 290. **2** *In ~o*, in safety: *ut in ~o sint* CI 381.

secus, *adv.* Differently, otherwise: *~us fit cum Dominus elevat aliquos* CI 35; *ac ~us nec potuisset loqui* ES 1864; *~us ac*, in distinction from, unlike: *quod homo, ~us ac bruta animalia, possit cogitare de coelo* AC 3747.2.

sed, *conj.* But: *qui non in bono charitatis vixerunt, sed in contrariis* AC 6692.1; (in aposiopesis) *fateor etiam ego, quod universa natura sit a Deo, sed...* VR 79.4.

sedatio ~onis, *f.* The act of quietening or allaying: *per ~onem venti et fluctuum maris* AE 514.22; *pro ~one turbarum intellectus* AM 285.1.

sedecim, *indecl. a.* Sixteen: *~im bases* Exod. 26.25 (AC).

sedeo ~dere ~di ~ssum, *intr.* **1** To be seated, sit: *ignis ad ~dendum coram eo* Isa. 47.14 (AC 6832.8); *quod felices... ~ssuri sunt super thronis* AM 3.5; *quare etiam Dominus ibi ~dit* SS 2.2. **2** (w. expressions implying a particular activity) To sit: (w. pple. or adj.) *~debit conflans et purgans argentum* Mal. 3.3 (AC 8159.2); *~det mutus* VR 111.1; (of judges) *cum judicibus... ~debant in portis* AC 7111.3; (w. acc.) *ut ~deant concilium* VR 506.2; (w. *super*) *a primogenito Pharaonis ~ssuro super throno illius* Exod. 11.5 (AC); (w. *ab*) *~dere a dextris Dei* AC 7281; (w. *in* + abl.) *sic ~deant in delitiis* ES 592. **3** To be mounted, sit (on a horse or other animal): *equus albus et ~dens super illo* Rev. 19.11 (AR); *vidi mulierem ~dentem super bestia coccinea* Rev. 17.3 (AR). **4** (of things) To be located, reside: *infime et proxime loquelae in mente ~dent* [*naturalia*] VR 147.

sedes ~is, *f.* **1** A place to sit down, seat: *quisque novit suam ~em in camera* ES 5991; (of an animal) *fila retiformia araneae ~i proxima* DP 107. **2** The location or spatial position of anything: *quod litigent quid anima, et ubinam ~es ejus* AC 6929; CI 602. **3** The proper position of anything, its place: *sol, luna stetit ~e sua* Hab. 3.11 (AC 2709.3); *unicuivis est suus locus seu sua ~es* VR 32.6; (fig.) *ideo est utriusque* [sc. *amoris et sapientiae*] *~es in effectu* AM 8.5. **4** The part of the body on which one sits, seat: *sub ~e seu clunibus* ES 3211.

sedile ~is, *neut.* A structure for sitting on, seat: *~ia formata ex...complicatis propaginibus arborum* AM 13.2.

sedimentum ~i, *neut.* Sediment: *~um aquarum* Ezek. 34.18 (AC 4769.4).

seditio ~onis, *f.* A rebellious movement, sedition: *ut ~o sedaretur* VR 830; ES 5426.

seditiosus ~a ~um, *a.* Mutinous, seditious: *spiritus qui rebelles vel ~i fuerunt* ES 5093.

sedo ~are ~avi ~atum, *tr.* **1** To allay (pain): *dolores ~abantur et aggravabantur* ES 153; to quench (thirst): *~are sitim* AE 455.7; to stave off (hunger): *ut ~ent famem* AC 987.2. **2** To reduce to a tranquil state, calm down: *utcunque exteriora... ~antur tranquillitatis causa* CI 380.3; *ut seditio ~aretur* VR 830.

seduco ~cere ~xi ~ctum, *tr.* To lead into error, cause to go astray: *hi sunt serpentes...qui ~cunt mundum* AC 206.2; *fallere et ~cere alios* AC 7356.1; *qui...facile se ~ci patiuntur* AC 8315; (of things) *sapientia tua, quae est ingeniositas scribendi, ~xit te* AM 380.6; VR 72.3.

seductio ~onis, *f.* The act of leading astray, seducing: AC 10641.

seductor ~oris, *m.* A seducer: *ad homines...qui sunt ~ores* ES 776; AC 3529.

sedule, *adv.* Diligently: *fideliter, sincere, et ~e suae functionis opus facere* AM 9.4.

sedulitas ~atis, *f.* Diligence, assiduity: AM 164.

sedulo, *adv.* Carefully, attentively: *observatum est ~o, quomodo homo seipsum devastat* ES 4679.

sedulus ~a ~um, *a.* Attentive, diligent: *qui sua sorte contenti sunt, in suo opere ~i et diligentes* CI 364; AM 220.3.

seges ~etis, *f.* A crop of grain: *~es stans* Exod. 22.6 (AC); CI 137.4; AM 134.1.

segmentum ~i, *neut.* A piece formed by cutting, section: *et arietem secabis in ~a sua* Exod. 29.17 (AC); (geom.) a segment (of a circle): *apparent tanquam ~um quoddam minus circuli efforment* ES 813.

segregatus ~a ~um, *a.* Formed into separate groups, segregated: *tandem ~i steterunt vicissim* VR 335.1.

seipsum, *acc. pron.* (abl. *~o*, acc. pl. *~os*, dat. and abl. pl. *~is*) Himself, herself, itself, oneself, etc.: *quod ~os...illuc conjecerint* AC 8275; *quod ducere ~um sit duci a proprio* CI 280; *malum contra ~um non potest agere* VR 68.2.

sejunctim, *adv.* Separately: *unum* [*genus concubinatus*] *conjunctim cum uxore, et alterum ~im ab uxore* AM 463.1.

sejunctio ~onis, *f.* The act of being kept apart, separation: *a significatione 'peccare' quod sit ~o, recessio et separatio a bono et vero* AC 7614; DP 326.5.

sejungo ~gere ~xi ~ctum, *tr.* To keep apart, separate: *inde est quod prorsus ~ctus sit a coelo* CI 531.2; *quoad amorem actualem se ~gunt ab uxore* AM 466.3.

selah, *indecl.* (Hebr.) A word of obscure meaning occurring in Hebr. poetry: *Deus a Temane veniet, et Sanctus de monte Paran, ~ah* Hab. 3.3 (AC 1675.6).

selav, *indecl.* (Hebr.) A Hebr. word for the bird quail: *et ascendit ~av* Exod. 16.13 (AC); *caro coturnicum seu ~av* AE 750.15.

selectio ~onis, *f.* That which is chosen, choice specimen: *omnes arbores Edenis, ~o et praecipuum Libani* Ezek. 31.16 (AC 7090.2).

selenites ~ae, *f.* (Gk.) A kind of crystalline gypsum, selenite: *~es seu lapides speculares* VR 35.2; AM 443 (*selemnites* erroneously in 1st and 2nd edns.).

seligo ~ligere ~legi ~lectum, *tr.* To pick out, select: *~ligam te in catino afflictionis* Isa. 48.10 (AC 1846.1).

sella ~ae, *f.* A chair, seat: *dum ad mensam sedent, non sedent super ~is aut scamnis* AC 8377; (used in obstetrics) *in obstetricando vos Hebraeis, et videritis super ~is, si filius ille, et occidetis illum* Exod. 1.16 (AC).

semel, *adv.* **1** On one occasion only, once: *quod sol ~l quovis die circum hanc tellurem feratur* AC 5084.2; DD 35.4. **2** (to denote the start of a state) Once: *quae ~l sibi acquisiverunt, illa retinent* AC 6812; *nisi sensus spiritualis ~l aperiretur, Verbum...foret clausum* SS 12.2. **3** On some previous occasion, once (upon a time): *narravi quod ~l cogitaverim de Dei essentia...ab aeterno* AM 328.3; *~l etiam ego in simili statu fui* VR 31.3.

semen ~inis, *neut.* **1** A seed of a plant: *ex ~inibus fructuum* AC 8326; *arbor in sua prima origine est ~en* FI 16; (prov.) *serere ~en in aquam* 'to sow seed on water' [i.e., waste one's labour] ES 2230. **2** (collectively) The seminal fluid of animals, semen: *~ini...patris inest anima* VR 92.1; ES 875. **3** (collectively) The progeny, offspring: *erigo foedus meum cum vobis, et cum ~ine vestro post vos* Gen. 9.9 (AC); *qui ex ~ine Jacobi sunt, ut Judaei* AC 788.2; (fig.) *estne universum genus humanum...~en illius amoris?* AM 113. **4** (transf.) Anything which gives rise to something, seed: *aptiores facti ad recipiendum ~en veritatis* AC 1366.2; *posteritas ...~en coeleste...per foedas cupiditates...perdidit* AC 726.

sementis ~is, *f.* (acc. sg. *~em* and *~im*) **1** The time of sowing, seed time: *~is et messis, et frigus et aestus...non cessabunt* Gen. 8.22 (AC); AE 610.2. **2** That which is sown, a crop: *egerminare...quasi ex pulvere humi seges et ~is laeta* ES 231.

semet, *refl. pron.* (acc. and abl. sg. and pl. *semet*, dat. sg. and pl. *sibimet*) Reinforced form of **se**: *hoc foret contra semet* AC 6779.

semetipsum, *refl. pron.* (acc. sg. *semetipsum*, abl. sg. *semetipso*, acc. pl. *semetipsos*, dat. pl. *sibimetipsis*, abl. pl. *semetipsis*) Reinforced form of **se** coupled with the appropriate forms of **ipse**: *quod ne hilum amoris... ex semetipsis habeant* AC 32; *quod ii sibimetipsis malum inferant* AC 592.2; *homo...semetipsum conjicit in infernum* CI 547.

semiapertus ~a ~um, *a.* Half-open: *apud quosdam ...id* [sc. *conjugiale*] *non occluditur, sed manet ~um supra* AM 203.

semichomer ~eris, *m.* also **semiḥomer**. Half a homer (see **chomer**): Hos. 3.2 (AC 8468.1).

semicorus ~i, *m.* Half a homer (see **corus**): *~um hordeorum* Hos. 3.2 (AE 374.13).

semideus ~i, *m.* A demigod: *~os tutelares* CO 43.

semidiabolus ~i, *m.* A half-devil: *alius qui erat quasi ~us* ES 1080.

semiḥomer: see **semichomer**.

semihora ~ae, *f.* A half-hour: *post ~am* AM 231.3.

semihorium ~i, *neut.* A period of half an hour: *spiritus momento eloqui possunt quae homo vix per ~um* AC 6987.2; VR 731.3.

semimortuus ~a ~um, *a.* Half-dead: *fui ~us cum saevo dolore* SE 114.1.

seminalis ~is ~e, *a.* Concerned with semen: *provinciam vesicularum ~ium* AC 5056.2.

seminarium ~i, *neut.* A seedbed (in quots. fig.): *genus humanum est ~um coeli* AC 6697; CI 315.

seminatio ~onis, *f.* Insemination: *quod sit correspondentia cum amore conjugiali, ~one, prolificatione* AM 116.

seminex ~ecis, *a.* Half-dead: *sic ut sibi ~eces videantur* AC 581.1.

seminifico ~are ~avi, *tr.* (of plants) To produce (seed): *herbam ~antem semen* Gen. 1.11 (AC).

semino ~are ~avi ~atum, *tr.*, *intr.* **1** To sow (seed): *qui ~at bonum semen est Filius Hominis* Matt. 13.37 (AC 264.2). **2** To plant (land with seed): *~abo domum Israelis...semine hominis* Jer. 31.27 (SS 51.8). **3** (intr.) To sow seed: *exivit ~ans ad ~andum* Matt. 13.3 (VI 2).

seminudus ~a ~um, *a.* Half-naked: *nudi coram omnibus aut ~i* AC 829.1; ES 1696.

seminulum ~i, *neut.* A small seed: *ex ~o jacto in terram* VR 12.2; *quod ~a in arbores crescant* CI 109.

semiplenus ~a ~um, *a.* Half-full: *ore ~o* 'with the mouth half-open' AM 115.4.

semirepletus ~a ~um, *a.* Half-filled: *sicut tota sphaera...falsitate ~a esset* ES 857.

semirotundus ~a ~um, *a.* Semicircular: *templum erat amplum... ~um* AM 23.

semissis ~is, *m.* A half: *per ~em horae* AM 24; *dimidium et ~is significat quantum correspondens* AE 488.

semita ~ae, *f.* A pathway, road: *visae ~ae obliquae sursum lente* AC 189; *erit ~a ex Aegypto in Aschurem* Isa. 19.23 (DD 4); (fig.) *transeuntem ~as marium* Ps. 8.8 (AC 52).

semivigil ~lis, *a.* Half-awake: *in statu ~li* ES(M) 4598; characterized by being half-awake: *in visione nocturna ~li* ES 3611.

semotus ~a ~um, *a.* Distant, remote: *abditi a Domino, seu ab oculis aliorum ~i* AE 392.3.

semper, *adv.* On all occasions, always: *quod causae justum ~er triumpharet* AC 7007.1; AC 10618.2.

sempiternus ~a ~um, *a.* Everlasting: *~a conservatio* AM 85; *in ~um*, for ever: Isa. 25.8 (AC 1736.2).

senarius ~a ~um, *a.* Of or relating to the number six: *triplicatio numeri ~i* AC 10217.8.

senator ~oris, *m.* (in ancient Rome) A member of the Senate: ES 5210; (in modern times) a member of a similar senior council of state, senator: ES 6047.

senatus ~us, *m.* (in ancient Rome) The body of senior citizens exercising control over the republic, senate: *regimini Romano...quando fuerunt consul, ~us et tribunus plebis* VR 141; any similar official body: *de pluribus hominibus qui simul unum ~um, synedrium aut concilium conformant* VR 16.3.

senecta ~ae, *f.* Old age: *ab infantia usque ad seram ~am* AM 102; VR 4.1.

senectus ~utis, *f.* Old age: *infantia, adolescentia, virilitas et ~us* CI 166; AM 90.2.

senesco ~nescere ~nui, *intr.* To grow old, age: *corvus ...albescit...cum ~nescit* AM 233.4; *quando... ~nueris* John 21.18 (AE 9.3).

senex ~is, *m.* (gen. pl. *~um*) An old man: *adolescentes et ~es simul* Jer. 31.13 (AC 8339.1); *multitudinem tam ~um quam juvenum* AM 8.2; (pl. as including women) *inter conjures ~es* AM 290; *~es mares et ~es mulieres* Zech. 8.4 (AC 2348.1).

seni ~ae ~a, *pl. adj.* Six each: *pones illas* [sc. *placentas*] *in duos ordines, ~os ordine* Lev. 24.6 (AC 7978.2).

senilis ~is ~e, *a.* Of advanced age, old: *quae ~es ac senio confectae mortuae sunt* AC 553.1; (of age) advanced: *ab infantia ad ~em aetatem* ES 2095.

senior ~oris, *m.* One of a class of men respected for their age, an elder: *~ores Israelis* AC 121; *sederunt... ~ores seu sapientiores ad latera* AM 207.2.

senium ~i, *neut.* Old age: *sepelieris in ~o bono* Gen. 15.15 (AC); *quae seniles ac ~o confectae mortuae sunt* AC 553.1; *ex provecto ~o* AM 473.

sensatio ~onis, *f.* **1** The act of receiving a sensory impression, feeling, sensation: *haec scientifica...ad ~onem seu perceptionem hominis...veniunt* AC 991; *duo illa jucunda amoris in subjectis...ex ~one illorum vocantur bona* VR 38.2; *ibi est ~o visus interni eorum* AE 8.2. **2** A sense impression, sensation: *corpus terrestre ...non recipit ab interiori...mundo primas ~ones et primos motus* CI 331; *ignis ~o* ES 1980. **3** Consciousness, feeling: *quod nullam ~onem habeant honoris pro facinorosis* ES(M) 4597.

sensibilis ~is ~e, *a.* (compar. *~ior*, superl. *~issimus*) **1** Apprehensible by the senses, perceptible: *quod activitatis hujus sphaera... ~is sistatur* AC 1504; *quod spiritus diabolici...etiam hominibus ~issimos cruciatus... inferrent* ES 376 titulus. **2** Capable of feeling, sensory: *in...visceribus...sunt fibrae ~es* ES 1758; (of persons) possessing senses: *multo promptiores et ~iores sunt... quam dum in corpore suo vixerunt* ES 2252.

sensibilitas ~atis, *f.* Sensitivity: ES 4348.2.

sensibiliter, *adv.* In a manner apprehensible by the senses, perceptibly: *tranquillitas...implebat ~er thoracem et cor* AC 8113; *animadverti...perceptibiliter et ~er influxum illum nunc per 25 annos continue* AM 419.

sensilis ~is ~e, *a.* Having sensation, sensory: *fibrillas ... ~es in organis* ES 1941.

sensim, *adv.* Little by little, gradually: *at haereses... ~im aberrabant ab hoc* AC 409; *sicut homo qui...ex vigilia in statum somni, ~im cadit* ES 319.

sensitivus ~a ~um, *a.* **1** Of or concerned with the senses, sensory: *quod spiritus multo excellentiores facultates ~as habeat* AC 321; *contra dulces ~as illecebras sui corporis* AM 426. **2** (neut. as sb.) A sensory impression, feeling: *quod obliteraretur omne ~um veri* AC 7671; *~um jucundi* AE 229.2; also, a sensory faculty: *aliquod vitale...ei* [sc. *animae*] *addicere, sed usque non ~um quale homini* CI 456.2.

sensorium ~i, *neut.* An organ of sense perception, sensory organ: *antrorsum in capitis facie sunt quinque hominis ~a* AM 315.5; *similiter...se habet...auditio quae est auris, ad intellectuale quod est ~i interni* AC 656;

(transf. of persons) *quod uxores sint illarum* [*delitiarum*] *receptacula et ~a* AM 155^{a}.3.

sensorius ~a ~um, *a.* Of or concerned with sense perception, sensory: *organo ~o* CI 217; VR 10.

sensuale ~is, *neut.* **1** A faculty of sense perception: *quod sit interius ~e quod correspondet coelo spirituum* AC 978.2; *~ia, nempe tactus, gustus, olfactus, auditus et visus* AC 1718; *quod* [*homo*]*...ex ~i suo capit* AC 6997.7; *supra ~e, quod est infimum intellectus, apparuit sicut velamen* VR 12.10. **2** (pl.) Objects as apprehended by the senses, sense perceptions: *explorare illa quae sunt fidei per ~ia et scientifica* AC 647; *pro scientificis infimis, quae sunt ~ia* AC 6726.

sensualis ~is ~e, *a.* **1** Apprehended by means of the senses, sensual: *vera ~ia quae sunt visus et auditus* AC 777; *bonum et verum...rationale, naturale et ~e* SS 18.3. **2** Characterized by concentration on the senses, sensual: (of persons) *qui ~is est seu sensibus modo credit* AC 196.2; *quod prorsus ~es et corporei fierent* AC 6959.1; (qualified by *corporeus*) *plerique ~es corporei sunt* CI 575; (of life or qualities) *vitam intime ~em* AC 978.3; *externum naturale seu ~e* AC 7041.1.

sensualitas ~atis, *f.* The quality of concentration on sense perceptions, sensuality: *ex mente naturali hominis, et ex ejus rationalitate et ~ate* AE 1210.3.

sensualiter, *adv.* By means of sense perceptions: *antequam ~er confirmatur* AC 7289; *cogitant ~er et materialiter* AM 416.3.

sensum ~i, *neut.* A perception in the mind: *exprimere ~a animi et ideas cogitationis* AC 7361.2; ES(M) 4548.

sensus ~us, *m.* **1** Any of the five bodily senses: *ex ~ibus externis, nempe ex visu, auditu, gustu, odoratu, tactu* AC 7038.2; *fallaciis sensuum plena* AC 7112. **2** A perception, feeling: *cogitat...absque aliquo ~u qui involvit cognitionem ejus* [sc. *Dei*] VR 4.2; *cum ~u...quod circumfunderer spiritibus* ES 243. **3** A meaning (of a word, phrase, sentence, etc.): *nam cuique tali voci sunt ~us contrarii seu oppositi* AC 1066.4; *unaquaevis litera in alphabeto significat ibi aliquem ~um* AM 326.5. **4** Any of the levels at which an utterance may be understood, sense: *in ~u interno* AC 6713; *~um spiritualem Verbi* DD 37.2; *quod sapientia...sub ~u literae jaceat recondita* AM 24; *in ~u abstracto* VR 76.4. **5** A complete utterance, sentence, phrase: *loquela illorum in fine cujusvis ~us terminatur quoad accentum in unum* VR 8.2; *non datur ibi ~us, imo non vox nec litera quae non aliquid Domini...in se continet* SS(P) 16 (= 6.1).

sententia ~ae, *f.* **1** A judgment, opinion: *qui... defendit ~am suam contra alios* AC 6663.2; *quarta cohors...enuntiavit suam ~am* AM 3.4. **2** A judicial sentence (on a malefactor): *mitior ~a* AC 5759; *suffragia ... ~ae affirmativae* AE 147.

sentica ~ae, *f.* A briar, bramble: *spina ~a ascendet* Isa. 32.13 (AC 273).

senticetum ~i, *neut.* A thicket of brambles: *~um et vepretum* Isa. 9.18 (AC 1861.2).

sentina ~ae, *f.* A lavatory, privy: *voluptatem...diu sedendi in ~is* ES 597; ES 377.

sentio ~tire ~si (*or* ~tivi) ~sum (*or* ~titum), *tr.*, *intr.* (*~tivi* and *~titus* are well attested in Autographs and 1st edns., but have frequently been emended by editors: e.g. VR 146; ES 408; AC 175; AC 10312; AM 266.3; VR 570.7. n.b. There is no reason to suppose these forms are from **sentisco***, which does not occur.) **1** To perceive by the bodily senses, feel: *~titus odor aromaticus* AC 175; *qui* [*calor*] *~titus est...sicut calor in balneis* VR 834; (w. *quod*) *per visionem spiritualem ~tivi quod rebelles dolore correpti sunt* ES 408. **2** To become mentally aware of, feel, experience: *ut aliquid de coelesti gaudio ~tiret* AC 537; *si...admitterentur in coelum, ~tirent infernum in se* AC 7439.3; *non ~tit praesentiam...Dei* VR 105.1; (w. *quod*) *quando homo apud se ~tit aut percipit quod cogitet bene de Domino* AC 1102.2. **3** (intr.) To hold an opinion, feel: *ridentur qui aliter ~tiunt* AC 6666.3; *ut male ~tiant et loquantur...de Ecclesia* AC 7747; *dum omnibus et singulis una sententia est, potest dici quod unum ~tiant* VR 16.3.

sentis ~is, *m.* A bramble, briar: *spina, carduus, ~is, vepris, urtica* AC 273; AM 526; VR 78.5.

seorsim, *adv.* **1** In a separate place, separately: *habitant ~im* CI 51; (in a book) *de qua turba... ~im* AC 581.1. **2** Taken separately, in isolation: *explicabant quid significarent ~im et quid conjunctim* SS 90.1.

seorsum, *adv.* Away, apart: *quod Jesus assumserit surdum aegre loquentem a populo ~um* AC 7430.1 (Mark 7.33).

separabilis ~is ~e, *a.* Separable: *separati et ~es ab homine* ES 164.

separatim, *adv.* (compar. *~ius*) Separately: *quod omnes ~im cum suis habitent* AC 8117; *fides scientifica ... ~im recondita* ES 3376; *~im ab*, apart from: *de solo Mosche...aut de populo ~im ab illo* AC 10571; *spiritus apud me ~ius a corpore agit quam apud alios* ES 4437.

separatio ~onis, *f.* Separation: *spiritus hominis post ~onem aliquantisper manet in corpore* CI 447; *ex fidei ~one a charitate* SS 112.1; (of married partners) *apud illos qui ~ones cogitant* AM 214.3. **b** (Bibl.) *aquae ~onis*, water used for ritual purification: Num. 19.21 (AE 79.4).

separatus ~a ~um, *a.* (pf. pple. of **separo**) **1** Physically separated: *spiritus...ex aliis telluribus omnes...inter se ~i sunt* AC 6701. **2** Not joined or shared with another, separate: *ab illis qui sunt in scientificis ~is* AC 6666.1; *propter favores ~os a conjuge* AM 282.2; *cuique [personae] ~as qualitates...attribuunt* VR 15.2.

separo ~are ~avi ~atum, *tr.* **1** To move or keep apart, separate physically: *ut nebulosum...quod circumcingit, et prorsus ~at a sereno* AC 6853; *[infernum hoc] ~atur ab infernis adulterorum per aquas quasi maris* AC 8099.2. **2** (transf.) To treat as distinct, keep apart, separate: *qui ~ant fidem a charitate* AC 916.3; *vera et bona non genuina inde ~antur et rejiciuntur ad latera* AC 7975.1.

sepelio ~lire ~livi (*or* ~lii) sepultum, *tr.* **1** To lay in the earth, bury (a corpse): *quos ita interemerunt, postea ~liunt* AC 7248; VR 10; cf. *tanquam aurum, argentum et lapides pretiosi sepulta inter ossa in valle Hinnomi* VR 619.1; *~livit Abraham Saram* Gen. 23.19 (AC); *~lieris in senio bono* Gen. 15.15 (AC). **2** (transf.) To lose sight of, bury: *ne...status vitae...post mortem nesciretur...ac tandem ~liretur in negatione* AM 39; *ita erat fides ejus sepulta in scientiis* ES 690 1/2.

sepelitio ~onis, *f.* Burial (of a corpse): *angeli, cum memoratur in Verbo ~o, non cogitant de corpore quod rejicitur sed de anima quae resurgit* AC 4621.

sepes ~is, *f.* A hedge: *plantavit vineam, et ~em ei circumposuit* Matt. 21.33 (AC 124).

sepio ~pire ~pivi ~pitum, *tr.* To build (a fence): *~pivistis sepem pro domo Israelis* Ezek. 13.5 (AC 1664.3); to repair by fencing, mend (a breach): *~piens rupturam* Isa. 58.12 (AC 613).

sepono ~nere ~sui ~situm, *tr.* To put apart, set aside: *ad ~sitos filios Israelis non misit manum Suam* Exod. 24.11 (AC); *ecce mina tua, quam habui ~sitam in sudario* Luke 19.20 (AE 193.10); *pro corpore...quod ~nitur illico* ES 379.

septem, *indecl. a.* Seven: *draco...habens capita ~m* Rev. 12.3 (AR); AM 20.1.

September ~bris, *m.* The month of September: ES 3073.

septempliciter, *adv.* Sevenfold: *omnis occidens Cain ~er vindicabitur* Gen. 4.15 (AC).

septenarius ~a ~um, *a.* Of or concerned with the number seven: *per ~os numeros* AC 728.2.

septendecim, *indecl. a.* Seventeen: *qui vixerunt ante ~im saecula* CI 363.

septeni ~ae ~a, *pl. a.* Seven each: *septem...lucernae ... ~a infundibula lucernis* Zech. 4.2 (AE 62.2).

septennium ~i, *neut.* A period of seven years: VR 279.1.

septentrio ~onis, *m.* The north as a point of the compass: *quatuor plagae, oriens, meridies, occidens et ~o* CI 141; also, the north as a region: *cum nominatur Europa, percipiunt ~onem* AE 21.

septentrionalis ~is ~e, *a.* Of the north, northern: *in plaga ~i* CI 513; (masc. as sb.) *caeperunt... ~es... aperire suam mentem* VR 48.10.

septies, *adv.* Seven times: *~es in die laudo te* Ps. 119.164 (VR 51).

septimalis ~is ~e, *a.* Of the seventh (month, day, etc.): *~e festum* 3AD 6026.

septimana ~ae, *f.* **1** A period of seven days, week: *non quidem per diem et ~am sed per menses et fere annum* AC 70; *quod jejunaret bis in ~a* VI 30.3 (Luke 18.12); *festum ~arum* Deut. 16.10 (AC 7093.4). **2** (Bibl.) Any long period of time: *tempora...vocabantur ~ae... septem annorum tempus vocatur ~a* AC 395.1.

septimus ~a ~um, *a.* Seventh: *in die ~o* Gen. 2.2 (AC); AM 2.3.

septingenti ~ae ~a, *pl. adj.* Seven hundred: *uxores ejus, quae numero ~ae fuerunt* DP 245.

septuagenarius ~a ~um, *a.* Of or concerned with seventy: *numerus ~us* AC 433.

septuagies, *adv.* Seventy times: *vindicabitur... Lamech ~es et septies* Gen. 4.24 (AC).

septuaginta, *indecl. a.* Seventy: *et vixit Kenan ~a annis* Gen. 5.12 (AC); CI 229.

septum ~i, *neut.* (anat.) The partition between the nostrils, septum: *evolvere tunicam oculi sinistri versus ~um nasi* AC 183.

septuplus ~a ~um, *a.* Seven times as great: *lux solis erit ~a* Isa. 30.26 (AC 395.1); (neut. as sb.) seven times as much: *retribue vicinis nostris ~um in sinum illorum* Ps. 79.12 (AC 6960.5).

sepulchralis ~is ~e, *a.* Of a tomb, sepulchral: *tumuli ~es* VR 110.8; *per ~es statuas* ES 2147.

sepulchrum ~i, *neut.* also **sepulcrum**. A place of burial, tomb, grave: *~is dealbatis* Matt. 23.27 (VI 30.1); *ut... ~a illorum sancta crederentur* FI 8.

sepulcrum: see **sepulchrum**.

sepultura ~ae, *f.* Burial: *Ipsius mors, ~a et resurrectio* AE 220.2; AC 901.4.

sepultus ~a ~um: pf. pple. of **sepelio**.

sequela ~ae, *f.* **1** The act of following: *vocavit eum ad ~am Sui* Isa. 41.2 (AC 2686.4; cf. AE 357.5). **2** The act of following mentally, apprehension: *si tunc facilis est ~a loquelae inductae, inde judicant quod tales sint* AC 5383. **3** That which follows logically, result, consequence: *voces sunt spontaneae ipsius sensus ~ae* AC 1648; *~ae ex confirmatione...sunt plures* VR 485.

sequens ~ntis, *a.* (pres. pple. of **sequor**) (abl. sg. *~nte* VR 9.2 or *~nti* VR 9.3) In senses of verb, esp. **1** Coming after in time, succeeding: *tempus ~ns* AC 6984; *in saeculo ~nte* VR 9.2. **2** Coming after in sequence, following, next: *ad finem ~ntis capitis* AC 6702; (neut. pl. as sb.) *antequam explicantur ~ntia* AC 7041.2; *in ~ntibus dicetur* CI 233.

sequor ~i ~utus sum, *tr., intr.* **1** (tr.) To walk behind, come after, follow: *veni, ~ere Me* Mark 10.21 (AC 8159.4); *~imini me, et introducam vos in gaudia vestra* AM 4.2. **2** (tr.) To follow as a guide or leader, be a follower of: *quod...Johannes ~utus sit Dominum, significabat quod qui in bonis charitatis sunt ~antur Dominum* AC 10087.4. **3** (intr.) To come after in sequence, follow: *praecedunt pisces et aves...et ~untur bestiae* AC 52. **4** (intr.) To follow as a consequence, result: *in intimis suis, et inde in ~entibus ex illis* AM 101; *ex una parabolica idea innumerabilia ~untur applicabilia* ES 4006; (impers., w. *quod*) it follows (that): *inde ~itur quod...quisque...sit proximus* AC 6706; *ex his ~itur, quod Divinum...descendat per tres gradus* SS 6. **5** To be inseparable from, attend upon, follow: (tr.) *quod bona opera usque sponte ~antur fidem* SE 46; *unumquodvis malum sua paena ~itur* DP 249.3; (intr.) *opera...illorum ~untur cum illis* Rev. 14.13 (AR). **6** (tr.) To follow with the mind, perceive, grasp: *~untur presse ejus cogitationem* ES 2201; *ut quicquid dicebatur ~erentur* ES 808. **7** To act in accordance with, conform to: *omnis Ecclesia ~ens intima Domini etiam est sabbathum* AC 85.2; *scribe de illo, et ~ere revelationem* AM 534; *~endo ideas sibi infusas* ES 3701.

sera ~ae, *f.* A bolt: *scrinia tribus ~is occlusa* VR 185.8.

seraphim, *indecl. pl.* (Hebr.) Seraphs, seraphim: Isa. 6.2 (AC 2921.5).

serenitas ~atis, *f.* A period of calm weather: *comparari...potest cum ~ate post tempestates* VR 304; (fig.) tranquillity: *apud Judaeos...quibus tunc ~as* AE 706.7.

sereno ~are ~avi ~atum, *tr.* To make tranquil, calm: *pax et tranquillitas ~ant mentes* AM 285.2; (pass.) to become calm: *constat ex turbulentis...aquis, quod sensim ~entur* ES 2089.

serenum ~i, *neut.* **1** Fine weather, clear sky: *per ~a, per tempestates* ES 196; clarity (of light): *auferunt lucis apricum et ~um* CI 549; AC 6853. **2** (fig.) A period of calm or peace: *est sicut ~um pacis* AM 155[a].5; *factum est tranquillum et ~um* VR 71.4.

serenus ~a ~um, *a.* **1** (of light, air, etc.) Unobscured, clear, fine: *vapor densus...in ~a aura* AC 6639.2; ES 4270; *in luce matutina et ~a* VR 77.1. **2** *Gutta ~a*, the eye disease amaurosis: VR 346.2.

sericatus ~a ~um, *a.* Ornamented with silk: *pileus ~us super capite doctoris* VR 673.

sericum ~i, *neut.* Silk: *transparent, sicut facies per tenue ~um* SS 55; *quod viles illi vermes...~o vestirent...faeminas* VR 12.9.

series ~ei, *f.* **1** An ordered arrangement of one thing after another, sequence: *secundum ~em rerum in sensu interno agitur de Ecclesia instaurata* AC 6639.1; *absque interruptione ~ei* AC 7933.3; *in sua ~e affectio veri existit* FI 13. **b** *in ~e* (w. gen.), in the course (of): *in ~e hujus operis* VR 20.1. **2** A coherent group, series: *scientifica...in continuas ~es disposita sunt, una ~es cum altera* AC 6690; *quod sint variae ~es in geometricis quae vadunt in infinitum* VR 32.8.

serio, *adv.* Seriously: *ex persuasione illa amplius loqui ~o interdictum est* VR 796.2; AM 280.

seriosus ~a ~um, *a.* (of persons) Concerned with serious matters, serious: *in societatem ~orum veniunt* ES 1125.

serius[1] ~a ~um, *a.* **1** Of serious import, serious: *hoc in ~am ventilationem missum est* AR 294.4; *per ~am poenitentiam* ES 4091; (neut. as sb.) *converti sermonem ad ~a* AM 521.5. **2** (of persons) Stern, severe: *inter judices istos maxime ~os* ES 3228.

serius[2], *compar. adv.*: see **sero**[2].

sermo ~onis, *m.* **1** The content of speech, talk, conversation: *affectationes elegantiae ~onis et eruditionis* AC 6924; *cum apud angelos ~o est de doctrinalibus* AC 3216; (pl.) *omnis qui venit ad Me, et audit ~ones Meos* Luke 6.47 (AC 8361.2); *per ~ones sapientiae protraxerunt diem* AM 18.3. **b** *communis ~o*, what is generally said: *in communi ~one est quod quisque sibimet proximus sit* AC 6933; FI 3. **2** A sermon: *cum ~ones suos seu praedicationes concinnarent* VI 7; VR 381.3.

sermocinatio ~onis, *f.* Conversation, talking: *status cogitationis et ~onis satanarum* VR 80.5; an instance of this: *a continuis ~onibus defatigati sumus* AM 5.2.

sermocinor ~ari ~atus sum, *tr., intr.* To say, talk about: *illa quae coram caetu ~ati sunt* VR 147; (intr.) *de his...~ati sumus* ES 222.

sero[1] ~rere ~vi satum, *tr.* **1** To sow (seed): *~verunt tritica* Jer. 12.13 (AC 3941.3); (prov., of wasted labour) *~rere semen in aquas*, to sow seed on water: AC 1874. **2** To sow (land) with seed, plant: *bestia est sicut humus jamdum sata* AM 134.1.

sero[2], *adv.* (compar. *~ius*) At a late time, tardily: *hoc non credit...nisi ~o cum judicio pollet* AC 1838.2; *facies hypocritarum ~ius mutantur quam facies reliquorum* CI 458.

serositas ~atis, *f.* A watery fluid in the body, serosity: *ubi ~ates influunt ab interstitiis fibrarum* ES 830; AC 4050.2.

serotinus ~a ~um, *a.* Late in a period of time; late in the year: *pluvia ~a* [i.e., spring rains] Hos. 6.3 (AC 93); *pluviam tempestivam et ~am* Deut. 11.14 (AE 644.6); late in the day: *per pluvias matutinas et ~as* VR 687.2.

serpens ~ntis, *m.* (gen. pl. *~ntum*) A snake: *et factus* [*baculus*] *in ~ntem aqueum* Exod. 7.10 (AC); *in Aegypto ...fuerunt in imagine vituli, boves, ~ntes* SS 23.1; (of evil spirits) *eorum qui ~ntes sunt seu qui in vita corporis dolosi fuerant* ES 2492.

serpentiformis ~is ~e, *a.* Snake-like, serpentine: *ut putarem eos...in ~es globos versos esse* ES 2492.

serpentinus ~a ~um, *a.* Of or connected with snakes: *sunt...iis oculi quasi ~i* AC 831.3; *poena eorum est ~a* ES 2867.

serpentulus ~i, *m.* A small snake: *sentiebam inter crines...sicut anguiculos seu ~os parvulos plures* ES 3810.

serpo ~ere ~si *intr.* To creep, crawl: *a peste quae in caligine ~it* Ps. 91.6 (AC 7102.10); to spread slowly: *gangraenae, quae ~it et putrefacit vicina* VR 120.2.

serra ~ae, *f.* A saw: *truncus securi aut ~a discinditur* CO 7.2; *per scissionem graminis per ~am* ES 575 titulus.

serrarius ~i, *m.* **1** A worker with a saw, sawyer: *lignarii, ~i* ES 3054. **2** One who mows (grass): *~i graminis* ES 3079.

serratio ~onis, *f.* **1** The act or motion of sawing: *ii per modum ~onis agunt, seu triturationis cis et ultra, cum quodam murmure ~onis* ES 1009; AC 5184. **2** The act of mowing (grass): *quod videantur sibi secare gramen...et per ~onem istam se calefacere student* AC 1111.

serrator ~oris, *m.* One who mows (grass): *quod videantur sibi secare gramen et vocantur graminis ~ores* AC 1111.

serro ~are ~avi ~atum, *tr.* To mow (grass): *secare ligna et ~are gramen* AC 6393.5.

serteus ~a ~um, *a.* Made of garlands: *~ae compages ornatissimae supra introitum* ES 4354; (neut. as sb.) a garland: *infantes nudi...cincti ~is* AC 165.

sertum ~i, *neut.* A garland: *florum ~is circum pectus cincti* AC 154; *flores diversicolores in ~o* VR 62.

sertus ~a ~um, *a.* Joined together: *ibi lecti ~i, unus superior altero* ES 3790.

serum ~i, *neut.* A watery fluid in the body, serum: *colligitur semen cum ~o conveniente* AC 5056.2; AM 374; ES 826.

serus ~a ~um, *a.* Advanced in time, late: *~a vespera* AM 23.

serva ~ae, *f.* A female servant, handmaiden (in quot. fig.): *sic philosophia potest adesse, quum ~a est* ES 650.

servatio ~onis, *f.* The act of keeping safe, preserving: *tutatio et ~o* AR 186.

servator ~oris, *m.* A preserver: *quia* [*Salvator*] *idem est cum omnium ~ore* ES 531.

servilis ~is ~e, *a.* Of or proper to a servant, servile: *amicitium ~em in conjugiis* AM 248.2.

serviliter, *adv.* In the manner of a servant, servilely: *hos et illos obsequia...non conjungunt nisi ~er* AM 250.

servio ~vire ~vivi (*or* ~vii) ~vitum, *intr.* (*tr.*) **1** To be a slave or servant: *et ~vire fecerunt Aegyptii filios Israelis* Exod. 1.13 (AC); (w. cognate acc.) *et ~vies servitium hoc in mense hoc* Exod. 13.5 (AC); (w. dat.) to be servant (to), serve: *nemo potest duobus dominis ~vire* Matt. 6.24 (VI 28). **2** (pass.) To be served (by): *volunt ut sicut supremi ab omnibus ~viantur* AC 8313.4; ES 592. **3** (w. dat.) To be of service (to), serve: *ut ~virent falsis* AC 7123; *vera induentia bonum, et ~vientia illi* AE 31.7; (w. *ad*) to serve (to): *satis ad illustrandum ~vire possunt illa* AM 314.1; (w. *pro*) to serve (as): *faciebant doctrinam ut ~viret pro norma* AC 519.1; CI 305.

servitas: see **servitus**.

servitium ~i, *neut.* **1** The condition of being a slave, slavery, servitude: *de servo qui non ~o exire vellet* AC 3869.11. **2** An act performed for another, duty, service: *inter eos qui vilia ~a praestare possint* AC 1095; *ad serviendum ~um Habitaculi* Num. 3.7 (AE 444.2). **3** A thing which performs a service, instrument, tool: *omnia quaecunque apud externum hominem sunt, non sunt aliud quam ~a, hoc est, ut inserviant interno homini* AC 1486; CI 347.2. **4** A person who serves another, servant: *quod...adhibeantur ad usus, sed ut ~a infima* AC 6389; (sg. as collective) *et fuit ei acquisitio gregis...et ~um multum* Gen. 26.14 (AC).

servitus ~utis, *f.* also **servitas** ~atis, *f.* The state of being a slave, slavery, servitude: *et amaram reddiderunt vitam illorum ~ute gravi* Exod. 1.14 (AC); (fig.) *primus horum status est ~utis, et alter est propriae voluntatis* VR 106.1.

servo ~are ~avi ~atum, *tr.* **1** To keep safe, preserve, save: *brachium illorum non ~avit illos* Ps. 44.3 (AC 8281.5); (w. *ab*) *tunc ab hostibus meis ~abor* Ps. 18.3 (AC 8261.6). **2** To act in accordance with, observe, keep (instructions, promises, etc.): *si quis amaverit Me, verbum Meum ~at* John 14.23 (AC 8269); *propter ordinem ~andum in rebus domesticis* AM 271.

servus[1] ~i, *m.* **1** A servant: *cum Abrahami et Isaci ~is* FI 50; *emisit ~os, et invitavit ad nuptias* AM 41.3 (Matt. 22.9). **b** (as describing the relationship of man to God, a subject to his king, etc.): *juravi Davidi ~o Meo* Ps. 89.3 (AC 6804.9); *quare facis sic ~is tuis?* Exod. 5.15 (AC); *ab Emanuele Swedenborg Domini Jesu Christi ~o* VR titulus. **2** A slave (as opposed to a free man): *carnes omnium liberorum et ~orum* Rev. 19.18 (AR). **3** (fig.) A person in a state of subjection, slave: *dominantur apud eum mala et falsa, et est ~us* AC 81.3; AC 6205.

servus[2] ~a ~um, *a.* In or associated with subjection, slavish, servile: *omne id quod trahit originem ex amore sui...non liberum est sed ~um* AC 8993.2; *cum abalienantur [vera et bona fidei] tunc in statum ~um veniunt* AC 8906.4. **b** (neut. as sb.) servitude, slavery: *quod liberum caeleste sit ipsum liberum, consequenter quod oppositum sit ~um utrique* DP 43.1; *non possunt esse in libero, sed in ~o* ES(M) 4655.

sescenti: see **sexcenti**.

sessio ~onis, *f.* The act of sitting: *de ~one Filii ad dextram Patris* VR 136.3.

seu, *conj.* **1** (to introduce an alternative expression) Or in other words, that is to say: *lex Divina seu verum Divinum* AC 6735; *ad affectionem et cogitationem, seu quod idem est, ad voluntatem et intellectum* AS 374. **2** (to introduce a correction or amplification of a preceding statement) Or rather: *quod...non detur una facies prorsus similis seu eadem cum alterius* VR 32.1. **3** (to put mutually exclusive alternatives) Or instead, or: *cultus idoli, sculptilis seu fusilis* AC 8943; *boni et veri, seu mali et falsi* AC 10623.2.

severe, *adv.* (compar. *~ius*, superl. *~issime*) **1** Strictly, sternly: *ideo tunc tam ~e interdictum fuit* AC 1003. **2** Severely, intensely: *si redit...castigator, ~ius punitur* AC 7808; ES 1977.

severus ~a ~um, *a.* Stern, severe: *apparet sicut vestitu obscuro, et ~us* ES 4402; (neut. as sb.) *exuit homo omne ~um, moestum et siccum senile* AE 1000.4.

sex, *indecl. a.* Six: *erant sex turmae* AM 2.3; AE 194.2.

sexagecuplus ~a ~um, *a.* Sixty times as much: *fructum fert...alius...centuplum, alius...~um* Matt. 13.23 (VI 2).

sexagesimus ~a ~um, *a.* Sixtieth: *ab anno aetatis vigesimo ad ~um* AC 10225.1.

sexaginta, *indecl. a.* Sixty: *per sex millia annorum seu ~a saecula* AM 182.5.

sexangularis ~is ~e, *a.* Having six angles, hexagonal: *octo insinuationes ~es* AM 151[a].2.

sexcentenus ~a ~um, *a.* Six hundred: *ex significatione numeri ~i* AC 893.2.

sexcentesimus ~a ~um, *a.* Six hundredth: AC 754.

sexcenti ~ae ~a, *a.* also **sescenti**. Six hundred: *sumsit ~os currus electos* Exod. 14.7 (AC); *invenimus ~os ex mille pro natura* VR 77.5.

sexcenties, *adv.* Six hundred times: ES 615.

sexies, *adv.* Six times: *a vespera ad mane, ut capite primo Geneseos ~es dicitur* AC 860.

sexto[1], *adv.* Sixthly: DP 157.9.

sexto[2] ~are ~avi ~atum, *tr.* To divide into six parts: *et reverti faciam te, et ~abo te* Ezek. 39.2 (AC 737.2).

sextus ~a ~um, *a.* Sixth: *dies ~us* Gen. 1.31 (AC); *in Decalogi ~o praecepto* VI 74.

sexus ~us, *m.* **1** Either of the male and female divisions of man and animals, sex: *quod ~us foemininus talis sit...ut voluntas...regnet prae intellectu* AC 568.2; *Ecclesia est ex utroque ~u* AM 21.3; (as a distinction absent from plants) *in arboribus...non sunt duo ~us, masculinus et faemininus* VR 585.1. **2** The opposite sex as the object of love: *igniculus libidinis ad ~um* AM 44.2; *amor ~us*, a general love for and attraction to the opposite sex: *amor ~us angelicus* AM 44.3; *nimia coercitio amoris ~us* AM 450; cf. *de modis amandi ~um* VR 48.8.

Shaddai: see **Schaddai**.

shalom: see **schalom**.

shittim: see **schittim**.

shoham, *indecl.* (Hebr.) The name of a precious stone: Gen. 2.12 (AC); Ezek. 28.13 (AC 114).

si, *conj.* **1** In the case that, if: *credit...si aliquid determinatum existit, quod sit prudentiae propriae* AC 6692.2; *si ita foret cum homine post mortem* AM 29. **2** (to amend a previous statement) If: *cum pauci si ulli norunt* AC 1707.2; *crusta quae parum si quicquam nexa est cum nucleo* ES 2947; (w. *non*) *per aliquot jam dies, si non septimanam* ES 708. **3** If for example: *sive septuaginta, sive septem, idem involvunt ut si septem dies* AC 728.4; (so, also) *si forte*, if perhaps: *et si forte hic* [sc. *amor caeli*] *adest, est sub illo* [sc. *amore sui*] *sicut servus* VR 424. **4** (introducing an indir. qu.) Whether: *dicebam iis, si non respectum haberent spiritualium peccatorum* ES 1788. **5** Even though: *si fuerint peccata vestra sicut coccinea, sicut nix albescent* Isa. 1.18 (AC 3300.5). **6** (Bibl.) *Si non* (as a strong assertion), surely, without fail: *in igne indignationis* *meae, si non in die hoc fuerit terrae motus magnus* Ezek. 38.19 (DD 4).

sibilaris ~is ~e, *a.* Like a whistle, sibilant: *sonus loquelae illorum erat ~is* AM 268.2.

sibilo ~are ~avi, *intr.* To signal by whistling: *et ~avit illi ab extremitate terrae* Isa. 5.26 (AE 355.32); *~abit Jehovah muscae quae in extremitate fluviorum Aegypti* Isa. 7.18 (AC 7441.2).

sibilose, *adv.* In a whistling manner: *~e susurrabant* ES 3469.

sibilosus ~a ~um, *a.* Whistling: (neut. as sb.) *auditum in Gehenna ~um quid* AC 826.

sibilum: see **sibilus**.

sibilus ~i, *m.* also **sibilum** ~i, *neut.* **1** A whistling noise, whistle: *ostensum...quod modo ~us eos in terrorem...ageret* AC 950; *per venti levis ~um in terrorem redacti* ES 3749; *~a gregum* Judg. 5.16 (AE 434.13). **2** A whistle uttered as a mark of derision: *responderunt ad haec cum ~o* AM 79.5; an object of derision: *ponam eos in desolationem, et in ~um* Jer. 25.9 (AC 1327.8).

sibimet: see **semet**.

sibimetipsis: see **semetipsum**.

sibylla ~ae, *f.* (Gk.) A female prophet in the ancient world, sibyl: ES 4094 titulus.

sibyllinus ~a ~um, *a.* Of a sibyl; *~a biblia*, the Sibylline books: *ex ~is bibliis* ES 4094.

sic, *adv.* **1** In the foregoing manner, thus: *fibrae... complicantur inter se, et sic complicatae tendunt ad utrumque oculum* VR 371.7; *status prior...inservit pro plano statui sequenti, et sic continue* AC 6645.2. **b** *et sic porro*, and so on: AM 376. **2** In the following manner, thus: *sic dixit Jehovah...Pasce oves occisionis* Zech. 11.4 (AC 6767.3); (w. clause) *annon sic conjunctio, quod homo voluntarie faciat secundum Verbum?* AR 417.8. **3** As a result of this, thus: *illi apparent prope sibi esse et sic mutuo cognoscunt se* AC 6806.3; *quod...provideatur, ut...innocentia infantiae fiat innocentia sapientiae ac ut sic infantes fiant angeli* AM 385. **4** *Sic ut*, in such a manner that, so that: *ut voluntas et intellectus...unum facerent, sic ut non aliud cogitaret quam vellet* AC 2930.1; CI 60.

sica ~ae, *f.* A dagger: *praeter aliquem cultrum, mucronem aut ~am* ES 4494.

sicarius ~i, *m.* A professional killer, assassin: AC 816; *fuerunt ~i et venefici* AE 659.5.

siccitas ~atis, *f.* Dryness, drought: *Jehovah ponit fluvios in desertum, et exitus aquarum in ~atem* Ps. 107.33 (AC 7324.2); *percutiet te Jehovah tabe...et ~ate* Deut. 28.22 (AC 8364.3).

sicco ~are ~avi ~atum, *tr.* To make dry: *fimis qui ~ati...odorem fragrantem spargunt* VR 324.

siccus ~a ~um, *a.* **1** Lacking moisture, dry, parched: *arida vocatur locus ~us* AC 6976; (neut. as sb.) dryness: *aequilibrium...inter ~um et humidum* CI 589.1; also, dry land: *quod...populus in ~o transiverit* VI 55.3. **b** (neut. pl. as sb.) dry commodities (as opposed to liquids): *per chomerem mensurabantur ~a* AC 8540.1. **2** Deprived of natural moisture, dried up: *ne...a ligno virente faciat illum ~um stipitem* AM 294.6. **b** (of cruelty) Unaccompanied by bloodshed: *in sua crudelitate ~a, quia absque sanguinis effusione* ES 1213. **3** (of fire, app.) Unaccompanied by flame or light: *vidi ignem foci ~um in carbonibus...cum maxime ~us, ad carbonarium colorem accedit, sic ut vix sit nisi niger carbo* ES 4047. **4** Devoid of pleasurable emotion, unfeeling, dry: *vitam torridam et ~am* AC 1964.2; *o quam ~um gaudium caeli* AM 44.3; *quod inde vir...sit torvus, austerus, ~us et inamabilis* AM 56.4.

sicera ~ae, *f.* Any alcoholic drink other than wine or beer, liquor: *amara erit ~a bibentibius illam* Isa. 24.9 (AC 1071.4); *sicut fermentat vinum aut ~a* DP 284; *quaesivi de vinis, ~is, cerevisiis* UJ(P) 292.

siclus ~i, *m.* (Hebr.) A Hebrew weight, shekel: *quod siclus esset pondus et argenti et auri* AC 10222.

sicut, *adv.* and *conj.* **1** After the fashion of, as: *apparuit Dominus ~t Homo* AC 49.1; *quod...visi sint ~t infantes nudi* AM 137.2. **2** *~t...ita*, as...so: *homo, ~t de coelo, ita de inferno, non habet ideam nisi communissimam* AC 692; CI 53; *~t...etiam*, as...so also: *fiat voluntas, Tua ~t in caelo etiam in terra* Matt. 6.10 (AR 839.5). **3** (to introduce an example of a preceding statement) As for instance: *a ritualibus...ubi septenarium toties occurrit, ~t 'quod de sanguine et oleo spargeretur septem vicibus'* AC 716.2; VR 71.2. **4** (to indicate similarity but not identity) As it were, as if: *ad latera graduum apparebant ~t leones cum catulis* AR 875.5; *quod...de Deo foveant ideam ~t nubeculae in medio* AS 11. **5** (conj. w. indic.) In proportion as, in so far as: *cuivis est affectio bona, ~t fugerat mala sicut peccata* DP 61; *receptaculum fit imago Dei ~t recipit* VR 48.7. **6** (conj. w. subj.) As if: *tunc apparet ~t externus homo vitam haberet ex se* AC 1603.1; *sunt ~t non videant illos* CI 438; *infundebatur ~t essent anthropophagi* ES 3994.

sicuti, *adv.* and *conj.* = **sicut**: AM 263.2; ES 797; ES 1520.

sidereus ~a ~um, *a.* Carrying stars, starry; *coelum ~um*, the starry sky (used to differentiate the physical sky and outer space from the spiritual realm of heaven): *separans...mundum nostrum solarem a mundis quibusdam coeli ~i* AC 9582; UJ 2.

siderulum ~i, *neut.* A small star: ES 3540.

Sidonius ~a ~um, *a.* also **Zidonius**. Of the city of Sidon: Ezek. 32.30 (AC 1201.2).

sidus ~eris, *neut.* A large celestial body, star: *quod ~era essent eorum* [sc. *coelicolarum*] *habitacula* AC 9408.2; (dist. from **stella**) *notum est...quod unumquodvis ~us sit instar solis...et quod distantia faciat ut appareat in parva forma sicut stella* AC 9441; (fig.) *~us ~erum* VR 759.2.

sigillo ~are ~avi ~atum, *tr.* To stamp with a seal, put a seal on: (in quot. fig.) *ut actualiter justitiam Filii inscribat, et constabilitam ~et* VR 177.1.

sigillum ~i, *neut.* **1** A sealstone, signet: *sculpturis ~i sculpes duos lapides* Exod. 28.11 (AC); AR 463.4. **2** The impression of a seal, sealing: *librum...obsignatum ~is septem* Rev. 5.1 (AR); *charta ~o obsignata* VR 48.1; (fig.) a token: *Sancta Coena est ~um illius conjunctionis* AC 10522.

signatio ~onis, *f.* The act of distinguishing with a mark, marking: *patet quid ~o manus et frontis significat* AC 396.2; (in a script) a mark, point: *sunt... plures punctationes et ~ones super literis* SS 72.

signatura ~ae, *f.* A distinguishing mark: *signa seu ~ae in imperiis...sunt tituli dignitatum* VR 680.1; *postquam receperunt ~am Christi* VR 683.2; SS(P) 32 (= 14.3); a diacritical sign in writing: *literis vetustis Hebraicis...cum ~is supra, inter et intra* VR 241.1.

signifer ~eri, *m.* A standard-bearer: *sicut ~er, qui cum vexillo abit* VR 681.

significatio ~onis, *f.* An idea conveyed by a word, meaning: *vocum varias ~ones norunt* [*spiritus*] AC 1638; esp. a meaning in the spiritual sense: *ex ~one baculi, quod sit potentia in naturali* AC 6954; *quod illa urbs absque illa repraesentatione et inde ~one nullatenus sancta fuerit* AE 223.11.

significativus ~a ~um, *a.* Having a special meaning, significant: *Verbum...conscriptum...literis inflexis cum corniculis et apicibus ~is* SS 90.2; esp. having a meaning in the spiritual sense: *historica vera...quae omnia repraesentativa sunt, et singula verba ~a* AC 1401; (w. gen.) *quod sensus literalis...sit ~us et repraesentativus rerum quae in sensu spirituali* AC 6996.3; (neut. as sb.) *repraesentativa et ~a Ecclesiae Antiquae...versa fuerunt in magica* AC 6692.1.

significatus[1] ~a ~um, *a.* (superl. *~issimus*) Capable of carrying much meaning, significant: *loquela angelorum expressivissima est et ~issima* ES 4411.

significatus[2] ~us, *m.* Signification, meaning: *in ~u interno* AC 2395.

significo ~are ~avi ~atum, *tr.* **1** (of persons) To convey, express (ideas): *quod antiquissimi per numeros ... ~averint status et mutationes statuum Ecclesiae* AC 575; *per illa* [sc. *hieroglyphica*] *~abant* [*Aegyptii*] *spiritualia* AC 6692.1. **2** (of words or expressions) To carry (a meaning), mean: *sunt duae voces in lingua originali quae ~ant hominem* AC 7120; *ens rationis quod ~at non aliquid* VR 11.2. **b** esp. to mean in the spiritual sense: *quod 'Hebraei' ~ent illa quae sunt Ecclesiae* AC 6738; *scientia correspondentiarum docet quid ~at 'equus albus'* SS 9. **3** (of things, actions, etc.) To have as meaning, stand for: *omnis affectio ~etur per incalescentiam* AC 2146; *hi sunt qui...per avem lapideam ~ati sunt* AC 7745; *quod sacrificia ~averint omnem cultum* AC 7393.

signo ~are ~avi ~atum, *tr.* **1** To place a mark upon, seal: *~a signum super frontes virorum* Ezek. 9.4 (AC 308.2); *et audivi numerum ~atorum* Rev. 7.4 (AR); to mark (in writing): *nomina personarum et locorum in Verbo ~ata sunt* VR 241.2. **2** To put on as a mark, make the sign of: *sacerdos crucem...digito ~at in fronte* VR 685.2.

signum ~i, *neut.* **1** A visible mark, sign: *et posuit Jehovah Caino ~um, ut non percuteret eum quisquam* Gen. 4.15 (AC). **b** a mark of punctuation: *in lingua originali antiquitus non distinguebantur sensus per ~a* AC 5578. **2** An object, flag, etc. hoisted as a signal: *~a...quae posita fuerunt super montibus, ad congregandum populum ad bellum* AE 706.26; ES 5055. **b** a military standard, ensign: *absque ~is, quae vocantur vexilla* VR 680.2; *eunt cum quodam ~o...rotunda forma* ES 5932. **3** Any action used as a signal, sign: *quod...ad datum ~um conveniant* AM 132.1; *quod... exporrigant...manum, quod est ~um* ES 5647. **4** Anything which is used as a token of something else, sign, mark: *'sanguis' erat foedus seu ~um foederis* AC 6804.11; *est...baptismus modo in ~um et memoriale quod homo regenerandus sit* CI 329. **5** A miraculous sign: *multi crediderunt in nomen Ipsius, videntes Ipsius ~a quae faciebat* John 2.23 (AC 6674.6); *apparebit ~um Filii Hominis in coelo* Matt. 24.30 (AC 4056); *artibus... illicitis, quibus solent ~a facere, sic per magicas artes* ES 401.

silentium ~i, *neut.* An absence of sound, silence: *factum est ~um in caelo* Rev. 8.1 (AR); an avoidance of speech, silence: *apud angelos...est sermocinatio de amore...et non tale ~um, sicut est...in terris* AM 258.

sileo ~lere ~lui, *intr.* To keep silent: *~lente vel etiam simul mentiente facie* AC 8250.1; *tunc ~let tota urbs* AM 17.2.

silex ~icis, *m.* Flint (as a material): *qui convertit... ~icem in fontem aquarum* Ps. 114.8 (AC 7324.2); *molle semen cadens super ~icem* AM 396.1.

silv-: see **sylv-**.

simia ~ae, *f.* A monkey: *sicut ~ae, facie torva...ac vultu horrido* AM 505.4; VR 113.1.

simila ~ae, *f.* Wheat-flour: *~a triticorum facies ea* Exod. 29.2 (AC).

similago ~inis, *f.* = **simila**: AC 9995.4; AE 324.14.

similaris ~is ~e, *a.* Similar: *filii et posteri ex uno patre, quorum animi, mores et facies ~es sunt* VR 15.1; (masc. as sb.) *quisque...adjungitur ~ibus* VR 447.

similis ~is ~e, *a.* (superl. *simillimus*) **1** Of similar nature, like: *nullus ~i modo recipit Dominum* AC 6706; (w. *ac*) *ut una societas non ~em perceptionem habeat ac altera* AC 483.1; (w. dat.) *scripturae...sunt ~es scripturis in mundo* CI 261; (neut. as sb.) *amor... crudelitatis, adulterii, et ~ium* AC 6872.2; *~e est hodie* VR 3.1. **2** (neut. as sb.) Similarity: *de ~i ejus [conjunctionis] cum conjunctione boni et veri* CI 423.

similiter, *adv.* In like manner, similarly: *non potestis fugere adulteria...nisi fugeritis reliqua mala ~er* AM 356; (w. *ac*) *illae, ~er ac nostra tellus, circum solem ferantur* AC 6697; (ellipt.) *in Verbo Novi Testamenti ~er* DD 22.

similitudo ~inis, *f.* **1** The quality of being like, likeness: *status ~o facit quod praesentes appareant* AC 6806.3; *tanta ~o intercedit inter cor et charitatem* FI 19.2. **2** That which resembles something else, an effigy, likeness: *spiritualis homo est imago, coelestis autem homo est ~o seu effigies* AC 51; *quod bonum procedens a Domino sit ~o Ipsius* CI 16; *~ines et comparationes desumptae ex talibus quae in natura sunt* SS 40.1.

simplex ~icis, *a.* (compar. *~icior*, superl. *~icissimus*) **1** Having a single nature, simple, uncomplicated: *infinita, quae homo non videt nisi sicut unum ~ex* VI 112; *quod sit [substantia] ita ~ex ut nihil ~icius* DP 6.1; *in mundo spirituali non est homini duplex loquela, sed ~ex* AR 294.1. **b** (w. the connotation of perfection) whole, undamaged: *si oculus ~ex (hoc est, bonus) est* Matt. 6.22 (VR 403.2); *omne ~ex quo ~icius, quia est perfectius, est immunius a damnis* AS 204. **2** (of good, faith, etc.) Uncomplicated, straightforward, simple: *in ~ici bono dicuntur esse qui in Ecclesiae externis sunt, ac simpliciter credunt Verbo quoad sensum ejus literalem* AC 6775; *in ~ici fide ex charitate* AM 115.2. **3** (of persons) Of a simple nature, not wise or learned: *quod Petrus fuerit homo admodum ~ex* AC vol. iii, praef.2; *creditur quod sapientes gloriam et eminentiam prae ~icibus in coelo habituri sint* CI 346; *sensus literae...est pro ~icissimis, et pro infantibus* AC 10441.1.

simplicitas ~atis, *f.* (of persons) Simplicity: *qui in ~ate, in amicitia, et in charitate mutua vixerunt* AC 1141; *in ~ate mea credidi...quod universum a Deo creatum sit* VR 79.4.

simpliciter, *adv.* **1** In the fashion of simple people, simply: *~er credunt Verbo* AC 6775; *qui ~er pii* ES 4681. **2** No more than, simply: *cum Dominum ~er nominarem* CI 325; ES 222.

simpulum ~i, *neut.* A small vessel, dish: *in ~o magnificorum attulit butyrum... ~um erat vas, quo utebantur in sacrificiis* 3AD 4812 (Judg. 5.25).

simul, *adv.* **1** At the same time: *quod sit in luce mundi et inde ~l in mundanis* AC 6686; *~l ac*, at the same time as: *incipit ~l ac ex fide, etiam ex amore agere* AC 12. **2** At the same place, together: *ibi ~l habitant in summa felicitate* AC 1115; *qui in vita corporis in amore conjugiali vixerunt, ii ~l sunt in altera vita* ES(M) 4604. **3** On an overall view, together: *societates...quae ~l sumtae formam caeli constituunt* DP 4.4; *de pluribus hominibus qui ~l unum senatum...conformant* VR 16.3. **4** As well: *quisque secundum vitam et ~l fidem suam* VR 22.

simulachrum ~i, *neut.* also **simulacrum**. **1** A likeness of a living creature, statue, image: *potuerunt confirmari a ~is...in templis, ubi angeli ut infantes exhibentur* CI 340; *~um ex ligno* VI 109; *~a pro diis colunt* VR 9.1; (as opposed to a real person) *qui noctu... videt... ~a, et credit esse homines vivos* SE 40. **b** *mortis ~um*, a likeness of a dead person, death mask: *sedentes ut mortis ~a in cruciatu* AC 830; AC 9281.2; ES 3811. **2** Any mere representation replacing the real thing: *quod nollet talis amoris ~um habere* ES 1082; *homo absque illo libero arbitrio non foret homo, sed modo typus et ~um* CO 28.1.

simulacrum: see **simulachrum**.

simulate, *adv.* By way of pretence: *is... ~e per nutus insinuabat quod multa haberet...* AC 816; *ut ~e faveat uxori* AM 286.

simulatio ~onis, *f.* Pretence: *~o fraudulenta ac dolus* AC 7360; *per ~onem innocentiae* AC 6914.2.

simulativus ~a ~um, *a.* Imitative: *alteram [sphaeram]... ~am boni* AC 1080; full of pretence: *inde vita eorum facta ~a et dolosa* AC 831.1.

simulator ~oris, *m.* One who pretends, dissembler: *moralis homo ~or, qui potest facere ut malum appareat sicut bonum* VR 160.3.

simulatorie, *adv.* By way of pretence: *cum hac [voluntate] non conjungit se [uxor] nisi ~e aut lusorie* AM 195.

simulatorius ~a ~um, *a.* Not genuine, pretended:

affectiones externae...vel ~ae AM 278; *poesi ~ae, in qua nihil nisi fictiones verbosae* ES 1045.

simulo ~are ~avi ~atum, *tr., intr.* **1** To exhibit as a false appearance, make a pretence of: *homo... ~at contrarium* AC 7795.3; *affectiones bonas... ~ant* AE 448.12. **b** (intr.): *qui a pueritia didicerunt ~are* AC 8247; (w. *quod*) *qui ~averunt...quod in bono amoris essent* AR 338. **2** To practise under a false appearance, employ pretence in: *~ant dolos sub velo innocentiae* ES 240. **3** To imitate deceitfully, simulate: *amicitia inter non bonos illum amorem... ~at* VR 44.2; *coelestes in vita corporis ~arunt* ES 1491.

simultanee, *adv.* Simultaneously: AM 447.2.

simultaneus ~a ~um, *a.* Existing or happening at the same time, simultaneous: *ordo successivus et ordo ~us* SS 38.1; (neut. as sb.) *quod non detur illa identitas in ~is* VR 32.1.

simus ~a ~um, *a.* (Gk.) Concave: *in superiore gibba parte...in parte ~a* AS 432.2.

sin, *conj.* *Sin aliter*, but if not, otherwise: *inter hos... procedere potest amor conjugialis in suo justo ordine ...sin aliter, juvenis non fuit juvenis* AM 322; ES 956; (so, also) *sin minus*: *resipisce et prima opera fac, sin minus veniam tibi cito* Rev. 2.5 (AR).

sinapi ~is, *neut.* (Gk.) Mustard: *simile est regnum coelorum grano ~is* Matt. 13.31 (AC 55.3).

sincere, *adv.* (compar. *~ius*) Without deceit, honestly: *~e et sedule suae functionis opus facere* VR 738.4.

sinceritas ~atis, *f.* Uprightness in dealings, honesty: *~atem in negotiis* VI 24.

sincerus ~a ~um, *a.* Free from deceit, upright, honest: (of persons) *qui ~i sunt nihil volunt loqui...nisi tale quod sciant alii* AC 7747; AM 286; (of actions) *non ~um est ita loqui* AC 7747; *ab amicitia ~a* CI 406.3; (neut. as sb.) *apud illum qui in ~o est* AC 7046.2.

sinciput ~itis, *neut.* The upper and front part of the head, sinciput: *supra frontis ~ut* ES 1199; ES 1701.

sindon ~onis, *f.* (Gk.) A fine woven material, muslin: *in vestibus albis ex ~one, bysso aut lino* AE 951.1; (pl.) linen garments: *removebit Dominus ornatum compedum,...et ~ones, et cidares...* Isa. 3.23 (AC 2576.11).

sine, *prep. w. abl.* Not accompanied by, without: *ignis nusquam potest esse sine lumine* AC 1666.2; AM 498.

singillatim, *adv.* One by one, individually, singly: *prolixum foret omnia ita ~im exponere* AC 1662; AM 457.

singularis ~is ~e, *a.* (compar. *~ior*, superl. *~issimus*) **1** One alone, individual, single: *non de ~i homine, sed de Ecclesia* AC 271; *angeli...nusquam determinant suas cogitationes ad ~es personas* AC 6804.2. **b** (neut. as sb., in grammar) the singular: *dicitur in ~i, Creabat Deus illum in imaginem Suam* AC 50.3. **2** Not general, restricted, particular: *didici per ~es quasdam experientias* ES 263; *vita primum communi, et postea ~iori secundum formationem...mentis* ES 168. **b** (neut. as sb.) a restricted part, particular, detail: *~ia fidei a parte hominis sunt* VR 3.2; *quod plures fallaciae impugnent providentiam Divinam in ~ibus* AC 7007.4. **3** (superl.) Of the smallest distinguishable size: *quod...homo ~issimis momentis regatur* ES(M) 4652; (neut. as sb.) the smallest part, tiniest detail: *quod Dominus...impleverit omnia Verbi, usque ad ~issima ejus* DD 11; *spiritus hominis agit in singula, imo in ~issima corporis* CI 453.2.

singulariter, *adv.* (superl. *~larissime*) In detail, in particular: *sic...universaliter rem comprehendunt, et simul tunc ~lariter illa quae ad rem pertinent* AC 6653; (superl.) in extreme detail: *quod Dominus singillatim, imo ~larissime in omne particulare hominis ...agat* DP 124.3.

singulatim, *adv.* Taken singly, individually: *haec ~im evolventur* VR 5; *in tres personas, quarum quaelibet per se aut ~im est Deus* VR 15.2.

singultim, *adv.* In gasps: *ii volumatim...exsurgebant, quasi ~im crasse, vocabam id kluncka* ES 3531 (J D Odhner).

singulto ~are ~avi, *intr.* To gasp: *sicut exantlatur aër, ~at [avis] et demum exspirat* VR 28.2.

singultus ~us, *m.* Laboured breathing, gasping: *quod praedicationes...non sint nisi ~us ex pectore* VR 798.8; *modus voluminis eorum ~ibus similis* ES 3531.

singulus ~a ~um, *a.* (usu. in pl.) Each of several: *sphaera...in ~is subjectis variatur* AM 925; *~is diebus* ES 3616; (sg.) *~o mane faciet illum* Ezek. 46.13 (AC 7839). **b** (masc. as sb.): *hoc bonum cum amatur, amantur ~i qui in bono* AC 6823. **c** (neut. as sb.) each detail: *in ~is ejus cogitationis* AC 1026; esp. *omnia et ~a*, each and every detail: *universale fidei est quod in omnibus et ~is erit* FI 35.

sinister ~tra ~trum, *a.* **1** Left (as opposed to right): *~ter oculus* AC 6923; *~tram aurem* AC 7359; (neut. as sb.) the leftwards direction, left: *antrorsum versus ~trum* AC 7077; *habitant ad ~trum* AE 107.2. **b** (fem. as sb.) the left hand: *misit... ~tram suam super capite Menaschis* Gen. 48.14 (AC); *a ~tra* or *a ~tris*, on or from the left: *fluctus...a ~tra versus dextram ferebantur* ES 243; *...Rex dicet similia ad hircos, qui a ~tris* Matt. 25.41 (VI 2); *apparuit...fulmen a ~tris* AM 316.5. **2** Perverted, improper, wrong: *per interpretationes ~tras et sic perversiones* AC 8149; *~tris opinionibus feruntur* ES 922; (neut. as sb.) *inde conjectarunt... ~trum* ES 2021.

sinistre, *adv.* Improperly, wrongly: *incipiunt ~e cogitare, et inde ~e velle* AC 7364; ES 760.

sinistrorsum, *adv.* Leftwards, towards the left: *via lata tendens ~um* CI 534.1; *~um a veteri Hierosolyma* ES 3100; on the left: *apparent nunc antrorsum, nunc ~um* AC 7078; ES 812.

sino ~ere sivi, *tr.* To allow, permit: (w. inf.) *~e mortuos sepelire mortuos* Matt. 8.22 (AC 3703.8); *~ite infantes venire ad Me* Mark 10.14 (CI 281).

sinuatio ~onis, *f.* An act of curving: *per varias plicationes et ~ones* AC 4799.1.

sinulus ~i, *m.* A small recess, nook: [*pulvisculum*] *exhalat ex ~o suo aliquod* VR 785.

sinuo ~are ~avi ~atum, *tr.* To move sinuously, wind: *locus ~atus in rotundum* TE 152; (refl.) *quae nubes tenuis se ~abat* ES 1233.

sinus ~us, *m.* **1** (anat.) A recess or blind passage, sinus: *~um longitudinalem qui in cerebro inter bina ejus haemisphaeria jacet* AC 7744; *per varios meatus, canales et ~us versus venam jugularem* ES 831. **2** The fold of a loose garment in which things can be carried, lap: *afferent filios tuos in ~u* Isa. 49.22 (AC 6740); *in ~um dabitur mensura bona* Luke 6.38 (CI 349); (fig.) bosom: *Filius qui in ~u Patris est* John 1.18 (DD 32.5). **3** *In ~u* [*suo*], in the interior, within: *lux...quae in ~u suo habet calorem* AC 1470; *unaquaevis vox...in ~u recondit aliquod Divinum* DP 231.1. **4** A fold or twist: *contorserunt et plicaverunt labia in plures ~us* VR 111.2.

sipho ~onis, *m.* (Gk.) A pneumatic apparatus, tube, pump: *~oni pneumatico* VR 28.2; *occlusio apparebat sicut pistillum injectum ~oni magno* ES 4952.

siquidem, *conj.* **1** (enlarging on a statement) For: *~em dicit, Nonne principes mei simul reges?* Isa. 10.8 (AC 2588.10). **2** (causal, explaining a previous point) Since: *verum pugnans repraesentatur per illa quae sunt acuminata instar ensium, ~em verum absque bono tale est, at cum bono est glomeratum et lene* AC 2799.21; AC 2708.6. **3** (explaining and reversing a previous misconception) Since in fact: *non propter multitudinem vestram prae omnibus populis desideravit Jehovah vos ut eligeret vos, ~em vos estis pauciores omnibus populis* Deut. 7.7 (AC 10217.4). **4** That, the fact that: *non celabimus a domino, ~em consumtum argentum* Gen. 47.18 (AC).

siren ~enis, *f.* (*m.*) (nom. sg. masc. *sirenis* ES 4430 Tafel and J D Odhner; Autograph unclear) (usu. occurs in pl.) **1** (pl.) Mythical female beings who lured sailors to their deaths, the Sirens: *sunt* [*duo amores*] *etiam sicut veterum ~enes, quae cantu allectabant homines, et per illum necabant* VR 533.1. **2** The name given to a class of evil spirits, usu. female: *hae sunt quae in altera vita fiunt magae...quarum quaedam sunt quae vocantur ~enes* AC 831.2; AM 433; VR 80.1; also male: *informatus...quod ~enes sint qui insinuant se* ES 2963; ES 4304.

sirenicus ~a ~um, *a.* Of or proper to sirens: *turba quae paene ~a* ES 5128.

sisto ~ere stiti, *tr.* **1** To cause to stand, place: *quod a tergo ~atur* AC 7078. **2** (pass.) To be brought to a halt, stop: *quod* [*vita*] *non quiescat quam in ultimo ordinis, ubi ~itur* AC 6451.2; *necessum est ut ~antur* [*veritates spirituales*] *nec penetrent* ES 249. **3** (w. dat.) To introduce, present (a person to another): *deduxerunt Ipsum in Hierosolymam ut ~erent Domino* Luke 2.22 (AC 6752.7). **4** To present in visible form, render visible, show: *repraesentative talem mulierem stiterunt* AC 4658.5; *~ere ei dabatur arborem* ES 2877; (refl.) *ut... stiterit se in alterius persona* ES 3003. **5** (w. predicate) To render, make: *quod natura modo creata sit ut...id* [sc. *spirituale*] *~at correspondens in ultimo ordinis* CI 102; (esp. refl. and pass.) to become: *bonum...certo modo se ~it videndum* VI 43.2; *hoc...dum ~itur videndum* AC 41; *cum ~untur a Domino parati ad recipiendum* AC 7000. **6** To cause to be present, bring about: *in subjectis quae concordant cum bono, ibi* [*Divinum Verum*] *~it vitam spiritualem* AC 6685; *notum est quod conatus...per eas* [*vires*] *~at motum* AS 218. **7** To render apprehensible, present: *per mutationes inductas faciei meae...stiterunt ideas ita vive ut pateret...cogitatio eorum* AC 1762; *quod verum quod procedit immediate a Divino non possit ~i alicui ut sermo aut loquela* AC 6982; (refl.) *Divina in mundo se ~unt per correspondentias* SS 20.3; (w. inf.) *~it angelis scire quantum vitae inest spiritui* ES 1884. **8** To present in words, describe, discuss: *~am illam* [sc. *fidem*] *in sua nuditate* FI 44; *publico ~enda sunt sequentia* DD praef.

sitibundus ~a ~um, *a.* Thirsting: *famelici et ~i* Ps. 107.5 (AE 223.5).

siticulosus ~a ~um, *a.* (of places) Lacking in water, dry, thirsty: *erit aridus locus in stagnum, et ~us in scaturigines aquarum* Isa. 35.7 (AC 6723.2); ES 299.

sitio ~tire ~tivi, *intr.*, *tr.* **1** (intr.) To feel thirsty, thirst: *recipit verum sicut ~tiens potum* AC 6829; *~tivi et potastis Me* Matt. 25.35 (VI 2); *quod esuriat et ~tiat... sicut prius in mundo* AM 182.3. **2** (tr.) To thirst for (in quot. fig.): *pauperes sunt illi qui ~tiunt et esuriunt bona et vera* ES(M) 4583; (w. inf.) *omnes spiritus quasi esuriunt et ~tiunt scire* ES 1055.

sitis ~is, *f.* A desire for drink, thirst: *adhaesit lingua lactentis palato ejus ob ~im* Lam. 4.4 (AC 6745.6); (fig.) *homo...est quasi in fame boni et in ~i veri* AC 6829.

situatus ~a ~um, *a.* Located, placed: *in organis generationi dicatis quae in sua regione... ~a sunt* AM 310.2.

situla ~ae, *f.* A bucket, pail: *defluent aquae e ~is* Num. 24.7 (AC 3079.2); *sicut gutta de ~a* Isa. 40.15 (AE 406.19).

situs[1] ~us, *m.* **1** Location in space (real or apparent), position: *~us illius caeli ibi est* AM 410; *mutationes ~us illorum* VR 77.5. **2** Alignment in a plane, attitude: *quod...sternantur horizontaliter et circumrotentur... dein transversim alio ~u* AC 829.1; *bestia ideo stat super pedibus in ~u paralelo cum terra* VR 69.1.

situs[2] ~a ~um, *a.* **1** Laid out, constructed, built: *ipsa civitas quadrangularis ~a* Rev. 21.16 (NH 1). **2** Placed in relation to its surroundings, positioned, situated: *si... novissem domos, quomodo ~ae...* AC 2485; *urbs...illa ~a erat sub monte* AC 2430; AC 2485.

sive, *conj.* **1** (introducing two alternative statements or questions) *Sive...sive...*, either...or...: *sive nunc id erit verum quod Ecclesia docet...sive quod mundus docet* DP 191.2; *quid nunc verum est, sive hoc sive illud?* DP 114.2. **2** (introducing an indir. qu.) Or if: *non curantes quali vita sint sive odia intestina foveant* AC 1844. **3** (introducing possible alternatives) *Sive...sive...* (w. subj.), irrespective of whether...or...: *quae in corpore fiunt, sive sit in facie, sive in loquela, sive in gestibus, vocantur correspondentiae* CI 91; *et hoc sive fidem, sive non fidem habeat* VR 480; (so, also) *sive...aut si...*: *absque delectu, sive sint viri...aut si pueri* ES 1093.

Smalcaldicus ~a ~um, *a.* Of Schmalkalden in Germany, Schmalkaldic; *Articuli ~i*, a document of early Protestantism: NE 31.

smaragdinus ~a ~um, *a.* (Gk.) Of or resembling emerald: *aspectu ~o* Rev. 4.3 (AE 253.4).

smaragdus ~i, *m.* (Gk.) The name of a precious stone of green colour, emerald: *fundamentum primum jaspis...quartum ~us* Rev. 21.19 (AR); *viridescens instar ~i* AR 232.

smegma ~atis, *neut.* (Gk.) A detergent substance: *parti interiori tabe infectae illinere ~a* VI 112; VR 673; *~a fullonum*, fullers' soap: Mal. 3.2 (AC 8159.2).

Smyrnensis ~is ~e, *a.* Of Smyrna: *angelum Ephesinae et ~is Ecclesiae* AE 130.1.

soboles ~is, *f.* also **suboles** (AC 5084.7 3rd edn., app. erroneously). Offspring (of either human beings or animals): *quod...jucundissimum illorum vitae fuerit procreare ~em* AC 1123; *inde illis* [sc. *apibus*] *nova ~es* VR 12.7; a generation of offspring: *si id non potest in prima ~e, praestat id in sequentibus* VR 103.2.

sobrietas ~atis, *f.* Avoidance of intoxication, sobriety: AM 164.

socer ~eri, *m.* A father-in-law: *Moscheh...reversus ad Jethronem ~erum suum* Exod. 4.18 (AC).

socia ~ae, *f.* A female companion: *petant vir ex socio suo, et mulier ex ~a sua* Exod. 11.2 (AC).

socialis ~is ~e, *a.* Of or relating to partners or companions, social: *destruere quicquid societas, ~e, et vinculum societatis audit* ES 2321.

societas ~atis, *f.* **1** Association with a group of people, society: *malorum...eae species, quae fiunt secundum ejus* [*hominis*] *~ates, actiones, cogitationes* ES 2425; *quod iis adimatur ~as cum spiritibus* ES 2468. **2** A group of people living together, community, society: *quid bonum et verum ~atis civilis* AC 495; *est... ~as minor et major, est patria, est Ecclesia* AC 6819; any kind of association: *qui ex ~ate Jesu se nominant* [sc. the Jesuits] VR 146. **b** a group of spirits or angels in the other world: *in coelo sunt, et ibi in ~ate angelica* AC 6629; *cum spiritus Mercurii ad alias ~ates veniunt* AC 6813.

Socinianus ~a ~um, *a.* Pertaining to Faustus Socinus, Socinian: *fides ~a* VR 339.1; *in abominatione... ~a* VR 380.3; (masc. as sb.) a follower of Socinus, Socinian: AC 7233.3; CI 3; DP 231.6.

socio ~are ~avi ~atum, *tr.* **1** To engage in jointly, share, communicate: *inter spiritus est et cum iis ~at vitam* AC 69; *cum spiritibus...planetae Jovis diutius ~are commercium datum est* AC 7799; *~are cogitationem* ES 3046; esp. *~are sermonem* or *sermones*, to engage in conversation: *per aliquot annos... ~are cum illis sermones* AC 1634; *petiit ut liceat illis etiam vobiscum ~are aliquem sermonem* AM 21.1. **2** (pass. w. dat.) To keep company (with): *~atus idolis Ephraim* Hos. 4.17 (AE 283.16).

socius ~i, *m.* A companion, fellow: *quare percutis ~um tuum?* Exod. 2.13 (AC); CI 270.2; *amant...suas nutrices, et infantes ~os* AM 395.

socors ~rdis, *a.* Slothful, lazy: *datur cibus...secundum usum...at nullus ~rdibus* AM 6.6.

Socraticus ~a ~um, *a.* Of Socrates; (masc. pl. as sb.) the followers of Socrates: AM 153[a].2.

socrus ~us, *f.* A mother-in-law: *Jesus vidit ~um Petri febri afflictam* Matt. 8.14 (AE 79.3).

sodalicium: see **sodalitium**.

sodalis ~is, *m.* A colleague: *nos convenimus cum ~ibus nostris ab occidente* VR 48.13.

sodalitium ~i, *neut.* also **sodalicium**. **1** A group of people sharing some common purpose, company: *legentes ex arboribus fructus, et in calathis portantes ad ~a* AM 8.2; *is in ~um Arianorum...se infert* VR

380.2. **2** A gathering for social purposes, party: *post hoc festivum ~um...abiverunt* AM 23.

sodomia ~ae, *f.* Sodomy: ES 2675 titulus.

sodomita ~ae, *m*. One who practises sodomy, sodomite: ES 1977; ES 3768.

sodomiticus ~a ~um, *a*. Sodomitical: *inferna ~a* AE 1006.2.

sol ~lis, *m*. **1** The sun of this world: *calor e ~le influit* FI 32; *sub ~le*, beneath the sun, anywhere on earth: *talis natio sub ~le non datur* ES 2261. **2** Any star in the universe capable of acting as a sun: *extra hujus ~lis mundum* AC 6696; *ex infinito numero stellarum, quae totidem ~les sunt* VR 32.5. **3** The sun of the spiritual world: *quod origo amoris et sapientiae sit e ~le mundi spiritualis, in cujus medio est Jehovah Deus* VR 41.1; *a Domino, ut a ~le sapientiae et intelligentiae* AC 1042.2. **4** (Bibl., as translation of Hebr. *shimshoth*) A window: *ponam pyropum ~les (fenestras) tuos* Isa. 54.12 (AC 655.1).

solaris ~is ~e, *a*. Of or belonging to the sun, solar: *lumen cum radii ~es aurei apparent* AC 455; *Divinum Bonum Divini Amoris est ipse ignis ~is in altera vita* AC 6834; *in mundo nostro ~i* CI 292.

solatium ~i, *neut*. Consolation, comfort: *appercipiunt aliquid... ~i* AC 2041.3; (pred. dat.) *vocantur...oves, quod iis quoque multo ~o est* ES 219.

solemniter: see **solenniter**.

solennis ~is ~e, *a*. also **sollemnis**, and **sollennis**. **1** Customary, usual: *'extendere coelos' est ~is loquutio apud Prophetas* AC 25; *voces in literato orbe ~es* CI 56; *~e est* (+ inf.), it is customary (to): *~e est pictoribus faciem deformem juxta formosam adponere* VR 61.1. **2** (neut. pl. as sb.) Customary rites or practices: *de...nuptiis, et quoque de ~ibus circa illas* AM 295.1.

solennitas ~atis, *f.* also **sollemnitas**. A customary rite: *per 'clangere tubis' significatur convocare ad ~ates* AR 391.

solenniter, *adv*. also **solemniter**. In due form ceremoniously: *ablegati...qui ~er illos introducerent* AM 207.1.

soleo ~lere ~litus sum, *intr*. (pf. is usually dep., but act. forms in *~lui* occur at VR 798.6, DP 289.1) **1** (w. inf.) To be constantly liable (to), be in the habit (of), happen regularly (to): *tenuis radius candidus, qualis ~let esse fulguris* AC 8112; *persuasiones captae... animos illos formare ~lent* AM 246.2. **2** (w. no inf.): *per pilorum derasionem, sicut ~lent sues, candidi sibi fieri videntur* AC 939; *lucrari voluerunt, et quidem ea arte qua ~lent industrii mercatores* ES 404.1.

solers ~rtis, *a*. also **sollers**. (compar. *~rtior*) **1** (of persons) Clever, skilful: *quod ille prae aliis ~rs in ratiocinando sit* AC 10236.7. **2** (of actions) Skilfully executed: *per ~rtes adductiones et insinuationes* AM 243.

solerter, *adv*. also **sollerter**. (compar. *~ius*, superl. *~issime*) In a clever fashion, skilfully: *hoc spiritus ~issime possunt facere* AC 6809; *si bestiae potuissent loqui, tam ~er ratiocinarentur...sicut homines* AM 151[a].4.

solertia ~ae, *f.* also **sollertia**. Cleverness: *inde... ~a in talibus quae sunt corporis* AC 8378; AM 164.

solicit-: see **sollicit-**.

solido ~are ~avi ~atum, *tr*. To make full and whole: *crevisti et adolevisti..., ubera ~ata sunt* Ezek. 16.7 (AC 3301).

solidus ~a ~um, *a*. (compar. *~ior*) **1** Of the same material throughout, solid: *auro ~o* Exod. 25.18 (AC). **2** Having no empty space inside, tightly packed, solid: *quod in fibris etiam minutissimis humanis nihil sit ~um seu cohaerens* ES 242; *punctum quasi ~um* ES 2087; (neut. as sb.) a solid: *in ~o ex tribus illis gradibus constante* AS 205. **3** (of proofs) Incontrovertible, solid: *argumentis...verosimilibus, in tuo judicio ~is* DP 213.

solitarie, *adv*. In isolation, by itself: *voces quae... ~e absque adjunctis aliis dicuntur* SS 84.2.

solitarius ~a ~um, *a*. Unaccompanied by others, alone, solitary: *qui ~i habitant* CI 50; *~a voluntas* VR 377.1; (masc. as sb.) ES 4852.

solito, *adv*. By custom, usually: *Mons Olivarum...ubi Dominus ~o commoratus est* DD 14.5.

solitudo ~inis, *f.* An uninhabited place, solitude: *Ephraim in ~inem erit* Hos. 5.9 (SS 79.3); *complanate in ~ine semitam Deo nostro* Isa. 40.3 (DD 6); *illico mihi ut ~o visum est* ES 3608.

solitus ~a ~um, *a*. (pf. pple. of **soleo**) Customary, usual: *contra morem ~um* AC 6811; *nuclei...circumdati sua crusta ~a et nativa* AM 364; (neut. as sb.) *apud quosdam ~um est sistere repraesentationes* ES 233; *facies... ~o minores* AC 8243; *ex ~o*, as a rule, usually: *ex qua viri ex ~o gloriantur* AM 288; AE 405.24.

solium ~i, *neut*. A chair: *reposuit se super ~o ad mensam* VR 35.4; (usu.) a chair of state, throne: *~um tres cubitos a terra elevatum* AM 7.2; *a ~o papali* VR 503.1.

sollemn-: see **solenn-**.

sollennis: see **solennis**.

soller-: see **soler-**.

sollicitatio ~onis, *f.* **1** Earnest request, demand: *quod significet ~onem ut consentiat* AC 6513. **2** Anxiety, worry: *augurati sumus praesentiam tuam ac ~onem de aperiendo adhuc unum arcanum* AM 208.1.

sollicite, *adv.* With anxious care, earnestly: *faciem suam... ~e conservant a solis aestu* AC 8245; *~e petebat ut...* ES 872.

sollicito ~are ~avi ~atum, *tr., intr.* To seek earnestly: (w. acc.) *qui absque successu ~averunt illud* [sc. *conjugium*] AM 54.3; (w. *ut*) *~abant ut intromitterentur* ES 706.

sollicitudo ~inis, *f.* also **soli-**. Care, concern, anxiety, worry: *absque omni ~ine de futuris* AC 7744; *non ~o illis de victu et amictu* CI 277.2.

sollicitus ~a ~um, *a.* also **soli-**. Anxious, worried: *quod de vita...parum ~i sint* AC 7802; *ne ~i estote* Luke 12.11 (DD 51.4); (of care) attentive, solicitous: *quod Gentiles...cum ~a cura ab angelis instruantur* CI 321; (neut. as sb.) a care: *in jucunda sua tranquillitate manent, sic absque ~is* ES 742.

solubilis ~is ~e, *a.* **1** Capable of being resolved or explained: *si...tunc plura influunt non ~ia* ES 2651. **2** (of marriages) Capable of being dissolved: *si conjugia inita non essent pacta usque ad finem vitae, sed ~ia ex arbitrio* AM 276.1.

solum[1] ~i, *neut.* The ground on which one walks: *hiabat ~um sub illis* VR 77.6; (in a building) the floor: *tectum ex ligno...thyino, ~um ex asseribus populi* AM 103.3.

solum[2], *adv.* **1** No more than, only, merely: *non bonum, ~um tale quod mentitur bonum* AC 1096.3; *velim ~um aliqua adducere* SS 15.1; *apparet...quod ~um sint formalia, quae possunt omitti* AM 306. **2** *Non* [or *nec*] *~um...sed etiam...*, (and) not only...but also...: *quod non ~um sint tellures...in hoc mundo sed etiam in universo* AC 6696; *nec ~um mundus naturalis in communi sed etiam in singulis* CI 89; *~um quod*, with the exception that, apart from the fact that, only that: *dictum...quod essent sui juris...~um quod spiritus cum illis loquerentur* AC 6212.5.

solummodo, *adv.* (reinforced form of **solum**[2]) also spelled as two words **solum modo**. Only, solely: *quod conjugiale Christianum ~o detur castum* AM 138; AM 44.5.

solus ~a ~um, *a.* (gen. sg. *~ius*, dat. sg. *~i*) **1** Unaccompanied by others, alone, by oneself (itself, etc.): *illi qui ~am fidem in mundo confessi sunt* AC 7112; *qui amant ~as cognitiones* AC 7748; *quod tales, cum ~i sunt, non possint aliquid cogitare* AM 233.6. **2** And no other, alone: *internus homo...est ~ius Domini* AC 1707.3; *illi se ~os amant* AC 8318.2.

solutio ~onis, *f.* The act of dissolving or releasing, dissolution: *quod non sit ulla pars...quae se non renovat, quod fit per ~ones* AM 171.2; the release (of the soul from the body): *post ~onem a corpore* CI 355.

solutus ~a ~um, *a.* (pf. pple. of **solvo**) (in senses of vb., esp.) Free from restraint, dissolute: *amor sexus...~us, promiscuus, et vagus* AM 107; *vitam ~am et meretriciam* ES 230.

solvo ~vere ~vi ~utum, *tr.* **1** To undo, break (a fastening, seal, etc.): *quis est dignus aperire librum et ~vere sigilla ejus?* Rev. 5.2 (AR). **2** To give liberty to, set free, release: *~ve quatuor angelos vinctos* Rev. 9.14 (AR); *quicquid ~veris in terra, erit ~utum in coelis* Matt. 16.19 (AE 206.3); *quod gentes e captivitate sua ~vendae* ES 214. **b** to release (a beast of burden) from its harness, loose: *et venit vir domum, et ~vit camelos* Gen. 24.32 (AC). **3** To unmake, break (a bond, connection): *si ~veretur ille nexus...caderet mortuus* CI 302; *vinculum conjugiale ~vere* VR 41.3; (transf.) *observavi quod plures ~verent consortia* AM 5.2. **4** To sever the connection between, take to pieces (a structure): *~vite templum hoc, et in tribus diebus exsuscitabo illud* John 2.19 (SS 47); *quod ibi conglutinatio picea ~vatur* VR 342.3; *manus...quae ~utae erant a corpore* ES 1373 ½. **b** (pass.) to be rendered incapable: *ut...ex gaudio intimo quasi ~verer* ES 293. **5** To render ineffective, abrogate: *ita ut non ~vatur Lex Mosis* John 7.23 (AC 6752.7); *quisquis...~verit praeceptorum horum minimum* Matt. 5.19 (VI 2); *cum...aufertur causa efficiens a suo effectu, tunc effectus ~vitur et dilabitur* CI 303.

somnio ~are ~avi, *intr.* (*tr.*) **1** To dream: *homo non regeneratus est sicut qui ~at* VR 606.1; (w. *quod*) *~avi quod pater meus...caderet in aquas* ES 4191; (w. cognate acc.) *~avi somnium sed vulgare* AC 1981. **2** To have fantastic ideas like dreamers: *sicut hodie ~ant et Romano-Catholici et Reformati* VR 82.3.

somnium ~i, *neut.* **1** A vision seen in sleep, dream: *per visiones et ~a a Domino* AC 597.2; *angelus Domini in ~o apparuit illi* Matt. 1.20 (DD 21). **2** A fantastic idea, dream: *respondebimus...ad ventosa vestra auguria et ~a* AM 79.10.

somnolentia ~ae, *f.* Sleepiness, somnolence: *effudit Jehovah super vos spiritum ~ae* Isa. 29.10 (AE 152.4).

somnus ~i, *m.* **1** Sleep: *cum in ~o essem* AC 831.3; *in statum quendam qui medius est inter ~um et vigiliam* CI 440. **2** A state resembling sleep, trance: *ad excitandum illos e ~o, diximus...* VR 160.7.

sonans ~ntis, *a.* (pres. pple. of **sono**) (compar. *~ntior*) Making a sound, sounding, loud: *est modo ~ns quid, et sicut vas vacuum* AC 2429.2; *quod sit* [*sonus*] *grandior et ~ntior* AC 8823.

sonanter, *adv.* (compar. *~ius*) With sound, loudly: *quod...talis loquela...~ius audiatur* AC 4657.

sonitus ~us, *m.* A sound: *~us equitum armatorum* AC 2128.2; *cum non attenderem ad campanae ~um* ES 2248.

sono ~are ~ui ~itum, *intr., tr.* **1** (intr.) To make a noise, sound: *campana quavis hora ~abat* ES 2248; *affectio ~at et cogitatio loquitur* AR 655.6; (often used pejoratively to mean an empty, meaningless sound) [*ranae*] *garrule ~ant, et coaxant* AC 7352; *nec potuisset loqui, sed solum ~are sicut bestia* DP 104.2; *vox* or *verbum ~ans*, an empty, meaningless expression: *si non vivat secundum illa, quid fides, nisi inane quid, et vox ~ans?* AC 1077.1; *annon absque sensu interiore forent aliud quam voces ~antes, cum tamen unaquaevis vox in Verbo pondus habet* AC 7729.4; *verba ~antia absque aliqiuo spiritu in illis* AC 10406.7. **2** (intr., of sounds) To be audible, ring: *haec...in templis ~ant et reverberantur e parietibus* VR 132.2; *~at* [*Natura*] *in auribus nostris* VR 159.6; *loquela angelorum coelestium ~at multum ex vocalibus U et O* CI 241. **b** (tr.) to make (a sound or word) audible (often used to imply a lack of deeper meaning): *Verbum ex quo ministri ~ant Deum* VR 14.3. **3** (tr.) To express in sound, make a sound expressive of: *non...potuisset cogitare, et ex cogitatione loqui, sed solum ~are suam affectionem* CC 14.4; AM 151[a].3; cf. *si arca...ut et diluvium, non plus quam ~at litera, significarent* AC 639.1.

sonor ~oris, *m.* A sound, noise: *~or inter spiritus correspondet cogitationi* ES(M) 4617; ES 3947.

sonore, *adv.* With audible sound: *quod homo possit articulate loqui, et bestia ~e* AM 521.2; AC 1635.

sonorus ~a ~um, *a.* **1** Making a sound, audible: [*loquela*] *non ~a, sed paene tacita* AC 7360; *per sonos articulatos aut voces ~as* AC 7361.2; (neut. as sb.) a sound: *loquela eorum est cogitativa absque ~o* AC 180. **2** Realized as sound, made audible: *cantus caelestes nec aliud sunt quam affectiones ~ae* AM 55.1. **3** Of or relating to sound, vocal: *provinciae ~ae* [sc. in the body] ES 1090.

sons ~ntis, *a.* Guilty: *sicut cum rege qui absolvit ~ntes* AC 8227.2; *hos declarabant insontes, illos autem ~ntes* AM 453.

sonticus ~a ~um, *a.* Important, serious, grave: *naevi ...quidam ~i, et quidam non ~i* AM 288; *quod causae ~ae hujus concubinatus sint reales et non reales* AM 471.

sonus ~i, *m.* A sound: *exterior loquela est ~i articulati labentis versus membranam auris externam* AC 7359; *ex ~o appercipiebatur quasi in statu somni esset* AC 7744; (as opposed to speech) *vox cultus ejus* [*comparari potest*] *~o, et non loquelae* FI 48.

sophisma ~atis, *neut.* (Gk.) A piece of clever argument, sophistry: *seductio multorum per ~ata* AE 581.8.

sophisticus ~a ~um, *a.* (Gk.) Of sophists; (neut. as sb.) a sophistic device, piece of sophistry: *per ratiocinia ex variis ~is* VR 375.2; VR 802.3.

sophus ~i, *m.* (Gk.) A wise man, sage: *sapientum, qui vocati sunt ~i, in Graecia et alibi* AM 73.1.

sopio ~pire ~pivi ~pitum, *tr.* To render insensitive as in sleep, make dormant, lull: *~piti...quoad corporea* AC 541; *memoria naturalis ~pitur* CI 467; *vigilias rationis ~piunt, et sic somnia vident* VR 37.3; cf. *inde alte ~piverunt dogmata sua* SE 20.

sopitio ~onis, *f.* The act of putting as it were to sleep, lulling: *non est remotio illarum cupiditatum, sed modo ~o* AC 2041.3; *~onem sensationum corporis* AS 257.4.

sopor ~oris, *m.* Profound sleep, unconsciousness: *et ~or cecidit super Abram* Gen. 15.12 (AC); *in plures status somni lenissimi, et dein ~oris* ES 319.

soporatus ~a ~um, *a.* Plunged in sleep, deeply asleep: *reduci...in speciem somni, ut nescirent quid facerent, ita ~i* ES 2575.

soporifer ~era ~erum, *a.* Soporific: *inde sentire potui vim ~eram* ES 3618.

soporo ~are ~avi ~atum, *tr.* To plunge in deep sleep: ES Index s.v. 'cogitatio' (p. 136 Tafel), referring to ES 2575.

sorbeo ~bere ~bui, *tr.* **1** To suck into the mouth, sup: *~bere fac me quaeso parum aquae e cado tuo* Gen. 24.17 (AC); *ex significatione '~bere' quod simile sit ac bibere, sed in diminutivo quia explorandum* AC 3089; *onagri...~buerunt ventum* Jer. 14.6 (AC 1949.3). **2** (transf.) To suck in, absorb: *ubi pleno ore circumflua gaudia in aeternum ~berent* AM 10.6.

sordeo ~dere, *intr.* To be dirty or soiled: *quod calceus* [*significet*] *omnium infima, quae ~dent* AC 2162.2.

sordes ~is, *f.* (more often used in the pl. than in the sg., with no change in meaning) (gen. pl. *~ium*) Dirt, filth: *quod peccata...abluantur sicut ~es ab aquis* AC 7318.2; *~es et quisquiliae omnis generis* AM 443.

sordesco ~ere, *intr.* To become dirty, turn to filth: *indigesta et maligna, qualia sunt ~entium ciborum in ventriculo* CI 299.

sordide, *adv.* In a sordid manner, foully: *qui ~e avari sunt* AC 8318.3.

sordidus ~a ~um, *a.* (superl. *~issimus*) **1** Unclean, dirty, filthy: *linteum ~um* AM 463.2; *in locis ~issimis* ES 4861; (neut. as sb.) *in spurca et ~a immundis illorum voluptatibus correspondentia* CI 401. **2** (transf.) Sordid, foul: *foeminae...ex ~a et vili conditione divites factae* AC 944; *~a avaritia* AC 7051.1; *amor pecuniae ...qui est ~issimus* ES 2910.

sorditas ~atis, *f.* Dirtiness: *in talibus ~atibus vivunt, ut sues* ES 3785.

soror ~oris, *f.* A sister: *cum...fratre, ~ore, patre, matre* AC 6653; AM 116.

sors ~rtis, *f.* **1** A lot, anything used to make a random selection: *dirimamus has lites per ~rtem et ~rti quae primum exit favebimus* CC 19.5; *~rtem jacere*, to cast lots: *super tunicam ~rtem jecerunt* AE 38 (John 19.24). **2** A piece of land assigned by lot, parcel: *communes ~rtes regni spiritualis Domini* AC 3238; *communes ~rtes dicuntur quia regnum Domini repraesentatur per 'terram', quae distribuitur per ~rtes* AC 3239.2. **3** A particular sort or kind: *servi...qui inferioris ~rtis sunt* AC 7396; *dum vestimenti talem ~rtem emerim* ES 817; *quod sirenes sint ex pluri ~rte* ES 4635. **4** The kind of life one experiences, lot, fate, destiny: *~rs eorum in altera vita multo pejor est* AC 593; *quod...non possint aliter quam ~rtem habere cum illis qui in inferno sunt* VI 63.2; *quod post duras illas ~rtes non concupiverint amplius caelum* AM 10.6.

sortior ~tiri ~titus sum, *tr., intr.* **1** (intr.) To decide by chance selection, cast lots: *ne dividamus eam* [sc. *tunicam*], *sed ~tiamur de illa cujus erit* John 19.24 (AE 64.3). **2** (tr.) To have allotted, be assigned: *locum... ~titi sunt* AC 7236.1; *ex affectione et secundum illam ~tiuntur vestes* AM 42.3; *antequam tunicas ovinas ~titi* ES 633.

sospes ~itis, *a.* Unscathed, safe and sound: *homo... continue ~es et stabili potitus valetudine* AM 107.

spargo ~gere ~si ~sum, *tr.* **1** To sprinkle (a liquid): *et accepit Moscheh sanguinem et ~sit super populum* Exod. 24.8 (AC); cf. *~sa est victoria eorum super vestes Meas* Isa. 63.3 (DD 14.2); to spread around (an odour): *foetor murium ~gitur ab illis* AC 1514. **2** (transf.) To spread around, scatter, throw out: *malis...inter jucundiora est falsa ~gere* AC 7356.1; *~gentes facetias* AM 8.2; *coram vulgo ~gere conjecturas* VR 57.1; to move in all directions, cast around: *oculos ingeniose ~gunt ad laedendum alios* ES 2245.

sparsim, *adv.* In a scattered fashion, discontinuously, disconnectedly: *quae in explicationibus ~im tradita sunt* AC 6627; *unam ideam communem tam ~im continuant* ES 1123; *facie erat brunea, ~im lutea* ES 3302.

sparsio ~onis, *f.* The act of sprinkling: *per ~onem sanguinis* AC 10047.4.

sparsus ~a ~um, *a.* (pf. pple. of **spargo**) (in senses of vb., esp.) Discontinuous, scattered: *non est* [*stylus*] *continuus...sed est ~us* AC 66.2; *societates...~ae per totum terrarum orbem* AC 7390; *sicut pulvis ~a, nullius cohaerentiae* ES 3891.

sparta ~ae, *f.* (a neologism of unknown origin, perhaps related to **sporta**) A contribution: *unicuique* [*angelo*] *est sua ~a in specie* CI 392; *sensus tactus...ex illis* [sc. *aliis sensibus*] *trahit ~as* AM 210; *conferre ~as xenodochiis* DP 83.4; VR 425.1; VR 459.8.

spatha ~ae, *f.* (Gk.) A broad leaf, frond, spathe: *~as palmarum* Lev. 23.40 (AC 7093.2).

spatiolum ~i, *neut.* A small space, gap: *mensae plenae ferculis, et ~a inter haec ornata parvis pyramidibus cum condituris* AM 6.2; ES 1280.

spatior ~ari ~atus sum, *intr.* To move in a leisurely fashion, progress: *quod...planetae...non sint moles vacuae, et creatae ut modo ~entur circum solem* AC 6697; CI 417.3.

spatiosus ~a ~um, *a.* (compar. *~ior*, superl. *~issimus*) Occupying much space, roomy, spacious: *via...erat lata et ~a* CI 534.1; *in gymnasio ejus, quod erat ~um, ambulavimus* AM 380.4; (fig.) *in ~iori campo libertatis* ES 2406; ES 4010.

spatium ~i, *neut.* **1** Space in abstract: *absque idea temporis et ~i* AC 7381.3; CI 143. **2** A spatial interval, space: *in mundo spirituali non sunt ~a, sed sunt apparentiae ~orum* AM 50. **3** An interval of time, space: *per octimestre ~um* 1AD 943.

specialis ~is ~e, *a.* **1** Restricted to a particular individual or group, special, specific, peculiar: *spiritus... assident capiti, et id ~i modo quasi implent* AC 7805; *mala quorum ~es formae sunt* CI 554; *~em Ecclesiam, quae est apud hominem in singulari* VR 245.1; (w. *pro*) *praesentia...solis mundi est modo ~is pro mundo naturali* SA 160 (= xii.3.[2]). **2** Regarded in detail, particular, special: *quod per singula quae nominantur* [*significetur*] *aliquid ~e* AC 426.1; (opposed to **generalis**) *societates generales...societates...~es* AC 7836.2; (opposed to **genericus**) *quoad differentias genericas et ~es perceptionum* AC 483.2; (opposed to **communis**) *per affluxum communem...ex coelis...et quoque per affluxum ~em e quolibet coelo* CI 543.

specialiter, *adv.* (compar. *~lius*) In a particular manner: *homo cujus internum constituit caelum...aut ~lius, cujus caput constituit caelum supremum* VR 119.1.

speciatim, *adv.* In detail: *plura quae ~im non ita dici possunt* AC 1511.

species ~ei, *f.* **1** Outward appearance, look: *non vocem Patris audivistis unquam, neque ~em Ipsius vidistis* John 5.37 (DD 32.5); *nemo credere potest in Deum ...quem non sub aliqua ~e comprehendere potest* AC 9356; (as opposed to reality) *frequens loquela ex memoria et reminiscentia...infert ~em fidei* VR 77.5; *hoc spirituale...~em inducit tanquam sit intimius* ES 241. **2** A species of plant or animal, kind: *arborem fructus facientem fructum secundum ~em suam* Gen. 1.11 (AC); *conjunctionibus diversarum ~erum animalium* *inter se, sicut ovium et hircorum* AM 246.3. **3** A kind, type, sort (of anything): *~es viperae* AC 259.2; *fides...est ~es persuasionis* FI 31; (dist. from **genus**) *secundum bonorum coelestium genera et ~es* CI 513. **4** *In ~e*, in particular, in detail, especially: *quod Moses repraesentaret Dominum quoad...Verbum, in ~e quoad Verbum historicum* AC 6723.3; *quae in ~e non nominantur, quia nota sunt* CI 104; (dist. from *in genere*) *ubicunque bestiae nominantur in genere et in ~e* AC 143; AM 202.1.

specifice, *adv*. In a specific manner: *in orbe Christiano generaliter notum est, et ~e in ordine ejus Ecclesiastico* VR 343; ES 1464.

specificus ~a ~um, *a*. (of a difference) Allowing classification as a species: *ut differentiae ~ae possint dici indefinitae* AC 775.1; (of things) restricted to a species, specific: *significatur...per unamquamvis tribum aliquod ~um Ecclesiae* SS 11; (neut. as sb.) a specific instance: *velim modo aliqua ~a adducere* CI 508.1.

specimen ~inis, *neut*. A piece intended to show the character of the whole, specimen: *~en et Sciagraphia Doctrinae Novae Ecclesiae in Summario* JU (Tafel, p. 15).

speciose, *adv*. In appearance (as opposed to in reality), apparently: *quod...in aliquid ~e pulchrum converti potuisset* ES 231.

speciosus ~a ~um, *a*. Fair-seeming: *erant omnes quoad faciem ~i ex vita in oculis* AR 939.4; *similes estis sepulchris dealbatis, quae foris apparent ~a* Matt. 23.27 (CI 505); specious: *ii qui ratiociniis ~is destruere conantur doctrinalia* AC 896.1.

spectabilis ~is ~e, *a*. Capable of being seen, visible: *interiora...angelorum sistuntur ita ~ia* AC 10227.24.

spectaculum ~i, *neut*. **1** A theatrical performance, show: *~a ex personatis* AM 3.3; *ludi et ~a* AM 6.1. **2** The act of viewing, spectacle: *dixit quod ~a punitionum quoad mortem ei jucunda fuerint* ES 2883.

spectator ~oris, *m*. A spectator: *cum scamnis...super quibus ~ores sedebant* AR 655.1; the name of an English journal, *The Spectator*: *erat Spectator Londini* ES 5565.

specto ~are ~avi ~atum, *tr., intr*. **1** To regard with the eyes, look at, view: *quod non ~are velint vaginam* AC 6816; *sollicite cavent...ne ~entur a tergo* AC 8373; (of the sight) *quod visus oculi tam crassus...sit, ut plura insectula ~et ut unum obscurum* VR 12.4. **2** (intr.) To direct one's gaze, look: *canes muti... ~antes, cubantes* Isa. 56.10 (AC 7784.4); (w. *ad*) *oculi ejus ad Sanctum Israelis ~abunt* Isa. 17.7 (DD 40); (w. *in*) *oculus ~ans in aërem* VR 61.1. **3** (intr., of places) To afford a view, face: *portam ~antem versus orientem* Ezek. 46.12 (AC 1250.2); *a parte planetae huc ~ante* AC 7246; *super montem ~antem ad mare* ES 2240. **4** To have in view as an end, aim at: *misericordia Domini involvit et ~at salvationem totius generis humani* AC 598.1; *quod sex dies laboris... ~ent septimum sanctum* AC 737.3; *usus qui a Domino ~atur* AC 1097.2; (w. inf.) *aedificare domos ~arunt* ES 3309. **b** (intr.) to direct one's attention: *quoad vitam solum ~arunt ad mundana* AC 6971.2. **5** To subject to mental scrutiny, consider, regard: *unumquodvis ~atur separatim* AE 17; (w. indir. qu.) *ut ~et num emendum* ES 3670. **6** To look on, consider (in a specified way): *~at ideas spatii sub se* VR 30.1; *repraesentativum... ~atum in forma externa* AC 6832.1; (w. *ex*) *cum ex veris ~atur bonum* AC 7839; *ille amor ex sua origine... ~atus* AM 57; (w. *ab*) *~at...illud* [sc. *Verbum*] *a stylo* SS 3. **b** *in se ~atus*, regarded in its essence: *Divinum in Se ~atum est supra coelos* AC 8328.1; *amor in se ~atus non est aliud quam...nisus ad conjunctionem* AM 37. **7** To consider (as): *intellectualia ~ant voluntaria sicut alia et distincta a se* AC 732; *Ipse ~andus...ut finis ad quem* AC 6824. **8** (of things) To have regard to, refer to: *vox 'creare' etiam ~at spiritualem hominem* AC 476. **9** (of things) To verge on: (tr.) *per 'femora' intelligitur pars inferior lumborum, quae ~at pedes* AC 9961.1; (intr.) *fastidiosum...quod ~at ad nauseam* AM 433.2.

spectrum ~i, *neut*. An insubstantial apparition of a person, ghost, spectre: *clamorem inconditum sicut ex ~is in sylvis* VR 71.1; VR 80.4.

specula ~ae, *f*. A lookout post, watchtower: *e ~a vidimus montem* AM 77.2.

specularis ~is ~e, *a*. *Lapis ~is*, a mirror-like mineral, prob. mica: *lapides ~es, selenites vocati* AM 443; VR 35.2; made of mica: *per ~es nostras fenestras* VR 80.3.

speculatio ~onis, *f*. **1** The action of mental contemplation: *percipit quod intus sit ~o, maxime intra frontem* AS 365. **2** A more interior kind of thought, contemplation: *pro interioribus inservire potest vox 'imaginatio', pro intimioribus '~o', pro intimis 'cogitatio'* ES 679; *per intensas ~ones, in quibus respiratio quiescit* ES 3464.2.

speculator ~oris, *m*. A watchman, lookout: *~ores ejus coeci omnes* Isa. 56.10 (AC 7784.4); *quod ~ores angeli vident* ES 1413.

speculatorius ~a ~um, *a*. Of or for watchmen; *turris ~a*, a watchtower: Isa. 23.13 (AC 1306.2).

speculor ~ari ~atus sum, *intr*. To keep watch: (w. indir. qu.) *custodes illi fuerunt super muris, ~antes num hostis veniret* AC 8211.5.

speculum ~i, *neut*. **1** A looking glass, mirror: *sicut in ~o videri potest* CI 56; (used to concentrate the sun's rays) *sicut lignum in foco magni ~i caustici* VR 370.1. **b** (fig.): *quod cognitiones de Deo sint ~a Dei* VR 11.3; VR 6.2. **2** (app.) A lookout post, watchtower (= **specula**): *qui...spectat alterum aut ex alto ~o videt illum* AC 4198.1.

specus ~us, *f.* A large hole in the ground, pit: *quod cavernae...appareant...sicut ~us tenebricosae* AE 526.9; ES 4910; (fig.) *libidinum erumpentium ex ~ubus mentis nondum defaecatis* AM 108.

spelta ~ae, *f.* A hardy European type of wheat, spelt: *ex significatione zeae vel ~ae* AC 7605.

spelunca ~ae, *f.* A cave, den, esp. used for living in: *~a latronum* Jer. 7.11 (VI 91); *inferna...similia lustris et ~is, quales sunt feris in sylvis* CI 586.

spermaticus ~a ~um, *a.* (anat.) *Vasa ~a*, the spermatic vessels: AC 5391; ES 960.

sperno ~ere sprevi spretum, *tr.* To reject with contempt, scorn, spurn: *ut spiritus boni prorsus ~ant jucunditates corporis* AC 996.1; *~unt alios qui non sibi similes sunt* CI 360.1; AM 263.2.

spero ~are ~avi ~atum, *tr.*, *intr.* **1** (tr.) To hope for, expect: *nihil inde ~antes* Luke 6.35 (AC 8002.7); *cum ~ata non obtinent* VR 441.1. **2** (intr.) To hope: *ut ~o* AE 1135.5; (w. *in* + abl.) *in Me insulae ~abunt* Isa. 51.5 (AC 1158.4); *~et Israel in Jehovah* Ps. 130.7 (DD 34.2).

spes ~ei, *f.* **1** Hope: *perducitur in statum ~ei* AC 8165.2; (w. gen.) *~e nuptiarum* AM 44.10. **2** A source of hope: *~es Israelis Jehovah* Jer. 17.13 (AE 222.6).

sphaera ~ae, *f.* (Gk.) **1** An area of physical activity surrounding anything, sphere: *~a nidoris cadaverosi* AC 1124; *Verbum...cinctum ~a lucis* VR 508.1; *sunt quatuor ~ae naturales a sole oriundae* ES 222. **2** The region in which a person or spirit lives: *quod spiritus aliarum tellurum non appareant intra ~am ubi spiritus nostrae telluris* AC 7078; *voces...crassius materiales, ut essent infra ~am eorum* AC 1876.2. **3** The region within which any activity takes place, range: *singularia...quae homo prorsus nescit, nam intra ejus captus et perceptionis ~am sunt* AC 868.2; *super omnem ~am mentis humanae* VR 370.1. **4** A sphere of influence of a particular type: *sunt ibi* [sc. *in coelo*] *~ae amoris et fidei, quae manifeste percipiuntur* AC 925.2; *quod ~a conjugialis sit, quae a Domino per caelum influit in omnia...universi* AM 209; (as the source of instinctive knowledge in animals) *animalia habent ~am temporum, in longinquum tunc evolandi* ES 3340. **5** A sphere of spiritual activity emanating from a person or spirit or from God: *sunt ~ae vitae spirituales quae procedunt ex unoquoque angelo* CI 17; *protectio...coeli per Divinam ~am boni et veri* AC 9502; *~a Divina procedens a Domino est perpetuus conatus salvandi omnes* CI 595.

sphaericus ~a ~um, *a.* (Gk.) Spherical: *ceram... compingunt...in ~am [formam]* VR 184.

sphaerula ~ae, *f.* A small sphere, globule: *compages ex globulis seu ~is contiguis* AS 32.2; *quod...in medulla spinae sint ~ae quasi moleculae* SA 72 (= ii.2.[3]).

sphincter ~eris, *m.* (Gk.) (anat.) The sphincter: AC 5389; ES 4281.

sphinx ~ngis, *f.* (Gk.) A kind of ape, the sphinx baboon: *~nges aut simias vestitas ut homines* VR 320; VR 274.

spica ~ae, *f.* **1** An ear (of grain crops): *primum herbam, dein ~am, deinde plenum frumentum in ~a* Mark 4.28 (AC 29.2); *triticum, hordeum et reliqua messis ex ~is* AE 405.48. **2** Anything shaped like an ear of corn, spike: *cum ~is in varias formas pulchras concinnatis* ES 2763.

spicilegium ~i, *neut.* The picking up of ears of corn, gleaning: *leges latae de ~is* AC 5212.4 (Lev. 19.9; 23.22).

spiculum ~i, *neut.* A sharp projection, spike: *pileo instructi acuto, ex quo ~um* AC 546; ES 1843; *~a salis crassa* ES(M) 4627.

spina ~ae, *f.* **1** A thorn: *ascendent in palatia ejus ~ae, carduus et sentis in munitiones ejus* Isa. 34.13 (AC 7293.4); *coronam ex ~is* DD 16.5. **2** (anat.) The spine: *medullam...per quam utrumque cerebrum continuatur in ~am* AM 315.6; *~am dorsi* ES 1289.

spinalis ~is ~e, *a.* Of the spine, spinal: *medulla ~is* AC 3745.

spineus ~a ~um, *a.* Of thorns: *~am coronam* AC 9144.10.

spinosus ~a ~um, *a.* = **spineus**: *~am coronam* DD 16.7.

spira ~ae, *f.* (Gk.) A convolution, coil: *contextus pulcher ex ~is mirabiliter consertis* AC 5559; *retorsio ~ae in oppositum* AS 254.2; *cidaris circumvoluta ~is tanquam colubri* AM 264.1; *serpens flexus in ~am* AM 521.1; *qui...feruntur quasi in ~am* ES 2846.

spiraculum ~i, *neut.* **1** Air breathed by the lungs, breath: *Jehovah...inspiravit in nares ejus ~um vitarum* Gen. 2.7 (AC); *per ventum Jehovae seu ~um Ipsius* AC 8286.2. **2** Air as carrying scents, breath: *calor vernalis cum ejus amaenis ~is sicut ex horto* AM 137.2; (fig.) *sphaera amoris...cum amaeno suo ~o* AM 321.3. **3** An air-hole, vent: *sicut athmosphaerae tempestate actae ex ~is draconum oriundae* VR 619.6.

spiralis ~is ~e, *a.* Convoluted, spiral: *quae [lux] per ~es flexus se devolvens* AM 461.8; ES 3495; (neut. as sb.) a spiral: *in ~is seu helicis formam* ES 1233.

spiratio ~onis, *f.* Breathing: *fides mortua, quae est sicut ~o pulmonaris absque anima ejus ex corde* VI 46.

spiratus[1] ~a ~um, *a.* Formed in a coil, coiled: *sunt illae* [sc. *substantiae*] *~ae antrorsum* DP 319.3.

spiratus[2] ~us, *m.* The act of breathing or blowing: *sic ut labia moveantur...per ~um talem, sic afflatum, intrinsecum pulmonicum* ES 3279.

spiritalis ~is ~e, *a.* (app.) Resembling breath, airy: *quod homo post mortem sit quoddam umbratile, ~e, ex aethere larva ineffigiata* AE 988.3.

spiritualis ~is ~e, *a.* (compar. *~ior* ES 3545) **1** Of or appropriate to the spirit, not natural or material, spiritual: *pugnae ~es* AC 6656; *quod haec non fides ~is sit* FI 1; *auferre illis omne lacticinium ~e et... cibatum ~em* VR 93.2. **b** (neut. as sb.) that which is spiritual: *hodie quid ~e pauci sciunt* AC 6685; *~e cujusvis hominis* UJ 25.1; (pl.) *comprehendere ~ia seu theologica* FI 3; *in ~ibus Ecclesiae* AM 10.1. **2** *Mundus ~is*, the non-material world in general, the spiritual world: *a mundo qui est supra naturam, qui mundus ~is vocatur* AC 4524; *dum intrant mundum ~em, quod ut plurimum fit tertio die post obitum* VR 138. **b** of or relating to the spiritual world: [*athmosphaerae*] *~es sunt quia oriuntur a sole ~i* AS 176. **3** *Sensus ~is*, the internal or spiritual sense (of the Word): *sensus ~is non apparet in sensu literae* SS 5; *de sensu interno seu ~i Verbi* AE 1. **4** (of persons) Made spiritual by regeneration: *quia tunc incipit simul ac ex fide, etiam ex amore agere, fit homo ~is* AC 12; *homo...nisi fiat ~is, non potest venire in caelum* DP 83.1; *quod* [*infantes*] *fiant aliis multo... ~iores* ES 3545; *Ecclesia ~is vocatur cum ex charitate...agit* AC 916.2. **5** Of or relating to the second of the three degrees of heaven, spiritual: *coelum distinguitur in duo regna...regnum coeleste...regnum ~e* CI 21; *quod homini sit mens naturalis, mens ~is et mens caelestis* DP 147; *bonum ~e et coeleste* AC 81.1; *vocatur id Divinum caeleste, ~e et naturale* VR 6.1; (neut. as sb.) *e coelesti nascitur ~e* AC 1025.7. **b** (combined with *coelestis* and *naturalis* to distinguish further): *scientifica a coelesti ~i origine* AC 91; *~es naturales vocantur, qui influxum recipiunt ex coelo medio* CI 31.

spiritualitas ~atis, *f.* The quality of being spiritual, spirituality: *qui in pueritia sua se confirmant contra ~atem charitatis* VR 796.5.

spiritualiter, *adv.* In a spiritual manner, spiritually: *in coelo omnia ~er intelliguntur, in terra autem naturaliter* AC 10215; [*homo*] *spiritualis ~er agit* AM 280.

spirituosus ~a ~um, *a.* Spirituous, volatile: *chylum ~um e cerebro* ES 1130; (neut. as sb.) *ubi pituitosa cum ~is* ES 1239.

spiritus ~us, *m.* **1** The air inhaled and exhaled by the lungs, breath: *athmosphaera fragranter olens, quae pleno ~u attrahitur* DP 296.9; *anhelo ~u et festino cursu aufugerunt* AM 6.4; *...vellem tenere ~um* ES 3320. **b** (as lost at the time of death): *quod homo dicatur emittere ~um, cum moritur* DD 47.1; *per ablationem ~us eorum* ES 623. **c** the breath (of the Lord): *Jehovah... ~u labiorum Suorum occidet impium* Isa. 11.4 (AC 1286.2). **d** the breath (of the wind): *~us (seu ventus) ubi vult spirat* John 3.8 (AC 97); *~um procellarum* Ezek. 13.13 (AC 739.2). **2** A vapour or volatile liquid given off by a physical substance: *~us vinosus alcohol dictus* VR 98.1; *fibrae e cerebro impletae ~u* AC 5951.2; *~us animalis*, animal spirits (conceived of as animating the person; cf. sense 5): *de sanguine, vel de ~u animali* ES 4525. **3** The intellectual and sentient part of the mind which animates the body and survives its death, spirit: *percipiunt quod dum in corpore vixerunt, fuerit ~us qui sensit* AC 322.2; *~us hominis seu internus homo* AC 4676.2; *per ~um hominis in concreto non aliud intelligitur quam mens ejus* VR 156.1; *oculis ~us sui* VR 400.3; *Jesus puer crevit, et corroboratus est ~u et impletus sapientia* Luke 2.40 (AC 9818.10). **b** *in ~u*, in the state of being withdrawn from bodily concerns, in the spirit: *cum in cogitatione abstracta est a corpore et quasi in ~u suo cogitat* AC 1015.2; *factus sum in ~u* VR 76.1; *per 'esse' in ~u...intelligitur status mentis separatae a corpore* VR 157.1. **4** The mind as the seat of intellectual pride: *beati pauperes ~u* Matt. 5.3 (AC 9818.7); *agitatus ~us illius* Gen. 41.8 (AC); *~um tuum in hunc gradum vesaniae evexeras, ut nunc credas quod sis ipse Deus* AM 264.2; (pl.) *in statu illo...est deficientia ~uum* AC 5323.1. **5** The active principle, spirit: *fidem...in qua ~us et vita unice est ex charitate* AR 875.3; SS 69; *~us propheticus* ES 2521. **b** (of God): *postquam ~us Dei seu misericordia Domini produxit in diem cognitiones veri et boni* AC 24.1; *super servos...effundam ~um Meum* Joel 2.29 (DD 4); *Ego rogabo Patrem, ut alium Paracletum det vobis... ~um veritatis* John 14.17 (AC 6788). **c** *~us Sanctus*, the Holy Spirit: *Paracletus, ~us Sanctus, quem mittet Pater* John 14.26 (AC 6788); *per ~um Sanctum proprie significatur Divinum Verum* VR 139.1. **6** A person who has after death passed into the spiritual world, spirit: *cum in alteram vitam veniunt, diu non sciunt quod ~us sint* AC 938; *angelici ~us* AC 394; *~us mali* AC 50.2; *~us infernales* AC 6724.2. **b** (as possessing a person in this world): *quando immundus ~us exit ab homine* Luke 11.24 (AE 731.1). **c** *mundus ~uum*, the part of the spiritual world into which newly arrived spirits are brought, the world of spirits: *mundus ~uum est locus medius inter coelum et infernum* CI 422.

spiro ~are ~avi, *tr.*, *intr.* **1** (intr., of winds) To blow: *~are facit ventum Suum* Ps. 147.18 (AC 8286.4); (of

God) *~asti vento Tuo* Exod. 15.10 (AC). **b** (tr.) to cause (a wind) to blow: *~abant ventum satis fortem* ES 2865. **2** (w. acc.) To be disposed towards, yearn for: *qui odium ...habent et inde vindictam ~ant* AC 814.1; *qui elato animo et alta ~ant* AC 1276; *vindictae quae ~ant necem* VI 67. **b** (w. inf.): *~at et cupit esse maximum* AC 452. **c** (w. *ad*): *subordinati continue ~ant ad dominium* AC 7773.

spissitudo ~inis, *f.* The quality of being glutinous, viscosity: *a nimia ~ine, tenacitate et acrimonia humorum* AM 253.2.

spissus ~a ~um, *a.* (compar. *~ior*) Dense, viscous, thick: *undae apparent tenuiores aut ~iores secundum falsorum quale* AC 6853; *per quod...sanguis fiat viscosus, tenax, ~us* AM 374.

spithama ~ae, *f.* (Gk.) The extended hand as a measure, span: *coelos ~a exaequavit* Isa. 40.12 (AE 373.4).

splendens ~ntis, *a.* (compar. *~ntior*) Shining, brilliant: *is nitentiori et ~ntiore facie erat* CI 75; *tota ejus facies fuit unus ~ns decor* AM 42.3.

splendeo ~dere ~dui, *intr.* To emit bright light, shine: *cum Jesus transformatus est, ~duit facies Ipsius sicut sol* AC 7083 (Matt. 17.2); *luna non ~dere faciet lucem suam* Isa. 13.10 (CI 119); *omnes usus boni in caelis ~dent et fulgent* AM 266.2.

splendescentia ~ae, *f.* (= **splendor**) Resplendence: AC 10536 (Autograph).

splendesco ~ere, *intr.* To be resplendent: *florum ex amaenissimis et coelestibus coloribus ~entium* CI 337; (fig.) *cum confirmata sunt, [falsa] possunt ~ere* CI 352.1.

splendide, *adv.* In a magnificent fashion: *oblectabat se quotidie ~e* Luke 16.19 (SS 40.3); *~e se vestiendo* AM 453.

splendidus ~a ~um, *a.* (compar. *~ior*, superl. *~issimus*) Brilliant, dazzling: *omnia ~a ex auro et lapidibus pretiosis* AM 266.2; *unum palatium ~ius quam alterum* CI 185.

splendor ~oris, *m.* The quality of emitting bright light, brilliance, brightness: *stellae contrahent ~orem suum* Joel 2.10 (SS 14.3); *lux seu ~or ignis* AM 383; *pro luminaribus, ex quibus templa...in ~ore sunt* VR 12.9.

spolio ~are ~avi ~atum, *tr.* To deprive of possessions, rob, despoil: *quod... ~arent Aegyptios* AC 1551.4 (Exod. 3.22); *alios defraudarent, diriperent et ~arent* CI 530.2; (w. abl.) *alios...suis bonis ~arunt* AC 1631.

spolium ~i, *neut.* Property taken in war or by violence, spoils, plunder: *fiet illi anima ejus in ~um* Jer. 21.9 (AC 7102.7); *cistas auferebat sicut ~a* ES 727; *~a opima,* (in antiquity) spoils taken from an enemy general defeated in single combat: (in quot. fig.) *gloriati sunt super furtis illis sicut super ~is opimis* AM 505.2.

sponda ~ae, *f.* A couch: *ut super ~is cubarent* AM 8.2; *in extremitate ~ae* Amos 3.12 (AE 163.3).

spondeo ~dere spopondi ~sum, *tr.* (pf. act. also *spospondi* ES 4412, perh. erroneously) To promise solemnly, pledge: *de duobus qui spoponderunt conjugium* AM 300.1; *ut...se humiliet et ~deat poenitentiam* ES 487; (w. *quod*) *~dentes quod non amplius cuperent altiora* CI 35; (w. *ut*) *spospondit ei, ut hoc obtineret* ES 4412.

spongia ~ae, *f.* (Gk.) A sponge (in domestic use): *sunt sicut ~ae quae imbibunt artificia nefanda* AC 831.2; ES 2743; (fig.) *quod homo...foret quoad carnem mera ~a* VR 364.1.

spongiosus ~a ~um, *a.* Resembling a sponge, spongy: *sicut lignum ~um ac porosum* CI 479.5.

sponsa ~ae, *f.* A woman promised in marriage (often at the time of a wedding), bride: *quod Dominus dicatur Sponsus et Maritus ac coelum ~a et quoque uxor* CI 371; *viderunt...sponsum et ~am tenentes se manibus* AM 20.2; *paratam sicut ~am ornatam marito suo* Rev. 21.2 (AR).

sponsalis ~is ~e, *a.* Of or belonging to betrothal; (neut. as sb.) betrothal: *quod per ~e et conjugiale... significetur...conjunctio Domini cum Ecclesia* AC 4434.2.

sponsio ~onis, *f.* A solemn promise, pledge: *~ones Dei irrefragabiles* AM 3.5.

sponsus ~i, *m.* A man engaged to be married, fiancé, (often at a wedding) bridegroom: *Josephus ~us ejus* Matt. 1.19 (DD 21); AM 20.2.

spontaneus ~a ~um, *a.* **1** Arising of one's own free will, spontaneous: *omnis correspondentia est naturalis et ~a* CI 262; *submissionem quasi ~am* ES 170; *ex ~o*, spontaneously: AM 511. **2** (Bibl., in uncertain sense): *~i populorum congregati sunt* Ps. 47.9 (SS 86).

sponte (abl. of obsolete noun used as adv.) Of one's (its) own accord, spontaneously: *~te enim terra fructum fert* Mark 4.28 (AC 29.2); *cadit cogitatio prompte et ~te in voces* AC 1638; *volupe...quod se ~te consumit* AM 482; (so, also) *~te sua* AC 6812.

sporta ~ae, *f.* (ad. Gk.) **1** A basket: *quod superessent septem ~ae plenae* AE 257.9 (Matt. 15.37). **2** A contribution, portion (cf. **sparta**): *conferre ~as aedificandis templis* AE 933.2; *Dominus implevit omnes Suo spiritu, sed quisque desumpsit inde ~am* VR 154.1.

spretus ~a ~um: pf. pple. of **sperno**.

sprevi: pf. of **sperno**.

spuma ~ae, *f.* Foam, froth: *utrumque cerebrum...in ~am abiret* VR 30.2; *sicut ~a super faciebus aquarum* Hos. 10.7 (AE 391.28); (pl.) *~as faeculentissimas* ES 585.

spuo ~ere ~i ~tum, *intr.* To expectorate, spit: *quod flagellaverint, ~erint in faciem* DD 16.6.

spurcities ~ei, *f.* Filth, dirt: *...intra quod reconditae sunt omnis generis ~es* CI 505; filthiness, foulness: *~em voluptatum amoris scortatorii* AM 424.

spurcus ~a ~um, *a.* (superl. *~issimus*) Morally foul, filthy, polluted: *~issimum malum* AC 1861.17; *amores ~os* AC 6832.8; *flagravissent in ~a adulteria* AM 342.4; (neut. as sb.) *lasciva loqui et ~a cogitare* SS 67.3.

spurius ~a ~um, *a.* **1** Illegitimate: *ab Antiquissimae Ecclesiae prole, quae ~a* ES 3353; (masc. as sb.) a bastard: *quod non veniret ~us in congregationem Jehovae* AC 8904.11 (Deut. 23.2). **2** Not genuine, spurious: *conscientia ~a vel falsa* AC 977.1; *quid vera intelligentia et sapientia, quid ~a, et quid falsa...dicetur* CI 351.1; *ab amore conjugiali ~o, falso et frigido* AM 224; *vitia quae vocantur ~a tubercula* AC 5188.1.

sputum ~i, *neut.* Spittle: *fecit lutum ex ~o* John 9.6 (AE 239.19).

squalidus: see **squallidus**.

squallidus ~a ~um, *a.* also **squalidus**. Dirty, filthy: *induti vestibus, sed laceris, ~is et tetris* CI 182; *intestina ~a* ES 3087.

squallor ~oris, *m.* also **squalor**. Dirt, filth: *vivunt demum in ~ore* AC 4054.2.

squalor: see **squallor**.

squama ~ae, *f.* **1** A scale on the skin of fish: *adhaerere faciam pisces fluviorum tuorum ~is tuis* Ezek. 29.4 (AC 6693.4). **2** A scale or shell on other creatures: *pili et ~ae cutis* AC 3527.2; *~a cochleae* AM 268.2. **3** Any worthless covering, husk: *horum sermo...est sicut ~a et palea respective ad nuclearia* AC 4957.

squamosus ~a ~um, *a.* Scaly: *ad provinciam cutis imprimis ~ae* AC 1385; AC 1500; ES 2656.

stabilimentum ~i, *neut.* **1** The act of establishing or supporting: *nox...et hyems non conferunt ad ~um mundi* CO 17.1. **2** That which establishes or supports: *pignora illa sunt ~a amoris conjugialis* AM 300.3; *illa tria ut ~a et firmamenta caelorum* SE 78.2.

stabilio ~lire ~livi ~litum, *tr.* **1** To set up securely, establish: *orbis ~litur, et non dimovetur* Ps. 96.10 (AC 8261.5); *sedebit...super regno ejus, ad ~liendum illud* Isa. 9.7 (SS 85). **2** To make certain, secure, establish (promises, propositions and sim.): *non ~liverunt verba foederis* Jer. 34.18 (AC 1362); *si...haec* [sc. *propositio*] *relinquitur inquisitioni ut assentiatur et ~liatur per confirmationes* AM 156.2; *quod infernalis amor per falsificata ~liatur* AE 177.10.

stabilis ~is ~e, *a.* **1** Standing firm, unshakeable: *~is erit mons domus Jehovae* Isa. 2.2 (AC 795.2). **2** Firmly established: *num faedus conjugiale...mansurum et ~e futurum sit post mortem* AM 45.

stabularius ~i, *m.* A stableman, ostler: VR 825.

stabulum ~i, *neut.* A building where horses or other animals are kept, stable: *instar praesepis in ~o* SS 26.3; AM 76.2; *cum irem circa ~um equorum* ES 3817.

stacte ~es, *f.* (Gk.) An aromatic substance, oil of myrrh: *cameli...ferentes aromata et resinam et ~en* Gen. 37.25 (AC); Gen. 43.11 (AC); another similar substance: Exod. 30.34 (AC); cf. AC 10292.3.

stadium ~i, *neut.* A Roman measure of length, approximately 185 m, sometimes translated as furlong: *et mensus est urbem calamo ad ~a duodecies mille* Rev. 21.16 (AR); *tam multi ut paene implerent spatium ~i* VR 665.1.

stagnans ~ntis, *a.* (of water) Stagnant: ES 2804.

stagnatus ~a ~um, *a.* Stagnant: *aquae impurae obturatae aut ~ae* DP 117.1; *nidores ex urinis ~is* AM 461.7.

stagneus ~a ~um, *a.* Stagnant: *mare ~um* ES 4453; (neut. as sb.) stagnant water: *in ~is, coenosis et excrementitiis degere* AC 1666.1.

stagno ~are ~avi, *intr.* (of liquids) To stagnate: *humores qui in cerebro ~ant* ES 1798.

stagnum ~i, *neut.* A pond, lake: *super fluvios et super ~a* Exod. 8.1 (AC); *apparent...monstra serpentum, qualium in ~is* AC 819; (of fire) *missi sunt...in ~um ignis ardens sulphure* Rev. 19.20 (AR); cf. *omnes facientes mercedem ex ~is animae* Isa. 19.10 (AC 7324.3).

stamen ~inis, *neut.* **1** A thread, filament: *quando* [*bombyx*] *extrahit ex se et evolvit ~ina serici* VR 571.2; (esp. of the earliest development of living creatures) *delineamenta primorum ~inum licet vascula appellare* AC 5726; AC 7408.2. **2** The initial stage of development of a life form, rudiments: *cui* [*formae*] *ut ~ini aut initiamento in utero successive accedunt substantiae* AS 6; *non...semen potuisset...excrescere...a primo ~ine usque ad fructus* VR 470.3; VR 687.2.

staminatum ~i, *neut.* A thread-like structure: *ut non sit fibrilla, ~um, aut minima tela ex illis* SA 101 (= vii.4.[1]).

stannum ~i, *neut.* Tin: *aes et ~um et ferrum et plumbum* Ezek. 22.18 (AC 8298.2); VI 10.

stapes ~idis (*or* ~edis), *m.*? **1** A stirrup, hence anything shaped like a stirrup; a bone in the tympanum of the ear: *nisi sit corpus consonans et ~es communicans* ES 2003 (J D Odhner). **b** a bridge-like structure serving to raise the occupant above ground level: *sicut galli qui super ~ide alta voce coram gallinis, quae humi gradiuntur, canunt* VR 839.2; *in medio* [sc. of a trap] *super ~ide ponit meretricem* CO 33.2. **2** (perh. an error) = **stipes**: *idem succus e radice per ~idem usque ad insitum aut inoculatum ascendit* VR 584.2.

stater ~eris, *m*. A Greek coin of high value, stater: *piscem tolle, et aperi os ejus, et invenies ~erem* Matt. 17.27 (AE 513.18).

statera ~ae, *f*. (ad. Gk.) A balance for weighing: *et sedens super illo* [*equo*] *habens ~am in manu sua* Rev. 6.5 (AR).

statim, *adv*. Immediately, at once: *quidam intra breviusculum tempus auferuntur in coelum, quidam ~im post mortem* AC 698; *si mittimus aliquem in infernum, diaboli ~im recipiunt illum* AM 264.2.

statio ~onis, *f*. **1** The act of standing: *~ones et sessiones sunt quietis hominis* AE 687.5. **2** A position occupied, place: *quod rotationes illae* [sc. *telluris*] *a ~one ad ~onem secundum zodiacum pergant* VR 29.1; *stant sub abruptis petris...; in tali ~one...* AE 411.26. **b** a position on a racetrack, esp. *prima ~o*, a starting point: *ubi excursus ~o seu carcer* ES 4652; (fig.) *amor procedit a sua ~one prima ad suam metam* AM 311.2. **3** A place for resting, stopping place: *quod Schechem sit prima quasi ~o in terra Canaane* AC 1441; AC 8103; (fig.) a stage: *ex significatione 'venire' quod sit ~o successivi quod per 'proficisci'...significatur* AC 8398. **4** Social position, situation in life: *vitae ~o* AC 6051; *ut quisque in sua ~one functionem suam rite obeat* AC 7338.1.

stationarius ~i, *m*. A soldier on guard duties, picket: *ubi erant quidam quasi ~i, qui me...tenerent vigilem* ES 2930; *quod...ad me miserunt ut essent eorum ~i* ES 2942; ES 3043; ES 3087.

stator ~oris, *m*. An upholder (in quots. as a title of the Lord): *a Domino Creatore et ~ore universi* AM 90.1; AM 238.2.

statua ~ae, *f*. **1** Anything which is set upon end as a sign or mark, pillar, upright: *et sumsit* [*Jacob*] *lapidem... et posuit illum ~am* Gen. 28.18 (AC); *lapides illos quos in terminis statuebant...~as vocabant* AC 3727.1; *Moscheh...aedificavit...duodecim ~as pro duodecim tribubus Israelis* Exod. 24.4 (AC); (of Lot's wife) *et facta ~a salis* Gen. 19.26 (AC). **2** A representation in the round of a living creature, sculpture, statue: *adorarunt aliquem deum sub imagine aut ~a* CI 326; *per sepulchrales ~as* ES 2147. **b** (as a type of inactivity): *sedent in judiciis muti sicut ~ae* AM 231.4; *si homo staret remissis manibus sicut sculpta ~a cum articulis mobilibus* [i.e., a puppet] VR 356.

statuo ~ere ~i ~tum, *tr*., *intr*. **1** To cause to stand, position, set: *~it illos coram Pharaone* Gen. 47.2 (AC); *~et oves a dextris et hircos a sinistris* Matt. 25.33 (DD 25). **2** To erect, set up: *in his lapidibus quos ~ebant* AC 3727.1; *longo palo seu ~to axi* ES 3006. **3** To reach a decision, decide: (w. inf.) *quod Deus Pater...~erit vindicare per ejus* [sc. *humani generis*] *damnationem* FI 44; (w. *quod*) *ex consulto ~erunt quod...in magnum auditorium ibi introducerentur* AM 207.1; (impers. pass.) *idcirco ~tum erat...quod...immundus esset* AC 6767.5. **b** (tr.) to decide on, fix, appoint: *tempus ~tum* Ps. 102.13 (AE 850.16). **4** To set up as a theory, suppose, assume: *qui salvationem ex sola fide...~unt* AC 8313.4; *qui...~unt internum, de illo...nullam...habent ideam* AC 8513.3; (w. *quod*) *illi qui ~unt...quod homo absque Verbo scire posset existentiam Dei* SS 115.1; (w. inf.) *quidam ~unt resurgere hominem post mortem* ES 1956.

statura ~ae, *f*. The height (of a person), stature: *viri et mulieres mediae ~ae* AM 75.4; *parvi quoad ~am* ES 460; VR 90.1.

status[1] ~a ~um, *a*. Unchanging, fixed, constant: *satellites...circum orbem suum ~is temporibus vagantur* AC 6697; *per ~as vices* CI 104; *ut...fiat ~a et sarta societas* AM 130.2; *sol...manet ~us in oriente* VR 29.2.

status[2] ~us, *m*. **1** The physical condition of a thing, state: *~us foveae seu carceris, squallidus et immundus* AC 5246.2; *quod affectiones...sint merae mutationes ~us substantiarum pure organicarum mentis* DP 279.6. **2** A mode of being, set of circumstances, condition: *qualitas formae est ~us ejus* VR 52; *~us diei sunt vesperae, noctis, matutae et meridiei* AC 1458.1; *illi in maximo angore sunt, et quamdiu in illo ~u, quasi in duro servitio sunt* AC 7218; *a primaevo ~u hominis in paradiso* VR 490.1. **b** *in ~u* (w. gen. of gerund), in a position (to): *non est in ~u exercendi charitatem* VR 406. **3** The state of a person's mind as subject to change: *homo...post mortem secum fert omnes vitae suae ~us* AC 4663.2; *~us prior tunc inservit pro plano ~ui sequenti* AC 5645.2; *quod tunc cogitatio illorum in ~u coacto sit* AC 7218; *in illo ~u, in quo fuerunt cum praelegerunt orationem* VI 7. **4** (w. gen.) A state characterized (by): *~us tentationum* AC 6726; *~us veri et boni* AC 8325.1; *fuerunt Ipsi* [*Domino*] *duo ~us, qui vocantur ~us humiliationis...et ~us glorificationis* DD 35.3. **5** A person's state or condition in the spiritual world as analogous to location in space or time: *ver et mane vertuntur in ideam ~us amoris et sapientiae* CI 166; *perductus sum...ad aliam tellurem...quod factum per mutationes ~us mentis meae* AC 10734; *idea spiritualis non trahit aliquid ex spatio, sed omne* *suum trahit ex ~u* AS 7. **6** The permanent condition of being, nature, state: *~us hominis talis est quod nusquam aliquod malum et falsum ita discuti possit ut aboleatur* AC 868.2; *solus...Dominus videt ~um cujusvis...tum qualis homo fuit* AR 262; *secundum ~um mentis, quem sibi homo...formavit* VR 6.2.

statutum ~i, *neut.* **1** A law or mandatory provision, statute (esp. in religious matters): *praecepta dicebantur quae erant vitae, judicia quae erant status civilis, et ~a quae erant cultus* AC 9972.2; *Ecclesiae ~a* CI 222. **2** (more generally) Any provision of authority: *Jehovah, dans... ~a lunae* Jer. 31.35 (AC 37); *invitabantur...sed cum ~o quod primo die comederent cum Abramo* AM 6.2. **b** a prescribed condition: *usque dum [Ecclesia] crescit ad suum ~um* AR 547.

stella ~ae, *f.* **1** A star (of the sky): *lumen...a luna et ~is* AC 7233.2; *equitare ad quendam asterismum in caelo, et inde captare ~am* VR 137.3; *~a caduca*, a falling star, meteorite: *dissipatur sicut ~a caduca in aërem* VR 82.1. **2** A small point of light, star: *~ae errantes circum spiritum significant...falsitates* AC 940.3; ES 1195; *cum recesserunt [angeli]...apparebant ~ae circum capita illorum* AC 875.3.

stellaris ~is ~e, *a.* Star-shaped: *in cerebris ejus sunt formae illae sicut ~es* AS 316.2.

stellatus ~a ~um, *a.* Covered with stars, starry: *facies ejus ~a apparuit non procul a facie mea* ES 1213.

stellifer ~era ~erum, *a.* (of the sky) Carrying stars, starry: *coelum ~erum* AC 1806; *in universo ~ero* ES 553; (of light) given by stars: *in luce nocturna seu ~era* ES 1195.

stellula ~ae, *f.* A small point of light, star: *umbrosum quoddam coloris coelestis cum ~a* AC 184; *nubes obscura cum ~is mobilibus in nube* AC 7803.

stellulosus ~a ~um, *a.* Composed of small stars: *multitudo...sicut ~a quasi Viae Lacteae* ES 5426.

stemma ~atis, *neut.* (Gk.) A line of descent, lineage, pedigree: *ex legitimo ~ate* AM 109; *nomen quod tulit...a patre aut ~ate* VR 300.1; *illi qui trahunt ~a per regenerationem a Domino* VR 724.

Stentorius ~a ~um, *a.* Of Stentor, a Greek hero famed for his loud voice, Stentorian: *stant qui ~ae tubae voce clamant, Ne accede propius* CO 38.

stercoreus ~a ~um, *a.* Of or resembling dung: *sordes ~as* AE 512.2; (neut. as sb.) *ut corvis, lupis, porcis, qui ex percepto nidore ad cadaverosa et ~a advolant et accurrunt* CI 429.

stercus ~oris, *neut.* A piece of excrement, dung: *placentam hordeorum cum ~ore fimi hominis* Ezek. 4.12 (DD 15.7); *~ora et caena* AM 430; (used as fertilizer) *in agris et vineis fimi et ~ora* AC 1103.2.

stereometricus ~a ~um, *a.* (Gk.) (neut. pl. as sb.) The science of solids, stereometry: *in geometricis, ~is, arithmeticis et physicis* VR 184.

sterilis ~is ~e, *a.* (compar. *~ior*) **1** (of persons or animals) Unable to produce young, barren: *canta, ~is, [quae] non pepererat* Isa. 54.1 (AE 223.16); *familiae alioquin ~es* AM 500.3. **2** (of land) Unproductive, barren: *deserta, ubi nihil nisi quam ~e et arenosum* CI 586. **3** (transf., of good and truth) Unproductive: *absque vita ex illis bona et vera sunt inanimata, et quoque sunt ~ia* VR 38.1.

sterilitas ~atis, *f.* Barrenness, sterility: *~atem, nempe doctrinae* AC 2586.1; *de agro et ejus ~ate* AE 374.4.

sterno ~ere stravi stratum, *tr.* **1** To spread as a covering, strew: *super illam [telam] stravimus plumas ex alis pavonum mutuatas* VR 487.2; *cur...straverint vestimenta super viam* AE 31.7 (Matt. 21.8). **2** (w. abl.) To bestrew, cover, pave (with): *planitiem stratam asseribus* AM 6.1; *planum lapillis...stratum* VR 48.1. **3** To cause to lie flat, lay down: (refl.) *si ~am me in inferno* Ps. 139.8 (VR 62); esp. to lay low (an enemy): *non cessare a pugnando usque dum strati hostes* AC 8294; ES 3145.

sterquilineum: see **sterquilinium**.

sterquilinium ~i, *neut.* also **sterquilineum**. A dunghill: *crabro...ubi videt ~um, involat* VR 69.2; *e ~o extollit egenum* 1 Sam. 2.3 (AE 253.6); ES 2185.

steti: pf.of **sto**.

stibium ~i, *neut.* Antimony: *ecce dispono cum ~o lapides tuos* Isa. 54.11 (AC 9407.8).

stigma ~atis, *neut.* (Gk.) A wound inflicted with a sharp point, prick, stab: (fig.) *naturalismus et Mahumedismus...duo ~ata mortifera ad avertendum voluntates* VR 137.12.

stilla ~ae, *f.* A drop (in quots. fig.): *quod...unaquaevis ~a affectionis vestrae sit dividua usque ad infinitum* AM 329.2; *si aliqua ~a ejus* [sc. *Domini justitiae*] *...tangeret illos* VR 641.3.

stillatio ~onis, *f.* The emission of drops, dropping: *dulcia prae melle et ~one favorum* Ps. 19.10 (AC 5620.10).

stillo ~are ~avi, *intr.*, *tr.* **1** (intr.) To fall in drops, rain down: *pluviam benevolentiarum ~are facis* Ps. 68.9 (AC 3753.2); *~abit sicut ros verbum Meum* Deut. 32.2 (AE 644.5); *quod illa* [sc. *pluvia aurea*] *~aret super aulam* AM 208.1. **2** (intr.) To shed drops, pour down rain: *etiam coeli ~arunt coram Deo* Ps. 68.8 (AC 8753.2). **3** (tr.) To allow to fall in drops, shed: *etiam* *nubes ~arunt aquas* Judg. 5.4 (AC 8753.3); *lachrymae sunt quae ~antur* AC 9223.2.

stilus: see **stylus**.

stimulus ~i, *m.* **1** A stinging organ, sting: *~i erant in caudis illarum* Rev. 9.10 (AC 6952.2). **2** Anything causing irritation, sting: *omnis dictio contra id est sicut ~us in naribus illorum* VR 110.1.

stipatus ~us, *m.* A concomitant crowd, throng: *Petrus spoliatus omni ~u* 2AD 1433.

stipendium ~i, *neut.* Regular payment for work performed, pay, wages: *quibus salaria et ~a ex publico aerario impendenda sunt* VR 430; *quod dederim ei* [sc. *famulo*] *~a* ES 4765.

stipes ~itis, *m.* A log of wood, stick: *sicut ~es injectus nudo soli* VR 641.1; esp. as a type of unresponsive object: *non sumus saxa et ~ites, sed perceptiones et affectiones vitae* AM 44.4; *annon homo concipit fidem actu sicut ~es...?* AR 675.4.

stipo ~are ~avi ~atum, *tr.* **1** To surround with a crowd, beset, throng: *praeparantur primum, et ~antur angelis intermediis* CI 35; 2AD 687; *facies...multis stellis errantibus ~ata* ES 1211. **2** (pass.) To be constipated: *quod torquerer...ventriculo, sic ut ~arer, cum intrinseco et muto dolore* ES 1272.

stips ~ipis, *f.* A small sum of money, pittance: *circumeunt sicut qui ~ipem quaerunt* AC 1631; CI 563.

stipula ~ae, *f.* The stalks of grain, esp. after reaping, stubble: *concipite quisquilias, parite ~am* Isa. 33.11 (AC 1297); *dispersit se populus...ad colligendum ~am ad paleam* Exod. 5.12 (AC).

stipulatum ~i, *neut.* An agreement, contract: *~a praestare* VR 432.

stipulor ~ari ~atus sum, *tr.* To enter into a contract, promise: *quod unus Deus cum altero Deo...potuerit talia ~ari* FI 46.

stirps ~irpis, *f.* **1** The trunk or bole of a tree: *excidite arborem...verum ~irpem radicum in terra relinquite* Dan. 4.15 (AE 650.29); *frons insita communi ~irpi fert suum fructum* AC 7343.2; (fig.) *Ego sum ~irps et progenies Davidis* Rev. 22.16 (AE 179.10; *radix* in AR). **2** The common source or origin of any descendant or derivative, stock, line: *sunt...gentium ~irpes seu radices* AC 1362; *distinguuntur inter se sicut facies humanae ex una ~irpe* CI 70; *...origo veri interioris ex ~irpe Divina* AC 4447.3.

sto stare steti, *intr.* **1** (of living creatures) To be in a standing position, stand up: *crederent...quod antipodes nusquam stare possent pedibus* AC 1378.2; *stant erecti* AC 7068; *apparebant...sicut stantes cum concludebant* AR 417.4. **2** To stand (in a specified place or manner): *angelus stans ad mensam* SE 120.10; *ubi stat miles armatus et clamat, Ne accede* VR 562.3; *in altiori...loco ...steti* ES 2240. **3** (of things) To be located, be placed, stand: *quintum gymnasium in ipsa umbra vesperae stetit* VR 136.1; (fig.) *inde totalis damnatio ante fores stetit et imminuit* VR 3.1. **4** To remain motionless, stand still: *et stetit sol in medio coeli* Josh. 10.13 (AE 401.18); (of warriors) to stand firm (in battle): *non stabunt in bello in die irae Jehovae* Ezek. 13.5 (DD 4); to remain inactive: *quod homo...non stet in fide impotentiae, et exspectet ut Deus...peccata abstergat* VR 71.2. **5** To be firm (in a resolution or opinion): *et stetit omnis populus in foedere* 2 Kgs. 23.3 (AC 6804.7); *qui...pro Trinitate Divina in tres personas divisa stant* VR 17.1.

stola ~ae, *f.* (Gk.) A long outer garment, robe: *induti ~is albis* Rev. 7.9 (AR); ES 710.

stolide, *adv.* Insensitively, dully: *fiunt vel sicut muti, vel loquuntur ~e* CI 3.

stolidus ~a ~um, *a.* Lacking quick perceptivity, dull, insensitive: *~us populus Meus, Me non norunt* Jer. 4.22 (AC 17); *et ille* [*vir*] *non sapiens est nisi sibi soli, et hic est ~us* AM 56.4.

stomachalis ~is ~e, *a.* Of or belonging to the stomach: *morbi ~es* VR 665.5.

stomachus ~i, *m.* (Gk.) (anat.) The digestive organ, stomach: *fastidit illos* [*cibos*] *~us* AM 6.4; *~us biliosis differtus* VR 42.2; (also, dist. from **ventriculus**) the oesophagus: *quod cibum...devolvat in ~um, et sic in ventriculum* DP 996.14.

storax ~acis, *m.* (Gk.) A fragrant gum: *cera aromatica, quae sicut ~ax* AC 5621.1.

storge ~es, *f.* (Gk.) The love of parents for their children: [*innocentia*] *facit amorem qui vocatur ~e* CI 277.4; *ex amore ~e exaltato* AM 109; ES 1201.

strabismus ~i, *m.* (Gk.) Squinting: *fides lusca... comparari potest cum vitio oculi quod vocatur ~us* VR 346.2.

strages ~is, *f.* Slaughter, massacre: *non ovat* [*dux exercitus*] *ex ~e hostium* CH 164 (= vii.[5]); *quali anathemate et ~e percussi fuissent Judaei* VR 691.4; AM 426.

stragula ~ae, *f.* A blanket: *quod ~am intinxerit aquis* ES 2791 (2 Kgs. 8.15).

stramen ~inis, *neut.* Straw: *pabulum...est cibus quo pascuntur asini et sunt ~en et palea* AC 5495; *leo sicut bos comedet ~en* Isa. 11.7 (AE 761.17).

stramentum ~i, *neut.* Straw: *Rachel...posuit illos* [sc. *theraphim*] *in ~o cameli* Gen. 31.34 (AC); *macerias hic ex juncis, hic ex ~is* AM 477.5.

stramineus ~a ~um, *a.* Made of straw; (neut. pl. as sb.) straw-producing plants: *herbacea...non aliud sunt, ut et ~a* AC 7112.

strangulo ~are ~avi ~atum, *tr.* To choke to death, strangle: *non volebant admittere ut diceretur quod vellent interimere, sed ~are ac ita suffocare* ES 3583.

stratim, *adv.* In a stratified manner, in layers: *quod fila ... ~im componant duplici ac triplici ordine* AC 10163; *~im succedunt montium expansa* AE 410.2; ES 5781.

stratum ~i, *neut.* A blanket for sleeping on, bedding: *~um meum ascendit* Gen. 49.4 (AC); (pl.) *accumbendo, sicut reginae, ~is* AC 944; AE 237.10 (1 Chron. 5.1).

stratus ~a ~um, *a.* (pf. pple. of **sterno**) (in senses of vb., esp.) Surfaced, paved: *terunt ~am viam* AM 380.1; *super pontem ~um longum* ES 4713.

stravi: pf. of **sterno**.

strenue, *adv.* Vigorously: *quatuor turmas spirituum, qui ~e confirmabant quod...* VR 159.2.

strenuitas ~atis, *f.* Briskness, energy, vigour: *viri ~atis* Gen. 47.6 (AC); AC 164.

strenuus ~a ~um, *a.* Vigorous, energetic: *defensores ~i fidei* ES 9383; (of sounds) shrill, bright: *cum instrumentis soni...vocis ~ae et vocis blandae* AM 17.1.

strepens ~ntis, *a.* Noisy, clamouring: *turbae ~ntes* ES 2856.

strepitus ~us, *m.* Meaningless sound, noise, din: *sicut ~um maris* VR 71.1; *magna erat copia [spirituum], sicut ex ~u...concludere potui* ES 243.

stria ~ae, *f.* A thin band, streak, stripe: *alis...aureis cum interspersis ~is et guttis...argenteis* VR 71.1; *~ae lucidae...sicut ~ae inflexae fulminis* ES 928.

striatim, *adv.* In streaks: *radii ~im transmicabant illas* [sc. *nubeculas*] AM 315.1.

striatura ~ae, *f.* A pattern of bands of light, striation: *qui in pariete vident ~as* DP 318.7.

striatus ~a ~um, *a.* **1** Having bands of different colours, striped: *apparuerunt in vestibus ~is ex lino* UJ(C) 77; *instar tenuis pluviae ~ae* AC 7747; *callositas eorum apparet...intus sicut ex tendinibus ~a* CI 466. **2** (of sound) Varying in intensity, vibrant: *coelestium loquela... est molliter fluens, nihil asperum aut ~um, hoc est, sonorum* ES 1108; ES 1109.

stricte, *adv.* Strictly, closely: *qui...admodum ~e observant externa Ecclesiae* AC 1103.1; AC 1200; *~e occlusa tenentur [inferna]* AC 7879.

strictim, *adv.* Cursorily, summarily: *idcirco...mox praecedentia tam ~im...explicata sunt* AC 3596.1.

strictura ~ae, *f.* **1** The stripping (of a tree of fruit): *sicut ~a oleae* Isa. 24.13 (AE 313.12). **2** Poss. error for **striatura**; cf. DP 318.7: *vident in pariete ~as...assimilanda sunt phantasmatis ac ~is in pariete* AC 6400.1.

strictus ~a ~um, *a.* (pf. pple. of **stringo**) (compar. *~ior*, superl. *~issimus*) In senses of vb., esp. **1** Restricted in width, narrow, strait: *via...erat angusta seu ~a* CI 534.1; ES 4216. **b** (of sounds) close: *i et e [dant] sonum ~um* SS(P) 14 (= 4.2). **2** (of choice) Restricted: *nec datur electio nisi ~a et limitata ad domus quae cognoscuntur* AM 49. **b** (of meaning) strict, rigorous: *in lato sensu...in ~o...et in ~issimo* AC 6752.1; AC 9295.3; VI 91.

stridens ~ntis, *a.* (of sounds) Harsh, jarring, grating: *loquela ejus erat ~ns* AC 8021; *erat ~ns quasi murmur* ES 1319; *audiebam eorum ~ntes gyros* ES 3405.

strideo ~dere, *intr.* To make a harsh sound, grate, jar: *omnia falsa in mundo spirituali ~dent* CI 575; *sonus ~det et laedit aures* VR 111.1.

stridor ~oris, *m.* **1** A harsh sound, grating: *~ores disharmonicos* AM 424; ES 1319. **2** The noise made by grinding teeth together, gnashing: *~orem dentium* AC 4175.2; CI 245.

stridule, *adv.* With a harsh sound: *in qua [voce] est aliquid sonans ~e* AC 1759; ES 3544.

stridulus ~a ~um, *a.* (of sound) Harsh, grating, jarring: *sonum edunt ~um et discretum* AC 9926.8; ES 3544.

stringo ~ngere ~nxi ~ctum, *tr.* **1** To press closely, pull tight: *ex tunica ~cta ad thoracem* AM 78.4. **2** To unsheathe, draw (a sword): *~cti gladii* Ps. 55.21 (AE 537.10). **3** (of light) To impinge upon, strike: *ex flammea luce quae... ~ngit aulaea tabernaculi nostri* AM 75.7; *ut primum lux coeli oculos illorum ~nxit* AE 865.1. **4** To touch so as to cause pain, strike, hurt: *super bestia quae...hominem sibi insidentem dentibus ~ngit, lacerat ac dilaniat* CO 33.3; *quod...putor sicut cadaveris ~nxerit nares meas* VR 569.5; *in...fletu...exit aqua, sed amara et ~ngens* AE 484.3.

stropha ~ae, *f.* (Gk.) A curved mark, curl, twist: *scriptura constabat modo ex aliquibus literis alphabeticis cum ~is supra* AM 326.5.

structura ~ae, *f.* The manner of building, construction: *et erat ~a muri ejus jaspis* Rev. 21.18 (AR); *accesserunt discipuli ad ostendendum Jesu ~am templi* Matt. 24.1 (AE 220.9); ordered form, structure: *~a corporis* ES 3148; ES 3605.

strues ~is, *f.* A heap, pile: *constabat [desertum] ex ~ibus lapidum* AM 79.4; VR 45.2; ES 4563.

struo ~ere ~xi ~ctum, *tr.* To construct, build: *qui*

palatium ~it, primum coacervat materialia AC 6486; *palatia ~cta ex marmore* AM 76.3; *quod... [aves] arte ~ant nidos* VR 12.5.

studeo ~dere ~dui, *intr.* **1** (w. dat.) To apply oneself (to), concentrate (upon): *sunt [mulieres] quae...solum ~duerunt sibi et mundo* AC 831.1; *cum homo Verbo ~det* AC 7012; *qui...soli memoriae ~duerunt* CI 466; (w. internal acc.) *qui non aliud ~dent et cupiunt quam ut hominem exstinguant* AC 660. **2** (w. inf.) To devote one's energies (to), aim (to): *quam [sphaeram]...exuere ~dent* AC 1508; *quod revocare in memoriam ~dere mihi visus* ES 3573.

studiose, *adv.* Assiduously: *quae meretricatui ~e operam dederunt* AM 459.5.

studiosus ~a ~um, *a.* (compar. *~ior*) (w. gen.) Applying oneself (to), devoted (to): *inde fit amantior veri et ~ior boni vitae* AM 94; *orthodoxiae hodiernae ~i* NE 23; ES 230.

studium ~i, *neut.* **1** Application, zeal, ardour: *quod... summo ~o formarent candelabrum* AC 552; *intensissimo ~o conquirunt sibi opes* AC 4293.2. **b** *~o*, zealously, enthusiastically: *quae ~o et ex voluntate fiunt sunt talia quae egrediuntur ex corde* AC 8925; *si ~o incumbit suae operae* VI 39. **2** (w. gen.) Strong desire, enthusiasm, eagerness (for): *~um vitae secundum praecepta fidei* AC 4638.10; *ex ~o explorandi illa* AC 7074. **b** (w. *ut*): *incumbere animo et ~o, ut ea sciantur* AE 102.1; *dirigebat navem ~o ut perirent qui in navi* ES 2240. **3** The direction of interest towards a particular object, interest, enthusiasm: *qui...nullo ~o, ne quidem domestico, dediti fuerint, sed solum voluptati* AC 5723; *labores et ~a quae pro fine habent illa quae mundi...sunt* AC 7893; *quod liberos suos suo ~o ex coelo excludant* CI 344. **4** An object of keen desire or interest, pursuit: *~um nostrae aetatis fuit studium veritatum* AM 76.4; *est itaque [requies aeterna] aliquod ~um et opus ex quo excitatur...mens* AM 907.7. **5** (pl.) Intellectual pursuits, studies: *perceptum quod is deditus fuerit ~is* AC 1769.1; *qui ~is delectatur legit et scribit sicut prius* CI 461.2.

stulte, *adv.* Foolishly: *quod...qui ~e agit stultus sit* DP 321.3.

stultesco ~ere, *intr.* To become foolish: *sic... ~erent magis et magis* AC 2477.

stultitia ~ae, *f.* Foolishness, folly: *actualis ~a et fatuitas* AM 252; *loco intelligentiae et sapientiae est insania et ~a* AE 118.1; (as something uttered) *omne os loquens ~am* Isa. 9.17 (AC 1861.2).

stultus ~a ~um, *a.* Lacking intelligence, stupid, foolish: *sapientes illi sibi visi ibi fiunt ~i* AC 7749; *apud quinque virgines ~as* AC 7778.4 (Matt. 25.2).

stupefactus ~a ~um, *a.* Stupefied, astonished: *ex his ~us dixi* AM 591.6; VR 72.2.

stupende, *adv.* In an astonishing manner: *omne...se fructificat et multiplicat...in altera vita ~e* AC 43.

stupendus ~a ~um, *a.* Astonishing, amazing: *cum ~a magnificentia et varietate* AC 1622.1; *cum ~o miraculo* AM 351.2; (neut. pl. as sb.) *quod...viderint et perceperint ~a* CI 411.

stupeo ~pere ~pui, *intr.* To be incapable of thought, be dull: *ex ignavia...et otio ~pet mens et torpet corpus* AM 249.2; to be astonished: *~pebis ad omnia* DP 3.3.

stupesco ~ere, *intr.* **1** To become dull or insensitive: *~unt aures nostrae...non auditur amplius vox* AM 9.2. **2** To become astonished: *quod... ~ant quando iis id monstratur* ES 792 titulus.

stupiditas ~atis, *f.* Lack of intelligence, stupidity: *in quo tam parum ex vita intelligentiae...ut dicas ~atem in effigie* AC 4221; an instance of this: *illi sunt obstipationes cerebri, et ~ates ei inducunt* AC 4054.2.

stupidus ~a ~um, *a.* (compar. *~ior*, superl. *~issimus*) Lacking intelligence, stupid: *spectant illos...ut ~os quia jugiter spectant ad se* CI 10; *quod homo ex sua natura ...omni bestia ~ior...sit* AM 151[a].4; (neut. as sb.) stupidity: *in singulis ejus cogitationis est ~um* AC 1040.2.

stupor ~oris, *m.* **1** Lethargy, stupor: *percutiam omnem equum ~ore* Zech. 12.4 (DD 4); *ex otio est mentis, et inde totius corporis, languor, torpor, ~or et sopor* AM 207.7. **2** Astonishment, amazement: *~ore perculsi sunt* AC 7077; *eram in ~ore de ingente multitudine hominum qui...* AM 380.1.

stuppa ~ae, *f.* (Gk.) Coarse flax, tow: *erit robustus in ~am* Isa. 1.31 (AC 1861.7); *quidam accendunt ~am* ES(M) 4551.

stuppeus ~a ~um, *a.* Of or resembling tow: *sic ut non facies, sed quoddam quasi ~um luridum* AC 816.

stupratio ~onis, *f.* An act of debauching: *~ones quae sunt violationes virginum* AM 459.5.

stupro ~are ~avi ~atum, *tr.* To induce (a woman) to have illicit intercourse, debauch: *uxores illorum ~abuntur* Isa. 13.16 (AC 3902.2); *cupidine...puellas parvas ~andi* ES 2711; *[uxorem] omni studio, vi et rapina conantur ~are* ES 3594.

stuprum ~i, *neut.* The sexual corruption of a woman, debauching: *commoverunt [aliquam uxorem] ad ~um* AC 2754; *qui pellexerunt virgines ad ~a* CI 462[a].4; *libido...cum virgine est ~um* AM 444[a].

Stygius ~a ~um, *a.* (Gk.) Of the river Styx, a river of hell in Greek mythology: *caeli...ex aquis ~is suffocantur* VR 119.3; (as typical of hell) *quod talia ratiocinia...sint*

~*a* AE 982.5.

stylobata ~ae, *m.* (Gk.) The horizontal member upon which a column or other upright rests, stylobate, plinth: *quibus haec innituntur sicut columnae suis ~is* AC 9163.4; *super solio, dum ejus ~ae auferuntur* VR 121.3.

stylus ~i, *m.* (spelling due to erroneous Gk. etymology) also **stilus**. **1** A pointed instrument for writing, stylus: *peccatum Jehudae scriptum est ~o ferri* Jer. 17.1 (AC 9416.3); (used as a weapon) *dolose homines occidunt, sicut ~is aut simili ferali instrumento* ES 1863. **2** A particular manner of expression, style in writing: *sunt in genere quatuor differentes ~i in Verbo* AC 66.1; *Verbum ...apparet sicut scriptum vulgare, ~o peregrino* SS 1.

suadeo ~dere ~si ~sum, *intr.* (*tr.*) **1** (intr., w. dat.) To persuade (someone): *~deo tibi emere a Me aurum* Rev. 3.18 (AR); (absol.) *prout calliditas ~det* AC 8247. **2** (w. acc.) To present persuasively, urge: *spiritus qui contraria ~dent* AC 7812; *in ea quae indoles eorum ~det* ES 295; (w. *quod*) *quod [modus] sit pellicatus, ~dent haec* AM 459.1.

suasio ~onis, *f.* The act of giving a suggestion or advice: *~o ad colendum alios deos* AC 3698.2.

suasus ~us, *m.* Persuasion, urging: *pelliciuntur [puellae] ad talia per ~us a laenis* AM 504.1; *Synodum Nicenam...Imperator Constantinus... ~u Alexandri... habuit* VR 632.1.

suaveolens ~ntis, *a.* Sweet-smelling, fragrant: *calor vernalis cum ~nte odore* AM 137.1.

suaveolentia ~ae, *f.* A sweet smell, fragrance: *discernit ignem...ab igne aromatis...usti ex ~a ejus* AM 439.

suaveolentus ~a ~um, *a.* = **suaveolens**; (neut. as sb.) a sweet smell: *ex quo [vase] aperto exspiratur ~um* VR 38.2.

suaviloquens ~ntis, *m.* Speaking sweetly, honey-tongued: *prae multis aliis... ~ntes sermonibus sunt* AM 514.1.

suavis ~is ~e, *a.* (compar. *~ior*, superl. *~issimus*) **1** Pleasing to the senses, sweet, pleasant: *~issimum melos* AM 55.1; *convivium vinorum ~ium* Isa. 25.6 (AC 2341.2); *odor [fimi] iis ~is est* ES 2901. **2** Pleasing to the mind, agreeable, sweet: *faciem et loquelam ~em praeferendo* AC 830; *in vita ~issima et dulcissima sunt* AC 5054; *in somnio ~i* ES 4133.

suavitas ~atis, *f.* Sweetness, agreeableness, pleasantness: *probitas per lenitudinem et ~atem in altera vita se manifestat* AC 8111; (w. pl.) an instance of this: *faciunt ut consortia inter sexus...sint ipsae ~ates caelestes* AM 44.3.

suaviter, *adv.* Sweetly, pleasantly: *loquuntur ~er* AC 4327.2; ES 634.

sub, *prep. w. acc.* or *abl.* **A** (w. acc.) **1** To (a position) underneath, beneath: *quod...dejiciatur...sub terram in infernum* VR 41.2; (fig.) *congerant frumentum sub manum Pharaonis* Gen. 41.35 (AC). **2** Towards the time of, around: *quod...surrexerint sub auroram* Josh. 6.15 (AC 728.5). **3** Under the control of, within the grasp of: *arcanum...quod...potest sub intellectum cadere* AS 221; ES 883; *[Dominus] redegit illud* [sc. *infernum*]*...sub Suam obedientiam* VR 2.2. **B** (w. abl.) **1** At a lower position, underneath, below: *in plano sub plantis* AC 6692.2; *patuit quod urbs sub urbe daretur* ES 5251. **b** (implying protection or exposure): *cubat sub pulchro velamento* VR 582.2; *Jehovah sub ala Sua obteget te* Ps. 91.4 (AC 8764.8); *...ara et pulpitum sub diu variis exposita violentiis* VR 55. **c** (implying subordination): *omne id extensum quod sub sole est* CI 89; *apud unumquemvis spiritum sub caelo* VR 30.1. **2** During the time of, under: *sub punitione dolos nexuit* ES 4461. **3** Subject to, under: *sub Ipsius conspectu et providentia* AC 1274; *quod non sub lege illa sint* VI 64; *vivit sub auspicio Domini* AS 252; *voluntatem sub ejus obedientia tenet* VR 588.1. **4 a** Under (a specified form): *sistunt sibi ideam Divini sub specie humana* AC 8705.5; *diaboli sub forma angelica* ES 5207. **b** under the form of: *sub Davidis ut regis persona...agitur de Domino* AC 66.2; *adorarunt aliquem deum sub imagine aut statua* CI 326; *in quas [opes] sub amicitia animum intendunt* ES 404.1.

subalternus ~a ~um, *a.* Of subordinate rank, minor: *amores ~os qui vocantur affectiones* DP 194.1; (masc. as sb.) a subordinate officer: *praesules Ecclesiarum...et inde ~i illorum* VR 644.

subcaelestis: see **subcoelestis**.

subcapitalia ~um, *neut. pl.* Something on which to rest one's head, pillow: *sumsit lapidem, quem posuit ~a sua* Gen. 28.18 (AC).

subcoelestis ~is ~e, *a.* also **subcaelestis**. Under the heavens: *quod redieritis in inferiorem hanc seu ~em terram* AM 10.1.

subdialis ~is ~e, *a.* Exposed to the sky, open-air: *inde eorum statuae ~es* AC 920.4.

subdiaphragmaticus ~a ~um, *a.* (anat.) Below the diaphragm: *provincia abdominis seu ~a* ES 3036.

subditus ~i, *m.* One who is under authority, a subject: *quod rex amet ~os* AM 34; VR 422.

subdivido ~dere ~si ~sum, *tr.* To divide further, subdivide: *in plures classes quas etiam ~debant* AC 7259.

subdivisio ~onis, *f.* A subdivision: *species innumerabiles...praeter ~ones plures* ES 906.

subdo ~ere ~idi ~itum, *tr.* To place (something)

under or below (something else): (w. *sub* + acc.) *qui non traderent collum suum sub jugum ejus, quod gladio, fame, et peste visitarentur, at qui ~erent collum suum, relinquerentur super terra* AC 3542.4.

subdole, *adv*. Deceitfully, craftily, slyly: *operatur ut ex instinctu et quidem ~e* ES 466; *insidiati sunt ~e* ES 727.

subdolus ~a ~um, *a*. Deceitful, crafty: *ex ~is ejus machinationibus* ES 1258; ES 4358.

subduco ~cere ~xi ~ctum, *tr*. **1** To take from underneath, draw up: *quod per corticem et librum ~catur succus* ES 251; to extract: *illa quae ibi confirmant per ignem amoris coelestis quasi sublimat et ~cit ac purificat usque in ideas spirituales* CI 356.2. **2** To withdraw from view, keep hidden: *utcunque satagebant cogitationes illi ~cere* AC 7746; *dejectis aut ~ctis oculis* AM 207.3. **3** (w. *ab* or *ex*) To make remote, withdraw (from): *cum ~cti a corpore erant* CI 119; *non potest homo a Domino ~ci ex proprio* SS 61.2. **b** (refl.) to withdraw oneself: *se ~cere in subtiliorem naturam* AC 960; *sic se ~cere quoad eam vicem* ES 415. **4** (w. *in* + acc.) To multiply (by): *computa ex uno semine millia, et ~c millia in millia decies, vigesies, ad centies* AS 318.1.

subductio ~onis, *f*. The act of taking away, withdrawal: *quandam speciem subtractionis seu ~onis* ES 300.

subeo ~bire ~bii (*or* ~bivi) ~bitum, *tr., intr*. **1** (intr.) To go up, climb: *spiritus mali...cupiunt...~bire in mundum spirituum* AC 1868.2; *descendebant in locum ex quo ~biverunt* ES 3387. **2** (tr.) To go underneath, submit to: *gens...quae non ~bivit jugum talis dominationis* DP 257.4. **3** (tr.) To undergo, suffer: *quod mali...~beant paenas* AC 7788; *~bire tentationes* AC 7861; *quod...pericula ~beant* AC 548.3; *sunt duo status quos homo post mortem ~bit* AM 47[a]. **4** (intr.) To present oneself, appear, come along: *et tunc alia ~beunt quae ministrant* ES 2477; *tunc solet tristitia ~bire* ES 972. **5** (intr., of ideas) To present themselves to the mind, occur: *cum loca excitantur, etiam ~beunt illa* [sc. those ideas] AC 6809; (w. *quod*) *tunc ~biit satis vive quod nullum alium...agnoscere possent* ES 169; (w. inf.) *~biit aliquid...proponere* ES 858.

subhalo ~are ~avi ~atum, *tr*. To emit (a gas, odour, etc.): *halitus faedi et putres ~ati ex apostematibus* AM 470.

subigo ~bigere ~begi ~bactum, *tr*. **1** To reduce to subjection, overcome: *de omnibus gentibus quas ~begit* 2 Sam. 8.11 (AC 6917.3); *magis proprium...remotum, ~bactum et in obsequium redactum est* AC 1042.2. **2** To knead, work (dough and sim.): *cessat excitator a ~bigendo massam ejus* Hos. 7.4 (AC 7356.2); *placentae melle ~bactae* Exod. 16.31 (AE 146.5).

subinde, *adv*. Repeatedly, time and again: *illorum...curam multam Dominus habet; et ad eos ~de mittit angelos* AC 1110; *certum est quod faeminae...~de repugnent* AM 512.2.

subintelligo ~ligere ~lexi ~lectum, *tr*. To contain as additional or hidden meaning, imply: *stylus propheticus est talis ut perplura ~lecta sint, quae ex verbis non apparent* 3AD 7704.

subintro ~are ~avi, *intr*. (*tr*.) To enter by stealth, steal in: *via inferior...per quam malum et falsum ~ant ab inferno* CI 430; *concupiscentiae...~ant...sicut in istius domus mansiones* VR 611.1. **b** (tr.): *haec* [*sphaera*] ... *~at ideas* VR 619.2.

subito, *adv*. Suddenly: *Dominus nusquam ~o, minus momento, destruere vult...cultum* AC 1992.4; CI 168.1; *~o aperuit se terra* AM 263.1.

subitus ~a ~um, *a*. Sudden: *variationes lentae fuerunt et ~ae* ES 215.

subjaceo ~cere, *intr*. To lie underneath: *quoniam haec* [*sol, calor et lux ejus, et athmosphaerae*] *sunt mortua, sunt etiam omnia et singula telluris, quae ~cent, et vocantur terrae, mortua* AS 158.

subjecte, *adv*. (superl. *~issime*) In the manner of a subject, submissively: *~issime obedire arbitriis illarum* [sc. *uxorum*] AM 292.1.

subjectio ~onis, *f*. Reduction in status, subjection: *abdicationem et ~onem omnium quae inserviunt Ecclesiae* AC 6143.

subjectum ~i, *neut*. **1** (in philosophy) That which is acted upon and is determined by something else, a subject: *quale ~um, tale praedicatum* AC 103; *voluntas est receptaculum et ~um omnium boni* VI 43.1; *lingua est ~um* [*gustus*] AS 41. **2** (in general) Any person or thing regarded as an object, member (of a class): *in ~is mortuis et in ~is vivis* AS 218; *in omnibus ~is trium regnorum naturae* VR 6.3. **3** A subject of discussion, topic, matter: *voces applicandae sunt suo ~o de quo agitur* AC 6844.1; *assumserunt primum ~um ventilationis* AM 132.3. **4** The name given to the emissary or representative of a community in the spiritual world: *fuerunt ~a integrarum societatum* AC 4403; AC 5856; CI 601.

subjicio ~jicere ~jeci ~jectum, *tr*. **1** To place as addition, add: *his ~jiciam duo memorabilia* AM 42.1. **2** (w. dat. or *sub*) To make subject, subordinate: *omnes qui se non ~jiciunt ei ut servos* AC 1594.3; *ne...sibi ~jiciant societatem* AC 7364; *ex omnibus visui ~jectis in mundo* DP 3.2; *Jehovah ~jiciet populos sub nos* Ps. 47.3 (SS 86).

subjugalis ~is ~e, *a*. Broken to harness, domesticated: (sb.) *super asina et super pullo filio ~is* Matt. 21.5 (AC 9212.5).

subjugatio ~onis, *f.* The act of bringing under control, subjugation: *de...illorum ~one a Philistaeis* AC 8093.1; *de ~one illorum* [sc. *infernorum*] DD 14.7.

subjugo ~are ~avi ~atum, *tr.* To bring under control, subdue, overcome: *implete terram et ~ate eam* Gen. 1.28 (AC); *mens ~ata...nullius voluntatis est* CI 380.2; *ut...inferna tunc dominantia ~aret* DD 3.2.

subjungo ~gere ~xi ~ctum, *tr.* To join on below or afterwards, append: *concioni ~xit votivam orationem* AM 24.

sublateo ~tere ~tui, *intr.* To lurk hidden: *contemtus, qui tametsi non apparet, usque ~tet* AC 2216.

sublatio ~onis, *f.* **1** The act of lifting up, raising: *~o et extensio manus* AC 878.5; *~o manuum mearum* Ps. 141.2 (AE 324.12). **2** The act of taking away, removal: *respirationis ~o per vices* AC 7810. **3** An offering lifted up, 'heave-offering': *armum ~onis* Exod. 29.27 (AC).

sublatus ~a ~um: pf. pple. of **tollo**.

sublestus ~a ~um, *a.* Weak, feeble: *quod trahunt ex ~is illorum dolis et incantationibus* CO 38.

sublevatio ~onis, *f.* **1** The act of raising, lifting up: *talis ~o cranii* ES 2468. **2** The raising of a person's spirits, encouragement: *ex significatione 'dare gratiam', quod sit ~o, in tentationibus enim 'gratiam dare' est consolari et spe sublevare* AC 5043.

sublevatura ~ae, *f.* A lifting up: *~a exterior capitis* ES 2469.

sublevo ~are ~avi ~atum, *tr.* **1** To lift up, raise: (in fig. phr.) *~at...se alternis* [*intellectus*] *sicut aquila* AM 495.2. **2** To encourage: *eos licuit ~are spe aliqua* ES 228.

subligaculum ~i, *neut.* A loincloth: *fecerunt sibi ~a* Gen. 3.7 (1AD 45).

sublimatio ~onis, *f.* The process of refining, purification, sublimation: *defaecatio...decantatio, ~o* AM 145.2; (transf.) *ex scientificis...fit quasi extractio, et si ita dicere liceat, quasi ~o* AC 5871.

sublimis ~is ~e, *a.* (compar. *~ior*, superl. *~issimus*) Lofty, grand, sublime: *ipsi philosophi etiam ~iores* AC 1919.4; *~iora...quam usquam mentes humanae capere possent* AC 1769.2; *stylo peregrino, non ~i nec lucente* SS 1.

sublimitas ~atis, *f.* Loftiness, sublimity: ES 4826.

sublimo ~are ~avi ~atum, *tr.* To refine, purify: *sicut ignis in retortis acuit, clarificat et ~at materias* VR 141; *quomodo cerebrum sanguinem ~at* DP 336; (transf.) *omnis idea hominis, etiam ~ata, est substantialis* AM 66.

sublunaris ~is ~e, *a.* Of or belonging to this earth, sublunary: *distantia quae apparet in ~i orbe nulla est in coelo* AC 1999.3.

submergo ~gere ~si ~sum, *tr.* To cause to plunge below the surface of water, submerge, sink, drown: *et electio ducum... ~si in mari Suph* Exod. 15.4 (AC); *aves quae super magno oceano volant...decidunt et ~guntur* VR 67.1; *...a procella...quae navem... ~get* VR 32.9.

submersio ~onis, *f.* Submersion, drowning: *per ~onem eorum in mare Suph* AC 6589.1; AC 8261.3.

subministro ~are ~avi ~atum, *tr.* To provide as a servant, supply: *memoria...propius ~at cogitationi objecta sua* AC 6814; *ex inductionibus quas ratio nobis ~avit* AM 182.6; *supplicantes...ut iis victus ~etur* ES 692.

submisse, *adv.* Submissively: *erga quem se... ~e gerit* AC 5066.

submissio ~onis, *f.* Self-abasement, submission: *'et incurvabimus nos' quod significet ~onem constare potest absque explicatione* AC 2794; ES 170.

submissus ~a ~um, *a.* (pf. pple. of **submitto**) (in sense of vb., esp.) Submissive: *eorum... ~am introductionem* AC 4361; *vel elati vel ~i* AC 7372.

submitto ~mittere ~misi ~missum, *tr.* (w. dat.) To make subject (to): *quia amor...disponat illa* [*vera*] *in ordinem ac ita ~mittat Domino* AC 6366; *dum...sensui literae...sensus internus... ~mittitur* AE 17; (esp. refl.) to submit: *quod se ~miserit* [*falsum*] AC 172; *quomodo potest ille, qui est imperator imperatorum, ita se ~mittere...?* AM 264.1.

submoveo ~vere ~vi ~tum, *tr.* also **summoveo**. To move out of the way, get rid of: *ut itaque ~veretur infernum...Dominus...venit* VR 579.2; *discordantiam apparenter ~tam* AE 786.1.

subnecto ~ctere ~xi ~xum, *tr.* To append, add on, subjoin: *quae...videas...et praemissa et ~xa unicuivis capiti* AC 1885.

subnervo ~are ~avi ~atum, *tr.* To hamstring: *quod equi ~abuntur* 3AD 4539.

suboles: see **soboles**.

subolfacio ~facere ~feci ~factum, *tr.* To perceive by smell, catch a sniff of: *ut...dum quasi ~faciunt quod inde bonum, illico illud* [*in malum*] *vertant* ES 3047.

subordinatio ~onis, *f.* Arrangement in descending rank, subordination: *sunt nempe dominationes et sunt ~ones* AC 7773; *in obedientia et ~one* CI 321.

subordinatus ~a ~um, *a.* (pf. pple. of **subordino**) Arranged in descending rank, subordinated: *omnia in coelis... ~a sunt* CI 389; *ei* [sc. *duci*] *praefecti ~i* VR 10.

subordino ~are ~avi ~atum, *tr*. (w. dat.) To make subordinate (to): *cum...sensuale conjunctum est cum interno, seu rite ~atum rationali* AC 6949; *ut...sic naturalia ~entur spiritualibus* AC 7990; *ut* [*alter*] *suis desideriis ~etur* AM 282.2. (n.b. *subordinati* in ES [6101.4] may be erroneous; perhaps *subornati* should be read.)

suborior suboriri subortus sum, *intr*. **1** (of the sun) To be about to rise: *in diluculo suboriente sole* VR 110.1. **2** To come into being, arise: *sensi anxietates ab illis subortas* CI 299; *statim suborta suspicio* ES 1260.

subpingo ~ngere ~nxi ~ctum, *tr*. To colour slightly: *amor... ~ngit faciem virginis nubilis quadam flamma* AM 382.

subrepo ~ere ~si, *intr*. To move stealthily, creep: *ex struibus lapidum...e quibus ~serunt hydrae et echidnae* AM 79.4; VR 57.1; (fig.) *insaniae quae ex frigore illo ~unt in cogitationes* AM 241.

subrideo ~dere ~si, *intr*. To smile: *ad hoc ~serunt angeli* AM 232.2; to express amusement: *quidam voce ~dente dixit* AM 105.

subruo ~ere ~i ~tum, *tr., intr*. **1** (tr.) To undermine: *hoc* [sc. *muro*] *sub pedibus ejus ~to cadit* VR 600; ES 5039. **2** (intr.) To collapse: *quae* [*columna*] *si avelleretur, ~eret illa sicut domus in qua fuerunt satrapae Philisthaeorum* VR 627.

subsannatio ~onis, *f*. Mocking, ridicule: *sic exponerer eorum ~oni* AC 448.2; CI 506.2.

subsannator ~oris, *m*. One who mocks: *~ores Divinae Providentiae* DP 208; ES 594.

subsanno ~are ~avi, *tr*. To expose to ridicule, mock: *quod... ~ent illa quae sunt sensus interni Verbi* AC 1877; *vera ~are* AC 7356.1; (absol.) *quotiescunque audiunt aliquem...apud se ~ant* AC 6907.2; *his ~ando addiderunt* AM 79.8.

subscribo ~bere ~psi ~ptum, *tr*. **1** To write underneath: *scio quod haec... ~pturus sit* [*angelus*] DP 213; *~bite initialem literam regni* AM 103.4. **2** (w. dat.) To give support (to), endorse: *quod...horum judicia allegent in copia et ~bant alicui* VR 814.

subsellium ~i, *neut*. A bench: *~a super quae congregati se reposuerunt* VR 503.1; (fig.) *illa quae... vocantur naturalia faciunt ~um illorum* AM 130.2.

subsequens ~ntis, *a*. Following in order, subsequent: *in versu ~nte* AC 1091; VI 22.

subsequor ~i ~utus sum, *tr., intr*. **1** (tr.) To follow: *virtus bona eorum opera semper antecedit, et comitatur, et ~itur* SE 5(e). **2** (intr.) To come next in sequence, follow: *quae violatio, quomodo fit, et a quibus, ex his quae ~untur aliquantisper patet* AM 517.

subsidentia ~ae, *f*. Lowering in position, dropping, subsidence: *hoc fit per ~am et appropinquationem caelorum* AR 343.1.

subsidium ~i, *neut*. Assistance, support: *mulos dederunt ~is tuis* Ezek. 27.14 (AC 1154).

subsido ~sidere ~sidi (*or* ~sedi), *intr*. To fall gently, sink down, subside: *in domo, cui non est fundamentum, quae... ~sidit* CI 528; *sicut columna graduum ~sidens fit corpus cohaerens in plano* SS 38.1; *sicut qui...in motu terrae ~sidens in statu absorptionis est* VR 31.2; *~siderunt...in sua inferna* AM 264.3; *~sederunt in terram portae* Lam. 2.9 (AC 5044.10).

subsilio ~lire ~lui, *intr*. To jump up and down, skip: *quare ~litis, montes...?* Ps. 68.16 (AE 405.13).

subsistentia ~ae, *f*. Continuation in existence, subsistence: *~a est perpetua existentia* AC 775.2; *~a seu conservatio* AM 86.

subsisto ~ere substiti, *intr*. **1** To remain in one's place, stay still, stop: *elongabant se adhuc magis, at usque ~ebant* AC 6811; *sublatus sum...in mansionem intimioris coeli, ubi...aliquantisper ~ere potui* ES 299. **2** To cease functioning, stop: *si hoc fieret, ~eret utrumque* [sc. *cor et pulmo*] VR 154.3; *si auferretur... hoc liberum homini, numne cogitatio ejus ~eret...?* VR 497.1. **3** To cease advancing (beyond a specified stage of development), stop: *quod nequaquam conveniat homini...in solis cognitionibus ~ere* AC 6815; *Divinus ordo nusquam ~it in medio* CI 315; *amor sexus...potest ~ere in facie faeminae* AM 55.4. **4** To continue in existence, remain, subsist: *~ere est perpetuo existere* CI 9.1; *amor et sapientia existunt et ~unt in usu* AM 16.3; *nomen personae significat...quod proprie ~it* VR 17.3.

substantia ~ae, *f*. **1** (in philosophy) The underlying constituent which receives attributes, substance: *quod ~a, quae ~a, sit modo unica et quod reliqua sint formationes inde* AC 7270.4; *~am simplicem Wolffianam* VR 90.2. **2** The basic constituent which characterizes a person or thing, essential quality: *voluntas est ipsa ~a hominis, seu ipse homo* AC 808; *humana Ipsius* [*Domini*] *~a seu essentia* DD 35.11. **3** A particular form of matter, substance: *subtilia organica, ~ae corticales dicta* AC 501; *aurum arte factum...non est bonum, non enim ~a auri in eo est* VI 10; *anima... obvelata ~is ex purissimis naturae* AM 183.4. **b** (in the spiritual world): *cum sola differentia quod ~ae et formae, quae sunt amor et sapientia, non existent coram oculis* AS 42.

substantialis ~is ~e, *a*. Composed of substance: *quod putatur existere absque subjecto ~i, hoc nihil est* CI 434; *Humanum ex Patre, quod in se simile Divino Suo et sic ~e* DD 35.2; (as opposed to **materialis**) *homo spiritualis seu ~is...homo naturalis seu materialis* AM 31. **b** (neut. as sb.): *quia separant illam* [sc. *cogitationem*] *a ~i, concludunt quod evanitura sit cum corpus exspirat* AC 196.3; *ipsum...Divinum Verum est unicum ~e* AC 7004.2; *est... ~e primitivum materialis* VR 79.7.

substantialiter, *adv.* In the manner of substance: *cum verum hoc influit in...primum coelum...recipitur ~er* AC 4411.

substantiatus ~a ~um, *a.* Given substance, substantiated: *sunt illae* [sc. *affectiones et perceptiones*] *~ae* AM 361.1; *~a et materiata* VR 30.2.

substantivus ~a ~um, *a.* That can stand alone; (neut. as sb.) a noun or a word playing the role of a noun, substantive: *numeri...in Verbo significant quale rerum cum quibus copulantur...sunt sicut quaedam adjectiva copulata ~is, aut sicut quaedam praedicata adjuncta subjectis* AR 738; AR 10.

substerno ~sternere ~stravi ~stratum, *tr.* To spread or place underneath: *dura mater...non supersternitur, sed ~sternitur iis* ES 1691; *quia sensualia interioribus ~strata sunt* AC 9214; *pedibus meis postea ~strati sunt* ES 169.

substituo ~ere ~i ~tum, *tr.* To put in place of something, substitute: *ubi haec trinitas ~ta est* DD 57; *~endo falsos testes* AE 160.1 (1 Kgs. 21.10).

substitutio ~onis, *f.* The act of putting one thing in place of another, substitution: *~o loco prioris* AC 9186.1.

substratio ~onis, *f.* Possibly error for **substructio**: IM 41.

substratus ~a ~um: pf. pple. of **substerno**.

substructio ~onis, *f.* A foundation course of a building, footing: *tres ~ones erant* [*templi Hierosolymae*] AC 655.2; *~o erat sub terra* AM 78.3.

substruo ~ere ~xi ~ctum, *tr.* To provide with foundations: *palatium...structum ex porphyrite, et ~ctum ex jaspide* AM 12.1; AM 315.1.

subsultim, *adv.* In a jumping fashion, in hops: *in altum se attollit, et sic ~im per vices* AM 495.2; *quod ~im vadant* ES 567.

subsulto ~are ~avi, *intr.* To jump, leap: *~ant super caput alterius* AC 822.

subsum subesse subfui, *intr.* To be underneath, underlie: *vitae expers quod subest...non apparet* AC 8250.1; *si malum subest* CI 132.

subtego ~gere ~xi ~ctum, *tr.* To form a covering beneath: *quod...succrescat infernum in tantum ut ~gat totum coelum angelicum* CO 12.

subtendo ~dere ~di ~sum, *tr.* To spread underneath: *eorum sphaera activitatis...se ~debat ad sinistrum latus* ES 3584.

subtensio ~onis, *f.* (in architecture) The lower part of a capital: *super qua* [sc. *columna*] *est coronamentum, sub hoc teres ~o* CO 17.1.

subter, *adv.* and *prep. w. acc.* **1** (adv.) At a lower level, below, underneath: *uxor amicta erat toga purpurea, et ~er tunica pectorali* AM 75.4; *ubi divites habitant ~er vel intus in illis* ES 5291. **2** (prep.) To below, underneath: *sumserunt lapidem et posuerunt ~er illum* Exod. 17.12 (AC); so, *ad ~er*: *clamabitis vir ad socium suum, ad ~er vitem* Zech. 3.10 (AC 488.2).

subterfugio ~gere ~gi, *tr.* To escape by stealth, evade: *cognitio illius se abscondidit ac ~git indagationes* AM 83.

subterraneus ~a ~um, *a.* Underground: *antra ~a* CI 586; *cellis ~is* ES 384 titulus.

subthoracicus ~a ~um, *a.* Under the thorax: *respirationem ~am* ES 445.

subtilis ~is ~e, *a.* (compar. *~ior*, superl. *~issimus*) **1** (of nets and sim.) Having a close mesh, fine: *involvebatur ~i reti* ES 745; (fig.) *per tam ~es transennas ...inspicere* VR 17.4; (of a microscope) having high resolution: *microscopio ~issimo* ES 2543. **2** Composed of very small particles, finely divided: *in cujus* [sc. *solidi*] *medio...sunt partes ~issimae...et in extremis... crassiores* AS 205; [*sensus cutis*] *imbibunt ~issima mundi* ES 1738; *aliquod ~e sicut effluvium* VR 585.4. **3** Capable of acute perception, penetrating, keen: *quod non aliquis tam ~i et limato ingenio sit, ut dispicere possit quid anima* AM 315.8; *ex ~issima et homini imperceptibili...imaginatione* ES 301. **4** Displaying acute perception, sharp: *quod homines...videant haec quae scripta sunt sicut ~ia et elevata* AC 6929; *undans eorum idearum loquela erat tam ~is ut mirarer* ES 3512. **5** Crafty, cunning: *~i dolo* AC 947; *in negotiis suis sunt ~es* AC 4630.

subtilisatio ~onis, *f.* The act or process of refining: *naturale nusquam per ~onem potest approximare ad spirituale* VR 280.2.

subtiliso ~are ~avi ~atum, *tr.* To render fine, refine: *in tantum ~ati erant ut vix eam* [*sphaeram*] *perciperem* ES 3512.

subtilitas ~atis, *f.* A subtle argument, subtlety: *post ~ates inaniter agitatas* AM 111; *extra ~ates illas video in clara luce quod...* VR 17.4.

subtiliter, *adv.* (compar. *~lius*) In a manner hard to perceive, subtilely: *qui influunt ~liter* ES 3466; penetratingly, acutely: *~lius et acutius possunt de illis loqui* AC 4214.2.

subtractio ~onis, *f.* Withdrawal, removal: *cum remotione affectionum et ~one cogitationum ab aliis* AC 7745; *viderunt...quosdam deliros oculis ex perpetua ~one illorum* AM 9.2.

subtraho ~here ~xi ~ctum, *tr.* To take away, withdraw: *alicubi se ~hit* ES 1697; (transf.) *quod... ~hant arte cogitationes suas ab aliis* AC 7745; *~xerunt se a praestigiis mundi* AM 155.3.

subtriplicatus ~a ~um, *a. Potentia ~a*, the power of one third (i.e., the cube root): VR 168.

subtus, *adv.* In a lower position, underneath, below: *benedicet tibi benedictionibus coeli desuper, benedictionibus abyssi jacentis ~us* Gen. 49.25 (AC 3969.6).

subula ~ae, *f.* An instrument for making small holes, awl: *perforabit dominus ejus aurem ejus ~a* Exod. 21.6 (AC); *omnis dictio contra id est...sicut ~a perforans aures illorum* VR 110.1.

subundatio ~onis, *f.* The sinking (of a ship): *ex ~one [navis] pereunt navarchae cum mercibus* CO 57.3.

suburbanus ~a ~um, *a.* In the vicinity of a town, suburban: *domos ~as* ES 3500.

suburbium ~i, *neut.* **1** An inhabited area surrounding a town, suburb: *Templum...cum atriis, conclavibus, ...~is* CI 197.2 (Ezek. 48); *est urbs antrorsum ad dextrum...sunt ibi ~a etiam* ES 4699. **2** An underground town: *urbs intra montem magna...sub illo ~o non erat alia urbs* ES 5270; ES 5273.

subvenio ~nire ~ni, *intr.* To come up, rise: *chylo ~nienti per ductum thoracicum* ES 831.

subversio ~onis, *f.* A turning upside down, inversion: *cum subiret similiter ~onem* ES 4366.

subverto ~tere ~ti ~sum, *tr.* To turn upside down, confound: *Jehovah...~tit cogitationes populorum* Ps. 33.10 (SS 86).

succedaneus ~a ~um, *a.* Succeeding, successive: *status mutationes...ordine ~o procedunt* AM 190.

succedo ~dere ~ssi, *intr.* **1** To come later in time, follow, succeed: *de Ecclesia Antiquissima, principali et parente reliquarum et ~dentium* AC 491; *~dente tempore* AC 8118.3; *post haec ~ssit altera ventilatio* SE 120.10. **2** To come after in order, proceed in sequence: *quae tentationes apud regenerandum ~dunt* AC 734; *omnia illa...~dunt ordine, ita ab intimo usque ad extimum* AC 6451.2; (w. dat.) *coelum quod ei [coelo] ~dit* AE 283.2. **3** To appear as a replacement, succeed: *loco perceptionis ~ssit conscientia* AC 573; *cessarunt miracula manifesta et ~sserunt miracula quae homini ignota sunt* ES 2434. **4** To advance towards completion, progress: *cum opus ~sserit usque ut fides conjuncta sit amori* AC 63; *quod omnia bene ~dant* AC 972. **5** To proceed well, go well, succeed: *cum videt quod ~dant machinationes* DP 237; (w. dat.) *ex eo quod talia ~sserint iis* AC 947; (impers.) *quod ~dat malis secundum artes* AC 10777.

succendo ~dere ~di ~sum, *tr.* To set on fire, set alight: *~dentur ambo pariter, et nemo exstinguens* Isa. 1.31 (AC 1861.7).

succenseo ~sere ~sui, *intr.* To be angry: *~sent si quis aliud cogitat* AC 2077.2; (w. dat.) *quis ~set captivo, qui se vindicat cum potest?* AM 79.5.

succenturiatus ~a ~um, *a.* Auxiliary, subsidiary: *quod quaedam animalia...bina quasi ~a cerebra... habeant* AC 4407; *sol mundi naturalis creatus est, ut ~am opem ferat* AS 153.

succenturio ~are ~avi, *intr.* To assist in a secondary capacity, act as auxiliary: *ex amore naturali... ~antibus sensibus corporis ejus* CC 15.5; (w. dat.) *ex calore corporis qui ex calore ejus spiritus exsuscitatur, et ei ~at* CI 567.1.

successio ~onis, *f.* **1** A following in order, succession: *illam ideam de ~one rerum habent* AC 10099.2; *secundum ordinem ~onis* AM 18.3. **2** A succeeding thing or stage, replacement: *quod continuae ~ones sint a Primo* AC 7270.3; *omnia...in universa natura...sunt derivationes et ~ones* AC 8603.2.

successive, *adv.* In a series of stages, successively: *homo...se ~e removit e coelo* CI 252; *ex frigoribus ~e post conjugium innatis* AM 234.

successivus ~a ~um, *a.* **1** Following after, succeeding: *de ejus inchoamentis et ~is statibus* AC 6713; *derivata non sunt nisi quam formae ~ae inde* AC 7004.2; (neut. as sb.) a succeeding state: *vitae ~um hic est elevatio ad interiorem...vitam* AC 7016; *quod nec detur identitas duorum effectuum in ~is in mundo* VR 32.1. **2** Arranged in sequence, successive: *~i status Ecclesiae...a principio ad finem ejus* SS 12.1; *per ~as progressiones* AM 17.5; (neut. as sb.) *quomodo cum ordine in ~is se habet* AC 7270.2. **3** (of order) Showing differences of degree, discrete: *prior ordo vocatur ordo ~us, hic autem simultaneus* AC 645.2; *quod mundus sit complexus usuum in ~o ordine pro humano genere* VR 13.2.

successor ~oris, *m.* One who takes another's place, successor: *in Petrum et inde in ejus ~ores* AE 114.9.

successus ~us, *m.* **1** The course, progress (of time, life, etc.): *sapientia illa antiqua ~u temporis decrevit* AC 6630; FI 49; *[ille amor] potest inscribi in ~u vitae* AM 531. **2** The fact of going well, prospering, success: *ex ~u omnia tribuerunt propriae prudentiae* AC 7296;

jucunditas ex ~u rerum CI 290; *pax...mundi est ex ~ibus ibi* AE 365.6.

succido ~dere ~si ~sum, *tr*. To cut down: (in quot. fig.) *vox Jehovae ~dens flammas ignis* Ps. 29.7 (AC 219).

succingo ~gere ~xi ~ctum, *tr*. To surround as with a girdle: *~gere Se Divino Vero et Divino Bono* AE 288.5.

succoth, *indecl*. (Hebr.) Transliteration of a Hebr. word for tents for slaves and animals: AC 4391.1.

succresco ~rescere ~revi, *intr*. **1** To increase in height, rise: *quod...inferna ~reverint in altum, usque ut implerent universum mundum spirituum* VR 121.1. **2** (of living things) To grow up, grow tall or long, increase: [*arbor*] *crescit et ~rescit* AM 185.1; *ibi ~rescunt sentes* VR 78.5; *illis* [sc. *capillis*] *~rescentibus* AE 66.2 (Judg. 16.22); (in mental qualities) *postea* [*Dominus*] *~reverit in intelligentia et sapientia* AC 7014.

succuba ~ae, *f*. A woman who sleeps with a man: *concubina est ~a lecti* AM 462.

succulentus ~a ~um, *a*. Full of juice, juicy: *concupiscentiae carnis comparari possunt cum torridis et ambustis uvis...at affectiones spiritus cum uvis ~is* VR 328.

succulus ~i, *m*. A fine liquid, juice: (in quot. fig.) *quomodo per putamen, ut ita dicam, novi insinuantur ~i* ES 1475.

succumbentia ~ae, *f*. The act or fact of yielding: *per ~am in statu tentationum* AC 8158.

succumbo ~mbere ~bui, *intr*. **1** To collapse, give away: *quidam deficientes anhelitu ~mbebant* VR 138.5. **2** To be overcome, yield the victory: *homo...paene semper ~mbit* AC 81.3; *qui in tentationibus ~buerunt* AC 7854; *is non vincit, sed ~mbit* AE 128.

succus ~i, *m*. also **sucus**. **1** The liquid found in plants, sap, juice: *cum fructibus, qui primum implentur ~o amaro* AC 3470.2; *~us arboris ut primum in frondem insitam influit* AC 7343.2; *sciunt illi* [sc. *vermiculi*] *se nutrire ~o ex suis foliis* CI 108.2. **2** Any fluid in living matter, juice: *in ciborum ~is* AC 5174; *ex cibo...evocant...fibrae nerveae suum ~um* SS 66.

suctio ~onis, *f*. The act of sucking: *ex continua ~one* [*infantis*] *in utero* AM 133.1; ES 1128.

sucus: see **succus**.

sudarium ~i, *neut*. A napkin: *ecce mina tua, quam habui sepositam in ~o* Luke 19.20 (AE 193.10).

sudo ~are ~avi, *intr*. **1** To perspire, sweat: *quod facies ejus incalescat et ~et* AM 363. **2** (fig.) To exert oneself violently, sweat: *quod mundus...sic ~aret in pulvere* AC 6326.2; *~avimus ibi in articulo de justificatione per solam fidem* VR 112.3; DP 241.2.

sudor ~oris, *m*. Perspiration, sweat: *factus...est ~or Ipsius ut guttae sanguinis* Luke 22.44 (AC 1573.5); (pl.) *per quas* [sc. *cuticulas*] *~ores...excernuntur* AC 5386; ES 364. **b** (as a figure expressing exertion): *in ~ore vultus tui edes panem* Gen. 3.19 (AC).

Suecanus ~a ~um, *a*. Swedish: *gens ~a* ES 5034.

suetus ~a ~um, *a*. Customary, usual: *~o eloquio...id defendit* DP 197.2; *ex ~is virorum nugis* AM 208.5.

suffero ~rre, *tr*. To tolerate, put up with: *quod spiritus praesentiam ejus* [sc. *angeli*] *non ~rre possent* AC 1398; (w. *ut*) *potest...~rre, imo amare, ut in intellectu sit* VI 45; ES 4079.

sufficienter, *adv*. Sufficiently: *quod omnis ordo procedat a primis ad ultima...ex cognitis et visibilibus in mundo ~er coram ratione potest confirmari ac illustrari* AM 311.2.

sufficientia ~ae, *f*. An adequate amount, sufficiency: *dantur illis opes in ~a* AM 250; adequate capacity or ability: *quod spiritualis illa ~a...nec defutura sit hodie* AM 433.

sufficio ~ficere ~feci, *intr*. To be enough, suffice: *si...hae* [*differentiae*] *recenserentur, non ~ficerent paginae* AM 291.3; (w. dat.) *ne forte non ~ficiat* [*oleum*] *nobis et vobis* Matt. 25.9 (AC 4635); (w. *pro*) *ut non ~ficerent volumina pro illis explicandis* AC 64; (w. *ad*) *Divinum Humanum...non amplius ~fecit ad sustentandum omnia* CI 101.

suffimentum ~i, *neut*. Incense: *et phialas aureas plenas ~is* Rev. 5.8 (AC 420.5); *unde erat quod ~um factum sit ex aromatibus fragrantibus* AE 324.1.

suffio ~fire ~fivi (*or* ~fii), *intr*. To burn incense: *et ~fiunt super lateribus* Isa. 65.3 (AE 324.19); *vanitati ~fiverunt* Jer. 18.15 (AE 411.28); *super montibus...~fierunt* AE 405.54.

suffitio ~onis, *f*. The burning of incense: *et facies altare ~onis suffimenti* Exod. 30.1 (AC).

suffitus ~us, *m*. The burning of incense: *altare aureum pro ~u* SS 46; *cum...~ibus fragrantissimis* AM 3.6; *~us ex thure* VR 108.

sufflamino ~are ~avi ~atum, *tr*. To apply a brake to, check, restrain: *cum...~antur* [*mali spiritus*] *ab amore sui et mundi* AC 4311.3; *bonum vel ~atur vel adulteratur* CO 12.

sufflatus ~us, *m*. A blowing, blast: *talia ludibria...~u risus abigimus* VR 80.3.

sufflo ~are ~avi ~atum, *intr*., *tr*. To aid as if by blowing, puff: (intr.) *cum amor sui et mundi ~ant* AC

362; *cum nihil lasciviae naturalis ~at* AC 829.1; *quoties idea...redit, spiritus mali ~ant* ES 4204; (tr.) *tale inhaerebat phantasiae, et a magicis aliis ~abatur* ES 4468.

suffocatio ~onis, *f.* Choking, suffocation: *exspiratio seu ~o eorum qui ibi* AC 662; (transf.) *captivitas et ~o cogitationum* AM 375.1.

suffocativus ~a ~um, *a.* Choking, suffocating: *talis persuasionis natura...est necativa seu ~a* AC 562; AC 581.1.

suffoco ~are ~avi ~atum, *tr.* **1** To stop the breathing of, stifle, choke, suffocate: *quod...videantur sibi non posse respirare, sed quasi ~ari* AC 3894; *quidam sicut inebriati, et quidam sicut ~ati* VR 72.2. **2** To stifle the growth of, choke (plants): *enatae spinae ~arunt illud* Luke 8.7 (VI 90); *humus jamdum sata... ~aret illa* [*semina*] VR 48.10. **3** To stop from acting, block, choke, stifle: *objecta quae ~ant lucem et pervertunt* AC 4320; *ut influxum Divini infringant, vel repellant vel ~ent* AC 8265.1.

suffragium ~i, *neut.* A vote: *quod...unanimis ~is illud decreverint* VR 634.2; *in judiciis colligebantur ~a per calculos* AR 121; (in fig. phr.) *quis non ex ~is per experientias collectis scit...?* CO 35.1.

suffragor ~ari ~atus sum, *intr.* To vote in favour, lend support: *si hoc diceretur, non ~aretur mere naturale lumen* AS 72; (w. dat.) *vera ~antia bono* AR 121; *hae experientiae ~antur illis qui dicunt...* AS 342.

suffulcimentum ~i, *neut.* A prop, support: *ultimum est quasi ~um interioribus* AC 9430.2.

suffulcio ~cire ~civi ~tum, *tr.* To prop up, support: *baculus instar pedis ~cit corpus* AC 6947; (transf.) *ex lite quae...tot ~ta fuit documentis experientiae* AC 6948.4; *Deus...adest ac ~cit* [*hominem*] VR 126.1.

suffundo ~ndere ~si ~sum, *tr.* To give a tinge to; (pass., w. abl.) to blush (for shame): *tanto pudore... ~si sunt, ut dicerent ad me ne hoc propalarem* AC 8544; VR 79.8.

suggero ~rere ~ssi ~stum, *tr.* **1** To provide, supply: *terra modo ~rit et latices et elementa* VR 491.2. **2** To put into mind, suggest: *spiritus mali...tot confirmantia ~runt ut non aliter videat* AC 1673.4; (absol.) *hae* [sc. *bestiae*] *feruntur a sensibus sui corporis, ~rente appetitu ac voluptate* VR 478.3.

suggestum ~i, *neut.* also **suggestus** ~us, *m.* (VR 697.9; abl. pl. *~ibus* VR 831). A platform for a speaker: *in medio orchestrae erat ~um ubi sedit vir sapiens* AM 315.2; (esp. in a church) a pulpit: *quid...e ~is frequentius praedicatur...?* VR 132.1.

suggestus: see **suggestum**.

sugillator ~oris, *m.* One who insults: *obtrectator aut ~or Verbi* BCP (VI 6).

sugillo ~are ~avi ~atum, *tr.* To insult, speak ill of: *~are et supplantare omne religionis* VI 31; *~avit illa* [*opera*], *vituperando et blasphemando* ES [6101.2].

sugo ~ere suxi, *tr.* To suck up (liquids): *affluentiam maris ~ent* Deut. 33.19 (AC 6745.2); *~es lac gentium* Isa. 60.1 (AC 6745.3); to suck at: *ubera regum ~es* Isa. 60.16 (AC 6745.3); (absol.) *quod modo sciat* [*infans*] *~ere* AM 133.1.

suillus ~a ~um, *a.* Of pigs: *amant sordes ~as* CI 488.4; *caro ~a*, pork: DP 254.4.

suisonus ~a ~um, *a.* Prob. erroneous reading, perh. for **suavisonus***: CN prologus.

sulcus ~i, *m.* A furrow: *quod...passus sit calamum suum arare ~um* VR 137.8.

sulfur: see **sulphur**.

sulfureus: see **sulphureus**.

sulphur ~uris, *neut.* also **sulfur**. Sulphur, brimstone (used to mean any highly inflammable material): *lignum gopher est lignum abundans ~ure* AC 643.1; *stagnum ignis ardens ~ure* Rev. 19.20 (AR).

sulphuratus ~a ~um, *a.* Treated with sulphur: *taedas ~as et bituminosas* AM 231.2.

sulphuree, *adv.* In a sulphurous manner: ES 5065.

sulphureus ~a ~um, *a.* also **sulfureus**. Of or resembling sulphur: *bitumen quia ~um et igneum* AC 1299; *fumus fornacis igne ~o mixtus* ES 4453.

sum esse fui, *intr.* (as in classical Latin; n.b. alternative impf. subj. *forem* as well as *essem*; imperative *esto*, *estote*, *sunto*; fut. pple. *futurus*, pres. pple. *ens entis*; alternative pres. pple. *essendo* AC 2226) **1** To have existence, exist, be: *Jehovah dicitur quia solus est aut vivit* AC 300; *si Ecclesia Domini...exstingueretur...genus humanum nequaquam potuisset esse* AC 637.1; *haec ita apparent sicut forent, sed sunt repraesentationes* ES 4214; *hoc internum erit, ut homo reformetur* DP 151.1. **b** *Sum*, (as divine title) I am: *Sum Qui Sum...Sum misit me ad vos* Exod. 3.14 (AC); *quod Jehovah siginificet Sum et Esse* VR 19.1. **2** (of events, processes) To take place, happen: *eo tempore fuit communicatio cum coelo* AC 6692.1; *cum dicere vellem quod in hac tellure sint bella* AC 8117; *si* [*influunt*] *in cogitationes est per affectiones* ES 4674; (impers.) *et erit, cum viderint te Aegyptii et dicent* Gen. 12.12 (AC). **3** (impers.) *Est*, there is, *sunt*, there are, etc.: *alioquin foret...repetitio* AC 1860.3; *sunt duo amores qui...generi humano irradicati sunt* VR 533.1; *est sicut horror invadat illos* VR 567.7; *est infernum antrorsum...ad distantiam* ES 4631. **b** (w. dat.) *est mihi* [etc.], I (etc.) have: *vitam quae est homini* VR 63; *non...ei religio est* VR 564.1. **4** (w. pred.) To be (as specified): **a** (w. adj. or sb.): *Aegyptii, qui hic sunt populus* AC 6692.1; *cum...angelis qui fuerant incolae ibi* AC 6695; *dicentes quod pessimus essem* AC 6811. **b** (w. prep. or adverbial phrase): *Ecclesia...apud illos fuerat* AC 6692.1; *cum in colloquutione...eram* AC 7745; *talis cooperatio est...in omni sensu* VR 577.3; *...quod forent sicut Deus* AC 204. **c** (Bibl., w. *in* + acc.) to turn into, become: *estote in viros* 1 Sam. 4.9 (AC 1343.4); *ero illis in Deum* Ezek. 37.27 (AC 6904.9); *erunt urbes refugii...in derelicta sylvae* Isa. 17.9 (DD 4); (so, w. *ad*) *tu eris illi ad deum* Exod. 4.16 (AC). **5** (as auxiliary vb. to form past tense of pass.): *ex quibus...confirmatus sum* DP 99; (also, w. pres. pple.) *videns fui in visionibus noctis* Dan. 7.13 (AC 1607.1).

summ-: see also **subm-**.

summa ~ae, *f.* **1** A total, sum: *cum sustuleris ~am filiorum Israelis* Exod. 30.12 (AC); *numerus tot hominum...in unam ~am collectus* CI 417.5. **2** A brief statement of a large subject, summary: *~a rerum traditur* AC 335; *collegi in ~am haec e loquela illorum* AM 183.2. **b** *in ~a*, in summary form, in brief: *agitur hic in ~a de Antiquissima Ecclesia* AC 290; *in ~a, quantum quis fugit mala ut peccata...tantum in charitate est* FI 23.

summarius ~a ~um, *a.* In condensed form, summary: *~a Expositio Doctrinae* SE titulus; *haec ~a etiam collata sunt cum Verbo in caelo* SS 97.5. **b** (neut. as sb.) a summary: *erant [illae leges] in brevi ~o complexus omnium religionis* VI 54; *fides in forma universali...praemittitur ut...sit ~um* VR 1.

summatim, *adv.* In summary form: *illustratur ejus primum...per haec ~im* SE 44.

summe, *adv.* In the highest degree, supremely: *quod illis ~e delectabile fuit* AC 403; *mens humana, etiam ~e analytica* VR 28.1; (w. sb.) *apud ~e hypocritas* AM 140.

summitas ~atis, *f.* The topmost point, summit, tip: *in ~atibus illorum* [sc. *montium*] *habitant* CI 207; *navis naufraga...super cujus mali ~ate stat nauclerus* VR 504.4; *circa hastae ~atem* ES 745.

summopere, *adv.* To the greatest extent, in the highest degree, extremely: *~e delectati sunt* CI 323; *licet ~e laboraverint* ES 154.

summoveo: see **submoveo**.

summus ~a ~um, *a.* **1** Highest in space: *termites versi sunt in aes nitidum, et ~i apices illorum in aurum* AM 77.7; (neut. as sb.) the highest point, top: *a ~o ad imum* AC 7774. **2** Highest in rank or status: *quod...crediderint in quendam ~um Creatorem* AC 7251; *~us sacerdos*, high priest: AM 266.1; *apud quos volunt ~i esse* ES 1822. **3** Extreme: *~us dolor* AC 8313.2; *~i adulteri* ES 4637; (neut. as sb.) the highest degree: *in ~o alicujus voluptatis* AC 541; *crescit...usque ad ~um intellectus* AS 237. **4** (neut. as sb., used as adv.) At the most: *dicebant...quod ~um 3 aut quatuor liberos habeant* ES 1679.

sumo ~ere ~(p)si ~(p)tum, *tr.* **1** To take hold of, pick up, take: *~e balsamum* Jer. 46.11 (AC 6729); *~ite vobis paleam* Exod. 5.11 (AC); *~ite quisque patellam* AM 16.1. **2** (w. ref. to source) To extract, derive, take: *homo ~tus de humo* AC 479; *aurum quod ~serat de gentibus quas subegit* AC 7770.5; *fidem sibi ~ere ex propria imaginatione* ES 257. **3** To take (vengeance): *quod... ~etur ultio* AC 8226.2; *vindictam ~et de hostibus suis* Jer. 46.10 (DD 4). **4** To take into use, employ, use: *nec usquam una [vox] loco alterius ~itur* AC 519.3; *terra pro ipsa voluntate hominis ~itur* AC 585; *non ~es nomen Dei tui in vanum* Exod. 20.7 (AC 6674.8); *Divinum...singulariter ~tum est Deus* VR 8.2. **5** To take into consideration, think about (an idea): *~e falsissimum* AS 267; *e regno animali ~e pisces maris* VR 32.3. **b** *simul ~(p)ti*, taken together: *societates...simul ~ptae* AC 7363; *angeli simul ~ti dicuntur coelum* CI 7.

sumptus: see **sumtus**.

sumtus ~us, *m.* also **sumptus**. Expense: *si ~us impendas hospitalibus* DP 326.8.

supellex ~ectilis, *neut.* (treated as if neuter, despite classical fem. gender; nom. pl. *~ectilia*, gen. pl. *~ectilium*) The movable furnishings of a house, equipment, household goods: *et oculus vester ne parcat super ~ectilibus vestris* Gen. 45.20 (AC); *horrea quae sunt ~ectilia illius* AE 336.7; (fig. in sg.) material for use: *confirmet se pro Divino, non deest ~ex* AS 357.

super, *prep. w. acc.* and *abl.*, and *adv.* **A** (w. acc.) **1** (expressing motion) To the top or surface of, onto: *omnis populus hic ~er locum suum veniet* Exod. 18.23 (AC); *descendit Jehovah ~er montem Sinai* Exod. 19.20 (AC); *quod illa [pluvia aurea] stillaret ~er aulam* AM 208.1; (fig.) *quod malum...relabatur ~er ipsos* AC 8223.3. **2** Across the top of, over: *dicitur...quod Jehovah vehatur ~er nubes* AC 8781; *caecus...qui...cadit ~er lapides* VR 90.2. **3** (w. no idea of motion) Close by, near: *omnis populus stans ~er te* Exod. 18.14 (AC); *habitationes illorum sunt a meridie ~er occidentem ad septentrionem* AM 77.1. **4** In authority over, in control of: *quod ordinati principes fuerint ~er mille* AC 8715; *potentia inferni valuit ~er potentiam caeli* VR 3.1; *erit Jehovah in regem ~er totam terram* Zech. 14.9 (VR 6.3). **5** With respect to, over: *judicium ~er eos* AC 1311.1; *et miserta ~er illum* Exod. 2.6 (AC); *absque ulla reflexione ~er differentiam* AC 10604.3. **B** (w. abl.) **1** In position on, on top of, on the surface of: *in mundo aut ~er tellure* AC 1361.1; *mimi ~er theatris*

DP 121.2; *planitiem... ~er qua positae erant mensae* AM 6.1; *~er cruce exclamavit [Dominus]* VR 104; *cum butyrum ~er pane ederem* ES 3894; (fig.) *sed ira Dei manet ~er illo* John 3.36 (VR 2.3). **b** *a ~er*, from upon: *removit Pharaoh annulum suum a ~er manu sua* Gen. 41.42 (AC). **2** By reason of, for: *et gavisus est Jethro ~er omni bono quod fecit Jehovah Israeli* Exod. 18.9 (AC); *eripe te ~er anima tua* Gen. 19.17 (AC). **C** (adv.) *Satis ~erque*, enough and more than enough: *quod significent persuasiones falsi...ostensum satis ~erque est ibi* AC 1673.1. (n.b. Other apparently adverbial uses may be regarded as part of compounds.)

superabundantia ~ae, *f.* Excessive quantity, superabundance: *qui ex ~a laborant aestro* AM 450.

superabundo ~are ~avi, *intr.* To be present in excessive quantities, be too abundant: *alioquin falsa ex malo ~arent* CI 540; *~anti sapientiae* AS 125.

superaddo ~ere ~idi ~itum, *tr.* To add in excess, pile on: *confirmat apud se id malum et quoque ex se ~it plura* NH 176; *quibus plures rationes ~ere non opus est* AM 276.2; *quod aliquid ~itum esset homini prae brutis* ES 3890.

superadjicio ~jicere ~jeci ~jectum, *tr.* To add on top: *ut prorsus supervacaneum sit aliquid ~jicere* AM 337; ES 662.

superbia ~ae, *f.* Pride: *super elationem animi... quae ~a vocatur* CI 555; a cause of pride: *dejicietur ~a Aschuris* Zech. 10.11 (AC 8185.2).

superbio ~bire ~bivi, *intr.* To display pride, pride oneself: *voluptates...quae sunt ~bientium* AC 6188.2; *qui ex scientiis ~biunt* AE 117.2; *ii qui ~biunt et phantasia se evehunt* ES 636.

superbus ~a ~um, *a.* (compar. *~ior*, superl. *~issimus*) **1** Proud, conceited: *erunt omnes ~i* Mal. 4.1 (CI 570); *ille prae omnibus... ~issimus interius fuit* ES 4748. **2** (of things) Indicative of pride, imposing: *palatia quae ~iora sunt quam usquam aliquis...sibi potest repraesentare* ES 2160.

supereminens ~ntis, *a.* (superl. *~ntissimus*) High-ranking, supereminent: *quod ~ns sapientia sit angelis* CI 266.2; *quae omnium societatum ~ntissima est* AM 263.2.

supereminentia ~ae, *f.* Supereminence: *sphaeram ~ae et auctoritatis contraxit* AC 1507.

supereminеo ~nere ~nui, *intr.* To be supereminent: *quisque ~nere vult et alteri auferre quae ejus sunt* AC 6832.9.

supereo ~rire ~rivi, *intr.* To go above, climb: *inde ~rire continuo affectant* ES 501 (J D Odhner; Autograph unclear).

superextendo ~dere ~di ~sum, *tr.* To spread above: *dura mater ~sa est* ES 1691.

superficialis ~is ~e, *a.* Superficial: *est sicut ~e, intra quod non aliquid est* AM 388.

superficies ~ei, *f.* **1** The outer boundary of a material object, surface: *quasi repunt in ~e hominis* AC 746; *opus cohaerens cum peripheriis a centro ad ~em* SS 38.1; *implerent ~em non modo unius telluris sed etiam plurium* VR 32.3. **2** The upper surface, top: *in ~e agri* Num. 19.16 (AC 6767.5).

superficietenus, *adv.* As regards the surface, superficially: *cum fructu ~us pulchro* DP 233.9; *[vera] non spectantur nisi extrorsum seu ~us* AR 436.

superfluo ~ere ~xi, *intr.* **1** To overflow: *mensura bona, pressa, agitata et ~ens* Luke 6.38 (AC 6960.3); *ad ejectionem spirituum infernalium ~entium in deserta* CI 594. **2** To be present in large amounts, abound: *quod falsitates adhuc ~erent* AC 875.1.

superfluus ~a ~um, *a.* Superfluous: *nusquam aliqua vocula est quae ~a et inanis* AC 734; *quod ~um sit dicere* AE 386.4.

supergredior ~di ~ssus sum, *tr.* To step beyond, overstep: *si quisquam ~deretur limitem* ES 4388.

super-illustris ~is ~e, *a.* More than brilliant, exceedingly bright: *super-regia magnificentia ac ~is splendor* AM 3.5; AM 7.1.

superimpono ~nere ~sui ~situm, *tr.* To place on top: *piscem ~situm foco* AC 7852.2; *Dominum...dejicere e throno et quendam suum clientem ~nere* VR 133.2; VR 336.2.

superinduco ~cere ~xi ~ctum, *tr.* **1** To cover with an outer layer, coat: *ex substantia lapidea... ~cta humo* AS 65; *ex lapidibus piceis, qui ~cti erant lamellis sicut vitreis* VR 35.2. **2** To induce in addition: *~citur iis sensus paene sicut corporeus* AC 969; *num amor conjugialis...possit separari, aut transcribi, aut ~ci* AM 317. (n.b. In VR 582.2 *superindueret* should probably be read for *superinduceret.*)

superindumentum ~i, *neut.* An additional garment, wrapper: *cum sola differentia quod accessorium, sicut ~um, ex sole mundi datum sit illis* AE 1218.3.

superinduo ~ere ~i ~tum, *tr.* **1** To put on (clothing) in addition: *sicut gremio foveret serpentem, et ~eret [superinduceret* 1st edn.] *vestem ne appareat* VR 582.2; (fig.) *quod Dominus...tertium illum gradum... ~erit* AS 234. **2** (pass. w. abl. or *cum*) To be clothed (with): *praeter quod non ~ti sint materiali corpore* CI 75; *ambulant...cum operculo laxo ~ti* ES 559.

superinfusio ~onis, *f.* A pouring (of something)

on (something else): *quid baptismus nisi ~o aquae super caput infantis...?* VR 667.

superinjectio ~onis, *f.* The act of throwing over, the draping: *~o veli* AC 963.

superinjicio ~jicere ~jeci ~jectum, *tr.* To throw on top, superimpose: *removebit obvelationes, si homo quas ~jeceret* CH 4 (= i.3); ES 3296; prob. reading in ES 1084.

superinsterno ~sternere ~stravi ~stratum, *tr.* To spread as a covering over, strew upon: (w. dat.) *quod pulvis ... ~stratus esset mari* UJ 61.

superinstructio ~onis, *f.* Superstructure: *fana... quorum substructio erat sub terra, et ~o supra* AM 78.3.

superinstructus ~a ~um, *a.* Built on top; (neut. pl. as sb.) superstructure: *ultimum planum cum ~is* AM 447.1.

superintego ~gere ~xi ~ctum, *tr.* To cover over: *id quod infossum est terrae ac ~ctum lapide* SE 107.

superinundo ~are ~avi, *intr.* (of water) To rise in flood, flood over: *inundatio aquarum validarum ~antium* Isa. 28.2 (AC 739.3).

superior ~or ~us, *compar. a.* **1** Higher in physical space, upper: *quoad ~orem partem corporis* AC 8373; *Deo...cujus robur in ~oribus nubibus* Ps. 68.34 (AE 36.4). **2** Previous in order, earlier: *ut in ~ore articulo dictum est* DD 8. **3** Higher in degree, superior: *verum aliquod ~us* AC 20; *prior seu ~or gradus* AC 6824; *cui...potentia ~or erat* DD 17.1; *angeli interiores et quoque ~ores* CI 22; *elevatio mentis in ~orem lucem* AM 184; (neut. pl. as sb.) *~ora, inferiora et infima Ecclesiae* SS 18.3.

superioritas ~atis, *f.* The fact or condition of being superior: *cum una [uxore]...foret...infestum ex velitatione de ~ate* AM 78.4; *primum Ecclesiae, cui prioritas et ~as* AE 434.6.

superirruo ~ere ~i, *intr.* To rush in as replacement or additionally: *si unum [infernum] superaretur, alterum ~eret* AC 1692.2.

superius, *compar. adv.* At a higher level, in the upper part, above: *Dagon...qui ~us fuit sicut homo, inferius sicut piscis* SS 23.2 (1 Sam. 5); *conjugium...unit animas, et mentes ~us ligat* AM 377.1.

superjaceo ~cere ~cui, *intr.* To lie on top: *vident focum positum, et pisciculum ~centem* John 21.9 (AC 7852.2).

superlativum ~i, *neut.* (in grammar) A superlative: *'valde valde', quod est ~um linguae originalis* AC 794.1.

superliminare ~is, *neut.* The lintel (of a doorway): *et accipient de sanguine, et dabunt super binos postes et super ~e* Exod. 12.7 (AC).

supernaturalis ~is ~e, *a.* Above the natural level, supernatural: *quod non aliquis possit comprehendere spiritualia...quia sunt ~ia* FI 3.

superne, *adv.* At the upper level, above: *fenestram facies arcae, et ad cubitum perficies illam ~e* Gen. 6.16 (AC); *per rimas ~e aliquid lucis...influit* CI 430.

supernumerarius ~a ~um, *a.* Additional to the fixed number, extra, supernumerary: *quod illis impossibile sit cogitare...de uxore aut foemina ~a* AE 1004.5.

supernus ~a ~um, *a.* Situated above, upper: *ad ~am palati regionem* ES 1181.

supero ~are ~avi ~atum, *tr.* **1** To be more powerful than, overcome: *cum actio ~at reactionem* AS 263.2; *tunc ~atura est mortales...anxietas* ES 218. **2** To be greater than, exceed: *aliquae [planetae] magnitudine ~ant hanc tellurem* AC 6697; *perfectio illorum immensum ~at perfectionem angelorum in medio coelo* CI 34.

superpondium ~i, *neut.* An excess weight, preponderance: *da modo ~um ab una parte* CI 592; *haec* [sc. *conjunctio mentium*] *tenet inclinationem sicut trutinam in bilance, et facit ~um* AM 318.1.

super-regius ~a ~um, *a.* Exceeding that of kings, super-royal: *~a magnificentia et super-illustris splendor* AM 3.5.

superscando ~ere, *tr.* To climb beyond, surpass, transcend: *amor qui omnes alios amores excellentia et amaenitate ~it* AM 333.1.

superscribo ~bere ~psi ~ptum, *tr.* To write above or at the top of (something): *super portis angelos duodecim, et nomina ~pta* Rev. 21.12 (AR); (neut. of pf. pple. as sb.) an inscription written above or at the top of (something): *si videret picturam unius Personae Divinae...cum ~pto, hic est noster Deus* VR 296.4.

supersedeo ~dere ~di ~ssum, *tr.* To dispense with, omit: *explicatio horum ~detur* AM 170; *haec... ~dentur et solum aliqua adducentur* AE 237.1; (impers. pass. w. inf.) *haec...singillatim explicare ~detur* AC 7231.1; CI 553.3.

supersterno ~sternere ~stravi ~stratum, *tr.* To spread over, overlay: *dura mater...non ~sternitur, sed substernitur iis* ES 1691.

superstes ~itis, *a.* Surviving, still alive: *manet usque radix in terra ~es* NE 22; *fuit...vix aliquid bonum et verum ~es* AC 637.2; *quae Ecclesia adhuc ~es erat* AE 443.7.

superstitio ~onis, *f.* A false religious system, superstition: *cum quibusdam e gente pontificia qui in illa ~one sunt* VR 824.2; *horum religio non fuit religio sed ~o* CO 51.2.

superstitiosus ~a ~um, *a.* Possessing a false

religion: *clamaret turbae ~ae* CO 54.2; (neut. pl. as sb.) false beliefs or practices: *facile abducuntur a ~is istius religionis* VR 821.1.

superstruo ~ere ~xi ~ctum, *tr*. To build on top of, found upon: *praeter quod talia etiam ~enda sint ideis veritatum naturalium* AC 3596.1.

supersubstantialis ~is ~e, *a*. Transcending material substance, supersubstantial: [*panis Sacrae Caenae*] *vocatur panis ~is* AR Doc RC.2.

supersum ~resse ~rfui, *intr*. **1** To be left over, remain: *hominem...internum, de quo parum ~rest* AC 270; *Ecclesia...in tantum consummata est ut vix aliquae reliquiae ejus ~rsint* VR 4.1. **2** To be left alive, survive: *nusquam aliquis homo hodie in tellure hac ~resset* AC 1673.2; *tantum in fluxio ~rerunt* [*ranae*] Exod. 8.7 (AC).

supertego ~ere, *tr*. To cover over: *per habitaculum significatur coelum...et per tentorium quod ~ebat illud, externum ejus* AC 9615.

supervacaneus ~a ~um, *a*. Superfluous, unnecessary: *singulos...gradus describere, et prolixum nimis et ~um foret* AC 789.

supervacuus ~a ~um, *a*. = **supervacaneus**: *quod apud illum...subtilitas ~is teratur* AM 315.8; 3AD 3102.

supervenio ~nire ~ni, *tr*., *intr*. **1** (tr.) To come upon, overcome: *~nit illos zelus* VR 48.6. **2** (intr.) To occur in addition, supervene: *quae* [*tentatio*] *si ~niret, gravior esset quam ut vivere possent* AC 270; CI 159.

supervivo ~vere ~xi, *intr*. To survive: *consolatio fuit quod ~veret et perstaret* [*Ecclesia*] AC 535.

supino ~are ~avi ~atum, *tr*. To throw on one's back, knock flat: *ibi ~antur ut caput oblique deorsum in linteis* ES 1203; (refl.) *se nudos ~averint super caput* ES 3717; (pf. pple.) *qui ~atus cadit* CI 510.

supinus ~a ~um, *a*. Lying on one's back: *projeci me ~um super humum* AM 10.4; *reversus ~o seu prono corpore, facie sursum* ES 753.

suppeditatio ~onis, *f*. The act of providing, supply: *per 'messem'* [*significatur*] *~o talium ibi quae applicuerunt* AE 811.28.

suppedito ~are ~avi ~atum, *tr*. To supply, provide: *signa quae ~arent illis recordationem* AC 1038.8; *quo... apes ~arent ceras pro luminaribus* AM 420.

suppetiae ~tiarum, *f. pl*. Aid, help: *qui ~tias fert bonis* AC 8120.

suppeto ~ere, *intr*. To be available, be sufficient: *rei familiaris amplificatio per opes...ut ~ant copiae* AM 274.

supplantativus ~a ~um, *a*. Treacherous: *~um cor prae omni, et desperatum id* Jer. 17.9 (AC 348).

supplanto ~are ~avi ~atum, *tr*. **1** To replace treacherously, supplant: *omnis namque frater ~ando ~at* Jer. 9.3 (AC 6756.3). **2** To make away with, oust: *sugillare et ~are omne religionis* VI 31; *quae... ~ant et proculcant* AM 231.4.

suppleo ~lere, *tr*. To make good (a deficiency): *angeli ...quae non vocibus loquelae suae exhauriunt, ~lent sono* CI 269.1; *~lere ignorantiam* ES 200.

supplex ~icis, *a*. Begging for mercy, suppliant: *quod ~ex sit* [*rex Sodomae*] AC 1740.1; *~ex esse voluit ad Dominum* ES 4314.

supplicatio ~onis, *f*. An appeal for mercy, begging, supplication: *sunt duo debita quae homini incumbunt facere... ~o et confessio* VR 539.1; *ad ~ones humiliores quam alii confugiunt* ES 149.

suppliciter, *adv*. With appeals for mercy: *spiritus ~er oravit ut liberaretur a carcere* ES 1259.

supplicium ~i, *neut*. Punishment: *quod homo damnatus sit ~o aeterno...sed quod...tandem auferatur damnatio, sed per vastationes et ~a* ES 2583.

supplico ~are ~avi ~atum, *intr*. (*tr*.) To make an earnest petition, appeal, beg: *qui ~at in humiliatione est* AC 7391; *~antes et adorantes illos venerunt* [*imperatores*] AM 265; (w. *ad*) *~abo ad Jehovam* Exod. 8.25 (AC); VR 73.2; (w. *ut*) *dum ~avit* [*Moses*] *ut videret gloriam Jehovae* VR 6.1. **b** (w. internal acc.) to utter earnestly, pray: *cum ~arem Orationem Domini* ES 3000. **c** (impers. pf. pass.): *de qua ~atum* AC 3061.

suppono ~nere ~sui ~situm, *tr*. **1** To substitute: *si ... ~neretur alius infans...loco genuini* AM 393.2; *tametsi loco Domini lignum ~ant* ES 536. **2** To suppose the existence of, imagine: *quod ~suerit opera inconspicua a Spiritu Sancto* VR 162.7.

suppositio ~onis, *f*. An assumption, supposition: *ex causa suarum ~onum de spiritu* AC 322.1.

supprimo ~rimere ~ressi ~ressum, *tr*. To inhibit, stifle (an utterance): *alius...vocem ejus per altiorem sonum ~ressit* VR 459.9.

suppuratio ~onis, *f*. An increase of pus under the surface, festering, suppuration: *exspectavit judicium sed ecce ~o, justitiam sed ecce clamor* Isa. 5.7 (AC 3654.2).

supputo ~are ~avi ~atum, *tr*. To calculate, reckon (a number): *ita antiquissimi ~abant suos numeros* AC 901.1.

supra, *prep*. and *adv*. **A** (prep. w. acc.) **1** At a higher level than, above: *quod...tres gradus altitudinis seu discreti sint, unus ~a aut intra alterum* AS 236; *ubi lutum ~a talos* ES 750. **2** To a greater extent than, above: *ut amet proximum plus quam se, et Dominum*

~a omnia AC 760; *filii hujus saeculi prudentiores sunt ~a filios lucis* Luke 16.8 (DP 250.5). **3** Beyond the reach or scope of: *Dominus...infinite ~a omnes infirmitates* AC 1093.1; *quae ~a perceptionem, dictamen et conscientiam sunt Domini* AC 1831; *dixerunt...quod hoc sit ~a vires illorum* VR 567.7. **B** (adv.) **1** At a higher level, above: *infra est infernum et ~a est caelum* VI 19; *qui ~a in inferno erant* DP 288. **2** At a previous place in a book, above: *videatur mox ~a* AC 6726; *ut ~a dictum est* CI 47. **3** In excess, beyond: *aetas hominum ibi est ut plurimum 30 annorum, qui ~a sunt, dicuntur esse indociles* ES 546.

supracaelestis: see **supracoelestis**.

supracitatus ~a ~um, *a.* Quoted above: AE 489.4.

supracoelestis ~is ~e, *a.* also **supracaelestis**. Higher than heaven, supercelestial: *anima, quae pure spiritualis est et ~is* 1AD 919; *veritates ~es* 1AD 933.1; *amor ~is et Divinus* 1AD 976.

supradictus ~a ~um, *a.* Above-mentioned: *in locis ~is* CI 519; (neut. pl. as sb.) *ex ~is comprehendi potest quod...* VR 29.3.

supralapsarius ~i, *m.* A person who believes the fall of Adam was predestined, Supralapsarian: VR 72.1.

supramemoratus ~a ~um, *a.* Mentioned above: *~ae operationes* VR 142.

supramoralis ~is ~e, *a.* More than moral, supermoral: *videbis quod sim ~is inter morales, suprarationalis inter rationales, imo supraspiritualis inter spirituales* AM 269.4. (n.b. The first two compounds are printed as one word, the last as two words, in 1st and 2nd edns.)

supranaturalis ~is ~e, *a.* Higher than the natural plane: *quod ideae spirituales essent ~es, inexpressibiles* AM 326.7.

supranominatus ~a ~um, *a.* Named above: *adulteria ~a* AM 496; CI 165.

supraostensus ~a ~um, *a.* Shown above: (neut. pl. as sb.) AM 222.3.

suprapondero ~are ~avi, *intr.* To weigh heavier, preponderate: *si malum ~aret, et sic praevaleret* ES 3726.

suprapondium ~i, *neut.* An excess weight, preponderance: *quando ~um est mali* AC 689.

suprarationalis ~is ~e, *a.* More than rational: AM 269.4 (see **supramoralis**).

suprarenalis ~is ~e, *a.* (anat.) Situated above the kidneys, suprarenal: *glandulae ~es* ES 970.

supraspiritualis ~is ~e, *a.* More than spiritual: AM 269.4 (see **supramoralis**).

supraspiritualiter, *adv.* In a manner above the spiritual: AC 10614.2.

supremus ~a ~um, *superl. a.* **1** Highest in position, topmost: *est enim caput ~um* AC 7859; *quia est [tectum] ~um seu altissimum* AC 10184.1. **2** Highest in rank, foremost, greatest: **a** (of persons): *volunt ut sicut ~i ab omnibus serviantur* AC 8313.4; ES 718. **b** (of things): *locus ubi sedet [dignissimus] est ~us* AC 1582; *bonum spirituale est ~um* VI 12; *qui in ~is [regiminibus]* AM 7.4; *gradum ~um naturalem* VR 34.3. **3** Highest as relating to the Divine, supreme: *si ipsum ~um Divinum influeret* AC 2716; *tertium seu ~um caelum* SS 6; (esp.) *~us sensus*, the most interior sense of the Word: *in ~o sensu per hominem...intelligitur Dominus* AC 49.2; *intimus seu ~us sensus* AC 6827.1.

surculus ~i, *m.* A side shoot of a plant, twig: *~um quem plantavit dextra Tua* Ps. 80.15 (AC 8281.4); *exibit virga de trunco Jischaji, et ~us e radicibus ejus fructum feret* Isa. 11.1 (DD 6); *haec duo conjugia, ex quibus ut ~us descendit amor conjugialis* AM 64.1.

surdesco ~ere, *intr.* To become deaf: *numne auris ~it ex uno tono continue stringente organa ejus...?* VR 763.1.

surditas ~atis, *f.* Deafness: *talis caecitas et ~as inducitur menti humanae per miracula* DP 130.2.

surdus ~a ~um, *a.* Deaf: *aures ~orum aperientur* Isa. 35.5 (AC 6989).

surgo ~gere ~rexi, *intr.* (fut. pple. *~recturus*) **1** To get up (from sitting or lying), arise: *cadebant...et cum ~rexerint percurrebant viam latam* CI 534.1; *sedentes ...e soliis ~rexerunt* VR 48.5; to climb (out of): *e quibus [foveis] non ~rexerunt* VR 621.4. **2** (implying starting on a course of action) Arise, set forth: *nonne subito ~gent mordentes te?* Hab. 2.7 (AC 6669.2); *in tempore illo ~get Michael princeps magnus* Dan. 12.1 (DD 4). **3** To rise (from the dead), be resurrected: *cum ~rexit [Dominus] ex mortuis* AE 28.2; *quod animae e sepulchris non ~recturae sint quam Ultimo Judicio* ES 2339. **4** To come into existence, originate, arise: *saeculo tertio, quando ~rexerunt Ariani* VR 94.2. **5** To reach a higher level, rise: (in quot. fig.) *cogitationes vanae non possunt altius ~gere quam in tertium coelum* ES 238.

surrepo ~ere ~si, *intr.* To crawl secretly, creep up: *vipera...quae ~serat in arborem* ES 3993; (fig.) *ex malis quae ex corpore...in mentem ~unt* 3AD 6666.

surripio ~ripere ~ripui ~reptum, *tr.* To take away secretly, steal: *qui astu ~ripiunt aliis sua bona* AM 268.3; *cum...scabellum pedum... ~reptum est* VR 121.3; (fig.) *callebant ~ripere aliis eorum ideas* AC 5573.1; ES 2012. **b** *se ~ripere*, to retire secretly, steal away: *se ~ripere volebant in naturam interiorem* AC 959; ES 3499.

sursum, *adv*. perh. also **sursus** (ES 586, ES 1346 Autographs). Upwards: *amare coelestia est spectare ~um* AC 760; *quae [directio] fuerat ~um elevata ad Deum a Deo* AM 153[a].2; *quod hoc ambiguum ferat mentem jam ~um, jam deorsum* VR 35.10. **b** (w. preps.) *in ~um*, upwards: *in ~um versus pectus* ES 1858; *de ~um*, from above: *quindecim cubitis de ~um superarunt aquae, et operuerunt montes* Gen. 7.20 (AC).

sursus: see **sursum**.

sus suis, *m.,f.* A pig or sow: *vapor ex suibus excoriatis in canali* AC 939; (dist. from wild boar) *dictum quod non sint apri, sed sues* ES 3785; *sus aper*, a boar: *talis manet in coeno sicut sus, quare...sus aper mihi repraesentatus sit* ES 1604.

susceptibilis ~is ~e, *a.* (compar. *~ior*) Capable of receiving, liable to be acted upon, susceptible: *formae illae...sunt vitales, et sic ~es* AM 189; (w. gen.) *Divinum non est ~e mali* AC 1573.7; *quo...aptiora sunt interiora, eo sunt ~iora recipiendi Divinum Bonum* AC 8114.

susceptibilitas ~atis, *f.* Liability to be acted upon, susceptibility: ES 987.

susceptio ~onis, *f.* The action of taking (a person) in, receiving: *illi mercedem accepturi secundum ~onem* AC 10683.5.

suscipio ~cipere ~cepi, ~ceptum, *tr.* **1** To lift off the ground, pick up: *ad latus ~cipiemini* Isa. 66.12 (AC 6745.5); *quisquis non ~cipit crucem suam* Matt. 10.38 (AC 8159.4). **2** To give hospitality to, take in, receive (a person): *quisquis ~cipit vos, Me ~cipit* Matt. 10.40 (AC 10683.5); *qui venientes ~cipiebant salutabant* AM 9.1. **3** To take upon oneself, assume: *quod Dominus in hac tellure ~ceperit Humanum* AC 6700; VR 2.2; *hanc potentiam ~cepit Dominus etiam quoad Divinum Humanum Suum* SS 49.1.

suscito ~are ~avi ~atum, *tr.* **1** To cause to stand up: *cubuit sicut leo...quis ~abit eum?* Gen. 49.9 (AC); to revive (the dead): *multa corpora dormientium sanctorum ~ata sunt* Matt. 27.52 (AC 8018.2). **2** To cause to arise, raise up: *~abo Davidi germen justum* Jer. 23.5 (CI 216).

suspendo ~dere ~di ~sum, *tr.* **1** To hang up: *passus Se ~di cruce* FI 44; *mandatum est ut capita populi ~derentur Jehovae coram sole* AE 141.2 (Num. 25.4); *~dunt eas ut sues nudas* ES 593. **2** To hold in suspense: *possunt ideas cogitationis suae tenere in alto, et sicut ~dere ne descendant* AM 55.4.

suspensio ~onis, *f.* The action of hanging: *~o super ligno* AC 5156; the action of keeping in suspense: *propter hebetudinem ex duorum dierum ~one mentis* AM 9.3.

suspicio[1] ~picere ~pexi, *intr.* To look up: *~pexi in caelum* AM 42.1; VR 25.1.

suspicio[2] ~onis, *f.* A suspicion: *inde suborta ~o quod aliquid lethale...patraverit* AC 817; AM 375.1.

suspiciosus ~a ~um, *a.* Prone to suspicion, suspicious: *qui ex natura ~i sunt* AM 357; ES 915; causing suspicion: *vitia mentis...inter quae primas tenet phantasia ~a* AM 374.

suspicor ~ari ~atus sum, *intr.* To harbour a suspicion, suspect: *~or etiam ego quod non aliquis tam subtili...ingenio sit* AM 315.8; (w. acc.) *ut nemo quid tale de illis ~ari posset* AC 5060.2.

suspiratio ~onis, *f.* Sighing (as an indication of pain, grief, etc.): *Jehovah, vocem meam audivisti, ne abscondas aurem Tuam ad ~onem meam* Lam. 3.56 (AC 3869.13).

suspirium ~i, *neut.* **1** A sigh: *~a ad Dominum* AE 389. **2** A longing, intense desire: *in una affectione hominis, imo in uno ejus ~o* AC 2209.2; *cum affectione, desiderio, jucundo aut sancto ~o* AC 5365.3; *~um est cordis cogitatio* ES 3308.

suspiro ~are ~avi, *intr.* To sigh (as an indication of pain, grief, etc.): *~abant filii Israelis e servitio* Exod. 2.23 (AC); *Jesus ~ans spiritu Suo* Mark 8.12 (DD 50.1); *orantes, ~antes, dicentes, Celebrate festum...* AM 9.3.

sustentaculum ~i, *neut.* That which holds something up, support, prop: *pondera absque ~is* AC 7545; *patinae...ex argento...cum ~is suis* AM 14.2; (fig.) *est verum ~um boni, sicut ossa sunt carnis* AC 3812.8.

sustentatio ~onis, *f.* The action or fact of being kept in existence or supported: *~o...est perpetua creatio, sicut subsistentia est perpetua existentia* DP 3.2; *quod sit [viaticum] ~o a vero et bono* AC 7981; AM 385.

sustento ~are ~avi ~atum, *tr.* **1** To hold up, support: *inde est quod baculus ~et manum et brachium* AC 7026. **2** To maintain in existence, sustain: *vita spiritualis ... ~atur illis quae sunt cognitionum fidei* AC 12; *quod unaquaevis voluptas non solum afficiat hominem, sed etiam ~et sicut cibus* AC 995.1; VR 12.1.

sustineo ~nere ~nui, *tr.* **1** To keep up, hold (an object): *excutit manus suas ne ~neant munus* Isa. 33.15 (VI 84.1). **2** To keep alive or active, sustain: *quod ~net hominem, est conjunctio ejus cum coelo* AC 661.3. **3** (w. inf.) To persist (in), keep on: *~nuit negare quod talis fuerit* AC 2483. **4** To undergo, suffer (pain, grief, etc.): *de pugna quam non possunt non ~nere* AC 59.2; *quas [paenas] cum saepe ~nuit* AC 6977; *dicebat se ingentes cruciatus ~nuisse* ES 4468. **5** To tolerate, endure, put up with: *quod praesentia Ipsius Divini talis sit ut nullus angelus illam ~neat* AC 6849.5; *hi illos admodum diu ~nebant* AC 8383. **b** (w. inf.): *minus adhuc audire ~nent aliquid rationale* AC 202; AM 241.

susurratio ~onis, *f.* A whispering: *quod...non conveniat in coelo talis ~o* ES 1149.

susurro[1] ~are ~avi, *intr., tr.* To speak in a whisper: *in angulis ~ant in aures* CI 488.2; *abivit ~ans cum sociis* VR 79.4; (tr.) to utter in a whisper: *~abant laudem votivam ad Dominum* AM 16.1.

susurro[2] ~onis, *m.* A whisperer: *manifestat quod ~ones fuerint* AC 4657; ES 1149.

susurrus ~i, *m.* A whispered utterance, whisper: *cur... attendis ad nostros ~os* AM 521.3; a rustling sound: *auditus est ~us tonans qui defluebat ex altiori* AC 4326.1.

sutor ~oris, *m.* A shoemaker, cobbler: *nec ~oros [percipiant] sphaeram [odoris] in qua sunt* ES 3349; ES(M) [4720].

sutorius ~a ~um, *a.* Of or belonging to a shoemaker, cobbler's: *duae stillae...atroris ~i* CO 22.

sutura ~ae, *f.* (anat.) A suture (at the junction of two bones): *supra caput, et quidem inter ~am transversalem ad sinistrum caput* ES 4098.

suus ~a ~um, *pron. adj.* **1** Belonging to a person or thing specified, his, her, its, their: *quisque enim...vitam ~am defendit* AC 6705; *spirituale in ~a prima origine est Divinum Verum* AC 6685; *cum [Dominus] Humanum ~um fecit Divinum Verum* AC 6750.2. **2** (emphatic) His (her, etc.) own: *inde est quod sibimet ~aeque prudentiae tribuant singularia* AC 7007.1; *[Dominus] redegit illud* [sc. *infernum*] *in ordinem et sub ~am obedientiam* VR 2.2. **b** (reinforced with *-met* or *-pte*): *obvelantur ~ismet falsis et malis* AC 8265.1; *omnis virgo vult...nubere, ut libere in ~amet domo agat* DP 148; VR 71.2; *~apte essentia* 3AD 2478. **c** (masc. pl. as sb.) one's own people: *omnis homo...post obitum ad ~os venerat* AM 28; *se contulerunt ad coelum unde erant, gavisi quod inter ~os venirent* CI 35; *quod... colligatur ad ~os* VR 14.4. **3** Under his own control: *quantum alter favet, hoc est, quantum is ~us est, tantum amatur* AC 6667; *quod quo propius aliquis conjunctus est Domino, eo minus ~us sit* DP 42; ES 2506. **4** Proper to or typical of a specified person or thing, peculiar: *qui...in magnificis palatiis habitarunt in talibus ~um coelum ponendo* AC 1631; *frons insita communi stirpi fert ~um fructum* AC 7343.2; *quod mala una cum inferno...exstiterint, ~o loco demonstrabitur* VR 53; *~o tempore cum vixerunt in mundo* AC 1123; ES 4679; (neut. as sb.) one's own property: *quod Dominus in ~o habitet apud angelos coeli* CI 12; *quod ~a...dare velit alteri* ES(M) 4607.

sycomorum ~i, *neut.* (Gk.) also **sycomorus** ~i, *m.* A kind of fruit tree, prob. *Ficus sycomorus*: *percussit... ~a illorum grandine gravi* Ps. 78.47 (AC 7553.4).

sycomorus: see **sycomorum**.

sycophanta ~ae, *m.* (Gk.) One who claims to be what he is not, trickster: *homo similiter potest ~am agere* DP 224.1; AM 267.3.

syllaba ~ae, *f.* (Gk.) A single sign in a script, letter: *dicunt...[Judaei] Divina arcana ibi* [sc. *in Verbo*] *usque in unaquavis ~a recondi* AC 10705; *explicabant... sensum Verbi...ex solis literis seu ~is* SS 90.1; *Alphah est prima et Omegah est ultima ~a in alphabeto Graeco* VR 19.2; *non ex vocibus sed ex ~is et earum flexionibus, curvationibus* ES 5578.

syllogismus ~i, *m.* (Gk.) (in logic) A syllogism: *philosophica...solum in terminis et ~o constiterunt* ES 866; ES(M) 4578.

syllogisticus ~a ~um, *a.* (Gk.) Of or concerned with syllogisms: *~a philosophia* ES 866; ES 2606; (neut. as sb.) syllogistic argument: AC 5128.3.

sylva ~ae, *f.* also **silva**. A piece of land covered by trees, wood, forest: *prata, novalia, hortos, ~as* AC 7071; *quod sint [equi] feri seu in ~is* AC 8381; *vidi ~am opacam* AM 521.1.

sylvestris ~is ~e, *a.* also **silv-**. Of the woods, woodland: *spectant paradisiaca haec non aliter quam ~ia* AM 13.3; (of wild animals) *equos...qui ~es sunt* ES 632; *sues ~es* ES 3785; cf. *vestitus...ex lanis ~ibus* ES 1547.

symbola ~ae, *f.* A contribution: *petiit ut liceret hujus [hominis] effatis aliquam ~am adjicere* VR 459.12.

symbolicus ~a ~um, *a.* (Gk.) **1** Serving as a token, symbolic: *alia externa successerunt, nempe loco sacrificiorum..., ~a* AC 1083.2. **2** Of or concerned with a creed: *per fidem...vulgus non aliam quam ~am intelligit, seu quam libri ~i docent* AC 4690.2; *ex ~a... confessione* VR 9.1.

symbolum ~i, *neut.* (Gk.) **1** A thing or action which serves as a token, symbol: *panis et vinum sunt ~a in Sancta Coena* AC 276.1; *baptismus sit ~um regenerationis hominis* AC 2702.17; ES 2409. **2** A brief statement of belief, creed: *in ~o Athanasiano* VR 4.3; SE 31.

symmetria ~ae, *f.* (Gk.) Due proportion, symmetry: *angeli ex modulationis ~a et profluentia percipiunt rem affectionis* AM 55.1.

symmetrice, *adv.* By reference to proportion: *sicut oculus videt...~e naturalia* VR 365.4.

sympathia ~ae, *f.* (Gk.) A feeling of harmony, agreement: *homogeneitates et heterogeneitates, seu ~ae et antipathiae* AM 273.1.

sympathicus ~a ~um, *a.* (Gk.) Acting in agreement, harmonious: *quae [inclinatio] si est concors et ~a vitam conjugialem continuant* AM 47[a]; (neut. as sb.) *~a ac nisus homogeneorum...ad conjunctionem non aliunde ducunt originem* VR 44.2.

symphonia ~ae, *f.* (Gk.) An orchestra: *saltantium ad modos ~arum et tibiarum* AM 3.3.

symphonicus ~a ~um, *a.* (Gk.) Harmonious: *audiebant cantum illum ut ~um et suavem* AM 55.2.

symphysis ~is, *f.* (Gk.) (as a medical term) The growing together of two parts of the body: VR 665.5.

synagoga ~ae, *f.* (Gk.) A synagogue: *Jesus intravit in ~am* Luke 4.16 (DD 11); AC 4859.1.

synchrone, *adv.* Synchronously, so as to keep time: *quod pulmo possit respirare non ~e cum corde* AS 405.2.

synchronus ~a ~um, *a.* (Gk.) Synchronous, keeping time: *ad conformes et ~as activitates* AM 310.1.

syncretismus ~i, *m.* (Gk.) An attempt to reconcile conflicting views, syncretism: *qui inter se de unione religionum seu ~o consultarunt* ES 5662[a].

syncretista ~ae, *m.* (Gk.) One who practises syncretism, syncretist: AR 386.3.

synedrium ~i, *neut.* (Gk.) **1** (Bibl.) The high court at Jerusalem, Sanhedrin: *obnoxious erit ~o* Matt. 5.21 (AC 374.1); Matt. 10.17 (AE 122.3). **2** Any council, esp. for religious matters: *audivi quod convocatum sit ~um ex famigeratis in scriptis* VR 137.1; ES 4551 titulus.

syngrapha ~ae, *f.* (Gk.) A written contract: *sume ~am tuam* Luke 16.6 (AC 2252.5).

synodicus ~a ~um, *a.* (Gk.) Of an ecclesiastical council or synod, synodal: *decretum ~um* VR 487.5.

synodus ~i, *f.* (Gk.) A meeting, council, synod: *a ~o Dordrechtana* VR 486.2; *~um Nicaenam* VR 632.1.

synonymus ~a ~um, *a.* (Gk.) Having the same name, synonymous: *quae apparent sicut ~a, cum tamen usque non sunt* SS 84.1; 3AD 4464.

Syriacus ~a ~um, *a.* Of the ancient language of Syria, Syriac: *Kephah significat petram in lingua ~a* AE 411.13.

syringicus ~a ~um, *a.* Exerted by means of a tube or syringe: *capiti inducunt dolorem tanquam attractionis ~ae* [i.e., suction] AC 1763.1; ES 1129.

syrtis ~is, *f.* (Gk. name of shallows off the coast of Libya) A sandbank: *navi quae...fertur in scopulos et ~es* VR 28.2; VR 127.

systema ~atis, *neut.* (Gk.) A coherent and ordered structure, system: *totius corporis ~a* AM 207.3; *hoc magnum ~a, quod vocatur universum* VR 13.1; *in toto ~ate mentis et corporis nostri* VR 159.3; (of abstract things) *integrum ~a doctrinae* AC 794.2; *~a theologicum* VR 75.7.

systematicus ~a ~um, *a.* Systematic: *in suo mundo ~o* ES 4627.1; (neut. as sb.) a systematic theory: *funes et palos per quos ~um suum sicut tentorium firmum aedificavit* VR 758.2.

systole ~es, *f.* (Gk.) The contraction of the heart muscle, systole: *motus cordis qui vocatur ~e et diastole* FI 19.1; VR 37.2.

systolice, *adv.* In a systolic manner: *si homo disponeret...interiora cordis ad ~e agendum* DP 180.8.

systolicus ~a ~um, *a.* (Gk.) Systolic: *motus...~i cordis* CI 445; VR 87.1.

T

tabacum: see **tabakum**.

tabakum ~i, *neut.* also **tabacum**. Tobacco (prob. in the form of snuff): *habebat...pyxidem ~i* [*tabaci* Tafel and J D Odhner] ES 5008.

tabella ~ae, *f.* A painting, picture: *flores...picti super ~a* AC 8480.1.

taberna ~ae, *f.* A shop: *ad ~as artificum qui capillamenta concinnant* VR 381.3; VR 834.

tabernaculum ~i, *neut.* **1** A temporary dwelling, booth, hut: *quam bona sunt ~a tua, Jacob* Num. 24.5 (AC 4286.7); *in ~o Davidis* Isa. 16.5 (DD 6). **b** *festum ~orum*, the Feast of Tabernacles: AC 7093.2. **2** The tent or booth made to house the Ark of the Covenant, the tabernacle (also called *habitaculum* Exod. 26.1 in AC): *haec* [sc. *arca*] *in intimo ~i* VI 55.1; (of similar structures in heaven) *apertum est Templum ~i Testimonii in caelo* Rev. 15.5 (AR); *repraesentabatur coram quibusdam ~um cum arca* AC 3478.

tabes ~is, *f.* A disease causing wasting, consumption: *percutiet te Jehovah ~e* Deut. 28.22 (AC 8364.3); *meretrix ...quae interius maligna ~e scatet* VI 46; *parti interiori ~e infectae illinere smegma* VI 112; *adulteria quae... ~e conficiunt corpora* AM 105.

tabula ~ae, *f.* **1** A large, flat piece of wood, plank, board: *ex abietibus...aedificarunt tibi omnes ~as* Ezek. 27.5 (AC 6385.2). **2** A board set up to display a written legend, noticeboard: *~a, cui inscriptio est* AM 75.8; *quibus ~a praefigitur in qua scriptum est quales sunt* ES 5984. **b** (to display a picture): *in ~a super altari videt pictum unum Deum* VR 15.2; *vidi in ~a opus acupicturae* ES 6019. **3** A tablet for writing, usually covered with wax: *monstravit nobis scripturas antiquissimorum, quod essent super ~is ligneis et lapideis* AM 77.6; *~a rasa, in qua non apparet aliquid scriptum* AR 461.2; esp. those delivered to Moses on Mount Sinai: *decem praecepta ~is lapideis...inscripta* AC 6752.1. **4** (app.) A potter's wheel: *ille* [sc. *figulus*] *fecit opus super ~a* Jer. 18.3 (AC 6669.5).

tabulatio ~onis, *f.* (app.) A structure, building: *sibi magnifica per varias artes fecerunt, tam quoad ~ones et quae ibi, quam quoad vestitus* ES [5765] 1/3 (Tafel).

tabulatus ~a ~um, *a.* Covered with planking, boarded: *turris immensa circumcirca transtris ~is, per quae ascenderetur* ES(M) 4601; *cavum ~um facies illud* [sc. *altare*] Exod. 27.8 (AC). **b** (neut. as sb.) a platform: *steterunt post ~um oblongum in palatio ante fores erectum alienigenae* AM 113; AC 10837; *per Gogum et Magogum etiam in lingua Hebraea significatur tectum et ~um* AR 859.3.

taceo ~cere ~cui ~citum, *intr.*, *tr.* **1** (intr.) To keep silent: *tota die...non ~cebunt commemorantes Jehovam* Isa. 62.6 (AC 8211.5); *quod faeminae non loquantur...sed in consortiis virorum... ~ceant* AM 165. **2** (tr.) To keep silent about: *ut ~ceam mirabilia in ipsis ovis* CI 108.3.

tacite, *adv.* Without audible sound, silently: *nec loquuti* [*angeli coelestes*] *nisi ~e* AC 180; AC 7320; AM 144.

taciturnitas ~atis, *f.* A tendency to keep silent, taciturnity: *signum quod viam ~atis et ignorantiae eant* UJ(P) 295.

taciturnus ~a ~um, *a.* Prone to keep silent, taciturn: UJ(P) 295.

tacitus ~a ~um, *a.* (pf. pple. of **taceo**) (superl. *~issimus*) **1** (of persons) Keeping silent: *angeli... ~issimi erant, modo communicantes sua cogitata cum facie* AC 173; (of sounds) barely audible, quiet: *loquela...non sonora, sed paene ~a* AC 7360; *mitis et ~us sonus* AC 7573.1. **2** (of actions) Unaccompanied by sound, inaudible, silent: *remanente respiratione interiore...cum tenui et ~a corporis* CI 449.1; *per ~am perceptionem* SS 44.3. **3** Not expressed in words, unspoken, tacit: *post conventionem inter illos ~am* AM 248.2.

tactilis ~is ~e, *a.* Apprehensible by the sense of touch: *omnia gaudia...fiunt perceptibilia, sensibilia, ~ia* AM

156^{a}.4; (neut. pl. as sb.) *quantum indulgent...lenociniis ~ium corporis* CI 462.2.

tactus ~us, *m*. The sense of touch: *ex visu, auditu, gustu, odoratu, ~u* AC 7038.2; AM 210; an instance of touching, touch: *ad primum ~um...aufugiunt* CI 18.

taeda ~ae, *f*. **1** A species of pine tree, pitch pine: *gloria Libani ad te veniet, abies, ~a, buxus simul* Isa. 60.13 (AC 2162.11). **2** A torch made of resinous wood: *focus in quem...injiciebant ~as sulphuratas et bituminosas* AM 231.2. **b** (fig.) a torch as a symbol of sexual love (used by the ancients in weddings): *praestat...ut ~a amoris sexus cum uxore primum accendatur* AM 460.5; *haec sphaera...exstinguit ~as conjugiales inter vera et bona* VR 619.4.

taedeo ~dere ~dui, *intr.*, *tr*. To be weary, tire: *is ~debat et desiderabat suorum consortium* ES 532. **b** (impers. w. acc.): *paullatim ~duit eum, et factum gaudium nullum* AC 455; (w. inf.) *illos ~det aedificare* VR 281.8.

taediosus ~a ~um, *a*. Wearisome, tiresome: *~us et ingratus factus est* [*status*] VR 79.8; *tristissima vita et ~a* ES 3985.

taedium ~i, *neut*. **1** A feeling of distaste induced by satiety, weariness: *qui non in bono est, ~um sentit cum de talibus cogitat* AC 3314.2; *~um ratiocinandi ex meris falsis* AC 7391; *ex ~o contulimus nos ad hanc portam* AM 5.2. **2** A source of weariness, bore: *at homini qui in sphaera naturali est...talia ~a sunt* AC 5221.2.

taeter: see **teter**.

taetre: see **tetre**.

talaris ~is, *m*. An outer garment reaching to the ankles, robe: *similem Filio Hominis, indutum ~i* Rev. 1.13 (AR); *princeps indutus erat ~i coloris purpurei* AM 15.

talentum ~i, *neut*. (Gk.) The major unit of weight in antiquity, frequently used as a unit of currency, a talent (= 60 *minae*): *in parabolis de ~is* AC 7984.4 (Matt. 25.14-30). **b** (fig.): *intellectum...non expolitum per ~a et minas eruditionis* VR 393.1.

talio ~onis, *f*. Retaliation: *jus ~onis antiquis notissimum* AC 1011; *in ~one seu vindicta* AC 8223.3; *se conjiciunt in paenam ~onis* AC 8214.

talis ~is ~e, *a*. **1** Of the kind just mentioned, such: *cum in ~i vel alio ordine nominantur* AC 6640.1; *in coelis inferioribus non ~es scripturae sunt* CI 261; *his et ~ibus phantasiis cruciant unus alterum* ES 4381; (masc. as sb.) *apud ~es magicum non potest existere* AC 6692.3; (neut. as sb.) *in odiis et ~ibus* AC 1277. **2** (accompanied by a gesture, illustration, etc.) Like this: *recipit unum puellum ~em in nomine Meo* Matt. 18.5 (AC 6674.5); *spicula salis crassa,* [*illustratio*] *~ia* ES(M) 4627. **3** (Further defined by context): **a** (correlated w. *qualis*) as...such: *qualis homo, ~is vita* AC 1005; AC 6684; (also, w. *sicut*) *quod ~es sint sicut fuerunt in cogitatione* ES 4318. **b** (w. rel. pron.): *pro ~ibus in quibus non aliquid verum datur* AC 6723.2; *scientia ~ium quae fidei sunt* AC 7039.2. **c** (w. *quod*): *principia falsi vertuntur...in ~es phantasias, quod videantur sibi secare gramen* AC 1111. **d** (w. *ut*): [sc. *religiosum*] *~e est ut nihil credatur nisi falsum* AC 6729; VR 4.2.

taliter, *adv*. **1** In the manner just mentioned, in that kind of way: *~er ii se habent* AC 546; *simplices multo clariorem perceptionem habent...quam ~er docti* ES(M) 4655. **2** (Correlated w. *qualis*): *qualis quisque est ~er sentit* ES 2640; (w. *ut*) *inducunt speciem suctionis... ~er ut locus...doleat* AC 5180.

talpa ~ae, *f*. A mole: *hominem cujus intellectus est sicut ~ae donare visu aquilae* VR 58.1; AE 410.2.

talus ~i, *m*. **1** The ankle: *in luto et coeno supra ~os* AC 940.2; *loco pedum erant ~i ossei absque carne* AM 263.1. **2** (pl.) The knuckle bones of an animal used for gaming, dice: *sume ~os aut chartulas lusorias* DP 212.1; CH 189 (= xi).

tam, *adv*. **1** To such an extent, so: *vix aliquis...potuisset credere, tam astuosa et artificiosa sunt* AC 6666.2; *hoc animalculum tam velox* AM 329.1. **b** (correlated w. *ac*): *visa sunt et audita tam sensibiliter ac in societate humana* ES 1532. **c** (w. *ut*): *influebant...tam graviter ut in vigilia iis non resistere potuissem* AC 1270.2; CI 228. **2** (correlated w. *quam*) As much...as, both...and: *tam tentationes quam desolationes in Verbo comparantur diluviis* AC 705.1; *est Dominus noster Jesus Christus, tam quoad Divinum a Quo, quam quoad Divinum Humanum* VR 25.4; *bestiae...tam nobiles quam ignobiles* VR 48.2. **b** (app. also w. *tum* or *sed*): *animae...feruntur ad cognoscendum Deum Messiam ...tam* [*tum* Tafel] *per instructiones vivas...tum per id, quod...* ES 342; *...rete hoc apparuit sicut album, tam quod veritates quidem essent, sed quod justificationem sui quoque significarent* ES 1629.

tamdiu, *adv*. For so long: **a** (correlated w. *quamdiu*): *quamdiu haec conjunctio perstat, ~u correspondentia est* CI 447; VR 182.2. **b** (w. *usque dum*): *ab iis cupit, et hoc ~u et toties, usque dum se associat talibus...* CI 450; ES 297.

tamen, *adv*. **1** (in a main clause) In spite of this, nonetheless, however: *at spirituales tale licet sciunt, non ~n agnoscunt* AC 981.3; *ut...appareat sibi in libero esse ...cum agnitione ~n...quod...* AC 6663.1; *potest bonum esse inter mala et falsa, et ~n in tuto esse* AC 6724.2; *quod sapientia in aeternum possit crescere, et ~n usque non longe ultra gradum primum perveniri* AC 6648; AM 478.3. **2** (in a subordinate clause) Nonetheless, however: **a** (w. rel.): *quod...Benjamin [nominetur] ante Danem...qui ~n ultimo natus est* AC 6640.2; CI 67. **b** *cum ~n*, when in fact: *cum ~n ita se res habet* AC 29.1; VR 94.1.

tametsi, *conj.* (w. indic.) Although: *neminem videbant... ~si magna multitudo erat* CI 35; SS 8. **b** (without a verb): *cingulum...lunare, quod multam lucem, ~si reflexam, telluri illi dat* AC 6697; VR 10.

tandem, *adv.* Finally, at last: *illustrabatur intellectus usque ~em ut perciperem quae non prius percepi* CI 130; *tandem post intervalla temporis eximitur* VR 448.1.

tango ~ere tetigi tactum, *tr.* **1** To come into physical contact with, touch: *cum spirituale ~it et videt spirituale* CI 461.1; (w. abl.) *ab illis quae...sensu tetigerat* AC 7381.2; *actutum cum tetigerunt terram pedibus* VR 77.6; (absol.) *ventus qui ~it et dissipatur* ES 227. **2** To have an influence upon, affect: *haec tentatio...ipsam... vitam hominis ~it* AC 760; *quod Deus... ~at liberum ejus arbitrium, sed nusquam violet* VR 74.3; (w. abl.) *admirationis stupore tacti et perfusi* AC 1756.3; *quod nullo amore proximi ~antur* ES 3501.

tanquam, *adv.* and *conj.* **1** (adv.) As it were: *audivi vocem... ~am vocem aquarum multarum* Rev. 14.2 (AR); *uterque ~am homo divisus* AM 37. **2** (conj. w. subj.) As if: *quod Dominus ducat omnes... ~am essent unus angelus* CI 52; *quod loquantur ~am sciant, cum tamen non sciunt* ES 1902.

tantillus ~a ~um, *a.* Of such small size or extent, so very small: *decima pars pro reliquiis ~is* AC 576.1; (neut. as sb.) *~um vitae vere humanae remanet* AC 827.

tantopere, *adv.* To such an extent, so much: *chori illi ~re oblectabant spiritus...ut...* AC 8115; *qui moraliter vivunt...nec ~re curant instrui* CI 33.

tantum, *adv.* To such an extent: *non ~um ac amor sui* AC 1594.1; (correlated w. *quantum*) to the extent that...to such an extent: *~um intrat felicitas coeli, quantum illi amores...removentur* AC 10724; AM 405.

tantummodo, *adv.* Exclusively, only: *~o inter te Deus, et praeterea non Deus* Isa. 45.14 (AR 962.3); *~o justificationi per solam fidem studium impendit, non autem charitati* VR 797.1.

tantus ~a ~um, *a.* So great, so large: *cum tamen illa doctrina tot et ~is arcanis abundat* AC 6632; *doctrina...quae ~i pretii fuerat* AC 6632; *~a similitudo intercedit inter cor et charitatem...ut...* FI 19.2. **b** (neut. as sb.) so great an amount: *~um temporis vobiscum sum, non nosti Me?* John 14.9 (AC 15). **c** *in ~um*, to such an extent: *omnes caeli labefactarentur in ~um ut angeli non potuissent subsistere* AM 352. **d** *~i esse*, to be of such value: *quod plura scire... ~i non sit* FI 71.

tantusdem ~tadem ~tundem, *a.* (neut. as sb.) The same quantity, just as much: *quod ~tundem sub altera specie atque sub utraque contineatur* AR 795.

tapete ~is, *neut.* (Gk. *tapes*) (gen. pl. *~um* AC 9751) **1** A large cloth used in a hanging or curtain: *~es centum longitudine* Exod. 27.11 (AC); *picti ~es parieti...multis clavis affixi* VR 639. **2** A floor covering, carpet: *vapor... qui versus terram delapsus, ubi ~e, erat visus* ES 397; *per convolutionem cujusdam ~is, qui sub pedibus jacere solet* ES 1144.

tarantula: see **taratantula**.

taratantula ~ae, *f.* also **tarantula** in later edns. A kind of poisonous spider, tarantula: *ex ictu ~ae* VR 367.7 (1st edn.); VR 566.2 (1st edn.); VR 574.2 (1st edn.).

tardatio ~onis, *f.* The action of delaying, delay: *cum status vitae est in statu dubitationis, tunc externum est in statu ~onis* AC 5163.

tarde, *adv.* Slowly: *quod non ~e sed festine fit* AC 9223.1.

tarditas ~atis, *f.* Slowness: *~as est illis in omnibus* AC 5562; ES 920.

tardo ~are ~avi, *intr.* To be slow, delay: *et non ~avit puer facere verbum* Gen. 34.19 (AC); *~ante...sponso dormitarunt omnes* Matt. 25.5 (AC 4635).

tardus ~a ~um, *a.* Slow: *erat loquela illorum ~a* AC 4658.1; *stulti et ~i corde ad credendum* Luke 24.25 (DD 11).

Tartara ~orum, *neut. pl.* (Gk.) see also **Tartarus**. The infernal regions in Greek mythology: *ita illi ad meridiem feruntur, hi autem ad ~a* AC 3708.22; AM 75.2; 3AD 3143.

Tartareus ~a ~um, *a.* Of Tartarus, infernal: *spectare ex umbra ~a lucem nostri caeli* AM 75.6.

Tartari ~orum, *m. pl.* The inhabitants of Tartary, Tartars: *quaerite de eo in China, et forte invenietis illud ibi apud ~os* AR 11.2.

Tartaria ~ae, *f.* *~a Magna*, the country lying to the west of China proper and the north of India, prob. including Sinkiang and Tibet, Great Tartary: *quod hoc [sc. Verbum] ibi adhuc reservatum sit apud populos qui in Magna ~a habitant* AR 11.2; AM 77.2. **b** *~a Minor*, the area nearest to China proper, prob. the western provinces of present-day China: ES 6077 titulus.

Tartarus ~i, *m.* (Gk.) see also **Tartara**. The infernal regions in Greek mythology: *sicut styx aut caligo in ~o* VR 20.2.

taurus ~i, *m.* A bull: [*quod sit zelotypia*] *etiam apud ~os, tametsi illis non vituli* AM 378.

taxus ~i, *m.* A badger (in quot. of its skin): *vestivi te* *acupicto, et calceavi te ~o* Ezek. 16.10 (AC 2576.27); AE 375.10; AE 1143.2.

techna ~ae, *f.* (Gk.) A ruse, trick: *~as condunt sub eo, quod vera loquantur* ES 1486.

technicus ~a ~um, *a.* (Gk.) (neut. as sb.) A piece of craftsmanship, design, pattern: *antithalamum ubi plura ~a super parietibus* AM 76.6.

tectum ~i, *neut.* The roof of a building: *removit Noach ~um arcae* Gen. 8.13 (AC); *templum...absque ~o et pariete* SS 33; *~um ex laminis auri* AM 12.1; (as a point of vantage) *quod...loquuti fueritis in cubiculis, praedicabitur in ~is* Luke 12.3 (AC 7795.2); Matt. 24.17 (CI 208).

tecum, *pron.* = *te* (see **tu**) combined with *cum* (see **cum**[1]). With you (sg.): VR 661.13.

tegillum ~i, *neut.* A small shelter, hut: *et hinc inde commovebitur [terra] sicut ~um* Isa. 24.20 (AE 304.4).

tegmen ~inis, *neut.* A covering: *immundum judicabitis ~en sculptilium argenti tui* Isa. 30.22 (AC 10406.3); *vermes qui...circumdant se ~ine...ut renascentur* VR 12.6.

tego ~gere ~xi ~ctum, *tr.* **1** To place a covering over, cover up: *~xerunt nuditatem patris sui* Gen. 9.23 (AC); *clavum...quo ~gerent excrementum suum* AM 431.2 (Deut. 23.14). **b** (refl. w. abl.) to clothe oneself (with): *~genti se antiquo* Isa. 23.18 (AC 6917.3); *~xit se sicut pallio zelo* Isa. 59.17 (DD 14.3); *~ctus* (w. abl.), clothed (with), dressed (in): *~cti pileis* VR 74.5. **2** To form a covering over, cover: *redundans super lateribus habitaculi...ad ~gendum illud* Exod. 26.13 (AC); *alae ~gentes corpora* Ezek. 1.23 (AC 8764.3); *sponsi caput ~gebat cidaris* AM 20.2. **3** To keep hidden, cover up: *naturale... ~git et claudit quod intra...est* AC 9544; *externa ~gunt et abscondunt interna* CI 497; *quod sensus literae ~gat interiora Verbi* SS 45. **b** *~ctus*, not openly declared, secret, hidden: *operiretur ille contumeliis ~ctis in caetibus virorum, et apertis in caetibus mulierum* AM 469.

tegula ~ae, *f.* A roofing tile: *amphitheatrum...tectum ~is nigris* AM 231.2.

tegumentum ~i, *neut.* A covering, integument: *corpus est modo quasi ~um seu quasi crusta* AC 1718; *cerebrum...absque communi ~o...quod vocatur cranium* SS 33.

teipsum: see **tu**.

tekel: see **thekel**.

tela ~ae, *f.* **1** A piece of woven material, web, cloth: *~ae eorum non erunt in vestem* Isa. 59.6 (AC 623.2); (in fig. phrase) *contexuimus et contorsimus ~am ex filis variorum colorum* VR 487.2. **2** A spider's web: *~as araneae texent* Isa. 59.5 (AC 251.2). **3** Any orderly construction, structure, web: *prima... ~a formae humanae...est ex principiis e cerebro* AS 388. **4** (transf.) An orderly arrangement, thread: *si non sequuntur ~am sui praejudicii* AM 231.4; *ut ~am sermonis finiti... iterum exorsurus esset* VR 796.1.

tellus ~uris, *f.* **1** Any heavenly body suitable for habitation, planet, earth: *cum ipsis incolis ~urum* AC 6695; *spiritus ~uris Mercurii* AC 6925; VR 32.5; *~us, sive planeta sit sive luna sive satelles* ES 3244. **b** *nostra* or *haec ~us*, our (this) earth, the planet Earth: *a nostrae ~uris spiritibus* AC 6700; *planetae quarum aliquae magnitudine superant hanc ~urem* AC 6697. **2** (without further definition) The planet Earth: *quia spectarent ad coelum et ad Dominum...et non ad ~urem et mundum* AC 7607.1; *~urem investitam terris* AS 314; *per quod ~us conglomerata sit in orbem* VR 29.1; *homines ~uris* VR 182.2.

telum ~i, *neut.* An arrow: *cujus ~a acuta et omnes arcus tensi* Isa. 5.28 (AC 8215.3); *sicut ~um ex arcu emissum* DP 202.3.

temerarie, *adv.* Rashly, recklessly: *visio de...~e desperatis* ES 3135 titulus.

temerarius ~a ~um, *a.* Rash, reckless: *annon hoc sit insolentia et audacia indecens et ~a* VR 162.1; *quidam...inter maxime ~os* ES 3136.

temere, *adv.* Without good cause: *quisquis irascitur fratri suo ~e, obnoxius erit judicio* Matt. 5.22 (AC 1010.2); *irasci ~e Domino* VR 311.

temero ~are ~avi ~atum, *tr.* To desecrate: *haec* [sc. *conjugia*] *simili notione ~ant* AM 453.

temet: see **tu**.

temperamentum ~i, *neut.* A person's characteristic combination of the humours, temperament, character: *hos, quemque secundum suum ~um...invadunt... phantasiae* VR 655.4.

temperantia ~ae, *f.* Avoidance of excessive emotion, moderation: *ex valetudine, vel ex ~a vitae* AM 79.10; AM 164; *remota intemperantia, intrat ~a* AE 790.6.

temperatio ~onis, *f.* The act of moderating, tempering: *semper directio adest...et sic ~o secundum hominem* ES 248.

temperatura ~ae, *f.* The modification of one thing by mixture with another, tempering: *per quorum mirabilem ~am apud hominem...iridis species repraesentari potest* AC 868.2; *cum radii lucis...incidunt, secundum variam ~am obscuri et nivei... existunt colores* AC 1042.2; *qui ignis talis ardoris est ut si absque intermedia ~a incideret in aliquem...is... periret* AC 6834; an instance of this: *per ~as species pulchras induunt* ES 1311.

temperatus ~a ~um, *a.* (pf. pple. of **tempero**) (in sense of vb., esp.) Of climatic zones, temperate: *in zonis ~is* ES 4380.

temperies ~ei, *f.* The state of being well-adjusted so as to avoid extremes, balance: *mala sanguinis et fluidorum corporis ~e* AC 847.2; *in ~e verna vivunt* CI 489.2; *secundum ~em caloris et lucis* AM 137.3; AS 105.

tempero ~are ~avi ~atum, *tr.* To reduce the strength of, moderate, modify, temper: *a Domino hi status per illos ~antur* AC 561; *mala...quae resolvenda et ~anda per bona* AC 719; *per nubem quae radios et calorem e sole illo ~at et moderatur* AC 6849.5; *status...caloris cum luce non ~ati* AM 137.3; *ii quos ~are volunt per cruciatum* ES 745.

tempestas ~atis, *f.* **1** A storm of wind, gale, tempest: *Jehovae in procella et ~ate via* Nahum 1.3 (AE 419.22); AE 419.2; ES 196; (fig.) *~ates in mentibus vestris obortas sedaturi* VR 335.2. **2** A climate: *quod in frigida ~ate vivant* [*incolae Saturnini*] ES 460.

tempestivus ~a ~um, *a.* Coming at the right time, seasonable: *dedit vobis pluviam ~am* Joel 2.23 (AE 375.29).

tempestuosus ~a ~um, *a.* Very rough or violent, stormy, tempestuous: [*ventus orientalis*] *erat... ~us,...et per vim suam confregit arbores, et in mari naves* AC 7679.1.

templum ~i, *neut.* A building set aside for divine worship: *apertum est ~um Dei in caelo* Rev. 11.19 (AR); *cantica ~i* Amos 8.3 (DD 4); (fig.) *qui non est ~um Domini, non potest esse quod per ~um significatur, quod est Ecclesia* AC 82. **b** (among pagans) a temple: *similia etiam posuerunt* [*antiqui*] *in suis ~is* DP 255.2; AC 7779.5. **c** (among the Jews) The Temple at Jerusalem: *~um Hierosolymae aedificatum est super monte* AC 6435.12; *Dominus Se dixit ~um quod in Hierosolyma* CI 187 (John 2.19, 21). **d** (among Christians) a church, place of worship: *frequentatio ~i* AC 7038.1; *ex oratione quae in ~is...legitur coram populo* VI 4; *~um Petri*, St Peter's (in Rome): ES 5408. **e** (in heaven): *est quoque hic aedificium quod vocamus ~um Sapientiae* AR 875.4; AR 962.1.

temporalis ~is ~e, *a.* Of or pertaining to time as the sphere of human life in the natural world, worldly, earthly, temporal (as opp. to spiritual and eternal): *nihil est nisi quod aeternum, reliquum omne quia ~e et momentaneum est nihil* ES 2257; *credere quod pro mercibus seu divitiis ~ibus et temporariis recipiant merces seu divitias spirituales ac aeternas* AR 789.1; *non modo liberant reos a paenis aeternis sed etiam a paenis ~ibus* AR 799.3.

temporarius ~a ~um, *a.* **1** Subject to time, temporal: *illa quae sunt vitae in mundo et quae ~a* AC 1854.1; (esp. neut. as sb.) *dicunt de illis qui moriuntur, quod relinquant ~a* CI 168.3; *excidit mentibus illorum idea aeterni, ac loco ejus ~i incidit* AM 216.2. **2** (of persons) Concerned only with the present: *non habent radicem in seipsis, verum ~i sunt* Mark 4.17 (AC 1846.4).

temporeus ~a ~um, *a.* Of or concerned with time: (neut. pl. as sb.) *quia ~a amant* DP 59.

tempus[1] ~oris, *neut.* **1** Time in the abstract, as a quality of the material universe: *quod Deus, postquam mundus factus est, sit in spatio absque spatio, et in ~ore absque ~ore* VR 30.1; *angelis nulla notio et idea ~oris est* CI 162; (pl.) instances of time, periods: *una cum illo mundo creata sunt spatia et ~ora* VR 27. **2** A period of time: *inde derivatum quod ~ora quoque assimilata fuerint eisdem metallis* AC 1551.1; *eo ~ore* AC 6692.1; *lunas quae...circum orbem suum statis ~oribus vagantur* AC 6697; *ultimum ~us Ecclesiae* SS 14.1; *~ore veris* FI 32; *meo ~ore*, in my lifetime: VR 110.2. **3** (pl.) The regular periods exhibited by a phenomenon: *~ora pulsus erant regularia* AC 3884.3; *pulmonica ~ora erant communia cordis* ES 1615. **4** The right moment in time, opportune moment: *de quibus multa referri potest sed nondum est ~us* AC 49.1; *~us cum apparere debuit* AC 6722; *reddent... fructus in ~ore suo* Matt. 21.41 (VI 65); *quia ~us prope* Rev. 1.3 (AR). **b** *plenum ~oris, plenitudo ~orum*, the fullness of time: *quod significet plenum ~oris quo non apparuit* AC 6721; *quod Dominus in mundum venerit in plenitudine ~orum* DD 3.1. **5** (in grammar) A tense: [*lingua Hebraea*] *non se finiri per ~ora et per distinctiones patitur* AC 618. **6** (phrases) **a** *~ore*, in course of time: *haec* [*conjunctio*] *a se mutuo ~ore dilabitur* VR 99.2. **b** *~ore a ~ore*, from time to time: VR 152. **c** *ad ~us*, for a time: [*diabolus*] *destitit ab Ipso ad ~us* Luke 4.13 (AC 1690.1). **d** *ex ~ore*, at once, immediately: *unde arefacta est ex ~ore ficus* Matt. 21.19 (AC 217).

tempus[2] ~oris, *neut.* (anat.) The area of the head between the forehead and the ear, temple: *se applicabant sinistro meo ~ori* AC 7359; *cui duae alae erant circa pedes et duae circa ~ora* AM 136.

temulentus ~a ~um, *a.* Intoxicated, drunk: *sumus sicut ~i, non ex vino, sed ex sermone hesterno istius viri* VR 73.1.

tenacesco ~ere, *intr.* To become clinging: *viscosa... quae tunc densantur et ~unt* ES 1267 (J D Odhner).

tenacitas ~atis, *f.* The quality of being clinging, adhesiveness: *a nimia spissitudine, ~ate, et acrimonia humorum* AM 253.1.

tenaciter, *adv.* (compar. *~cius*, superl. *~cissime*) Tenaciously: *quod...obnixitatibus suis possint ~citer inhaerere* AM 292.1; *arripiunt...ideam et eam detinent ~citer* ES 1132; ES 4227.

tenax ~acis, *a.* (superl. *~acissimus*) **1** Clinging, adhesive: *per quod...sanguis fiat viscosus, ~ax, spissus, lentus, acer* AM 374. **2** Not easily influenced or dispelled, tenacious: *odia ~acia* ES 1276; (w. gen.) clinging (to): *illi tres ~aces sententiae suae* VR 17.4. **3** Unwilling to part with money, miserly, niggardly: *qui multum solliciti fuerunt de futuris, et magis qui ideo ~aces et avari facti sunt* AC 5177; ES 908.

tendicula ~ae, *f.* The cord of a snare: *num cadet avis super laqueum terrae si ~a illi non?* Amos 3.5 (AC 9348.5).

tendinosus ~a ~um, *a.* Sinewy: *correspondent... carni, usque ad ~a ibi* ES 5575.

tendo[1] ~inis, *f.* (anat.) A sinew, tendon: *callositas... apparet dura, ac intus sicut ex ~inibus striata* CI 466; AM 329.1.

tendo[2] ~dere tetendi ~sum, *tr., intr.* **1** (tr.) To stretch, extend, distend: *nervi...se ~dunt ad aspectum uxoris* AM 44.7; *humores isti collecti ~dunt cava* ES 1805. **b** to draw (a bow): *~dunt arcum suum* Ps. 37.14 (AE 238.3). **c** to pitch (a tent): *tetendit tentorium* Gen. 12.8 (AC); Exod. 33.7 (AC). **2** (intr.) To extend, stretch out: *cavernae...deorsum ~dentes* AC 814.2; CI 429; *lata via quae ad infernum ~dit* ES 4216; (fig.) *primum per medium ~dit et vadit ad suum ultimum* SS 38.2. **3** (intr. w. *ad* or *in* + acc.) To exhibit a tendency (towards), tend (to): *a principio illo ~dit status ad mane* AC 7844.2; *ex proprio ~dunt omnes ad infernum* CI 592; *omne Divinum...in formam humanam ~dit* DD 32.8.

tenebrae ~rarum, *f. pl.* Darkness: *e... ~ris oculi coecorum videbunt* Isa. 29.18 (AC 6989); *vox per quam ...exprimitur caligo significat ~ras densissimas* AC 7711.1; *ex luto ac e ~ris inferni ascendere* AM 415.1. **b** (as a symbol of lack of mental illumination): *dilexerunt homines magis ~ras quam lucem* John 3.19 (VI 2); *qui...in ~ris quoad veritates fidei sunt* AC 1605.

tenebricosus ~a ~um, *a.* Poorly illuminated, dark: *quae inordinata sunt, ~a sunt et opaca* AC 6406; AC 4319.2; *specus ~ae* AE 526.9.

tenebrositas ~atis, *f.* The quality of being dark, darkness: *lux mundi...est angelis sicut densa ~as* AC 1521.

tenebrosus ~a ~um, *a.* (superl. *~issimus*) Poorly illuminated, dark: *sopor est status ~us respective ad vigiliam* AC 1838.1; *luna [apparet] ut ~um quid* CI 122; (neut. as sb.) *in umbroso sunt et ~o* AC 6400.1.

tenellus ~a ~um, *a.* Delicate, soft: *sicut specie ~i vasis seu corporis* AC 3299; *~a corpora [infantum]* ES 971; ES 2477.

teneo ~nere ~nui ~ntum, *tr.* **1** To grasp, hold: *~nens septem stellas in dextra Sua* Rev. 2.1 (AR); *quod rex... ~neret dextra sceptrum* AE 31.6. **b** *in ore ~nere*, to have it on the tip of one's tongue: *~nuit in ore quod illos vocaret insanos* VR 80.5. **2** To occupy, keep to (a position): *~nens altitudinem collis* Jer. 49.16 (AE 410.4); *scientifica quasi ~nentia superficiem* ES 295; *tales ~nent locum supra caput* ES 3843. **3** To hold back, restrain: *ut ne quidem risum ~nere potuissem* ES 169. **b** (w. inf.) to keep under constraint, compel (to): *quisque ~netur loqui sicut cogitat* DP 262.8; *mulieres... ~nentur in rebus judicii consulere viros* AM 175.2. **4** To keep in being, preserve: *et ~nes nomen Meum* Rev. 2.13 (AR). **5** To keep (the eye, mind, attention, etc.) concentrated (upon): *cum homo in talibus chartis ~neret oculum* AC 6930; *quamdiu mens seu cogitatio ~netur in historicis* AC 4989.2; *quod tenerent alterius auditum et sic mentem...in verbis...suis* AR 462.2. **b** *~nendum est quod*, it must be grasped that: *~nendum quod omnes qui in coelis...sunt haeredes regni Domini* AC 1802.1; *~nendum est quod ignis ille...vertatur in intensum frigus* CI 572. **6** (w. predicate) To keep (in a specified state): *ut conjunctio sarta ~neatur* AC 6804.5; *spiritus... ~nebant faciem meam continue hilarem* AC 7807. **7** To keep, hold (a person in a specified state): *quoad internum suum ~netur a Domino in bono et vero* AC 6724.2; *~nentur in simulatione honesti* AC 6914.3; *non ~nerentur in vinculis* CI 220.

tener ~era ~erum, *a.* (compar. *~erior*, superl. *~errimus*) **1** Soft by reason of immaturity, tender: *accepit filium bovis ~erum et bonum* Gen. 18.7 (AC); *circum ~era eorum [sc. infantum] brachia* CI 337. **2** (of sounds) Soft-sounding, gentle: *quod...sit...mulier...loquela ~eriore* CI 368; AM 218.1. **3** (of mental qualities) Delicate, gentle, tender: *in ~eras et novitias illorum ideas* AC 2290; *intelligentia faeminarum...cedens, mollis, ~era* AM 218.1; *amores ~errimi* AM 155[a].3.

tenere, *adv.* (compar. *~ius*, superl. *~rime*) Tenderly: *infantum quos ~rime amant* AC 8380; *apud conjuges qui se ~e amant* AM 158.2.

teneritas ~atis, *f.* Tenderness: *pulchritudo faeminae habitat in molli ~ate* AM 330.2; ES 3496.

teneritudo ~inis, *f.* Tenderness, gentleness, delicacy: *appercepi ~inem laetitiae ab illis talem ut exprimeret lachrymas ex oculis meis* AC 7251; *similis [infantibus] ~o omnium* CI 330; *ex ~ine materna* AM 410.

tenia ~ae, *f.* A narrow band of cloth, ribbon: *sigillum significat consensum; ~a vero sacerdotalia* AC Codex 8, p. 76 (as a substitute for *panniculus* in Gen. 38.18).

tenor ~oris, *m.* A regular way of proceeding, course, tenor: *destrueret [homo] omnem ordinem et ~orem progressionis Divinae Providentiae* DD 180.1; AM 320.1; *tunc in ~ore loquutus est* VR 796.1.

tensibilitas ~atis, *f.* The quality of being capable of stretching: *ex jactura ~atis et elasticitatis nervorum* AM 253.2; VR 665.4.

tensio ~onis, *f.* The act of stretching, tension: *quid in expansione et ~one tenet totius corporis systema...?* AM 207.3.

tentamen ~inis, *neut.* An attempt, effort: *ut respondeat eorum facinorosis ~inibus* ES 264; (w. gen.) *~en angeli per correspondentias agendi* ES 2208 titulus.

tentatio ~onis, *f.* The state or fact of being tempted, temptation: *ne inducas nos in ~onem* Matt. 6.13 (AC 1875); *cum...homo...in ~onem venit* AC 6657.2; *status ~onis* AC 6828; *per ~ones in Humanum Suum admissas* VR 2.2.

tentator ~oris, *m.* A tempter: *Schaddai...proprie significat ~orem, et post tentationes benefactorem* AC 1992.5.

tento ~are ~avi ~atum, *tr.* **1** To subject to trial, put to the test: *aliqui...dixerunt, '~emus illos'* VR 111.2; *ex causa ~andi venenum* ES 1260. **2** To subject to temptation, tempt: *Dominus fuit in deserto quadraginta diebus cum ~atus* AC 6828 (Matt. 4.2); *qui credit, cum ~atur, quod resistere possit* AC 8172; (absol.) *quod puniat [Dominus], dejiciat in infernum, ~et* SS 94. **3** To attempt, try: *hoc ~atum est, sed non potuerunt* CI 237; *~arunt multa, sed in occulto* ES 3762. **b** (w. inf.) to try (to): *~ant ab inferno isto emergere* AC 1267; AC 6677.

tentorio ~are ~avi, *intr.* To pitch a tent, camp: *~avit usque ad Sodomam* Gen. 13.12 (AC).

tentorium ~i, *neut.* A tent: *antiquitus in ~is suis cultum sanctum peregerunt* AC 414.3; *~a habent, superne rotundata, ac protensa in longum* AC 8379; esp. the tent over the Ark of the Covenant: *facies aulaea... ad ~um super habitaculo* Exod. 26.7 (AC). **b** (fig.) a dwelling: *est unio inter nos sicut est duorum ~orum in pectore, quae vocantur cor et pulmo* AM 75.5.

tenuesco ~ere, *intr.* To become thin: ES 1267 (Tafel).

tenuis ~is ~e, *a.* (compar. *~ior*, superl. *~issimus*) **1** Lacking in solidity, unsubstantial, fine, thin: *obvelantur ... ~i et conveniente nube* AC 6849.1; *per ~e sericum* SS 55; *species humanas, sed ~es quia spirituales* AM 182.6. **2** Lacking in depth, shallow: *undae apparent ~iores aut spissiores* AC 6853; AC 8026.

tenuitas ~atis, *f.* Lack of substance, thinness: *nubes ...in varia forma, et in densitate et ~ate secundum quale veritatum* AC 8443.3.

tenuiter, *adv.* (superl. *~nuissime*) Thinly, finely, without much depth: *quod sphaera illa circumstipet hominem...sed ~nuiter a tergo* AM 171.2; *corpora... ~nuissime striata* ES 1058.

tenus, *prep. w. abl.* (always following the sb.) **1** Up to the point of, as far as: *haerent [vera] solum superficie ~us seu in memoria* AC 875.2; *capite ~us usque ad pedes* ES 1850. **2** In respect of, as regards: *quae...non memoria ~us sciuntur sed sunt in corde ejus* AC 1798.4; *haec discunt memoria ~us* AE 115; *verum... origine ~us non est sanctum* AC 3207.2; *uxores non nomine ~us, sed actualiter* AM 217; cf. *proprias oves vocat nomine ~us* John 10.3 (DP 230.4).

tepefactus ~a ~um, *a.* Warmed: *terra aestu ejus* [sc. *solis*] *~a semina educit* VR 80.2.

tepens ~ntis, *a.* Warm: *tactum ~ntis aquae* AC 7768.

tepesco ~ere, *intr.* To become warm: *quod [homo] secundum amoris augmenta ~at, incendatur et inflammetur* DA 58 (= xx.[1]).

tepidus ~a ~um, *a.* Lukewarm: *quia ~us es, et nec frigidus nec calidus* Rev. 3.16 (AR); AC 1513.

tepor ~oris, *m.* Warmth: *sicut est primus ~or ad frigus mediae hyemis* AM 449.

ter, *adv.* Three times: *in hunc statum modo ter aut quater immissus sum* AC 1883; *ter quaterve* CI 222.

teraphim: see **theraphim**.

tercenties, *adv.* Three hundred times: *numne potest intra diem septuagies aut intra septimanam ~es cogitare de Deo, de Domino, de Spiritu Sancto?* VR 480.

terebinthinus ~a ~um, *a.* (Gk.) Of the turpentine tree, pistachio: *nuces ~as* Gen. 43.11 (AC).

terebra ~ae, *f.* A boring tool, drill: *~as quibus crudeliter unus alterum tractat* AC 824; *quod [caput] rotabatur circum sicut ~a* ES 3657.

terebratio ~onis, *f.* The act of drilling: *per speciem ~onis* ES 3218; ES 3968.

terebro ~are ~avi ~atum, *tr.* To bore, drill; (pass.) to be rotated like a drill: *videbantur dextrorsum et sinistrorsum circumflecti et quasi ~ari* ES 3743.

terebrosus ~a ~um, *a.* Produced by drilling: *auditus est sonus ~us, sicut multae terebrae magnae forent* AC 1270.3; ES 3367.

teredo ~inis, *f.* A woodworm: *sicut ~o domui Jehudae* Hos. 5.12 (AC 5354.4).

tergalis ~is ~e, *a.* Of the back: *applicant se parti ~i* AC 958; AC 1120; *ad collum ~e* ES 2974.

tergiversatio ~onis, *f.* Reluctance: *intolerantia et ~o ad actualem amorem* AM 473; AR 461.

tergiversor ~ari ~atus sum, *intr.* To show reluctance, hang back: *mandatur exire, et si ~atur, dejicitur* VR 110.1; ES [6106.2]; (w. inf.) to be reluctant (to): *quod*

... *~entur reflectere super mala apud se* AR 710.

tergum ~i, *neut.* **1** The back (of the body): *vertit ~um ad Illum* [sc. *Dominum*] AC 10420.2; *quod duo conjuges...jaceant obversi, ~o ad ~um* AM 171.2; *circa partem ~i, supra coxendicem* ES 884. **b** *ad* or *in ~um*, towards the back, backwards: *apparent nunc antrorsum, nunc sinistrorsum, nunc paulo ad ~um* AC 7078; *religionem a pectore in ~um rejecerunt* VR 9.1. **c** *a ~o*, at one's back, behind: *planeta illorum sistitur spiritibus a ~o* AC 7078: *unus portabat alterum a ~o* AC 9233; CI 123. **2** The rear part, back (of anything): *quasi in ~um capitis* ES 2207; *a ~o*, on the back: *librum scriptum intus et a ~o* Rev. 5.1 (AR). **3** Some part of a wheel: *rotae aeris...manus illarum, et ~a illarum, et canthi illarum* 1 Kgs. 7.33 (AC 8215.5).

termes ~itis, *m.* A twig, branch (of a tree): *sumserunt ~ites palmarum* John 12.13 (AC 8369.2); *rami, ~ites, folia* VR 12.2.

terminatio ~onis, *f.* An ending: *statuum illorum determinationes et ~ones* AC 1866.1; *quod Verbum in lingua sua originali careat ~onum signis* [i.e., punctuation] AC 7191.

terminor ~ari ~atus sum, *a.* To reach a final stage, be bounded, end: *omnia quae sunt interni hominis ~antur in externis* AC 1083.1; *quod dictatur a Domino transit omnes coelos ordine, ac ~atur apud hominem* CI 259; *necessum est ut omnes gradus...bene ~ati sint* AC 5145.3.

terminus ~i, *m.* **1** A boundary marker: *et ~os ponas populo circumcirca* Exod. 19.12 (AC). **2** A boundary, frontier: *mare et Jordanes erant ~i* AC 1444.3; *sistit se ad ~um Moabi* Num. 21.15 (SS 103.1). **b** the edge, end (of anything): *duas catenulas auri puri, a ~is facies illas* Exod. 28.14 (AC). **3** The border region (of an extent or territory), bounds: *ad illos qui in ultimis ~is coeli sunt* AC 7926.2; *binae statuae...locatae in ~o universi creati* AC 8325.3. **b** (as implying the territory within it): *Ego afficiam omnem ~um tuum ranis* Exod. 7.27 (AC); *omnes ~i nostri caeli a polygamis... custoditi sunt* AM 77.5. **4** A point not to be passed, final stage, limit: *~um ultimum Antiquissimae Ecclesiae* AC 812; *omne malum habet suos ~os, quousque vadere permittitur* AC 1311.2; *amor...et sapientia absque usu non habent ~um aut finem* AS 230. **5** A linguistic expression, term: *~is orbi erudito familiaribus* AC 129; *philosophi...de spiritu per ~os loquuntur quos ipsi non sciunt* AC 196.2; *meris ~is scholasticis* ES 3960.

ternarius ~a ~um, *a.* Of three: *numerus ~us* AC 482.1.

ternus ~a ~um, *a.* Three apiece, three in a set: *in novo templo erunt thalami portae tres hinc et tres illinc, mensura una ~is illis* Ezek. 40.10 (AC 2788.10).

tero ~ere trivi tritum, *tr.* **1** To wear out by use, use up: *apparent modo calcare et ~ere unam glebam et non progredi* AM 232.2; *libellus qui...tritus est a manibus puerorum* VR 14.3; VR 35.1; cf. *in dicto hodie in Ecclesia trito* VR 338.2. **2** To destroy little by little, nibble away: *qui...ea quae sunt veritatum ~unt, sicut mures frumenta* ES 3425. **3** To expend in vain, waste: *quod... subtilitas supervacuis ~atur* AM 315.8.

terra ~ae, *f.* **1** The earth (as the place inhabited by people and animals): *~a in literali sensu est ubi homo* AC 585; *distinguitur...inter bestias et feras ~ae ac inter bestias et feras agri* AC 46.3. **b** *~ae motus*, an earthquake: *si non...fuerit ~ae motus magnus* Ezek. 38.19 (DD 4); VR 79.2. **2** *Orbis ~arum*, the world, the globe: *antiquissimi hoc bene norunt...sed in ~arum orbe nullus adhuc* AC 97; *in universo hoc ~arum orbe* CI 415. **3** The earth (as the medium in which plants grow): *semina...ceciderunt...alia in ~am bonam* Matt. 13.8 (VI 2); *victus ex messibus agri, fructibus ~ae* VR 12.9; (dist. from **humus**) *in Verbo accurate distinguitur humus a ~a* AC 566.1. **4** (pl.) Various kinds of earth, terrestrial components: *lapides pretiosi...ac ~ae varii generis* CI 104; AS 173. **b** earth (as the material for making pottery): *argentum conflatum in catino ~ae* Ps. 12.6 (AC 1551.4). **5** The ground (as the surface on which people live), the surface of the earth: *descendere fecerunt quisque manticam suam ~am* Gen. 44.11 (AC); *prosternebant se faciem premendo in ~am* AC 2327.1; *subito aperuit se ~a* AM 263.1; (pl.) *speluncae seu cavernae sub ~is* FI 48. **6** Dry land (as opposed to sea): *ut non flaret ventus super ~am, neque super mare* Rev. 7.1 (AR). **7** A particular part of the earth's surface, land, country: *~ae et regiones quae extra* [*Europam*] *sunt* AC 567; *~am Aegypti* Exod. 8.1 (AC); *pro ~a Canaane* SS 71.2. **b** (standing for its inhabitants): *et omnis ~a venerunt Aegyptum ad emendum* Gen. 41.57 (AC). **8** Earth (as opposed to heaven): *facilius est coelum et ~am transire* Luke 16.17 (AC 7933.3); *qui in ~a violenti fuerunt* ES 377; (esp. pl.) *in coelis et in ~is* AC 648.1; *in Ecclesia Domini in ~is* AC 1103.1. **9** *~a inferior*, the lower earth (a region of the spiritual world nearest to hell): *dejectus in ~am inferiorem* AC 539; *in ~a inferiore, quae proxime est super infernum* VR 71.1.

terraqueus ~a ~um, *a.* (of the globe) Covered by land and sea: *universo orbi ~o* VR 29.1; ES 222.

terrefacio ~facere ~feci ~factum, *tr.* To frighten, terrify: *habitabunt confidenter, et non ~faciens* Ezek. 34.28 (AE 388.8).

terrenus ~a ~um, *a.* Made of material substance, earthly: *nubes opaca, in qua quasi ~um* AC 1524; *tunc ~a ejus repraesentantur per tale solidum punctum* ES 2087.

terreo ~rere ~rui ~ritum, *tr*. To frighten badly, scare, terrify: *internus homo non timet mala nec ~retur pro falsis* AC 986.2; *habitatores ~riti facti aufugerunt* AM 79.11; *sedebunt vir sub vite sua...non ~rens* Mic. 4.4 (VR 304).

terrestris ~is ~e, *a*. (compar. *~ior*) Of or peculiar to the earth, earthly: *quod corpora ~is materiae sint* AC 6697; *cogitatio hominis non est nisi ~is, corporea et materialis* AC 1072.1; (neut. as sb.) *qui ~ia et mundana pro fine habent* AC 8783.

terreus ~a ~um, *a*. Of the earth; (neut. pl. as sb.) objects upon earth: *non vident nisi universaliter ~a ut lucidum lunare, et aquea ut maculas* VR 22.3.

terribilis ~is ~e, *a*. Frightening, terrifying: *magnus dies Jehovae et ~is valde* Joel 2.11 (DD 4); *~es canes quorum aliqui erant tricipites* AM 79.2.

terricola ~ae, *m*. An inhabitant of the earth: *non ex ore alicujus ~ae, sed ex oribus caelicolarum* AM 178.1; VR 80.3.

terrifico ~are ~avi ~atum, *tr*. To frighten badly, terrify: *quod... ~ent illos, tametsi nihil nocent* AC 8381; ES 931.

terrificus ~a ~um, *a*. Terrifying: *quod...contraxerint pro uxoribus ~um timorem* AM 292.1.

terrifio ~fieri, *intr*. (pass. of **terrefacio**) To be frightened, terrified: *vidi impios... ~fieri sicut ipsam mortem viderent ante oculos suos* VR 691.2.

territo ~are, *tr*. To frighten: *parum ~ant, sed nihil mali inferunt* ES Index s.v. 'doctus, eruditus, doctrina' (p. 216 Tafel), referring to ES 545.

territorium ~i, *neut*. Territory: *omnes qui communicabant cum illis qui infra, quia extra ~um suum* ES [5759] ½.

terror ~oris, *m*. A state of strong fear, terror: *quod...in continuo ~ore sint* AC 390; *~orem incutiunt* AC 8021; (w. gen.) *ex ~ore paenarum* AC 7280.2. **b** *~ori esse*, to be a source of fear: *ne consociis ~ori sint* AM 510.2.

tersus ~a ~um, *a*. (pf. pple. of **tergeo***) Polished so as to shine, glittering: *gladius exacutus, et etiam ~us ad mactandum mactationem* Ezek. 21.14-15 = EVV 21.9-10 (AC 309); *ferrum ~um* Ezek. 27.19 (AC 426.1). **2** (of a light) Bright: *vidi lumen candelae illuc inferri, et inde lux satis ~a* ES 4863.

tertianus ~a ~um, *a*. Standing in the third degree: **a** Of the third generation: *visitare iniquitatem super ~os et quartanos* AR 322 (Num. 14.18); Gen. 50.23 (AC). **b** of the third highest rank: *~i duces super omnes illius* Exod. 14.7 (AC). **c** (fem. pl.) a third storey (in Noah's ark): *infimas, secundanas et ~as facies illam* [sc. *arcam*] Gen. 6.18 (AC).

tertio, *adv*. For the third time: *cecidit super terram et oravit...hoc secundo, et hoc ~o* AC 1787.2 (Mark 14.41).

tertius ~a ~um, *a*. Third: *est ~us status qui... describitur* AC 6750.1; *tradidit ~o tunicam* AM 315.7; (of the highest heaven) *in intimo seu ~o coelo* AC 6701. **b** *~us decimus*, thirteenth: *~o decimo anno rebellarunt* Gen. 14.4 (AC).

terumah: see **theruma**.

tessela ~ae, *f*. also **tessella**. (cf. **tesselo**) A small square piece: *patina panum scissorum in quadrates ~as* [*tesseras* Tafel; *tessellas* J D Odhner] ES 2626 (Autograph).

tesselatus ~a ~um, *a*. Chequered: *tunicam ~am* Exod. 28.4 (AC).

tessella: see **tessela**.

tessello: see **tesselo**.

tesselo ~are ~avi ~atus, *tr*. also **tessello**. To make in a chequered pattern: *~abis tunicam byssi* Exod. 28.39 (AC).

tessera ~ae, *f*. A small square block, split into two to serve as a token of recognition, (hence) a token: *quod dona illa sint confirmationes, est quia sunt ~ae consensuum* AM 300.1.

tessula: see **tessela**.

testa ~ae, *f*. **1** An earthenware vessel, pot: *num argilla increpatura est figulum, quod ex se ~am lotii faciat?* VR 72.1 (cf. Isa. 45.9). **2** The external carapace of a crustacean, egg, nut, etc., shell: *sicut ~ae seu crustae illorum* AM 364; *ovo putido intra ~am albam* VR 593.1.

testaceus ~a ~um, *a*. Made of earthenware: (neut. as sb.) *baptizationes poculorum et ~orum* Mark 7.4 (AC 5120.7).

testamentum ~i, *neut*. **1** A document disposing of the goods of a deceased person, will: *disponit in puncto mortis de iis, per ~um et similia* ES 1235. **2** Each of the two divisions of the Word, testament: *in Verbo Veteris ~i* AC 45; *Verbum utriusque ~i* AC 9548.3.

testatio ~onis, *f*. An act of bearing witness, attestation: (w. gen. as object) *est...verum ~o boni et quoque revelatio boni* AC 9474.2; *haec...mala in se recondunt ~onem falsi* VR 321; (w. gen. as subject and *quod* clause as object) *~o Domini in caelo quod* [*quidam*] *sit Ipsius, et sic quod sit in caelo unus inter angelos ibi* AR 819.

testator ~oris, *m*. One who bears witness: *falsus ~or* DP 95.

testatus ~a ~um, *a*. (pf. pple. of **testor**) (compar. *~ior*, superl. *~issimus*) **1** Well attested, clearly evidenced:

dictum...mihi est e coelo, et quoque per multam experientiam ~um factum est CI 554; *veritas irrefragabilis est et per experientiam ~issima* ES 300; ES 356. **2** *Ex ~o*, from experience: *quare hoc dico ex ~o* AM 419; VR 12.8.

testiculus ~i, *m.* (anat.) A testicle: *provinciam in vico ~orum* ES 3152; ES 5216.

testificatio ~onis, *f.* The bearing of witness, attestation: *foedus significat conjunctionem, ac testimonium ~onem ejus* VI 57; *in ~onem quod a Domino liberati sint* AC 8018.2.

testifico ~are ~avi ~atum, *tr.* also **testificor** ~ari. To give evidence of, attest: **a** (act.): *~ata fuit laetitia cordis...per cantus* AC 8339.1. **b** (dep.): *his modis ~ari gaudium* AC 8339.1; AM 56.5; (absol.) to bear witness: *Jehovah ~atus est inter te et inter uxorem* Mal. 2.14 (AC 255).

testificor: see **testifico**.

testimonium ~i, *neut.* **1** Evidence given in a court of law, witness: *non falsum ~um profert* CI 531.1. **2** (more generally) A piece of evidence: *talia mihi fuerunt ~a influxus spiritualis in mundum naturalem* AM 419; *theatrum super quo ~a quod Deus sit...continue exhibentur* VR 12.1. **3** (Bibl.) **a** The divine law of the Ten Commandments: *et dabis ad arcam ~um, quod dabo ad te* Exod. 25.16 (AC); also, divine law in general: *custodientibus foedus Ipsius et ~a Ipsius* Ps. 25.10 (AC 6804.10). **b** the witness borne by Jesus Christ: *habentibus ~um Jesu Christi* Rev. 12.17 (AR); Rev. 19.10 (AR).

testis[1] ~is, *m.* **1** One who provides legal evidence, witness: *en ~em populi dedi Ipsum* Isa. 55.4 (AC 6804.3); *ero ~is festinans contra praestigiatores* Mal. 3.5 (AC 7297.3); *falsum ~em agere* VI 87; (to a contract) *quod...faedus conjugiale pangendum sit in praesentia ~ium* AM 295.3. **2** Anything which serves as evidence, witness: *quod erigerent lapides in ~es quod ita* AC 1298.1; *suntne sensus corporis nostri ~es veritatum?* VR 77.2.

testis[2] ~is, *m.* A testicle: *qui ~ibus correspondent* AC 5060.1; AM 316.4; (sg.) *contusus ~e* Deut. 23.1 (AC 2468.15).

testor ~ari ~atus sum, *tr., intr.* **1** (w. acc.) To bear witness to: *quod quisque ~etur amorem per...facere quae alter vult* CI 16; *qui ~atus est Verbum Dei* Rev. 1.2 (AR). **2** (intr.) To bear witness: *false ~ari* VI 53; (w. *de*) *Ille ~abitur de Me* John 15.26 (AC 6788); *illae* [sc. *scripturae*] *~antur de Me* John 5.39 (DD 11); *ille sensus potest de Verbi Divinitate...~ari* SS 4; (w. *quod*) *quod amor vere conjugialis sit a Domino, ~antur omnes angeli caeli* AM 131.

testudo ~inis, *f.* **1** A tortoise: *se recondere sicut ~o suum caput in concha* VR 443.3. **2** A turtle: *exspectamus videre pulchras nostras ~ines (sköldpadda)* AR 463.1.

teter ~tra ~trum, *a.* also **taeter**. (compar. *~trior*, superl. *~terrimus*) Offensive to the senses, foul, hideous, abominable: *vertunt...lucem in colores injucundos et ~tros* AC 681; *apparuerunt aliquoties, sunt ~tri et aversatiles* AC 7419; *ructus ~tri* AM 253.2; *reptilia nidoris ~tri* VR 38.2; *~terrimum animal venenosum* ES(M) 4569.

tetre, *adv.* also **taetre**. Foully, abominably, hideously: *ut stomachum ~e afficerent* ES(M) 4574; *in igne ~e flammante* AE 1015.2.

texo ~ere ~ui ~tum, *tr.* **1** To weave: *tunica... ~ta* AC 9942.1; *telas araneae ~ebant* Isa. 59.5 (AE 581.4). **2** To construct, weave (any elaborate or complicated structure): *in talibus porticibus, ~tis, arcuatis* ES 2160; (fig.) *voluntarium influit in intellectuale, et ~it illud* AC 9915.2.

textor ~oris, *m.* A weaver: *~ores aulaeorum* Isa. 19.9 (AC 7601.7).

textura ~ae, *f.* A complex structure, web: *usque adeo ut illa quae in intellectuali sint ~ae ex voluntario* AC 9915.2; *~ae musculares* ES 1060.

textus ~us, *m.* **1** A complex structure, web: *~us interiores omnes resolverentur* AS 260.1. **2** The text (of a book, document, etc.): *in ~u Verbi* AC 71; *~us... internus* AC 7933.3; ES 4671.

thalamus ~i, *m.* (Gk.) **1** A room in a building: *angelus mensus est murum, portas, ~os* AE 223.10 (Ezek. 40.7). **2** A bedroom, chamber: *cum intrat* [*sponsus*] *~um cum sponsa* AM 10.2; VR 73.2; (fig.) *quod amor...habitet...in ~o seu conclavi voluntatis* AM 270.5. **3** (anat.) **a** A chamber of the brain from which the optic nerves were believed to originate, optic thalamus: *vadunt versus conjunctionem ~orum opticorum, ubi nervus alterius oculi concurrit* ES 1354. **b** a ventricle (in the heart): *cor e dextro suo ~o infundit sanguinem in pulmonem* VR 371.5.

thalassius ~i, *m.* (Gk., = English 'marine') The name of a precious stone (*tharschcish* in AC): *~us, sardius et jaspis, quartus ordo* Exod. 28.20 (SS 44.2).

thau, *indecl.* (Hebr.) The last letter of the Hebr. alphabet, taw: AR 38.

the: see **thea**.

thea ~ae, *f.* (poss. French) also **the**, and **thee**. Tea: *quaesivi de vinis, siceris, cerevisiis...thea* [*thee* Rogers] UJ(P) 292 (Tafel, p. 88); *parva vascula...quae usitabantur circa the* ES 3753; ES 3894.

theatralis ~is ~e, *a.* **1** Of or in a theatre, theatrical: *scenae ~es* AR 655.2; *vestes ~es* VR 381.4; *ludum ~em* ES 1880; (neut. as sb.) *per ~ia abducunt a vero cultu Divino* VR 320. **2** (of persons) Delighting in pretence, acting a part: *qui ~es sunt* ES 1882; (of things) hypocritical, insincere: *vocabant talia absona, ludicra et ~ia* AC 446.

theatrum ~i, *neut.* (Gk.) **1** An open area used for the presentation of plays, auditorium, theatre: *planum, super quo stabant, mutabatur in ~um* AM 55.3; *lucus cujus arbores...formabant sicut ~um* AM 132.1. **2** A stage (in a theatre): *spectacula comaedorum super ~is* AM 17.5; VR 173.2; *ecce erat ~um histrionum* SA 69 (= i.[5]). **3** A scene upon which any spectacle may be viewed: *ut universum...nihil aliud sit quam quoddam ~um repraesentativum gloriae Domini* AC 3000; *estne totus mundus sicut ~um, super quo quisque agit suam scenam...?* VR 665.3.

theca ~ae, *f.* (Gk.) A case for holding or displaying gems: *a...~is, in quibus nobiles gemmae...reconduntur* AM 389.2; [*sensus literae Verbi*] *est sicut ~a continens pretiosa, quae sunt sensus spiritualis ejus* VR 192; cf. *quod pomum contineat intus in se... seminum ~as* ES 3738.

thee: see **thea**.

thekel, *indecl.* (Hebr.) also **tekel**. Thekel, a word in the handwriting on the wall (cf. Dan. 5.25) meaning 'weighed' or 'to weigh': *per ~el seu appendere* AR 313.

thema ~atis, *neut.* (Gk.) A subject for discussion: *ad demonstrationem duorum ~atum hujus capitis* VR 367.7.

theologia ~ae, *f.* (Gk.) A particular system of theology: *universa doctrina salvationis hominis, quae vocatur ~a* AR 133; *aperi quae tua ~a* CC 20.5; (as the subject of a book) *plures qui ~am naturalem scripserunt* AC 8944.1.

theologicus ~a ~um, *a.* (Gk.) Of or concerned with theology: *tunc erant in zelo ~o* AM 354.1; *systema ~um* VR 75.7; (neut. as sb.) *omne ~um illis non aliud est quam sicut idolum* VR 7; FI 3.

theologus ~i, *m.* (Gk.) A theologian: AM 313.1; ES 1244.

theorema ~atis, *neut.* (Gk.) A demonstrable proposition, argument: *quid mihi juveni cum tam sublimi ~ate?* AM 315.7; *secundum ~a notum in orbe erudito* VR 473.

theoretice, *adv.* Theoretically: *moralia... ~e lustrata* VR 186.1.

theoreticus ~a ~um, *a.* Theoretical: *omnia ~a haurienda...sunt ab experientiis* UJ(P) 323.

theraphim, *pl.* (Hebr.) also **teraphim**. Images of deities, household gods: Gen. 31.19 (AC).

thermae ~marum, *f. pl.* (Gk.) A place for taking hot baths, bathhouse: *dissolutus eram in delitiosa lenocinia, sicut ~marum dulcium* ES 379.

theruma ~ae, *f.* (Hebr.) also **terumah**, and **thruma**. A choice offering: *quod omnis vir...adduceret ~am Jehovae* VR 495 (Exod. 35.21, where AC has *oblationem*); *ex thruma seu collecta quam facerent ad tabernaculum* AC 1947.4.

thesaurarium ~i, *neut.* A treasury: *~a sunt ubi opes reponuntur* AC 6661.2; *in ~a colligunt clenodia auri et argenti* VR 527.2.

thesaurarius ~i, *m.* A treasurer: *amicos faciunt coquos, tum ~os* ES 2500.

thesaurus ~i, *m.* (Gk.) **1** A collection of precious objects or money, treasure: *si aliqui ~i...latent reconditi* AM 267.3; *cui usui sunt tanti reditus, ~i et possessiones...?* AR 759.2. **2** A place for hoarding treasure, treasury: *nonne istud absconditum apud Me, obsignatum in ~is Meis?* Deut. 32.34 (AC 7051.3); (fig.) *bonus homo ex bono ~o cordis sui emittit bona* Matt. 12.35 (VI 28); *quod...illa quae intimae sapientiae sunt e ~is suis educat* VR 35.3.

thesis ~eos, *f.* (Gk.) (acc. sg. *~in*) A position adopted in an argument, proposition, thesis: *quamcunque ~in... homo arripit ut principium* ES 1312; *dum suas ~es seu fidei articulos affirmare volunt* ES 1737.

Thessalonicensis ~is ~e, *a.* Of or belonging to Thessalonica, a city of northern Greece: *ab Ecclesia ~i* UJ(P) 360.

thoracicus ~a ~um, *a.* (anat.) Of or belonging to the thorax: *per ductum ~um* DP 164.6; *provincia ~a* ES 3036.

thorax ~acis, *m.* **1** (anat.) The thorax: *pectoris seu ~acis* ES 870; *ex tunica stricta ad ~acem* AM 78.4. **2** A piece of armour to protect the chest, breastplate: *et habebant thoraces sicut ~aces ferreos* Rev. 9.9 (AR).

Threni ~orum, *m. pl.* (Gk.) The book of Lamentations: AC 6729; AE 357.24.

thronus ~i, *m.* (Gk.) A chair of state occupied by a ruler, throne: *scandere...in ~um Dei* AC 7375; *super ~o Davidis* Isa. 9.6 (CI 216); *vocabunt Hierosolymam ~um Jehovae* Jer. 3.17 (DD 4); *sedemus ibi super ~is ~orum* AM 263.2.

thruma: see **theruma**.

thum, *indecl.* (Hebr.) Transliteration of a Hebr. word (see quot.): *~um in lingua Hebraea legitur, per quod significatur integrum seu integritas* AC 9905.3.

Thumim, *indecl.* (Hebr.) also **Thummim**. One of two Hebrew terms which Swedenborg took to mean the twelve precious stones on Aaron's breastplate, Thummim: *duodecim lapides, qui Urim et ~m dicebantur* AC 9873.2; Exod. 28.30 (AC); cf. AC 9905.

Thummim: see **Thumim**.

thurcicus ~a ~um, *a.* also **tur-**. *Lapis ~us*, turquoise: AC 9870.

thuribulum ~i, *neut.* also **turibulum**. A vessel in which incense is burnt, censer: *vasa suffitus dicebantur ~a* AC 10296.2.

thus ~uris, *neut.* also **tus**. Frankincense: *aurum et ~us portabunt* Isa. 60.6 (AC 113); *suffitus ex ~ure* VR 108.

Thyatirensis ~is ~e, *a.* also **Thyatiriensis**. Of Thyatira: *Ecclesiae...~i* AE 108.1; (masc. pl. as sb.) its inhabitants: *~ium Ecclesiam* AR 124.

Thyatiriensis: see **Thyatirensis**.

thyinus ~a ~um, *a.* (Gk.) Of an African juniper (*callitris quadrivalvis*), thyine: *lignum ~um ad tabulas* AR 463.1; *tectu ex ligno nobili ~o* AM 103.3.

thymiama ~atis, *neut.* (Gk.) The use of incense, censing: *vestes, lumina, ~ata, pompae processionum* SE 107.

thymus ~i, *m.* (Gk.) (anat.) The thymus gland: *ad provinciam glandulae ~i* ES 1049.

tiara ~ae, *f.* A close-fitting headdress, cap: *quatuor viri in candidis vestibus, et in ~is* AM 9.4; *vir...cui ~a super capite, et pileus super illa* VR 137.12.

tibia ~ae, *f.* A flute, pipe: *canit uno tono ~ae* FI 42; AM 3.3.

tibialia ~um, *neut. pl.* Stockings: *tunicae...ex serico ...similiter femoralia et ~a* AM 15; AM 42.3; UJ(P) 325.

tibialis ~is ~e, *a.* Of a flute or pipe: *loquela eorum fuit sicut ~is, unius toni* CI 327; ES 489; ES 4507.

tibicen ~inis, *m.* A flute player: *vox citharoedorum, et musicorum, et ~inum* Rev. 18.22 (AE).

tigillum ~i, *neut.* A small beam or plank: *argentum vivum [mittere] in ~um candens in camino* CO 51.1.

tignum ~i, *neut.* A beam, plank: *hae [domus] constructae ex lateribus, interjectis ~is* AM 78.3; ES 5958.

tigris ~idis, *m.* or *f.* (Gk.) also **tigris** ~is, *f.* A tiger: *ut leones, ~ides, ursos* AM 378; (as a type of savagery) *fiunt ... ~ides quoad saevitiam* VR 13.4; *dolosi ~es* AC 8623.4.

tilia ~ae, *f.* A lime tree: *nemora plena castaneis, palmis, ~is* VR 78.1.

timeo ~mere ~mui, *tr., intr.* **1** (w. acc.) To be afraid of, fear: *et ~mebant obstetrices Deum* Exod. 1.17 (AC); *quod nec ~meant mortem* AC 8113; *jacturam ~met* AM 282.2; (pass.) *~mendus Ille super omnes deos* Ps. 96.4 (AC 7401). **2** (intr.) To be afraid: *et ~muit Moscheh* Exod. 2.14 (AC); *ne ~me* Isa. 7.4 (AC 6952.6). **b** (w. gen.) to be afraid (of), afraid (for): *maxime ~ment vitae* AC 939; ES 1293; *~mens damni proximi sicut sui* VI 72; *quod ~meat suae impuritatis* 3AD 707. **c** (w. *ab*): *quod...homo sic ~meat a malo et faciat bonum* AC 589; (w. dat. of refl. pron.) *ne ~mete vobis ab iis qui occidere corpus possunt* Matt. 10.28 (AC 7021.2). **d** (w. *ut*): *valde ~ment ut spectentur in luce coeli* CI 131; (w. *quod*) *pecuniae, quas ~mebant quod fures auferrent* ES 469.

timiditas ~atis, *f.* Fearfulness, timidity: *ex connata ~ata* AM 292.3.

timidus ~a ~um, *a.* (compar. *~ior*, superl. *~issimus*) Fearful, timid: AC 7111.3 (Deut. 20.8); (w. gen.) *~i sunt mortis* AC 821.2; CI 325.

timor ~oris, *m.* Fear, dread: *ex ~ore omnia faciunt* AC 6997.3; *quantum ~ores externi non inhibent* AC 7007.2; (w. gen.) *principium sapientiae ~or Jehovae* Ps. 111.10 (AR 527); *ex ~ore legis* VI 111; (w. *pro*) *aversatio conjuncta ~ori pro morte spirituali* AC 8162.

tinea ~ae, *f.* A grub, maggot: *in terra, ubi aerugo et ~a corrumpit* Matt. 6.19 (DP 217.6); ES 2673.

tingo ~gere ~xi ~ctum, *tr.* **1** To dye: *vestimento ~cto sanguine* Rev. 19.13 (AR). **2** To colour as with a dye, tinge: *calor... ~git lucem...colore suo, qui est aureus* AM 75.7.

tinnio ~nire ~nii (*or* ~nui), *intr.* **1** To make a metallic sound, ring: *status uxor Lothi, ~niens ex mero sale stricta penna scribae* AR 484.6 (Luke 17.32). **2** To vibrate, tremble: *~nuerunt* [*~nierunt* Autograph rough draft] *labia mea* Hab. 3.16 (AE 622.9).

tinnula ~ae, *f.* (app.) A bell: [*sirenes*] *habent certas boum ~as, ad quas loqui adigunt spiritum* ES 4601.

tinnulus ~a ~um, *a.* Making a bell-like sound, ringing, jangling: *voces ~ae afficientes aurem* ES 5835.

tintinnabulum ~i, *neut.* A bell: *super ~is equorum* Zech. 14.20 (DD 4).

tiro ~onis, *m.* also **tyro**. A novice, apprentice: [*status*] *cujusvis ~onis antequam fit mercator* VR 106.1; *ex membranis...ex scriptis a ~onibus* VR 137.1.

titillatio ~onis, *f.* Sensual excitement, tickling: *hujus* [sc. *sensus tactus*] *amaenitates sunt ~ones* AM 210; ES 4035.

titillo ~are ~avi ~atum, *tr.* To excite sensually, tickle: *immunda quae fibras corporis illorum ~ant* DP 38.2; (absol.) *quod* [*scabies*] *a nefandis insectis plena esset, quae ~abant* ES 4466.

titio ~onis, *m.* A piece of burning wood used to start a fire, torch, firebrand: *propter duas caudas ~onum fumantium istorum* Isa. 7.4 (AC 6952.6); *intuli ignem per ~onem* VR 159.1.

titubo ~are ~avi, *intr.* 1 To walk unsteadily, stagger: *ita ~abant ut clamarent quod angerentur* AC 1271. 2 To make mistakes, stumble: *~at voce et desperat* CI 35; *~ant judicio* Isa. 28.7 (AE 235.7).

titularis ~is ~e, *a.* Conferring an honorific title: *affectant dignitates, et quoque ~es* ES 5462.

titulus ~i, *m.* 1 An honorific title: *signa...in regnis sunt ~i dignitatum* VR 680.1. 2 A pretext: *qui...* [*aliorum bona*] *abstulerunt quoties ~o aliquo specioso potuerint* AC 949; ES 909.

toga ~ae, *f.* A full-length dress, robe, gown: *induunt illum ~a sua domestica* DP 109.2; *aulici erant in ~is coloris badii* AM 15; *sponsa...amicta erat chlamyde, et sub illa ~a acupicta, continua a collo ad pedes* AM 20.2; *in bursa ~ae* VR 137.3.

tolerabilis ~is ~e, *a.* (compar. *~ior*) Tolerable, bearable: *~ius erit terrae Sodomae et Gomorrhae* Matt. 10.15 (AC 7418.2).

tolerantia ~ae, *f.* Ability to endure, endurance: *novi opera tua, et laborem tuum, et ~am tuam* Rev. 2.2 (AR); AC 10622.1.

tolero ~are ~avi ~atum, *tr.* To allow to exist, tolerate: *cujus mentio...non ~atur in coelo sed illico respuitur* AC 1007; *quod ideo in populosis civitatibus lupanaria ~entur* AM 444[a].

tollo ~ere sustuli sublatum, *tr.* 1 To raise up, lift (persons): *quidam in primum atrium coeli sublati* AC 65; *tunc subito sublatus est in altum* AC 1769.1; *ego inde eum sustuli* ES 4191. 2 To raise, lift (things): *quando ~etur signum montium, aspicite* Isa. 18.3 (AE 55.2); *baculus ejus super mari, quem ~et in via Aegypti* Isa. 10.26 (SS 15.1). 3 To take up with the hand, pick up: *ne descendat ad ~endum quid e domo sua* Matt. 24.17 (AC 7857.1); *sustulit chartam, ex qua legit haec* AM 112. 4 To lift up (parts of the body so as to bring them into use): *~at Jehovah facies Suas super te* Num. 6.26 (AC 6674.8); *dictum est Moschi...quod ~eret manum* AC 6947; *sustuli oculos meos et vidi* Dan. 10.5 (AE 69.3); *sustulit super Me calcaneum* John 13.18 (DD 11). 5 To raise, set up (a lament): *~e lamentum super principibus Israelis* Ezek. 19.1 (AC 1069.4). 6 To take away, remove: *quod Dominus...illa* [sc. *omnia peccata*] *sustulerit* AC 7318.2; *~ite ab eo talentum, et date habenti decem talenta* Matt. 25.28 (AC 7770.2); *amor dominii...prorsus ~it amorem conjugialem* CI 380.1.

tonans ~ntis, *a.* (pres. pple. of **tono**) Resembling thunder, thunderous: *est loquela ~ns* CI 244; [*zelus*] *est extrinsecus laevis, glaber, ~ns et flagrans* VR 155.2.

tondeo ~dere totondi ~sum, *tr.* 1 To cut the hair of: *vocavit Josephum...et totondit et mutavit vestes suas* Gen. 41.14 (AC); Mic. 1.16 (SS 35.4); to cut (hair): *~de crinem* Jer. 7.29 (AE 66.5). 2 To shear (sheep): *iverat ad ~dendum gregem* Gen. 31.19 (AC).

tonitru ~ui (*or* ~u), *neut.* (gen. sg. usually *~ui*, but once *~u* AC 7573.4; nom. and acc. pl. *~ua*; gen. pl. usually *~uum*, but twice *~uorum* AE 854, AE 1216.1; abl. pl. *~ibus*) A peal of thunder: *pluviae, fulgura, ~ua* CI 105; *audivi sicut ~u crepans* AM 415.1; *a voce ~ui* Ps. 104.9 (AE 405.21); *Boanerges, hoc est, Filii ~ui* Mark 3.17 (AR 236.2); *audivi...tanquam vocem ~uum* Rev. 19.16 (AR); *constat a significatione 'vocum' quae ~uum* AC 7573.1.

tonitruo ~are, *intr.* To thunder: *post illa etiam ~abat, quod erat lene murmur* AM 316.5.

tonna ~ae, *f.* A large cask, barrel: *in ~is urinosis dicebat se morari velle* AC 820; *~a infernalis* AC 947; *quatuor arbores in quadam ~a plantatae* ES 2611.

tono ~are ~ui, *intr.* To thunder: *Deus gloriae ~are facit* Ps. 29.3 (SS 18.4); *~uit de coelo Jehovah* 2 Sam. 22.14 (AE 2735); *ut quasi ~aret* ES 3242 1/2.

tonsio ~onis, *f.* Shearing (of sheep): *lavatio apud ovem...ante ~onem* VR 673.

tonsor ~oris, *m.* 1 One who cuts hair, barber: *novaculam ~orum* Ezek. 5.1 (DD 15.5). 2 One who shears sheep, shearer: *sicut ovis coram ~oribus suis* Isa. 53.7 (DD 12).

tonsorius ~a ~um, *a.* Of or belonging to a barber: *sume tibi gladium acutum, novaculam ~am accipias tibi, quam traduces super caput tuum et super barbam tuam* Ezek. 5.1 (AC 3301.7).

tonsura ~ae, *f.* The product of shearing, clip: *primitiae ~ae pecoris* AC 9223.2.

tonus ~i, *m.* 1 The pitch of a sound, musical note: *loquela eorum fuit sicut tibialis, unius ~i* CI 327; *varii ~i discordes* AM 243. 2 A particular manner of speaking, tone: *loquitur...~o alto et elato* AR 692.2; *respondent ~o interno paene tacito* VR 35.1; *~o auctoritatis loquutus* VR 112.2.

topazius ~i, *m.* (ad. Gk.) A precious stone, topaz: [*fundamentum*] *nonum ~us* Rev. 21.20 (AR).

torcular ~aris, *neut.* A wine press: *~ar calcavi solus* Isa. 63.3 (AC 8273.2); *vindemiavit vineam terrae, et conjecit in ~ar irae Dei magnum* Rev. 14.19 (AR); also for oil: *exundant ~aria mustum et oleum* Joel 2.24 (AE 922.6).

tormentum ~i, *neut.* Torment: *non audent pedem ex illis efferre...propter ~um et cruciatum si hoc faciunt* AR 339.

tormina ~um, *neut. pl.* Griping pains: *~a et dolores apprehendunt* Isa. 13.8 (AC 8313.2).

torosus ~a ~um, *a.* Muscular, brawny: *corpus... ~um nudum ad limbos* ES 1084.

torpedo ~inis, *f.* An absence of activity, lethargy: *sphaerae dantur omnium, tam quoad activitates quam quoad ~ines* ES 1846.

torpeo ~pere ~pui, *intr.* To be inactive: *si ex sole luci non inest calor...omnia inde ~pent et moriuntur* AC 1577.2; *ex...otio stupet mens, et ~pet corpus* AM 249.2.

torpesco ~ere, *intr.* To become inactive, become dulled: *autumno, cum incipiunt* [*omnia*] *~ere* AC 1837; *omne delitium...elanguescit et ~it* AM 8.4.

torpor ~oris, *m.* Inactivity, inertia, sluggishness: *ex ~ore otii* DP 98.2; *totius corporis languor, ~or, stupor et sopor* AM 207.7; (w. gen.) reluctance (to): *inducunt ~orem faciendi bonum* ES 2502.

torqueo ~quere ~si ~tum, *tr.* **1** To subject to physical pain, torture, torment: *nisi fugiant, ~quentur et cruciantur* AC 6784.2; *~quentur...sicut pisces extra aquas* CI 54; *spiritualia...ambirent et ~querent illos* AM 352; *~quendo ~quebat corpus, sicut prorsus frangerer* ES(M) 4658. **2** To subject to mental torture, rack: *spiritus maximopere se ~quent, quomodo id intelligant* ES 2161. **3** To impart a circular motion to, twist: *cum talia alluunt...humorem talem ~quent* ES 1807; (refl. and pass.) *spirae ~quenti seu circumflectenti se sursum* AS 263.4; *serpentem in spiram ~tum* VR 122. **4** To distort, twist (the meaning of words): *ne lectores ~querent sensum* ES 2414; ES 2041.

torques ~is, *m.* A collar of twisted metal, torque: *sculpti sapphiri e collo ex aureo ~e pendentes* AM 15; *dedi... ~em super guttur tuum* Ezek. 16.11 (AE 126.3).

torrefacio ~facere ~feci ~factum, *tr.* To make hot, heat: *fornicationes...sunt sicut incendia... ~faciunt fibras* AM 456.

torrens ~ntis, *m.* **1** A powerful stream, current: *diabolici spiritus, in quorum consortio et quasi ~nte est* AC 892.1; *a fluminis magnitudine et ~nte judicare potui* AC 6699. **2** A rapidly flowing stream, torrent: *sicut ~ntem inundantem* Isa. 66.12 (AC 6745.5); *justitia sicut ~ns fortis* Amos 5.24 (SS 85).

torridus ~a ~um, *a.* Dried by heat, parched: *latuerunt sicut ignes in lignis ~is cortice obductis* VR 455[a]; (of the sense of taste) dried up: *cibi facti sunt nobis insipidi, ac gustus ~us* AM 6.4.

torris ~is, *m.* (abl. sg. ~*e*) A piece of burning wood used for starting a fire, firebrand: *~es ex quo incendium* AC 1327.2; *cinis sub quo prunae et ~es* ES 4563; (used to provide light) *cum luce ~is in manu viatoris* VR 348.2; (as building material) *macerias...hic ex stramentis, et hic ex ~ibus* AM 477.5.

torsio ~onis, *f.* A severe pain: *eorum tortura similis est ~oni sphincteris* ES 867.

tortuosus ~a ~um, *a.* Winding, sinuous: *Leviathanem serpentem ~um* Isa. 27.1 (AC 42.2); VR 74.2; *vias ~as* Judg. 5.6 (AC 8753.3).

tortura ~ae, *f.* Torture: *quod...cruciatus et ~as inferrent* ES 376; ES 867.

torus ~i, *m.* **1** A couch, bank: *quisque ad suam mensam accedens se reposuit super ~o ad caput ejus* AM 6.2. **2** A raised bank of earth: *vireta distincta in areas et ~os* AM 13.2; *non sedent super sellis...aut elevatis ~is gramineis* AC 8377. **b** a protuberance, lobe: *gibba pars...erat etiam divisa in binos quasi ~os* AS 432.2; *quod dextra pars sit torus seu receptaculum amoris* SA 79 (= iii.4.[1]). **3** The marriage bed: *illi* [sc. *filii ancillae*] *ex inferiore ~o sunt* AC 9281.1; *proles ex ~o non legitimo procreatae* SE 54; (fig.) *sunt enim* [*bonum et verum*] *consortes ~i seu conjuges* DP 233.1.

torvus ~a ~um, *a.* Grim, severe, stern: *quod inde vir ...sit ~us, austerus, siccus et inamabilis* AM 56.4.

tostus ~a ~um, *a.* (pf. pple. of **torreo***) Roasted, parched: *~us panis hordeorum* Judg. 7.13 (AC 7602); *spicam ~am* Lev. 23.14 (AC 9295.1).

tot, *indecl. a.* So many: *universum...tot innumerabilibus astris illustre* AC 6698; *a quo tot docti e clero...se dicunt duci* AR 962.8; (correlated w. *quot*) *quot capita tot animi* VR 32.2.

totalis ~is ~e, *a.* Complete, utter, total: *inundationem ~em* AC 660; *ad cessationem ~em cordis* CI 447; *~is damnatio* VR 3.1.

totaliter, *adv.* Completely, totally: *hoc ~er repugnat ordini* VR 110.3.

totidem, *indecl. a.* To the same number, as many: *per nomina...significantur ~em Ecclesiae* AC 483.1; *non dii, sed ~em proprietates...unius Dei* VR 9.3; (correlated w. *quot*) *~em infantes sunt...quot...desiderat* CI 332; VR 74.5.

toties, *adv.* So many times: *inde est quod in Verbo ~es nominentur arbores* CI 111; (correlated w. *quoties*) *quod ~es remitterent quoties peccat* AC 433.

totus ~a ~um, *a.* (gen. sg. ~*ius*, dat. sg. ~*i*) **1** The whole of, all: *super ~am terram Aegypti* AC 6643; *hic 'Lex' in lato sensu pro ~o Verbo* AC 6752.2; *Deus ~ius terrae* Isa. 54.5 (DD 41). **2** In respect of every part, wholly: *sic ut dicas illos* [sc. *angelos*] *~os non esse nisi amores* AC 6872.3; *quod in Sancta Caena sit ~us Dominus* VR 716.1; *~us dissolutus eram in delitiosa lenocinia* ES 379. **b** (reinforced by *quantus*): *~us quantus ad infernum rueret* AC 35; *corvus est ~us quantus albus*

AM 233.4; (also w. *tantus*) *nisi in corporeis ~us tantus esset ut nihil credat* AC 227.

toxicatus ~a ~um, *a.* Poisonous, toxic: *aliquae herbae ~ae* VR 78.5; CO 40.

toxicum ~i, *neut.* (Gk.) A poison: *apparent etiam [in inferno] ~a, et cicutae omnis generis et aconita* AS 339.2.

trabs ~bis, *f.* A balk of timber, beam: *eam vero quae in oculo tuo ~bem non intelligis?* Matt. 7.3 (AC 9051.3); *serpens...crassus instar ~bis* ES(M) 4700; Hab. 2.11 (AE 1145.8).

trachea ~ae, *f.* (Gk.) (anat.) The trachea, windpipe: *progressionem...per ~am in laryngem versus linguam* DP 180.3; ES 3324.

tracta ~ae, *f.* A loaf: *~am panis unam* Exod. 29.23 (AC).

tractatio ~onis, *f.* Rough treatment: *eorum ~ones malae sunt diversi modi* ES 453.

tractatus ~us, *m.* A section of a written document, chapter: DO 2.

tractio ~onis, *f.* The act of drawing, pull: *ut non aliter exprimi possit [amor] quam per ~onem* ES 322.

tracto ~are ~avi ~atum, *tr.* To treat roughly, manhandle: *crudeliter unus alterum ~at* AC 824; *quod Ipsum similiter ~arent [Judaei]* DD 15.2; *sicut feles ~ant mures* ES 4369.

tractus ~us, *m.* **1** A piece of ground, area, region: *omnis illa regio vocatur ~us Ecclesiae* AC 567; *~us horti* ES 2072. **2** *Temporis ~us*, the passage of time: *quod temporis ~u [Ecclesia] ab illa* [sc. *charitate*] *deflectat* AE 104; *post ~um temporis* AC 69; so, *~us* alone: *quae [memoria] mollescere ~u debet* ES 358.

traditio ~onis, *f.* A belief or opinion passed on by others, tradition: *secundum quorundam ~ones* AM 29; AC 259.2.

trado ~ere ~idi ~itum, *tr.* **1** (w. dat.) To give (a thing) into the possession (of): *quod decalogus ~atur omni puero et omni puellae in manum* DP 258.4; *~itus est Ipsi liber Esaiae prophetae* Luke 4.17 (DD 11). **2** To transfer control of, hand over (a person): *~et frater fratrem in mortem* Mark 13.12 (AC 6767.4); *quod ad instantias rogationis virorum se sicut victas ~iderint [uxores]* AM 297. **3** To pass on (information), relate, recount: *quae in explicationibus sparsim ~ita sunt* AC 6627; *differentias ~ere prolixum foret* CI 157; (w. indir. qu.) *licet breviter ~ere qualis unus et qualis alter* AC 81.1. **b** to hand down by tradition: *a conciliis...Ecclesiarum ~itum est quod...* VR 520.1.

traduco ~cere ~xi ~ctum, *tr.* **1** To cause to pass across, take across: *per mare Suph, per quod tuto ~cti filii Israelis* AC 8125; *per quod novaculam tonsorum ~ceret super caput suum* Ezek. 5.1 (DD 15.5); *tres advenae...per medium auditorii ~cti sunt* AM 207.2. **b** (app.) to cause to open (a door): *fracta est, januae populorum, ~cta est ad me* Ezek. 26.2 (AE 208.11). **2** To transfer, to carry over: *proclivitas ad mala a parentibus ~cta in liberos* VR 521.3.

traductio ~onis, *f.* The act of taking across, transfer: *de ~one illorum per medium infernum* AC 8125; ES 4362.

tradux ~ucis, *m.* **1** A part of a plant grafted onto another, graft: *quod...animalia et vegetabilia...mediate per semina, ova aut ~ucem propagentur* AS 347. **2** (fig.) An offshoot, graft: *qui...ex aliis per ~ucem sciverunt ex Verbo, quod Deus sit* DP 254.1; *amor parentum regnans per ~ucem derivatur et transcribitur in prolem* AE 989.3.

tragicus ~a ~um, *a.* (Gk.) Of or proper to a tragedy, tragic: *conjugia verterentur in scenas ~as* AM 297; (neut. as sb.) *tunc comaedum eorum fit ~um* VR 148.2.

traho ~here ~xi ~ctum, *tr.* **1** To pull, draw: *currus ab equis ~cti* ES 688; (absol.) *quod una [vis] ~hat et altera retrahat* AC 8168; (w. *ad*) *omnes...salvare vult et ad Se ~here* AC 1032.1. **b** *animam* or *spiritum ~here*, to draw breath, breathe: *inibi quasi animam ~here nequeunt* ES 210; *~here spiritum* AC 9281.3; also, to breathe with difficulty, gasp for breath: *~hunt ibi animam et torquentur* CI 54; *sicut suffocatus continue ~hens animam* DP 227.2. **2** To pull abusively, drag: *canibus ad ~hendum* Jer. 15.3 (AC 988); *se...lacerant, capillamentis ~hunt* ES 593; to force to go: *si quis te velit in jus ~here* Matt. 5.40 (AC 9942.11). **3** (w. *secum*) To bring along, bring with one: *homo...~hit secum in alteram vitam...innumera mala et falsa* AC 698; *animae mortuorum secum a corpore ~hunt omnem naturam* ES 333. **4** To impel, force, drive: *nihil...datur ...quod non...eum ad mortem ~hit* AC 1850.5; *amor voluntatis...~hit intellectum in consensum* AM 498. **5** To distort the meaning of, twist: *talia...quae absque sensu interno Verbi ad favorem cujuscunque opinionis ~hi queunt* AC 7127.2. **6** To acquire, get (a characteristic): *omne malum quod per habitum ~xerat quasi naturam* AC 8550; *~hunt quasi notam, sicut Cainus* ES 1248. **7** (w. *ab* or *ex*) **a** To derive, draw (its origin from): *verum...originem ~hit ex bono* AC 6717.1; *~hit...vox 'spiritus' derivationem suam a 'respiratione'* DD 47.1; *illud religiosum...~hit suum ortum ex amore imperandi* FI 49. **b** to derive (other things from): *plus ~hunt a corpore* AC 45; *unaquaevis affectio...~hit suam existentiam et naturam ex ejus intellectualibus* AC 803.1. **c** (absol.) to be derived (from): *haec* [sc. *voluntas externa*] *saepius ~hit ex simulatione et dissimulatione* AM 195.

trajicio ~jicere ~jeci ~jectum, *intr.* To pass through, cross over: *quod per ignem seu fornacem ignitam ~jecerit, hoc negatur* ES 2641.

trames ~itis, *m.* **1** A path, track: *ascenderunt per ~item clivosum in quendam collem* AM 11; *in quo purum reddet puer ~item suum?* Ps. 119.9 (AC 1288.2). **2** The course, route (of a moving object): *sequutus sum ~item soni* VR 72.1; ES 3490 1/2.

tranquille, *adv.* (compar. *~ius*) Quietly, calmly: *~e vivunt, nullum alicui incommodum afferunt* AC 1125.

tranquillitas ~atis, *f.* Freedom from disturbance, quiet, calm: *non amant jucundum ~atis sicut illi* AC 8115; *propter pacem et ~atem* AM 280.

tranquillo ~are ~avi ~atum, *tr.* To make quiet, calm: *mens per hoc ~at se, et satisfacit sibi* AM 6.6.

tranquillus ~a ~um, *a.* Free from disturbance, calm, quiet: *status post tentationem est ~us* AC 8370; *consortiis ~is, securis, amabilibus* AM 290; (neut. as sb.) a calm: *tumultus...cessavit, et factum est ~um et serenum* VR 71.4; *jucundum et ~um animi* AC 7364.

trans, *prep. w. acc.* **1** Across, through: *a corde usque ad cutem trans viscera est continuus nexus* AC 10044.9; *haec trans tectum infra audivimus* VR 71.1. **2** (w. no idea of motion or extension) On the other side of, across, through: *cis et trans Jordanem* CI 327; *apparuit uxor trans parietem* AM 56.6; *vidi trans fenestram...fulgur* VR 77.1.

transactio ~onis, *f.* A section of a book devoted to a particular subject, treatise, chapter: *in ~onibus...quae erunt...de Divina Providentia, Omnipotentia, Omnipraesentia...* SS 32; *in limine hujus ~onis* AM 48.

transcendo ~dere ~di ~sum, *tr.*, *intr.* also **transs-**. **1** (intr.) To pass beyond or across: *non ultra terminos acquisitos licet ei ~dere* AC 6977; *quod hi per mortem e suo* [*mundo*] *in alterum ~dant* VR 76.2; *quod parentium mala... ~dant in liberos* ES 1310; (impers. pass.) *sic ~ditur a mundo spirituum in coelum angelicum* ES 1958. **2** (tr.) To exceed, surpass: *misericordia Domini...infinite ~dit omnem intellectum hominis* AC 588.1; *infinitas ~dit finitum* VR 27.

transcribo ~bere ~psi ~ptum, *tr.* also **transs-**. To transfer: *quod Dominus desumpserit pulchritudinem ...a viro, et ~pserit in faeminam* AM 56.4; to change: *quod vita mala in bonam...nullatenus ~bi possit* CI 527; NH 239.

transcriptio ~onis, *f.* The action of transferring, transfer: *de ~one posterioris* [*amoris*] *in mulierem* AM 88.2; AM 194.1.

transcurro ~ere, *intr.* To change quickly or easily from one mode to another, switch: *hariolus super theatro qui potest duas personas agere, ~endo ab una parte in alteram* VR 173.2.

transcursus ~us, *m.* A cursory treatment: *sed haec in ~u* [i.e., in passing] 3AD 1399.

transenna ~ae, *f.* A screen of latticework (fig. to denote unclear vision): *solum in obscuro et sicut per ~am videri potest* DD 37.2; AM 132.4; *ego non volo per tam subtiles ~as hanc supremam rem inspicere* VR 17.4.

transeo ~sire ~sivi (*or* ~sii), *intr.* (*tr.*) **1** To pass across or through: *licet illis extra hujus solis mundum ~sire in alios* AC 6696; *Divinum Verum... ~sibit ad hominem per mediationes* AC 6996.2; *per mediam damnationem incolumes ~sibunt* AC 7889. **b** (Bibl., w. hostile intent): *~sibo per terram Aegypti in nocte illa, et percutiam omne primogenitum* Exod. 12.12 (AC); Zech. 9.8 (AC 6852). **2** To pass (to a different state), change: *quando illis* [sc. *malis*] *patrocinantur, ~seunt ad partes illorum* AC 7766; *paradisus terrestris ~sire potest in coelestem* ES 155. **3** To cease to exist, pass away: *coelum et terra ~sibunt* Matt. 24.35 (AC 1288.4); *felicitas ...temporaria, quae finitur et ~sit* AM 16.2. **4** (tr.) **a** To cross: *antequam ~sirent Jordanem* AC 7111.3 (Josh. 1.11). **b** to pass through (states): *Ecclesia Christiana... ~sierat aetates ab infantia ad ultimam senectam* VR 4.1.

transfero ~ferre ~tuli ~latum, *tr.* (*intr.*) **1** To take to another place, move, transfer: *~fer calicem a Me hunc* Mark 14.36 (AC 1787.2); *potentia totius hominis se ~fert in brachia* CI 231; *~ferre illuc milites per naves* VR 84. **b** (intr.) to take oneself, move (elsewhere): *et ~tulit inde in montem* Gen. 12.8 (AC). **2** To transfer possession or control of, give away, take over: *si divitiae...quae apud malos ~feruntur ad bonos* AC 6917.1; *quod peccata illorum...in Se ~tulerit* DD 15.1. **3** (app.) To change (into another state): *per vermiculos qui in nymphas ~feruntur* ES 877.

transfigo ~gere ~xi ~xum, *tr.* To drive a pointed object through, transfix, pierce: *qui Ipsum ~xerunt* Rev. 1.7 (AR).

transfiguratio ~onis, *f.* A change in the appearance, transformation: *propter hanc ~onem et defigurationem coelestium* CO 43.

transfluo ~ere ~xi, *intr.* To flow through: *Divinum quod per coelum ~it est bonum* AC 6720; CI 336.

transfluxus ~us, *m.* A flowing through: *hic ~us fuit Divinum Humanum* AC 6720; *per ~um innocentiae a Domino* CI 282.

transfodio ~dere ~di ~ssum, *tr.* To run through, pierce: *videbunt quem ~derunt* John 19.37 (DD 11); *Pinchasus... ~dit in lupanari virum ex Israele* AE 141.2 (Num. 25.8).

transformatio ~onis, *f.* **1** An alteration of form, transformation: *ex ~one vermiculorum in nymphas* AC 2758; *~o fidei naturalis in fidem spiritualem* VR 8.1. **2** The Lord's transfiguration before three disciples: *Dominus in hac ~one Se videri fecit ut Verbum* AR 24.7.

transformo ~are ~avi ~atum, *tr.* To change the form of, transform; esp. of the Lord's transfiguration: *cum ~atus Dominus* AC 6752.9; VR 104.

transfundo ~ndere ~di ~sum, *tr.* To infuse by a change, transfuse: *quod Deus Se ~derit et transscripserit in homines* CC 11.6; CO 38.

transgredior ~di ~ssus sum, *tr.* To go beyond (limits): *unumquodvis malum habet suum terminum... quem terminum ~di non licet* AC 1857.2; to break (a covenant): *quia ~ssi sunt foedus Meum* Hos. 8.1 (AE 55.2).

transgressio ~onis, *f.* The breaking of an agreement, breach of faith: *'rebellare' dicitur cum defectio et ~o* AC 9156.3; *ad has ~ones avertendas ipsa societas tutelam illius faederis in se suscepit* AM 307.

transigo ~sigere ~segi (*or* ~sigi) ~sactum, *tr.* **1** To cause to pass, put through: *quod ipsa vasa quae immunda facta sunt... ~sigerentur per aquas* AE 475.5 (Lev. 11.32). **2** To spend, pass (time): *in odiis...vitam ~segerunt* AC 968; ES 4471; (pass., of time) to pass: *~sacto integro anno* AC 893.2. **3** (impers. pass., w. *de*) There is a written discussion (about), it is treated (of): *nisi...de duobus illis arcanis ~sigatur* AM 70; *de Libero Arbitrio... ~sigendum est* VR 371.2.

transilio ~lire ~livi, *tr.* To leap to the other side of, jump over: *~liam murum* 2 Sam. 22.30 (AC 4402.10).

transitio ~onis, *f.* The act of passing, passage: *mors seu ~o ad patres* AC 1853; *~onem per mare Suph* AC 8039; *~ones in illas aetates non apparent* AM 185.1.

transitorius ~a ~um, *a.* Short-lived, transitory: *discessiones quae non sunt... ~ae* AM 289; *aegritudines ~ae* AM 474.

transitus ~us, *m.* **1** The act of crossing, passage: *~us Jordanis* AC 901.4; *~um...tuto per infernum* AC 8191; cf. *reges insulae quae in ~u maris* Jer. 25.22 (AE 406.12). **2** The possibility of crossing, passageway, opening: *clauditur ~us pro luce coeli* AC 6971.2; *existit liber ~us a primis usque ad ultima pro vena amoris* AM 293.4. **3** The passage from one state to another: *mors modo est ~us* CI 493.

translatio ~onis, *f.* **1** The act of transferring, relocation, transfer: *ad ~onem aliquorum ab uno inferno in aliud* CI 594; AM 207.2; *ejus* [sc. *potentiae*] *communicatio et ~o* AE 79.2. **2** The act of translating into another language, translation: *in ~one Scripturae Sacrae laborarunt* ES 1950.

translator ~oris, *m.* A translator: *~ores Mosis et Prophetarum* ES 2040.

translucens ~ntis, *a.* (pres. pple. of **transluceo**) Translucent: *fila illa instar filorum sericorum apparent ...pulchre ~ntia* AC 7601.3; AC 9407.5.

translucentia ~ae, *f.* Translucence: *apparuit* [*aedicula*] *ut una ex ~a* AM 56.2; AE 268.3.

transluceo ~cere ~cui, *intr.* To shine through, be translucent: *apud quos Verbum lucet et ~cet* SS 57; AM 192.

translucidus ~a ~um, *a.* Translucent: *per parietem ~um* AM 56.2; ES 4245.

transmeo ~are ~avi, *intr.* To pass across or through: *per succum ~antem alunt id* [sc. *semen*] AC 9258.2.

transmico ~are ~ui, *tr.* To glitter through: *radii striatim ~abant illas* [sc. *nubeculas*] AM 315.1.

transmigratio ~onis, *f.* Removal to live in another place, migration: *agnosco ~onem Jehudae in terram Chaldaeorum, in bonum* Jer. 24.5 (AE 403.18); ES 4232.

transmigro ~are ~avi, *intr.* To change one's residence, migrate: *quod ~averint modo ab uno mundo in alterum* CI 312.4; VR 160.2.

transmissio ~onis, *f.* The act of being sent: *~o per mediam damnationem significatur per transitionem per mare Suph* AC 8039.

transmitto ~mittere ~misi ~missum, *tr.* **1** To send across: *~misit ad me cochleare ebenum* AM 344; to pass across: *accipe novaculam et ~mitte super caput* Ezek. 5.1 (AE 66.5). **2** To allow to pass through, transmit: *quia memoria eorum interior lucis radios ~mittit in exteriorem* CI 466; ES 4457. **3** To transfer to another place or state, relocate: *quod homo in vitam boni ~mitti possit momento* AC 7439.3; *Dominus...potest illos ~mittere in societates coelestes* AE 1164.3. **4** To give in turn, pass on: *concentrant...influxum felicis e coelo in se, nec illum ~mittunt ad alios* AC 6388.2; *inque haereditatem ~mittatis eos filiis vestris* Lev. 25.46 (AC 8002.6).

transmutatio ~onis, *f.* A change into something different, transformation: *hanc ~onem et versuram* [*apparentiarum*]...*saepius animadverti* VR 650.

transmuto ~are ~avi ~atum, *tr.* To change into something different, transform, transmute: *licuit repraesentare illis prata...sed illico ~abant illa* AC 7071; *spiritus draconis... ~are in angelos Michaelis* VR 58.1.

transparens ~ntis, *a.* Transparent: *in membranam ~ntem* VR 34.4.

transparentia ~ae, *f.* Transparency: *tale est Verbum in suo sensu literae ex ~a* SS 42; the fact of shining through: *quod albedo et candor* [*significent*] *verum ex ~a lucis* AE 67.1.

transpareo ~rere ~rui, *intr*. **1** To shine through, penetrate: *miraretur quod usquam possent...~rere radii lucis* AC 1043.3; *fuligo, per quam ignis sicut foci furve ~ruit* AM 264.1. **2** To be visible through: *per illam* [sc. *faciem*] *mens quasi ~ret* AC 8243; *~rent, sicut facies per tenue sericum* SS 55.

transpicio ~picere ~pexi, *intr*. also **transs-**. To look through: *foramina...per quae ~picerent versus me* ES 4027; ES 5875.

transpiratio ~onis, *f*. also **transs-**. The act of oozing through, osmosis, transpiration: *ex ~one affectionis domini sui sciunt* [*canes*] *tanquam nutus ejus* AE 1198.2; AE 1191.2.

transpiro ~are ~avi, *intr*. also **transs-**. To ooze through, transpire: *serositas...cujus...pars aliunde ~at* ES 831; *vas in quo sunt tetra et sordida quae ~ant* AE 126.2.

transplantatio ~onis, *f*. Transplantation (in quot. fig.): *inde est insitio ejus* [sc. *religionis*], *et quoque ~o ejus a generatione in generationem* AM 466.2.

transplanto ~are ~avi ~atum, *tr*. To transplant (in quot. fig.): *malum... ~atur in liberos* AC 494.1; *quod religio ~ata sit in universum orbem ex Verbo Vetusto* DP 254.2.

transpono ~nere ~sui ~situm, *tr*. To place instead, relocate: *eos...in quoddam habitaculum melius ~nere* ES 308.

transportatio ~onis, *f*. The act of carrying away: *per ~onem Judaeorum in terram Chaldaeorum* AE 403.18.

transporto ~are ~avi ~atum, *tr*. To carry away, transport: *quod rex Aschuris ~averit filios Israelis in Aschur* AC 1189.

transs-: see **trans-**.

transtrum ~i, *neut*. A horizontal beam, cross-beam: *per ~um coeruleum ex fasciolis* ES 4379; *turris immensa circumcirca ~is tabulatis, per quae ascenderetur* ES(M) 4601. **b** a horizontal member of a trained tree: *arbores...combinatae in ~a* CI 176; ES 4354. **c** a thwart (in a boat): *navigia magna et parva...et super ~is sedentes pueri* VR 462.1.

transubstantialitas ~atis, *f*. also **transs-**. Transubstantiality: ES 3960.

transubstantiatio ~onis, *f*. also **transs-**. Transubstantiation: AR 751.2.

transudo ~are ~avi, *intr*. To pass through as by sweating, transpire: *sic ut ~averit aliquid boni* ES 807.

transumo ~ere ~psi ~ptum, *tr*. also **transsumo** ~ere ~si ~tum, *tr*. To take over, copy: *haec...sunt ~pta ex Formula Concordiae* VR 463.

transversaliter, *adv*. Sideways: *circumvolvuntur a capite et pedibus in modum axeos ~er* AC 829.1.

transversim, *adv*. At right angles, crosswise: *quod... circumrotentur sicut volumen...dein ~im alio situ, et sic in alio* AC 829.1; *parietes formantur...per flores...et similia...quae se extendunt ~im per parietem* ES 878; *non deorsum et sursum, verum ~im* ES 1693.

transversus ~a ~um, *a*. Placed crosswise, horizontal: *demiserunt contum ~um pendentem e fune* ES 1553.

transvibro ~are ~avi ~atum, *tr*. To flash (light) on and off through (something), transmit intermittently: *quod per Urim et Thumim transmicuerit ac ~ata fuerit lux* AC 6335.2.

trecenti ~ae ~a, *pl. a*. Three hundred: *~os et nonaginta dies* Ezek. 4.5 (DD 15.7); AM 264.2.

tredecim, *indecl. a*. Thirteen: *et hoc per ~im annos* CI 1.

tremefacio ~facere ~feci ~factum, *tr*. To cause to tremble: *qui ~facit terram e loco suo* Job 9.6 (AE 219.4).

tremefactio ~onis, *f*. The act of causing to tremble; quaking: *sub pedibus meis... ~o perstabat* ES 375.

tremefio ~fieri ~factus sum, *intr*. To be caused to tremble: *terrentur et ~fiunt* [*tremiscunt* Tafel] *ad judicium veritatis* ES 149.

tremiscenter, *adv*. In a quivering manner: *percipiebantur per crines et supremam capitis mei cutem quam ~er movebant* ES 3206.

tremisco ~ere, *intr*. To quiver, quake: *~ebat totus mons valde* Exod. 19.18 (AC).

tremo ~ere ~ui, *intr*. To tremble, quake: *fundamenta montium ~uerunt* Ps. 18.7 (AE 400.6).

tremor ~oris, *m*. A trembling, quivering: *incidebant in me aliqui spiritus tali vehementia ut ~orem incuterent nervis et ossibus* AC 3219; AC 8261.3.

tremulatio ~onis, *f*. Trembling, quivering: *cum tali ~one et anxietate* ES 3586.

tremulo ~are ~avi, *intr*. To tremble, quiver: *incipiebant ~are crasse* ES 3586.

trepidatio ~onis, *f*. A quaking: AE 677.6.

trepido ~are ~avi, *intr*. To quake in fear: *vox Jehovae ~are facit desertum* Ps. 29.8 (AC 6971.4); *commovebo caelum, et ~abit terra e loco suo* Isa. 13.13 (DD 4).

tres ~es ~ia, *pl. a*. Three: *per ~es gradus* SS 6; *de angelis ~ium coelorum* CI 435.

trias ~adis, *f.* A group of three: *~ades et ~ades ac decades et decades* AM 8.2.

triangularis ~is ~e, *a.* Triangular: *quasi ~e spatium* AC 941.1; ES 4357.

triangulum ~i, *neut.* A triangle: *sic ut ~um efficiatur* ES 750.

triarchia ~ae, *f.* (Gk.) The rule of three persons, triumvirate: VR 171.1.

tribula ~ae, *f.* A threshing sledge: *posui te in ~am ~ae recentis* Isa. 41.15 (AE 405.48).

tribulatio ~onis, *f.* Severe punishment, tribulation: *tradent vos in ~onem* Matt. 24.9 (AC 3486); *ex ~one magna* Rev. 7.14 (AE; *afflictione* AR).

tribulum ~i, *neut.* A threshing sledge: *quid ~a, vide prius, nempe quod sint vasa trituratoria olerum cum instrumentis triturantibus ibi ferreis* ES 2638.

tribulus ~i, *m.* (Gk.) A thistle: *~us et spina ascendet super altaria illorum* Hos. 10.8 (AC 9144.7).

tribunal ~lis, *neut.* A court of justice, tribunal: *dicebatur mihi, quod illud vocarent ~l* AM 231.2.

tribunus ~i, *m.* An officer: *sicut ~us equitans super generoso equo* CO 40; *~us plebis*, the title of a magistrate in ancient Rome, Tribune of the Plebs: VR 141.

tribuo ~ere ~i ~tum, *tr.* To ascribe, attribute: *sibi applicare et ~ere verum* AC 878.1; *doctrinae ~unt amaenum et jucundum* AC 7002; CI 130.

tribus ~us, *f.* A division of a people, tribe: *plangent omnes ~us terrae* Matt. 24.30 (AC 1984.3); *per dispositionem angelorum...in classes et quasi ~us* ES 212; esp. of the twelve tribes of Israel: *ex duodecim ~ubus Israelis* AC 577.

tributarius ~a ~um, *a.* That pays taxes or tribute; (fem. as sb.) a tributary nation: [*urbs*] *quae dominata est in provincias, facta est in ~am* Lam. 1.1 (AC 6394).

tributum ~i, *neut.* Tribute: *et erit ~o serviens* Gen. 49.15 (AC); *principes ~orum* Exod. 1.11 (AC).

triceps ~ipitis, *a.* Three-headed: *canes quorum aliqui erant ~ipites* AM 79.2.

tricesimus: see **trigesimus**.

triclinium ~i, *neut.* A dining room: *sequuti sunt in ~um* AM 14.2; *contignat aquis ~a sua* Ps. 104.3 (AE 283.8).

Tridentinus ~a ~um, *a.* Of Trent in Austria: *ex Concilio ~o* AR 738.3; *ex Synodo ~a* VR 640.2.

triduum ~i, *neut.* A period of three days: *post ~um coeperunt faustitates illae hebescere* AM 8.3.

triennis ~is ~e, *a.* Three years old: *accipe tibi vitulam ~em* Gen. 15.9 (AC).

triennium ~i, *neut.* A period of three years: *me persequutus est jam paene per ~um* ES 461.

triental ~lis, *neut.* A measuring vessel (holding one third of a major unit): *complexusque est in ~li pulverem terrae* Isa. 40.12 (AE 373.4).

trigecuplus ~a ~um, *a.* Thirty times as much: *dederunt fructum, aliud centuplum...aliud ~um* Matt. 13.8 (AC 3310.2).

trigesimus ~a ~um, *a.* also **tricesimus**. Thirtieth: *quovis ~o die* AC 10833.

triginta, *indecl. a.* Thirty: *distantia inter solem et lunam ibi est ~a graduum* CI 146.

trihorium ~i, *neut.* A period of three hours: *post ~um* AM 7.3.

trinitas ~atis, *f.* A threefold entity: *quis...non potest percipere Trinitatem in Domino, ex ~ate in unoquovis homine?* VR 169; esp. of the Divine Trinity: *quod Deus sit unus essentia et persona, in quo est Divina ~as* VR 2.2.

trinum ~i, *neut.* A threefold entity, trinity: *quod in omni re completa sit ~um* SS 28; esp. of the Divine Trinity: *quod in Domino omne ~um sit perfectum, nempe Pater, Filius et Spiritus Sanctus* AC 6993.2.

trinus ~a ~um, *a.* Threefold: *~a dimensio omnium est in terrestribus* AC650; *quod non detur...perfectum nisi sit ~um* AR 875.7; *omnis Ecclesia est ~a* CO 39.

tripartitio ~onis, *f.* A division into three parts: *de ~one etiam coeli* AC 9992.1.

tripartitus ~a ~um, *a.* Divided into three parts: *de secundo statu, qui ~us* AC 834; *quod* [*unitas Dei*] *non sit ~a in personas* VR 138.

tripersonalis ~is ~e, *a.* Relating to three persons (in God), tri-personal: *quod credatur in Ecclesia quod ~is ejus fides in illo dicto a Paulo intellecta sit* VR 338 (Rom. 3.28).

triplex ~icis, *a.* Occurring three times, triple: *in ~ice ordine repositi erant panes* AM 20.1; of three kinds: *vera sunt ~icis generis* CI 468.1; *in ~ici sensu* VI 87.

triplicatio ~onis, *f.* Multiplication by three, tripling: *~o numeri senarii involvit etiam finem* AC 10217.8.

triplicatus ~a ~um, *a.* Multiplied by three, tripled: [*adulterium*] *simplex, duplicatum et ~um* AM 478.3; ES 289; composed of three parts, triple: *pleraque inferna sunt ~a* CI 586.

triplicitas ~atis, *f.* Threefold nature: *quod duplicitas et ~as sit in omni creato* VR 147.

triplico ~are ~avi ~atum, *tr.* To multiply by three, triple: *~atur ille numerus* AE 847.1.

triplo, *adv.* Three times: *hoc adulterium... ~o gravius est* AM 484.

tripos ~odis, *f.* (Gk.) also **tripus** ~odis, *m.* (VR 17.4 Worcester). A three-legged cauldron, such as was used in giving oracles in antiquity at Delphi: *~os, ex qua responsa vellent dare* VR 17.4 (1st edn.).

tripudio ~are ~avi, *intr.* To dance in a rollicking, joyful, triple time rhythm: *David, cum arca deduceretur ...in urbem Davidis, ~abat et saltabat coram Jehovah* 2 Sam. 6.16 (AC 10416.3).

tripus: see **tripos**.

tristis ~is ~e, *a.* (compar. *~ior*, superl. *~issimus*) **1** (of persons or their state) Sad, gloomy, miserable: *percipiunt ...quam ~is et quam lamentabilis vita sit illorum* AC 2363.2; *ivi ~is in excandescentia spiritus mei* Ezek. 3.14 (DD 48.4); *~i et gemente facie* CI 358. **b** (neut. as sb.) sadness: *haec sunt quae inducunt ~e et anxium animis* AC 8247; ES 4439. **2** (of things) Causing sadness, depressing: *ex insaniis, etiam quae ~issimae sunt et summe injucundae* ES 231; *in colores...nigrescentes aliosque ~es* ES 2876; (neut. as sb.) *postquam haec ~ia et atrocia mihi visa sunt* AM 266.1.

tristitia ~ae, *f.* Sadness, depression: *fugient ~a et gemitus* Isa. 35.10 (AC 8339.2); *dolor animi et ~a interior quae melancholia vocatur* CI 299; (w. pl.) an instance of this: *opposita sunt gaudia et luctus, ac laetitiae et ~ae* AM 425.1.

triticum ~i, *neut.* **1** Wheat as a crop: *sevit zizania inter ~um* Matt. 13.25 (AE 187.8). **2** Wheat as grain: *panes ex ~o* AC 1002; *separantur paleae a ~o* VR 26.2. **b** (pl. in same sense): *semina...hordea, ~a et similia* AC 7112.

tritura ~ae, *f.* The process of threshing: *fustibus ~ae* VR 331.2.

trituratio ~onis, *f.* The act of threshing or crushing: *per modum serrationis agunt, seu ~onis cis et ultra* ES 1009.

trituratorius ~a ~um, *a.* Of or concerned with threshing or crushing: *vasa...quasi ~a sicut quae sunt olerum* AC 824; *de ~a undulatione* ES 3218 titulus.

trituro ~are ~avi ~atum, *tr.* To thresh: (absol.) *surge et ~a, filia Zionis* Mic. 4.13 (AC 7770.5); to pound, pulverize: *~ant et cruciant quos possunt* AC 824.

tritus ~a ~um: pf. pple. of **tero**.

triumpersonatus ~us, *m.* A word coined on the analogy of **triumviratus** to express the concept of God as three Persons, triumpersonate: *pro triumviratu vocari potest ~us* VR 133.2.

triumpho ~are ~avi, *tr.* To be victorious, triumph: *quod causae justum semper ~aret* AC 7007.1; *ut injustitia... ~et super justitiam* VR 72.1.

triumphus ~i, *m.* A victory parade, triumph: *quis in ~o non aspicit victorem...?* VR 660.2.

triumviratus ~us, *m.* The rule of a group of three persons, triumvirate: *sicut de ~u, qualis semel fuit Romae* VR 133.2.

triunus ~a ~um, *a.* (of God) Three-in-one, triune: *Deus Trinus aut Deus ~us...est...Ille cui Trinum aut ~um in una Persona est* AR 490.3; VR 135.1.

Trojanus ~a ~um, *a.* Of Troy, Trojan: *per equum ~um* AC 2762.4.

trucido ~are ~avi ~atum, *tr.* To massacre, butcher: [*praedones*] *irruunt et ~ant* CI 560.

truculentus ~a ~um, *a.* Aggressive, fierce: *visi sunt sicut variae ferae ~is oculis* AM 264.4.

trudo ~dere ~si ~sum, *tr.* To force to go, push: *~dere camelum per foramen acus netoriae* VR 481.1; *quod Dominus nullum ad infernum ~dat* ES 4344.

trulla ~ae, *f.* A dish to catch and carry away the consumed portion of a lamp's wick, snuff-dish: *ex significatione forcipum et ~arum, quod sint emunctoria, ita purificatoria et evacuatoria* AC 9572 (Exod. 25.38).

trunco ~are ~avi ~atum, *tr.* To maim, mutilate: *eum ~are et occidere* VR 169.

truncus ~i, *m.* **1** The trunk (of a tree): *arbor cum ~o, ramis, foliis et fructibus* SS 66; *exibit virga de ~o Jischaji* Isa. 11.1 (DD 6). **2** The torso of a human body, trunk: *quod...fiat sicut ~us humanus* VR 23.2.

trutina ~ae, *f.* (Gk.) The pointer in a balance: *hoc* [sc. *aequilibrium*] *ad ~am moderari et aequare* CI 593; *conjunctio mentium...tenet inclinationem sicut ~am in bilance* AM 318.1. **b** (transf.) a delicate judgment, balance: *exquisitior ~a in his est quam usquam aliquis credere potest* AC 3110.2.

trutinatio ~onis, *f.* Weighing: *sicut nulla ~o nisi lances ex aequilibrio possint utrinque protendi* AM 438; AE 373.1.

trux ~ucis, *a.* Fierce, savage: *~ucibus oculis nos... aspectabant* AM 79.2.

tu, *pers. pron.* (acc. *te*, gen. *tui*, dat. *tibi*, abl. *te*) You (sg.): *num...vocabo tibi mulierem nutricem?* Exod. 2.8 (AC); (reinforced w. *-met*) *cur Dominus...elegerat piscatores...quod etiam temet* CC 20.4; (w. *ipse*) *sicut teipsum* Matt. 22.39 (AC 6632).

tuba ~ae, *f.* **1** A trumpet: *emittet angelos cum ~a et voce magna* Matt. 24.31 (SS 14.1); AM 2.1. **2** (anat.)

~a Eustachiana, the tube connecting the pharynx with the ear, Eustachian tube: *per quoddam ibi quod vocatur hodie ~a Eustachiana* AC 1118; AC 7359.

tuber ~eris, *neut.* A swelling on the body, lump: *~era lethalia capitis intra cranium* AC 5717.2; ES 5925.

tuberculum ~i, *neut.* A small excrescence: *in parvo ~o inter cerebrum et cerebellum* AM 315.4.

tuberositas ~atis, *f.* A swelling on the body: *apparet ~as deprimi et cava fieri* AC 5188.2.

tubulatus ~a ~um, *a.* Equipped with tubes: *receptacula illa non sunt ~a aut insinuata sicut vascula* SA 78 (= iii.4.[1]).

tubulus ~i, *m.* A small pipe or tube: *ex...voce receptaculi facile incidit idea vasculi seu ~i* SA 78 (= iii.4.[1]); ES 2216.

tubus ~i, *m.* *~us opticus*, a telescope: *qui per ~os opticos vident circumjacentia* VR 61.2; VR 808.

tueor tueri tutus sum, *tr.* **1** To look at, contemplate: *ut mens...queat...tueri coelum* 1AD 1148. **2** To protect: *haec* [sc. *bona*] *tuta sunt a Domino* AC 6677; see also **tutus**.

tuguriolum ~i, *neut.* A small hut: *~a lutea* ES 392.

tugurium ~i, *neut.* A crude dwelling, hut, shack: *tunc inde vacillat* [*terra*] *sicut ~um* Isa. 24.20 (AC 1066.1).

tulipa ~ae, *f.* A tulip: *efflorescentiae ~arum tempore veris* VR 316.

tum, *adv.* In addition, besides, also: *vices...caloris et lucis, tum fructificationum terrae* AC 37; *apparet...ut lux, tum sicut splendor...lucis* AC 8267.1; VR 42.2. **b** (reinforced w. *quoque*): *bini fluvii...tum quoque mare* AC 1585.2; (w. *etiam*) *sensum delitiarum coelestium, tum etiam sensum delitii conjugialis* ES 399. **c** *tum... tum*, both...and at the same time: *constat tum quam incomprehensibiles sunt, tum quam crassae* ES Index s.v. 'loqui, loquela' (p. 20 Tafel), referring to ES 2211-20.

tumeo ~mere ~mui, *intr.* **1** To be swollen: *pectus ~mens in rhombum* AM 263.1. **2** To be puffed up, be conceited: *pro iis qui amore sui ~ment* AC 290.

tumescentia ~ae, *f.* A puffing up, inflation, swelling: *ex his est ~a pectoris eorum dum in fastu sunt* AE 1057.6.

tumescibilis ~is ~e, *a.* Capable of swelling up: [*membrana*] *~is* AC 5378.2.

tumesco ~ere, *intr.* To become swollen, swell up: *coeperunt ~ere facie* AM 7.2; *coepit is ~ere, et ita magnus fieri, ut...* ES 991.

tumidus ~a ~um, *a.* Swollen, puffed up: *sunt ~i, sicut colon suo vento* AC 5379; *amore sui ~i* ES 2336.

tumor ~oris, *m.* A swelling (on the body): *ulcera leprae, ut ~or, abscessus...* AC 7524.3; ES(M) [4740].

tumulo ~are ~avi ~atum, *tr.* To bury, inter: *externae ...affectiones...sequuntur corpus et ~antur cum illo* AM 320.3; ES(M) [4725].

tumultuatio ~onis, *f.* Violent disturbance, uproar: *in die illo erit ~o Jehovae magna* Zech. 14.13 (DD 4); *~o ista maris* ES 243.

tumultuor ~ari ~atus sum, *intr.* **1** (of the sea) To be violently disturbed, be rough: *mare...~ans cum magnis fluctibus* AC 953; ES 179; (also, of other things) *in statu quieto, utcunque ~atur cerebrum utrinque* AC 7744. **2** (of persons) To create a violent disturbance, be in an uproar: *pueri...colludebant ~ando* AM 218.2; ES 4683.

tumultuosus ~a ~um, *a.* Violently agitated, seething: *Divinum Verum et Divinum Bonum...sunt...cum delabuntur versus inferiora...impacifica et tandem ~a* AC 8823; *mare ~um* ES 243.

tumultus ~us, *m.* A violent disturbance, uproar, tumult: *~us sicut internecinus auditur* AC 4951; *dies ~us et conculcationis* Isa. 22.5 (DD 4).

tumulus ~i, *m.* A mound: *acervi qui...sicut ~i sepulchrales super terra illa eminebant* VR 110.8; (fig.) *sicut in ~o jacet absconditum, quid bonum charitatis* AM 126.

tunc, *adv.* **1** At that time, then: *~c potentia inferni valuit super potentiam caeli* VR 3.1; (reinforced w. *temporis*) *per hominem significatur hic genus humanum ~c temporis* AC 564; AC 2868. **2** After this, next, then: *at ~c auditum est tonitru* AR 417.4. **3** At that stage, then: *postquam rationale...conceptum est, ~c per ancillam etiam intelligitur tenerum illud rationale* AC 1920; *post mortem, quia ~c non amplius reformari ...potest* DP 17. **4** Under those circumstances, then: *si homo nullo haereditario malo imbutus esset, ~c nasceretur rationale* AC 1902.1.

tundo ~ere tutudi tusum, *tr.* To pound, beat, crush: *oleum olivae purum, tusum* Exod. 27.20 (AC); Exod. 30.36 (AC).

tunica ~ae, *f.* **1** An inner garment, tunic, shirt: *fecit Jehovah Deus homini et uxori ejus ~as pellis* Gen. 3.21 (AC); *per vestimentum ejus intelligitur ~a* AC 9942.7; *amictus erat toga...et ~a...sub illa* AM 266.1. **2** (anat.) The outer layer or integument of an organ, tunic: *cutes seu ~ae quae cingunt corpus* AC 8980; *omnis arteria* [*consistit*] *ex ~is in triplici serie* VR 147; (of the eye) *evolvere ~am oculi* AC 183; ES 1106; (of the afterbirth) *uterinis e matre post partum elapsis ~is* SE 67. **b** (in plants) an exterior layer, tunic: *quod per libros, philyras et ~as fiunt vegetationes* AS 314.

turba ~ae, *f.* **1** An unorganized group of people, crowd, mob: *~a mixta multa ascendit cum illis* Exod. 12.38 (AC); *affluebat ~a* CI 344; *audivi clamorem ~ae circum vos* AM 232.2. **b** (esp. of devils): *associari ~ae diabolicae in inferno* AC 7097.1; *Diabolus...cum ~a sua* CI 311.1. **c** (of things): *propter malorum ~am in cujus medio est* AC 7090.4. **2** A disturbance, upset: *quod...mali spiritus...se quandoque in cohortes consocient et sic ~as excitent* AC 842.2; *contentio...cum aliis est intranquillum, quia est ~a animi* AC 5963.

turbatio ~onis, *f.* Disturbance: *absque ullius societatis ~one* AC 8985.2.

turbidus ~a ~um, *a.* Murky, opaque, turbid: *bonum... fit ~um et tetrum, sicut infermentatum vinum* DP 284.

turbo[1] ~inis, *m.* A whirlwind: *sicut gluma e ~ine abigitur ex area* Hos. 13.3 (AC 1861.6); *fiebat ~o venti magnus* Mark 4.37 (AE 419.24).

turbo[2] ~are ~avi ~atum, *tr.* **1** To disturb (physical objects): *~abantur aquae* Ps. 46.3 (AE 304.17). **2** To disturb mentally, disorder: *Ecclesia ~atur et discerpitur* AC 6822; *nunc anima Mea ~ata est* John 12.27 (DD 13); *sic ut angeli...non potuissent inde laedi aut ~ari* ES 313.

turbulentus ~a ~um, *a.* Much disturbed, agitated: *post turbam seu ~um statum oritur quasi serenum* AC 842.2; *sicut ~um magnum volumen* AC 1271.

turcicus: see **thurcicus**.

turibulum: see **thuribulum**.

turma ~ae, *f.* **1** A band of armed men, squadron, troop: *qui se...contra ~am hostilem conjicit* AC 8282; *~as exercitus* VR 160.2; (of bandits) *diffundit se ~a foras* Hos. 7.1 (AE 193.8). **2** Any organized body of people or animals, band, troop: *vidi duas ~as a septentrione* AM 2.3; *examen se primum colligit in ~am, ne consociatio divellatur* VR 12.7.

turmatim, *adv.* In organized bodies, in bands: *deturbati a coelo isto ~im* ES 409; *~im et agminatim circum volitant [spiritus]* ES 2393.

turpis ~is ~e, *a.* (superl. *~issimus*) Unpleasing to the senses, ugly, foul: *sunt quae...[radios solis] in ~issimos colores vertunt* AC 1589.3; *~ia falsitatum* AC 1665; AC 5981.

turpitudo ~inis, *f.* Ugliness, foulness: *pulchritudo externi hominis...~o ejus* AC 1598; AC 5433.6.

turris ~is, *f.* (acc. sg. *~im*) A tower: *aedificemus nobis urbem et ~im* Gen. 11.4 (AC); *olim urbes muniebantur ~ibus* AC 1306.3; ES 3734.

turritus ~a ~um, *a.* Equipped with a tower; (of hats) having a high extension, 'top': *habuerunt pileum rotundum nigrum protensum, quasi ~um antrorsum* AC 1272; AC 8738; AM 78.4.

turtur ~uris, *m.* A turtle dove: *a significatione avium in genere, ac ~urum et columbarum in specie* AC 1826; AM 137.1.

tus: see **thus**.

tusus ~a ~um: pf. pple. of **tundo**.

tutamen ~inis, *neut.* That which keeps safe, protection: *[clypeus] ~en pectoris fuit* AC 1788.2; *praecipuum ~en religionis istius fuit ignorantia veri* FI 8; *vir...fuit ejus...~en* AM 325.1.

tutatio ~onis, *f.* The act of making safe, safe keeping, protection: *~onem contra mala et falsa* AC 1784; *~oni veri et boni* AM 127; (w. *ne*) *~onem ne falsum mali in voluntarium influeret* AC 8191.

tute, *adv.* Safely: *~e habitare* AC 7750.1.

tutela ~ae, *f.* Safe keeping, protection: *Divinum...pro fine habet ~am ac salvationem bonorum* AC 8227.1; *pupillus, cujus ~am gessimus* VR 17.1.

tutelaris ~is ~e, *a.* Concerned with protection, tutelary: *deus ~is illius urbis* AM 78.3.

tuto[1], *adv.* (compar. *~ius*, superl. *~issime*) In safety, safely: *ut...~ius adulterantur* AC 827; *quod...~o transiverint inferni illius regionem* AC 8324; ES 853.

tuto[2] ~are ~avi ~atum, *tr.* = **tutor**[2]: *quod 'obtegere' sit ~are* AC 6848; *a Domino ~ati* AC 7090.1; ES 2035.

tutor[1] ~oris, *m.* A protector, defender: *defensor et ~or amoris* AM 358; *~ores Trinitatis personarum* VR 17.1.

tutor[2] ~ari ~atus sum, *tr.* see also **tuto**[2]. To keep safe, protect: *si Dominus non ~aretur hominem omni momento* AC 59.2; *genus humanum se ~andi causa congregavit in regna* AC 8118.3; *vera ~antia illam [doctrinam]* CI 307.2; (w. *ab*) *patria...ipsum...ab injuriis ~atur* AC 6821; (w. *contra*) *~ari suam patriam... contra invasores hostes* DP 252.2.

tutudi: pf. of **tundo**.

tutus ~a ~um, *a.* (pf. pple. of **tueor**) (superl. *~issimus*) Unharmed, protected, safe: *illum ita ~um reddunt ut spiritus infernales ne hilum damni queant inferre* AC 6724.2; AC 8311.2; (w. *pro*) *ut ~i pro latronibus in urbem hanc...veniant* AC 941.1. **b** *in ~o*, in safety: *potest bonus esse inter mala et falsa, et tamen in ~o esse* AC 6724.2.

tuus ~a ~um, *a.* Of or belonging to the person addressed, your: *per ~am dextram* AR 417.9; *non quaeritur qualis ~a fides fuerat...sed quae ~a vita* DP 100.3.

tympanizo ~are ~avi, *intr.* (Gk.) To play small

drums: *in medio puellarum ~antium* Ps. 68.25 (AC 6742).

tympanum ~i, *neut.* (Gk.) **1** A small drum, tambourine: *et sumsit Mirjam... ~um in manu sua* Exod. 15.20 (AC); *cessabit gaudium ~orum* Isa. 24.8 (AC 8261.6); *genera instrumentorum...ut...cymbala, ~a, buccinae* AE 323.1. **b** (used in an army) kettledrum: *antequam auditur ~um, quod desistendum sit* VR 498.3. **2** (anat.) *~um auris*, the eardrum: AC 1118.

typicus ~a ~um, *a.* (Gk.) Symbolic, emblematic: *quod omnes Ecclesiae ante Dominum fuerint repraesentativae et ~ae* VR 291; (neut. as sb.) a token: *~a ejus* [sc. *amoris*] *sistuntur in exaltationibus illorum* [sc. *subjectorum regni mineralis*] VR 44.2.

typographicus ~a ~um, *a.* (Gk.) Of printing, typographical: *similes literis ~is* SS 71.1.

typographus ~i, *m.* (Gk.) A printer: VR 123.1.

typus ~i, *m.* (Gk.) **1** An object serving to represent an abstract concept, symbol, token, emblem: *antiquissimis mos erat omnia sub ~is repraesentativis historice concinnare* AC 403; *mores et facies sunt interiorum ~i* AC 788.2; *ut in ~o particulari videas creationem universalem* VR 78.3. **2** A pattern, model: *ante cujus* [sc. *simiae*] *vultum appositus est ~us faciei hominis* VR 148.1; [sc. *vegetabilia*] *suo modo, in ~o, referunt corpora vivorum* ES 1714. **3** (usu. pl.) Type used in printing: *charta...sicut impressa ~is qualibus in hac tellure* AC 6930; CI 258; (sg.) *ex membranis ~o impressis* VR 137.1.

tyrannus ~i, *m.* (Gk.) A tyrant: *inter duos monarchas quorum unus est rex et simul ~us, et alter ~us cujus potestas ligata est* VR 57.2.

tyro: see **tiro**.

tziim, *indecl. pl.* (Hebr.) also **tzjim**. Hebr. word of doubtful meaning: Isa. 23.13 (AC 1306.2); Isa. 34.14 (AR 458.2); *aves ochim et tziim vocatae* AM 430.

tzjim: see **tziim**.

U

uber[1] ~eris, *neut.* (anat.) A teat, nipple: *~er regum suges* Isa. 60.16 (AC 425); *quod infans ne quidem ex connata scientia queat ad ~er matris semet admovere* AM 133.1; *circumcinctum ad ~era zona aurea* Rev. 1.13 (DD 27).

uber[2] ~eris, *a.* (compar. *~erior*, superl. *~errimus*) Rich in produce, fruitful: *arbores ~errimas fructibus* AM 13.1; *quae [delitiae] interiores et ~eriores amaenitate sunt quam ut possint describi* AM 44.5.

ubi, *interrog.* and *rel. adv.* **1** (interrog.) In what place, where? **a** (w. direct qu.): *et dixit ei, Ubi tu?* Gen. 3.9 (AC); AM 521.1. **b** (w. indirect qu.): *indica...ubi illi pascentes* Gen. 37.16 (AC); also, to what place: *recedere volebant...sed nesciebant ubi* ES 3842. **2** (rel.) At the place in which, where: *in solitudinem, ubi sunt casae* AR 153.7; *cum intimis Verbi, ubi Deus in suo Esse...est* VR 6.1; (in a book) *per stellas ubi nominantur non aliud significatur* AC 4060.4. **3** (as a sb. to translate Gk. *pou*) Somewhere: *dicitur de animabus post mortem, quod sint in pu seu ubi* VR 29.2; *quod...sit in ubi, et exspectet judicium* AE 988.3.

ubicumque: see **ubicunque**.

ubicunque, *rel. adv.* also **ubicumque**. Wherever: *cum sui similibus, ~que sunt* AM 10.6; (w. ellipse of vb.) *quod homines sint ~que aliqua tellus* AC 6697; *ab omni spiritu, ~que natus* ES 1123.

ubinam, *interrog. adv.* At what place, where: *quod litigent quid anima, et ~m sedes ejus* AC 6929; *nescitur ~m honores et opes sunt* DP 216.2; to what place: *spiritus mirati ~m detruderetur* ES 3859.

ubique, *adv.* Everywhere: *antiqui in suis scriptis ~que assignant magis baculos* AC 7026.

ubivis, *adv.* Anywhere you like, everywhere: *nihil refert, quod bonum illud ~vis differat* CI 51; *[Deus] est idem ~vis* VR 25.3; *locustae quae... ~vis fecerunt desertum* VR 71.1.

ulcerosus ~a ~um, *a.* Full of sores: *Lazarus, qui projectus ad vestibulum ejus ~us* Luke 16.20 (SS 40.3).

ulciscor ~i ultus sum, *tr.* To take revenge on: *ut... ~atur omnes contra quos odium habet* AC 10618.2; (w. cognate acc.) *adducam super vos gladium ~entem ultionem faederis* Lev. 26.25 (AC 7102.5); (absol.) *de Jehovah ibi dicitur, quod... ~atur, puniat* AM 366.

ulcus ~eris, *neut.* An ulcer, sore: *~era dolorifica* AC 7768; *~us modo exterius sanatum* VI 110.

ullatenus, *adv.* To any extent, at all: *ita vincti ut se non queant ~us movere* ES 589; *quae non confundi ~us debent* ES 974.

ullibi, *adv.* (w. neg. or virtual neg.) Anywhere: *quid vix ~bi videant lucem* AS 188; *non legitur ~bi in Vetere Faedere* SE 120.9.

ullus ~a ~um, *a.* (gen. sg. *~ius*, dat. sg. *~i*) (w. neg. or virtual neg.) Any: *absque ~a misericordia* AC 7032.3; *nec ~us homo...id negat* DD 45.1; *num illis... ~a veritas sit* FI 70; (masc. as sb.) anyone: *haec nec ~us intellecturus esset* SS 13.1; *quaerebant num ~us angelorum... esset ab aeterno* ES 2941.

ulmus ~i, *f.* An elm tree: VR 94.2.

ulna ~ae, *f.* **1** The forearm: *applicant se sinistro lateri sub ~a* AC 1763.2; *stans porrectis ~is* ES 753; (as the part used in grasping or carrying) *cum libris sub ~is* AM 151[a].2; VR 74.5; *suscepit [infantes] in ~as* Mark 10.16 (AE 79.3). **2** A linear measure equivalent to the length of the forearm, cubit, ell: *spatium 3 ~arum cubicarum* TE 126.2.

ulterior ~or ~us, *compar. a.* Going beyond the present stage, more complete, further: *progressus ~ores faciet, nam homo successive illustratur* AC 6766.2; *absque ~ore explicatione* AC 7405; *tutationem...a talium ~ore invasione* VR 117.

ulterius, *compar. adv.* To a more advanced stage, further: (in space) *apparuerunt quidam... ~us ire* ES 5247; (in time) *ab Abrahami tempore et ~us* AC 66.2;

(abstractly) *angeli ex sapientia sua adhuc ~us progrediuntur* CI 9.1.

ultimo, *adv.* Finally, lastly: *arcanum quoddam... velim ~o dare* CI 460; *primum...dein...postea...et ~o...* VR 48.2.

ultimus ~a ~um, *superl. a.* **1** Most remote from the principal part, outermost, furthest: (neut. as sb.) *brachia et manus sunt ~a hominis* CI 65; *quod Dominus glorificaverit ipsum corpus Suum usque ad ~a ejus, quae sunt ossa et caro* AC 10125.4; *si vel forent in ~o universi* ES 4016. **2** Last in time, latest, final: *indicium est quod ~um ejus tempus instet* AC 6666.3; *cum... ~us dies cuique sit cum moritur* AC 5078.6. **b** (neut. as sb.) the last period: *a primo vitae stamine usque ad ~um hominis* AC 5894; (pl.) *tametsi in ~is...persuasus fuerit a sacerdote* ES 792. **3** Last in sequence, final, ultimate: *ad finem capitum ~orum Exodi* AC 8183; *Alphah est prima et Omegah est ~a syllaba in alphabeto Graeco* VR 19.2; (w. ref. to other senses) *Ego sum Alpha et Omega, Primus et ~us* Rev. 1.11 (AR). **b** (neut. as sb.) the last stage, end: *quod ~um sit damnatio* AC 7766. **c** *~um Judicium*, the Last Judgment: *tempus ~i Judicii* AC 8211.4. **d** (neut. as sb.) the ultimate: *quia ~um est continens et basis, est etiam firmamentum* SS 27. **4** Last in rank, lowest: *quod ~o loco sederent cum imperarent* ES 4839; *in coelo primo seu ~o* CI 267; (masc. as sb.) *in ordine...ab Abramo ad ~um Apostolorum* AM 6.2. **5** Most remote from a source, ultimate: *fructus...sunt ~i effectus conatus fructificandi in arbore* FI 16; *orbis terraqueus... est ~um opus in quod omnia desinunt* AS 165. **6** Beyond which no increase is possible, utter, extreme: *~a illarum* [sc. *tentationum*] *fuit passio crucis* VR 2.2; *plagas septem ~as* Rev. 15.1 (AR); *ex necessitate ~a* ES 2998.

ultio ~onis, *f.* The taking of revenge: *dies ~onis Jehovae* Isa. 34.8 (AC 6724.1); *dies ~onis, vindictam sumet de hostibus suis* Jer. 46.10 (DD 4).

ultor ~oris, *m.* An avenger: *ubi Deus dicitur Vindex, ~or, Zelotes* AE 778.2.

ultra, *prep. w. acc.* Beyond, above: **a** (in space): *deductus sum ~a illum ambitum* ES 5244. **b** (in time): *~a binos annos* ES 258; ES 546. **c** (in number): *plures myriades, ~a centenos* ES 5250. **d** (in degree): *quod sapientia...possit crescere, et tamen usque non longe ~a gradum primum perveniri* AC 6648; *luna ~a modum exsplenduit* CI 159; *si ~a fidem humanam dicere liceat* ES 2062.

ultro, *adv.* *Cis et ~o*, to and fro: *quod...sic ferretur cis et ~o* ES 4515.

ultroneus ~a ~um, *a.* Acting on one's own initiative: *~a...terra fructum fert* Mark 4.28 (AE 153.5).

ultus ~a ~um: pf. pple. of **ulciscor**.

ulula ~ae, *f.* A tawny owl: *ova in quibus latet ~a, bubo* DP 292.2; *in nube volabant ~ae et vespertiliones* AM 233.7.

ululatus ~us, *m.* Howling: *catervae canum cum rictibus apertis ~u et furore inani* VR 680.2.

ululo ~are ~avi, *intr.* To howl, hoot, screech: *~abant aves noctis ferales* AM 521.1; VR 45.2.

ulva ~ae, *f.* (collectively) Rushes, sedge: [*arcula*] *posita in ~a juxta litus fluminis* AC 639.2 (Exod. 2.3).

umbilicalis ~is ~e, *a.* Of the navel, umbilical: *ligamenta ~ia* ES 867.

umbilicus ~i, *m.* (anat.) The navel: *ab ~o versus pectoris interiorem regionem* AC 1120; *quod nostrae telluris incolae modo ad ~um eorum pertingant* AC 7249.

umbo ~onis, *m.* A knob or button fixed on the point of a sword: *Divinum Bonum...est sicut ~o ensis rotundus* VR 86.

umbra ~ae, *f.* **1** Comparative darkness, shade, shadow: *~a vesperae* AC 7844.1; *nonne mutatur lux in ~am...?* AM 233.3; *in ~a lucis*, in a place shaded from the light: AM 79.6; ES 5225; (transf.) *non scit id aliter quam in ~a* VI 76. **2** The shadow cast by an object: *venerunt in ~am trabis meae* Gen. 19.8 (AC); *in ~a ejus vivemus* Lam. 4.20 (AE 175.7); (transf.) *in terra ~ae mortis* Isa. 9.2 (AC 6854.5). **3** A shadowy entity, shade: *apparent sicut ~ae quae volitant* [*volutant* 1st edn., *volitarent* Autograph] AC 5977.2; *sunt in intellectu sicut ~ae* CI 265; SS 33.

umbraculum ~i, *m.* A shelter from light or heat, shade: *Jehovah Deus... ~um ab aestu* Isa. 25.4 (AC 739.2); *~um fulgurans ex igne infernali* VR 77.6; (transf.) [*apparentiae*] *sunt...sicut ~um et velamen veris* AC 7392.2.

umbratilis ~is ~e, *a.* Dimly perceived, shadowy: (neut. pl. as sb.) *dictum quod mali spiritus fingant ~ia* ES 4102.

umbratiliter, *adv.* In a dim manner, obscurely: *ordinem...nemo mortalium novit, ne quidem angeli nisi ~er* AC 1554; *vix observavi modo ~er* ES(M) 4556.

umbro ~are ~avi ~atum, *tr.* To put in the shade: *sic ut tandem ita ~etur et obtegatur veritas ut ne hilum appareat* ES 2313.

umbrosus ~a ~um, *a.* Full of shade, shady: *sylva ~a* Ezek. 31.3 (AE 388.28); dim, obscure: *aliquid ~ae lucis...immittit* CI 549; ES 1115.

umecto: see **humecto**.

umeralia: see **humeralia**.

umerus: see **humerus**.

umquam: see **unquam**.

una, *adv*. Together: *num...separentur, vel num ~a vivant* AM 45; *Jehovah Deus...rediit in Suum Divinum ... ~a cum et in glorificato Humano* VR 3.1.

unanimis ~is ~e, *a*. (= **unanimus**) Of one mind: *cogitationes angelorum concordes et ~es sunt* ES 199; ES 2092.

unanimitas ~atis, *f*. The quality of being of one mind, unanimity: *ex pluribus...qui ex harmonia et ~ate constituunt sicut unam personam* AC 684; *~as, quia est consensus plurium...non concordat cum unitate Dei* VR 25.2.

unanimiter, *adv*. (superl. *~missime*) With one mind, unanimously: *Antiquissima Ecclesia ~miter agnovit Dominum* AC 1343.1; *ut ~missime [unanissime* 1st edn.] *conspiret ad commune unum* AC 684.

unanimus ~a ~um, *a*. (compar. *~ior*) Of one mind, concordant: *formis...connexis in ~a serie* AC 1876.2; *quod sic uxores vitam ~am, et successive ~iorem cum maritis ducant* AM 172; (neut. as sb.) unanimity: *quo plures eo veniunt...inde ~um fortius* AC 2130.2.

unctio ~onis, *f*. The act of anointing: *externa cultus fuerunt excelsa, luci, statuae, ~ones* AC 1241; AE 324.26.

unctus ~i, *m*. (pf. pple. of **ungo**) The Anointed: *~us Jehovae, seu Dominus* AC 96; *quod Dominus dicatur Rex et ~us* DD 42.

unculus ~i, *m*. A small link in a chain: *catena ex ~is auri* AM 7.2.

uncus ~i, *m*. A link in a chain, hook: *spectant se mutuo, sicut ~us ~um in catena* DP 4.2; *pendet sicut longa catena ab ~o fixo* VR 627.

unda ~ae, *f*. **1** A wave (on the sea or other body of water): *~ae apparent tenuiores aut spissiores* AC 6853; (pl.) water (collectively), the waves: *immersus ~is* AC 6853; *alte sub ~is* AE 235.3. **2** A body of water: *ut claram ~am me spectare non vellent* ES 1422. **3** A wave in the air: *sicut tenuis ~a seu athmosphaera circumfluens* CI 240.

undans ~ntis, *a*. Moving as in waves, streaming: *per influxum molliusculum quasi ~ntem* AC 2733.1; CI 385; *ex sphaera ~nte ex illis* AC 9297.4; ES 2001.

undatio ~onis, *f*. A wave motion, undulatory movement: *eadem sphaera spiritualis...manifestat se coram visu sicut ~o* AE 822.3.

unde, *interr*. and *rel. adv*. **1** (interr.) From what place, whence: **a** (in direct qu.): *~e venis? et quo vadis?* Gen. 16.8 (AC). **b** (in indirect qu.): *non scis ~e venit* John 3.8 (AC 6686). **2** (interr.) From what source: *intelligere ...quid et ~e correspondentiae* CI 38.3; AM 461.6. **3** (rel.) For which reason, wherefore: *Jehovah robur meum... ~e cantico confitebor Ipsum* Ps. 28.7 (AC 8261.6).

undecim, *indecl*. Eleven: *per ~im plagas Aegyptiis... illatas* AC 7264.

undecimus ~a ~um, *a*. Eleventh: *ab hora... ~a* AE 194.2 (Matt. 20.6).

undecumque: see **undecunque**.

undecunque, *rel. adv*. also **undecumque**. From whatever source: *quod cogitatio, ~que sit, appareat in illo* DP 321.4.

undenam, *interr. adv*. From what place, whence: *scire...datum...quando, ~nam...et quomodo...spiritus ...influxerunt* AC 751.3; CI 109; *urbane quaesivi, ~nam essent* AM 293.1.

undequaque, *adv*. In all directions: *circumspicere ~que* CI 184; *cor emittit sanguinem ~que* VR 154.3; (transf.) *quod a falsis detenti fuerint ~que* AC 8191.

undequavis, *adv*. In any direction: *quae ~vis circum* AC 9484.

undique, *adv*. All around, on every side: *indefinita... consociata a malis ~que* ES 2292; *ab* or *ex ~que*, from all sides: *congregabantur ab ~que omnes spiritus* AC 10810; *quod falsa malevola ex ~que...erumperent* AC 7433; ES 3893 (Tafel).

undulatio ~onis, *f*. A wave-like movement or progress: *appercipiebatur loquela eorum, quia plurium simul, sicut ~o* AC 6923; ES 894.

undulatorie, *adv*. In a wave-like motion: *loquebantur ~e* AC 950; ES 1682.

undulatorius ~a ~um, *a*. Having a wave-like motion, undulatory: *agebant per ~am vibrationem* ES 3741; (neut. as sb.) *est sicut molle ~um usque audibile* ES 5521.

undulo ~are ~avi, *intr*. To progress or change as in waves, alternate: *apud eas ~are igneum et frigidum ab uno extremo ad alterum* AC 825.

ungo ~gere ~xi ~ctum, *tr*. also **unguo** ~guere. To anoint: *~xit me Jehovah* Isa. 61.1 (AC 6854.5); *omnia sancta Ecclesiae Israeliticae oleo ~gebantur* SS 17.3.

unguentarius ~i, *m*. A maker of unguent: *opus ~i* Exod. 30.35 (AC).

unguentosus ~a ~um, *a*. Resembling unguent: *quod illa ~a seu crasse oleosa* AC 5620.1.

unguentum ~i, *neut*. Ointment, unguent: *de muliere quae ~o lavit pedes Ipsius* VI 51 (Luke 7.46); ES 809.

unguis ~is, *m*. The nail of a finger or toe: *faciet ~es* *suos* Deut. 21.12 (AC 3703.16); *ad extrema corporis illorum usque ad ~es* AM 75.9; *veritates ne quidem tangitis ~e* VR 333.4; *in ~em pollicis pedis sinistri* ES 3453. **b** a nail's breadth, 'inch' (in quot. fig.): *quod...nec inde ~em discedant* AC 5860.

ungula ~ae, *f.* The hoof (of a horse or sim.): *non relinquetur ~a* Exod. 10.26 (AC); *quod perruptus sit* [*fons*] *ab ~a equi Pegasi* AM 182.2.

unguo: see **ungo**.

unice, *adv.* To the exclusion of all else, solely: *sensus Verbi internus, qui ~e spectat Dominum* AC 49.4; *mens formatur ~e ex veris et bonis* CI 375.

unicornis ~is, *m.* A mythical animal with a single horn, unicorn: *robora ~is* Num. 24.8 (AC 3812.9); *vidi... cervos...et quoque ~es* VR 78.1.

unicors ~rdis, *a.* Having a single heart, concordant: *propter curam infantum et erga liberos ~rdem* AM 271; AM 284.

unicus ~a ~um, *a.* **1** One and one only, sole, single: *in illa ~a lege ut ament Dominum* AC 548.1; *agnoscunt Dominum pro ~o Deo* AC 6700. **2** Having no equal, unparalleled, unique: *aedificia...quae putant ~a dari* ES 4303.

uniformis ~is ~e, *a.* Of a single form, uniform: *tametsi extrinsecus apparent ~ia, usque intrinsecus sunt multiplicia* VR 365.4.

unigenitus ~a ~um, *a.* Only-begotten: *~us Filius* AC 6716.3; John 3.16 (VR 107.2); (masc. as sb.) *gloriam ut ~i a Patre* John 1.14 (AC 6723.4); as the title of a Papal Bull of 1713: ES 5841.

unio[1] ~onis, *f.* **1** The state of being united, union: *propter ~onem Ipsius Divini et Divini Humani in Domino* AC 7605; *de ~one charitatis et fidei* AM 24. **2** A pearl: *athmosphaerae sicut ~onum...pellucentium* AC 1621; *collarium ex ~onibus* AM 20.3.

unio[2] unire univi (*or* unii) unitum, *tr.* (compar. of pf. pple. *unitior*) To join into one, unite: *univit Essentiam Humanam Divinae* AC 6834; *duo conjuges...uniuntur conjugio boni et veri* AM 44.9; *omnis civis aut subditus unitur regi* VR 131.

unitas ~atis, *f.* **1** The quality of being one, oneness, singularity: *de ~ate Dei* VR 5 titulus; cf. *quod ~as in Trinitate, et Trinitas in ~ate colenda sit* Sym. Ath. (DD 56.3). **2** An instance of this, a unit: [*voces spirituum*] *desinunt in ~ates, utplurimum simplices* AC 1648; ES 3423.

unitim, *adv.* In a united fashion, as one: *illa duo* [sc. *sapientia et amor*] *~im procedunt a Domino* CC 14.2.

unitio ~onis, *f.* The act of uniting: *glorificatio est ~o Divini et Humani* DD 13; the state of being united, union: *a Domino et Ipsius Humanae Essentiae ~one quasi conjugio cum Divina* AC 1432.

universalis ~is ~e, *a.* (compar. *~ior*, superl. *~issimus*) **1** Not admitting exceptions, all-embracing, universal: *nusquam intelligitur hic aliquod diluvium, minus diluvium ~e* AC 662; *~is lex est, quod prima existant... ab ultimis* AM 44.8. **2** Shared by all, universally used or admitted: *loquela spiritus...est loquela ~is* AC 6987.2; *scientia correspondentiarum...tam ~is ut omnes illorum...libri per correspondentias scripti sint* SS 20.1; *secundum doctrinam ~em Ecclesiae* AE 26. **3** Not closely defined or distinguished, general: *recensebat modo genera ~issima gaudiorum* AC 457; *quod sibimet... tribuant singularia, et Divino solum regimen ~e* AC 7007.1; *fides in forma ~i et singulari* VR 1; *Esse est ~ius quam Essentia* VR 18. **b** (neut. as sb.): *cogitationem humanam, quae non extenditur ad ~ia* AC 6804.2; *in ~i*, in general: *regnum Domini in ~i* AC 402.1.

universaliter, *adv.* (superl. *~lissime*) **1** Without exception, universally: *~liter notum est quod omnia se referant ad bonum et verum* VR 38.1; VI 3. **2** At the general level, generally: *quod Deus unus sit, Scriptura Sacra non modo ~liter...docet, sed etiam particulariter* VR 6.3; *in sensu adhuc inferiori* [*Verbi est*] *~lissime Ecclesia Domini* ES 2539.

universim, *adv.* In every way: *quod prolifica impensa a maritis recipiantur ~im ab uxoribus* AM 172.

universum ~i, *neut.* **1** The universe as God's creation, thus the spiritual world as well as the natural: *Patrem Creatorem ~i* AC 7097.4; *omnia in ~o quae secundum ordinem Divinum sunt* VI 43.1. **b** (distinguished into the natural and the spiritual universes): *~um hoc spirituale non potest existere absque ~o naturali* VR 76.3. **2** The material universe, space: *nisi Divinum in forma sit...dissiparetur idea, sicut visus in ~o* AC 6700; *de planetis et telluribus in ~o* DD praef.

universus ~a ~um, *a.* The whole of, all: *~a natura est theatrum repraesentativum mundi spiritualis* AC 7384; *in ~o terrarum orbe* CI 312.5; *anima...est intima forma omnium formarum ~i corporis* AM 315.11.

univocus ~a ~um, *a.* Having a single significance, simple: *objecta...apparent ita ~a, sicut nihil illis inesset praeter tale quod oculo conspicitur* AS 184.1.

unoculus ~a ~um, *a.* Having but one eye, one-eyed: *quisque novit...quod nemo ~us ingrediatur in regnum Dei* AC 9051.2 (Matt. 5.29).

unquam, *adv.* also **umquam**. Ever: *Deum nemo vidit ~m* John 1.18 (AC 10579.1); *quis ~m cogitare potest quod...?* AC 6698.

unus ~a ~um, *a.* (gen. sg. *~ius*, dat. sg. *~i*) **1** One (as opposed to plurality), one and only one: *totum coelum repraesentat sicut ~um hominem* AC 2057.2; *quod Deus sit ~us essentia et persona* VR 2.2; (w. pl. sb.) *fuit tota terra labium unum, et verba ~a* Gen. 11.1 (AC); (w. *cum*) one (with): *quod internus esset ~us cum externo* AC 159. **b** (masc. or fem. as sb.) a single individual, one man or woman: *ut amor universalis ad sexum determinetur ad ~um seu ~am e sexu* AM 301. **c** (neut. as sb.) a single unit or entity: *quod omne ~um formetur ex harmonia plurium* AC 457; *apparent sicut forent ~um* AC 2021; *~um facere*, to make up a single unit: *quod supremum, medium et ultimum faciant ~um* VI 14; *~um agere*, to act as one: *caelum...et Ecclesia ... ~um agunt* VR 1. **2** *~us et idem* or *idemque*, one and the same: *repetitio ~ius ejusdemque personae* AC 435; *putant [internum hominem et externum] esse ~um et eundem* AC 978.1. **3 a** *~us...alter*, one... another: *delectantur...cruciare ~us alterum* AC 391; *pugnat vita ~ius contra vitam alterius* AC 6677. **b** *~us et alter*, the one and the other, both (of a pair): *videbant qualis ~us et alter esset homo Ecclesiae* AC 6705; *intelligentia et sapientia, quarum ~a et altera crescere potest* VR 32.4. **4** Any one (of a set): *consociationes angelicae sunt quae ~i membro correspondent* CI 418; (esp. as sb.) *quantum fecerint ~i ex fratribus suis* Matt. 25.40 (AC 6711); *debent omnino esse in ~a provinciarum* ES 666. **5** A certain, some: *visa est charta demissa...in ~am societatem in mundo spirituum* VR 389.1; (masc. as sb.) someone: *pulsavimus, et mox ~us aperuit januam* VR 35.3.

unusquilibet unaquaelibet unumquodlibet, *a.* Any whatsoever, each: *custodiuntur [homines] a malis spiritibus unoquolibet momento* ES 185.

unusquisque unaquaeque unumquodque, *a.* Each severally: *quod...unaquaeque domus per se habitaret* AC 8118.2; *agnoscere unamquamque Personam per Se esse Deum* Sym. Ath. (DD 56.2); (masc. as sb.) *unusquisque est proximus* AC 6707; *Dominus per Verbum unumquemque docet* SS 26.2.

unusquivis unaquaevis unumquodvis, *a.* also spelled as two words **unus quivis**. Each severally: *unus lapis pro unaquavis tribu* AC 6640.2; *Dominus...in unoquovis homine est ut in Suo coelo* AC 8269; (masc. as sb.) *haec progressio est apud unumquemvis in mundo* FI 25.

upharsin: see **perizin**.

urbane, *adv.* Politely: *~e quaesivi, undenam essent* AM 293.1.

urbanitas ~atis, *f.* Politeness, culture: *ut vocaret viros ~atis et affabilitatis* AM 16.3.

urbanus ~a ~um, *a.* **1** (masc. as sb.) An inhabitant of a town, townsman: *~i fame perituri sunt* VR 117; VR 388.4. **2** Cultured, polite: *loquuntur cum consociis ~is* VR 22.3.

urbs ~bis *f.* A large town, city: *~bes cum palatiis magnificis* AC 1626; *ideam ~bis natatilis* CI 325.

uredo ~inis, *f.* A blight on plants, scorching: *percussi vos ~ine et rubigine* Amos 4.9 (AC 1069.3); Deut. 28.22 (AC 8364.3).

ureter ~eris, *m.* (Gk.) (anat.) The ureter: *spiritus qui repraesentant renes, ~eres et vesicam in homine* ES 825; ES 870; AE 167.6.

urethra ~ae, *f.* (Gk.) (anat.) The urethra: *qui referunt sphincterem cervicis seu introitus versus ~am* ES 867; ES 3453.

urgeo ~gere ~si, *tr.*, *intr.* **1** (tr.) To exert pressure on, push, pull, drive: *qui valida vi brachii ~gent remos* AR 756; [*pastor*] *~get illas* [sc. *feras*] *in stagna* VR 122; (intr.) to press (against): *~gebant in praesidia, et abigebant illa* AM 9.2. **2** (intr.) To exert moral pressure, be insistent, urge: *exactores ~gentes* Exod. 5.13 (AC); *non potest auxilium ferre, ~gente et resistente fine* AC 7877.5; (w. *ut*) *quod... ~gerent ut discederent* AC 7946; ES 244. **3** (tr.) To urge (a course of action): *quod...haec ~serint et praedicaverint* ES 3105.

Urim, *indecl.* (Hebr.) One of two Hebrew terms which Swedenborg took to mean the twelve precious stones on Aaron's breastplate, Urim: *duodecim lapides, qui ~m et Thumim dicebantur* AC 9873.2; Exod. 28.30 (AC); cf. AC 9905.

urina ~ae, *f.* Urine: *in ~ae matulam* ES 4490; (pl.) *nidores ex ~is stagnatis* AM 461.7.

urinarius ~a ~um, *a.* Of or for urine: *in tonnam ~am* ES 4492; (anat., of the kidneys) concerned with the production of urine: *renes tam ~i quam succenturiati* ES 960.

urinatorius ~a ~um, *a.* **1** = **urinarius**: *e provincia vesicae ~ae* AC 956. **2** For diving; *campana ~a*, a diving bell: VR 125.

urinosus ~a ~um, *a.* (compar. *~ior*) Abounding in urine: *in tonnis ~is* AC 820; (neut. as sb.) *amant ~a* CI 488.4; *profundius, eo ~ius* ES 3186.

urna ~ae, *f.* An urn: *sententiam inscribite chartae, et immittite in argenteam ~am* AM 103.4; *quot possunt ~ae impleri aquis* VR 57.1.

uro ~ere ussi ustum, *tr.* To burn: *odor...panis...usti* ES 1046; (absol.) *quod illa flamma non ~at* AM 359.1.

ursa ~ae, *f.* A she-bear: *discerpti sunt quadraginta duo pueri a duabus ~is* SS 35.2 (2 Kgs. 2.24); *apud leones et leaenas, ursos et ~as* AM 392.2.

ursinus ~a ~um, *a.* Of a bear: *pelle ~a* UJ(C) 47.

ursus ~i, *m.* A bear: *~i ad sinistrum, et leopardi ad dextrum* AM 78.2.

urtica ~ae, *f.* A stinging nettle: *campestria obsita arbustis cum intermixtis spinis et ~is* AM 231.1.

usitatus ~a ~um, *a.* (superl. *~issimus*) Commonly used, familiar: *voces in literato orbe solennes et ~ae* CI 56; ES 890.

uspiam, *adv.* (w. neg.) In any way, at all: *nec simulare ~am possunt* ES 574.

usquam, *adv.* **1** At any time, on any occasion, ever: *quod nemo viderit ~am Jehovam Patrem* AC 10579.1 (John 1.18); *raro si ~am deest* AM 200. **2** Under any circumstances, ever: *conjugia, et quicquid ~am assimilari potuit conjugiis* AC 54; *quis ~am dicturus est...?* CI 108.4; *plures...quam ~am potui credere* ES 3700.

usque, *adv.* and *prep.* **1** (adv.) In spite of this, nonetheless, still: *reliquiis, quae tametsi manent, ~que non possunt produci* AC 571; *cum pugnat sicut a se, et ~que credit quod a Domino* AC 8179.2; *si non in filiis ~que in nepotibus* AM 206. **2** (adv., w. *ad* or *in*) Even, right (up to or into): *tentationes...admissas ~que ad ultimam illarum* VR 2.2; *illud* [sc. *Verbum*] *transivit caelos ~que in mundum* VR 85.2. **b** *~que adeo ut*, even to such an extent that: *ne fastus...infatuet virum ~que adeo ut credat se intelligere...ex se* AM 353. **c** *~que dum*, until: see **dum**, sense 4. **3** (prep. w. acc.) Up to: *percusserunt Rephaim...et Choritas in monte eorum Seir, ~que Elparan* Gen. 14.6 (AC); *~que Beerschebam* 2 Sam. 3.10 (AC 1710).

usquedum, *conj.* also spelled as two words **usque dum**. see also **dum**, sense 4. Up to the time when, until: *~um consummarentur mille anni* Rev. 20.3 (AC 8715).

ustio ~onis, *f.* The act of burning: *~onem pro ~one* Exod. 21.25 (AC); *non...aliquam ~onem ibi sentiunt, sed modo calorem* CI 571.

ustus ~a ~um: pf. pple. of **uro**.

usufruor ~i ~ctus sum, *intr.* To make use (of): *quod talia data sint homini ad ~endum* AS 334.

usura ~ae, *f.* **1** Enjoyment, use: *angeli...qui dant ei lucis ~am* AC 182; CI 450. **2** The lending of money at interest, usury: *foenerator concredit pecunias alteri propter ~am* AC 9210.1.

usurarius ~a ~um, *a.* **1** For use or enjoyment: *est... faemina sicut uxor ~a* AM 465. **2** (masc. as sb.) A moneylender, creditor: *quis est de ~is Meis cui vendiderim vos?* Isa. 50.1 (AC 5886.2).

usurpatio ~onis, *f.* The act of using, enjoyment: *post ~onem eorum libertatis imaginariae* ES 638; *memoriae istius ~onem habent omnem* ES 2989.

usurpo ~are ~avi ~atum, *tr.* To make use of, employ: *nomen...Dei...jugiter ~andum est* VR 297.1; *quod memoriam corpoream ~are spiritui non liceat* ES 3783.

usus ~us, *m.* **1** The act of using, employment, use: *ut conservaretur in ~um generi humano* AC 398; *ut...voluptatem habeat in dignitatum ~u* AC 5025.1; *quod...modo in ~um veniant quae homo...hausit* CI 464.2. **b** *~us fructus* (also spelled as one word), benefit, enjoyment: *~us fructus Sanctae Caenae* VR 698 titulus; CH 127 (= vi.1); DA 32 (= xii.[1]). **2** Frequent use, habit, custom: *aliter facere nequeunt ex continuo ~u* AC 7074; *~u receptum est dicere...* DP 165. **3** The quality of being of use, usefulness: *quo insignior ~us ejus est, eo jucundum est majus* AC 997.2; (gen.) of use: *illi fines sunt nullius ~us quia non conducunt proximo* AC 5214; *arbores ~us* VR 38.2; (pred. dat.) *tunc primum apud eum sunt ei...~ui et saluti* AC 1197.1. **4** A particular purpose served, service, use: *~us quos praestant, sunt vilissimi* AC 1097.2; *loquela illorum* [sc. *angelorum*] *non est rerum...sed est finium et inde ~uum* AC 1645; *causae...inservriturae indagandis ~ibus qui vitae erunt* AC 6815.

ususfructus: see **usus**, sense 1 b.

ut, *adv.* and *conj.* **A** (as adv.) **1** In the same manner as, as: *quod simile sit cum charitate et fide...ut est cum voluntate et intellectu* AS 427.1; *baptismus ut regeneratio repraesentatur...per multa* VR 687.1. **b** *ut et*, as also: *alta spirarunt...ut et qui dolosi fuerunt* AC 1380; AC 1612. **c** (parenthetically): *angeli...dicuntur elohim ...ut quoque patebit a locis infra...adductis* AC 4402.5; *angeli...id ut credo apperceperunt* ES 241.1; *ut dictum est* VR 399.7. **2** As for instance: *posteri, ut gentes* AC 921.1; *leges...de...conjugiis...ut quod unam solam uxorem ducerent* AC 4434.9; *crustae alicujus fructus, ut aurantii, pomi* VR 109.3; *ut pro exemplo* VR 399.2. **3** As being: *illis ut remoris et impedimentis...remotis* AC 1389; *nemo in coelo percipit bonum in se ut bonum* NH 268; *illos ibi qui se non ut numina colunt* CI 354. **b** (w. vbs. of appearing): *intelligentia veri...quae coram oculis angelorum ut lux apparet* AC 441 3; CI 69. **4** As if, as it were: *quod haec* [sc. *bona*] *facienda sint ab homine ut ab ipso* VR 3.2; *ex quibus omnia bona et vera, ut ex ipsis suis fontibus, existunt* VR 399.6. **5 a** *Ut primum,* as soon as: *quod...ut primum dissentiunt, disparentur* CI 194; *quod amor conjugialis frigeat, ut primum dividitur* AM 147. **b** *ut plurimum*, for the most part: see **utplurimum**. **B** (conj. w. subj.) **1** (final) In order that, for the purpose that: *ut instruantur, elevantur ad societates coelestes* AC 4415; (preceded by *ideo*) *ideo ut cultus repraesentativus...restauraretur* AC 4449.3. **b** (Bibl., w. inf.): *et filii Jacobi venerunt ab* *agro, ut audire illos* Gen. 34.7 (AC). **2** (to introduce a necessary condition) That: *ut fiat* [*homo*] *intelligens et sapiens, oportet addiscere multa* CI 351.3; *quod fides et charitas non possint separari, ut homini vita spiritualis sit* VR 393.1. **3** (introducing nominal clauses, where inf. is more frequent) That: **a** (where the clause explains a preceding word): *in unica lege ut ament Dominum supra omnia* AC 1038.5; *'adduc tibi natum hunc' significat ut illum adjungeret sibi* AC 6728; *illa... formant ea ad correspondentiam, hoc est, ut secum unum agant* CI 351.2. **b** (w. expressions denoting causation or necessity): *bini...amores...faciunt ut homo sit naturalis* VR 399.8; *quod Ipse Dominus...baptizatus sit...fuit causa, ut...institueret baptismum* VR 684; *docti sunt ut inducerent speciem lavacri* ES 403; *necessum est ut mala et falsa illa revelentur* AC 7122.2. **c** (w. expressions of wishing): *num velitis ut de illa re loquar vobiscum* AR 463.6; *haec est voluntas Ipsius qui misit me, ut omnis...habeat vitam aeternam* John 6.40 (AC 2343.4); ES 2937. **d** (w. expressions denoting fear, liability, etc.): *valde timent ut spectentur in luce coeli* CI 131; *tunc* [*partes*] *magis sunt frangibiles, et obnoxiae ut disperdantur* ES 242. **e** (following *esse* as predicate): *natura mali est ut unumquemvis lacessere velit* AC 1683; *ex more illorum est ut non directe ad quaestiones respondeant* AC 7172; *ut diceretur quomodo sancta prophanis misceant prolixum foret* ES 4450. **4** (w. consecutive force) With the result that, so that: *bona...non dari queunt homini...ut sint propria* AC 8497; *solent insenescere in cupiditatibus ut in iis tenaces sint* ES 893; (in neg. *ut non*) *homo...non ita sed amplo cerebro pollet, ut non intellectuale ejus a visu pendeat* AC 4407. **b** (following a compar.) *quam ut*, than so that: *haec plura arcana continent quam ut possint edici* AC 1708; *ea quae minutiora sunt quam ut oculus videret* ES 2298. **c** (w. expressions implying a comparison) so...that: *fit lumen illorum tenebricosum, adeo ut plane nihil videre possint* AC 4417.2; *ita obscura ut vix intelligibilia* AC 4402.3; *quod tam malitiosi sint...ut non satis describi possit* ES 248; *Ecclesia...in tantum consummata est, ut vix aliquae reliquiae ejus supersint* VR 4.1. **d** *ut ita dicam* (and sim.), so to speak, if I may so put it: *naturam ut ita dicam, innaturalem contraxerat* ES 1663; *quasi facientia nucleum, ut ita dicere liceat* ES 295.

utcumque: see **utcunque**.

utcunque, *conj. w. indic.* also **utcumque**. **1** In whatever way, however: *putant...esse quoddam gaudium in quod intromitti queant, ~que vixerunt* AC 547. **2** To whatever extent, however much: *sunt mere sensuales, ~que eruditi et docti...creduntur* CI 353.1; *cohabitatio spiritualis, quae datur apud conjuges... ~que distant corpore* AM 158.2; *ita cogitat internus ejus homo ~que aliter loquitur externus* VR 14.4.

utensilis ~is ~e, *a.* For use, useful: *formae ~es* DP 220.10; (neut. pl. as sb.) objects for use, utensils, furniture: *ornata habitacula cum ~ibus* AC 995.2; *super quibus* [*mensis*] *erant varia ~ia ex lapidibus pretiosis* AM 12.1.

uter[1] utris, *m.* A bottle, jar: *lux influens in utrem* VR 38.2; *utres repleti ramentis ferri* VR 113.2; *sicut fractura utris figulorum* Isa. 30.14 (AE 177.7).

uter[2] utra utrum, *a.* Which of two?: *utrum majus est, aurum an templum...?* Matt. 23.17 (AC 9714.2).

uterinus ~a ~um, *a.* Of the womb: *~o morbo affectae* VR 759.3.

uterlibet utralibet utrumlibet, *a.* Whichever one chooses, whichever you like: *quod rationale humanum se vertere possit ad utramlibet partem* AM 436.

uterque utraque utrumque, *a.* and *pron.* **1** (as adj.) Either of the two: *in utroque sensu* AC 6661.1; *ab utraque parte* AC 6804.5; *cum utroque mundo, spirituali et naturali* AM 24. **2** (as pron.) Each (of the two): *memoratur uterque* [sc. *Moses et Elias*] *apud Malachiam* AC 6752.10; *quod et Divinum et Humanum sublatum sit in caelum, et quod quoad utrumque sedeat ad dextram Dei* DD 60; (pl.) *sphaerae...spirituales quae ex utrisque exhalantur sunt paene contrariae* AC 6816.

uterus ~i, *m.* **1** (anat.) The womb: *~us maternus* AC 1803.3; *ex formatione in ~o* CI 99; *ab ~o* [i.e., from birth] Judg. 16.17 (SS 49.3). **2** (fig.): *amor sapientiae... nihil amaenius sentit, quam illa recipere quasi ~o, et sic concipere* AM 115.5; *vermes qui...mittunt se in ~um ut renascantur* VR 12.6.

uti, *adv.* = **ut**, sense A: *uti in corpore humano* ES 1712.

utilis ~is ~e, *a.* (compar. *~ior*) Serving a purpose, useful: *bestiarum mundarum et ~ium* AC 1823.2; *quod cibus ~is illis sapidus sit* AC 8378; (w. *ad*) *inanime corpus quod, quia ad nihil ~e, projiceretur* VR 10.

utilitas ~atis, *f.* The quality of being useful: *quod talia in se infelicitates...etiam essent ~ati* ES 231; (w. pl.) a useful quality: [*voluptas*] *~atum ex cibis et potulentis* AC 994.2; AM 271.

utiliter, *adv.* Usefully, profitably: *a Divinae justitiae timore, quo ~er concutiuntur* Council of Trent in SE 4(c).

utinam, *particle.* (followed by impf. or plupf. subj. to express a wish) Would that: *~nam auscultasses praeceptis Meis* Isa. 48.18 (AC 1803.2); *~nam adessent discipuli* AM 182.8; *~nam liceret nobis cum angelis caeli loqui* VR 77.1.

utique, *adv.* Without doubt, certainly: *si per digitum Dei ejicio daemonia, ~que pervenit ad vos regnum Dei* Luke 11.20 (AC 7430.1); *simile accidesset etiam iis... sic ~que prophanavissent...sancta* 3AD 5420.

utor ~i usus sum, *intr.* (w. abl.) To make use (of), resort (to), employ: *~untur...omni malitia* AC 6666.2; *a hieroglyphicis Aegyptiorum, quibus...in sacris ~ebantur* AC 6692.1; *~ere rationalitate tua* DP 123.2.

utplurimum, *adv.* also spelled as two words **ut plurimum**. In most cases, for the most part: *dispelluntur per alias cohortes...a dextra ~um* AC 842.2; *illi ~um simplices...apparent* CI 278.2; *quod duo conjuges ~um post mortem conveniant* AM 45.

utpote, *particle.* As for instance: *non potuerunt interiora Ecclesiae...revelari, ~te de coelo et inferno, de resurrectione...* CO 54.2.

utprimum: see **ut**, sense A 5 a.

utrimque: see **utrinque**.

utrinque, *adv.* also **utrimque**. **1** In both places: *miratus quod potuissem esse ~que* ES 1879. **2** In either direction, on either side: *utcunque tumultuatur cerebrum ~que* AC 7744; *cardo qui ~que potest vertere januam, aliter dum intrat quam dum exit* DP 235; (fig.) *~que pendere non concessum est* AC 1857.3; ES 4564. **3** On the part of either, on both sides: *quod...dum juvenis videt virginem...~que sentiant conjugiale incendi* AM 44.6; *quod Romano-Catholici ac Reformati concordent...est quia ~que agnoscuntur Tria Symbola* SE 22.

utrobique, *adv.* In either place: *in statu medio, sicut ~que...in coelo ut angelus, et extra coelum ut spiritus* ES 1332.

utrobivis, *adv.* In either place: *putant quod infernum sit simile unicuivis et quod coelum sit simile unicuivis, cum tamen ~vis indefinitae diversitates... sint* AC 457; VR 95.

uva ~ae, *f.* A grape: *neque ex rubo vindemiant ~am* Luke 6.44 (VI 28); *ex mustis delicatissimis ~arum* AM 8.1.

uvea ~ae, *f.* (anat.) The middle coat of the eye, uvea: *ex obstipatione inter tunicam scleroticam et ~am* VR 346.2.

uxor ~oris, *f.* A wife: *virum et ~orem ejus* Gen. 7.2 (AC); *ut acciperet sibi meretricem in ~orem* SS 16 (Hos. 1.2).

uxoratus ~a ~um, *a.* Having a wife: *si ~i [sunt], ex ipsa castitate amant conjugem* DP 110; (masc. as sb.) *dum ~us...committit adulteria* AM 255.1.

uxoreus ~a ~um, *a.* Of a wife, wifely: (neut. as sb.) *quod virgineum mutetur in ~um apud faeminas* AM 199.1.

V

vacca ~ae, *f.* A cow: *de ~a rufa* AC 716.4; ES 2973.

vacillo ~are ~avi, *intr.* To be unsteady: *cum...basis non correspondet, coelum angelicum ~at* AE 397.3; (fig.) *haec fides ~at...apud illos* VR 116.4.

vaco ~are ~avi, *intr.* **1** (w. abl.) To have time (for), devote oneself (to): *dicebat se piam vitam egisse, precibus ~avisse* AC 952; *ut... ~arent piis meditationibus* CI 360.1; *ut ~ent Divino cultui* AM 155.2. **2** (impers. w. inf.) There is time (to): *mutationes illas hic describere non ~at* AM 190; AE 23.1.

vacue, *adv.* Without an offering, empty-handed: *et non videbuntur facies Meae ~e* Exod. 23.15 (AC); cf. *'non videri ~e' seu non absque munere* AC 9293.1.

vacuitas ~atis, *f.* Emptiness: *et terra erat ~as et inanitas* Gen. 1.2 (AC); cf. SS 84.1.

vacuus ~a ~um, *a.* **1** (of vessels) Unfilled, empty: *reversa sunt vasa eorum ~a* Jer. 14.3 (AE 71.2); (neut. as sb.) a vacuum: *abstractum a materiali apparuit vobis sicut nihilum, ita sicut ~um* AM 207.5. **2** (of places, seats) Empty of people, unoccupied: *terra ~a et inanis* AC 17 (Gen. 1.2); *quod...planetae...non sint moles ~ae* CI 417.3; *invitabant nos ad solia adhuc ~a* AM 132.2; cf. *internum hoc...vocatur a Domino ~um* AC 7045 (Matt. 12.44). **3** (of people) Carrying or possessing nothing, empty-handed: *non ibitis ~i* Exod. 3.21 (AC). **4** (fig.) Lacking substance, empty: *fides prorsus ~a et inanis non datur* FI 28; cf. *o dementes, ~i spiritu* VR 72.3.

vadimonium ~i, *neut.* A formal promise, guarantee, pledge: *sponsio seu ~um non ultra vadit* AC 5610.

vado ~ere, *intr.* **1** To move oneself, go: *illi in tuto sunt, ubicunque ~unt* AC 6769; *~o ad Patrem* John 16.28 (DD 35.11); *dum quis ~it in arena profunda* ES 2391; (of a river) to flow: *is ~it orientaliter* Gen. 2.14 (AC). **2** To go away, depart: *ecce uxor tua, accipe et ~e* Gen. 12.19 (AC); Exod. 4.12 (AC). **3** (transf.) To proceed, progress, advance: *simplices...ultra cognitiones ex sensualibus vix ~unt* AC 926; *omne...jucundum tale est ut vilius sit quo magis ad externa ~it* AC 996.1; *visus...rationalis...illuc ~it* AM 168; *series in geometricis quae ~unt in infinitum* VR 32.8. **b** to proceed (in a specified manner): *omnes extensio affectionum... ~it secundum illam formam* CI 49; *primum ~it per medium ad ultimum* SS 27. **4** (w. *in* + acc.) To turn into, become: *simulatio ~it in apertum odium* ES 611.

vadum ~i, *neut.* A ford: *~um seu transitus Jabbok* AC 4270 (Gen. 32.22).

vae, *particle w. dat.* Woe (to): *vae vobis, Scribae et Pharisaei* Matt. 23.25 (SS 40.2); (treated as a sb.) *vae unum praeteriit, ecce veniunt adhuc duo vae post haec* Rev. 9.12 (AR).

vafer ~fra ~frum, *a.* Artful, cunning: (neut. as sb.) *quod [Deus]...passus sit illos per blanda et ~fra illaqueari* CO 33.1.

vafre, *adv.* (compar. *~ius*) Artfully, cunningly: *captiosa ...callidius et ~ius componere* AE 978.2.

vagabundus ~a ~um, *a.* Having no fixed abode, wandering, itinerant: *inter spiritus ~os* ES 1136; ES 3035; (masc. as sb.) *nec apparent ~i* AM 17.1; (fig.) *vir qui ~us spiritu* Mic. 2.11 (DD 48.5).

vagatio ~onis, *f.* A wandering: *ex ~one filiorum Israelis in deserto* AE 730.31.

vage, *adv.* With no fixed objective, in a roving fashion: *fornicator spectat ~e et promiscue ad sexum* AM 448; 4AD Isa. 16.11 (= EVV 16.2).

vagina ~ae, *f.* A sheath (for a sword or other object): *circumcingit illud...sicut ~a ensem* AM 449; ES 1434.

vagor ~ari ~atus sum, *intr.* (*tr.*) **1** To go in an irregular fashion, wander: *quod spiritus illi ~entur per universum* AC 6926; *~ati sumus per vias* AM 8.3; (of the movement of heavenly bodies) *satellites...circum orbem suum... ~antur* AC 6697. **b** (tr.) to wander over: *foeminae quae exteras regiones ~antur* ES 3611. **2** (of immaterial things) To stray, wander: *est quoddam...quod* *tenet cogitationes intra certos limites, ut non possint ultra eos ~ari* ES 2001.

vagus ~a ~um, *a.* Having no fixed objective, wandering: *mens... ~a et incerta* SS 52; *quod amor sexus...sit ...quia est ~us et illimitatus, scortatorius* AM 48; (masc. as sb.) a wanderer, vagrant: *cum ~is extra urbes* VR 841.

valde, *adv.* (shortened form of **valide**) Very much, extremely, exceedingly: *spiritus...mirantur ~e* CI 66; *uxores ~e indignatae sunt* AM 199.2; (Bibl., repeated) *corroboratae sunt aquae ~e ~e* Gen. 7.19 (AC); (so, also) *in ~e ~e* Exod. 1.7 (AC).

vale, *indecl.* see also **valeo**. A goodbye: *cum ~e dicerem* VR 76.5; *fletus...significat ultimum ~e* AC 4565.

valens ~ntis, *m.* (pres. pple. of **valeo**) A person in good health: *non opus habent ~ntes medico* Matt. 9.12 (AC 8365).

valeo ~lere ~lui, *intr.* **1** To have power, be strong, prevail: *argumentationes ex fallaciis per quas pugnant et ~lent* SS 13.3; *quamdiu ~let* [*amor*] AM 331.3; (w. *contra*) *quid exercitus ~leret contra hostes...?* VR 10; (w. *super*) *potentia inferni ~luit super potentiam caeli* VR 3.1; (w. *supra*) *quod verum scientificum ~leat supra potentiam doctrinae falsi* AC 6784.2; (w. *prae*) *is ~let prae aliis* AC 6784.1. **2** (of statements) To be valid: *quod sic ~leat hoc in Symbolo Athanasiano* VR 4.3. **3** To be able (to do something): *ut homo...quantum ~let rationaliter cogitet illas* [*veritates*] VR 73.2. **4** (imperative) Be well, i.e., goodbye: *~ete* AM 107.

valete: see **valeo**.

valetudo ~inis, *f.* Good health: *salutem in mundo seu ~inem* AC 4681; AM 79.10.

valide, *adv.* Strongly: *ubi ~e stabilitur...quod humana Christi natura...exaltata sit* VR 101.1.

validus ~a ~um, *a.* (compar. *~ior*) **1** Possessing physical strength, powerful: *populus ~us* Isa. 25.3 (SS 86); *confidunt...super equitibus quod ~i sint* Isa. 31.1 (VI 30.2). **2** (of things) Potent, strong: *detentio a malo... et quidem ~a* AC 929; *argumentis coram ratione sapientis ~is* AM 466.1.

vallatus ~a ~um, *a.* Surrounded by a wall of earth: *cisterna fontis circum ~a* VR 814.

vallis ~is, *f.* A valley: *~is est humile quoddam inter montes* AC 1292.2; *mundus spirituum apparet sicut ~is inter montes et petras* CI 429.

vallum ~i, *neut.* An artificial mound or barrier of earth, rampart: (in sieges) *quod...poneret obsidionem, et daret ~um et aggerem contra illam* [sc. *Hierosolymam*] DD 15.7 (Ezek. 4.2); (to control water) *oceanum ...irrumpentem in regiones...disruptis ~is* VR 123.5.

valor ~oris, *m.* **1** Worth, value: *discrimen sicut inter ~orem sicli et ~orem talenti* VR 413; (of a person) [*spiritus*] *exploratur quali astutia est, et inde quali ~ore* CI 574.2; *excellens ~ore* Gen. 49.3 (AC). **2** (transf.) The force, validity (of an argument and sim.): *similes aliae* [*causae*] *nullius ~oris* AM 474; *talis est istius sphaerae ~or* ES 152.

valvatus ~a ~um, *a.* Provided with doors: *parietibus qui ~i sunt* ES 1681.

valvae ~varum, *f. pl.* A pair of doors, double door: *interiora non mihi patuerunt, praeter ~vas* ES 1681; Ezek. 41.25 (AE 458.4).

vampirus ~i, *m.* A vampire: *cogitavisse narrabant de ~is* ES 1289.

vane, *adv.* In vain, idly: *quod...affectent ~e gaudium coeleste* AC 1675; *cum...cogitant ~e in absentia facultatis* AM 256.

vaniloquium ~i, *neut.* Idle talk: *omnia illa sunt ~a* VR 502.

vanitas ~atis, *f.* A matter of no consequence, idle talk: *omnes dii populorum ~ates* Ps. 96.5 (AC 8261.5); *~atum ludibria et ludicra* AM 16.3; AM 268.3.

vanus ~a ~um, *a.* Impossible of fulfilment, vain, empty: *illa exspectatio ~a sit* AC 7051.2; *quod imputatio illius fidei sit ~a* VR 627; *quod ~um sit velle cognoscere qualis Deus est* VR 28.2. **2** Lacking in serious import, idle: *nulla vox ibi est ~a* SS 9; *~as ideas mentis* AM 4.2; (neut. as sb.) *~a et inania, sicut sunt illa quae sunt gloriae mundi et sui* AC 3603.4. **b** *ad ~um* or *in ~um*, to no purpose, idly: *non feres nomen Jehovae Dei tui ad ~um* Exod. 20.7 (AC); *diu meditatus sum, sed in ~um* VR 76.2.

vapor ~oris, *m.* An exhalation, mist, vapour: *~orem ascendere fecit e terra* Gen. 2.6 (AC); *sicut ~or densus terrestris in serena aura* AC 6639.2; *~ores noxii* AM 253.1; ES 397.

vaporosus ~a ~um, *a.* Vaporous: SA 120 (= x.3).

vappa ~ae, *f.* An empty husk: *semina a pluvia tumescunt, et fiunt ~ae* VR 347.3; a person of no consequence, nobody: *sic ut facti sint sicut ~ae* AM 292.1.

variabilis ~is ~e, *a.* Liable to variation, variable: *quod omne varium et ~e sit in recipiente* AR 961.4.

varians ~ntis, *a.* (pres. pple. of **vario**) Variant: *~ntes lectiones autorum classicorum* ES 805.

variatio ~onis, *f.* The introduction of differences, variation: *per ~ones lucis et umbrae* AC 7381.3.

varicus ~a ~um, *a.* Varicose; (neut. pl. as sb.) varicose veins: [*facies*] *ex pustulis, ~is, et ulceribus enormes* CI 553.2.

varie, *adv*. In different ways: *apparent...quidam infra caput ~e ad corpus* AC 7111.2; *omnes... ~e seu dissimiliter recipiunt unicum Domini Bonum* AC 10261.2.

variegatio ~onis, *f.* The splitting of white light into different colours: *colores illi sunt ex... ~one lucis spiritualis* AC 1053.2; an effect of colour so produced: *illi sunt repraesentati per flammeum colorum ~onibus pulchre coruscum* AC 7743.

variegatus ~a ~um, *a*. (pf. pple. of **variego**) Striped in different colours, variegated: *capros ~os et maculosos* Gen. 30.35 (AC); *excelsa ~a* Ezek. 16.16 (AE 195.7).

variego ~are ~avi ~atum, *tr*. To diversify with colours: *lux...quae inde lucidior fit et ~atur coloribus* AC 1043.2; *ex rosis pulchre ~antibus colores* VR 78.1. **b** (transf.) to modify with variations: *ex sonoro ~ato per ideas in vocibus* CI 269.2.

varietas ~atis, *f.* **1** Variation, differentiation: *hoc [fit] cum pluri ~ate* AC 6639.2; AC 7236.2. **2** A difference produced by change, variation: *sonorum harmonicum et ejus ~ates correspondent statibus gaudii* AC 8337.2; *candidum...et album correspondent vero, et colores ~atibus ejus* CI 179.

vario ~are ~avi ~atum, *tr*. **1** To make different, vary: *verum tam multiplex sit et varium ut... ~are queat bonum* AC 7236.3; (esp. pass.) to be varied: *quae respiratio ~ata fuit secundum omnes status interni hominis* AC 805.2; [*vita*] *in subjectis ~atur secundum formam* AC 6685. **2** To take or adopt different (members of a series), change: *etiam ~ant societates* AC 273; *quod...commessationes renovarent ~ando sedes* AM 6.2.

variola ~ae, *f.* A mark left by smallpox or similar diseases, pock: *ex superficie corporis sunt malignae ~ae, verrucae, pustulae* AM 253.1.

varius ~a ~um, *a*. **1** Of more than one kind, varied, diverse: [*bonum*] *~um erit ut unumquodvis per se subsistat* AC 6706; *in ~o sensu* AC 7021.1; *~i generis bona* AC 7850.2. **2** (esp. pl.) Different in kind, diverse: *post ~os status in deserto* AC 6639.3; *ut constare potest ex ~is haeresibus* AC 6765; (neut. as sb.) *intellectus... versat ~a* AM 285.1.

varix ~icis, *m*. or *f.* A varicose vein: *Quis amat virginem...quae malignis inescata est, aut pustulis et ~icibus obsita...?* VR 331.3.

vas ~sis, *neut.* (nom. and acc. pl. *~sa*, gen. pl. *~sorum*, dat. and abl. pl. *~sis*) **1** A container for liquids, vessel, jar: *per quisquilias immundas ex ~se* AC 1644; *~sa argenti et ~sa auri* Exod. 12.35 (AC); *~s quod ille* [sc. *figulus*] *faciens* Jer. 18.4 (AC 6669.5). **b** a boat (made of reeds): *in ~sis junci* Isa. 18.2 (AC 6723.1). **2** (pl.) Baggage: *~sa migrationis fac tibi* Jer. 46.19 (AC 6729); *et ~sa ejus in domo, ne descendat ad tollendum ea* Luke 17.31 (CI 208). **3** (anat.) A blood vessel: *~sorum sanguineorum* CI 63; *magnum ~s aorta vocatum* AM 315.7; VR 12.4. **4** (transf.) Anything which serves as a container, vessel: *non sunt vera...sed modo sunt ~sa recipientia* AC 1469; *sunt spiritus ~sa* ES 3759; *memoria corporea, in cujus ~sis seu ideis fundantur ideae interiores* ES 4037.

vasculum ~i, *neut.* **1** A small vessel for liquids: *bina parva ~a, nivea, quae usitabantur circa the* ES 3753; used as a collecting box: *habent unum cum ~o et petunt eleemosynam* ES 431. **2** (anat.) A small tube or vessel in the body: *minima et invisibilia ~a* AC 5726; *fibrae et ~a in omni viscere* AS 207.

vastatio ~onis, *f.* **1** The act of ruining, ruination, laying waste: *dies angustiae et coarctationis, dies ~onis et devastationis* Zeph. 1.15 (DD 4). **2** The laying waste (of immaterial things): *~o mali et falsi, et ~o boni et veri* AC 7984.2. **3** The process undergone by spirits to prepare them for heaven or hell, purgation, vastation: *post ~ones in damnatione sunt* AC 7766; *~o non est nisi immissio in interna* CI 551; (also of a church) *tempore ~onis Ecclesiae cum non amplius aliqua fides quia non charitas* AC 6767.2.

vastator ~oris, *m*. One who lays waste, destroyer: *super omnes colles...venerunt ~ores* Jer. 12.12 (AE 131.5); (immaterial things) *de ~ore veri agitur* AC 8715.3.

vastitas ~atis, *f.* **1** The quality of being laid waste, devastation: *dies ~atis et devastationis* Zeph. 1.15 (AC 7711.3); *~as et solitudo* SS 84.1. **2** A wasteland, waste: *qui in ~atibus gladio morientur* Ezek. 33.27 (AC 7102.3); *posui montes Esavi ~atem* Mal. 1.3 (AC 7293.4).

vasto ~are ~avi ~atum, *tr*. **1** To render unfit for use, ruin, destroy: *profunditates maris...quae exsiccantur, seu ~antur* AC 18; *~atus est ager...quia ~atum est frumentum* Joel 1.10 (AC 3941.4). **b** to damage, destroy (a person): *~abit Jehovah Philisthaeos* Jer. 47.4 (FI 53); *~antur usque ad ossa* ES 4085. **2** To ruin or destroy (immaterial things): *verum tunc dicitur ~atum quando non bonum amplius in illo est* AC 2455.1; *spiritus...cupiditatibus corporeis polluti, quae ~andae sunt* ES 1435. **3** To reduce (a church) to a state of spiritual devastation, vastate: *cum Ecclesia prorsus perit ...dicitur ~ata seu vasta* AC 2959.1. **4** To submit to the process of vastation (see **vastatio**, sense 3): *de malorum ...spirituum...cupiditate ~andi et cruciandi hominem* ES 189 titulus; (esp. pass.) to undergo vastation: *sunt quidam qui libenter volunt ~ari* AC 1107; (w. *quoad*) *~ari quoad verum* AC 3268.5.

vastus ~a ~um, *a*. (superl. *~issimus*) **1** Laid waste, desolate: *cum Ecclesia prorsus perit...dicitur vastata seu ~a* AC 2959.1. **2** Of great extent or amount, vast:

regnum Domini, quod tam ~um est...ut nusquam aliquis credere possit AC 1810; *~issimi est operis* ES 1741.

vates ~is, *m.* A source of authoritative statements, authority: *ubinam ejus* [sc. *animae*] *aula est, eruditi ~es divinarunt* AM 315.4.

vaticinium ~i, *neut.* An authoritative statement, pronouncement: *hoc meum ~um est* AM 315.7.

vaticinor ~ari ~atus sum, *intr.* To utter prophecies, predict: *ii qui ~antur...de venturis* ES 1580; to pronounce authoritatively: *~or quod* [*sedes animae*] *sit in corde* AM 315.7; VR 181.

-ve, *enclitic particle.* Or: *per unam alteramve horam* AC 552; *nebulosum magis minusve furvum* AC 6853; *bis terve* ES 651.

vecordia ~ae, *f.* Mental disturbance, frenzy: *ex intestina ~a* AM 339.3.

vecors ~rdis, *a.* Mentally deranged, mad: *hic est ~rs et stultus* AM 77.4.

vectigal ~lis, *neut.* A tax: *in pendendis tributis et ~libus* VR 317; VR 430.

vectio ~onis, *f.* The act of being carried, riding: *et ~one in curru magnifico* AM 478.1.

vectis ~is, *m.* A door-bar: *portas aeris confringam, et ~es ferri concidam* Isa. 45.2 (AC 9496.3); *~es portarum* Ps. 147.13 (AE 374.12); a carrying pole: *~es quibus portabatur arca* AC 9496.3.

vector ~oris, *m.* A rider or driver, coachman: *~or tenens lora palmis illos* [sc. *equos*]...*impellebat* VR 185.2.

vegetabilis ~is ~e, *a.* Of or concerned with plants, vegetable: [sc. *regna mundi*] *sunt tria, nempe minerale, ~e, et animale* CI 589.1; (neut. as sb.) a plant: *in productionibus tam ~ium quam animalium* VR 12.2; ES 2830.

vegetatio ~onis, *f.* The growth of plants, vegetation: *calor...influens in arboreta et floreta producit ~onem* CI 569; SS 109.

vegetativus ~a ~um, *a.* Of plants, vegetative: *anima seu vita ~a* AC 1632; *odor ~us* [*incipit*] *circumspargi ex rore* CI 289.

vegetatum ~i, *neut.* A plant: *sol qui praesens est calore et luce in ~is mundi* AC 2706.

vegeto ~are ~avi ~atum, *tr.*, *intr.* **1** (tr.) To cause (plants) to grow: *non radix ~at arborem...absque foliis* VR 585.2; (pass., of plants) to grow: *omnia inde ~antur et vivunt* AC 1577.2. **2** (intr., of plants) To grow: *nisi spirituale...intus continue ageret...nusquam ~arent et crescerent* AC 3648.1; ES 4105; *facultas ~andi* FI 16.

vegetus ~a ~um, *a.* Vigorous, lively: *qui...amores coelestes sunt, apparent ~i, lucidi, candidi, et pulchri* CI 481.2.

vehemens ~ntis, *a.* Energetic, violent: *quod sonus loquelae ejus sit altus, ~ns, acer et asper* AM 363; *vocem tonitruum ~ntium* Rev. 19.6 (AR).

vehementer, *adv.* (compar. *~ius*) Violently, forcefully: *zelamus pro uxoribus nostris tam ~er ut non sinamus alicui intrare domos nostras* AM 78.6; *incipiunt illum infestare...successive acrius et ~ius* CI 574.2.

vehementia ~ae, *f.* Violence, vigour, force: *agitabit manum Suam super fluvium cum ~a spiritus Sui* Isa. 11.15 (SS 15.2); *vidi hircos cum duobus cornibus, quibus cum ~a ferierunt oves* FI 63.4; *vir...in ~a accurrit* AM 82.1.

vehiculum ~i, *neut.* A means of transport, vehicle: *datur animae transferri sicut ~is circumcirca* ES 299.

veho ~here ~xi ~ctum, *tr.* **1** To convey in a vehicle or on an animal, carry: *per currus per quos ~hebantur merces significabantur doctrinalia veri* AC 8215.1; (cf. of animals) *equi ~hentes currus et onera* ES 2862. **2** (pass.) To travel in a vehicle or on an animal, ride: *dispergam...currum et ~ctum in eo* Jer. 51.21 (AC 8226.2); *~cti in curru* AM 42.5; *~ctus super alis venti* Ps. 18.10 (AE 282.2). **3** (transf.) To act as a carrier for, convey: *per affectiones...quae implent aut ~hunt voces* AC 1758; *qui potuisset eum ad honores ~here* ES 4375.

vel, *particle.* **1** (to introduce an alternative) Or: *in tali vel alio ordine* AC 6640.1; *ut diceret...num joculetur, vel num credat* AM 233.5. **b** (in indirect qu.): *adeo ut vix scirent num in vita essent vel non* CI 35; VR 113.5. **2** *Vel...vel...*, either...or...: *leges doctrinae in sui favorem vel explicat vel immutat* AC 6705; *non infestatur ita, vel enim mens ejus tunc adhaeret falsis, vel discutit illa* AC 6757. **3** (to qualify a particular word) Even, it may be: *dum vel minimum a bono amoris...recedunt* AC 155.2; *qui callus vel leniendus est, sed non frangendus* ES 862. **4** *Si vel*, even if: *quod sola fides salvet si vel nullum opus charitatis facit* AC 1017; *ut non impleri possit* [*coelum*]...*si vel darentur plures myriades tellurum* CI 419.

velamen ~inis, *neut.* A covering: *nudi...usque tamen cum ~ine circum lumbos* AC 8375; *apparuit sicut ~en fulgurans* VR 12.10; (transf.) *amor, et ~en hujus sapientia* AM 32.

velamentum ~i, *neut.* (anat.) An integument: *in homine...ubi innumerabilia...sunt distincta per ~a, ac unita per ligamenta* DP 4.5.

velificatio ~onis, *f.* The management or trimming of sails: VR 381.3.

velitatio ~onis, *f.* Skirmishing; (transf.) quarrelling: *infestum ex ~one de superioritate* AM 78.4.

velito ~are ~avi, *intr.* To skirmish: *inter binos exercitus ~are cum sua turma* VR 437.

velle (inf. of **volo**, used as sb.) The act of willing: *homo ...a ~le est homo* AC 585; *influit...Dominus...in ~le hominis* CI 26; *Ipsius* [*Dei*] *posse et ~le unum sunt* VR 56.1.

vellico ~are ~avi ~atum, *tr.* To pull or tweak (a person's ears to call attention or express anger): *influxit in loquelam humanam, ~are aurem pro facere ut attendat* AC 8990.4; *in indignatione concluserunt... dicendo etiam quod ~arent aures nostras* AR 839.5; VR 136.4; (also, the cheeks) *corpus meum dedi...maxillas meas ~antibus* Isa. 50.6 (AC 1793.3).

vello ~ere vulsi vulsum, *tr.* To pull hair from, pluck: *sicut ~et caput* ES 1748.

vellus ~eris, *neut.* A fleece: *ex totidem ~eribus aureis Jasonis* AM 504.1.

velo ~are ~avi ~atum, *tr.* To cover with a cloth, veil: *quod ~aret faciem cum loqueretur cum populo* AC 6752.9; *~avi te serico* Ezek. 16.10 (CI 180).

velocitas ~atis, *f.* Swiftness, speed: *~as in Verbo... significat affectionem veri* AE 281.7.

velociter, *adv.* (superl. *~cissime*) Swiftly: *~citer extuli me domo* AM 381; VR 77.2.

velox ~ocis, *a.* Swift, fast: *prae aquilis ~oces fuerunt* 2 Sam. 1.23 (AE 278.10); *lingua balborum ~ox erit ad loquendum* Isa. 32.4 (AE 455.19); (neut. as sb.) a racer: *sic vestiti ut ~oces* AM 103.1.

velum ~i, *neut.* **1** A large piece of fabric used as a curtain, veil: (in the tabernacle) *et facies ~um hyacinthino et purpura* Exod. 26.31 (AC); SS 16; (in the Temple at Jerusalem) Matt. 27.51 (AC 2576.5); (in the spiritual world) *in medio templi erat adytum, ante quod ~um, sed nunc sublatum* VR 508.1. **b** (used as a punishment in the spiritual world): *paenae sub ~is* AC 955; *superinjectio ~i* AC 963; (also, as a protection) *solent Judaei, quum aliquem...tutari velint...superinjicere ~um* ES 434. **2** Anything resembling or serving as a curtain: *sicut ~um album in atmosphaera* ES 2681. **3** (transf.) A pretence, veil: *simulant dolos sub ~o innocentiae* ES 240. **4** A sail: *sicut ~um utrinque potest vertere navem* DP 235; VR 381.3.

velut, *adv.* also **veluti**. As it were, as if: *quod ~ut ex gravi delabitur* [*malum*] AC 8298.1; *est ~ut reminiscentia rei* CI 256; *quod Ecclesiae...sint ~uti totidem clenodia in corona regis* VR 763.2.

veluti: see **velut**.

vena ~ae, *f.* **1** (anat.) A blood vessel returning blood to the heart, vein: *noxiis quae influunt in sanguinem, et pervadunt ~as et arterias* AC 1877; *ex azyga seu ~a cava* AS 405; *versus ~am jugularem* ES 831. **2** An aperture from which water emerges in a spring, source, outlet: *sicut ~a fontis cujus aquis nullus effluxus* AC 4618.2; *sicut fons cujus aqua est impura ex ~a* VI 25; (fig.) *unde est ipsa ~a fontis, ex qua talis abominatio desolationis...scaturivit?* VR 181. **3** A current of moving water: *latens ~a fluvii quae trahit et aufert* AC 8855; *urgent remos contra ~am fluvii torrentis* AR 756.2; *sicut flumen latens aut ~a secunda* [*ducit*] *navem* DP 186. **4** (transf.) Any attractive force, current, vein: *est aliqua ~a in affectione voluntatis...latens* AM 6.6; *quo...in amoris conjugialis ~a et potentia sit* AM 183.6; *~am attractionis non sequi possunt angeli* VR 350.1.

venalis ~is ~e, *a.* For sale, venal: *illi qui justitiam ~em faciunt* AE 976.3.

venatio ~onis, *f.* **1** Hunting: *is fuit potens ~one* Gen. 10.9 (AC). **2** The produce of hunting, game: *edam e ~one filii mei* Gen. 27.25 (AC).

venator ~oris, *m.* A hunter: *mittam ad multos ~ores* Jer. 16.16 (AC 3309.3).

venditatio ~onis, *f.* The act of making a parade of, vaunting: *~ones falsorum* AE 141.3.

venditio ~onis, *f.* The act of selling: *quod in mundo spirituali non sit emtio et ~o* AC 5886.1.

vendito ~are ~avi ~atum, *tr.* **1** To make a parade of, vaunt: *qui falsas monetas cudunt...et ~ant pro puris* VR 320; *qui propter lucra facerent et ~arent bonum et verum* AC 7997. **2** (refl. w. pred.) To represent oneself boastfully (as): *ii qui se sanctos ~ant* ES 2941; *ii qui se maxime pro spiritu sancto ~ant* ES 3684.

vendo ~ere ~idi ~itum, *tr.* **1** To put on sale, sell: *quaecunque habes, ~e, et da pauperibus* Mark 10.21 (VI 66.1); *quod non plura exemplaria... ~ita sint quam quatuor* ES 4422. **2** (transf.) To betray, beguile: *~entis gentes per scortationes suas* Nahum 3.4 (AC 6978).

veneficium ~i, *neut.* **1** The use of drugs, poisoning: *si aliqua uxor meretrix... ~is accendit virum* AM 488. **2** The use of magical arts, sorcery (in antiquity, hardly distinguished from sense 1): *~o tuo seductae sunt omnes gentes* Rev. 18.23 (AR); AE 1191.1.

veneficus ~a ~um, *a.* **1** Poisoning: *de ~o homicida* ES 3559 titulus; (masc. as sb.) a poisoner: *~us amice... loquutus est et porrexit poculum* CI 462[a].7. **2** Of witchcraft, magic: *suis ~is artibus...loquuti sunt* ES 2744.

venenatus ~a ~um, *a.* (compar. *~ior*, superl. *~issimus*) **1** Equipped with poison, poisonous: *serpentes ~i* VR 45.2; *eo serpentes sunt ~iores* ES 2857; *potio ~a* ES 3486.

2 Having the effect of poison, poisonous: *sphaera persuasionum ~issima* AC 581.1; *intus ~os dolos recondendo* AC 830.

venenosus ~a ~um, *a.* 1 Equipped with poison, poisonous: *sphaera serpentum ~orum* ES 3690. 2 Having the effect of poison: *persuasio quaedam ~a de vita* ES 775.

venenum ~i, *neut.* Poison: *~um serpentis* CI 278.2; AM 521.1; (transf.) a deadly influence: *quibus* [sc. *malis spiritibus*] *permissum ~a sua effundere et me infestare* AC 59.2; AC 1820.5.

venerabundus ~a ~um, *a.* Deserving of respect; (neut. as sb.) veneration: *illa vita...producit sanctum et ~um ibi pro Domino* AC 9051.1.

veneratio ~onis, *f.* Reverence, veneration: *inducebantur ad agnoscendum Jehovam ex coeca ~one pro patribus suis* AC 6877; AM 6.2.

venereus ~a ~um, *a.* Related to sexual concupiscence, venereal: *lues ~ae* AM 253.1; *oestro... ~o* ES 3206; (neut. as sb.) ES 3899.

veneror ~ari ~atus sum, *tr.* To revere, venerate: *quis sicut Tu... ~andus laudibus* Exod. 15.11 (AC); *formae... minarum contra illos qui se non ~antur* CI 553.1; VR 803.

venia ~ae, *f.* Willing consent, favour: *quod percipiant num a Domini voluntate, num ex ~a, et num ex permissione* AC 1384; *ex data nobis ~a* AM 42.1; (w. gen.) *non data est copia et ~a cogitandi de eo* AM 19.1.

venialis ~is ~e, *a.* Forgivable, pardonable, light: *quod justi in levia et ~ia peccata cadant et quod usque sint justi* AR Doc RC.5.

venio ~nire ~ni, *intr.* 1 (of physical movement) To come, arrive: *homo...recens e mundo ~niens* AC 6639.2; *aliqui...ad me ~niebant missi ab aliis* AC 7074; *nisi Dominus in mundum ~nerit* VR 2.2. 2 (absol.) To present oneself, appear: *Ego ~ni ut vitam habeant* John 10.10 (AC 6767.4); *~nturus est Filius Hominis in gloria Patris Sui* Matt. 16.27 (VI 2). 3 (w. gerundive, of topics) To come up (for): *ibi ostendendum ~nit quod...talia significentur* AC 1182; *hic nunc demonstrandum ~nit, quod mens naturalis reagat contra mentes superiores* AS 260. 4 To come in the process of time, happen, succeed: *quod unum discedat ~niente altero* AC 1047; *annus redemptorum Meorum ~nerat* Isa. 63.4 (AC 8273.2). b (fut. pple.) *~nturus*: *qui fuerunt, et qui ~nturi* AC 1605; *per Novam Hierosolymam quae...praedicitur ~ntura* DD praef.; *cum scriberem aliquid de ~nturis* AC 6811. 5 To advance (to a specified stage), arrive (at a state): *cum...magis ad lucem ~nit* [*homo*] AC 20; *qui... ~nirent in statum recipiendi vera* AC 6989; *quod homo nascatur in nullam scientiam, ut possit ~nire in omnem* VR 48.15. 6 To be derived, come (from): *omne essentiale a voluntate ~nit* AC 809; *quod inde ~nit, quia ex spiritibus illis influebat idea* AC 8243; *quia mutationes locorum ex mutationibus societatum ~niunt* ES 3942.

veno, *adv.* For sale: *in popinis ubi esculenta faetida ~o exstant* VR 834.

venor ~ari ~atus sunt, *tr.* To hunt (wild animals): *ivit Esau agrum ad ~andum venationem* Gen. 27.5 (AC); (also, other things) *animas ~amini populo Meo* Ezek. 13.18 (AC 1178.2).

venosus ~a ~um, *a.* Veinous: *per...fibras quasi ~as* ES 1035.

venter ~tris, *m.* (*f.*) (anat.) The abdomen, belly: *coarctatio dolorifica circa medium ~trem* AC 7810; *flumina e ~tre illius fluent* John 7.38 (DD 32.6); *super ~tre tuo ambulabis* Gen. 3.14 (AC). b (as the organ of digestion) Stomach: *indulserunt gulae et ~tri* CI 488.5; *ut gravedine infestaret ~trem meum* AM 431.2. (n.b. App. fem. in AM 510.3 *a regione imae ventris,* unless *ima* be read.)

ventilabrum ~i, *neut.* A winnowing shovel: *separantur paleae a tritico ex ~o agitato* VR 26.2; *cujus ~um in manu Ipsius* Matt. 3.12 (AE 374.14).

ventilatio ~onis, *f.* The 'airing' or discussion (of a topic): *assumserunt primum subjectum ~onis* AM 132.3.

ventilator ~oris, *m.* One who operates a fan or other implement to create a current of air: *quod...dissipet peccata sicut ~or fumum e fornace* VR 16.1; a winnower: *spargere sicut ~or paleas in aërem* VR 90.2.

ventilo ~are ~avi ~atum, *tr.* To expose to consideration, discuss, 'air' (a topic): *~ate hunc amorem* AM 55.3; to hold (a discussion): *liceat...vobiscum ~are aliquem sermonem* AM 232.2.

ventosus ~a ~um, *a.* Consisting of wind; (neut. as sb.) a draught: *sicut ~um e folle* VR 154.5; puffed up, empty, vain: *respondebimus...ad ~a vestra auguria et somnia* AM 79.10; VR 487.3.

ventriculus ~i, *m.* 1 The stomach: *habebat effectum in ~um ut evomerem* AC 814.1; CI 299; *~um ruminatorium* VR 146. 2 (anat.) A ventricle (of the heart or brain): *per sinistrum cordis ~um* DP 296.14; *in tribus ~is cerebri* AM 315.5.

venturus ~a ~um: fut. pple. of **venio** (see esp. sense 4 b).

ventus ~i, *m.* 1 A wind: *sicut palea in ~o* AC 6631; *ambulat super alis ~i* Ps. 104.3 (AE 36.3). 2 Any of the four winds as representing the points of the compass:

tertiam [*partem*]...*in omnem ~um dispergam* Ezek. 5.12 (AC 7102.6); *a quatuor ~is veni* Ezek. 37.9 (AC 8286.2); *omnes cupiditates...dissipantur in omnes ~os* AM 16.3. **3** Any current of air, puff, breath: *~o narium Tuarum coacervatae sunt aquae* Exod. 15.8 (AC); *per ~um oris* AC 9327.3; *animosi, sicut colon suo ~o* ES 993.

venula ~ae, *f.* A small vein: *quod in vesiculis...sint in multa copia ~ae* AS 420.2.

Venus ~eris, *f.* **1** The Roman goddess of love, Venus: *Mercurio et ~eri* VR 17.2; cf. *de ludis ~eris et Cupidinis* AM 461.2. **2** The name of a planet, Venus: *in planeta ~eris* AC 7246. **3** Sexual activity: *datur ~eris licentia* AM 376; *talis ut cuperet promiscuam ~erem* ES 3307.

venustas ~atis, *f.* Charm, attractiveness: *~as faciei, corporis et morum* AM 297.

venustus ~a ~um, *a.* (superl. *~issimus*) Charming, attractive: *in aliquibus pulchris et ~is facie* CI 99; *~um ruborem* AM 192.

vepretum ~i, *neut.* A cluster of thorn bushes, thorny thicket: *senticetum et ~um comedit* Isa. 9.18 (AC 1861.2); *ascendit leo ex ~o* Jer. 4.7 (AE 223.7).

vepris ~is, *m.* A thorn bush: *urtica haereditabit eos, ~is in tentoriis eorum* Hos. 9.6 (AC 273).

ver veris, *neut.* **1** The season of spring: *anni tempora, nempe ver, aestatem, autumnum et hyemem* AC 6697. **2** The time of youth, springtime of life: *apparent omnia ...ut in suo pulcherrimo vere et flore* AC 1622.1.

verax ~acis, *a.* Truthful: *obsignavit quod Deus ~ax sit* John 3.33 (AC 9503.3).

verbalis ~is ~e, *a.* Relating to words, verbal: *Verbum Domini est spirituale, non ~e* AC 426.1; *nullum alium sensum quam ~em seu literalem* ES 1789.

verber ~eris, *neut.* A blow with a whip, stripe: *ex...timore ~erum a famulis* AM 153.2; *mulctantur ~eribus* ES 658.

verberatio ~onis, *f.* A flogging, whipping: *rixae, inimicitiae ~ones, et dilaniones* CI 586.

verbero ~are ~avi ~atum, *tr.* To whip, flog: *pugnando, ~ando, projiciendo lapides in alterum* AM 218.2.

verbo, *adv.* (abl. of **verbum**) In a word, in short, briefly: *in rapinis, in adulteriis, ~o in omnibus contrariis charitati* AC 1077; VR 105.

verbosus ~a ~um, *a.* Containing many words, prolix, verbose: *nihil nisi fictiones ~ae* ES 1045.

verbotenus, *adv.* Word for word: *quae... ~us explicata videantur* SE 73; *quod ~us recitare potuissent singulas voces* ES 2155.

verbulum ~i, *neut.* A small word: *quod...ne ~um in Verbo potest scriptum esse quod non demissum sit e coelo* AC 1659.2; *quod opus nisi ~o ad hoc?* VR 72.1.

verbum ~i, *neut.* **1** The expression of an idea in language, an utterance, word: *non e pane solum vivit homo, sed ab omni ~o quod exit ex ore Dei* Matt. 4.4 (AC 1288.4); *~a increpationis* AC 6682. **b** (as distinct from thought or sense): *cogitatio est et voluntas quae conjungunt, non autem ~a* AC 4126; *elegantiam ~orum* ES 805. **c** (pl.) a particular expression, wording: *quae ~a iis solum applicabilia sunt* AC 312; *ipsa... ~a quae scriberent in auribus illorum enuntiabantur* AC 7055.3. **2** (as conveying information or orders) A message, command: *vade quaeso...et reduc mihi ~um* Gen. 37.14 (AC); *~um ad me factum a Jehovah* DD 53 (Jer.); (pl.) *qui audit ~a Mea, et facit illa* Matt. 7.24 (VI 2); *secundum Ipsius ~a* AM 406. **b** *decem ~a*, the Decalogue or Ten Commandments: Exod. 34.28 (AC). **3** (pl.) Language: *fuit tota terra labium unum, et ~a una* Gen. 11.1 (AC). **4** The revelation of divine truth in inspired writings, the Word: *~um non solum scriptum pro homine sed etiam pro angelis* AC 1025.2; *in historicis ~i* AC 6683. **5** The Word as the Lord: *in principio erat ~um* John 1.1 (SS 2.3); *apud Dominum...qui solus est Sermo et ~um* AC 1642; *~um significat Divinum Verum...et Dominus est ipsum Divinum Verum* DD 1. (n.b. In senses 4 and 5 *Verbum* is written with a capital letter.) **6** (as translation of Hebr. *dabar*) A thing, matter: *in lingua originali res per ~um exprimitur* AC 5272.1; *propter ~um Sarai* Gen. 12.17 (AC); *ne forte obliviscaris ~a, quae viderunt oculi tui* Deut. 4.9 (AC 1288.5).

vere, *adv.* (compar. *~ius*) Truly, really: *amor ~e conjugialis* CI 281; ES 3254.

verecunde, *adv.* Modestly: *~e rubescit superior* AM 250.

verecundus ~a ~um, *a.* Modest, shy: *num amicum ex corde num ~um* AC 1640.3.

veredarius ~i, *m.* (app.) A fast riding camel, dromedary: *super mulis et super ~is* Isa. 66.20 (AE 355.15).

vereor vereri veritus sum, *intr.*, *tr.* To be concerned, fear: *at vereor quod cordis tui confessio sit, quod nullus Deus sit* VR 110.7; VR 137.8; (tr.) to be afraid of: *quod nusquam verendi sunt...cupiunt...ut timeantur et eos vereantur alii* ES 2302.

vergo ~ere, *intr.* **1** To lie obliquely, slope: *literae... inflexae cum corniculis sursum ~entibus* SS 90.1. **2** (of periods of time) To draw near, be at hand: *reversum est mare ad ~ere mane* Exod. 14.27 (AC). **3** To exhibit a tendency (towards), verge (on): *cultus ~ens ad idololatricum* AC 1351; *decrescentia lucis ~entis ad umbram* CI 275; *quod libido fornicandi gravior sit, sicut ~it ad cupidinem varietatum* AM 444[a].

verifico ~are ~avi ~atum, *tr.* To make true: *canon*

est quod...falsa apud illos qui in bono vitae sunt ~entur AC 8149.

verisimilis: see **verosimilis**.

verisimilitudo: see **verosimilitudo**.

veritas ~atis, *f.* **1** The quality of being true: *ex his patet ~as hujus rei* DP 233.3. **2** Truth as an abstract entity, esp. as identified with the Lord: *omnes viae Jehovae misericordia et ~as* Ps. 25.10 (AC 6804.10); *Ego sum via, ~as, et vita* John 14.6 (AE 10.2). **3** An instance of truth, a particular truth: *verum fidei, hoc est, ipsa ~as est quod Dominus pugnet* AC 1813.2; *quod ~as sit quod humana prudentia sit nulla* DP 197.1; (pl.) *quod hujus regni leges sint ~ates aeternae* AC 548.1; *~ates quas ex Verbo discit* VR 6.2. **4** Acting in accordance with perceived truth, sincerity: *in ~ate non stetit* John 8.44 (AC 7051.3); *adorabunt Patrem in spiritu et ~ate* John 4.23 (AM 49); *patet quod fides et ~as unum sint* FI 6. **5** An action characterized by truth: *qui...facit ~atem, venit ad lucem* John 3.21 (VI 2).

vermicosus ~a ~um, *a.* In CO 22 *~a* is prob. erroneous for *verminosa* or *vermiculosa*. (It is quite possible that *~a* was not the original reading. The author's original is no longer extant; all extant versions of CO are based on handwritten copies made after the author's death.)

vermicularis ~is ~e, *a.* Of or relating to grubs, worms or other insects: *~ibus exuviis* ES 1672 1/2.

vermiculo ~are ~avi ~atum, *tr.* To breed or bring forth (grubs or worms): (w. cognate acc.) *quod ex manna nihil residuum facerent ad mane, et quod residuum ~aret vermes et putresceret* AC 8480.3 (Exod. 16.20); AC 8476; (pf. pple.) infested with grubs or worms: *nuclei... ~ati* AM 364.

vermiculosus ~a ~um, *a.* Full of worms: *fructu... qui intus ~us et putris est* DP 233.9.

vermiculus ~i, *m.* A small worm, grub or similar insect: *~i qui vocantur insecta* AM 133.2.

verminosus ~a ~um, *a.* Infested with grubs: *quod contineret spurcum, sicut ~um* ES 1386.

vermis ~is, *m.* Any small insect, worm, grub: *corpora a ~ibus exesa* CI 312.2; *viles ~es, qui sunt apes* AM 420; *cum... ~e alato et non alato* VR 145. **b** (as a term of reproach): *ne timeto, ~is Jacobi* Isa. 41.14 (AE 328.20).

verna ~ae, *m.* A slave born in the household: *~ae domus sunt ultima servitia* 3AD 5971.

vernaculus ~a ~um, *a.* Belonging to one's own country or community; *lingua ~a*, a mother tongue: *cum me loqueris lingua mea ~a* AM 326.3; so also fem. as sb.: *quod loquela spirituum cum homine sit in ejus ~a* AC 1637.

vernalis ~is ~e, *a.* Of springtime: *lux ~is* AC 7056.2; AM 137.2.

verno ~are, *intr.* To be in a condition proper to springtime, be verdant: *~at humus continue* TE 177.

vernus ~a ~um, *a.* Typical of springtime: *media temperie ~a* CI 289; *redeunt in ~am suam juventutem* AM 44.9. **b** (neut. as sb.) springtime: *ad ~um adolescentiae suae pergunt* AC 553.1; *quod...me efflaverit ~um* AM 137.2.

vero, *particle.* (introducing a qualification of a previous statement, placed as second word in a clause) However: *Angeli intimi coeli Divina Vera non reponunt in memoria...aliter ~o res se habet cum angelis ultimi coeli* CI 271; *duos conjuges quorum unus est spiritualis, alter ~o naturalis* AM 281.1.

verosimilis ~is ~e, *a.* also **verisimilis**, and spelled as two words **vero similis**. Probable, likely: *hoc...sicut verum aut ~e apparuit multis* AM 315.4; *videtur ~e quod in tellure Jovis nati sint* ES 1672 1/2; *historiam vero similem concinnare* AC 755.1.

verosimilitas ~atis, *f.* Probability: *~as quae ei inducitur* AC 9424.9.

verosimilitudo ~inis, *f.* also **verisimilitudo** (VR 35 1st edn.). A likeness: *imagines...erant enim ~ines, quae per confirmationes factae sunt fallaciae* AM 380.4.

verro ~ere ~i, *tr.* To clean with a broom, sweep: *et ego ~i domum* Gen. 24.31 (AC); *dicunt...quod quisque ad suam januam ~ere debeat* ES 5070.5.

verruca ~ae, *f.* A wart: *~ae, pustulae* AM 253.1.

verrucosus ~a ~um, *a.* Covered in warts: *facies... ~ae et pustulatae* AC 8246.

versatilis ~is ~e, *a.* **1** Capable of being turned, revolving: *non plus ~is quam janua absque cardine* CO 28; *rota ~is* ES 4696; (transf.) *hic* [sc. *externus ejus homo*] *~is circum internum* VR 373.1. **2** (of persons) Inconstant, variable: *circumrotabatur, quod significabat quod ~is esset* ES 1259; ES 4696.

versatio ~onis, *f.* A perversion, distortion, twist: *potest usque ille per ~ones sibi suetas...Divinam illam legem circumducere* AM 332.2.

versiculus ~i, *m.* A verse (in Scripture): *quantum arcanorum continetur in unoquovis ~o* AC 167; VR 137.5.

versio ~onis, *f.* A change of circumstances, reversal: *quod ~o fiat* ES 214.

versipellis ~is, *m.* Someone with the ability to metamorphose into someone else: *~is, qui se fingunt alios* ES Index s.v. 'versipellis' (vol. 6, p. 319 J D Odhner), referring to ES 937.

verso ~are ~avi ~atum, *tr.* **1** To turn over: *dum volvis talos et ~as chartulas* [sc. *lusorias*] DP 212.1. **2** To turn over in the mind, consider, think about: *de Divina ope... ~at dubium* AC 8179.3; *homo...mente sua plura intra minutum potest ~are, evolvere, et concludere* CI 576; *apud se ~at astutias et dolos* CI 577.4. **3** To turn away, twist, deflect: *cum omni cogitatione, intentione, jucundo, timore quae tunc una ~abant eorum animos* CI 462ª.2; *hoc ~are in utramque partem* AM 232.4. **4** (pass.) To be situated, live, be: *quod mens...e superiori videat illa quae in mente inferiori... ~antur* VR 603; *sphaerae...ubi ~antur animae humanae post mortem corporis* ES 270.

versura ~ae, *f.* **1** The act of turning: *hoc fit in omni ~a corporis eorum* CI 17; *quae* [*togae*] *ex filis intextis auri secundum ~am exsplenduerunt* AM 381. **2** Change, reversal: *interiora...apud hominem hanc ~am habuerunt* AC 4823.2; *cum...status vitae hominis invertendus est,...et haec ~a non dari potest momento* DP 233.6.

versus[1] ~us, *m.* **1** The direction of turning: *amota sunt* [*interiora ejus*] *a spectare sursum...nam in ~u contrario sunt* AC 7693; *binae rotae in contrario ~u* VR 57. **2** A verse (in Scripture): AC 6742; *singulos ~us lustrare* DD 37.1.

versus[2], *prep. w. acc.* In the direction of, towards: *cum approximant ~us coelum* AC 1321.2; *progredi ad sinistrum ~us lunam coeli* CI 159; *amor ille ~us animas ascendit* AM 302.1.

versutus ~a ~um, *a.* Cunning, crafty: *nisi latrones ~i sunt, non sunt latrones diu* ES 1155; ES 4359.

vertebra ~ae, *f.* One of the segments of the spinal column, vertebra: *supra cervicis ~as* ES 2812; AS 408.

vertex ~icis, *m.* **1** The highest part, top: *gradus scalae in cujus ~ice est Dominus* AC 6819; *in ~ice arboris* AM 15; *super capite seu ~ice collis* VR 48.1. **2** The highest part of the body, crown: *a vola pedis tui usque ad ~icem tuum* Deut. 28.35 (AC 8364.3). **3** A point directly overhead, the zenith: *nec supra caput seu in ~ice, sed ante angelorum facies* CI 118; *sub ~ice coeli paene* ES 1129.

verticalis ~is ~e, *a.* Overhead: *~em locum occupat* ES 469.

verticaliter, *adv.* In a vertical position: *prope me ~er positum revolvebatur* ES 1412.

verticillus ~i, *m.* A whorl on a spindle: *poena...quae vocari potest poena ~i, quod nempe circumrotentur sicut axis* ES 1485; a similar ornament worn by women on their heads: *secum habentes ~um qualem mulieres super capita habent, sed qui pulchre circumrotaretur* ES 1183.

vertigo ~inis, *f.* A spinning sensation, dizziness: *mentem ejus delirium aut ~o invaderet* VR 57; *sphaerae, ut ita dicam, ~inis seu ~inum* ES 2310.

verto ~tere ~ti ~sum, *tr.* **1** To reverse the direction of, turn around: *~sa pagina* 'on the back of the page' ES 240; *~sus ita ut quod extra esset intra* ES 4367; *ne* [*porci*] *~si lacerent vos* Matt. 7.6 (AE 1044.4); (transf.) *hic potest leges justitiae ~tere sicut suas palmas* VR 73.1. **2** To direct, turn (in a specified direction): *stuppa ignis ~tebatur in ejus palmam* ES(M) 4552; (esp. refl. of parts of the body) *ut in libero se possit ~tere quo velit* AC 5650; *faciem ~tere ad orientem* AC 101. **b** (refl.) to direct one's attention, turn (to): *ne se ~tant ad vera* AC 7106. **3** To change to its opposite, reverse: *illico...ut ~titur status periculi* ES 150; ES 6089. **b** (esp. w. *in* + acc.) to change (into): *quod Dominus omnia mala... ~tat in bonum* AC 6663.2; *vera... ~tunt in falsa* FI 71; (pass.) *~tentur* [*aquae*] *in sanguinem* Exod. 7.17 (AC); *~sane est* [*sapientia*] *in ingeniositatem fatuam?* AM 152ª.1. **4** To direct to another purpose, twist: *qui ~tit fines ad se* AC 6938; *quod ille sensus* [sc. *literae Verbi*] *possit huc illuc ~ti* SS 97.1. **5** *Vitio ~tere*, to reckon as a fault: see **vitium**.

vertumnus ~i, *m.* A Roman god of change, used as a type of varying form or inconstancy: *non sum ludio, nec ~us, sed sum alternus, nunc in luce vestra, et nunc in umbra vestra* AM 326; *erant...quoad fidem sicut ~i* VR 77.5; *se...vertunt in varias formas sicut ~i* ES 1000.

verum[1] ~i, *neut.* **1** Truth in an absolute sense, esp. of the Divine: *quod ~um ex Divino esset* AC 6728; *quod Jehovah Deus...sit Ipsum Bonum et Ipsum ~um* VR 3.1; *ex Divino ~o est angelis lux* CI 127. **b** *~o similis*, probable: see **verosimilis**. **2** Truth as being capable of distinction into various kinds: *aliud est ~um scientificum, aliud ~um rationale, et aliud ~um intellectuale* AC 1496; *aliud...est coeleste ~um et aliud ~um coeleste* AC 1545; *quod detur ~um boni et ex hoc bonum ~i* AM 83. **3** Truth as belonging to a system of thought, a church, etc.: *spirituale est verum, quod nusquam fit ~um fidei nisi in illo sit bonum fidei* AC 880.2; *in ignorantia ~i fidei vivunt* AC 1059.3; *~um Ecclesiae, ita Verbum* DD 16.7. **4** (w. pl.) A particular true thought or utterance, truth: *omne ~um quod cogitant* AC 874; *quod omnia ~a quae apparent immergerent falsis* AC 6691.

verum[2], *conj.* **1** But, however: *uxor* [*repraesentat*] *sapientiae ejus amorem, ~um hic amor non est prior, sed est amor secundarius* AM 21.2; CI 222; *non deorsum et sursum, ~um transversim* ES 1693. **2** *~um enim vero*, however: *~um enim vero...volo solum aliqua memorabilia afferre* VR 75.7.

verumtamen, *conj.* also **veruntamen**, and spelled as two words **verum tamen**. All the same, in spite of this: *non reputavimus illum; ~en morbos nostros Ipse tulit* Isa. 53.4 (AC 1846.3); DD 45.1.

veruntamen: see **verumtamen**.

verus ~a ~um, *a.* (superl. *~issimus*) **1** (of statements, ideas, etc.) In accordance with fact, true: *quod incredibile forte sed usque ~issimum* AC 41; *credit quod ~um sit, quia ita a Domino dictum* AC 1911.6; *annon possum ~um facere quodcunque volo?* DP 286.1; *haec verba ~a sunt Dei* Rev. 19.9 (AR). **2** Properly so called, genuine, real, true: *inde ~a intelligentia, et inde ~a scientia, et inde ~a cognitio* AC 1226; *~us cultus consistit in praestatione usuum* AC 7038.1; *Ipse erat lux ~a* John 1.9 (AC 20). **3** Characterized by truth, truthful: *justae et ~ae viae Tuae* Rev. 15.3 (AR). **4** (as a title of the Lord): *haec dicit Sanctus ~us* Rev. 3.7 (AR); *sedens super illo* [sc. *equo albo*] *vocatur Fidelis et ~us* Rev. 19.11 (AR).

vesane, *adv.* Without soundness of mind, madly: *ne homo... ~e intret in mysteria fidei* AC 308.1.

vesania ~ae, *f.* Lack of sound mind, madness: *juvenes qui ex ~a aetatis et pruritu conceperunt principia nefanda* AC 829.2; *~a quod adulteria non sint mala religionis* AM 243.

vesanus ~a ~um, *a.* Lacking soundness of mind, mad: *sicut ~us alterius bona depraedatur* AC 7046.1; AM 152[a].1; *suis ~is cupiditatibus* AC 571.

vescor ~i, *intr.* To receive food, be fed: *vestiuntur gratis ~untur gratis* CI 393.3; (w. abl.) to feed (on): *~entes fructibus* AM 3.4; *pulvis, quo serpentes ~untur* VR 94.

vesica ~ae, *f.* (anat.) A bladder, sac: *e provincia ~ae urinatoriae* AC 956; *~as seminales* ES 884 (n.b. elsewhere Swedenborg uses *vesiculae*); *de ~a fellis* ES 1012 titulus.

vesicatorium ~i, *neut.* An ointment causing blisters: *per emplastra et ~a* VR 665.6.

vesicula ~ae, *f.* A small bladder, sac: *provinciam ~arum seminalium* ES 875; AE 167.6; *a me etiam ~as abstulere similes* ES 433.

vespa ~ae, *f.* A wasp: *talpis et ~is* Isa. 2.20 (AC 9424.6) emended in the 3rd edn. to *talpis et vespertilionibus*, in conformity with other places where Swedenborg quotes Isa. 2.20.

vespera ~ae, *f.* see also **vespere**. The evening: *mane, meridiem, ~am et noctem* AC 6697; *avium ~ae et noctis* AM 231.2; *quadam ~a* 'one evening' ES 618.

vespere, *adv.* also **vesperi**. An evening: *cum noctuis et vespertilionibus, quae noctu* [*et*] *~e vident tam clare objecta* DP 167; *mortua uxor mea ~i* Ezek. 24.18 (AC 7844.6).

versperi: see **vespere**.

vespertilio ~onis, *f.* (masc. in classical Latin) A bat: *ululae et ~ones* AM 233.7; *similis ~oni qui* [*quae* 1st edn.]...*noctu volat* CC 4; DP 167.

vespertinus ~a ~um, *a.* Of the evening: *matutinis horis, et ~is quoque* ES 514.

Vestalis ~is ~e, *a.* Of the goddess Vesta: *virgines quae ~es dictae sunt* AC 6832.7.

vester ~tra ~trum, *a.* Of you (in pl.), your: *ex zelo amoris pro ~tra felicitate et simul nostra* AM 208.2; *sic essentiam ~tram* [sc. which you assert] *Divinam dividitis* VR 16.3.

vestibulum ~i, *neut.* An enclosure in front of a door, porch: *Lazarus, qui projectus ad ~um ejus* Luke 16.20 (SS 40.3); AE 208.1.

vestigium ~i, *neut.* **1** A footprint: *ut vix ~i locus daretur inter duos* VR 160.2. **b** (transf.) a trace: *ita ut ne quidem aliquod ~um appareret* AC 635. **2** A movement of the feet, pace, step: *in primo ~o...repellitur* VR 108; (fig.) *omne ~um et omnis gressus ex religione et in religionem* AM 80.2.

vestimentum ~i, *neut.* A piece of clothing, garment: *vincens induetur ~is albis* Rev. 3.5 (AR); *dum ~i talem sortem emerim* ES 817.

vestio ~tire ~tivi ~titum, *tr.* To clothe, dress: *~tiuntur gratis* [*angeli*] CI 266.3; *quod...bombyces serico ~tiunt ...et faeminas et viros* VR 12.9; (transf.) to cover as with clothing: *bonum coeleste est quod non ~titur* AC 297; *non nuda vera, sed ~tita* SS 51.1.

vestis ~is, *f.* A piece of clothing, garment: *~es in Verbo etiam significant vera* NH 129; (fig.) *amicitia est sicut facies illius amoris et quoque sicut ~is ejus* AM 214.2.

vestitus ~us, *m.* Clothing, apparel: *hic honorabilis in ~u suo* Isa. 63.1 (AC 8273.2); *ea quae ad ~um hominis pertinent* ES 817.

veteramentum ~i, *neut.* A worn-out garment: *per ~a extractorum et ~a detritorum* AE 537.17 (Jer. 38.11).

veterasco ~rascere, *intr.* (fut. pple. *~raturus*) To become old, wear out: *terra sicut vestis ~rascet* Isa. 51.6 (AE 539.11).

veternus ~i, *m.* Torpor, lassitude: *numne ~us occuparet et caput et corpus ejus* AM 207.3.

veto ~are ~ui ~itum, *tr.* To prohibit, forbid: *~or quidem ab uxoribus...conjugia illa in lucem publicam sistere* AM 292.1; (pass.) *~itum fuit illis...maledicere surdo* AC 6989 (Lev. 19.14); *lectio Verbi...~abatur* FI 8.

vetula ~ae, *f.* An old woman: *per ~am faciei indecorae* AC 1774; VR 109.3.

vetulus ~a ~um, *a.* Of an advanced age, old: *~ae anus* AM 137.7; *leo ~us* Gen. 49.9 (AC).

vetus ~eris, *a.* **1** Of early date, old, ancient: *Ecclesia ~us* AC 6895.2; (masc. pl. as sb.) the ancients (usually Greeks and Romans): *hoc philosophicum ~erum* AM 185.3; VR 33. **2** *~us Testamentum*, the Old Testament: *propter Verbum ~eris Testamenti* AC 7051.4; *in ~eri Testamento* VI 2; cf. *ideo vocatur* [*Verbum*] *Faedus ~us et Novum* AM 128.

vetustas ~atis, *f.* The state of having existed for a long time, extreme age, antiquity: *usus duorum...sacramentorum comparari possunt templo quod ex ~ate in terram subsiderat* VR 669; ME 11.

vetustus ~a ~um, *a.* (compar. *~ior*, superl. *~issimus*) **1** Of advanced age, old: *quasi hominem ~um barbae canae* AC 1124. **2** Of ancient times, old: *adhuc...libri ~i exstant* AC 1756.2; *linguas ~as* CI 464.3; *fabulosa ~issimorum* SS 20.2; *ex usu ~o* AE 422.17.

vexatio ~onis, *f.* **1** A breaking up, harrying: *tales ~ones* [sc. *cibi*] *repraesentantur per primas vexationes spirituum* AC 5174. **2** Annoyance: *~o est similis coactioni ad loquendum citius quam cogitat* ES 1014.

vexator ~oris, *m.* One who annoys or hurts, tormentor: *spiritus ~ores...eum misere vexabant* ES 1013 1/2.

vexillum ~i, *neut.* A flag, ensign: *piratae qui appendunt ~um regni pacis* VR 380.4.

vexo ~are ~avi ~atum, *tr.* **1** To break up, disintegrate: *quod alimenta seu cibi in ventriculo multis modis ~entur* AC 5174. **2** To distress, annoy, torment: *~ati a falsis, hoc est, ab infernalibus* AC 7090.1; *interiora iis ~ant et inquietant* ES 744.

via ~ae, *f.* **1** A road, path: *alia semina ceciderunt super ~am duram* Matt. 13.4 (VI 2); *~a Lactea*, the Milky Way: AC 10587. **2** A journey, way: *ad custodiendum te in ~a* Exod. 23.20 (AC); *in ~a domum* 'on the way home' VR 160.8; (transf.) *in ~a mutatur* [*conjugiale*] *ab ipso homine* AM 203. **b** (Bibl.) a course of conduct: *omnes ~ae Jehovae misericordia et veritas* Ps. 25.10 (AC 6804.10). **3** A direction or course followed, route: *quod per illam ~am veniant qui e mundis* AC 6699; *mali spiritus eunt ~as quae tendunt ad infernum* CI 590; *sicut navis in torrente contra ~am ejus agente* VR 57; (transf.) *fides Dei intrat in hominem per ~am priorem* VR 11.3. **4** (of the Lord): *Ego sum ~a, Veritas et Vita* John 14.6 (SS 2).

viaticum ~i, *neut.* Food for a journey, provisions: *parate vobis ~um* Josh. 1.11 (AC 901.4).

viator ~oris, *m.* A traveller: *quod...abiturus sit ~or in Tartara* AM 75.2; ES 2862.

vibratilis ~is ~e, *a.* Moving rapidly to and fro, fluttering: *quoddam quasi alatum ~e se manifestat* CI 339; [*stellae*] *~es et e locis suis mobiles* ES 998.

vibratio ~onis, *f.* The sudden appearance and disappearance (of light), flash: *~o lucis sicut fulguris* AM 415.1; AE 131.19.

vibratiuncula ~ae, *f.* A shaking, fluttering: *quod stridule sicut alatis ~is citis erumpant* ES 3544.

vibratorius ~a ~um, *a.* Proceeding in short bursts, staccato: *loquela angelorum coelestium est...mollis et quasi continua, sed loquela angelorum spiritualium est paulum ~a et discreta* CI 241.

vibro ~are ~avi ~atum, *tr.* **1** To move rapidly to and fro, shake, wave: *~abant pileos suos* AR 417.10; *dextram manum ~abat* ES 723; (pass. and refl.) *brachia eorum pendent et ~antur* CI 3; AE 131.18. **2** (refl., of light) To flash: *hoc rutilum ex oculo in oculum se ~at* AM 384.

vicariatus ~us, *m.* The office of deputy or substitute: *propter ~um stabilitum ex verbis Domini ad Petrum* DP 264.2; VR 634.

vicarius ~a ~um, *a.* Taking the place of another person or thing, substituted: *potentia ~a, quod idem est cum mediate* AC 7619; (masc. as sb.) a person or thing substituted for another, replacement: *ipse Mahumedes nusquam adest, sed ~us loco ejus substitutus est* AM 344; *non potuisset Papa ~us ejus esse in terra* ES 4551; *amor vitae...ponit ~um infra se, qui vocatur amor mediorum* DP 109.1.

vicem, *acc. f.* (abl. sg. *~e*, acc. pl. *~es*, abl. pl. *~ibus*) **1** An instance of a repeated event, occasion, time: *altera ~e* 'a second time' AC 1030.1; *tertia ~e* AC 1328; *unitio non facta est simul et una ~e sed successive* AC 1926; *qui ad problema illa ~e responderunt* AM 315.2; (pl.) *binis ~ibus postea* AC 1770; *hoc aliquoties occurrit... ~es non possum numerare, nam tot sunt* ES 2957. **b** (w. compar. to express multiplication): *ut...is permultis ~ibus doctior sit* ES 2482. **2** (pl.) Regular changes or alternating states: *~es spiritualium...quae comparantur ~ibus dierum* AC 37; *statae ~es ortus et occasus solis et lunae* DP 190.1; *~es pulsus* AC 3884.3. **b** *per ~es*, from time to time, occasionally: [*Ecclesia*] *novos status per ~es subit* AC 6645.2; *redi per ~es et forte plura detegentur* AM 155[a].5; (also, abl. pl.) *per totam noctem in qua ~ibus evigilabam* ES 2273. **3** The function of a person or thing, role, part: *ii qui ~em eorum sustinerent in interiori coelo* ES 281; *hepar...agit ~em plurium viscerum* ES 368. **b** *~e* (w. gen.), in place (of): *unus a principe missus ~e ejus etiam acclamavit* AM 20.3; *facit ut* [*arbores*] *germinent,* *florescant et fructificent, quae ~e beatitudinis sunt in animatis* VR 44. 4 *~e versa*, with the terms reversed, conversely: *cum illa quae fidei, excitantur illa quae charitatis, et ~e versa* AC 6690.

vicesimus: see **vigesimus**.

vicina ~ae, *f.* A female neighbour: *petat mulier e ~a sua* Exod. 3.22 (AC).

vicinia ~ae, *f.* The adjacent district, neighbourhood: *exeuntes ex urbe et a ~is* AM 151[a].2; VR 144.

vicinus ~a ~um, *a.* (compar. *~ior*, superl. *~issimus*) 1 Situated close, neighbouring: *ne quidem illis qui in proximo seu ~issimo [inferno]* AC 8237.2; CI 236.1. 2 (masc. as sb.) A neighbour: *ille et ~us illius propinquus ad domum ejus* Exod. 12.4 (AC). b (neut. as sb.) neighbourhood: *implent omne ~um [viciniam* Rogers] *idea et imagine sui* UJ(P) 233 (Tafel, p. 76).

vicissim, *adv.* 1 Reciprocally, mutually: *omnis cogitatio...et omnis affectio...se extendunt...in coelum ...et mirabiliter communicant cum societatibus quae ibi, et hae ~im cum illo* CI 203.1; *expende...annon intus in media via unum expungit alterum ~im* VR 4.2. 2 In the opposite case, conversely: *ab illis qui in coelo sunt videri possunt inferna...non autem ~im* AC 8237.2; *Dominus secundum conjunctionem... propior apparet, et ~im secundum rejectionem... remotior* DP 33.4; AM 31. 3 On the other hand, on the contrary: *cum videt impios ad honores evehi...et ~im cultores Dei in contemtu* DP 237; *formae illae fiunt pellucidae...per fidem in unum Deum, at ~im fiunt opacae...per fidem in plures Deos* VR 8.4.

vicissitudo ~inis, *f.* Alternation or succession of changes: *hic potest per ~ines illas videre insanias suas* AM 48[a].3; *~ines annorum, tum dierum* ES 2294.

victima ~ae, *f.* A sacrificial animal, victim: *culter qui adhibebatur in sacrificiis ad ~as* AC 2799.1.

victor ~oris, *m.* One who wins a battle or contest, winner, victor: *pugna spiritualis in qua pugnans fit ~or* AC 6663.1; *sicut ~or post stragem destruit...castra* AM 426; (as adj.) victorious: *terror pro hoste ~ore* AC 8318.1.

victoria ~ae, *f.* A victory in battle: *pugnae, ~ae, clades submersiones* AC 8261.3; (Bibl.) *sparsa est ~a illorum super vestes Meas* Isa. 63.3 (AC 8273.2); (transf.) *~am super hostes spirituales* AC 8261.5; *de ~is super illa* [sc. *mala*] VI 99.

victrix ~icis, *f.* A female victor: AM 248.2.

victurus ~a ~um: fut. pple. of **vivo**.

victus[1] ~us, *m.* Food, nutriment: *curae pro ~u et amictu* AC 6648; *~u amaeno...ex floribus se nutriunt [papiliones]* VR 12.6.

victus[2] ~a ~um: pf. pple. of **vinco**.

vicus ~i, *m.* A narrow street in a town, lane, alley: *dixit servo ut abiret in plateas et ~os urbis* AE 118.3 (Luke 14.21); *in speciem urbis, cum ~is et plateis* CI 586; *in ~is et compitis* ES 420; (in the Grand Man) *provinciam in ~o testiculorum* ES 3152.

videlicet, *adv.* That is to say, namely: *concludi potest, quod simile sit cum castis, ~et, quod apud hos casta sint omnia* AM 140.

video ~dere ~di ~sum, *tr.* 1 To experience visually, see: *tales erant ut quicquid usquam ~dissent in mundo ...quidem ~debant, sed cogitabant de coelestibus* AC 241; *quae oculus nusquam ~derit* AC 7381.2; *fasciculatio illa...sistitur ~denda in cerebro* AC 7408.1. b (w. pred.) to see (in a stated condition): *cum quis... ~det aliquem in miseria* AC 6737; *~si sunt Moses et Elias cum Ipso colloquentes* AC 6752.9; (w. inf.) *quod mater potius famem patiatur quam ut ~deat infantem esurire* AC 548.3. 2 (absol.) To possess the faculty of sight, see: *aquilae...acute ~dent* AC 3901.1; *oculi coecorum ~debunt* Isa. 29.18 (AC 6989); *spirituales ~dent ex suo sole* CI 128. 3 To catch sight of, see: *sustulit Abraham oculos suos, et ~dit locum e longinquo* Gen. 22.4 (AC); *aliquoties ~di sicut flumen* AC 6699; (w. indir. qu.) *num ~disti...quae seniores filiorum Israelis faciunt?* Ezek. 8.12 (AC 7353). 4 To look for, search out: *~deat Pharaoh virum intelligentem* Gen. 41.33 (AC); (absol.) to look: *attolle oculos tuos circumcirca et ~de* Isa. 60.4 (AC 6740); *~dete et cavete a fermento Pharisaeorum* Matt. 16.6 (AC 7906.1). b (used in quoting references in a book): *de his ~deantur quae prius...dicta sunt* AC 6643; *quid...correspondentia, ~deri potest in opere De Caelo et Inferno* SS 7. 5 To have experience of, meet with: *qui vero non credit Filio, non ~debit vitam* John 3.36 (AC 30.1); *quod ~suri effectum Divinum ex Divino Humano Domini* AC 8137.1; *Ipse Deus, qualis est in intimis Verbi, non potest ab ullo creato ~deri* VR 6.1. 6 To become mentally aware of, perceive: *si malum apud aliquem ~dent* AC 6655; *quod ~derit [Jehovah] afflictionem illorum* Exod. 4.31 (AC); *hoc...conceptores Symboli Athanasiani e longinquo ~derunt* VR 110.3. b (w. indir. qu.): *~debant qualis...esset* AC 6705; *~debo num adhuc illi vivunt* Exod. 4.18 (AC); (w. *quod*) *omnis ratio sana...~det quod omne divisum...ex se dilabatur* VR 10; *et ~dit Deus lucem, quod bona* Gen. 1.4 (AC). 7 (pass. w. pred.) To appear, seem: *ita ut sibi ~derentur quasi ligati* AC 8393; *sibi ~sus est...in tristitia* AM 461.1; (w. inf.) *ut ~derer mihi in spiritu...esse* AM 293.1; *~deri coram hominibus quod probi* ES 4396; (impers.) *~debatur mihi, quod me prorsus oppressissent* ES 817. b to seem to be true, be one's opinion: *quod vobis ~detur de Christo?* Matt. 22.42 (DD 35.5). 8 (pass.) To be highly regarded, be conspicuous: *cultus eorum internus in externo fuerat vel ut ~derentur mundo, vel ut obtinerent mundana* AC 1094.2.

vidua ~ae, *f.* A widow: *status conjugii...juvenis cum ~a* AM 317; ES 1328.

viduitas ~atis, *f.* The fact of being a widow, widowhood: *causae...quae ~atem faeminae aggravant* AM 325.3.

viduo ~are ~avi ~atum, *tr.* To make a widow, bereave; (pf. pple.) bereft (of): *verum... ~atum bono* AC 7910.

viduus ~i, *m.* A widower: *status conjugii... ~i cum virgine* AM 317.

vigeo ~gere ~gui, *intr.* **1** (of plants) To flourish, grow: *nihil ~get et excitatur ad fructificandum* AM 223.2. **2** (transf.) To be strong, flourish: *adulteria, quae ibi ~gent plus quam alibi* AC 6666.3; *qualis opinio ad hodiernum diem ~get* ES 2387.

vigesies, *adv.* Twenty times: *numerus...excedit numerum...decies ad ~es* ES 5315.

vigesimus ~a ~um, *a.* also **vicesimus**. Twentieth: *usque ad annum ejus ~um* AC 2280.

vigil ~lis, *a.* **1** Awake: *expergiscitur a somno et ~l fit* AC 147; (of sleep) similar to wakefulness: *fui in somno dicto ~li* ES 4398; (masc. as sb.) watchman, guard: *cum duobus ~libus armatis* ES 3880. **2** Mentally alert, wide awake: *putant se plus ~les esse aliis* AC 1072.6; *nec adhuc ~les facti sunt ex Verbo* VR 82.

vigilans ~ntis, *a.* Alert, watchful: *a videntibus et ~ntibus...potest perspici* VR 30.3.

vigilatio ~onis, *f.* The state of being watchful, vigilance: (w. *super*) *pro ~one super illo* [sc. *vero interiore*] AC 5622.2.

vigilia ~ae, *f.* **1** The state of being awake, wakefulness: *datum est illos videre in plena ~a* CI 74.1. **2** The time of awaking: *in prima ~a* AC 184; *circa ~am, antequam vigilarem* ES 2436. **3** One of the periods into which the night was divided, watch: *ad principium ~arum* Lam. 2.19 (AE 187.7).

vigilo ~are ~avi, *intr.* **1** To be awake: *cerebellum... tempore somni ~at* AC 1977.2. **2** To be alert: *beatus qui ~at* Rev. 16.15 (AR); *quare ~ent homines* ES 259.

viginti, *indecl. a.* Twenty: *quod...dies* [*distinguitur*] *in ~ti quatuor horas* CI 168.2.

vigor ~oris, *m.* Energy, vigour: *homo...non deficitur ~ore* AM 107.

vilesco ~ere, *intr.* To become worthless: *quod jucundum vitae... ~eret* CI 158; *quae faciunt ut matrimonia ~ant* ES 3613.

vilipendo ~dere ~di ~sum, *tr.* To consider worthless, disparage: *vera doctrinae omittunt aut ~dunt* AR 108; *famuli...quos dominus ~dit* CI 472.2; (neut. of pf. pple. as sb.) *voluptas...loquendi non nisi quam ~sa et nugas* AM 252.

vilis ~is ~e, *a.* (compar. *~ior*, superl. *~issimus*) **1** Of low rank or esteem, humble, mean: *infimos seu ~es in Ecclesia* AC 7784.3; *in regno animali ~issima sunt* [*vermiculi*] CI 108.2; *status ejus ~ior foret* AM 29. **2** Lacking value, worthless, vile: *panem ~em* AC 276.2; *excrementa ~issima* ES 3572; *in vestibus obscuris, ~ibus, laceris* AE 195.5.

villa ~ae, *f.* A village: *intra...civitatem aut ~am nativitatis* AM 49; *urbes et ~ae* AM 182.3; Isa. 42.11 (AE 405.12).

vinarius ~a ~um, *a.* Concerned with the making of wine: *in cellis ~is* VR 834; ES 4053.

vincio ~cire ~xi (*or* ~civi) ~ctum, *tr.* **1** To fasten with bonds, bind, tie up; (esp. pf. pple.) bound, prisoner: *tenentur...sicut ~cti* AC 6757; *ad educendum e carcere ~ctum* Isa. 42.7 (AC 6854.4); *hanc filiam Abrahami, quam ~xit Satanas* Luke 13.16 (AR 591); *~civit illum* Gen. 42.24 (AC). **b** (w. dat.) to fasten, attach (to): *quomodo ~ciret alios spiritus mihi* ES 4504; *~ctus infernis* ES 4679. **2** To place under restraint, constrain, force: *leges et normae, quae ~ciunt homines* AM 130.2; *ad ~ciendum plebem ad obedientiam* VR 14.3.

vinco ~ncere ~ci ~ctum, *tr., intr.* **1** (tr.) To overcome by force, defeat: *solum Divinum potest ~ncere inferna* AC 8175; *quod...se sicut ~ctas tradiderint* [*uxores*] AM 297; *dum* [*navis*] *~ncitur a procella...fertur in scopulos* VR 28.2. **2** (intr.) To prove superior, win: *postquam pugna exstiterat ac verum ~cerat* AC 7906.2; *cum Dominus pugnat pro homine, ~ncit homo in omnibus* AC 8159.5; (in a game) *quod nullatenus ille ~ncere posset* ES 4567.

vinculum ~i, *neut.* **1** A physical means of restraint, bond, fetter: *quod faceret sibi ~a et juga* AC 3542.4 (Jer. 27.2). **2** Anything which imposes restraint, bond, curb: *~a ejus sunt externa, ut timor legis jacturae vitae* AC 81.3; *in ~is conscientiae* AC 7090.4. **3** Anything which joins or links, tie, bond: *quod ~um universale sit Dominus, ita amor ab Ipso* AC 9613.3; *~um conjugiale* VR 41.3.

vindemia ~ae, *f.* The harvesting of grapes, vintage: *quando consummata est ~a* Isa. 24.13 (AE 313.12).

vindemiatio ~onis, *f.* The harvesting of grapes: AE 919.2.

vindemiator ~oris, *m.* A grape harvester: *si ~ores venerint tibi* Obad. 5 (AC 5135.8).

vindemio ~are ~avi ~atum, *tr.* To harvest (grapes): *neque ex rubo ~ant uvam* Luke 6.44 (VI 28).

vindex ~icis, *m.* An avenger: *sciendum quod... Jehovah...dicatur zelotes aut ~ex* AC 8875.8; AE 778.2.

vindicatio ~onis *f.* **1** The claiming (of what is not one's own): *furtum significat ~onem aliorum* AC 5135.1. **2** Deliverance, rescue: *de ~one Lothi per Abramum* AC 1659.1; *~onem a malis et liberationem a falsis* AE 328.19. **3** Revenge: *talis ~o ne quidem datur apud ullum angelum* AE 805.3.

vindicativus ~a ~um, *a.* Avenging, retributive: *ex justitia, quae ab aliquibus etiam vocatur ~a* DD 18.1; FI 39.

vindicator ~oris, *m.* An avenger: *ardens ~or* VR 518.2.

vindico ~are ~avi ~atum, *tr., intr.* **1** (tr., w. *sibi*) To claim (for oneself): *qui ex propria justitia ~ant sibi coelum* AC 942; *non aliquid auferre Domino et id sibi ~are* AC 7089.1; (also w. other dat.) *concilium Nicaenum ad ~andum divinitatem Domino finxerunt Filium Dei natum ab aeterno* VR 94.2. **2** (tr.) To rescue, save: *sic a servitute in libertatem ~entur* ES 244. **3** (intr.) To exact retribution, take vengeance: *sumetur ultio ac ~abitur* AC 8226.2; *quod Deus...ex justitia statuerit ~are per ejus* [sc. *generis humani*] *damnationem* FI 44.

vindicta ~ae, *f.* An act of vengeance, revenge: *ob astus, dolos... ~as* AC 6666.3; *amores ~ae, crudelitatis* AC 6832.8; *in illos ~as exercent* CI 220.

vinea ~ae, *f.* A plantation of vines, vineyard: *~ae et laurus correspondent affectioni veri* CI 520; *in parabola de agricolis in ~a* VI 2 (Matt. 21.33-44).

vinitor ~oris, *m.* A vine dresser: *Ego sum vitis...et Pater Meus ~or* John 15.1 (VI 2).

vinosus ~a ~um, *a.* Of wine: *odor ~us* AC 1517; *spiritus ~us alcohol dictus* VR 98.1.

vinum ~i, *neut.* Wine: *~um est bonum fidei* DD 27; (w. pl.) a kind of wine: *nobile ~um* SS 40.1; *commiscant illa...sicut quisquilias cum ~is in uno poculo* AM 453.

violabilis ~is ~e, *a.* Susceptible to violation, violable: *quod* [*conjugium coeleste*] *sit non ~e* AC 8895.

violatio ~onis, *f.* Sexual violation, rape: *per libidinem ~onis non intelligitur libido deflorationis* AM 511.

violator ~oris, *m.* A violator, rapist: *ex zelotypia contra ~ores* AM 106.

violatrix ~icis, *f.* Violating: *contra conatus scorti ~icis* AM 379.2.

violenter, *adv.* Violently: *quandoque ~er renuimus* AM 294.2.

violentia ~ae, *f.* The use of immoderate force, violence: *~am illatam charitati* AC 7326; *ex influxu et ~a activitatis oppositi in oppositum* AM 10.8; *ara et pulpitum sub diu variis exposita ~is* VR 55; *qui contra alios ~a utuntur* ES 391 titulus.

violentus ~a ~um, *a.* Prone to the use of force, violent: *qui in terra ~i fuerunt* ES 377.

violina ~ae, *f.* A violin: *clavichordium, ~a et similia* ES 4482.

violo ~are ~avi ~atum, *tr.* **1** To injure, damage, break down, violate: *conatus... ~andi conjugia* CI 384; *vincula non ~anda* AM 257.1; *quod Deus...tangat liberum ejus arbitrium, sed nusquam ~et* VR 74.3. **2** To violate sexually, rape: *ardor ~andi faeminas* AM 511.

vipera ~ae, *f.* A poisonous snake, viper: *mala...quae circumspargunt sicut ~ae venena* CI 578; *tali pedum sicut duae ~ae* AM 264.1.

viperinus ~a ~um, *a.* Resembling vipers: *per serpentes diversi generis, ~os, aliter maculatos* ES 4470.

vir viri, *m.* **1** A male person, man: *cum cornu ferierit bos virum aut mulierem* Exod. 21.28 (AC); *quod... praedicetur tam de viro quam de foemina* AC 478. **b** (w. special reference to sexual function): *duae filiae, quae non cognoverunt virum* Gen. 19.8 (AC). **2** (as opposed to wife) Husband: *de praerogativa viri et obedientia uxoris* AC 568; *cum non nominatur maritus, sed dicitur 'vir'* AC 1468. **3** (combined w. other nouns) Male: *de omni bestia munda accipias tibi septena septena, virum et uxorem ejus* Gen. 7.2 (AC); (so, perh.) *rarum reddam virum hominem prae auro* Isa. 13.12 (AC 4287.5). **4** Man (as opposed to child or old man), adult: *adolescens, vir, senex* CI 330. **5** A man (as opposed to an animal): *et omnibus filiis Israelis non movebit canis linguam suam, ad a viro usque ad bestiam* Exod. 11.7 (AC). **6** (w. gen.) A man (of a specified kind), man, figure: *viros strenuitatis* Exod. 18.21 (AC); *dictatum a viro auctoritatis* VR 42; (of the Lord) *Vir bellorum* Isa. 42.13 (DD 14.9).

virectum: see **viretum**.

virens ~ntis, *a.* (of plants) Showing green shoots, flourishing: *ne...a ligno ~nte faciat illum siccum stipitem* AM 294.6.

virescentia ~ae, *f.* The turning green of a plant: *arboris... ~a ex foliis* AC 5116.1.

viretum ~i, *neut.* also **virectum**. An area of green grass, lawn, meadow: *ostia quae patebant in floreta, et ab his in ~a* AM 13.2; *campi et ~a* FI 63.1.

virga ~ae, *f.* **1** The shaft or trunk of a plant: *effloruit ~a* Ezek. 7.10 (DD 4); *primum producit radicem, et ex illa ~am seu caulem cum ramis et foliis* FI 16; (Bibl., in quot. fig.) *Aschur ~a irae Meae* Isa. 10.5 (SS 86). **2** A rod made from the stem of a plant, wand: *palmas...modo ~as, nempe absque foliis* ES 2295; *quod* *haec* [sc. *Medea*] *Ulyssis comites...contigerit ~a magica* AM 521.4; (as a means of punishment) *unum ceciderunt ~is* Matt. 21.35 (AE 122.3).

virgineus ~a ~um, *a.* Of a young woman, girlish: *puellam in sua prima ~a aetate* AC 1774; *sexus ~i* ES 4377; (neut. as sb.) *quod ~um mutetur in uxorem* AM 199.1.

virginitas ~atis, *f.* The state of being a virgin, virginity: *perpetuam ~atem voverant* AM 155.3; *haec libido* [sc. *deflorationis*] *est violatio ~atum, non autem virginum dum fit ex consensu* AM 511.

virgo ~inis, *f.* **1** A young woman before marriage, girl: *infantes...una cum ~inibus in horto* CI 337; *parabola de decem ~inibus* SS 17.1. **2** A woman without sexual experience, virgin: [*Dominus*] *a ~ine muliere natus* AC 1414; *~o filia Aegypti* Jer. 46.11 (AC 6729); *de statu ~inis seu faeminae illibatae* AM 502.1. **3** (in Greek mythology) *Novem ~ines*, the nine Muses: [*fons*] *consecratus novem ~inibus* AM 182.2.

virgultum ~i, *neut.* A large plant, shrub, bush: *et nullum ~um agri adhuc erat in terra* Gen. 2.5 (AC); *sylvae cum arboribus et ~is* FI 63.3; VR 54.

viridesco ~ere, *intr.* To turn green: *stagnum ex ovulis ranarum ~ens* VR 120.1; AR 232.

viridis ~is ~e, *a.* Of a green colour: *pupilla oculi in plano ~i* AM 268.2; esp. w. ref. to vegetation: *campi floridi et ~es* FI 63.3; (neut. as sb.) greenery: *et omni ferae terrae, et omni avi coelorum...omne ~e herbae in escam* Gen. 1.30 (AC).

viriditas ~atis, *f.* Greenness: AE 507.9.

virilis ~is ~e, *a.* Of a man, male: *quod...seminatio ~is ex origine spirituali sit* AM 220.1.

virilitas ~atis, *f.* **1** Virility: *encomia ~atis* AM 75.9. **2** The period of a man's full potentiality, manhood: *infantia, adolescentia, ~as, et senectus* CI 166.

virtus ~utis, *f.* **1** Power, strength, force: *ex significatione ~utis, quod sit vis et potentia* AC 8266; *quod delitiae illae quoad copiam, gradum et ~utem, praestantes et eminentes sint* AM 75.7; *hujus* [sc. *solis*] *objecta non sunt in ~ute ejus* VR 70.2; *Filium Hominis venientem in nubibus coeli cum ~ute et gloria* Matt. 24.30 (AC 49.4). **b** (pl.) sources of power: *~utes coelorum commovebuntur* Matt. 24.29 (AC 32). **2** (w. pl.) An exercise of power: *in nomine Tuo ~utes multas fecimus* Matt. 7.22 (AC 6806.2); *hae sunt...~utes quas Dominus operatur* VR 142; cf. *quod Divina Trinitas sit...sicut anima, corpus, et ~us procedens apud...hominem* VR 138. **3** Male sexual potency: *forte uxor se unit cum ~ute viri* AM 331.1; *in statu adolescentiae, et inde in ~ute aetatis illius* AM 356; (w. *virilis*) *facultas et ~us, quae vocatur virilis* AM 433. **4** Manly courage, bravery: *Romani erant fortiores eo; sed ostensum quod Romanorum ~us erat vesana* ES 3394. **5** A valuable quality, excellence, virtue: *describere illa* [sc. *justitiam, sinceritatem, castitatem*] *ut ~utes morales et spirituales* AS 416.2; *varias vitae moralis honestates et ~utes* AM 17.5.

virulentus ~a ~um, *a.* Poisonous: *scabies ~a* AM 253.1.

virus ~i, *neut.* (acc. sg. *~us*) **1** Poison (in quot. fig.): *amor...effutiendi ~us contra Deum* DP 38.1. **2** An offensive odour, stench: *nidoribus tetris...spiritus diabolici...delectantur, sicut illis animalia quibus ~us inest* AS 339.3.

vis, *f.* (acc. sg. *vim*, dat. and abl. sg. *vi*, nom. and acc. pl. *vires*, gen. pl. *virium*, dat. and abl. pl. *viribus*) **1** Capacity for action, power: *putant...vim baculis inesse* AC 4936; *ex conatu est vis, et ex vi effectus* AC 5116.2; *utrique nulla vis sit, quia similis potentia utrinque est* CI 537.1. **2** (pl.) Strength, ability, powers: *qui credit...quod resistere possit ex propriis viribus* AC 8172; *brachia...vibrantur sicut expertia virium in internodiis* CI 3. **3** The exercise of force, violence: *mulieres vim patientur* Zech. 14.2 (AE 555.9); *vi*, forcibly: *ut discederent vi unus ab altero* ES 2177. **4** A particular manifestation of power, force: *corpus vires et potentias suas exercet per brachia et manus* AC 4933; *si vis viva hujus Solis retraheretur ...sol ille collaberetur* AS 157; *vis haec propagativa seu plastica in seminibus...non aliunde est* AM 238.2. **5** A thing capable of exerting force, power: *sunt enim* [*spiritus*] *modo vires passivae* AC 5557; *athmosphaerae sunt vires activae* AS 178; *vires vivae in homine sunt quae intus constituunt ejus corpus* AS 219.1.

viscera: see **viscus**.

viscerulum ~i, *neut.* A small internal organ: *homo, in quo...tot viscera, et tot ~a intra viscera* AC 1285.2; [*insectulum*] *praeditum...corculis, fistulis pulmonicis, ~is ac cerebris* AS 352.

viscidus ~a ~um, *a.* Sticky, glutinous: *objecta...quae adhaerent sicut gluten seu ~um* ES 685 (J D Odhner).

viscositas ~atis, *f.* The quality of being sticky, viscosity: *sic ut quaedam ~as quoque insit* ES 826.

viscosus ~a ~um, *a.* (superl. *~issimus*) Sticky, viscous: *ex ~o et bilioso sanguine* AM 357; ES 810; *~issima cerebri* AC 5717.1.

viscus ~eris, *neut.* Any one of the internal organs of the body: *cuivis membro, organo, et ~eri* AC 6698; CI 405; (esp. pl.) the viscera: *e ~eribus matris meae* Ps. 71.6 (AC 8043.4); *super cor et super ~era corporis* AM 315.6; (as the seat of emotions) *videns eum ~eribus commotus est* Luke 10.33 (AE 444.14).

visibilis ~is ~e, *a.* Capable of being seen, visible:

planetae qui coram oculis nostris ~es sunt AC 6697; *Deus... ~is sub humana forma* CI 514; (neut. pl. as sb.) *ex cognitis et ~ibus in mundo* AM 311.2.

visibiliter, *adv.* Visibly: *quod malae parentum inclinationes ~er maneant in liberis* AC 313; *ex lateritiis lapidibus, ~er distinctis* ES 2386.

visio ~onis, *f.* **1** The power of seeing, sight: *ubi illustratio, ibi etiam contrariorum ~o erit* ES 4772. **2** The state of seeing with other than physical eyes, the ability to see visions: *tunc est illuminatus...estque tunc in ~one Divina* AC 1584; *cum fuerunt [prophetae] in ~one, non erant in suo corpore sed in suo spiritu* DD 52; *sunt...in ~one posteriore* AM 233.7. **3** An appearance as if of something seen, vision: *Antiquissima Ecclesia revelationem...habuit...per ~ones et somnia* AC 597.2; *secedam ergo, et videbo ~onem magnam hanc* Exod. 3.3 (AC); *~ones sunt duplicis generis, Divinae et diabolicae* DP 134.1. **b** (esp. of false appearances): *asseverare possum quod illa non sint ~ones, sed quod sint visa in omni vigilia* UJ(C) 35; *illa erant solum ~ones* AR 7; *quod illa essent ~ones et non realia* ES 5896.

visionarius ~a ~um, *a.* **1** Prone to see visions, visionary: *tales sunt ~i et enthusiastae* CI 249; *secundum ~os, qui vocantur idealistae* DP 46.2. **2** Typical of visions, imaginary: *in concupiscentia ~a seu phantasia possessionis omnium opum* AM 268.1; *quod Verbum...sit ~um et congestum quid* VR 14.3.

visitatio ~onis, *f.* A visitation (by the Divine): *quid facietis die ~onis?* Isa. 10.3 (AC 6767.3); AE 129.

visito ~are ~avi ~atum, *tr.* **1** To go to see, call upon, visit (a person): *quod ~averit Jehovah filios Israelis* Exod. 4.31 (AC); *aegrotus fui et ~astis me* Matt. 25.36 (VI 2); *incolae quos ~abimus* AM 79.3. **b** to see to, tend (a thing): *vide, et ~a vitem hanc* Ps. 80.14 (AC 8281.4). **2** To submit to trial, test: *postquam primum ~ati sunt, hoc est, explorati* AC 7273.1; *quod...missi simus, ad ~andum num apud vos sit religio* VR 113.5. **3** (Bibl., absol. w. *super*) To execute judgment (upon): *~abit Jehovah super exercitum altitudinis* Isa. 24.21 (AC 566.2); *super hircos ~abo* Zech. 10.3 (FI 68); (also, w. acc.) *~abo super orbem malitiam* Isa. 13.11 (SS 14.3).

viso ~ere ~i, *tr.* To catch sight of, espy: *quod cum ~untur [equi], terrificent illos* AC 8381; ES 4683.

visualis ~is ~e, *a.* **1** Of sight, visual: *ex ~i experientia* CI 526.3. **2** Visible: *haec sphaera est quae...fit ~is per arcum* AC 1048.

visualiter, *adv.* By means of sight, visually: *ne aliquid ~er detegatur* AM 376.

visus ~us, *m.* **1** The faculty of seeing, sight: *ex ~u, auditu, gustu, odoratu, tactu* AC 7039.2; *apparetne corvus niger coram ~u* AM 233.4; *~um noctuarum similem* VR 7. **2** The use of sight, look: *dissiparetur idea, sicut ~us in universo* AC 6700; *ad primum ~um* AC 6631. **3** The power of perceiving with the mind, perception, sight: *nec dubitari potest quin Dominus...in tali Divino ~u fuerit* AC 1584; *~ui intellectuali* AC 7078; *mentis ~us* VR 11.2.

vita ~ae, *f.* **1** The state of being alive, life: *~a consistit in sensu* AC 322; *~a quae non aeterna non est ~a* AC 726; *sunt tres gradus... ~ae...apud unumquemvis angelum* CI 267. **2** Life on earth (as opposed to life after death): *bini quos in ~a cognovi* ES 268; ES 1045. **3** *~a post mortem*, life after death: AC 3957.8; (so, also) *~a aeterna*, everlasting life: John 6.40 (VR 2.3); *altera ~a*, the other life: AC 6681. **4** Life on earth regarded as a period of time, lifetime: *anni ~ae Levi septem et triginta et centum anni* Exod. 6.16 (AC); *per totum ~ae Suae curriculum* AC 2776.2; (pl.) *hi dies annorum ~arum Abrahami* Gen. 25.7 (AC). **5** A person's life on earth regarded historically, the events of one's life, biography: *in Verbo ~ae Domini apud Evangelistas* AC 1690.1; *audivi angelos detegentes alterius ~am solum ex illo audito* CI 236.4; *quod id traxerint a ~is in corpore* ES 1794. **6** A person's life regarded as a series of actions, way of living: *~a absque vicibus et varietatibus foret una, ita nulla* AC 37; *confirmatus per multum ~ae* AC 2715.6; *quod omnis religio sit ~ae* VI 1 titulus. **b** (w. epithet) a particular way of living, a life: (w. gen.) *in ~a...mali sunt* AC 2357.3; *de ~a charitatis* FI 59; (w. adj.) *~a moralis* AC 3690:3; *~a spiritualis* AC 6685. **7** Life as a faculty possessed by a person: *sunt in homine binae ~ae, una est voluntatis, altera est intellectus* AC 652; *nisi homini propria ~a foret, sicut est...propria facies* AM 524.2. **8** The state of being spiritually alive, real life: *ut homo novam ~am accipiat, seu potius ut ~am* AC 848.1; *nullius ~ae sunt* AC 30.2; *~a consistit in intellectu veri et voluntate boni* ES 3756. **9** Life regarded as a force derived from the Lord: *in bono et jucundo est ~a, non autem in vero* AC 668; *anima Domini fuit ipsa ~a* AC 2025.4; *in Ipso ~a erat, et ~a erat lux hominum* John 1.4 (AC 3195.4); *verba quae Ego loquor vobis spiritus sunt, et ~a sunt* John 6.63 (SS 2.2); *calor et lux e sole mundi naturalis nihil ~ae in se habent* VR 360.1; (Bibl., in pl.) *et inspiravit [Jehovah Deus] in nares ejus spiraculum ~arum* Gen. 2.7 (AC). **10** The vital principle or vivifying force of anything: *ipsa essentia et ~a fidei est solus Dominus* AC 30.1; *sensus Verbi internus ipsissima illius ~a* AC 64; *succus, qui est ~a plantae et arboris* ES 251.

vitalis ~is ~e, *a.* Of or concerned with life, life-giving, vital: *calor ~is hominis* AC 7082; *quod amores sint ignes ~es* AC 7324.4; *~es motus* CI 446. **b** (neut. as sb.) the vital principle or force, vitality: *amor mutuus est* *ipsissimum ~e quod accipiunt ab essentia Domini* AC 1802.4; *anima non cogitatur...nisi sicut purum quid...in quo ~e est ex rationalitate* AM 315.9.

vitiligo ~inis, *f.* A disease of the skin, psoriasis: *ulcera leprae, ut...ustio, porrigo, ~o* AC 7524.3.

vitio ~are ~avi ~atum, *tr.* To corrupt, spoil: *ex ~ato sanguine aut ex ~ata lympha* AM 253.2; ES 1335.

vitiositas ~atis, *f.* The state of being corrupt: *ex ~ate sanguinis* AR 678.1; an instance of this: *quod ~ates... repraesententur per velum* ES 1413.

vitiosus ~a ~um, *a.* Full of corruption, faulty: *tunc deploret ~am suam naturam* BCP (VI 6); (neut. as sb.) *comparantur illi ~is et noxiis quae influunt in sanguinem* AC 1877.

vitis ~is, *f.* A grapevine: *arbores...ut olea, ~is, cedrus, populus* SS 18.2; *elevatae orchestrae circumductae cancellis consertis ex ~ibus* AM 17.1; (of the Lord) *Ego sum ~is* John 15.1 (VI 2); also, a vine-like plant: *~em agri* 2 Kgs. 4.39 (AC 8408.5).

vitium ~i, *neut.* A fault, defect, disorder: *~a et mala vitae spiritualis* AC 8364.5; *~um mentis* AM 234. **b** *~o vertere*, to reckon as a fault, hold against: *quidam spiritus volunt appellari scientiae...quibus non ~o vertitur n.598* ES Index s.v. 'intellectus' (p. 455 Tafel), referring to ES 598.

vito ~are ~avi ~atum, *tr.* To move away from, avoid: *hi ~aturi lupum inciderunt in leonem, aut sicut dicitur in proverbio, cupiens ~are Charybdin incidit in Scyllam* VR 637.

vitreus ~a ~um, *a.* Made of glass: *lamellae sicut ~ae ex auro et argento quasi micantes* AM 380.2; resembling glass, glassy: *mare ~um simile chrystallo* Rev. 4.6 (AR).

vitrum ~i, *neut.* Glass: *mole nigrum lapidem aut ~um in tenuem pulverem* AM 233.4; *influxu lucis in ~um* VR 34.4.

vitula ~ae, *f.* A female calf, heifer: *accipe tibi ~am triennem* Gen. 15.9 (AC).

vitulinus ~a ~um, *a.* Resembling young oxen, calf-like: *viginti ut satyros ~os* AM 521.3.

vitulus ~i, *m.* A young ox, calf: *cum pararent ~os in conviviis charitatis* AC 7779.5; SS 18.2; (of the golden calf worshipped by the Israelites) *fecit illud ~um fusilis* Exod. 32.4 (AC).

vituperatio ~onis, *f.* The uttering of insults, vituperation: *absque ~one sinite ut sacerdotes praedicent illa* VR 160.6; an instance of this, insult: *audivi recensitas in ordine ~ones* CI 462[a].5.

vituperium ~i, *neut.* An insult: *Dominus moderatur ne in ~a se effundant* AC 7250; *calcitrant, pugnant inter se ~is* AR 421.3.

vitupero ~are ~avi ~atum, *tr.* To attack with insults: *nisi detur iis copia ~andi verum* AC 1695.1; *~are alios pro nihilo reputavit* CI 462[a].5.

vivacitas ~atis, *f.* Liveliness: *omnis alacritas, ~as et perceptibilitas jucundi* AM 359.2.

vivarium ~i, *neut.* A place for keeping wild animals, zoo, reserve: *sicut cervi in ~is detenti ut serviant principi* VR 815.1.

vivax ~acis, *a.* Lively: *non sicut mulieres Aegyptiae Hebraeae, nam ~aces hae, antequam venit ad illas obstetrix et pepererunt* Exod. 1.19 (AC 4588.2).

vive, *adv.* In a lifelike manner: *ita ~e coram visu eorum externo ut videant non solum, sed etiam percipiant singula...* AC 1622.1; *somniavi ~e* ES 4142; ES 4354.

vivens ~ntis, *a.* (pres. pple. of **vivo**) Living, alive: *et factus homo in animam ~ntem* Gen. 2.7 (AC); *daret tibi aquam ~ntem* John 4.10 (SS 2); (masc. as sb.) *adorabant ~ntem in saecula saeculorum* Rev. 4.10 (AR).

viventer, *adv.* (compar. *~ius*) In a lifelike manner: *quod ita vive, et ~ius illa percipiant* ES 4354.

vivide, *adv.* (compar. *~ius*) In a lifelike manner, vividly: *ut...percipiant singula ~ius multo quam visus oculi capit talia* AC 1622.1.

vividus ~a ~um, *a.* (compar. *~ior*) (of light) Brilliant, vivid: *lux candidior et ~ior* ES 712.

vivificatio ~onis, *f.* The act of making lively: *~o illorum qui ab Ecclesia spirituali a Domino* AC 8018.3; *paralelismus est inter ~onem hominis et vegetationem arboris* FI 32; an instance of this: *a ludis et spectaculis ...quae in se sunt dulcedines, quia ~ones* AM 256.

vivifico ~are ~avi ~atum, *tr.* **1** To endow with life, make to live: *lux vernalis cui calor ~ans omnia telluris unitus est* AC 7056.2; *est idem Deus qui ~at omnem bestiam, qui hominem* VR 8.3. **2** (Bibl.) To keep alive: *occident me, et te ~abunt* Gen. 12.12 (AC); *timebant obstetrices Deum...et ~abant pueros* Exod. 1.17 (AC). **3** (transf.) To make lively, enliven, vivify: *fides...~ata per amorem* AC 30.2; *ille sensus est spiritus qui ~at literam* SS 4; *influxus a Deo...~at illa secundum receptionem* VR 8.1.

vivo ~vere ~xi ~ctum, *intr.* (*tr.*) **1** To be alive, live: *cum ~xit in mundo* AC 6929; *anima sua quae ~ctura post mortem* CI 86.1. **2** To spend one's life, live (in a specified manner): (w. pred.) *~xerint distincti in gentes* AC 8118.2; *quod homo non ~cturus sit homo* AM 17; (w. adv.) *qui male ~vit* VI 1; (w. prep.) *tametsi ~verent* *in odiis* AC 7272.1; *si... ~xissent secundum genium suum* AC 6963.2; (w. dat.) *~xerunt genio et solum studuerunt sibi et mundo* AC 831; *qui soli corpori ~vunt* ES 2330; (w. abl. *vita*) *unusquisque sua vita ~vere autumat* ES 720; ES 1313. **3** (w. acc.) To express in one's life, live according to: *quod pauci sint qui ~vunt religionem suam* DP 238; *inversum ~vunt ordinem* ES 169. **b** to spend (one's life): *~vunt meram vitam corporis et mundi* AC 1200. **4** To have spiritual life, be really alive: *tunc incipit* [*externus homo*] *primum ~vere* AC 39.1; *rationale in se nullum est nisi affectio...faciat illud activum utque ~vat* AC 1589.2.

vivus ~a ~um, *a.* **1** Living, alive (as opposed to dead): *ut descendant ~i in infernum* Num. 16.30 (AC 8306); *in subjectis mortuis et in subjectis ~is* AS 218; (masc. pl. as sb.) the living: *venturus est ad judicandum ~os et mortuos* Sym. Ath. (VI 3). **2** Endowed with physical life, animate: *illa* [*decoramenta*] *se moventia sicut ~a* AC 1627; *per animam in Verbo intelligitur omne ~um* AC 7021.1; *respiratio...quae non dari potest in aliquo ~o sed solum in automato* FI 19.2. **3** Lively, active, vivid: *color fit in quibusdam ~us et lucidus, in quibusdam quasi mortuus et fuscus* AC 6991; *motus ~us in homine est actio* AS 219.2. **b** *~a vox*, direct speech: *effulgurationes varias lucis tulerunt responsa, quibus adjuncta fuit vel ~a vox vel perceptio interna* AC 6640.2; *mihi dicebatur e coelo ~a voce* ES 331. **c** *argentum ~um*, mercury, quicksilver: VR 11.3. **d** *ad ~um*, in a vivid or lifelike manner: *quod mihi ostensum est ad ~um* AC 33; *quod ita sit, ad ~um mihi scire datum est* VR 65. **4** Endowed with spiritual life, really alive: *proprie anima ~a est quod vitam accipit a Domino, hoc est, regeneratum est* AC 1040.1; *quod angelus sit ~us secundum studium mentis* AM 207.7; VR 48.20. **b** (neut. as sb.) the vital principle: *ipsa vita hominis seu ipsum ejus ~um est ex amore coelesti* AC 1436. **5** (of mental concepts) Having spiritual life, life-giving, alive: *quia angelicae ideae tales sunt, etiam ~ae sunt* AC 7847.1; *quamdiu homo non vult illa* [sc. *vera*]*...non fiunt ~a* AC 8881; *fides fit ~a et salvifica* VR 74.3. **b** (of things in the spiritual world): *vocant* [*angeli*]*...sua* [*habitacula*] *~a et vera, quia a Domino* AC 1628; *quod absque bino sole, uno ~o et altero mortuo, non detur creatio* AS 163 titulus. **c** (Bibl., of water): *exibunt aquae ~ae ex Hierosolyma* Zech. 14.8 (DD 4); *Agnus...deducet eos ad ~os fontes aquarum* Rev. 7.17 (AR).

vix, *adv.* Hardly, scarcely: *vix apparent ut homines* CI 80; *vix aliquis*, hardly any: *pro Divino...cui parum et vix aliquid essent millia...tellurum* AC 6698; *vix aliquae reliquiae* VR 4.1; (so, also) *nemo vix*, hardly anyone: *neminem vix potuit laudare* ES(M) 4676.

vobiscum, *pron.* = *vobis* (see **vos**) combined with *cum* (see **cum**[1]). With you (pl.): AM 7.3.

vocabularium ~i, *neut.* The study of a collection of terms: *solum sit* [*Philosophia mundi*] *~um, nam agitur ibi de qualitatibus accidentibus, viribus, substantiis et similiter* ES 2263.

vocabulum ~i, *neut.* A word: *quid opus est nisi duobus ~is, 'omnipotentia' et 'fides'* VR 57; VR 80.2.

vocalis ~is, *f.* (sc. *litera*) A vowel: *~es tres primae* [i.e., A, E, I] AC 793; *loquela angelorum coelestium sonat multum ex ~ibus U et O* CI 241; VR 19.2.

vocatio ~onis, *f.* **1** A summoning, calling: *causa ~onis erat destruere vera* AC 6681 (w. ref. to Exod. 1.18); *annihilare ~onem, quae facta est ad omnes...ex genere humano* VR 134.3. **2** A title, name: *Verbum habent Antiquae Ecclesiae cujus ~onem partim Moschlim vocant* ES 5605.

vociferatio ~onis, *f.* A loud exclamation, shout, cry: *quondam audivi ~ones* AM 231.1.

vociferor ~ari ~atus sum, *intr.* To exclaim, cry out, shout: *sicut vir bellorum... ~abitur* Isa. 42.13 (AC 1664.10); *pueri...colludebant tumultuando, ~ando* AM 218.2; *ad haec reliqui ~abantur, Bravo* AM 521.2.

voco ~are ~avi ~atum, *tr.* **1** To ask to come, invite, summon: *num... ~abo tibi mulierem nutricem?* Exod. 2.7 (AC); *ut ~aret viros urbanitatis* AM 16.3; (w. *ad*) *beati qui ad caenam Agni ~ati sunt* Rev. 19.9 (AR); (w. *in* + acc.) *populos in montem ~abunt* Deut. 33.19 (AC 6745.2). **2** (w. pred.) To give a name to, call: *~abitur uxor, quia ex viro sumta illa* Gen. 2.23 (AC); *quod universum coelum referat hominem, qui Maximus Homo ~atus est* AC 6807; *Ego Jehovah, qui ~averim te nomine tuo* Isa. 45.3 (AC 7091.3). **b** (Bibl.) to give (a name): *et ~abat homo nomina omni bestiae* Gen. 2.20 (AC); *~abitur tibi nomen novum* Isa. 62.2 (DD 64.2). **3** To refer to as, address as, call: *hos fratres ~ant* AC 6710; *arca ~abatur arca foederis* AC 6804.6 (Deut. 31.9); *quod caetera ~ent fortunam ac casum* AC 7007; *Ecclesiae illius temporis ~atae sunt Ecclesiae repraesentativae* CI 306.

vocula ~ae, *f.* A small unit of which speech is composed, word: *nusquam aliqua ~a est quae superflua et inanis* AC 734; *quod...toties interponatur ~a 'Et'* CI 241; also, a single sound in a word: *ex Jehovae nomine est sumta ~a 'h' in Abrahamo* AC 1416.2.

vola ~ae, *f.* The hollow of the hand: *imple ~as tuas prunis ignis* Ezek. 10.2 (AC 308.2); *omnes arbores agri plaudent ~a* Isa. 55.12 (AC 368); [*serpens*] *factus in baculum in ~a illius* Exod. 4.4 (AC); *adhaesit* [*flammeum*]*...palmae seu ~ae* AC 7620; *pulsum agebant... plenius, ut impleret pulsus ~am* ES 1693. **b** *~a pedis*, the hollow in the sole of the foot: *non invenit columba quietem ~ae pedis sui* Gen. 8.9 (AC); *illotus a capite* *ad ~am pedis* DP 278ᵃ.1. **c** *~a femoris*, the hollow of the thigh: Gen. 32.25 (AC).

volatilis ~is ~e, *a.* **1** Capable of flight, flying: *~ia animalcula* ES 2475. **b** (neut. as sb.) a flying creature: *aliud [semen] cecidit super viam...et ~ia caeli comederunt* Luke 8.5 (VI 90); *connubia ~ium et animalium* AM 137.5; (sg. collectively) *et descendit ~e super corpora, et abegit illa Abram* Gen. 15.11 (AC). **2** Liable to fly away: *amor et sapientia absque usu sunt modo ~ia rationis, et quoque evolant* VR 67.1.

volatus ~us, *m.* The act of flying, flight: [*angelus*] *indutus erat chlamyde, quae ex ~u fluebat retrorsum* AM 2.1; *aves...lassae ~u* VR 67.

volito ~are ~avi, *intr.* To fly about, flit: *avis ~et super terra* Gen. 1.20 (AC); *insecta ~antia in aëre* AC 7441.2; *num animae Adami et Evae...adhuc ~ent in universo* AM 182.5.

volo[1] ~are ~avi, *intr.* **1** To move through the air, fly: *apparet sicut ignis ~ans* AC 7812; *angelus sub caelo orientali ~ans* AM 2.1. **2** To move rapidly, 'fly': *quod ~avit [foemina] ad eum et osculata eum* ES 4494.

volo[2] velle ~ui, *intr.* (*tr.*) (2nd, 3rd pers. pres. ind. sg. *vis, vult*, 2nd pl. *vultis*; pres. subj. *velim, velis*, etc.; impf. subj. *vellem, velles*, etc.) **1** To wish, desire, want: **a** (w. inf.): *quod...necare ~uerint infantes pueros* AC 6639.1; *velim ipsas experientias adducere* AC 6806; *si vultis videre* AM 380.3. **b** (w. *ut* + subj.): *~unt ut...ab omnibus serviantur* AC 8313.4; *~uerunt omnes ut...fieret conclusum* VR 48.15. **c** (absol.): *agunt hominem ad cogitandum, ~endum* AC 7935; *velle est mentis intimioris* ES 1568. **2** (w. *in* + acc.) To wish to go (to): *qui in coelum ~unt* ES 2519. **3** (w. acc.) To will, wish for: *liberum cogitandi ~endique malum* AC 6657.1; *quod alter cum altero unum velit* VR 99; *instruebar...quid vellet cohors ista* ES 2123. **4** (in a weakened sense) To be willing, consent: (w. inf.) *vis mecum ire in nostrum paradisum?* AR 875.4; *ille sensus potest...convincere etiam hominem naturalem, si vult convinci* 554; (w. *ut*) *vis ut propius adveniamus?* AM 42.2. (n.b. *Non volo* is sometimes used in place of **nolo**: *non ~unt recedere* AR 710; *non ~ebant ut converterem me* ES 587.)

volubilis ~is ~e, *a.* **1** Moving in coils, rolling: *gyrus non est simplex gyrus, sed ~is circumcirca* ES 1036. **2** (of speech) Fluent, flowing: *quod...terminetur [loquela]...in molle quasi murmur quod intus ~e est* AC 8733; ES 1113.

volubilitas ~atis, *f.* Fluency (of speech): *erat ~as ejus* [sc. *sermonis*] *sicut aurae tenuis* AC 8025.

volubiliter, *adv.* In a flowing manner, fluently: *potuit ...loqui ~er, fluvii instar* AC 5388.

volucris ~is, *f.* **1** A flying creature, bird: *hic nominantur avis, et ~is, et alatum* AC 776.1; *sancta...a bestiis terrae, et a ~ibus caeli violarentur* SS 33. **2** (as fem. adj.) Bird-like, flighty: *ex...regione, in qua ~es ideae mentium illorum volant* AM 79.9.

volumatim, *adv.* (= **voluminatim**) In a rolling fashion: *loquebantur ~im* AC 6923; *ii ~im ita exsurgebant* ES 3531; ES 4304.

volumen ~inis, *neut.* **1** An ancient book in the form of a roll, scroll: *cum vidit [Sacharias] ~en volans et epham* DD 52 (Zech. 5.1); *~en libri* Ezek. 2.9 (CI 258). **2** A modern book, volume: *quod de illis ~ina possint conscribi* AC 7131; *exsurgeret hoc opusculum in grande ~en* AM 209. **3** Anything made by rolling, a roll, fold: *intra piam meningem inter ~ina* ES 1239; *apparebat cohors illa tunc sicut ~en* AC 7077; *~en longum rotundum...conformatum a baculis longis* ES 2821. **4** A rolling movement like a breaking wave: *loquela... undulans instar ~inis* AC 1763.1; *ii [spiritus] agunt quasi ~en maris* ES 2678. **5** A mass, volume: *dum pusillum nigri in aquam mittitur, unde aquae ~en obscuratur* AC 1008.3; *simile sibi est in parvo ~ine, ut in magno* VR 103.3; also, a large volume: *congeries idearum in ~ine* VR 154.5.

voluminatim, *adv.* see also **volumatim**. In a rolling fashion: *audivi spiritus... ~im loquentes* ES 3233; *quos salutabant ~im, per undulationis species sicut fluctus in medio subsidendo et [se] elevando* ES 3284.

voluntarie, *adv.* Of one's own accord, voluntarily: *sed usque ~e separantur* ES 294.

voluntario, *adv.* At will: *vidi infra navem istam a gubernatore ~o circumagi* ES 2240.

voluntarius ~a ~um, *a.* **1** Of or controlled by the will, voluntary: *respirationem ~am* AC 3351; *solum quoad partem intellectualem, non autem quoad partem ~am* AC 6854.1; *de ~is bonis* AC 734; *~um malum* AC 7032.2; *uxor nata est ~a* AM 195. **2** (neut. as sb.) The voluntary faculty of a person, will: *quando... ~um hominis prorsus corruptum factum est* AC 1023.2; *externum et internum...se habent sicut ~um et ejus intellectuale apud hominem* CI 32. **b** (Bibl.) A free-will offering: *in ~o sacrificabo Tibi* Ps. 54.6 (AC 1947.4).

voluntas ~atis, *f.* **1** The voluntary faculty of a person, will: *intellectus agnoscit et ~as facit* AC 6717.2; *duo regna, unum est ~atis et alterum est intellectus* CI 95. **2** An act of the will, willing: *ut sit praesentia Domini...in omni ~ate et in omni cogitatione* AC 1038.8; *haec vocantur bona fidei, nam sunt ~ates* AC 8362; (w. gen.) *non...per ~atem boni, sed per intellectum veri* AC 640; AC 9799. **3** The wishes of a person, his will: *fiat ~as Tua* Matt. 6.10 (AR 839.11); *quisquis...*

fecerit ~atem Patris Mei Matt. 12.50 (AC 6756.5); *non... ex ~ate carnis, neque ex ~ate viri, sed ex Deo nati sunt* John 1.13 (DD 18); (pl.) *ut non facias ~ates tuas in die sanctitatis Meae* Isa. 58.13 (AC 8495.3).

volupe ~is, *neut. adj.* (originally an adv., but used adjectivally) Agreeable, pleasing: *quod homo amat, ac jucundum et ~e sentit* CI 500; *ex suo proprio amore, et ejus jucundo et ~i* CI 508.7; *conferre posset omnia beata, fausta, jucunda, et ~ia* AM 180.

voluptarius ~a ~um, *a.* Of or concerned with sensual pleasure: *Antiquissimi sensualia hominis et ~a ejus compararunt...reptilibus et repentibus* AC 746.

voluptas ~atis, *f.* The lower kind of pleasure, especially of a sensual nature: *duplicis generis ~ates sunt, nempe voluntariorum et intellectualium* AC 994.2; *ut ditescat...solum divitiarum causa, vel ~atis causa, vel eminentiae causa* AC 6935; *plures ~ates quae sunt sensualium corporis* CI 304.2.

voluptuosus ~a ~um, *a.* Devoted to sensual pleasure; (masc. as sb.) a voluptuary: ES 4547; ES 4629.7.

volutio ~onis, *f.* The act of rolling: *per... ~onem ibi in pulvere* AC 7418.3; *percipere...mihi dabatur ~onem quandam mollem, super caput* ES 255; (w. gen.) *per formationes vultus et ~ones labiorum* AC 7745.

voluto ~are ~avi, *tr.* (refl.) To lie down and turn over, roll: *in cinere ~ant* [*volvent* Autograph] *se* Ezek. 27.30 (AC 7418.3); *porci ~antes se in stercoribus* AM 500.1. (n.b. In AC 5977.2 *volitant* should be read for *volutant*; cf. AC 5977.2 Autograph where *volitarent* is used.)

volvo ~vere ~vi ~utum, *tr.* **1** To make to turn over, roll: *dum ~vis talos* DP 212.1; (refl.) to proceed with a rolling movement: *respiratio...se ~vens sursum per pectus* AC 7362; cf. [*voces*] *per accentum ~vunt se in sequentem* AC 1648. **2** To turn over in the mind, reflect on, consider: *in via continue ~vebant et intendebant mala* AC 814.2; *haec...cum ephebus cogitationibus suis ~vit* AM 111; (of the heart) *~vit cor meum verbum bonum* Ps. 45.1 (AC 1288.3).

volvulus ~i, *m.* A small cylindrical package, roll: *tanquam bombyx in ~o serico* [sc. a cocoon] VR 80.3; *quidam...in collariis ex ~is* [i.e., rolled collars] VR 137.1.

vomitalis ~is ~e, *a.* Of vomited matter: *nidor ~is* AC 1514.

vomitio ~onis, *f.* Vomiting: *effectus erat ~o* ES 1278.

vomitus ~us, *m.* **1** The act of vomiting: *post ~um* ES 1045. **2** Vomited matter, vomit: *seducitur ebrius in ~u suo* Isa. 19.14 (AE 235.4); AM 482.

vomo ~ere, *tr.* To vomit: *bibite et inebriamini et ~ite et cadite* Jer. 25.27 (AR 721).

vorago ~inis, *f.* **1** A deep opening, chasm: *tales hiatus et ~ines* UJ(P) 141; AC 9582; CI 585. **2** A quagmire: *in ~ines quae apparent sicut paludes immerguntur* CI 354; AM 339.3.

vorax ~acis, *m.* **1** A glutton: *comparari possunt cum ~acibus, qui cibaria...ingerunt in buccam* VR 527.3. **2** A chasm: *apertus est ~ax inferni* ES 4582.

voro ~are, *tr.* To devour: *cupiditas insectandi et ~andi aves* VR 334.4.

vortex ~icis, *m.* A whirlpool, vortex: *natura... convolvit se in ~ices* VR 79.2; *erat forma illa activa sicut ~ex* ES 4686.

vorticalis ~is ~e, *a.* Of or resembling a vortex: *fluxio ~is* ES 402.

vorticillaris ~is ~e, *a.* Of or resembling a vortex: *ingyrationes et egyrationes ~es* DP 319.2.

vos vestrum, *m.* and *f. pl.* (dat. and abl. *vobis*) You (of more than one person): *amen dico vobis* Matt. 5.18 (AC 6752.2); *vos prorsus nihil scitis* AM 208.2; (combined with **cum**[1]) *vobiscum*: AM 7.3.

votivus ~a ~um, *a.* **1** Offered as a prayer: *susurrabant laudem ~am ad Dominum* AM 16.1. **2** (neut. as sb.) An earnest wish, prayer: *'Vade in pace' quod significet assensum et ~um* AC 7018; *post ~um pacis* AM 261.3.

votum ~i, *neut.* **1** A vow: *ex ~is* AC 6905; *redde ~a tua* Nahum 1.15 (AC 7093.5). **2** An earnest wish, desire: *quando illis succedit ex ~o* CI 290; AM 10.1.

voveo ~vere ~vi ~tum, *tr.* To promise upon oath, vow: *~vendo perpetuum caelibatum* AM 155; (w. *quod*) *~vit quod mundus talia agnoscere...velint* ES 676; (absol.) *~vit Forti Jacobi* Ps. 132.2 (DD 39).

vox vocis, *f.* **1** The distinctive sound made by the vocal organs, voice: [*os*] *est organum vocis* AC 6985; *oves vocem illius audiunt* John 10.3 (AC 9310.3). **b** the collective voice of a group of people as expressing their opinion or feelings: *respondit...populus voce una* Exod. 24.3 (AC); *audivit Joschua vocem populi in vociferatione ejus* Exod. 32.17 (AC). **2** The distinctive sound made by other things, esp. musical instruments: *vox buccinae* Exod. 19.19 (AC); *vox alarum illarum* [sc. *locustarum*] *sicut vox curruum equorum multorum* Rev. 9.9 (AR); *cum instrumentis soni vocis altae et vocis humilis* AM 17.1. **3** An expression in language, word: *sonis articulatis seu vocibus* AC 607.2; *nec distinguit* [*lingua Hebraea*] *inter voces* AC 618; *quod in Hebraea lingua veritas et fides una vox sunt* FI 6.

vulgaris ~is ~e, *a.* Of the common sort, ordinary: *non aliam ideam de Ipso quam sicut de ~i homine fovent* CI 321; *Verbum...apparet sicut scriptum ~e* 551; *~is idea* VR 33.

vulgo ~are ~avi ~atum, *tr*. To make public, publish: *quod talia ~are vellem in nostra tellure* AC 8385; *chartae...typis ~atae* CI 258; *cupiditas ~andi secreta domus* AM 252.

vulgus ~i, *neut.* (acc. sg. *~us*, dat. and abl. sg. *~o*) The common people, the public: *sicut ~us opinatur* AC 1850.1; *~us ineruditum* CI 464.5; *in ~o notum est* AM 171.1.

vulnero ~are ~avi ~atum, *tr*. To wound: *quod percuteretur et ~aretur* DD 15.7 (1 Kgs. 20.37); (masc. of pf. pple. as sb.) *de Samarita, qui misericordiam fecit ~ato a latronibus* VR 410.3.

vulnus ~eris, *neut.* A wound: *Samarita postquam obligavit ~era* AC 6708; *sanies in ~ere solum extrinsecus sanato* AM 149.

vulpinus ~a ~um, *a*. Of or typical of a fox: *pellis ~a* ES 4151; *si in hoc est sicut...vulpis, est omne ejus opus interius... ~um* VR 373.1.

vulpis ~is, *f.* A fox: *~es foveas habent, et volucres nidos* Matt. 8.20 (DD 27); as a type of cunning: *fiunt... ~es quoad astutiam* VR 13.4; *~is est ~is in omni suo* VR 373.1.

vulsi: pf. of **vello**.

vulsus ~a ~um: pf. pple. of **vello**.

vultur ~uris, *m*. A vulture: *sicut sentiret ~urem in sinu pectoris sui* VR 123.4.

vultus ~us, *m*. The expression of the face, countenance, look: *nusquam potuerunt alium ~um praeferre quam secundum illa quae cogitabant* AC 7361.2; *discunt inducere faciebus ~us, per quos affectiones... abscondunt* AM 192; *ad hoc...expandimus ~us facierum nostrarum* VR 159.4.

vulva ~ae, *f.* The womb: *lati a ~a* Isa. 46.3 (AC 4918.2); *aperta ~a* ES(M) 4575.

vunar A misreading of Swedish *winnar* 'gains' (A W Acton): ES 395 (Tafel).

W

Wolffianus ~a ~um, *a.* Of or postulated by Christian Wolff: VR 90.2.

X

xenodochium ~i, *neut.* (Gk.) A hostel for travellers, hospice: *conferre spartas ~is* DP 83.4.

xiphoides ~is, *a.* (Gk.) (acc. fem. sg. *~en*) Sword-shaped, xiphoid: *cartilaginem scutiformem seu ~en* AC 9236; TE 111.

xylinum ~i, *neut.* (Gk.) Fine linen or cotton, lawn: *facies tegumentum...ex hyacinthino et purpura, et coccineo dibapho, et ~o intertexto* Exod. 26.36 (AC 2576.6); cf. AC 114.

Y

Y, *indecl.* The Gk. letter pronounced like French *u* or German *ü*: *quod [angeli tertii caeli]...non possent enuntiare vocales* i *et* e, *sed pro illis* y *et* eu VR 278; ES 5622.

Z

zea ~ae, *f.* (Gk.) A hardy kind of wheat, spelt: (sg.) *ex significatione '~ae' vel speltae* AC 7605; 7502.1; (pl.) *quod tritica, hordea, fabae, lentes, milium, ~ae, sint talia quae significent panem, sed cum differentia in specie* AC 3332.3; VR 130.1.

Zebaoth, *indecl.* (Hebr.) A title of Jehovah taken from a Hebr. word for armies or legions and usually translated 'of Hosts': *Redemptor noster Jehovah ~th* Isa. 47.4 (AC 7091.4); *Jehovah ~th, hoc est, Jehovah Exercituum* VR 116.3.

zelo ~are ~avi, *intr.* To be jealous: *~avit Rachel in sororem suam* Gen. 30.1 (AC); *~amus pro uxoribus nostris* AM 78.6.

zelosus ~a ~um, *a.* Jealous: *dantur... ~i, qui continue cogitant de uxoribus quod sint infidae* AM 374.

zelotes ~is, *m.* (Gk.) (acc. sg. *~em* and *~en*, nom. pl. *~es*) **1** A person full of zeal, zealot: *audies illum plus rationalem ~en, quam quempiam alium* AM 499. **2** (as a title of Jehovah) Jealous: *inde etiam est quod [Jehovah] nuncupetur ~es* AM 366.

zelotypia ~ae, *f.* (Gk.) The desire to protect that which is loved, jealousy: *Lex...de ~a* DD 9 (Num. 5.29); *ex ~a contra violatores* AM 106; *zelus amoris conjugialis... novo nomine appellatur ~a* AM 367.

zelotypicus ~a ~um, *a.* (Gk.) Of jealousy: *ignis ~us* AM 370.

zelotypus ~a ~um, *a.* (Gk.) Jealous: *quod qui tenere amat conjugem etiam ~us sit* AM 371.

zelus ~i, *m.* (Gk.) **1** Excited enthusiasm, zeal: *aliquem vera Ecclesiae profitentem non ex officio sed ex ~o* AC 6907.2; *ex quadam indignatione ~i pro veritate* VR 35.6; *~us...in se spectatus est excandescentia naturalis hominis* VR 146. **2** (Bibl.) Jealous anger: *in igne ~i Mei comedetur tota terra* Zeph. 3.8 (AC 6997.4); *texit Se sicut pallio ~o* Isa. 59.17 (DD 14.3).

zenith, *indecl.* (app. Arabic) The point in the sky directly overhead, zenith: *sol...stat jugiter in medio inter ~th et horizontem* AM 137.5; *in ~th seu prorsus super caput* ES 461; *sublatus supra caput in linea ~th* ES 3089.

Zidonius: see **Sidonius**.

ziim, *indecl. pl.* App. variant spelling of **tziim**: Isa. 13.21 (AC 1326.3); Ps. 74.14 (AC 7293.3).

zizania ~ae, *f.* = **zizanium**: *~ae perdunt omne bonum semen* AC 408; AC 731; DP 292.1.

zizanium ~i, *neut.* (Gk.) A weed found in wheat fields, tare: *Dominus dicit quod ~a in fasciculos colligenda sint* VR 38.3. (Matt. 13.30); Matt. 13.38 (AE 63.9).

zodiacus ~i, *m.* (Gk.) The zodiac: *quod illi* [sc. *planetae*]*...progrediantur via ~i* TE 3; VR 29.1.

zona ~ae, *f.* (Gk.) **1** A belt, girdle: *praecinctum ad mamillas ~a aurea* Rev. 1.13 (AR); AM 15. **2** A maidenhead, hymen: *postquam ~a adempta est ac virginitas libata* AM 503. **3** An area enjoying the same climatic conditions, zone: *qui in ~is illorum calidis vivunt nudi vadunt* AC 8375; ES 4383.

Zwinglianus ~a ~um, *a.* Of the Swiss reformer Ulrich Zwingli (1484-1531), Zwinglian; (masc. as sb.) a follower of Zwingli, Zwinglian: VR 378.2.

Proper Nouns

A

Abaddon, *m.* (Hebr.) (generally indeclinable, but twice nom. pl. ~*nes* SE 93, VR 182.3). Abaddon, the Destroyer: Rev. 9.11 (AR).

Abdeel, *indecl.* also **Adbeel**, *indecl.* Adbeel, son of Ishmael: Gen. 25.13 (AC).

Abdon ~onis, *m.* Abdon, a judge of Israel: Judg. 12.14 (AC 2781.6).

Abel: see **Habel**.

Abel Mizraim: see **Avel Misraim**.

Abiasaph, *indecl.* Abiasaph, third son of Korah and great-great-grandson of Levi: Exod. 6.24 (AC).

Abida: see **Abidah**.

Abidah, *indecl.* also **Abida**, *indecl.* Abida, fourth son of Midian and grandson of Abraham: Gen. 25.4 (AC).

Abiel, *indecl.* One of Saul's ancestors: 1 Sam. 9.1 (AC 7836.3).

Abihu, *indecl.* Abihu, a son of Aaron killed for offering strange fire: Exod. 28.1 (AC).

Abimael, *indecl.* Abimael, son of Joktan and descendant of Shem: Gen. 10.28 (AC).

Abimelech[1], *indecl.* also **Abimelechus** ~i, *m.* The king of Gerar: Gen. 20.2 (AC).

Abimelech[2] ~chi, *m.* The king of the Philistines: Gen. 26.1 (AC).

Abimelechus: see **Abimelech**[1].

Abischai ~i, *m.* also **Abishai** ~i, *m.* Abishai, nephew of David and brother of Joab: 1 Sam. 26.9 (AC 9954.18).

Abishai: see **Abischai**.

Abisina: see **Abyssinia**.

Abraham ~mi, *m.* Abraham, the new name of Abram: Gen. 17.5 (AC).

Abram ~mi, *m.* Abram, son of Terah: Gen. 11.26 (AC).

Absalom: see **Abschalom**.

Abschalom ~omis, *m.* also **Absalom** ~omis, *m.*, and **Abshalom** ~omi, *m.* Absalom, third son of David: 2 Sam. 13.23-24 (AC 4110).

Abshalom: see **Abschalom**.

Abysina: see **Abyssinia**.

Abyssina: see **Abyssinia**.

Abyssinia ~ae, *f.* also **Abisina** ~ae, *f.* (ES 5947 Autograph, UJ(P) 122 Rogers), **Abysina** ~ae, *f.* (SS(P) 46 (= 18.2) Rogers), and **Abyssina** ~ae, *f.* (SS 108 1st edn.). Abyssinia, Ethiopia: ES 5947.

Acatiani ~orum, *m. pl.* The name of a body of heretics, Acatians: VR 378.2.

Accad: see **Akkad**.

Achabus ~bi, *m.* also **Ahab** ~bi, *m.*, and **Aḥabus** ~bi, *m.* Ahab, seventh king of Israel and husband of Jezebel: 1 Kgs. 21.27 (AC 4779.6).

Achan ~anis, *m.* Achan, a man of the tribe of Judah who hid part of the spoils of Jericho: AC 5135.6.

Achbor, *indecl.* Achbor, father of the seventh king of the Edomites: Gen. 36.39 (AC).

Acheron ~ntis, *m.* (Gk.) Acheron, one of the rivers of hell in Greek mythology: CO 38.

Achia ~ae, *m.* also **Achiah** ~ae, *m.*, **Achija** ~ae, *m.*, **Aḥija** ~ae, *m.*, and **Aḥijah** ~ae, *m.* Ahijah, the prophet: AC 4763.

Achiah: see **Achia**.

Achija: see **Achia**.

Achimelech, *indecl.* also **Aḥimelech**, *indecl.* Ahimelech, a Hittite officer of David: 1 Sam. 26.6 (AC 2913).

Achisamachus ~i, *m.* Ahisamach, father of Aholiab: Exod. 31.6 (AC).

Achischus ~i, *m.* also **Achisus** ~i, *m.* Achish, king of Gath in the time of David: 1 Sam. 27.12 (AC 7161.2).

Achisus: see **Achischus**.

Achitophel, *indecl.* Ahithophel, David's counsellor who joined Absalom: 2 Sam. 16.21 (AC 7161.2).

Achor ~oris, *m.* Achor, the valley in which Achan was destroyed: Isa. 65.10 (AC 10609.3).

Achusath ~athi, *m.* also **Aḥuzzath** ~ati, *m.* Ahuzzath, a friend of Ahimelech: Gen. 26.26 (AC).

Adah[1], *indecl.* Adah, a wife of Lamech: Gen. 4.19 (AC).

Adah[2] ~ae, *f.* Adah, a wife of Esau: AC 4643.

Adam: see **Adamus**.

Adamantini ~orum, *m. pl.* The followers of Origen (from his other name Adamantius), Adamantines: VR 378.2.

Adamus ~i, *m.* also **Adam**, *indecl.* and **Adam** ~ae, *m.* (SE 3). Adam, the first man: SS 97.2; (form *Adam*) AC 478; VR 48.13.

Adbeel: see **Abdeel**.

Adma ~ae, *f.* Admah, a town destroyed along with Sodom and Gomorrah: Gen. 14.2 (AC).

Adolphus: see **Gustavus Adolphus**.

Adonajus ~i, *m.* (Hebr.) Latinized form of the Hebr.ew word *Adonai*, a divine epithet: CO 51.2.

Adonia, *indecl.* also **Adonijah**, *indecl.* Adonijah, fourth son of David: AC 2252.4.

Adonijah: see **Adonia**.

Adulla, *indecl.* also **Adullam**, *indecl.* Adullam, a royal city near Jerusalem: AC 4816.

Adullam: see **Adulla**.

Adullamita ~ae, *m.* An inhabitant of Adullam, Adullamite: Gen. 38.1 (AC).

Aegyptus ~i, *f.* (Gk.) Egypt: CI 327.

Aeneas ~ae, *m.* Aeneas, the hero of Vergil's *Aeneid*: ES(M) 4815.

Aeolus ~i, *m.* (Gk.) The Greek god of the winds: VR 15.2.

Aethiopia ~ae, *f.* A land to the south of Egypt, Ethiopia: *terra Cush seu Aethiopia abundat quoque auro* AC 117.

Aethiops ~opis, *m.* An Ethiopian, negro: AC 876.

Aetna ~ae, *f.* A volcano in Sicily, Mount Etna: CO 38.

Africa ~ae, *f.* The continent of Africa: SS 117.

Africus ~i, *m.* An African: AM 114.

Agagus ~i, *m.* Agag, king of the Amalekites: *ad ~um regem Amalekitarum* 1 Sam. 15.22 (AC 8593.4).

Ahab: see **Achabus**.

Aḥabus: see **Achabus**.

Aharon ~onis, *m.* Aaron: DD 14.

Aḥija: see **Achia**.

Aḥijah: see **Achia**.

Aḥimelech: see **Achimelech**.

Aholiab: see **Aholiabus**.

Aholiabus ~bi, *m.* also **Aholiab** ~bi, *m.* Aholiab, a Danite who helped prepare the tabernacle: Exod. 31.6 (AC).

Aḥuzzath: see **Achusath**.

Ai, *indecl.* also **Aia** ~ae, *m.*, **Aja** ~ae, *m.* Ai, a city near Bethel: Gen. 12.8 (AC).

Aia: see **Ai**.

Aiah: see **Ajah**.

Aiath: see **Ajath**.

Aja: see **Ai**.

Ajah, *indecl.* also **Aiah**, *indecl.* Aiah, son of Zibeon: Gen. 36.24 (AC).

Ajalon ~onis, *m.* Aijalon, a valley in Dan: Josh. 10.12 (SS 103).

Ajath, *indecl.* also **Aiath**, *indecl.* Aiath, feminine form of Ai but not necessarily the same place: Isa. 10.28 (AC 1888.2).

Akan, *indecl.* Akan, a son of Ezer and grandson of Seir: Gen. 36.27 (AC).

Akkad, *indecl.* also **Accad**, *indecl.* Accad, a city in the land of Shinar near Babel: Gen. 10.10 (AC).

Alcimus ~i, *m.* Alcimus, a high priest of Israel: ES 6082.

Alemannia: see **Allemannia**.

Alexander ~dri, *m.* **1** Alexander the Great: VR 74.2. **2** Alexander, Bishop of Alexandria: VR 632. **3** *~der Jannaeus*, Alexander Jannaeus, king of Judea and high priest of Jerusalem 103-76 BC: ES 6082.

Algerianus ~i, *m.* An inhabitant of Algeria, Algerian: ES 5667[a].

Algiriensis ~is, *m.* An Algerian: VR 829.

Allemannia ~ae, *f.* also **Alemannia** ~ae, *f.* Germany: AR 484.1.

Allon Bacuth, *indecl.* Allon Bacuth, the place near Bethel where Deborah was buried: *Allon Bacuth in lingua originali significat quercum fletus* AC 4565.

Almodad, *indecl.* Almodad, a son of Joktan and descendant of Shem: Gen. 10.26 (AC).

Alogiani ~orum, *m. pl.* A sect of second-century heretics, Alogians: VR 378.2.

Alva, *indecl.* also **Alvah**, *indecl.* Alvah, a descendant of Esau: Gen. 36.40 (AC).

Alvah: see **Alva**.

Alvan, *indecl.* Alvan, a son of Shobal and descendant of Seir: Gen. 36.23 (AC).

Amaleck: see **Amalekus**.

Amalek: see **Amalekus**.

Amalekita ~ae, *m.* An Amalekite, an arch-enemy of the children of Israel: Gen. 14.7 (AC).

Amalekus ~i, *m.* also **Amaleck**, *indecl.*, and **Amalek**, *indecl.* Amalek, often used collectively to refer to the Amalekites: Exod. 17.9 (AC).

Amaziah, *indecl.* and ~ae, *m.* Amaziah, an idolatrous priest in Bethel: Amos 7.12 (AC 1453.3).

America ~ae, *f.* The Americas, America: ES 3867; DP 330.7.

Aminadabus ~i, *m.* also **Amminadabus** ~i, *m.* Amminadab, Aaron's father-in-law: AC 7230.

Ammi: see **Benammi**.

Amminadabus: see **Aminadabus**.

Ammon ~onis, *m.* Ammon, father of the Ammonites: Gen. 19.38 (AC).

Ammonita ~ae, *m.* An inhabitant of Ammon, Ammonite: Deut. 23.3 (AC 576.2).

Amon ~onis, *m.* Amon, a sun god of ancient Thebes: Jer. 46.25 (AC 6015.3).

Amora: see **Gomorrha**.

Amorra: see **Gomorrha**.

Amorrha: see **Gomorrha**.

Amos: see **Amosus**.

Amosus ~i, *m.* also **Amos** ~si, *m.* The prophet Amos: DD 4.

Amram, *indecl.* also **Amramus** ~i, *m.* Amram, father of Aaron, Moses, and Miriam: Exod. 6.18 (AC).

Amramus: see **Amram**.

Amraphel ~lis, *m.* Amraphel, king of Shinar in Abraham's time: Gen. 14.1 (AC).

Amstelodamum ~i, *neut.* Amsterdam: VR 20.

Ana ~ae, *f.* Anah, daughter of Zibeon and mother-in-law of Esau: Gen. 36.2 (AC).

Anabaptismus ~i, *m.* The heresy of the Anabaptists: DP 259.1.

Anabaptistae ~tarum, *m. pl.* An heretical sect, the Anabaptists: VR 378.2.

Anah ~ae, *m.* **1** Anah, son of Seir: Gen. 36.20 (AC). **2** Anah, son of Zibeon and grandson of Seir: Gen. 36.24 (AC).

Anakus ~i, *m.* also **Enakus** ~i, *m.* **1** (sg.) Anak, son of Arba and ancestor of the Anakim: Num. 13.33 (AC 567). **2** (pl.) The Anakim, giants: AC 2909.

Anamim, *indecl.* Anamim, a Mizraite people, probably of northern Egypt: Gen. 10.13 (AC).

Anathoth: see **Anatoth**.

Anathus ~i, *m.* Anath, the father of Shamgar: AC 8753.3.

Anatoth, *indecl.* also **Anathoth**, *indecl.* Anathoth, a Levitical city in Benjamin: Jer. 32.9 (AC 755).

Andreas ~ae, *m.* Andrew: AE 821.3.

Aner ~eri, *m.* Aner, brother of Mamre: Gen. 14.13 (AC).

Anglia ~ae, *f.* England: VI 4.

Anglus ~i, *m.* An inhabitant of England, Englishman: AM 28.

Antetrinitarii ~orum, *m. pl.* also **Antitrinitarii** ~orum, *m. pl.* A sect of heretics, Antitrinitarians: VR 378.2.

Antigonus ~i, *m.* Antigonus the Hasmonean, king of Judea 40-37 BC: ES 6082.

Antiochus ~i, *m.* Antiochus Epiphanes, a king of Syria from 175-163 BC: ES 6082.

Antipas ~atis, *m.* Antipas, a martyr of Pergamos: Rev. 2.13 (AR).

Antitrinitarii: see **Antetrinitarii**.

Antonius ~i, *m.* Anthony of Padua: *~us Paduae* ES 4402; ES(M) 4565.

Aphiach, *indecl.* Aphiah, one of Saul's ancestors: 1 Sam. 9.1 (AC 7836.3).

Aphra ~ae, *f.* Aphrah, a city of Benjamin near Philistia: Mic. 1.10 (AC 7418.3).

Apollo ~inis, *m.* The Greek god Apollo: VR 17.2; (pl. as a type) SE 93.

Ar, *indecl.* and Arem (Deut. 2.18 (AC 2468)). Ar, a dwelling on the border of Moab: Num. 21.15 (AC 2897).

Arabia ~ae, *f.* The Arabian peninsula, Arabia: *desertum ~ae* VR 38.2.

Arabs ~bis, *m.* An inhabitant of Arabia, Arab: AM 326.4.

Arafna ~ae, *m.* also **Arnan** ~anis, *m.* Araunah, a Jebusite from whom David bought an altar site: 2 Sam. 24.24 (AC 2252.4).

Aram, *indecl.* and ~mi, *m.* also **Arom**, *indecl.* (AR 707). **1** Aram, son of Shem: Gen. 10.22 (AC). **2** Syria: AC 1232.

Aram Naharaim, *indecl.* Mesopotamia, the area between the Tigris and Euphrates rivers: Gen. 24.10 (AC).

Aran, *indecl.* Aran, descendant of Seir: Gen. 36.28 (AC).

Ararat: see **Ararath**.

Ararath, *indecl.* also **Ararat**, *indecl.* Ararat, a district of Armenia where Noah's ark landed: Gen. 8.4 (AC).

Archita: see **Arkita**.

Ard: see **Arde**.

Arde, *indecl.* also **Ard**, *indecl.* Ard, a son of Benjamin: Gen. 46.21 (AC).

Areli, *indecl.* Areli, a son of Gad: Gen. 46.16 (AC).

Argus ~i, *m.* (in Gk. mythology) Argus, a fabulous creature possessing a hundred eyes: *credit se...plus ocularem quam ~us* VR 165.3.

Ariani ~orum, *m. pl.* also **Arriani** ~orum, *m. pl.* The followers of the heretic Arius, Arians: VR 94.

Arianismus ~i, *m.* The Arian heresy: VR 94.

Ariochus: see **Arjochus**.

Arisippus ~i, *m.* (Gk.) also **Aristippus** ~i, *m.* Aristippus, ancient Greek philosopher who held that the pursuit of pleasure tempered by prudence was the best way to live happily: VR 692.1.

Aristippus: see **Arisippus**.

Aristobolus ~i, *m.* also **Aristobulus** ~i, *m.* Aristobulus, king and high priest of Judea 104-103 BC: ES 6082; also, Aristobulus II, king and high priest of Judea 66-63 BC: ES 6082.

Aristobulus: see **Aristobolus**.

Aristoteles ~is, *m.* Aristotle, ancient Greek philosopher: VR 273.

Arius ~i, *m.* Arius, the 4th cent. heretic who denied the divinity of Christ: VR 159.6.

Arjochus ~i, *m.* also **Ariochus** ~i, *m.* Arioch, king of Ellasar in Assyria: Gen. 14.1 (AC).

Arkita ~ae, *m.* also **Archita** ~ae, *m.* An Archite, the patronymic of David's friend Hushai: 2 Sam. 15.32 (AC 4763.5).

Arkus ~i, *m.* A member of a Syrian tribe descended from Canaan, Arkite: Gen. 10.17 (AC).

Armageddon, *indecl.* Armageddon: Rev. 16.16 (AR).

Armageddoni ~orum, *m. pl.* The inhabitants of a place in the Spiritual World called Armageddon (cf. Rev. 16.16): VR 113.9.

Arnan: see **Arafna**.

Arnon ~onis, *m.* Arnon, a river and valley that form the southern boundary of Canaan: Num. 21.14 (AC 2897).

Arodi, *indecl.* Arodi, a son of Gad: Gen. 46.16 (AC).

Arom: see **Aram**.

Arpachsad: see **Arphachschad**.

Arpachschad: see **Arphachschad**.

Arpachshad: see **Arphachschad**.

Arphachsad: see **Arphachschad**.

Arphachschad, *indecl.* also **Arpachsad**, *indecl.*, **Arpachschad**, *indecl.*, **Arpachshad**, *indecl.*, **Arphachsad**, *indecl.*, and **Arphakschad**, *indecl.* Arphaxad, a son of Shem: AC 1230.

Arphakschad: see **Arphachschad**.

Arriani: see **Ariani**.

Arvad ~di, *m.* and *indecl.* **1** An island near Sidon: Ezek. 27.8 (AR 406). **2** A member of a tribe descended from Canaan, Arvadite: Gen. 10.18 (AC).

Asariah, *indecl.* also **Azariah**, *indecl.* Azariah, a man who was carried to Babylon with Daniel: Dan. 1.19 (AC 5223.4).

Aschbel, *indecl.* also **Ashbel**, *indecl.* Ashbel, a son of Benjamin: Gen. 46.21 (AC).

Aschdodae ~darum, *f. pl.* The inhabitants of Ashdod: DP 326.11.

Aschdodus ~i, *m.* also **Asdodus** ~i, *m.* Ashdod, a chief city of the Philistines: VR 203.

Ascher ~eris, *m.* also **Asher** ~eris, *m.* Asher, eighth son of Jacob: Gen. 30.13 (AC).

Aschkenas, *indecl.* also **Aschkenaz**, *indecl.*, **Ashkenaz**, *indecl.*, and **Askenas**, *indecl.* Ashkenaz, grandson of Japheth: AC 1154.

Aschkenaz: see **Aschkenas**.

Aschur ~uris, *m.* also **Asshur** ~uris, *m.* Assyria: *erit semita ex Aegypto in ~urem* Isa. 19.23 (DD 4); an Assyrian: Mic. 5.5 (AC 1186.5).

Aschurim, *indecl.* also **Asshurim**, *indecl.* Asshurim, son of Dedan and great-grandson of Abraham: Gen. 25.3 (AC).

Asdodus: see **Aschdodus**.

Aseka ~ae, *m.* Azekah, a town of Judah: Josh. 10.11 (AC 7553.7).

Asenath, *indecl.* Asenath, daughter of Potiphera and wife of Joseph: Gen. 41.45 (AC).

Ashbel: see **Aschbel**.

Asher: see **Ascher**.

Ashkelon: see **Askalon**.

Ashkenaz: see **Aschkenas**.

Ashtaroth: see **Astaroth**.

Ashteroth Karnaim: see **Asteroth Karnaim**.

Asia ~ae, *f.* The continent of Asia, regarded as including part of North Africa: *in multis regnis ~ae* SS 21; the Roman province of Asia (a part of Asia Minor): Rev. 1.4 (AR).

Askalon ~onis, *m.* also **Ashkelon** ~onis, *m.*, and **Askelon** ~onis, *m.* Ashkelon, a city of the Philistines: 2 Sam. 1.20 (AC 3024.3).

Askelon: see **Askalon**.

Askenas: see **Aschkenas**.

Assa ~ae, *f.* also **Azza** ~ae, *f.* Gaza or Azzah, a city of the Philistines: Gen. 10.19 (AC).

Asshur: see **Aschur**.

Asshurim: see **Aschurim**.

Assir, *indecl.* Assir, son of Korah: Exod. 6.24 (AC).

Assyria ~ae, *f.* Assyria: AC 1186.1; CI 327.

Astaroth, *indecl.* also **Ashtaroth**, *indecl.* An idol of the Philistines: AC 1094.2; VR 292.

Asteroth Karnaim, *indecl.* also **Ashteroth Karnaim**, *indecl.*, and **Asteroth Karnajim**, *indecl.* Ashteroth Karnaim, a city in the territory of Manasseh across the Jordan: AC 1669.

Asteroth Karnajim: see **Asteroth Karnaim**.

Atad, *indecl.* Atad, the place across the Jordan where Joseph grieved his father's death: Gen. 50.10 (AC).

Athanasius ~i, *m.* Athanasius, Bishop of Alexandria in 4th century: DD 55.6.

Athenae ~narum, *f. pl.* Athens, esp. of the classical Greek period: *ut ~nis et Romae* AS 11.

Athenaeum ~i, *neut.* The name of a city in the spiritual world: AM 151[a].1.

Atheneides ~um, *f. pl.* (Gk.) Athenian (cf. **Athenaeum**) maidens: AM 207.6.

Atlas ~antis, *m.* (in Gk. mythology) Atlas, a giant who held up the sky: *sicut gigas seu ~as* ES 991; VR 822.

Augustinus ~i, *m.* St Augustine, Bishop of Hippo: VR 840.

Augustus ~i, *m.* see also **Octavius**. (used alone or with Octavius) The Roman Emperor Augustus, also known as Octavian (63 BC–AD 14): *agere absolute sicut Octavius ~us* VR 73.1; ES 4418; ES 6082.

Avaeus ~i, *m.* One of the Avim, a tribe destroyed before Moses' time: Deut. 2.23 (AC 1868).

Avel Misraim, *indecl.* also **Abel Mizraim**, *indecl.*, and **Avel Mizraim**, *indecl.* Abel Mizraim, a place near Hebron: Gen. 50.11 (AC).

Avel Mizraim: see **Avel Misraim**.

Aven, *indecl.* Aven, an Egyptian city: Hos. 10.8 (AC 273).

Avith, *indecl.* Avith, Hadad's capital city: Gen. 36.35 (AC).

Azariah: see **Asariah**.

Azza: see **Assa**.

B

Baal ~lis, *m.* also **Bal** ~lis, *m.* (gen. pl. *~lium*, acc. pl. *~les* , but acc. pl. *~lim* Jer. 2.23 in AC 4715.4) (sg.) Baal, chief male god of the Canaanites: *fides gentilium...in Baalem* VR 655; (pl.) Baals, Canaanite gods: *gentes quoque in terra Canaane quae coluerunt Bales et alios deos* AC 1094.3; *induere inaurem Balibus est colere deos Baales, ac obedire illis* AC 10402.2.

Baal-Chanan, *indecl.* also **Baal-Ḥanan**, *indecl.* Baal Hanan, a king of Edom: Gen. 36.38 (AC 4650).

Baalchazor, *indecl.* also **Baalḥazor**, *indecl.* Baal Hazor, a place near Ephraim: 2 Sam. 13.23 (AC 4110.3).

Baal-Ḥanan: see **Baal-Chanan**.

Baalḥazor: see **Baalchazor**.

Baalpeor ~oris, *m.* Baal of Peor, a Moabite god: VR 655.

Baal-Zephon, *indecl.* Baal Zephon, a place close to the Israelites' crossing of the Red Sea: Exod. 14.2 (AC).

Babel ~lis, *f.* (Hebr.) Babel, Babylon: Gen. 10.10 (AC); AC 1303.

Babylon ~onis, *f.* Babylon: *~on magna* Rev. 18.2 (AR).

Babylonia ~ae, *f.* The Land of Babylon, Babylonia: CI 508.3; (as representing those who arrogate divine power) *Ecclesia...descivit in ~am, quae in se potestatem Divinam Domini transtulit* DP 262.8.

Babylonii ~orum, *m. pl.* The inhabitants of Babylon, esp. in spiritual sense (see **Babylonia**): AC 3419.3.

Bacuth: see **Allon Bacuth**.

Bajith, *indecl.* Bajith, a temple for the Moabite gods: Isa. 15.2 (AC 3301.9).

Bal: see **Baal**.

Balaam: see **Bileamus**.

Balacus ~i, *m.* also **Balakus** ~i, *m.* Balak, the king of Moab who hired Balaam to curse the Israelites: AR 114.

Balakus: see **Balacus**.

Baptista ~ae, *m.* (Gk.) *Johannes ~a*, John the Baptist: AC 6752.1.

Barak: see **Barakus**.

Barakus ~i, *m.* also **Barak**, *indecl.* Barak, a Naphtalite who helped Deborah the prophet in her fight against Sisera: AC 1756.3.

Bared, *indecl.* Bered, a place to one side of the well Beer-Lahai-Roi: Gen. 16.14 (AC).

Baruchus ~i, *m.* Baruch, Jeremiah's scribe: Jer. 36.15 (AC 9397.2).

Baschan ~anis, *m.* also **Bashan** ~anis, *m.* Bashan, a region to the east of the Jordan river: Deut. 33.22 (AC 3923.3).

Basemath, *indecl. f.* Basemath, daughter of Elon the Hittite and one of two wives of Esau by the same name: Gen. 26.34 (AC).

Basematha ~ae, *f.* Basemath, daughter of Ishmael and one of two wives of Esau by the same name: Gen. 36.3 (AC).

Bashan: see **Baschan**.

Batavia ~ae, *f.* The Netherlands, Holland: VR 35.3.

Batavus ~i, *m.* A Dutchman: VR 72.1.

Bathscheba ~ae, *f.* also **Bathsheba** ~ae, *f.* Bathsheba, wife of Uriah taken by David: AC 2913.2.

Bathsheba: see **Bathscheba**.

Bazar ~aris, *m.* (Hebr.) Bazar or Bazir, possibly a place or a forest associated with Bashan (although English translations of Zech. 11.2 have no place name, reading instead 'forest of the vintage' or 'thick forest'): *ejulate quercus Baschanis, quia descendit sylva ~aris* Zech. 11.2 (AC 4552.5).

Becher, *indecl.* Becher, a son of Benjamin: Gen. 46.21 (AC).

Bechorath, *indecl.* Bechorath, an ancestor of Saul: 1 Sam. 9.1 (AC 7836.3).

Bedad, *indecl.* Bedad, father of Hadad: Gen. 36.35 (AC).

Beelschebub: see **Beelsebub**.

Beelsebub, *indecl. m.* (Hebr.) also **Beelschebub**, *indecl. m.*, **Beelzebub**, *indecl. m.*, and **Beelzebul** ~lis, *m.* The lord of flies, a false god: AE 740.10; VR 292.

Beelzebub: see **Beelsebub**.

Beelzebul: see **Beelsebub**.

Beer, *indecl.* Beer, a place with a well where the Children of Israel stopped: Num. 21.16 (AC 2702.2).

Beeri, *indecl.* Beeri, Hittite father of Judith and father-in-law of Esau: Gen. 26.34 (AC).

Beer-lachai-roi, *indecl.* (Hebr.) also **Beerlachai roi**, *indecl.*, and **Beer-laḥai-roi**, *indecl.* Beer-Lahai-Roi, a well between Kadesh and Bered: Gen. 24.62 (AC).

Beerlachai roi: see **Beer-lachai-roi**.

Beer-laḥai-roi: see **Beer-lachai-roi**.

Beerscheba ~ae, *f.* also **Beerschebah** ~ae, *f.* and *indecl.*, **Beersheba** ~ae, *f.* and *indecl.*, and **Beershebah** ~ae, *f.* Beersheba, the southernmost point in Canaan: Gen. 21.14 (AC).

Beerschebah: see **Beerscheba**.

Beersheba: see **Beerscheba**.

Beershebah: see **Beerscheba**.

Bel ~lis, *m.* Bel, the Babylonian name for Baal: Jer. 51.44 (AR 717).

Bela ~ae, *m.* **1** Bela, a place also called Zoar: Gen. 14.2 (AC). **2** Bela, first king of Edom: Gen. 36.32 (AC). **3** Bela, a son of Benjamin: Gen. 46.21 (AC).

Belschazar: see **Belschazzar**.

Belschazzar ~aris, *m.* also **Belschazar** ~aris, *m.*, **Belshazar** ~aris, *m.*, and **Belshazzar** ~aris, *m.* and *indecl.*, **Belthschazar** ~aris, *m.*, and **Beltschazar** ~aris, *m.* and *indecl.* Belshazzar, son of Nebuchadnezzar, last king of Babylon: UJ 54.

Belshazar: see **Belschazzar**.

Belshazzar: see **Belschazzar**.

Belthschazar: see **Belschazzar**.

Beltschazar: see **Belschazzar**.

Benammi, *indecl.* also **Ammi**, *indecl.* (AC 1364), and **Ben-Ammi**, *indecl. m.* (Gen. 19.38 (AC)). Ben Ammi, brother of Moab and father of the Ammonites: Gen. 19.38 (AC).

Ben-Ammi: see **Benammi**.

Benhadadus ~i, *m.* Ben-Hadad, a king of Damascus: *accendam ignem in murum Damasci, qui comedet palatia ~i* Jer. 49.27 (AC 6419.5).

Benjamin ~inis, *m.* and *indecl.* Benjamin, the youngest son of Jacob and the tribe and territory named after him: Gen. 35.18 (AC).

Benoni, *indecl.* (Hebr.) Ben-Oni, Rachel's name for her second son, whom Jacob named Benjamin: Gen. 35.18 (AC).

Beor ~oris, *m.* Beor, father of King Bela of Edom: Gen. 36.32 (AC).

Bera, *indecl.* Bera, king of Sodom in Abram's time: Gen. 14.2 (AC).

Beria ~ae, *m.* also **Beriah** ~ae, *m.* Beriah, a son of Asher: Gen. 46.17 (AC).

Beriah: see **Beria**.

Beseth: see **Bi-Pesech**.

Bethaven, *indecl.* Beth Aven, a town near Bethel: Hos. 5.8 (AC 4592.10).

Bethchoron ~onis, *m.* Beth Horon, one of two places, an upper and a lower, in Ephraim: Josh. 10.11 (AC 7553.7).

Bethdiblathaim, *indecl.* Beth Diblathaim, a Moabite town: Jer. 48.22 (AC 2468.17).

Bethel ~lis, *m.* and *indecl.* (gen. sg. app. *~li* in the phrase *ab oriente Betheli* Gen. 12.8 (AC)) Bethel, a holy place in Benjamin, where Jacob's name was changed to Israel: Gen. 31.13 (AC).

Bethesda ~ae, *m.* Bethesda, a pool near Jerusalem: DP 231; John 5.2 (AC 10083).

Bethgamul, *indecl.* Beth Gamul, a Moabite town: Jer. 48.23 (AC 2468.17).

Beth Kerem, *indecl.* Beth Kerem (see quot.): *domus vineae seu Beth Kerem* Jer. 6.1 (AC 4592.8).

Bethlechem, *indecl. f.* (Hebr.) also **Bethleem**, *indecl. f.*, **Bethlehem**, *indecl. f.*, and **Bethlehemus** ~i, *m.* Bethlehem: VR 845.

Bethlechemita ~ae, *m.* (Hebr.) An inhabitant of Bethlehem: *pater Davidis ~a fuit* AC 4594.4.

Bethleem: see **Bethlechem**.

Bethlehem: see **Bethlechem**.

Bethlehemus: see **Bethlechem**.

Bethmeon, *indecl.* Beth Meon, a Moabite town: Jer. 48.23 (AC 2468.17).

Bethogarma: see **Beththogarmah**.

Bethsaida, *indecl.* Bethsaida, native city of Andrew and Peter in Galilee: Matt. 11.21 (AR 492). (n.b. *Bethsaidae* in AE 163.7 Hindmarsh should read *Bethesdae*.)

Bethschemita ~ae, *m.* An inhabitant of Beth-shemesh: 1 Sam. 6.13 (AR 529.3).

Beththogarmah ~ae, *f.* also **Bethogarma** ~ae, *f.*, and **Bethtogarmah** ~ae, *f.* Beth Togarmah, the house of Togarmah, son of Gomer: Ezek. 27.14 (AC 1154).

Bethtogarmah: see **Beththogarmah**.

Bethuel ~lis, *m.* Bethuel, nephew of Abraham and father of Rebekah: Gen. 22.22 (AC).

Bethynia: see **Bithynia**.

Bezaaleel: see **Bezaleel**.

Bezaleel ~lis, *m.* also **Bezaaleel** ~lis, *m.* Bezaleel, chief artisan for the tabernacle: Exod. 31.2 (AC).

Bileamus ~i, *m.* also **Balaam**, *indecl.* Balaam: AC 2898.

Bilha: see **Bilhah**.

Bilhah ~ae, *f.* also **Bilha** ~ae, *f.* Bilhah, Rachel's handmaiden and mother of Dan and Naphtali: Gen. 30.3 (AC).

Bilhan, *indecl.* Bilhan, grandson of Seir: Gen. 36.27 (AC).

Bi-Pesech, *indecl.* (Hebr.) also **Pi-Beseth**, *indecl.* Pi Beseth, a capital city in lower Egypt: Ezek. 30.17 (AC 8398).

Birscha, *indecl.* also **Birsha**, *indecl.* Birsha, king of Gomorrah in Abram's time: Gen. 14.2 (AC).

Birsha: see **Birscha**.

Bithynia ~ae, *f.* also **Bethynia** ~ae, *f.* Bithynia, an area on the north-western coast of Asia Minor: VR 632; SE 31.

Boanerges, *indecl.* (Gk.) Boanerges, epithet for the disciples James and John (see quot.): *a Domino vocati sunt ~es, hoc est, filii tonitrui* Mark 3.17 (AR 236).

Boas[1], *indecl.* Boaz, the name of the left-hand pillar in the porch of Solomon's temple: 1 Kgs. 7.22 (AE 219.5).

Bochim, *indecl.* also **Bochin**, *indecl.* Bochim, a place west of the Jordan river near Gilgal: Judg. 2.1 (AC 4539.2).

Bochin: see **Bochim**.

Bozra ~ae, *f.* also **Bozrah** ~ae, *f.* Bozrah, a city in Edom: Jer. 49.13 (AC 5376.11).

Bozrah: see **Bozra**.

Britannia ~ae, *f.* Britain: VR 161.1.

Britannus ~i, *m.* An inhabitant of Britain, Briton: VR 72.1.

Buz, *indecl.* Buz, a son of Nahor and Milcah: Gen. 22.20 (AC).

C

Cain, *indecl.* also **Cainus** ~i, *m.*, and **Kainus** ~i, *m.* Cain, son of Adam and Eve: Gen. 4.1 (AC).

Cainita ~ae, *m.* A follower of Cain, Cainite: AC 407.

Cainus: see **Cain**.

Calaḥ: see **Kalach**.

Calebus: see **Chalebus**.

Calmucki ~orum, *m. pl.* A people of Asia, the Calmucks: ES 3411.

Calneh: see **Kalneh**.

Calvinianus ~i, *m.* A follower of Calvin, Calvinist: SE 18.

Calvinismus ~i, *m.* The heresy of Calvin, Calvinism: VR 94.1.

Calvinista ~ae, *m.* A follower of Calvin, Calvinist: AC 1799.4.

Calvinus ~i, *m.* John Calvin (1509-64), the Swiss Protestant theologian: UJ(C) 54.

Canaan ~anis, *m.* The ancient name of Palestine, Canaan: *per terram ~anem* CI 327; also, the son of Ham: Gen. 9.18 (AC).

Canaanita ~ae, *m.* A Canaanite: Gen. 10.18 (AC).

Canneh: see **Channeh**.

Caphtor, *indecl.* also **Kaphtor** ~oris and *indecl.* Caphtor, primary seat of the Philistines that was situated in or near Egypt: Jer. 47.4 (AC 1201.1).

Caphtoraeus ~i, *m.* A person from Caphtor: Deut. 2.23 (AC 1868.3).

Caphtorim: see **Kaphthorim**.

Capucini ~orum, *m. pl.* The Capuchin friars: ES 4681.

Carmel ~lis, *m.* and *indecl.* also **Carmelus** ~i, *m.* Carmel, the mountain on the west coast of Canaan that juts out into the Mediterranean Sea: AC 5201.5.

Carmelus: see **Carmel**.

Carmi: see **Karmi**.

Carolus ~i, *m.* A personal name, Charles: (of Charles XI, king of Sweden) ES 6019.

Cartesianus ~i, *m.* A follower of Descartes, Cartesian: VR 696.1.

Cartesius ~i, *m.* Latinized form of the name of the 17th-century philosopher Descartes: CC 19.1.

Cartush, *indecl.* Probably for Cartouche, a notable robber executed in Paris: ES 5560.

Casluḥim: see **Kasluchim**.

Cataphryges ~um, *m. pl.* A 2nd-century AD sect of heretics, Cataphrygians or Montanists: VR 378.2.

Cathari ~orum, *m. pl.* (Gk., = English 'pure') A name given to the followers of Novatianus, Catharans: VR 378.2.

Catholico-Romani ~orum, *m. pl.* Roman Catholics: SS(P) 40 (= 17.1).

Catholismus ~i, *m.* Catholicism: *doctrinalia ex ~o papali* AR 751.

Cerberus ~i, *m.* (in Gk. mythology) Cerberus, the three-headed dog which guarded the entrance to the underworld: *canes quorum aliqui erant tricipites sicut ~i* AM 79.2; ES 2614.

Cerinthus ~i, *m.* An error for **Corinthus**: VR 378.2 (2nd edn.).

Chabor, *indecl.* also **Ḥabor**, *indecl.* Habor, a region of Assyria: 2 Kgs. 17.6 (AC 1189).

Chadar, *indecl.* also **Ḥadad**[2], *indecl.* Hadad, a son of Ishmael: Gen. 25.15 (AC).

Chaggi, *indecl. m.* also **Ḥaggi**, *indecl. m.* Haggi, a son of Gad: Gen. 46.16 (AC).

Chaiva ~ae, *f.* (Hebr.) see also **Evah**. Eve: DP 275.

Chaja ~ae, *f.* see also **Evah**. Chaja, a Hebrew word meaning life from which Eve was named: AR 239.1.

Chaldaea ~ae, *f.* A land in the south of Assyria (modern Iraq), Chaldaea: SS 21.

Chaldaeus ~i, *m.* An inhabitant of Chaldaea, Chaldaean: Ezek. 23.14 (VI 79.2).

Chalebus ~i, *m.* also **Calebus** ~i, *m.*, and **Kalebus** ~i, *m.* Caleb, one of the twelve chiefs sent to spy out Canaan and one of two who brought back a favourable report: AC 2909.

Cham, *indecl.* also **Chamus** ~i, *m.*, and **Ḥam**[2], *indecl.* Ham, a son of Noah: Gen. 5.32 (AC).

Chamath, *indecl.* also **Ḥamath**, *indecl.* Hamath, a city of upper Syria: Isa. 11.11 (AC 1259.2).

Chamathus ~i, *m.* also **Ḥamathus** ~i, *m.* A member of a tribe descended from Canaan living in the far north of the Holy Land, Hamathite: Gen. 10.18 (AC).

Chamor ~oris, *m.* also **Ḥamor** ~oris, *m.* Hamor, father of Schechem: Gen. 33.19 (AC).

Chamul, *indecl.* also **Ḥamul**, *indecl.* Hamul, a son of Perez and grandson of Judah: Gen. 46.12 (AC).

Chamus: see **Cham**.

Chanamel ~lis, *m.* also **Ḥanamel** ~lis, *m.* Hanameel, a cousin of Jeremiah: Jer. 32.9 (AC 755).

Chananeel, *indecl.* also **Ḥananeel**, *indecl.* Hananeel, the builder of a tower in Jerusalem: Zech. 14.10 (AC 4592.12).

Chanania ~ae, *m.* also **Ḥananiah** ~ae, *m.* Hananiah, the Hebr. name of Shadrach: Dan. 1.19 (AC 5223.4).

Channa ~ae, *f.* also **Channah** ~ae, *f.*, and **Ḥannah** ~ae, *f.* Hannah, mother of Samuel: AC 66.

Channah: see **Channa**.

Channeh, *indecl.* also **Canneh**, *indecl.* Canneh, a place on the south coast of Arabia: Ezek. 27.23 (AC 2967.3).

Chanoch, *indecl.* also **Chanochus** ~i, *m.*, **Ḥanoch**, *indecl.*, and **Ḥanochus** ~i, *m.* **1** Enoch, son of Cain: Gen. 4.17 (AC). **2** Enoch, son of Jared and descendant of Seth, who 'walked with God and was no more': Gen. 5.24 (AC). **3** Hanoch, son of Midian: Gen. 25.4 (AC). **4** Hanoch, son of Reuben: Gen. 46.9 (AC).

Chanochus: see **Chanoch**.

Chanun, *indecl.* also **Ḥanun**, *indecl.* Hanun, a king of the Ammonites: 2 Sam. 10.1 (AC 4763.7).

Charan ~anis, *m.* and *indecl.* also **Ḥaran**[2] ~anis, *m.* and *indecl.* **1** Haran, brother of Rebekah: Gen. 27.43 (AC). **2** Haran, a place in Paddan Aram to which Abram moved from Ur: Gen. 11.32 (AC 1375).

Charites ~um, *f. pl.* (Gk.) (in Gk. mythology) The three Graces: AC 4966.2.

Charon ~ntis, *m.* (Gk.) (in Gk. mythology) Charon, the ferryman who carried the dead over the river Styx: VR 453.2.

Charybdis ~eos, *f.* (Gk.) Charybdis, the famous whirlpool of antiquity: *cupiens vitare ~in incidit in Scyllam* VR 637.

Chasael ~lis, *m.* Hazael, a king of Syria: 1 Kgs. 19.15 (AC 9954.9).

Chaso, *indecl.* also **Ḥazo**, *indecl.* Hazo, a son of Nahor: Gen. 22.22 (AC).

Chavah: see **Evah**.

Chavillah[1], *indecl.* also **Ḥavilah**, *indecl.* **1** Havilah, son of Cush: Gen. 10.7 (AC). **2** Havilah, son of Joktan: Gen. 10.29 (AC). **3** Havilah, a region east of Amalek: Gen. 25.18 (AC).

Chavillah[2], *indecl.* also **Ḥavillah**, *indecl.* Havilah, a land that was a source of gold: Gen. 2.11 (AC 9881); (AC 115 identifies it with **Chavillah**[1], sense 3 q.v.).

Chazarmaveth, *indecl.* also **Ḥazarmaveth**, *indecl.* Hazarmaveth, a son of Joktan of the family of Shem: Gen. 10.26 (AC).

Chazeroth, *indecl.* also **Ḥazeroth**, *indecl.* Hazeroth, a stopping point of the Israelites in their wandering: Num. 12.16 (AC 2714.4).

Chazezon Thamar, *indecl.* also **Ḥazezon-Tamar**, *indecl.* Hazezon Tamar, dwelling place of the Amorites: Gen. 14.7 (AC).

Chazor ~oris, *m.* and *indecl.*, and **Ḥazor** ~oris, *m.* Hazor, kingdoms in the east of Arabia: Jer. 49.28 (AC 3048.5).

Cheber, *indecl.* also **Ḥeber**, *indecl.* Heber, a son of Beriah and grandson of Asher: Gen. 46.17 (AC).

Chebron[1], *indecl.* Hebron, son of Kohath and grandson of Levi: Exod. 6.18 (AC).

Chebron[2], *indecl.* and ~onis, *f.* also **Ḥebron**, *indecl.* and ~onis, *f.* see also **Kiriath Arba**. Hebron, a city of Judah not far from Jerusalem: Gen. 23.2 (AC).

Chelbon: see **Chesbon**[1].

Chemdan, *indecl.* also **Ḥemdan**, *indecl.* Hemdan, a son of Dishon and grandson of Seir: Gen. 36.26 (AC).

Chemos: see **Kemosch**.

Cheran, *indecl.* Cheran, son of Dishon and grandson of Seir: Gen. 36.26 (AC).

Cheres: see **Ir Cheres**.

Chermon ~onis, *m.* also **Ḥermon** ~onis, *m.* Hermon,

a mountain at the north-east corner of the land of Canaan: Ps. 133.3 (AC 3579.5).

Chermonim, *indecl. pl.* also **Ḥermonim**, *indecl. pl.* Hermonites, inhabitants (or perh. areas) of Mt. Hermon: Ps. 42.6 (AC 4255.3).

Chesbon[1] ~onis, *m.* also **Chelbon** ~onis, *m.*, and **Ḥelbon** ~onis, *m.* Helbon, an ancient village near Damascus famous for its wine: AC 4453.3.

Chesbon[2] ~onis, *m.* also **Cheschbon** ~onis, *m.*, **Ḥesbon** ~onis, *m.*, and **Ḥeshbon** ~onis, *m.* Heshbon, a Levitical city of Reuben and Gad that first belonged to Moab and then to Ammon: Num. 21.27 (VR 265).

Cheschbon: see **Chesbon**[2].

Cheth, *indecl.* also **Chethus** ~i, *m.*, **Ḥeth**, *indecl.*, and **Ḥethus** ~i, *m.* Heth, son of Canaan and ancestor of the Hittites: Gen. 23.3 (AC).

Chethus: see **Cheth**.

Chezron, *indecl.* also **Ḥezron**, *indecl.* Hezron, a son of Reuben: Gen. 46.9 (AC).

Chiddechel, *indecl.* also **Chiddekel**, *indecl.*, and **Ḥiddekel**, *indecl.* Hiddekel, the ancient name of the Tigris river that flowed eastward out of Eden towards Assyria: Gen. 2.14 (AC).

Chiddekel: see **Chiddechel**.

Chilkia ~ae, *m.* also **Ḥilkiah** ~ae, *m.* Hilkiah, the high priest in the time of Josiah who rediscovered the sacred book: AC 9396.6.

China ~ae, *f.* China: AR 11.

Chinenses ~ium, *m. pl.* The inhabitants of China, Chinese: CI 325.

Chirach: see **Chirah**.

Chirah ~ae, *m.* also **Chirach** ~ae, *m.*, and **Ḥirah** ~ae, *m.* Hirah, an Adullamite friend of Judah: Gen. 38.12 (AC).

Chir Charesch, *indecl.* also **Kir-Chareseth**, *indecl.*, **Kir-Cheres**, *indecl.*, and **Kir Ḥareseth**, *indecl.* Kir Hareseth, a fortified city of Moab that may be the same as **Kir**, sense 1, q.v.: Isa. 16.7 (AC 2608).

Chiroth: see **Pi-Chiroth**.

Chittita ~ae, *m.* also **Ḥittita** ~ae, *m.* A Hittite, a descendant of Heth and inhabitant of the mountainous regions of Judah: Gen. 15.20 (AC).

Chivita ~ae, *m.* see also **Chivus**. The Hivite (collective sg.), a people descended from Canaan: Exod. 33.2 (AC).

Chivus ~i, *m.* also **Ḥivus** ~i, *m.* see also **Chivita**. A member of a tribe descended from Canaan, Hivite: AC 1205.

Chobah ~ae, *m.* also **Ḥobah** ~ae, *m.* Hobah, a place just north of Damascus: Gen. 14.15 (AC).

Cholon ~onis, *m.* also **Ḥolon** ~onis, *m.* Holon, a city of Moab: Jer. 48.21 (AC 2468.17).

Chorazin, *indecl.* Chorazin, a city near Capernaum: Matt. 11.21 (AR 492).

Choreb: see **Chorebus**.

Chorebus ~i, *m.* also **Choreb**, *indecl.*, **Ḥoreb**, *indecl.*, and **Ḥorebus** ~i, *m.* Horeb, the mountain range that includes Sinai: Exod. 3.1 (AC).

Choresch ~schi, *m.* also **Choreschus** ~i, *m.*, **Choresh** ~shi, *m.*, **Koresch** ~schi, *m.*, and **Koresh** ~shi, *m.* Cyrus, founder of the Persian Empire, who conquered Babylon and assisted the Jews: Isa. 45.1 (AC 2851.14).

Choreschus: see **Choresch**.

Choresh: see **Choresch**.

Chori, *indecl.* also **Ḥori**, *indecl.* Hori, a son of Lotan and grandson of Seir: Gen. 36.22 (AC).

Chorita ~ae, *m.* also **Ḥorita** ~ae, *m.* A Horite, an inhabitant of Mt. Seir in Moab: Gen. 14.6 (AC).

Chorma ~ae, *m.* Hormah, a Canaanite capital city in the southern part of the land: Num. 14.45 (AC 8593.2).

Chormah ~ae, *m.* also **Ḥormah** ~ae, *m.* Prob. an error for **Ramah**: Isa. 10.29 (AC 1888.2).

Choronaim, *indecl.* also **Ḥoronaim**, *indecl.* Horonaim, a town of Moab: Jer. 48.3 (AC 2608).

Chul, *indecl.* also **Ḥul**, *indecl.* Hul, a son of Aram and grandson of Shem: Gen. 10.23 (AC).

Chuppim, *indecl.* also **Ḥuppim**, *indecl.* Huppim, a son of Benjamin: Gen. 46.21 (AC).

Chur[1] ~uris, *m.* Hur, an associate of Aaron's who helped him hold up Moses' hands: Exod. 17.10 (AC).

Chur[2] ~uri, *m.* Hur, grandson of Caleb and father of Bezaleel: Exod. 31.2 (AC).

Chuschai, *indecl.* also **Ḥushai**, *indecl.* Hushai, a friend of David: 2 Sam. 15.32 (AC 4763.5).

Chuscham, *indecl.* also **Ḥusham**, *indecl.* Husham, a Temanite king of Edom: Gen. 36.34 (AC).

Chuschim, *indecl.* also **Ḥushim**, *indecl.* Hushim, son of Dan: Gen. 46.23 (AC).

Cicero ~onis, *m.* Marcus Tullius Cicero (106-43 BC), Roman statesman, orator, and philosopher: CI 322.1.

Cingliani ~orum, *m. pl.* Prob. an error for **Zwingliani** (cf. VR 378.2): AR Doc Ref.10.

Cocceiani: see **Coccejani**.

Coccejani ~orum, *m. pl.* also **Cocceiani** ~orum, *m. pl.* The followers of the 17th-century Dutch theologian Cocceius: VR 803.

Colonia ~ae, *f.* Cologne (Köln) in Germany: *trium sapientum ~ae* NE 46.

Colossae ~sarum, *f. pl.* A city of Anatolia: UJ(P) 359.

Constantinopolis ~eos, *f.* The city of Constantinople (now Istanbul): DP 312.2; (in the world of spirits) DC 302.H.

Constantinus ~u, *m.* *~us Magnus*, the Emperor of Rome, Constantine the Great (AD 274-337): VR 137.11.

Corinthus ~i, *m.* Corinth, an ancient city of southern Greece: VR 378.2 (1st edn.).

Cusch: see **Kusch**.

Cuschus: see **Kusch**.

Cush: see **Kusch**.

Cushim: see **Kusch**, sense 3.

Cushus: see **Kusch**.

Cyclops ~opos, *m.* (Gk.) (in Gk. mythology) A fabulous giant with one eye: CO 38.

Cynosura ~ae, *f.* (Gk., = English 'dog's tail') The name of the constellation Ursa Minor; hence, a guiding star in navigation: *apparet hoc illi sicut ~a, ad quam omnia vela...dirigit* VR 165.3.

D

Damascenus ~i, *m.* An inhabitant of Damascus: Gen. 15.2 (AC).

Damascus ~i, *m.* The city of Damascus in Syria: *~us erat urbs principalis Syriae* AC 1715.

Dan, *indecl.* and ~nis, *m.* **1** Dan, The northernmost city in Canaan: Gen. 14.14 (AC). **2** Dan, a son of Jacob, after whom a tribe was named: Gen. 30.6 (AC).

Danemarchia ~ae, *f.* also **Danemarkia** ~ae, *f.* Denmark: VR 161.1.

Danemarkia: see **Danemarchia**.

Dania ~ae, *f.* Denmark: VI 4.

Daniel ~lis, *m.* Daniel, the prophet taken to Babylon and the book named after him: AC 1990.2.

Danita ~ae, *m.* A member of the tribe of Dan, Danite: CI 324.

Danus ~i, *m.* An inhabitant of Denmark, Dane: AM 103.2.

Daphne ~es, *f.* (Gk.) (in Gk. mythology) A maiden who was changed into a laurel tree: VR 58.2.

Dardaus ~i, *m.* Darda, a wise man around the time of Solomon: 1 Kgs. 4.31 (AC 5223.2).

Darius ~i, *m.* Darius the Mede, who took over Babylon after Belshazzar: VR 292.

Dathan ~anis, *m.* Dathan, a Reubenite who conspired against Moses in the wilderness: Num. 16.25 (AC 8306).

David ~idis, *m.* (Hebr.) David: CI 326; VI 55.2; as the author of the Book of Psalms: VR 748.3.

Davus ~i, *m.* The name often given to slaves in comedy, used as a type of stupidity with ref. to Terence, *Andria* 194: *auscultatori ~o infundere intelligentiam antistitis Oedipi* CO 54.3.

Deborah ~ae, *f.* **1** Deborah, Rebekah's nurse: Gen. 35.8 (AC). **2** Deborah, a female prophet and judge: AC 8753.3.

Dedan ~anis, *m.* **1** Dedan, son of Raamah and the territory named for him: Gen. 10.7 (AC). **2** Dedan, son of Jokshan and grandson of Abraham: Gen. 25.3 (AC). **3** A district near Edom: Jer. 25.23 (AC 3268.6).

Dedanim, *indecl. pl.* The Dedanim, descendants of Raamah: AC 3268.5.

Delilah ~ae, *f.* Delilah, a Philistine woman who betrayed Samson: AC 5247.4.

Delphi ~orum, *m. pl.* (Gk.) Delphi, a town in central Greece, the site of the ancient oracle of Apollo: *qui originem illius amoris vult...educere...adeat ~os* AM 111.

Democritus ~i, *m.* A Greek philosopher of the 5th century BC: AM 182.8.

Demosthenes ~is, *m.* A Greek orator and statesman of the 4th century BC: AM 182.1.

Deucalio ~onis, *m.* (myth.) The Greek figure corresponding to Noah, who survived a flood and subsequently repeopled the earth, Deucalion: VR 58.2.

Diahabah ~ae, *f.* also **Dinhabah** ~ae, *f.* Dinhabah, the capital city of Bela, king of Edom: Gen. 36.32 (AC).

Diana ~ae, *f.* The Roman goddess Diana, equivalent to the Greek Artemis: VR 17.2.

Dibon ~onis, *m.* Dibon, a city south-west of Heshbon: Num. 21.30 (AC 2897).

Diklah, *indecl.* Diklah, a son of Joktan: Gen. 10.27 (AC).

Dimon ~onis, *m.* Dimon, a city of Moab (prob. same as Dibon): Isa. 15.9 (AC 4735.12).

Dinah ~ae, *f.* Dinah, daughter of Jacob: Gen. 30.21 (AC).

Dinhabah: see **Diahabah**.

Diogenes ~is, *m.* Diogenes, the 4th-century BC Greek philosopher: VR 693.

Dischan ~anis, *m.* also **Dishan** ~anis, *m.* **1** Dishan, youngest son of Seir: Gen. 36.21 (AC). **2** Dishan, son of Anah and grandson of Seir: Gen. 36.25 (AC).

Dischon ~onis, *m*. also **Dishon** ~onis, *m*. Dishon, son of Seir: Gen. 36.21 (AC).

Dishan: see **Dischan**.

Dishon: see **Dischon**.

Dodanim, *indecl*. Dodanim, a son of Javan: Gen. 10.4 (AC).

Dodrechtum: see **Dordrectum**.

Dodrectum: see **Dordrectum**.

Donatista ~ae, *m*. A follower of the 4th-century heretical bishop named Donatus: VR 378.2.

Dordrechtum: see **Dordrectum**.

Dordrectum ~i, *neut*. also **Dodrechtum** ~i, *m*., **Dodrectum** ~i, *m*., and **Dordrechtum** ~i, *neut*. Dodrecht or Dort in the Netherlands: VR 487.1.

Dothan, *indecl*. and ~anis, *m*. Dothan, a city of Manasseh west of the Jordan: Gen. 37.17 (AC).

Dumah ~ae, *m*. Dumah, son of Ishmael: Gen. 25.14 (AC).

E

Ebal, *indecl.* **1** Ebal, a mountain in Ephraim: Deut. 11.29 (AC 1443). **2** Ebal, a son of Shobal: Gen. 36.23 (AC).

Ebed, *indecl.* (Hebr.) Ebed, father of Gaal: Judg. 9.28 (AC 4430.3).

Eben Eser, *indecl.* Ebenezer, (see quot.): *illud dogma osculati sunt, sicut Philistaei idolum Dagonis in fano Eben Eser* [*Eban Eser* 1st edn.] *Asdodi* VR 759.2.

Eberus ~i, *m.* also **Heberus** ~i, *m.* Eber, a son of Salah and and great-grandson of Shem: Gen. 10.24 (AC).

Echi, *indecl.* also **Eḥi**, *indecl.* Ehi, a son of Benjamin: Gen. 46.21 (AC).

Eden, *indecl.* and ~enis, *neut.*? Eden: *hortum in Eden* Gen. 2.8 (AC); *per hortum ~enis* SS 42.

Edenis: see **Eden**.

Eder, *indecl.* Eder, a place near Ephrath: Gen. 35.21 (AC).

Edom: see **Edomus**.

Edomita ~ae, *m.* An inhabitant of Edom, Edomite: Deut. 23.7 (AC 3322.6).

Edomus ~i, *m.* also **Edom**, *indecl. m.* The land of Edom: *~us et Moabus* Isa. 11.14 (SS 15.2); Isa. 63.1 (DD 6).

Eglaim: see **En-Eglaim**.

Eḥi: see **Echi**.

Eislebia ~ae, *f.* (locative *~ae*) Eisleben, Germany, home of Martin Luther: VR 796.1.

Ekron ~onis, *m.* or *f.*? A city of Philistia, Ekron: VR 71.3 (cf. 1 Sam. 5.10).

Ekronita ~ae, *m.* An inhabitant of Ekron: AR 529.3 (1 Sam. 5 and 6).

El-Bethel, *indecl.* El Bethel, the place where God appeared to Jacob: Gen. 35.7 (AC).

Elah, *indecl.* Elah, a leader of Edom: Gen. 36.41 (AC).

Elam, *indecl.* and **Elamus** ~i, *m.* Elam, a son of Shem and the Persian region inhabited by his descendants: Gen. 10.22 (AC); Gen. 14.1 (AC).

Elamus: see **Elam**.

Eldaah, *indecl.* Eldaah, a son of Midian: Gen. 25.4 (AC).

Elealeh, *indecl.* Elealeh, a place on the east of the Jordan river: Jer. 48.34 (AC 1825).

Eleasar ~aris, *m.* also **Eleazar** ~aris, *m.* Eleazar, a son of Aaron: Exod. 6.23 (AC).

Eleazar: see **Eleasar**.

Eli, *indecl.* Eli, a high priest and judge of Israel: AC 6148.5.

Eliakimus ~i, *m.* Eliakim, the son of Hilkiah who was in charge of Hezekiah's household: AR 174.

Elias ~ae, *m.* The prophet Elijah: *vecti in curru igneo sicut ~as* AM 266.5.

Elieser: see **Eliezer**.

Eliezer, *indecl. m.* also **Elieser**, *indecl. m.* **1** Eliezer, Abram's servant from Damascus: Gen. 15.2 (AC). **2** Eliezer, a son of Moses: Exod. 18.4 (AC).

Elihu, *indecl.* Elihu, great-grandfather of Samuel the prophet: AC 7836.3.

Elim, *indecl.* Elim, a place with twelve springs and seventy palm trees where the Israelites camped: Exod. 15.27 (AC).

Eliphas ~si, *m.* also **Eliphaz** ~zi, *m.* Eliphaz, a son of Esau: Gen. 36.4 (AC).

Eliphaz: see **Eliphas**.

Elisabetha ~ae, *f.* Elizabeth, mother of John the Baptist: Luke 1.41 (DD 51.5).

Elisaeus ~i, *m.* also **Elischah**[2] ~ae, *m.*, **Elishah**[1] ~ae, *m.*, and **Elisseus** ~i, *m.* The prophet Elisha: SS 35.2.

Elischah[1] ~ae, *m.* and *indecl.* also **Elishah**[2] ~ae, *m.* and *indecl.* Elishah, a son of Javan: Gen. 10.4 (AC).

Elischah[2]: see **Elisaeus**.

Elischeba ~ae, *f.* The wife of Aaron: Exod. 6.23 (AC).

Elishah[1]: see **Elisaeus**.

Elishah[2]: see **Elischah**[1].

Elisseus: see **Elisaeus**.

Elkanah ~ae, *m.* **1** Elkanah, a son of Korah: Exod. 6.24 (AC). **2** Elkanah, father of Samuel: 1 Sam. 1.1 (AC 7836.3).

Ellasar, *indecl.* Ellasar, a Chaldean town: Gen. 14.1 (AC).

Elon ~onis, *m.* **1** Elon, Hittite father-in-law of Esau: Gen. 26.34 (AC). **2** Elon, a son of Zebulun: Gen. 36.14 (AC).

Elparan, *indecl.* also **El-Paran**, *indecl.* El Paran, dwelling place of the Horites in the south of Canaan and the west of Edom: Gen. 14.6 (AC).

El-Paran: see **Elparan**.

Elzaphan, *indecl.* Elzaphan, a son of Ussiel and grandson of Levi: Exod. 6.22 (AC).

Emim, *indecl.* The Emims, a race of giants: Gen. 14.5 (AC).

Emoraeus: see **Emorraeus**.

Emorita ~ae, *m.* also **Emorrita** ~ae, *m.* An Amorite: Gen. 15.21 (AC).

Emorraeus ~i, *m.* also **Emoraeus** ~i, *m.* An Amorite: Gen. 15.16 (AC); Exod. 3.17 (AC).

Emorrita: see **Emorita**.

Emorus ~i, *m.* An Amorite: Gen. 10.16 (AC).

Enachim: see **Enakim**.

Enakim, *m. pl.* (Hebr.) also **Enachim**, *m. pl.* A race of giants, the Anakim: VR 87.

Enakus: see **Anakus**.

Encratita ~ae, *m.* A member of an early Christian heretical sect, an Encratite: VR 378.2.

En-Eglaim, *indecl.* En Eglaim, a place near the salt sea: Ezek. 47.10 (AC 40).

Engedi, *indecl.* En Gedi, a town on the west shore of the salt sea: Ezek. 47.10 (AC 40).

En mischpath, *indecl.* also **En-mishpat**, *indecl.* En-mishpat, another name for Kadesh: Gen. 14.7 (AC).

En-mishpat: see **En mischpath**.

Enosch, *indecl.* (Hebr.) also **Enoschus** ~i, *m.*, **Enosh**, *indecl.*, and **Enoshus** ~i, *m.* See quot.: *sunt duae voces in lingua originali quae significant 'hominem', una est Adam, et altera Enosch* AC 7120.

Enoschus: see **Enosch**.

Enosh: see **Enosch**.

Enoshus: see **Enosch**.

Ephah, *indecl.* Ephah, a son of Midian and grandson of Abraham: Gen. 25.4 (AC).

Epher, *indecl.* Epher, a son of Midian and grandson of Abraham: Gen. 25.4 (AC).

Ephesus ~i, *f.* A city in Asia Minor, Ephesus: Rev. 1.11 (AR).

Ephraim, *indecl.* also **Ephraimus** ~i, *m.* Ephraim, a son of Joseph and the territory given to his descendants: Gen. 41.52 (AC).

Ephraimus: see **Ephraim**.

Ephrata ~ae, *f.* also **Ephrath**, *indecl. f.* A region of Palestine: Ps. 132.6 (AC 9485.1).

Ephrath: see **Ephrata**.

Ephron ~onis, *m.* Ephron, a Hittite, from whom Abraham purchased a field as a burial place: Gen. 23.8 (AC).

Epicurus ~i, *m.* A Greek philosopher of the 4th to 3rd centuries BC: AM 182.1.

Er Eri, *m.* Er, firstborn son of Judah: Gen. 38.3 (AC).

Ereb, *indecl. f.* (app.) Hebr. = foreigners: Ezek. 30.5 (AC 1164.2).

Erech, *indecl.* Erech, a city in the land of Shinar: Gen. 10.10 (AC).

Eri, *indecl. m.* Eri, a son of Gad: Gen. 46.16 (AC).

Eris ~idis, *f.* (Gk.) Strife (personified): *pomum ~idis* VR 112.1.

Esaias ~ae, *m.* also **Esajas** ~ae, *m.* The prophet Isaiah: DD 2.1.

Esajas: see **Esaias**.

Esau: see **Esavus**.

Esavus ~i, *m.* also **Esau**, *indecl. m.* Esau: Gen. 25.25 (AC).

Esbon, *indecl. m.* also **Ezbon**, *indecl. m.* Ezbon, a son of Gad: Gen. 46.16 (AC).

Eschban, *indecl.* also **Eshban**, *indecl.* Eshban, a son of Dishon and grandson of Seir: Gen. 36.26 (AC).

Eschkol: see **Esckol**.

Eschol: see **Esckol**.

Esckol, *indecl.* also **Eschkol** ~li, *m.* and *indecl.* (acc. *~lem* AE 403 Worcester), **Eschol** ~li, *m.*, **Escol**, *indecl.*, **Eshkol** ~li, *m.* and *indecl.* (AC 3rd edn.), and **Eskol**, *indecl.* (acc. ~*len* AE 403 1st edn.). Eshcol, an Amorite ally of Abraham: AC 1751.

Escol: see **Esckol**.

Esek, *indecl.* Esek, a well in the valley of Gerar: Gen. 26.20 (AC).

Eser: see **Eban Eser**.

Eshban: see **Eschban**.

Eshkol: see **Esckol**.

Eskol: see **Esckol**.

Esrachita ~ae, *m.* also **Ezrachita** ~ae, *m.* An Ezrahite (the patronymic of Ethan and Heman): 1 Kgs. 4.31 (AC 5223.2).

Etham, *indecl.* Etham, a place where the Israelites camped on the edge of the wilderness: Exod. 13.20 (AC).

Eunomiani ~orum, *m. pl.* The followers of the heretic Eunomius, Eunomians: VR 378.2.

Euphrates ~is, *m.* The river Euphrates: *juxta ~em* SS 16 (Jer. 13.5).

Europa ~ae, *f.* The continent of Europe: *~a ubi nunc Ecclesia Christiana* AC 567.

Eva: see **Evah**.

Evah ~ae, *f.* also **Chavah** ~ae, *f.*, **Eva** ~ae, *f.*, and **Ḥavah** ~ae, *f.* see also **Chaiva** and **Chaja**. Eve, the wife of Adam: AE 388.22.

Evil: see **Evilmerodachus**.

Evilmerodachus ~i, *m.* also spelled as two words **Evil** (*indecl.*) **Merodachus** ~i, *m.* Evil Merodach, son and successor of Nebuchadnezzar: Jer. 52.31 (AC 5124.1).

Ezbon: see **Esbon**.

Ezechiel ~lis, *m.* also **Hezechiel** ~lis, *m.* The prophet Ezekiel: SS 16.

Ezer, *indecl. m.* Ezer, a son of Seir: Gen. 36.21 (AC).

Ezrachita: see **Esrachita**.

F

Fock, *indecl. m.* Martin Folkes (1690-1754), vice-president of the Royal Society of London 1722-41: *audivi binos praesides Societatis Anglicanae, Sr. Sloan et Sr. Fock, in mundo spirituali inter se colloquentes* AS 344.

Franciscus ~i, *m.* A personal name, Francis: (of Francis Xavier) ES(M) 4570.

Francus ~i, *m.* An inhabitant of France, Frenchman: *~i seu Galli* AM 103.2.

Futziani ~orum, *m. pl.* also **Voëtiani** ~orum, *m. pl.* The followers of the Dutch theologian Gisbert Voëtius (1588-1676): ES [6099.10].

G

Gaal, *indecl. m.* Gaal, a son of Ebed: Judg. 9.28 (AC 4430.3).

Gabriel ~lis, *m.* (Hebr.) The angel Gabriel: AM 26; VR 43.2; (as the name of ministries in heaven) AR 548.

Gacham, *indecl. m.* also **Gaḥam**, *indecl. m.* Gaham, a son of Nahor: Gen. 22.24 (AC).

Gad, *indecl.* and ~adis, *m.* **1** Jacob's son by Zilpah: Gen. 30.11 (AC); (as the name of one of the twelve tribes) AR 349.3. **2** David's seer: 2 Sam. 24.11 (AE 453.2); DP 236.

Gaddita ~ae, *m.* also **Gadita** ~ae, *m.* A member of the tribe of Gad, Gadite: AC 8623.

Gadita: see **Gaddita**.

Gaetam: see **Gaetham**.

Gaetham, *indecl. m.* also **Gaetam**, *indecl. m.* Gatam, a son of Eliphaz and grandson of Esau: Gen. 36.11 (AC).

Gaḥam: see **Gacham**.

Galeed, *indecl. m.* Galeed, a heap of stones marking Jacob's covenant with Laban: Gen. 31.48 (AC).

Galilaea ~ae, *f.* The land of Galilee: *Dominus...ivit... in ~am* AE 50.1.

Gallia ~ae, *f.* France: AM 380.3.

Gallim, *indecl.* Gallim, a city of Benjamin north of Jerusalem: Isa. 10.30 (AC 1888.2).

Gallus ~i, *m.* A Frenchman: *Franci seu ~i* AM 103.2.

Gamadaeus ~i, *m.* also **Gammadaeus** ~i, *m.* One of the Gammadim, a Hebr. term whose meaning has been lost: Ezek. 27.11 (AC 3448.8).

Gammadaeus: see **Gamadaeus**.

Gareb, *indecl.* Gareb, a hill near Jerusalem: Jer. 31.39 (AC 9603.3).

Gath, *indecl.* Gath, one of five Philistine royal cities: 2 Sam. 1.20 (AC 3024.3).

Gebal ~lis, *m.* **1** Gebal, a region inhabited by Edom: Ps. 83.7 (AC 2468.14). **2** Gebal or Bibylus, a city between Beirut and Tripolis: Ezek. 27.9 (AC 6385.2).

Gebim, *indecl.* Gebim, a city of Benjamin: Isa. 10.31 (SS 15.1).

Genoveva ~ae, *f.* Geneviève, the patron saint of Paris, who lived in the 5th century: VR 826; UJ(C) 67.

Genua ~ae, *f.* Genoa: ES 5648.

Genuenses ~ium, *m. pl.* The people of Genoa, Genoese: *nauclerus factus, tunc captus a ~ibus* UJ(P) 80.

Gera, *indecl. m.* Gera, a son of Benjamin: Gen. 46.21 (AC).

Gerar, *indecl.* and ~aris, *m.* Gerar, an ancient city south-east of Gaza: Gen. 20.1 (AC).

Gerisim, *indecl.* also **Gerizim**, *indecl.* Gerizim, a mountain near Mt. Ebal: AC 3862.4.

Gerizim: see **Gerisim**.

Germania ~ae, *f.* Germany: VI 4; AM 380.3.

Germanus ~i, *m.* A native of Germany, German: VR 112.2.

Gerschom, *indecl. m.* also **Gershom**, *indecl. m.* Gershom, a son of Moses: Exod. 2.22 (AC).

Gerschon ~onis, *m.* also **Gershon** ~onis, *m.* Gershon, a son of Levi: Gen. 46.11 (AC).

Gerschonita ~ae, *m.* A Gershonite, a descendant of Gershon son of Levi: AC 3708.15.

Gershom: see **Gerschom**.

Gershon: see **Gerschon**.

Geschurita ~ae, *m.* A Geshurite, a member of a tribe that lived between Arabia and Philistia: 1 Sam. 27.8 (AC 1928.3).

Gethsemane, *indecl.* (Hebr.) A place close to Jerusalem: *de ultima tentatione in ~e* AC 1690.1.

Gibea ~ae, *m.* also **Gibeah** ~ae, *m.* Gibeah, a city in the mountains of Judah: Isa. 10.29 (AC 1888.2).

Gibeah: see **Gibea**.

Gibeon ~onis, *f.* A city in Palestine: Josh. 10.12 (SS 103.3).

Gibeonita ~ae, *m.* A Gibeonite, an inhabitant of Gibeon: AC 1097.2.

Gichon, *indecl.* also **Giḥon**, *indecl.* **1** Gihon, a river in the garden of Eden: Gen. 2.13 (AC). **2** Gihon, a place near Jerusalem: 1 Kgs. 1.45 (AC 2781.6).

Gideon ~onis, *m.* also **Guideon** ~onis, *m.* Gideon, the son of Joash: Judg. 8.13 (AC 1925.3); DP 96.6; AE 412.15.

Giḥon: see **Gichon**.

Gilead, *indecl.* and ~adis, *m.* A region, also a mountain, east of the Jordan: *ad terram ~adis* Zech. 10.10 (AC 8185.2); *montem ~ad* Gen. 31.21 (AC).

Gilgal, *indecl.* and ~lis, *m.* Gilgal, a place west of the Jordan river near Jericho: 2 Kgs. 4.38 (AC 3316.3).

Girgasaeus ~i, *m.* = **Girgaschita**: 3AD 4474.

Girgaschita ~ae, *m.* also **Girgashita** ~ae, *m.* An inhabitant of Girgash, Girgashite: Gen. 15.21 (AC).

Girgaschus ~i, *m.* also **Girgashus** ~i, *m.* = **Girgaschita**: Gen. 10.16 (AC).

Girgashita: see **Girgaschita**.

Girgashus: see **Girgaschus**.

Gisrita ~ae, *m.* also **Gizrita** ~ae, *m.* A Gezrite or Girzite, an inhabitant of Gezer: 1 Sam. 27.8 (AC 1928.3).

Gitthaeus ~i, *m.* A Gittite, an inhabitant of Gath: 2 Sam. 15.18 (AC 6180.2).

Gizrita: see **Gisrita**.

Goah, *indecl.* Goah, a place near Jerusalem to its east: Jer. 31.39 (AC 9603.3).

Godoschalcus ~i, *m.* also **Godoschalkus** ~i, *m.*, and **Godoskalchus** ~i, *m.* Gottschalk, a German theologian of the 9th century: VR 486.2.

Godoschalkus: see **Godoschalcus**.

Godoskalchus: see **Godoschalcus**.

Gog: see **Gogus**.

Gogus ~i, *m.* also **Gog**, *indecl. m.* Gog, the prince of Meshech and Tubal: Ezek. 38.18 (AE 400.9); Rev. 20.8 (AR).

Goliath: see **Goliathus**.

Goliathus ~i, *m.* also **Goliath**, *indecl. m.* Goliath, the giant from Gath whom David killed: FI 52.

Gomer, *indecl.* and ~eris, *m.* also **Gomerus** ~i, *m.* Gomer, a son of Japheth: Gen. 10.2 (AC).

Gomerus: see **Gomer**.

Gomorrha ~ae, *f.* also **Amora** ~ae, *f.*, **Amorra** ~ae, *f.*, and **Amorrha** ~ae, *f.* The city of Gomorrah: Isa. 13.19 (AE 357.17).

Gosan, *indecl.* also **Gozan**, *indecl.* Gozan, a river in Assyria: 2 Kgs. 17.6 (AC 1189).

Goschen, *indecl.* and ~enis also **Goshen**, *indecl.* and ~enis, *m.* Goshen, the part of Egypt where the Israelites lived during their long sojourn: Gen. 45.10 (AC).

Goshen: see **Goschen**.

Gothoburgus ~i, *m.* The city of Gothenburg or Göteborg in southern Sweden: VR 137.12.

Gozan: see **Gosan**.

Graecia ~ae, *f.* Greece: SS 21; AM 73.1.

Guideon: see **Gideon**.

Guni, *indecl. m.* Guni, a son of Naphtali: Gen. 46.24 (AC).

Gustavus ~i, *m.* Gustav I, king of Sweden from 1523-60: ES 3191; NE 24.

Gustavus (~i, *m.*) **Adolphus** ~i, *m.* Gustavus Adolphus, king of Sweden from 1611-32: ES 3191; NE 24.

H

Habakkuk: see **Habakuk**.

Habakuk, *indecl.* also **Habakkuk**, *indecl.* The prophet Habakkuk: DD 4.

Habel ~lis, *m.* also **Abel** ~lis, *m.* Abel, brother of Cain and son of Adam and Eve: Gen. 4.2 (AC).

Ḥabor: see **Chabor**.

Hadad[1], *indecl.* Hadad, a son of Bedad and a king of Edom: Gen. 36.35 (AC).

Ḥadad[2]: see **Chadar**.

Hadad-Eser ~eris, *m.* also spelled as two words **Hadad** (*indecl.*) **Ezer** ~eris, *m.* Hadadezer, king of the Zobah region in Syria: 2 Sam. 8.10 (AC 6917.3).

Hadad Ezer: see **Hadad-Eser**.

Hadadrimmon, *indecl.* Hadadrimmon, a place in the valley of Megiddo where Josiah died: Zech. 12.11 (AR 707.2).

Hadar, *indecl.* Hadar, the last of the ancient kings of Edom: Gen. 36.39 (AC).

Hadoram, *indecl.* Hadoram, a son of Joktan of the family of Shem: Gen. 10.27 (AC).

Hagar ~aris, *f.* The slave girl who bore Ishmael to Abram: Gen. 16.3 (AC).

Haggaeus ~i, *m.* The prophet Haggai: AE 365.34.

Ḥaggi: see **Chaggi**.

Hagraei ~orum, *m. pl.* The Hagrites or Hagarenes: Ps. 83.6 (AC 2468.14).

Ham[1], *indecl.* The name of a place where Chedorlaomer defeated the Zuzim: Gen. 14.5 (AC).

Ḥam[2]: see **Cham**.

Ḥamath: see **Chamath**.

Ḥamathus: see **Chamathus**.

Hamburgenses ~ium, *m. pl.* The inhabitants of Hamburg: VR 816.

Ḥamor: see **Chamor**.

Ḥamul: see **Chamul**.

Ḥanamel: see **Chanamel**.

Hanan: see **Baal-Chanan**.

Ḥananeel: see **Chananeel**.

Ḥananiah: see **Chanania**.

Ḥannah: see **Channa**.

Ḥanoch: see **Chanoch**.

Ḥanochus: see **Chanoch**.

Ḥanun: see **Chanun**.

Haran[1] ~anis, *m.* Haran, youngest brother of Abram and father of Lot: Gen.11.26 (AC).

Ḥaran[2]: see **Charan**.

Ḥareseth: see **Chir Charesch**.

Ḥavah: see **Evah**.

Ḥavilah: see **Chavillah**[1].

Ḥavillah: see **Chavillah**[2].

Ḥazarmaveth: see **Chazarmaveth**.

Ḥazeroth: see **Chazeroth**.

Ḥazezon-Tamar: see **Chazezon Thamar**.

Ḥazo: see **Chaso**.

Ḥazor: see **Chazor**.

Ḥeber: see **Cheber**.

Heberus: see **Eberus**.

Ḥebron: see **Chebron**[2].

Hecateus ~a ~um, *a.* (Gk.) Of Hecate, a Greek goddess of the underworld: *quod...Ulyssis comites...consperserit herbis ~is* AM 521.4.

Heerenhuteri: see **Herrenhuteri**.

Ḥelbon: see **Chesbon**[1].

Helicon ~onis, *m.* (Gk.) A mountain in Boeotia regarded as the home of the Muses: *quod gentiles in Graecia ~onem posuerint in alto monte* AE 405.54; VR 276.

Heliconeum ~i, *neut.* A mountain in the spiritual world named after Mount Helicon: *clivus...altior [vocatur] ~um* AM 151[a].1; VR 693.1.

Heliconides ~um, *f. pl.* A title of the Muses, maidens of Helicon: *ludi...literarii, quorum aliquos vocabant ~um* AM 207.6.

Hemam, *indecl.* Hemam, a son of Lotan and grandson of Seir: Gen. 36.22 (AC).

Heman ~anis, *m.* Heman, a wise man in the time of Solomon: 1 Kgs. 4.31 (AC 5223.2).

Ḥemdan: see **Chemdan**.

Heraclitus ~i, *m.* A Greek philosopher of the 6th-5th centuries BC: AM 182.8.

Ḥermon: see **Chermon**.

Ḥermonim: see **Chermonim**.

Herodes ~is, *m.* **1** Herod the Great, son of Antipater: Matt. 2.15 (AC 1462.6). **2** Herod Antipas, the son of Herod the Great: Mark 6.20 (AR 173.4).

Herrenhuteri ~orum, *m. pl.* also **Heerenhuteri** ~orum, *m. pl.* (AR Doc Ref.10 1st edn., UJ(C) 86 1st edn.), and **Herrnhuteri** ~orum, *m. pl.* (UJ(C) 86 Elliott). The members of the Moravian Church who built the town of Herrnhut in Saxony (1722-7): *cum Moravianis, qui etiam ~i vocantur* UJ(C) 86; VR 378.2.

Herrnhuteri: see **Herrenhuteri**.

Ḥesbon: see **Chesbon**[2].

Ḥeshbon: see **Chesbon**[2].

Ḥeth: see **Cheth**.

Ḥethus: see **Cheth**.

Hezechiel: see **Ezechiel**.

Hezekiah: see **Hiskias**.

Ḥezron: see **Chezron**.

Ḥiddekel: see **Chiddechel**.

Hierosolyma ~ae, *f.* (Gk. after Hebr.) also **Jerusalem**, *indecl.* **1** The city of Jerusalem: *urbs ~ae tempore Salomonis* VR 23.2. **2** *Nova ~a*, the New Jerusalem: *quae [Ecclesia] per Novam ~am in Apocalypsi intelligitur* AM 1. **3** The name of two cities in the world of spirits: UJ(C) 79; ES 3042.

Ḥilkiah: see **Chilkia**.

Hinnom, *indecl.* also **Hinnomus** ~i, *m.* Hinnom, a person whose name, or whose nameless son, was associated with a valley near Jerusalem where filth and human remains were burned: VR 619.1.

Hinnomus: see **Hinnom**.

Hiob: see **Hiobus**.

Hiobus ~bi, *m.* also **Hiob** ~bi, *m.* see also **Jobus**. Job: *liber ~bi...correspondentiis plenus est* SS 20.1.

Hippo ~onis, *m.* The name of a city, in full Hippo Regius, in modern Algeria: VR 840.

Ḥirah: see **Chirah**.

Hircanus ~i, *m.* John Hyrcanus, a Hasmonean ruler and high priest of Judea 134-104 BC: ES 6082.

Hischias: see **Hiskias**.

Hiskiah: see **Hiskias**.

Hiskias ~ae, *m.* also **Hezekiah** ~ae, *m.*, **Hischias** ~ae, *m.*, **Hiskiah** ~ae, *m.*, and **Hizkiah** ~ae, *m.* Hezekiah, king of Judah after his father Ahaz: 2 Kgs. 20.7 (AE 403.17).

Hispania ~ae, *f.* Spain: AR 752.2.

Hispanus ~i, *m.* An inhabitant of Spain, Spaniard: AM 103.2.

Ḥittita: see **Chittita**.

Ḥivus: see **Chivus**.

Hizkiah: see **Hiskias**.

Ḥobah: see **Chobah**.

Hollandia ~ae, *f.* The Netherlands, Holland: AM 521.4.

Hollandus ~i, *m.* An inhabitant of the Netherlands, Dutchman: VR 800.

Holmia ~ae, *f.* Stockholm: ES 3626.

Ḥolon: see **Cholon**.

Ḥoreb: see **Choreb**.

Ḥorebus: see **Choreb**.

Ḥori: see **Chori**.

Ḥorita: see **Chorita**.

Ḥormah: see **Chormah**.

Ḥoronaim: see **Choronaim**.

Hoscheas ~ae, *m.* also **Hosea** ~ae, *m.*, **Hoseas** ~ae, *m.*, and **Hosheas** ~ae, *m.* The prophet Hosea: DD 15.6; VI 79.3.

Hosea: see **Hoscheas**.

Hoseas: see **Hoscheas**.

Hosheas: see **Hoscheas**.

Ḥul: see **Chul**.

Hungaria ~ae, *f.* Hungary: ES 6059.

Ḥuppim: see **Chuppim**.

Ḥushai: see **Chuschai**.

Ḥusham: see **Chuscham**.

Ḥushim: see **Chuschim**.

Hymenaeus ~i, *m.* (Gk.) A man's name (see 2 Tim. 2.17): VR 378.2.

I

Ignatius ~i, *m.* Ignatius Loyola, founder of the Jesuit order: UJ(P) 67.

Iisaschar: see **Isaschar**.

Iishaius: see **Jishajus**.

Iiska ~ae, *f.* also **Jiskah** ~ae, *f.* Iscah, a daughter of Haran and sister of Lot: Gen. 11.29 (AC).

Immanuel, *indecl.* (Hebr.) Immanuel (meaning 'God with us'): *vocabit nomen ejus ~el* Isa. 7.14 (AC 2184.1); Isa. 8.8 (AE 304.28).

Indi ~orum, *m. pl.* The people of India, Indians: VR 64.1.

India ~ae, *f.* The Indian subcontinent, India: *unus...in ~a et alter in Europa* AC 1277; (pl.) South-East Asia generally, the Indies: *gentes et populi in Asia et in ~is* SS 105.3; *in ~as et illarum insulas* SS 117.

Indiani ~orum, *m. pl.* Indians: ES 6067.

Indus: see **Indi**.

Irad ~di, *m.* Irad, son of Enoch and grandson of Cain: Gen. 4.18 (AC).

Ir Chaeres: see **Ir Cheres**.

Ir Cheres, *indecl.* (Hebr.) also **Ir Chaeres**, *indecl.* Transliteration of Hebrew words meaning city of sunbeams (see quots.): *erunt quinque urbes in terra Aegypti loquentes labio Canaanis, et jurantes Jehovae Zebaoth, Ir Cheres dicetur cuique* Isa. 19.18 (AC 1462.2); *ir...est urbs,...cheres est coruscatio ut solis* AE 391.13; *cheres...in lingua Hebraea significat solem et ejus jubar* AE 654.7.

Irlandia ~ae, *f.* Ireland: AE 1070.2.

Isaac: see **Isacus**.

Isaacus: see **Isacus**.

Isabel: see **Jesabel**.

Isac: see **Isacus**.

Isacus ~i, *m.* also **Isaac**, *indecl.*, **Isaacus** ~i, *m.*, **Isac**, *indecl.*, **Isakus** ~i, *m.*, **Jischak**, *indecl.*, **Jischakus** ~i, *m.*, **Jishak**, *indecl.*, and **Jishakus** ~i, *m.* Isaac: *epulationes cum Abrahamo, ~o, et Jacobo* AM 3.3; SS 71.2; (form *Isac*) AM 29.

Isakus: see **Isacus**.

Isaschar, *indecl.* and ~aris, *m.* also **Iisaschar** ~aris, *m.*, **Jisaschar**, *indecl.* and ~aris, *m.*, **Jisascher**, *indecl.*, **Jischaskar** ~aris, *m.*, and **Jissascha**, *indecl.* Issachar, the son of Jacob: Gen. 30.18 (AC); as the name of one of the twelve tribes: Rev. 7.7 (AR).

Iscariot: see **Ischarioth**.

Ischajus: see **Jishajus**.

Ischarioth, *indecl.* and ~tis, *m.*, also **Iscariot**, *indecl.* and ~tis, *m.* Surname of the Judas who betrayed Jesus: AC 4751.3; AE 1145.9.

Ishmael: see **Jischmael**.

Ismael: see **Jischmael**.

Ismaelitae ~tarum, *m. pl.* also **Jischmaelitae** ~tarum, *m. pl.*, and **Jishmaelitae** ~tarum, *m. pl.* The descendants of Ishmael, Ishmaelites: AC 1358.

Israel ~lis, *m.* **1** The name given to Jacob, Israel: Gen. 32.28, 35.10 (AC); *filii ~lis*, the children of Israel: *nomina superscripta, quae sunt duodecim tribuum filiorum ~lis* Rev. 21.12 (AR). **2** The descendants of Israel, the Israelites: *audi ~l* Deut. 6.4 (VR 6.3); *praevaricationes ~lis* Amos 3.14 (DD 4).

Israelitae ~tarum, *m. pl.* The Israelites: AC 7272.1; AM 380.12.

Itali ~orum, *m. pl.* The people of Italy, Italians: AM 103.2; DP 212.2.

Italia ~ae, *f.* Italy: AM 521.4; SS 117.

Ithamar ~aris, *m.* Ithamar, a son of Aaron: Exod. 28.1 (AC).

Ittaeus: see **Itthaeus**.

Itthaeus ~i, *m.* also **Ittaeus** ~i, *m.* Ittai the Gittite, a Philistine in David's army: 2 Sam. 15.19 (AC 6180.2).

J

Jabal, *indecl.* Jabal, a son of Lamech: Gen. 4.20 (AC).

Jabbok, *indecl.* Jabbok, a small brook running from the hills of Bashan to the Jordan river: *~ok...terminus erat terrae Canaanis* Gen. 32.22 (AC).

Jabesch, *indecl.* also **Jabesh**, *indecl.* Jabesh, short for Jabesh Gilead, a city in Gad: 2 Sam. 2.5 (AC 6180.2).

Jabesh: see **Jabesch**.

Jachebed, *indecl. f.* also **Jochebed**, *indecl. f.* Jochebed, mother of Miriam, Aaron, and Moses: Exod. 6.20 (AC).

Jachin, *indecl.* **1** Jachin, a son of Simeon: Gen. 46.10 (AC). **2** The name of the right-hand pillar in the porch of Solomon's temple: 1 Kgs. 7.21 (AE 219.5).

Jachleel, *indecl.* also **Jaḥleel**, *indecl.* Jahleel, a son of Zebulun: Gen. 46.14 (AC).

Jachzeel, *indecl.* also **Jaḥzeel**, *indecl.* Jahzeel, a son of Naphtali: Gen. 46.24 (AC).

Jacob: see **Jacobus**.

Jacobus ~bi, *m.* also **Jacob** ~bi, *m.* and *indecl.* **1** Jacob, the son of Isaac: AC 6804.1; AM 6.1; (as a name for the people of Israel) Num. 24.5 (AE 799.3). **2** James, the disciple: *de Domino coram Petro, ~bo et Johanne transformato* SS 48; AE 8.2.

Jael ~lis, *f.* Jael, the wife of Heber and assassinator of Sisera: Judg. 5.6 (AC 10422.3).

Jaelam, *indecl.* Jalam, a son of Esau: Gen. 36.5 (AC).

Jaeser ~eris, *m.* and *indecl.* Jaazer, a city in Gilead: Isa. 16.18 = EVV 16.9 (AC 5480).

Jahaz, *indecl.* also **Jahzah** ~ae, *m.* Jahaz, a Levitical city in Reuben: Jer. 48.34 (AC 1825).

Jaḥleel: see **Jachleel**.

Jahzah: see **Jahaz**.

Jaḥzeel: see **Jachzeel**.

Jair ~iri, *m.* Jair, a Gileadite who was a judge over Israel: Judg. 10.3 (AC 2781.6).

Jamin, *indecl.* Jamin, a son of Simeon: Gen. 46.10 (AC).

Janitzares ~um, *m. pl.* also **Janitzari** ~orum, *m. pl.* The bodyguards of the Sultan of Turkey, Janissaries: ES 5062; UJ(P) 86.

Janitzari: see **Janitzares**.

Jannaeus: see **Alexander**, sense 3.

Jansenistae ~tarum, *m. pl.* The followers of Cornelius Jansen, Catholic Bishop of Ypres in early 17th century, Jansenists: AR 740.3.

Japheth, *indecl.* also **Japhethus** ~i, *m.*, and **Japhetus** ~i, *m.* Japheth, a son of Noah: Gen. 5.32 (AC).

Japhethus: see **Japheth**.

Japhetus: see **Japheth**.

Japonia ~ae, *f.* Japan: ES 857.

Jardenes: see **Jordanes**.

Jareb, *indecl.* Jareb, a king of Assyria: Hos. 5.13 (AC 5354.4).

Jared ~di, *m.* and *indecl.* Jared, a son of Mahalaleel: Gen. 5.15 (AC).

Jason ~onis, *m.* (in Gk. mythology) The hero who brought back the golden fleece, Jason: *quod glorientur ex numero virginitatum, sicut ex totidem velleribus aureis ~onis* AM 504.1.

Javan ~anis, *m.* and *indecl.* Javan, a son of Japheth: Gen. 10.2 (AC).

Javanimi ~orum, *m. pl.* (Hebr. pl. w. Lat. termination) The Greeks: *filios Hierosolymae vendidistis filiis ~orum* Joel 3.6 = Hebr. Bible 4.6 (AC 1151.6, AC 1197.4).

Jebusaeus ~i, *m.* A member of the Jebusites, a people of Canaan: Exod. 3.17 (AC).

Jebusita ~ae, *m.* = **Jebusaeus**: Exod. 34.11 (AC).

Jebusus ~i, *m.* A Jebusite: Gen. 10.16 (AC).

Jegar Sahadutha, *indecl.* Jegar Sahadutha, the name given by Laban to the heap of stones Jacob called Galeed: Gen. 31.47 (AC).

Jehoiachin ~ni, *m.* Jehoiachin, a son of Jehoiakim and a king of Judah: 2 Kgs. 25.27 (AC 5124.1).

Jehoiakimus: see **Jojakimus**.

Jehoramus ~i, *m.* Jehoram, a son of Ahab: 2 Kgs. 9.12 (AC 9188.5).

Jehoschua: see **Joschua**.

Jehosephus: see **Joseph**.

Jehoshua: see **Joschua**.

Jehu, *indecl.* **1** Jehu the prophet: 1 Kgs. 16.7 (AC 7619). **2** Jehu, king of Israel after Ahab: 2 Kgs. 9.22 (AR 134.3).

Jehuda: see **Jehudah**.

Jehudaeus: see **Judaeus**.

Jehudah ~ae, *m.* also **Jehuda** ~ae, *m.*, **Jehudas** ~ae, *m.*, **Judah** ~ae, *m.*, and **Judas** ~ae, *m.* **1** One of Jacob's sons, Judah: Gen. 29.35 (AC); AC 768.2. **2** The name of one of the twelve tribes of Israel: *ex tribu ~ae* Rev. 7.5 (AR).

Jehudas: see **Jehudah**.

Jehudith, *indecl. f.* Judith, a wife of Esau: Gen. 26.34 (AC).

Jehudius ~i, *m.* Jehudi, a man sent by the princes of Judah to fetch Baruch: Jer. 36.23 (AC 4763.2).

Jeminita ~ae, *m.* Someone of the tribe of Benjamin, a Benjamite: 1 Sam. 9.1 (AC 7836.3).

Jemuel, *indecl.* Jemuel, a son of Simeon: Gen. 46.10 (AC).

Jephuneh, *indecl.* also **Jephunneh**, *indecl.* Jephunneh, father of Caleb: Num. 14.6 (AC 4763.2).

Jephunneh: see **Jephuneh**.

Jerabal: see **Jerubbaal**.

Jerach, *indecl.* also **Jeraḥ**, *indecl.* Jerah, a son of Joktan of the family of Shem: Gen. 10.26 (AC).

Jeraḥ: see **Jerach**.

Jeremias ~ae, *m.* The prophet Jeremiah: SS 16; (as the name of a book of the Word) AC 6729.

Jericho, *indecl.* and ~untis, *gender uncertain.* The city of Jericho: *cum ceperunt urbem ~o* AE 55.2; *muri ~untis* VI 55.3.

Jerobabel: see **Jerubbaal**.

Jeroboam: see **Jeroboamus**.

Jeroboamus ~i, *m.* also **Jeroboam** ~mi, *m.* Jeroboam, the first king of the ten tribes of Israel: AC 878.8.

Jerochamus ~i, *m.* Jeroham, a grandfather of Samuel: 1 Sam. 1.1 (AC 7836.3).

Jerubaal: see **Jerubbaal**.

Jerubbaal ~lis, *m.* also **Jerabal** ~lis, *m.* (AC 4430.3 1st edn.), **Jerobabel** ~lis, *m.* (AC 4430.3 Autograph), and **Jerubaal** ~lis, *m.* (AC 4430.3 Tafel). Jerubbaal, the name given to Gideon by his father: Judg. 9.28 (AC 4430.3 3rd edn.).

Jerusalem: see **Hierosolyma**.

Jesabel ~lis, *f.* and *indecl.* also **Isabel** ~lis, *f.*, and **Jezabel** ~lis, *f.* and *indecl.* Jezebel: *vocatur Ecclesiae ...mulier Jesabel, ex eo quod per Isabelem, uxorem Achabi in Verbo* AE 159.1; AR 132.1.

Jeschurun, *indecl. m.* also **Jeshurun**, *indecl. m.* Jeshurun, a poetical collective name for the Israelites: *~un quem elegi* Isa. 44.2 (AC 8043.2); *Deus ~un* Deut. 33.26 (AE 36.4).

Jeshurun: see **Jeschurun**.

Jesuita ~ae, *m.* A member of the Roman Catholic order of the Society of Jesus, Jesuit: *qui se ex societate Domini seu ~as vocant* AC 8383; ES 4681.

Jesus ~u, *m.* (Gk. after Hebr.) (acc. *~um*, abl. *~u*) The name of the Lord in His incarnation, Jesus: *Filius Dei...vocatur Salvator, et in mundo ~us, hoc est, Salus* VR 135.5.

Jetheth, *indecl.* Jetheth, a leader in Edom: Gen. 36.40 (AC).

Jethro ~onis, *m.* Jethro, the father-in-law of Moses: Exod. 3.1 (AC).

Jetur, *indecl.* Jetur, a son of Ishmael: Gen. 25.15 (AC).

Jeusch ~schi, *m.* also **Jeush** ~shi, *m.* Jeush, a son of Esau: Gen. 36.5 (AC).

Jeush: see **Jeusch**.

Jezabel: see **Jesabel**.

Jezer, *indecl.* Jezer, a son of Naphtali: Gen. 46.24 (AC).

Jidlaph, *indecl.* Jidlaph, a son of Nahor and a nephew of Abraham: Gen. 22.22 (AC).

Jimna, *indecl.* also **Jimnah**, *indecl.* Imnah, a son of Asher: Gen. 46.17 (AC).

Jimnah: see **Jimna**.

Jisaschar: see **Isaschar**.

Jisascher: see **Isaschar**.

Jischaius: see **Jishajus**.

Jischajus: see **Jishajus**.

Jischak: see **Isacus**.

Jischakus: see **Isacus**.

Jischaskar: see **Isaschar**.

Jischbakus ~i, *m.* also **Jishbakus** ~i, *m.* Ishbak, a son of Abraham: Gen. 25.2 (AC).

Jischmael ~lis, *m.* and *indecl.* also **Ishmael** ~lis, *m.*, **Ismael** ~lis, *m.*, and **Jishmael** ~lis, *m.* and *indecl.* Ishmael: AC 8314.3; Jer. 41.2 (AE 374.6).

Jischmaelitae: see **Ismaelitae**.

Jischva, *indecl.* also **Jishvah**, *indecl.* Ishvah, a son of Asher: Gen. 46.17 (AC).

Jischvi, *indecl.* also **Jishvi**, *indecl.* Ishvi, a son of Asher: Gen. 46.17 (AC).

Jishaius: see **Jishajus**.

Jishajus ~i, *m.* also **Iishaius** ~i, *m.*, **Ischajus** ~i, *m.*, **Jischaius** ~i, *m.*, **Jischajus** ~i, *m.*, and **Jishaius** ~i, *m.* Jesse: *exibit virga de trunco ~i* Isa. 11.1 (DD 6).

Jishak: see **Isacus**.

Jishakus: see **Isacus**.

Jishbakus: see **Jischbakus**.

Jishmael: see **Jischmael**.

Jishmaelitae: see **Ismaelitae**.

Jishvah: see **Jischva**.

Jishvi: see **Jischvi**.

Jiskah: see **Iiska**.

Jisreel, *indecl.* and ~lis, *m.* (Hebr.) also **Jizreel** ~lis, *m.* Jezreel, the son of Hosea: Hos. 1.4 (DD 15.6).

Jissascha: see **Isaschar**.

Jithran, *indecl.* Ithran, a son of Dishon and a grandson of Seir: Gen. 36.26 (AC).

Jizhar ~aris, *m.* Izhar, a son of Kohath and a grandson of Levi: Exod. 6.18 (AC).

Jizreel: see **Jisreel**.

Joabus ~i, *m.* Joab, a nephew of David and a captain in his army: AC 9014.5.

Joachus ~i, *m.* also **Joaḥus** ~i, *m.* Joah, a son of Asaph and attendant to Hezekiah: AC 4763.1.

Joaḥus: see **Joachus**.

Joas, *indecl.* also **Joash**, *indecl.* Joash, a son of Jehoahaz and a king of Israel: AC 2709.3.

Joash: see **Joas**.

Job, *indecl.* Job, a son of Issachar: Gen. 46.13 (AC).

Jobab, *indecl.* also **Johab**, *indecl.* **1** Jobab, a son of Joktan of the family of Shem: Gen. 10.29 (AC). **2** Jobab, a son of Zerah and a king of Edom: Gen. 36.33 (AC).

Jobus ~i, *m.* see also **Hiobus**. Job: ES 4367; (as the name of a book) AC 46.2.

Jochebed: see **Jachebed**.

Jochschan ~anis, *m.* also **Jokshan** ~anis, *m.* Jokshan, a son of Abraham: Gen. 25.3 (AC).

Joel ~lis, *m.* The prophet Joel, esp. as the title of a book of the Word: DD 4.

Johab: see **Jobab**.

Johannes ~is, *m.* **1** The disciple John: AM 6.2; (as the author of the fourth Gospel) VR 2.3; (as the author of Revelation) AR 5. **2** John the Baptist: AM 117.

Jojakimus ~i, *m.* also **Jehoiakimus** ~i, *m.* Jehoiakim: AE 481.4.

Jokshan: see **Jochschan**.

Joktan ~anis, *m.* and *indecl.* Joktan, a son of Eber of the family of Shem: Gen. 10.25 (AC).

Jonas ~ae, *m.* Jonah: SS 29; (as the name of a book) AC 6726; (as the father of the apostle Simon) John 1.42 (AE 411.13).

Jonathan ~anis, *m.* Jonathan: SS 29.

Jordan: see **Jordanes**.

Jordanes ~is, *m.* also **Jardenes** ~is, *m.*, and **Jordan**, *indecl.* The river Jordan: VI 55.3; Gen. 13.10 (AC).

Joschia ~ae, *m.* also **Joshiah** ~ae, *m.*, and **Joshias** ~ae, *m.* Josiah: AC 6804.7 (2 Kgs. 23.2).

Joschua ~ae, *m.* also **Jehoschua** ~ae, *m.*, **Jehoshua** ~ae, *m.*, **Joschuah** ~ae, *m.*, **Joshua** ~ae, *m.*, and **Josua** ~ae, *m.* **1** Joshua: Deut. 34.9 (DD 48.1); (as the name of a book) AC 6752.6. **2** Joshua the high priest: Zech. 3.1 (AE 740.16).

Joschuah: see **Joschua**.

Joseph, *indecl.* also **Jehosephus** ~i, *m.*, and **Josephus** ~i, *m.* **1** Joseph the son of Jacob: Gen. 30.24 (AC); as a synonym for the tribe of Ephraim: Rev. 7.8 (AR). **2** Joseph the husband of Mary: Matt. 1.18 (DD 21).

Josephus: see **Joseph**.

Joshiah: see **Joschia**.

Joshias: see **Joschia**.

Joshua: see **Joschua**.

Josua: see **Joschua**.

Jubal, *indecl*. Jubal, a son of Lamech: Gen. 4.21 (AC).

Judaea ~ae, *f.* The land of the Jews, Judaea: AC 3654.1.

Judaeus ~i, *m.* also **Jehudaeus** ~i, *m.* A Jew: *Israelitae et ~i* AC 6997.3; *quis non ex aspectu cognoscit ~um?* AM 202.2.

Judah: see **Jehudah**.

Judas ~ae, *m.* **1** Judah, one of Jacob's sons: AC 3858.6; VR 845. **2** Judas Iscariot, the traitorous disciple: DD 13; AE 433.37. **3** The apostle Jude: AE 735.4.

Juno ~onis, *f.* The Roman goddess Juno: VR 17.2.

Jupiter Jovis, *m.* **1** The principal god of the ancient Romans, Jupiter: *Jovem, ita forte vocatum a Jehovah* VR 9.3. **2** The planet Jupiter: *incolis planetae Jovis* AC 7751; ES 1113.

K

Kadesch, *indecl.* and ~schi, *m.* also **Kadesh**, *indecl.* and ~shi, *m.* Kadesh, a place comprising the southern border of Canaan and the western one of Edom: Gen. 14.7 (AC).

Kadesh: see **Kadesch**.

Kadmonita ~ae, *m.* (Hebr.) A Kadmonite: Gen. 15.19 (AC).

Kainus: see **Cain**.

Kalach, *indecl.* also **Calaḥ**, *indecl.* Calah, an ancient Assyrian city: Gen. 10.11 (AC).

Kalebus: see **Chalebus**.

Kalkol ~lis, *m.* Chalcol, a wise man in the time of Solomon: 1 Kgs. 5.11 (AC 5223.2).

Kalneh, *indecl.* also **Calneh**, *indecl.* Calneh, a place near Babylon: Gen. 10.10 (AC).

Kana ~ae, *f.* Cana of Galilee, the village where Jesus turned water into wine: AR 316.3.

Kaphtor: see **Caphtor**.

Kaphthorim, *indecl. pl.* also **Caphtorim**, *indecl. pl.* The Caphtorim, people from Caphtor: Gen. 10.14 (AC).

Karmi, *indecl.* also **Carmi**, *indecl.* Carmi, a son of Reuben: Gen. 46.9 (AC).

Karnaim: see **Asteroth Karnaim**.

Kasluchim, *indecl.* also **Casluḥim**, *indecl.* The Casluhim, a tribe descended from Mizraim son of Ham: Gen. 10.14 (AC).

Kebar, *indecl.* Chebar, a Chaldean tributary of the Euphrates river: Ezek. 3.15 (AC 728.3).

Kedar ~aris, *m.* Kedar, a son of Ishmael: Gen. 25.13 (AC); Ps. 120.5 (AC 3268.5); (standing for Arabia) *quod ~ar sit Arabia ex sequentibus locis patet* AC 3268.3.

Kedemah: see **Kedmah**.

Kedmah, *indecl.* also **Kedemah**, *indecl.* Kedemah, a son of Ishmael: Gen. 25.15 (AC).

Kedorlaomer ~eri, *m.* Chedorlaomer, a king of Elam in the time of Abraham: Gen. 14.4 (AC).

Kehath ~thi, *m.* and *indecl.* Kohath, second son of Levi and an ancestor of Moses: Gen. 46.11 (AC).

Kehathita: see **Kehatita**.

Kehatita ~ae, *m.* also **Kehathita** ~ae, *m.* A descendant of Kohath son of Levi, Kohathite: AC 3708.15.

Kemosch ~schi, *m.* also **Chemos**, *indecl.*, and **Kemosh** ~shi, *m.* Chemosh, a national idol of the Moabites and Ammonites: Num. 21.29 (SS 103).

Kemosh: see **Kemosch**.

Kemuel, *indecl.* Kemuel, a son of Nahor and nephew of Abraham: Gen. 22.21 (AC).

Kenan ~anis, *m.* and *indecl.* Kenan, son of Enosh and grandson of Seth: Gen. 5.9 (AC).

Kenas, *indecl.* also **Kenaz**, *indecl.* Kenaz, a son of Eliphaz and grandson of Esau: Gen. 36.11 (AC).

Kenaz: see **Kenas**.

Kenissita ~ae, *m.* also **Kenizzita** ~ae, *m.* A Kenizzite, member of one of the ten tribes in Canaan in the time of Abraham: Gen. 15.19 (AC).

Kenita ~ae, *m.* A Kenite, member of one of the ten tribes in Canaan in the time of Abraham: Gen. 15.19 (AC).

Kenizzita: see **Kenissita**.

Kephah ~ae, *m.* (Syriac) The name given to Simon Peter: *tu vocaberis ~ah* John 1.42 (AE 411.13); *~ah significat petram in lingua Syriaca* AE 411.13.

Kerem: see **Beth Kerem**.

Kerethim, *indecl.* The Cherethites, a Philistine tribe in southern Canaan: Zeph. 2.5 (AC 2323.3).

Kerioth, *indecl.* also **Kirioth**, *indecl.* Kerioth, a city of Moab: Jer. 48.24 (AC 2608).

Kesed, *indecl.* Chesed, a son of Nahor and nephew of Abraham: Gen. 22.22 (AC).

Kesib, *indecl.* also **Kezib**, *indecl.* Chezib, a Canaanite town that afterwards belonged to Judah: Gen. 38.5 (AC).

Keturah ~ae, *f.* Keturah, Abraham's second wife, whom he married after Sarah had died: Gen. 25.1 (AC).

Kezib: see **Kesib**.

Kibroth Thaavah, *indecl.* Kibroth Hattaavah, the first stop after Mt. Sinai in the Israelites' wanderings: Deut. 9.22 (AC 8588.3 Autograph).

Kiiun: see **Kijun**.

Kijun, *indecl.* also **Kiiun**, *indecl.* Chiun, an idol worshipped by the Israelites: Amos 5.26 (AC 1715).

Kilmad, *indecl.* Chilmad, a region between Assyria and Arabia: Ezek. 27.23 (AC 9854.2).

Kir, *indecl.* **1** Kir, a city of Moab that may be the same as **Chir Charesch** q.v.: Isa. 15.1 (AC 6000.8). **2** Kir, the name of an Assyrian district between the Caspian Sea and the Black Sea, and the name of its inhabitants: Isa. 22.6 (AC 2851.13); AC 9340.6.

Kir-Chareseth: see **Chir Charesch**.

Kir-Cheres: see **Chir Charesch**.

Kir Ḥareseth: see **Chir Charesch**.

Kiriath Arba ~ae, *f.* and *indecl.* see also **Chebron**[2]. Kiriath Arba, a city in the hill country of Judea south of Jerusalem, also called Hebron: Gen. 23.2 (AC).

Kiriathaim, *indecl.* Kiriathaim, a city of Reuben east of the Jordan: Jer. 48.1 (AC 2468.7).

Kiriathaim, Shave: see **Schave Kirjathaim**.

Kirioth: see **Kerioth**.

Kisch, *indecl.* Kish, the father of Saul: 1 Sam. 9.1 (AC 7836.3).

Kittaeus: see **Kitthaeus**.

Kitthaeus ~i, *m.* also **Kittaeus** ~i, *m.* see also **Kitthim**. An inhabitant of Cyprus, Cypriot: Jer. 2.10 (AC 3268.6).

Kitthim, *indecl.* also **Kittim**, *indecl.* see also **Kitthaeus**. **1** Kittim, a son of Javan: Gen. 10.4 (AC). **2** The Chittim or Cypriots: AC 1156.

Kittim: see **Kitthim**.

Korach[1] ~chi, *m.* Korah, a son of Izhar and great-grandson of Levi: Exod. 6.21 (AC).

Korach[2] ~chi, *m.* and *indecl.* also **Koraḥ** ~ḥi, *m.* and *indecl.* Korah, a son of Esau: Gen. 36.5 (AC).

Korachita ~ae, *m.* Korahite, a descendant of Korah son of Izhar: Exod. 6.24 (AC).

Koraḥ: see **Korach**[2].

Koresch: see **Choresch**.

Koresh: see **Choresch**.

Kub, *indecl.* Chub, a people in alliance with Egypt in the time of Nebuchadnezzar: Ezek. 30.5 (AC 1164.2).

Kusch, *indecl. m.* also **Cusch**, *indecl. m.*, **Cuschus** ~i, *m.*, **Cush**, *indecl. m.*, **Cushim**, *indecl. pl.*, **Cushus** ~i, *m.*, **Kuschim**, *indecl. pl.*, **Kuschus** ~i, *m.*, **Kush**, *indecl. m.*, and **Kushus** ~i, *m.* **1** Cush, a son of Ham: Gen. 10.6 (AC). **2** Ethiopia: *per Kusch seu Aethiopiam* AC 1163.6. **3** Ethiopians (Hebr. pl. *Kuschim*): Dan. 11.43 (AC 1164.6).

Kuschan ~anis, *m.* also **Kushan** ~anis, *m.* Cushan, a place in the land of Midian: Hab. 3.7 (AC 3242.5).

Kuschim: see **Kusch**.

Kuschus: see **Kusch**.

Kush: see **Kusch**.

Kushan: see **Kuschan**.

Kushus: see **Kusch**.

L

Laban ~anis, *m.* and *indecl.* Laban, brother of Rebekah and father of Leah and Rachel: Gen. 24.29 (AC).

Laḥai: see **Beer-lachai-roi**.

Laish: see **Lajish**.

Lajisch: see **Lajish**.

Lajish, *indecl.* also **Laish**, *indecl.*, and **Lajisch**, *indecl.* Laish, a Sidonian city at the extreme northern end of the Holy Land: Isa. 10.30 (SS 15.1).

Lamech ~chi, *m.* and *indecl.* **1** Lamech, son of Methushael and descendant of Cain: Gen. 4.18 (AC). **2** Lamech, son of Methuselah and descendant of Seth: Gen. 5.26 (AC).

Laodicea ~ae, *f.* A city of Asia Minor: Rev. 1.11 (AR).

Lappones ~um, *m. pl.* The inhabitants of Lapland, the Lapps: ES 419.

Lapponia ~ae, *f.* Lapland: ES 419.

Lascha, *indecl.* Lasha, a place at the southernmost part of the Holy Land: Gen. 10.19 (AC).

Lazarus ~i, *m.* Lazarus who was raised from the dead by the Lord: John 11.1 (AC 9231.3); also, the beggar in the parable: Luke 16.22 (AC 6804.2).

Lea: see **Leah**.

Leah ~ae, *f.* also **Lea** ~ae, *f.* Leah, Laban's older daughter and Jacob's first wife: Gen. 29.16 (AC).

Lehabim, *indecl.* Lehabim, a son of Mizraim: Gen. 10.13 (AC).

Leibnitius: see **Leibnitzius**.

Leibnitzius ~i, *m.* also **Leibnitius** ~i, *m.* The philosopher Gottfried Wilhelm von Leibniz (1646-1716): DP 289.2.

Letuschim, *indecl.* also **Letushim**, *indecl.* Letushim, a son of Dedan and great-grandson of Abraham: Gen. 25.3 (AC).

Letushim: see **Letuschim**.

Leumim, *indecl.* also **Leummim**, *indecl.* Leummim, a son of Dedan and great-grandson of Abraham: Gen. 25.3 (AC).

Leummim: see **Leumim**.

Levi, *indecl. m.* (Hebr.) (acc. *Levin* AC 7231.1) **1** Levi: Gen. 29.34 (AC). **2** App. for the man's name Lewis: ES 5987.

Levita ~ae, *m.* A member of the tribe of Levi, Levite: Exod. 6.25 (AC).

Libanon: see **Libanus**.

Libanus ~i, *m.* also **Libanon**, *indecl.* The mountain of Lebanon: *~us per Magnificum cadet* Isa. 10.34 (SS 15.1).

Libni, *indecl.* Libni, a son of Gershon and grandson of Levi: Exod. 6.17 (AC).

Libya: see **Lybia**.

Lilith, *indecl. f.* (Hebr.) Lilith, a female evil spirit of ancient Semitic legend: *satyrus socio suo obviabit, imo quiescet ibi ~ith* Isa. 34.14 (VR 575).

Lipsia ~ae, *f.* (locative *~ae*) Leipzig, a city in Germany: SE 9.

Londinum ~i, *neut.* London in England: *in opere... ~i...edito* SS 10; *Angli e ~o* ES 5012; also, a city of the same name in the world of spirits: UJ(P) 292. (n.b. There seems to be no example of the usual form *Londinium.*)

Loretto, *indecl.* Loreto, a Roman Catholic episcopal see and pilgrimage resort in the Marches region of Italy, in the province of Ancona: AR 752.2.

Lot: see **Lothus**.

Lotan ~anis, *m.* Lotan, a son of Seir the Horite: Gen. 36.20 (AC).

Loth: see **Lothus**.

Lotharingia ~ae, *f.* Lorraine, a former province of north-east France: *cardinalis e ~a* AR 914.2.

Lothus ~i, *m.* also **Lot**, *indecl.*, **Loth**, *indecl.*, and **Lotus** ~i, *m.* Lot: *amici uxoris ~i* AM 232.4; AC 598.3; AC 1428.

Lotus: see **Lothus**.

Lubim, *indecl.* The Lubim, inhabitants of an area of North Africa west of Egypt: Dan. 11.43 (AC 1164.4).

Luca ~ae, *m.* The evangelist Luke: AC 29.2.

Luchith, *indecl.* also **Luḥith**, *indecl.* Luhith, a city of Moab: Isa. 15.5 (AC 1825.2).

Lud, *indecl.* Lud, a son of Shem: Gen. 10.22 (AC).

Ludim, *indecl.* **1** Ludim, a son of Mizraim: Gen. 10.13 (AC). **2** The Ludim, descendants of Lud (see also **Ludius**): AC 1195.

Ludovicus ~i, *m.* Louis the Fourteenth (1638-1715), king of France (1643-1715): *datum est loqui cum ~o XIV., avo regis Galliarum hodie regnantis* UJ(C) 60.

Luḥith: see **Luchith**.

Lus, *indecl.* also **Luz**, *indecl.* Luz, a city in Canaan that was later named Bethel: Gen. 28.19 (AC).

Lutherus ~i, *m.* Martin Luther (1483-1527), the German reformer: AM 28.

Luz: see **Lus**.

Lybia ~ae, *f.* (ad. Gk.) also **Libya** ~ae, *f.* The country to the west of Egypt, Libya: AC 1163; CI 327; AE 391.31.

M

Maacah: see **Maachah**.

Maachah, *indecl.* also **Maacah**, *indecl.* Maachah, a son of Nahor and nephew of Abraham: Gen. 22.24 (AC).

Mabara ~ae, *f.* also **Mebara** ~ae, *f.* Transliteration of a Hebr. word which Swedenborg, prob. following Schm., takes to be a proper name, but which appears as 'passage', 'pass', or 'ridge' in English translations of the Bible: Isa. 10.29 (AC 1888.2); SS 15.1.

Macchiavelista: see **Machiavellista**.

Macedoniani ~orum, *m. pl.* The Macedonians, a heretical sect founded by Macedonius, Bishop of Constantinople (AD 352-62): VR 378.2.

Machalath, *indecl. f.* also **Maḥalath**, *indecl. f.* Mahalath, a daughter of Ishmael and one of Esau's wives: Gen. 28.9 (AC).

Machanaim, *indecl.* also **Maḥanaim**, *indecl.* Mahanaim, a town east of the Jordan river and south of the Jabbok brook: Gen. 32.2 (AC); *~im in lingua originali significat bina castra* AC 4237.

Machiavellista ~ae, *m.* also **Macchiavelista** ~ae, *m.* A follower of Machiavelli: VR 462.5.

Machiavellus ~i, *m.* The Italian writer Machiavelli (1460-1527): AR 578.2.

Machir, *indecl.* Machir, a son of Manasseh and grandson of Joseph: Gen. 50.23 (AC).

Machli, *indecl.* Mahali, a son of Merari and grandson of Levi: Exod. 6.19 (AC).

Machpela ~ae, *f.* and *indecl.* also **Machpelah** ~ae, *f.* and *indecl.* Machpelah, Abraham's burial place: AC 2935.1.

Machpelah: see **Machpela**.

Madai, *indecl.* Madai, a son of Japheth and grandson of Noah: Gen. 10.2 (AC).

Magdiel, *indecl.* Magdiel, a leader of Edom: Gen. 36.43 (AC).

Magog, *indecl.* also **Magogus** ~i, *m.* Magog, a son of Japheth, and the descendants named for him who inhabited Scythia in northern Europe and Asia: Gen. 10.2 (AC).

Magogus: see **Magog**.

Mahalalel ~lis, *m.* and *indecl.* Mahalaleel, a son of Kenan and great-grandson of Seth: Gen. 5.13 (AC).

Maḥalath: see **Machalath**.

Maḥanaim: see **Machanaim**.

Mahumedes ~is, *m.* Mohammed, the founder of Islam (AD 570-632): UJ 50.2; (of a spurious Mohammed) UJ(P) 81.

Malachias ~ae, *m.* The prophet Malachi, esp. as the name of a book of the Word: *a primo capite Esajae usque ad ultimum ~ae* SS 113.

Malchiel: see **Malkiel**.

Malchizedech: see **Malkizedech**.

Malchizedek: see **Malkizedech**.

Malkiel, *indecl.* also **Malchiel**, *indecl.* Malchiel, a son of Beriah and grandson of Asher: Gen. 46.17 (AC).

Malkizedech ~chi, *m.* and *indecl.* also **Malchizedech** ~chi, *m.*, **Malchizedek** ~ki, *m.*, **Malkizedechus** ~i, *m.*, and **Malkizedeck** ~ki, *m.* and *indecl.* Melchizedek, a priest and king in Abraham's time: Gen. 14.18 (AC).

Malkizedechus: see **Malkizedech**.

Malkizedeck: see **Malkizedech**.

Mamre[1], *indecl. m.* Mamre the Amorite, an ally of Abram: Gen. 14.13 (AC).

Mamre[2], *indecl.* Mamre, another name for Hebron, or part of Hebron: Gen. 23.19 (AC).

Manachath, *indecl.* also **Manaḥath**, *indecl.* Manahath, a son of Shobal and grandson of Seir: Gen. 36.23 (AC).

Manaḥath: see **Manachath**.

Manichaei ~orum, *m. pl.* The name of a heretical sect, the Manichees: VR 378.2.

Manoach ~chi, *m.* also **Manoachus** ~i, *m.*, and **Manoahus** ~i, *m.* Manoah, father of Samson: AC 8581.6.

Manoachus: see **Manoach**.

Manoahus: see **Manoach**.

Maphaata ~ae, *m.* also **Mephaata** ~ae, *m.* Mephaath, a Levitical city in Reuben: Jer. 48.21 (AC 2608).

Marah, *indecl.* Marah, the first stop of the Israelites east of the Red Sea: Exod. 15.23 (AC).

Marcionita ~ae, *m.* A follower of Marcion, a heretic of the 2nd century: VR 378.2.

Marcus ~i, *m.* Mark, the author of the second gospel: VI 66.1.

Marescha, *indecl.* Mareshah, a fortified city in the plain of Judah: Mic. 1.15 (AC 4816).

Maria ~ae, *f.* Mary, the mother of Jesus: AM 119; VR 94; also, Mary Magdalene and other women: Matt. 28.1 (AE 400.14); *Marthae soror ~a* Luke 10.39 (2IB s.v. 'audire', p. 167 Tafel).

Mars ~rtis, *m.* The planet Mars: *planeta ~rtis* AC 7171; *spiritus ~rtis* AC 7475.

Martha ~ae, *f.* Martha, sister of Mary and Lazarus: John 11.27 (AC 3008.1).

Masch, *indecl.* also **Mash**, *indecl.* Mash, a son of Aram and grandson of Shem: Gen. 10.23 (AC).

Mash: see **Masch**.

Masoretae ~tarum, *m. pl.* also **Masorethae** ~tharum, *m. pl.* The Massoretes, the Jewish scholars who preserved the traditional text of the Old Testament: SS 13.4.

Masorethae: see **Masoretae**.

Masrekah ~ae, *m.* Masrekah, a place in Edom between Petra and Shobek: Gen. 36.36 (AC).

Massah, *indecl.* see also **Meribah**. Massah, a place also called Meribah where the wandering Israelites grumbled about the lack of water: *~ah...in lingua originali significat tentationem* Exod. 17.7 (AC).

Matred, *indecl. f.* Matred, mother of Mehetabel: Gen. 36.39 (AC).

Matthaeus ~i, *m.* The author of the first gospel, Matthew: AC 34.1.

Mebara: see **Mabara**.

Mechujael, *indecl.* also **Meḥujael**, *indecl.* Mehujael, son of Irad and great-grandson of Cain: Gen. 4.18 (AC).

Medan ~anis, *m.* Medan, a son of Abraham: Gen. 25.2 (AC).

Medba ~ae, *f.* also **Medeba** ~ae, *f.* Medeba, a plain and city in Reuben south-east of Heshbon: Isa. 15.2 (AC 3301.9).

Medea ~ae, *f.* (Gk.) In Gk. mythology, the princess of Colchis who was famous as a sorceress; but in AM 521.4 this name is apparently an error for Circe.

Medeba: see **Medba**.

Media ~ae, *f.* The country of the Medes: *regum ~ae* Jer. 51.11 (DD 48.2).

Mediolanum ~i, *neut.* see also **Milanum**. A city of northern Italy, Milan: ES 5648.

Medus ~i, *m.* An inhabitant of Media, Mede: *ecce Ego excitans contra eos ~um* Isa. 13.17 (AE 242.16).

Medusa ~ae, *f.* (Gk.) The Gorgon credited by Greek mythology with the power to turn to stone: SE 66.2.

Megiddon ~onis, *m.* and *indecl.* Megiddo, a city in the plain of Jezreel north-east of Mt. Carmel: *amor ex celsitudine [significatur] per ~onem in lingua vetusta Hebraea, ut patet a significatione ejus in lingua Arabica* AR 707.2.

Mehetabel, *indecl. f.* Mehetabel, wife of King Hadar of Edom: Gen. 36.39 (AC).

Meḥujael: see **Mechujael**.

Melanchthon: see **Melanchton**.

Melanchthonismus: see **Melanchtonismus**.

Melanchton ~onis, *m.* also **Melanchthon** ~onis, *m.*, **Melancthon** ~onis, *m.*, and **Melancton** ~onis, *m.* Melanchthon (1497-1560), the leading Protestant: AM 28; VR 64.1.

Melanchtonismus ~i, *m.* also **Melanchthonismus** ~i, *m.* The doctrine of Melanchthon: AE 1176.2.

Melancthon: see **Melanchton**.

Melancton: see **Melanchton**.

Meletiani ~orum, *m. pl.* The followers of the schismatic Meletius: VR 378.2.

Menasche ~is, *m.* (acc. *~en*) (Hebr.) also **Menascheh**, *indecl.*, **Menashe** ~es, *m.* (gen. also *~is*, dat. *~i*, acc. *~en*, abl. *~e*), **Menasheh**, *indecl.*, **Menasse** ~es, *m.* and *indecl.* (acc. *~en*, abl. *~e*), **Menasseh**, *indecl.*, and **Menassis** ~is, *m.* The name of Joseph's elder son: Gen. 41.51 (AC); the name of one of the twelve tribes of Israel, Manasseh: Rev. 7.6 (AE 39.3); Rev. 7.6 (AR).

Menascheh: see **Menasche**.

Menashe: see **Menasche**.

Menasheh: see **Menasche**.

Menasse: see **Menasche**.

Menasseh: see **Menasche**.

Menassis: see **Menasche**.

Menius ~i, *m.* (?) (Hebr. *meni*) Destiny as the name of a god: *impletis ~o libamen* Isa. 65.11 (AC 4581.7).

Mephaata: see **Maphaata**.

Mephiboschetus ~i, *m.* also **Mephiboshethus** ~i, *m.* Mephibosheth, a son of Jonathan and grandson of Saul: AC 2165.1.

Mephiboshethus: see **Mephiboschetus**.

Merari, *indecl.* Merari, a son of Levi: Gen. 46.11 (AC).

Merarita ~ae, *m.* A descendant of Merari, Merarite: AC 3708.15.

Mercurius ~i, *m.* **1** The god of the Romans corresponding to Gk. Hermes, Mercury: VR 17.2. **2** The planet Mercury: *de spiritibus planetae ~i* AC 6702.

Meribah, *indecl.* (pl. **Meriboth** AC 1678.2) see also **Massah**. Meribah, a place also called Massah between Sin and Mt. Sinai: Exod. 17.7 (AC).

Meriboth: see **Meribah**.

Merodachus: see **Evilmerodachus**.

Mesahab, *indecl.* also **Mezahab**, *indecl.* Mezahab, parent of Matred and grandparent of Mehetabel: Gen. 36.39 (AC).

Mescha, *indecl.* and ~ae, *f.* also **Mesha**, *indecl.* and ~ae, *f.* Mesha, a place in south-east Arabia: Gen. 10.30 (AC).

Meschech, *indecl.* and ~chi, *m.* also **Meshech**, *indecl.* and ~chi, *m.* Meshech, a son of Japheth: Gen. 10.2 (AC).

Mesha: see **Mescha**.

Meshech: see **Meschech**.

Mesopotamia ~ae, *f.* (Gk.) The country between the rivers Tigris and Euphrates, Mesopotamia: SS 102.1.

Messias ~ae, *m.* The Messiah: *sciunt etiam Judaei quod venturus ~as* AC 250; *Deus ~as*, God the Messiah (used in AD and early part of ES in place of *Dominus*): ES 154; 1AD 1515.

Methuschael, *indecl.* also **Methushael**, *indecl.* Methusael, a son of Mehujael and father of Lamech: Gen. 4.18 (AC).

Methuschelach ~chi, *m.*, **Methushelaḥ** ~ḥi, *m.* Methuselah, a son of Enoch and father of Lamech: Gen. 5.22 (AC).

Methushael: see **Methuschael**.

Methushelaḥ: see **Methuschelachus**.

Meusal, *indecl.* Transliteration, app. as a name, of an obscure Hebr. word in Ezek. 27.19: *Dan et Javan, et Meusal, in negotiationibus tuis* AC 426. (n.b. This passage is rendered quite differently elsewhere: *Dan et Javan adveniens in nundinis tuis* AC 3923.5; *Dan et Javan netum in negotiationibus tuis* AC 10256.3; AC 10258.2.)

Mezahab: see **Mesahab**.

Mibsam, *indecl.* Mibsam, a son of Ishmael: Gen. 25.13 (AC).

Mibzar, *indecl.* Mibzar, a leader of Edom: Gen. 36.42 (AC).

Micah: see **Micha**.

Micha ~ae, *m.* also **Micah** ~ae, *m.*, and **Michah** ~ae, *m.* The prophet Micah: CI 324.

Michael ~lis, *m.* (Bibl.) The name of an angel, Michael: *~l et alii angeli in Verbo* AC 1705; cf. *credebant se ~les et Raphaeles futuros* SS 61.1; (as the name of an angelic society) AR 839.5.

Michah: see **Micha**.

Michal, *indecl. f.* Michal, a daughter of Saul and wife of David: AC 4111.5.

Michmasch, *indecl.* also **Michmash**, *indecl.* Michmash, a city in Benjamin: Isa. 10.28 (SS 15.1).

Michmash: see **Michmasch**.

Midian ~anis, *m.* One of the peoples of Arabia, Midian: *~an et Amaleck, et filii orientis* Judg. 6.33 (AC 3242.5); also, their eponymous ancestor: Gen. 25.4 (AC).

Midianita ~ae, *m.* A person from the land of Midian, Midianite: Num. 31.7 (AE 55.2).

Midianitis ~idis, *f.* A woman of Midian: Num. 25.6 (AE 746.3).

Migdal[1], *indecl.* Migdol, a place west of the Red Sea: Exod. 14.2 (AC).

Migdal[2], *indecl.* also **Migdol**, *indecl.* Migdol, a city in north-eastern Egypt: Jer. 46.14 (AC 2799.13).

Migdol: see **Migdal**[2].

Migron ~onis, *m.* Migron, a city in Benjamin near Gibeah: SS 15.1.

Milanum ~i, *neut.* (Ital.) see also **Mediolanum**. The city of Milan in northern Italy: ES 3729.

Milchom, *indecl.* also **Milkom**, *indecl.* Milcom, national god of the Ammonites also called **Molech** q.v.: *deus filiorum Ammonis [fuit] Molech et ~om* AC 2468.16.

Milckah: see **Milkah**.

Milkah ~ae, *f.* also **Milckah** ~ae, *f.* Milkah, wife of Nahor: Gen. 11.29 (AC).

Milkom: see **Milchom**.

Minerva ~ae, *f.* The Roman goddess of the intellect, Minerva: VR 17.2; (of an apparition in the spiritual world) *vocatae Pallades, non ~ae* ES 3952.

Minni, *indecl.* Minni, the district of Manavas in what later became Armenia: Jer. 51.27 (AC 1154).

Miriam: see **Mirjam**.

Mirjam, *indecl.* also **Miriam** ~amis, *f.* Miriam, a prophet and sister of Aaron and Moses: Exod. 15.20 (AC).

Mischael, *indecl.* **1** Mishael, a son of Uzziel and grandson of Kohath: Exod. 6.22 (AC). **2** Mishael, a companion of Daniel who was renamed Meshach: Dan. 1.19 (AC 5223.4).

Mischma: see **Mischmah**.

Mischmah, *indecl.* also **Mischma**, *indecl.* Mishma, a son of Ishmael: Gen. 25.14 (AC).

Mischpath, *indecl.* also **Mishpat**, *indecl.* see also **En mischpath**. Part of the name En-Mishpat: *quod En Mischpath seu fons judicii aut fons ~ath Kadesch significet contentionem de veris* AC 1678.4.

Misgab, *indecl.* Misgab, the mountainous region of Moab: AC 2468.7.

Mishpat: see **Mischpath**.

Missa, *indecl.* also **Mizzah**, *indecl.* Mizzah, a son of Reuel and grandson of Esau: Gen. 36.13 (AC).

Mizpah, *indecl.* Mizpah, a city of Gad in Gilead where Jacob and Laban once made a covenant, also called Galeed: Gen. 31.49 (AC); *nomen ~ah...in lingua originali a spectare dictum est* AC 4198.2.

Mizraim, *indecl.* see also **Avel Misraim**. Mizraim, a son of Ham whose name is synonymous with Egypt: Gen. 10.6 (AC); *per ~im seu Aegyptum* AC 1163.

Mizzah: see **Missa**.

Moab: see **Moabus**.

Moabita ~ae, *m.* A person of Moab, Moabite: AC 1360.

Moabus ~i, *m.* or **Moab**, *indecl. m.* Moab: Gen. 19.37 (AC); (as the name of a people) *de ~bo* 2 Sam. 8.12 (AC 6917.3).

Mogol ~lis, *m.* The country of the Moguls, Mongolia: *de regno ~lis* AR 655.7; *apud imperatores ~lis et Chinae* VR 245.2.

Mogolenses ~ium, *m. pl.* The people of Mongolia: ES 5729.

Molech, *indecl. m.* also **Molechus** ~i, *m.* see also **Milchom**. The pagan god Molech: *Molech erat deus filiorum Ammonis* AE 768.25 (1 Kgs. 11.7).

Molechus: see **Molech**.

Moph, *indecl.* see also **Noph**. Memphis, a city in central Egypt: AC 273.

Moravianismus ~i, *m.* The Moravian heresy, Moravianism: DP 259.1.

Moreh, *indecl.* Moreh, a place in Ephraim near Gilgal and Mt. Gerizim: Gen. 12.6 (AC).

Moriah ~ae, *f.* Moriah, the hill north-west of what was to become Jerusalem, on which Solomon's temple was built: *quod in monte ~ae sit aedificatum a Davide altare, et postea a Salomone templum* AC 2775.

Moronus ~i, *m.* Giovanni Morone (1509-80), president of the Council of Trent: *praeses ~us* AR 914.2.

Moscheh ~is, *m.* (Hebr.) (acc. *~en*) The Hebrew form of the name Moses: *vocavit nomen illius ~eh* Exod. 2.10 (AC).

Moses ~is, *m.* Moses: AC 6752.1; (as the author of the first five books of the Bible) *apud ~en* AC 6745.2; *incipiens a ~e* Luke 24.27 (AC 6752.6).

Muppim, *indecl.* Muppim, a son of Benjamin: Gen. 46.21 (AC).

Muschi, *indecl.* Mushi, a son of Merari and grandson of Levi: Exod. 6.19 (AC).

N

Naamah, *indecl. f.* Naamah, daughter of Lamech: Gen. 4.22 (AC).

Naaman[1], *indecl. m.* Naaman, a son of Benjamin: Gen. 46.21 (AC).

Naaman[2], *indecl. m.* and ~nis, *m.* Naaman, a Syrian captain who was healed of leprosy: AC 4255.5; AE 475.

Naboth ~thi, *m.* Naboth, a Jezreelite with a vineyard which Jezebel coveted: 1 Kgs. 21.7 (AR 132).

Nachaschon ~onis, *m.* Nahashon, brother of Elisheba and brother-in-law of Aaron: Exod. 6.23 (AC).

Nachath, *indecl.* also **Naḥath**, *indecl.* Nahath, son of Reuel and grandson of Esau: Gen. 36.13 (AC).

Nachor ~oris, *m.* also **Naḥor** ~oris, *m.* **1** Nahor, a grandfather of Abraham: Gen. 11.22 (AC). **2** Nahor, a brother of Abraham: Gen. 11.26 (AC).

Nachum: see **Nahum**.

Nadab, *indecl.* also **Nadabus** ~i, *m.* Nadab, a son of Aaron: AC 9375.2.

Nadabus: see **Nadab**.

Naepheg, *indecl.* Nepheg, a son of Izhar: Exod. 6.21 (AC).

Naharaim, *indecl.* Part of the name **Aram Naharaim** q.v.: *a ~im seu fluviis* AC 3051.

Naḥath: see **Nachath**.

Naḥor: see **Nachor**.

Nahum, *indecl. m.* also **Nachum**, *indecl. m.* The prophet Nahum: AC 6669.2.

Naphisch, *indecl.* also **Naphish**, *indecl.* Naphish, a son of Ishmael: Gen. 25.15 (AC).

Naphish: see **Naphisch**.

Naphtali, *indecl. m.* also **Naphtalim**, *indecl. m.*, and **Naphthali**, *indecl. m.* Naphtali, the son of Jacob: Gen. 30.8 (AC); as the name of one of the tribes of Israel: Rev. 7.6 (AR).

Naphtalim: see **Naphtali**.

Naphthali: see **Naphtali**.

Naphthuchim, *indecl.* also **Naphtuḥim**, *indecl.* The Naphtuhim, inhabitants of central Egypt, said collectively to be the 'son' of Mizraim or Egypt: Gen. 10.13 (AC).

Naphtuḥim: see **Naphthuchim**.

Nathan ~anis, *m.* Nathan, a prophet in the time of David: AC 2781.6.

Nathanael ~lis, *m.* Nathaniel, one of Jesus' twelve disciples: John 1.48 (AR 624.1).

Nazareth, *indecl.* and **Nazarethus**, *m.*? (acc. *~thum*) The town of Nazareth in Galilee: *propheta a ~th* Matt. 21.11 (DD 15.3); *relinquens ~thum* Matt. 4.13 (AE 447.5).

Nazarethus: see **Nazareth**.

Naziraeatus ~us, *m.* The fact or period of being a Nazirite: AE 66.2 (Num. 6.5).

Naziraeus ~i, *m.* A Nazirite: *~us...in lingua Hebraea significat comam* SS 35.3.

Neapoli, *f.*? (app. pl.) (Gk.) (abl. *~is*) Naples in Italy: AM 451.

Nebaioth: see **Nebajoth**.

Nebajoth, *indecl.* also **Nebaioth**, *indecl.* Nebaioth, a son of Ishmael: Gen. 25.13 (AC).

Nebon ~onis, *m.* Nebo, a city in Reuben east of the Jordan river: Jer. 48.22 (AC 2468.17).

Nebucadnezar: see **Nebuchadnezar**.

Nebuchadnezar ~aris, *m.* also **Nebucadnezar** ~aris, *m.*, and **Nebuchadnezzar** ~aris, *m.* The king of Babylon, Nebuchadnezzar: AC 395.2; AM 78.1.

Nebuchadnezzar: see **Nebuchadnezar**.

Nephilim, *indecl. m. pl.* (Hebr.) Nephilim, a kind of giant (see quots.; cf. Gen. 6.4): *turmam spirituum infernalium apparentium sicut Enakim et ~im, hoc est,* *sicut gigantes* VR 87; *Sirenes quae sunt proprie ~im intus spurcissimae* ES 4448.

Neptunus ~i, *m.* The Roman god of the sea, Neptune: VR 17.2.

Nestoriani ~orum, *m. pl.* The followers of the 5th-century heretic Nestorius: VR 378.2.

Newton ~onis, *m.* also **Newtonus** ~i, *m.* The English scientist Sir Isaac Newton (1642-1727): UJ(P) 289; AS 82; ES 6064.

Newtonus: see **Newton**.

Nicaea: see **Nicea**.

Nicea ~ae, *f.* also **Nicaea** ~ae, *f.* Nicaea, a city of northwest Anatolia, now Isnik, where a Council was held in AD 325: *in Concilio Niceae urbis Bithyniae habito* SE 31.

Nicodemus ~i, *m.* Nicodemus, a rabbi who came to Jesus by night: AC 675.

Nicolaita ~ae, *m.* (Gk.) A Nicolaitan, a follower of Nicolas the proselyte from Antioch: Rev. 2.6 (AR).

Nicolaus ~i, *m.* Nicolas, a proselyte from Antioch for whom the Nicolaitans were named: *a ~o, a quo Nicolaitae ita dicti* Acts 6.5 (VR 378.2).

Nilus ~i, *m.* The river Nile in Egypt: AC 6975.

Nimrim, *indecl.* Nimrim, waters on the borders of Gad and Moab: Isa. 37.27 (AC 7571.2).

Nimrod ~di, *m.* also **Nimrodus** ~i, *m.* Nimrod, a son of Cush and grandson of Ham: Gen. 10.8 (AC).

Nimrodus: see **Nimrod**.

Ninevita: see **Ninivita**.

Ninive ~es, *f.* also **Niniveh** ~es, *f.* (also gen. sg. *~ae* AC 588.2; dat. sg. *~e* AE 401.36) Nineveh, the ancient capital of Assyria: Gen. 10.11 (AC).

Niniveh: see **Ninive**.

Ninivita ~ae, *m.* also **Ninevita** ~ae, *m.* An inhabitant of Nineveh, Ninevite: AC 9437.2.

Nisroch, *indecl.* Nisroch, an Assyrian idol with a temple in Nineveh: AC 1188.3.

No, *indecl.* No, the capital city of Upper Egypt also known as Thebes: AC 8398.

Noa ~ae, *m.* = **Noach**: ES 4154.

Noach ~chi, *m.* also **Noachus** ~i, *m.*, and **Noaḥ** ~ḥi, *m.* Noah the son of Lamech: Gen. 5.29 (AC).

Noachus: see **Noach**.

Noaḥ: see **Noach**.

Nob, *indecl.* Nob, a Levitical city in Benjamin just north of Jerusalem: Isa. 10.32 (SS 15.1).

Nod, *indecl.* Nod, a land east of Eden: Gen. 4.16 (AC); *a significatione vocis ~od quod est vagus et profugus esse* AC 398.

Noe, *indecl. m.* = **Noach**: Matt. 24.37 (AC 4332).

Noëtiani ~orum, *m. pl.* (Gk., w. Latin ending) The followers of Noëtus, a heretic of the 3rd century AD: VR 378.2.

Noph, *indecl.* see also **Moph**. Noph, a city in Egypt also called Memphis: AC 5044.4.

Nophach, *indecl.* also **Nophaḥ**, *indecl.* Nophah, a city in the kingdom of Sihon near Medeba: Num. 21.30 (VR 265.2).

Nophaḥ: see **Nophach**.

Nun Nunis, *m.* Nun, the father of Joshua: AC 10556.

O

Obadias ~ae, *m.* The prophet Obadiah: *prophetica... ~ae* AC 2606; DD 4; NH 266.

Obal, *indecl.* Obal, a son of Joktan: Gen. 10.28 (AC).

Obed Edomus ~i, *m.* Obed Edom, a Levite in whose house the Ark lay for three months: 2 Sam. 6.12 (AC 10416.3).

Ochad, *indecl.* also **Ohad**, *indecl.* Ohad, a son of Simeon: Gen. 46.10 (AC).

Octavius ~i, *m.* Octavius (63 BC-AD 14), who took the title Augustus when he became Emperor of Rome: *agere absolute sicut ~us Augustus* VR 73.1.

Oedipus ~i, *m.* (Gk. w. Latin declension) (in Gk. mythology) Oedipus, the king of Thebes who solved the riddle of the Sphinx: *auscultatori Davo infundere intelligentiam antistitis ~i* CO 54.3.

Ogus ~i, *m.* Og, the king of Bashan: Deut. 3.11 (AE 163.8).

Ohad: see **Ochad**.

Ohola, *indecl. f.* also **Oholah**, *indecl. f.* Oholah, a symbolic name for Samaria: *~a pro Ecclesia perversa spirituali, quae est Samaria* Ezek. 23.5 (AC 6534.5).

Oholah: see **Ohola**.

Oholiba, *indecl. f.* also **Oholibah**, *indecl. f.* Oholibah, a symbolic name for Jerusalem: *~a pro Ecclesia perversa coelesti, quae est Hierosolyma* Ezek. 23.11 (AC 6534.5).

Oholibah: see **Oholiba**.

Oholibamah ~ae, *f.* or *m.* **1** Oholibamah, a wife of Esau: Gen. 36.2 (AC). **2** Oholibamah, a leader of the children of Esau: Gen. 36.41 (AC).

Olympus ~i, *m.* (Gk.) Mount Olympus in northern Greece, the fabled home of the gods: SS(P) 18 (= 7.3).

Omar, *indecl.* Omar, a son of Eliphaz and grandson of Esau: Gen. 36.11 (AC).

On, *indecl.* On, capital of lower Egypt: AC 5330.

Onam, *indecl.* Onam, a son of Shobal and grandson of Seir: Gen. 36.23 (AC).

Onan ~anis, *m.* and *indecl.* Onan, a son of Judah: Gen. 38.4 (AC); AC 4836.

Ophir[1], *indecl. m.* Ophir, a son of Joktan: Gen. 10.29 (AC).

Ophir[2] ~iris, *m.* and *indecl.* also **Ophirus** ~i, *m.* Ophir, a famous gold-producing region: Ps. 45.9 (AC 490).

Ophirus: see **Ophir**[2].

Oreb, *indecl.* Oreb, a prince of the Midianites killed on a rock just east of the Jordan river: Isa. 10.26 (SS 15.1).

Origenistae ~tarum, *m. pl.* Followers of the 3rd cent. theologian Origen: VR 378.2.

Ovidius ~i, *m.* The Roman poet Ovid (43 BC-AD 17): *fabulosa...ab ~o in ejus Metamorphosi...collecta* SS(P) 18 (= 7.3).

P

Pachad, *indecl.* also **Paḥad**, *indecl.* The name of Isaac's God: *Jischak* [*elegit*] *Deum qui dictus Pachad seu Pavor* AC 6003.

Padan Aram: see **Paddan Aram**.

Paddan Aram ~nis Aram, *m.* (Hebr.) also **Padan Aram** (both *indecl.*), **Paddan Aram** (both *indecl.*), and **Paddan-Aram**, *indecl.* Paddan Aram, the plains of Mesopotamia between the Tigris and Euphrates rivers: *vade ~nem Aram* Gen. 28.2 (AC).

Padua ~ae, *f.* Padua, a town in northern Italy, now Padova: *Antonius ~ae* ES 4402.

Paeneach: see **Zaphenath Paeneach**.

Paḥad: see **Pachad**.

Palaestina ~ae, *f.* The country of Palestine: ES 2256.

Pallu: see **Phallu**.

Paran, *indecl.* (Hebr.) see also **Elparan**. Paran, the wilderness to the south and south-west of Canaan and to the west of Edom: Hab. 3.3 (AC 2714.1).

Parcita: see **Parsita**.

Paris, *indecl.* François de Pâris (1690-1727), a French Jansenist: CS i.31 (Tafel, p. 139); CS iii.18 (Tafel, p. 141); NE 55.

Parisienses ~ium, *m. pl.* The inhabitants of Paris, Parisians: VR 826.

Parisii ~orum, *m. pl.* Paris in France: AM 451.

Parmos: see **Patmos**.

Parnassium ~i, *neut.* The name of a place for meetings in the spiritual world: *vocatur...clivus humilior ~um* AM 151[a].1; VR 693.1.

Parnassus ~i, *m.* (Gk.) **1** A mountain in central Greece, reputed home of the Muses: *si stylus impletus esset meris nominibus poeticis, ut ~o* ES 1989; *virgines ~i* [sc. the Muses] VR 58.

Parsita ~ae, *m.* (Hebr.) also **Parcita** ~ae, *m.*, and **Parzita** ~ae, *m.* A Pharzite, a descendant of Pharez the son of Judah: Num. 26.20 (AC 4818.2).

Parzita: see **Parsita**.

Pathros, *indecl.* (Hebr.) Pathros, upper Egypt: Isa. 11.11 (AC 1259.2).

Pathrusim, *indecl.* (Hebr.) Pathrusim, a people of upper Egypt: Gen. 10.14 (AC).

Patmos ~i, *f.* An island in the eastern Aegean where the Revelation was given to St John: Rev. 1.9 (AR). (n.b. Both here, in AR 34, and in AE the name is incorrectly read as *Parmos.*)

Pau, *indecl.* (Hebr.) Pau, the city of Hadar king of Edom: Gen. 36.39 (AC).

Paulus ~i, *m.* The apostle Paul: *~us dicit quod in Jesu Christo omnis plenitudo Divinitatis habitet corporaliter* Col. 2.9 (VR 101.2); ES 4412.

Pegasus ~i, *m.* (Gk.) The winged horse of Greek mythology, Pegasus: *per equum alatum ~um intellexerunt intellectum veri* AM 182.2; ES 1989.

Pekin, *indecl. neut.* The Chinese capital, Peking: ES 3066.

Peleg ~gi, *m.* and *indecl.* (Hebr.) Peleg, a son of Eber: Gen. 10.25 (AC).

Pelishtim: see **Pelisthim**.

Pelisthim, *indecl. pl.* (Hebr.) also **Pelishtim**, *indecl. pl.* The Philistines, descendants of the Casluhim 'son' of Mizraim: Gen. 10.14 (AC).

Pen, *indecl.* also **Penn**, *indecl.* William Penn (1644-1718), English Quaker colonizer in America and founder of Pennsylvania: UJ(C) 84.

Peniel, *indecl.* (Hebr.) also **Penuel**, *indecl.* Peniel, the place where Jacob wrestled the angel, south of the Jabbok brook: AC 4310.

Penn: see **Pen**.

Pennsylvania: see **Pensylvania**.

Pensilvania: see **Pensylvania**.

Pensylvania ~ae,*f.* also **Pennsylvania** ~ae,*f.*, and **Pensilvania** ~ae,*f.* The American colony of Pennsylvania: VR 515; ES 3814.

Penuel: see **Peniel**.

Perez, *indecl.* (Hebr.) also **Perezus** ~i, *m.* Perez, son of Tamar and Judah: *in lingua originali Perez est ruptura* AC 4927; AC 367.1.

Perezus: see **Perez**.

Pergamus ~i, *m.* A city of Asia Minor, Pergamum, now Bergama: *angelo in ~o Ecclesiae* Rev. 2.12 (AR).

Perisaeus ~i, *m.* also **Perizzaeus** ~i, *m.* A Perizzite: Josh. 17.15 (AC 1574).

Perisita ~ae, *m.* also **Perizzita** ~ae, *m.* = **Perisaeus**: Gen. 13.7 (AC).

Perizzaeus: see **Perisaeus**.

Perizzita: see **Perisita**.

Persa ~ae, *m.* A Persian: Dan. 5.28 (AR 313).

Persia ~ae,*f.* The ancient kingdom of Persia: *reges Mediae et ~ae* Dan. 8.20 (FI 66); the modern kingdom of Persia or Iran: VR 515.

Petrus ~i, *m.* (Gk.) The disciple Peter: *Tu es ~us, et super hanc petram aedificabo Ecclesiam Meam* Matt. 16.18 (AC 8304).

Phaebus ~i, *m.* (Gk.) also **Phoebus** ~i, *m.* The Greek sun god, also called Apollo: *~us solem equis suis ferens circum orbem* VR 822.

Phallu, *indecl.* (Hebr.) also **Pallu**, *indecl.* Pallu, a son of Reuben: Gen. 46.9 (AC).

Pharao ~onis, *m.* also **Pharaoh** ~onis, *m.* The ruler of Egypt in antiquity, Pharaoh: *~o, rex Aegypti* AC 42.1; *et praecepit ~o omni populo suo* Exod. 1.22 (AC).

Pharaoh: see **Pharao**.

Pharisaeus ~i, *m.* A member of the Jewish sect of Pharisees: *vae vobis, scribae et ~i!* Matt. 23.25 (SS 40.2).

Phichol: see **Phicol**.

Phicol ~lis, *m.* (Hebr.) also **Phichol** ~lis, *m.* Phichol, the leader of Abimelech's army in Abraham's time: Gen. 21.22 (AC).

Philadelphia ~ae,*f.* A city of western Asia Minor in antiquity: Rev. 1.11 (AR).

Philetus ~i, *m.* A man's name (see 2 Tim. 2.17): VR 378.2.

Philippinus ~i, *m.* A follower or imitator of Philip (see quot.): *illi qui separant Divinum...a Domino... dicendi sunt ~i, ex Philippo qui petiit a Domino videre Patrem* AT 160.

Philippus ~i, *m.* also **Philipus** ~i, *m.* The disciple Philip: John 1.45 (AC 6752.6).

Philipus: see **Philippus**.

Phoebus: see **Phaebus**.

Phrath, *indecl.* The Euphrates river: *~ath seu Euphrates* Gen. 2.14 (AC).

Pi-Beseth: see **Bi-Pesech**.

Pichiroth: see **Pi-Chiroth**.

Pi-Chiroth, *indecl.* (Hebr.) also **Pichiroth**, *indecl.* Pi Hahiroth, a place on the west side of the Red Sea: Exod. 14.2 (AC).

Pilatus ~i, *m.* Pontius Pilate, the Roman governor of Judaea: John 18.37 (AE 27.4).

Pildasch, *indecl.* (Hebr.) also **Pildash**, *indecl.* Pildash, a son of Nahor and nephew of Abraham: Gen. 22.22 (AC).

Pildash: see **Pildasch**.

Pinchasus ~i, *m.* (Hebr.) also **Pinḥasus** ~i, *m.* Phinehas, a son of Eleasar and grandson of Aaron: Exod. 6.25 (AC).

Pindus ~i, *m.* A large mountain range in northern Greece: *ex... ~o juxta Athenas* SS(P) 18 (= 7.3).

Pinḥasus: see **Pinchasus**.

Pinon, *indecl.* (Hebr.) Pinon, a leader of Edom: Gen. 6.41 (AC).

Pischon, *indecl.* (Hebr.) also **Pishon**, *indecl.* The Pison river, one of the four rivers of Eden: Gen. 2.11 (AC).

Pisgah ~ae,*f.* (Hebr.) Pisgah, the ridge of mountains across the Jordan river from Jericho whose highest point is Mt. Nebo: Deut. 34.1 (AC 4117.2).

Pishon: see **Pischon**.

Pithom, *indecl.* (Hebr.) Pithom, a city in lower Egypt east of the Nile river in Goshen: AC 6662.

Plato ~onis, *m.* The Greek philosopher Plato: AM 151[a].1; VR 9.3.

Platonicus ~i, *m.* A follower or student of Plato, Platonist: *inter illos erat quidam ~us* AM 153[a].2.

Plejades ~um,*f. pl.* (Gk.) The constellation of the Pleiads: *navigare ad ~es* SE 98.

Poloni ~orum, *m. pl.* The people of Poland, Poles: AM 103.2.

Polonia ~ae, *f.* Poland: AM 521.4.

Pompeius ~i, *m.* Pompey the Great (106-48 BC), politician and military leader of the Roman Republic: ES 6082.

Portugallia ~ae, *f.* Portugal: ES 6059.

Portugisus ~i, *m.* An inhabitant of Portugal, Portuguese: *Judaei qui nuncupantur ~i* VR 841.

Potiphar ~aris, *m.* Potiphar, an officer of Pharaoh and captain of the guard to whom Joseph was sold: Gen. 37.36 (AC).

Potiphaera ~ae, *m.* Potiphera, a priest of On who became father-in-law of Joseph: Gen. 41.45 (AC).

Praga ~ae, *f.* A city in what is now the Czech Republic, Prague: ES 3411; ES 3729.

Priapus ~i, *m.* The name of the Roman god of fertility, used as a designation of lascivious male spirits: *apparent ...aliis e longinquo sicut ~i* DP 117.2; *quod viderint satyros aut ~os* AM 44.4.

Protestantes ~ium, *m. pl.* Protestants: *omnes ~es, sive dicantur Evangelici sive Reformati* VR 154.2.

Pua: see **Pujva**.

Puah, *indecl. f.* (Hebr.) Puah, a Hebr. midwife at the time of Moses: Exod. 1.15 (AC).

Pujva, *indecl.* (Hebr.) also **Pua**, *indecl.*, **Puva**, *indecl.*, and **Puvah**, *indecl.* Puvah, a son of Issachar: Gen. 46.13 (AC).

Pul, *indecl.* (Hebr.) Pul, a place or tribe in Africa near Libya: AC 1158.5.

Put: see **Puth**.

Puth, *indecl.* (Hebr.) also **Put**, *indecl.* Put, a son of Ham and the tribe and the country of Libya that were named for him: Gen. 10.6 (AC).

Putiel ~lis, *m.* (Hebr.) Putiel, father-in-law of Eleazar: Exod. 6.25 (AC).

Puva: see **Pujva**.

Puvah: see **Pujva**.

Pyris, *indecl.* A name belonging to spiritual language: *quod...discipuli Godoskalchi...congregentur in loco qui vocatur lingua spirituali Pyris* VR 798.2.

Pyrrha ~ae, *f.* In Gk. mythology, the wife of Deucalion: VR 58.2.

Pythagoras ~ae, *m.* The Greek philosopher of the sixth century BC: AM 151[a].1.

Q

Quakeri: see **Quaqueri**.

Quaqueri ~orum, *m. pl.* also **Quakeri** ~orum, *m. pl.* The Quakers: ES 3011.

Quaquerianismus ~i, *m.* The Quaker sect: *cum ~us incepit* UJ(C) 83.

Quaquerismus ~i, *m.* The Quaker system of belief, Quakerism: DP 259.1.

Quartodecimani ~orum, *m. pl.* also spelled as two words **Quarto** (*indecl.*) **Decimani** ~orum, *m. pl.* A sect which kept Easter on the 14th day of the month Nisan, Quartodecimans: VR 378.2.

R

Raamah ~ae, *m.* (Hebr.) Raamah, a son of Cush and grandson of Ham: Gen. 10.7 (AC).

Raamses, *indecl.* (Hebr.) see also **Rameses**. Raamses, a treasure city built by the Israelites in Egypt: Exod. 1.11 (AC).

Rabbah ~ae, *m.* (Hebr.) Rabbah, a chief city in Ammon: Ezek. 25.5 (AC 2468.12).

Rabschake ~es, *m.* (Hebr.) also **Rabshakeh** ~es, *m.* Rabshakeh, an officer to King Sennacherib of Assyria: AC 2588.11; AC 5321.10.

Rabshakeh: see **Rabschake**.

Rachab, *indecl. f.* (Hebr.) Rahab, a woman in Jericho who helped two Israelite spies: AC 9468.8 (Josh. 2.1).

Rachel ~lis, *f.* Rachel, daughter of Laban and the wife of Jacob: Gen. 29.6 (AC).

Rahaba ~ae, *f.* (Hebr.) Rahab, a poetic name for Egypt: Ps. 87.4 (AC 1164.7).

Ramah, *indecl.* (Hebr.) Ramah, a city in Benjamin north of Jerusalem on the border between Judah and Israel: AC 4592.10.

Rameses, *indecl.* (Hebr.) see also **Raamses**. Rameses, possibly equivalent to Raamses (see quot.): *~es...erat tractus terrae optimus in terra Goschen* AC 6104.

Raphael ~lis, *m.* The name of an angel: *intelligitur... integra societas angelica, ut per Michaelem, Gabrielem, ~lem* AE 302.

Rebecca ~ae, *f.* (Hebr.) Rebekah, daughter of Bethuel and wife of Isaac: Gen. 22.23 (AC).

Rechoboth, *indecl.* (Hebr.) also **Reḥoboth,** *indecl.* **1** Rehoboth, a city in Assyria: Gen. 10.11 (AC). **2** Rehoboth, a well dug by Isaac: Gen. 26.22 (AC).

Rechobus ~i, *m.* (Hebr.) Rehob, father of King Hadadezer, king of Zobah: 2 Sam. 8.12 (AC 6917.3).

Rehabeam ~mi, *m.* (Hebr.) Rehoboam, son and successor of Solomon: 1 Kgs. 12.12 (AC 4495.5).

Reḥoboth: see **Rechoboth**.

Remaliah ~ae, *m.* (Hebr.) Remaliah, father of Pekah: AC 6952.6.

Rephaim, *indecl. pl.* (Hebr.) The Rephaim, a race of people descended from the Nephilim: *posteri eorum* [sc. *Nephilim*] *dicti sunt Enakim et ~im* AC 581.2.

Rephidim, *indecl.* (Hebr.) Rephidim, a place in the desert where the Israelites fought the Amalekites: Exod. 17.1 (AC).

Resen, *indecl.* (Hebr.) Resen, a city between Nineveh and Calah: Gen. 10.12 (AC).

Reu, *indecl.* (Hebr.) Reu, a son of Peleg: Gen. 11.18 (AC).

Reuben: see **Ruben**.

Reubenita: see **Rubenita**.

Reuel ~lis, *m.* (Hebr.) **1** Reuel, a son of Bashemath and Esau: Gen. 36.4 (AC). **2** see **Reul**.

Reul ~lis, *m.* also **Reuel** ~lis, *m.* Father, or probably grandfather, of Moses' wife: Exod. 2.18 (AC).

Reumah, *indecl.* (Hebr.) Reumah, a concubine of Nahor: Gen. 22.24 (AC).

Rezinus ~i, *m.* Rezin, the king of Syria: Isa. 7.4 (AC 6952.6).

Riphath, *indecl.* (Hebr.) Riphath, a son of Gomer and grandson of Japheth: Gen. 10.3 (AC).

Roi: see **Beer-lachai-roi**.

Roma ~ae, *f.* The city of Rome in Italy: DP 312.2; (as the seat of the ancient Roman Empire) *apud gentiles, imprimis in Graecia, et ~ae* AC 2724.3; (as the seat of the Papacy) AM 265.

Romano-Catholici ~orum, *m. pl.* The Roman Catholics: *vocant se... ~os* AC 1799.4; VR 82.3.

Rosch, *indecl.* (Hebr.) also **Rosh,** *indecl.* Rosh, a son of Benjamin: Gen. 46.21 (AC).

Rosh: see **Rosch**.

Ruben ~enis, *m*. also **Reuben** ~enis, *m*. The name of one of the sons of Jacob: Gen. 29.32 (AC); also, one of the twelve tribes of Israel: Rev. 7.5 (AR).

Rubenita ~ae, *m*. also **Reubenita** ~ae, *m*. A member of the tribe of Reuben: AE 911.10.

Russi ~orum, *m. pl*. The people of Russia, Russians: ES 5949.

Russia ~ae, *f*. Russia: *Verbum...parum legitur in ~a* SS(P) 39 (= 16).

S

Saavan *indecl.* (Hebr.) Zaavan, a son of Ezer and grandson of Seir: Gen. 36.27 (AC).

Sabaeus ~i, *m.* also **Sebaeus** ~i, *m.* A Sabean, one of the descendants of Seba inhabiting northern Ethiopia: Isa. 45.14 (AC 1164.5).

Sabelliani ~orum, *m. pl.* A sect of heretics, followers of Sabellius (3rd cent. AD): VR 378.2.

Sabtah: see **Sabtha**.

Sabteca: see **Sabtheka**.

Sabtha, *indecl.* (Hebr.) also **Sabtah**, *indecl.* Sabtah, a son of Cush: Gen. 10.7 (AC).

Sabtheka, *indecl.* (Hebr.) also **Sabteca**, *indecl.* Sabtecha, a son of Cush: Gen. 10.7 (AC).

Sacharias: see **Zacharias**.

Sadducaei ~orum, *m. pl.* The name of a Jewish sect, Sadducees: *cavete a fermento Pharisaeorum et ~orum* Matt. 16.6 (AC 7906.1).

Sahadutha: see **Jegar Sahadutha**.

Salomo ~onis, *m.* (Hebr.) also **Schelomo** ~onis, *m.*, **Schelomoh** ~onis, *m.*, and **Solomo** ~onis, *m.* King Solomon: *hic ~o ita loquitur* AC 6804.6; *in templo ~onis* AC 7847.4.

Samaria ~ae, *f.* A city and region in the north of Palestine, Samaria: *mulier e ~a* John 4.7 (AE 71.2).

Samarita ~ae, *m.* A man from Samaria, Samaritan: Luke 10.33 (AC 6708).

Samgar: see **Schamgar**.

Samlah, *indecl.* (Hebr.) Samlah, an ancient king of Edom: Gen. 36.36 (AC).

Samosateni ~orum, *m. pl.* The followers of Paul of Samosata (3rd cent. AD): VR 378.2.

Samsumim, *indecl.* (Hebr.) also **Zamzumim**, *indecl.* Zamzummim, a tribe of the Rephaim living in the region afterwards occupied by the Ammonites: Deut. 2.20 (AC 2468.5).

Samuel ~lis, *m.* (Hebr.) also **Schemuel** ~lis, *m.* The prophet Samuel: SS 29; (as the name of two books of the Word) *in Libro 2 ~lis* AC 6804.3.

Sancheribus ~i, *m.* also **Sanḥeribus** ~i, *m.* Sennacherib, king of Assyria: Isa. 37.37 (AE 131.14).

Sanḥeribus: see **Sancheribus**.

Sarah ~ae, *f.* Sarah, the new name given to Sarai when Abram received the new name Abraham: Gen. 17.15 (AC); AM 6.1.

Sarai, *indecl. f.* Sarai the wife of Abram: Gen. 11.29 (AC).

Sarchita ~ae, *m.* (Hebr.) also **Zarḥita** ~ae, *m.* A member of the family of Zerah, son of Judah: Num. 26.20 (AC 4818.2).

Sardes ~ium, *f. pl.* An ancient city in Lydia, Sardis: *et angelo in ~ibus Ecclesiae scribe* Rev. 3.1 (AR).

Sarepta ~ae, *f.* (Gk.) Sarepta, a city midway between Tyre and Sidon: Luke 4.26 (AC 9198.1).

Saturnus ~i, *m.* **1** The name of one of the ancient Roman gods, Saturn: VR 17.2. **2** The name of the sun's sixth planet: AC 6697.

Saul: see **Schaul**.

Saxonia ~ae, *f.* The district of Saxony in Germany: VR 112.2.

Schalem, *indecl.* (Hebr.) also **Schalemus** ~i, *m.*, and **Shalem**, *indecl.* Salem, the city of Melchizedek: Gen. 14.18 (AC).

Schalemus: see **Schalem**.

Schamgar ~aris, *m.* (Hebr.) also **Samgar** ~aris, *m.* Shamgar, son of Anath and judge of Israel: Judg. 5.6 (AC 8753.3).

Schammah, *indecl.* (Hebr.) also **Shammah**, *indecl.* Shammah, a son of Reuel and grandson of Esau: Gen. 36.13 (AC).

Schaphan ~anis, *m.* (Hebr.) also **Shaphan** ~anis, *m.* Shaphan, a scribe at the time of King Josiah: DD 9.

Scharon ~onis, *m.* (Hebr.) also **Sharon** ~onis, *m.* Sharon, the rich plain on the west coast of Canaan between Joppa and Caesarea: AC 10609.6.

Schaul ~lis, *m.* (Hebr.) also **Saul** ~lis, *m.*, **Schaulus** ~i, *m.*, and **Shaul** ~lis, *m.* **1** Shaul, an ancient king of Edom: Gen. 36.37 (AC). **2** Shaul, a son of Simeon and a Canaanite woman: Gen. 46.10 (AC). **3** Saul the king of Israel: 2 Sam. 5.2 (AC 6983.2).

Schaulus: see **Schaul**.

Schaveh, *indecl.* (Hebr.) also **Shaveh**, *indecl.* Shaveh, a valley in Salim near Aenon: Gen. 14.17 (AC).

Schave Kirjathaim, *indecl.* (Hebr.) also **Shave Kiriathaim**, *indecl.* Shaveh Kiriathaim, a place in Reuben inhabited by the Emim: Gen. 14.5 (AC).

Scheba ~ae, *m.* (Hebr.) also **Sheba** ~ae, *m.* **1** see **Schebah**. **2** Sheba, a son of Raamah and grandson of Cush: Gen. 10.7 (AC). **3** Sheba, a son of Joktan: Gen. 10.28 (AC). **4** Sheba, a son of Jokshan and grandson of Abraham: Gen. 25.3 (AC).

Schebah ~ae, *m.* (Hebr.) also **Scheba** ~ae, *m*, and **Sheba** ~ae, *m.* Sheba, a wealthy area of south-western Arabia: Ezek. 27.22 (AC 10199.6).

Schechem, *indecl.* (Hebr.) also **Schechemus** ~i, *m.*, **Sechemus** ~i, *m.*, **Shechem**, *indecl.*, **Shechemus** ~i, *m.*, and **Sichemus** ~i, *m.* **1** Shechem, a place near Mt. Ephraim: Gen. 12.6 (AC). **2** Shechem, son of Hamor and violator of Dinah: Gen. 34.2 (AC).

Schechemus: see **Schechem**.

Schelach ~chi, *m.* (Hebr.) also **Shelaḥ** ~ḥi, *m.* Salah, son of Arphaxad: Gen. 10.24 (AC).

Schelah ~ae, *m.* and *indecl.* (Hebr.) also **Shelah** ~ae, *m.* and *indecl.* Shelah, a son of Judah: Gen. 38.5 (AC).

Scheleph, *indecl.* (Hebr.) also **Sheleph**, *indecl.* Sheleph, a son of Joktan: Gen. 10.26 (AC).

Schelomo: see **Salomo**.

Schelomoh: see **Salomo**.

Schelonita ~ae, *m.* (Hebr.) also **Shelonita** ~ae, *m.* An inhabitant of Shiloh, Shilonite: AC 7619.

Schem ~mi, *m.* also **Sem** ~mi, *m.*, and **Shem** ~mi, *m.* The son of Noah: Gen. 5.32 (AC); AC 9960.16; ES 4106.

Schemeber, *indecl.* (Hebr.) also **Shemeber**, *indecl.* Shemeber, king of Zeboiim in the time of Abraham: Gen. 14.2 (AC).

Schemuel: see **Samuel**.

Schepho, *indecl.* (Hebr.) also **Shepho**, *indecl.* Shepho, a son of Shobal and grandson of Seir: Gen. 36.23 (AC).

Scheth ~thi, *m.* and *indecl.* (Hebr.) also **Sheth** ~thi, *m.* and *indecl.* Seth, a son of Adam and Eve: Gen. 4.25 (AC).

Schibba, *indecl.* (Hebr.) also **Shiba**, *indecl.*, and **Shibeah**, *indecl.* Shebah, a well that Isaac's servants dug in Judah: Gen. 26.33 (AC).

Schibna, *indecl.* (Hebr.) also **Shibna**, *indecl.* Shebna, the scribe or secretary to King Hezekiah: 2 Kgs. 18.37 (AC 4763.1).

Schichor ~oris, *m.* (Hebr.) also **Shiḥor** ~oris, *m.* Sihor, a river on the southern boundary of Canaan: AC 9295.7.

Schillem, *indecl.* (Hebr.) also **Shillem**, *indecl.* Shillem, a son of Naphtali: Gen. 46.24 (AC).

Schiloach, *indecl.* (Hebr.) also **Shiloaḥ**, *indecl.* Shiloah, a fountain between the upper and lower parts of Jerusalem: Isa. 8.6 (AC 790.2).

Schiloh ~untis, *m.* (Hebr.) also **Shilo** ~untis, *m.* and *indecl.* Shiloh, a city in Ephraim and an epithet for the Messiah: Gen. 49.10 (AC).

Schimei, *indecl.* (Hebr.) **1** Shimei, a son of Gershon and grandson of Levi: Exod. 6.17 (AC). **2** Shimei, a Benjamite who cursed David: 2 Sam. 19.21 (AC 9954.18).

Schimeon ~onis, *m.* and *indecl.* (Hebr.) also **Shimeon** ~onis, *m.* and *indecl.*, and **Simeon** ~onis, *m.* and *indecl.* Simeon, the son of Israel: Gen. 29.33 (AC); (as the name of one of the twelve tribes) Rev. 7.7 (AR); also, in form *Simeon*, the name of a man of Jerusalem: Luke 2.25 (AC 3007.1).

Schimron, *indecl.* (Hebr.) also **Shimron**, *indecl.* Shimron, a son of Issachar: Gen. 46.13 (AC).

Schimson: see **Simson**.

Schinaar: see **Schinear**.

Schineab, *indecl.* also **Shinab**, *indecl.* Shinab, king of Admah in the time of Abram: Gen. 14.2 (AC).

Schinear, *indecl.* also **Schinaar**, *indecl.*, **Shinar**, *indecl.*, and **Shinear** ~aris, *m.* Shinar, the name for Babylonia in its fullest extent: Gen. 10.10 (AC 1180).

Schiphra, *indecl.* (Hebr.) Shiphrah, a Hebr. midwife at the time of Moses: Exod. 1.15 (AC).

Schirion: see **Schirjon**.

Schirjon ~onis, *m.* (Hebr.) also **Schirion** ~onis, *m.* Sirion, the Sidonian name for Mt. Hermon: Ps. 29.6 (SS 18).

Schittim, *indecl.* (Hebr.) A place in the Negeb: Num. 25.1 (SS 101).

Schobal ~lis, *m.* (Hebr.) also **Shobal** ~lis, *m.* Shobal, a son of Seir: Gen. 36.20 (AC).

Schua ~ae, *m.* (Hebr.) also **Shua** ~ae, *m.* Shua, Canaanite father-in-law of Judah: Gen. 38.12 (AC).

Schuachus ~i, *m.* (Hebr.) also **Shuaḥus** ~i, *m.* Shuah, a son of Abraham and Keturah: Gen. 25.2 (AC).

Schuni, *indecl.* (Hebr.) also **Shuni**, *indecl.* Shuni, a son of Gad: Gen. 46.16 (AC).

Schur, *indecl.* (Hebr.) also **Shur**, *indecl.* Shur, the desert between Egypt and Canaan: Exod. 15.22 (AC).

Schwengfeldianus: see **Swenckfeldianus**.

Scotia ~ae, *f.* Scotland: VR 812.

Scylla ~ae, *f.* A fabulous monster of Greek fable: *sicut dicitur in proverbio, cupiens vitare Charybdin incidit in ~am* VR 637.

Seba ~ae, *m.* (Hebr.) Seba, a son of Cush and his land in northern Ethiopia: Gen. 10.7 (AC).

Sebaeus: see **Sabaeus**.

Sebaita ~ae, *m.* A Sabean or Shebaite, one of the descendants of Sheba, son of Jokshan: Joel 3.8 (AC 5886.3).

Sebul, *indecl.* (Hebr.) also **Zebul**, *indecl.* Zebul, an officer of Abimelech and governor of Shechem: Judg. 9.28 (AC 4430.3).

Sebulon: see **Sebulun**.

Sebulun ~onis, *m.* also **Sebulon** ~onis, *m.*, **Zebulon** ~onis, *m.*, and **Zebulun**, *indecl.* One of the sons of Israel: Gen. 30.20 (AC); as the name of one of the tribes: Rev. 7.8 (AR).

Sechemus: see **Schechem**.

Seir, *indecl.* (Hebr.) **1** Seir, a mountain south of the salt sea: Gen. 14.6 (AC). **2** Seir, ancestor of the Horites: Gen. 36.20 (AC).

Sem: see **Schem**.

Semiariani ~orum, *m. pl.* The name of a heretical sect: VR 378.2.

Semisocinianus ~i, *m.* Half a follower of Socinus, half-Socinian: ES [6101.1].

Seneca ~ae, *m.* The Roman philosopher L Annaeus Seneca (*c.* 3 BC–AD 65): SS 115.3.

Sephar ~aris, *m.* (Hebr.) Sephar, a mountain in south-western Arabia: Gen. 10.30 (AC).

Sepharad, *indecl.* (Hebr.) Sepharad, an ancient name for Iberia or Georgia: Obad. 20 (AC 1458.4).

Serach[1], *indecl.* (Hebr.) also **Zeraḥ**, *indecl.* **1** Zerah, a son of Reuel and grandson of Esau: Gen. 36.13 (AC). **2** Zerah, father of Jobab: Gen. 36.33 (AC).

Serach[2], *indecl.* (Hebr.) also **Serah**[2], *indecl. m.*, and **Serachus** ~i, *m.* Zerah, a son of Judah by his daughter-in-law Tamar: Gen. 38.30 (AC).

Serachus: see **Serach**[2].

Seraḥ[1]: see **Serech**.

Serah[2]: see **Serach**[2].

Serech, *indecl. f.* (Hebr.) also **Seraḥ**[1], *indecl. f.* Serah, a daughter of Asher: Gen. 46.17 (AC).

Sered, *indecl.* (Hebr.) Sered, a son of Zebulun: Gen. 46.14 (AC).

Serubabel ~lis, *m.* (Hebr.) also **Serubbabel** ~lis, *m.* Zerubbabel, son of Shealtiel and leader of the first returning band of exiles: Zech. 4.9 (AR 43.4).

Serubbabel: see **Serubabel**.

Serug: see **Serugus**.

Serugus ~i, *m.* (Hebr.) also **Serug**, *indecl.* Serug, son of Reu and father of Nahor: Gen. 11.20 (AC).

Seveneh ~es, *m.* Syene, the southernmost town in Egypt: *a turri ~e* Ezek. 29.10 (AC 1164.3).

Shalem: see **Schalem**.

Shammah: see **Schammah**.

Shaphan: see **Schaphan**.

Sharon: see **Scharon**.

Shaul: see **Schaul**.

Shaveh: see **Schaveh**.

Shave Kiriathaim: see **Schave Kirjathaim**.

Sheba: see **Scheba** or **Schebah**.

Shechem: see **Schechem**.

Shechemus: see **Schechem**.

Shelah: see **Schelah**.

Shelaḥ: see **Schelach**.

Sheleph: see **Scheleph**.

Shelonita: see **Schelonita**.

Shem: see **Schem**.

Shemeber: see **Schemeber**.

Shepho: see **Schepho**.

Sheth: see **Scheth**.

Shiba: see **Schibba**.

Shibeah: see **Schibba**.

Shibna: see **Schibna**.

Shiḥor: see **Schichor**.

Shillem: see **Schillem**.

Shilo: see **Schiloh**.

Shiloaḥ: see **Schiloach**.

Shimeon: see **Schimeon**.

Shimron: see **Schimron**.

Shimshon: see **Simson**.

Shinab: see **Schineab**.

Shinar: see **Schinear**.

Shinear: see **Schinear**.

Shobal: see **Schobal**.

Shua: see **Schua**.

Shuaḥus: see **Schuachus**.

Shuni: see **Schuni**.

Shur: see **Schur**.

Siberia ~ae, *f.* Siberia: *sciebant de China et de ~a* ES 6077.

Sibmah ~ae, *m.* (Hebr.) Sibmah, a city in Reuben: Jer. 48.32 (AC 2468.7).

Siccuth, *indecl.* Sikkuth, a pagan deity: Amos 5.26 (AC 1715).

Sichar, *indecl.* Sychar, a city of Samaria: AC 4430.4.

Sichemus: see **Schechem**.

Sichon ~onis, *m.* (Hebr.) also **Siḥon** ~onis, *m.* Sihon, an Amorite king in Heshbon: Num. 21.27 (VR 265.2).

Sichri, *indecl.* (Hebr.) Zichri, a son of Izhar and great-grandson of Levi: Exod. 6.21 (AC).

Sicilia ~ae, *f.* Sicily: ES 5648.

Sicilianus ~i, *m.* A Sicilian: ES 5658.

Siddim, *indecl.* (Hebr.) Siddim, the region on the shores of the Dead Sea that included Sodom, Gomorrah, Admah, and Zeboiim: Gen. 14.3 (AC).

Sidon: see **Zidon**.

Siḥon: see **Sichon**.

Siloah, *indecl.* (Hebr.) also **Siloam**, *indecl.* Siloam, a pool at the king's gardens, south of Jerusalem: John 9.11 (AR 378.2).

Siloam: see **Siloah**.

Silpah ~ae, *f.* (Hebr.) also **Zilpah** ~ae, *f.* Zilpah, handmaid of Leah and mother of Gad and Asher: Gen. 29.24 (AC).

Simeon: see **Schimeon**.

Simon ~onis, *m.* Simon (see quot.): *tu es ~on Jonae filius, tu vocaberis Kephah, quod si interpreteris, est Petra* John 1.42 (AE 411.13); also, Simon Magus (Acts 8.9): VR 378.2.

Simran ~anis, *m.* (Hebr.) also **Zimran** ~anis, *m.* Zimran, a son of Abraham and Keturah: Gen. 25.2 (AC).

Simri, *indecl.* also **Zimri**, *indecl.* Zimri, an unknown place: Jer. 25.25 (AC 3240.4).

Simson ~onis, *m.* (Hebr.) also **Schimson** ~onis, *m.*, and **Shimshon** ~onis, *m.* Samson: *per ~onem, de quo dicitur, quod Naziraeus esset ab utero matris* SS 49.2.

Sin, *indecl.* (Hebr.) also **Zin**, *indecl.* Sin, a desert in southern Judah west of the southernmost part of the Dead Sea: Exod. 16.1 (AC).

Sinai, *indecl.* The name of a mountain, Sinai: *e monte ~i* AC 6723.3; *tota extensio montis illius vocabatur Chorebus, et mons editior in medio ejus vocabatur mons ~i* AC 10608.1.

Sinim, *indecl.* Sinim, a people in the far east: Isa. 49.12 (AC 3708.6).

Sinus ~i, *m.* A member of a Canaanite tribe, Sinite: Gen. 10.17 (AC).

Sion: see **Zion**.

Sisera ~ae, *m.* (Hebr.) Sisera, captain of the army of Canaanite King Jabin: Judg. 5.28 (AC 3391.3).

Sithnah, *indecl.* (Hebr.) also **Sitnah**, *indecl.* Sitnah, the name of a well that Isaac's servants dug in Gerar: Gen. 26.21 (AC).

Sithri, *indecl.* (Hebr.) Zithri, a son of Uzziel and grandson of Kohath: Exod. 6.22 (AC).

Sitnah: see **Sithnah**.

Sixtus ~i, *m.* A name adopted by Popes: *cum Pontifice ~o Quinto* AR 752.1.

Sloan, *indecl.* Sir Hans Sloane (1660-1753), physician, botanical collector, and president of the Royal Society of London (1727-41): AS 344.

Smidius ~i, *m.* Sebastian Schmidt or Schmidius, professor at Strasbourg and translator of the Bible into Latin: *ex versione ~i* 1AD Gen. 1.6 (Tafel, p. 2).

Smyrna ~ae, *f.* A Greek city of Asia Minor, now Izmir in Turkey: *ad Ecclesiam in ~a* VI 99 (Rev. 2.8).

Smyrnaeus ~i, *m.* An inhabitant of Smyrna: *et angelo Ecclesiae ~orum scribe* Rev. 2.8 (AR).

Socinianismus ~i, *m.* The heresy of Socinus, Socinianism: VR 94.1.

Socinus ~i, *m.* An Italian theologian of the 16th century, Faustus Socinus (1539-1604), who was influenced by his uncle Laelius Socinus (1525-62) in denying the

Divinity of Christ: *num...videritis ~um, qui solum Deum Patrem agnovit* VR 159.6.

Socrates ~is, *m.* The Greek sage of the 5th century BC: *veteres sapientes in Graecia, ut Pythagoras, ~es* AM 151[a].1.

Sodoma ~ae, *f.* A city of Canaan, Sodom: *veniendo ad ~am et Amoram* Gen. 10.19 (AC); DD 64.2; applied to Jerusalem: Rev. 11.8 (AR).

Solifidiani ~orum, *m. pl.* Those who hold that faith alone justifies, Solifidians: VR 812.

Solomo: see **Salomo**.

Stockholmia ~ae, *f.* The city of Stockholm in Sweden: ES 4142; (in the spiritual world) ES 5035.

Stoicus ~i, *m.* (Gk.) A Greek philosopher of the school of Zeno, a Stoic: ES 3952.

Styx ~ygis, *f.* (Gk.) The chief river of hell in Greek mythology, the Styx: *apud tales est omne Ecclesiae sicut ~yx aut caligo in Tartaro* VR 20.2; *fidem nostram... projecit in ~ygem* VR 137.2; (applied to certain hells) *illi etiam inferna illorum vocaverunt Tartara...ac profunda ibi ~ygem* CO 38.

Succoth, *indecl.* (Hebr.) **1** Succoth, a place east of the Jordan river where Jacob went after Esau had departed from him: Gen. 33.17 (AC). **2** Succoth, the first stopping place of the Israelites after they had left Egypt: Exod. 12.37 (AC).

Suecia ~ae, *f.* also **Sveria** ~ae, *f.* Sweden: *in Germania, ~a et Dania* VI 4.

Suecus ~i, *m.* also **Sverus** ~i, *m.* An inhabitant of Sweden, Swede: *ab Emanuele Swedenborg, ~o* AM title page.

Suionia ~ae, *f.* Sweden: *illi ex ~a et Danemarchia* VR 161.1.

Suph, *indecl.* The Hebr. name for the Red Sea: *conjecit illam* [sc. *locustam*] *mare Suph* Exod. 10.19 (AC); (in the spiritual world) *in mare, quod ibi vocatur mare Suph* VR 71.4.

Supha, *indecl.* also **Suphah**, *indecl.* Suphah, an obscure place name: Num. 21.14 (VR 265.1).

Suphah: see **Supha**.

Susimi ~orum, *m. pl.* also **Zuzim**, *indecl. pl.* The Zuzim, a primitive race of giants: Gen. 14.5 (AC).

Sveria: see **Suecia**.

Sverus: see **Suecus**.

Swammerdam ~mi, *m.* Jan Swammerdam (1637-80), Dutch anatomist and entomologist: VR 585.3.

Swenckfeldianus ~i, *m.* also **Schwengfeldianus** ~i, *m.* A follower of the Silesian Protestant mystic Caspar Schwenkfeld (1490-1561), Schwenkfeldian: VR 378.2.

Synergistae ~tarum, *m. pl.* (Gk.) Synergists, believers in the cooperation of the human will with divine grace: VR 378.2.

Syria ~ae, *f.* The country to the north of Canaan, Syria: *in ~a incepit cultus quidam externus* AC 1238.2; *per Assyriam, Mesopotamiam, ~am, Aethiopiam* CI 327.

Syrophaenissa ~ae, *f.* (Gk.) also **Syrophoenissa** ~ae, *f.* A woman of the Phoenician area of Syria: Mark 7.26 (AC 7784.3).

Syrophoenissa: see **Syrophaenissa**.

Syrus ~i, *m.* An inhabitant of Syria, Syrian: *~os e Kir* Amos 9.7 (AC 9340.6); DP 251.3.

T

Tabera, *indecl.* (Hebr.) Taberah, a place three days' journey north of Sinai where the Israelites were punished: Deut. 9.22 (AC 8588.3, Autograph and 3rd edn.).

Taḥash: see **Thachasch**.

Tamar: see **Thamar**[1] or **Thamar**[2].

Tarshish: see **Tharschisch**.

Tebach: see **Thebach**.

Tebaḥ: see **Thebach**.

Tekoa: see **Thekoa**.

Tel-Abib: see **Thelabib**.

Tema: see **Thema**.

Teman: see **Theman**.

Teraḥ: see **Therach**.

Thaavah: see **Kibroth Thaavah**.

Thachasch, *indecl.* (Hebr.) also **Taḥash**, *indecl.* Thahash, a son of Reumah and Nahor: Gen. 22.24 (AC).

Thachpanchesus ~i, *m.* also **Thechapneches**, *indecl.* Tahpanhes, a city in Egypt on the Nile: Jer. 43.9 (AC 7519.10).

Thamar[1], *indecl.* (Hebr.) also **Tamar**, *indecl.* see also **Chazezon Thamar**. Tamar, a city in the south of Judah near the Dead Sea: Ezek. 47.19 (AC 1678.2).

Thamar[2] ~aris, *f.* (Hebr.) also **Tamar** ~aris, *f.* **1** Tamar, Judah's daughter-in-law whom he unknowingly violated: Gen. 38.11 (AC). **2** Tamar, David's daughter whom Amnon knowingly violated: 2 Sam. 13.18 (AC 9942.8).

Tharschisch, *indecl.* and ~schi (Hebr.) also **Tarshish**, *indecl.* and ~shi. **1** The name of a people of the western Mediterranean: *et filii Javan; Elischah et ~sch* Gen. 10.4 (AC); *naves ~schi* Isa. 23.1 (AC 1156). **2** The name of a precious stone, beryl: Exod. 28.20 (AC); Ezek. 28.13 (AC 114); Dan. 10.6 (AE 69.3).

Thebach, *indecl.* (Hebr.) also **Tebach**, *indecl.*, and **Tebaḥ**, *indecl.* Tebah, a son of Reumah and Nahor: Gen. 22.24 (AC).

Thechapneches: see **Thachpanchesus**.

Thekoa, *indecl.* (Hebr.) also **Tekoa**, *indecl.* Tekoa, a city south-east of Bethlehem and south of Jerusalem: Jer. 6.1 (AC 3708.18).

Thelabib, *indecl.* (Hebr.) also **Tel-Abib**, *indecl.* Tel Abib, a high point alongside the river Chebar: Ezek. 3.15 (AC 728.3).

Thema ~ae, *m.* and *indecl.* (Hebr.) also **Tema** ~ae, *m.* and *indecl.* Tema, a son of Ishmael and a region named for him: Gen. 25.15 (AC).

Theman ~anis, *m.* also **Teman** ~anis, *m.* Teman, a grandson of Esau: Gen. 36.15 (AC); also, the territory of north-eastern Edom named for him: Hab. 3.3 (AC 1675.6).

Themanita ~ae, *m.* An inhabitant of north-eastern Edom, Temanite: Gen. 36.34 (AC).

Themis ~is, *f.* (Gk.) A Greek goddess, the personification of justice: VR 159.5.

Therach ~chi, *m.* (Hebr.) also **Teraḥ** ~ḥi, *m.* Terah, father of Abram, Nahor, and Haran: Gen. 11.26 (AC).

Thesbita ~ae, *m.* Tishbite, the obscure epithet for Elijah: 2 Kgs. 1.8 (AC 3301.2).

Thideal ~lis, *m.* (Hebr.) also **Tidal** ~lis, *m.* Tidal, a king of Goiim in the time of Abram: Gen. 14.1 (AC).

Thimna[1], *indecl. f.* (Hebr.) also **Timna**, *indecl. f.* **1** Timna, a concubine of Eliphaz: Gen. 36.12 (AC). **2** Timna, a daughter of Seir: Gen. 36.22 (AC).

Thimna[2], *indecl. m.* (Hebr.) also **Timna**, *indecl. m.* Timna, a leader of Edom: Gen. 36.40 (AC).

Thimnata ~ae, *m.* also **Timnatha** ~ae, *m.* Timnah, a city in Judah two miles west of Beth-shemesh: Gen. 38.12 (AC).

Thiras, *indecl.* also **Tiras**, *indecl.* Tiras, a son of Japheth: Gen. 10.2 (AC).

Thogarmah, *indecl.* also **Togarmah**, *indecl.* Togarmah, a son of Gomer and grandson of Japheth: Gen. 10.3 (AC).

Thola, *indecl.* (Hebr.) also **Tola**, *indecl.* Tola, a son of Issachar: Gen. 46.13 (AC).

Thomas ~ae, *m.* The disciple Thomas: *per Domini verba ad ~am* AC 7290.2.

Thrismegisthus ~i, *m.* (Gk.) also **Trismegistus** ~i, *m.* A title of Hermes in ancient Egypt: *~us in Aegypto Mosis tempore...creditur invenisse exprimere animi sensa per imagines bestiarum* ES 6083.

Thubal ~lis, *m.* and *indecl.* also **Tubal** ~lis, *m.* and *indecl.* Tubal, a son of Japheth: Gen. 10.2 (AC).

Thubal Cain, *indecl.* also **Tubal-cain**, *indecl.* Tubal Cain, a son of Zillah and Lamech: Gen. 4.22 (AC).

Thyatira ~orum, *neut. pl.* A city of ancient Lydia: Rev. 1.11 (AR).

Tidal: see **Thideal**.

Timna: see **Thimna**[1] or **Thimna**[2].

Timnatha: see **Thimnata**.

Timotheus ~i, *m.* (Gk.) Timothy, a convert and travel companion of Paul: VR 378.2.

Tiras: see **Thiras**.

Tochu, *indecl.* (Hebr.) Tohu, an ancestor of the prophet Samuel: 1 Sam. 1.1 (AC 7836.3).

Togarmah: see **Thogarmah**.

Tola: see **Thola**.

Tophet: see **Topheth**.

Topheth, *indecl.* (Hebr.) also **Tophet**, *indecl.* Tophet, a place in the valley of Hinnom where sacrifices were offered to Molech and the dead bodies were buried or consumed: Isa. 30.33 (AR 748.1).

Toscana ~ae, *f.* A region of northern Italy, Tuscany: ES 5648.

Transmontana ~ae, *f.* The northern region of Italy: *qui e Toscana, Genua, Venetiis, Milano et ~a* ES 5648.

Trismegistus: see **Thrismegisthus**.

Tubal: see **Thubal**.

Tubal-cain: see **Thubal Cain**.

Turca ~ae, *m.* A Turk: *convoluto pileo sicut ~arum quorundam* ES 723; ES 4777.

Tyrus ~i, *f.* A city of Phoenicia, Tyre: *filia ~i* Ps. 45.12 (AC 6729); AC 8093.2; CI 327.

U

Ulysses ~is, *m*. The king of Ithaca in Greek mythology, Odysseus, known in Latin as Ulysses: *fabulae de ~e et Medea* AM 521.4.

Uphasus ~i, *m*. also **Uphazus** ~i, *m*. Uphaz, a place in southern Arabia known for its gold: Dan. 10.5 (AC 3021.7).

Uphazus: see **Uphasus**.

Ur Chaldaeorum, *indecl*. (Hebr.) Ur, a city or district of northern Mesopotamia: Gen. 11.28 (AC).

Uriah, *indecl*. (Hebr.) Uriah, Hittite husband of Bathsheba: 2 Sam. 11.13 (AC 2913.2).

Urus ~i, *m*. (Hebr.) Uri, father of Bezaleel: Exod. 31.2 (AC).

Usa ~ae, *m*. also **Uzzah** ~ae, *m*. Uzzah, a son of Abinadab who died for touching the Ark: AC 4926.6; VI 59 (2 Sam. 6.6).

Usal, *indecl*. (Hebr.) also **Uzal**, *indecl*. Uzal, a son of Joktan: Gen. 10.27 (AC).

Ussiel, *indecl*. (Hebr.) Uzziel, a son of Kohath and grandson of Levi: Exod. 6.18 (AC).

Uz, *indecl*. (Hebr.) **1** Uz, a son of Aram and grandson of Shem: Gen. 10.23 (AC). **2** Uz, a son of Nahor and Milcah: Gen. 22.21 (AC). **3** Uz, a son of Dishon of the family of Seir: Gen. 36.28 (AC). **4** Uz, a region south of Edom and west of the great Arabian desert: Lam. 4.21 (AC 1073).

Uzal: see **Usal**.

Uzzah: see **Usa**.

V

Vahebam, *indecl.* also **Vahebum**, *indecl.* Waheb, the name of a place yet to be identified: *~am in Supha* Num. 21.14 (AC 2897); SS 103; VR 265.1.

Vahebum: see **Vahebam**.

Valentiniani ~orum, *m. pl.* The followers of the gnostic heretic Valentinus (2nd cent. AD): VR 378.2.

Venetiae ~tiarum, *f. pl.* The city of Venice in northern Italy: AM 451; ES 5648.

Versailles: see **Versaliae**.

Versaliae ~liarum, *f. pl.* (French) also **Versailles**, *indecl.* Versailles, a place near Paris known for its magnificent palace built by Louis XIV: *audivi illum* [sc. *Ludovicum XIV*] *dicentem quod videretur sibi sicut ~liis esset* UJ(C) 60.

Vespasianus ~i, *m.* The Roman Emperor (AD 69-79) who was responsible for the suppression of the Jewish revolt and the destruction of the Temple at Jerusalem: VR 23.2.

Vesta ~ae, *f.* A priestess of the Roman goddess Vesta, Vestal: *sicut ~a antiquorum, quae exstinxit ignem sacrum* VR 137.4.

Vesuvius ~i, *m.* A volcano in southern Italy: VR 79.3.

Vienna ~ae, *f.* The capital of Austria, Vienna: AM 451.

Vitus ~i, *m.* A Roman saint, after whom St Vitus's dance is named: *assimilari potest saltui S. ~i seu Guy* VR 367.7; ES 3895 (Tafel).

Voëtiani: see **Futziani**.

Vulcanus ~i, *m.* The Roman god of smiths, used as an expression for fire or flames: *si tunc scivisset, qualis illa blasphemia est, sane discerpsisset illam* [sc. *epistolam*] *digitis, et tradidisset ~o ad comburendum* VR 137.12.

W

Warsovia ~ae, *f.* The capital of Poland, Warsaw: VR 515.

Wolfius ~i, *m.* **1** The philosopher Christian Wolff (1679-1754), a follower of Leibniz: TE 38; VR 335.7. **2** Johan Christoph Wolf (1683-1739), pastor and theologian: ES 5850; ES 4550.

X

Xaverius ~i, *m.* Francis Xavier (1509-52, canonized in 1622): UJ(C) 65; VR 824.2.

Xenophon ~ntis, *m.* The Greek writer of the early 4th century BC: AM 151[a].1.

Z

Zachar ~aris, *m.* also **Zaḥar** ~aris, *m.* An unknown place that produced wool: Ezek. 27.18 (AC 9470.4).

Zacharias ~ae, *m.* also **Sacharias** ~ae, *m.* **1** The prophet Zechariah: AC 6852. **2** The father of John the Baptist: Luke 1.67 (DD 51.5).

Zadochus ~i, *m.* (Hebr.) also **Zadok** ~ki, *m.* Zadok, a priest in the time of King David: AC 9959.4.

Zadok: see **Zadochus**.

Zaḥar: see **Zachar**.

Zamzumim: see **Samsumim**.

Zaphenath Paeneach, *indecl.* (Hebr.) also **Zaphenath Paneaḥ**, *indecl.* Zaphnath Paaneah, the name given to Joseph by Pharaoah: *Zaphenath Paeneach in lingua sua originali significat revelatorem occultorum et aperitorem futurorum* AC 5331.

Zaphenath Paneaḥ: see **Zaphenath Paeneach**.

Zarḥita: see **Sarchita**.

Zebedaeus ~i, *m.* (Gk. from Hebr.) Zebedee, husband of Salome and father of the apostles James and John: Mark 10.35 (AC 1812.2).

Zeboiim: see **Zeboim**.

Zeboim, *indecl.* also **Zeboiim**, *indecl.* Zeboiim, one of three cities in the valley of Siddim destroyed along with Sodom and Gomorrah: Gen. 10.19 (AC).

Zebul: see **Sebul**.

Zebulon: see **Sebulun**.

Zebulun: see **Sebulun**.

Zedekias ~ae, *m.* also **Zidkiah** ~ae, *m.* Zedekiah, the king of Judah: Jer. 21.7 (AC 7102.7).

Zedkiah, *indecl.* (Hebr.) Zedekiah, a false prophet who encouraged Ahab to attack the Syrians: DD 15.7. (1 Kgs. 22.11).

Zemarus ~i, *m.* A member of a tribe that lived near Lebanon, Zemarite: Gen. 10.18 (AC).

Zephanias ~ae, *m.* The prophet Zephaniah: AC 6997.4.

Zepho, *indecl.* Zepho, a son of Eliphaz and grandson of Esau: Gen. 36.11 (AC).

Zephon: see **Baal-Zephon**.

Zeraḥ: see **Serach**[1].

Zeror, *indecl.* (Hebr.) Zeror, father of Abiel and ancestor of Saul: 1 Sam. 9.1 (AC 7836.3).

Zibeon ~onis, *m.* (Hebr.) **1** Zibeon, a Hivite grandfather of Oholibamah wife of Esau: Gen. 36.2 (AC). **2** Zibeon, a son of Seir: Gen. 36.20 (AC).

Zidkiah: see **Zedekias**.

Zidon ~onis, *m.* also **Sidon** ~onis, *m.* **1** Firstborn son of Canaan: Gen. 10.15 (AC). **2** A city in Phoenicia: Gen. 10.19 (AC).

Zillah, *indecl.* and ~ae, *f.* (Hebr.) Zilla, a wife of Lamech: Gen. 4.19 (AC).

Zilpah: see **Silpah**.

Zimran: see **Simran**.

Zimri: see **Simri**.

Zin: see **Sin**.

Zinzendorfiani ~orum, *m. pl.* The followers of Zinzendorf: ES 5995.

Zinzendorfius ~i, *m.* Count Nikolaus von Zinzendorf (1700-60), restorer of the Moravian Church: UJ(C) 89.

Zion ~onis, *m.* also **Sion** ~onis, *m.* The name of a hill at Jerusalem, Mount Zion: *tunc venit ~oni Redemptor* Isa. 59.20 (DD 14.3); AM 21.3.

Ziphion, *indecl.* (Hebr.) also **Zipion**, *indecl.* Ziphion, a son of Gad: Gen. 46.16 (AC).

Zipion: see **Ziphion**.

Zippora ~ae, *f.* (Hebr.) Zipporah, wife of Moses: Exod.

2.21 (AC).

Zoan ~anis, *m.* and *indecl.* Zoan, a capital city in Egypt: Isa. 19.11 (AC 1482).

Zoar, *indecl.* and ~aris, *m.* (Hebr.) Zoar, a small city at the south-east corner of the Dead Sea: Gen. 13.10 (AC).

Zoba ~ae, *m.* Zobah, a district in Syria: 2 Sam. 8.12 (AC 6917.3).

Zochar, *indecl.* (Hebr.) also **Zoḥar**, *indecl.* **1** Zohar, father of Ephron the Hittite: Gen. 23.8 (AC). **2** Zohar, a son of Simeon: Gen. 46.10 (AC).

Zoḥar: see **Zochar**.

Zorpa ~ae, *f.* Zarephath, a Phoenician city between Tyre and Sidon: 1 Kgs. 17.9 (AC 9995.6).

Zuph, *indecl.* (Hebr.) Zuph, an ancestor of Samuel: 1 Sam. 1.1 (AC 7836.3).

Zuzim: see **Suzimi**.

Zwingliani ~orum, *m.pl.* The followers of the Swiss reformer Ulrich Zwingli (1484-1531): VR 378.2.

Appendices

APPENDIX I:
CHRONOLOGICAL LIST OF THE LATIN WORKS OF SWEDENBORG

Published by Swedenborg

Arcana Coelestia [AC], 8 vols. ([London: John Lewis,] 1749-56); 2nd edn., ed. J F I Tafel, 13 vols. (Tubingae: in Bibliopolio Zu-Guttenberg, 1833-42); 3rd edn., ed. P H Johnson, E C Mongredien, Erik Sandström, John Elliott, Norman Ryder, 8 vols. (London: Swedenborg Society, 1949-73).

De Telluribus in Mundo nostro Solari [TE] (Londini: [John Lewis,] 1758); 2nd edn., ed. F. B. (London: Swedenborg Society, 1934); 3rd edn., ed. Lisa Hyatt (Bryn Athyn, PA: The Academy of the New Church Press, 1980); 4th edn., ed. John Elliott (London: Swedenborg Society, 2007).

De Coelo et ejus Mirabilibus, et de Inferno, ex auditis et visis [CI] (Londini: [John Lewis,] 1758); 2nd edn., ed. J F I Tafel (Boston: Wm. Carter & br., London: Swedenborg Society and Tubingae: Verlags-Expedition, 1862); 3rd edn., ed. S H Worcester (New York: American Swedenborg Printing and Publishing Society, 1890).

De Ultimo Judicio, et de Babylonia destructa [UJ] (Londini: [John Lewis,] 1758); 2nd edn., ed. S H Worcester (New York: American Swedenborg Printing and Publishing Society and London: Swedenborg Society, 1889); 3rd edn., ed. John Elliott (London: Swedenborg Society, 2007).

De Nova Hierosolyma et ejus Doctrina Coelesti [NH] (Londini: [John Lewis,] 1758); 2nd edn., ed. S H Worcester (New York: American Swedenborg Printing and Publishing Society, 1885); 3rd edn., ed. John Elliott (London: Swedenborg Society, 2004).

De Equo Albo [EA] (Londini: [John Lewis,] 1758); 2nd edn., ed. F. B. (London: Swedenborg Society, 1934); 3rd edn., ed. John Elliott (London: Swedenborg Society, 2004).

Doctrina Novae Hierosolymae de Domino [DD] (Amstelodami, 1763); 2nd edn., ed. L Hofaker and G Werner in *Scripta Novae Domini Ecclesiae,* sec. i (Tubingae: in libraria Guttenberg, 1834); 3rd edn., ed. S H Worcester in *Quatuor Doctrinae* (New York: American Swedenborg Printing and Publishing Society and London: Swedenborg Society, 1889).

Doctrina Novae Hierosolymae de Scriptura Sacra [SS] (Amsteoldami, 1763); 2nd edn., ed. L Hofaker and G Werner in *Scripta Novae Domini Ecclesiae*, sec. ii (Tubingae: in libraria Guttenberg, 1835); 3rd edn., ed. S H Worcester in *Quatuor Doctrinae* (New York: American Swedenborg Printing and Publishing Society and London: Swedenborg Society, 1889).

Doctrina Vitae pro Nova Hierosolyma [VI] (Amstelodami, 1763); 2nd edn., ed. L Hofaker and G Werner in *Scripta Novae Domini Ecclesiae*, sec. iii (Tubingae et Lipsiae: in libraria Guttenberg, 1835); 3rd edn., ed. S H Worcester in *Quatuor Doctrinae* (New York: American Swedenborg Printing and Publishing Society and London: Swedenborg Society, 1889).

Doctrina Novae Hierosolymae de Fide [FI] (Amstelodami, 1763); 2nd edn., ed. L Hofaker and G Werner in *Scripta Novae Domini Ecclesiae*, sec. iv (Tubingae et Lipsiae: in libraria Guttenberg, 1835); 3rd edn., ed. S H Worcester in *Quatuor Doctrinae* (New York: American Swedenborg Printing and Publishing Society and London: Swedenborg Society, 1889).

Continuatio de Ultimo Judicio [UJ(C)] (Amstelodami, 1763); 2nd edn., ed. J F I Tafel (Tubingae: Curam Administrat 'Verlagsexpedition', 1846); 3rd edn., ed. S H Worcester (New York: American Swedenborg Printing and Publishing Society and London: Swedenborg Society, 1889); 4th edn., ed. John Elliott (London: Swedenborg Society, 2007).

Sapientia Angelica de Divino Amore et de Divina Sapientia [AS] (Amstelodami, 1763); 2nd edn., ed. J F I Tafel (Stuttgardiae: Ebner et Seubert, 1843); 3rd edn., ed. S H Worcester (New York: American Swedenborg Printing and Publishing Society, 1899); 4th edn., ed. N Bruce Rogers (Bryn Athyn, PA: Academy of the New Church, 1999).

Sapientia Angelica de Divina Providentia [DP] (Amstelodami, 1764); 2nd edn., ed. J F I Tafel (Tubingae: Curam Administrat 'Verlagsexpedition' and Londini: Swedenborg Society, 1855); 3rd edn., ed. S H Worcester (New York: American Swedenborg Printing and Publishing Society, 1899); 4th edn., ed. N Bruce Rogers (Bryn Athyn, PA: Academy of the New Church, 2003).

Apocalypsis Revelata [AR] (Amstelodami, 1766); 2nd edn., ed. S H Worcester, 2 vols. (New York: American Swedenborg Printing and Publishing Society, 1881).

Delitiae Sapientiae de Amore Conjugiali [AM] (Amstelodami, 1768); 2nd edn., ed. Ludovicus Hofaker (Tubingae et Lipsiae: Verlagshandlung Zu-Guttenberg, 1841); 3rd edn., ed. S H Worcester (New York: American Swedenborg Printing and Publishing Society, 1889); 4th edn., ed. N Bruce Rogers (Bryn Athyn, PA: Academy of the New Church, 1993, 1995).

Summaria Expositio Doctrinae Novae Ecclesiae [SE] (Amstelodami, 1769); 2nd edn., ed. J F I Tafel (Tubingae: Curam Administrat 'Verlagsexpedition' and Londini: Swedenborg Society, 1859).

De Commercio Animae et Corporis [CC] (Londini, 1769); 2nd edn., ed. J F I Tafel (Stutgardiae: Ebner et Seubert and Tubingae: in bibliopolis Zu-Guttenberg, 1843); 3rd edn., ed. F. B. and L. G. (London: Swedenborg Society, 1935).

Responsum ad Epistolam ab Amico ad me scriptam [RA] (Londini, 1769); 2nd edn. in *The Aurora*, no. xx, November 1, 1800, pp. 224-8; 3rd edn., ed. J F I Tafel in *Arcana Coelestia* (Tubingae: in Bibliopolio Zu-Guttenberg, 1838), vol. vi; 4th edn., ed. John Elliott in *Small Theological Works and Letters* (London: Swedenborg Society, 1975).

Vera Christiana Religio [VR] (Amstelodami, 1771); 2nd edn., ed. J F I Tafel, 2 vols. (Tubingae: Curam Administrat 'Verlagsexpedition' and Londini: Swedenborg Society, 1857-8); 3rd edn., ed. S H Worcester, 2 vols. (New York: American Swedenborg Printing and Publishing Society, 1906).

Index Memorabilium in Vera Christiana Religione [IM] in *Vera Christiana Religio* (Amstelodami, 1771); 2nd edn., ed. J F I Tafel in *Vera Christiana Religio*, vol. II (Tubingae: Curam Administrat 'Verlagsexpedition' and Londini: Swedenborg Society, 1858); 3rd edn., ed. S H Worcester in *Vera Christiana Religio*, vol. I (New York: American Swedenborg Printing and Publishing Society, 1906).

Responsum ad Dr Ernesti [RE] (1771); 2nd edn., ed. John Elliott in *Small Theological Works and Letters* (London: Swedenborg Society, 1975).

Published posthumously

Adversaria [AD] (1745-7), ed. J F I Tafel, 4 pts. (pt. 1 split over six vols.) and a Supplement (Tubingae: Curam

Administrat 'Verlagsexpedition'/in Bibliopolio Zu-Guttenberg, Londini: William Newbery, and Stuttgardiae: Ebner et Seubert, 1842-54).

Index Biblicus [IB] (1746-8), ed. J F I Tafel (vols. 1-3) and A Kahl (vol. 4), 4 vols. (Tubingae: Curam Administrat 'Verlagsexpedition' and Londini: Swedenborg Society, and Lundae: ex officina Lundbergiana, 1859-68).

Experientiae Spirituales [ES] (1745-65), ed. J D Odhner, 6 vols. (Bryn Athyn, PA: Academy of the New Church, 1983-97); also, entitled *Diarium Spirituale*, ed. J F I Tafel, 7 parts (Tubingae: Curam 'Verlagsexpedition' and Henricus Lauppius, Londini: William Newbery and Swedenborg Society, and Stuttgardiae: Ebner et Seubert, 1843-60).

Autograph MS of *Arcana Coelestia* [AC Codex 8] (1749) (a rough draft of *Arcana Coelestia*, Gen. 16 to Exod. 40) forming Codex 8 in the library of the Royal Academy of Sciences, Stockholm.

Experientiae Spirituales (Minores) [ES(M)] (*c.* 1749-51), ed. J D Odhner in *Experientiae Spirituales*, vol. III (Bryn Athyn, PA: Academy of the New Church, 1991); also, entitled *Diarium Minus*, ed. J F I Tafel in *Diarium Spirituale*, pt. 4 (Londini: William Newbery and Tubingae: Henricus Lauppius, 1843).

De Miraculis [MI] (1750), ed. P H Johnson (London: Swedenborg Society, 1943, rev. 1947).

Arcana Coelestia Indexes [AC Index] (*c.*1756), ed. John Elliott (London: Swedenborg Society, 2004); first published as *Index Verborum, Nominum et Rerum in Arcana Coelestibus*, ed. J A Tulk (Londini: Typis T Bensley, Bolt-Court, Fleet Street, impensis Joh. Aug. Tulk, 1815) from a copy of the MSS by A Nordenskjöld, including material imported from Gabriel Beyer's *Index Initialis in Opera Swedenborgii Theologica* (Amstelodami: A D Sellschop & P Huart, 1779); this was followed by a revised edn., ed. R L Tafel (Londini: Swedenborg Society, 1890).

Apocalypsis Explicata [AE] (1757-9), ed. H Peckitt, W Spence, G Adams, B Chastanier and R Hindmarsh, 4 vols. (Londini: typis Robert Hindmarsh, 1785-9); 2nd edn. (nos. 1-532 only), ed. J F I Tafel, 3 vols. (Tubingae: 'Verlagsexpedition' and Londini: Swedenborg Society, 1861-4); 3rd edn., ed. S H Worcester, 6 vols. (New York: American Swedenborg Printing and Publishing Society, 1884-5).

De Athanasii Symbolo [AT] (1759), ed. J J G Wilkinson and Revd M Sibly (Londini: James S Hodson and William Newbery and Manchester: Edward Baylis, 1840); 2nd edn., ed. S H Worcester (New York: American Swedenborg Printing and Publishing Society, 1884); 3rd edn., ed. Doris H Harley with John Chadwick (London: Swedenborg Society, 1954). The author's original manuscript is no longer extant; all extant versions of AT are based on handwritten copies made after the author's death.

De Domino [DO] (1760), ed. J J G Wilkinson and Revd M Sibly (Londini: James S Hodson and William Newbery and Manchester: Edward Baylis, 1840); 2nd edn., ed. S H Worcester (New York: American Swedenborg Printing and Publishing Society, 1884); 3rd edn., ed. John Elliott in *Small Theological Works and Letters* (London: Swedenborg Society, 1975). The author's original manuscript is no longer extant; all extant versions of DO are based on handwritten copies made after the author's death.

Summaria Expositio Sensus interni Librorum Propheticorum ac Psalmorum Veteris Testamenti [PP] (1761), ed. R Hindmarsh (Londini: Robert Hindmarsh, 1784); 2nd edn., ed. J F I Tafel (Tubingae: in der 'Verlagsexpedition' and Londini: Swedenborg Society, 1860); 3rd edn., ed. E J E Schreck (New York: American Swedenborg Printing and Publishing Society, 1900).

De Scriptura Sacra seu Verbo Domini [SS(P)] (1762), ed. J F I Tafel in *Diarium Spirituale*, pt. vii, sec. i and ii (Tubingae: Curam Administrat 'Verlagsexpedition' and Londini: William Newbery, 1846-54); 2nd edn., ed. N Bruce Rogers, B Erikson Odhner, Prescott A Rogers et al in *Tria Opuscula* (Bryn Athyn, PA: Academy of the New Church, 1997).

De Praeceptis Decalogi [PD] (1762), ed. J F I Tafel in *Diarium Spirituale*, pt. vii, sec. i and ii (Tubingae: Curam Administrat 'Verlagsexpedition' and Londini: William Newbery, 1846-54); 2nd edn., ed. John

Elliott in *Small Theological Works and Letters* (London: Swedenborg Society, 1975); 3rd edn., ed. N Bruce Rogers, B Erikson Odhner, Prescott A Rogers et al in *Tria Opuscula* (Bryn Athyn, PA: Academy of the New Church, 1997).

De Ultimo Judicio (Posthumous) [UJ(P)] (1762), ed. J F I Tafel in *Diarium Spirituale*, pt. vii, sec. i (Tubingae: Curam Administrat 'Verlagsexpedition' and Londini: William Newbery, 1846); 2nd edn., ed. N Bruce Rogers, B Erikson Odhner, Prescott A Rogers et al in *Tria Opuscula* (Bryn Athyn, PA: Academy of the New Church, 1997).

De Divino Amore [DA] (1762), ed. H Peckitt, W Spence, G Adams, B Chastanier and R Hindmarsh in *Apocalypsis Explicata*, vol. IV (Londini: Robert Hindmarsh, 1789); 2nd edn., ed. S H Worcester (New York: American Swedenborg Printing and Publishing Society, 1884).

De Divina Sapientia [SA] (1763), ed. H Peckitt, W Spence, G Adams, B Chastanier and R Hindmarsh in *Apocalypsis Explicata*, vol. IV (Londini: Robert Hindmarsh, 1789); 2nd edn., ed. S H Worcester (New York: American Swedenborg Printing and Publishing Society, 1884).

Colloquia cum Angelis [CA] (1766), ed. J F I Tafel in *Diarium Spirituale*, pt. vii, sec. i (Tubingae: Curam Administrat 'Verlagsexpedition' and Londini: William Newbery, 1846); 2nd edn., ed. John Elliott in *Small Theological Works and Letters* (London: Swedenborg Society, 1975).

De Charitate [CH] (1766), ed. J J G Wilkinson and Revd M Sibly (Londini: James S Hodson and William Newbery and Manchester: Edward Baylis, 1840); 2nd edn., ed. S H Worcester (New York: American Swedenborg Printing and Publishing Society, 1878).

[*Quinque*] *Memorabilia* [ME] (1766), ed. J F I Tafel in *Diarium Spirituale*, pt. vii, sec. i (Tubingae: Curam Administrat 'Verlagsexpedition' and Londini: William Newbery, 1846); 2nd edn., ed. John Elliott in *Small Theological Works and Letters* (London: Swedenborg Society, 1975). The author's original manuscript is no longer extant; all extant versions of ME are based on handwritten copies made after the author's death.

De Conjugio [CJ] (1766), ed. J F I Tafel (Tubingae: 'Verlagsexpedition' and Londini: Swedenborg Society, 1860); 2nd edn. as *De Conjugio II*, ed. John Elliott in *Small Theological Works and Letters* (London: Swedenborg Society, 1975).

Pro Memoria [PM] (1767), a letter (written in Swedish) to Dr Gabriel Beyer. Published in: 'Utdrag af några bref från Emanuel Svedenborg til åtkillige des vänner', in *Samlingar för Philantroper* (Stockholm, 1787), pt. i; 2nd edn., ed. John Elliott in *Small Theological Works and Letters* (London: Swedenborg Society, 1975).

De Justificatione [JU] (*c.* 1768), ed. J F I Tafel (Tubingae: in der 'Verlagsexpedition' and Londini: Swedenborg Society, 1860); 2nd edn., ed. John Elliott in *Small Theological Works and Letters* (London: Swedenborg Society, 1975).

Canones Novae Ecclesiae [CN] (1769), ed. J J G Wilkinson and Revd M Sibly (Londini: James S Hodson and William Newbery and Manchester: Edward Baylis, 1840); 2nd edn., ed. S H Worcester (New York: American Swedenborg Printing and Publishing Society, 1885). The author's original manuscript is no longer extant; all extant versions of CN are based on handwritten copies made after the author's death.

Appendix ad codicillum de Equo Albo [EA(A)] (1769), ed. G E Klemming in *Svedenborgs Drömmar, 1744* (Stockholm: P A Norstedt & Söner, 1859), pp. 73-7; 2nd edn., ed. A Kahl and J A Sevén in *Swedenborgs Drömmar, 1744* (Stockholm: Tryckt Hos J. & A. Riis, 1860), pp. 73-7; 3rd edn., ed. J F E Le Boys des Guays in *Du Cheval blanc* (Saint-Amand (Cher): La Librairie de la Nouvelle Jérusalem, Paris: M Minot and Treuttel and Wurtz, and London: Swedenborg Society, 1859); 4th edn., ed A W Acton in *De Equo Albo* (London: Swedenborg Society, 1934); 5th edn., ed. John Elliott in *Small Theological Works and Letters* (London: Swedenborg Society, 1975).

Dicta Probantia Veteris et Novi Testamenti [DI] (1769), ed. J F I Tafel (Tubingae: Curam Administrat 'Verlagsexpedition', 1845).

Index ad Formulam Concordiae [FC] (1769), ed. John Elliott in *Small Theological Works and Letters* (London: Swedenborg Society, 1975).

Historia Ecclesiastica Novae Ecclesiae [HE] (1770), ed. S H Worcester and L H Tafel in *Words for the New Church*, vol. I (Philadelphia: J B Lippincott & Co., 1877), pp. 57-9; 2nd edn., ed. John Elliott in *Small Theological Works and Letters* (London: Swedenborg Society, 1975).

Fragmentum de Miraculis [MI(F)] (1770), ed. S H Worcester in *Coronis seu Appendix* (New York: American Swedenborg Printing and Publishing Society and London: Swedenborg Society, 1884).

Quaestiones Novem de Trinitate [QN] (1771), ed. Robert Hindmarsh (Londini: Robert Hindmarsh, 1785); 2nd edn., ed. J F Potts (New York: American Swedenborg Printing and Publishing Society, 1904); 3rd edn., ed. John Elliott in *Small Theological Works and Letters* (London: Swedenborg Society, 1975). The author's original manuscript is no longer extant; all extant versions of QN are based on handwritten copies made after the author's death.

Coronis seu Appendix ad Veram Christianam Religionem [CO] (1771), ed. A Nordenskjöld (Londini, 1780); 2nd edn. ('Summaria' and 'Ultimo de Miraculis' only), ed. J F I Tafel in *Diarium Spirituale*, pt. vii, sec. i (Tubingae: Curam Administrat 'Verlagsexpedition' and Londini: William Newbery, 1846); 3rd edn., ed. S H Worcester (New York: American Swedenborg Printing and Publishing Society and London: Swedenborg Society, 1884). The author's original manuscript is no longer extant; all extant versions of CO are based on handwritten copies made after the author's death.

De Consummatione Saeculi [CS] (1771), ed. J F I Tafel in *Diarium Spirituale*, pt. vii, sec. i (Tubingae: Curam Administrat 'Verlagsexpedition' and Londini: William Newbery, 1846); 2nd edn. (including only *Invitatio ad Novam Ecclesiam*), ed. S H Worcester in *Coronis seu Appendix* (New York: American Swedenborg Printing and Publishing Society and London: Swedenborg Society, 1884). The author's original manuscript is no longer extant; all extant versions of CS are based on handwritten copies made after the author's death.

Invitatio ad Novam Ecclesiam [NE] (1771), ed. J F I Tafel in *Diarium Spirituale*, pt. vii, sec. i (Tubingae: Curam Administrat 'Verlagsexpedition' and Londini: William Newbery, 1846); 2nd edn., ed. S H Worcester in *Coronis seu Appendix* (New York: American Swedenborg Printing and Publishing Society and London: Swedenborg Society, 1884). The author's original manuscript is no longer extant; all extant versions of NE are based on handwritten copies made after the author's death.

Miscellaneous composite volumes

Documents concerning Swedenborg [DC], 3 vols. tr., ed. and comp. R L Tafel (London: Swedenborg Society, 1875-7).

Small Theological Works and Letters [ST], ed. John Elliott (London: Swedenborg Society, 1975).

APPENDIX II: NOTES TO THE LATIN TEXTS OF SWEDENBORG

1. Repeated section numbers.

In keeping with eighteenth-century practice Swedenborg appended section numbers to his published texts. These section numbers have been followed in nearly all subsequent editions. Unfortunately in a few of these works he repeated numbers with the result that, in one work, two (or sometimes more) different sections are identified by the same number. Different editors and translators have dealt with this problem in different ways. Here, in this Lexicon, a single system has been applied. The first repetition of a section number is identified by a superscript letter 'a' immediately following the number, e.g. AM 156^{a}.1. A second repetition will be identified by a superscript letter 'b', e.g. AM 156^{b}.1, and so on.

An additional problem occurs in Swedenborg's posthumously published works, in that, as well as repeating section numbers, Swedenborg in places numbered sections with fractions, $^{1}/_{2}$, $^{1}/_{3}$, $^{1}/_{4}$, etc., sometimes repeating the previous section number, sometimes only using the fraction. So references to a work such as *Experientiae Spirituales*, i.e. ES 2093, might be followed by a repetition of the number 2093 (which in this Lexicon would be treated as ES 2093^{a}) or by ES 2093 $^{1}/_{2}$ or just by $^{1}/_{2}$. These fractions are retained in this Lexicon. Where, in the manuscripts, only a fraction is given, this is given with the previous section number in square brackets, e.g. ES [2093] $^{1}/_{2}$.

2. Experientiae Spirituales (ES) numbering.

Experientiae Spirituales or *Diarium Spirituale* (*Spiritual Experiences* or *The Spiritual Diary* in English), has been treated as 2 works, hence the abbreviations ES and ES(M). ES(M) forms part of *The Spiritual Diary* but Swedenborg wrote it in a separate volume, repeating the section numbers 4545-4715 that he had already used in the codex he kept the rest of his Diary in. Rather than treating all of these numbers as repeated section numbers and identifying them with superscript letters, we have given this volume its own title, *Experientiae Spirituales (Minores)* with abbreviation ES(M). At the end of both ES and ES(M), where there are long sections that were left unnumbered by Swedenborg, we have followed J D Odhner in giving these sections identifying numbers placed in parentheses. See 'Repeated section numbers' above for a further explanation of the fractions, square brackets, and superscript letters in ES references.

3. Adversaria (AD) numbering.

J F I Tafel's edition of *Adversaria* was published in loose fascicles non-sequentially over a period of twelve years and has come to be bound in different ways and orders by its owners. References in this Lexicon to a 1AD, 2AD, 3AD, and 4AD are therefore to the Autograph tomes of Swedenborg. 1AD = Hyde 483 (covering Gen. ch. 1-35.15, nos. 1-1713), 2AD = Hyde 484 (covering Gen. 35.16-50.26 and Exod. ch. 1-14.28, nos. 1-2476), 3AD = Hyde 485 (covering Exod. 14.29-36.5 and Josh., Judg., Ruth, 1 Sam., 2 Sam., 1 Kgs., 2 Kgs., 1 Chr., 2 Chr., Lev., Num., and Deut., nos. 1-7762), 4AD = Hyde 499 (covering Isa. and Jer.).

4. De Charitate (CH), De Divina Sapientia (SA), De Divino Amore (DA), and De Scriptura Sacra seu Verbo Domini [posth.] (SS(P)) numbering.

These four posthumously published works are given references with two numbering systems. The first follows immediately after the two letter abbreviation for the work and the second follows after the first, enclosed in parentheses and preceded by an equals sign:

CH 78 (= iv.2); SA 124 (= x.6.[1]); DA 14 (= v.[3]); SS(P) 33 (= 14.4).

For all four of these works the first set of numbers (78, 124, 14, and 33 in the examples above) refer to section numbers, as is usual for Swedenborg's works. However, these section numbers have all been supplied by editors and translators, Swedenborg himself not using his customary section numbering system in these unpublished works, instead giving chapter numbers in Roman (or Arabic, in the case of SS(P)) numerals and then, sometimes, numbering portions of the text within the chapters. Unfortunately, not all of the Latin editions and printings of these works have applied the section numbers of the later editors and translators, so for the aid of the reader, we have included Swedenborg's chapter numbering and subdivisions in parentheses (iv.2, x.6.[1], v.[3], and 14.4 in the examples above). The numbers in square brackets within the parentheses represent editorial subdivisions, as opposed to those of Swedenborg himself. These subdivisions were devised by J F Potts in his *The Swedenborg Concordance*, and are now common to many modern editions and translations.

5. De Ultimo Judicio (Posthumous) (UJ(P)) numbering.

The numbering for references to UJ(P) in this Lexicon refer to the edition of Rogers et al published in *Tria Opuscula* (Bryn Athyn, PA: Academy of the New Church, 1997). The previous edition, found in J F I Tafel's *Diarium Spirituale*, pt. vii, sec. i, did not (like Swedenborg himself in the manuscript) supply section numbers.

6. Citations from Scripture (and other works)

When Swedenborg cites from Scripture (or from other works, such as Symbolum Athanasii (the Athanasian Creed), Papal Bulls, the Council of Trent, etc.), the reference is given first, followed by the reference to where the citation is found in Swedenborg's works, usually in parentheses: Matt. 5.29 (AC 10061.5); Sym. Ath. (DD 56); Council of Trent in SE 3(a).

Where Swedenborg makes a more allusive reference to Scripture, etc., then the reference to Swedenborg's work is given first, followed by the reference to Scripture in parentheses: AC 3301.2 (Matt. 3.4); SE 3(a) (Council of Trent).

7. Alternative forms of verbs

Alternative forms of verbs are presented in two ways to give an approximation of their frequency of use. When the alternative past participle or perfect form is fairly common in Swedenborg's writings it is given in parentheses, preceded by an italicized 'or', after the usual past participle or perfect:

assequor ~qui ~quutus (*or* ~cutus) sum, *tr*.
cupio ~pere ~pivi (*or* ~pii) ~pitum, *tr*.

However, when the alternative form is significantly rarer (less than 3% of Swedenborg's usage of the word), it is given later in the entry, again in parentheses—but this time preceded by 'also'—following after the indication of whether the verb is transitive or intransitive. Particularly rare forms will also be accompanied by a reference to where the form can be found in Swedenborg's works:

exeo exire exivi exitum, *intr*. (pf. act. also *exii*)
redeo ~dire ~dii, *intr*. (pf. also *~divi*)
illino ~linere ~livi ~litum, *tr*. (pf. act. also *~levi* VR 797.3)
inhabito ~are ~avi, *intr*. (*tr*.) (pf. pple. *~atus* VR 466)

8. Alternative spellings

As stated in the Editor's Introduction, alternative spellings decline/conjugate in the same way as the main spelling, unless stated otherwise. However, in the section entitled Proper Nouns, where oftentimes the proper names have many different alternative spellings—some of which inflect, and some of which do not—an indication of inflectional type is given for all alternative spellings, regardless of whether they match that of the headword.

APPENDIX III: NOTE TO THE LATIN BIBLE OF SEBASTIAN SCHMIDT

Born in 1617 in Alsace, Sebastian Schmidt received a broad education at various German-speaking universities, after which he become a Lutheran pastor and then a Professor of Theology at the University of Strasbourg. He wrote a number of books on religious, biblical, and theological subjects, some in German, others in Latin; and he produced a Latin translation of the Bible. But Schmidt never saw the first printed edition of his translation, published in Strasbourg in 1696, for he died while seeing it through the press.

Swedenborg's own copy of this first edition of the Schmidt version was found among his possessions after his death in 1772, and it is now lodged in the library of the Royal Swedish Academy of Sciences, Stockholm. Although a large number of pages are missing from it, this copy is of great importance, since it contains numerous marginal annotations in Swedenborg's own hand. In 1872 a photolithographic reproduction of this much annotated, but defective, copy of what had been printed in 1696 was published in Stockholm, the editor being Rudolph L Tafel, who added from another copy of the 1696 edition some of the missing pages. Before 2005 Tafel's reproduction had been long out of print, but in that year The Academy of the New Church, Bryn Athyn, Pennsylvania, brought out a new edition, which also includes certain pages, notably those containing the Books of Samuel, which had been accidentally omitted by Tafel or his printer.

When quoting texts or passages from the Sacred Scriptures to illustrate or confirm some point he was making, Swedenborg usually relied on the Schmidt Latin version; but he did not always reproduce the exact wording. Frequently he used expressions which were different from, though nonetheless synonymous with, Schmidt's. He often omitted a word or two, sometimes a whole phrase, or even an entire sentence. And in some instances his understanding of the original Hebrew or Greek Scriptures may well have influenced his different wording from that contained in the Schmidt version. Some slight variations from that version however may have been attributable to Swedenborg's quoting roughly from memory rather than precisely from a printed page in front of him. All of this suggests that Swedenborg did not share our present-day urge to be verbally precise when quoting from another's work. But how many eighteenth-century authors felt the need for such precision?